DATA STRUCTURES

FORM AND FUNCTION

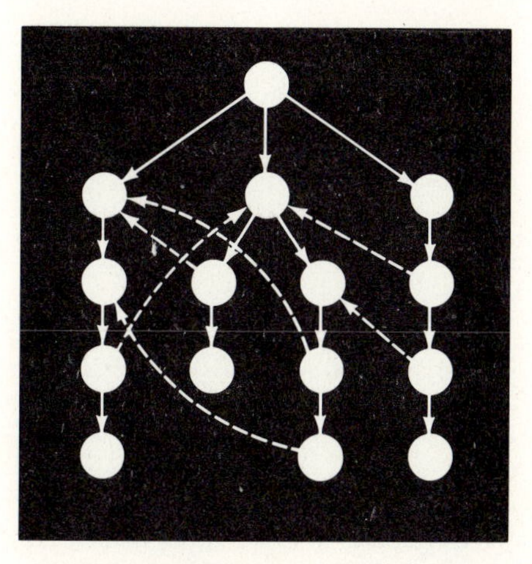

HARRY F. SMITH

IBM Scientific Center, Palo Alto

California State University, San Jose

Harcourt Brace Jovanovich, Publishers
and its subsidiary, Academic Press

San Diego New York Chicago Austin Washington, D.C.
London Sydney Tokyo Toronto

ISBN: 0-15-516820-7

Library of Congress Catalog Card Number: 86-83142

Printed in the United States of America

The camera-ready pages for this book were produced with the IBM 4250 Page Printer. The text is set in Monotype Times Roman, the figures in Helvetica, and the algorithms in Univers.

The illustrations are by House of Graphics.

To Mary

Author of Contentment

PREFACE

The subject of data structures is a rich treasure house of basic concepts, clever tricks, the power of abstraction, numerous algorithms, and – implicit or explicit throughout – means of evaluation and comparison of alternative approaches. It is good that, by now, almost every student of computer science or data processing takes an explicit data structures course; most programmers of earlier vintage learned of these matters imperfectly from sketches on the backs of computer listings. The topic has become so fundamental, in fact, that whereas it was once presented as an upper division course, it is now presented in the lower division, very often in a "softened" form. But at the same time that the initial presentation has "moved down," the subject has "moved up" both in depth and scope, so that now a second course is usually needed by serious students.

This book is designed primarily to respond to this need for additional coverage; it contains a considerable amount of advanced and up-to-date material. With reference to the guidelines of ACM Curriculum '78 [1979], the material herein is centered on CS7 (Data Structures and Algorithm Analysis). However, ACM Curriculum '78 also treats data structures in CS2 (Computer Programming), CS5 (Introduction to File Processing), and CS13 (Algorithms). We share the view that it is desirable to have a unified treatment of these topics. In any advanced treatment, it is difficult to do equal justice to several different aspects of the subject, including:

- the enormous amount of invention in the field;
- the increasing importance of abstraction in discussing data structures;
- the analysis of structures and algorithms in terms of complexity theory.

We have elected to present the latter two aspects, but not with consistent emphasis, thereby maximizing the opportunity to dwell upon the first aspect. One objective of this approach is to make the book useful as a text for a second course, either at the upper division or graduate level; another objective is that the book should be valuable as a reference for the professional programmer. Partly for this second reason, the book is complete and self-contained with respect to the subject matter; this has the added consequence that some number of teachers and students might find it to their liking in the context of a first course in data structures. In summary, we have striven to make this an eminently *useful* book. The following paragraphs describe some of the ways in which the style of the book is designed to respond to these multiple intentions.

1. In most of the chapters, the material is organized in the logical sequence: basic notions, several applications of these notions, advanced notions. Thus, readers having no prior familiarity with data structures would very likely wish to skip the latter portions of the chapters, and knowledgeable readers might prefer to skip or skim the initial portions. At an earlier point in time, the sections were marked in a manner to indicate whether the material was introductory, intermediate, or advanced. Two things caused that to change. One was the maturing

realization that our primary audience consists of those pursuing the subject a second time. Related to this is the second reason that for such an audience, there is great divergence in what can be considered as basic and already known. The present point of view is that the unmarked sections are all significant for a second course in data structures, but that most students in such a course would be able to skim through the initial parts of most chapters. On the other hand, there are numerous sections marked with a †, indicating that the material is more advanced, or less fundamentally significant, or both. There are two or three special sections at the end of each chapter. One of these, the Reference to Terminology, might seem somewhat inappropriate for a second-level text. But we are convinced of its utility. Although more advanced readers may not be overwhelmed by the proliferation of terminology, experience firmly indicates that they still appreciate tools that are helpful in organizing concepts.

2. We have tried to provide a treatment that is more complete than usual, even though – in such a dynamic subject area – that goal is ephemeral at best. Related to this aim are the extensive bibliographic references. In order to reduce the element of distraction for the more casual reader, multiple references are usually removed to the Bibliographic Notes section at the end of the chapter, with [§] left to signal their occurrence.

3. In order to make the book accessible to a wide audience, only a modest level of mathematics is employed. In Chapter 1, we review the necessary competence on the reader's part. For readers who wish to see detailed analyses of algorithms or learn how to perform their own analyses of algorithms, the original treatment of these matters by Knuth [1973a, 1973b] is still incomparable. An excellent treatment with a different point of view is that of Aho, Hopcroft, and Ullman [1974].

4. We concur with the widespread use of Pascal for representing data structures and algorithms. The issue is not without debate, however, as we discuss in Chapter 1. In addition to the usual reasons for choosing Pascal, we find it comforting that all the algorithms are in executable form, except for the necessity to transpose a few lines of text in some cases. As a sample of the clarity that can be brought to exposition by Pascal, readers already acquainted with the Schorr-Waite algorithm for marking a List are invited to examine the procedure MARK_LIST (Algorithm 4.7) on page 154.

5. It is relatively easy and can be quite informative to read a text such as this. But the real transfer of knowledge in Computer Science comes with mastering examples and doing exercises. We have sought to have a variety of examples that are both interesting and meaningful, but to avoid the appearance of presenting a cookbook of code. On occasion, minor details of efficiency in an algorithm are suppressed in favor of clarity; in almost all cases, an algorithm appears on one page. With regard to exercises, we have sought to have enough to satisfy a wide range of interests and abilities among readers. The exercises at the end of each chapter are classified at three of levels. Those marked with † should be considered as intermediate, and those marked with †† should be considered as

advanced. Note, however, that these ratings reflect not one but several factors – level of the corresponding text, depth of requisite understanding, amount of work required, etc. The language to be used for implementing algorithms is deliberately not specified, being left to the reader and/or the instructor. For obvious reasons, however, Pascal is a strong candidate.

6. The organization of the chapters in this book reflects the title *Data Structures: Form and Function*:

   - Chapters 1 – 8 are about the individual data structures.
   - Chapter 9 is a brief coda to the first eight chapters, presenting some summary ideas about the use of structure in dealing with complexity.
   - Chapters 10 – 13 address the topics of searching, memory management, files, and sorting.

   Although there are many examples relating to individual data structures in the first eight chapters, there is much to be gained by having the dedicated discussions of the last four chapters. If the reader's interest is pragmatic, he[1] can more readily make comparisons between methods – some of which do not neatly fall into any of the earlier chapters. If his interest is more theoretical, he can more readily appreciate the effects of choosing and commingling among the various data structures.

It is definitely not trite to acknowledge the relevance of experience in using earlier versions of these notes while teaching Data Structures courses at San Jose State University. Over and over again, student reactions have shown that an apparently good way of explaining something could be made better, and so this effort owes much to those who have stumbled and complained. The teaching experience is also valuable because it seems to confirm the viability of writing one book that could serve multiple audiences. These notes have been used more often in teaching a graduate course in Data Structures, but they have been used just as successfully in teaching an undergraduate, first course in the subject. In fact, the same precaution needs to be observed at either level – to be careful about which material should be covered and which should be omitted, depending upon the background of the audience. Although there is not a great deal of latitude in picking material that should be covered in a first course, there is for a second course; my own custom has been to vary the latter by about 20 percent each time I teach it, which helps keep the subject fresh. Specific suggestions for syllabi that are appropriate for both first and second courses are given in the Instructor's Manual.

It is sobering to recount the number of people to whom I am indebted in the course of finishing this project. Sincere thanks go to all those who have read or reviewed the work over the past years. Some of them are still nameless to me.

---

[1] Throughout this book, the use of the pronoun "he" has no intended prejudice. It should be construed as a reduction of "she" or "he."

However, it is a pleasure to be able to acknowledge contributions from Joel Aron, Marilyn Bohl, and Tony Hassit of IBM; from Henson Graves, John Mitchem, and Jeff Smith of San Jose State University; and from Robert Tarjan of Princeton University. I am particularly grateful to Cliff Hollander for his perceptive and encouraging commentary when the manuscript was being launched, to William Topp at University of the Pacific for offering valuable ideas that led to an important mid-course correction, and to Christopher Brown at the University of Rochester and David Frisque at the University of Michigan for their constructive encouragement in bringing the book to completion.

The experience with Academic Press and Harcourt Brace Jovanovich has been uniformly a rewarding one. On the editorial side, Richard Bonacci, Dale Brown, and Jack Thomas were all extremely helpful. On the production side, Lynn Edwards and Don Fujimoto demonstrated a marvelous mixture of support and trust with regard to the uncommon manner of producing camera ready masters. Alex Teshin and Romaine Lo Prete from the House of Graphics were wonderfully patient in rendering the line art.

There is an immense debt of gratitude of a different sort to the IBM Corporation for enabling both the authorship and the computerized typesetting of this book. None of this is to be construed, however, as an endorsement by IBM of any of the views expressed herein. Over the past few years, numerous managers at the Palo Alto Scientific Center have endured the traumas associated with this book; I am particularly grateful to Pat Smith for his role in initiating this support. In carrying out the typesetting, I received valuable help from Bob Creasy, Kathy Cruz-Young, Mike Kay, and Art Schmidt.

CONTENTS

DATA STRUCTURES

FORM AND FUNCTION

1

PRELIMINARIES

"Not only does one not retain all at once
the truly rare works, but even within such works,
it is the least precious parts that one perceives first.
Less deceptive than life, the great masterpieces
do not give us their best at the beginning."

Proust,
Remembrance of Things Past,
Within a Budding Grove, Part I

As with the mastery of any discipline, one must have a set of basic skills before he can begin. For this book, that set of skills should be within the proximate grasp of most programmers or students of programming. These skills include:

1. A modest competence in mathematics, including ordinary algebra and finite mathematics. A knowledge of vector spaces and of some basic combinatorial analysis is also helpful.
2. An appreciation of the use of algorithms, as distinct from a familiarity with the nuts and bolts of a programming language.
3. A familiarity with a high-level programming language. Pascal is optimal for our purposes; Ada, ALGOL, Modula, or PL/I should also provide adequate background. Readers who know only BASIC, C, or FORTRAN will most likely need to consult one of the scores of tutorial texts on Pascal.

After an initial discussion of something old (computing machines) and something new (data abstraction), most of this chapter is devoted to setting forth some details in each of these three areas. Less advanced readers may prefer to skirt the issue of complexity, which is addressed in Section 1.3.2. In a sense, reading a chapter of this nature resembles taking vitamins — not as tasty as subsequent fare, but a sensible means of averting a painful deficiency later on. It is addressed to the reader who doesn't already have everything in these areas.

1.1 REAL MACHINES AND ABSTRACT DATA

Even as computing machines become ever more prevalent, most users are blissfully unaware of how they really operate at their native level; indeed, they are much happier in not needing that knowledge. By the native level of operation, we refer to machine instructions that, for example:

- add the contents of a memory location, which typically might be a word of 16 or 32 bits, to the contents of a designated machine register of the same size;
- move a byte of 8 bits from one memory location to another memory location;
- test the result of the last preceding arithmetic operation and take the next machine instruction out of sequence if that result is negative or zero.

It is certainly possible to program a computer at this level of detail and many people do, by either choice or necessity. Even in this case, however, most such users actually write their programs in *assembly language* rather than in machine language. By using assembly language, the programmer gains numerous advantages; primarily he is relieved of the responsibility for keeping track of where the instructions and the data are within the memory of the machine.

Nonetheless, at this level of assembly programming, he must still be aware of the nature of each machine instruction (and some of these can be quite difficult to master and remember) and each machine register. Most machines have quite a bit of idiosyncrasy at this level of detail. The stroke that finally frees most users from having to contend with these details is the use of a *high-level language* (*HLL*) such as Ada, ALGOL, APL, BASIC, COBOL, FORTRAN, LISP, Modula, Pascal, PL/I, etc. We assume that any reader of this book is well acquainted with the state of affairs that we have just summarized, and is comfortable using the machine in some HLL, thereby suppressing irrelevant details. By using *control structures*, such as

```
if ... then ... else ...
while ... do ...
   etc.
```

he has acquired a powerful abstraction away from the necessity of composing equivalent sequences of machine instructions.

1.1.1 Data Type and Data Structure

Now, what is the situation with regard to the manipulation of data, as opposed to the composition of instruction sequences? The answer varies according to the HLL that we examine. In many cases the facilities for abstraction are rather limited. We can employ the *primitive data types*:

boolean	corresponding to one bit of computer memory
character	typically one byte (8 bits) of computer memory
integer	typically one word (4 bytes) of computer memory
real	typically two words (8 bytes) of computer memory

and we can employ arrays of any of these types. The integer and real types are imperfect *models* of the integers and the real numbers from mathematics. The modelling process has many nuances and pitfalls, which would merit an entire chapter if this were a treatise in numerical computation. The heart of the matter is that integers and real numbers in mathematics can have an unbounded number of digits (or other symbols) in their representation; but with computers, integers are represented by *fixed-point numbers* of a fixed size, and real numbers are represented by *floating-point numbers*, also of a fixed size. The number of bits actually employed varies with the machine, and it is common for a given manufacturer to have machines accommodating a variety of data sizes. Some representative values for both number types are shown in Table 1.1.

computers	integers (fixed)	reals (floating)
Burroughs	40 bits	48, 88 bits
Control Data	18, 48, 60 bits	60, 108 bits
DEC	16, 36 bits	32, 36, 64, 128 bits
IBM	16, 32 bits	32, 64, 128 bits

Table 1.1 Number Sizes for Typical Computers

The situation with regard to floating-point numbers is much worse than that of fixed-point numbers. It depends, for example, upon how many bits are allocated to the mantissa, how many bits are allocated to the exponent, and what number base is used with the exponent. But no matter what choices are employed for these three parameters, floating-point numbers are poor models of real numbers, for several reasons:

- For any two distinct real numbers u and v, there are always other real numbers w such that $u < w < v$; but with the finite representation of floating-point numbers, this fundamental property does not always hold.
- If we plot the finite set of all floating-point numbers for a given machine on the real number line, we find that the gaps between the numbers are very uneven in length (see Exercise 1.3).
- Although addition and multiplication are associative and distributive for real numbers, the same operations on floating-point numbers are not!

Bounded representation has some peculiar hazards. For example, since $2^{10} > 10^3$ we would expect that a computing machine could faithfully represent any three-digit number by the use of ten bits. Thus the largest three-digit integer 999 can be represented by the ten-bit number 1111100111. However, let us consider the 100 distinct decimal numbers in the range 9.00, 9.01, ... , 9.99. For each of these numbers, the first four of the ten binary bits would have to be 1001, leaving just six bits for the fractional parts. But these six bits yield only 64 distinct binary values into which to map the 100 decimal numbers, so that in the binary representation over two thirds of the numbers will be indistinguishable from neighboring values. Many other examples of numerical pitfalls due to bounded representation can be exhibited [§].

With regard to representing characters in computing machines, there are peculiarities of a different and lesser kind. The characters of interest are mapped, via a *character code*, onto arbitrary bit patterns. On most machines, a character code pattern occupies one byte of storage; thus, in the common EBCDIC code, the bit configuration 11000001 corresponds to the character 'A', 11110101 corresponds to '5', etc. Complications can arise with respect to an insufficient number of bits for the entire set of characters, and also with respect to the arbitrariness of the code. These matters will be discussed in detail in Section 8.2.1.

It would be logical to ask, from what we have said so far, how a computing machine "knows" whether a sequence of bits such as 11000001 is:

- a sequence of boolean values – true, true, false, etc.,
- a short integer value of $2^7 + 2^6 + 2^0 = 193$,
- the character 'A'
- or even something else.

The answer is that the machine does not "know" at all, from the bits themselves.[1] Rather, the programmer – by operating upon the bits in a certain way – causes them to be treated in the desired manner. At the level of assembly language, this is controlled by the choice of machine operation codes. At the level of an HLL, it is controlled by declaring items to be of the desired types, which in turn causes the compiler or interpreter of the HLL to employ the proper operation codes.

Since the proper interpretation of data generally depends upon factors extrinsic to its raw form in bits, what is the most appropriate manner in which to present arbitrary data from a machine to a human when those factors are unknown? If we consider a typical machine word of 32 bits under its alternate interpretations, then:

- 11000011 11110011 11010111 11010110 is obviously awkward,
- 3,287,537,622 obscures boolean and character data values,
- 'C3PO' obscures boolean and integer data values,
- and similar remarks apply for displaying real number data.

A very convenient solution to this dilemma is to group four bits at a time and to display data in *hexadecimal* notation. Just as binary notation uses base 2 for numbers and decimal notation uses base 10, so hexadecimal uses base 16. Hexadecimal needs sixteen symbols for its digits; these symbols are by convention

0 1 2 3 4 5 6 7 8 9 A B C D E F

corresponding to the decimal values

0 1 2 3 4 5 6 7 8 9 10 11 12 13 14 15

Thus, we have

$$11000001_2 = (1100\ \ 0001)_2 = (12\ \ 1)_{16} = \mathrm{C1}_{16} = 12 \times 16^1 + 1 \times 16^0 = 193_{10}$$

and also

---

[1] At least, this is the situation in the von Neumann style of computing machine, which prevails so widely today. There are various exceptions, for example machine architectures in which the data words have associated *tags* that make the data self-describing, to various degrees.

$$11000011\ 11110011\ 11010111\ 11010110_2 = C3F3D7D6_{16}$$

It is often important to be able to do a limited amount of hexadecimal arithmetic by hand. For instance, raw data is usually displayed or dumped from a machine in hexadecimal form; and we must be able to translate this to binary or decimal numeric values or to characters, as the case may require. When this involves too much effort, either precomputed tables or subroutines are commonly used. Also, we sometimes need to do hexadecimal addition or subtraction; an example of this is combining offsets with the contents of registers in a memory dump. These operations are easily performed, as we can see from the examples:

$$845A + 1A6B = (8\ 4\ 5\ 10) + (1\ 10\ 6\ 11) = (9\ 14\ 12\ 5) = 9EC5$$

$$845A - 1A6B = (8\ 4\ 5\ 10) - (1\ 10\ 6\ 11) = (6\ 9\ 14\ 15) = 69EF$$

The primitive types that we have been discussing are just one *attribute* of data. An attribute is a generic quality used to describe an object, and a given attribute may have several possible values. For instance, a person has the attribute of sex, with the two possible values of male and female; some other attributes of persons are height, weight, and age – with the values measured in inches, pounds, and years, respectively. We have seen that in computing, data has the attribute of type, with possible values of boolean, character, integer, and real. However, data can also have other attributes. One is precision, for example 32 or 64 bits for reals; another is number base, either binary or decimal.

The attribute of data that is the principal concern of this book is that of structure, or "shape." Structures are obtained by taking collections of primitive data items and grouping them together in particular ways. From familiarity with HLL's, you know about one such structure, the array. Others that we will investigate are: sets, records, lists, stacks, queues, trees, graphs, and strings. As we will point out repeatedly, each of these is a *logical structure*, and it is convenient to think about them without regard to how they are actually represented in a machine. Yet, the issue of their *physical representation* is an important one that we need to address explicitly in each case. As illustrated in our earlier discussion of integers and reals, the process of modelling an abstraction (that is, choosing a representation) can have many ramifications. We will see further evidence of this point in Section 1.4.1.

1.1.2 Abstract Data Types

We have seen that the use of control structures for execution sequencing is of great advantage in HLL's. The ability to define and use functions and procedures is perhaps even more important. In an arithmetic expression, we are initially restricted to the operators +, -, *, and /. These are then augmented by system functions for absolute value, modulus, square root, etc. Beyond that, we can define any function that we like, and then invoke it at any point within our program; thus, we can effectively expand upon the primitive operators with arbitrarily defined ones. If such a function is properly defined (that is, programmed), then anybody who uses it can be unconcerned with numerous details of its implementation. In fact, it can be implemented in many different ways, all of which are correct from the point of view of the user, who simply presents input arguments and obtains output values in return.

A powerful concept for data is to provide a similar definitional facility for data structures. When this idea is carried out completely, an *abstract data type* (*ADT*) is defined. Such a definition specifies both the set of permissible values that a variable (or parameter) of this type may assume and also the permissible operations on instances of ADT's. The manner in which the ADT is represented is hidden from the user, and he can only operate upon instances of ADT's via procedure or function calls. This mechanism also ensures that no illegitimate values can ever be created. Several advantages accrue from the methodology of ADT's. First, just as the user of an ordinary program function can trust in its correctness, so the user of an ADT can trust in the correct consequences of its use. Also, a program written in terms of ADT's is completely portable to any machine, as long as correct implementations of the ADT's exist for that machine. A simple instance of an ADT might be for complex numbers, with functions to perform addition, multiplication, conjugation, etc. The actual representation could be in terms of polar coordinates or rectangular coordinates, or it might even switch from one to the other, but such considerations would be transparent to the user.

The current state of computer science is such that the concepts just cited are not yet all formally available in most programming languages. However, the notion of an ADT is still of great utility in the first stages of a programming project. By using it, a programmer can effectively distill the essential logic of a data structure from the details of its possible representations. To put it positively, he should first specify *what* he wants with his structures, and only after that take into consideration *how* to implement them. To put it appositively, his design may profit from his awareness of representation issues, but such issues should not distort the design. In this book, we choose to approach data structures by asking what and then how in an informal and unsystematic manner, rather than by defining and using ADT's in any rigorous fashion. However, since any serious student should be conversant with the more formal approach, these matters are discussed in Chapter 9.

The programming language Pascal does provide some of the definitional power that we have just described. A programmer can define and subsequently use arbitrarily complex data structures of his choosing; but Pascal does not provide any means for ensuring that these data structures will always be used correctly. In a language that truly supports ADT's, it is as if the implementation details are hidden in a black box; but the analogy in Pascal is that they are enclosed within a clear glass box, thus leaving open the possibility of misuse. More recent HLL's such as Ada [U.S. Dept. of Defense 1983] and Modula [Wirth 1985] fully support the ADT concept, but they are yet to become the lingua franca that Pascal is. We will discuss the facilities of Pascal for data typing in Section 1.4.2.

1.2 MATHEMATICAL BACKGROUND

The level of mathematics that we need is modest, since we will usually analyze algorithms in only modest detail. By analyzing algorithms, we basically mean finding quantitative results about the time or the memory requirements for their execution; this matter will be explained in Section 1.3.2.

A. To begin with, we will need some concepts that are very simple but possibly unfamiliar to some readers.

1. $y = \lfloor x$ is the *floor* of x; that is, y is the greatest integer such that $y \leq x$. Thus,

$$\lfloor 3.2 = 3 \qquad \lfloor 7 = 7 \qquad \lfloor -5.8 = -6 \quad (\text{not } -5)$$

2. $y = \lceil x$ is the *ceiling* of x; that is, y is the least integer such that $y \geq x$. Thus,

$$\lceil 3.2 = 4 \qquad \lceil 7 = 7 \qquad \lceil -5.8 = -5 \quad (\text{not } -6)$$

3. From the operation of dividing z by y to obtain an integer-valued quotient, we get the two operations

$$v = z \text{ div } y = \lfloor (z \div y), \quad \text{and} \quad u = z \bmod y = z - v \times y \tag{1.1}$$

The operator *div* yields the integer quotient and the operator *mod* yields the *modulus*, or remainder. For example,

$$\begin{array}{lll} 13 \text{ div } 5 = 2 & 60 \text{ div } 12 = 5 & -19 \text{ div } 4 = -5 \\ 13 \bmod 5 = 3 & 60 \bmod 12 = 0 & -19 \bmod 4 = \ \ 1 \end{array}$$

We should caution you that there are alternative definitions of div and mod, based on using truncate in lieu of floor. For example, in certain implementations of Pascal, -19 **div** $4 = -4$ and -19 **mod** $4 = -3$.

B. Familiarity with *logarithms* is presumed. The usual notation is

$$\log_{10} u = v, \text{ or } \log u = v, \text{ for } u = 10^v \tag{1.2}$$

If, more generally, the base value is b, then the notation is

$$\log_b u = v, \text{ for } u = b^v = b^{\log_b u} = \log_b (b^u) \tag{1.3}$$

Two base values that are important for our purposes are $b = 2$ and $b = e = 2.718281828\ldots$. For the former, the common notation is

$$\lg u = v, \text{ for } u = 2^v \tag{1.4}$$

The latter case yields the natural logarithm, wherein

$$\ln u = v, \text{ for } u = e^v \tag{1.5}$$

To convert logarithms from one base b to another base a simply requires multiplication by a constant, since

$$\log_a u = \log_a b \times \log_b u = \frac{\log_b u}{\log_b a} \tag{1.6}$$

C. The *factorial* of a non-negative integer n is $n!$, defined as follows:

$$\begin{aligned} &\text{for } n = 0, \ n! = 1 \\ &\text{for } n > 0, \ n! = n \times (n-1)! = n \times (n-1) \times (n-2) \times \cdots \times 1 \end{aligned} \tag{1.7}$$

Related to the factorial are the *binomial coefficients*, denoted by either $C(n,r)$ or $\binom{n}{r}$, where for $n \geq r \geq 0$

$$\binom{n}{r} = \frac{n \times (n-1) \times (n-2) \times \cdots \times (n-r+1)}{1 \times 2 \times 3 \times \cdots \times r} = \frac{n!}{(n-r)!\, r!} \tag{1.8}$$

$C(n,r)$ is the number of *combinations*, or ways in which r objects can be selected from n (distinct) objects; for example, $C(7,2) = 21$, $C(7,3) = 35$, etc. The binomial coefficients get their name from the fact that they occur as the coefficients in the familiar binomial expansion

$$(a+b)^n = \sum_{r=0}^{n} \binom{n}{r} a^{n-r} b^r \tag{1.9}$$

There are numerous identities relating the binomial coefficients. Some of the more significant ones, all with simple proofs, are:

$$\binom{n}{0} = \binom{n}{n} = 1 \tag{1.10a}$$

$$\binom{n}{1} = \binom{n}{n-1} = n \tag{1.10b}$$

$$\binom{n}{r} = \binom{n}{n-r} \tag{1.10c}$$

$$\binom{n}{r} = \binom{n-1}{r} + \binom{n-1}{r-1} \tag{1.10d}$$

and, for $r \neq 0$

$$\binom{n}{r} = \frac{n}{r} \times \binom{n-1}{r-1} \tag{1.10e}$$

Also, related to the factorial and the binomial coefficients are the *permutations* of r objects out of n, defined by

$$P(n,r) = r! \times C(n,r) = \frac{n!}{(n-r)!} \tag{1.11}$$

In a combination the order among the selected elements is irrelevant; in a permutation, however, the order is significant. Thus, $P(7,2) = 42$, $P(7,3) = 210$, etc. In particular, $P(n,n) = n!$, and it represents all the different orders in which n distinct elements can be arranged in n distinct positions.

D. There are two common ways to represent a permutation of n elements. The first is illustrated by

$$\begin{pmatrix} a & b & c & d & e & f & g \\ d & f & g & b & e & a & c \end{pmatrix} \tag{1.12}$$

This signifies that the element in the first position goes to the fourth position (a replaces d), the element in the second position goes to the sixth position (b replaces f), etc. Typically, the first row of such a representation is implied rather than given explicitly; so, for example, $(d\ f\ g\ b\ e\ a\ c)$ would suffice for Eq. 1.12.

The second common way to express a permutation is in *cycle notation.* Our same example would, in this style, be represented by

$$(d\ b\ f\ a)\ (g\ c)\ (e) \tag{1.13}$$

In each cycle $(x_1, x_2, \ldots, x_k)$, the element x_k replaces x_1, and for all $i < k$ the element x_i replaces x_{i+1}. When representing permutations in cycle notation, it is often desirable to obtain a unique representation by either of two sets of transformation rules. The first of these sets is:

I.1 Arrange each cycle so that the smallest element in that cycle is the first element in the cycle.

I.2 Delete any singleton cycles, such as (e) in Eq. 1.13.

I.3 List the remaining cycles in order of their first elements.

When these steps are applied to Eq. 1.13, we obtain the notation

$$(a\ d\ b\ f)\ (c\ g) \tag{1.14}$$

On the other hand, the following set of rules is frequently more useful for working with permutations:

II.1 Arrange each cycle so that the smallest element in that cycle is the first element in the cycle.

II.2 Retain any singleton cycles.

II.3 List the cycles in *decreasing* order of their first elements.

When these steps are applied to Eq. 1.13, we obtain the *canonical form*

$$(e)\ (c\ g)\ (a\ d\ b\ f) \tag{1.15}$$

With the canonical form, the parentheses around the cycles can be omitted, yielding

$$e\ c\ g\ a\ d\ b\ f \tag{1.16}$$

It is safe to omit the parentheses because they can easily be reconstructed by the following rule: Insert a left parenthesis preceding any global left-to-right minimum. Thus, in reconstructing Eq. 1.15 from Eq. 1.16, there are minima at e, c, and a.

E. The *Fibonacci numbers* are the sequence of integers F_n, as follows:

1, 1, 2, 3, 5, 8, 13, 21, 34 ...

and defined by the relationship

$$F_1 = 1, \quad F_2 = 1$$
$$F_n = F_{n-1} + F_{n-2} \qquad (n = 3, 4, \ldots) \tag{1.17}$$

They describe a pattern of growth frequently found in nature. Examples include population growth in idealized situations, spatial arrangement of leaves and flowers in plants, etc. Closer to our purpose, they also describe various phenomena in the analysis of data structures and algorithms.

F. Some basic concepts from set theory are also important for our purposes. However, we will examine them in situ when we discuss sets as data structures in Section 2.4.

The concepts that we have described to this point are essential for our purposes. Some less elementary ones will be introduced as needed; they include linear algebra, recurrence relations, harmonic numbers, generating functions, and elements of graph theory. Readers who are unfamiliar with these areas should not be concerned about losing very much of the overall presentation. Background material can be found in [§] if needed.

1.2.1 *O*-Notation

It is common to have a quantity whose value depends upon some parameter n. A simple example of this is $V(n)$, the sum of the first n integers

$$V(n) = \sum_{i=1}^{n} i = 1 + 2 + 3 + \cdots + n \tag{1.18}$$

It is easy to show that $V(n)$ has the exact value $V(n) = \frac{1}{2}n \times (n+1)$. This is often not as pertinent, however, as the simpler fact that, as n increases, $V(n)$ is of the *order of magnitude* of n^2, or $V(n) = O(n^2)$. This idea can be made both more general and more precise at the same time. The generality comes from speaking about $O(f(n))$, where f may be any function of n. Thus, for the sum of squares

$$W(n) = \sum_{i=1}^{n} i^2 = 1 + 4 + 9 + \cdots + n^2 = \frac{n \times (n+1) \times (2n+1)}{6} \tag{1.19}$$

the pertinent fact is that $W(n) = O(n^3)$. We obtain precision from the definition:

$$r(n) = O(f(n)) \text{ iff there are two constants } C \text{ and } n_0,$$
$$\text{such that } |r(n)| \le C \times |f(n)| \text{ whenever } n > n_0. \tag{1.20}$$

This is read as "$r(n)$ is order of $f(n)$," or "$r(n)$ is big Oh of $f(n)$," if and only if ...

By way of illustration, for $r(n) = V(n)$, then $f(n) = n^2$. If $n_0 = 2$ then $C = 0.7$ will work, and if $n_0 = 5$ then $C = 0.6$ will work, etc.; actually, for n_0 sufficiently large, we can get C as close to 0.5 as we like. Although O-expressions are used in equations – as in $V(n) = O(n^2)$ – such equations have the peculiar property of being "one-sided"; they are formal means for conveying information from the right hand side about the left hand side, as in Eq. 1.20. An alternative point of view that makes this one-sidedness more explicit is to interpret Eq. 1.20 as saying that $r(n)$ is included (in a set theoretic sense, see Section 2.4) among those functions that are asymptotically dominated by $f(n)$. O-notation is very useful in contexts that have nothing to do with machine computation [Knuth 1973a]; it is also a very important tool for analyzing and describing the behavior of algorithms, as we will see in Section 1.3.2.

1.3 ALGORITHMS

In many ways, the study of data structures and the study of algorithms are complementary. Indeed, this entire book could be rewritten with the emphasis upon algorithms and yet cover many of the same topics. Therefore, it behooves us to review just what an algorithm is. An algorithm can be defined as an unambiguous specification of the steps to follow in order to solve a general problem, with the assurance that the process will terminate after a finite number of steps. This statement is straightforward, but we should be sure that we understand all that is implied by the definition.

General solution. An algorithm specifies how to solve some general problem. The problem may have one input or several, or even none; but there is no solution without at least one output. On the other hand, for many algorithms, just one bit of output (true or false) is sufficient – for example, is n a prime number? An algorithm that solved the same problem every time would not be very useful; rather it should solve a general class of problems, such as finding the square root of x, as opposed to the square root of 3.

Unambiguous. The steps to be followed must be unambiguous. There must be a determinism about the entire set of steps, and none of them can invoke any magic. Thus, most kitchen recipes resemble algorithms but fall short in terms of ambiguity, due to phrases such as: add a pinch of salt, stir over medium heat, etc. In some cases, though, this ambiguity is less apparent, as in a computational "recipe" that instructs us to choose an element x such that ..., or to choose the best (?) route from A to B.

Termination. Finally, algorithms must be guaranteed to terminate. Herein arises the principal distinction between an algorithm and a procedure. It is quite easy to have a procedure that will run forever (until interrupted), as most beginning programmers discover, or as in the case of an operating system. Sometimes, it can be difficult to decide whether or not a computational procedure satisfies this criterion. There is, for instance, the following famous "algorithm," which takes a positive integer n as input and computes a sequence of integers from it.

```
while n > 1 do
   if (n mod 2) = 0 then
      n := n div 2
   else
      n := n * 3 + 1;
```

As an example, starting with $n = 7$, the following sequence is computed:

$$7, 22, 11, 34, 17, 52, 26, 13, 40, 20, 10, 5, 16, 8, 4, 2, 1$$

No one has been able to prove as yet that this process will terminate for all positive integers n. There's no need to expend machine cycles, however, since its termination has been established for all values of n up to an extremely large limit.

The comparison between algorithms and programs is reminiscent of the comparison between abstract data types and their representations. The essence of an algorithm is independent of any particular machine or programming language. Yet we can only capture the algorithm by expressing it in some particular language. We will take up the subject of representing algorithms in Section 1.4. The remainder of this section deals with algorithms in more general terms.

When considered in their own right, algorithms have a curious taxonomy. Some useful characterizations that are employed to describe them are: deterministic, nondeterministic, probabilistic, greedy, oblivious, on-line, off-line, recursive, etc. We will be concerned almost exclusively with deterministic algorithms, although we will discuss the nondeterministic case in Chapter 6. The descriptions greedy, oblivious, and on-line and off-line are modestly significant, and will be illustrated subsequently. Recursion, however, is of fundamental importance and will be discussed in the next section. A distinct and very important issue is the characterization of algorithms in terms of the amount of time and the amount of memory space that they require for execution; we will expand on that in Section 1.3.2.

1.3.1 Recursion

Recursion is the phenomenon wherein an object is defined in terms of itself. We can find recursion in many guises. It describes, for instance, the infinite series of reflections that we see when we stand between two mirrors that are not quite parallel to each other. It also occurs commonly in mathematics. Examples of this are Eq. 1.7 for factorials, Eq. 1.10d for binomial coefficients and Eq. 1.17 for Fibonacci numbers. Another example from mathematics is found in the inductive definition of the natural numbers:[2]

(a) 1 is a natural number, and

(b) if n is a natural number, then so is $n + 1$.

---

[2] This common, intuitive definition by clauses (a) and (b) has several technical deficiencies. They can be redressed by using a more detailed set of specifications known as the *Peano postulates*.

Our interest in recursion, of course, is that many algorithms (and data structures!) employ it in their definition. Note that, in order to avoid infinite regress, a recursive definition will have two parts: (a) a basis clause that specifies some initial value(s), and (b) an inductive clause that specifies how to obtain subsequent values.

```
function ALGOR_A (n: integer): integer;

var     i,p,q,r: integer;

begin
  if n <= 2 then
     ALGOR_A := 1
  else begin
     q := 1; r := 1;
     for i := 1 to n - 2 do begin
        p := q;  q := r;  r := p + q;
     end;
     ALGOR_A := r;
  end;
end;
```

Algorithm 1.1 ALGOR_A

Recursion is especially useful because it often leads to definitions that are concise and intuitive. In demonstration of this point, consider the function ALGOR_A (Algorithm 1.1), which uses *iteration* rather than recursion. Can you recognize what it is computing? You should experiment with it for several values of n before comparing it with the definition given in Eq. 1.17. On the other hand, recursive definitions are not always easier to comprehend. Consider, for example, the function ALGOR_B (Algorithm 1.2). What is a simpler way to specify its effect? If it is not obvious to you, then try the algorithm for some sample set of values, such as $p = 0$, $m = 7$, $n = 4$.

```
function ALGOR_B (p,m,n: integer): integer;
begin
  if n = 0 then
     ALGOR_B:= p
  else
     ALGOR_B := ALGOR_B (p + m,m,n - 1);
end;
```

Algorithm 1.2 ALGOR_B

Expressing an algorithm in a manner that enhances insight and expressing it in a manner that maximizes computational efficiency often represent conflicting goals.

As an example, the computation of F_7 by applying Eq. 1.17 would expand into the set of evaluations in Figure 1.1; a direct computation by ALGOR_A would be much more efficient, particularly as n becomes large. In Section 5.4 we will discuss the transformation of an algorithm between equivalent (that is, producing the same answers for all inputs) non-recursive and recursive forms. In this section our objective has been simply to elucidate the basic nature of recursion, since it occurs in both the algorithms and the data structures that we will be studying. The subject is a large one in its own right, and we will return to it from time to time, beginning in Chapter 4.

$$
\begin{aligned}
F_7 &= F_5 + F_6 = (F_3 + F_4) + (F_4 + F_5) \\
&= ((F_1 + F_2) + (F_2 + F_3)) + ((F_2 + F_3) + (F_3 + F_4)) \\
&= ((1 + 1) + (1 + (F_1 + F_2))) + ((1 + (F_1 + F_2)) + ((F_1 + F_2) + (F_2 + F_3))) \\
&= (2 + (1 + (1 + 1))) + ((1 + (1 + 1)) + ((1 + 1) + (1 + (F_1 + F_2)))) \\
&= (2 + (1 + 2)) + ((1 + 2) + (2 + (1 + (1 + 1)))) \\
&= (2 + 3) + (3 + (2 + (1 + 2))) = 5 + (3 + (2 + 3)) \\
&= 5 + (3 + 5) = 5 + 8 = 13
\end{aligned}
$$

Figure 1.1 Evaluation of F_7 by Eq. 1.17

1.3.2 Analysis of Algorithms

Discovering that a particular algorithm can solve some problem is just part of the story. A significant consideration beyond its capability is its cost. In real life, computing costs can be measured in many different ways: coding time, debugging time, dollars expended, physical resources required, etc. In discussions of data structures and algorithms, however, cost is considered to have two principal components: the amount of computer time (in milliseconds, minutes, months, etc.), and the amount of computer memory required for the execution of the algorithm. By memory we mean primarily that which is required for the data, including temporary or working values, and not that which is required for the program itself.

All of the problems that we will be considering have some size n associated with them. What is meant by size? In many problems, this is easy to decide. If we are doing a calculation involving an input of n items, then the size is often just n. Assuming that we can abstract such a value of n from all the details of a problem, the analysis proceeds from the observation that, as n increases, so may the costs, both in time and in memory space. Analyzing an algorithm means trying to estimate these costs as a function of the size. Often one cost can be traded off against the other. For instance, a simple loop to add a set of n numbers in memory would require relatively less space but more time than would a program that added them via a succession of n add instructions without a loop. However, most of the significant trade-offs between time and memory are not so simple, and involve swapping time for a choice of data structure, as opposed to space for instructions. Our discussions of algorithmic complexity will primarily be in terms of time, since that is usually the more critical resource, but space will enter the discussion in some cases.

In this section, we first describe the insights to be gained by classifying algorithmic costs in broad categories of *algorithmic complexity*. Next we consider some of the problems associated with trying to measure that complexity for a given algorithm. In all of these discussions of the effectiveness of algorithms, the reader might plausibly associate computational efficiency solely with choosing a good algorithm. Such a belief would be very misguided. The choice of an appropriate representation (that is, data structure) for a problem is, in many cases, the most significant choice to be made for reducing computational effort. Although the corroboration of that claim depends upon the rest of this book, we can find another, dramatic illustration in astronomy. For hundreds of years, early scientists used the model devised by Ptolemy to describe the apparent motions of the planets in the heavens. The key assumption of this model held that the planets and the sun move around the earth; and this necessitated the use of epicycloids (circles with loops around their circumference) to make the observed data fit the theory. By contrast, Copernicus and Kepler developed a model in which the planets move around the sun; in this representation, planetary motions are much more simply explained by using ellipses. Not only that, but it was this basic model of planetary motion which led Newton to formulate his epochal Law of Gravitation. Imagine the state of science today if we were still laboring under the weight of the earlier model.

1.3.2.1 Complexity Classes. In analyzing an algorithm, we do not try to estimate precise costs. Too many factors are hard to quantify: how efficiently the algorithm is expressed in a program, how efficiently the compiler or interpreter will translate the program, what machine the program is run on, etc. Instead we try to find some expression that depends upon an obvious, explicit parameter (or parameters) n, and that can be used to approximate the performance of the algorithm. This is the reason why the O-notation of Section 1.2.1 is of such importance for computation.

With regard to the definition given by Eq. 1.20, although there are algorithms for which the value of the constant C is of interest, the nature of the expression $f(n)$ is much more significant. Why is this type of analysis so important, given that it is often so crude? In most of the algorithms that we will study, a major consideration is the feasibility of applying them to problems with larger and larger values of n. As n grows, how does the time to execute an algorithm increase, if its complexity is proportional to $f(n)$? Some common functional forms of $f(n)$, and their values as n increases, are illustrated in Table 1.2.

The importance of these effects can be demonstrated more effectively by changing the point of view. Let us associate with each form of $f(n)$ a constant that hypothetically allows us to measure elapsed time for some algorithm of that complexity class in units of milliseconds, that is $T = C \times f(n)$. Then, for each $f(n)$, we can invert this equation to find $n = s(T)$, the largest size problem that can be handled for any time interval. Moreover, we will "load the dice" by assigning constants that discriminate against those $f(n)$ with lower growth rates. The results of this exercise are shown in Table 1.3.

$f(n)$	$n = 3$	$n = 10$	$n = 30$	$n = 100$	$n = 300$	$n = 1000$
$\lg n$	1.6	3.3	4.9	6.6	8.2	10
n	3	10	30	100	300	1000
$n \lg n$	4.8	33	147	664	2469	9966
n^2	9	100	900	10000	90000	10^6
n^3	27	1000	27000	10^6	2.7×10^7	10^9
2^n	8	1024	10^9	10^{30}	10^{90}	10^{300}
10^n	1000	10^{10}	10^{30}	10^{100}	10^{300}	10^{1000}

Table 1.2 Growth of Various $f(n)$ with n.

The most important feature of Table 1.3 is that, whereas with algorithms A1 – A4 it is feasible to solve problems of larger and larger size by making longer computations, that is not the case for algorithms A5 and A6. Increasing the time available for computation pays off for the former, where there is a multiplicative factor between successive columns; but it has relatively little effect on the latter, where there is an additive factor between successive columns. Thus it is far more effective to find a faster algorithm than it is to compute for a longer time, or even to acquire a faster machine. This is true even though we have chosen constants that favor the latter algorithms. The benefit of these biased constants makes A5 and A6 competitive for small problems, but that benefit is of no avail as n increases.

$f(n)$	1 second	1 minute	1 hour	1 week	1 year
A1: $300 \times n$	3	180	10800	2×10^6	10^8
A2: $100 \times n \lg n$	4	91	3103	3.3×10^5	1.3×10^7
A3: $30 \times n^2$	5	44	346	4489	32377
A4: $10 \times n^3$	4	18	70	390	1454
A5: 3×2^n	8	14	20	27	33
A6: 1×10^n	3	4	6	8	10

Table 1.3 Attainable Problem Size n for Given $f(n)$ in Given Time T

It is clear from Tables 1.2 and 1.3 that an algorithm with *exponential complexity* (A5,A6) is far less satisfactory than one with *polynomial complexity* (A1 – A4). In fact, if the only algorithms that are known for solving a problem are all of exponential complexity, then that problem is often said to be *intractable*. For large values of n, such a problem may be solvable in theory, but it is not solvable in practice, since we cannot wait years or millennia for the calculation to terminate. Is it really reasonable to make such a distinction between polynomial and exponential algorithms? After all, how feasible is a computation of $O(10^6 \times n^{1000})$? There seem to be two answers confirming the value of the distinction. One is that useful polynomial algorithms are, in practice, always of quite low degree. Another reason, significant for analysis, is that the class of polynomial algorithms is closed under composition. We will have more to say about the gap between polynomial and exponential complexity in Chapter 6.

1.3.2.2 Measuring Complexity. It is conventional to denote the amount of work, or time, required to solve a problem of size n with a particular algorithm, by $T(n)$. Analyzing an algorithm to determine its performance means determining that $T(n) = O(f(n))$, for some $f(n)$ like those of the preceding section. Thus, Eq. 1.19 could represent a generic example wherein the terms of the series $W(n)$ correspond to the work required to compute successive values $s_1, s_2, \ldots$ in some other series S, and where the work for the term s_i is proportional to i^2. In this case the complexity $T(n)$ of computing S is $O(n^3)$.

More typically, we have to start our analysis at a lower level, by counting how many times each step of the algorithm is executed. A more refined measure might take into account the different amounts of time required by different steps, but we sweep that under the rug by choosing a sufficiently large value for the constant C. In fact, all that really matters is the time required for the steps that dominate the computation. These steps might be multiplications for one problem, data comparisons for another, data moves for yet another, etc. Having identified these, we proceed by trying to estimate their frequency of execution. In the next paragraphs, let P_i and P_j represent blocks of algorithmic steps that are executed in some approximate times, and let $P_{i,j}$ represent a sub-block of algorithmic steps within P_i.

If we have an algorithm of the general form P_i followed by P_j, such that P_i executes in time $T_i = O(f(m))$ and P_j executes in time $T_j = O(g(n))$, then the overall time complexity for executing P_i followed by P_j is

$$\begin{aligned} T_i + T_j &\leq C_1 |f(r)| + C_2 |g(r)| \qquad \text{for } r > m_0 \text{ and } r > n_0 \\ &\leq (C_1 + C_2) \max(|f(r)|, |g(r)|) \end{aligned}$$

In other words,

$$T = T_i + T_j = O(\max(f(m), g(n))) \tag{1.21}$$

This is the additive property of O-notation. In the case of two successive definite iterations

```
for i := 1 to m do begin
  ...
end;
for j := 1 to n do begin
  ...
end;
```

Eq. 1.21 reduces to max (m,n).

Next, consider the case of an algorithm P containing parts P_i and sub-parts $P_{i,j}$, with the properties:

- the outermost steps P_i execute in time $T_i = O(f(m))$, and
- the innermost steps $P_{i,j}$ execute in time $T_{i,j} = O(g(n))$ for each single outermost step P_i.

Then the overall time complexity for executing P is determined by the product of the two:

$$T = O(f(m) \times g(n)) \tag{1.22}$$

by an appropriate choice of constants. This is the multiplicative property of O-notation. In the case of two nested definite iterations

```
for i := 1 to m do begin
  ...
  for j := 1 to n do begin
    ...
  end;
  ...
end;
```

Eq. 1.22 reduces to $m \times n$.

Although estimations for definite iteration are easy, estimations in the cases of indefinite iteration (for example, **while** ... **do** ... or **repeat** ... **until** ...) or in the cases of alternate path selection (for example, **if** ... **then** ... **else** ... or **case** ... **of** ...) require more elaborate analysis methods. As an extreme example, Knuth uses properties of the gamma function and complex-variable theory when analyzing radix exchange sorting [Knuth 1973b].

Note from Eq. 1.20 that an estimate in terms of O-notation represents an upper bound analysis for a particular algorithm. A different point of view is to look for a lower bound analysis, as represented by Ω-notation:

$$\begin{gathered} r(n) = \Omega(g(n)) \text{ iff there are two constants } C \text{ and } n_0, \\ \text{such that } |r(n)| \geq C \times |g(n)| \text{ whenever } n > n_0. \end{gathered} \tag{1.23}$$

Although Ω-analysis can be applied to an algorithm, the more interesting and difficult question is to apply it to a problem. In other words, we would like to know the lower bound for the complexity of solving a problem, using *any* algorithm, and this requires some fundamental insight into the nature of the problem. It is usually easy to obtain a trivial estimate for Ω. For instance, we would expect any problem that has m inputs and n outputs to require at least $\Omega(m + n)$ work, by virtue of the usual necessity to read each input and write each output. However, depending upon the nature of the problem, the complexity may be inherently greater than this. Although we will mainly characterize results in terms of O-notation, there will be a few instances of Ω-notation, for example, with matrix multiplication, sorting, etc.

If we have an algorithm to compute $r(n)$, there is also the felicitous possibility that $C_1 f(n) \leq r(n) \leq C_2 f(n)$, for some $f(n)$ and for appropriate constants C_1 and C_2. Thus, our algorithm is both $\Omega(f(n))$ and $O(f(n))$, denoted by $r(n) = \Theta(f(n))$. If a problem has complexity $\Omega(f(n))$, and if we have an algorithm for solving it with complexity $\Theta(f(n))$, then the only possible room for improvement lies in improving the constant factor.

The actual values of the input, as opposed to just n, the number of such items, constitute another important factor for the performance of an algorithm. When the performance of an algorithm does not depend upon the actual values, then that algorithm is said to be *oblivious*, which greatly simplifies the analysis. When an algorithm is not oblivious, then the worst-case complexity that we obtain using O-notation may be very infrequent. It may be much more meaningful to try to estimate its average performance. However, this estimation depends upon knowing the probability distribution for all the possible sets of input values. This can usually only be guessed at, and a uniform distribution is often employed, but such an assumption is patently unjustified in many cases.

Analysis of algorithms is a very active area in computer science, and the use of O, Θ, and Ω is poorly standardized [Knuth 1976a]. In particular, it is common to find $O(f(n))$ employed when one of the other measures is more appropriate. Further discussion of these issues can be found in Weide [1977].

†1.3.2.3 Recurrence Relations. Let's suppose that you and an acquaintance are having a friendly game of chance, such as matching pennies. He starts with 38¢ and you start with 12¢. At every play the two of you simultaneously flip a coin and look for heads and tails. In the two cases that the coins match one of you keeps both coins, and in the two cases that they do not match the other keeps both coins. Thus, at every play one of you wins 1¢ from the other. What are the probabilities that: (a) he wins all the money, (b) you win all the money, or (c) the game never ends? We'll begin by using the variable p_j to denote your expectation of winning all 50¢, starting with j pennies. Note that, with equal likelihood after the first play, you will have either $j - 1$ pennies or $j + 1$ pennies, and be confronted with the new expectation p_{j-1} or p_{j+1}. The only two ways that you can start with j pennies and win everything are via these other states, and so we have the *recurrence relation*

$$p_j = \frac{p_{j-1} + p_{j+1}}{2}, \quad \text{or} \quad p_j - p_{j-1} = p_{j+1} - p_j$$

We can spell out the latter formula for $j = 1, 2, \ldots, 49$ as follows:

$$p_1 - p_0 = p_2 - p_1 = \cdots = p_{50} - p_{49} = d$$

for some constant difference d. Summing these 50 individual formulas, we obtain $p_{50} - p_0 = 50d$. But observe that $p_{50} = 1$ (you did it) and $p_0 = 0$ (hope is lost), so that $d = .02$. It is now easy to find that $p_{12} = .24$. Moreover, the analysis from your opponent's point of view is complementary, with the result that he will win with probability $p_{38} = .76$. Thus, even though there are an infinite number of intermediate possibilities, it is a statistical certainty that one of you will eventually experience the painful condition known as *Gambler's Ruin*.

Many phenomena in mathematics are most naturally expressed in terms of a recurrence relation between values of a function for some integer values of its arguments. Some examples include the binomial coefficients, the Fibonacci numbers, etc. If the recurrence relation is not too complicated, we may be able to solve it, thereby obtaining a closed form solution. The complexity analysis of recursive algorithms in turn depends upon the ability to formulate and solve such recurrence relations. To illustrate these points, let us take Eq. 1.17, the definition of the Fibonacci numbers, and rewrite it as

$$F_n - F_{n-1} - F_{n-2} = 0 \tag{1.24}$$

This is a particularly simple form of recurrence in that it is linear, with constant coefficients (that is, all 1's), and *homogeneous* (that is, the linear combination sums to zero). As with solving a linear differential equation, this homogeneous equation has homogeneous solutions of the form $F_n = r^n$. Substituting this in Eq. 1.24 and cancelling powers of r yields the *characteristic equation*

$$r^2 - r^1 - r^0 = 0 \tag{1.25}$$

By the quadratic formula, this equation has two distinct roots

$$r_1 = \frac{1+\sqrt{5}}{2}, \quad \text{and} \quad r_2 = \frac{1-\sqrt{5}}{2} \tag{1.26}$$

The linear homogeneous form of Eq. 1.24 then guarantees that the complete solution to it is a linear combination of the solutions corresponding to the two distinct roots:

$$F_n = A_1 r_1^n + A_2 r_2^n \tag{1.27}$$

with the constants A_1 and A_2 to be determined from the initial values $F_1 = 1$ and $F_2 = 1$. It simplifies matters to define $F_0 = 0$, and then use Eq. 1.27 with F_0 and F_1, whence we have

$$F_0 = 0 = A_1 + A_2$$

$$F_1 = 1 = A_1 r_1 + A_2 r_2 = \frac{A_1(1+\sqrt{5})}{2} + \frac{A_2(1-\sqrt{5})}{2}$$

These yield

$$A_1 = 1/\sqrt{5}, \quad \text{and} \quad A_2 = -1/\sqrt{5} \tag{1.28}$$

from which, finally, the nth Fibonacci number is given by

$$F_n = \frac{(r_1^n - r_2^n)}{\sqrt{5}} \tag{1.29}$$

with r_1 and r_2 as in Eq. 1.26.

We now have a closed form solution for F_n. Let us compare our two original algorithms for computing F_n, ALGOR_A and the method of Eq. 1.17. ALGOR_A is clearly $O(n)$. From Figure 1.1, we observe that the recursive algorithm is $O(F_n)$, which we have just seen is $O(r^n)$. Even though the iterated algorithm is dramatically better than the recursive one, it is not optimal; as we will see in Section 5.4.2, there is an $O(\lg n)$ algorithm for computing Fibonacci numbers.

Several more complicated possibilities can arise in solving recurrence relations: non-homogeneity, non-linearity, repeated roots, complex roots, etc. In this book, we will employ some of these other solution techniques in an ad hoc manner, for example in Section 2.5.1. A more systematic treatment of the topic can be found in Lueker [1980].

1.4 LANGUAGES AND PROGRAMS

Computing has its own Tower of Babel, which forces most programmers to become multilingual out of sheer necessity. There have been repeated attempts to lessen these effects and to make the representation of algorithms relatively independent of particular programming languages. We have elected to use none of these, but rather to employ the language Pascal to represent the algorithms in this book. Some of the reasons for this choice will be discussed in the next section.

The remainder of this preliminary material about languages and programs is devoted to two other issues. One of these has to do with something comparatively new; it centers on the facilities in Pascal for defining and then using data of arbitrary type and structure. The other deals with something that should be old to most readers, the nature of procedures, functions, and parameters.

1.4.1 Representation of Algorithms

Methods that have been used to represent algorithms independently of particular programming languages include:

A. natural language such as English
B. flowcharts
C. decision tables
D. a semi-formal "Knuth" style
E. pseudo-code

Let us look at each of these briefly.

A. Natural language represents an ideal in that it shifts the burden of unfamiliarity from the user to the computer, where it belongs. Unfortunately, the ideal of unrestricted natural language has been all but abandoned in the face of two overwhelming obstacles. First, specifying the steps of an algorithm in natural language often results in verbosity; consider, for example, the ease of doing arithmetic in FORTRAN as compared with COBOL. An even bigger drawback is the unremitting presence of ambiguity in natural language. Examples of this abound, but the following will suffice: "I saw the man on the hill with the telescope." Does "with the telescope" apply to I, the man, or the hill?

B. Flowcharts have been used with some success, but they are used less commonly now, due to several shortcomings. These disadvantages include the following: there is very little standardization in the manner of drawing them; they all too often look like spaghetti, obscuring rather than clarifying matters; they fail to convey essential global and descriptive facts about an algorithm; it is hard to be certain that all logical possibilities have been provided for; the translation from a flowchart to a program must be done entirely by hand.

C. The use of decision tables represents a relatively small but well established tradition. Since we will be discussing them subsequently, in Chapters 2 and 6, it is sufficient for now to remark that their special form makes them unsuited for representing algorithms in all of their generality.

D. The style that Knuth uses in his monumental set of volumes has been imitated by many other writers. Basically, it consists of a set of numbered steps. Each step is written in a mixture of plain English and program-like notation, as is most convenient. Most steps include commentary in brackets that assist in understanding what is happening, and sequencing is accomplished by conditional and unconditional jumps to other numbered steps. There are two principal drawbacks associated with this style. First, since no control structures are used (we will discuss these shortly), the logical structure of the algorithm is obscured. Second, the translation from this representation to a program is again a manual process; this introduces the hazard that the algorithm cannot be implemented and tested directly, leading to a higher risk of incorrectness. In fact, although we have not ourselves found such an error in Knuth's algorithms, he does discuss their occurrence [Knuth 1974]. Moreover, we have found errors wherever other writers have used that style in books on data structures. In summary, it would be preferable if readers could be spared the possibility of such occurrences.

E. There is not just one single form of pseudo-code. Rather, every author who uses such a method devises what he likes, although the results usually bear a strong resemblance to either ALGOL, Pascal, or PL/I. The author gains several advantages by this method: his algorithms are technically language-independent, he is free to simplify his syntax compared to what is required in a real language, and he is also free to introduce mechanisms that he feels are helpful. The disadvantages will seem rather familiar. First, since there is no standard pseudo-code, the reader must be prepared to learn a different one with each author (and slight differences between authors can be the source of disproportionate confusion). Second, since pseudo-code is, by definition, not immediately executable, but must be translated, there is less reason to be confident as to correctness. With regard to the latter point, we have commonly found such errors when authors have employed this method.

It has been very easy to find fault with each of these five approaches. Indeed, no method is immune to criticism, and this is equally true of the one we will now discuss, the use of Pascal. We do not describe Pascal in any great detail here, nor even provide an appendix on the subject. One reason is that so many books are already available for this purpose. Also, for those who have little prior familiarity with the language, we do provide some help as we go along. The remainder of this chapter, in fact, is designed to accomplish two purposes in overlapping fashion:

- to provide some initial coaching in Pascal, and
- to review the use of procedures and parameters in HLL's.

In standard Pascal [Jensen and Wirth 1984], there are seven sections to a program, ordered as follows:

1. **program** { a header statement }
2. **label** { declaration of program labels (for **goto**'s) }
3. **const** { declaration of program constants }
4. **type** { declaration of program data types }
5. **var** { declaration of program variables }
6. { declaration of **procedure**'s and **function**'s }
7. { executable code, the main body of the program }

Only the first and seventh sections are strictly necessary, but a fifth section is also needed for any practical computation. The declarations of procedures and functions are each, in turn, given using the same seven sections, except that **procedure** or **function** is written instead of **program**. Since procedures (and functions) can themselves have nested procedures, we see that the schema introduced above is a recursive one. In some extended versions of Pascal, the rigid ordering of the seven sections is somewhat relaxed.

The unit of program in any HLL is the statement. Broadly speaking, this includes declarative statements, assignment statements, control statements, and compound statements. In Pascal, the **label**, **const**, **type**, and **var** sections are entirely declarative in nature; we will talk about the **type** and **var** sections in Section 1.4.2. Assignment statements are presumed to be familiar. (Note that the assignment operator is ':=' and not '='.) As far as control statements are concerned, this is where the reader unfamiliar with Pascal is apt to feel the most pain, until he becomes accustomed to the syntax.

Pascal has one construct for definite iteration:

```
for <simple assignment statement> to <limit> do
   <statement>;
```

and two constructs for indefinite iteration:

```
while <condition> do
   <statement>;
```

and

```
repeat
   <statement>;
   <statement>;
     ...
until <condition>;
```

Note the asymmetry between the **repeat** ... **until** construct and the other two. This is certainly bothersome, although minor. For selecting alternative actions, Pascal has the following constructions:

```
if <condition> then
   <statement>;
```

and

```
if <condition> then
   <statement>
else
   <statement>;
```

and

```
case <identifier> of
   <subcase>;
   <subcase>;
      ...
end;
```

The items in angle brackets are to be interpreted as meaning "any instance of that class of object." Thus < statement > might be a simple assignment statement, an iteration control statement, a selection control statement, etc. In any of these preceding "blueprints" of control structures, < statement > could, in addition to the instances cited above, be a *compound statement*:

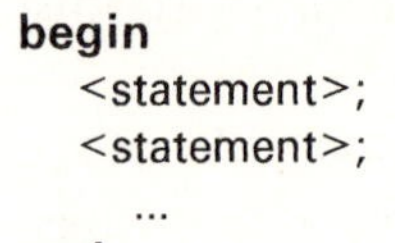

```
begin
   <statement>;
   <statement>;
      ...
end;
```

that is, a group of statements delimited by **begin** and **end**. In this situation, the use of **begin** and **end** for grouping of statements is analogous to the use of parentheses within statements for delimiting of expressions. Note that if a **for**, **while**, or **if** statement is to apply to more than a single consequential statement, then the consequence must be a compound statement.

Readers who are unfamiliar with Pascal-like syntax often find it difficult to know when a control statement ends. Rather than giving a detailed exposition of the syntax, we have two brief comments that are helpful here. One significant cue is that in HLL's of this sort, statements are delimited by semi-colons. The second point has to do with the systematic manner in which we employ indentation in the text of the algorithms in this book. You will find that the scope or the extent of a control statement can always be found by reading downwards until the text is no longer indented inside what is employed for the initial part of that statement. Whereas the use of semi-colons is rigidly prescribed by the language, the use of indentation is quite arbitrary; it is just an effective visual aid, of no significance to the compiler.

The virtues and defects of Pascal as a programming language have been thoroughly explored elsewhere [§], and we will not rehash them here. Our interest in Pascal has to do mainly with its power for representing algorithms. That these representations are directly executable is a significant plus, since it provides a measure of confidence as to their correctness; the principal issue, however, is that of clarity of representation. To this end, we do not hesitate to sacrifice secondary details of efficiency if we can thereby enhance clarity. In almost every case, an algorithm is exhibited on one page. On the other hand, there are few comments, since this sort of information is provided in the text describing the algorithm. With regard to **goto**'s and the controversy surrounding them [Knuth 1974], we avoid them in most cases. However, there are instances where they cannot be eliminated except through the introduction (and excessive setting and testing) of boolean variables. In such cases, we have not hesitated to use an occasional **goto**.

The reader should be aware of a few particular points throughout the remainder of this book. First, we will represent algorithms by procedures or functions where it is important to emphasize the role of parameters, but we may simply represent algorithms by programs where this simplifies matters. Second, we consistently use semi-colons as statement *terminators* rather than statement *separators*. Although the definition of Pascal specifies the latter usage, the former usage does no harm, and we have preferred to employ it consistently. The compiler easily accommodates the former usage by treating affected parts of the program text as null statements.

Finally, we occasionally take some minor liberties with the text of algorithms in order to facilitate exposition. These liberties, which violate Pascal rules, are of the following nature:

- employing variables as array bounds instead of constants;
- placing type definitions for the parameters of a procedure within the procedure;
- placing declarations of global variables within the procedure;
- placing the text of large sub-procedures outside a procedure.

The adjustments, if any, that are required to transform an algorithm to a syntactically correct Pascal program will always be trivial.

1.4.2 Data Typing in Pascal

Different HLL's exhibit different philosophies with regard to declaring the attributes of data:

- In APL, attributes are always inferred, never declared.
- In FORTRAN and PL/I, some attributes must be declared, but others may be either declared or left for the compiler to assign default values.
- In Pascal, all attributes must be declared.

The fact that all attributes are declared in Pascal, thus communicating the programmer's intent to the compiler (or interpreter), enables many programming errors to be detected at translation time rather than at execution time. Detection of errors at this stage is more efficient and also makes debugging easier.

What we have called attributes are subsumed in Pascal under the **type**. Every variable must be declared, along with its type, as in

```
var     s: integer;
        t: char;
        u,v: real;
```

The type information that appears after the colon may be as simple as one of the primitive data types — boolean, character, integer, or real — that we discussed in Section 1.1.1. It may also include structural information, as we will see in the ensuing chapters. In addition, it is possible to employ two special types.

The first of these is the *enumerated type*, as in the declaration

```
var     day: (Sun,Mon,Tues,Wed,Thurs,Fri,Sat);
        color: (red,orange,yellow,green,blue,purple);
```

where a list of arbitrary, distinct names can be given in a list within parentheses. In some other HLL's, the user would have to make an implicit association between the numbers 1 to 7 and the days of the week, and also between the numbers 1 to 6 and the colors, and then use such integer values in his program. With enumerated types, it is possible to deal explicitly, and more naturally, with meaningful symbols, as in the examples

```
day := Mon; color := blue;
```

The second special type is the *subrange type*, as in the declaration

```
var     interest: 7 .. 20;
        digit: '0' .. '9';
```

by which it is specified that the permissible values for the variable *interest* are the integers between 7 and 20, and that the permissible values for the variable *digit* are the characters '0' through '9'. Subrange specifications are particularly useful for declaring the bounds of arrays, as we will see.

The items discussed so far in this section are useful. However, the primary attractive feature of Pascal for the study of data structures is that the user can define a "template" or type of data structure in the **type** section of his program, and give it any name that he wishes. He may then use that defined type, by name, elsewhere in the program as often as he chooses. This has great value both as a mnemonic device and for purposes of guaranteeing consistency of structure definition. By way of illustration, consider the fragment

```
type    day = (Sun,Mon,Tues,Wed,Thurs,Fri,Sat);
        food = (cocktail,soup,salad,entree,dessert,nuts);
        work = Mon .. Fri;

var     holiday,vacation: work;
        menu: soup .. nuts;
        week: day;
```

Note that *day*, *food*, and *work* are definitions, with an '=' and not a ':'; they are *not* data variables.

The type of a variable determines the set of values that that variable may assume. In many cases, the number of such values is a constant, the *cardinality* of the type. As examples of this, the cardinality of type boolean is 2, that of char is 256 (in EBCDIC), that of *day* is seven, etc. The use of types can be carried to arbitrarily many levels of definition, as long as no type is used before it is defined. The utility of these methods will be more apparent as we begin to use structural information as well as type information in the type definitions.

1.4.3 Functions, Procedures, and Parameters

Almost all HLL's have two distinct categories of subroutines, the *procedure* and the *function*. Their usage in Pascal presents nothing essentially new, just the detail that the declarations of the parameters must include type information. Not only that, but since a function returns a value, then the type of that value must be declared also. In the remainder of this chapter, when we speak of procedures, we are really referring to both procedures and functions.

Recall that, in the text defining a procedure, three categories of variables may be employed:

1. *Formal parameters* occur in the procedure heading.
2. *Global variables* are declared outside the procedure text, usually but not always in the main program itself.
3. *Local variables* are declared within the text of the procedure itself. It is important to realize that a local variable may be declared with a name identical to that of some global variable; in such a case, the global variable then becomes hidden and inaccessible while the procedure is executing, and the use of the duplicate name refers to the local variable. This *hiding* of one variable by another also occurs when a formal parameter has a name identical to that of a global variable.

When a procedure is invoked from some point, the invocation specifies some *actual parameters.* There must be the same number of actual parameters as there are formal parameters in the procedure header, and each actual parameter must have the type that was specified for it in the header. There are two principal ways in which parameters can be passed to a procedure:

1. In *call-by-value*, the value of the actual parameter is copied from its memory location in the calling program to a private location in the procedure, where it is subsequently used.
2. In *call-by-reference*, the address of the actual parameter is passed from the calling program to the procedure, so that the procedure operates upon the original value and not a copy.

There are other parameter passing techniques, but they are neither present in Pascal nor relevant to our presentation. How does the user control whether a parameter is passed by value or by reference? This varies with the HLL; in some cases, it is not even possible to do so. In Pascal, if a parameter is to be called by reference, the formal parameter is preceded by **var** in the procedure heading. The ability to pass parameters by reference is very important. Otherwise, except for the single value that a function returns, we would have no satisfactory mechanism for making permanent changes to the value of data with a procedure. (Of course, one can still change the values of global variables, but that is a separate consideration.)

This brief discussion of procedure variables and parameters might seem rather pointless. After all, we would not commonly reuse the names of variables, thereby introducing needless confusion. But if we think about what happens with recursive procedures – wherein both parameters and local variables are reused, perhaps many times – it becomes clear that these issues are very relevant indeed. Readers not already familiar with the issues would be well-advised to become so, in order to avoid difficulties in comprehending the algorithms that we will be studying.

1.5 OVERVIEW

This chapter has been concerned with the two related subjects of data structuring and algorithms. Even though the various individual data structures have yet to be broached, it is apparent that the tool of abstraction can be as powerful for describing data structures as it is for expressing algorithms. The language Pascal is very useful for this purpose in that it provides syntactic mechanisms for expressing such abstraction.

We cannot speak quantitatively about data structures and algorithms without employing some tools of a mathematical nature. Some examples of these include logarithms, combinations and permutations, Fibonacci numbers, etc. Many of these tools already convey the notion of recursion; and recursion permeates the subject matter of this book, both with regard to data structuring and algorithms.

Another significant topic in this chapter has been that of complexity of computational methods, and techniques for characterizing and measuring complexity. The focus of this book is primarily on data, and so the subject of complexity is not treated in depth. However, no student of data structures can afford to ignore these matters, though the less experienced might reasonably choose to postpone attention to them at first reading.

1.6 BIBLIOGRAPHIC NOTES

- Some useful books on the subject of numerical analysis are Dahlquist and Björck [1974], Forsythe et al. [1977], and Hamming [1971].

- Among the many excellent treatments of combinatorial mathematics are Liu [1968], Roberts [1984], and Tucker [1984].

- The virtues and defects of Pascal as a programming language are argued in Haberman [1973], Lecarme and Desjardin [1974], Welsh et al. [1977], and Wirth [1975].

1.7 REFERENCE TO TERMINOLOGY

1.8 EXERCISES

Sections 1.1 – 1.2

1.1 What is (a) $693\text{B}_{16} + 3585_{16}$? (b) $58\text{A}4_{16} - 29\text{B}5_{16}$?

1.2 Convert (a) 9255_{10} to hexadecimal; (b) $35\text{D}9_{16}$ to decimal.

†1.3 Suppose that binary floating-point numbers $m \times 2^e$ are represented by using three bits plus sign for the mantissa m and two bits plus sign for the exponent e, with $0.5 \leq m < 1.0$. Plot the positive numbers in this representation on the real line. How many distinct real numbers are there in this representation?

1.4 Pick some object from everyday life and list several of its attributes, and also some representative values for each attribute.

1.5 Prove the identity given in Eq. 1.6.

1.6 Prove the identities given in Eqs. 1.10a – 1.10e.

†1.7 Use Eq. 1.10d to compute all the non-zero values of $C(n,r)$ for $n = 1 \mathinner{..} 8$ and $r = 0 \mathinner{..} 8$, and arrange them in a table of rows by n and columns by r. The table so constructed is *Pascal's triangle.* Now consider the sums of the entries on diagonals running from the lower left to the upper right. What do you find? Prove the observed relationship.

†1.8 Prove the following identities *without* using Eq. 1.19:

(a) $\binom{r}{r} + \binom{r+1}{r} + \binom{r+2}{r} + \cdots + \binom{n}{r} = \binom{n+1}{r+1}$

(b) $1^2 + 2^2 + \cdots + n^2 = 2\binom{n+1}{3} + \binom{n+1}{2}$

†1.9 For the Fibonacci numbers,

(a) prove that $F_{n+1}F_{n-1} - F_n^2 = (-1)^n$;

(b) derive the value of $\sum_{k=1}^{n} F_k$;

(c) derive the value of $\sum_{k=1}^{n} F_k^2$.

Section 1.3

1.10 Under what conditions might a musical score be considered an algorithm for performing a piece of music?

1.11 Given F and G as defined below, compute the value of $G(4)$. Show your intermediate evaluations.

```
function F (x: integer): integer;
begin
  if x <= 1 then F := 2
  else F := 3 * F (x - 2) + G (x - 1);
end;

function G (x: integer): integer;
begin
  if x <= 1 then G := 3
  else G := 2 * F (x - 1) + 3 * G (x - 2);
end;
```

1.12 Given the following recursive definition:

```
function F (m,n: integer): integer;
begin
  if n = 0 then F := m
  else F := F (m,n - 1) + F (m + 1,n - 1);
end;
```

compute $F(1,3)$. Show your intermediate evaluations.

†1.13 A *partition* of an integer n is a decomposition of n into summands. For example, the integer 4 can be partitioned in five distinct manners, as follows:

$$1+1+1+1 \quad 1+1+2 \quad 2+2 \quad 1+3 \quad 4$$

The number of partitions of n is denoted by $P(n)$, and we see that $P(4) = 5$. In general, $P(n)$ can be computed recursively via the introduction of $Q(m,n)$, as follows:

```
function Q (m,n: integer): integer;
begin
   if (m = 1) or (n = 1) then
      Q := 1
   else if m <= n then
      Q := 1 + Q (m,m - 1)
   else
      Q := Q (m,n - 1) + Q (m - n,n);
end;

function P (n: integer): integer;
begin
   P := Q (n,n);
end;
```

Compute $P(7)$, showing your intermediate evaluations.

††1.14 Given the following recursive definition:

```
function F (m,n: integer): integer;
begin
   if m * n = 0 then F := m + n + 1
   else F := F (m - 1,F (m,n - 1));
end;
```

compute $F(4,1)$. Show your intermediate evaluations.

†1.15 Given two functions $f(n)$ and $g(n)$, prove or disprove the necessity that either $f(n) = O(g(n))$, or $g(n) = O(f(n))$, or perhaps both.

1.16 Write an efficient function in Pascal for computing the nth power of a number, where n is a non-negative integer that may be quite large in practice. (Do not use logarithms.) Test your program with several moderate examples, such as 3^{23} and 2^{77}. What is the complexity of your algorithm?

†1.17 [Dijkstra 1976] Write an efficient procedure to find all the distinct integer solutions of the equation $x^2 + y^2 = r$. Test your program by applying it to $r = 9425$. What is the complexity of your algorithm?

††1.18 The complexity classes discussed in Section 1.3.2.1 are adequate to encompass the great majority of situations. But there are other possibilities as well. Classify the following functions into complexity classes, arranged from low to high. A class might contain more than one function; that is, it might contain f and g such that $f = \Theta(g)$.

$\log n$	$\log \log n$	$n^{\log \log n}$
n	$(\lg n)^{1/2}$	$n^{(\lg n)^2}$
$n \lg n$	$(\log n)^{10}$	$n^{(\lg n)^{1/2}}$
n^2	$\lg n^2$	$n^{1/2}$

Section 1.4

1.19 Give a brief comparison of the control structures in Pascal with those in any other language of your choosing. If the language you choose for comparison does not have the control structures **repeat** ... **until**, **while** ... **do** ..., or **case** ... **of** ... **end**, sketch how their effects could be obtained with the control structures that your language does have.

1.20 Discuss the distinctions between the typing facilities in Pascal and the typing provided with ADT's.

†1.21 For the following program:

```
program FRAGMENT;

var     u,v,w: integer;

procedure JUNK (p,q: integer; var r,s: integer);
begin
   r := p * q;
   s := (p + q) * r;
end;

begin
   u := 4;  v := 3;  w := 7;
   JUNK (u,v,v,w);
end.
```

(a) What will be the final value of *w*?

(b) What will be the final value of *w* if the header for JUNK is changed as follows:

```
procedure JUNK (p: integer; var q,r,s: integer)
```

2

ARRAYS and SETS

"Now go, write it before them in a table, and note it
in a book, that it may be for the time to come ..."

Isaiah 30: 8

Imagine a deck of playing cards in a neat pile. Then imagine that same deck of cards scattered over the floor. What is the essential difference? Succinctly, in the first case the cards form an array, with an associated sequence; and in the second case the cards form a set, without any order. In this chapter we will examine both of these data structures, with an emphasis on the array.

The array is a data structure that is undoubtedly familiar to most readers. There are two reasons for this:

- Arrays are a very natural and efficient structure for many operations with data, as witness tax tables, time schedules, etc.
- Almost all HLL's reflect this fact by providing constructs that facilitate operations on arrays.

Sets, on the other hand, tend to be disquieting to most non-mathematical readers, and they are seldom supported directly in HLL's.

This chapter begins with some very basic material on arrays, after which some examples of array usage are covered. Sets are then discussed, and some relationships between these data structures are developed. Their placement at this point in the book reflects our desire to be able to:

- talk about sets in terms of arrays, and then immediately
- talk about arrays in terms of sets.

Finally, the last half of the chapter has a broader treatment of the nature and utility of arrays than an ordinary programming course might provide. Although most of our presentation of arrays is in terms of Pascal, we will also call attention to ways of thinking about arrays that are not possible in most programming languages.

2.1 ONE-DIMENSIONAL ARRAYS

The basic concept of an array suggests an ordered list, such as *scores*: 75, 90, 63, 82, 74, 88. In this simple example, we see three important features of an array:

1. It can have an arbitrary name, in this case *scores*.
2. It contains some definite number of elements of the same type, which in this case is integer.
3. The elements of the array have a de facto ordering, so that we can refer, for example, to the third score as being 63.

Unfortunately, the reasonable notion of a one-dimensional array as a "list" is sure to engender confusion when we come to Chapter 4. Thus we will eschew the term list in our discussion of arrays in this chapter.

A mathematician or a scientist would most likely refer to the third score as $scores_3 = 63$, using a *subscript* value of 3. However, programming languages do not admit subscripts, superscripts, and other elements of general mathematical notation; instead, for referencing an element of an array, they usually employ one or the other of the notations *scores* (3) or *scores* [3], which are referred to as both subscripts and *indices*. Parentheses are employed in some languages, such as BASIC and FORTRAN, and brackets are employed in some other languages, such as APL and Pascal.

If we think about it, our example is implicitly a set of ordered pairs of

scores: (1,75), (2,90), (3,63), (4,82), (5,74), (6,88)

except that we do not need the first member of each pair as long as we keep elements in their proper sequence. In many cases in both mathematics and computing, it is desirable to start counting with zero (*0-origin*) rather than one (*1-origin*). A compelling example of this is the memory of a computer. Addresses or locations in memory always start with the value of zero. If a hypothetical computer had 100 memory locations, we would reference them as *memory* [0], *memory* [1], ... , *memory* [99].

In our example, using 0-origin, the ordered pairs would be

scores: (0,75), (1,90), (2,63), (3,82), (4,74), (5,88)

A potential problem here is to know what is meant by *scores* [3]. Does it refer to 63 or to 82? A language that allows these two interpretations will also provide a means for specifying which meaning is intended. Even more generally, we can allow the first members of our pairs to begin with any integer value, as in

scores: (6,75), (7,90), (8,63), (9,82), (10,74), (11,88)

or in

scores: (−2,75), (−1,90), (0,63), (1,82), (2,74), (3,88)

Although this may seem strange, it means that we can now label the elements of our array in a possibly more natural manner. For example, we may have an array of loan payment amounts versus interest rates, in which it is realistic to speak of rates of 7, 8, ... , 20 (percent). With such flexibility, there must be some means of specifying the intended index values. In Pascal, the declaration of an array always includes this information, as in

scores: **array** [6 .. 11] **of** integer, or *scores*: **array** [−2 .. 3] **of** integer.

Note that the declaration of an array contains the composite specification of two types, the *index type* and the *base type*. The base type may be of a very general nature. It is integer in the above examples, but it might have been character or real or even some user-defined type. However, the index type must be that of a set of ordinal values. As in the previous examples, it is usually a subrange type, but it may also be an enumerated type, as in

```
type    workweek = (Monday,Tuesday,Wednesday,Thursday,Friday);
        activity = (reports,plans,laboratory,study,meetings,travel);
var     schedule: array [workweek] of activity;
```

so that we might, for example, encounter *schedule* [*Tuesday*] := *study*.

The basic operations with arrays are very simple. The index, or subscript, is used to select a position within the array; and either the value in that position is retrieved, or a value is assigned to that position. An important aspect of these operations is that the index may be an integer constant, an integer-valued variable, or even an integer-valued expression. Alternatively, retrieval or assignment can be applied to the entire array, treated as one composite value (see Section 2.3.1).

2.1.1 Sequential Storage Allocation

Since the one-dimensional arrays that we have described so far are sequences of elements, and computer memory is itself a sequence of locations, it is simple and natural to accommodate arrays in computers by mapping one sequence to the other. Thus, if the array *soup*: **array** [2 .. 11] **of** char is stored in memory beginning at location 1210, then *soup* [2] will be in 1210, *soup* [3] will be in 1211, ... , *soup* [11] will be in 1219. (This presumes that each addressable memory location holds one character, as is the case in byte-oriented computers.) More generally, if x: **array** [s .. t] **of** char with lower index bound s and upper index bound t is stored in memory beginning at location b, then

$$\text{loc}\,(x\,[i]) = b + (i - s) \tag{2.1a}$$

However, other base types may require more than a single byte of storage per element. Let us denote by *int_size* and *real_size* the amount required for integers and reals. As we cited in Section 1.1.1, these would commonly be 4 and 8 bytes, respectively. Thus, if y: **array** [s .. t] **of** integer is stored in memory beginning at location b, then

$$\text{loc}\,(y\,[i]) = b + (i - s) \times int\_size \tag{2.1b}$$

and if z: **array** [s .. t] **of** real is stored in memory beginning at location b, then

$$\text{loc}\ (z\ [i]) = b + (i - s) \times real\_size \qquad (2.1c)$$

2.1.2 Searching an Array

An array is very commonly used for storing groups of related values as a table. In a table there is usually one value from each related group that uniquely identifies the group. This is sometimes called the *argument*, but the term *key* is used more commonly in computing. The notion is that one searches the table to see if an input value (the key) is present, and if so, where it is in the table. By finding where the key is located in the table, one can also locate the data related to the key. A familiar example of this process is that of finding the address and telephone number of a person by looking-up his name in a directory. In a vastly simplified fashion, these few sentences represent what Chapter 10 (Searching) is about. They are presented here as background for the function SEARCH_A (Algorithm 2.1), which searches for a key in an array of unordered numerical values. It takes two arguments, *tbl* for the name of the array to be searched, and an input value of *key*. If *key* is present, SEARCH_A returns its index within *tbl*; otherwise, it returns the value 0. Note that SEARCH_A violates Pascal syntax (see Section 1.4.1) by having the type *table* defined within the function rather than previous to it. SEARCH_A scans the table from the bottom to the top, which is slightly faster with some computers; however, that is of minor importance.

```
function SEARCH_A (tbl: table; key: integer): integer;
type    table = array [1 .. n] of integer;
var     i: 0 .. n;
begin
   i := n;
   while (key <> tbl [i]) and (i <> 1) do
      i := i - 1;
   if key = tbl [i] then SEARCH_A := i
                    else SEARCH_A := 0;
end;
```

Algorithm 2.1 SEARCH_A

To illustrate matters, suppose that we have a table *t*: **array** [1 .. 9] **of** integer containing the values 22, 17, 5, 65, 48, 83, 19, 28, 52. Then SEARCH_A (*t*,65) returns the value 4, SEARCH_A (*t*,34) returns the value 0, SEARCH_A (*t*,52) returns the value 9, etc. Note the compound test for termination either upon finding *key* in *tbl* or upon reaching the end of the table; similarly, it is necessary to discriminate between these causes after leaving the iteration.

Even as simple an algorithm as SEARCH_A can be made more efficient via a simple modification. Most of the work in SEARCH_A is done in the **while** loop.

However, the decrementing of the variable *i* will, on most machines, take much less time than the double test for termination. This situation can be improved by the tactic illustrated in the function SEARCH_B (Algorithm 2.2). Here, a 0'th location is maintained at the head of the table for storing the value of *key* prior to iteration. Since this guarantees that *key* will always be found, only a single termination condition is required. We are also able to dispense with the test after termination. It is very common to use a special value in a last or first position of a data structure as a signal that we have reached the boundary of the structure. A data value used in this fashion is called a *sentinel.* What are the complexities of SEARCH_A and SEARCH_B? Indefinite iteration is used in both cases; however, the maximum number of iterations is bounded by *n*, the size of the table, in both cases. Thus the complexity is $O(n)$ for the two algorithms, although the second one is superior because of its smaller constant factor.

```
function SEARCH_B (tbl: table; key: integer): integer;

type    table = array [0 .. n] of integer;

var     i: 0 .. n;

begin
   i := n;
   tbl [0] := key;
   while key <> tbl [i] do
      i := i - 1;
   SEARCH_B := i;
end;
```

Algorithm 2.2 SEARCH_B

2.2 MULTI-DIMENSIONAL ARRAYS

The preceding sections treated one-dimensional arrays, so called because they can be represented by listing their elements in one dimension, as in a line or a row. It is very common, however, to deal with information that is most naturally represented via arrays with two dimensions, as in the typical tax table shown in Figure 2.1, or even three or more dimensions. Arrays of more than three dimensions can be awkward to visualize or to represent in a drawing; but these perceptual issues are largely irrelevant to computers and programming languages. First, we will consider how arrays of progressively higher dimension generalize Eqs. 2.1; then we will examine the effects of using some special kinds of arrays.

Income (to nearest $1000)	Number of Dependents 2	3	4	5	6
10	900	720	550	390	240
11	1090	900	720	550	390
12	1310	1090	900	720	550
13	1530	1310	1090	900	720
14	1760	1530	1310	1090	900
15	2000	1760	1530	1310	1090
16	2240	2000	1760	1530	1310
17	2480	2240	2000	1760	1530

Figure 2.1 A Table of Tax Liability

2.2.1 Storage Allocation Functions

Look at Figure 2.1 and you will note that it can be regarded in three different ways:

1. as a two-dimensional array of integers

   array [10 .. 17,2 .. 6] **of** integer

2. as a one-dimensional array of rows of integers

   array [10 .. 17] **of array** [2 .. 6] **of** integer

3. as a one-dimensional array of columns of integers

   array [2 .. 6] **of array** [10 .. 17] **of** integer

Indeed, in Pascal and in some other programming languages, it is quite possible to define multi-dimensional arrays recursively, as in methods 2 and 3 above. Method 1 seems more natural, however, and we will adhere to it in this book.

Although we will be using the first method, the ambivalent views suggested by the other two methods raise a problem. How should an array that is two-dimensional be stored in computer memory, which is one-dimensional? Should we store all the first row, then all the second row, etc. (*row-major order*); or should we store all the first column, then all the second column, etc. (*column-major order*)? FORTRAN employs column-major order, but almost all other programming languages employ row-major order. You may wonder why this would matter, and why it would not be transparent in an HLL. The problem is that it occasionally ceases to be transparent. For example, in an I/O operation of an entire array, the default sequence in which the elements appear would reflect their internal storage allocation.

Let us suppose now that an array

$$x\text{: }\mathbf{array}\ [s_1 \,..\, t_1, s_2 \,..\, t_2]\ \mathbf{of}\ \mathit{base\_type}$$

with lower/upper index bounds s_i/t_i is stored in row-major order beginning at location b. In this declaration, *base_type* denotes character, integer, real; correspondingly, *base_size* denotes the size of one element of that type. The storage allocation function is then

$$\text{loc}\ (x\ [i,j]) = b + [n_2(i - s_1) + (j - s_2)] \times base\_size \qquad (2.2a)$$

where $n_2 = t_2 - s_2 + 1$ is the number of elements in any row. This equation states that, in order to find the location of the element in the ith row and the jth column, we must start at b, increment sufficiently to step over $(i - s_1)$ rows, and then increment past $(j - s_2)$ elements in the next row. If, on the other hand, the array is stored in column-major order, then the storage allocation function is

$$\text{loc}\ (x\ [i,j]) = b + [n_1(j - s_2) + (i - s_1)] \times base\_size \qquad (2.2b)$$

where $n_1 = t_1 - s_1 + 1$ is the number of elements in any column. Note that for an array with m rows and n columns, stored in row-major order (with 1-origin indexing) the subscripts of array elements as they occur in storage sequence are $11, 12, \ldots, 1t_2, 21, 22, \ldots, 2t_2, \ldots, t_11, t_12, \ldots, t_1t_2$. In other words, the rightmost subscript varies most rapidly and the leftmost subscript varies least rapidly, in the manner of an odometer. You should be able to easily satisfy yourself of the truth of Eqs. 2.2.

If we consider next a three-dimensional array

x: **array** $[s_1 .. t_1, s_2 .. t_2, s_3 .. t_3]$ **of** *base_type*

with lower/upper index bounds s_i/t_i, and stored in row-major order beginning at location b, then

$$\text{loc}\ (x\ [i,j,k]) = b + [n_2n_3(i - s_1) + n_3(j - s_2) + (k - s_3)] \times base\_size \qquad (2.3)$$

where $n_d = t_d - s_d + 1$ is the number of elements in the dth dimension. As we proceed to higher dimensions, the term row-major order is conventionally extended to again mean that the subscripts vary with rapidity which diminishes as we read from right to left; and the term column-major order is extended to signify the opposite, that the rapidity diminishes as we read from left to right. This is so despite the fact that for purposes of translating three-dimensional array notation to a picture, it is conventional to regard the first subscript as selecting a plane, the second subscript as selecting a row, and the third subscript as selecting a column.

A better term for describing this odometer type of storage allocation is *lexicographic ordering*. This term signifies that, in comparing two sequences

$$A: a_1, a_2, \ldots, a_n \quad \text{and} \quad B: b_1, b_2, \ldots, b_n$$

to determine whether A precedes B or B precedes A, we start with a_1 and b_1 and examine successive pairs, a_i and b_i, until the first pair is found for which $a_i \neq b_i$. The order between A and B is then the same as the order for that pair. Note that this is the same rule used to order words in a dictionary. To illustrate matters more concretely, if we have

```
y: array [3 .. 4,1 .. 3,-2 .. 2] of integer
```

2040 3,1, – 2	2044 3,1, – 1	2048 3,1,0	2052 3,1,1	2056 3,1,2
2060 3,2, – 2	2064 3,2, – 1	2068 3,2,0	2072 3,2,1	2076 3,2,2
2080 3,3, – 2	2084 3,3, – 1	2088 3,3,0	2092 3,3,1	2096 3,3,2

2100 4,1, – 2	2104 4,1, – 1	2108 4,1,0	2112 4,1,1	2116 4,1,2
2120 4,2, – 2	2124 4,2, – 1	2128 4,2,0	2132 4,2,1	2136 4,2,2
2140 4,3, – 2	2144 4,3, – 1	2148 4,3,0	2152 4,3,1	2156 4,3,2

Figure 2.2 Lexicographic Allocation

stored in row-major order beginning at location 2040, then Figure 2.2 shows the correspondence between subscripts and memory locations.

For the general case of an r-dimensional array

$$x\text{: } \mathbf{array}\ [s_1 \,..\, t_1, s_2 \,..\, t_2, \ldots, s_r \,..\, t_r]\ \mathbf{of}\ base\_type$$

stored in row-major order beginning at location b, then

$$\text{loc}\ (x\,[i_1, i_2, \ldots, i_r]) =$$
$$b + \left[(i_1 - s_1) \times \prod_{d=2}^{r} n_d + (i_2 - s_2) \times \prod_{d=3}^{r} n_d + \cdots + (i_r - s_r) \right] \times base\_size \tag{2.4}$$

where $n_d = t_d - s_d + 1$ is the number of elements in the dth dimension.

The formulas in this section are useful for several reasons. You may have to identify array elements in an unformatted printout, or perhaps write programs to perform array manipulations in a language without array facilities (such as assembly language), or even write a compiler for a language that supports arrays. In the latter two cases, the preceding formulas can be usefully rearranged. As an example of this, consider Eq. 2.3. It can be rewritten as

$$\begin{aligned}\text{loc}\ (x\,[i,j,k]) &= (b - [n_2 n_3 s_1 + n_2 s_2 + s_3] \times base\_size) + (n_2 n_3 \times base\_size) \times i \\ &\quad + (n_3 \times base\_size) \times j + base\_size \times k \qquad (2.5) \\ &= p + q \times i + r \times j + s \times k\end{aligned}$$

where p,q,r,s are constant values that can be pre-computed once the array has been allocated in storage. For the example array in Figure 2.2, Eq. 2.5 would reduce to

$$\text{loc}\ (x\,[i,j,k]) = 1848 + 60 \times i + 20 \times j + 4 \times k$$

In practice, compilers pre-compute these constant values wherever possible – for example, if the array bounds are constants. These and other constants associated with the array, such as array dimensioning information, are stored within the compiled program as a *dope vector* for that array. The dope vector facilitates rapid reference to arbitrary elements of an array during program execution. Note that in Eq. 2.5 it costs just three multiplications and three additions to compute the location of an array element, as compared with four multiplications and six additions in Eq. 2.3. The savings rapidly become more significant as the number of dimensions in an array increases.

2.2.2 Triangular Arrays

Conventional arrays have some shortcomings as structures for describing and representing data in computers. We will explore these shortcomings and some remedies in the last half of this chapter; however, it is worth considering one particular situation at this point. Note that the cardinality of an array is the product of its dimensions. In the array of Figure 2.2, for instance, the cardinality is $2 \times 3 \times 5 = 30$. These numbers were deliberately chosen to be small, but arrays of just a few dimensions of moderate size can easily swamp the memory of a small computer.

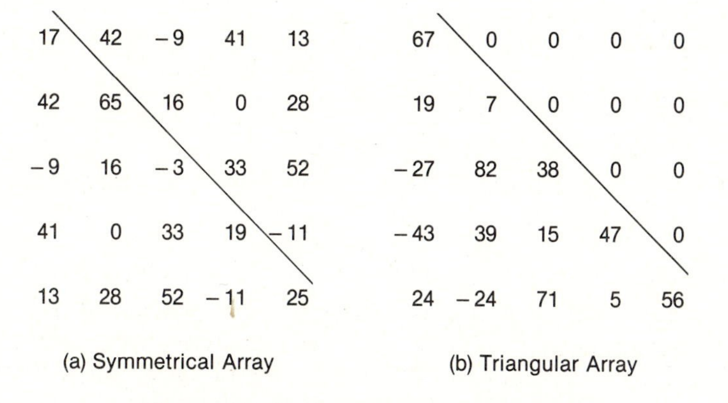

Figure 2.3 Redundant Array Elements

In real life applications, however, arrays often have special structures that allow the storage requirement to be reduced. Two such cases are illustrated in Figure 2.3, where we see

(a) a *symmetric array*, in which $a_{i,j} = a_{j,i}$, and

(b) a *triangular array*, in which $a_{i,j} = 0$ for $i < j$.

In both cases, it would be redundant to allocate storage for the entire square two-dimensional array; there is no essential information above the diagonal from element $a[1,1]$ to element $a[n,n]$.

In allocating storage for triangular arrays (and for symmetric arrays, which can be represented by triangular arrays), we can place the rows one after the other – the first requiring one location, the second requiring two locations, ... , up to the ith with i locations. This means that the ith row begins after the

$$1 + 2 + 3 + \cdots + i - 1 = \frac{i \times (i-1)}{2}$$

locations needed for the preceding $i - 1$ rows, so that the storage allocation function becomes

$$\text{loc}\ (x\ [i,j]) = b + \left[\frac{i \times (i-1)}{2} + j \right] \times base\_size \tag{2.6}$$

Although our storage allocation function is still fairly simple, it is nonetheless quadratic in i instead of linear; moreover, such a mapping into memory is not supported by most general purpose HLL's. Thus, in order to obtain this saving, the user would have to declare a one-dimensional array and then explicitly employ the indices i and j to compute the offset into that array, using Eq. 2.6.

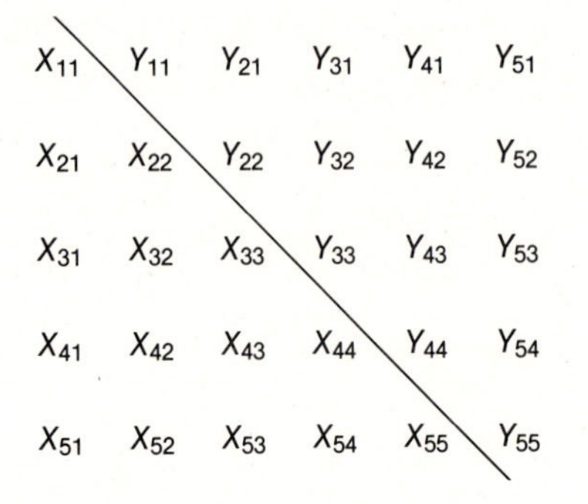

Figure 2.4 Two Triangular Arrays

It is also possible for a problem to have a pair of triangular arrays, x and y, of the same size n. In that case, they can be placed in memory together as one rectangular array of size $n \times (n + 1)$, as shown in Figure 2.4. The composite two-dimensional array z can be declared in a straightforward manner, and then

$$x_{i,j} = z_{i,j} \quad \text{and} \quad y_{i,j} = z_{j,i+1} \tag{2.7}$$

It is possible to generalize the ideas of this section to arrays of higher dimensions. In this case they are called *tetrahedral arrays* (see Exercise 2.21).

2.3 EXAMPLES OF ARRAY USAGE

Since arrays are so widely used in computing, a thorough survey of their applications would be very large indeed. We will endeavor to convey some of this variety by considering arrays from three different points of view. First, we look at arrays from the point of view of geometry and information content. Second, we address a few of the vast number of algebraic techniques for dealing with two-dimensional arrays. And lastly, anticipating some special techniques for dealing with arrays of boolean base type, we look at the nature and implementation of decision tables.

2.3.1 Cross Sections

Let us suppose that we have taken a survey of a group of persons with respect to their sex, education, and marital status. The expected responses to these queries are as follows:

sex	male or female
education completed	primary, secondary, or college
marital status	single, married, divorced, widowed, or other

The responses are totalled and then recorded in

```
survey: array [1 .. 2,1 .. 3,1 .. 5] of integer
```

In accordance with the conventional view of subscripts in three-dimensional arrays, as cited in Section 2.2.1, we interpret our array as having two planes, three rows, and five columns. The actual data is as shown in Figure 2.5, and a pictorial representation is given in Figure 2.6.

	single	married	divorced	widowed	other
male					
primary	20	17	9	11	14
secondary	32	13	7	5	10
college	11	9	11	8	12
female					
primary	33	28	6	14	17
secondary	21	24	13	8	15
college	19	17	4	5	20

Figure 2.5 Example Data in Three Dimensions

From *survey* [1,2,3] = 7, we can then, for instance, read that there are 7 male high school graduates that are divorced. When dealing with arrays, it is common to be concerned with all the elements in a *cross-section* or *hyperplane*, in which some indices are held constant and the remaining indices range over all their permissible

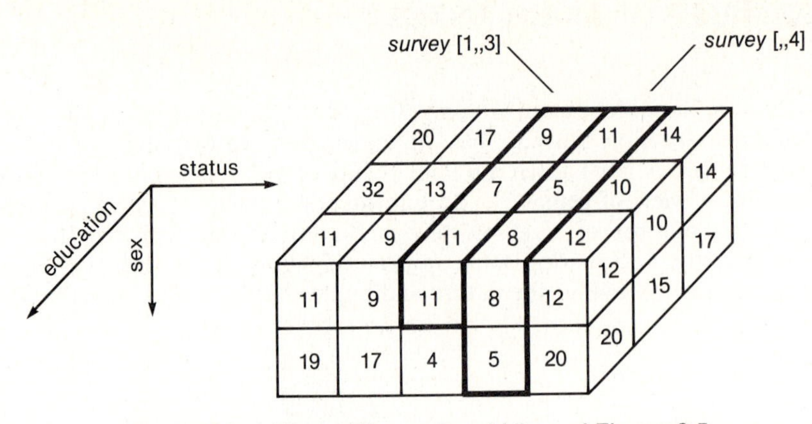

Figure 2.6 A Three-Dimensional View of Figure 2.5

values. Thus, by *survey* [,,4] we signify all elements in the fourth column, over all planes and all rows; this corresponds to the plane of elements

11	14
5	8
8	5

namely, all the widowed persons. Or, by *survey* [1,,3] we signify all the elements in the first plane and the third column; this corresponds to the line of elements

9 7 11

namely, all the divorced males. Our first example is a two-dimensional cross-section, and the second example is a one-dimensional cross-section. In arrays of higher dimension, the geometrical analogy falters, and we simply speak of hyperplanes.

Note that the notations *survey* [,,4] and *survey* [1,,3] are not supported in Pascal. Hyperplane notation is permitted in Pascal only when trailing consecutive subscripts are omitted – for example, *survey* [1] or *survey* [2,1] – and then only within simple assignment statements. However, more general use of cross-sections is allowed in some other programming languages, such as PL/I and APL.

2.3.2 Linear Algebra

Linear algebra deals extensively with properties of one-dimensional arrays, called *vectors*, and two-dimensional arrays, called *matrices*. These structures are fundamental to all of engineering and scientific computation.

The (*inner*) *product* of two vectors u and v is defined as the sum of products $\sum u_i \times v_i$. Thus, for $u = (11, 5, -7, -2)$ and $v = (1, -3, 9, -27)$, their product is

$$11 \times 1 + 5 \times -3 + -7 \times 9 + -2 \times -27 = -13$$

Note that two vectors can be multiplied in this fashion only if they have the same number of elements. Inner products are a useful way of expressing many common situations. For example, the preceding multiplication could represent the evaluation of the polynomial

$$f(x) = a_0x^0 + a_1x^1 + a_2x^2 + a_3x^3$$

where the u_i are the coefficients a_i and the v_i are the powers x^i, for $x = -3$.

```
program MAT_VEC;

{computes product of matrix A and vector u, in vector v}

var     i,j: integer;
        sum: real;
        A: array [1 .. m,1 .. n] of real;
        u: array [1 .. n] of real;
        v: array [1 .. m] of real;

begin
   for i := 1 to m do begin
      sum := 0;
      for j := 1 to n do
         sum := sum + A [i,j] * u [j];
      v [i] := sum;
   end;
end.
```

Algorithm 2.3 MAT_VEC

This concept extends with beautiful simplicity to the multiplication of a matrix A by a vector u, as long as the matrix has dimensions $m \times n$ and the vector has dimension n. Thus, the matrix has m rows, each of which can be regarded as a vector of dimension n; and we can then multiply A [1,] by u to obtain a value, multiply A [2,] by u to obtain another value, etc. These values taken together constitute a new vector v, of dimension m, with one element corresponding to each row of A. This is illustrated by the program MAT_VEC (Algorithm 2.3).

These ideas can be generalized yet again to yield the product of two matrices $C = A \times B$, if the dimensions of A and B are *conformable*, that is, if they match up properly. For instance, if A has dimensions $m \times n$ and B has dimensions $n \times p$, then they can be multiplied to yield C with dimensions $m \times p$. To see this, regard the p columns of B as p vectors, and then multiply $A \times B$ [,1] to obtain the vector C [,1], followed by $A \times B$ [,2] to obtain the vector C [,2], etc. In general, the element C [i,j] is obtained by taking the vector product of the ith row of A and the jth column of B. This is illustrated by the program MAT_MAT (Algorithm 2.4).

If you are not already familiar with these basic concepts from linear algebra, then you might consult one of numerous books on the subject, such as Birkhoff and MacLane [1977]. Our principal concern here is to call attention to the manner in which the computational complexity increases in the preceding sequence of processes. For a vector of n elements and a matrix of $n \times n$ elements, we see that:

- to multiply a vector by a vector is $O(n)$;

```
program MAT_MAT;

{computes product of matrix A and matrix B, in matrix C}

var     i,j,k: integer;
        sum: real;
        A: array [1 .. m,1 .. n] of real;
        B: array [1 .. n,1 .. p] of real;
        C: array [1 .. m,1 .. p] of real;

begin
  for i := 1 to m do
    for j := 1 to p do begin
      sum := 0;
      for k := 1 to n do
        sum := sum + A [i,k] * B [k,j];
      C [i,j] := sum;
    end;
end.
```

Algorithm 2.4 MAT_MAT

- to multiply a matrix by a vector is $O(n^2)$;
- to multiply a matrix by a matrix is $O(n^3)$.

These three values reflect the customary practice of equating the size of a matrix problem to the length along one dimension. Note that this convention conflicts with another, which measures the size of a problem by the amount of associated input data. With the latter convention, since the amount of data increases as $O(n^2)$ and the work increases as $O(n^3)$, we would be led to say that the complexity of matrix multiplication is $O(n^{3/2})$.

There are many other basic and useful operations in linear algebra in addition to those shown in Algorithms 2.3 and 2.4. Perhaps the most common is that of solving a set of simultaneous linear equations, such as the following

$$\begin{aligned} a_{1,1}x_1 + a_{1,2}x_2 + \cdots + a_{1,n}x_n &= b_1 \\ a_{2,1}x_1 + a_{2,2}x_2 + \cdots + a_{2,n}x_n &= b_2 \\ \cdots \\ a_{n,1}x_1 + a_{n,2}x_2 + \cdots + a_{n,n}x_n &= b_n \end{aligned} \tag{2.8}$$

These can be written (and thought of!) much more simply as $Ax = b$, where

A is the (square) matrix of coefficients $a_{i,j}$
x is the vector of unknowns x_j
b is the vector of right-hand sides of the equations b_i

There are several methods for solving such a set of simultaneous equations. One that is commonly taught and fairly easily understood is known as *Gaussian elimination*. The basic idea is to use the first equation to eliminate the first unknown from all succeeding equations, then use the second equation to eliminate the second unknown from equations below it, etc. These eliminations are accomplished by repeatedly transforming the coefficients of matrix A and vector b to new values A' and b' until the matrix is triangular. In this process, if the ith equation is being eliminated from those below it, then the element $a_{i,i}$ is the *pivot element*; the basic elimination step, to be applied for all $i < j$ and $i \leq k$, is

$$\begin{aligned} a'_{j,k} &= a_{j,k} - a_{j,i} \times a_{i,k} \,/\, a_{i,i} \\ b'_j &= b_j - a_{j,i} \times b_k \,/\, a_{i,i} \end{aligned} \tag{2.9}$$

For $k = i$, it is easy to see that the coefficients below the pivot element vanish, so that the matrix of coefficients becomes triangular. At that point it is possible to solve the last of the equations for $x_n = b_n \,/\, a_{n,n}$. This value of x_n can then be substituted in the next-to-last equation to solve for x_{n-1}; both of these values can then be substituted in the equation before that to solve for x_{n-2}; and so on, up to x_1. Thus Gaussian elimination consists of two processes: a forward elimination step to bring the coefficients to triangular form, and a backward substitution step to solve for the values of the unknowns. In this method the forward elimination step has a complexity of $O(n^3)$, and the backward substitution step has a complexity of $O(n^2)$. The details of an algorithm to accomplish a solution in this manner are left as an exercise (see Exercise 2.10).

Matrix multiplication and the solution of systems of linear equations are operations of pervasive significance throughout scientific and engineering computation. These operations also serve as paradigms for other computations. In particular, the complexity of $O(n^3)$ for matrix multiplication will be cited several times in this book as a paradigm of the performance of various other algorithms.

2.3.3 Decision Tables

In Section 1.4.1 we alluded to decision tables as an alternative formalism for representing the logic of algorithms. Their utility in this regard traditionally has been more apparent in business data processing than in scientific computation. In our case, it is the techniques for manipulating decision tables that are of most interest. For the reader unfamiliar with decision tables [§], we present some introductory material in the next few pages. Knowledgeable readers may wish to skip to the next section.

By well established convention, *decision tables* are drawn, as in Figure 2.7, with four quadrants containing the following parts: a *condition stub* (northwest), *condition entries* (northeast), an *action stub* (southwest), and *action entries* (southeast). This table illustrates how a student might decide algorithmically whether to study and/or watch television and/or sleep and/or walk the dog, when confronted with the circumstances for an evening and the next day in school.

The columns in the entries half of the table correspond to different *decision rules* to be applied. In any given situation, each condition stub evaluates to Yes/True or No/False; the rule to be applied is then that for which the column of condition entries matches the actual vector of condition values. In operational terms, the condition values in different rows and the same column are combined

	*R*1	*R*2	*R*3	*R*4	*R*5	*R*6	*R*7	*R*8	*R*9	*R*10	*R*11	*R*12
*C*1: homework	Y	Y	Y	Y	Y	Y	Y	Y	N	N	N	N
*C*2: test day	Y	Y	Y	Y	N	N	N	N	N	N	N	N
*C*3: good TV	Y	Y	N	N	Y	Y	N	N	Y	Y	N	N
*C*4: tired	Y	N	Y	N	Y	N	Y	N	Y	N	Y	N
*A*1: study	X	X	X	X	X	X		X				
*A*2: watch TV					X	X			X	X		
*A*3: sleep							X				X	
*A*4: walk dog												X

Figure 2.7 Decision Table (Limited Entry)

with logical AND; the rule to be applied corresponds to that column for which this logical AND evaluates to True. Reading down that column, we then perform those actions for which there is an X; note that there should be just one final rule, but that this rule may entail more than one action. Thus, in the table, if conditions *C*1 and *C*3 are true and conditions *C*2 and *C*4 are false, then we should perform rule *R*6, invoking actions *A*1 and *A*2.

school	test	test	test	test	hw	hw	hw	hw	none	none	none	none
TV fare	good	good	poor	poor	good	good	poor	poor	good	good	poor	poor
energy	down	up	down	up	down	up	down	up	down	up	down	up
school	work	work	work	work	work	work		work				
other					TV	TV	sleep		TV	TV	sleep	dog

Figure 2.8 Decision Table (Extended Entry)

The decision table in Figure 2.7 is called a *limited entry decision table*. Figure 2.8 shows the same problem expressed in a different form, which is called an *extended entry decision table* – wherein entries can be more general than Y,N,X, or blank. Note that extended entries allow a decision table to be compressed vertically. Both limited entry and extended entry tables are widely used, with limited entry being somewhat more common. The choice is primarily one of convenience, since it is simple to transform from extended entry to limited entry.

Obviously, if we have n independent limited entry conditions to be tested, then there are 2^n possible columns of rules; thus, decision tables can rapidly become unwieldy with even a modest number of conditions. Fortunately, it is usually possible to apply the process of *condensation* to decision tables, shrinking them horizontally by means of *don't-care* entries, denoted with "–". Thus, in Figure 2.9, note that when conditions *C*1 and *C*3 are true, then condition *C*2 is irrelevant. The form in Figure 2.9 is termed a fully expanded decision table. Using don't-care entries, it can be condensed to the form shown in Figure 2.10(a). The table also illustrates the use of the ELSE rule, to be applied when the given values of the conditions match none of the sets of condition values in the other rules.

	R1	R2	R3	R4	R5	R6	R7	R8
C1	Y	Y	Y	Y	N	N	N	N
C2	Y	Y	N	N	Y	Y	N	N
C3	Y	N	Y	N	Y	N	Y	N
A1		X		X		X		
A2	X		X					
A3					X		X	X

Figure 2.9 A Decision Table to be Condensed

	R1	R2	R3	ELSE
C1	Y	N	Y	
C2	–	Y	–	
C3	N	N	Y	
A1	X	X		
A2			X	
A3				X

(a)

	R1	R2	R3	ELSE
C1	–	Y	Y	
C2	Y	N	–	
C3	N	N	Y	
A1	X	X		
A2			X	
A3				X

(b)

Figure 2.10 Two Condensations of Figure 2.9

Unfortunately, the process of condensation may not be unique, as shown by Figure 2.10(b). Systematic techniques for performing condensation, based on Karnaugh maps and Quine-McCluskey simplification, are discussed in Shwayder [1975]. Applying condensation to a decision table in an ad-hoc manner is also hazardous. The resulting table runs the risk of having one or more of the following properties:

1. *Redundancy*. A rule (that is, a set of condition entries along with a set of action entries) may be repeated or subsumed in another rule.
2. *Inconsistency*. There may exist rules having identical condition entry values but different action entries;
3. *Incompleteness*. Some possible set(s) of condition values may not be covered by the rules in the table.

It is easy to check for these properties in a fully expanded decision table, and there are also techniques to check for them in condensed tables.

However, there is another issue that is not as readily verified by machine. Suppose that some of the condition stubs are not logically independent, as in Figure 2.11, which indicates how bus fare is to be charged. If condition *C1* is true, then condition *C3* cannot be true; this means, in turn, that a fully expanded form of Figure 2.11 should have less than 2^n rules. So, in a given decision table in

	*R*1	*R*2	*R*3	*R*4	*R*5
*C*1: senior citizen	Y	Y	N	N	N
*C*2: handicapped	–	–	Y	N	N
*C*3: child	–	–	–	Y	N
*C*4: commute hour	N	Y	–	–	–
*A*1: ride free	X				
*A*2: pay reduced fare		X	X	X	
*A*3: pay full fare					X

Figure 2.11 Non-Independent Conditions

condensed form and with dependent condition stubs, confirming that there are no ambiguous situations in the table is a more subtle process.

2.3.3.1 The Rule-Mask Technique. As stated previously, our interest is discovering how to convert a decision table array to a machine computation. To this end, we are not concerned with the specifics of the action entries, but only with the determination of the proper rule, given a set of conditions. There are two general methods for converting a set of conditions to the correct rule. The first of these is the *rule-mask* technique, which we will discuss in this section. The second method is based upon decision trees, and so is deferred to Chapter 6.

	*R*1	*R*2	*R*3	*R*4	*R*5
*C*1	Y	Y	N	N	–
*C*2	Y	N	N	Y	N
*C*3	–	Y	Y	–	N

Figure 2.12 A Decision Table to be Evaluated

Suppose that we have the condition entries from a decision table, as shown in Figure 2.12. In order to use this method, we need to perform three actions, as follows:

1. Convert the decision table into two boolean matrices: the truth matrix, with a value of 1 (True) where the decision table has either "Y" or "–" and a value of 0 (False) where it has "N"; and the falsity matrix, with a value of 1 (True) where the decision table has either "N" or "–" and a value of 0 (False) where it has "Y." For the data of Figure 2.12, the result of this process is illustrated in Figure 2.13.

2. Evaluate all the conditions and generate a boolean vector in which the *i*th bit is 1/0, corresponding to the truth/falsity of the *i*th condition.

3. Finally, apply the algorithm shown by the program RULE_MASK (Algorithm 2.5). Observe that it first generates a rule vector of all True's, and then for each condition AND's it against a corresponding row of one of the matrices *truth* or *falsity*, according to the value of that condition. At the conclusion, the vector *rule* will have the value True for all rules that match the actual condition values.

	R1	*R2*	*R3*	*R4*	*R5*
C1	1	1	0	0	1
C2	1	0	0	1	0
C3	1	1	1	1	0

truth

	R1	*R2*	*R3*	*R4*	*R5*
C1	0	0	1	1	1
C2	0	1	1	0	1
C3	1	0	0	1	1

falsity

Figure 2.13 Expansion of Figure 2.12 for RULE_MASK

As an example, suppose that the conditions *C*1,*C*2,*C*3 had the respective values: True, False, True. Then the vector *rule* would go from 11111 to 11001 to 01001 to 01000, indicating that rule 2 is to be applied. This formulation of the rule-mask technique has the advantage that it can also be used for decision tables in which more than one rule may satisfy a particular set of conditions. Moreover, the resultant rule vector(s) can be AND'ed with the rows of the action entries, for the case where multiple actions are indicated.

```
program RULE_MASK;

{evaluates rule as a function of cond, falsity, and truth}

var     i,j: integer;
        cond: array [1 .. m] of boolean;
        rule: array [1 .. n] of boolean;
        falsity,truth: array [1 .. m,1 .. n] of boolean;

begin
   for j := 1 to n do
      rule [j] := true;
   for i := 1 to m do
      if cond [i] then
         for j := 1 to n do
            rule [j] := rule [j] and truth [i,j]
      else
         for j := 1 to n do
            rule [j] := rule [j] and falsity [i,j];
end.
```

Algorithm 2.5 RULE_MASK

The rule-mask technique is naturally efficient in terms of storage utilization, and it can also be made efficient via the use of parallel bit operations, as we will illustrate in Section 2.5.2. Although the rule-mask computation is simple, the calculation of the values of the conditions may be rather costly. In many cases the proper rule could be determined without evaluating every condition. A variant known as the interrupt rule-mask technique relaxes this requirement, but at the expense of added computational complexity [King 1966].

2.4 SETS

We now turn and examine the nature of sets. We have not given them a chapter of their own for reasons having to do with emphasis and sequencing of topic material. Specifically, we are concerned with sets as data structures more than as mathematical objects. Thus, we wish to be able to talk about sets that are implemented as arrays; in turn, this representation of sets is central to some methods to be explained in Section 2.5. Therefore, we have placed the discussion of sets at this juncture. First, we give some background about sets as mathematical objects; next, we discuss them in the light of data structures for program manipulation.

2.4.1 Sets in Mathematics

A set is a collection of entities. In mathematics, there are two methods for defining what constitutes a set. With *extension* the members are explicitly exhibited, as in

workdays = {Tuesday,Friday,Monday,Wednesday,Thursday}

or

colors = {blue,green,orange,purple,red,yellow}

A more powerful concept is that of *intension*, whereby members are defined in terms of a property that they possess, as in

prime_numbers = {all positive integers *n*, such that the only divisors of *n* are 1 and *n*}

In mathematical notation it is conventional to denote set membership with braces, as in the examples. As we pointed out at the very beginning of this chapter, there is no notion of sequence among the elements of an ordinary set; they are like objects jumbled together in a bag. In this sense, sets are particularly distinct from arrays, where elements reside in sequential slots.

There is another consequence of the lack of order in sets. By way of example, consider the cases of the array (4, 7, 5, 19, 7, 6, 4) and the set {4, 7, 5, 19, 7, 6, 4}. There is no difficulty with having repeated values in the array, since they are distinguishable by their positions. In the case of the set, however, repeated values can lead to confusion. In point of fact, many treatments of sets do not allow such duplication. Nonetheless, it is useful to be able to speak of cases such as: three red balls, two white balls, and seven blue balls. Sets in which repetition is allowed are termed *multisets*.

Up to this point, our examples have been of sets whose members are simple entities: days of the week, colors, integers, etc. Much of the power of set theory, however, comes from being able to deal with sets whose members may themselves be composite items, such as other sets. Thus, consider the set

```
fruit = {apple,banana,orange}
```

and the following set of *subsets* of *fruit*.[1]

```
salad = { { }, {apple}, {banana}, {orange}, {apple,banana},
          {apple,orange}, {banana,orange}, {apple,banana,orange} }
```

Since there are three fruits and each may or may not be present when we construct a subset, then there are of course $2^3 = 8$ possible subsets, the collection of which defines the set *salad*. The possibilities for sets of more elaborate nature are not confined to the case just illustrated; but this construction of a set B of subsets of another set A is particularly important. The set B is called the *powerset* of the set A, sometimes denoted by $B = 2^A$. Since 2^A counts the number of possible values that can be assumed by a variable whose type is "set of A," it is also the *cardinality* for that type. Be careful not to confuse this type cardinality for a variable of type **set** with the cardinality of the set itself, which is the number of objects in the set.

Given a set S and an object t, a basic consideration is whether the object is in the set, expressed as $t \in S$. A related but distinct question arises when we are dealing with two sets. The question then is whether one set is contained in the other or not, denoted by the (proper) *inclusion* operator $\subset$ rather than the *membership* operator $\in$. For example, $\{a,c\} \subset \{a,b,c\}$. The operator $\subset$ is analogous to the operator $<$ in ordinary arithmetic, while the operator $\subseteq$ is analogous to the operator $\leq$.[2]

Given two sets A and B, there are three basic binary operations that can be performed upon them. Using $A = \{p,q,r\}$ and $B = \{r,s\}$ as examples:

1. *Set intersection*, $A \cap B$, yields the set consisting of all those entities that are in both A and B; thus $A \cap B = \{r\}$.

2. *Set union*, $A \cup B$, yields the set consisting of all those entities that are in A or in B or in their intersection; thus $A \cup B = \{p,q,r,s\}$.

3. *Set difference*, $A - B$, yields the set consisting of all those entities that are in A but not in B; thus $A - B = \{p,q\}$, and $B - A = \{s\}$.

---

[1] The set { } with no members is called the empty set. Note that {*apple*} is not the same as *apple*. The former is a set with one member, *apple*; the latter is not a set but rather just itself. This distinction may seem nitpicking, but it is highly significant.

[2] These analogies are imperfect because with the arithmetic operators we have a total order, whereas with the set operators we have a partial order. This matter is addressed in Section 7.4.5.

These basic notions that we have cited about sets may seem almost trivial. Nonetheless, they have been employed as the foundation for all of modern mathematics, as we will illustrate in the next section. As a conclusion to this section, we should point out a hazard of combining two concepts introduced herein:

- defining members of a set by intension, and
- allowing members of a set to be sets.

Imagine that we have a set U of persons in a town, and that one of them is a barber. Now define the set X to be the subset of U consisting of those people who do not shave themselves. If we assert that the barber shaves just those persons in set X, does he shave himself or not? If we say that he does, then since he shaves himself he cannot be in X, and so cannot shave himself. If we say that he does not shave himself, then he must be in X, which would mean that he does shave himself. This paradox, in different terminology, was known to the Greek philosophers. In the stated form, we can resolve it by insisting that since the hypothesis of such a barber introduces a contradiction, then no such barber can exist, and therefore there is no paradox. However, when expressed more carefully in terms of the class of all classes that are not members of themselves, the paradox is much harder to deal with. It was Bertrand Russell who finally proposed to resolve it with his Theory of Logical Types, in which sets are constrained from having members of unrestricted type [Quine 1962].

2.4.1.1 Relations and Functions. Consider now the set S, whose members are pairs of objects

$$S = \{<a,b>, <c,d>, <e,f>, \ldots\}$$

Such pairs are commonly called *tuples*, and the order within the pairs is important; thus, $<a,b>$ is not the same as $<b,a>$. A common way to obtain a set of tuples is via the set operation of *Cartesian product* of two other sets, where $A \times B$ denotes all tuples $<a_i,b_j>$, with $a_i \in A$ and $b_j \in B$. If there are m objects in set A and n objects in set B, then there are $m \times n$ distinct tuples in the set $C = A \times B$. A pervasive instance of the notion of Cartesian product is the following. Let A and B be the same (infinite) set Z, consisting of all the real numbers. Then $Z \times Z$ corresponds to all the points in the plane, with tuple values $<x,y>$ corresponding to coordinates at those points.

More pertinently, consider the example of the set $A = \{2, 3, 4, 6, 8, 12, 24\}$ and the set of tuples

$$D = \{<2,4>, <2,6>, <2,8>, <2,12>, <2,24>, <3,6>, <3,12>, <3,24>, <4,8>, <4,12>, <4,24>, <6,12>, <6,24>, <8,24>, <12,24>\}$$

The set of tuples D, which is a subset of $A \times A$, can be said to define a *relation* R on the set A, in that, for certain values of i and j, we have $<a_i,a_j> \in D$, or $a_i \mathrm{R}\, a_j$. In our example, the relation $a_i \mathrm{R}\, a_j$ corresponds to the fact that a_i is a proper divisor of a_j. It is perhaps more natural to think of relationships as being defined intensively − that is, in terms of some property such as "divides," "is greater than," "is brother of," etc. But the important point is that relations *can* be defined extensively, through the use of tuples, and sometimes this is a more desirable method.

Consider next a set of tuples based on the sets A and B, and let $<a_i,b_i>$ denote the ith tuple value. Then, if these tuple values are constrained so that all the values a_i are distinct, we have a theoretical basis for another powerful concept in mathematics, that of the *function*. Given a value a_i, we simply need find the unique tuple containing a_i as its left hand member, and then we have $b_i = f(a_i)$. This corresponds to the manner in which, for example, the function $y = \sin(x)$ is expressed in tabular form for discrete values of the independent variable x.

These points will not be discussed further; our intention has been simply to indicate the fundamental importance of sets in mathematics.

2.4.2 Ordered Sets and Set Representations

When we began our discussion of sets, we stressed that sets are intrinsically unordered. In some cases, however, we prefer to think of members of a set as possessing a natural order, in which case the set is conventionally written, for example, as

workdays = <Monday,Tuesday,Wednesday,Thursday,Friday>

instead of with braces. In still other cases, even though sets may not be intrinsically ordered, ordering of the elements is de facto present, particularly when we are using computing machines with their sequential memories. This, in turn, has a bearing upon the methods used for representing sets in computers.

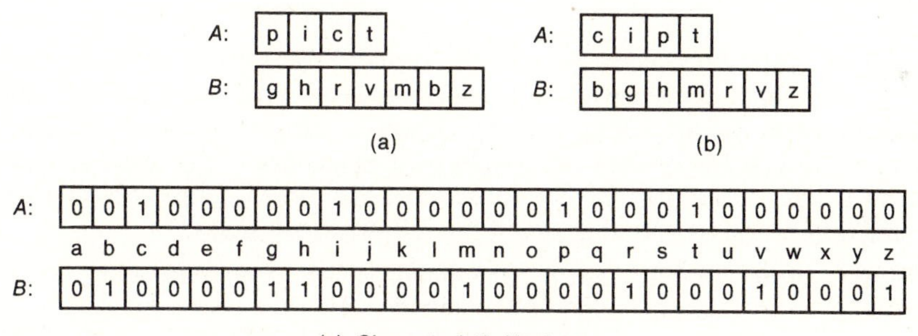

(c) Characteristic Vectors

Figure 2.14 Alternate Set Representations

When we considered how arrays are represented in computers, we found it very natural and efficient to map successive array elements into successive memory locations. In many other data structures, however, there is not one best method for mapping the logical structure into a physical representation in computer memory. This is the case for sets. We will illustrate it by showing two methods for representing the sets $A = \{p,i,c,t\}$ and $B = \{g,h,r,v,m,b,z\}$. One possibility is to simply list all the members of a set as elements of a one-dimensional array, or vector. In such a case, A and B might appear as in Figure 2.14(a). There are several points to be made about this choice of representation:

- There is an ordering of the elements, but it is a de facto one. A and B might equally well be represented as in Figure 2.14(b), or in several other sequences.
- Such representations require arrays of varying length, according to the cardinality of the set.
- Such a representation is adequate for the sets A and B, and also for $fruit = \{apple,banana,orange\}$; but it is not adequate for sets whose members are not simple objects, as in the case of the powerset of fruit.

In many problems involving sets, there are only a definite number of objects that can be members, and the set containing all of these candidate members is called the *universal set*. Since membership is a boolean valued attribute, we can characterize any particular set over this universe by a boolean vector, called the *characteristic vector* of the set. If we suppose that our universe in Figure 2.14 consists of all the lower case letters of the alphabet, then the sets A and B can be represented as in Figure 2.14(c). Note that the characteristic vector requires that the set be an ordered one; the ith boolean value in the vector indicates the absence/presence of the ith object in the set. As long as the universe is not large, the characteristic vector is quite efficient in terms of storage requirements. However, over a large universe, the storage utilization is poor, particularly if most of the sets encountered in practice have cardinality much smaller than the size of the universe. There are still other methods for representing sets, as we will see later (see Section 6.6.5).

2.4.3 Sets in Programming Languages

Few programming languages have direct support for sets as data structures [§]. The user with such a need usually must represent sets in some manner similar to that illustrated in the preceding section. However, there are exceptions. For example, sets are directly supported in Pascal at a modest level. Therein, the universe of members is constrained to be some ordered collection of simple objects, delimited by enumeration or as a subrange, as in the following examples:

```
type   colors = set of (red,orange,yellow,green,blue,violet);
       extent = set of min .. max;
       ...
var    flag: colors;
       ...
  flag := [red,yellow];
       ...
```

The symbols $\in$, $\subset$, $\cap$, and $\cup$ of mathematics are usually not available to computer users. In Pascal, the corresponding symbols in Table 2.1 are employed.

The definition of Pascal does not prescribe how sets are to be represented, but in fact the exclusive method of choice has been the characteristic vector. Most Pascal implementations restrict the number of bits in the vector to the maximum number of bits that can be conveniently manipulated with one machine instruction, which is commonly 60, 64, or 256 bits. Thus, it is common to have the pragmatic restriction that sets in Pascal consist of objects from a universe that is isomorphic to

Operator	Set Notation	Pascal Operator
membership	$\in$	**in**
inclusion	$\subset$	<
intersection	$\cap$	*
union	$\cup$	+
difference	$-$	-

Table 2.1 Pascal Symbols for Set Operations

the subrange 0 .. 59 or 0 .. 63 or 0 .. 255. There are several significant consequences of this choice:

- Membership can be determined efficiently at the machine language level via a shift instruction.
- Intersection maps to logical AND.
- Union maps to logical OR.

```
program SIEVE;

{as prime numbers are found in prospects, they are recorded
  in primes and their multiples are deleted from prospects}

var     i,next: integer;
        primes,prospects: set of 2 .. n;

begin
   prospects := [2 .. n];
   primes := [ ];
   next := 2;
   repeat
      while not (next in prospects) do
         next := next + 1;
      primes := primes + [next];
      i := next;
      while i <= n do begin  {delete multiples of this prime}
         prospects := prospects - [i];
         i := i + next;
      end;
   until prospects = [ ];
end.
```

Algorithm 2.6 SIEVE

An illustration of the use of the set data structure is given by the program SIEVE (Algorithm 2.6), which mimics the action of the *sieve of Eratosthenes* for finding the prime numbers between 2 and n. The method commences with the set *prospects*, containing all the numbers 2 .. n, and the empty set *primes*. Whenever a number i is found to be prime, it is added to the set *primes*, and all of its multiples are deleted from the set *prospects*. The generalization of this technique to allow for arbitrarily large n is left as an exercise (see Exercise 2.13).

2.5 REDUCING ALGORITHMIC COMPLEXITY

There are many problems involving two-dimensional arrays for which the straightforward algorithms are $O(n^3)$. We have seen this, for instance, with matrix multiplication and the solution of simultaneous linear equations in Section 2.3.2. What are the possibilities for reducing this complexity? This section explores several techniques. Before considering these, however, a very significant practical possibility occurs when the matrix can be partitioned into blocks of submatrices, as in Figure 2.15, such that the blocks off the diagonal can be ignored as a first approximation. (That is, they contain values sufficiently small that their effects can be accounted for as second-order corrections.) If the original matrix is of dimension $n \times n$, and if it is partitioned into $m \times m$ submatrices, each of dimension $(n/m) \times (n/m)$, we may then have to deal only with the m sub-problems on the diagonal, each of complexity $O((n/m)^3)$; in other words, we may be able to improve matters by a factor of m^2.

Splitting a large problem into smaller ones may yield improved performance even in cases where none of the subsets of data can be ignored. This is the subject of the next section. In the case that the base type of the arrays is boolean, and when there is access to the underlying capabilities for parallel bit processing that exist with most computers, there is another avenue for improvement. Section 2.5.2 presents this technique in simpler terms. Finally, in 2.5.3, we will see an illustration of applying both methods for the reduction of complexity.

2.5.1 Divide-and-Conquer

Suppose that we have an array of n numbers, and that we wish to find both the smallest and the largest values in the array. A direct solution would be to loop through the entire array and find the smallest value with $n - 1$ comparisons, and likewise find the largest value with another $n - 1$ comparisons. A solution requiring fewer comparisons is illustrated by the procedure MIN_MAX (Algorithm 2.7). Using this method, we split the array in half in order to solve the original problem with both halves; from these solutions, we find the overall minimum and maximum by comparing the minima/maxima from the two halves. By applying this technique recursively, we obtain a solution that requires $(3/2)n - 2$ comparisons rather than $2n - 2$ comparisons.

In order to demonstrate this, we have to deal with the recursive nature of MIN_MAX by finding and solving the corresponding recurrence relation, as in Chapter 1. For this particular case, we see that the work $T(n)$ for an array of size n

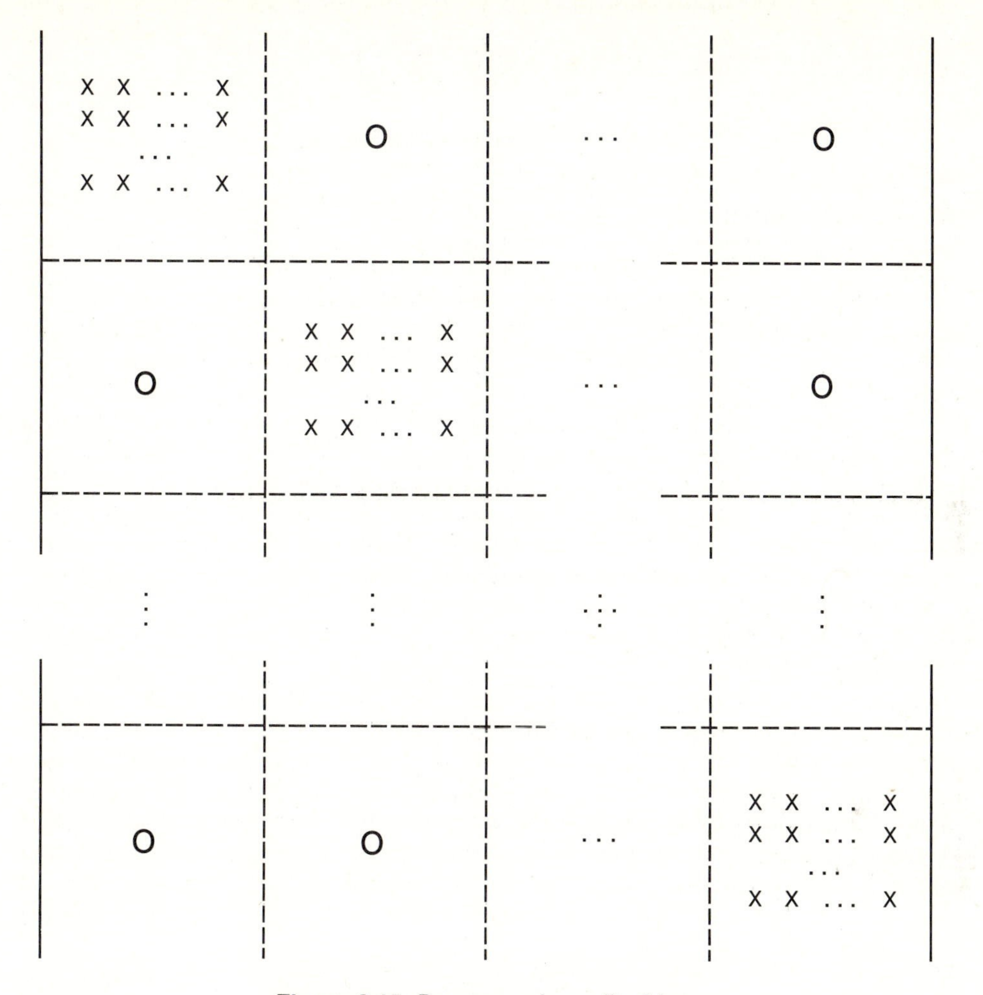

Figure 2.15 Decomposing a Problem

is twice the work, $T(n/2)$, for an array of size $n/2$, followed by two comparisons using those results:

$$T(n) = 2T(n/2) + 2 \tag{2.10}$$

This recurrence relation really applies only if the size of the original array is a power of two; but we can expect to interpolate fairly closely for intermediate sizes. The solution of a non-homogeneous recurrence relation, as in Eq. 2.10, can be expressed as the sum of a homogeneous solution plus a *particular* solution. We have illustrated a little bit about the first of these solutions in Section 1.3.2.3. Obtaining the latter is a bit more complicated, and requires a different tack. A method that is simple and commonly effective, if inelegant, is to guess at the general form of the solution using unknown coefficients. One can then try to determine the

```
procedure MIN_MAX (lo,hi: limit; var mini,maxi: integer);

{finds mini and maxi values between lo and hi in data}

type    limit = 1 .. n;

var     mid,min1,min2,max1,max2: integer;
        data: array [limit] of integer;

begin
  if ((hi - lo) < 2) then begin
    if data [lo] < data [hi] then begin
      mini := data [lo];  maxi := data [hi];
    end else begin
      mini := data [hi];  maxi := data [lo];
    end;
  end else begin
    mid := (lo + hi) div 2;
    MIN_MAX (lo,mid,min1,max1);
    MIN_MAX (mid+1,hi,min2,max2);
    if min1 < min2 then mini := min1
                   else mini := min2;
    if max1 > max2 then maxi := max1
                   else maxi := max2;
  end;
end;
```

Algorithm 2.7 MIN_MAX

unknown coefficients by substituting the general form in the original equation. It is reasonable to expect that the solution must be $O(n)$, or

$$T(n) = An + B \tag{2.11}$$

and substituting this in Eq. 2.10 yields

$$An + B = 2\,[A(n/2) + B] + 2 = An + 2B + 2 \tag{2.12}$$

whence $B = -2$. Finally, since we know that $T(2) = 1$, then $A = 3/2$. Thus, we have shown that

$$T(n) = (3/2)n - 2 \tag{2.13}$$

proving the earlier claim about MIN_MAX.

This technique for reducing complexity is called *divide-and-conquer*. The recurrence relation in Eq. 2.10 expresses the fact that we have divided the original problem into two parts, wherein the first term on the right describes the effort to solve the subproblems, and the second term on the right describes the effort to synthesize the subproblem results. The first term leads to the homogeneous solution, and the second term leads to the particular solution. A generic equation for the divide-and-conquer technique is

$$T(n) = cT(n/d) + f(n) \tag{2.14}$$

Solutions corresponding to different values for the constants c and d and the function f are illustrated in Aho et al. [1983] and Tucker [1984].

It is important to realize that our analysis of MIN_MAX is predicated upon the assumption in Eq. 2.10, that the dominant factor in the algorithm is the number of comparisons between elements of the array, ignoring even the **div** operation. Such an assumption might in many cases be justified by taking note of factors such as: the other costs in the algorithm are proportional to this dominant factor, and so can be subsumed in the constant of proportionality; the comparisons may be between large items, so that the cost of these comparisons really does dominate the computation; etc. Unfortunately, MIN_MAX improves only the constant factor, not the complexity class. In fact, even though it invokes only 75 percent as many comparisons of array elements, the associated overhead will usually cause it to be slower than the naive approach.

More commonly, divide-and-conquer can be very effective in that it may lower the complexity class. We shall see examples of this in the next section and throughout this book (see also Exercise 2.19).

†2.5.1.1 Strassen's Algorithm. A remarkable result by Strassen [1969] gave the first demonstration that matrices can be multiplied with complexity less than $O(n^3)$. To begin with, consider the case of multiplying two 2×2 matrices A and B to produce the 2×2 product matrix C. By the conventional method, the four elements of C are obtained using 8 multiplications and 4 additions, as follows:

$$\begin{aligned}
c_{11} &= a_{11}b_{11} + a_{12}b_{21} \\
c_{12} &= a_{11}b_{12} + a_{12}b_{22} \\
c_{21} &= a_{21}b_{11} + a_{22}b_{21} \\
c_{22} &= a_{21}b_{12} + a_{22}b_{22}
\end{aligned} \tag{2.15}$$

However, consider the unobvious sequence of multiplications:

$$\begin{aligned}
m_1 &= (a_{12} - a_{22})\ (b_{21} + b_{22}) \\
m_2 &= (a_{11} + a_{22})\ (b_{11} + b_{22}) \\
m_3 &= (a_{11} - a_{21})\ (b_{11} + b_{12}) \\
m_4 &= (a_{11} + a_{12})\ b_{22} \\
m_5 &= a_{11}\ (b_{12} - b_{22}) \\
m_6 &= a_{22}\ (b_{21} - b_{11}) \\
m_7 &= (a_{21} + a_{22})\ b_{11}
\end{aligned} \tag{2.16}$$

followed by the sequence:

$$\begin{aligned}
c_{11} &= m_1 + m_2 - m_4 + m_6 \\
c_{12} &= m_4 + m_5 \\
c_{21} &= m_6 + m_7 \\
c_{22} &= m_2 - m_3 + m_5 - m_7
\end{aligned} \tag{2.17}$$

Using Eqs. 2.16 and 2.17, the product of A and B is obtained with a total of 7 multiplications and $k = 18$ additions.

Crucial to Strassen's method is the fact that these same equations can be used when $n \times n$ matrices A,B,C are decomposed into $n/2 \times n/2$ submatrices $A_{i,j}$, $B_{i,j}$, $C_{i,j}$ for $i,j = 1,2$. (Matrices with dimensions that are not powers of two can be accommodated in several ways.) The recurrence equation for the number of multiplications is then $T(n) = 7\ T(n/2)$, with solution

$$T(n) = 7\ T(n/2) = 7^2\ T(n/4) = \cdots = 7^j\ T(n/2^j) = \cdots = 7^{\lg n}\ T(1) \tag{2.18}$$

In other words, since $T(1) = 1$

$$T(n) = 7^{\lg n} = n^{\lg 7} \approx n^{2.81} \tag{2.19}$$

The number of additions can actually be reduced from $k = 18$ to $k = 15$. More significantly, however, it can be shown that the number of additions by this method, for any constant k, is likewise asymptotically $O(n^{2.81})$, whereas the number of additions with the conventional method is $O(n^3)$. Nevertheless, the constant factor associated with this method is rather large, and so n must be sizeable (>40) before the method becomes profitable.

With regard to the inherent complexity of matrix multiplication, there are two interesting postscripts (see also Exercise 2.16). One is that Strassen's method is known not to be optimal. Algorithms of even lower complexity have been exhibited; an example is that of Coppersmith and Winograd [1982] with complexity less than $O(n^{2.5})$. The other comment has to do with the best-case analysis of the problem. It is easy to see that since the product matrix has n^2 elements, then it must require at least that many multiplications. Surprisingly, however, the best theoretical lower bound is still no better than $\Omega(n^2)$. As simple as one might suppose it would be, the question of the complexity of matrix multiplication is still open.

2.5.2 Parallel Bit Operations

At the assembly language level, there is no problem in using parallel bit operations if they exist in system hardware. In Pascal, we have seen that there is the data type **set**, and that a set is virtually always represented as a vector of bits. We can thus obtain access to parallel bit operations in Pascal by letting the truth/falsity of the ith logical value correspond to the presence/absence of i in a set.

When applied to the procedure RULE_MASK (Algorithm 2.5) for dealing with decision tables, this would cause both inner loops to be replaced by single statements, using the set intersection operator. We would then have

`rule := rule * truth [i] ,` and `rule := rule * falsity [i]`

Rather than setting out the other changes to RULE_MASK, we investigate the more general issue: What would it take to multiply two boolean matrices in Pascal, representing them via sets? In fact, this process can be represented in several manners that appear quite different. A method that is both efficient and instructive

```
program BOOL_MULT;

{computes boolean matrix product, C = A × B}

const  u = {# of rows in A and C}
       v = {# of columns in A and # of rows in B}
       w = {# of columns in B and C}

type   setv = set of 1 .. v;
       setw = set of 1 .. w;

var    i,k: integer;
       A: array [1 .. u] of setv;
       B: array [1 .. v] of setw;
       C: array [1 .. u] of setw;

begin
  for i := 1 to u do begin
    C [i] := [ ];
    for k := 1 to v do
      if k in A [i] then
        C [i] := C [i] + B [k];
  end;
end.
```

Algorithm 2.8 BOOL_MULT

is given by the procedure BOOL_MULT (Algorithm 2.8), for matrices of arbitrary but conforming dimensions. We see that the ith row of the product matrix C is obtained as the union of various rows of B, according to the members of the set in the ith row of A. The situation is illustrated in Figure 2.16 for $u = 3$, $v = 4$, $w = 5$; there, for example, since the first row of A is 0101, the first row of C is obtained by OR'ing the second and fourth rows of B. The net result is that BOOL_MULT performs $O(uv)$ set unions instead of $O(uvw)$ individual bit multiplications.

$$\begin{pmatrix} 0 & 1 & 0 & 1 \\ 0 & 0 & 1 & 1 \\ 1 & 1 & 0 & 0 \end{pmatrix} \times \begin{pmatrix} 0 & 0 & 1 & 0 & 0 \\ 0 & 1 & 0 & 0 & 1 \\ 0 & 0 & 0 & 1 & 0 \\ 1 & 0 & 0 & 0 & 1 \end{pmatrix} = \begin{pmatrix} 1 & 1 & 0 & 0 & 1 \\ 1 & 0 & 0 & 1 & 1 \\ 0 & 1 & 1 & 0 & 1 \end{pmatrix}$$

$A: u \times v$ $B: v \times w$ $C: u \times w$

Figure 2.16 Boolean Matrix Multiplication

†2.5.3 Four Russians' Algorithm

When the base type is boolean, there is a method of matrix multiplication that is $O(n^{3/\lg n})$, without reference to parallel bit processing. This method is called the Four Russians' algorithm [Arlazarov et al. 1970; Baase 1978], and it operates by partitioning the two matrices to be multiplied. When this technique can be combined with that of the previous section, then the cost is $O(n^{2/\lg n})$. For simplicity, we will illustrate the method with the two square matrices shown in Figure 2.17. For A and B of dimensions $n \times n$, we would have $m = \lfloor \lg n$ and $p = \lceil (n/m)$. A is then partitioned into p submatrices A_h, and B is partitioned into p submatrices B_h, as shown in the figure. If m does not divide n evenly, it is necessary to pad A with extra columns of zeros and B with extra rows of zeros, so that the submatrices are of the same size.

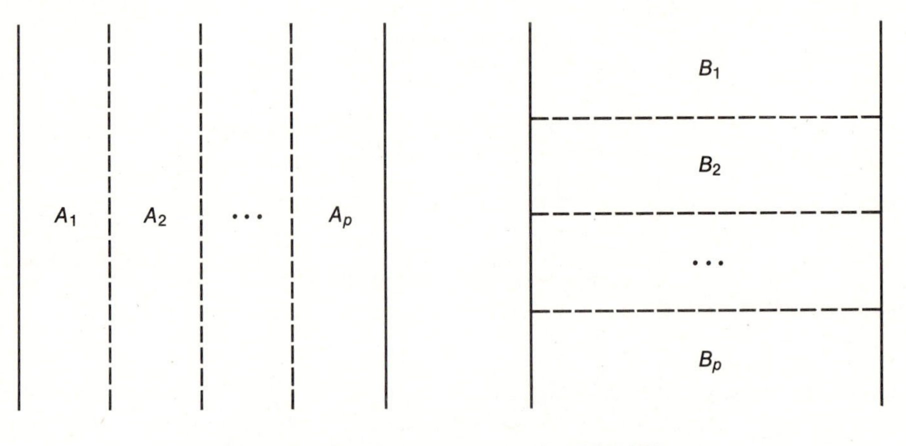

Figure 2.17 Partitioning for RUSSIANS

As a result of the manner of partitioning, the product matrix is given by $C = A \times B = \sum A_h \times B_h$, where each product $A_h \times B_h$ is itself an $n \times n$ matrix. In the preceding section, we have seen that the ith row of the boolean product $C = A \times B$ can be developed by OR'ing rows B_k such that $k \in A_i$. The situation here is exactly analogous, except that the partitioning now causes us to have p submatrices both for A and for B. The resulting reference for A then needs to be $A_{h,i}$ corresponding to the ith row of the hth submatrix of A, and the reference for B needs to be $B_{h,k}$ corresponding to the kth row of the hth submatrix of B.

However, there are just m elements in any row of a submatrix A_h, so that there can be only $2^m = q \leq n$ *distinct* rows in any submatrix A_h. The trick with the Four Russians' algorithm is, for each $1 \leq h \leq p$, to precompute and store in a table the q possibly needed combinations of the rows from B_h, and to use the value of each entire row of A_h as an index into this table. This is illustrated in the program RUSSIANS (Algorithm 2.9), where the boolean combinations of the rows $B[h,k]$ are computed and stored in the array *BCOMB*. Subsequently, each row $A[h,i]$ is interpreted as an integer for indexing into *BCOMB* to find the correct contribution to the sum of products which is C. In reading the algorithm, be careful to realize

```
program RUSSIANS;

const  m = {⌊lg n}
       n = {order of square matrices A, B, C}
       p = {the partitioning factor, ⌈(n/m)}
       q = {2^m-1 (for 0-indexing)}

type   setm = set of 1 .. m;
       setn = set of 1 .. n;

var    h,i,j,k,u: integer;
       A: array [1 .. p,1 .. n] of setm;
       B: array [1 .. p,1 .. m] of setn;
       BCOMB: array [0 .. q] of setn;
       C: array [1 .. n] of setn;

function SET_TO_INT (s: setm): integer;
var    i,j: integer;
begin
  i := 0;
  for j := m downto 1 do
    i := 2 * i + ord (j in s);
  SET_TO_INT := i;
end;

begin
  for i := 1 to n do
    C [i] := [ ];
  for h := 1 to p do begin
    BCOMB [0] := [ ];
    j := 0;
    k := 1;
    u := 1;
    for i := 1 to q do begin      {generate BCOMB from B}
      BCOMB [i] := BCOMB [j] + B [h,k];
      j := j + 1;
      if j = u then begin
        j := 0;
        k := k + 1;
        u := i + 1;
      end;
    end;
    for i := 1 to n do      {index BCOMB by A and apply to C}
      C [i] := C [i] + BCOMB [SET_TO_INT (A [h,i])];
  end;
end.
```

Algorithm 2.9 RUSSIANS

that $A[h,i]$ and $B[h,k]$ do not refer to bits in A and B, but rather to rows (that is, sets) in the hth partitions of A and B.

Two points about the algorithm need amplification. First, it computes each row of *BCOMB* as the boolean sum of a row $B[h,k]$ with a row of *BCOMB* already in hand. This is accomplished by using the variables j,k,u to count in the appropriate manner. Second, the interpretation of the set $A[h,i]$ as an integer is trivial in assembly language, but may or may not be trivial in an HLL. To isolate this consideration, it is depicted in RUSSIANS as the function SET_TO_INT, which is $O(m)$ in time as shown. Note in this function that **ord** (*j* **in** *s*) will have the value 0 or 1, from the definition of the Pascal built-in function **ord**.

What is the complexity of RUSSIANS? It depends upon the implementation. As shown, the outer loop with h is executed p times, the two inner loops with i are executed n times, and within the second inner loop SET_TO_INT is $O(m)$. Thus, the complexity is $O(mnp) = O(n^2)$. In Section 3.2.2 we will see how in Pascal to overcome the bottleneck introduced by this version of SET_TO_INT, and how to achieve the performance $O(np) = O(n^{2/\lg n})$. More generally, it can be shown that no method based upon row-unions can attain a lower complexity, except in the sense of having a smaller constant factor [Angluin 1976].

```
0 0 0 0|0 0 0 0|1 0 0 1
1 1 0 0|1 1 0 0|1 1 0 0
0 0 0 0|0 0 0 0|1 1 0 0
1 1 0 0|0 0 0 0|0 1 0 0
1 0 0 1|0 0 0 1|1 0 0 0
0 0 0 0|0 1 0 1|0 0 0 0
1 0 0 1|0 0 0 0|0 0 0 0
0 0 0 0|0 0 0 1|0 0 0 0
0 0 1 0|0 0 0 0|0 0 0 0
1 0 0 1|0 1 1 1|0 1 1 1
1 0 0 0|0 0 0 1|0 0 0 0
1 0 0 0|0 1 0 0|0 0 0 0
```

(a) *A*

```
0 0 0 0 0 1 1 0 1 0 0 0
1 1 0 0 1 1 0 0 1 0 0 0
0 1 1 0 1 0 0 0 0 0 0 1
-----------------------
0 1 0 0 0 0 1 0 0 0 1 0
0 0 0 0 1 0 0 0 0 0 0 1
0 0 0 1 0 0 1 0 0 0 0 1
-----------------------
0 0 0 0 0 0 1 0 0 0 0 0
0 1 0 0 0 1 0 0 0 0 0 1
0 0 0 0 0 0 0 0 1 1 0 0
-----------------------
0 1 0 0 0 0 1 0 0 0 0 0
0 1 0 0 1 0 0 1 0 0 0 0
0 0 0 0 0 1 0 0 0 0 0 1
```

(b) *B*

```
0 0 0 0 0 0 0 0 0 0 0 0
0 0 0 0 0 1 1 0 1 0 0 0
1 1 0 0 1 1 0 0 1 0 0 0
1 1 0 0 1 1 1 0 1 0 0 0
0 1 1 0 1 0 0 0 0 0 0 1
0 1 1 0 1 1 1 0 1 0 0 1
1 1 1 0 1 1 0 0 1 0 0 1
1 1 1 0 1 1 1 0 1 0 0 1
```

(c) *BCOMB*

```
0 0 0 0 0 0 0 0 0 0 0 0
1 1 0 0 1 1 1 0 1 0 0 0
0 0 0 0 0 0 0 0 0 0 0 0
1 1 0 0 1 1 1 0 1 0 0 0
0 0 0 0 0 1 1 0 1 0 0 0
0 0 0 0 0 0 0 0 0 0 0 0
0 0 0 0 0 1 1 0 1 0 0 0
0 0 0 0 0 0 0 0 0 0 0 0
0 1 1 0 1 0 0 0 0 0 0 1
0 0 0 0 0 1 1 0 1 0 0 0
0 0 0 0 0 1 1 0 1 0 0 0
0 0 0 0 0 1 1 0 1 0 0 0
```

(d) *C*

Figure 2.18 Trace of Algorithm RUSSIANS (see Figure 2.17)

To illustrate the algorithm, consider the matrices A and B, as shown in (a) and (b) of Figure 2.18. Here we have $n = 12, m = 3, p = 4$; note that the index type of $BCOMB$ is 0 .. 7 rather than 1 .. 8, to allow 0-origin indexing. For the submatrices A_1 and B_1, the computed value of $BCOMB$ is shown in (c), and the corresponding first value of C is shown in (d). New values for $BCOMB$ and updated values for C would have to be computed for $h = 2,3,4$ to complete the calculation.

2.6 ADVANTAGES AND LIMITATIONS OF ARRAYS

In Chapter 1, we cited the distinction between a logical data structure and its physical realization in storage. Most HLL's explicitly provide the array as a data structure for the user, thereby allowing references of the form $x\,[i,j,\ldots]$ without any need to think about how the references are carried out. In actual practice, as we saw in Section 2.2.1, the compiler usually makes such a reference by storing the array in row-major order, and then employing a storage allocation function that reduces to the formula

$$\text{loc}\,(x\,[i,j,\ldots]) = p + q \times i + r \times j + \cdots \tag{2.15}$$

employing the values p,q,r, etc. from the dope vector for that array. From this point of view, the physical storage structure of an array is not radically different from its logical data structure; it just involves "unravelling" along the dimensions.

Implemented in this fashion, arrays are the most natural and efficient data structure for many applications. They have the following advantages:

A1. They are well suited to random access; that is, any element $x\,[i,j,\ldots]$ can be referenced as directly as any other element, using Eq. 2.15.

A2. If we have located $x\,[i,j,\ldots]$, then it is very easy to traverse to any of the neighbor elements $x\,[i-1,j,\ldots]$, $x\,[i+1,j,\ldots]$, $x\,[i,j-1,\ldots]$, $x\,[i,j+1,\ldots]$, ... ; from Eq. 2.15, it simply requires incrementing loc $(x\,[i,j,\ldots])$ by $-q$ or $+q$, or $-r$ or $+r$, etc.

A3. If the elements of an array have independent values and so must all be retained, the use of storage is very efficient. The only overhead, in fact, is that required for the elements of the dope vector.

On the other hand, arrays as we have described them thus far have several inflexibilities that make them unsuitable for storage of data in numerous applications. Some of these limitations are as follows:

L1. Arrays are required to have a homogenous base type in most HLL's. We cannot, for example, have an array in which one element is a character, another element is a number, and still another element is a sub-array.

L2a. It is very awkward to insert or delete new elements (as opposed to modifying existing values) in an array. Thus, in our survey of persons with respect to sex, education, and marital status in Section 2.3.1, suppose – after all the data was recorded in our array – that there were no widowed persons and that we wished to delete that category. Or suppose that we needed to add to the educational dimension the category of post-graduate attainment. Either of these would change the dimensions of the array, and would necessitate reshuffling all or most of the elements in storage. This reshuffling, since it involves a change in the total storage requirement, could force other data objects to be relocated as well.

L2b. Even more drastically, suppose that we wish to add another dimension to an array. Imagine in our survey that we now need to tabulate results by political affiliation as well as by sex, education, and marital status. This could cause reshuffling, as before; but now, all the code for processing these results must be changed as well, since references to *survey* with three subscripts will no longer be valid.

L3. It is quite common to have arrays in which a high percentage – 90%, 99%, or even more – of the elements are zero in value. It can obviously be quite inefficient to store such *sparse arrays* in conventional lexicographic order.

There are several answers to these difficulties. For the first point, the inability to store heterogeneous data in an array, we will find an answer primarily in Chapter 3, with records; another point of view is presented in Section 2.9. We address the second point in the next section and also in Section 2.9. The topic of sparse arrays is treated in Section 2.8.

†2.7 ALTERNATIVE STORAGE SCHEMES

As we stated, arrays are ill suited to problems in which their dimensions tend to vary. Nonetheless, it is possible to reduce this disadvantage in some cases by storing the array in memory in a manner that compromises one or more of the advantages listed in Section 2.6. We will describe some of these approaches in this section; later, in Chapter 4, we will revisit the subject of arrays to see what can be gained by using lists and pointers.

For ease of discussion throughout this section, let us now restrict our attention to two-dimensional arrays; there is no intrinsic difficulty in extending these concepts to arrays of higher dimension. First, we will consider how such an array could be enlarged or extended without having to reshuffle any of its elements. Of course, the total storage requirement increases in such a case, but we will assume that such growth has been anticipated in the initial allocation of storage.

Consider an array $A\,[1\,..\,m,1\,..\,n]$ and imagine the two following situations:

(a) that we wish to add another row $A\,[m+1,\,]$, or

(b) that we wish to add another column $A\,[,n+1]$

How feasible are either of these two extensions to A? Fairly obviously, if A is stored in row-major order, then (a) is easy and (b) is impossible without complete reshuffling; if A is stored in column-major order, then (b) is easy and (a) is impossible without reshuffling. Thus, it is quite easy to extend an array in just one dimension, as long as it has been stored in a manner that anticipates growth in that dimension. Moreover, the storage allocation function remains linear in all the indices.

What can be done about extending arrays in more than one dimension? Also, as we look at the consequences of mapping array elements into memory space, how does this affect the proximity, in that memory space, of neighboring elements in each of the dimensions? These questions have been investigated in depth [§]. In the next two sections, we describe several techniques, primarily of theoretical interest, for dealing with these matters. Our discussion is restricted to the case of main memory, which is one-dimensional in nature. It is interesting to speculate on the effect of memories with higher dimensional address structure, such as disk drives.

†2.7.1 Shell Storage

In this section, we describe two storage allocation methods that provide extendibility in more than one dimension, at the expense of ease of random access. They correspond to growth taking place in shells. It sometimes happens that we have a square array in which it is natural to think of both growth and traversal as taking place in *cubic shells* that expand in one quadrant. This is shown in Figure 2.19, where (a) depicts the elements partitioned into shells, and (b) depicts the locations in which elements of A are stored. It is now easy to traverse successive shells by accessing elements in consecutive memory locations; moreover, it is straightforward to annex another shell without having to reshuffle any elements already in storage. What has been lost is the ability to easily access elements at random, since the corresponding allocation function is

$$\text{loc}\,(A\,[i,j]) = b + (\max(i,j) - 1)^2 + (\max(i,j) - 1) + (j - i) \tag{2.21}$$

which is equivalent to

$$\begin{aligned} \text{loc}\,(A\,[i,j]) &= b + i^2 - 2i + j \quad (i > j) \\ \text{loc}\,(A\,[i,j]) &= b + j^2 - i \qquad\quad\;\; (i \le j) \end{aligned} \tag{2.22}$$

In general, the storage allocation function for cubic shells of dimension n is a polynomial of nth degree in the subscripts, which complicates both random access and also traversal to neighbors along the dimensions.

Reminiscent of the triangular arrays of Section 2.2.2 are *diagonal shells*, as illustrated in Figure 2.20. Again, (a) depicts the elements partitioned into shells, and (b) depicts the locations in which elements of A are stored. Both traversal and growth are easy in the diagonals, but random access is again more complicated, given by

$$\text{loc}\,(A\,[i,j]) = b + \binom{i+j}{2} - i = b + \frac{(i^2 + 2ij + j^2 - 3i - j)}{2} \tag{2.23}$$

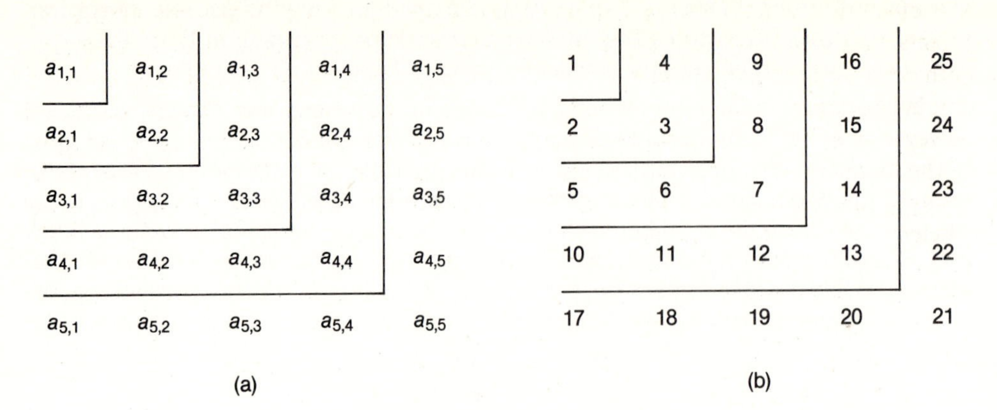

Figure 2.19 Cubic Shells

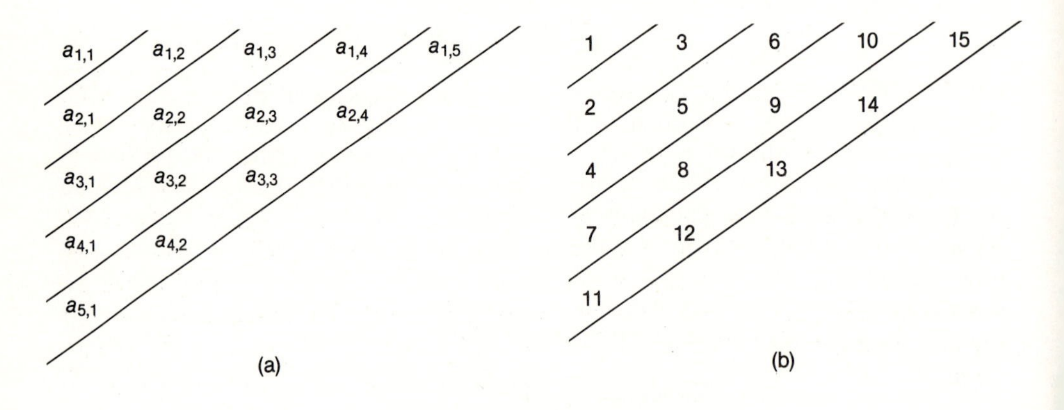

Figure 2.20 Diagonal Shells

Note that Eq. 2.23 has a term with both i and j. Because storage allocation functions for diagonal shells contain such multivariate terms, traversal to neighbors along the dimensions is even less convenient than it is for cubic shells.

†2.7.2 Arbitrary Extendibility

Allocating array elements in shells provides a degree of multi-dimensional extendibility, but only for certain preferred patterns of traversal. This causes both random access and traversal to neighbors along the dimensions to be awkward. We now examine two storage allocation functions that allow both very general extendibility and relative ease of access to these neighbors.

The first method uses the function

$$\text{loc}\ (A\ [i,j]) = b + 2^{i-1} \times 3^{j-1} \tag{2.24}$$

The effect of this is shown is Figure 2.21, where (a) depicts the array A, and (b) depicts the memory locations obtained via Eq. 2.24. It is now possible to annex both rows and columns in any arbitrary sequence. Also, traversals to neighbors are obtained by multiplying or dividing by 2 or 3. To reference a random element, however, requires computing exponential terms. In addition, only a small fraction of the available memory locations is "hit" by Eq. 2.24. For an $m \times n$ array A, the storage utilization is $(m \times n) \div (2^{m-1}3^{n-1})$; in Figure 2.21, this corresponds to an efficiency of 5 percent.

a_{11}	a_{12}	a_{13}	a_{14}	1	3	9	27	1	2	4	8
a_{21}	a_{22}	a_{23}	a_{24}	2	6	18	54	3	6	12	24
a_{31}	a_{32}	a_{33}	a_{34}	4	12	36	108	5	10	20	40
a_{41}	a_{42}	a_{43}	a_{44}	8	24	72	216	7	14	28	56
a_{51}	a_{52}	a_{53}	a_{54}	16	48	144	432	9	18	36	72
	(a)				(b)				(c)		

Figure 2.21 Arbitrary Extendibility

The inefficiency associated with Eq. 2.24 is due in part to the fact that it maps the subscripts *into* the integers rather than *onto* the integers. Therefore, one would hope that an allocation function mapping onto rather than into the integers would give better results. This possibility can be realized, in the two-dimensional case at any rate, by means of the observation that any integer can be uniquely expressed as the product of an odd integer, $2i - 1$, and some power of two, 2^{j-1}. Accordingly, let

$$\text{loc}\,(A\,[i,j]) = b + (2i - 1) \times 2^{j-1} \tag{2.25}$$

The effect of this mapping upon the array elements in Figure 2.21(a) is shown in Figure 2.21(c). Traversal to neighbors in columns is obtained by addition, and traversal to neighbors in rows is obtained by multiplying or dividing by a power of 2 (which is particularly easy to do on almost all computers). Although this method is superior to the preceding one in both ease of traversal and in storage efficiency (28 percent in the figure), the exponential term in j still causes terms to be allocated in a manner sufficiently non-compact that extension of A by columns is impractical.

Although the two schemes described in this section allow for arbitrary extendibility and also afford relative ease of access to neighbors, the cost of random access is high, and storage efficiency is poor. Section 4.3.3 discusses an alternative, more practical solution to the problem of arbitrary extendibility.

2.8 SPARSE MATRICES

We have defined sparse arrays as those containing relatively few elements (10 percent or less) that are non-zero in value. Such arrays are particularly common in the solutions of large systems of equations. Thus, for reasons of relevance as well as convenience, we will restrict our discussion to the two-dimensional case of sparse matrices. Even a modest system of simultaneous equations of order 100 would entail 10,000 real coefficients, or 80,000 bytes if storage were allocated for all of them. For larger systems, it becomes still more imperative to suppress the storage of full matrices consisting largely of zeros (not to mention saving the time that would be wasted in processing these zeros). Several techniques have been employed to effect this suppression [§]. Our objective here is mainly to describe what issues are involved in choosing one method over another.

The important issues are as follows:

1. *Density.* Each of the methods to be described shortly suppresses zero elements at the expense of carrying along information to identify the coordinates of the retained elements. The storage efficiency of these techniques varies considerably as a function of the density ρ, defined as the proportion of non-zero elements.

2. *Access requirements.* Applications of sparse matrices may require easy random access to elements, easy traversal to elements in both rows and columns, or easy traversal along one dimension only. These issues are reminiscent of those discussed in Section 2.7.

3. *Insertion and deletion.* Although there are many problems in which the locations of the non-zero elements do not change, there are also processes wherein elements may change from zero to non-zero, and vice-versa. Thus, it may be important to employ a technique that facilitates the continual insertion and deletion of elements in the matrix.

4. *Special formats.* It is useful to distinguish three different types of sparsity, as illustrated in Figure 2.22. Here, (a) corresponds to random sparsity, (b) corresponds to band sparsity, and (c) corresponds to block sparsity. In cases (b) and (c), it is common to employ special techniques to exploit the regularity of the matrix structure. All of the methods that we will describe here, however, are for the more general case of randomly sparse matrices.

To facilitate the description and comparison of the methods, we will use the sparse matrix M of Figure 2.23. It is actually rather far from being sparse according to most criteria, but it serves the purpose of providing a good example. In brief succession, we will consider the following methods – bit maps, address maps, delta-skips, and triples – for storing sparse matrices. None of these methods are directly supported in HLL's. Although it is possible to carry them out within an HLL, the attendant overhead can be high. There is thus a strong implicit assumption, with all of these methods, that they are implemented in assembler language.

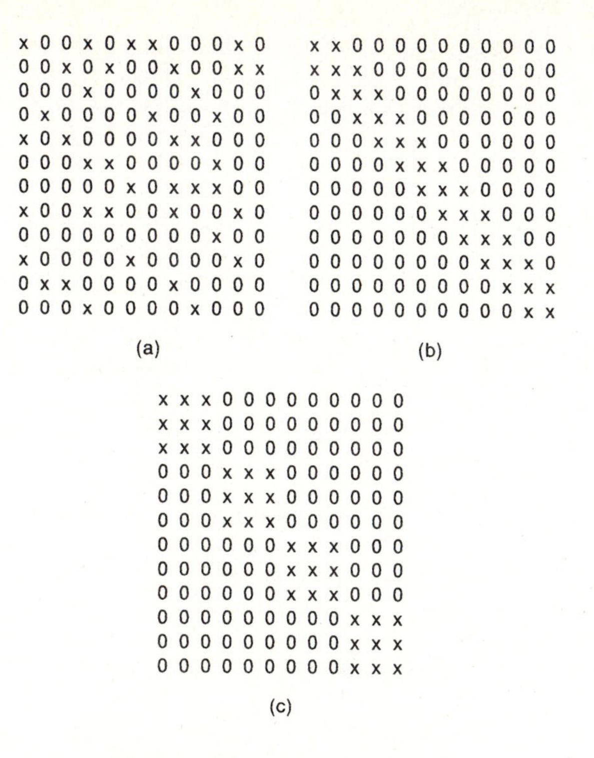

Figure 2.22 Types of Sparsity

The *bit map* scheme would represent the sample matrix M by the three items shown in Figure 2.24. The items are an array B of bits with values of 1/0 corresponding to non-zero/zero elements of M, a vector Z containing the non-zero elements of M, and a vector R containing the relative locations of the first element of each row of M in Z. The bit values of B would really be packed into machine words – typically 32 bits at a time, in row-major order – to match the sequence of elements of M in Z. The vector R is somewhat optional; its inclusion would depend upon the application. Let us compute the storage requirement S (in bytes) for this method. If we presume that the elements of M are real and require 8 bytes each, and that the addresses in R require 4 bytes each, then S depends upon the size of M, which is n^2, and its density ρ. It is seen to be

$$S = 8\rho n^2 + \frac{n^2}{8} + 4n \tag{2.26}$$

where the three terms correspond to the storage requirements for Z, B, and R. Succinctly, the bit map method has good storage efficiency for matrices that are not overly sparse. However, as the density becomes very small, then for large matrices the middle term in Eq. 2.26 causes the method to have excessive overhead compared with other methods. With respect to accessing array elements from Z using B and R, the method makes it fairly easy to traverse along rows of M, but considerably more costly to traverse along columns of M. (It would be possible to make traversal easy along columns as well as rows; however, this would entail the expense of storing, in addition to B and R, the transpose of B and a vector C of column origins.)

```
0 5 0 0 2
4 0 9 0 0
0 0 0 6 0
1 0 0 0 3
0 8 0 0 0
```

Figure 2.23 An Example Sparse Matrix

```
0 1 0 0 1
1 0 1 0 0
0 0 0 1 0      5 2 4 9 6 1 3 8      1 3 5 6 8
1 0 0 0 1
0 1 0 0 0             Z                 R

    B
```

Figure 2.24 Bit Map Allocation

```
0 1 0 0 2
1 0 2 0 0
0 0 0 1 0      5 2 4 9 6 1 3 8      0 2 4 5 7
1 0 0 0 2
0 1 0 0 0             Z                 R

    A
```

Figure 2.25 Address Map Allocation

The *address map* method is similar to the bit map method. As applied to the sample matrix M, it entails the three items of Figure 2.25. The items are an array A (to be described), a vector Z (as before), and a vector R (almost as before). In this scheme, the zero elements of A correspond to zero elements in M; non-zero elements in A are displacement values to be added to the elements of R, in order to access the corresponding elements in Z. The storage requirements for this method are quite a bit higher than in the bit map method. The saving observation is that, depending upon the size of M, a small number of bits, perhaps just a byte, will probably be sufficient to indicate the displacement in any one row. With such an assumption, we find for this method that

$$S = 8\rho n^2 + n^2 + 4n \qquad (2.27)$$

In exchange for this greater storage requirement, the address map method offers improved traversal capability, assuming that the underlying machine has reasonable character or byte operations. In particular, it becomes reasonable to traverse along both rows and columns, without the necessity of storing the transpose of A.

In the *delta-skip* method, the matrix M is represented by the items in Figure 2.26. Here, C is the vector of relative locations of the first element of each column of M in X (4 bytes should be adequate again). An element of X is either a non-zero element of M, or a count of intervening zero elements in a column of M until the next non-zero element. In the use of this method for solving large sets of equations via a relaxation method, double precision integers were employed; for each element of X the least significant bit was used to signify the proper interpretation of the element. The storage requirements for this scheme depend upon a somewhat unpredictable factor, namely the degree to which non-zero elements and zero elements in M tend to be separately clustered. In the most favorable case, this could require just two delta elements for each column of M, for

$$S = 8\rho n^2 + 16n + 4n \tag{2.28a}$$

In other cases this could require for each column of M as many delta elements as there are non-zero elements, giving

$$S = 8\rho n^2 + 8\rho n^2 + 4n \tag{2.28b}$$

except that Eq. 2.28a is a lower bound for Eq. 2.28b. For large systems of very sparse equations, the effect of the middle term in Eq. 2.28 makes the storage requirement of the delta-skip method superior to that of the bit map method. In terms of traversal, the delta-skip method is extremely fast in traversing the selected dimension (columns, in this case) since no scanning of a map is required; however, it is useless for traversing the other dimension.

```
X = (1) 4 (1) 1 (1) / 5 (3) 8 / (1) 9 (3) / (2) 6 (2) / 2 (2) 3 (1)
C = 1 6 9 12 15
```

Figure 2.26 Delta-Skip Allocation

```
R = 1 1 2 2 3 4 4 5
C = 2 5 1 3 4 1 5 2
Z = 5 2 4 9 6 1 3 8
```

Figure 2.27 Triples Allocation

In addition to their properties already cited, the bit map, address map, and delta-skip methods all have the limitation that they are ill suited to problems in which non-zero elements may vanish and/or appear, necessitating deletion and insertion. With the last method that we will illustrate here, the *triples* method, such a capability is at least possible, albeit somewhat awkwardly. For this method, the sample matrix M is represented by the items in Figure 2.27, where R is a vector of row indices, C is a vector of column indices, and Z is a vector of the non-zero values of M. Clearly, the array elements $R[i]$, $C[i]$, and $Z[i]$ specify the non-zero element $Z[i] = M[R[i], C[i]]$. The storage required for elements of R and C depends, of course, upon the maximum subscript value to be accommodated. Supposing that we generously allow 2 bytes, or 16 bits, for the subscript range, then we find that

$$S = 8\rho n^2 + 2\rho n^2 + 2\rho n^2 \tag{2.29}$$

For not very sparse matrices, the overhead with this method is quite high. However, since all the terms in Eq. 2.29 are proportional to ρ, the triples method becomes more storage-efficient than any of the preceding methods for low values of ρ. Like the preceding methods, the triples method has a bias for traversal in one dimension over the other. Along the preferred dimension, traversal with triples is not as fast as with delta-skip, but faster than with either map method.

Finally, it is possible, although slightly awkward, to accommodate insertions and deletions via the following strategy:

1. Make the dimensions of the vectors R,C,Z somewhat greater than what is needed to accommodate all the initially non-zero elements of M; these extra positions then become an overflow area.
2. As elements of M vanish, simply allow those Z-values to go to zero.
3. As new elements need to be inserted in M, post them as they occur in the unused overflow positions of R,C,Z.
4. Any processing of the elements of M using R,C,Z must take the overflow area into special account.
5. Periodically, the elements of R,C,Z can be sifted to discard zero values in Z and to re-establish them in sequence as desired – say, row-major order, as they are in Figure 2.27.

This almost concludes our discussion of sparse matrices. To illustrate the relative storage efficiencies of the four methods described, we give in Table 2.2 the storage requirements (in bytes) for a sparse matrix of dimensions 100×100, with values of ρ from .1 down to .003. For this purpose, Eq. 2.28 was evaluated by computing the geometric mean of Eqs. 2.28a and 2.28b – that is, the square root of their product.

Density ρ	.1	.03	.01	.003
Bit-Map	9650	4050	2450	1890
Address-Map	18400	12800	11200	10640
Delta-Skip	11978	4670	2331	1260
Triples	12000	3600	1200	360

Table 2.2 Storage Requirements for Sparse Matrices

There are two remaining points that should be mentioned here. First, there is another very important method of representation, using linked lists, that must be deferred to the appropriate point in Chapter 4. Second, we have characterized the methods solely in terms of various criteria cited at the beginning of this section. In a given case, however, the type of array processing required by an application may substantially influence the choice of representation. For example, it might be important to compare two matrices of equal size to determine when corresponding elements are non-zero. For such a case, it is easy to see that the bit map method would be uniquely effective.

†2.9 EXTENDED SEMANTICS FOR ARRAYS

In the two preceding sections, we discussed various alternative techniques for representing arrays in storage, focusing primarily on ways to compensate for some of the shortcomings listed in Section 2.6. In the present section, we deal with arrays at a much higher level, briefly citing some ways in which the ordinary concept of an array as a logical data structure has been extended.

Recall that the indices into an array may be constants, variables, or even expressions; but they must evaluate to integer values. Some HLL's, such as REXX, support arrays with a more general form of subscripting wherein the indices may be non-numeric symbols, such as "cow," "moon," "spoon," etc. This effect is called *associative indexing*.

A different and even more powerful generalization is found in the the language APL. It was originally invented by Iverson [1964, 1980] for notational purposes, but has since been widely implemented on many different computers [Falkoff and Iverson 1973]. The language has many novel features, and we will not try to describe APL in any detail in this brief space. From our perspective, the significant point is that it employs the array as its single, native data structure. However, arrays are completely dynamic with regard to both size and base type in APL. Whereas all type attributes must be explicitly given in Pascal, all attributes are implicitly deduced in APL. Moreover, there are a great number of both arithmetic and structuring operators. For most computations, these can be applied directly to arrays without the necessity of any explicit indexing. This dispenses with the usual necessity to visualize array operations as being performed one element at a time, with index variables varying simultaneously and correctly over their appropriate domains. By way of illustration, the entire process for multiplying two matrices A and B (see Algorithm 2.4) is expressed in APL simply as `C←A+.×B`. This relative brevity of programs in APL as compared with other languages is very typical. Such brevity can make it possible to conceptualize problems and their solutions in global terms, without regard for irrelevant and specific details.

The diversity of data structures in this book reflects the fact that no single data structure is best for all purposes. Nonetheless, it is possible to construct models of computation in which a single data structure is sufficiently powerful to accommodate everything else, as we will see on several occasions. It is worth comparing such models for computation with the ideas expressed in Section 2.4.1, wherein the development and elaboration of set theory in the last century has provided the theoretical underpinnings of almost all of modern mathematical analysis. *Array Theory* illustrates the analogous idea of a generic basis for computation based upon the array data structure [More 1973]. It is not a programming language, but rather a large body of axioms and proofs. As the theory has evolved, however, it has been translated into various experimental programming systems, notably APL2 and NIAL (Nested Interactive Array Language). One of the important features of these developments is that they allow the elements of an array to be heterogeneous in nature. The notations of both Array Theory and its programming derivatives are largely based upon that of APL.

2.10 OVERVIEW

When data is of homogeneous type and has a highly regular, fixed shape, then the array serves very well as a structure onto which to map the data. Under these circumstances, it offers maximum storage efficiency and very good access times. Thus, it is not surprising that the array is the first (and sometimes only) data structure discussed in beginning programming courses.

In this chapter we explored the types of calculations for which arrays are particularly well suited, of which linear algebra is a prime example. From this starting point, we followed three paths that point the way to recurrent themes in this book. One important direction deals with attaining more flexibility in data structures. Sparse arrays illustrate a significant instance of this by relaxing the regularity of arrays. Another important goal is to reduce the complexity of a computation on a given data structure; the technique that is often appropriate for doing this with arrays is divide-and-conquer. A third theme investigates ways to generalize what can be done with the array as a logical data structure, leading to the topics of associative arrays, APL, and Array Theory.

2.11 BIBLIOGRAPHIC NOTES

- Extended treatments of decision tables can be found in Montalbano [1974], Pollack et al. [1971], and Pooch [1974]. For an interesting discussion of the comparative power of decision tables versus other methods for representing algorithms (for example, flowcharts and structured programs), see Lew [1982].

- Closely related variations of the rule-mask technique can be found in Barnard [1969], Kirk [1965], and Muthukrishnam and Rajaraman [1970]. An additional feature of the method is that it can be implemented in a manner to detect decision table ambiguities at run-time, as well as at compile time [Imbrasha and Rajaraman 1978].

- Two programming languages that are primarily set-oriented are LEAP and SETL. LEAP is a language similar to ALGOL, but containing several built-in set operations as well [Feldman and Rovner 1969]. A primary objective in its design was efficiency of searching in sets; it has been used primarily for work in graphics and in artificial intelligence. SETL has been used for a variety of combinatorial problems. It primarily employs a set representation [Kennedy and Schwartz 1975] based upon hashing (see Section 10.4); however, a significant objective in the design of the SETL compiler [Schwartz 1975] is that it should select the best representation for a given problem (see Section 9.3).

- The issues of array extendibility and the resulting proximity of neighbor elements are explored in DeMillo et al. [1978], Rosenberg [1975], and Solntseff and Wood [1977]. Methods for both shell storage and for arbitrary extendibility are given in Rosenberg [1974], along with analyses thereof.

- Discussions of sparse matrix representations and of basic methods of operations using them, can be found in MacVeigh [1977] and Pooch and Nieder [1973]. The delta-skip representation and its use in solving large systems of linear equations is described in Smith [1965].

2.12 REFERENCE TO TERMINOLOGY

2.13 EXERCISES

Sections 2.1 – 2.2

2.1 What is the cardinality of the array A declared by

```
A: array [-3 .. 7,9 .. 13,4 .. 17,-1 .. -1] of real
```

2.2 [Wirth 1973] M and N are 3×3 arrays of integers, with M initially as follows:

$$M = \begin{pmatrix} 2 & 1 & 3 \\ 1 & 3 & 2 \\ 3 & 1 & 2 \end{pmatrix}$$

(a) What is the value of N after executing

```
for i := 1 to 3 do
   for j := 1 to 3 do
      N [i,j] := M [M [i,j],M [j,i]];
```

(b) What is the value of M after executing

```
for i := 1 to 3 do
   for j := 1 to 3 do
      M [i,j] := M [M [i,j],M [j,i]];
```

2.3 Stored in row-major order starting at location 376 is

```
V: array [0 .. 5,-2 .. 2,-3 .. 8,4 .. 7] of real
```

(a) What is the location of the element V [2,1,3,6]?

(b) What are the coefficients of the dope vector for V?

†2.4 Suppose that we have T: **array** [1 .. n] **of** integer with ordered elements. Write a function SEARCH_C that has as input parameters an argument key and a table such as T, and that does the following. If the argument is already present, it should return the index of its location; if the argument is not present, it should insert it — relocating array elements as necessary so that the ordering will be maintained — and then return the index of the argument in the rearranged table. What is the computational complexity of your algorithm? What might be the hazards in using an algorithm with this specification?

Sections 2.3 – 2.4

2.5 Consider the problem of evaluating a polynomial

$$y(x) = a_n x^n + a_{n-1} x^{n-1} + \cdots + a_1 x + a_0$$

for integer a_i and real x, and with each a_i stored as the ith entry of an array of coefficients. Assume that there is no exponentiation operator, so that the high degree terms must be obtained by repeated multiplication by x. Write a function to do this, and test it against

$$y(x) = x^7 + 6x^6 - 7x^5 + 12x^4 + 2x^2 - 3x + 8$$

for several values of x, such as 1.7 and −7.2. How many multiplications and how many additions does your method require, as a function of the degree of the polynomial? What can you say with regard to the minimum complexity of an algorithm for this problem?

2.6 For a matrix A of dimensions $m \times n$, define the vector R by $r_i = \min(a_{i,s})$ for $s = 1 .. n$, and the vector C by $c_j = \max(a_{t,j})$ for $t = 1 .. m$. A is then said to have a *saddle point* if $\max(r_i) = \min(c_j)$. Write a procedure to test for the presence of a saddle point in a matrix, and apply it to several 5×7 matrices of your choosing.

††2.7 [Knuth 1973a] In Exercise 2.6, assume that the $m \times n$ elements of a matrix have distinct values and that all permutations of these elements in the matrix locations are equally likely. What is the probability of there being a saddle point?

†2.8 The array shown in Figure 2.28 is an example of a *magic square of order n*. It has the property that its entries consist of the numbers from 1 to n^2, and that the sums along any row, any column, or the two diagonals all add up to $\frac{1}{2} \times n \times (n^2 + 1)$. For n an odd number, a long known method of construction is as follows. Start with 1 in the middle of the top row, and always record the next integer diagonally to the left and above the previous integer. If this causes you to fall off an edge of the square, then "wrap around" modulo n; if the sought-after square is already occupied, then drop down one row and proceed. Write a procedure to generate magic squares for odd values of n, and use it to compute the magic square of order 13.

†2.9 Permutations form a group. The product $P_a \times P_b$ signifies the result of applying first P_a and then P_b. The inverse P^{-1} is a permutation with the property that $P \times P^{-1}$ leaves the elements in their original arrangement. Thus, for P analogous to Eq. 1.12, P^{-1} is found by first transposing the two rows and then reordering the columns with respect to the new first row, as follows:

$$\begin{pmatrix} 4 & 6 & 7 & 2 & 5 & 1 & 3 \\ 1 & 2 & 3 & 4 & 5 & 6 & 7 \end{pmatrix} = \begin{pmatrix} 1 & 2 & 3 & 4 & 5 & 6 & 7 \\ 6 & 4 & 7 & 1 & 5 & 2 & 3 \end{pmatrix}$$

Write a procedure that computes the inverse of P in situ; that is, it replaces the elements of P by the elements of P^{-1} as it executes. Assume that P is given as in the second line of Eq. 1.12, but output P^{-1} in cycle notation (canonical form is not required).

28	19	10	1	48	39	30
29	27	18	9	7	47	38
37	35	26	17	8	6	46
45	36	34	25	16	14	5
4	44	42	33	24	15	13
12	3	43	41	32	23	21
20	11	2	49	40	31	22

Figure 2.28 Magic Square of Order 7

††2.10 Write a procedure that takes as input parameters the coefficient matrix and the vector of right hand sides for a set of simultaneous linear equations, as in Eqs. 2.8, and then solves these equations by Gaussian elimination, returning the solution vector as an output parameter. Test your program by using it to solve the set of equations

$$\begin{aligned} .410x_1 + .123x_2 + .368x_3 + .294x_4 &= .404 \\ .365x_1 + .192x_2 + .378x_3 + .064x_4 &= .424 \\ .178x_1 + .400x_2 + .279x_3 + .393x_4 &= -.256 \\ .225x_1 + .387x_2 + .402x_3 + .113x_4 &= .155 \end{aligned}$$

and printing out the transformed coefficients at each iteration. What is the complexity of your algorithm?

Straightforward Gaussian elimination has a serious potential hazard because the forward step involves repeated divisions by the pivot elements $a_{i,i}$. It should be apparent that a small pivot value (perhaps even zero) is an invitation to disaster as far as accuracy is concerned. One resolution is to inspect all of the coefficients $a_{i,i}, a_{i+1,i}, \ldots, a_{n,i}$ to find the $a_{j,i}$ that is greatest in magnitude. The ith and jth equations can then be swapped, in a technique known as *partial pivoting*. Revise your algorithm to incorporate partial pivoting, and use it to solve the same equations again. Under what circumstances will pivoting be important?

††2.11 The *transpose* of a matrix M, denoted by M^T, is such that $M^T[i,j] = M[j,i]$. It is possible to transpose a matrix in memory by permuting its elements in situ, as opposed to getting a block of storage and copying from M to M^T. Write a procedure to transpose a matrix in this fashion. To accomplish this, you should subvert the normal automatic mapping of arrays into sequential storage by declaring a one-dimensional array A and then mapping M into A in lexicographical order. Then apply your program to obtain M^T in A. Test your program by using it against the following 5×7 matrix, wherein the values of the elements correspond in fact to the indices of the elements:

11	12	13	14	15	16	17
21	22	23	24	25	26	27
31	32	33	34	35	36	37
41	42	43	44	45	46	47
51	52	53	54	55	56	57

What can you say about the complexity of your program?

2.12 For the decision table of Figure 2.11, construct the matrices *truth* and *falsity*, and apply the algorithm RULE_MASK to them. Trace the values assumed by the vector *rule*, for a rider who is a non-handicapped child during the commute hour.

2.13 Rewrite the algorithm SIEVE, employing arrays of sets, and use it to search for prime numbers over a reasonable range.

Section 2.5

†2.14 Simulate the application of the algorithm MIN_MAX to the following array of data:

267 399 67 871 59 767 755 599 619 879 163 71

For each call to MIN_MAX, trace the following information: the input parameters *lo* and *hi*, and the output parameters *mini* and *maxi*.

†2.15 What is the recurrence relation for the number of additions with Strassen's algorithm? What is its solution?

†2.16 [Winograd 1970] Strassen's algorithm reduces the complexity of matrix multiplication from $O(n^3)$ to $O(n^{2.81})$; however, it also has a large constant factor. A method by Winograd does not attain a lower complexity, but it *does* have a smaller constant factor (less than one) than that of Algorithm 2.4. By way of introduction, suppose that we wish to multiply two vectors, $U = (u_1, u_2, u_3, u_4)$ and $V = (v_1, v_2, v_3, v_4)$. We can write the product as

$$U \times V = (u_1 + v_2)(u_2 + v_1) + (u_3 + v_4)(u_4 + v_3) - [u_1u_2 + u_3u_4] - [v_1v_2 + v_3v_4]$$

In the general case, and restricting attention to the case $n = 2m$, we have

$$U \times V = \sum_{i=1}^{m}(u_{2i-1} + v_{2i})(u_{2i} + v_{2i-1}) - \sum_{i=1}^{m}[u_{2i-1}u_{2i}] - \sum_{i=1}^{m}[v_{2i-1}v_{2i}]$$

This requires $3n/2$ multiplications rather than n, so it is not very profitable. However, note that the bracketed terms can be precomputed for U and for V. Similarly, in multiplying two matrices A and B, the bracketed terms can be precomputed for each row of A and each column of B; this gives us the basis for Winograd's algorithm.

(a) Write a procedure to multiply matrices using this technique; for simplicity, let the matrices all be of order $n = 2m$. Test your program against Algorithm 2.4, both for correctness and for performance.

(b) Analyze your program to determine the total number of multiplications required. Also, how does the number of additions for this algorithm compare with the number of additions in Algorithm 2.4? Finally, how do the numbers of storage accesses (for elements of A and B) compare in the two methods?

†2.17 Continue the application of the algorithm RUSSIANS to the multiplication of the boolean matrices 2.18(a) and (b); that is, compute the matrix *BCOMB* and the updated value of C, for $h = 2$.

†2.18 Strassen's algorithm and the Four Russians' algorithm provide two different approaches that can be used to multiply boolean matrices with complexity less than $O(n^3)$. Describe as precisely as possible the circumstances under which one would be preferred over the other.

††2.19 Assume that we have a vector V containing both positive and negative integer values, and we wish to find a contiguous sub-vector of V such that the sum of its elements is the maximum over all possible sub-vectors. Write a procedure for doing this with complexity that is less than $O(n^2)$. (*Hint*: Try divide-and-conquer.) Test your program against the input vector

$$29 \quad -38 \quad 46 \quad -30 \quad 35 \quad -52 \quad 49 \quad -43 \quad 78 \quad 26 \quad -53 \quad 58 \quad 67 \quad -11$$

What can you say about the complexity of your algorithm?

Sections 2.7 – 2.8

†2.20 A common type of sparse matrix is the *tridiagonal matrix*, with non-zero coefficients on the main diagonal and the two adjacent diagonals, and with zeros elsewhere, as illustrated in the following sketch. Derive a storage allocation formula that will map the non-zero elements of a tridiagonal matrix A into consecutive memory locations, with A [1,1] in the first location.

```
x x 0 0 0 ... 0
x x x 0 0 ... 0
0 x x x 0 ... 0
      ...
0 ... 0 x x x 0
0 ... 0 0 x x x
0 ... 0 0 0 x x
```

††2.21 Eq. 2.6 gives a sequential storage allocation formula for a triangular matrix, with indices $1 \le j \le i \le n$, as

$$\text{loc } (x\,[i,j]) = b + \left[\frac{i \times (i-1)}{2} + j\right] = b + f(i) + g(j)$$

Derive a sequential storage allocation formula for a 3-dimensional *tetrahedral* array, with indices $1 \le k \le j \le i \le n$ such that

$$\text{loc } (x\,[i,j,k]) = b + f(i) + g(j) + h(k)$$

(*Hint*: Use the results of Exercise 1.8.)

†2.22 Assume that we have a sparse matrix in the triples representation, with the triples stored in row-major order. Write a procedure to transpose the matrix (see Exercise 2.11), obtaining the triples of the transposed matrix in the new row-major order, and test your program against the sparse matrix of Figure 2.23. Do not simply switch the indices and then sort. As an example, the original list of triples (see Figure 2.27) is

1,2,5; 1,5,2; 2,1,4; ... ; 5,2,8

and the transposed set of triples would be

1,2,4; 1,4,1; 2,1,5; ... ; 5,4,3

What is the computational complexity of your algorithm?

††2.23 [Pfaltz 1977] Assume that we have two square, sparse matrices A and B, with $\rho_A = \text{Prob}\ (a_{i,j} \neq 0)$ and $\rho_B = \text{Prob}\ (b_{i,j} \neq 0)$.

(a) For $S = A + B$, what is $\rho_S = \text{Prob}\ (s_{i,j} \neq 0)$?

(b) For $T = A \times B$, what is $\rho_T = \text{Prob}\ (t_{i,j} \neq 0)$?

(c) How do the preceding results change if the elements $a_{i,i}$ and $b_{i,i}$ are known to be zero? non-zero?

3

RECORDS

"Yea, from the table of my memory
I'll wipe away all trivial fond records."

Shakespeare
Hamlet, act I, scene 5

Records may indeed be trivial or complex, fond or bitter, but the need to transcribe and retain information in a usable form matters to all of us – the householder with a checkbook, the personnel manager, the accountant, the college registrar, even the bookie and the loan shark. In essence a record is a composite of data; typically, it may be a mixture of elements of alphabetic, numeric, and logical base types. The fact that the data elements may be of heterogeneous types precludes the use of an array structure, and we are thus led to using records. In this chapter, we will first look at ordinary record structures and then at means of generalizing them, all within the framework of HLL's, Pascal in particular. The last section describes some other techniques for dealing with variability in records; these latter methods are more suited to assembler language programming.

3.1 FIXED LENGTH RECORDS

Suppose that we have a personnel record as follows:

name	John Jones
birthday	03-31-46
wage	$ 1237.82
marital status	S(ingle), M(arried), D(ivorced), or W(idowed)

This record is one of many, and we wish to retain all the personnel records in a computer in some coherent manner. It would be convenient to represent them by

```
var     employee: array [1 .. n,1 .. 4] of base_type
```

Then, if John Jones were the *i*th employee, we might have:

```
employee [i,1] = 'John Jones'
employee [i,2] = 03,31,46
employee [i,3] = 1237.82
employee [i,4] = 'M'
```

However, this choice of data structure is not possible because the elements are, respectively, a vector of characters, a vector of integers, a real number, and a character; and arrays must have a homogeneous base type. Of course, one solution to this difficulty is to replace the array *employee* with four distinct arrays, as follows:

```
employee_name:   array [1 .. n,1 .. 20] of char
employee_bday:   array [1 .. n,1 .. 3] of integer
employee_wage:   array [1 .. n] of real
employee_status: array [1 .. n] of char
```

Indeed, such an approach is not uncommon; but it is unappealing. It forces us to think of several distinct arrays when dealing with what is logically one item. If employees are to be added or deleted in our personnel file, the programming overhead is both burdensome and error-prone.

A better approach is to explicitly aggregate the attributes for each employee. In Pascal, it would be natural to do this for the preceding example via the definition in Figure 3.1. This would cause *employee* to be a new, user-defined type, always consisting of the four *fields* as shown. With this definition as a template, we might then declare

```
var personnel: employee
```

whereby we could refer to any of the following: *personnel.name*, *personnel.bday*, *personnel.wage*, *personnel.status*.

```
type   employee = record
          name: array [1 .. 20] of char;
          bday: array [1 .. 3] of integer;
          wage: real;
          status: char;
       end;
```

Figure 3.1 Employee Record Format, Version 1

These composite identifiers, selecting variable and field within the variable, are called *qualified names*. The only permissible operations with a record are those of retrieving from or storing into a particular field (or else the entire record) as in:

```
personnel.wage := worker.wage
test := worker.status
personnel.bday [2] := 18
personnel := worker
```

where *worker* is another record of type employee. In these selection operations, the use of qualified names is more descriptive than the analogous use of subscripts for an array. However, note that in effect qualifiers are always constants. Since they cannot be variables or expressions, as subscripts can be for arrays, record operations tend to be rather mundane. Of course, the names of fields within a record must be distinct. However, the same name may be freely used as an identifier of a field within several types of records.

Records are available as data structures in some languages (for example, PL/I and COBOL) and not in others (for example, FORTRAN and BASIC). In those languages that support them, the syntax for declaring them and using them varies considerably. For example, in PL/I they are simply called structures, and the syntax for declaring them is quite different from that in Pascal; yet the use of qualified names for referencing fields is the same in the two languages.

In some assembly languages, such as that for the IBM 370, a record template can be defined very nicely with a dummy control section, whereby the fields are listed in sequence. Subsequently, by loading a base register with the origin of an actual record and by using the field name as a displacement, the effect of a qualified name is obtained. In fact, this suggests to us how records are mapped into storage in Pascal, PL/I, etc. Assuming that characters, integers, and reals occupy 1, 4, and 8 bytes respectively, the storage mapping for our employee record of Figure 3.1 would be as shown in Figure 3.2. That is, a personnel record of this type would require 41 bytes, and the offsets from the beginning of the record to the four fields would be 0, 20, 32, and 40.

Field	Location	Length
name	0	20
bday	20	12
wage	32	8
status	40	1

Figure 3.2 Storage Allocation Corresponding to Figure 3.1

3.1.1 Multiple Qualification

In the example of the employee record, we found it natural to define fields that are arrays. We might also have chosen to declare

```
var personnel: array [1 .. n] of employee
```

whereby we could refer to any of the following: *personnel* [*i*].*name*, *personnel* [*i*].*bday*, *personnel* [*i*].*wage*, *personnel* [*i*].*status*. An array in which every element is a record of the same type is sometimes called a *file*.[1] The use of one type

---

[1] The term file has other meanings as well. In particular, it is often understood to be a sequence of items of indefinite cardinality, and stored on some secondary medium such as tape or disk. With this definition, a file may not have an index type that can be used to select an item from it. We will discuss this more common usage in Chapter 12.

within another type may be carried to many levels. In particular, just as arrays of more than one dimension can be viewed as (recursive) arrays of arrays, so we can have records with fields that are themselves records.

As an example, suppose that we wished to include with each employee some data about his spouse. Such a record definition might look like Figure 3.3. If *worker* is a variable of type *employee*, then we could use *multiple qualification*, in a manner analogous to multiple subscripts, to reference fields of fields. Thus, for instance, *worker.spouse.name* = 'Elizabeth' and *worker.spouse.age* = 32. With regard to the field identifiers *name* and *age*, we have two different situations. *Name* is used in both the outer and inner record definitions, and so *worker.name* and *worker.spouse.name* refer to distinct items. On the other hand, it would be sufficient to refer to *worker.age* without any ambiguity, since *age* is not a field identifier in the outer record definition. This is called *elision*. Languages that support records tend to have somewhat different rules about which elisions are permitted. We will always use fully qualified names (with no elision) when dealing with records.

```
type    employee = record
          name: array [1 .. 20] of char;
          bday: array [1 .. 3] of integer;
          wage: real;
          status: char;
          spouse: record
             name: array [1 .. 10] of char;
             age: integer;
          end;
        end;
```

Figure 3.3 Employee Record Format, Version 2

Nonetheless, qualification, especially if it is multiple, can cause the names of program variables to become tediously long. Pascal has the construction **with**, which offers some relief in this regard. For instance, if it were necessary to revise each field of the variable *personnel* [*i*], we could write

```
with personnel [i] do begin
   name := ...
   bday := ...
   wage := ...
   status := ...
   spouse := ...
end;
```

(Note that *spouse* is of type record and that we can update the last field of *personnel* [*i*] with one assignment statement, presuming that we have a suitable variable of type *spouse* for the right hand side.) The **with** construction is also important because it can reduce the amount of computation required during execution. Thus, in the preceding example, the indexing required to address *personnel* [*i*] need only be performed once instead of for each field.

```
type  spouse = record
         name: array [1 .. 10] of char;
         age: integer;
      end;
      employee = record
         name: array [1 .. 20] of char;
         bday: array [1 .. 3] of integer;
         wage: real;
         status: char;
         spice: array [1 .. n] of spouse;
      end;
```

Figure 3.4 Employee Record Format, Version 3

To carry our example one step further, suppose we are in a culture that practices polygamy. In this case, we could employ the definitions of Figure 3.4. If *worker*, of type employee, is a variable that contains the data for Mr. Jones, we might then have:

```
worker.name = 'John Jones
worker.bday = 03,31,46
worker.wage = 1237.82
worker.status = 'P'
worker.spice [1].name = 'Elizabeth  ';  worker.spice [1].age = 32
worker.spice [2].name = 'Ann        ';  worker.spice [2].age = 28
worker.spice [3].name = 'Susan      ';  worker.spice [3].age = 43
      etc.
```

The foregoing suggests that there are some practical difficulties associated with fixed length records. Wherever a field is an array, we must decide on a maximum bound for the array. This constitutes a dilemma. Just as soon as we decide on a maximum – for example, that no name should require more than 30 characters – and lay out our data accordingly, we will surely find an exception that forces us to revise our plan. Moreover, the more that we attempt to forestall this possibility by making a generous initial definition, the more we then exacerbate the problem of wasted space in the majority of cases.

Note that the extra blanks in the name fields are at the right, with the significant data all the way to the left. Data recorded in this manner is said to be left justified. However, if the data corresponds to numeric values of varying sizes, such *justification* to the left would cause the corresponding fields in a succession of records to appear as

```
12
4872
3
```

so numeric data is always right justified, which causes the preceding values to appear, more appropriately, as

```
  12
4872
   3
```

The dilemma cited for the case of the name fields in our employee record example becomes even worse when we consider the effects of marital status upon the array spice. Just how much polygamy should we allow for? And what about the total waste of this space when an employee is single? Two approaches to overcoming the rigidity of fixed length records will be discussed subsequently under the topics of variant records and variable length records. First, however, we give a few other illustrations of the utility of fixed length records.

3.1.2 Examples of Record Usage

Even though the use of records is largely motivated by the desire to compose data of different base types, their structuring effect can also be useful with data elements of the same type. For instance, in the situation depicted in Figure 3.5, we can operate with complex numbers as generic entities, rather than having to keep track of their real and imaginary parts.

```
procedure COMPLEX_MULT (a,b: complex; var c: complex);

type    complex = record
            real_part: real;
            imag_part: real;
        end;

begin
   c.real_part := a.real_part * b.real_part - a.imag_part * b.imag_part;
   c.imag_part := a.real_part * b.imag_part + b.real_part * a.imag_part;
end;
```

Figure 3.5 Complex Numbers as Records

Another useful record structure is

```
date = record
   month: (Jan,Feb,Mar,Apr,May,June,July,Aug,Sept,Oct,Nov,Dec);
   day: 1 .. 31;
   year: 1980 .. 1999;
end;
```

The cardinality of a record structure is the product of the cardinalities of its fields. Thus, the cardinality of the type *date* is $12 \times 31 \times 20 = 7440$. Of these 7440 distinct values, there are 135 that are illegal, such as Feb. 29, 1983. Such possibilities for inconsistent sets of values are common in record structures. Note that if *date* were implemented as an ADT, then consistency checks would be built into the procedures that operated on values of this type. In more conventional programming, it falls upon the user program to provide these checks. As another instance of potentially inconsistent data values, consider the case of a record for a single employee that contains data for a spouse.

```
function BRIDGE_PLAYER (lead,follow: card): boolean;

{compares lead and follow and decides the winner;
 takes into account trump/notrump circumstances}

type    shdc = (spade,heart,diamond,club);
        card = record
           suit: shdc;
           rank: (two,three,four,five,six,seven,eight,nine,ten,
              jack,queen,king,ace);
        end;
var     notrump: boolean;
        trump: shdc;

function FACEOFF: boolean;
begin
   if lead.suit <> follow.suit then FACEOFF := true
   else FACEOFF := lead.rank > follow.rank;
end;

begin
   if notrump then BRIDGE_PLAYER := FACEOFF
   else begin
      if lead.suit <> trump then begin
         if follow.suit <> trump then BRIDGE_PLAYER := FACEOFF
         else BRIDGE_PLAYER := false;
      end else begin
         if follow.suit <> trump then BRIDGE_PLAYER := true
         else BRIDGE_PLAYER := lead.rank > follow.rank;
      end;
   end;
end;
```

Algorithm 3.1 BRIDGE_PLAYER

The function BRIDGE_PLAYER (Algorithm 3.1) is a more substantial example of computation based upon the record type. It compares two playing cards, *lead* and *follow*, and returns True if *lead* beats *follow* or False if *follow* beats *lead.* The determination is made according to the rules of bridge. Readers who are familiar with the game will easily recognize the various conditions. For those who are not, the following (non-independent) conditions determine the result:

1. There is a global boolean variable *notrump*; if *notrump* is false, then one of the four suits – spade, heart, diamond, or club – is a trump suit.

2. If *notrump* is true, then the determination of the winning card depends upon two factors, whether the cards are of the same suit, and which of the two has the higher rank.
3. If *notrump* is false, then the determination of the winning card is slightly more complicated, as elaborated in the algorithm.

For the cases where the determination has been reduced to evaluating the relative ranks of the two cards, BRIDGE_PLAYER calls the function FACEOFF to establish the result.

3.2 VARIANT RECORDS

There are several motivations for generalizing the fixed record format that we have considered so far. For example, suppose that we wish to have a single record structure for maintaining data about auto, home, and life insurance policies. Some information pertaining to the policy holder – name, address, amount, premium, etc. – would be the same for all these kinds of insurance. But other information would be specific to the kind of insurance: data about the insured car, or the insured home, or the type of life insurance and the beneficiary, etc. This situation can be accommodated by placing all the common information at the beginning of each record in a *fixed part*, and placing all the unique kinds of information at the end of each record in a *variant part*. In addition, so that we can later distinguish what kind of record we are dealing with, we must include a *tag field* in the fixed part. In this example, the tag would have one of the values (*auto, home, life*) This technique is known as the *discriminated union*.

The storage requirements for the three cases in this example will probably not be identical. However, the fixed fields can always be in the same locations, and the variant fields can be overlaid, since by the nature of our data a given record will have just one of the three variants. In terms of storage allocation, we have two possibilities:

1. At compile time, we can statically allocate for each record a total amount of storage matching the requirement for the largest variant. During execution, the fixed fields will then be assigned their values, and the variant fields will also be assigned values consistent with their tag value. For some policies, we expect to have wasted space at the end of the record.

2. Alternatively, during execution, we can determine what kind of policy we are dealing with and dynamically allocate just the proper amount of space for that variant. We then go on to assign the information to the fields of the record. There is never any wasted space.

Note that in both of these cases, but particularly in the latter, we can cause a disaster by reassigning the value of the tag in a record that already contains data corresponding to a particular variant.

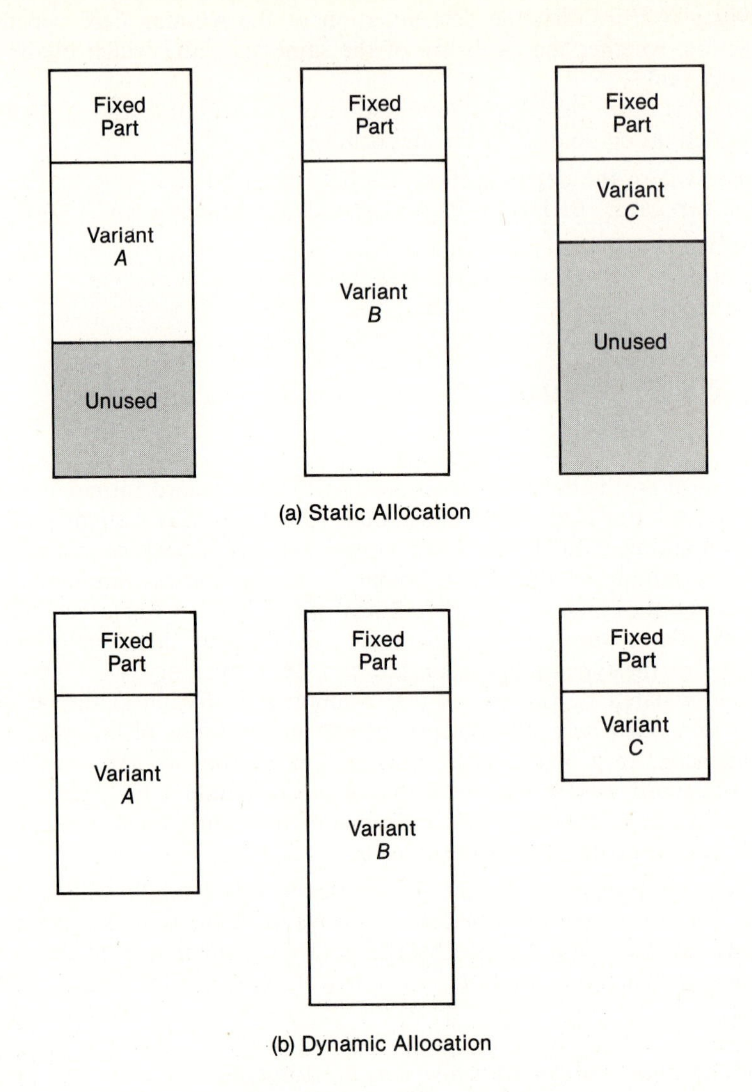

Figure 3.6 Variant Records

With the first allocation policy cited, we obtain the advantage that we can have one record type with alternative formats, as illustrated in Figure 3.6(a). With the second allocation policy, we obtain this plus an additional advantage; namely, we can have maximal thrift in our use of storage, as illustrated in Figure 3.6(b). Both of these policies are available in Pascal, but we need some tools from Chapter 4 before we can illustrate how to accomplish the latter alternative. In all, it is possible to identify three uses for variant records. We have already cited alternate formats and storage economy. In Section 3.2.2 we will describe an additional one, for type conversion.

3.2.1 Field Discrimination

Variant records are supported in Pascal. To illustrate their use, let us return to our employee record example, defining the format this time as in Figure 3.7. Here, the tag field is *status*, and its value is used, via the **case** construction, to selectively describe the format of the balance of the record. There are two significant differences between the use of **case** to discriminate record variants and its use to control program statement sequencing. One is that this **case** is not closed with an **end**; rather the **end** that closes the **record** definition also closes the **case**, since the end of the variant definitions is necessarily the end of the record definition as well. The other difference is that discrimination is really based, not upon the possible values of a variable, but upon the possible values of a type.

```
type    spouse = record
           name: array [1 .. 10] of char;
           age: integer;
        end;
        employee = record
           name: array [1 .. 20] of char;
           bday: array [1 .. 3] of integer;
           wage: real;
           case status: char of
              'M': (bliss: spouse);
              'P': (tally: 1 .. n;
                 spice: array [1 .. n] of spouse);
        end;
```

Figure 3.7 Employee Record Format, Version 4

If *worker* is a variable of this type and is monogamous, we might refer to *worker.bliss.name*; if *worker* is polygamous, we might refer to *worker.spice* [2]*.age*. Note that records for single, divorced, or widowed employees would have no spouse data at all; we might want to revise our definition, however, to include next-of-kin information for such persons.

There is still some inflexibility in the scheme as shown. Although we can discriminate on the basis of marital status, we are forced to allocate, at the outset, an array *spice* with the maximum foreseeable bounds 1 .. *n*. However, this is really a limitation of Pascal; in PL/I, for instance, it is possible under certain circumstances to allocate the array *spice* with bounds of 1 .. *tally* rather than 1 .. *n*, as long as *tally* precedes *spice* in the record specification.

In Pascal, the concept that a record consists of a fixed part followed by a variant part can be extended recursively. That is, any variant can itself contain a fixed part (with a tag) followed by a variant part, as illustrated in Figure 3.8. In this example, the record of type *r* has a fixed part (*d,e,a*) and three variants. The first variant *x* has a fixed part (*f,g,b*) with two variations (*h,i*) or *j*; the second variant *y* has only a fixed part (*k,l*); and the third variant *z* has a fixed part *c* with two

```
type   typea = (x,y,z);
       typeb = (u,v);
       typec = (s,t);

       r = record
          d,e: integer;
          case a: typea of
          x: (f: char;
             g: real;
             case b: typeb of
                u: (h: integer;
                   i: boolean);
                v: (j: array [1 .. 3] of char));
          y: (k,l: boolean);
          z: (case c: typec of
                s: (m: real;
                   n: char;
                   o: integer);
                t: (p: array [3 .. 7] of integer));
       end;
```

Figure 3.8 Recursively Variant Records

variations (*m,n,o*) or *p*. As you can see, the correct placement of parentheses is vital for distinguishing where variants begin and end. Also, one must not use the same field identifier within variants at the same level.

†3.2.2 Type Conversion

We have presented variant records as being primarily motivated by the need to discriminate among several formats that might apply to part of a record. In order to signal the correct format, a tag field is then required. This capability of applying alternate formats to data is also useful for converting between the various primitive (boolean, character, integer, real) types. In such a case, no tag field is required, and the structure is called a *free union*. Type conversions in this fashion are commonly useful, for example, in transmitting parameters across interfaces, or in I/O operations; however, they must be used with care. Reading data as characters, operating upon it as integers, and then interpreting it as characters again would be likely to yield meaningless results. In assembly language, it is trivial to read data as characters and then access it as numerical values. In an HLL like Pascal, the user must be cautious, because the results can depend upon various details of compiler implementation.

As an illustration of this technique, we might have the definition

```
type    word = record case boolean of
          true: (int: integer);
          false: (c1,c2,c3,c4: char);
        end;
```

Then, if *data* is a variable of type word, we might read four characters (in EBCDIC code) into its four bytes, as follows:

```
data.c1 := 'A'    {= C1₁₆ = 193₁₀}
data.c2 := 'T'    {= E3₁₆ = 227₁₀}
data.c3 := 'O'    {= D6₁₆ = 214₁₀}
data.c4 := 'Z'    {= E9₁₆ = 233₁₀}
```

Then, a reference to *data.int* would immediately evaluate to

$$3252934377_{10} \ \{ = 193 \times 256^3 + 227 \times 256^2 + 214 \times 256 + 233\}$$

Since the example has only two possibilities, it is sufficient to use the type boolean which has only the two possible values True and False. This, by the way, emphasizes the point made previously, that the **case** discrimination for record variants is based upon values of a type, not values of a variable.

As another example of this technique, let us recall from Section 2.5.3 the program RUSSIANS (Algorithm 2.9), for fast boolean matrix multiplication. The algorithm requires the ability to take the value of a set variable and convert it to an integer value. This conversion was performed in RUSSIANS by the function SET_TO_INT. Unfortunately, the complexity of SET_TO_INT is $O(m)$, causing the overall time complexity of RUSSIANS to be $O(n^2)$. By using a variant record, however, we can express this function so that it has complexity $O(1)$, thereby reducing the overall time complexity of RUSSIANS to $O(n^{2/\lg n})$.

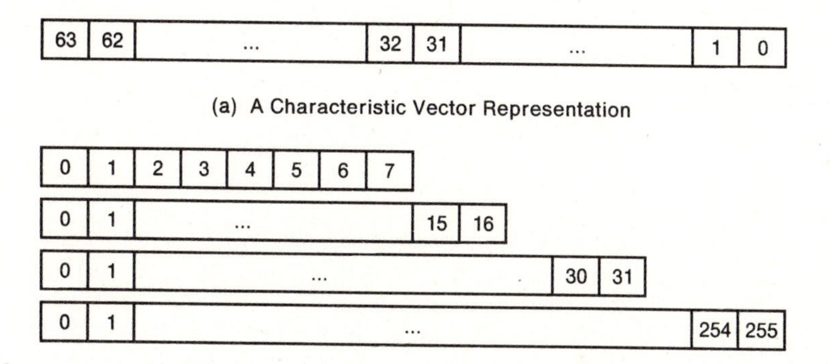

Figure 3.9 Alternative Set Representations

In the original conversion routine, SET_TO_INT, we did not have to be concerned with the manner in which sets are implemented by our Pascal compiler. In the mapping of the original boolean input into the matrices A and B, it was natural to associate the *i*th set element with the value in the *i*th column of the input. This led to the corresponding "natural" function SET_TO_INT. But now, in using variant records, we are escaping the consistency safeguards of Pascal typing, so that we must discern (by testing, for example) just how the compiler implements sets. One common scheme is, for *a* and *b* in the range 0 .. 63, to map set elements *a* .. *b* to the 64 bits of a double word, as shown in Figure 3.9(a). In discussing RUSSIANS, we did not worry about the issue of mapping the original boolean rows into sets, but it is rather natural to map the value in the *i*th column of a row onto the *i*th element of a set. With this implementation, the elements of the set appear in reversed order in the double word, leading to the function SET_TO_INT_V1 (Algorithm 3.2). Here, although there are again just two variants, we have arbitrarily used an enumerated type with two mnemonic values, *bit* and *int*, instead of the type boolean. The former refers to one set of 64 bits (*b*) and the latter refers to two integers of 32 bits each (*i*1, *i*2). However, we presume that the parameter *m* in RUSSIANS is such that the high order integer *i*1 is always zero. Since our sets in RUSSIANS were defined in terms of 1 .. *m* rather than 0 .. *m*, we must use the integer division operator **div** to discard the least significant bit.

```
function SET_TO_INT_V1 (s: setm): integer;

type    flag = (bit,int);
        setm = set of 1 .. m;

var     view: record case flag of
           bit: (b: setm);
           int: (i1,i2: integer);
        end;

begin
   view.b := s;
   SET_TO_INT_V1 := view.i2 div 2;
end;
```

Algorithm 3.2 SET_TO_INT_V1

A different, common manner of representing sets is, for *a* and *b* in the range 0 .. 255, to map the set elements *a* .. *b* onto the smallest unit of storage that will suffice − 8, 16, 32, or 256 bits − as shown in Figure 3.9(b).[2] In the problem at hand, we expect *m* to be small, so one byte is all that is required. To obtain conversion in $O(1)$ time with this representation, we need to number the columns of our *A* matrix from right to left when mapping rows onto sets. In turn, this impacts the original conversion routine (SET_TO_INT). We can adjust to the change in representation via the conversion function SET_TO_INT_V2 (Algorithm 3.3), which uses an integer variant with just one byte. Since the set elements are not reversed in

---

2 For $31 < b < 256$, this is not quite accurate; however, that is irrelevant to our purpose here.

this representation, and since $m = 3$ in our problem, we have to divide by 16 to shift off the last 4 bits.

The preceding paragraphs have been concerned with details that we would rather be able to ignore when discussing algorithms. If nothing else, they dramatize the advantages of being able to represent algorithmic processes without having to worry about the operations of an underlying machine. On the other hand, a conversion routine of this nature would in practice probably be implemented in machine language anyway. In the present example, it is almost a tour-de-force to be able to obtain executable algorithms in an HLL.

```
function SET_TO_INT_V2 (s: setm): byteint;

type   byteint = packed 0 .. 255;
       flag = (bit,int);
       setm = set of 1 .. m;

var    view: record case flag of
          bit: (b: setm);
          int: (i: byteint);
       end;

begin
   view.b := s;
   SET_TO_INT_V2 := view.i div 16;
end;
```

Algorithm 3.3 SET_TO_INT_V2

3.3 VARIABLE LENGTH RECORDS

As we have seen in the preceding section, variant records offer some solution to the problem of adjusting the size of a record to fit the data. However, the solution is only partial. In the case of a polygamist with m wives, some HLL's (such as PL/I) allow the construction of a record containing an array of m elements for the m wives; other HLL's (such as Pascal) insist that the array must have a pre-defined maximum number of elements, some of which will probably be unused. But what if, in such a record, we need to deal with n children as well as m wives? HLL's generally are not equipped to cope with even this modest amount of variability. Therefore, the techniques that we will describe for coping with truly variable length records are generally implemented in assembly language.

The way to cope with extreme variability is to make each record *self-describing* by interspersing control information with the rest of the data. A program to process such a record must then start at the beginning of the record and scan fields from left to right, interpreting them according to the control information that is recognized during the scan. This control information can have either of two forms: separators as in the next section, or counts as in Section 3.3.2. The data that we will use in our examples represents the polygamous employee of Section 3.1.1. It is reproduced here for convenience:

```
John Jones    033146    1237.82    P
          Elizabeth    32
          Ann          28
          Susan        43
```

Before embarking on the details, however, we should remark that it is possible, after all, to carry out such a scheme in an HLL, by the following technique. In lieu of all other data structures, declare

```
var    memory: array [0 .. memsize] of char  {or integer}
```

Then process the variable length records within this large array by scanning the data from left to right and interpreting it. Note that we must settle on a homogeneous base type for the array *memory*, and then perform type conversions as needed, perhaps using variant record techniques. It would be sensible to choose the base type corresponding to that of the majority of the actual data, in order to minimize the number of cases requiring conversion. The manner in which this method would work will become apparent in the next sections. Still another technique for handling variable length records using an HLL will be seen in Section 11.3.1.3.

3.3.1 Field Demarcation by Separators

This method is basically quite simple, as illustrated by the fragment

```
John Jones/033146/1237.82/ ...
```

There are two points to be observed in this fragment:

1. The real data is uniformly written in a homogeneous base type (character, in this case).
2. The individual fields of the data are separated by some special *separator* value from that base type ('/', in this case).

Thus, the nth field can be found by counting forward past $n-1$ separators; the contents of that field can be read directly if the type of the field is character, or otherwise it may need to be converted.

Usually, it is important that the separator value should not be present in any of the data fields. With the base type of character, this is fairly easy to ensure, since the set of character values is so rich. Typical characters used as separators are

/ , . : ; ' " @ # $ % ¢ & * ! etc.

In the rarer case when the base type is integer, it can be much harder to find distinctive values to use as separators. Moreover, even when safe values are available (for example, 0 or −1) we observe that they require the standard memory space for an integer, usually four bytes, which is uneconomical.

Applying this technique to the personnel data for our polygamous employee, we might obtain

```
John Jones/033146/1237.82/P:Elizabeth/32
/Ann/28/Susan/43/;   (next record)
```

Note that we actually used three separator characters for three different logical functions: '/' to separate fields within a record, ';' to separate records, and ':' to indicate the beginning of optional data pairs following the marital status field. It is important to realize that the choices of which characters to employ as separators, and what logical functions to ascribe to them for decoding the data are arbitrary. In addition, such a scheme is only meaningful when coupled with a program that has been written to process such a variable length record. There are likely to be occasions when you come across a variable length record that you need to decode by hand without being fully aware of the rules. When the fields are demarcated by separators, as in the example above, it is fairly easy to guess at the separators and read the record.

The use of separator characters for variable length records is fairly congenial to human processing of data, because the eye can easily scan and recognize where fields begin and end. But this is not true for machines. If, for instance, it wished to find the next record after that of Mr. Jones in this example, a program would have to scan every character, one at a time, until it encountered the ';' that signalled the end of the record. Another problem with separators is that in general they must not occur within the data. A way of handling exceptions to this rule is illustrated by the usual manner of allowing quote characters to be included within quoted character strings. Although we will not cover the string data structure until Chapter 8, most readers probably already have an acquaintance with literal data strings, as in

```
'Hello there'   and   'I''m tired of computing'
```

Here, a single quote indicates either the beginning or the end of a string of characters; two quotes indicates the occurrence of a single quote within a quoted string of characters. The program that reads such literal character constants contains the necessary logic to discriminate what is intended and to adjust the data in the machine; for example, it would change the latter to

```
I'm tired of computing
```

Although the preceding use of double separators is workable, it is awkward. It also is at variance with another conventional usage for repeated separator characters. Suppose that we have the following alterations to our personnel record for Mr. Jones: he is retired and thus salary does not apply, Elizabeth's age is obscure, and we are not sure of the second wife's name. The available data would then typically be recorded as

```
John Jones/033146//P:Elizabeth///28/Susa
n/43/;   (next record)
```

That is, fields for which data are missing or null are conventionally indicated by multiple separators.

In summary, encoding of variable length records using separators to demarcate the fields is commonly used where there is an interface to people, as in data entry or text editing, or where the data sizes are small enough that the scanning does not become too burdensome. However, this method is ill suited to the internal processing of large volumes of records by machines.

3.3.2 Field Demarcation by Counts

As an alternative to the use of separators, it is common to precede each data field with a fixed length count field. For data fields that are long and variable, the overhead is reasonable. For data fields that are short or intrinsically of fixed length, the overhead would seem to be unreasonable. Nonetheless, in the interest of uniformity and to make the record truly self-describing with fewer hidden assumptions, it is common practice to attach counts to every field.

If the record is regarded as a succession of characters, as in the preceding section, then we are faced with the decision of how many character positions, or bytes, to allow for the count fields themselves. Of course, this depends upon the data sizes in the application; regardless of size, however, the necessity to convert between character data and numeric count data remains. For illustrative purposes, we use the same personnel record as before. In this case, one byte would be sufficient, since we can then count to 255. Unfortunately, many of the corresponding character codes would be gibberish to the eye, or even unprintable. Although this is irrelevant for internal processing of variable length records, it does complicate our attempts to illustrate the method. Accordingly, we will allow two character positions for counts, but presume that only recognizable digit values are recorded therein. However, you should recognize that this is not a faithful representation of the actual internal record processing.

Of course, when we precede a data field of n characters with a count field of 2 characters, this makes the total space requirement $n + 2$ characters. Should the count field value be n, or include itself and be $n + 2$? It is more common to use n, but the decision really rests with the program for processing the record. In this regard, if we have a file of variable length records, it is very convenient to be able to skip over an entire record without having to skip over each individual field within the record. For this purpose, it is usual to precede each record with a count of the total number of characters in the record. To be useful, this count must be a sum of the lengths of all the data fields and their count fields.

With all the preceding description in mind, we arrive at the record for Mr. Jones, as follows:

```
7310John Jones06033146071237.8201P1509El
izabeth02320903Ann02281105Susan0243
```

Your first impression is probably that this is harder to read than when separators were used. And so it is, for humans; but a program can now skip from one field to the next, or from one record to the next, without the necessity of reading each individual character and interpreting it. Note that the scheme of preceding each record with a count of the total record length is also applied to the sub-records for each of the spouses.

The story of demarcating fields by counts does not end quite yet. Another kind of count field is commonly employed in variable length records. In cases where a field is an array of dimension 1 .. n, a count field containing the value of n may be inserted in the record before the array. In scanning an unfamiliar record of this type from left to right by hand, it can be unclear whether we are looking at a field size count, a record size count, a dimension count, or perhaps even data! This makes such variable length records even more difficult for humans to read. A program will necessarily contain logic to discriminate between these possibilities at each juncture. For a person attempting to read a memory dump containing such records, however, it often resembles solving a puzzle – making guesses as to what certain character positions signify, and occasionally revising guesses and partially restarting when the interpreted values become meaningless. (Note that with encryption, where no clues are to be found in the data itself, the puzzle may become extremely difficult.) With this embellishment of a third kind of count, the variable length record for Mr. Jones might now look as follows:

```
7510John Jones06033146071237.8201P031509
Elizabeth02320903Ann02281105Susan0243
```

At the beginning of this section, we cited the importance of using counts systematically if they are to be used at all. What would this record look like if the same data values were null or missing (salary, age of Elizabeth, and name of Ann) as in the example of the preceding section? It would appear as follows:

```
6310John Jones060331460001P031309Elizabe
th00060002281105Susan0243
```

Although the scheme of using count fields within records to handle variable length is much faster for machine processing than the scheme using separators, it is still necessary, for example, to skip over $i-1$ records one at a time in order to reach the ith record. A variation of the scheme using counts is to remove the record counts from the data and to place them in an array A, such that the value of A_i is the count of the size of the ith record. This can speed up access to the ith record to a moderate degree; however, the records are no longer self-describing, which may be too substantial a penalty. To make access to the ith record very fast, we could even use array B (compare Figure 3.2), defined by

$$B_i = \sum_{j=1}^{i-1} A_j \tag{3.1}$$

However, such a scheme would be very inflexible with respect to insertions or deletions into the file of records. All in all, the scheme of having the counts in the records and in front of their data fields seems to be a good compromise between flexibility and performance.

3.4 OVERVIEW

Beginning with the next chapter, we will be examining data structures that are much more glamorous than records. Nonetheless, we will see that this proletarian structure, the record, greatly facilitates construction of the more advanced ones. With records, we are completely relieved of one shortcoming of arrays, the restriction to a homogeneous base type. In variant records we also find a moderate degree of relief from another shortcoming of arrays, the restriction to one predefined size. If we need to escape this latter restriction entirely, we can do so via variable length records, using either separators or count fields. But variable length records require attention to a very low level of detail, one that is unsuited as a base for building higher data abstractions.

3.5 REFERENCE TO TERMINOLOGY

3.6 EXERCISES

Section 3.1

3.1 On the left in Figure 3.10 is the logical description of a data structure in Pascal syntax, and on the right are some values for the same data structure. Give the program "name" of each of the following values from that figure (that is, how you would refer to it in a program statement). Use full names, not elided ones.

(a) 13

(b) 2.718

(c) 10

(d) ' '

(e) 13.9

3.2 For the structure in Figure 3.10, compute two vectors − one containing the locations, or offsets, for each field, and the other containing the lengths for each

```
m: record
   n: char;                              'Z'
   o: record
      n: array [-1 .. 2] of integer;     59, 54, 13, 86
      p: record
         q: char;                        '.'
         r: real;                        2.718
      end;
   end;
   p: array [0 .. 1] of record
      q: array [5 .. 7] of integer;      10, 104, 15    27, 66, 85
      n: record
         o: array [-7 .. -6] of char;    'Y', 'Z'       ' ', '5'
         r: real;                        13.9           0.0
      end;
   end;
end;
```

Figure 3.10 Record for Exercises 3.1 and 3.2

field. Assume that the primitive data types character, integer, and real require 1, 4, and 8 bytes respectively.

3.3 Devise a structure that might be used to capture the information for a student's college transcript. Such a structure might need to include a small amount of personal data about the student, as well as data about courses, units, instructors, grades, etc.

†3.4 The procedure shown in Figure 3.5 for performing complex multiplication requires 4 multiplications and 2 additions. Find a procedure that requires 3 multiplications, albeit at the expense of more additions. Under what circumstances is your revised method a practical one?

†3.5 Convert the logic of the function BRIDGE_PLAYER to a decision table with five condition stubs:

- *C*1: contract = notrump
- *C*2: lead.suit = follow.suit
- *C*3: lead.suit = trump
- *C*4: follow.suit = trump
- *C*5: lead.rank > follow.rank

and two action stubs:

- *A*1: lead wins
- *A*2: follow wins

Discuss the relative merits of the function and the decision table for representing this algorithm.

Sections 3.2 – 3.3

3.6 Design a structure with variant records that might be suitable for the problem, cited at the beginning of Section 3.2, of handling various types of insurance policies that have a common fixed part.

3.7 Decode the following variable length record and rewrite it in a format appropriate for humans.

```
E30BMATHEMATICS044606LEHMER0307ALGEBRA07MWF090009P
ROJ GEOM08TUTH101508TOPOLOGY09TUWTH14003108BOURBAK
I0208ANALYSIS06MW13300ACATEGORIES05F14450905POLYA0
04C07RUSSELL0305LOGIC0BMTUWTHF11000EABELIAN GROUPS
06MF091509DIFF EQNS08TUTH1415
```

†3.8 We have the following variable length records:

```
A.  8706234A5708WING NUT0513/1703122031604ACME0211043.
    191907WINSTON0245042.541406HOOVER022300
B.  170532GPA0000025400
C.  470558BCZ12CONFABULATOR000218011607BARSTOW0003138
D.  6906909FF008HEXAFLEX0518/35018021605JIFFY015047.1
    11907RALSTON0245042.54
```

(a) Decode them and rewrite them in a format appropriate for humans.

(b) Rewrite them using separator characters instead of counts.

4

LISTS

"He's got 'em on the list – he's got 'em on the list;
and they'll none of 'em be missed."

W.S. Gilbert,
The Mikado, act I

From the humdrum – eggs, milk, rhubarb, flour – to the fanciful – a partridge in a pear tree, two turtle doves, ... , twelve drummers drumming – lists pervade our lives. They are also pervasive in computational processes, to the extent that the subject matter of this book could be entitled "Lists" rather than "Data Structures." For example, an array of integers is a species of list; likewise, the employee record of the preceding chapter is a list; and so also are queues, stacks, trees, graphs, and strings, as we will see.

However, the notion of a list as a structured collection of items is too general for our purposes; in any computer-oriented discussion that employs the term list, the reader must be careful to ascertain what is actually being described. In this chapter, we will first refine the notion by discussing lists that incorporate explicit information for specifying the next item on the list. In common parlance, the items on a list are variously called nodes, cells, elements, etc.; and the explicit data that specify "next" are commonly called pointers or links.

After illustrating the utility of this form of data structure with some applications, we will look at two generalizations of the concept. The first of these is obtained by building structures that can specify many next values. The second, more powerful generalization is obtained by employing recursion in the definition of "List structures."

4.1 THE FLEXIBLE NATURE OF LISTS

The essential aspect of a list is that we may wish to vary the sequence in which we consider its items. Thus, if we have the list shown in Figure 4.1(a), it may happen that we would really like to insert 65 as the fourth item, to obtain the list in (b); another possibility is that we would like to delete 29 from (a), to obtain the list in (c). If we record the list values in an array, then we can achieve the effects of insertion/deletion by moving blocks of values away from/toward the array origin. However, this can be an expensive solution for a large array. Moreover, since the array has a fixed size, this solution also fails to reflect the fact that the list has changed in a more fundamental fashion (that is, its length has changed).

(a)	(b)	(c)
24	24	17
29	29	14
14	14	32
32	65	59
59	32	40
40	59	
	40	

Figure 4.1 Insertion and Deletion in a List

The difficulty lies in the fact that, in Figure 4.1, physical sequence implies logical sequence. The essential notion of a list for our purposes is that it should contain explicit information for logical sequencing. This information is commonly termed a *link*, and the two fundamental operations on a list are:

first(p) – to access the first item on the list referenced by p;
next(r) – to access the item that follows r in the list.

Normally, however, we prefer to think in terms of higher-level operations, such as:

locate(p,t) – to finds the first item containing t in the list referenced by p;
retrieve(p,s) – to find the sth item in the list referenced by p;
insert(p,t) – to insert an item with value t in the list referenced by p;
delete(p,t) – to delete the first item with value t from the list referenced by p.

The descriptions of some of these operations lack precision. This is most evident in the case of insertion. Where in the list should the new item be placed? We will resolve such issues in the discussions that follow.

If we reflect upon the example cited in Figure 4.1, we see that there are two distinct problems that we would like to solve with lists:

1. to be able to alter logical sequencing of list items without extensive physical reordering, and
2. to be able to handle lists whose lengths may vary widely and unpredictably.

We will begin by discussing a method for implementing lists that works in all general purpose HLL's. It solves the sequencing problem but is weak with respect to the variable length problem. Accordingly, most of our discussion has to do with a more dynamic method that completely solves both problems. This method is available in some languages, such as Pascal and PL/I, but not in others, such as FORTRAN and BASIC.

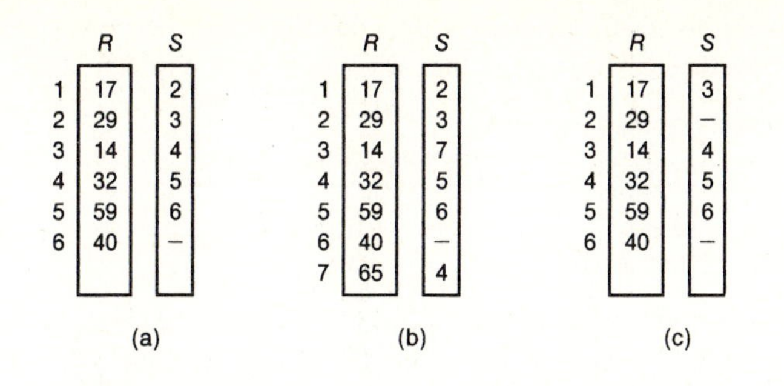

Figure 4.2 Insertion and Deletion Using Links

4.1.1 Array Indices as Links

In Figure 4.2(a), we have redrawn Figure 4.1(a). By annexing to the array *R* another array *S*, we have made explicit what was implicit in Figure 4.1; for the *i*th element in *R*, the location of the next element in *R* is indicated by the value of the *i*th element in *S*. Although this additional information may be unnecessary baggage in Figure 4.2(a), its utility is apparent in Figure 4.2(b) and (c), where it enables us to perform the insertion of Figure 4.1(b) and the deletion of Figure 4.1(c) simply by adjusting one or two link values instead of by moving blocks of data.

More generally, suppose that we have an array *A*, each of whose elements is an arbitrarily large aggregate of data. Then, let us supplement the data with linking information in one of two ways:

(a) by treating the data aggregates as records and by including a new link field in each record, or

(b) by introducing a new array *B* of link values.

It is then possible to thread the data aggregates in *A* into any number of disjoint lists; all that is required is some indication of where a particular list starts and where it ends. The starting locations must be supplied separately, but the end of a list is indicated by the occurrence of an illegal index value, usually zero. Thus, in Figure 4.3, let *list*1 = 20 be the beginning of one list and *list*2 = 25 be the beginning of another list, in an array containing character data. Then *list*1 yields "HAPPY" and *list*2 yields "HOUR."

	...	18	19	20	21	22	23	24	25	26	27	...
A	...	A	R	H	O	Y	–	P	H	P	U	...
B	...	24	0	18	27	0	–	26	21	22	19	...

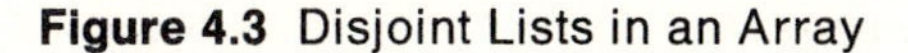

Figure 4.3 Disjoint Lists in an Array

To illustrate how easily insertions and deletions can be performed at arbitrary points in lists constructed in this manner, let us define list nodes by

```
type    node = record
            data: {whatever is required}
            next: 0 .. n;
        end;
var     list: array [1 .. n] of node;
```

Then, in Figure 4.4(a), suppose that we wish to insert the single node at *list* [*n*] between the logically successive list nodes at *list* [*i*] and *list* [*j*]. This is accomplished by

```
list [n].next := list [i].next;  list [i].next := n
```

On the other hand, to delete the node at *list* [*s*], which logically falls between the nodes at *list* [*r*] and *list* [*t*], we simply write

```
list [r].next := list [s].next
```

The combined effect of this insertion and this deletion is shown in Figure 4.4(b). That the deletion operation leaves *list* [*s*].*next* = *t* is irrelevant for the immediate purpose of logically resequencing *t* after *r*. This illustration is sketchy, and it glosses over several aspects of using links that we prefer to defer until later sections.

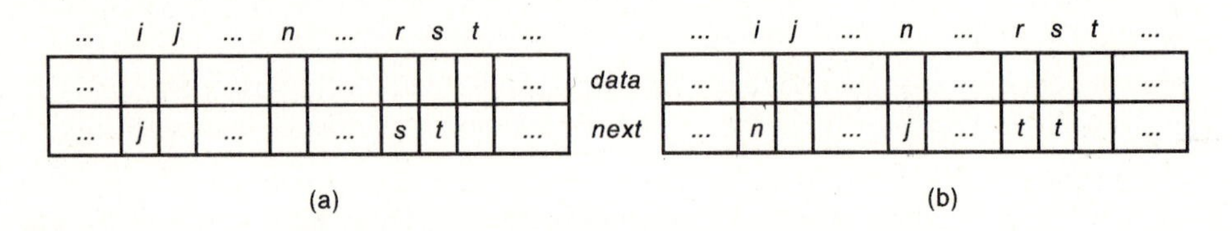

Figure 4.4 Implementing Lists with Cursors

Associating link information with a node is easily understood in terms of index values, and indices used for this purpose are sometimes called *cursors*. How useful are cursors, and why might we wish to have a more complicated approach? In brief, if we are dealing with lists that contain a single type of node, then cursors may be satisfactory. Moreover, whether we have one type of node or several, if we can safely estimate the maximum number of required nodes of each type, then cursors may still be satisfactory. However, if there are several node types, we will need a separate array for the lists of each type. Arrays must be declared with their dimensions at the outset. If even one of our estimates of dimensionality is too low, our program can fail during execution.

4.1.2 Pointer Variables as Links

The solution to the problem of lack of generality with the preceding approach is as follows. We will not declare any space for list nodes before such space is required; when it is required, we will ask for it via a system procedure. This procedure will acquire just the amount of space that we need and then tell us where it is via another primitive type of data, a *pointer variable*. Such a variable is not so mysterious when we realize that it must correspond to an address in the computer memory.[1]

This pointer variable opens the door to potentially serious programming hazards; we will discuss these at the end of the chapter (see Section 4.5.1), by which time the nature of the problems may be more easily appreciated. For now, suffice it to say that some of the problems associated with pointers can be avoided by insisting that a particular pointer variable can point only to a particular type of data object. For example, the Pascal definition

```
type    link = ↑node;
        node = record
           data: char; {for example}
           next: link;
        end;
```

asserts that any variable of type *link* is a pointer, but only to a variable of type *node*. Accordingly, in Figure 4.5(a) and with the preceding **type** definition, we have

```
var     p,q,s: link;
        a,b,c,h: node;
```

The notation for using pointers to access data varies considerably among those HLL's that support them; for p a pointer to a node and x a field in that node, the syntactic styles employed to reference the x pointed to by p include:

```
p↑.x,  p→x,  x(p),  [p].x,  etc.
```

Pascal employs the first of these styles. As examples of its use, with reference to Figure 4.5(a),

```
p↑ = a;  p↑.data = 'A';  p↑.next↑ = b;  p↑.next↑.data = 'B'
```

It is essential to distinguish between the value of a pointer p and the value of $p\uparrow$, the object to which it points. By way of illustration, if we started with Figure 4.5(a) again, then $q := p$ would yield (b) of the figure; however, $q\uparrow := p\uparrow$ would yield (c) of the figure. In the former case, we replicated the pointer value (address) of p into q; in the latter case, we copied the contents of the list node at p's location into the

---

[1] You have likely encountered pointer variables already, although you may not have realized it (and, in any event, could not explicitly manipulate them). Specifically, in using "call by reference" (see Section 1.4.3) for passing a parameter to a procedure, you are in fact causing the compiler to transmit a pointer to the value rather than a copy of the value.

list node at *q*'s location. With this background in hand, let us now explore the subject of sequential linked lists.

4.1.2.1 Simple Lists. Suppose that some list nodes have been allocated, forming the two lists shown in Figure 4.5(a). The objects *a,b,c,h* are of type node, according to the definitions of the preceding section, and the objects *p,q,s* are of type link. When dealing with a list of linked nodes, or a linked list, there is no name for the entire list as there is for an array or a record. Rather, one retains in some pointer variable a pointer value to the first node on the list. Such a variable is commonly called a list head, or *header*; *p* and *q* are headers in Figure 4.5(a). Many operations with lists involve linking or "chaining" from one node to the next, until the end of the list is recognized via a special pointer value called **nil**. In pictorial representations, **nil** is usually indicated as shown in nodes *c* and *h*, but sometimes the symbol Λ is used.

If we wish to insert the node *h* pointed to by *q* into the list pointed to by header *p*, what is required? It is very simple to insert *h* at the head of the list, as shown in Figure 4.5(d), via the two pointer changes

```
q↑.next := p; p := q;
```

It is more expensive to insert *h* at the end of the list because, in order to find the end of the list, it is first necessary to chain from the head to the end by performing *p* := *p*↑.*next* until the **nil** is encountered. What if we wish to insert *h* at an arbitrary point in the list, say with regard to *b* pointed to by *s*? In this case, it is straightforward to insert it after *b*, again with two pointer changes

```
q↑.next := s↑.next; s↑.next := q;
```

as shown in Figure 4.5(e). There is a difficulty, however, if we wish to insert *h* before *b*. That would require altering the pointer from node *a*, and we cannot get to it by just using the pointer values of *q* and *s*.

One solution to this problem is to chain from the head of the list until we find a node pointing to *b*, then make our insertion after that node. But note that this may require $O(n)$ chaining operations, not a very satisfactory situation. Another possible approach might be as follows:

```
temp := q↑.data;
q↑ := s↑;        {copy entire record from b to h}
s↑.data := temp;
s↑.next := q;
```

In other words, insert the node pointed to by *q* after the node pointed to by *s*, but then interchange their data. In the general case, however, this latter approach can involve copying too much data.

At this point, it is important to make an observation about the labels in Figure 4.5. There, we have labelled the nodes *a,b,c,h* in order to facilitate talking about them. But it would be misleading, for instance, to then characterize inserting node *h* after node *b* by

```
h.next := b.next; b.next := q;
```

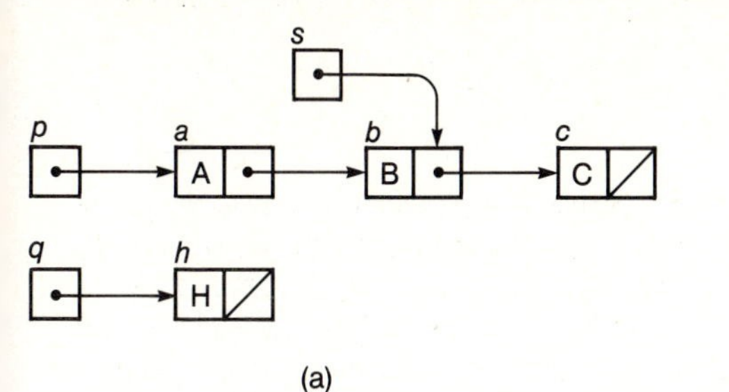

(a)

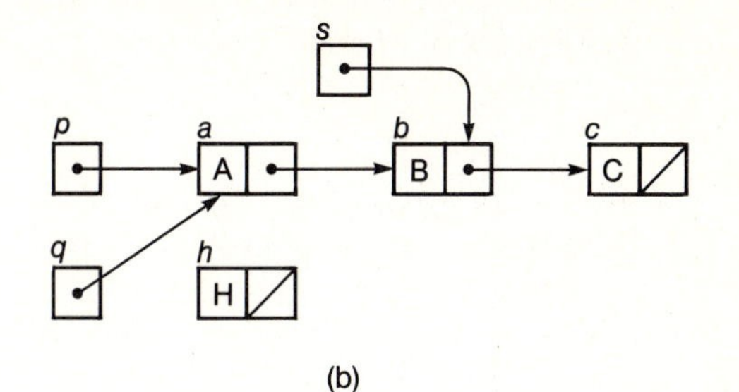

(b)

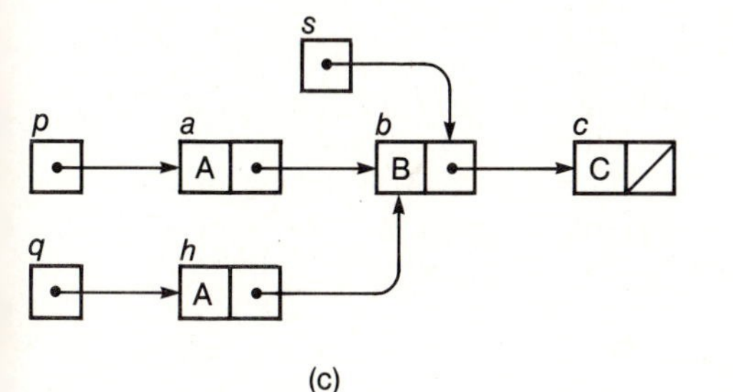

(c)

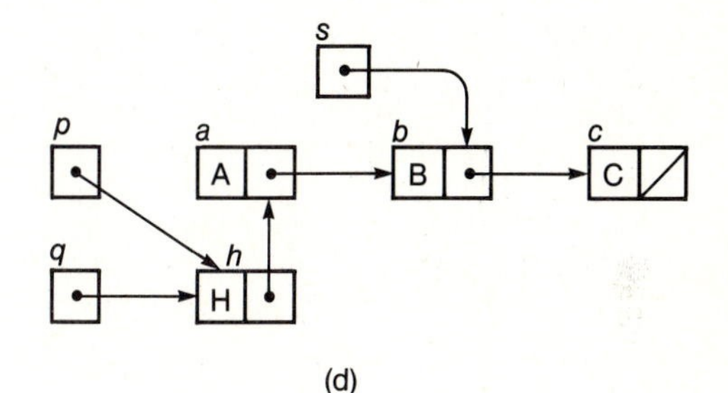

(d)

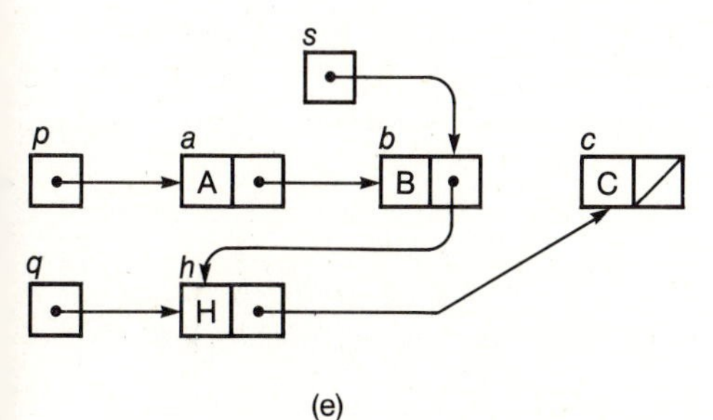

(e)

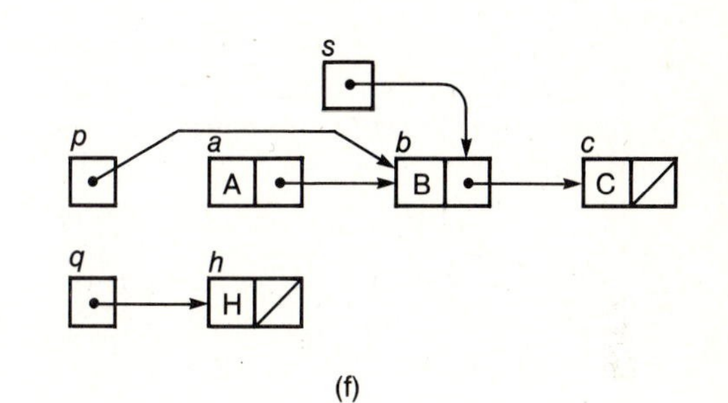

(f)

Figure 4.5 Implementing Lists with Pointers

In actual situations that involve computing with such nodes, they would not have any labels and would not be known to the program except via pointer variables that reference them. For our discussion, the pointers *p,q,s* fortuitously have meaningful values; we will see in Section 4.2 how pointer variables acquire meaningful values in practice.

Next, let us look at the operation of deletion, which is the converse to that of insertion. It is very easy to delete the first node in a list by $p := p\uparrow.next$, as shown in Figure 4.5(f). To delete the last node in a list is more work for the same reason as it was to insert a node at the end – it requires chaining from the head to find the end. More generally, suppose that we wish to delete the node pointed to by *s*. We encounter the same difficulty as in the case of inserting a node before *b*. Namely, the pointer from node *a* must be altered, but we do not have a means of accessing it. We can attempt a similar trick of copying $s\uparrow := s\uparrow.next\uparrow$. However, in addition to potential copying overhead, there is the fundamental problem that this won't work if *s* points to the last node on the list.

4.1.2.2 Circular Lists. A serious shortcoming associated with the simple form of list discussed in the preceding section is that, given a pointer value into the middle of such a list, we can access all the nodes from that point to the end, but cannot access any of the preceding nodes. A simple modification solves this problem. We can replace the **nil** pointer value in the last node by a pointer to the first node, thereby creating a *circular list*.

Figure 4.6(a) shows Figure 4.5(a) redrawn as circular lists. For this style of circular list, remarks about programming techniques would be similar to those made previously about simple lists. However, a modest change makes it easy to insert a node at either the first *or* the last position of a circular list. Namely, let the list header point to the *last* node rather than to the *first* node. This is shown in Figure 4.6(b). Therein, to insert *h* at the front of the first list, we need

```
q↑.next := p↑.next;  p↑.next := q;
```

and to insert *h* at the rear of the first list, we need

```
q↑.next := p↑.next;  p↑.next := q;  p := q;
```

That is, we insert *h* at the same place in the circle in both cases, but in the latter case we then move the header around the circle by one position. You should redraw Figure 4.6(b) for these two cases to convince yourself of this.

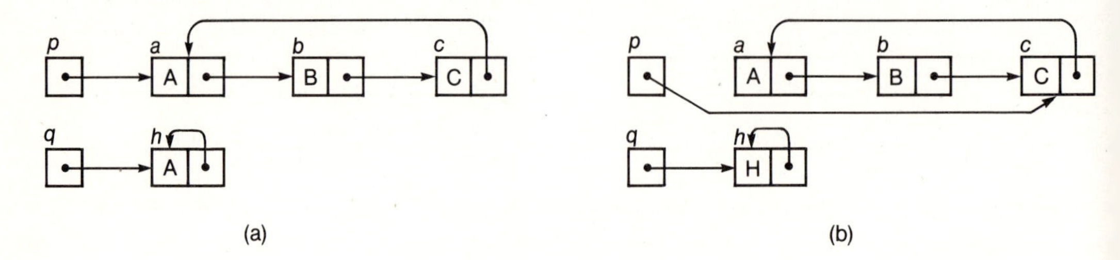

Figure 4.6 Circular Lists

Suppose that we have list *A* with nodes $a_1, a_2, \dots, a_m$ and list *B* with nodes $b_1, b_2, \dots, b_n$. A particular virtue of using circular lists as in Figure 4.6(b) is that it is then quite easy to concatenate *A* and *B* into one list *C* with nodes $a_1, a_2, \dots, a_m, b_1, b_2, \dots, b_n$ (see Exercise 4.3). With regard to the problems of insertion before an arbitrary nodeand deletion of an arbitrary node, we can now find the predecessor of a node by chaining all the way around the circle, although this solution is rather expensive.

There are two pitfalls in what we have said so far concerning lists:

1. If we are chaining around a circular list, how can we distinguish the first node from all the others?

2. What happens, in either a simple or a circular list, when there is only one node and we delete it?

In answer to the first pitfall, we could insist upon always having the header available for comparison, but this is clumsy. In answer to the second pitfall, we could test for, respectively, $p\uparrow.next =$ **nil** or $p\uparrow.next = p$, and then set $p :=$ **nil** if so. However, a better solution to both of these problems is to expand the header into a node of the same format as the other nodes in the list. Henceforth, we will refer to the term header as having this expanded sense.

In spite of the overhead, an extra node is worthwhile for several reasons, many of which apply to simple lists as well as to circular lists:

- It can be used for recognizing when we are at the beginning of a circular list.
- It simplifies the representation of empty lists. For instance, there may be many references to a list from within a program. Without a header node, if the list becomes empty we must change each of these pointer references to **nil**.
- It is often necessary in list operations to operate on a pointer that points to an arbitrary node r. If there is a possibility that r is the first one on a list, then all references to r must test for that possibility and do something different if it applies. The use of a header node removes the need for all these tests by standardizing the treatment of such pointers.
- When we have a header node, there is often extra space (where data is stored in non-header nodes) that can profitably be used to keep other information, such as extra pointers, the number of nodes on the list, etc.

With the inclusion of header nodes, Figure 4.5(a) becomes Figure 4.7(a) and Figure 4.6(a) becomes Figure 4.7(b). However, the literature on lists and headers is lacking in consistency and preciseness; for example, the term header is applied sometimes to p and q in Figure 4.7, and sometimes to what we call the header nodes pointed to by p and q.

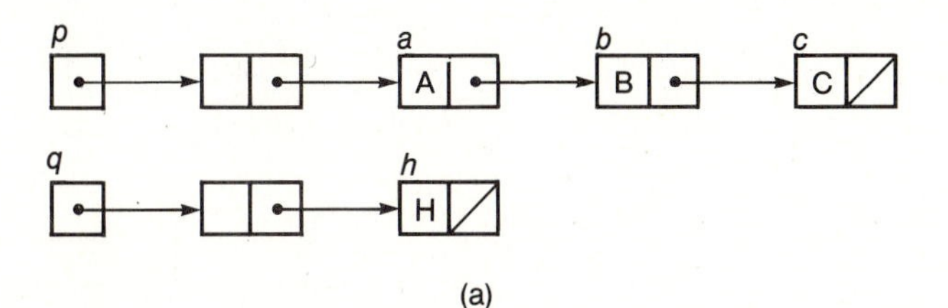

(a)

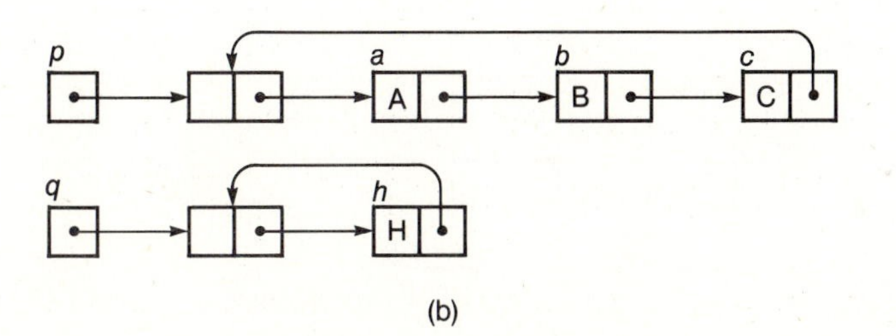

(b)

Figure 4.7 Header Nodes

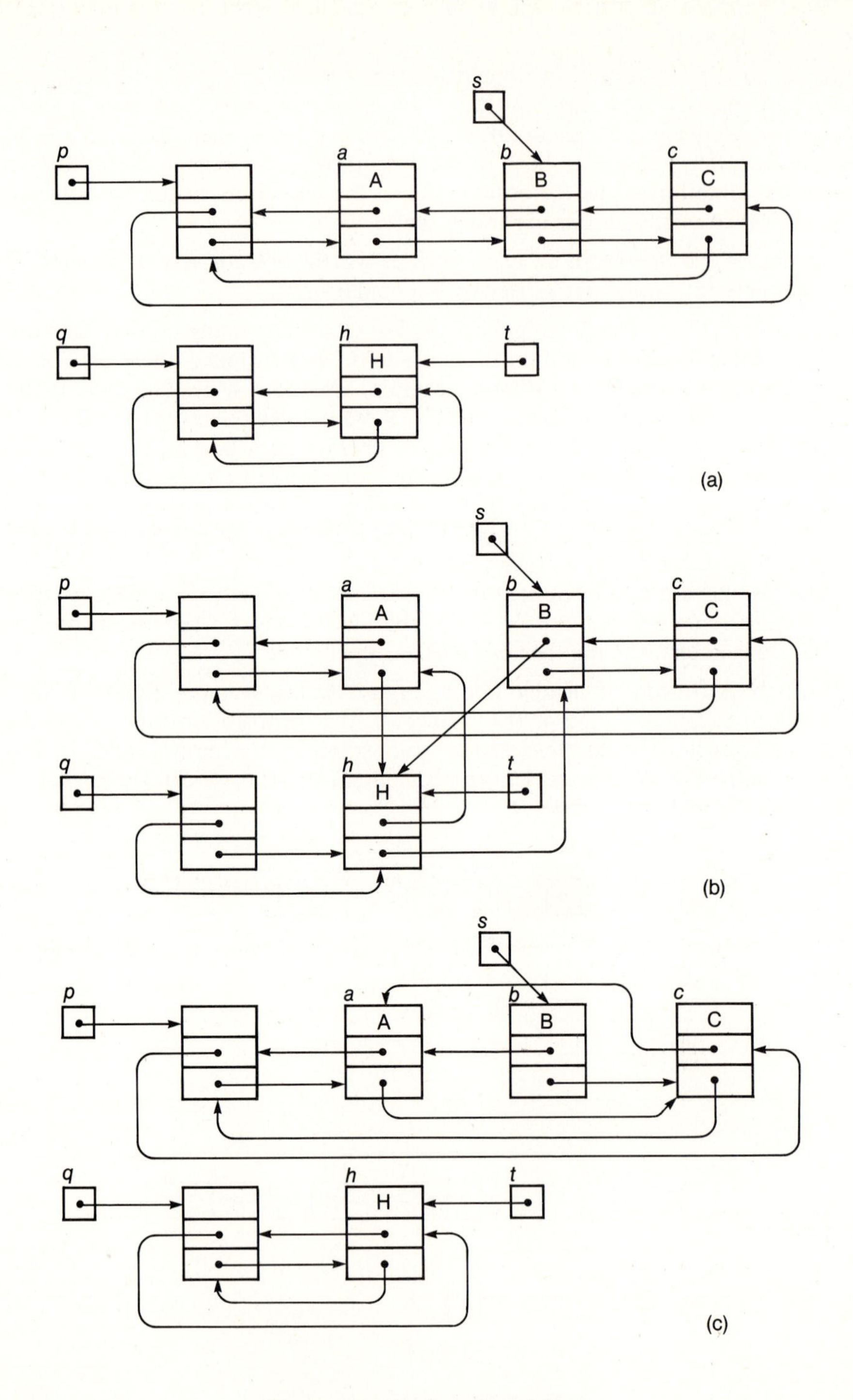

Figure 4.8 Bi-directional Lists

4.1.2.3 Bi-directional Lists. We encountered two problems with simple forms of lists, one having to do with inserting a node before an arbitrarily specified node in a list and another having to do with deleting an arbitrary node. In principle, these shortcomings can be overcome with a circular list; however, it is not realistic to chain all the way around a circular list in order to find the predecessor of a node. A much better resolution for both of these problems comes from introducing the list operation:

previous(r) – to access the item that precedes r in the list.

This is easily accommodated via the *bi-directional list*, in which two links are maintained at each node – one to that node's predecessor and one to its successor, as shown in the template:

```
type   link = ↑node;
       node = record
          data: char;      {for example}
          pred,succ: link;
       end;
```

Figure 4.8(a) shows Figure 4.5(a) redrawn as bi-directional lists. Note that we have employed header nodes again, and that both the forward and backward lists are circular. This would frequently be the preferred method, but it is also possible to have bi-directional lists that are not circular and/or do not have header nodes. It is now a simple matter to insert node h either before or after node b. The logic is similar, requiring four pointer changes in either case. For instance, in order to insert node h before node b, we would need

```
t↑.pred := s↑.pred;
t↑.succ := s;
s↑.pred↑.succ := t;
s↑.pred := t;
```

as shown in Figure 4.8(b). Thus, not only do bi-directional lists require space for extra pointers; they also require twice as much work for insertions. However, the situation with respect to deleting the arbitrary node b is much more elegant. It requires just the two pointer changes

```
s↑.pred↑.succ := s↑.succ; s↑.succ↑.pred := s↑.pred;
```

as shown in Figure 4.8(c).

To conclude these discussions of simple, circular, and bi-directional lists, what would empty lists look like in each of the three cases? They would have the forms shown, respectively, in (a), (b), and (c) of Figure 4.9.

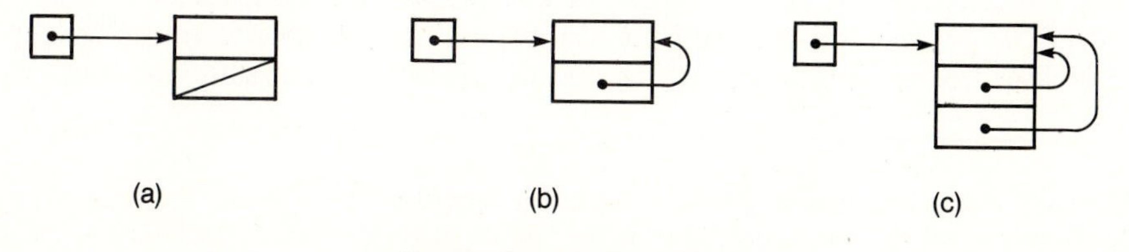

Figure 4.9 Empty Lists

4.1.3 The Free Storage Pool

In the beginning of our discussion of pointer variables, we said that the space for list nodes is acquired via system processes. More precisely, these processes cause the allocation and de-allocation of *free space*. The ramifications to this group of processes cause it to be a topic in its own right, called memory management; it will be elaborated upon in Chapter 11. For now, we will consider some of the basic issues. First, is the rationing of free space done explicitly by the user, does the system do it automatically, or is it a joint venture? In APL and LISP, for example, it all happens automatically; in Pascal and PL/I, on the other hand, it is done jointly. Second, what is the amount of free space required for list nodes? Is the size always the same, or does it vary? In LISP there is just one size of list cell; in APL and Pascal the amounts of space can vary in size. In this section we will do two things. We will cite the system routines by which a Pascal user controls free space. Then we will make a simplifying assumption, and illustrate how these system routines might operate under that assumption.

In Pascal, free space is obtained from a memory area called the *heap*. A block of free space is acquired from the heap by invoking **new**(*p*) , where *p* is a pointer variable of a specified type. After **new**(*p*) is executed, *p* will be pointing to a block of the appropriate size (since the compiler can detect the size from the type definition). Assuming that characters, integers, pointers, and reals require 1,4,4, and 8 bytes respectively, then in Figure 4.10, *p* would contain the address of a block of 33 bytes. Having obtained the space via **new**(*p*), we might then proceed to fill it, for example:

```
p↑.a := 'X'; p↑.b [2] := 7; p↑.d := 3.14; p↑.e := nil;
```

Figure 4.10 illustrates an important additional point. Note that *r* and *s* are pointers for a variant type record, with variants of unequal size. The invocation **new**(*r*,*case*1) yields a block of 52 bytes, and the invocation **new**(*s*,*case*2) yields a block of 24 bytes. You may recall from Section 3.2 that one of the reasons for using variant records is to economize on space by not allocating more than is needed for that particular variant. In Pascal, we can obtain this economy by invoking **new** with variant discriminators as additional parameters.[2]

The converse of space allocation is space de-allocation. The system procedure for this in Pascal is **dispose**, as in **dispose**(*p*), **dispose**(*r*,*case*1), **dispose**(*s*,*case*2), etc. Note that in many implementations of Pascal, the system procedure **dispose** is not supported; rather a more primitive de-allocation scheme is provided via the system procedures **mark** and **release**.

In order to convey some idea of what **new** and **dispose** do, let us assume that our list nodes are all of the same size. In this simple environment, let P_NEW and P_DISPOSE (for pseudo-new and pseudo-dispose) be routines to ration free space. In this case, free space can be one simple list of cells of the standard size, with a

---

[2] In reality, when a compiler allocates space for records such as these, the final sizes may be slightly greater. The usual cause is that fields of records are constrained to begin at memory locations that are some power of two, leaving "holes."

```
program ...

type    fptr = ↑fnode;
        fnode = record
           a: char;
           b: array [1 .. 3] of integer;
           c,d: real;
           e: fptr;
        end;
        rectype = (case1,case2);
        vptr = ↑vnode;
        vnode = record
           f: array [1 .. 4] of char;
           case rectype of
              case1: (g: real;
                         h: array [1 .. 10] of integer);
              case2: (i,j,k: integer;
                         m: real);
        end;

var     p: fptr;
        r,s: vptr;

begin
   ...
   new (p);
   new (r,case1);
   new (s,case2);
   ...
end.
```

Figure 4.10 Space Allocation from the Heap

header cell *Free* that points to the front of the list. Then the action of P_NEW is given by

```
procedure P_NEW (var x: link);
begin
   x := Free;
   Free := Free↑.next;
end;
```

and the action of P_DISPOSE is given by

```
procedure P_DISPOSE (x: link);
begin
   x↑.next := Free;
   Free := x;
end;
```

In other words, memory management in this simple case consists of nothing more than removing and adding cells at the front of a list. In Figure 4.11, P_NEW(*q*) yields (b) from (a), and P_DISPOSE(*q*) yields (a) from (b). (Whether

P_DISPOSE(q) actually sets q to **nil** would depend upon the implementation.) Simple as this technique may be, it is all that is required in many cases. In particular, when list processing must be performed in languages such as BASIC or FORTRAN, this technique can be used to maintain a pool of available nodes linked by cursors.

When de-allocating cells on a list, it is common to wish to free an entire list at one time. The use of circular lists allows this operation to be performed in constant time – that is, independently of the number of cells on the list (see Exercise 4.4).

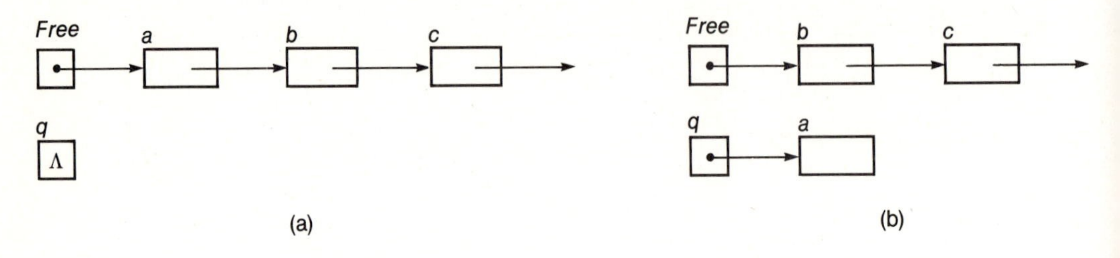

Figure 4.11 Free Space as a Simple Linked List

4.1.4 The Economy of Pointers

Before embarking on applications of linked lists, let us consider one last basic issue. The use of links requires extra space. Just how much of a problem is this? Their overhead is really a percentage of all the other space required in the list node or cell or record. If that space is rather large, then the incremental cost for pointer space should not be significant. Also, the amount of space required for a single pointer might be 32 bits on some machines, but only 16 bits or less on others; this is a function of the available addressing space on the underlying machine.[3] In the case of sequential lists, there is a trick that can be used. Bi-directional lists would seem to require twice as much link space as simple or circular lists. But two links can be fitted into the space required for one! We will describe two techniques for doing this, using the list of Figure 4.12(a), where each cell has both a backward and a forward link.

In Figure 4.12(b), the cell at address a_i is given the composite link value a_{i-1} XOR a_{i+1}, where XOR is the exclusive-or operation, available on many computing machines. Then, to go forward from a_i, we combine the predecessor location a_{i-1} with the ith composite link

$$a_{i-1} \text{ XOR } (a_{i-1} \text{ XOR } a_{i+1}) = a_{i+1} \tag{4.1}$$

---

[3] With the List structures that we will discuss in Section 4.4, fixed-size cells are packed in various ways with data and/or pointers. At the assembly language level, it is often possible to use ingenuity in this packing to maximize storage efficiency.

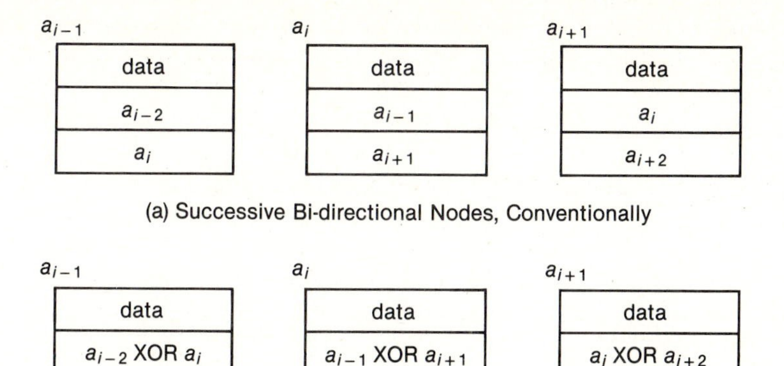

(a) Successive Bi-directional Nodes, Conventionally

(b) Successive Bi-directional Nodes, Encoding Links with XOR

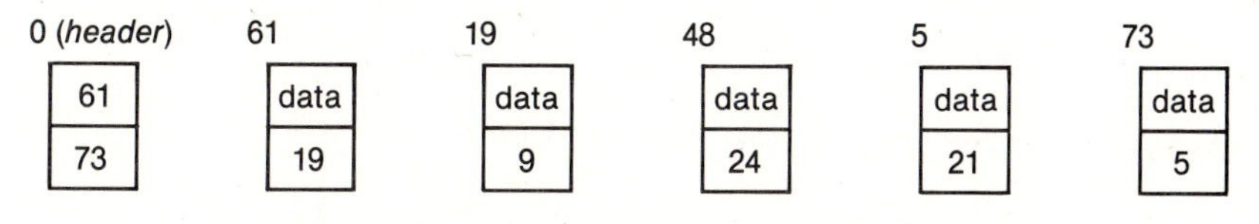

(c) An Example, Encoding Links with MOD (r = 100)

Figure 4.12 Bi-directional Lists with Just One Link per Node

to yield the location of the successor cell. We can also go backward from a_i by combining the successor location a_{i+1} with the ith composite link

$$a_{i+1} \text{ XOR } (a_{i-1} \text{ XOR } a_{i+1}) = a_{i-1} \tag{4.2}$$

to yield the location of the predecessor cell.

If the exclusive-or operation is not available, another possibility is obtained by computing the ith link value as $(a_{i-1} + a_{i+1})$ MOD r, where r is any sufficiently large number. In this case, we can go forward from a_i by computing

$$((a_{i-1} + a_{i+1}) - a_{i-1}) \text{ MOD } r = a_{i+1} \tag{4.3}$$

and we can go backward from a_i by computing

$$((a_{i-1} + a_{i+1}) - a_{i+1}) \text{ MOD } r = a_{i-1} \tag{4.4}$$

This latter variant is illustrated in more detail in Figure 4.12(c) by using arbitrary values for the a_i, and with $r = 100$.

Of course, these methods cannot be used with Pascal pointer variables, although the MOD technique could be used with cursors. Also, one needs two successive location values to start off rather than just one location value; however, it is then easy to scan the list and to have arbitrary alternations in direction as that scan proceeds. On the other hand, if insertions or deletions are common, then the adjustments that must be made to the composite link values are costly. This method has been characterized as referencing a list by its edges rather than its nodes, and has been shown to be effective for a variety of applications [Wise 1976].

4.2 EXAMPLES OF SEQUENTIAL LIST USAGE

It is worth repeating the caveat from the beginning of this chapter, that lists may mean many different things. Our discussion so far has been restricted to sequential lists; we will soon move on to other forms. Even so, the simple forms of lists that we have described thus far are already extremely useful, as the following three examples illustrate.

4.2.1 Maintenance of an Ordered List

In Section 2.1.2 we presented two short, simple functions SEARCH_A (Algorithm 2.1) and SEARCH_B (Algorithm 2.2) for scanning the elements of an unordered array in search of an input value. Both functions terminated with one of two values: zero if the sought after value was not in the array, or the index of the sought after value if it was in the array.

We will now look at an algorithm for searching an ordered list. This time, we will return a pointer to the node containing the input argument if it is there; and if it is not already there, we will insert it in the list in the correct location to maintain the order of the list. The list is assumed to have a header node that contains a dummy value less than any data value in the list. With such an algorithmic capability, it is easy to describe the construction and use of a dictionary, or a concordance, or a symbol table for a compiler or assembler. Instead, however, we will illustrate a capability that is common to all of these. Our list searching function SEARCH_LIST (Algorithm 4.1) takes two input arguments:

head – a pointer to the header node of a list (presumed to be in order), and
id – a key value to be searched for in the list.

It returns False if the key value was not in the list and has been inserted, or True if the key was in the list originally; it also has as an output argument:

loc – a pointer (in either case) to the location of the node containing the key.

Thus, in SEARCH_LIST the boolean result is returned by the function itself, and the pointer result is returned as a **var** parameter. Although it violates mathematical purity to have a function return a result via a call by reference, it is convenient for the typical manner in which SEARCH_LIST might be used, as in

```
if SEARCH_LIST (...) then
   {do one kind of processing if the key was already there}
else
   {do another kind of processing if it was inserted}
```

```
function SEARCH_LIST (head: ptr; id: integer; var loc: ptr): boolean;

{look for id in the ordered linked list with header node head (containing
  key less than any id) and returns true/false according as it is/isn't
  already there; if it isn't there, insert it in a new node in proper
  sequence; in any event, set loc to point to node containing id}

type    ptr = ↑node;
        node = record
           key: integer;
           next: ptr;
        end;

var     q,r: ptr;
        state: (append,found,insert,scan);

begin
   loc := head;
   state := scan;
   while state = scan do begin
      if loc↑.key = id then
         state := found
      else if loc↑.key > id then
         state := insert
      else if loc↑.next = nil then
         state := append
      else begin           {keep looking}
         q := loc;
         loc := loc↑.next;
      end;
   end;
   if state = found then
      SEARCH_LIST := true
   else begin
      new (r);
      r↑.key := id;
      case state of
         append: begin
            loc↑.next := r;
            r↑.next := nil;
         end;
         insert: begin
            q↑.next := r;
            r↑.next := loc;
         end;
      end;
      loc := r;
      SEARCH_LIST := false;
   end;
end;
```

Algorithm 4.1 SEARCH_LIST

The finished algorithm SEARCH_LIST masks some tricky details. For instance, one common mistake in writing this algorithm is to use

```
while (loc <> nil) and (loc↑.key < id) do
```

to control the scanning loop. At the end of the list, however, *loc* = **nil**, and the expression *loc↑.key* will cause a run time error with many compilers. To see a more subtle problem, note that just one of three things must be true when the scanning loop terminates:

(a) the variable *id* is already in the list, or

(b) a node with *id* is to be inserted between two other nodes, or

(c) a node with *id* is to be inserted after the last node.

It is very easy to confuse the last two cases and either cause a run-time error or insert a node at the wrong place in the list. Wirth [1976] gives an excellent exposition of some of the hazards involved in solving what seems like an innocuous problem.

In our solution, these difficulties are nicely finessed by the use of the variable *state*, of enumerated type. This technique [Atkinson 1979, 1984] makes explicit which conditions apply while searching through the list; it also provides an elegant way to discriminate what must be done when the scanning terminates. You should satisfy yourself how the algorithm works by trying it against a list of values (see Exercise 4.9).

4.2.2 Polynomial Addition

Lists provide a very natural representation for symbolic manipulation of algebraic terms. Each term can be represented by a list node; and a polynomial of such terms is then represented by a list of terms ordered on the values of the exponents of the variables. Under such operations as polynomial addition, polynomial multiplication, and differentiation, it is characteristic that terms with given exponents are created and destroyed in an unpredictable manner. Thus, the ability to insert and delete terms is essential.

For example, with the definition

```
type  link = ↑term;
      term = record
         expon: integer;
         coeff: real;
         next: link;
      end;
```

the polynomial $P = 8.1x^{11} + 3.2x^7 - 15$ would appear as in Figure 4.13. This representation employs a simple list with a header node. Our discussion will be restricted to polynomials with positive, integer exponents, which enables us to denote nodes as headers by employing exponent values of -1.

The procedure POLYADD (Algorithm 4.2) takes as input *p* and *q*, pointers to the header nodes of polynomials *P* and *Q*. *Q* is added to *P*, with *Q* being

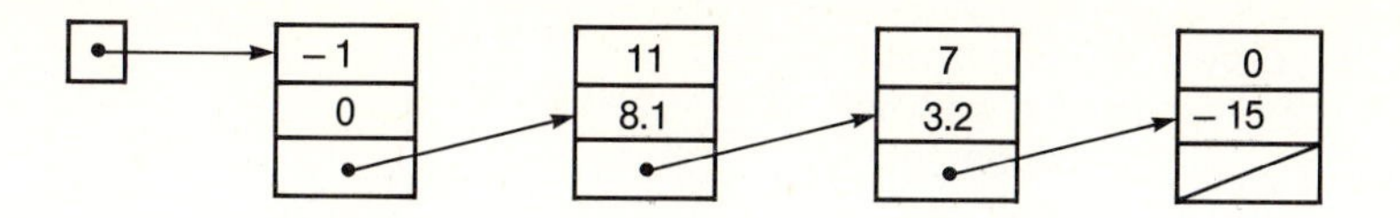

Figure 4.13 A Polynomial as a Linked List

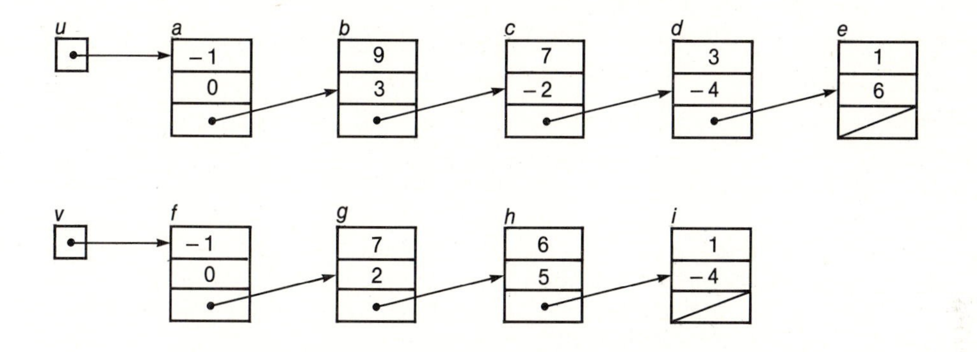

Figure 4.14 Polynomial Inputs to Algorithm POLYADD

unchanged but P being changed "in place" to reflect the sum. Our purpose in doing this rather than developing the sum in a third polynomial R is to demonstrate some important aspects of typical list processing. Note that POLYADD employs two working pointer variables $p1$ and $p2$. The first is used to retain the previous value of p, as p chains forward through P. This solves the problems of insertion before a given node and deletion of an arbitrary node. The second is used whenever we find a term in Q with no corresponding term in P. In such cases, we cannot simply relink that term from Q into P, for that would alter Q, contrary to the declared effect of POLYADD. Rather, we must get space for a new node via $p2$, copy over the data from the term in Q, and then adjust the pointers. To illustrate the operation of POLYADD, assume that we have

$$U = 3x^9 - 2x^7 - 4x^3 - 6x, \quad \text{and} \quad V = 2x^7 + 5x^6 - 4x$$

as shown in Figure 4.14. We have labeled the nodes for purposes of exposition, even though the labels are meaningless for the algorithm. A trace of POLYADD(u,v) is shown in Figure 4.15, and the resultant form of U is shown in Figure 4.16.

Suppose that we had not chosen to represent polynomials as lists, but had instead employed arrays, such as

```
a,b: array [0 .. n] of real
```

in which $a[i]$ contained the coefficient of x^i in $A = a_0 + a_1x^1 + a_2x^2 + \cdots + a_nx^n$, and $b[i]$ contained the coefficient of x^i in $B = b_0 + b_1x^1 + b_2x^2 + \cdots + b_nx^n$. In this case, the addition could be carried out much more simply by

```
procedure POLYADD (p,q: link);

type    link = ↑term;
        term = record
           expon: integer;
           coeff: real;
           next: link;
        end;

var     p1,p2: link;
        state: (add,delete,done,insert,qonly,skip);

begin
   state := add;
   repeat
      if state in [add,skip] then begin
         p1 := p;
         p := p↑.next;
      end;
      if state <> skip then
         q := q↑.next;
      if q = nil then state := done
      else if p = nil then state := qonly
      else begin
         if p↑.expon < q↑.expon then state := insert
         else if p↑.expon > q↑.expon then state := skip
         else begin        {exponents must be equal}
            state := add;
            p↑.coeff := p↑.coeff + q↑.coeff;
            if p↑.coeff = 0 then begin
         {delete term from P:  fix up links for P, free space}
               state := delete;
               p2 := p;
               p := p↑.next;
               p1↑.next := p;
               dispose (p2);
            end;
         end;
      end;
      if state in [insert,qonly] then begin
   {insert term in P:  get space via p2, copy q↑, fix up links for P}
         new (p2);
         p2↑.expon := q↑.expon;
         p2↑.coeff := q↑.coeff;
         p2↑.next := p;
         p1↑.next := p2;
         p1 := p2;
      end;
   until state = done;
end;
```

Algorithm 4.2 POLYADD

state	*p*	*p*1	*p*2	*q*
	$\uparrow a$			$\uparrow f$
add	$\uparrow b$	$\uparrow a$		$\uparrow g$
skip	$\uparrow c$	$\uparrow b$		
add				
delete	$\uparrow d$		$\uparrow c$	$\uparrow h$
insert		$\uparrow r$	$\uparrow r$	$\uparrow i$
skip	$\uparrow e$	$\uparrow d$		
add	Λ	$\uparrow e$		Λ
done				

Figure 4.15 Trace of Algorithm POLYADD

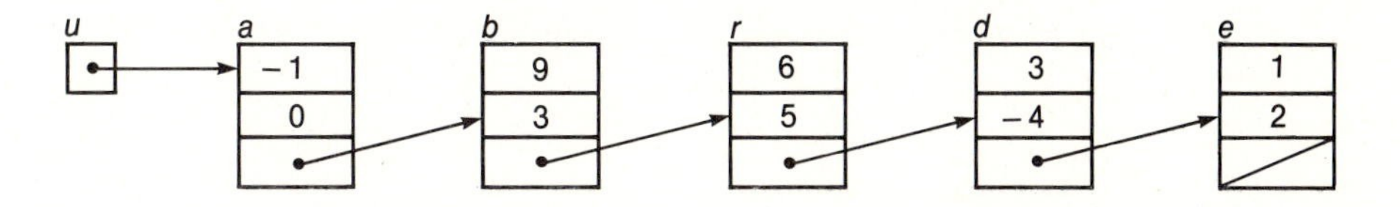

Figure 4.16 Output of Algorithm POLYADD

```
for i := 0 to n do
    a [i] := a [i] + b [i];
```

However, in actual situations where symbolic algebraic manipulation is needed, the range of the exponents is often much larger than the number of terms in any single polynomial. This is particularly true for polynomial multiplication, where it would be necessary to pre-allocate arrays of large dimension to anticipate extreme cases. In these cases, the arrays a and b would be sparse, and we would expend much space and time on zero terms. Thus, depending upon the sparsity, the list representation will almost certainly save space and, in many cases, time also.

The inappropriateness of arrays for representing symbolic polynomials is emphasized when we consider polynomials in several variables, because then the range of potential exponent combinations explodes. An array would have to have as many dimensions as there are variables. For lists, we can accommodate multivariate polynomials by placing an ordering on the variables, and then retaining terms according to lexicographical ordering of the corresponding exponents. As an example

$$R(x,y,z) = \mathrm{A}x^3y + \mathrm{B}x^3z + \mathrm{C}xy^2z^3 + \mathrm{D}y^2z^3 + \mathrm{E}y^2 + \mathrm{F}y + \mathrm{G}z^2 \tag{4.5}$$

could be represented as shown in Figure 4.17. Another approach to handling multivariate polynomials will be discussed in Section 4.4.3.3.

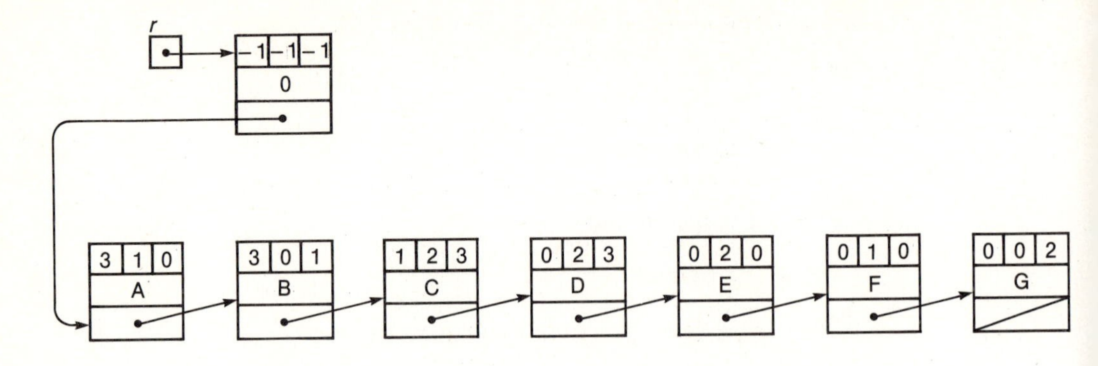

Figure 4.17 A Multivariate Polynomial as a Linked List

4.2.3 Equivalence Classes

Consider the following problem. We have a set of n objects $\{a_i\}$. We are also given m statements of equivalence between pairs of members of this set, such as $a_2 = a_5$, $a_3 = a_8$, etc. Let us assume that the objects can be mapped into the integers $1 \mathinner{..} n$ in an efficient manner. If such a mapping is not already at hand by the nature of the data, then we will discover how to do so in Chapter 10, when we talk about hash functions. For definiteness, suppose that, with $n = 19$ and $m = 16$, we have the following objects and relationships:

$$\begin{array}{rrrr} 18 = 12 & 16 = 14 & 8 = 18 & 16 = 6 \\ 6 = 10 & 9 = 1 & 17 = 4 & 16 = 17 \\ 8 = 2 & 3 = 13 & 9 = 11 & 3 = 8 \\ 11 = 5 & 7 = 19 & 3 = 9 & 19 = 15 \end{array} \tag{4.6}$$

By the nature of equivalence, we can easily determine that for this example there are really just three equivalence classes, as follows:

(1,2,3,5,8,9,11,12,13,18) (4,6,10,14,16,17) (7,15,19)

It is frequently necessary to discover equivalence classes by processing equivalent pairs. The problem arises naturally in assembling programs, when different symbols may be declared to be synonymous, or with EQUIVALENCE statements in FORTRAN [Arden et al. 1961; Galler and Fisher 1964]. It can also arise when performing set operations that are unrelated to language translation.

A naive first approach might simply be to use an array of n slots, as follows. For each pair,

(a) If the slots for both members are empty, then label both slots with a new class-id number.

(b) If the slot for one member is empty and the slot for the other member is occupied, then copy the label from the occupied slot to the empty slot.

```
program EQUIV;

const   listsize = 32;  pairsize = 16;  setsize = 19;

type    cellndx = 0 .. listsize;
        setndx = 0 .. setsize;
        cell = record
           valu: setndx;  link: cellndx;
        end;

var     i,cellnum,classnum: integer;
        flag: array [1 .. setsize] of boolean;
        head: array [1 .. setsize] of cellndx;
        classid: array [1 .. setsize] of integer;
        cells: array [1 .. listsize] of cell;

procedure ADDCELL (u,v: setndx);
begin
   cellnum := cellnum + 1;  cells [cellnum].valu := v;
   cells [cellnum].link := head [u];  head [u] := cellnum;
end;

procedure DOPAIR;
var     i,j: setndx;
begin
   read (i,j);  ADDCELL (i,j);  ADDCELL (j,i);
end;

procedure DOLIST (i: setndx);
var     j: cellndx;  k: setndx;
begin
   j := head [i];
   while j <> 0 do begin
      k := cells [j].valu;
      if not flag [k] then begin
         flag [k] := true;  classid [k] := classnum;  DOLIST (k);
      end;
      j := cells [j].link;
   end;
end;

begin
   for i := 1 to setsize do begin
      flag [i] := false;  head [i]:= 0;
   end;
   cellnum := 0;  classnum := 0;
   for i := 1 to pairsize do
      DOPAIR;
   for i := 1 to setsize do
      if not flag [i] then begin
         flag [i] := true;  classnum := classnum + 1;
         classid [i] := classnum;  DOLIST (i);
      end;
end.
```

Algorithm 4.3 EQUIV

(c) If the slots for both members are occupied, then select the label for one of the members and, for all members of the array having that label, change their labels to that of the other member of the pair.

As the slots become occupied, this method will be forced to execute case (c) for most instances of processing a pair. With a simple array structure, that will mean scanning the entire array to find all members having a particular label, an operation $O(n)$ in time. If m is of the same order of magnitude as n, then the total complexity will be $O(n^2)$.

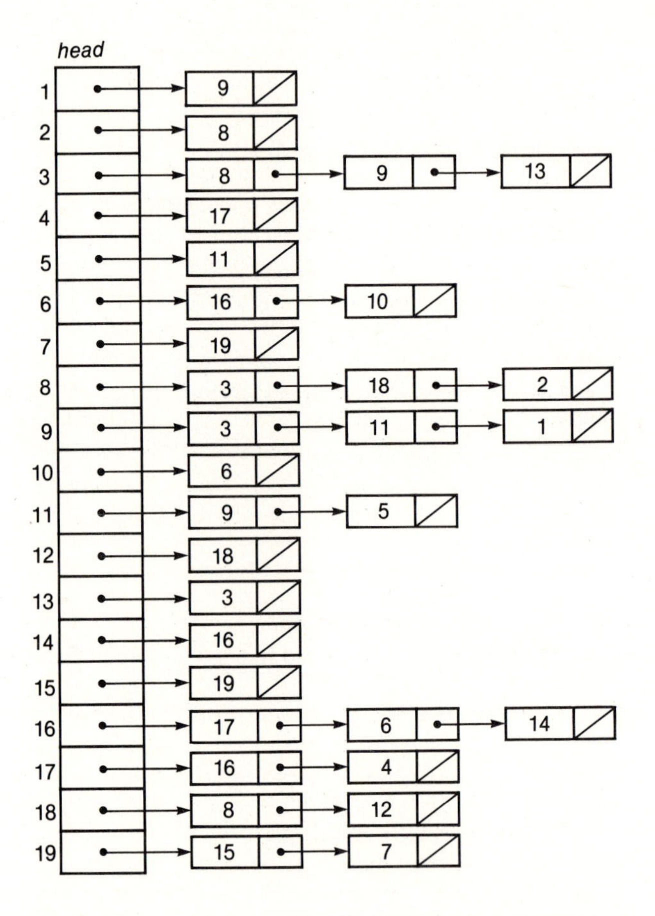

Figure 4.18 Action of First Phase of Algorithm EQUIV

A much more efficient method comes from maintaining the equivalence classes in lists. When the situation corresponding to case (c) above arises, one need only relabel all the items on the shorter list, and then concatenate the two lists. It is fairly easy to show [Aho et al. 1974] that with this technique, the resulting algorithm is $O(n \lg n)$. Rather than pursue this, however, we will describe yet a third approach, also using lists. In this method, we maintain the lists by using an array called *cells* as a Free-list (in the manner of Figure 4.11), and using cursors rather than pointer variables.

In the program EQUIV (Algorithm 4.3) we maintain a list head for each member of the set. Then, in the first stage, we process each pair in constant time, adding each member of the pair to a list for the other member. The effect of the first stage on the pairs in Eqs. 4.6 is illustrated in Figure 4.18; the total effort for this is $O(m)$. In the second stage, we process each member and its list, assigning class-id numbers. This is done via the recursive procedure DOLIST, which is executed just once for each member, so that the second stage is $O(n)$. In our example, DOLIST is called directly three times – for members 1, 4, and 7 – and recursively 16 times; it processes the members in the sequence

1 9 3 8 18 12 2 13 11 5 / 4 17 16 6 10 14 / 7 19 15

Combining the work in the first and second stages (and the initialization phase) we find that EQUIV is $O(m + n)$. Any algorithm for deciding equivalence classes must look at each pair at least once and at each member at least once, so that EQUIV is optimal with respect to time, at least within a constant factor. However, EQUIV also requires arrays of $O(n)$ space and list cells of $O(2m)$ space, for $O(m + n)$ space in total. Moreover, suppose that the problem is somewhat different, and that the pairs come intermixed with queries about equivalence classes that are knowable from the preceding pairs. EQUIV does not provide answers to such queries until all the pairs have been processed. In Section 6.6.5 we will present another algorithm for this problem that overcomes both of these deficiencies; it is $O(n)$ in space, is almost optimal in time, and allows intermixing of pair declarations and queries.

4.3 MULTIPLE LINKING

Our use of lists so far has involved maintaining data items in sequence. That sequence has usually been dictated by the value of a single key field within the item. In this section, we discuss some departures from this. Consider the problem of maintaining items in sequence on several lists simultaneously. We need a set of links for each of the lists. Two structures that provide this facility are the inverted list and the multilist. Note at the outset that these structures are very different from a bi-directional list. Even though the latter has two links for each node, they both have to do with sequence in a single list.

Inverted lists and multilists are used primarily when recording large amounts of data. Real applications may have numerous variations of these structures in response to the characteristics of the data, on the one hand, and the storage devices, on the other hand. Our program is to discuss the basic ideas here and then pursue them in greater detail in Chapter 12. In Section 4.3.3, as an illustration of multiple linking techniques, we will reconsider the subjects of arrays in general, and sparse matrices in particular.

4.3.1 Inverted Lists

In Section 2.3.1 we were concerned with the results of a survey summarizing the sex, education, and marital status of a group of people. These results were summarized in an array of dimension $2 \times 3 \times 5$, shown in Figure 2.5 and reproduced here as Figure 4.19. Typical questions that we could answer from this array are:

- How many married males are there who have not completed high school?
- How many single females are there?
- How many people have finished high school but not college?

We might also wish to ask other kinds of questions, such as:

- Who are all the widowed persons?
- Who are all the divorced males?
- What are the values of the attributes (sex, education, marital status) for a given individual who responded to the survey?

	single	married	divorced	widowed	other
male					
primary	20	17	9	11	14
secondary	32	13	7	5	10
college	11	9	11	8	12
female					
primary	33	28	6	14	17
secondary	21	24	13	8	15
college	19	17	4	5	20

Figure 4.19 The Three-Dimensional Array of Figure 2.5

For the second group of questions, the data in the array structure of Figure 4.19 is of no use. To answer those questions, we would most likely begin by having a record for each person, wherein these attribute values would be transcribed. Suppose that we have such an array of records as shown in Figure 4.20 and containing *name*, *age*, *sex*, *education*, and *marital status*. In this figure the records have a de facto ordering, and we can specify a particular record by its numerical index. It is often more useful, though, to be able to specify a record by its primary key value. In this case, the names can serve as such key values; in real situations, of course, names would not be unique, and social security numbers, employee numbers, etc. would be used instead.

We can regard these records as representing a function F, such that F(*name*, *attribute*) = *value*, as in the examples

F(Delilah, *status*) = single , and F(Roscoe, *education*) = secondary

If we now ask for the names of all the single persons, we can think of this question as inverting the function F to obtain F^{-1}(*attribute*, *value*) = *names*, as demonstrated by the example

record	name	age	sex	education	status
1	Archie	33	male	primary	divorced
2	Beulah	23	female	secondary	widowed
3	Caspar	25	male	secondary	single
4	Delilah	46	female	college	single
5	Egbert	52	male	primary	married
6	Gertrude	32	female	secondary	widowed
7	Hector	18	male	primary	single
8	Jezebel	41	female	primary	married
9	Maisie	32	female	college	divorced
10	Olaf	29	male	primary	married
11	Roscoe	49	male	secondary	single

Figure 4.20 Some Example Data

$$F^{-1}(\textit{status}, \text{single}) = \text{Caspar, Delilah, Hector, Roscoe}$$

This suggestive viewpoint is the origin of the term *inverted list*. There is one inverted list (possibly empty) for every combination of an attribute with its possible values, and this list will generally yield not one, but several names. The set of all the lists is called an *inverted file*. An inverted file for the data of Figure 4.20, except for the attribute of age, is shown in Figure 4.21. The list entries are recorded as names; the entries might alternatively have been record numbers or locations. In essence, however, an inverted list is a list of list pointers.

Sex

male	Archie, Caspar, Egbert, Hector, Olaf, Roscoe
female	Beulah, Delilah, Gertrude, Jezebel, Maisie

Education

primary	Archie, Egbert, Hector, Jezebel, Olaf
secondary	Beulah, Caspar, Gertrude, Roscoe
college	Delilah, Maisie

Marital Status

single	Caspar, Delilah, Hector, Roscoe
married	Egbert, Jezebel, Olaf
divorced	Archie, Maisie
widowed	Beulah, Gertrude
other	none

Figure 4.21 Inverted File of Data in Figure 4.20

An example of an inverted list that usually employs locations is the index of a book. In this book, for example, we find that the term "inverted list" is referenced on pages 132 – 134, 140, 303, 450, 551, and 656 – 658. Here, using page references serves very well because they apply just to this book, and they will change only in the infrequent case of a new edition. On the other hand, consider the Bible or the works of Shakespeare; these have been published in hundreds of editions, rarely with identical pagination. In such a case, it is more appropriate to have a concordance that is valid for all editions, referring to occurrences of words or phrases by their logical locations, as exemplified by:

perverseness: Isaiah – 30,12
Proverbs – 2,14; 11,3; 15,4
Psalms – 101,4

and

perturbation: Henry IV (2nd) – I,ii,132; IV,v,23
Macbeth – V,i,10
Much Ado About Nothing – II,i,268
Richard III – V,iii,161

4.3.2 Multilists

Although we can use inverted lists to find those records having certain values of attributes, we cannot dispense with the original data records. We thus have two files in place of one – the original file and the inverted file. In our example of Figures 4.20 and 4.21, however, we find that no individual has more than one value for a single attribute; the inverted lists for a given attribute are all disjoint. This suggests the possibility of combining the lists for each attribute within a single list, similar to that which we saw in Figure 4.3.

record	name	age	sex	education	status	link fields			
1	Archie	33	M	primary	divorced	8	3	5	9
2	Beulah	23	F	secondary	widowed	3	4	3	6
3	Caspar	25	M	secondary	single	10	5	6	4
4	Delilah	46	F	college	single	11	6	9	7
5	Egbert	52	M	primary	married	0	7	7	8
6	Gertrude	32	F	secondary	widowed	9	8	11	0
7	Hector	18	M	primary	single	2	10	8	11
8	Jezebel	41	F	primary	married	4	9	10	10
9	Maisie	32	F	college	divorced	1	0	0	0
10	Olaf	29	M	primary	married	6	11	0	0
11	Roscoe	49	M	secondary	single	5	0	0	0

Figure 4.22 Multilist of Data in Figure 4.20, Version 1

Such an organization of the data is called a *multilist*, and is illustrated for the data of our example by Figure 4.22. A multilist is a set of records wherein each record is simultaneously on r sequential lists. These unrelated list sequences are expressed by including r link fields in each record. In this instance, we have used record indices rather than name keys for the links; but they are in fact pointers to the next record on the list having the same value for that attribute. For our small example, it is not very helpful to maintain distinct values of age on distinct lists.

However, an easy and useful alternative is to incorporate a link field in the multilist structure for accessing the persons in increasing order of age, as shown in the figure. Finally, we no longer need to maintain the original file, as with inverted lists. However, we do need a set of list headers, one for each value of each attribute; these are shown in Figure 4.23.

Age	7	***Sex***	
		male	1
Marital Status		*female*	2
single	3		
married	5	***Education***	
divorced	1	*primary*	1
widowed	2	*secondary*	2
other	0	*college*	4

Figure 4.23 Headers for Multilist

With the annexation of the link field, the information in each record becomes somewhat redundant. For instance, starting with the fact that Caspar has completed high school, and then following the link to Gertrude, we can know that that is her educational level also. Indeed, it appears that we can compress out much of the original data from Figure 4.22 to yield Figure 4.24, thus saving some storage. Unfortunately, although we can find all the high school graduates by following the list header value of 2, we can now no longer access an arbitrary record and ascertain that person's educational level. A final adjustment that solves this problem is to replace the **nil** link at the end of each list by a circular link back to the header node for that attribute value. By such a strategy, we can always chain far enough to identify any attribute value for a randomly accessed record. This is illustrated in Figure 4.25.

record	name	age	sex	education	status
1	Archie	8	3	5	9
2	Beulah	3	4	3	6
3	Caspar	10	5	6	4
4	Delilah	11	6	9	7
5	Egbert	0	7	7	8
6	Gertrude	9	8	11	0
7	Hector	2	10	8	11
8	Jezebel	4	9	10	10
9	Maisie	1	0	0	0
10	Olaf	6	11	0	0
11	Roscoe	5	0	0	0

Figure 4.24 Multilist of Data in Figure 4.20, Version 2

In practice, it may be far more economical to retain all the data, as in Figure 4.22, than to pay the cost of chaining around a large list. This is just one of many pragmatic details that we will defer to Chapter 12. There is one final point to be made here concerning inverted lists and multilists. What if we were also maintaining a list of each person's citizenship? And what if Archie had dual citizenship in both Egypt and Israel? There is no problem with inverted lists if attributes have multiple values, but this feature cannot be accommodated with multilists.

record	name	age	sex	education	status
1	Archie	8	3	5	9
2	Beulah	3	4	3	6
3	Caspar	10	5	6	4
4	Delilah	11	6	9	7
5	Egbert	0	7	7	8
6	Gertrude	9	8	11	(widowed)
7	Hector	2	10	8	11
8	Jezebel	4	9	10	10
9	Maisie	1	(female)	(college)	(divorced)
10	Olaf	6	11	(primary)	(married)
11	Roscoe	5	(male)	(secondary)	(single)

Figure 4.25 Multilist of Data in Figure 4.20, Version 3

4.3.3 Arrays Revisited

In the discussion of arrays in Chapter 2, we saw that the usual sequential storage allocation method, while highly satisfactory for many applications, is too restrictive for cases wherein:

(a) the array has an irregular shape, or

(b) the array is sparse.

We will illustrate two manners in which linked lists can be used to facilitate operations on arrays of an arbitrary shape or density.

The first technique starts from the observation that a multi-dimensional array can be regarded as a vector of vectors ... of vectors. Rather than unravel such an array into a one-dimensional representation, we can employ vectors of pointers into all dimensions except the last, where we finally have vectors of data values. To be specific, let us consider again the array of Figure 4.19. In the new scheme illustrated in Figure 4.26, we have vector x with pointers to the vectors y_1 and y_2; the latter, in turn, contain pointers to the vectors $z_{i,j}$ $(i = 1,2;\ j = 1,2,3)$. Each z vector contains one row of actual data.

The number of pointers required for this representation (8 in our example, for an array of 30 elements) may seem to be excessive. But consider the general case of a hypercube of k dimensions, with n elements on a side, and such that n is of respectable size. Then it can be shown [Standish 1980] that the excess space for pointer storage is almost independent of k and is of proportion $1/(n-1)$. Moreover, on many machines, random access to an arbitrary element of the array by following pointers may be even faster than when using a dope vector, as in ordinary sequential allocation. However, this representation does have a bias toward access-

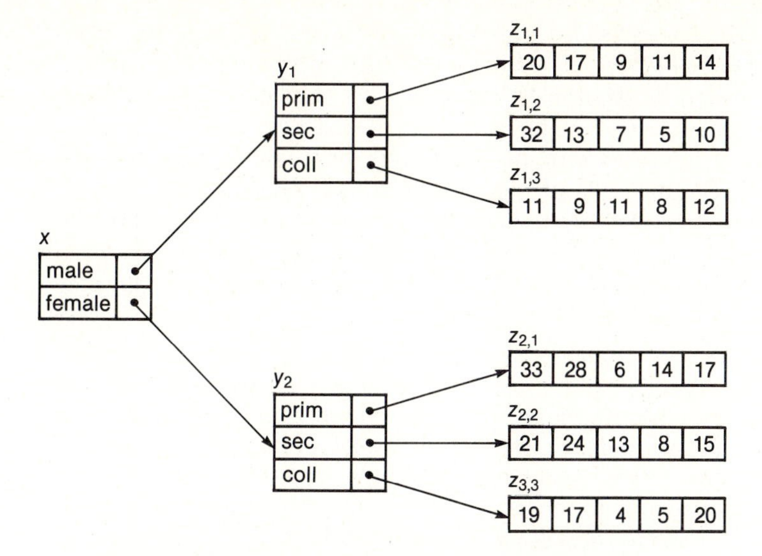

Figure 4.26 A Pointer-Based Array Representation

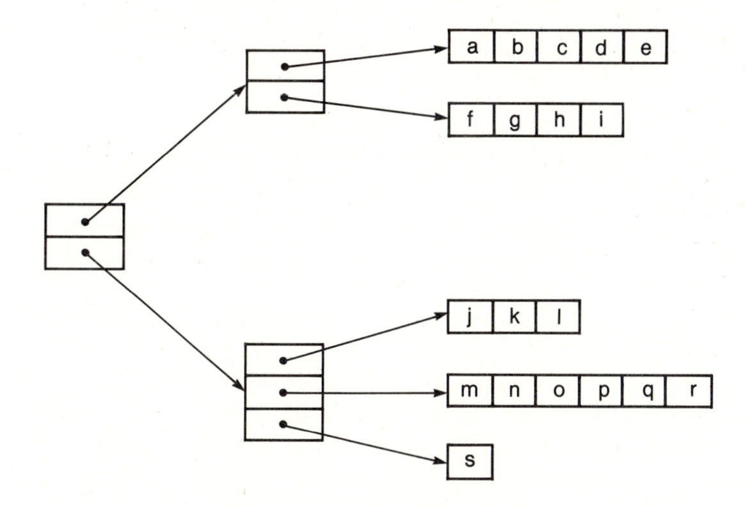

Figure 4.27 A Ragged Array

ing neighbors in the last dimension, with access to neighbors in the other dimensions being more costly.

There are two situations in which the vector of pointers method is particularly advantageous. One is when the array is large, so that there is a need to segment it, or divide it up into logical parts. The other is in the case of a *ragged array*. This term signifies an array in which, for example, not all planes have the same number of rows and/or not all rows have the same number of columns. An illustration of this is given in Figure 4.27. Overall, this solution to the problem of arbitrary extendibility is more practical than those presented in Section 2.7.2.

As a second illustration of the utility of linked lists for dealing with arrays, we return to the subject of sparse matrices. Recall that these are typified by an array of coefficients, mostly zero in value, for the solution of a set of simultaneous equations. The methods of representation that we described in Section 2.8 – bit map, address map, delta skip, and triples – are all related in approach in that they:

1. place the non-zero elements in sequential positions in a vector of data Z, and
2. employ auxiliary vectors to map the row and column indices of the original matrix to indices in Z.

These methods all achieve the primary goal of conserving storage, but they are ill suited to dynamic situations. For example, in solving a set of simultaneous equations by a relaxation method, where we repeatedly use an unaltered set of coefficients, the previously cited methods can work quite well. However, in solving the same equations by Gaussian elimination (see Section 2.3.2), coefficients appear and disappear throughout the matrix. Although the triples method allows for modest flexibility in dynamic situations, a better approach is to represent individual array elements as list nodes, in the form shown in Figure 4.28. With this method, each node is orthogonally linked in the row and column dimensions, using the pointer fields *Right* and *Down*.

<table>
<tr><td colspan="4">Coefficient</td></tr>
<tr><td>Down</td><td>Row</td><td>Col</td><td>Right</td></tr>
</table>

Figure 4.28 Node Structure for Sparse Array Elements

0	5	0	0	2
4	0	9	0	0
0	0	0	6	0
1	0	0	0	3
0	8	0	0	0

Figure 4.29 The Example Sparse Array of Figure 2.23

We will apply this method to the matrix of Figure 2.23, reproduced here as Figure 4.29. In so doing, we have to confess that we avoided an important detail when discussing sparse matrices in Chapter 2. Extremely sparse matrices usually have missing rows and columns consisting entirely of zero elements. In Chapter 2, we ignored this and treated the row and column numbers as consecutive values. But the fact that row j or column k is missing is important in a real problem. To redress matters, we now posit some non-consecutive row and column values for Figure 4.29. Applying the format in Figure 4.28 to this matrix, we obtain the structure in Figure 4.30. Note that both the row lists and the column lists are circular lists, and that there are header nodes for each row and column. In practice, the header nodes might have distinctive formats; we have chosen to give them the same format as data nodes.

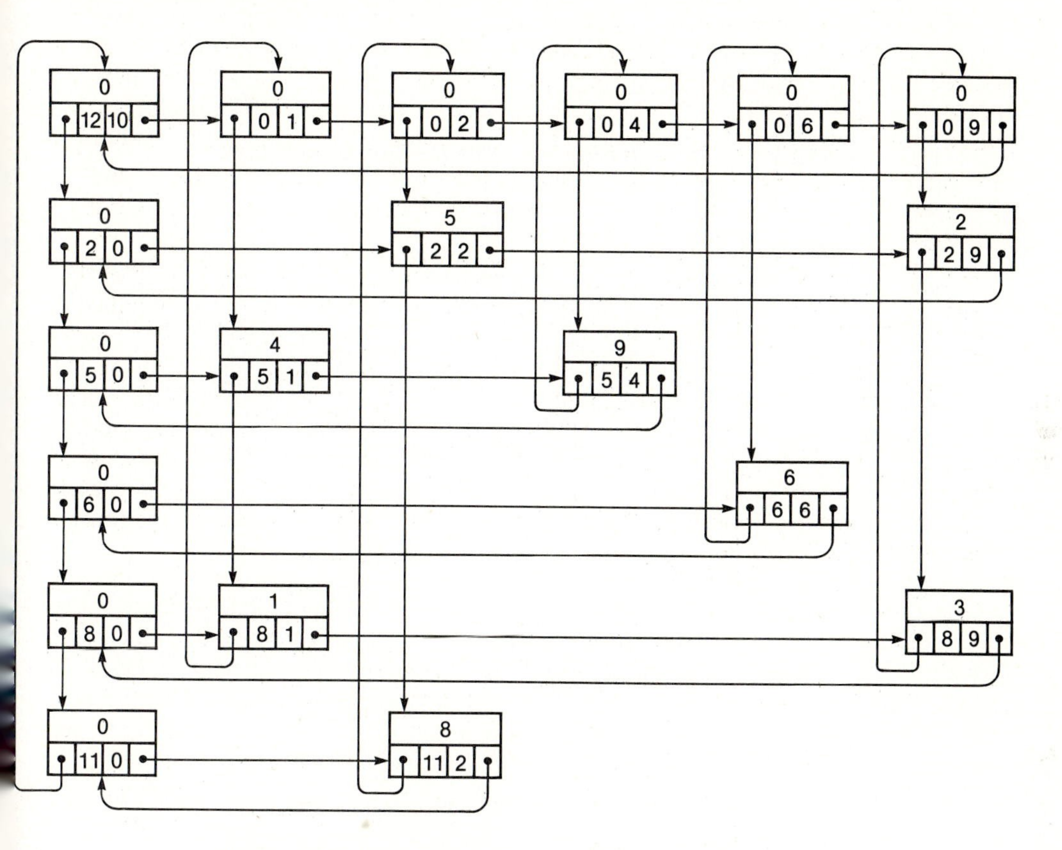

Figure 4.30 The Sparse Array of Figure 4.29 as a List

How do orthogonal lists compare with other methods for representing sparse matrices in terms of storage efficiency? To estimate this in a manner analogous to that employed in Section 2.8, assume that each node requires

8 bytes for the coefficient
4 bytes for two subscript values (should be adequate)
8 bytes for two pointer values (possibly overgenerous)

or 20 bytes in all. The total space requirement is then given by

$$S = 20\rho n^2 + 40n \tag{4.7}$$

where ρ is density, and the two terms correspond to the data nodes and the header nodes. Finally, let us assume that $n = 100$ and then carry forward Table 2.2 as Table 4.1, with a row appended for orthogonal links.

Density ρ	.1	.03	.01	.003
Bit-Map	9650	4050	2450	1890
Address-Map	18400	12800	11200	10640
Delta-Skip	11978	4670	2331	1260
Triples	12000	3600	1200	360
Linked List	24000	10000	6000	4600

Table 4.1 Storage Requirements for Sparse Matrices

Not too surprisingly, the overhead for the pointers places orthogonal linking at a disadvantage with respect to storage efficiency. However, there are many cases where this is much less significant than the capacity for dynamically inserting and deleting elements in the array. We will explore one example of this in depth in the next section. But first, let us recall the discussions of the preceding two sections. What, in fact, are the vectors of pointers in Figures 4.26 and 4.27? They are inverted lists. And what is the orthogonally linked structure of Figure 4.30? It is another multilist.

†4.3.3.1 Sparse Matrix Operations. Computations with sparse matrices are fairly common, and the subject has a fairly specialized literature, for example Bunch and Rose [1976]. Most of these treatments are directed at the efficient solution of large, sparse sets of equations. Since the associated issues are fairly complicated, and since we have not presented the graph-theoretical tools that underlie them, we will pursue the less complex issue of multiplying sparse matrices.

In implementing the multiplication process, we need to employ a variety of utility routines: for input and output, for conversion between the linked list format and others (such as triples format), for initializing the various header nodes, etc. Although important, such routines are straightforward to implement, and so we will presume their availability in what follows. The Pascal syntax corresponding to Figure 4.28 is

```
type  ptr = ↑node;
      node = record
         row,col: integer;
         coeff: real;
         rowptr,colptr: ptr;
      end;
```

We assume that we can employ the following subroutines:

1. SPARSE_SETUP (*a*,*b*: *ptr*; VAR *c*: *ptr*) – taking pointers to the headers of the matrices *A* and *B* as input parameters, and returning a pointer to the header of the matrix *C*. This initialization generates one row header in *C* corresponding to each non-zero row header in *A* and one column header in *C* corresponding to each non-zero column header in *B*. These are obviously the only positions

where we can develop a product in C; moreover, even some of these rows or columns may turn out to be empty when we are finished.

2. SET_NODE (*q*: *ptr*; *r*,*c*: integer; *valu*: real; *rp*,*cp*: *ptr*) – which assigns the last five parameters to the fields of the node pointed at by the first parameter.
3. SPARSE_TRIM (*q*: *ptr*) – which scans the row and column headers of the sparse matrix corresponding to q, and deletes header nodes for those rows or columns that are empty.

The most natural approach to the problem is to mimic the sequence of computation in MAT_MAT (Algorithm 2.4), as reproduced here:

```
for i := 1 to m do
   for j := 1 to p do begin
      sum := 0;
      for k := 1 to n do
         sum := sum + A [i,k] * B [k,j];
      C [i,j] := sum;
   end;
```

By transliterating this logic, we obtain the procedure SPARSE_MULT (Algorithm 4.4). Although the amount of code is substantially larger with lists than it is with arrays, the pattern of scanning the elements of A and B is identical. A significant source of inefficiency comes from having to chain from the ith row header and the jth column header of C in order to insert $C[i,j]$. Since the elements of C are developed a row at a time, we mitigate this by using the variable q to remember the previous point of insertion in the ith row. However, we are still forced to chain down the jth column using the variable s.

Algorithm 4.4 reflects a respectable, workman-like approach to the problem of multiplying sparse matrices, but it is possible to do far better by analyzing where it spends its time. Two things cause it to be inefficient. The first of these is that in inserting $C[i,j]$ into two linked lists, we are able to use the variable q to expedite row insertion, but are unable to expedite column insertion. Another, less obvious shortcoming is that in the simultaneous traversal of a row in A and a column in B, the statement

```
while (x <> u) and (y <> v) do begin
```

is executed with a frequency proportional to the sum of the densities of A and B, or $\rho_A + \rho_B$. Thus there are far more comparisons than multiplications! A pretty resolution for this by Schoor [1982] is to perform the multiplication by the unobvious sequence:

```
for i := 1 to m do
   for k := 1 to n do
      for j := 1 to p do
         C [i,j] := C [i,j] + A [i,k] * B [k,j];
```

where there is no need to initialize C in the list representation.

In other words, we pick an element $A[i,k]$ and then scan the kth row of B to see where there are any multiplications to be performed. As we repeat this operation for the successive elements in the ith row of A, we accumulate contributions to the ith row in C. As a consequence, the number of comparisons is reduced to the product of the densities of A and B, or $\rho_A \times \rho_B$. We still have to contend with the

```
procedure SPARSE_MULT (a,b: ptr; var c: ptr);

var   p,q,r,s,t,u,v,x,y: ptr;
      sum: real;

begin
  SPARSE_SETUP (a,b,c);
  u := a↑.rowptr;                {set to first row in A}
  p := c↑.rowptr;                {set to first row in C}
  while u <> a do begin
    q := p;               {remember beginning of ith row in C}
    v := b↑.colptr;              {set to first col in B}
    r := c↑.colptr;              {set to first col in C}
    while v <> b do begin
      x := u↑.colptr;          {begin ith row in A: a [i,1]}
      y := v↑.rowptr;          {begin jth col in B: b [1,j]}
      sum := 0;
      while (x <> u) and (y <> v) do begin
        if x↑.col < y↑.row then
          x := x↑.colptr
        else if x↑.col > y↑.row then
          y := y↑.rowptr
        else begin
          sum := sum + x↑.coeff * y↑.coeff;
          x := x↑.colptr;
          y := y↑.rowptr;
        end;
      end;
      if sum <> 0 then begin
        new (t);
        s := r;
        while s↑.rowptr <> r do
          s := s↑.rowptr;        {find ith row in jth col of C}
        SET_NODE (t,p↑.row,r↑.col,sum,r,p);
        q↑.colptr := t;
        s↑.rowptr := t;
        q := t;                {remember this entry in ith row of C}
      end;
      v := v↑.colptr;              {go to next col in B}
      r := r↑.colptr;              {go to next col in C}
    end;
    u := u↑.rowptr;                {go to next row in A}
    p := p↑.rowptr;                {go to next row in C}
  end;
  SPARSE_TRIM (c);
end;
```

Algorithm 4.4 SPARSE_MULT

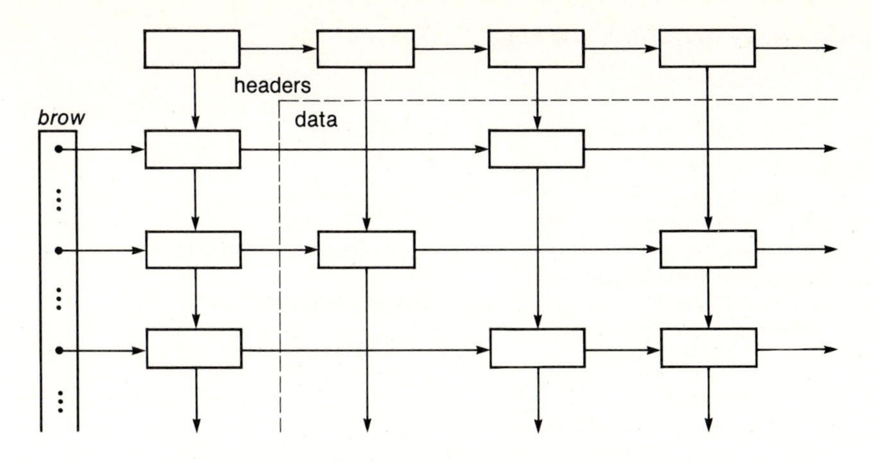

(a) Use of *brow* for Fast Access to Rows of *B*

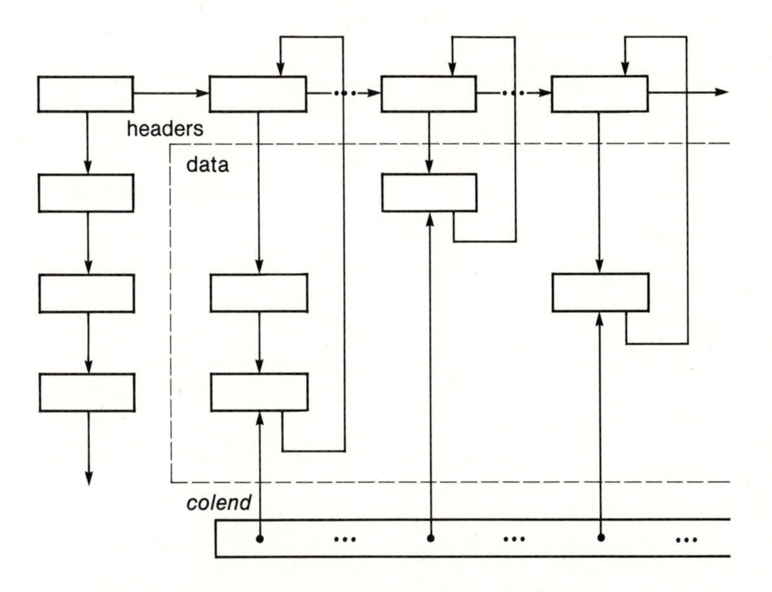

(b) Use of *colend* for Fast Access to Columns of *C*

Figure 4.31 Structures for Algorithm SPARSE_MULT_A

inefficiency of random insertion into two linked lists. The resolution for this is as follows:

1. Maintain an array of pointers *brow* to the beginning of each row in *B*, as illustrated in Figure 4.31(a). We can then index this array with the column index *k* of *A*, in order to begin processing the row of *B* that corresponds to *A* [*i*,*k*]. Note that *brow* must have an entry for the entire subrange 1 .. *n*.

```
procedure SPARSE_MULT_A (a,b: ptr; var c: ptr);

const  max = {maximum s ze of auxiliary arrays}

var    p,q,u,v,x,y: ptr;
       s: real;
       brow,colend,rowend: array [1 .. max] of ptr;

begin
  SPARSE_SETUP_A (a,b,c);
{Phase I: Generate the columns of matrix C}
  u := a↑.rowptr;                          {set to first row in A}
  while u <> a do begin
    x := u↑.colptr;                        {begin ith row in A: a [i,1]}
    while x <> u do begin
      v := brow [x↑.col];                  {find kth row in B}
      if v <> nil then begin
        y := v↑.colptr;                    {begin kth row in B: b [k,1]}
        while y <> v do begin
          s := x↑.coeff * y↑.coeff;
          p := colend [y↑.col];            {find end of jth col in C}
          if p↑.row = u↑.row then
            p↑.coeff := p↑.coeff + s
          else begin
            new (q);
            SET_NODE (q,u↑.row,p↑.col,s,p↑.rowptr,q);
            p↑.rowptr := q;
            colend [y↑.col] := q;
          end;
          y := y↑.colptr;                  {step along kth row in B: b [k,j]}
        end;
      end;
      x := x↑.colptr;                      {step along ith row in A: a [i,k]}
    end;
    u := u↑.rowptr;                        {go to next row in A}
  end;
{Phase II: Scan the columns of matrix C and link the rows}
  p := c↑.colptr;                          {set to first col in C}
  while p <> c do begin
    x := p; q := p↑.rowptr;                {begin jth col in C: c [1,j]}
    while q <> p do begin
      if q↑.coeff = 0 then begin
        q := q↑.rowptr;
        dispose (x↑.rowptr);
        x↑.rowptr := q;
      end else begin
        y := rowend [q↑.row];              {find end of ith row in C}
        q↑.colptr := y↑.colptr;
        y↑.colptr := q;
        rowend [y↑.row] := q;
        x := q; q := q↑.rowptr;
      end;
    end;
    p := p↑.colptr;                        {go to next col in C}
  end;
  SPARSE_TRIM (c);
end;
```

Algorithm 4.5 SPARSE_MULT_A

2. Do not attempt to maintain both row and column links for C throughout the multiplication. Rather, (a) develop C as a set of nodes linked along their columns only, and then (b) scan these column-lists and insert the row links after the multiplications are finished.
3. For use during 2(a) above, maintain an array of pointers *colend* to the last element in each column of C, as illustrated in Figure 4.31(b). We can then index this array with the column index j of B, and directly find where to apply the next product term in C. Note that *colend* need have just one entry for each column in B (and C).
4. For use during 2(b) above, maintain an array of pointers *rowend* to the last element in each row of C. We can then index this array with the row index j of C, and directly find where to row-link the next term in C. Note that *rowend* need have just one entry for each row in A (and C).

When we put these elements together, we obtain the procedure SPARSE_MULT_A (Algorithm 4.5). It employs the same auxiliary procedures SET_NODE and SPARSE_TRIM as before. However, it employs SPARSE_SETUP_A, in order to include the initialization of the arrays *brow*, *colend*, and *rowend*.

If we contemplate the multiplication of matrices that are sparse and very large, the effect of the difference between $\rho_A + \rho_B$ and $\rho_A \times \rho_B$ can be substantial. To confirm this effect, we tested the two algorithms rather carefully. To begin with, in dealing with matrices where the product of density and size is small, so that the number of non-zero terms is small in an absolute sense, then the savings in the number of comparisons is lost in the overheads of setup, loop initializations, and trimming. But if the matrix sizes are truly large, or (paradoxically) if the densities are not too small, then the time ratios are indeed commensurate with the comparison ratios. All in all, SPARSE_MULT_A is a nice illustration of the effectiveness of choosing the right combination of algorithm and data structures.

4.4 LIST STRUCTURES

We will now consider list structures that are more powerful than any of those that we have discussed so far. Whereas the lists of Section 4.3 achieved generality by the use of multiple links, the lists in this section achieve generality through the use of recursion. The term most commonly applied to this type of list is list structure, although other terms, notably List, have been applied as well. Since "list structure" is more useful when speaking and "List" is more useful when writing, we will think of them as *List structures*, but commonly revert to the use of List throughout the remainder of this text.

Definition: A List is a finite sequence (possibly empty) of elements, each of which is either atomic or a List.

The nature of an *atom* is not well specified, other than that it is not itself a List.

Several specialized programming languages have been developed for List processing, which is a generic term for performing computations with List structures.

We will examine these somewhat in Section 4.4.4, but the bulk of our discussion of Lists reflects the following perspectives:

- The typical application user's point of view of Lists and List processing is via some special HLL.
- Nonetheless, our discussion will begin with some details about List structure implementation, which is presumably carried out in assembly language. These details provide interesting examples of representation choices; they also provide insight for the List processing algorithms that we will study subsequently.
- In order not to burden many readers with an extra, unfamiliar language, these List processing algorithms are presented in Pascal. For those readers who are already familiar with a List processing language, the correspondence should be straightforward.

4.4.1 Representation Issues

The basic way of representing a List is illustrated pictorially in Figure 4.32(a). The elements of the outer List are *r*,*s*,*t*; *r* is itself the List consisting of *u* and *v*; *t* is the List consisting of *w*; *w* is the List consisting of *x*; and *s*,*u*,*v*,*x* are atomic. Another conventional manner of representing the same List is with parentheses, as ((A,B),C,((D))).

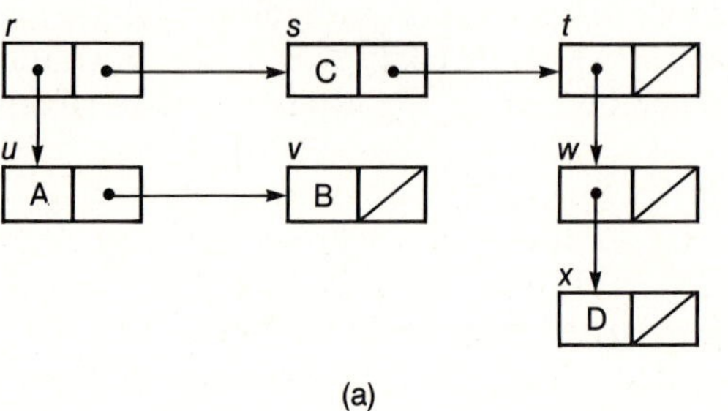

(a)

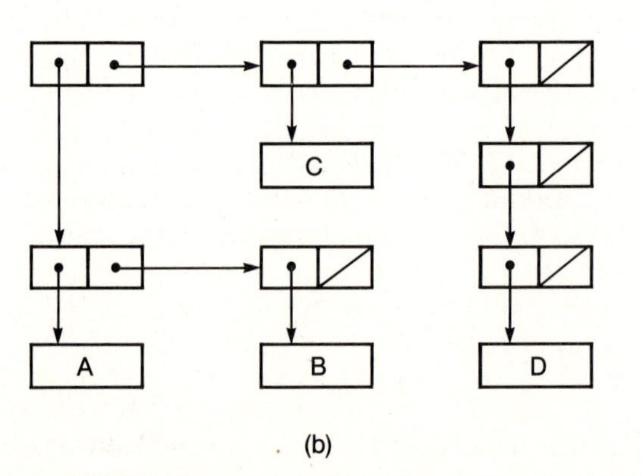

(b)

Figure 4.32 Two Pictorial Conventions for List Structures

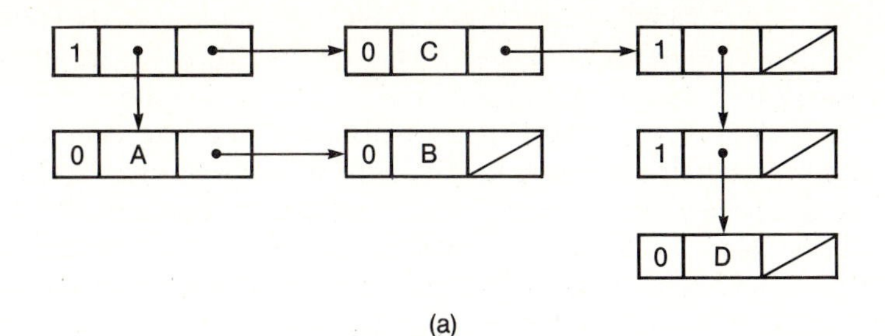

(a)

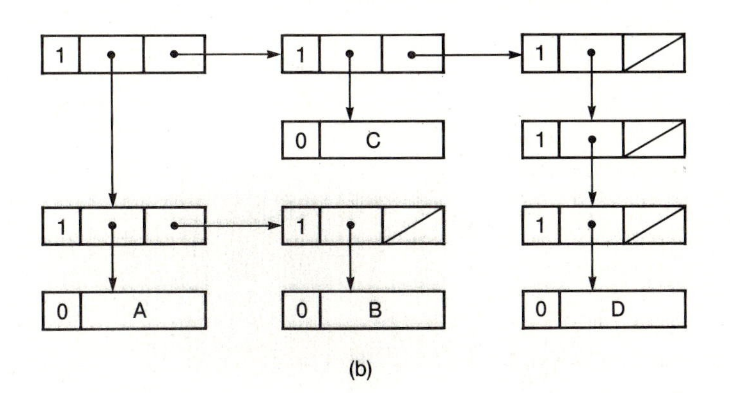

(b)

Figure 4.33 Implementing the Conventions of Figure 4.32

An alternate pictorial scheme for this same List is shown in Figure 4.32(b). The distinction between (a) and (b) reflects some important points to remember when representing List structures. List elements are almost always mapped into cells of a fixed size large enough to hold two pointer values. The right field always represents a List, denoted by NIL if it is empty or by a pointer otherwise. The left field may represent either another List, denoted by a pointer, or else an atomic value. Since many atomic values require no more space than does a pointer value, it is common to store them directly in the (available) left field. However, to complete that choice of representation, a tag field must then be added to each List node so that the nature of the left field can be discerned; this yields a structure like that shown in Figure 4.33(a).

In other cases, necessarily so if the atomic value will not fit, the left field has a pointer to the atom, and the use of tags for discrimination might result in the structure of Figure 4.33(b). There are still other possible representations; the actual choice depends upon machine architecture and other factors. Of course, an implementation of Lists would very likely incorporate header nodes, for the same reasons cited in Section 4.1 about simple lists: to facilitate selecting the first item of a List, to ease the problems that arise when a List changes and there are multiple pointers to it, etc. For our investigations, however, we find it sufficient and simplest to employ the representation of Figure 4.33(b). We will draw upon these important considerations for representing Lists as necessary, but suppress them where possible.

In any List there are two fundamental operations: to select the *head* of the List (referenced by the left pointer) and to select the *tail* of the List (referenced by the right pointer). As an example, the head of the List (A,(B),C) is the atom A and its tail is the List ((B),C); for the List ((D,E),F,(G)), the head is the List (D,E) and the tail is the List (F,(G)). For reasons that are historical and now irrelevant, the head and tail selector functions are commonly termed, respectively, CAR and CDR. From the point of view of a user of a List processing language, CAR and CDR extract sub-Lists from any List that is non-atomic; note that CAR may return an atom and CDR may return NIL. Of course, from the implementation point of view, as well as from the point of view to be discussed in Section 4.4.3, we are dealing not with Lists but with pointers to these Lists.

Note that the issue of representation has soiled the purity of the List concept. In the definition of Lists and in high-level operations on them, we speak of the empty List, NIL. In the machine, however, we cannot represent the nothingness of the empty list except by using the explicit pointer value **nil**. We can think of NIL in the List processing environment as being a special atom that denotes the empty List; however, this loses some of the simple elegance of the definition.

4.4.2 Reentrant and Recursive List Structures

The List structure in Figures 4.32 and 4.33 is, more precisely, a *pure List*. There are other possibilities, as illustrated in Figure 4.34. The List in (a) is termed a *reentrant List*, or *shared List*, because the element x is referred to more than once. The List in (b) is termed a *recursive List*, or *cyclic List*, because element y refers to itself directly, and element z refers to itself indirectly. Note that there is an important distinction between the use of the term recursive as applied to a List and to an algorithm. The latter usage necessarily implies a criterion for termination, whereas the former usage does not.

One consequence of having these less restricted Lists is that they cannot be simply represented with parentheses as in the case of pure Lists. The usual way of coping with this situation is to label the Lists and then refer to the labels. Using lower case letters as labels, we could write for the List of Figure 4.34(a)

u: (v,C,v) $\qquad$ v: (A,B)

and for the List of Figure 4.34(b) we could write

r: (s,B,(t)) $\qquad$ s: (s,A) $\qquad$ t: ((C,t))

Much more serious than the issue of representing these more general Lists by a string of symbols, however, are the complexities involved in computing with such structures. We will see how this is so in the next section.

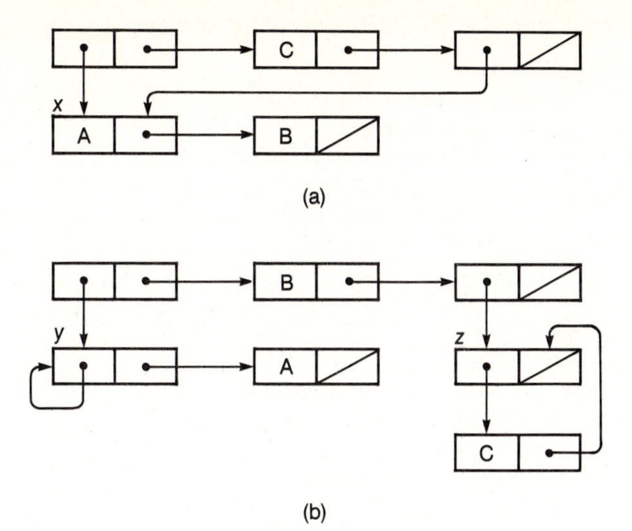

Figure 4.34 Reentrant and Recursive List Structures

†4.4.3 Operations with List Structures

It is difficult to convey the full flavor of List processing without going into details that are beyond the scope of this book. However, there are some very pretty and important ideas that can be expressed within the framework of two examples. The first of these has to do with the most basic operation that one can conceive of for a List: to traverse it, visiting each node without getting caught in an infinite excursion. This capability serves as a crucial first step in the process of reclaiming List cells, to be discussed in Section 11.2.[4] After the example of traversing a List, we will take a different tack and illustrate the use of a more special sort of List structure, appropriate for the problem of adding multivariate polynomials.

†4.4.3.1 Traversing a List Structure. The basic problem in traversing a List is that it may be reentrant and cause us to visit some nodes more than once, or even recursive and cause us to visit some nodes an infinite number of times, unless we employ some strategy to block repeated visits. The strategy used for this purpose is to *mark* nodes as they are visited, and then to follow links only to unmarked nodes. Suppose that our objective is to count how many nodes there are in a List. For this purpose, we will employ the recursive function COUNT_LIST (Algorithm 4.6), and use the marking technique just described. In this procedure, the type definition for a cell corresponds to Figure 4.33(b), augmented with a mark bit. To illustrate the

---

[4] As a matter of fact, the techniques that are discussed in Chapter 11 provide a wealth of instructive examples of List processing. But they belong there and not here.

```
function COUNT_LIST (list: link): integer;

type    link = ↑cell;
        cell = record
           mark: boolean;
           case isatom: boolean of
              true: (data: {atom});
              false: (head,tail: link);
           end;

var     cnt: integer;

begin
   cnt := 0;
   if not list↑.mark then begin
      list↑.mark := true;
      cnt := 1;
      if not list↑.isatom then begin
         cnt := cnt + COUNT_LIST (list↑.head);
         if list↑.tail <> nil then
            cnt := cnt + COUNT_LIST (list↑.tail);
      end;
   end;
   COUNT_LIST := cnt;
end;
```

Algorithm 4.6 COUNT_LIST

action of COUNT_LIST, consider the List of Figure 4.35, wherein pointer values are represented symbolically rather than with arrows, and the *mark* and *isatom* fields are not shown. Then the recursive sequence of visiting the cells is illustrated in Figure 4.36. In this figure, the vertical axis indicates chronological sequence and the horizontal axis indicates the depth of the recursive calls. Each entry in the figure consists of the label of a visited cell, along with the count of all the cells seen from it. Thus, cell *c* is the fourth cell to be visited. From it, we do not see cell *c* (since it is already marked), but we do see cell *f*, which in turn sees cell *h*; that line of inspection ends at cell *h*, since cell *b* has already been visited. So the count for cell *c* is 1 (for itself) plus 0 (looking along its head pointer) plus 2 (looking along its tail pointer), for a total of 3.

We have earlier, in Section 1.3.1, seen some evidence that recursive algorithms are likely to lose some efficiency in exchange for elegance of expression. Since the capability to visit the nodes of a List is so basic, several faster, non-recursive algorithms have been developed for this purpose. In Section 6.4.1, in our treatment of trees, we will see one such approach. However, since Lists are more general than trees, and in order to illustrate several other points, we will base our discussion upon a well-known algorithm by Schorr and Waite [1967]. In this example, we omit the counting and concentrate upon the marking, since it is the more essential issue. This algorithm uses the technique known as *link inversion*, whereby pointer

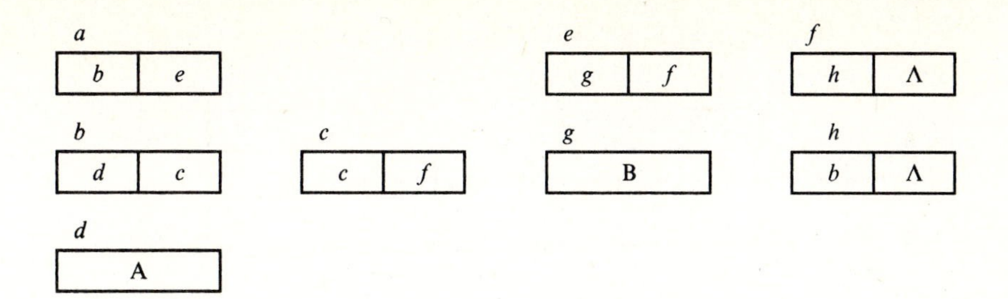

Figure 4.35 An Example List

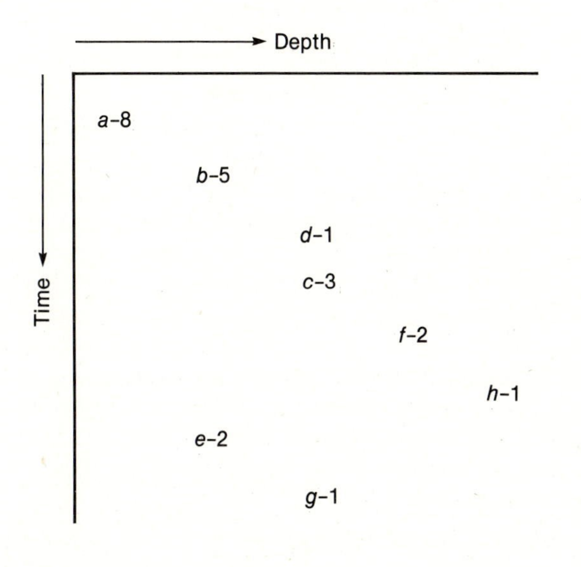

Figure 4.36 Trace of Algorithm COUNT_LIST

values are swapped back and forth between List cells in a systematic manner. To illustrate this, Figure 4.37 shows a portion of a List at one instant in time, and then again after a link inversion has been performed. In (a), the work cells *P* and *Q* point to cell *x* and its left successor *y*, respectively. Via the sequence of operations

```
t := Q↑.head; Q↑.head := P;
P := Q; Q := t {old value of Q↑.head}
```

we have in (b) that *P* and *Q* point, respectively, to *y* and its left successor *z*. The fact that *x* is the predecessor of *y* has been retained by inverting the left pointer in *y* to point at *x*. The restoration of (b) to (a) can be obtained via the complementary sequence of operations

```
t := P↑.head; P↑.head := Q;
Q := P; P := t {old value of P↑.head}
```

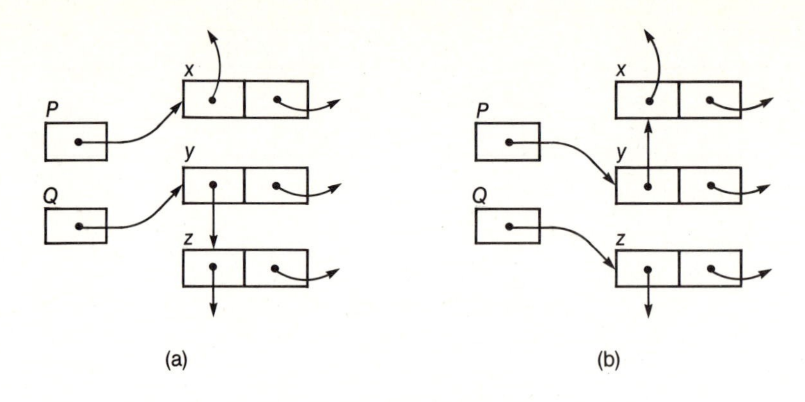

Figure 4.37 Link Inversion

When we begin to implement a traversal marking procedure based on link inversions, we discover a complication. Namely, upon ascending to a predecessor node, we need to know if we are ascending from the head (left or CAR) direction or from the tail (right or CDR) direction. In the former case, we should investigate the other pointer field in the cell; in the latter case, we should ascend further. Accordingly, in some implementations of the Schorr-Waite algorithm, every List cell needs a *tag bit* in order to make this discrimination, as well as a mark bit. For example, a tag bit is necessary if the List cells are represented as in Figure 4.33(a). However, if the List cells are represented as in Figure 4.33(b), we can avoid this – instead inverting the tag information in the bit field that is used to distinguish atoms from List cells, in analogy to the inversion of the pointers in the other two fields! We will see how this works shortly when we look at the algorithm.

Before we consider the algorithm, however, let us reflect upon what we are doing. By altering pointer values, we are radically, although systematically, distorting the topology of the List structure. Throughout the execution of this algorithm, the structure will be ill formed from the point of view of any other process that might inspect it. To compound the problem, the pointer values are reassigned one at a time, so that a totally inconsistent state will obtain during the middle of an inversion. The concept of a *pointer rotation*, which treats a set of pointer value exchanges as an indivisible action, is very useful in situations such as this [Suzuki 1982]. Chiefly, it allows algorithms to be expressed more concisely, and it reduces the likelihood of inadvertently coding an inconsistent set of individual pointer assignments.

Rotations can be specified among two values (that is, a swap), three values, or more. For the present case, we need consider just rotations among three pointer values. Even acquiring a node from the head of Free-list and inserting it at the head of another list, as in Section 4.1.3, has the effect of such a pointer rotation. This is illustrated in Figure 4.38, where (a) illustrates the pointer values before such a sequence, and (b) illustrates the pointer values after such a sequence. Deleting a node from the head of a list and returning it to the head of a Free-list would yield exactly the opposite rotation. As another example, the link inversions from (a) to

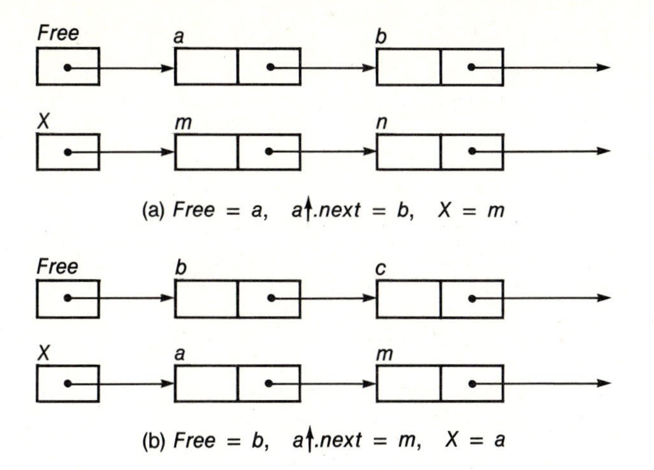

Figure 4.38 Pointer Rotations Illustrated with Free-List

(b) and back from (b) to (a) in Figure 4.37 can be expressed as the complementary rotations

ROTATE (Q↑.head,P,Q), and ROTATE (P↑.head,Q,P)

We are now ready to consider the Schorr-Waite algorithm, MARK_LIST (Algorithm 4.7). It takes a single parameter, which is a pointer to the origin of the list. For each value of the variable *pres*, it marks the node *pres*↑ (if not already marked), and then explores the cells accessible through *pres*↑*.head* (down left) and, subsequently, those accessible through *pres*↑*.tail* (down right). The algorithm retains the information for backing up to parents of cells by link inversions; these link inversions are performed by calls upon the procedure ROTATE_3. The logic for detecting if the search should be extended further in the head (tail) direction is expressed in the function GO_HEAD (GO_TAIL). Note that these functions reflect the logical nature of LISP-like cells as represented in Figure 4.33(b). A different set of conventions about List cells would probably require a different implementation for GO_HEAD and GO_TAIL; however, the logic for MARK_LIST might be identical, or almost so.

Note the manner in which the tag information is retained in the field *isatom*; that field contains the value True for atoms and False otherwise. Whenever the algorithm descends to the right, it first sets *isatom* to True in the List cell. Ascents from the left will find that value to be False, informing the algorithm to investigate the tail pointer; ascents from the right will find that value to be True, informing the algorithm to reset the value to False (it can't really be an atom, since it has descendants) and then to continue ascending.

The operation of MARK_LIST can best be understood by following its operation upon a List such as that of Figure 4.35. In order to represent the trace of MARK_LIST, the List representation is altered to the form of Figure 4.39(a), displaying the values of *mark*, *isatom*, *head*, and *tail* for each cell. Figure

```
procedure MARK_LIST (list: link);

type    link = ↑cell;
        cell = record
           mark: boolean;
           case isatom: boolean of
              true: (data: char);
              false: (head,tail: link);
        end;

var     pres,prev: link;

function GO_HEAD (ptr: link): boolean;
begin
   if ptr↑.isatom then GO_HEAD := false
   else GO_HEAD := not ptr↑.head↑.mark;
end;

function GO_TAIL (ptr: link): boolean;
begin
   if ptr↑.isatom then GO_TAIL := false
   else if ptr↑.tail = nil then GO_TAIL := false
   else GO_TAIL := not ptr↑.tail↑.mark;
end;

procedure ROTATE_3 (var p,q,r: link);
var     t: link;
begin
   t := p;  p := q;  q := r;  r := t;
end;

begin
   prev := nil;  pres := list;
   repeat
      if not pres↑.mark then
         pres↑.mark := true;
      if GO_HEAD (pres) then                          {down left}
         ROTATE_3 (prev,pres,pres↑.head)
      else if GO_TAIL (pres) then begin               {down right}
         pres↑.isatom := true;
         ROTATE_3 (prev,pres,pres↑.tail);
      end else if prev↑.isatom then begin             {up right}
         ROTATE_3 (pres,prev,prev↑.tail);
         pres↑.isatom := false;
      end else if GO_TAIL (prev) then begin           {switch}
         prev↑.isatom := true;
         ROTATE_3 (prev↑.head,pres,prev↑.tail);
      end else                                        {up left}
         ROTATE_3 (pres,prev,prev↑.head);
   until prev = nil;
end;
```

Algorithm 4.7 MARK_LIST

	a: F F b e		e: F F g f	f: F F h #
(a)	b: F F d c	c: F F c f	g: F T B	h: F F b #
	d: F T A	prev: #	pres: a	
	a: T F # e		e: F F g f	f: F F h #
(b)	b: F F d c	c: F F c f	g: F T B	h: F F b #
	d: F T A	prev: a	pres: b	
	a: T F # e		e: F F g f	f: F F h #
(c)	b: T F a c	c: F F c f	g: F T B	h: F F b #
	d: F T A	prev: b	pres: d	
	a: T F # e		e: F F g f	f: F F h #
(d)	b: T T d a	c: F F c f	g: F T B	h: F F b #
	d: T T A	prev: b	pres: c	
	a: T F # e		e: F F g f	f: F F h #
(e)	b: T T d a	c: T T c b	g: F T B	h: F F b #
	d: T T A	prev: c	pres: f	
	a: T F # e		e: F F g f	f: T F c #
(f)	b: T T d a	c: T T c b	g: F T B	h: F F b #
	d: T T A	prev: f	pres: h	
	a: T F # e		e: F F g f	f: T F h #
(g)	b: T T d a	c: T T c b	g: F T B	h: T F b #
	d: T T A	prev: c	pres: f	
	a: T F # e		e: F F g f	f: T F h #
(h)	b: T T d a	c: T F c f	g: F T B	h: T F b #
	d: T T A	prev: b	pres: c	
	a: T F # e		e: F F g f	f: T F h #
(i)	b: T F d c	c: T F c f	g: F T B	h: T F b #
	d: T T A	prev: a	pres: b	
	a: T T b #		e: F F g f	f: T F h #
(j)	b: T F d c	c: T F c f	g: F T B	h: T F b #
	d: T T A	prev: a	pres: e	
	a: T T b #		e: T F a f	f: T F h #
(k)	b: T F d c	c: T F c f	g: F T B	h: T F b #
	d: T T A	prev: e	pres: g	
	a: T T b #		e: T F g f	f: T F h #
(l)	b: T F d c	c: T F c f	g: T T B	h: T F b #
	d: T T A	prev: a	pres: e	
	a: T F b e		e: T F g f	f: T F h #
(m)	b: T F d c	c: T F c f	g: T T B	h: T F b #
	d: T T A	prev: #	pres: a	

Figure 4.39 Trace of Algorithm MARK_LIST

4.39(b) – (m) displays these values as the algorithm executes; in each of these displays, the values that have just changed are circled for emphasis.

Techniques for marking Lists have a great deal of relevance, as we will see in Section 11.2.1.1. In general, for marking unrestricted Lists, we can expect to need either more than linear time, or more than bounded workspace. In MARK_LIST, we got around the need for $O(n)$ separate tag bits by taking advantage of a particular representation for Lists. An interesting question remains: Is it possible to mark unrestricted Lists in linear time and with bounded workspace, if we disregard the possibility of such tricks of implementation?

†4.4.3.2 Multivariate Polynomial Addition. In Section 4.2.2 we illustrated the use of sequential lists for polynomial addition. Although the discussion and the algorithm POLYADD were centered on polynomials in one variable, we cited how the method using sequential lists could be extended to polynomials in several variables. Figure 4.17 depicted how the polynomial $R(x,y,z)$ of Eq. 4.5 might be represented in this fashion.

The method described in that section has the drawback that space for exponents must be allocated in each node for every variable that may be present, even though many terms may have zero exponents in most of the variables. An elegant alternate approach comes from noting that $R(x,y,z)$ may be regarded as a polynomial $U(x)$, wherein the coefficients of U are polynomials $V_i(y)$, and the coefficients in each V_i are in turn polynomials $W_{i,j}(z)$. This may be seen by factoring R as

$$\begin{aligned} R(x,y,z) &= \mathrm{A}x^3y + \mathrm{B}x^3z + \mathrm{C}xy^2z^3 + \mathrm{D}y^2z^3 + \mathrm{E}y^2 + \mathrm{F}y + \mathrm{G}z^2 \\ &= (\mathrm{A}y + (\mathrm{B}z))x^3 + ((\mathrm{C}z^3)y^2)x + ((\mathrm{D}z^3 + \mathrm{E})y^2 + \mathrm{F}y + (\mathrm{G}z^2)) \end{aligned} \tag{4.8}$$

From this insight, we see that we can use a List structure of polynomials with generalized terms, such that the coefficients of any of these terms can themselves be List structures of the same form. A suitable template for this is shown in Figure 4.40, where a tag value of 0/1 would indicate a constant/polynomial coefficient. The resulting form of $R(x,y,z)$ is shown in Figure 4.41, with the tag fields suppressed since their values may easily be inferred.

Tag	Coefficient	Exponent	Link

Figure 4.40 Node Structure for Term of Multivariate Polynomial

This representation may be just as significant for saving time as it is for saving space. To demonstrate this, let us consider the general nature of an algorithm that would add two polynomials P and Q in this representation, replacing P with the sum. For every generalized term in P such that Q does not have a corresponding term (say for x^2), the algorithm can skip that term and its entire sub-List in P. By contrast, with the structure suggested in Section 4.2.2, it would be necessary to step through every individual term in P that had a factor of x^2, even though there were no such terms in Q. In multivariate polynomials, the possibility of skipping over sub-Lists in this fashion can be very common. An algorithm for adding multivariate polynomials represented with a comparable but different List structure can be found in [Knuth 1973a]. Not surprisingly, it is considerably more elaborate than POLYADD.

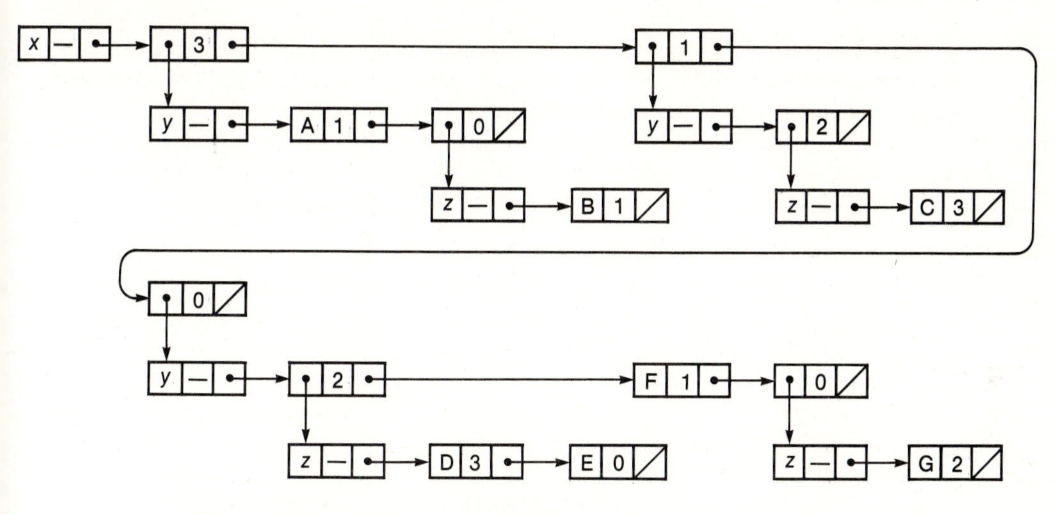

Figure 4.41 A Multivariate Polynomial as a List Structure

†4.4.4 List Processing Languages – LISP

The 1960's saw the invention of several languages whose sole or principal data structure was the List. These were devised to attack problems that are characterized by manipulation of symbols more than by numeric calculations. You have seen relatively simple examples of this for the case of polynomial algebra. The languages COMIT, IPL, and SLIP have largely disappeared as the language LISP [McCarthy 1960] has come to dominate List processing. To grossly oversimplify matters, COMIT was oriented more to sequential lists than List structures; IPL and SLIP burdened the user with responsibility for maintaining the free storage pool; SLIP was based on FORTRAN, with its attendant restrictions; and finally, none of the three has the expressive power of LISP [Bobrow and Raphael 1964].

The principal manner of expressing Lists in LISP is very similar to that employed in Section 4.4.1, except that List items are separated by blanks instead of commas, as in ((A) B (C D (E))). Although the empty List is usually denoted by NIL, it can also be denoted by ( ). We have already talked about CAR and CDR for taking Lists apart. There are also built-in functions for extracting particular parts of a List and for constructing a new List out of other Lists. There are even functions for replacing the CAR and CDR fields of a List cell in order to obtain reentrant or recursive Lists. The unit of program, or user function, in LISP is also a List; in it, the first element denotes the function to be performed and all subsequent elements of the List are parameters for that function. Some simple examples of this are the LISP functions:

```
(PLUS X1 X2 ... XN)      {= ΣXi}
(SUB1 7)                 {= 7 − 1 = 6}
(DIFFERENCE X 3.2)       {= X − 3.2}
```

For general computation, we need the ability to test conditions and take alternate actions depending upon the results. For testing purposes, LISP uses *predicate* functions. These examine an argument and return the value T (for true) or NIL (for false). Some basic predicates are ATOM and NULL; they test for atomic Lists and empty Lists, respectively. Another is EQ, which tests for equality between two atoms. Predicates and actions are combined in LISP via the function

$$(\text{COND } (p_1\ e_1)\ (p_2\ e_2)\ \ldots)$$

where the p_i are predicates and the e_i are actions. COND examines each List $(p_i\ e_i)$ from left to right. As soon as it finds a p_i that is not NIL, it returns the value of the corresponding e_i. If no such p_i is found, it returns the value NIL.

```
(DEFINE (COUNT L)
        (COND ((NULL L) 0)
              ((ATOM L) 1)
              (T (PLUS (COUNT (CAR L))
                       (COUNT (CDR L))))))
```

Figure 4.42 A LISP Function for Counting Cells

In addition to using built-in functions like those we have described, a user can define his own functions via the LISP function DEFINE. An example of this is the function COUNT, for counting the number of non-NIL items in a List, as shown in Figure 4.42. It is instructive to compare the LISP version of this function with the Pascal version, COUNT_LIST (Algorithm 4.6). Except for the fact that the Pascal function deals with Lists that may be reentrant or recursive, the two are very similar. DEFINE always takes two lists as arguments. Here, the first of these lists, (COUNT L), declares a function COUNT with one parameter L; it serves the role that a procedure heading has in more conventional programming languages. The second list corresponds to the body of the function definition. Here, it specifies how COUNT is to be computed for the three cases: if L is empty, if L is an atom, or (otherwise) if L is a List. Since it can be difficult to keep track of parentheses in LISP, expressions are commonly printed in an indented format such as this in order to assist the eye.

In the preceding remarks, we have not intended to convey more than a glimpse of a novel and very powerful language. The point we wish to make is that the List structure provides a very powerful means for expressing an algorithmic process, and that LISP does this without requiring *any* other data structures. Even more remarkably, the semantics of LISP can be expressed with a function (called EVAL) that is itself written in LISP! This is in marked contrast to the situation with other HLL's, where it is necessary to employ either a meta-language or natural language in order to express the effect of executing a program in the HLL.

4.5 OVERVIEW

We have discussed lists and also Lists, both of which are logical structures. Perhaps more than with any other data structure in this book, we have wedded the logical structure to a particular physical representation, based on the pointer variable. The pointer is, in fact, the only tool that is usually available to us for building such dynamic data structures. We will elaborate upon this point in a moment, after first surveying the significant features of lists and Lists.

The simple sequential list allows for flexibility of sequencing. When it is implemented with a free storage pool, we can "grow" one dimensional structures of arbitrary size. Lists of this sort are well-suited to diverse applications such as maintaining a directory in proper sequence, performing symbolic polynomial arithmetic, etc. If we also allow for more than one pointer from a node to other nodes, then we can create data structures of arbitrary shape as well as size. There are two ways to obtain this generality. One way is to simply allow a node to contain as many pointers as required by the situation, as with inverted lists and multilists. Although lists like these work very well for some applications with a database flavor, a more powerful technique has been to define List cells with just two pointers, and then employ recursion. The significant difference is that the first approach requires the user to anticipate any structures that may be needed, whereas the second approach allows a program to compute its own data structure requirements.

Interestingly, on the one hand, List structures are the premier vehicle for dealing with a significant class of problems; on the other hand, they have given rise to a whole new category of problems to be solved. These new problems have to do with administering the pool of Free storage used by List cells. In fact, the subjects of Lists and the management of memory are so closely related that many authors treat them together; however, Memory Management is broader than just the administration of List cells, and so our treatment of it is deferred to Chapter 11.

4.5.1 The Hazards of Pointing

The pointer variable is dangerous because it is a "bare" address. With an address, we expect to retrieve or store data – whatever data! – at that location. If our program has an error, then we may easily try to retrieve nonsensical data from an incorrect memory location; even worse, we might easily overwrite and destroy good data via a wrong address. To make matters more complicated, the use of pointers implies that nodes will be deleted at times, and their space returned (for example, via **dispose**) for recycled usage. However, once a program has acquired an address value for a pointer variable, there is nothing to prevent it from using that value even though the space has been recycled. Just how easily this can happen is illustrated by the sequence

```
new(p); q := p; dispose(p);
```

Even if the procedure **dispose** sets p to **nil**, there is nothing to prevent the program from subsequently using the invalid value contained in q. A situation like this, in which a pointer variable has a value that is no longer valid, is termed a *dangling reference*. The hazards of using pointer variables as data are analogous to the hazards of using GOTO's in program sequencing [Berry et al. 1976].

Pointer variables are really a means to an end – a tool for synthesizing data structures of arbitrary size and connectivity. Thus, it has been suggested [Kieburtz 1976] that programming languages should provide either ADT's or recursive data structures for attaining these ends without recourse to explicit pointers. Unfortunately, such proposals can be criticized as having two principal defects:

1. They do not remove all the negative effects, particularly with respect to performance degradation, since some of these effects just get hidden under the covers; for example, implicit pointers can confound pipelining and caching mechanisms just as much as do explicit pointers.
2. They simply do not allow for the generality and the control over data that a user may need for some applications.

The remedy provided by Pascal – that all pointer variables must themselves be typed – imposes a significant amount of discipline. But the programmer needs to augment this with his own measure of disciplined use, of which pointer rotations are an excellent example.

4.6 REFERENCE TO TERMINOLOGY

4.7 EXERCISES

Section 4.1

4.1 Suppose that we have a multiply-linked structure according to the Pascal syntax on the left, and that there are several such items as shown linked together (symbolically) on the right. What is *e.ptry↑.ptrw↑.ptrz↑.ptrx↑.data*?

```
link = ↑item
item = record
   data: integer;
   ptrw: link;
   ptrx: link;
   ptry: link;
   ptrz: link;
end;
```

a:	13	*c*	*e*	*d*	Λ
b:	4	*c*	*f*	*g*	*b*
c:	24	*c*	*g*	*e*	*f*
d:	72	*b*	*h*	Λ	*e*
e:	11	*a*	*d*	*g*	*h*
f:	35	*d*	Λ	*a*	*b*
g:	19	*b*	*d*	*c*	*h*
h:	40	Λ	*g*	*c*	*d*

4.2 For the lists in Figure 4.5(a), write the statements required to insert node *h* *after* the node pointed by *s*.

4.3 Suppose that we wish to concatenate two sequential lists *A* and *B* to obtain a list *C* that consists of all of the nodes from *A* followed by all the nodes from *B*.

(a) Write an algorithm to perform this in the case that *A* and *B* are simple lists.

(b) Write an algorithm to perform this in the case that *A* and *B* are circular lists.

4.4 Suppose that we must return all the nodes on a sequential list to Free storage.

(a) Write an algorithm to perform the deallocation for the case of a simple list.

(b) Write an algorithm to perform the deallocation for the case of a circular list.

†4.5 Write a procedure that has as its parameter a pointer to the beginning of a simple, sequential list without a header node, and that reverses the order of the nodes in the list. Your algorithm should operate on the list in situ by reversing the directions of the pointers, as opposed to making a reversed copy. Verify that your algorithm works properly for degenerate cases, such as the list being empty or containing just a single node.

†4.6 Suppose that we have two non-empty circular lists *without* header nodes, and with *p*1 pointing to the last node in one list and *p*2 pointing to the last node in the other list.

(a) What is the effect of the following sequence?

```
t := p1↑.link; p1↑.link := p2↑.link; p2↑.link := t;
```

(b) What effect does the preceding sequence have if *p*1 and *p*2 point to two different nodes in the same list?

4.7 You and some friends are suddenly rounded up into a circle. You are told that, starting from the head of the circle, They will count to *m*, execute that *m*th person, close the circle, and repeat this process until just one person is left to escape. Given that there are *n* persons and that the rule is to execute every *m*th person, you need to decide which position to take in the circle if you are to remain alive. This is the famous *Josephus problem.* Write a Pascal program to solve it, using a circular list with pointer variables. Begin by initializing your list header with the number of persons n, and your list nodes with the identifiers 1,2,3, ... Then proceed to count around the circle. As your program executes (literally!), have it print out the identity of each person as he is eliminated. Write a simple function to generate a circular list of size n, and use it in conjunction with your program to solve the Josephus problem for $(m,n) = (7,11)$, and for several other pairs of your own choosing. Verify that it works properly for $m = 1$.

†4.8 Consider a linked list such that the physical sequence of its nodes in memory is given by the locations

52 34 117 43 95 123 88

Using the MOD operator as in Section 4.1.4, and assuming a value of $r = 128$, compute the composite forward-backward link values for each node and for the header of this list.

Section 4.2

4.9 Trace the operation of the algorithm SEARCH_LIST by starting with an empty list, and then presenting to it the eight input arguments: 4 4 2 5 3 1 1 3.

(a) For each argument, trace the distinct values assumed by the variables *state*, *loc*, q, r.

(b) Draw the list as it appears when SEARCH_LIST terminates.

†4.10 Just as the introduction of a sentinel node in SEARCH_B (Algorithm 2.2) caused that algorithm to be more efficient than SEARCH_A (Algorithm 2.1), so can a sentinel node be employed in SEARCH_LIST. Rewrite SEARCH_LIST to incorporate this change, and test it against the input of Exercise 4.9.

†4.11 Starting with the functionality in SEARCH_LIST, write a program that will compute a concordance, or cross-reference listing, for a set of alphabetic symbols. The input to your program would be a symbol and its numeric location within some text. The output of your program would be a listing of all the symbols, in alphabetic order, along with all the locations at which each symbol was used.

4.12 Draw pictures of the following polynomial as (a) a simple list, (b) a circular list, and (c) a bi-directional list – all with header nodes.

$$V = 4x^{10} - 7.1x^9 + 3.9x^5 + 13$$

4.13 Compute POLYADD(u,v) where

$$U = 2.4x^{10} + 3.1x^5 + 3.6x^3 - 1.7x$$

$$V = 3.7x^{20} - 2.4x^{10} + 1.8x^5 + 4.5x^2 + 1.7x + 8.3$$

Trace the values assumed by the variables *state* and $p, p1, p2, q$ as the algorithm executes. Also, draw the structure corresponding to U upon termination of the algorithm.

4.14 Write a function that takes as input a value of x and a polynomial $U(x)$ represented as in Figure 4.13, and that for output evaluates $U(x)$ at x.

†4.15 Write a procedure that differentiates a polynomial $U(x)$ represented as in Figure 4.13, and replaces $U(x)$ with $U'(x)$.

†4.16 Write a procedure to multiply two polynomials U and V as represented in Figure 4.13. Your algorithm may invoke POLYADD as a sub-procedure. The product of U and V should be placed in W, a new list. What is the computational complexity of your algorithm?

†4.17 Simulate the application of the algorithm EQUIV to the following sixteen relationships:

1. 5 = 8	5. 2 = 13	9. 19 = 15	13. 17 = 1
2. 7 = 10	6. 3 = 17	10. 2 = 9	14. 9 = 16
3. 16 = 18	7. 14 = 11	11. 14 = 5	15. 4 = 14
4. 12 = 6	8. 12 = 4	12. 7 = 19	16. 16 = 7

(a) Show the resulting lists after the first stage, as in Figure 4.18.

(b) List the contents of each equivalence class, in the order in which they are determined in the second stage.

†4.18 Section 4.2.3 describes a different approach to the equivalence problem that leads to an $O(n \lg n)$ algorithm. In this method, separate lists are maintained for equivalence classes. Upon encountering a statement of equivalence for two items such that both have already been assigned to classes, we first relabel all the items on the shorter list, and then concatenate the two lists. Write a program to compute equivalence classes by this method, and test it against the data of Exercise 4.17.

††4.19 Consider the problem of finding the largest item in a list and also the runner-up (the second largest). It is simple to perform $n-1$ comparisons to find the largest, and then another $n-2$ comparisons to find the second largest, for $2n-3$ comparisons altogether. However, it is possible to find both items with $n+\lg n-2$ comparisons, by the following observation. The runner-up item *must* have been involved in a comparison (and lost) with the largest item. If we think in terms of a tournament, where the number of players, or items to be compared, is halved at each stage, then

(a) the largest item need have been involved in only $\lg n$ comparisons;

(b) the runner-up must have been the loser in one of these comparisons;

(c) we need only search the list of losers to the largest item in order to find the runner-up.

Write an algorithm to accomplish what has just been described. Note that we need the flexible sequencing of lists, but not the dynamic size. Therefore, it is sufficient and also much simpler to use cursors rather than pointer variables. You will need lists for keeping track of two categories of items: the locations of the winners at each stage of the comparison tournament (they will participate in the next stage of the tournament), and the locations of the losers to each winner (the loser list for the final winner is the source for the runner-up). Test your program against the following list of items:

267 399 67 871 59 767 755 599 619 879 163 71

Section 4.3

4.20 Construct an inverted file for the following records.

name	sex	politics	religion
Abigail	female	Democrat	Jewish
Andrea	female	Democrat	Moslem
Elizabeth	female	Republican	Christian
Foster	male	independent	Jewish
Harry	male	independent	other
Jennifer	female	Democrat	Moslem
Kendrick	male	Republican	Jewish
Malachy	male	Democrat	Christian
Mary	female	Republican	Christian
Pamela	female	independent	other

4.21 Construct a multilist for the records of Exercise 4.20, using the format employed in the ultimate version in Section 4.3.2.

4.22 Compare bi-directional lists, inverted lists, and multilists.

†4.23 Compare inverted files and multilists for ease of performing the standard operations: looking up, inserting, deleting, and updating a value. Find some parameters for characterizing the problem, and then perform your analysis in terms of these parameters.

†4.24 Write the utility routines required to perform sparse matrix multiplication with Algorithms 4.4 and/or 4.5. Input one or both of those algorithms along with your routines, and test the package by multiplying some sparse matrices. You should construct test matrices having about a dozen non-zero elements apiece, and with row and column indices such that the product matrix has a comparable number of non-zero elements. Your program should read two sparse matrices in triples format, translate them to linked list format, multiply them, squeeze out non-zero rows and columns, and then print the product matrix in triples format.

††4.25 Build on Exercise 4.24 by writing a procedure that constructs a random sparse matrix with the parameters:

m – range of the row index of the matrix
n – range of the column index of the matrix
ρ – the density of the matrix

via the use of a random number generator. Then generate a series of pairs of input sparse matrices for various combinations of m,n,ρ and multiply them by both Algorithms 4.4 and 4.5. Obtain timings for the two multiplication methods, and distill your experimental results in a table. Also, have your program measure the observed density ρ for each product matrix. How do these observed densities compare with the theoretical values of Exercise 2.23?

Section 4.4

4.26 Draw the List represented by (((A),((B),C,(D)),E),(F,(G)),(H,I)) in the style of Figure 4.32(a).

†4.27 Write a non-recursive procedure to perform the transformation as in Exercise 4.26 – that is, to read a List specification in parenthesis notation and produce the corresponding List structure – but in the representation of Figure 4.33(b). Test your program by running it against the List of Exercise 4.26.

†4.28 Write a procedure that takes a pure List, represented as in Figure 4.33(b), and reverses the order of the cells at each level; for example, it converts ((A,B),C,((D))) to (((D)),C,(B,A)). Your algorithm should operate on the List in situ, as opposed to making a reversed copy.

†4.29 Trace the operation of the algorithm MARK_LIST on the following List, in the manner employed in Figure 4.39.

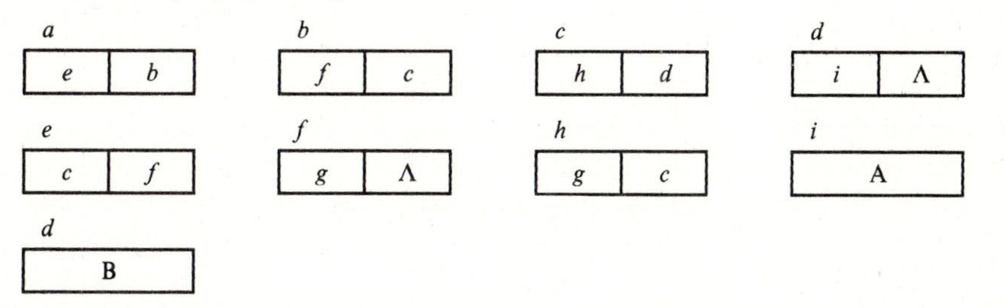

††4.30 Write a recursive function that examines a List and provides one or more messages indicating whether that List is pure, reentrant, or recursive. The messages should specify where reentrancy and/or recursiveness occurs. (*Hint*: What other information might be needed, and how might it best be represented?) Test your program against the Lists of Figures 4.32(b), 4.34(a) (in the alternate format for nodes), and 4.35.

†4.31 Represent the following polynomial in a List structure, employing the scheme illustrated by Figures 4.40 and 4.41.

$$R(x,y,z) = \mathrm{A}x^4y^2 + \mathrm{B}x^4yz + \mathrm{C}x^2yz^3 + \mathrm{D}x^2y^2 + \mathrm{E}y^2z + \mathrm{F}y^3z + \mathrm{G}y^3$$

5

QUEUES and STACKS

"And, behold, there are last which will be first,
and there are first which will be last."

Luke 13: 30

In our discussions of array, record, and list structures, we have seen the need for a more general data structure in order to overcome various limitations. Lists actually have such generality, but they are more complicated to use and also more costly, both in time and space. Queues and stacks represent compromise solutions. They allow for more flexibility than is possible with arrays; yet their implementations can be relatively simple, and they can have performance characteristics as good as those of arrays. This happy situation is obtained by restricting the notion of a linked list so that we can reference only those data nodes at one or both of its two ends, but not in the middle. Thus, queues and stacks are sometimes called restricted access data structures.

In a sense, we cheated in Chapter 4. Several of the list manipulations there already corresponded to queue and stack manipulations, but we did not disclose the fact! By way of compensation, you should find the early material in this chapter that much easier to understand. We begin with a discussion of queues and then a discussion of stacks – presenting their logical properties, physical representations, and examples of usage. The latter part of the chapter is devoted principally to the use of stacks for recursive algorithms, in a sense continuing the discussion of this topic in Section 1.3.

5.1 QUEUES

The queue is a familiar if not popular structure in everyday life. We spend much of our lives waiting in queues, comforted by the fact that they are "fair" – we are served in the order of our arrival. Every new arrival must go to the end of the queue and wait there until all who have arrived before him have been served, at which time he is at the front of the queue and so is the next to be served. This concept is captured in the acronym *FIFO*, or "First In, First Out." We will first model the use of a queue in an abstract manner, in the style of an ADT; subsequently, we will demonstrate two alternate manners of realizing the model; finally, we will discuss some uses of queues for computation.

5.1.1 Logical Data Structure

Logically speaking, a queue is a structure with several associated actions, predicates, and conditions. By an *action* we mean an operation involving the queue and the objects (people, cars, programs, etc.) that enter and leave it; our primary examples of actions for a queue are:

create(x) – to bring into existence an empty queue x;

enqueue(x,r) – to add the object r to the rear of queue x;

dequeue(x,s) – to remove the object at the front of queue x and assign it to s.

However, one can arbitrarily define other actions for a queue, such as:

count(x,c) – to assign to c the number of objects in the queue x;

head(x,t) – to assign to t the value of the object at the front of queue x, without removing the object from the queue;

tail(x,t) – to assign to t the value of the object at the rear of queue x, without removing the object from the queue.

By a *predicate* we mean a functional test that can be applied to a queue to yield an answer of either True or False. Our principal example is:

empty(x) – to ascertain if queue x is empty or not.

Whereas a predicate is a boolean function that is executed under user control, a *condition* is a boolean flag that is set by the underlying implementation (hardware and/or software) in response to an exceptional situation. Our primary examples of conditions are:

overflow(x) – to recognize when an attempt to enqueue an object on queue x has failed because of insufficient space for the enlarged queue;

underflow(x) – to recognize when an attempt to dequeue an object from queue x has failed because the queue is empty.

There are several points that should be made about the preceding definitions. The number of operations required of queues is fairly small. It is particularly easy, in this case, to characterize the logical structure of queues in an abstract fashion that says nothing about how they will be implemented. Although the preceding definitions lack some important elements that are needed for ADT's, they do convey much of the flavor. Note also the conventional use of the terms *head* and *tail* to refer to the front and rear of a queue, respectively. Finally, be careful not to confuse the semantics of these terms for queues with their semantics for Lists. The term head has analogous meanings for the two structures, whereas the meanings of the term tail in these cases are very different.

Figure 5.1 illustrates the use of this structure. On the left side of the figure are a series of queue operations applied to an initially empty queue x; for simplicity, the objects in the queue are designated by single character identifiers. On the right

Operation	Contents of Queue
enqueue (*x*,*A*)	*A*
enqueue (*x*,*B*)	*A B*
dequeue (*x*,*s*)	*B*
enqueue (*x*,*C*)	*B C*
enqueue (*x*,*D*)	*B C D*
enqueue (*x*,*E*)	*B C D E*
dequeue (*x*,*s*)	*C D E*
dequeue (*x*,*s*)	*D E*
enqueue (*x*,*F*)	*D E F*
dequeue (*x*,*s*)	*E F*
dequeue (*x*,*s*)	*F*

Figure 5.1 Example of Operations with a Queue

side of the figure are the states of the queue after each operation, with the head at the left and the tail at the right.

5.1.2 Physical Representation

It is fairly obvious that we can implement a queue as a linked list, with the enqueue and dequeue operations being applied to opposite ends, and so this method is shown first. It provides a pretty illustration of the use of a circular linked list. After that we describe a second method that is less obvious; in compensation, it yields the advantages of simplicity and efficiency that were touted at the beginning of this chapter.

5.1.2.1 Using a Linked List. Our representation using a circular linked list demonstrates the necessary type definitions and also the procedures for initializing a queue (that is, setting it to the empty state), for enqueuing, for dequeuing, and for testing for emptiness. These elements are lumped as QUEUE_L (Algorithms 5.1). In this representation, the circular list has a header node, which allows us to easily recognize an empty queue as one in which the solitary header node points to itself. Also, we do not need separate working pointers for the current first and last nodes; following the technique of Section 4.1.2.2, a single pointer to the last node suffices. Several comments should be made about QUEUE_L:

- The representation is not complete; it does not, for instance, spell out in detail the treatment of an underflow in DEQUEUE_L.
- In practice, DEQUEUE_L might be implemented as a function that returns the dequeued value rather than as a procedure. However, this will work only if the objects on the queue are single-valued (such as scalars or pointers).
- Note that each call to ENQUEUE_L causes three pointer values to be changed, as indicated by the dashed lines in Figure 5.2(a).

```
program QUEUE_L;

{algorithms for maintaining queues as circular link-lists;
 items on the queue are of type qobj; the
 parameter fifo points to the last item in the queue}

type   qobj = ...
       qptr = ↑cell;
       cell = record
          item: qobj;
          succ: qptr;
       end;

procedure INITQ_L (var fifo: qptr);
begin
   new (fifo);
   fifo↑.succ := fifo;
end;

function EMPTYQ_L (fifo: qptr): boolean;
begin
   EMPTYQ_L := (fifo = fifo↑.succ);
end;

procedure ENQUEUE_L (var fifo: qptr; data: qobj);
var      p: qptr;
begin
   new (p);
   p↑.item := data;
   p↑.succ := fifo↑.succ;
   fifo↑.succ := p;
   fifo := p;
end;

procedure DEQUEUE_L (var fifo: qptr; var data: qobj);
var      p,q: qptr;
begin
   if fifo = fifo↑.succ then
      {Underflow}
   else begin
      p := fifo↑.succ;
      q := p↑.succ;
      data := q↑.item;
      p↑.succ := q↑.succ;
      if q = fifo then  {header is only cell left in queue}
         fifo := p;
      dispose (q);
   end;
end;

begin
   ...
end.
```

Algorithms 5.1 QUEUE_L – Implementing a Queue as a Linked-List

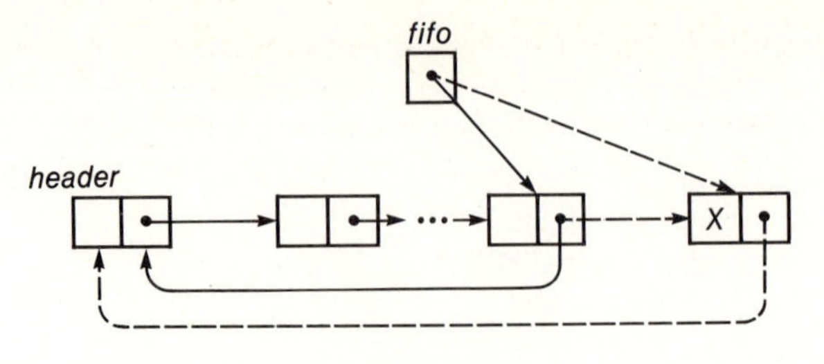

(a) Enqueuing X

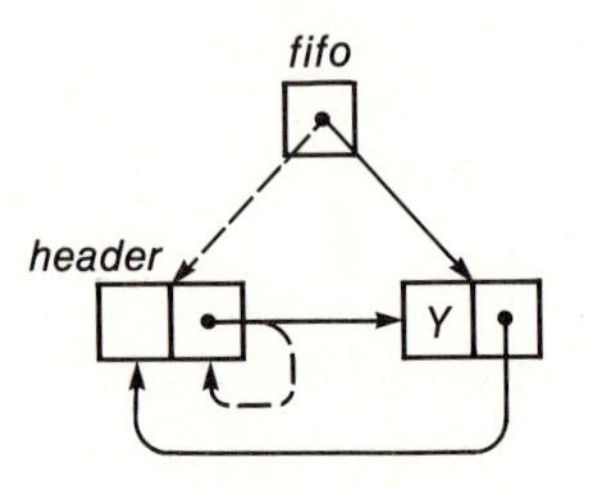

(b) Dequeuing Y

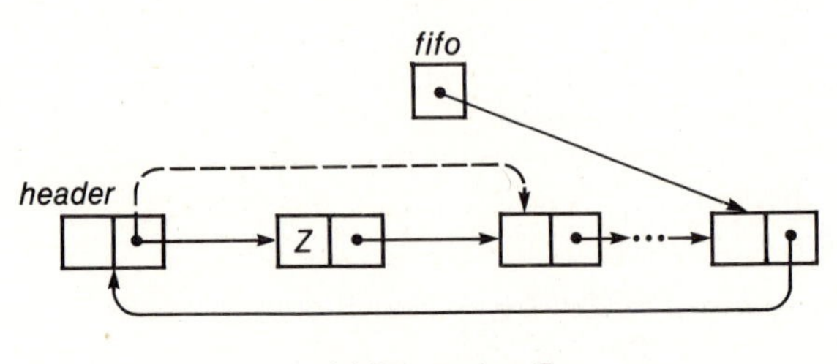

(c) Dequeuing Z

Figure 5.2 A Queue as a Linked List

- In the procedure DEQUEUE_L, it is necessary to make a distinction between the cases when the queue thereby becomes empty, and when it does not. In the former case, as shown in Figure 5.2(b), two pointer values must be changed; in the latter case, as shown by Figure 5.2(c), only one pointer value needs to be changed.

5.1.2.2 Using an Array as a Circular Queue. If we naively visualize a queue in a one-dimensional array, we see what has been described as a rubber snake, with its head and its tail both steadily progressing, though at different rates, from one end of the array to the other. Obviously, the definite, limited size of an array makes this representation infeasible. However, let us declare an array large enough to accommodate the maximum size of the queue at any one instant, and then imagine that this array is bent to form a circle. Letting the "rubber snake" chase its tail around the circle indefinitely, we have a viable representation termed a *circular queue*. This is illustrated in Figure 5.3, where the shaded/unshaded portions of the array indicate the occupied/empty portions of the queue at an instant in time. It is clear that we really need two distinct pointers, *head* and *tail*, in this scheme. In other words, our definition of a queue in this manner includes not just the array itself, but rather

```
type  qobj = ...
      queue = record
         head,tail: 0 .. qsize;
         item: array [1 .. qsize] of qobj;
      end;
```

The queue be may empty, of course, and there are several techniques for representing this in practice:

- adding another field to the definition, such as *state*: (*empty*, *occupied*);
- adding to the definition a count field that contains the number of elements in the queue;
- denoting emptiness by the condition, *head* = 0;
- denoting emptiness by the condition, *head* = *tail*.

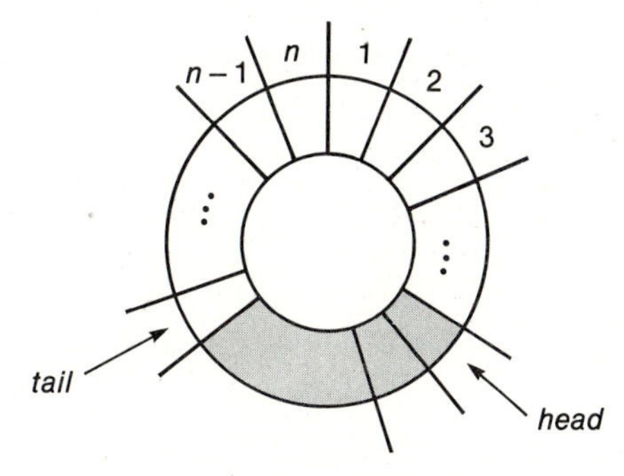

Figure 5.3 A Queue as an Array

Our form of circular queue representation is given in QUEUE_A (Algorithms 5.2); it employs the second of the above alternatives, a count field. With this alternative, it is convenient to have the variable *tail* refer to the *next* position in the queue for enqueuing, as indicated in Figure 5.3. As with the algorithms of QUEUE_L, the representation is not quite complete, and DEQUEUE_A might in practice be a function rather than a procedure. To illustrate the use of QUEUE_A, Figure 5.4 tabulates a sequence of (E)nqueue and (D)equeue operations for a circular queue of size 4, along with the corresponding sequences of values for the queue variables *head* and *tail*.

```
program QUEUE_A;

{algorithms for maintaining queues as circular arrays; items
 in the queue are of type qobj; head points to the next
 position for dequeuing, and tail points to the next
 position for enqueuing; an empty queue has count = 0}

const  qsize = {the size of the circular queue}

type   qobj = ...
       queue = record
          count,head,tail: 0 .. qsize;
          items: array [1 .. qsize] of qobj;
       end;

procedure INITQ_A (var fifo: queue);
begin
   with fifo do begin
      count := 0;
      head := 1;
      tail := 1;
   end;
end;

function EMPTYQ_A (fifo: queue): boolean;
begin
   EMPTYQ_A := (fifo.count = 0);
end;

procedure ENQUEUE_A (var fifo: queue; data: qobj);
begin
   with fifo do
      if (count = qsize) then
         {Overflow}
      else begin
         items [tail] := data;
         tail := tail mod qsize + 1;
         count := count + 1;
      end;
end;

procedure DEQUEUE_A (var fifo: queue; var data: qobj);
begin
   with fifo do
      if count = 0 then
         {Underflow}
      else begin
         data := items [head];
         head := head mod qsize + 1;
         count := count - 1;
      end;
end;

begin
   ...
end.
```

Algorithms 5.2 QUEUE_A — Implementing a Queue as an Array

	E	E	D	E	E	D	E	D	E	E	D	E	D	D
head	1	1	1	2	2	2	3	3	4	4	4	1	1	2	3
tail	1	2	3	3	4	1	1	2	2	3	4	4	1	1	1

Figure 5.4 Trace of Activity with a Circular Queue

5.1.3 The Use and Behavior of Queues

If we consider that the output of a queue is identical with the input to the queue, then we might reasonably conclude that queues are uninteresting data structures. Nonetheless, they are important as basic tools in larger problems. We will see examples of this in later chapters (Section 6.8.1, for example) and so we will not pursue that subject here. Instead we comment upon a class of applications where the queue is not just a utilitarian structure, but rather an essential aspect of the system being studied. These are applications involving *simulation*, where we examine the behavior of a model of some particular situation instead of examining the actual situation. It is often advantageous to study the former instead of the latter, as in the examples:

- designing an airplane;
- assessing the likely results if various traffic control parameters – one-way streets, traffic light cycles, etc. – are modified;
- assessing the effects of algorithms that might be used in a computer operating system to schedule various tasks;
- predicting the outcome of applying various tactics of business or war.

We may be able to make hundreds of simulated experiments far more cheaply, quickly, and safely than we could perform one real experiment. Typically, we need to make some simplifying assumptions to reduce the real process to a simulated one. So the caveats that we encountered in Chapter 1 about modeling apply here also: If the simulated process is not faithful to the true situation, then the answers from the simulation can be quite misleading.

In the usual paradigm of simulation, a series of events takes place in some time sequence. Each event is represented as a node, with time as the key value, and the event-nodes are kept in a queue. It is possible to drive the simulation with a clock that is regularly compared against the item at the head of the queue. However, it is often more efficient to drive the simulation with a loop that removes the first item from the queue, inspects the time at which it is to be performed, and then updates the clock to that value and proceeds. In all, a program for simulation would contain at least:

- queue data structures;
- procedures to generate and enqueue new event-nodes with the appropriate values of the time;
- procedures to dequeue event-nodes and perform the appropriate actions;
- procedures to capture various statistical data about the process;

- a main program to drive all the above components.

For many simulations, the effort of writing a program as just described is moderate, but not unreasonable. For a very large simulation, one might prefer to use one of a variety of general purpose simulation packages such as GPSS, SIMSCRIPT, SIMULA, etc.

†5.1.3.1 Queue Parameters

In analyzing the behavior of a queue, it is conventional to speak of the items of input – people, vehicles, messages, etc. – as *customers*. These customers are seeking some service which they may be able to obtain immediately or for which they may have to wait in a queue. There may be one or several *servers*, all taking their next customer from the common queue. In addition to n, the number of servers, two other important parameters that characterize such a system are:

arrival times – the distribution of times between successive customer arrivals;

service times – the distribution of times required to provide the services that customers are seeking.

It is conventional to use *Kendall notation* to succinctly characterize a given queuing system [Kendall 1953]. In its briefer and more common form, it is written as $A/S/n$, where A and S have symbolic values that specify the arrival and service time distributions, respectively, and n is the number of servers. Two common symbolic values for both A and S are M, for an exponential distribution, and D, for a deterministic (constant) distribution. As an example, the queuing model $M/D/3$ would describe a system with three servers, whose customers have exponential inter-arrival time, and with a constant amount of time required for service.

Given values for the parameters A,S,n we then wish to determine various properties such as:

- average and maximum queue lengths;
- average and maximum waiting times in the queue;
- traffic intensity, which determines the minimum number of servers that are required in order to keep up with the arriving customers;
- server utilization, or the probability that any given server is busy.

For some combinations of values for A,S,n – for example, $M/M/1$ – Queuing Theory is able to derive exact analytical solutions for many of these properties. These matters are described comprehensively by Kleinrock [1975], and succinctly by Allen [1975]. For other combinations of values for A,S,n it may be necessary or convenient to simulate the system with a program containing the components outlined in the previous section [§]. To relate these matters to our earlier discussion of queues, the movement of a tail pointer is determined by the parameter A, and the movement of a head pointer is determined by the parameter S.

5.1.4 Generalizations of Queues

By relaxing the logical characterization in Section 5.1.1, we can obtain other sorts of data structures that are related to queues. One of these is the *deque*, or double-ended queue. In this structure, insertions can be made at either end (enqueue-left or enqueue-right) and likewise deletions (dequeue-left or dequeue-right). A deque resembles a deck of cards in the hands of a sharp dealer; indeed, it even has the same pronunciation. It also resembles a necklace with beads that can be added and/or removed at either end, or the railway network of Figure 5.5. Two variants of the deque are the *input-restricted deque*, wherein the input (but not the output) is restricted to one end, and the *output-restricted deque*, wherein the output (but not the input) is restricted to one end.

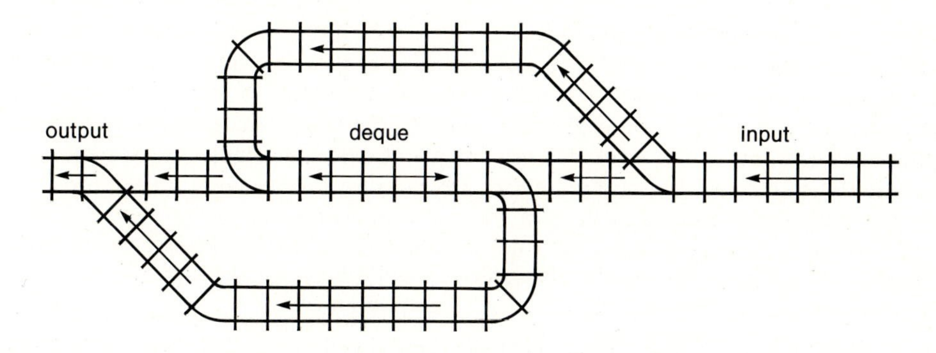

Figure 5.5 A Railroad Model of a Deque

Note that if a deque is implemented as a linked list, then the functional requirements dictate that it should be a bi-directional list. We observed earlier that the output of a queue is not a permutation of the input; however, this is not true for a deque (see Exercise 5.2). Situations that call for deques are somewhat infrequent. An example of their use is given in Section 8.6.2.

An important generalization of queues is the *priority queue*, in which each object that is enqueued has a priority. It is the ranking of the priorities that primarily determines the order of dequeuing, except that in the case of equal priorities, the order of enqueuing may be used to resolve ties. We have already seen a need for such a structure in our discussion of simulation in Section 5.1.3. Namely, when an event-node (corresponding to an event that is to occur at a definite time) is generated, then we need a priority queue discipline rather than a FIFO discipline in order to ensure sequencing of events in the proper chronology. It is straightforward, though not efficient, to base a priority queue upon an ordinary queue by either of the following two methods:

1. Items are inserted in the queue in order of their priority, analogous to SEARCH_LIST (Algorithm 4.1), and then dequeued in normal fashion. The times required for this are $O(n)$ for insertion and $O(1)$ for deletion.

2. Items are enqueued in normal fashion, and then the queue is searched for the item with lowest priority when a dequeuing operation is to be performed. This times required for this are $O(1)$ for insertion and $O(n)$ for deletion.

Priority queues can be implemented more efficiently than this, however. If there are relatively few levels of priority, a technique to be described in Section 5.3 may suffice. More generally, an entirely different sort of data structure is required, and this will be discussed in Section 6.6.4.

5.2 STACKS

A stack is a linear list that can be accessed for either input or output at just one of its two ends. One example of this model of access can be found in a stack of plates on a kitchen shelf or in a spring-loaded dispenser in a cafeteria. In both cases, the only two logical possibilities are to add a plate to the top of the stack or to remove a plate from the top of the stack. A stack is also exemplified by a railroad spur, as illustrated in Figure 5.6(a). In this model, we can insert a boxcar from the input to the open end of the spur, and we can remove a boxcar from the open end of the spur to the output, mixing insertions and deletions as we wish. The essence of these examples is that the next object to be removed will always be the last one that was added, whence the acronym *LIFO*, or "Last In, First Out."

In our example of the plates, the physical behaviors on the shelf and in the cafeteria are notably different. With the former, the stack contents do not shift with insertions and deletions; with the latter, the entire stack moves with each operation. By analogy with the cafeteria example, stacks are sometimes referred to as *push-down stores*. However, as we will see when we discuss the implementation of stacks, that term can be misleading; in a computer, we do not want to imitate the cafeteria case and relocate the entire stack with each operation upon it.

5.2.1 Logical Data Structure

The basic actions with a stack are as follows:

create(x) – to bring into existence an empty stack x;

push(x,r) – to add the object r to the top of stack x;

pop(x,s) – to remove the object at the top of stack x and assign it to s.

Another action that is sometimes defined for a stack is:

top(x,t) – to assign to t the value of the object at the top of stack x, without removing the object from the stack.

The important predicate for a stack is, as with a queue:

empty(x) – to ascertain if the stack x is empty or not;

and the important conditions are:

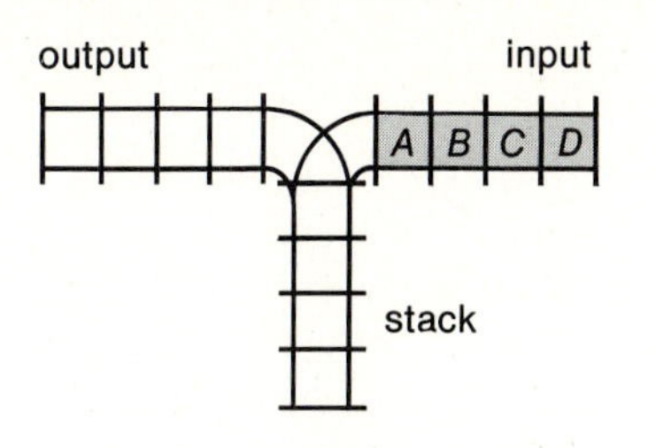

(a) Initial

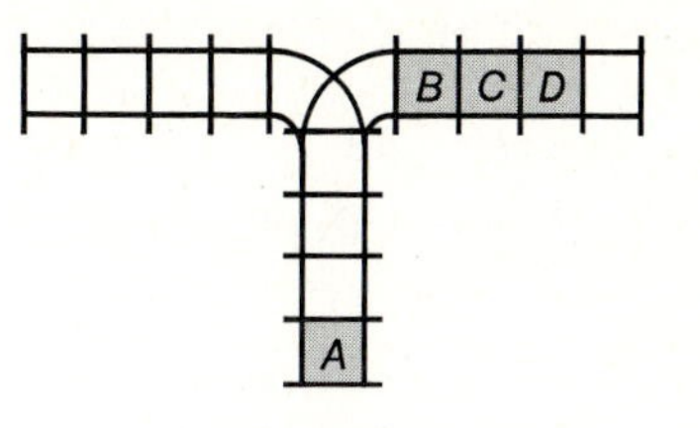

(b) Push *A*

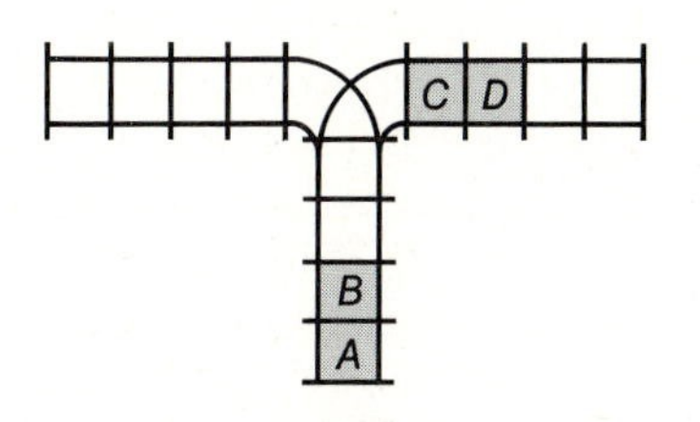

(c) Push *B*

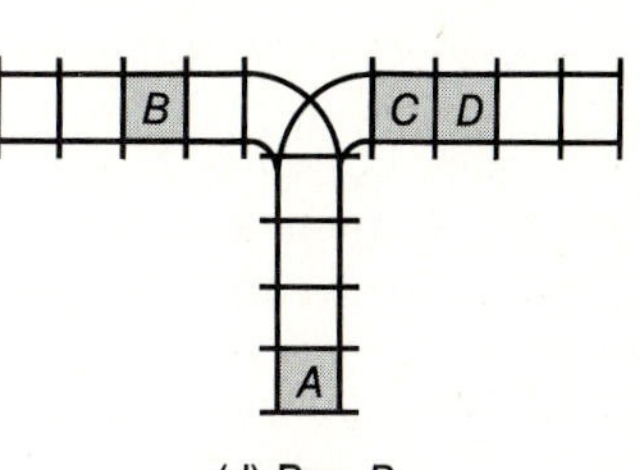

(d) Pop *B*

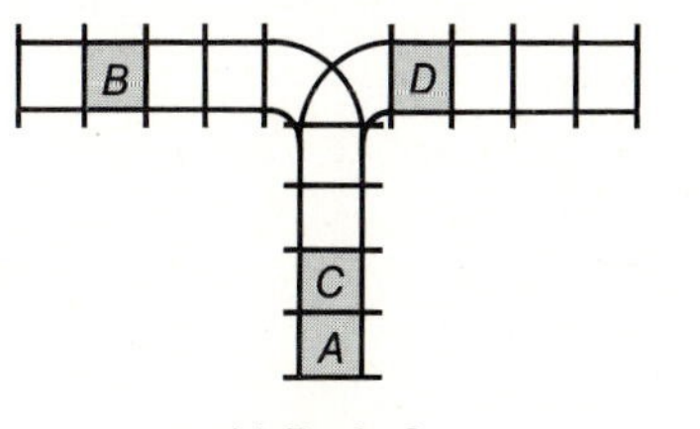

(e) Push *C*

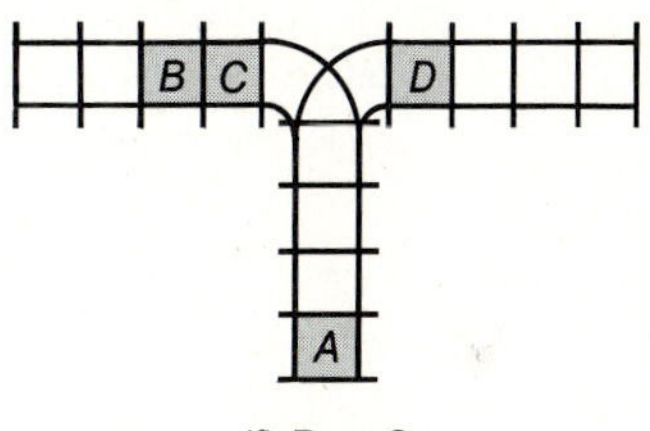

(f) Pop *C*

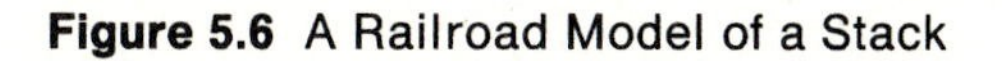

Figure 5.6 A Railroad Model of a Stack

overflow(x) – to recognize when an attempt to push an object on stack x has failed because of insufficient space for the enlarged stack;

underflow(x) – to recognize when an attempt to pop an object from stack x has failed because the stack is empty.

Note the conventional use of the term *top* to refer to the position in a stack where the last item was inserted.

Once again, these logical characterizations do not include any suppositions about how the structure and its operations are to be implemented. As in the previous case of the queue structure, this informal description of the stack structure has much of the flavor of the specification of an ADT. (A more formal specification of the stack as an ADT can be found in Section 9.2.1.) Figure 5.6 illustrates the stack notions in terms of a railroad spur model. Initially, (a) the input contains boxcars labeled *A*, *B*, *C*, *D*. Subsequent configurations for an arbitrary sequence of pushes and pops are then shown in (b) – (f). Since P(ush) and P(op) are indistinguishable, we will adopt the convention of using S(tack) and U(nstack) to describe a sequence of operations with a stack.

5.2.2 Physical Representation

Stacks are easier to implement than queues. By anchoring the closed end of the stack at some fixed location in memory, we need only keep track of the position of the top. Thus, it is easy to implement a stack with an array, as shown in Figure 5.7. (In figures such as this, stacks are sometimes grown like stalactites, sometimes like stalagmites, and sometimes horizontally; the choice is arbitrary, based on convenience.) Our only concern is that the array be large enough to accommodate the maximum potential size of the stack; we do not have to worry about the stack "crawling" through memory. The typical declaration of a stack and some basic operations upon it are illustrated in STACK_A (Algorithms 5.3). Similar observations apply here as cited in our discussion of queue representations in Section 5.1.2. One is that we have not spelled out the manner in which underflow and overflow would need to be handled. Another is that, for convenience, POP may often be a function that returns the popped object, as long as that object is a scalar.

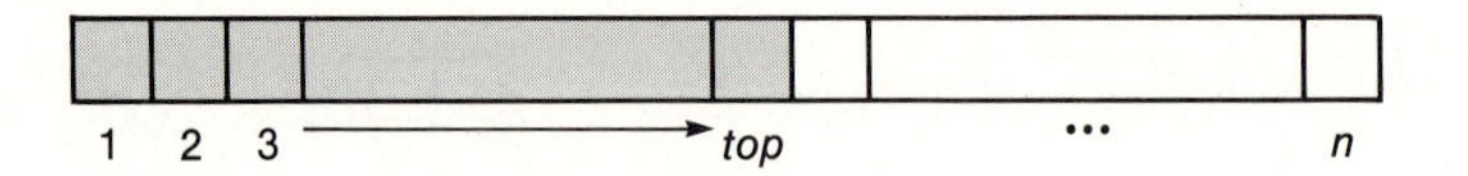

Figure 5.7 A Stack as an Array

Would we ever wish to represent a stack with a linked-list? The answer may occasionally be yes, as we will see in Section 5.3. However, this choice is less common and is also trivially easy to implement, so we will not elaborate upon it here. In point of fact, we have already illustrated such a representation of stacks. In the program EQUIV (Algorithm 4.3), there is one stack for each set member, and the procedure ADDCELL is used to push *v* onto the *u*th stack.

5.2.3 Applications of Stacks

A basic point about a stack, as opposed to a queue, is that it can be used to transform an input sequence into a different output sequence. If we do nothing more than a series of S(tack) and U(nstack) operations upon the input sequence *ABC*, the possibilities that can occur are those shown in Figure 5.8. Note that of the six permutations on these three symbols, we are unable to attain *CAB* by any series of basic stack operations. The permutations of 1 .. *n* that can be obtained via a single stack are called *stack permutations*; the characterization of those permutations that cannot be obtained using a stack is left as an interesting exercise (see Exercise 5.7).

```
program STACK_A;

{algorithms for maintaining stacks as arrays; items on the
  stack are of type stkobj; top points to the position of the
  accessible item on the stack; an empty stack has top = 0}

const  stkmax = {the maximum size of the stack }

type   stkobj = ...
       stack = record
          top: 0 .. stkmax;
          items: array [1 .. stkmax] of stkobj;
       end;

procedure INIT_STK (var lifo: stack);
begin
  lifo.top := 0;
end;

function EMPTY_STK (var lifo: stack): boolean;
begin
  EMPTY_STK := (lifo.top = 0);
end;

procedure PUSH (var lifo: stack; data : stkobj);
begin
  with lifo do
    if top = stkmax then
      {Overflow}
    else begin
      top := top + 1;
      items [top] := data;
    end;
end;

procedure POP (var lifo: stack; var data : stkobj);
begin
  with lifo do
    if top = 0 then
      {Underflow}
    else begin
      data := items [top];
      top := top - 1;
    end;
end;

begin
  ...
end.
```

Algorithms 5.3 STACK_A – Implementing a Stack as an Array

Operation Sequence	Output Sequence
S U S U S U	A B C
S U S S U U	A C B
S S U U S U	B A C
S S U S U U	B C A
S S S U U U	C B A

Figure 5.8 Example of Operations with a Stack

Stacks have many and varied uses. We will discuss two of these uses in general terms – for accomplishing procedure call and return, and for the evaluation of arithmetic expressions. Then we will illustrate in more concrete terms their use for the transformation of arithmetic expressions. Stacks are also important because of their role in dealing with recursive algorithms and backtracking algorithms. The first of these roles is dealt with in Section 5.3, and the topic of backtracking is explored in Section 6.8.2.

5.2.3.1 Procedure Call and Return. Suppose that we have the situation exhibited in Figure 5.9, with three procedures *P*, *Q*, and *R* residing in memory, such that:

P calls *R* from location *s*
P calls *Q* from location *t*
Q calls *R* from locations *u* and *v*

Control would be passed from one procedure to another in the sequence of the numbering on the branches in the figure. Whenever there is such a transfer of control, there must be some mechanism to remember where the call was issued from, so that control can be returned to the proper point in the calling procedure when the called procedure has terminated. This corresponds to a LIFO discipline. For example, when *P* calls *Q*, *Q* calls *R*, and *R* returns, the return must be to *Q*, to resume what *Q* had been doing. In a HLL, the compiler provides this mechanism without any explicit awareness on the user's part by (i) pushing information onto a stack at call-time, and (ii) popping this information off the stack upon return.

The amount of information that needs to be kept on the stack can be as little as a return address, but it might also involve the contents of machine registers, the values of local variables, etc. In fact, since the values of local variables are required only during the invocation of a procedure *A*, and since it is possible that *A* is recursive, then it makes much more sense to allocate space for these local variables directly on the stack when *A* is called. With the alternative course of allocating space within the procedure *A* itself, every recursive call would necessitate copying out these values to the stack to allow for fresh values in the new invocation.[1] Since

---

[1] In fact, the reduction in the amount of memory that is pre-allocated for local data may be more significant than the time that is saved in copying. We discuss such matters in Chapter 11.

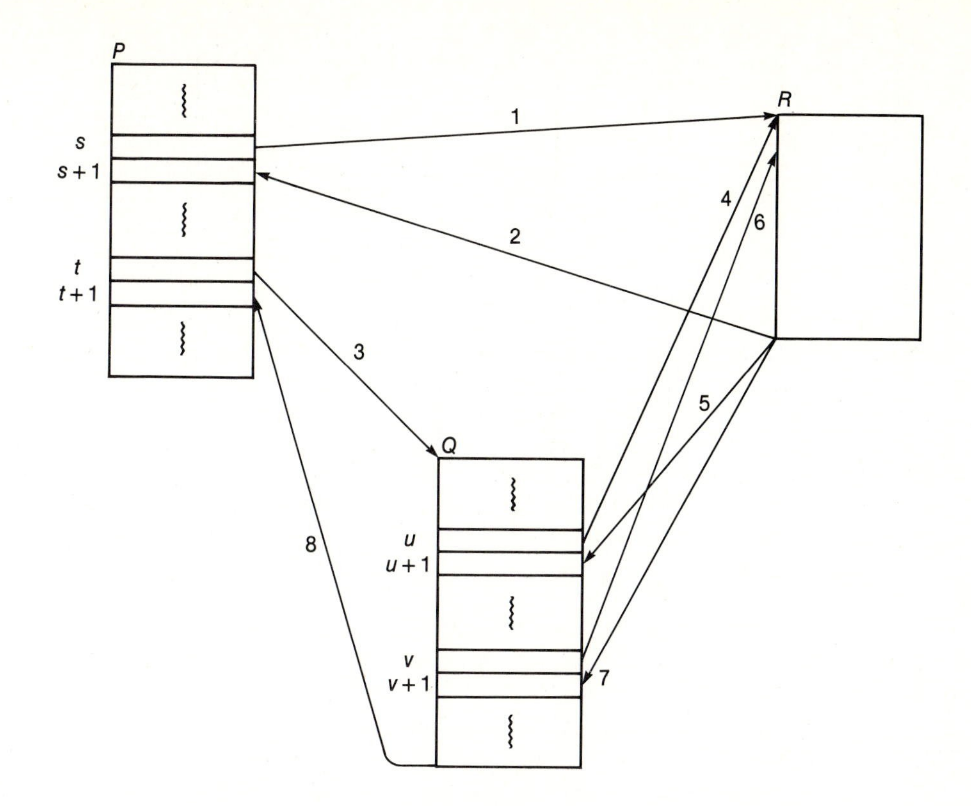

Figure 5.9 Procedure Segments with Procedure Calls

procedures will in general require different amounts of space on the stack for their local data, we encounter the additional twist that the amount by which to pop the stack – that is, reset the top-of-stack pointer – on a procedure return is known only by the called procedure. Thus, one of the values that needs to be stacked is the previous value of the stack pointer itself. Note that if we are talking about non-recursive procedures, then we may need to save and restore just a return address and the values of some machine registers. But if we are talking about recursive procedures, then we may need to preserve much more. Since the depth of recursion is unpredictable, the stack is a structure perfectly suited to the problem of allocating this storage in a dynamic fashion.

As the program in Figure 5.9 executes, the stack would contain a block of information for each active or suspended procedure, and each block would contain a return address, the value of the previous top-of-stack pointer, and values of local variables, as shown in Figure 5.10:

(a) *P* calls *R*	(e) *R* returns
(b) *R* returns	(f) *Q* calls *R*
(c) *P* calls *Q*	(g) *R* returns
(d) *Q* calls *R*	(h) *Q* returns

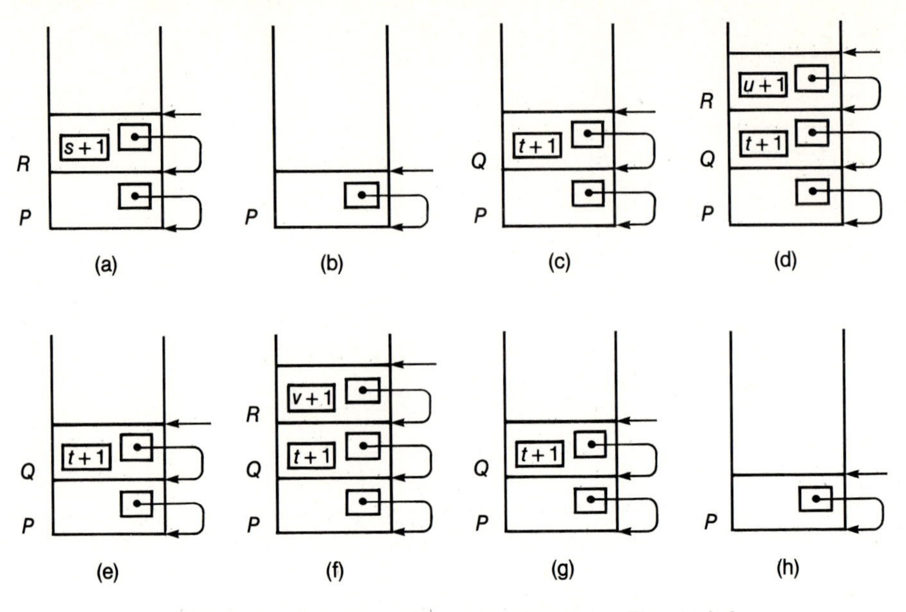

Figure 5.10 Trace of the Call Stack for Figure 5.9

The figure reflects the assumption that *P* was itself called from a main program.

5.2.3.2 Evaluation of Expressions. In ordinary arithmetic, we are used to the fact that $5 + 3 \times 7 = 26$, and not 56. In other words, we have learned that the multiplication operator always has a higher *precedence* than an addition operator, and so should be performed first in the evaluation of an expression. If we want the addition to be done before the multiplication, we can modify the precedence by rewriting the expression as $(5 + 3) \times 7$.

This use of parentheses poses no difficulty to humans, but their presence in expressions is inconvenient with computing machines. Fortunately, it is possible to write arithmetic expressions in such a fashion that parentheses are never required. In fact, any expression can be written in three equivalent manners, as follows:

prefix notation	$\times + 5\ 3\ 7$	(operator precedes its operands)
infix notation	$(5 + 3) \times 7$	(operator between its operands)
postfix notation	$5\ 3 + 7 \times$	(operator follows its operands)

Note that parentheses are required only in the notation most familiar to us, which is infix. Prefix and postfix notations were first introduced by the Polish logician Łukasiewicz in order to simplify expressions in propositional calculus. This causes prefix notation to be known also as Polish notation, and postfix notation to be known as reverse Polish notation. Unfortunately, terminology occasionally gets sloppy, so that postfix, which is particularly convenient for computation, is sometimes referred to simply as Polish notation.

To see why postfix notation is so convenient, suppose that we have a computing machine with a stack. The machine would operate on a postfix expression in the following manner:

1. When the next item in the input is an operand, it is stacked.
2. When the next item in the input is an operator, then the two top operands on stack are unstacked, the operation is performed, and the result is stacked.

Let us trace the operation of this machine upon the expression

9 3 5 * + 10 6 – /

for which the equivalent infix expression is

(9 + 3 * 5) / (10 – 6)

The trace is shown in Figure 5.11, and we see that a machine with a stack can indeed correctly evaluate an arithmetical expression in postfix notation. A stack used for this purpose is commonly called an evaluation stack, to distinguish it from the procedure-call stack of the preceding section.

Compilers almost always get rid of parentheses, translating infix expressions into postfix notation as an intermediate representation of the source code. What happens next in the compilation process depends upon the circumstances. Most often, the postfix expressions undergo further translation into code for direct execution on some target machine, but sometimes the code is left in the intermediate form. For example, some machines have a stack architecture, as opposed to a register architecture, so that the machine can execute such code directly. (The relative advantages of stack and register architectures is a subject of contention.) Even when the underlying machine does not have a stack architecture, it is possible to use an interpreter that simulates the actions of a stack machine. In fact, this is the manner in which small machines commonly support Pascal – by interpreting the intermediate code on a simulated stack machine.

Input Expression	Stack Contents
9 3 5 * + 10 6 – /	
3 5 * + 10 6 – /	9
5 * + 10 6 – /	9 3
* + 10 6 – /	9 3 5
+ 10 6 – /	9 15
10 6 – /	24
6 – /	24 10
– /	24 10 6
/	24 4
	6

Figure 5.11 Stack Evaluation of a Postfix Expression

5.2.3.3 Translation of Expressions. We have seen that a machine with a stack can directly evaluate expressions that are in postfix notation. But people generally prefer infix notation, so how is the translation from infix to postfix accomplished? With a stack again! In order to discuss how this is performed, we need to make a few background remarks concerning this common situation in computing. The text of a program in its source language is almost always treated as an array of characters. Within this text are program *tokens* of various types: constants (numeric or character), operators, identifiers, and delimiters.[2] Almost all operators and delimiters and some constants and identifiers require just one character in the program text, but most constants and identifiers consist of several characters.

To a compiler or other language translating program, the length of a token is far less significant than its type; therefore, the first phase of compilation usually decouples these aspects by scanning the text and extracting tokens for the next phase. To keep our illustration of translating infix to postfix as simple as possible, we will restrict our input expressions as follows:

- The tokens in an expression include just operands, parentheses, and the operators for add, subtract, multiply, and divide.
- The operand tokens are single characters.
- The special character '#' is used as a sentinel.

By making these restrictions, we can compute the token types via the function TOKENIZE (Algorithm 5.4).

```
function TOKENIZE (ch: char): token;

type    token = (null,opnd,asop,mdop,lpar,rpar);

begin
   TOKENIZE := opnd;                    {default assumption}
   case ch of
      '#':       TOKENIZE := null;      {to mark the end}
      '+', '-':  TOKENIZE := asop;      {add or subtract}
      '*', '/':  TOKENIZE := mdop;      {multiply or divide}
      '(':       TOKENIZE := lpar;      {left parenthesis}
      ')':       TOKENIZE := rpar;      {right parenthesis}
   end;
end;
```

Algorithm 5.4 TOKENIZE

We will translate infix to postfix via two structures. One of these is a stack and the other is a *precedence matrix*. The latter contains pre-encoded values that reflect what action should be performed next, depending jointly upon the next token in the input and the token at the top of the stack. The type of the former token is used to select a column of the matrix, and the type of the latter token is used to select a row of the matrix. The precedence matrix is shown in Table 5.1. Each of its entries is one of the possible actions to be taken, according to the row and column indices.

---

2 *Identifier* is the generic term applied to symbolic names of variables, procedures, keywords, etc. *Delimiters* are the punctuation of programs, such as parentheses, brackets, commas, periods, quote marks, etc.

The matrix with its action-valued entries is used in conjunction with the procedure IN_TO_POST (Algorithm 5.5).

	null	opnd	asop	mdop	lpar	rpar
null	done	pass	save	save	save	errr
opnd	errr	errr	errr	errr	errr	errr
asop	pop1	pass	pop1	save	save	pop1
mdop	pop1	pass	pop1	pop1	save	pop1
lpar	errr	pass	save	save	save	pop2
rpar	errr	errr	errr	errr	errr	errr

Table 5.1 Precedence Matrix for IN_TO_POST Algorithm

In IN_TO_POST, *defer* is a stack as defined in Algorithms 5.3, and PUSH and POP are likewise defined therein. (In a real situation, one would probably choose to implement PUSH and POP in-line rather than as distinct procedures.) As the input line *infix* is scanned, operands are copied directly to the output line *postfix*, the parentheses are removed, and the operators are relocated via the interaction of *defer* and *precedence*. Note that the logic of the algorithm requires a usual type of pop operation *pop*1 and a second type of pop operation *pop*2. The latter just corresponds to discarding a left parenthesis when the corresponding right parenthesis is encountered. Note also, in the action for *pop*1, that it is necessary to go back and reuse the precedence matrix with the same value from the input, but the uncovered value from the stack. These details may become clearer through examining Figure 5.12, which contains a trace of IN_TO_POST operating upon the input expression '(A+B*C)/(D−E)#'.

In the translation from infix to postfix notation, the stack is essential. The precedence matrix is not, however. It is common to achieve the same effect by employing two precedence functions − one applied to the input token and another applied to the token on top of the stack (see Exercise 5.11). The appropriate action is then determined by comparing the values of these two functions, $f(input\_token)$ versus $g(stack\_token)$. Whereas the precedence matrix requires $O(n^2)$ space for n tokens, the use of precedence functions require $O(n)$ space. On the other hand, if we wish to make IN_TO_POST more realistic by extending the variety of tokens that it will handle, it is simpler to add extra rows or columns to the precedence matrix (with no alteration to the code) than it is to reconsider the interaction of the precedence functions and the code in the light of these new token types. The precedence matrix also facilitates the detection of erroneous input expressions, as in the case of unbalanced parentheses.

```
procedure IN_TO_POST (infix: line; var postfix: line);

{IN_TO_POST operates on lines of characters, transforming
  an expression from infix notation to postfix notation}

label  1,2;

const  linmax = {maximum size of input and output lines}

type   line = array [1 .. linmax] of char;
       token = (null,opnd,asop,mdop,lpar,rpar);
       action = (pass,save,pop1,pop2,done,errr);

var    indx,pndx: 1 .. linmax;
       cndx,rndx: token;
       defer: stack;
       precedence: array [token,token] of action;

begin
   pndx := 1;
   defer.top := 0;
   PUSH (defer,'#');
   for indx := 1 to linmax do begin
      cndx := TOKENIZE (infix [indx]);
1:    rndx := TOKENIZE (defer.items [defer.top]);
      case precedence [rndx,cndx] of
         pass: begin
            postfix [pndx] := infix [indx];
            pndx := pndx + 1;
         end;
         save: PUSH (defer,infix [indx]);
         pop1: begin
            POP (defer,postfix [pndx]);
            pndx := pndx + 1;
            goto 1;
         end;
         pop2: begin
            if defer.top = 0 then
               {Underflow}
            else
               defer.top := defer.top - 1;
         end;
         done: goto 2;
         errr: {erroneous situation}
      end;
 2: end;
 end;
```

Algorithm 5.5 IN_TO_POST

indx	*top*	*action*	*stack*	*postfix*
1	1	save	#	
2	2	pass	# (	
3	2	save	# (	*A*
4	3	pass	# (+	*A*
5	3	save	# (+	*A B*
6	4	pass	# (+ *	*A B*
7	4	pop1	# (+ *	*A B C*
7	3	pop1	# (+	*A B C* *
7	2	pop2	# (	*A B C* * +
8	1	save	#	*A B C* * +
9	2	save	# /	*A B C* * +
10	3	pass	# / (	*A B C* * +
11	3	save	# / (	*A B C* * + *D*
12	4	pass	# / (−	*A B C* * + *D*
13	4	pop1	# / (−	*A B C* * + *D E*
13	3	pop2	# / (	*A B C* * + *D E* −
14	2	pop1	# /	*A B C* * + *D E* −
14	1	done	#	*A B C* * + *D E* − /

Figure 5.12 IN_TO_POST Operating upon '(A+B*C)/(D−E)#'

†5.3 MULTIPLE QUEUES AND STACKS

Our discussion of queues and stacks up to this point has been somewhat unrealistic, for two reasons. First, we have glossed over the important issue of what do to in the case of Overflow.[3] Second, we often need several of these data structures simultaneously. If they are implemented in terms of linked lists, then these issues do not arise. But if the implementation is in terms of arrays, then our alternatives may be either to abort a calculation, or else to dynamically reallocate space for the arrays as their dimensions vary, and then shuffle their contents in memory. Garwick [1964] has given an algorithm for accomplishing this, which we will discuss shortly. However, we will present some other comments first. Evidently, the issue can be finessed by using a linked list representation; so why bother with an array representation that is prone to these difficulties? Efficiency is one very good reason, both in terms of time and space. Another reason is that pointer variables may not be available, so that arrays are the only choice. In fact, Garwick's method was originally devised for the problem of handling the many one-dimensional tables needed by a FORTRAN compiler (with which there are no dynamic pointer variables), where it

---

[3] Underflow is less important to us. It reflects a possible aberration in the calling program rather than in the implementation of the queue or stack. Moreover, it is quite legitimate to keep deleting items from a queue or stack *until* an underflow is detected.

was not possible to know in advance how these tables would grow for various source programs.

There is another important point. If an application requires just two stacks, then it is a simple matter to share the entire pool of free memory between them, so that no Overflow will occur until that entire pool is exhausted. This is accomplished by anchoring the bases of the stacks at opposite ends of the memory pool and growing them toward each other, as illustrated in Figure 5.13 for stacks *U* and *V*. In fact, this is just the scheme that is employed in the run-time environments generated by many Pascal compilers. There is always a procedure-call stack such as described in Section 5.2.3.1; and when **mark** and **release** are used instead of **dispose**, for deallocating space from the heap, then the heap can be implemented as a stack growing from the opposite end of available memory, as in the figure. However, no such simple scheme is possible when there are more than two stacks.

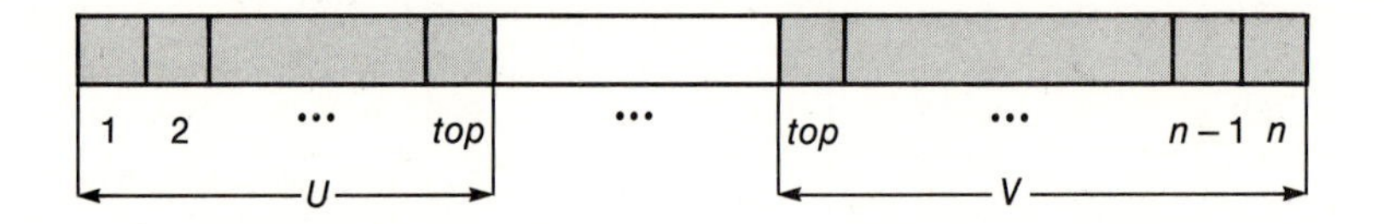

Figure 5.13 Two Stacks Grown in Opposite Directions

Let us consider now the dynamic solution given by the procedure REPACK (Algorithm 5.6). The strategy here is to anticipate future changes in stack size on the basis of past history. By reallocating the stacks on the basis of this predictive information, we hope to reduce the likelihood of future Overflows that must call on REPACK. In order to do this, we need the global declarations reproduced here.

```
var   Base,Oldtop,Top: array [1 .. n+1] of integer;
      Mem: array [lomem .. himem] of ...
```

The stacks are all allocated in *Mem*, with the *i*th stack located from $Mem\,[Base\,[i]] + 1$ to $Mem\,[Top\,[i]]$. Note that with this convention an empty *i*th stack corresponds to $Base\,[i] = Top\,[i]$. REPACK is called when a condition $Top\,[stkno] = Base\,[stkno + 1] + 1$ signals that an Overflow has occurred. In order for this condition to be valid for the *n*th stack, $Base\,[n + 1]$ (and $Newbase\,[n + 1]$) must contain the value of *himem*. The strategy in REPACK is to compare the growth of the stacks since the last time it was called, by computing any positive differences $Delta\,[i] := Top\,[i] - Oldtop\,[i]$. Thus, initially, we need to have $Oldtop\,[i] = Top\,[i]$. The variables *freemem* and *deltasum* are used to calculate, respectively, the total currently unused space and the total (positive) growth. From these data, new values for the stack limits are calculated, as follows:

(a) Divide some fraction (commonly 0.1) of the unused space evenly among all of the stacks.

(b) Reallocate the remainder of the unused space among the stacks according to their individual growths.

After the values of $Newbase\,[i]$ have been computed, the contents of the stacks are shifted up or down in memory accordingly, with due care not to overwrite items

```
procedure REPACK (stkno: 1 .. n);

const  alpha = 0.1;

var    deltasum,freemem,i,j,k,t: integer;
       p,q,r,s: real;
       Base,Newbase,Delta,Oldtop,Top: array [1 .. n+1] of integer;
       Mem: array [lomem .. himem] of ...

begin
  deltasum := 0;  freemem := himem - lomem;
{gather statistics}
  for i := 1 to n do begin
    freemem := freemem - (top [i] - Base [i]);
    if Top [i] <= Oldtop [i] then
      Delta [i] := 0
    else begin
      Delta [i] := Top [i] - Oldtop [i];
      deltasum := deltasum + Delta [i];
    end;
  end;
{compute new stack limits}
  if freemem < 0 then
    {No more Memory!}
  else begin
    p := alpha * freemem / n;
    q := (1 - alpha) * freemem / deltasum;
    r := 0;
    Newbase [1] := Base [1];
    for i := 2 to n do begin
      s := r + p + q * Delta [i - 1];
      t := trunc (s) - trunc (r);  r := s;
      Newbase [i] := Newbase [i - 1] + Top [i - 1] - Base [i - 1] + t;
    end;
{relocate the stacks}
    Top [stkno] := Top [stkno] - 1;
    for i := 2 to n do
      if Newbase [i] < Base [i] then begin
        k := Base [i] - Newbase [i];
        for j := Base [i] + 1 to Top [i] do
          Mem [j - k] := Mem [j];
        Base [i] := Newbase [i];
        Top [i] := Top [i] - k;
        Oldtop [i] := Top [i];
      end;
    for i := n downto 2 do
      if Newbase [i] > Base [i] then begin
        k := Newbase [i] - Base [i];
        for j := Top [i] downto Base [i] + 1 do
          Mem [j + k] := Mem [j];
        Base [i] := Newbase [i];
        Top [i] := Top [i] + k;
        Oldtop [i] := Top [i];
      end;
    Top [stkno] := Top [stkno] + 1;
  end;
end;
```

Algorithm 5.6 REPACK

before they have been relocated. Note the necessity to adjust the value of *Top* [*stkno*], since it has already been incremented by PUSH; when REPACK returns to PUSH, the item that caused the Overflow can then be placed on its stack. Note also that REPACK never relocates the first stack. This suggests that it would be more efficient to make the largest stack the first one, thereby reducing the time spent in relocating items.

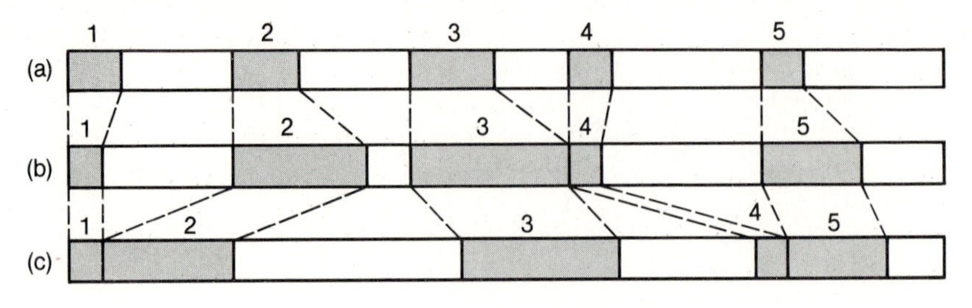

Figure 5.14 Effect of Algorithm REPACK

The following example helps to convey the action of REPACK. Suppose that we have 100 units of *Mem*, and that we have allocated 20 units each to five stacks. Moreover, for some initial values of *Oldtop*, let the actual sizes be: 7,5,14,4,4. These conditions are illustrated in Figure 5.14(a), and also displayed on the left of Figure 5.15. Now suppose that a series of pushes and pops on the five stacks cumulates with an overflow in the third stack, and with the *Delta* values illustrated in the middle of Figure 5.15. (Here, negative values of *Delta* are also shown.) The corresponding picture of *Mem* is shown in Figure 5.14(b). REPACK will compute the values shown on the right of Figure 5.15 (with *deltasum* = 18 and *freemem* = 51); the readjusted picture of *Mem* is shown in Figure 5.14(c).

	Base	*Oldtop*	*Space*	*Size*	*Delta*	*Newbase*	*Top*	*Space'*	*Size'*
1	100	107	20	7	−2	100	105	6	5
2	120	125	20	5	9	106	120	37	14
3	140	154	20	14	7	143	164	40	21
4	160	164	20	4	−1	183	186	4	3
5	180	184	20	4	2	187	193	13	6

Figure 5.15 Action of Algorithm REPACK

How effective is Garwick's method? Some detailed analysis can be found in Knuth [1973a]. Most importantly, it depends upon there being sufficient space to accommodate the overall maximum requirement. If the ratio of *deltasum* to *freemem* is nearly equal to 1.0 in value, then space is being released at about the same rate that it is being requisitioned. If *deltasum* is smaller than *freemem*, the method works well; if *deltasum* is generally larger than *freemem*, our efforts are almost certainly wasted, since space will soon be exhausted. Moreover, as the point of exhaustion is approached, REPACK will be invoked more and more frequently to reapportion smaller and smaller amounts of free space. This suggests that a test for such a condition would likely save time, by terminating an untenable situation earlier rather than later.

Another factor has been noted in the effectiveness of Garwick's method. If the values of the *Delta* [*i*] reflect too small a sample of the history, then the algorithm may oscillate wildly before arriving at stable values for the limits of the stacks. One proposed solution to this problem is to retain more change history, so that better predictive calculations can be performed [Wise and Watson 1976]. However, this may be insufficient, particularly when the sequence of stack alterations exhibits flurries of activity with just a few of the stacks over a period of time. This can cause the values of the *Delta* [*i*] to be even more misleading. A suggestion for coping with this is to incorporate the relative stack sizes in the reapportionment calculation, since the sizes are more stable than the changes in size [Standish 1980]. The two refinements of Garwick's method that we have just described are effective because they provide more stable solutions. An orthogonal enhancement that can significantly reduce the frequency of reorganization is to alternate the direction of growth of the stacks, so that they occur in pairs, with each pair allocated as in Figure 5.13 [Fraenkel 1979; Korsh and Laison 1983].

Although the motivation for REPACK is to accommodate multiple growing and shrinking stacks, it can be adjusted to handle other instances of dynamically varying tables of information, such as queues or deques. In particular, suppose that we wish to implement a priority queue, and that there are only a modest number of priority levels. We could associate one ordinary queue with each level, and then have enqueuing and dequeuing procedures that administer the collection of queues. Each individual queue might be implemented as a circular queue within the bounds of an overall array.

5.4 RECURSION REVISITED

In Section 1.3.1 we discussed the issue of choosing between iteration and recursion for expressing an algorithm. We saw there that recursion often provides a more concise and intuitive definition of a quantity or a process than does iteration. In the first of the following sections, we call attention to a very important instance of this in computer science. We also saw in Chapter 1 that recursion may be dramatically less efficient than iteration for actual computation. Accordingly, we examine in Section 5.4.2 some ways to systematically transform recursive programs to more efficient, non-recursive ones. Finally, in the last section, we point out some interesting and somewhat intricate relations between the subject of recursion and the subject of what is fundamentally computable. We introduce these topics at this point because there is a close connection between recursion and the capabilities provided by the stack data structure. Although this connection is not relevant for Section 5.4.1, it is very much so for the subsequent two sections.

5.4.1 Backus-Naur Form

In programming as well as in ordinary discourse, we have arrived at a variety of notations to express our ideas. Any such notation can be regarded as a first level of communication. However, it is frequently necessary to communicate at a second level, about the notation itself. Two examples of this are defining the nature of arithmetic expressions and characterizing the nature of English phrases and sentences. At the higher level we are no longer dealing with specific arithmetic factors or terms, or with specific words from a dictionary. Rather, we are dealing with entire *syntactic categories* of such objects. Two significant problems in such an endeavor are:

1. How do we discriminate between the levels of communication? Is "object" an ordinary variable at the first level of discourse, or is it the name of a category at the second level of discourse?
2. At the second level, how do we manage to specify every possible way of constructing an instance of a category?

For the first problem, one device is to enclose names of categories in angle brackets. Thus "object" is an ordinary variable at the first level, and "<object>" is a category at the second level. For the second problem, we should not be surprised to find that recursion provides the answer.

For the specification of arithmetic expressions, the combination of these two techniques leads to the scheme shown in Figure 5.16. This manner of notation is known as *Backus-Naur Form* (*BNF*). It was first used to describe the language ALGOL [Backus 1960; Naur et al. 1960], wherein it yielded a description that is formal, remarkably brief, and almost (but not entirely) free of ambiguity.

```
<expression> ::= <term> | <expression> + <term> | <expression> - <term>
<term>       ::= <factor> | <term> * <factor> | <term> / <factor>
<factor>     ::= <variable> | ( <expression> )
```

Figure 5.16 Example of BNF

What we see in Figure 5.16 are *productions*, wherein each syntactic category[4] – <expression>, <term>, and <factor> – is defined in terms of the following: other categories (possibly including itself), various literal values, and various *metalinguistic symbols*. Two of the latter, illustrated in this example, are '::=' (with the interpretation "is defined as") and '|' (with the interpretation "or"). Such symbols as '+' and '(', on the other hand, stand for themselves; that is, they are literal values from the first level of communication. To paraphrase the last of the three productions in the figure, a factor is either a variable or an expression enclosed within parentheses.

---

4 You may recognize this notational device from our discussion of Pascal control structures in Section 1.4.1.

Examination of Figure 5.16 reveals some important regularities of form. The left hand side of a production always contains a syntactic category, and is an instance of a *non-terminal symbol* – that is, one defined in terms of other symbols. The right hand specifies one or more alternative definitions, separated by '|'. These definitions may contain literal values, meta-linguistic punctuation, other non-terminal symbols, or *terminal symbols*, which are syntactic categories that are not further defined. In the figure, <*variable*> is allowed to remain as a terminal symbol. This is not very realistic. In practice, the productions would be comprehensive enough so that all the terminal symbols corresponded to literal values.

This example merely touches upon a topic of substantial depth and importance. We will have a little more to say about the matter when we discuss parse trees in Section 6.6.2, and still more in Section 8.6 when we talk about languages and grammars. For now, the important points are as follows:

- Recursion is essential in order to specify an infinite set of possibilities without constructing infinite lists, such as

```
<expression> ::= <term> | <term> + <term>
            | <term> + <term> + <term> | ...
```

- Note how the issue of precedence in arithmetic expressions is accounted for by the dependency among the productions.

In all of this, there is an important distinction between what we are trying to accomplish and how we do it. BNF notation in the form illustrated here is the original, pioneering tool for responding to the two issues raised at the beginning of this section. Variations of BNF notation are widely in use, and so are flowchart-like syntax diagrams.

†5.4.2 Transformation of Programs

As we saw in Section 5.2.3.1, stacks play an important role in the implementation of recursive procedures. However, there is an even broader relation between stacks and recursion. It is often possible to improve the performance of an algorithm by transforming a recursive function (with an implicit stack) to an equivalent iterative function employing an explicit stack. This improvement comes about because the amount of information that needs to be remembered may be much less than what is automatically saved and restored during procedure call and return. In such a transformation, each recursive call causes a value of the function parameter to be pushed onto the stack, and built around this are stack initialization and a loop that pops values off the stack umtil it is empty.

Indeed, program transformations are not limited to just this type of conversion; that is, the elimination of recursion may not be the primary goal. An important goal in computer science is to be able to perform these transformations automatically. With such an automatic system, we could hope to express an algorithm in a concise, intuitive, recursive fashion and then ultimately obtain an efficient counterpart with minimal human intervention. Even more significantly, it might be possible to compose a recursive algorithm that is clearly correct; then, if the transformation process were error-free, the resulting program would also be correct [Burstall and Darlington 1977].

A catalogue of program transformations would take us too far afield. Instead, let us consider the *program schema* of Figure 5.17. Such a schema is a generalized description of many recursive algorithms; it can be particularized by supplying *interpretations* to the predicate $p(x)$ and to the functions N, S, T, U, v, w. (There are alternative forms of recursive schemas, but this one is adequate for our purposes here and in what follows.) Since F calls itself twice, we might expect that a corresponding iterative program G would need to employ a stack at both of those points. But suppose now that we had an interpretation such that $U(x)$ was void. A very useful rule in this case is that we can eliminate the *tail-recursion* expressed by $F(w(x))$, since it is the last step within F. Thus, we can transform F to F', with only one recursive call, wherein the values of pertinent variables are reassigned, and then a branch is taken back to an early step in F'. Analogously, the iterative program G would need to employ a stack only for the transformation of the call $F'(v(x))$.

```
procedure F(x);
begin
   if p(x) then N(x)
   else begin
      S(x);  F(v(x));  T(x);  F(w(x));  U(x);
   end;
end;
```

Figure 5.17 A Recursive Schema

The preceding rather abstract discussion may become much clearer with the following example. Recall that the Fibonacci numbers are defined by the equation $F_n = F_{n-1} + F_{n-2}$. It is straightforward to translate the corresponding recursive function to an iterative one, wherein a call to $F(n)$ causes the values $n - 1$ and $n - 2$ to be stacked, unless $n \leq 2$. The result is FIB_STK_A (Algorithm 5.7). However, in comparing the Fibonacci definition with the recursive schema of Figure 5.17, we see that $U(x)$ is essentially void (as are $S(x)$ and $T(x)$). So the tail-recursion can be eliminated, yielding the more efficient function FIB_STK_B (Algorithm 5.7).

Automatic program transformations are a significant issue, but for the present transformations by hand are the norm. With regard to the particular issue of converting recursion to iteration via the introduction of a stack, the details can become somewhat tedious [§]. We are content to make these general observations:

- Our expressed motivation is that of efficiency, but we should realize that these transformations are also fundamentally important for languages that do not support recursion, such as FORTRAN.
- Transformations typically involve several steps until a "finished" program is obtained. Throughout this book, we will see numerous instances of algorithms that can be represented either recursively or else iteratively with a stack; in the latter cases, we will expeditiously present finished programs.

```
function FIB_STK_A (n: integer): integer;

var     defer: stack;
        sum: integer;

begin
   sum := 0; INIT_STK (defer);
   PUSH (defer,n);
   repeat
      POP (defer,n);
      if n <= 2 then
         sum := sum + 1
      else begin
         PUSH (defer,n - 1);
         PUSH (defer,n - 2);
      end;
   until EMPTY_STK (defer);
   FIB_STK_A := sum;
end;


function FIB_STK_B (n: integer): integer;

var     defer: stack;
        sum: integer;

begin
   sum := 0; INIT_STK (defer);
   PUSH (defer,n);
   repeat
      POP (defer,n);
      while n > 2 do begin
         PUSH (defer,n - 2);
         n := n - 1;
      end;
      sum := sum + 1;
   until EMPTY_STK (defer);
   FIB_STK_B := sum;
end;
```

Algorithms 5.7 FIB_STK

- The exchange of recursion for an explicit stack has the effect of reducing the constant factor in the complexity of an algorithm; it will not of itself reduce the complexity class of the algorithm.

†5.4.2.1 Tabulation and Other Speed-Ups. The final point in the previous section raises an interesting question. In Chapter 1 we saw both a recursive definition (Eq. 1.17) and an iterative function ALGOR_A (Algorithm 1.1) for computing Fibonacci numbers. The latter did not require a stack; moreover, it reduced the complexity from exponential to linear (see Section 1.3.2.3). How is this possible?

The answer has to do with the great number of redundant evaluations that occur when applying the recursive definition, as illustrated in Figure 1.1. Such redundancy is fairly common, and it can be avoided by the technique known as *tabulation*. In this method, as applied to the Fibonacci calculation, a table is maintained for the values of F_n. We initialize the table entries to zero; thereafter, when a value of F_n is sought, we check the corresponding entry in the table. If it is zero, we perform the evaluation and then store that value of F_n in the table for possible future use; otherwise, we retrieve the desired value directly from the table with no further evaluation. In the general method of tabulation, we need to maintain a table with as many entries as there are values of F_n. But in the case of ALGOR_A, we were able to do better by allocating storage for just two values at any one time – for F_{n-1} and F_{n-2} – and then reusing that storage at each iteration.

The use of tabulation is independent of the exchange of recursion for an explicit stack; that is, it is easy to find examples where either just the former, or just the latter, or both together might be employed. Tabulation can be an extremely effective tool for reducing complexity by eliminating redundancy [§]. The principal hazard in its use is that, in the general case, it may not be possible to predict a pattern of reusage, and so a large amount of storage may be required for the table entries. This is particularly true when the recursion is defined in terms of two or more parameters, so that the table becomes multi-dimensional.

We conclude this discussion by noting an ultimate transformation, whereby it is possible to compute F_n in $O(\lg n)$ time [§] rather than in $O(n)$ time, as with ALGOR_A. The Fibonacci recurrence can be expressed in matrix form as

$$\begin{pmatrix} F_n \\ F_{n-1} \end{pmatrix} = \begin{pmatrix} 1 & 1 \\ 1 & 0 \end{pmatrix} \times \begin{pmatrix} F_{n-1} \\ F_{n-2} \end{pmatrix} \tag{5.1}$$

Applying this recurrence $n-2$ times, we obtain

$$\begin{pmatrix} F_n \\ F_{n-1} \end{pmatrix} = \begin{pmatrix} 1 & 1 \\ 1 & 0 \end{pmatrix}^{n-2} \times \begin{pmatrix} 1 \\ 1 \end{pmatrix} \tag{5.2}$$

But the matrix product can be computed as a product of factors, each a power of 2 of the original matrix A, in $O(\lg n)$ time (see Exercise 1.16), giving us our promised result. By way of illustration, suppose that we wish to compute F_{15}. Then we need the matrices A, A^4, A^8 as follows:

$$A = \begin{pmatrix} 1 & 1 \\ 1 & 0 \end{pmatrix}, \quad A^4 = \begin{pmatrix} 5 & 3 \\ 3 & 2 \end{pmatrix}, \quad A^8 = \begin{pmatrix} 34 & 21 \\ 21 & 13 \end{pmatrix}$$

whence

$$\begin{pmatrix} F_{15} \\ F_{14} \end{pmatrix} = \begin{pmatrix} 377 & 233 \\ 233 & 144 \end{pmatrix} \times \begin{pmatrix} 1 \\ 1 \end{pmatrix} \tag{5.3}$$

so that $F_{15} = 610$.

†5.4.3 Recursive Schema and Computability

Figure 5.17 in the preceding section gave an example of a recursive schema which is one model of recursive computation. To express the full power of recursion would require a more generalized recursive schema R. Rather than pursue this, we note that it is also possible to express iteration with a generalized iterative schema I. The question then arises, is R more powerful than I; in other words, are there functions that we can compute with R but not with I? The answer is a bit subtle, and it depends upon certain other factors. It is always possible to transform an iterative calculation to a recursive one (see ALGOR_B, Algorithm 1.2), and it is often possible to transform a recursive calculation to an iterative one [Strong 1971]. An important feature for enabling this is that the iterative calculation should be able to employ "counter" variables, such as the variable i of ALGOR_A (Algorithm 1.1). However, there are cases wherein a recursive schema cannot be transformed to an equivalent iterative schema because the iterative computation would require an infinite set of locations for recording intermediate results. In other words, iteration is strictly less powerful than recursion [Paterson and Hewitt 1970]! However, if we amend our iterative schema I to I', allowing it to have two pushdown stores (unbounded stacks), then we find that I' is as powerful as R.

The preceding result has both practical and theoretical significance. The practical aspect is that it confirms the importance of the stack as a data structure. The theoretical significance derives from the following facts:

- It has been proven that any of several models of computation – among them generalized recursion, the use of a Turing machine, or the use of a finite machine with two pushdown stores – all yield computational capabilities that are equivalent.
- No one has been able to find a notion of effective computability that cannot be expressed in one of these provably equivalent models.

As a result, we have the *Church-Turing Thesis*: There is no function that is effectively computable that cannot be obtained via any one of these equivalent mechanisms! In this discussion, we have overlooked numerous details in the interest of conveying the broader picture. These deeper matters are explored in Beckman [1980] and Minsky [1967].

5.5 OVERVIEW

One theme that the queue and stack data structures clearly illustrate is the power of thinking in terms of Abstract Data Types, whereby the implementation of a structure becomes a separate issue from its functional specification. They also demonstrate that in programming, as in everyday life, a specialized solution to a problem can be more cost-effective than a generalized one. Thus, these structures can be used for many useful purposes, with significant savings in both space and time compared with that required for ordinary linked lists.

The great utility of both queues and stacks will become even more apparent as they are used in algorithms in subsequent chapters. In the case of stacks, however, the examples in this chapter have already conveyed some of their importance, both practical and theoretical. The practical importance was shown primarily in the manipulation of expressions; the theoretical significance is most evident in the relationship between recursion and the use of stacks.

5.6 BIBLIOGRAPHIC NOTES

- Examples of queue-like data structures for simulation that are superior to ordinary linked lists can be found in Franta and Maly [1977] and Wyman [1975]. Extensive comparisons of data structures for representing queues of simulation events are given in Jones [1986], McCormack and Sargent [1981], and Vaucher and Duval [1975].

- Examples and "recipes" for transformations between recursive and iterative forms of programs can be found in Auslander and Strong [1978], Bird [1977a, 1977b], and Horowitz and Sahni [1976].

- Two excellent accounts of the benefits that can be obtained with tabulation are Bird [1980] and Cohen [1979b]. The technique for computing Fibonacci numbers with $O(\lg n)$ complexity is described in Miller and Brown [1966] and Shortt [1978].

5.7 REFERENCE TO TERMINOLOGY

5.8 EXERCISES

Section 5.1

5.1 Assume a circular queue of length 5, with index variables *head* and *tail*, as used in Algorithms ENQUEUE_A and DEQUEUE_A. Tabulate the values of *head* and *tail*, as in Figure 5.4, under the following sequence of E(nqueue) and D(equeue) operations:

E E D E E D E E E D D E E E D D E D D

If an E/D operation would cause an overflow/underflow condition, ignore it and continue tabulating with the next E/D operation.

†5.2 Suppose that we have a sequence of four input symbols, *A B C D*.

(a) Which permutations of the four symbols cannot be obtained using an input-restricted deque, such that items can be inserted at just one end but removed from either end?

(b) Which permutations of the four symbols cannot be obtained using an output-restricted deque, such that items can be inserted at either end but removed from just one end?

†5.3 Write a set of routines to implement a deque as a linked list, analogous to Algorithms 5.1. For the four operations

DL – dequeue from the left	EL (*x*) – enqueue *x* on the left
DR – dequeue from the right	ER (*x*) – enqueue *x* on the right

test them against the command sequence

EL (*A*), ER (*B*), DL, ER (*C*), EL (*D*), DR, EL (*E*), DR, DL, DR,
ER (*F*), EL (*G*), DR, DL, EL (*H*), EL (*I*)

displaying the contents of the deque after each of the commands.

†5.4 Write a set of routines to implement a deque as a circular array, analogous to Algorithms 5.2. Test them against the command sequence of Exercise 5.3.

Section 5.2

5.5 With input *A B C D E F*, what will be the output under the following S(tack) and U(nstack) sequences?

(a) S S U S S U S U U S U U

(b) S S S U S U S U U S U U

5.6 With input *A B C D E F* and for each of the following permutations, either indicate that it cannot be obtained by using a stack, or show how it can be obtained via a sequence of S's and U's.

(a) *B D C F E A*

(b) *B A F D C E*

(c) *C B D A F E*

†5.7 Given an input sequence $A = a_1, a_2, \dots, a_n$ and some permutation of it A', how can you tell by looking at A' whether it could have been obtained from A by using a stack?

5.8 Simulate the operation of the algorithm IN_TO_POST in translating the following infix expression to postfix:

'(A−B−C)/D+E*(F−G*(H−I))*J#'

Show the contents of the stack, the action taken, and the output contents as the program executes, as in Figure 5.12.

†5.9 Rewrite the precedence matrix of Table 5.1 to include additional operators, and then apply the new matrix, as follows:

(a) Rewrite the precedence matrix to include the operators '←' ("gets") for assignment and '↑' ("exop") for exponentiation.

(b) Simulate the operation of IN_TO_POST, using this extended precedence matrix, on the following expression:

'A←(B−C*D↑E↑(F/(G/H+I)))#'

Show the contents of the stack, the action taken, and the output contents as the program executes, as in Figure 5.12.

†5.10 We have seen how to use stacks both for the evaluation of postfix expressions and for the translation of infix expressions to postfix notation. In this problem, you are to combine these processes by using two stacks − one for operators and one for operands − in order to read an infix expression from left to right, translating and evaluating simultaneously. For example, in processing the expression (11 − 7) * 6, we would have the parallel trace shown in Figure 5.18. Trace the contents of the two stacks when operating upon the expression:

$$((11 - 15 + 6) \uparrow 3 \uparrow 2 - 36) \,/\, 17 \,/\, (34 - 5 * 6)$$

where ↑ denotes exponentiation.

Operator Stack	Operand Stack
(	
(	11
(−	11
(−	11 7
(	4
	4
*	4
*	4 6
	24

Figure 5.18 Parallel Stack Contents

††5.11 The problem of converting an infix expression to a postfix expression is commonly solved by using two precedence functions rather than a precedence matrix. These two functions, commonly called f and g, directly reflect, for example, that '*' and '/' have higher precedence than '+' and '−'. Both f and g take a token as input and return an integer precedence value; both functions, in fact, can be represented as tables of *value* corresponding to *token*. The function f is used for examining the next position in the input, and the function g is used for examining the top of the stack. The corresponding algorithm is driven principally by whether $f < g$, $f = g$, or $f > g$.

(a) Construct the two precedence functions, taking into account the following operators and delimiters, according to the usual mathematical interpretation of precedence:

+ − * / ( ) #	as before
←	the assignment operator (':=')
↑	the exponentiation operator
< = ≠ >	the relational operators
& | ¬	the logical operators **and**, **or**, **not**

(b) Rewrite the algorithm IN_TO_POST to use these precedence functions. (You may have to make some arbitrary character substitutions in order to do this, such as '!' for '↑', etc.)

†5.12 We have seen that it is relatively straightforward, using a stack, to translate an infix expression to the corresponding postfix expression. What can be done for the problem of translating an infix expression to the corresponding prefix expression?

Sections 5.3 – 5.4

††5.13 Rewrite the algorithm REPACK to incorporate the improvement mentioned at the conclusion of Section 5.3; that is, have the stacks grow in alternating pairs, as in Figure 5.13.

†5.14 The following function was encountered in Exercise 1.12.

```
function F (m,n: integer): integer;
begin
   if n = 0 then F := m
   else F := F (m,n - 1) + F (m + 1,n - 1);
end;
```

Transform it to a function that computes F using a stack instead of recursion, and test your program by computing $F(1,3)$.

††5.15 A sequence of parentheses is said to be balanced when the numbers of left and right parentheses are equal, and when each left parenthesis can be matched against some later right parenthesis. For three pairs, there are five possibilities:

()()() ()(()) (())() (()()) ((()))

The goal of generating all balanced sequences of parentheses can be characterized in BNF notation by

$$S ::= (S) S \mid \varepsilon$$

where ε denotes the empty sequence. Write a recursive procedure to generate all balanced sequences for n pairs; then write an iterative program to generate the same sequences. What observations do you have about the relative ease of composing the two programs?

††5.16 The following function was encountered in Exercise 1.14.

```
function F (m,n: integer): integer;
begin
   if m * n = 0 then F := m + n + 1
   else F := F (m - 1,F (m,n - 1));
end;
```

Transform the function F from recursive form to (a) iterative form, and then (b) a form employing tabulation. After establishing that your programs are correct, try both of them, as well as the original function, for computing $F(4,1)$. What do you observe about the relative performance of these three programs?

6

TREES

"A fool sees not the same tree that a wise man sees."

Wm. Blake,
Marriage of Heaven and Hell, Proverbs of Hell

Just as Moliere's M. Jourdain was surprised to learn that he habitually spoke prose, many people would likely be surprised to realize how commonly they deal with trees. Yet they pervade all aspects of everyday life, as witness genealogical charts, hierarchical organizations of management, the Dewey decimal system for books, etc. They occur more overtly in various aspects of computation such as parse trees, sort trees, decision trees, etc.

Sometimes we think of trees in a graphical manner, and sometimes we use schemes that convert the graphical representation to a sequential structure. Thus, note that all the forms in Figure 6.1 are logically equivalent. In this figure, (a) displays a tree in record format (akin to the Table of Contents for a book), (b) displays the tree as a List structure via the use of parentheses, (c) displays the tree as a map, and (d) displays the tree in the convincingly tree-like format typically employed for discussions of this data structure.

Figure 6.1(d) clearly delineates the appropriateness of the term tree, since it highlights the branching nature of the structure. Note that, contrary to nature's canonical form for trees, with the root at the bottom, in computer science the root is generally at the top. However, this is not universally so, and one can still find books and articles wherein trees are drawn with the root placed at the bottom, or even at the left. In the next chapter, on graphs, we will see that a tree is a restricted form of graph, and we will characterize this assertion more precisely. For now, let us consider the following terminology and definitions.

6.1 DEFINITIONS AND TERMINOLOGY

A tree, in the most general sense, is a set of *vertices*, or *nodes*, and a set of *edges*, where each edge connects a pair of distinct vertices, such that there is one and only one connecting path on these edges between any pair of vertices. A tree in this

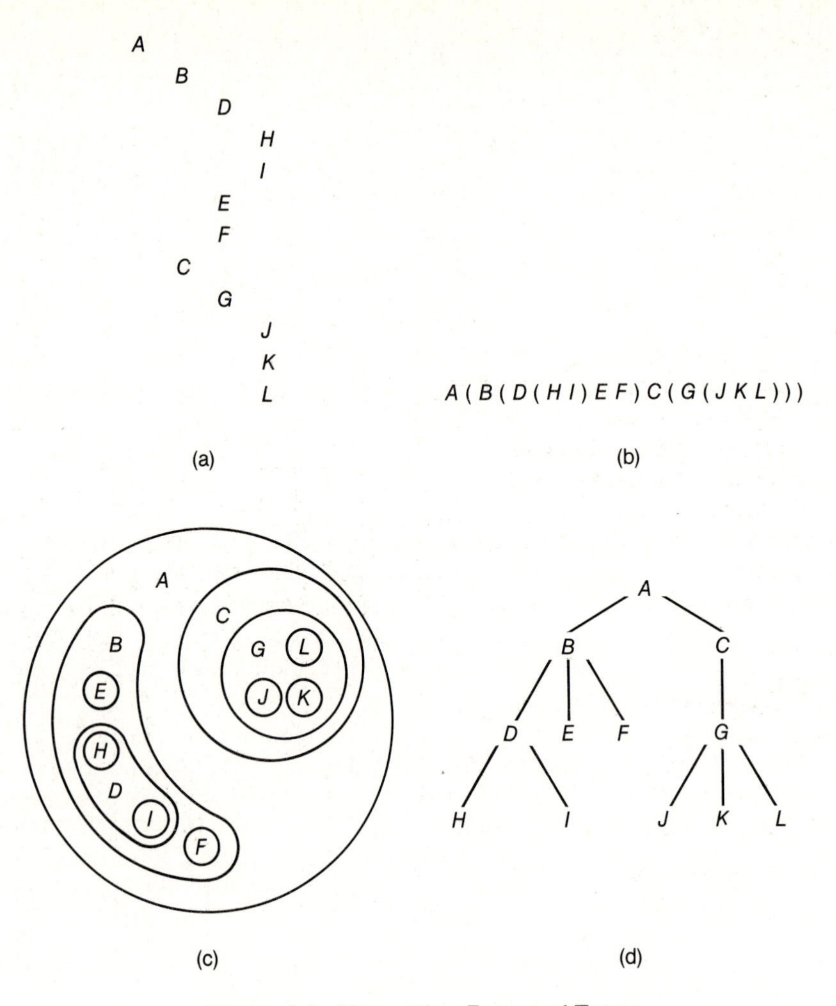

Figure 6.1 Alternative Forms of Trees

most general sense is called a *free tree*, as in Figure 6.2(a) However, it is more common to impose the notion that there is a distinguished vertex, called the *root*. In this case, we have an *oriented tree*, as in Figure 6.2(b). One can imagine picking up (a) at vertex *A* and shaking it until the structure sags into the shape of (b). Note that, except in the most trivial case, there are numerous oriented trees corresponding to a given free tree, according to which vertex is distinguished.

In Figure 6.2, the trees shown in (b), (c), and (d) are all equivalent in the sense of oriented trees. However, it is sometimes important to consider the edges from a vertex as having a left to right order. In this case, we have an *ordered tree*, and (b), (c), and (d) are all distinct. Note that, in the tree representations of Figure 6.1, (c) is an oriented tree while the other three cases are ordered trees. Ordered trees are more natural in computing, since most representation schemes for trees have, by

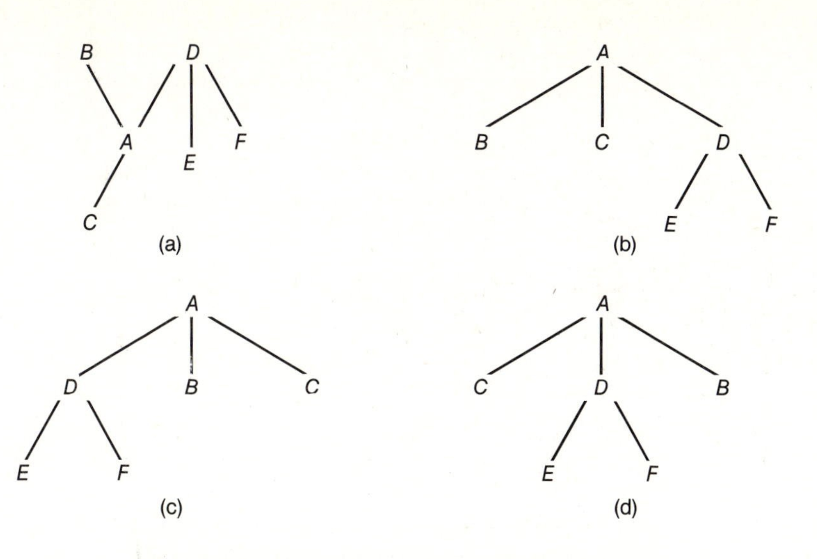

Figure 6.2 Free, Oriented, and Ordered Trees

default, an ordering among the branches. In most published allusions to tree structures, and in this book, the term tree without any qualifiers implicitly signifies an ordered tree.

The *degree* of a node is the number of edges that impinge on it. Except for free trees, it is common to associate a direction with each edge, usually away from the root. We also distinguish between the *in-degree* and the *out-degree*. But since the in-degree is always one, except for the root, it is usual with trees to refer to the out-degree simply as the degree. Thus, in Figure 6.3, node *A* has degree 3 and nodes *D*,*F*,*O*,*S* have degree 1.

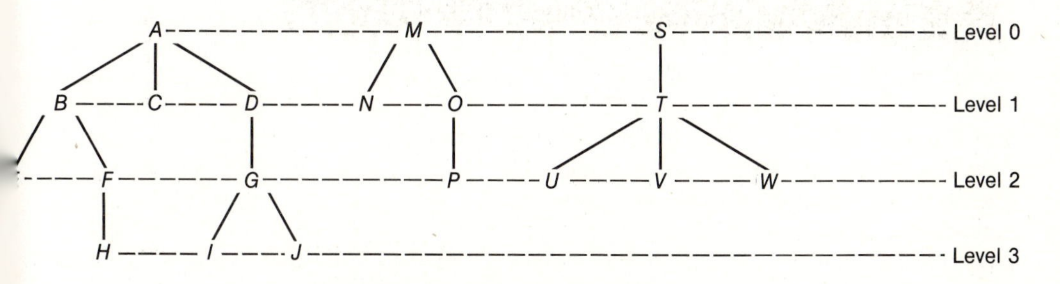

Figure 6.3 Basic Tree Definitions

Tree terminology borrows from both genealogy and horticulture. Thus, edges are sometimes called *branches*; also, *terminal nodes*, or nodes of zero out-degree, are usually called *leaves*. Note how Figure 6.3 is drawn so that nodes that are the same number of edges distant from the root are at the same vertical displacement, or *level*. The *height* of a tree corresponds to the level of the leaf or leaves that are most distant from the root. The vertical predecessor of a node is its *parent*, or father; the vertical successors are *children*, or sons, proceeding from the eldest at the left to the youngest at the right; and nodes that have the same immediate parent are *siblings*, or brothers. In addition, it is common to speak of a descendant of a node, where the progeny may be more than one level distant, and also an ancestor of a node, where the patrimony may be more than one level distant. It is sometimes convenient to be able to compare the positions of any two nodes of a tree. In order to do this, we extend the notion of order among siblings to encompass that of "cousins." Then, for nodes X and Y, the possibilities (as illustrated in Figure 6.3) are:

- X and Y have an *ancestor-descendant* relationship; for example, B is an ancestor of H, and J is a descendant of A.
- X and Y have a *left-right* relationship, either as siblings or as "cousins"; for example, I is left of J, and D is right of B; but also B is left of G, and C is right of H.

Note that a tree is a recursive structure. It can be thought of as a root node with zero or more children nodes, each of which is a tree. Thus, the structures beginning at nodes B,C,D in Figure 6.3 are called *subtrees* of the tree rooted at node A. The *weight* of the subtree at a node is the number of nodes in the subtree, not counting the node itself. Thus, node A has weight 9 and nodes B,D,M,T have weight 3. When there are disjoint trees, as in Figure 6.3, they are called a *forest*. A forest can readily be converted to a tree by introducing one extra node as a parent to all of the roots of the trees in the forest.

6.2 LINKED REPRESENTATION AND BINARY TREES

How should trees be represented physically in computer memory? The most common case is to make each node a separate List item, and to employ pointer variables to make the branches explicit. There is a problem, however, in that nodes do not all have the same number of children. One solution to this problem, shown in Figure 6.4(a), is to allocate for each node a number of pointer locations equal to the maximum out-degree for the application at hand, and to employ **nil** pointers as necessary. Another solution, shown in Figure 6.4(b), is to have variable-size nodes, allocating in each of them a number of pointer locations equal to the actual out-degree. If there is a large amount of data associated with each node, so that the memory required for the pointers is a small percentage of the memory required for the entire node, then the first solution is feasible. But there are many cases when this is not so, and it becomes highly inefficient. The second solution is likely to be shunned because of the complications associated with having variable length items.

The most common resolution for this representation problem is the following simple and ingenious construction. In Figure 6.5(a),

1. retain branches from parents to eldest (leftmost) sons, but delete branches to other children;

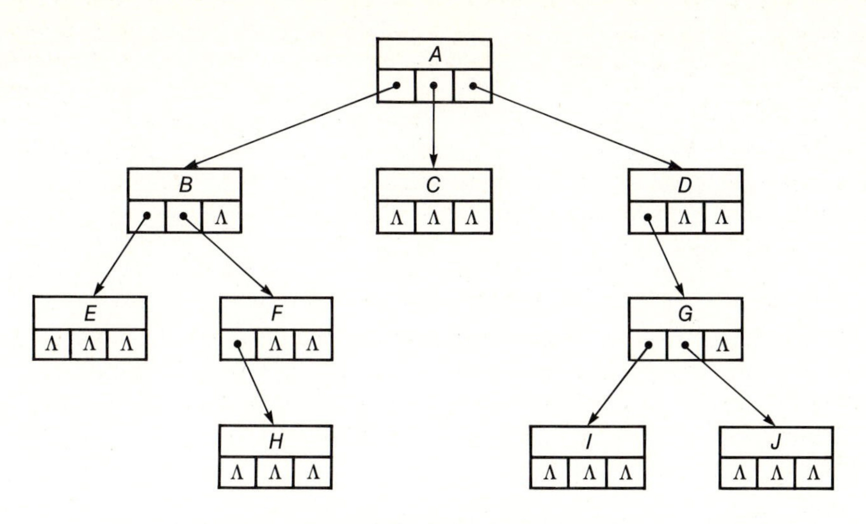

(a) Fixed Size Nodes

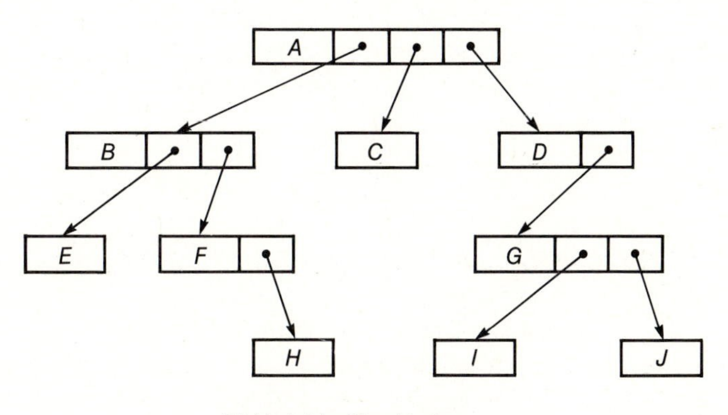

(b) Variable Size Nodes

Figure 6.4 Tree Representations

2. introduce branches from eldest children to their next youngest siblings.

In this manner, we obtain Figure 6.5(b). If we now tilt (b) by 45 degrees, we obtain (c), which looks like a tree again. It is, but of a special kind called a *binary tree*. Note that a node in a binary tree always has just 0, 1, or 2 children, so that it is feasible to allocate all nodes with just two pointer fields. However, a binary tree is distinct from an ordered tree of maximum degree 2, because the *left child* and the *right child* pointers have special significance. Thus, in Figure 6.6, the three structures are all equivalent as trees, although (b) is the preferred way of drawing it; however, as binary trees, (b) is ambiguous and (a) and (c) represent the distinct cases of **nil** right and **nil** left pointers for node *C*.

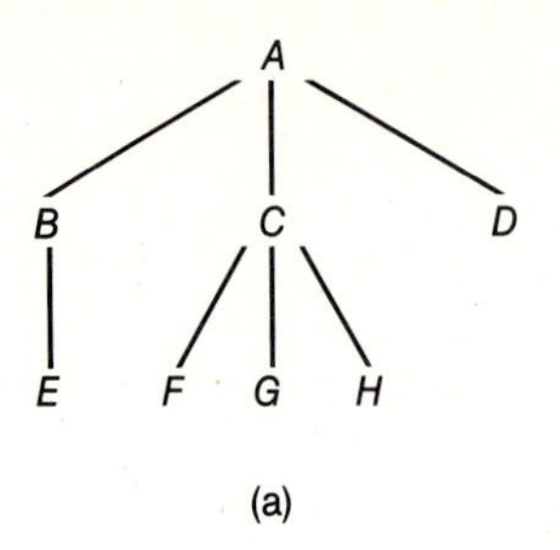

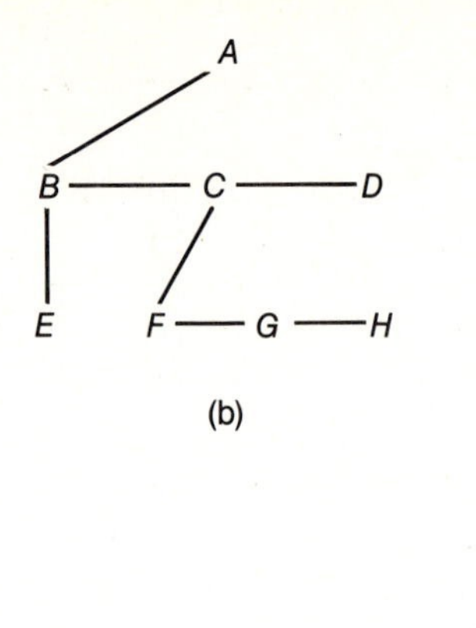

A
B
E
C
F
D
G
(c)
H

Figure 6.5 Ordered Tree – Binary Tree Correspondence

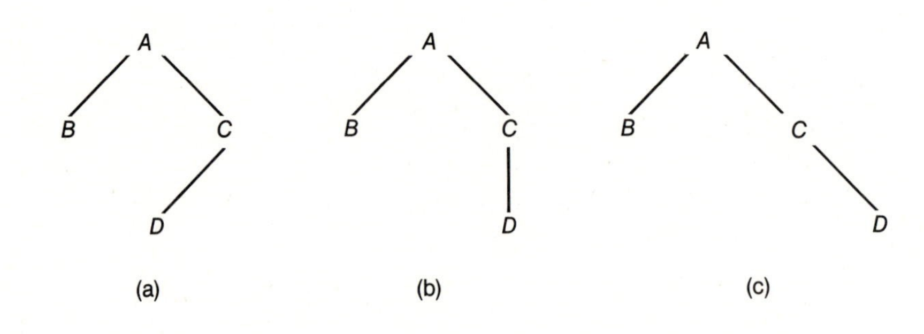

Figure 6.6 Branch Direction is Significant

Note that the transformation from tree to binary tree has a unique inverse process. Thus in Figure 6.7(a), by interpreting left pointers as child pointers and right pointers as sibling pointers, we obtain Figure 6.7(b) as the corresponding ordered forest. Be careful of truly ambiguous cases where a given drawing might be either a tree or a binary tree. For example, in Figure 6.8, what is (b)? It could be either the binary tree corresponding to (a) or a tree whose binary tree is (c).

Apropos of binary trees, a significant observation is that they correspond to pure Lists. Another important remark is that we sometimes deal with binary trees wherein each node has either no children or two children; in a case of this sort, we have a *strictly binary tree* (sometimes called a full binary tree). Most of this chapter will focus on binary trees rather than on trees, partly because of their storage efficiency. However, the reader should not infer that the only significance of binary trees is as efficient representations of ordered trees. Binary trees are important in their own right; they are commonly the natural data structure for a problem, as we will see in Section 6.6.

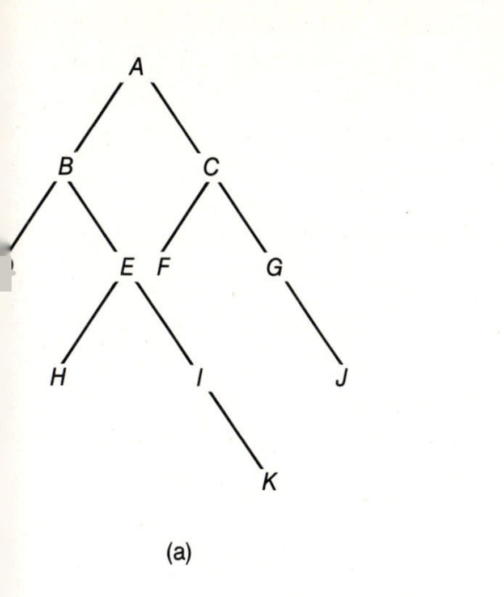

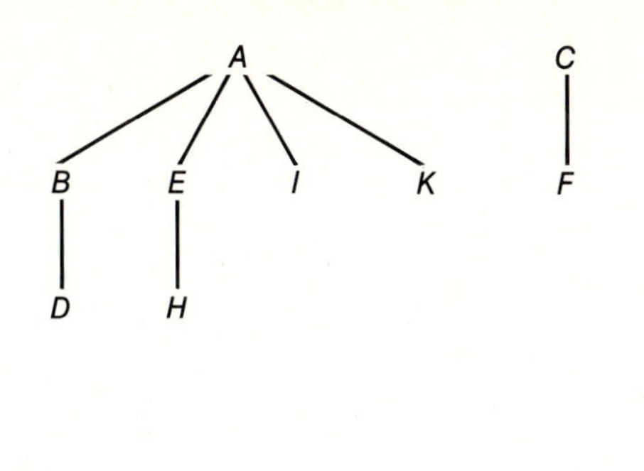

Figure 6.7 Binary Tree – Ordered Forest Correspondence

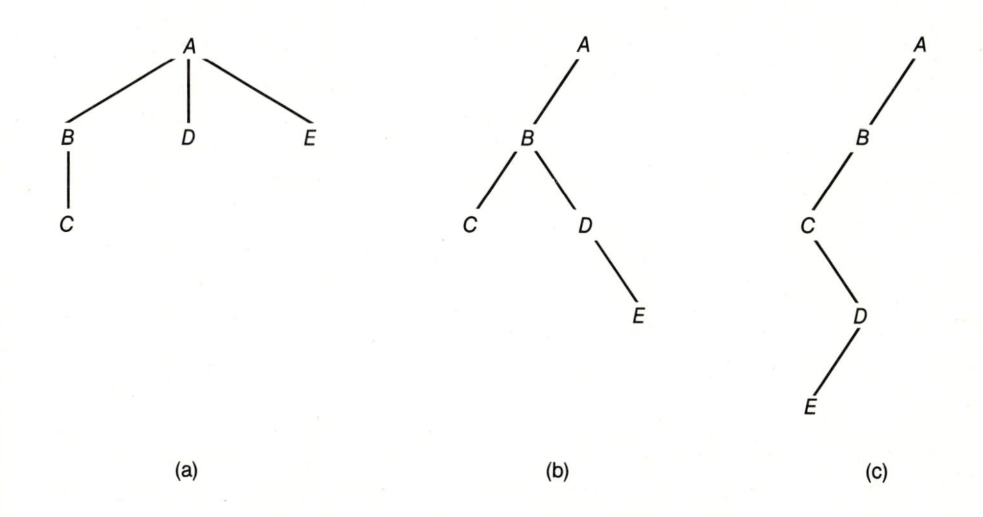

Figure 6.8 Ordered Tree or Binary Tree?

6.3 TREE OPERATIONS – TRAVERSAL SEQUENCES

Recall that the primitive operations for "crawling" through a list are *next*(*r*) and *previous*(*r*). It is apparent that for a tree the analogous operations are *oldest_child*(*s*), *next_sibling*(*s*), and *parent*(*s*). Using these as a basis, the following common operations are useful things that we can do with trees:

traverse(*r*)	– to systematically "visit" each node of the tree rooted at *r* in some order, being certain to include each node in the tour once and only once;
search(*r*)	– to examine some or all of the nodes of a tree rooted at *r* until some result is obtained, such as a maximum or minimum value;
look-up(*r*,*key*,*p*)	– to determine whether the data *key* is located in the tree rooted at *r*, and to return a reference *p* to its location if it is;
insert(*r*,*key*)	– to insert a node containing *key* at some appropriate location in the tree rooted at *r*;
delete(*r*,*p*)	– to delete the node referenced by *p* from the tree rooted at *r*;
split(*r*,*key*)	– to split the tree rooted at *r* into subtrees, with the form of the split dependent upon the location of *key* in the tree.

This list is not a complete one; also, it lacks precision, which cannot be fully supplied until we specify which of many kinds of trees we intend to employ.

Our initial objective is to master that operation upon which all the others depend, that of traversal. We will first concentrate upon traversal of binary trees, and then indicate the analogous process for ordered trees. Imagine that we have a compulsive squirrel who must visit each node of a binary tree once and only once, in order to gather every available nut with no wasted motion. Obviously, he can arrange to visit terminal nodes just once, but he must pass through non-terminal nodes three times: coming into the left branch, going from the left branch to the right branch, and leaving the right branch. But at only one of these transits does he really "visit," or do the meaningful task associated with being at the node.

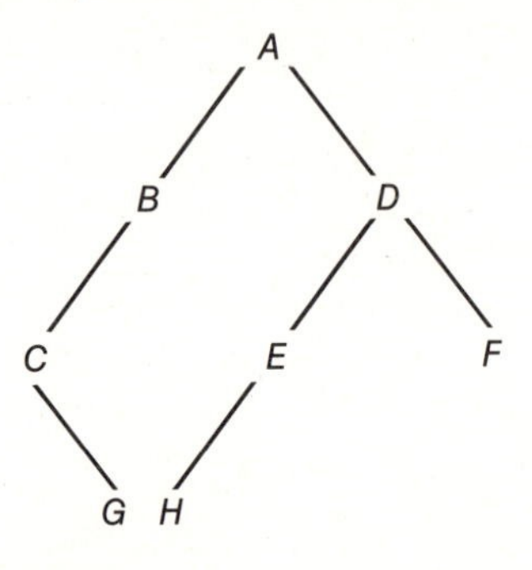

Figure 6.9 Tree Traversal

If we stipulate that the left branch should always be visited before the right branch, then the three cases just cited lead to three sequencing schemes for traversing a tree, as illustrated by reference to Figure 6.9:

- *preorder traversal*: At a given node, visit the Node itself, then the Left branch, then the Right branch (*NLR*) – *A B C G D E H F*.
- *inorder traversal*: At a given node, visit the Left branch, then the Node itself, then the Right branch (*LNR*) – *C G B A H E D F*.

- *postorder traversal*: At a given node, visit the Left branch, then the Right branch, then the Node itself (*LRN*) – *G C B H E F D A*.

Note that the leaves occur in their left-to-right order in all three sequences.

Since the tree structure is recursive, we can transliterate these three schemes into recursive procedures. In order to do this we first define a tree node as

```
type    link = ↑node;
        node = record
          data: {depends upon the application}
          left,rite: link;
        end;
```

The corresponding procedures are then PREORDER_R, INORDER_R, and POSTORDER_R (Algorithms 6.1). The lines "//...//" are used to indicate that, in practice, code would need to be inserted to accomplish the purpose of the traversal.

```
procedure PREORDER_R (ptr: link);
begin
  // visit the node ptr↑ //
  if ptr↑.left <> nil then
    PREORDER_R (ptr↑.left);
  if ptr↑.rite <> nil then
    PREORDER_R (ptr↑.rite);
end;

procedure INORDER_R (ptr: link);
begin
  if ptr↑.left <> nil then
    INORDER_R (ptr↑.left);
  // visit the node ptr↑ //
  if ptr↑.rite <> nil then
    INORDER_R (ptr↑.rite);
end;

procedure POSTORDER_R (ptr: link);
begin
  if ptr↑.left <> nil then
    POSTORDER_R (ptr↑.left);
  if ptr↑.rite <> nil then
    POSTORDER_R (ptr↑.rite);
  // visit the node ptr↑ //
end;
```

Algorithms 6.1 PREORDER_R, INORDER_R, POSTORDER_R

Preorder traversal corresponds to the sequential listing of a table of contents. It also corresponds to the notion of dynastic succession, whereby when a nobleman (at a node) dies, the title passes to his eldest son, and then to his eldest son, etc. – with younger children being considered only if there are no progeny along the line of eldest succession.

Inorder traversal corresponds to the way in which people construct algebraic expressions. Thus, in Figure 6.10, each operator at a non-terminal node is scanned between its left operand and its right operand, where an operand can itself be an expression subject to the same manner of scanning.

Postorder traversal corresponds to the way in which we recursively decompose tasks into subtasks. When, for instance, we are assembling some object and each of its components must also be assembled, we cannot put the object together until we have finished putting together all of the individual components.

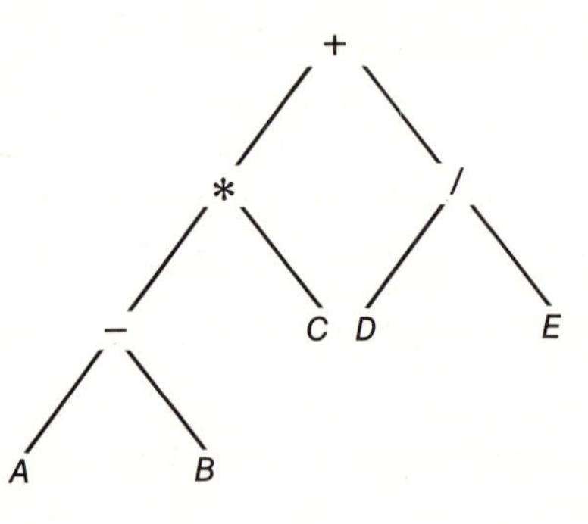

Figure 6.10 Algebraic Expressions via Inorder Traversal

Traversal of a tree is a way of imposing a linear structure upon something that is inherently non-linear. This notion of forced linearization occurs in other contexts too. For instance, the activity of thought would seem to depend a great deal upon extensive logical connectivity among ideas. However, when we need to communicate our ideas, the sequential nature of language forces us to impose a linear ordering on these elements. English, being highly uninflected, relies upon close adherence to the ordering: <subject phrase> <verb phrase> <object phrase>, which can be regarded as an inorder traversal of a tree with <verb phrase> at the root. It is interesting to note that other languages allow both preorder and postorder traversals of the same tree. Thus, in German we can have:

preorder	Gestern kletterte ich auf den Baum.
inorder	Ich kletterte gestern auf den Baum.
postorder	(Er weiss dass) ich gestern auf den Baum kletterte.

Traversal, by linearizing a tree, loses information. Section 6.7 addresses the question of how the information present in the original branching structure might be recovered.

6.4 EFFICIENT TRAVERSAL SCHEMES

For a variety of reasons having to do with efficiency, the preceding algorithms for traversing a binary tree are not likely to be used in practice. Recall from Section 5.2.3.1 that procedure calls require a variety of bookkeeping activities to take place. The calling environment must be saved on a stack and the called environment must be initialized; the converse must take place on procedure return. The amount that must be saved and restored can be large if the procedures involved are recursive. Because of this, several alternative methods have been developed for traversing binary trees; we will describe them in varying detail in this section. At the outset, note that all of these methods go down each tree branch just once, and visit each node just once, so that they are all $O(n)$ in time, for a tree with n nodes.

One consideration for choosing one method over another is of course the relative sizes of their constant factors; we have already commented that this factor tends to be large for the recursive solution. Another motif is to find the minimum amount of working storage that is required. The traversal methods of the first two ensuing sections – using a stack and using threads – are practical in orientation; on the other hand, those of Section 6.4.3 – using tree transformations – have a more theoretical flavor.

Whereas the three recursive traversal procedures (Algorithms 6.1) are symmetrical, the corresponding non-recursive procedures are not. In all of these alternative traversal schemes, we will restrict our attention to the case of inorder traversal, since it is almost always more complicated than preorder traversal, but less complicated than postorder traversal. The extensions of the ensuing methods to the other two traversal schemes are left as exercises.

Before we consider these methods, however, let us recall the ordered trees with which we started. What relationship, if any, do these three orders for traversing a binary tree have to do with the orders in which we might traverse an arbitrary tree? There is a very simple relationship, as follows:

1. There is a preorder traversal, defined by recursively visiting first the node and then all the children from eldest to youngest. Moreover, preorder traversal of a tree and preorder traversal of the corresponding binary tree access the nodes in identical sequence.
2. There is no inorder traversal for trees, since there is generally no definite middle position between a left and right branch.
3. There is a postorder traversal, defined by recursively visiting first all the children from eldest to youngest and lastly the node itself. Moreover, postorder traversal of a tree and inorder traversal of the corresponding binary tree access the nodes in identical sequence.

6.4.1 Traversal via a Stack

The most straightforward response to the inefficiency associated with recursive traversal is to transform the algorithm so that it uses an explicit stack. As the resulting iterative procedure traverses downward in the tree, it can record the location that it came from in the stack, and this information can be used subsequently to climb back up. Since the recursive algorithm for inorder traversal calls itself twice, it would appear that we would need to push items onto the stack at two points in the iterative algorithm. However, note that INORDER_R (Algorithm 6.1) is an instance of the recursive schema of Figure 5.17, with $U(x)$ void. As discussed in Section 5.4.2, the resulting tail-recursion can be eliminated, and information for just one of the calls in INORDER_R need be pushed on the stack. A "finished" and efficient algorithm is the procedure INORDER_S (Algorithm 6.2). It employs the same type definition for a node as previously, and it takes as parameter a pointer to the root of the tree.

```
procedure INORDER_S (ptr: link);

var     top: 0 .. smax;
        stk: array [1 .. smax] of link;

begin
   top := 0;
   while ptr <> nil do begin        {go to extreme left}
      top := top + 1;
      stk [top] := ptr;
      ptr := ptr↑.left;
   end;
   while top > 0 do begin
      ptr := stk [top];
      top := top - 1;
      // visit the node ptr↑ //
      if ptr↑.rite <> nil then begin
         ptr := ptr↑.rite;
         while ptr <> nil do begin     {go to extreme left}
            top := top + 1;
            stk [top] := ptr;
            ptr := ptr↑.left;
         end;
      end;
   end;
end;
```

Algorithm 6.2 INORDER_S

This is a fundamental scheme for traversing trees, and you should trace its operation on, for example, the tree of Figure 6.9. The essential feature of INORDER_S is that pointers are pushed onto the stack far enough ahead so that when a pointer p is popped off the stack, its left subtree has already been processed;

thus, we can immediately process p and then go to its right subtree. For a discussion of the systematic transformation of INORDER_R to INORDER_S, consult Horowitz and Sahni [1976] and Knuth [1974]. Note that whereas we used calls to PUSH and POP in transforming the Fibonacci examples of Algorithms 5.7, we expose the stack as part of the process in INORDER_S. Since the trade-off is between two lines of code and one procedure call, this is a realistic approach that one would often choose to use. In subsequent algorithms, we will have frequent instances of both of these approaches.

Two key issues arise in attempting to improve upon INORDER_S. One, of course, is that we would like to further reduce the constant factor associated with the $O(n)$ complexity. More significantly, in the worst case, the stack may need to be as large as the tree, or $O(n)$. So an important concern is to find a technique for traversing a tree such that the requirements for working storage are bounded and minimal. The methods to be described in the following sections place different emphases upon these issues.

6.4.2 Traversal via Threads

A binary tree of n nodes has $2n$ link fields, but each node except the root is pointed to exactly once. This means that there are $(n - 1)$ non-**nil** pointers, leaving $(n + 1)$ **nil** pointers in the binary tree representation. This is rather wasteful, and so it was proposed that the unused pointer fields should be used to assist in the traversal by storing appropriate pointer values in them [Perlis and Thornton 1960]. What are the appropriate values? That depends upon the desired order of traversal. We confront here the tension between two notions, alluded to in Section 6.3. On the one hand we want to retain information in a tree structure; on the other hand, we must process that information in some linear sequence.

If there is a preferred sequence in an application, then we can use the otherwise empty link fields in the binary tree to store *threads* to point to predecessors and successors in that sequence; this can enable us to do away with a stack entirely. However, since a given link field may contain either a child pointer or a thread pointer, it becomes necessary to associate boolean tag fields with the two link fields, to enable the correct interpretation. In Figure 6.11, (a) shows a binary tree with unused link fields, and (b) shows the same tree with tags and threads suitable for inorder traversal. In (b), child pointers are shown as solid lines with tag values of zero; predecessor threads are shown as dashed lines with left tag values of one; and successor threads are shown as dashed lines with right tag values of one. Note that node D has no predecessor and node K has no successor; the corresponding fields might contain **nil**'s. Alternatively, a threaded tree is often implemented with a header node, and in that case these fields in D and K would point to the header.

An algorithm for inorder traversal of a threaded binary tree is the procedure INORDER_T (Algorithm 6.3). In lieu of a stack of pointers, a single pointer variable is all that is required for remembering enough information to perform the traversal. This version of the algorithm does not assume the existence of a header

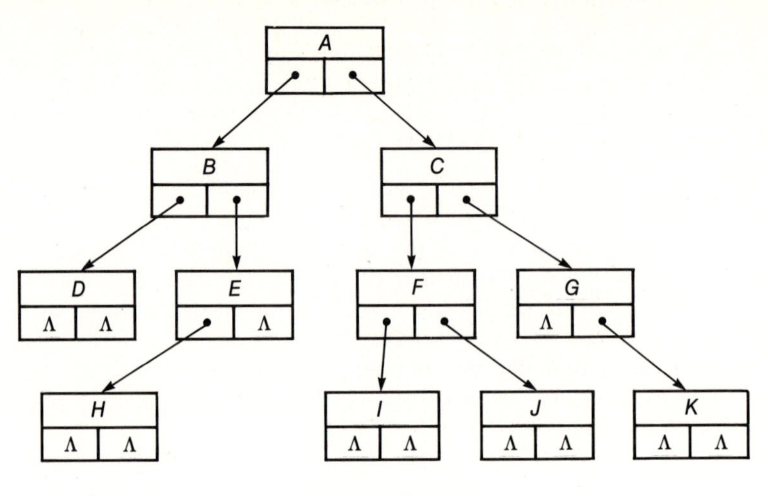

(a) Without Threads

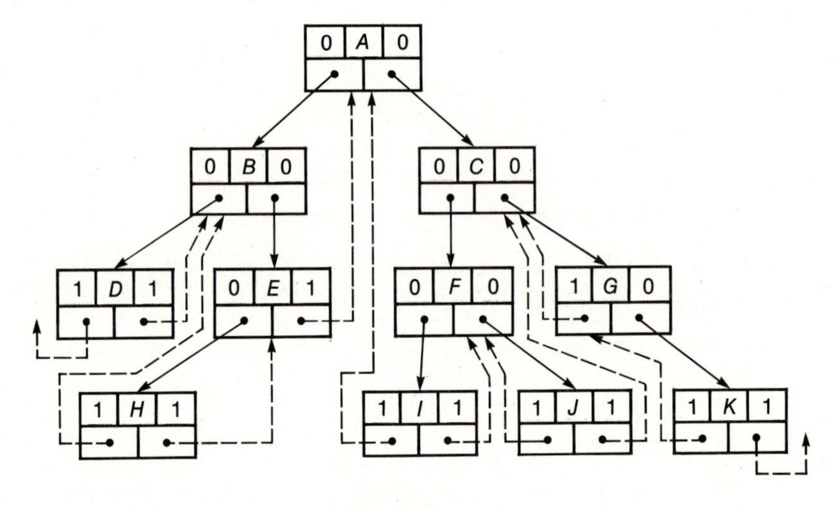

(b) With Threads

Figure 6.11 Threads for Inorder Traversal

node; that is, the left pointer field of node D and the right pointer field of node K are assumed to contain **nil**.

There are other possibilities for using threads to assist in traversal. For instance, the threads to the predecessor nodes are commonly less useful, and so may be omitted, yielding a right-threaded binary tree. Similarly, one can have a left-threaded binary tree, with threads to predecessors but not to successors. In any

```
procedure INORDER_T (ptr: link);

type    link = ↑node;
        node = record
           data: {depends upon the application}
           ltag: boolean;
           left: link;
           rtag: boolean;
           rite: link;
        end;

var     tptr: link;

begin
   while not ptr↑.ltag do
      ptr := ptr↑.left;
   while ptr <> nil do begin
      // visit the node ptr↑ //
      tptr := ptr;
      ptr := ptr↑.rite;
      if not tptr↑.rtag then
         while not ptr↑.ltag do
            ptr := ptr↑.left;
   end;
end;
```

Algorithm 6.3 INORDER_T

event, with threads, we can traverse a tree with reductions in both time and space over that required to stack traversal. Threads do require memory for the tag fields. Depending upon the data stored at a node and whether the algorithm is coded in an HLL or in assembler language, it may be trivial to find space for the tags, or it may increase memory requirements inordinately.

Note that threads do not make life simpler in all cases. For instance, consider the binary tree of Figure 6.12, which is threaded for postorder traversal, and observe the complexity of finding the successor to node *B*. More generally, if a tree is threaded for postorder traversal, it is awkward to discern the successor of a node with a right child without traversing the tree from the root; likewise, if a tree is threaded for preorder traversal, it is awkward to discern the predecessor of a node with a left child without traversing the tree from the root. However, if a tree is threaded for inorder traversal, one can easily discern both the predecessor and the successor of any node in all cases. The predecessor (successor) is either pointed to directly by the left (right) link, or else it can be found by following the left (right) child link. You should satisfy yourself that this is so by studying Figure 6.11. Inorder threading has still another virtue; it can be used to expedite preorder traversal as well as inorder traversal (see Exercise 6.9).

Given their orientation toward preferred traversal sequences, threads provide a mechanism that is both simple and fast for finding a desired node in a tree. On the

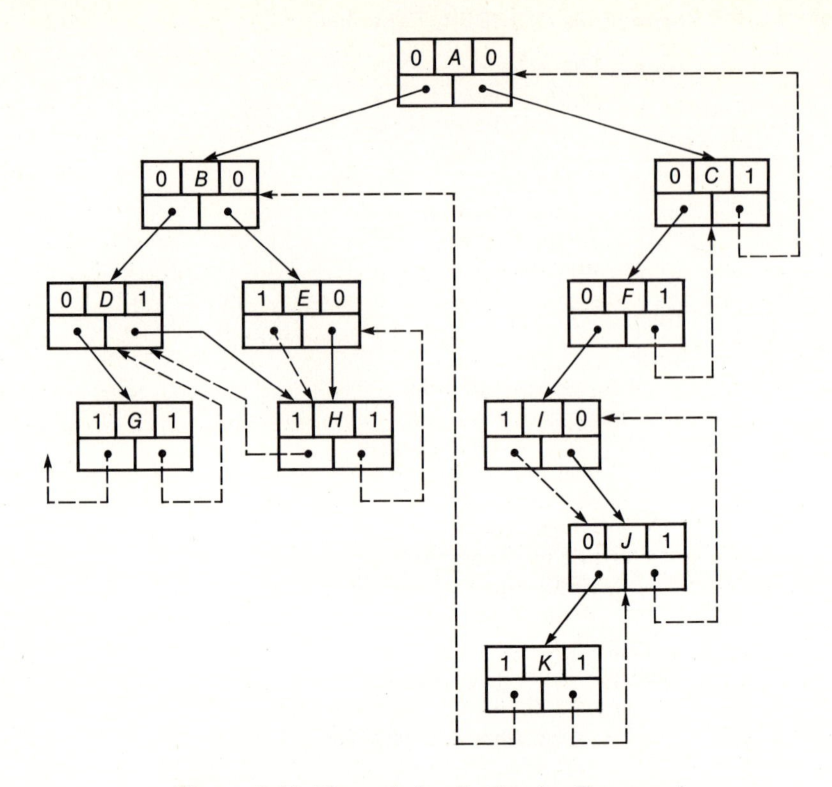

Figure 6.12 Threads for Postorder Traversal

other hand, if the operations of inserting or deleting nodes in a tree occur relatively frequently, then the additional overhead of updating the threads will be counterproductive. Perhaps even more important is the issue of *incremental traversal*, which is the capability of finding the successor of an arbitrary node without starting the search from the root every time, as alluded to in the preceding paragraphs. Except for the case of postorder traversal, threads provide this capability easily, whereas stack-based techniques do not. A thorough analysis of the relative efficiency of using stacks and threads can be found in Brinck and Foo [1981].

†6.4.3 Traversal via Tree Transformations

Traversing a tree via threads substitutes the requirement of two additional bits at each tree node for the requirement of an arbitrarily large working stack. Is is possible to reduce this requirement to just one additional bit, or no additional bits, and yet not need a stack? A moment's reflection upon the technique of MARK_LIST (Algorithm 4.7) suggests that the answer is yes. If we can traverse a possibly recursive List with minimal additional storage, we can certainly traverse a binary tree, or pure List, with minimal additional storage. However, there is an important difference between the situation in Section 4.4.3.1 and the situation here. In the former case, we were able to use the *isatom* bit to discriminate between ascents from the left and the right, without introducing an explicit additional tag bit. Here, the data structure is different. We can essentially use MARK_LIST, but must introduce an additional bit in each tree node. (It is possible to do even better and get by with a working bit stack; the size of this stack would need to be equal to the height of the tree being traversed.)

Are there any alternative approaches, such that *no* tag bits are needed, either in the tree nodes or in a working stack? There are several, and most of them employ the techniques of link inversion and pointer rotation discussed in Section 4.4.3.1. Lindstrom [1973] discusses several procedures for this type of traversal. A particularly simple case is that where the tree is strictly binary and the objective is to visit each node at least once, but it doesn't matter if some nodes are visited more than once. This is actually the case, for example, in some methods for doing garbage collection during memory management (see Section 11.2.1.1).

```
procedure LINDSTROM (ptr: link);
var     pres,prev: link;
begin
   pres := ptr;  prev := nil;
   while pres <> nil do begin
      if ATOM (pres) then begin
         // visit the node pres↑ //
         ROTATE_2 (pres,prev);
      end;
      // visit the node pres↑ //
      ROTATE_4 (pres↑.left,pres↑.rite,prev,pres);
   end;
end;
```

Algorithm 6.4 LINDSTROM

The procedure LINDSTROM (Algorithm 6.4) proceeds via two simple rules, which may best be understood by translating the strictly binary tree in Figure 6.13(a) to the maze in Figure 6.13(b). A guaranteed way to get out of the maze is to proceed with our right hand always in contact with the wall. This corresponds to turning right at intersections and turning around at dead ends. In LINDSTROM, it corresponds to:

(a) cyclically permuting pointer values at each non-terminal node, and

(b) swapping two pointer values at each terminal node.

The operations of permuting and swapping are expressed with pointer rotations (see Section 4.4.3.1). The algorithm is written with the assumption that non-terminal and terminal nodes have different structures (since the latter have no need for link fields), and that this difference can be detected with the functional test ATOM (*ptr*). If this is not true, then terminal nodes can be identified as those having two **nil**

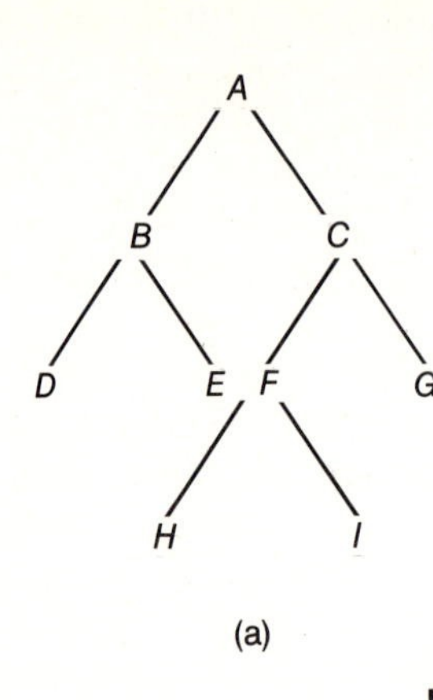

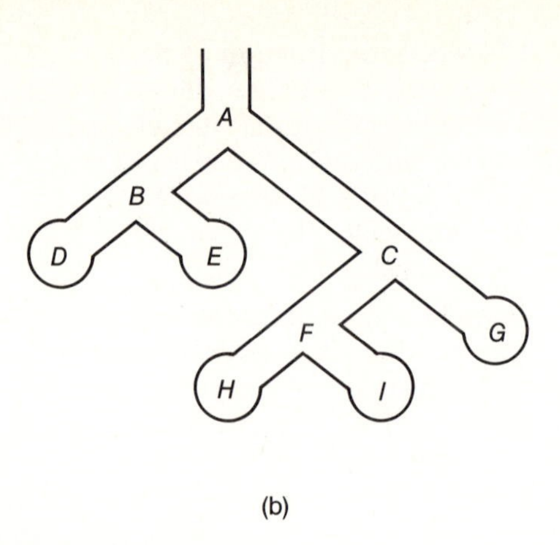

Figure 6.13 Lindstrom Traversal

pointers. Using these rules, the algorithm LINDSTROM actually visits each terminal node once and visits each non-terminal node three times.

There are a variety of other link inversion traversal schemes [§]; we will describe one very briefly and then another in more detail. The first one employs link inversions in the usual manner and also uses the empty pointer fields of the leaf nodes to maintain a stack [Robson 1973]. This stack contains just those nodes possessing a non-**nil** left subtree that has been visited and a non-**nil** right subtree currently being visited. (The traversal of the left subtree will always find leaf nodes that are available for the stack before they are actually needed.) On ascent, if the parent node has either a **nil** left or a **nil** right pointer, there is no ambiguity. If both pointers in the parent are non-**nil**, then a comparison of the parent pointer with the value at the top of the stack resolves the ambiguity.

In answer to the question at the beginning of this section concerning the minimum necessary amount of working storage for tree traversal, Morris [1979] found a fairly simple and extremely elegant solution requiring just two temporary registers and no tags. Suppose that we wish to do an inorder traversal of a tree rooted at *pres*↑, as shown in Figure 6.14(a). Here, the circles P_i correspond to individual nodes, and the triangles ST_j correspond to subtrees (possibly empty). If the tree were such that *pres*↑.*left* = **nil**, then (A) we could simply visit the node *pres*↑ and apply the process to the subtree *pres*↑.*rite*. But what if, as in the figure, *pres*↑.*left* ≠ **nil**? In that case, (B) we seek to transform the original tree T_0 to another form T_1 such that:

1. The number of left edges in T_1 is less than in T_0.
2. The inorder traversal of T_1 is the same as that of T_0.
3. The transformation is reversible.

If we can find such a transformation, then we can apply it until we have situation (A), and the problem is solved. In fact, we can obtain T_1 by finding the rightmost edge of T_0 – that is, by following right edges in the subtree *pres*↑.*left* – and then adding the wiggly edge from p_r to *pres* in Figure 6.14(b) and deleting the edge *pres*↑.*left*. T_1 has the same inorder traversal sequence as T_0 and also has one less left edge (and one more right edge) than T_0. Finally, in order to obtain reversi-

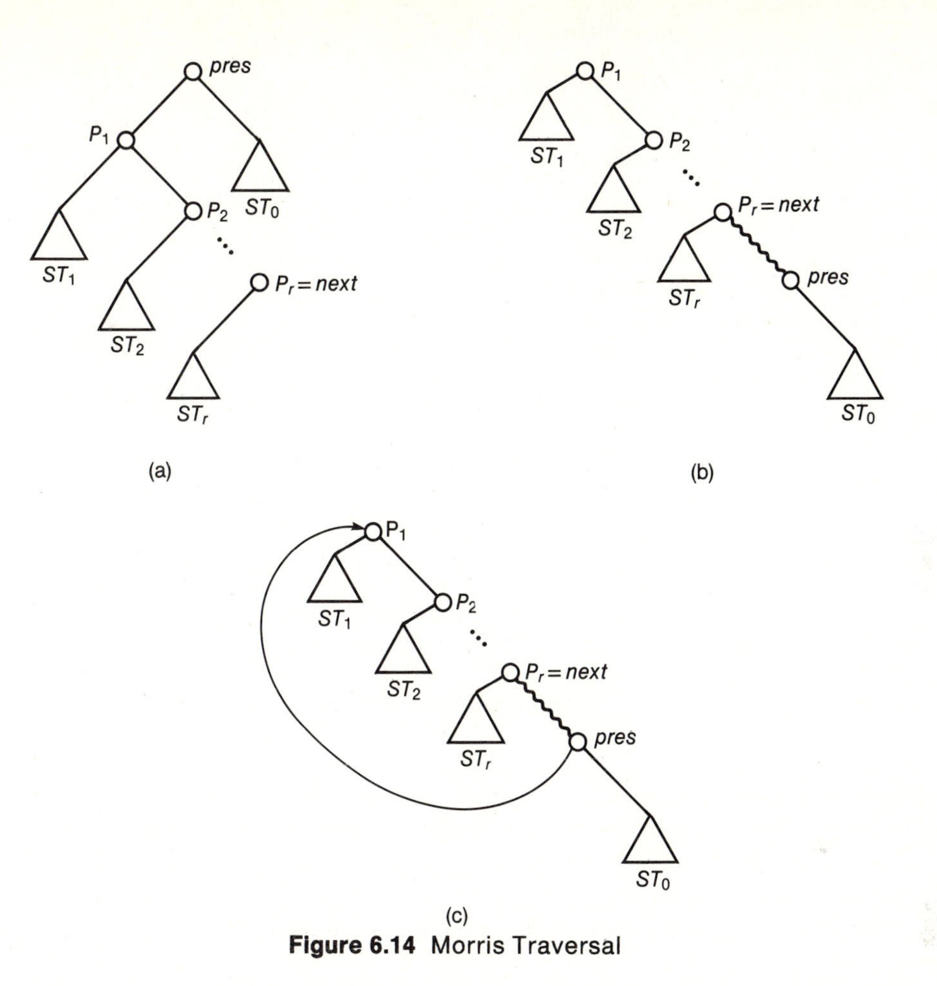

Figure 6.14 Morris Traversal

bility (without a stack), we do not actually delete *pres*↑.*left*; rather, we transform T_0 to T_2, as shown in Figure 6.14(c). This introduces a cycle, so that T_2 is not really a tree. However, we can use the predicate

pres↑ is right-reachable from *pres*↑.*left*

as a boolean signal to treat *pres*↑.*left* as though it were **nil**! This logic is embodied in the procedure MORRIS (Algorithm 6.5). Note therein that when a node is visited, we reverse the transformation simply by erasing *next*↑.*rite*. Variations on this technique suitable for preorder and postorder traversal are left as exercises.

As you can see, with all of these methods, a given link field may point, at various instants, to a child or to a parent or even to a "cousin." This means that the original structure of the tree is lost until the algorithm has terminated and restored all links to their original values. Accordingly, traversal via tree transformations precludes reentrant traversal by more than one user at the same time. In addition, these techniques do not afford incremental traversal. Finally, most such methods

```
procedure MORRIS (ptr: link);

var     next,pres: link;

begin
   pres := ptr;
   while pres <> nil do
      if pres↑.left = nil then begin
         // visit the node pres↑ //
         pres := pres↑.rite;
      end else begin
         next := pres↑.left;
         while (next↑.rite <> nil) and (next↑.rite <> pres) do
            next := next↑.rite;            {find "rightmost" node of tree}
         if next↑.rite = nil then begin       {mark unmarked node}
            next↑.rite := pres;
            pres := pres↑.left;
         end else begin                       {unmark marked node}
            // visit the node pres↑ //
            next↑.rite := nil;
            pres := pres↑.rite;
         end;
      end;
end;
```

Algorithm 6.5 MORRIS

are rather complicated, with high constant factors. Morris's algorithm is noteworthy for its simple elegance, and is comparable in speed to traversal with a stack.

In conclusion, we mention another traversal scheme that operates by a different principle. In Section 4.1.4 we discussed the use of the operators XOR or MOD to combine two pointers in one physical location. If we have a tree whose structure will not vary, then we can map it into read-only storage, and use this same technique to compute the addresses for the traversal. In addition to the two pre-computed link values, each node requires a single, constant bit value that indicates whether that node is a left or a right child of its parent. Further details can be found in Siklóssy [1972].

6.5 OTHER TREE REPRESENTATIONS

The entire preceding discussion has been based upon the premise that trees are to be represented as binary trees with two distinguished pointers, left and right. In practice, although this is very common, there are many other ways in which tree structures are represented in machine computation. We will briefly indicate some of these ways and also cite instances where they are used in subsequent sections.

6.5.1 Other Linked Representations

A little reflection suggests that the complication in tree traversal algorithms is due to the fact that it is easier to "climb down" than it is to "climb up." If space for pointers is not too tight, then the simplest solution is just to add to each node a third pointer, to the parent of that node (see also Exercise 6.15). In this case, a binary tree might appear as in Figure 6.15(a). This representation also yields the capability for incremental traversal. As we have seen, threads make it easy to find the preorder or inorder successor of an arbitrary node, but are not very helpful for the postorder case. Triply-linked binary trees provide a mechanism that does not have a preferred traversal sequence and that works for all three orderings [Fenner and Loizou 1981].

As we will see, there are many applications of binary trees in which the distinguished links, left and right, have interpretations that are different from those originally introduced, eldest child and next sibling. But if we are using a binary tree to represent an ordered tree, note the asymmetry: It is easy to find younger siblings of a node, but not easy to find older siblings of a node. A representation that solves this problem is illustrated in Figure 6.15(b) – (d). The tree in (b) of the figure has been converted to a binary tree in (c), with the siblings arranged in a circular list. In addition, if we apply the same idea to the left links that we applied in (c) to the right links, we obtain Figure 6.15(d). In this *ring* structure, there are circular lists both for the relationships "next younger sibling" and "eldest child."

In the representations shown in Figure 6.15, the effect has been that of replacing sequential lists with the bi-directional lists and circular lists. The figure illustrates three such possibilities; there are several others. The choice among such representations would depend upon the relative importance of the operations of insertion, deletion, traversal, backing-up, etc. As a final observation about linked representations, consider the following. All of our schemes have employed at least two link fields. Is it possible to represent a tree with just one link field? Yes, if we are dealing with an oriented tree rather than an ordered tree! In such a case, we can redraw the tree of Figure 6.15(a) as Figure 6.16, employing with each node a single pointer to its father. Such a representation is the basis of an important application in Section 6.6.5.

†6.5.2 Sequential Storage Schemes

If we are dealing with a tree structure that is fairly static, it may be worthwhile to dispense with pointer fields altogether. Rather, the nodes can be retained in a vector, and additional information that encodes the tree structure can be retained in parallel vectors. How much additional information is required? In Figure 6.17, comparison of (a) and (b) suggests that two bits will suffice, as they are just enough to allow for the association of two binary markers, analogous to left and right parentheses, with each node. Figure 6.17(c) illustrates such a scheme, called *marked preorder sequential* representation, wherein the markers for a node indicate whether it has (i) younger siblings and (ii) any children. Note that although the nodes are

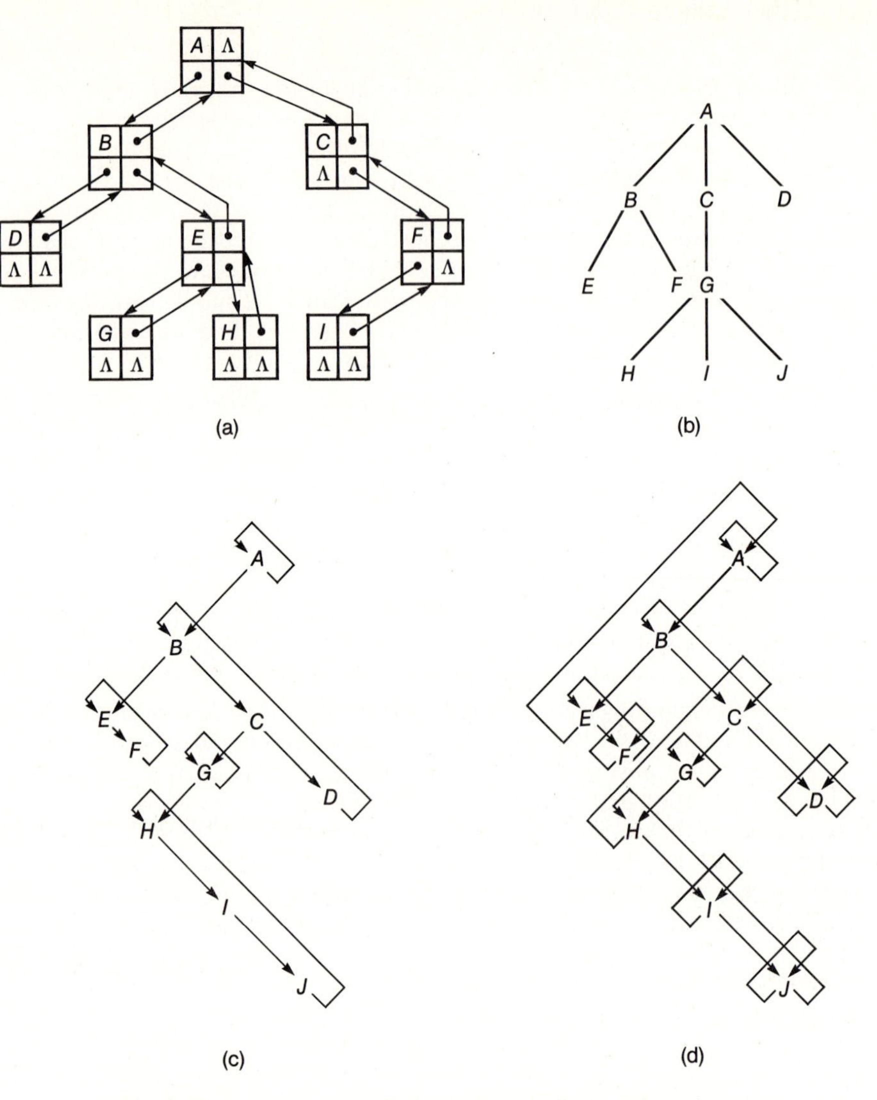

Figure 6.15 Alternative Pointer-Based Representations

fixed in preorder sequence, the two bits of information with each node are sufficient to allow construction of the underlying tree (see Exercises 6.16 and 6.17).

Another possibility is to associate with each node a single number that specifies the structure relative to that node. Such a number might be the degree of the node, as in Figure 6.17(d); this is referred to as *preorder sequential with degrees*. Alternatively, recalling the definition of the weight of a node and retaining that number with each node, we obtain Figure 6.17(e); this is referred to as *preorder sequential with weights*. Preorder sequential with degrees allows a subtree to be modified without having to alter parent nodes of the subtree, but it requires some computation to

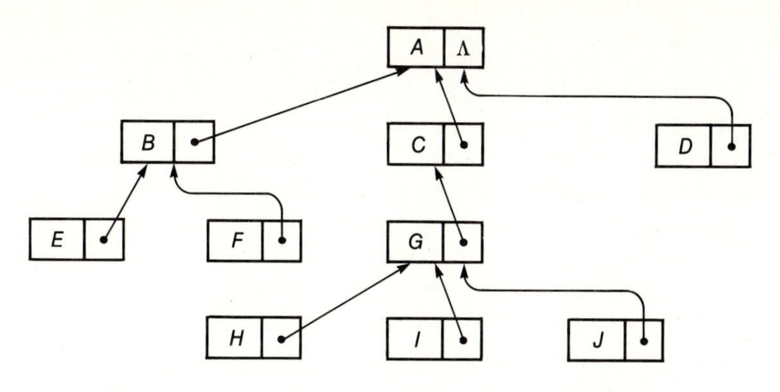

Figure 6.16 Trees with a Single Pointer per Node

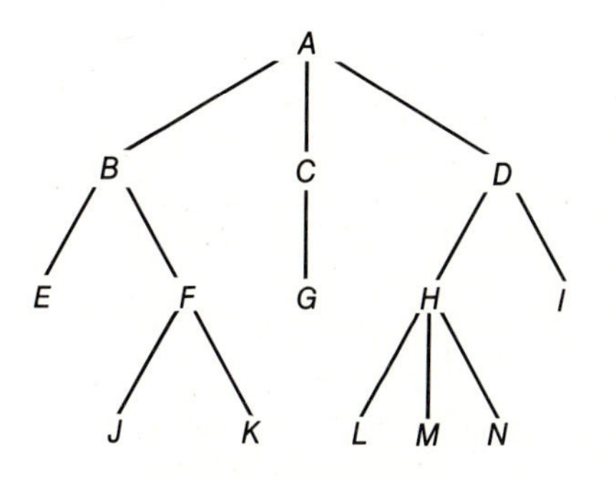

(a) An Ordered Tree

A(*B*(*EF*(*JK*))*C*(*G*)*D*(*H*(*LMN*)*I*))

(b) Corresponding List

Node	*A*	*B*	*E*	*F*	*J*	*K*	*C*	*G*	*D*	*H*	*L*	*M*	*N*	*I*
Sibling	0	1	1	0	1	0	1	0	0	1	1	1	0	0
Child	1	1	0	1	0	0	1	0	1	1	0	0	0	0

(c) Marked Preorder Sequential Representation

Node	*A*	*B*	*E*	*F*	*J*	*K*	*C*	*G*	*D*	*H*	*L*	*M*	*N*	*I*
Degree	3	2	0	2	0	0	1	0	2	3	0	0	0	0

(d) Preorder Sequential with Degrees

Node	*A*	*B*	*E*	*F*	*J*	*K*	*C*	*G*	*D*	*H*	*L*	*M*	*N*	*I*
Weight	13	4	0	2	0	0	1	0	5	3	0	0	0	0

(e) Preorder Sequential with Weights

Figure 6.17 Sequential Representations for Trees

determine the extent of the subtree from the degree information. On the other hand, preorder sequential with weights makes it trivial to determine the extent of a subtree, but modification of a subtree makes it necessary to update the weights of all its parent nodes. (These concepts are reminiscent of the discussion of encoding of variable length records in Section 3.3.) The preceding schemes apply to preorder enumeration of the nodes of a tree; it is straightforward to devise analogous sequential representations for postorder enumeration of nodes.

Just as oriented trees have a simple linked representation, as we saw in the preceding section, they also have a simple sequential representation. One simply need represent their fathers via a vector of pointers or cursors.

6.5.3 Complete *t*-ary Trees

The rest of the chapter following this section is concerned with two issues – the use of trees in a variety of applications, and means of obtaining efficient tree manipulation algorithms. With regard to efficiency, a very effective strategy is to restrict the variability in the tree structure, using a variety of means. Much of Chapter 10 will be concerned with several such strategies. One such restriction is so fundamental, however, that we introduce it here. With this technique it is possible to represent trees in sequential storage much more simply than in the preceding section.

A *complete t-ary tree* is one with the following structure:

1. All non-terminal nodes have degree t, except possibly the last one.
2. All leaves are on at most two levels, k and $k-1$.
3. Leaves at level k are to the left of leaves at level $k-1$.

Thus, in Figure 6.18, (a) is a complete ternary tree and (b) is a complete binary tree. Complete t-ary trees admit to a particularly simple sequential storage scheme, as may be seen in the figure, where the information depicted at each node is the relative storage address of the node. In any complete t-ary tree, the number of nodes at successive levels is $1, t, t^2, t^3, \ldots$. It is straightforward to compute the location of the parent, the children, and the siblings of a given node at location j, as demonstrated by the following equations:

parent of j	$\lfloor(t+j-2) \div t$		
ith child of j	$t \times (j-1) + i + 1$	(for $1 \leq i \leq t$)	(6.1)
left sibling of j	$j-1$	(only if $((j-2) \bmod t) \neq 0$)	
right sibling of j	$j+1$	(only if $((j-1) \bmod t) \neq 0$)	

The complete binary tree is a particularly important case. Since each of us has exactly two natural parents, it has obvious practical value for storing a family tree in a compact manner. We will also see its utility in the discussion of priority queues in Section 6.6.4. For a complete binary tree, Eqs. 6.1 reduce to Eqs. 6.2:

parent of j	$\lfloor(j \div 2)$	
left child of j	$2j$	
right child of j	$2j+1$	(6.2)

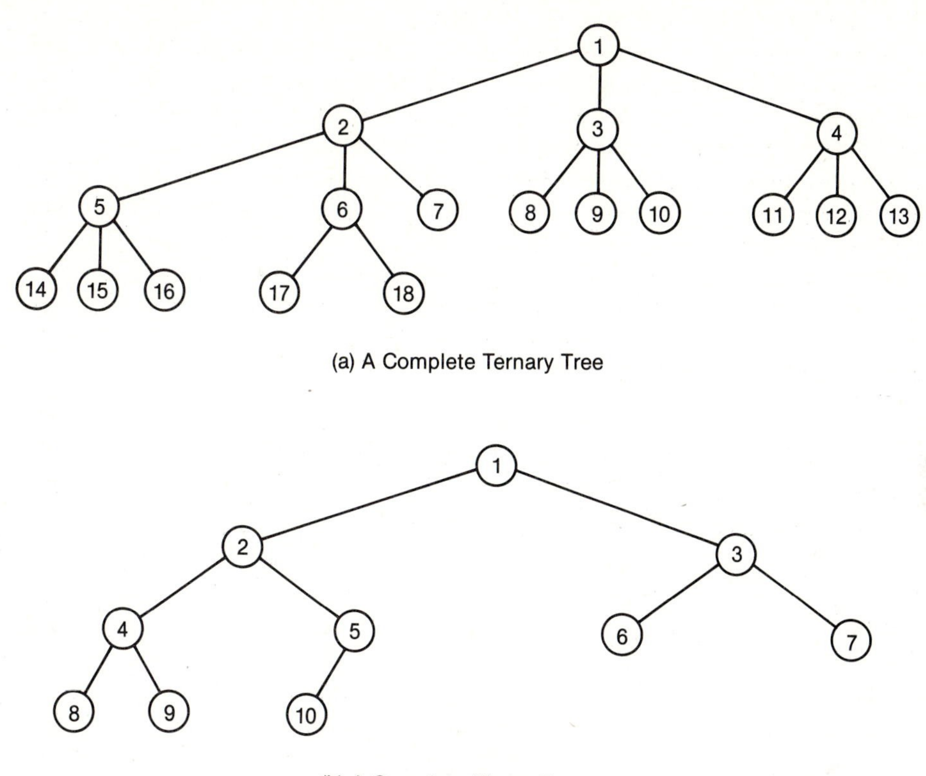

Figure 6.18 Complete *t*-ary Trees

left sibling of j	$j-1$	(only if j is odd)
right sibling of j	$j+1$	(only if j is even)

Complete *t*-ary trees are important for another reason besides their simplicity of representation. The regularity of a complete tree causes it to be a *balanced tree*: It has the minimum height for a tree of that degree with a given number of nodes. At this point, we are satisfied to use the term balance in a general, descriptive manner; for example, in terms of balance, the trees of Figure 6.18 are optimal, the tree of Figure 6.11 is (subjectively) not bad, and the right subtree of Figure 6.12 is quite degenerate. In Chapters 10 and 12 we will see how the concept of balance is made more precise in a variety of manners.

6.6 APPLICATIONS OF TREES

As cited at the beginning of this chapter, tree structures pervade both everyday experience and computing applications. This section expounds on some of these applications. A significant factor is the manner in which meaning is attached to the nodes and to the branches; this varies with the application, as we will see.

First, we look at the use of binary trees for maintaining a sorted list. We will introduce the concept here and explore it in a more quantitative form in Chapter 10. Then we look at expression trees and, more generally, parse trees. When they have been constructed according to a set of grammatical rules, a compiler can use these trees to explicitly analyze and record the component structure of a program. We then return to issues from earlier chapters, first examining the relation between decision tables (Section 2.3.3) and decision trees, then showing how to implement priority queues (Section 5.1.4) via complete binary trees, and finally illustrating the use of oriented trees for solving the equivalence problem (Section 4.2.3). Since we do not call attention to the fact each time, it is well to note at the outset that trees are used in many of these applications as efficient representations for sets. We will see this accomplished in three different manners in Sections 6.6.1, 6.6.4, and 6.6.5.

6.6.1 Binary Search Trees

Imagine the following scenario. We are receiving data $x_1, x_2, x_3, \ldots$ sequentially in time. Our objective is to maintain a list of the x's that is always in order according to the values of the x_i that have arrived. Specifically, suppose that the data consists of the winners of the Academy Award for Best Actress, as given in Figure 6.19, and that we wish to maintain them in alphabetical order.

1961	Loren	1966	Taylor	1970	Jackson
1962	Bancroft	1967	Hepburn	1971	Fonda
1963	Neal	1968	Hepburn	1972	Minnelli
1964	Andrews	1968	Streisand	1973	Jackson
1965	Christie	1969	Smith	1974	Burstyn

Figure 6.19 Academy Awards for Best Actress

One approach would be to use an array $A[1 .. n]$ with constant rearranging, as follows. First we have $A[1] = \text{Loren}$; when Bancroft arrives, we shuffle and get $A[1] = \text{Bancroft}$, $A[2] = \text{Loren}$; $A[3]$ becomes Neal; when Andrews arrives, we shuffle and get $A[1] = \text{Andrews}$, $A[2] = \text{Bancroft}$, $A[3] = \text{Loren}$, $A[4] = \text{Neal}$; and so forth. This process actually corresponds to sorting by insertion, as we will see in Chapter 13. It is not a very good method for a large list, since it requires $O(n)$ comparisons and $O(n)$ rearrangements for each new item. We have already encountered a better solution using a linked list, as exemplified by the function

SEARCH_LIST (Algorithm 4.1) in Section 4.2.1. In that approach, the amount of rearrangement for each new item is $O(1)$, since it requires changing just two links; however, there are still $O(n)$ comparisons for each new item.

```
function BST_INSERT (nptr,rptr: link): link;

{nptr points to node to be inserted, rptr points to root}

type    link = ↑node;
        node = record
           key: {the value to be used for ordering}
           left: link;
           rite: link;
        end;

var     tptr: link;

begin
   if rptr = nil then
      rptr := nptr;
   tptr := rptr;
   while nptr↑.key <> tptr↑.key do
      if nptr↑.key < tptr↑.key then begin  {go left}
         if tptr↑.left <> nil then
            tptr := tptr↑.left
         else begin                  {insert nptr↑ here}
            tptr↑.left := nptr;
            tptr := nptr;
         end;
      end else begin                 {go right}
         if tptr↑.rite <> nil then
            tptr := tptr↑.rite
         else begin                  {insert nptr↑ here}
            tptr↑.rite := nptr;
            tptr := nptr;
         end;
      end;
   BST_INSERT := tptr;
end;
```

Algorithm 6.6 BST_INSERT

Our example is somewhat fanciful. However, problems of this type, with the items arriving considerably faster than once a year – for example, cataloging the identifier symbols in a program during its compilation or assembly – are very common. So it is important to find a solution that overcomes the $O(n)$ complexity. A common, useful method is to build a *binary search tree* (*BST*), with the property that the value of every node is greater than that of its left child and less than that of its right child. The function BST_INSERT (Algorithm 6.6) uses such an interpretation of left and right to insert new nodes into the appropriate place in a constantly growing binary tree. It combines within one function the tree operations of look-up and insertion cited in Section 6.3, but it is specific to BST's. The algorithm reflects the usual assumption that a data item is generally a record containing a key, whose value determines the ordering, and other pertinent information as well. We assume that all this data is already present in the node pointed to by *nptr*, and that the two link fields in that node are both preset to **nil**. The input parameters are *nptr*, pointing at the new node, and *rptr*, pointing at the root of the tree. Upon completion, the function returns a pointer to the location of the node in the BST containing $nptr\uparrow.key$.

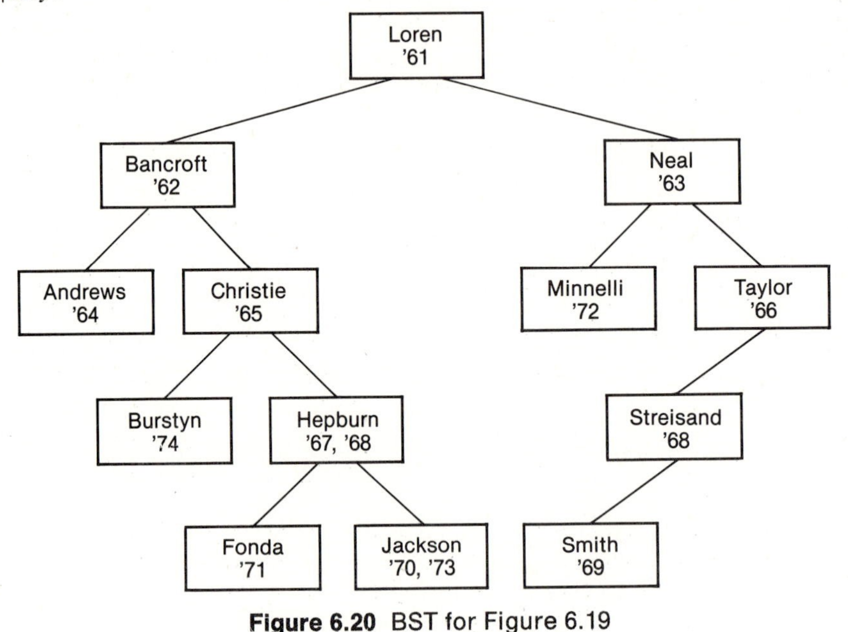

Figure 6.20 BST for Figure 6.19

The algorithm proceeds by forking to the left or right, as determined by the outcomes of comparisons between the key of the new item and keys of nodes in the tree, until either a match or a **nil** pointer is found. In the former case, the key value is already present in the tree; in the latter case, it is not present and so it is inserted. In successive years, using the data from Figure 6.19 with actress name as key, our tree would grow to that shown in Figure 6.20. In the figure we have simply allocated space in each node to record the award years, including repetition. The actual processing requirements in real cases involving repetition would vary with the application.

The binary search tree is a very important data structure. It will occupy much of our attention in Chapter 10, where we will also learn how to delete items from BST's. One of the reasons for its importance is that it allows us to read off the values in order at any time during its construction simply by doing an inorder traversal! Whether a BST efficiently serves its purposes of look-up, insertion, deletion, etc. depends greatly upon its balance (see Section 6.5.3). We will need to learn some additional properties of trees, in Section 10.1.2, before we can characterize the efficiency of BST's for these operations. For now, making the commonly safe assumption that the tree is not badly imbalanced, we can say that the times are proportional to the "average" height of the BST, which is $O(\lg n)$.

6.6.2 Recognizing Grammatical Structure with Trees

In Section 5.2.3 we illustrated the use of stacks both to evaluate a postfix expression and to convert an algebraic infix expression to postfix form. The latter conversion corresponds to a limited form of language translation. The translation process that a compiler must perform is considerably more complicated; it is common for this process to be conducted by:

1. constructing a tree that represents what the program intends, and
2. traversing the tree to cause the proper machine code to be generated.

The compiling process is a large subject in its own right [Aho and Ullman 1977; Gries 1971]. Here, we will simply illustrate here how tree structures are commonly used therein.

6.6.2.1 Expressions. In this instance, the information associated with a node is an operator, and the children of a node are the operands for the operator, with leaves corresponding to input data. If a program contains the expression '(A+B*C)/(D−E)', then the compiler might generate the tree shown in Figure 6.21(a). If we perform a postorder traversal, we obtain 'ABC*+DE−/', which you should recognize as the postfix form of our original expression. If we perform a preorder traversal, we obtain '/+A*BC−DE', which corresponds to the prefix form of the original expression.

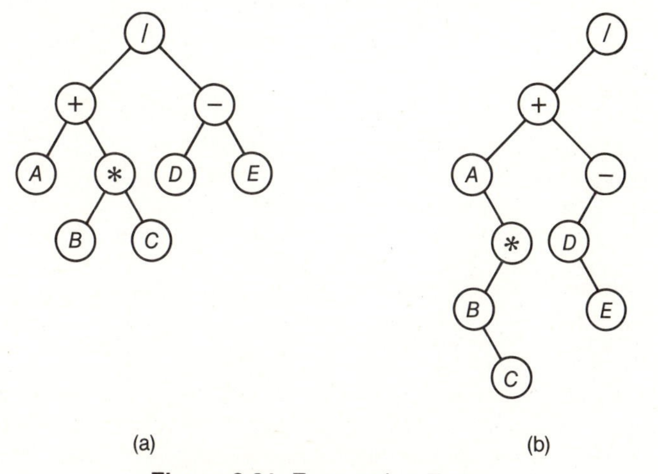

Figure 6.21 Expression Trees

If we perform an inorder traversal, we obtain 'A+B*C/D−E'. This is similar to the original expression but algebraically different, because of the conventional precedence rules. For inorder traversal to work properly, it must parenthesize subtrees before incorporating them at the next level. With this proviso, inorder traversal yields '((A+(B*C))/(D−E))'. Note that we now have superfluous parentheses, some of which can be pruned out. An advantage of both prefix and postfix notations is that parentheses in expressions simply disappear as an issue.

All the discussion of this section has been predicated on the use of binary operators such as +,−,*,/ of ordinary arithmetic. The unary minus sign, as in $-X$, can be treated as $0 - X$. However, this raises the question of what to do with nonbinary operators in general. Such might be the case, for instance, in subscripting an array or with a procedure call, as in the examples:

$$a\,[5, 2 * j, k]\ , \text{ or } \quad \text{SUB1}\ (s, A, y + t, \text{SUB2}\ (nn\ [z]))$$

In such cases, the ordered tree corresponding to the expression might have been converted to a binary tree, as in Section 6.2. In Figure 6.21, if (a) is now regarded as such an ordered tree and converted to the binary tree in (b), recall that the postfix expression is then obtained by an inorder traversal of the binary tree.

Note that during compilation, expressions are being manipulated symbolically; they are not being evaluated. Such manipulation of expressions is not limited to the process of compiling. Expression trees are also used for other symbolic manipulations, such as polynomial arithmetic, differentiation, etc.

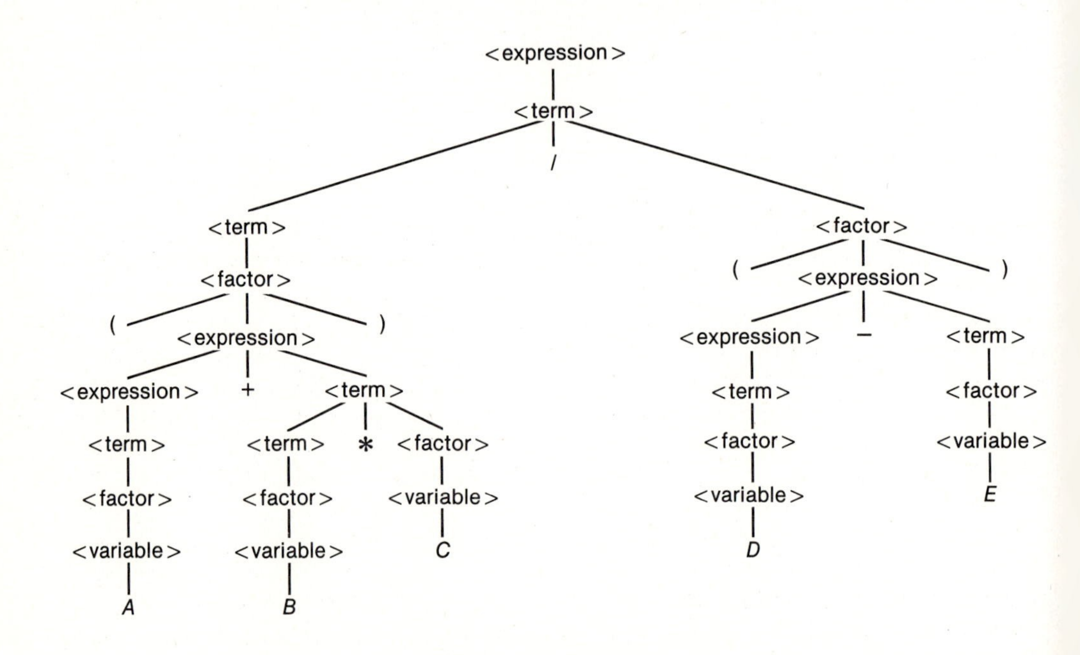

Figure 6.22 Parse Tree for the Expression '(A+B*C)/(D−E)'

6.6.2.2 Parse Trees. We have alluded to the fact that a compiler constructs expression trees from a source program. It does this by having at hand a formal set of rules that enables it to recognize which portions of the input text correspond to meaningful syntactic categories in the language. As described in Section 5.4.1, a very common way of specifying these rules is via BNF productions. The portion of compiling that has to do with comparing program text against these rules is called *parsing*. The parsing process produces an explicit *parse tree* to describe the intent of the program. We will say more about this in Section 8.6.3. For now, consider the application of the BNF productions of Figure 5.16 to the expression '(A+B*C)/(D−E)'. With these productions, a compiler would determine the parse tree of Figure 6.22. Note that the leaves of a parse tree are always terminal symbols, and that they correspond to tokens in the source program.

In a programming language with keywords − such as **if** ... **then** ... **else** ..., **for** ... **to** ... **do**, and the like − parsing is much more complicated than simply recognizing expressions and their components. In practice, the number of productions required to specify expressions down to their terminal parts is more likely to be about half a dozen (rather than the three shown in Figure 5.16). In contrast, the number of productions required to characterize programs properly written according to the grammar of that language is commonly two hundred or so. By way of illustration, Figure 6.23 shows a typical parse tree for the following Pascal program fragment:

```
for i := 1 to 12 do
  if a [i] < 0 then
    x := x - a [i];
```

6.6.3 Decision Trees and Decision Tables

Suppose that we have eight coins a,b,c,d,e,f,g,h and that we are told they are all of equal weight except for a counterfeit one, which is lighter. With an ordinary balance scale, how can we determine the bad coin in just two weighings? It is fairly easy and very natural to depict the solution to this type of problem as a *decision tree*, as in Figure 6.24. In this figure $abc : def$ represents balancing a,b,c against d,e,f. There are just three possibilities − $(a + b + c)$ is less than, equal to, or greater than $(d + e + f)$ in weight. Corresponding to each of these possibilities, we make the appropriate second weighing at the next level of the tree. The labels on the leaves identify the coin that has been determined to be light, according to the outcomes of the weighings.

Decision trees have many uses beyond that illustrated by this simple puzzle. Common examples include diagnosing situations or identifying objects, designing logic circuits or programs, analyzing algorithms, converting decision tables to machine code, etc. [Moret 1982]. In this section we confine our attention to the latter application. The material in Section 6.8 uses trees for analyzing more complicated situations.

Decision tables were introduced in Section 2.3.3. There are two principal methods for converting decision tables to executable code. One of these, the rule-mask

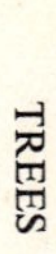

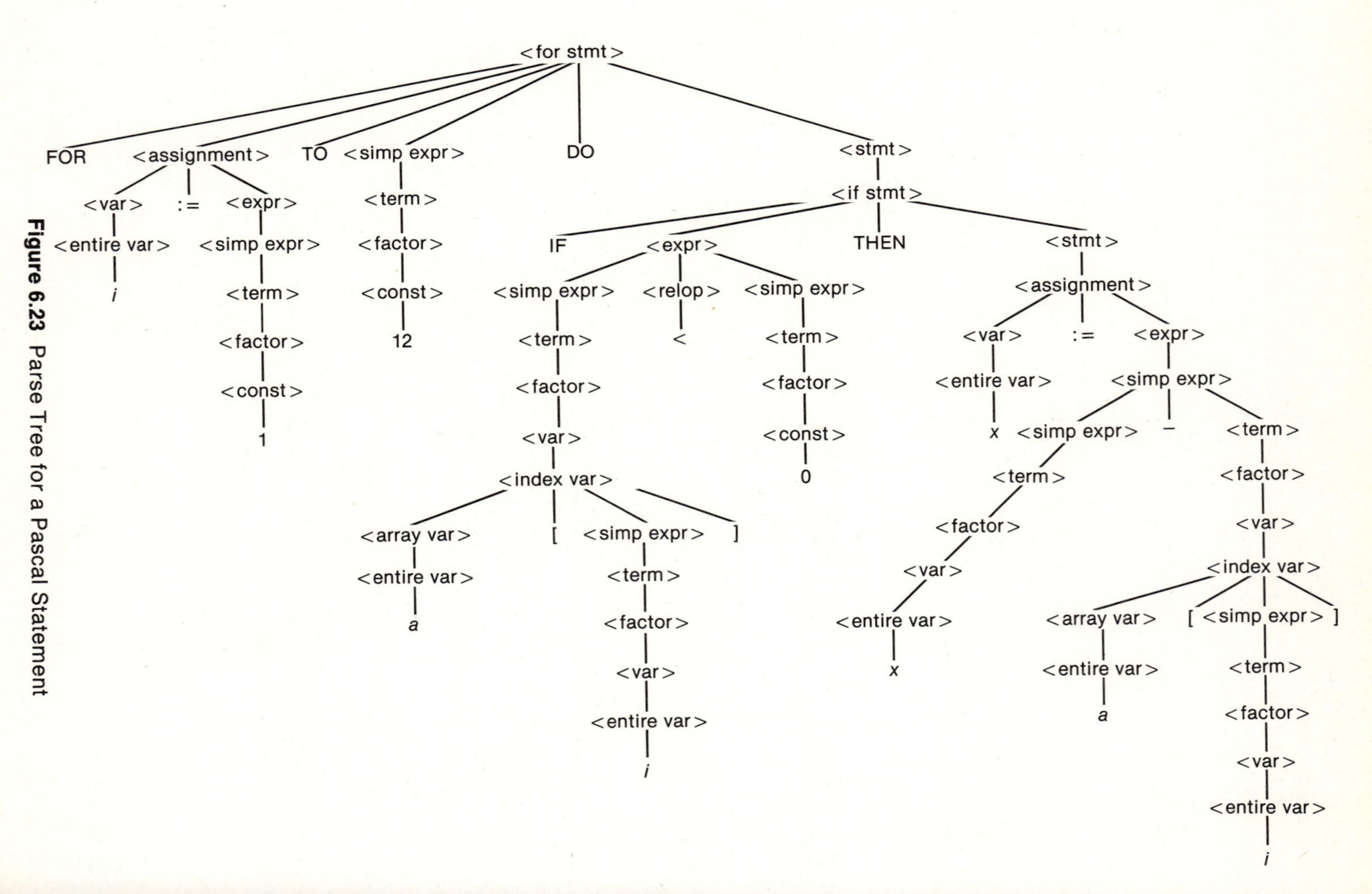

Figure 6.23 Parse Tree for a Pascal Statement

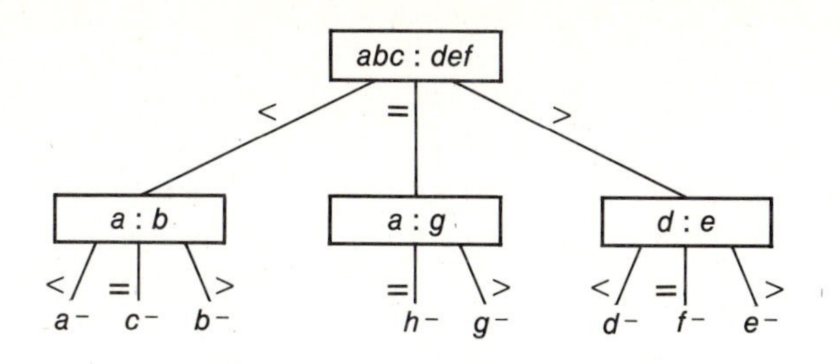

Figure 6.24 A Decision Tree

method, was illustrated in Section 2.3.3.1. This method is highly efficient in terms of storage utilization, but it generally requires that all the conditions be evaluated at the very beginning of the calculation, which may be unnecessary and wasteful. The second general method for translating a decision table does not have this drawback. It generates code for evaluating conditions sequentially, as needed; in fact, it constructs a decision tree. Sometimes this is done interpretively, via a special decision-table language; sometimes it is done via translation to another language, such as COBOL or FORTRAN. In choosing among the various alternatives, a variety of other factors relating to efficiency are likely to be of overriding importance. However, our discussion is confined to the nature of the translation from decision table to decision tree.

In deciding which decision tree is preferable, we must choose what measure to apply. In fact, there are several measures that can be applied, and they often yield different decision trees. The two most common ones are minimum time and minimum storage. These measures become both more realistic and more complicated when information is available about:

p_i = the probability of occurrence of rule R_i, and/or
t_j = the cost (time) for evaluating condition C_j.

The extent to which this additional information is useful is a moot point. The decision table user must balance a potential increase in efficiency against the difficulty or inconvenience of providing such data.

A more serious problem is that the determination of the best decision tree, by any of these measures, is an intractable (that is, exponential) problem [Hyafil and Rivest 1976]. We can easily see the plausibility of this claim via the following argument. Let $f(n)$ be the number of complete decision trees on n conditions. For one condition, $f(1) = 1$. For n conditions, there are n ways of choosing the condition at the root, and there are $f(n-1)$ possibilities for both of the subtrees. Since the two subtrees can be determined independently, we obtain for $n > 2$ the recursive equation

$$f(n) = n \times 2 \times f(n-1) \tag{6.3}$$

with solution

$$f(n) = 2^{n-2} \times n! \tag{6.4}$$

Because the function $f(n)$ grows exponentially, it is important to find better approaches to determining the best decision tree than the brute-force method of simply testing all possible candidates. There are two algorithmic methods that we will encounter soon in this text, and that are commonly useful for coping with intractable problems such as this. One is the technique known as branch-and-bound, (see Section 6.8.3), and the other is dynamic programming (see Section 7.4.2.1). Good results have been obtained with both of these methods for the decision tree problem. Yet another possibility is to apply one of a variety of faster heuristic methods; these may often yield results that are within a few percent of the optimum [§].

	*R*1	*R*2	*R*3	*R*4	*R*5
C1	Y	Y	N	N	–
C2	Y	N	N	Y	N
C3	–	Y	Y	–	N

Figure 6.25 Conditions from a Decision Table

In the interest of simplicity, we will just describe the following two heuristics [Montalbano 1962]:

- the *quick-rule method*, which is to make those tests that will isolate a rule as quickly as possible; and
- the *delayed-rule method*, which is to delay the tests that will isolate rules as long as possible.

The quick-rule method is storage-efficient because it minimizes the number of conditional tests to be generated; the delayed-rule method, on the other hand, minimizes the average number of conditional tests to be executed. It is more common to assume that time is the critical resource, and to therefore use the delayed-rule method. Suppose, for example, that we have the decision table with the conditions shown in Figure 2.12, reproduced here as Figure 6.25, and that we are not using values for p_i or t_j. Then the delayed-rule technique would cause *C*2 to be evaluated first, since it has the least number of don't-care entries. Figure 6.26 illustrates how this causes the original decision table to be factored into two sub-tables, corresponding to the values of *Y* and *N* for *C*2. The process of selecting conditions and factoring tables continues until all the rules have been reached. As a condition is selected for testing, it becomes a node in a decision tree, with branches corresponding to *Y* and *N*. If a table is factored on a condition that has a don't-care entry, then the rule corresponding to the don't-care entry must be entered in both sub-tables. Thus, in Figure 6.26, if *C*1 had been selected first, then the left and right sub-tables would have had columns for *R*1, *R*2, *R*5 and *R*3, *R*4, *R*5.

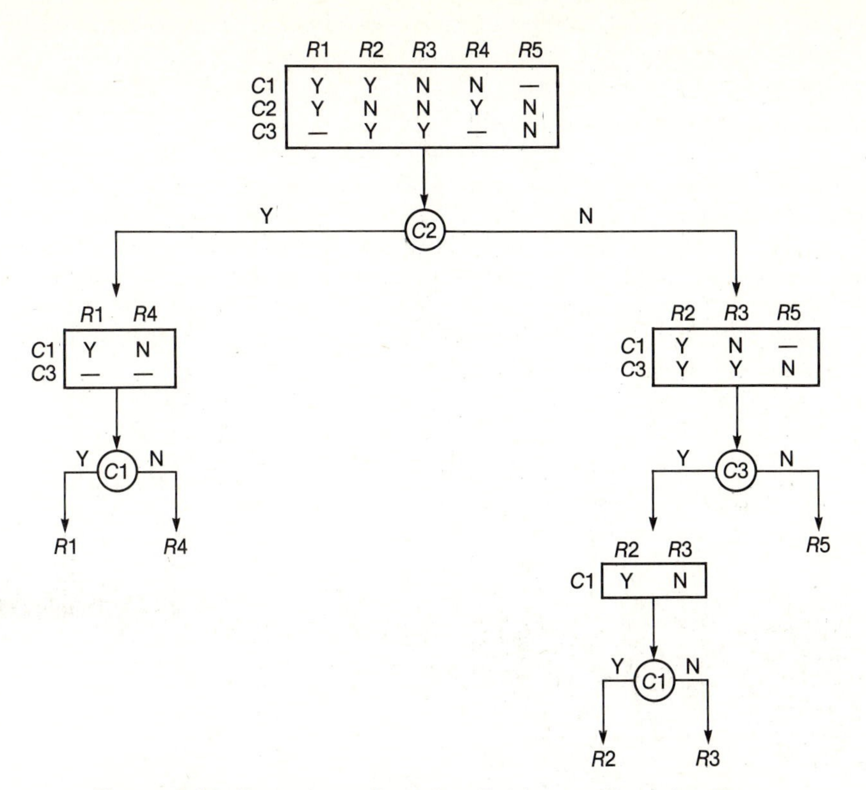

Figure 6.26 Factoring a Decision Table as a Decision Tree

6.6.4 Heaps and Priority Queues

Consider a data structure for a set of items, such that we can perform the following operations:

insert(*x*,*priority*) – to add an item with value *priority* to the set referenced by *x*;

remove(*x*,*s*) – to remove the item with largest (or smallest) priority value from the set referenced by *x* and assign it to *s*.

Such a structure is called a *priority queue* and is useful, for example, in job scheduling, in discrete simulations based upon event times, and within numerous algorithms. We will encounter several of these latter applications in subsequent sections (see Section 6.8.3 and Section 7.4.1). The priority queue was mentioned originally in Section 5.1.4; however, at that point we did not know how to implement it so that it would be efficient both for enqueuing and for dequeuing.[1] We will now discover how to do this by means of a binary tree. With a BST each node is

---

[1] Note that if successive items in time always have lower priorities, then the resulting priority queue functions as an ordinary queue. On the other hand, if successive items always have higher priorities, then the resulting priority queue functions as a stack.

intermediate in value to the values of its two children. For the priority queue, we maintain the binary tree such that the value of each node is *not less* in value than the values of either of its children.

Suppose that our initial set of items is as follows:

32 41 7 15 46 87 33 55 28 9 22

We begin by placing the items at sequential locations representing the nodes of a complete binary tree (see Section 6.5.3), as in Figure 6.27(a). We then promote large values by comparing each non-terminal node with its two children. If any parent is less than either of its children, we exchange the parent with the larger child. Moreover, if a parent is demoted, we also compare it with its two new children, in case there is a downward ripple. The application of this rule to the original tree yields the following series of exchanges:

15 and 55, 7 and 87, 41 and 55, 32 and 87, 32 and 33

as shown in (b) of the figure, with the final form shown in (c) of the figure. Note how 32, after being demoted from the root by 87, is then further demoted by 33.

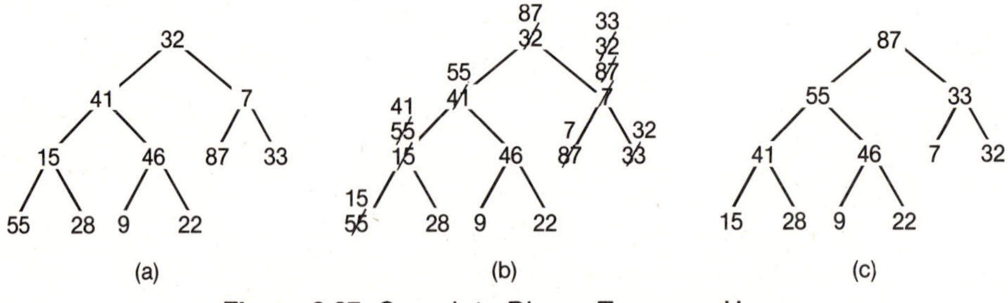

Figure 6.27 Complete Binary Tree as a Heap

A complete tree with the order property among its nodes as in Figure 6.27(c) is called a *heap*;[2] this use of the word heap has no relation whatsoever to its other meaning (a pool of storage for dynamic memory allocation, as discussed in Section 4.1.3). A heap is useful for many applications; in particular, it provides a good representation for a priority queue. This is so because if we already have a heap, then either operation – inserting or removing an item in the heap – can be performed (and the heap property maintained) in $O(\lg n)$ time. (Note that we could also have implemented a priority queue in an ordinary binary tree, without recourse to the complete binary tree representation. The choice to use a complete binary tree is based upon its guaranteed efficiency.) The procedures for insertion and removal in a heap, and for initializing it as a priority queue, are shown in P_QUEUE_H

---

2 The series of promotion decisions that transforms a complete binary tree to a heap should be carried out by proceeding in reverse sequential order from the last non-terminal node to the root. Thus, in Figure 6.27(b), we began by considering 46 in location 5 and ended by considering 32 in location 1. We will address this issue more directly in Section 13.2.1.2.1. Our present point of view is that the heap already exists, and our only concerns are how to insert another item or how to effect the removal of an item.

(Algorithms 6.7), analogously to the manner in which similar operations for an ordinary queue were shown in Chapter 5.

For insertion, the procedure INSERT_PRQ_H takes as parameters the address of the heap and the value of the new object. It "activates" the next array location, and then shuffles objects downward in the enlarged heap until it finds the proper location for inserting the new object. If we originally have the heap of Figure 6.27(c), and then insert the value 51, the node contents are exchanged as shown in Figure 6.28(a):

7 and 51, 33 and 51

It is important that the comparisons cease when the root is reached. An effective technique for guaranteeing this is to place a large sentinel value in the 0'th location of the array, as illustrated by the action of INIT_PRQ_H.

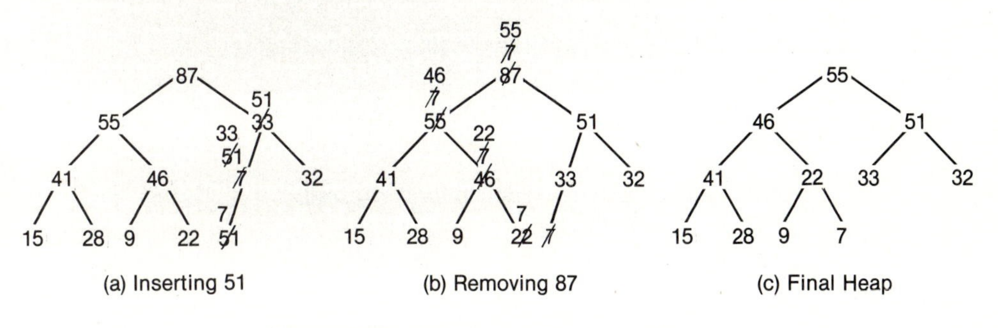

Figure 6.28 A Heap as a Priority Queue

For removal, the procedure REMOVE_PRQ_H takes as one parameter the address of the heap, and returns as another parameter the object originally at the root of the heap. Since the heap is now smaller, the last item in the array must be moved. We find the proper new location for it by comparing it against the other heap values, starting just below the root and shuffling items upward in the heap as needed. The effect is the same as if we inserted the last array item at the root, destroying the heap property, and then restoring it via a series of comparisons and exchanges down just one path in the tree. We illustrate this in Figure 6.28(b) by starting with the final heap of (a), removing the largest value (87), and then applying the changes as shown:

7 and 55, 7 and 46, 7 and 22

The final, restored heap is shown in (c) of the figure.

Several minor points should be noted about the implementation shown in Algorithms 6.7. First, we of course have to preallocate an array adequate for the largest anticipated queue size; we have not spelled out the obvious necessity to guard against overflow. Second, we have assumed that highest priority means largest key value; the changes required for implementing highest priority in the sense of smallest key are trivial. Finally, in a real application, one might prefer to include a level of indirection to the actual queue objects, to avoid exchanging large records during insertion and removal.

```
program P_QUEUE_H;
const  inf =  {a large number, forcing INSERT to terminate at root}
       prqsize =  {the size of the priority queue}
type   prqobj = record
          priority: integer;
          data: ...
       end;
       prq = record
          count: 0 .. prqsize;
          items: array [0 .. prqsize] of prqobj;
       end;

procedure INIT_PRQ_H (var heap: prq);
begin
   heap.count := 0;
   heap.items [0].priority := inf;
end;

procedure INSERT_PRQ_H (var heap: prq; data: prqobj);
var    i,j: integer;
begin
   with heap do begin
      count := count + 1;
      i := count;  j := i div 2;
      while items [j].priority < data.priority do begin
         items [i] := items [j];
         i := j;  j := i div 2;
      end;
      items [i] := data;
   end;
end;

procedure REMOVE_PRQ_H (var heap: prq; var data: prqobj);
label  1;
var    i,j: integer;
       temp: prqobj;
begin
   with heap do begin
      data := items [1];
      temp := items [count];
      count := count - 1;
      i := 1;  j := 2;
      while j <= count do begin
         if j < count then                 {check if node has right sibling}
            if items [j].priority < items [j + 1].priority then
               j := j + 1;
         if temp.priority >= items [j].priority then
            goto 1;
         items [i] := items [j];
         i := j;  j := 2 * i;
      end;
1:    items [i] := temp;
   end;
end;

begin
   ...
end.
```

Algorithms 6.7 P_QUEUE_H — Implementing a Priority Queue as a Heap

†6.6.4.1 Alternative Implementations of Priority Queues. The preceding heap implementation of priority queues is hard to beat in terms of its simplicity and efficiency, but several factors can cause other implementations to be preferred in some cases. For example, suppose that there are objects with equal priorities; it might be important to treat them with a FIFO discipline. However, it is easy to see that the heap implementation gives us no guarantee of such behavior. We could remedy the situation by including in each queue object another field that reflects its order of accession, so that priority then becomes a compound value, but this solution is likely to be undesirable.

There is another, more fundamental problem. Our application may need priority queue operations other than just *insert* and *remove*, as listed at the beginning of Section 6.6.4. A common requirement is for the operation of

merge(x,y) – to combine the priority queues referenced by x and y into one priority queue referenced by x.

We could certainly accomplish this by repeatedly removing items from the priority queue at s and inserting them into the priority queue at r; but that method would be $O(n \lg n)$, using heaps. So we seek implementations of priority queues that can perform all three operations in $O(\lg n)$ time.

Alternative implementations of priority queues include *p-trees*, (see Exercise 6.25), *leftist trees* [Knuth 1973b], and some of the forms of balanced trees that we will discuss in Chapter 10. For the case that the priorities are integers in the range $0 .. n$, there is an elegant, but fairly complicated implementation in which these values are kept as leaves in an *unconstructed* complete binary tree. It can be shown that this technique allows any of a variety of priority queue operations (including insert, remove, and merge) to be performed in $O(\lg \lg n)$ time [Johnson 1982; van Emde Boas et al. 1977].

Rather than pursue these, we will outline an implementation based upon *binomial trees* [Vuillemin 1978], which have interesting combinatorial properties in their own right. One manner of defining them is as follows:

D.1 A binomial tree B_0 is a single node.

D.2 If U and V are binomial trees B_{k-1}, then by adding an edge to make U the leftmost son at the root of V, we obtain a B_k tree.

An alternate definition is:

D.′ A binomial tree B_k has k children, of which the first is a B_{k-1} tree, the next is a B_{k-2} tree, ... , and the last is a B_0 tree.

Both of these definitions are apparent in Figure 6.29, displaying B_0 through B_4. The figure also illustrates some of the properties of binomial trees, as follows:

- B_k has height k and 2^k nodes.
- B_k has $\binom{k}{j}$ nodes on level j (whence the name).

The next step is to generalize binomial trees to binomial forests. After that, we can represent a priority queue by a binomial forest that satisfies the heap condition (that is, the priority of a node is not lower than the priorities of any of its children). Two such priority queues, P of size 3 and Q of size 6, are illustrated in Figure 6.30(a). Now, two B_{k-1} trees satisfying the heap property can be merged into one B_k tree satisfying the heap property simply by comparing their root nodes. The generalized merge operation for two binomial forests representing priority queues is carried out by merging their constituent trees, from smaller to larger, and employing "carries" that are themselves binomial trees. This is diagrammed in Figure 6.30(b), where P and Q of (a) are combined to form the priority queue R.

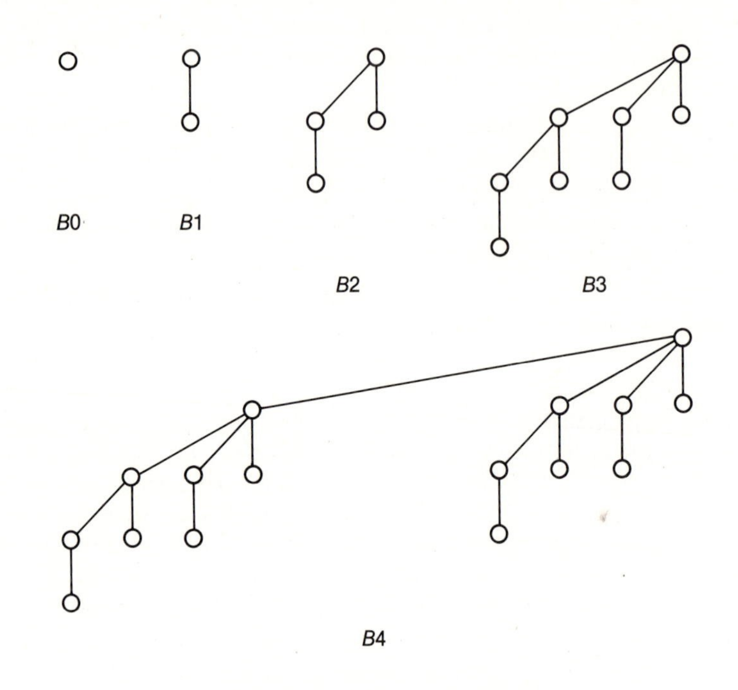

Figure 6.29 Binomial Trees

Not only does this construction give us our merge operation in $O(\lg n)$ time; it also becomes the basis for the insertion and removal operations! Insertion, for example, is a special case of merging a B_0 tree with the current binomial forest representation. For removal, we first scan the forest to find the tree B_j with the highest priority root; then, we separate that tree from the forest and remove the root, splitting that tree into its children, which constitute a binomial forest of $2^j - 1$ nodes; finally, we merge this forest with the original (reduced) forest.

Binomial trees provide an effective as well as pretty implementation for priority queues. Their principal disadvantage is one that is shared in varying degree by all of the alternatives to heaps − namely, the requirement for additional storage to carry along various pointers. The precise amount of extra storage depends upon various details of implementation. For binomial trees, a discussion of these details and a detailed analysis of their performance as priority queues can be found in Brown [1978].

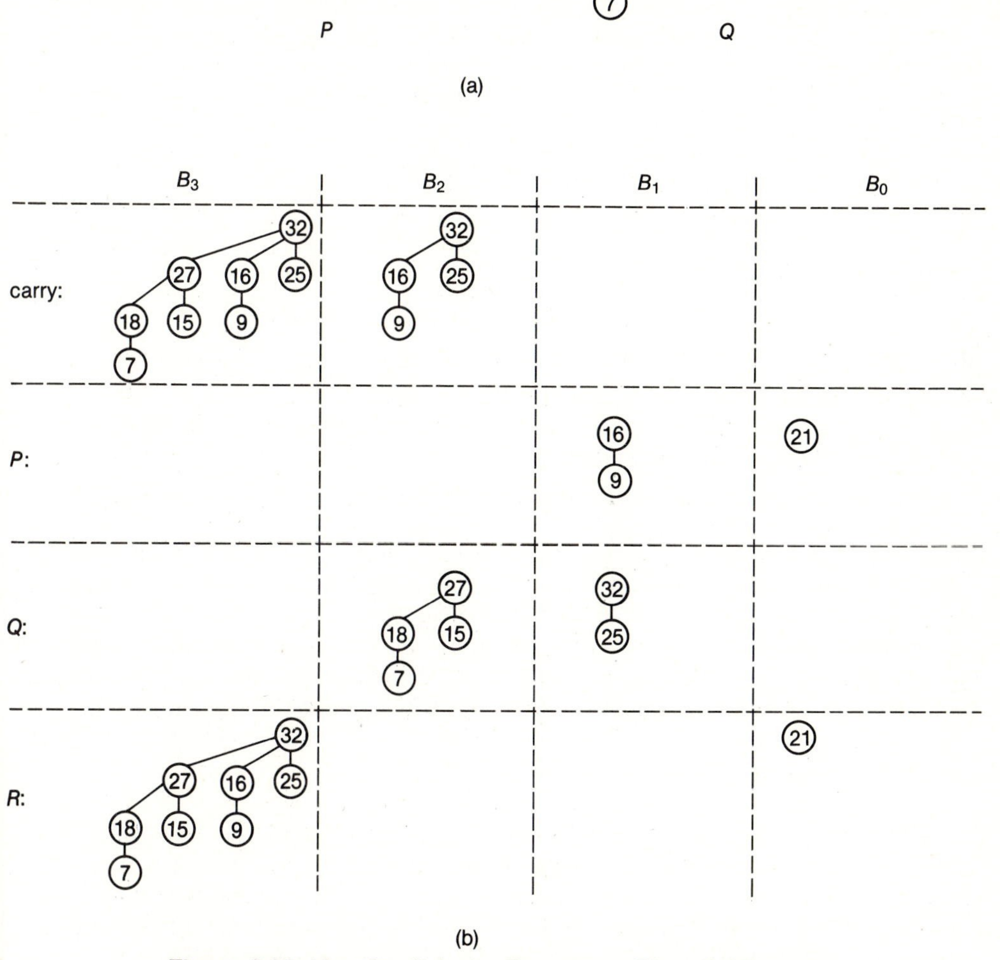

Figure 6.30 Merging Priority Queues as Binomial Forests

6.6.5 Equivalence Relations

In the beginning of this chapter, we made the distinction between oriented trees and ordered trees, and the subsequent discussion has been preoccupied exclusively with the latter and with binary trees. A representation for ordered trees requires at least two pointers at each node, in order to allow correct discrimination of children and siblings. Recall from Figure 6.16, however, that an oriented tree can be represented using just one pointer from a node to its father; alternatively, we can use an array and indices instead of pointer variables. Such an economical representation turns out to be entirely adequate for a variety of operations on sets. In this section, we will start with two very simple algorithms that provide an $O(n^2)$ solution to the equivalence problem, and then show how simple modifications to them improve performance, first to $O(n \lg n)$ and then to essentially $O(n)$.

Suppose that we have the same set of n objects, and m pairwise equivalence relationships between the objects, that we discussed in Section 4.2.3. Those relationships (Eqs. 4.6) are reproduced here for convenience:

$$\begin{array}{llll} 18 = 12 & 16 = 14 & 8 = 18 & 16 = 6 \\ 6 = 10 & 9 = 1 & 17 = 4 & 16 = 17 \\ 8 = 2 & 3 = 13 & 9 = 11 & 3 = 8 \\ 11 = 5 & 7 = 19 & 3 = 9 & 19 = 15 \end{array} \qquad (6.5)$$

We saw from the earlier discussion that there are really just three equivalence classes, as follows:

(1,2,3,5,8,9,11,12,13,18) (4,6,10,14,16,17) (7,15,19)

In a typical application, two things are needed:

1. to process the m statements of equivalence; and
2. to ascertain some number of times, usually proportional to n, to which equivalence class a given object belongs.

We will express the fact that objects are in the same equivalence class by maintaining them in an oriented tree, and will represent oriented trees via indices in an array. The basic construction for building this tree will be called UNION(i,j), which takes two oriented trees with roots identified by indices i and j and combines them into one oriented tree. We assume, for brevity, that the class of an object is synonymous with the index of its root node in the array, and that root nodes are distinguishable by having index fields of zero. The basic construction for deciding to which equivalence class an object belongs will be called FIND(i), which takes the index of an object i and returns the index of the root of its tree. The **type** and **var** information for this development are as follows:

```
type   index = 1 .. n;
       extent = -n .. n;
var    father: array [index] of extent;
```

To illustrate these processes, we will use the procedure UN (Algorithm 6.8(a)) as our first approximation to UNION and the function FI (Algorithm 6.8(b)) as our first approximation to FIND. By way of example, consider Figure 6.31. If we have the array shown in (a) representing the trees in (b), and if we then perform UN(FI(2),FI(4)), the resulting array values and tree structure would become as shown in (c) and (d). Let us apply these algorithms to Eqs. 6.5, having first initialized all the array values to zero. This would require the sequence of calls shown in Figure 6.31(e), and would yield the array shown in (f) of the figure, representing the oriented trees in (g) of the figure.

Note that UN requires a constant amount of work each time it is used, and so the work to process m equivalence statements is simply $O(m)$. The work for FI, on the other hand, depends upon how far one must search to find the root. Thus, if we have the following sequence of operations:

```
procedure UN (i,j: index);
begin
   father [i] := j;
end;
```

Algorithm 6.8(a) UN

```
function FI (i: index): index;
var     k: index;
begin
   k := i;
   while father [k] > 0 do
      k := father [k];
   FI := k;
end;
```

Algorithm 6.8(b) FI

$$\text{UN}(1,2)\ \text{FI}(1)\ \text{UN}(2,3)\ \text{FI}(1)\ \text{UN}(3,4)\ \text{FI}(1)\ \ldots\ \text{UN}(n-1,n)$$

we will grow the degenerate tree shown in Figure 6.32(a), and the work to perform the FIND's will be $1 + 2 + 3 + \cdots + (n - 1)$, or $O(n^2)$.

There are two very simple modifications that greatly improve matters. The first is to revise UN so that it always appends the tree of lesser weight as the child of the other tree. In order to accomplish this, we include with each root node the number of nodes in its tree; note that this is one more than the usual definition of the weight of a tree, wherein the root is excluded from the count. The procedure UNION (Algorithm 6.9(a)) incorporates this feature by interpreting a positive value $+k$ of *father* [i] as a pointer to the father k of node i, and a negative value $-k$ of *father* [i] as meaning that node i is a root with a count of $+k$. With this simple device, UNION is always able to append the smaller tree to the larger tree. If in the previous sequence of operations we now replace UN by UNION and initialize the elements of father to be -1 in value, we then grow the tree shown in Figure 6.32(b). The more typical result of using UNION is demonstrated by replacing UN by UNION in our processing of Eqs. 6.5; this yields the array values in Figure 6.32(c), representing the trees in (d) of the figure. It is easy to show by induction that a tree of n nodes grown with this weighting rule will always have maximum depth $\lg(n + 1)$. As a consequence, the work to perform the same sequence of FI's is now $O(n \lg n)$.

We can enhance performance even more by making another modification, this time changing FI to the function FIND (Algorithm 6.9(b)). In it, we *compress* the path from a node to its father whenever a FIND(i) operation is performed, so that after the root has been determined, the father pointers of all the nodes on the path from the root to node i are set to point directly to the root. In other words, if we originally had the tree of Figure 6.33(a), where the circles are nodes and the triangles are subtrees, then a FIND operation on the node D would have the side effect

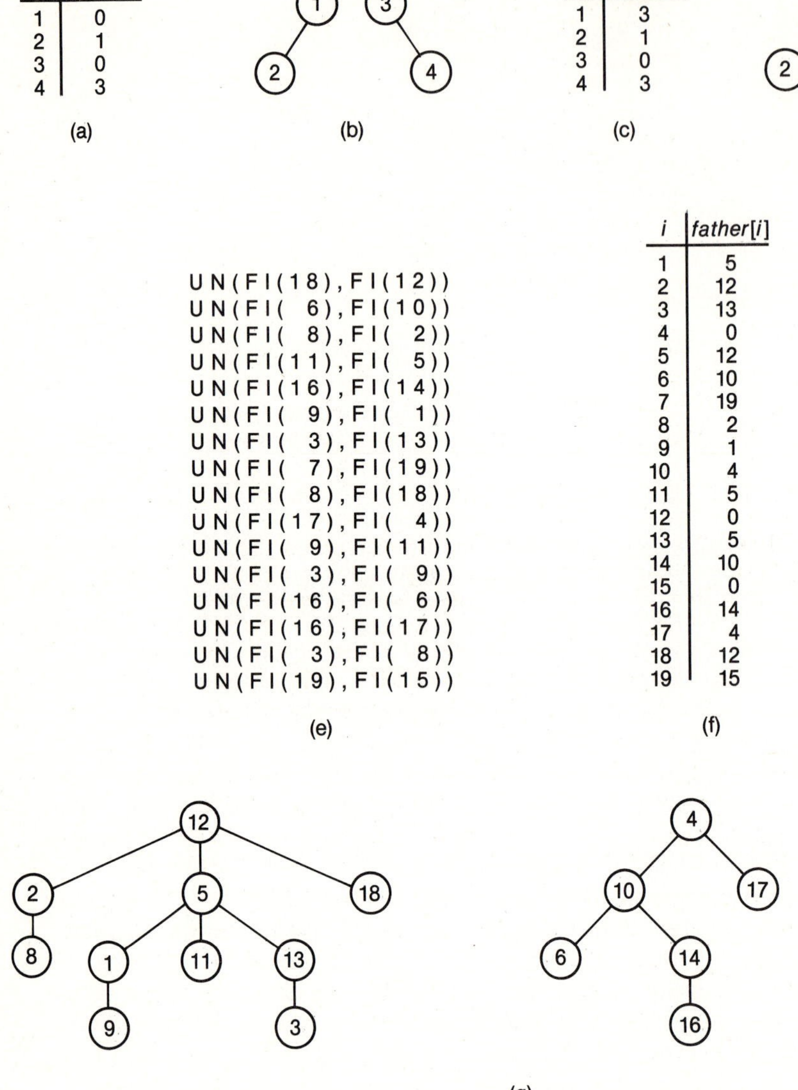

i	*father*[i]
1	0
2	1
3	0
4	3

(a)

(b)

i	*father*[i]
1	3
2	1
3	0
4	3

(c)

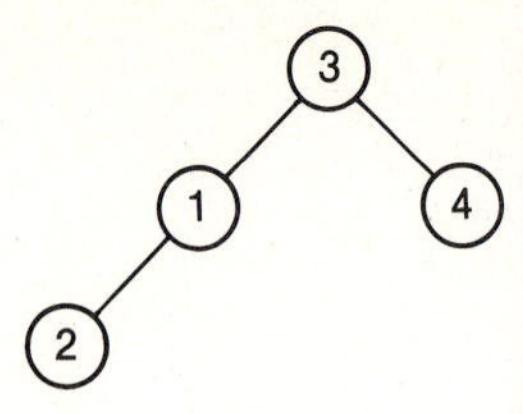

(d)

```
UN(FI(18),FI(12))
UN(FI( 6),FI(10))
UN(FI( 8),FI( 2))
UN(FI(11),FI( 5))
UN(FI(16),FI(14))
UN(FI( 9),FI( 1))
UN(FI( 3),FI(13))
UN(FI( 7),FI(19))
UN(FI( 8),FI(18))
UN(FI(17),FI( 4))
UN(FI( 9),FI(11))
UN(FI( 3),FI( 9))
UN(FI(16),FI( 6))
UN(FI(16),FI(17))
UN(FI( 3),FI( 8))
UN(FI(19),FI(15))
```

(e)

i	*father*[i]
1	5
2	12
3	13
4	0
5	12
6	10
7	19
8	2
9	1
10	4
11	5
12	0
13	5
14	10
15	0
16	14
17	4
18	12
19	15

(f)

(g)

Figure 6.31 Action of Algorithms UN and FI on Eqs. 6.5

of transforming the tree to the form in (b) of the figure. If where we originally applied UN and FI to Eqs. 6.5, we now apply UNION and FIND, having first initialized all the array values to -1, we obtain the array in Figure 6.34(a), representing the oriented trees in (b) of the figure.

```
procedure UNION (i,j: index);

var     k: extent;

begin
   k := father [i] + father [j];
   if father [i] < father [j] then begin
      father [j] := i;  father [i] := k;
   end else begin
      father [i] := j;  father [j] := k;
   end;
end;
```

Algorithm 6.9(a) UNION

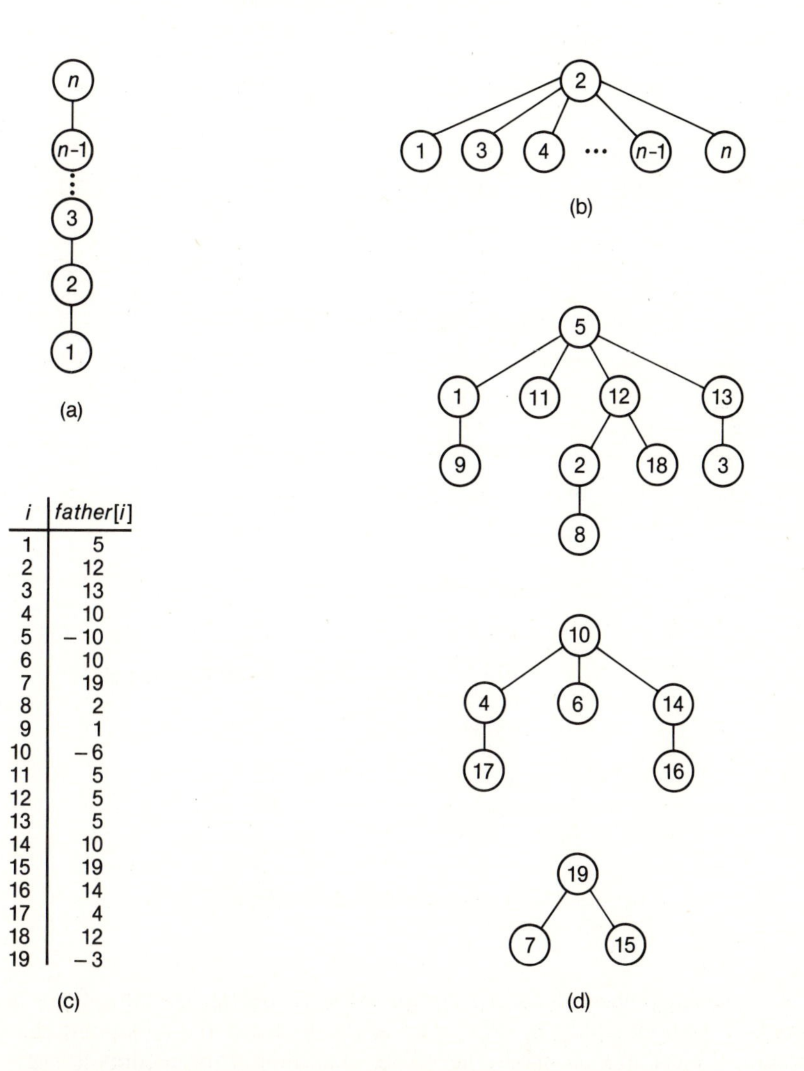

i	$father[i]$
1	5
2	12
3	13
4	10
5	−10
6	10
7	19
8	2
9	1
10	−6
11	5
12	5
13	5
14	10
15	19
16	14
17	4
18	12
19	−3

Figure 6.32 Action of Algorithms UNION and FI on Eqs. 6.5

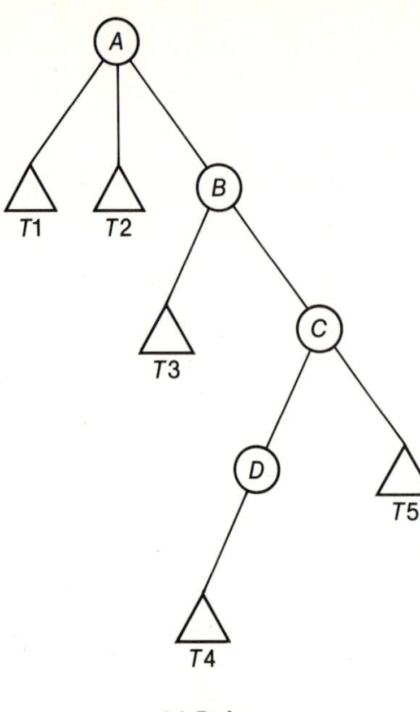

(a) Before

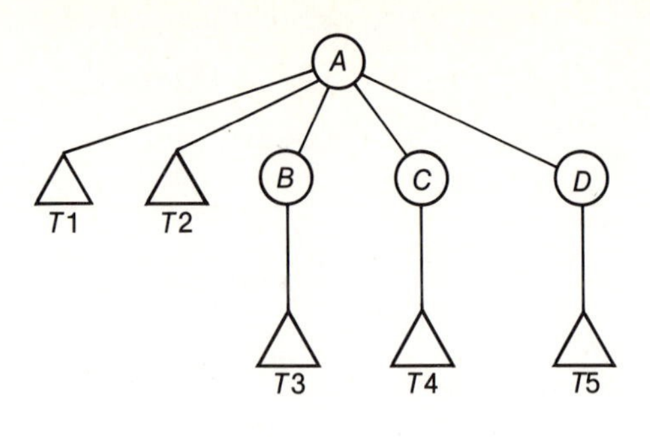

(b) After FIND'ing *D*

Figure 6.33 Path Compression

```
function FIND (i: index): index;

var     j,k,t: extent;

begin
   j := i;
   while father [j] > 0 do
      j := father [j];
   k := i;
   while j <> k do begin     {compress path}
      t := father [k];
      father [k] := j;
      k := t;
   end;
   FIND := j;
end;
```

Algorithm 6.9(b) FIND

As a consequence of adding compression to FIND, the time for a given FIND operation is about doubled. However, since the times for all subsequent FIND's to the same object are reduced, the effect of adding compression is very significant when, as is common, the application has many more FIND's than UNION's. The

i	*father*[i]
1	5
2	12
3	5
4	10
5	−10
6	10
7	19
8	12
9	5
10	−6
11	5
12	5
13	5
14	10
15	19
16	10
17	4
18	12
19	−3

(a)

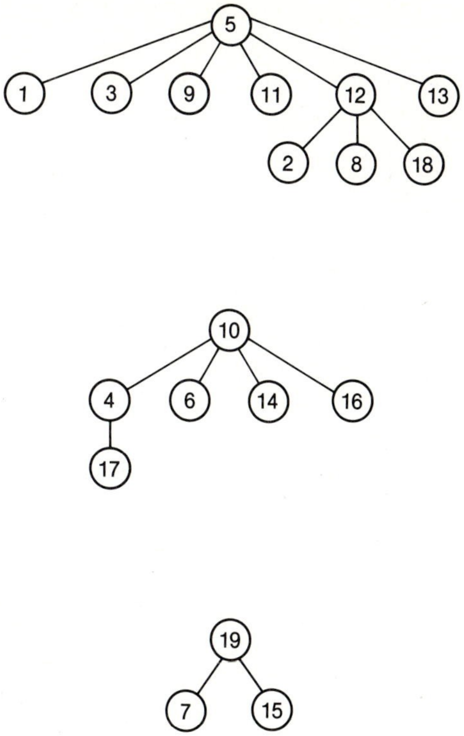

(b)

Figure 6.34 Action of Algorithms UNION and FIND on Eqs. 6.5

combined effect of UNION and FIND has been analyzed and shown to yield a performance that is not quite as good as $O(n)$, but very nearly so. We will spell this matter out in the next section; some other comments should be made at this point:

- The program EQUIV (Algorithm 4.3) is inferior to the UNION-FIND algorithm because, although they have the same time complexity, the former has space complexity $O(m + n)$, as opposed to $O(n)$ for the latter.
- In using EQUIV, we cannot answer any questions about which objects are equivalent until all the relationships have been processed. When, as with EQUIV, we must read all the input before being able to obtain any answers, we have an *off-line algorithm*. By contrast, UNION-FIND constitutes an *on-line algorithm* because we can freely intersperse FIND's with UNION's without waiting for the end of the input.
- This topic was originally motivated by the problem of determining equivalent sets of identifiers in a program. There are other useful applications for UNION-FIND, as we will see in the next chapter.

†6.6.5.1 The Ackermann Function. It is easy to show that the weighting rule for UNION in the preceding section yields $O(n \lg n)$ performance (see Exercise 6.27). By using path compression with FIND as well, we obtain a complexity $O(n\,f(n))$, for some function $f(n)$ that grows extremely slowly; however, it is considerably harder to demonstrate this fact. One such demonstration obtains the specific result $O(n\,G(n))$, where

n	2	3 .. 4	5 .. 16	17 .. 2^{16}	$2^{16}+1$ .. 2^{65536}	...
$G(n)$	1	2	3	4	5	...

so that $G(n) \leq 5$ for all practical purposes [Hopcroft and Ullman 1973].

An even more dramatic result is obtained by using a variant of the Ackermann function [Beckmann 1980]. This well-known example from recursive function theory is usually defined to be $A(m,n)$ as follows:

```
if m = 0 then A := n + 1
else if n = 0 then A := A (m - 1, 1)                    (6.6)
else A := A (m - 1, A (m, n - 1));
```

It is also conventional to define an Ackermann function of a single variable by $A(n) = A(n,n)$. The double recursion causes this function to grow extremely rapidly. Thus, $A(1) = 3$, $A(2) = 7$, and $(3) = 61$. But remarkably, considering that the only increasing arithmetic operation is $n + 1$,

$$A(4) = 2{\uparrow}2{\uparrow}2{\uparrow}2{\uparrow}2{\uparrow}2{\uparrow}2 - 3 > 10^{19199}$$

where $\uparrow$ denotes exponentiation. This latter number vastly exceeds the estimated number of particles in the universe!

Tarjan [1975] defines an even faster growing variant of the Ackermann function to be $A'(m,n)$ as follows:

```
if m = 0 then A' := 2n
else if n = 0 then A' := 0
else if n = 1 then A' := 2                               (6.7)
else A' := A' (m - 1, A' (m, n - 1));
```

For $A'(n) = A'(n,n)$, as before, we find that $A'(4) > 2{\uparrow}2{\uparrow}2{\uparrow} \ldots {\uparrow}2$ for a stack of 65536 2's! Finally, he introduces an inverse:

$$\alpha(n) = \text{the least } r \text{ such that } n \leq A'(r) \tag{6.8}$$

His net result is that the UNION-FIND algorithm has a complexity that is $\Theta(n\,\alpha(n))$. We see that $\alpha(n) \leq 4$, for all practical purposes, with α growing fantastically more slowly than even $G(n)$.

†6.7 ENUMERATION OF TREES

The question of how many different trees there are of a specific kind with just n nodes is fascinating in its own right. But also, for combinatorial applications involving searches in tree structures, it is important to know a priori just how large the search space is. By way of introduction, we address an issue that was alluded to when first discussing traversal. Traversal linearizes a tree structure; how can that structure then be recovered? Consider a binary tree with preorder traversal *A B D E H I C F J G* and with inorder traversal *D B H E I A F J C G*. Its root must then be *A*, and its left subtree must contain *D B H E I*. In the left subtree, *D* must be the left child of *B*, and the right subtree of *B* must contain *H E I*. Going on in this fashion, we discover that the original tree must be as shown in Figure 6.35.

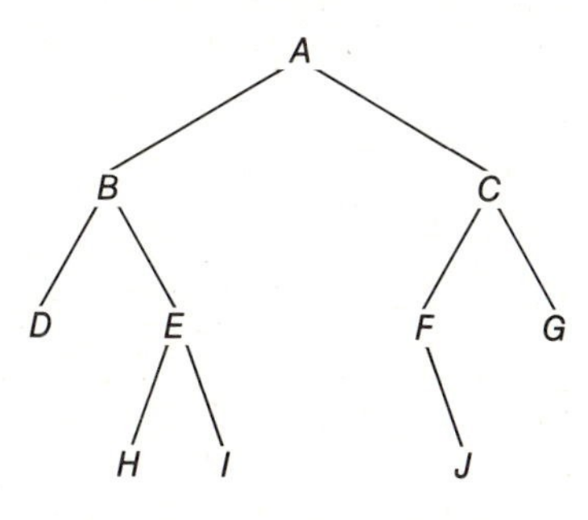

Figure 6.35 Reconstruction of a Binary Tree From Its Traversals

So we see that knowledge of the inorder traversal of a binary tree along with knowledge of the preorder traversal (or of the postorder traversal) is sufficient to allow reconstruction of the original binary tree. If we have a preorder traversal that is 1,2, ... ,n, then the inorder traversal is just some permutation of the first n integers. How many of the $n!$ possible permutations correspond to attainable binary trees on n nodes? For $n = 3$, we find that the possibilities are just those in Figure 6.36(a), with inorder traversals shown in (b). It may seem surprising, at first, that these traversals are exactly the same as the output sequences that can be obtained using a stack on the input sequence 1,2,3 – that is, the stack permutations (see Section 5.2.3). But this is not surprising after all, when we recognize that the stacking and unstacking sequences (c) used to obtain the outputs (b) are exactly the same as the stacking and unstacking sequences used in INORDER_S (Algorithm 6.2), when traversing the corresponding binary tree in (a).

To generalize our result from three nodes to n nodes, let b_n be the number of possible trees on n nodes. The number of such binary trees is the sum of all possible binary trees containing a root and a left subtree of j nodes and a right subtree of $n-1-j$ nodes. This can be expressed as

$$b_n = b_0 b_{n-1} + b_1 b_{n-2} + \cdots + b_{n-1} b_0 \qquad (6.9)$$

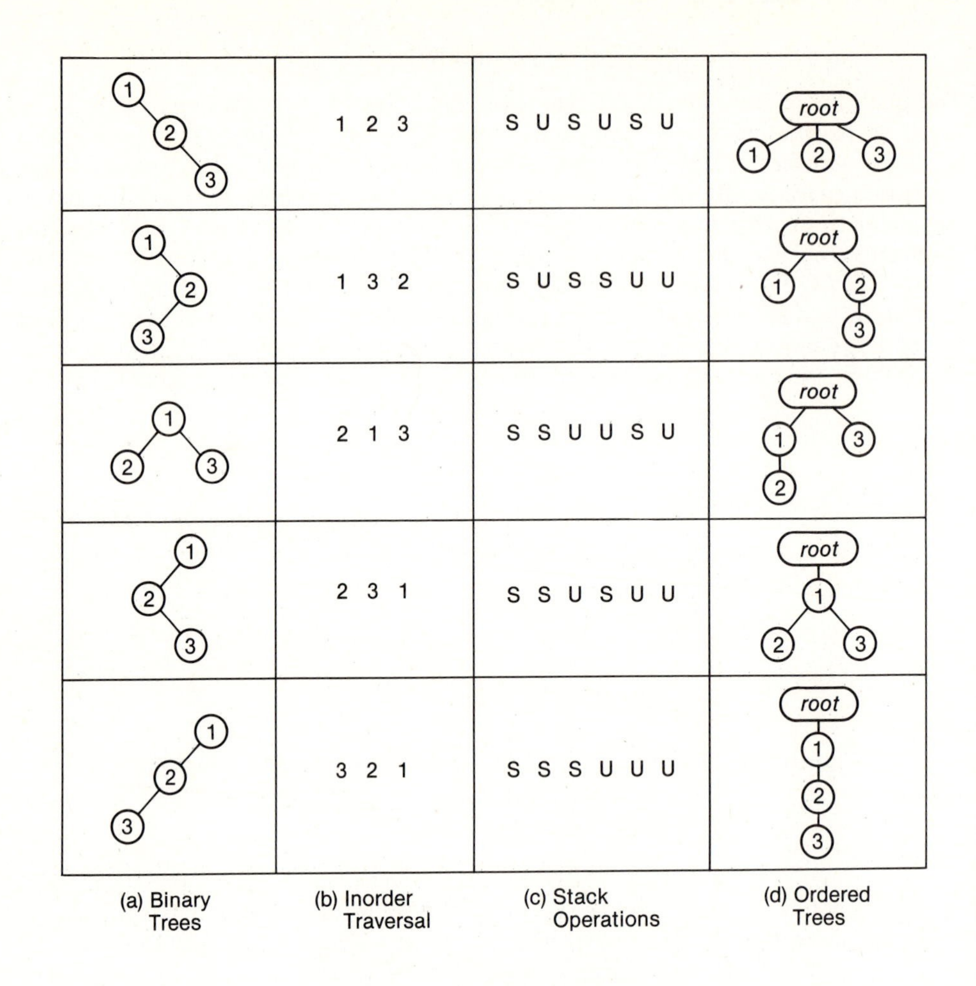

Figure 6.36 Stack Permutations

An explicit solution for this recurrence equation can be obtained through the use of *generating functions* [Knuth 1973a; Liu 1968]. In this approach we try to find a polynomial in the variable x, such that the coefficient of x^n is the desired number b_n. The method proceeds along the following lines. Let

$$B(x) = \sum b_n x^n \tag{6.10}$$

be the generating function for the number of binary trees on n nodes. Then, we observe that

$$B^2(x) = (b_0 + b_1x + b_2x^2 + \cdots)(b_0 + b_1x + b_2x^2 + \cdots)$$
$$= b_0b_0 + (b_0b_1 + b_1b_0)x + (b_0b_2 + b_1b_1 + b_2b_0)x^2 + \cdots \tag{6.11}$$
$$= \sum_{n\geq 0}\sum_{j=0}^{n} b_jb_{n-j}x^n$$

Comparing this with the equations for $B(x)$ and b_n, we see that the coefficient of x^n in $B^2(x)$ is the same as b_{n+1}. This leads us to

$$xB^2(x) = B(x) - 1 \tag{6.12}$$

A solution for this quadratic equation in $B(x)$ is

$$B(x) = \frac{1}{2x}\left(1 - \sqrt{(1-4x)}\right) \tag{6.13}$$

Finally, use of the binomial theorem to expand $\sqrt{(1-4x)}$, followed by various simplifications, yields

$$B(x) = \sum_{n\geq 0}\binom{1/2}{n+1}(-1)^n 2^{2n+1}x^n = \sum_{n\geq 0}\left(\frac{1}{n+1}\binom{2n}{n}\right)x^n \tag{6.14}$$

$$= 1 + x + 2x^2 + 5x^3 + 14x^4 + 42x^5 + \cdots \tag{6.15}$$

The coefficients b_n are the intriguing *Catalan numbers* [Cohen 1978], which occur in the solutions to numerous problems of a combinatorial nature.

Recall that there is a one-to-one correspondence between binary trees on n nodes and ordered forests on n nodes. If now, for each such forest on n nodes, we connect the root of each tree in the forest to a common parent node, then we obtain all ordered trees on $n + 1$ nodes. Thus, the number of ordered trees on $n + 1$ nodes is the same as the number of binary trees on n nodes. These are shown, for $n = 3$, in Figure 6.36(d).

What about oriented trees and free trees? For a given number of nodes n, what is the distinct number of each of these? These trees specify less information than is contained in the ordered trees on n nodes. The answers can be obtained by generating functions again [Knuth 1973a]. The results are:

$$C(x) = x + x^2 + 2x^3 + 4x^4 + 9x^5 + \cdots \tag{6.16}$$

for the number of oriented trees on n nodes, and

$$D(x) = x + x^2 + x^3 + 2x^4 + 3x^5 + \cdots \tag{6.17}$$

for the number of free trees on n nodes. Figure 6.37 depicts the 14 ordered trees on 5 nodes (remember that the number of ordered trees on n nodes is the same as the number of binary trees on $n - 1$ nodes). They are arranged in 9 boxes correspond-

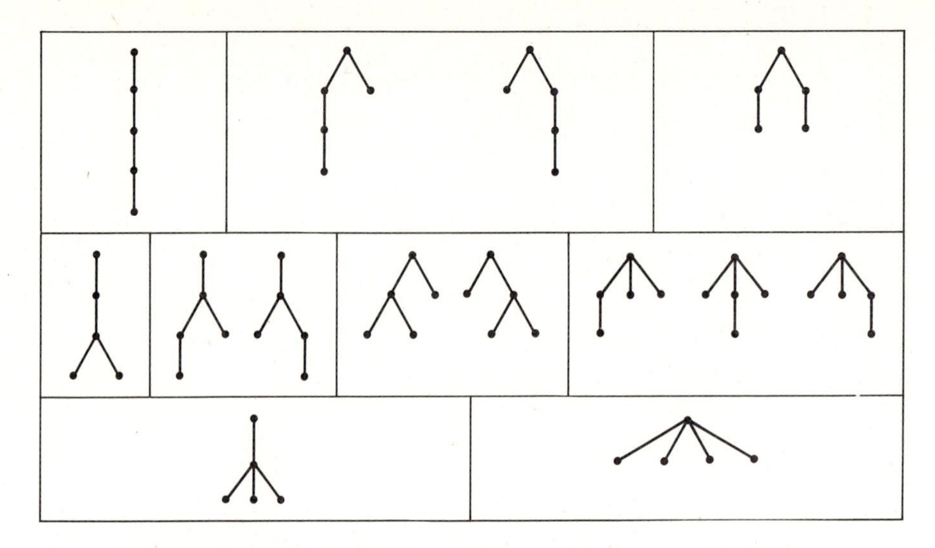

Figure 6.37 Free, Oriented, and Ordered Trees on 5 Nodes

ing to the distinct oriented trees on 5 nodes, and in 3 rows corresponding to the distinct free trees on 5 nodes.

All of the preceding discussion presumes that the n nodes are indistinguishable. However, there are cases where this is not so, when the tree nodes are *labeled.* The enumerations in these cases are fairly simple to derive. For ordered trees, each of the $n!$ labelings of the b_{n-1} trees is unique, so that there are $n!b_{n-1}$ labeled, ordered trees on n nodes. The formula for the case of labeled free trees was discovered by Cayley, one of the earliest investigators of trees, in 1889. It states that the number of distinct labeled, free trees on n nodes is n^{n-2}. We will conclude this section by deriving Cayley's formula. But first we observe that, having this formula in hand, the n choices of a root yield n distinct oriented trees for each free tree; thus the number of distinct, labeled oriented trees on n nodes is n^{n-1}. Table 6.1 illustrates the six cases that we have discussed, for several values of n.

Cayley's formula can be proved by demonstrating a one-to-one correspondence between the labeled free trees on n nodes and the sequences of length $n-2$ over the set of integers $\{1 .. n\}$. To do this, we systematically delete leaves and edges from a labeled free tree, as follows:

(a) Find the leaf with smallest label, output the label of its father, and delete the leaf and the edge to its parent.

(b) If there are just two nodes remaining, stop; otherwise, repeat step (a).

When applied to the tree of Figure 6.38, this procedure deletes the edges in the order shown in the figure, and generates the sequence 7, 1, 2, 6, 7, 1, 6.

On the other hand, any sequence S of $n-2$ values from the set $\{1 .. n\}$ can be used to generate a unique labeled, free tree. In the case of a free tree, the degree of a node corresponds to the total number of edges impinging on the node, and this value will be one more than the number of occurrences of that node label in S; to

n	labeled ordered	labeled oriented	labeled free	ordered	oriented	free
2	2	2	1	1	1	1
3	12	9	3	2	2	1
4	120	64	16	5	4	2
5	1680	625	125	14	9	3
6	30240	7776	1296	42	20	6
7	665280	117649	16807	132	48	11
8		2097152	262144	429	115	23
9			4782968	1430	286	47
10				4862	719	106

Table 6.1 Number of Trees of Each Type

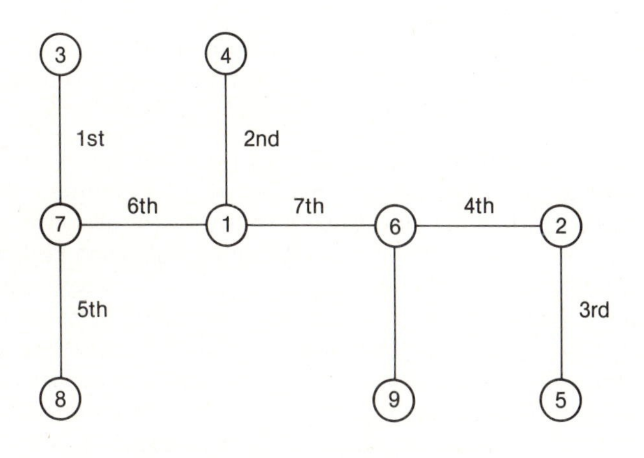

Figure 6.38 Cayley's Construction

see this, note that a node label is recorded in S only when that node is non-terminal at some point. This leads to the process:

(c) Let $N = \{1 .. n\}$, and let $S = s_1, s_2, \dots, s_{n-2}$.

(d) For i the smallest value from the set N that does not occur in the sequence S, construct an edge between node i and node s_1, and then delete i from N and s_1 from S.

(e) If S is non-empty then repeat step (d) with the reduced values of N and S; otherwise, construct an edge between the two nodes left in N, and then stop.

By referring to Figure 6.38, we see that the application of this process to the sequence $S = 7, 1, 2, 6, 7, 1, 6$ causes edges to be introduced with the same unique ordering and generates the original labeled, free tree. Thus, by the uniqueness of this correspondence, we have a canonical representation for free trees, and therefore also for oriented trees.

†6.7.1 Ranking Functions for Trees

The preceding section dealt with one aspect of combinatorial reasoning about a set of objects, that of counting how many such objects there are. Having determined that there are N such objects, a further objective is to derive a correspondence between the values 1 .. N and the objects themselves. In other words, we would like to be able to find a ranking function from the domain of trees to the range of integers, so that we could refer to the ith tree of a certain type. This capability has several practical consequences:

- If many trees must be stored or archived, there can be substantial savings in memory requirements.
- We can be sure to generate all of the trees $T_1, T_2, \dots, T_N$.
- Moreover, we can generate the trees "in order."
- We can compare two trees T_i and T_j by applying the ranking function ϕ to both of them, and comparing $\phi(T_i)$ and $\phi(T_j)$.
- We can obtain a random tree by first generating a random number i between 1 and N, and then using the inverse ranking function ϕ^{-1} to construct the tree $T_i = \phi^{-1}(i)$.

We begin by noting that for free or oriented trees with labels, the Cayley correspondence already gives an encoding whereby we can compute the kth Cayley sequence, and then construct the corresponding tree. However, we are more often interested in unlabeled ordered trees or, equivalently, unlabeled binary trees. There are actually several very different correspondences between these trees and subranges of the integers. A natural ordering on binary trees T_i and T_j can be obtained by recursively comparing the sizes of their left and their right subtrees. This serves as the basis for a scheme that orders binary trees lexicographically by their shapes, and then relates these shapes to various permutations. Such an ordering is illustrated by the vertical sequence of trees in Figure 6.36(a). Whereas, in that figure we labeled the nodes in preorder and read them in inorder, it is instructive now to label them in inorder, in Figure 6.39(a). Then if we read them in preorder, we obtain the *tree permutations*, as shown in (b) of the figure; and if we read them in postorder, we obtain the stack permutations again (though in a different sequence) in (c) of the figure. Both of these sets of permutations, and others as well, have been used as the bases of ranking functions for binary and t-ary trees [§]; that is, they are used to exhibit a correspondence between the ith permutation and the ith (unlabeled) tree.

By using the level numbers of the leaves of a tree, we can obtain an entirely different ranking function. We begin by appending leaf nodes to the original nodes of the tree wherever it is possible to do so, creating an *extended tree* from the original tree. For the five binary trees of Figure 6.36(a), we obtain the five extended (and strictly binary) trees of Figure 6.40, with the original *internal nodes* as circles, and the appended *external nodes* as squares. It is not hard to see that, if the original tree had n nodes, then the extended tree has $n+1$ leaves. (Why?) In Figure 6.40, each leaf is labeled with its level, and the level sequences are shown below each tree. Now suppose that we are given a set of positive integers $\{a_i\}$. Under what circumstances can these values, for some orderings, represent the level

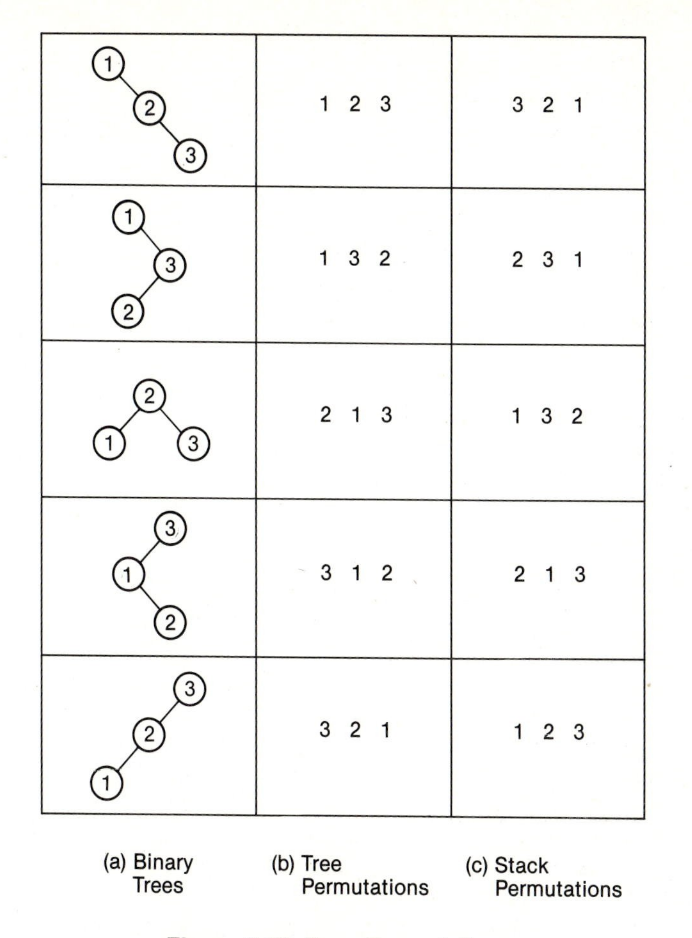

Figure 6.39 Tree Permutations

numbers of the leaves of a strictly binary tree? It can be shown (see Exercise 6.30) that a necessary and sufficient condition is that

$$\sum 2^{-a_i} = 1 \tag{6.18}$$

An ordering of the set $\{a_i\}$ for which this condition holds is called a *feasible sequence*, and it is fairly straightforward to construct ranking functions based upon such sequences [§].

There are many variations to the solution of the ranking problem, and the best method is not easily chosen. Note, though, that there are three aspects to the use of these methods:

1. to be able to compute $i = \phi(T)$, for a tree T;
2. to be able to compute $T = \phi^{-1}(i)$, for an index value i;

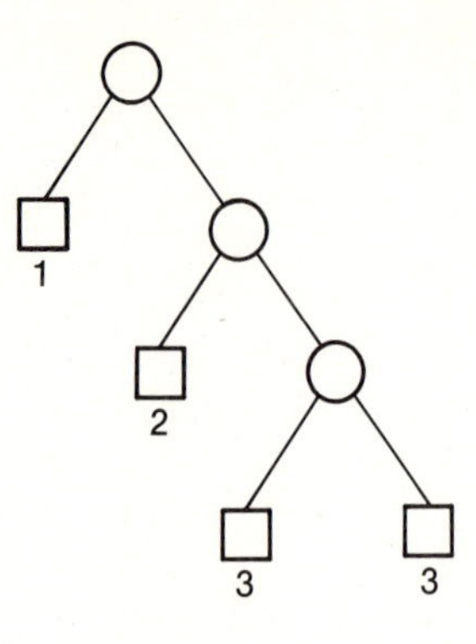

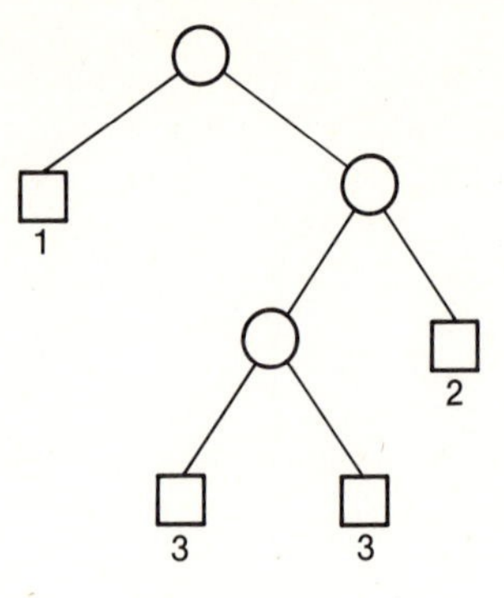

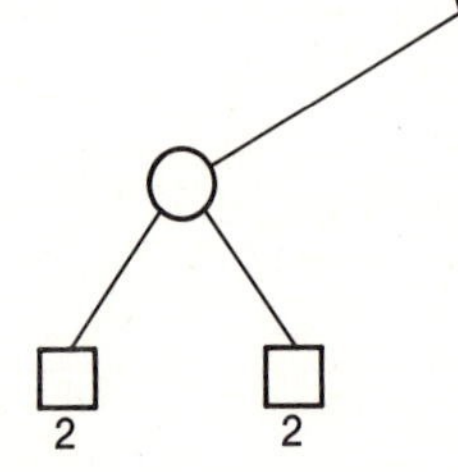

2 2 2 2

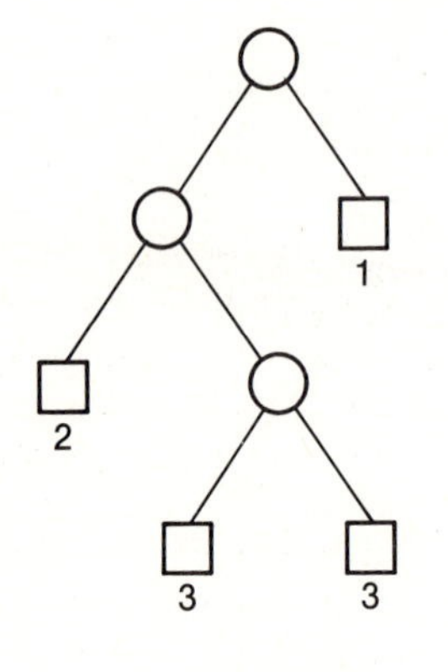

2 3 3 1

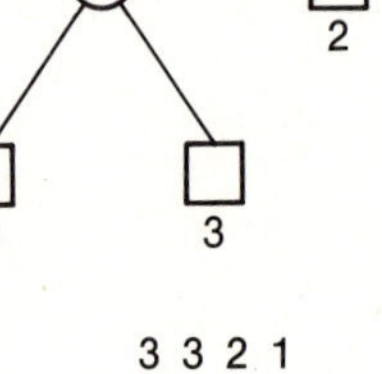

3 3 2 1

Figure 6.40 Feasible Sequences

3. to be able to compute the next encoded representation (tree permutation, stack permutation, feasible sequence, etc.), in order to generate the next tree.

Several of the methods cited provide these capabilities in $O(n)$ time, and they have been applied, for example, to the detection of isomorphic subtrees.

6.8 SEARCHING FOR SOLUTIONS IN TREES

For a large class of problems, the method of solution is to search among the nodes of a tree. This is not the same as traversing all the nodes of a tree, since we may be able to find the solution without visiting some of the nodes. Nor is it like searching for a specific item, such as a name in a telephone directory, since the criteria for having a solution can be much more complicated, involving various global features of the tree space. Problems of the sort that we are describing are particularly common in the area of endeavor known as Artificial Intelligence (AI) [Nilsson 1980; Raphael 1976; Winston 1977]. Examples include: proving theorems, playing non-trivial games, "understanding" natural language, "understanding" pictures, controlling robots, and diagnosing illness in humans.

As a first attempt for solving such problems, we can systematically visit every node in the tree. After such an exhaustive search, we may know more than we need to know, but we will by then have found the solution. However, since a t-ary tree of depth d has $O(t^d)$ nodes, this brute-force approach is not feasible for many large, real-life problems. In such cases, techniques for focusing and restricting the search are crucial. We will begin by examining two comparatively simple approaches; this material leads us, in Section 6.8.2, to the topic of backtracking. Section 6.8.3 presents the very useful branch-and-bound technique for restricting the search space. Finally, we discuss the use of trees as applied to game playing.

6.8.1 Exhaustive Search Strategies

Let us consider the problem of finding the shortest path from the root of a tree to a leaf, where the branches have associated weights that we can regard as distances. The tree in Figure 6.41 will serve as an example. To begin with, we might look at all the nodes at level 1 to see if any of them are leaves. If so, we would then pick the leaf at minimum distance. If none of the nodes at level 1 are terminal, we could then examine all the nodes at level 2 and again check for any leaves, repeating this process for successive levels until we finally found a leaf. Of course, if the distances were all the same, the task would really reduce to finding the leaf at the shallowest level, and we would then have obtained our objective. However, the distances in the figure are not equal, and we do not obtain a solution so easily. Instead, we will examine all those non-terminal nodes with partial distances less than that of the leaf. For these nodes, we will keep extending them by their descendants until either we find a leaf that is closer, or else none of the partial distances is less than that of the best leaf found so far.

This method, known as *breadth-first search* (*BFS*), can be viewed as search that proceeds in ever-broadening concentric circles. It calls for the use of a queue; with it, as nodes on level k of the tree are removed for processing, their descendants on level $k + 1$ are inserted for subsequent processing. In this approach, we can use the current best leaf value to restrict the search in two ways:

- to bypass enqueuing nodes whose distance already exceeds that value;

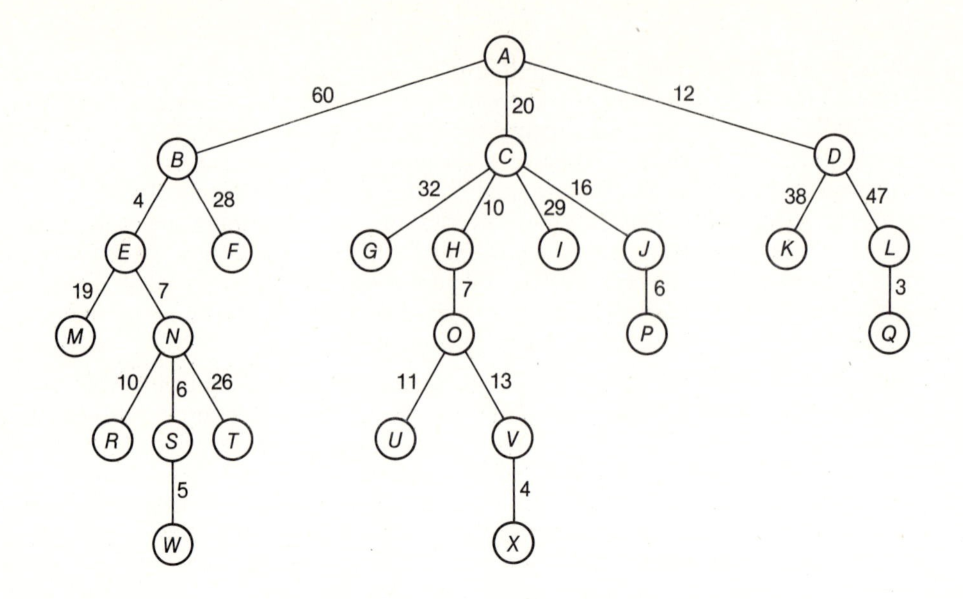

Search	Discard	Bypass	Minimum	At
A B C D E F			88	*F*
G			52	*G*
H I			49	*I*
J	*K L M N*		49	*I*
O P		*Q R S T*	42	*P*
	U	*V W X*	42	*P*

Figure 6.42 Breadth-First Search

- to discard dequeued nodes whose distance exceeds that value.

If we apply BFS to our tree of Figure 6.41, we will examine the nodes as shown in Figure 6.42. We know, for instance, to discard the nodes *K,L,M,N*, since they are all at a greater distance than the current best leaf value of 49 at *I*. We later know to bypass the nodes *R,S,T*, since they are already at a greater distance than the current best leaf value of 42 at *P*. On the other hand, even after *P* has been located, we must still examine some nodes in the subtree at node *O* with a distance of 37, until it is certain that there are no leaves with lesser distances at deeper levels. Note that when *O* is searched *I* is still the best leaf; thus *U* at 48 is enqueued and later discarded, whereas *V* at 50 is bypassed immediately.

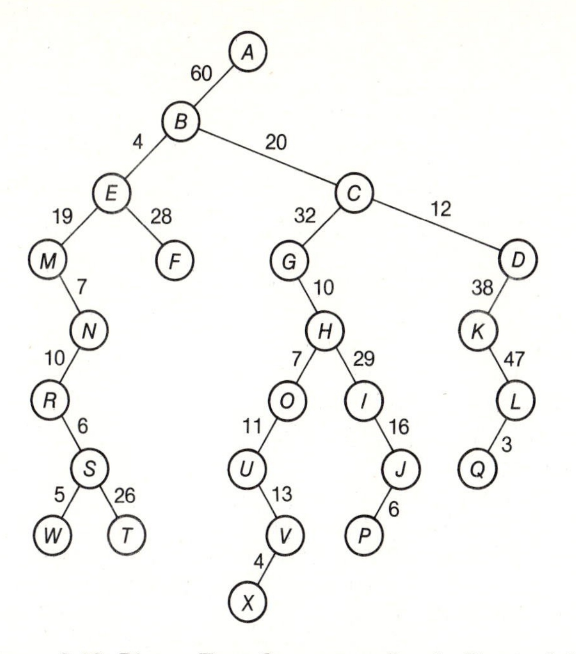

Figure 6.43 Binary Tree Corresponding to Figure 6.41

Let us consider how BFS might be implemented. First, we decide to represent the tree of Figure 6.41 as the corresponding binary tree, as shown in Figure 6.43.[3] In so doing, we associate distances with nodes rather than branches; namely, the distance from a node to its *i*th child is uniquely associated with that child. The corresponding node definition is then

```
type  link = ↑node;
      node = record
         cost: integer;
         left,rite: link;
      end;
```

Next, for obtaining the queue functions, we can employ either of the queue implementations, Algorithms 5.1 or 5.2. The final procedure is BFS_TREE (Algorithm 6.10), with input parameter *root* pointing at the tree to be searched, and output parameters *goal* and *best* identifying the location and distance of the winning leaf.

With breadth-first search, if you imagine yourself to be the searcher and the tree to represent alternate paths through a maze, then while you will certainly find your way out, it may cost incessant tracing and retracing of your steps. A different (more reckless? more optimistic?) method is *depth-first search* (*DFS*). It presumes that the tree to be searched is of bounded depth, and it proceeds as far as it can

---

[3] Note that our search really applies to an oriented tree, and that the de facto ordering is not significant.

```
procedure BFS_TREE (root: link; var goal: link; var best: integer);

type    qobj = record
            base: integer;
            ptr: link;
        end;

var     datum,defer: qobj;
        next: link;
        total: integer;
        wait: {queue type}

begin
   best := maxint;
   INITQ (wait);
   defer.base := 0;  defer.ptr := root;
   ENQUEUE (wait,defer);
   repeat
      DEQUEUE (wait,datum);
      if datum.base < best then                    {test for discard}
         if datum.ptr↑.left = nil then begin       {a leaf}
            best := datum.base;  goal := datum.ptr;
         end else begin                            {process children}
            next := datum.ptr↑.left;
            repeat
               total := datum.base + next↑.cost;
               if total < best then begin          {test for bypass}
                  defer.base := total;  defer.ptr := next;
                  ENQUEUE (wait,defer);
               end;
               next := next↑.rite;
            until next = nil;
         end;
   until EMPTYQ_L (wait);
end.
```

Algorithm 6.10 BFS_TREE

down one sequence of branches until reaching a leaf. With that leaf value in hand, it begins backing up and exploring other possibilities, except where the partial distance at a node is already greater than the distance to the best leaf so far.

Whereas the technique of BFS called for a queue, the technique of DFS calls for a stack, in order to remember where to back-up to. This time the current best leaf value can be used to limit the work by indicating when entire subtrees should be *pruned* and not searched further. When applied to the same tree in Figures 6.41 and 6.43, DFS causes the nodes to be examined as shown in Figure 6.44. We know, for instance, to prune the nodes W,T,F, since they are all at a greater distance than the current best leaf value of 81 at R. Later we prune the entire subtree at node V, since its distance of 50 is greater than the current best leaf value

Search	Prune	Minimum	At
A B E M		83	M
N R		81	R
S	W T F	81	R
C G		52	G
H O U		48	U
J P	V (X) I	42	P
D	K L (Q)	42	P

Figure 6.44 Depth-First Search

We eventually locate P at 42, but must still search the subtree of distance 12 at D to ensure that there is not a better solution therein.

An implementation of DFS for this problem is the procedure DFS_TREE (Algorithm 6.11), with input parameter *root* pointing at the tree to be searched, and with output parameters *goal* and *best* indicating the location and the distance of the winning leaf. Since it is natural to express depth-first search with a stack, it should not be surprising that it can also be expressed recursively (see Exercise 6.32). We choose to employ a stack not so much for reasons of efficiency as to expose the nature of the *backtracking* that takes place in DFS. In this process, we alternate our direction of tree exploration between forward and backward. A handy device to control this is the familiar use of a variable *state* to control the flow of calculation. As a minor point, note that a boundary value of $stack\,[0].base = 0$ is used. There is much more to be said about backtracking per se, but that is the subject of the next section.

It is easy to see that DFS can be just as inefficient as BFS, although in a different manner – in this case, by wasting a lot of time exploring sub-optimal branches. From the advantage of a global point of view, it is too easy to see wherein these methods are inefficient in the tree of Figure 6.41. But when such a perspective is not possible – for example, if the figure is made more complicated by several orders of magnitude – then our view of the problem comes closer to the myopic view of a computer, and it is not so easy to be so wise. Much of the remainder of Section 6.8 addresses ways to try to attain some of the wisdom of this global perspective. What can be said, in the meanwhile, about BFS versus DFS? The most important point is that one should try to suit the method to the problem. In our example, for instance, if all the distances were the same, then the problem would reduce to finding a leaf of minimum depth, for which BFS would clearly be superior. BFS is also a good method where it is possible to employ parallel search, and it is safer than DFS in that it will always succeed eventually (even if much later in some cases). The shape of the search tree is extremely significant. If problem states can recur, as in searching a maze, then DFS can completely fail, unless there is a solution along the leftmost branch. Nonetheless there are other situations wherein DFS will be superior. A distinct and important consideration, also, is the amount of working storage required. For a t-ary tree of depth d, the size of the DFS stack is just $O(d)$, but the size of the BFS queue is $O(t^d)$. Finally, we have illustrated BFS and DFS with the particular example of finding the shortest path

```
procedure DFS_TREE (root: link; var goal: link; var best: integer);

type    stkobj = record
          base: integer;
          ptr: link;
        end;

var     datum: stkobj;
        next: link;
        state: (frwd,bkwd,done);
        stack: array [0 .. smax] of stkobj;
        top: 0 .. smax;

begin
  state := frwd;
  best := maxint;  next := root;
  stack [0].base := 0;  top := 1;
  datum.base := 0;  datum.ptr := root;
  stack [top] := datum;
  repeat
    case state of
      frwd: begin
        if datum.base >= best then           {test for pruning}
          state := bkwd
        else if datum.ptr↑.left = nil then begin
          best := datum.base;  goal := datum.ptr;
          state := bkwd;
        end else begin                        {look deeper in tree}
          next := datum.ptr↑.left;
          datum.base := datum.base + next↑.cost;
          datum.ptr := next;
          top := top + 1;  stack [top] := datum;
        end;
      end;
      bkwd: begin
        while (top > 0) and (stack [top].ptr↑.rite = nil) do
          top := top - 1;
        if top = 0 then
          state := done
        else begin              {adjust value on top of stack and retry}
          datum := stack [top];
          next := datum.ptr↑.rite;
          datum.base := stack [top - 1].base + next↑.cost;
          datum.ptr := next;
          stack [top] := datum;
          state := frwd;
        end;
      end;
    end;
  until state = done;
end;
```

Algorithm 6.11 DFS_TREE

from the root to the leaf in a tree. Such search methods can be applied to many other problems where the criteria for a solution may be very different; correspondingly, the details of the new algorithms may be different. There may not even be a tree data structure, as we will see in the next section! Yet the paradigms of BFS in a *solution tree* (with a queue) and DFS in a solution tree (with a stack) will remain, causing the new algorithms to have some essential similarities.

†6.8.2 Backtracking

Consider the following generalized problem:

1. We have m sets $X_1, X_2, \ldots, X_m$ with respective cardinalities $N_1, N_2, \ldots, N_m$.
2. We wish to find an m-tuple of values $x_{1,i}, x_{2,j}, \ldots$ from the sets $X_1, X_2, \ldots,$ such that some *criterion function* $\Phi(x_{1,i}, x_{2,j}, \ldots)$ is satisfied; for example, Φ is true, Φ is maximized, etc.

There may in fact be no such m-tuples, or one, or many. We can certainly express the solution in terms of nested iterations, as follows:

```
for i := 1 to N [1] do
   for j := 1 to N [2] do
   ...
      {Test that Φ (x [1,i], x [2,j], ...) is satisfied}
```

We can represent the course of the computation as a tree wherein the index i varies on level 1, the index j varies on level 2, etc. The complexity of such a solution will be $O(N_1 N_2 \ldots N_m)$, corresponding to the number of leaves that are on the bottom level of the tree.

In a sense, we could say that backtracking is taking place in the process just described, but it is backtracking of a very rigid sort. The true sense of the term refers to the case where various *constraint functions* are used to restrict the search by pruning subtrees, as in the preceding section. As we examine the members of the sets in lexicographical order, if we have determined candidates for the first $k-1$ positions of our n-tuple, and if the next candidate for the kth position of the tuple can be rejected out of hand, then we have saved $N_{k+1} \ldots N_m$ evaluations. The constraint functions will be very different for different problems and can also vary considerably at the various levels of the tree for any given problem. There is a trade-off between the complexity of computing constraints to avoid computation and the complexity of simply evaluating a subtree. In the extreme case, with sufficiently sophisticated constraints, we may not have to backtrack at all! The more common case is that it will be feasible and worthwhile to compute some constraints, and that some backtracking will take place [§]. We will confine our attention to two issues in the ensuing sections. The first is to illustrate some issues about backtracking that did not appear in our discussion of DFS and to consider the efficiency of the method. The second is to relate backtracking to the concept of nondeterministic algorithms.

†6.8.2.1 Systems of Distinct Representatives. Suppose that we have the sets

$$S_1 = \{2,3,4,5\},\ S_2 = \{3,5\},\ S_3 = \{1,2\},\ S_4 = \{2,5\},\ S_5 = \{2,3\} \qquad (6.19)$$

and that we wish to pick one element as a representative from each set, but that the representatives of the sets must all be distinct. Such a situation might arise when an organization has many committees with overlapping memberships. If this organization must send a representative from each committee to general meetings scheduled in parallel, then the lack of a *System of Distinct Representatives* (*SDR*) will cause the organization to be unrepresented in some matters. The SDR problem certainly fits into the general backtracking scheme that we described in the previous section. The criterion function in this case is that each committee should have a representative, and the constraint is that no two representatives can be the same member. Let us see how the backtracking solution proceeds in this case. An important consideration at the outset is whether we wish to look for just one solution, or all possible solutions. Here, we will look for all of them.

Using the backtracking technique, we generate elements $x_{1,i}, x_{2,j}, \ldots$ of our m-tuple solution in succession. When we have candidates in the first $k-1$ positions, but cannot find a candidate in the kth position, then we need to discard the current candidate in the $(k-1)$th position and try again. However, we may have to discard much more than the current value of the $(k-1)$th candidate; the values of many other variables may have been affected also. Sometimes we can reverse all the necessary calculations to undo matters. It is often easier and safer to save on a stack the values of variables subject to change, and simply restore them from the stack when backtracking.

For the SDR problem, we can expect to find cases where there is no available candidate from the kth set, consistent with the first $k-1$ choices. Although it is simple, in this case, to delete a member from a set in order to restore matters, it is more instructive to imagine that we maintain a global variable *active* that records which members of the universal set have already been assigned. When making a forward step, we stack the value of the index in the current set and the value of *active*; when making a backward step, we restore the previous values of the index and of *active* from the stack. Whichever method is used to restore the previous environment, the solution tree for finding SDR's for the sets of Eqs. 6.19 is shown in Figure 6.45, where the O's indicate nodes that are expanded, and the X's indicate nodes where pruning occurs.

One of the problems associated with backtracking is the large uncertainty about how effectively the constraints will prune subtrees. Apparently trivial tinkering with a backtrack program can cause orders of magnitude difference in their efficiency. Since in some problems we do not know if there exists even one solution, there is the prospect of having a machine run for hours, and then not knowing if an answer is minutes or centuries away. Some relief from this dilemma can be obtained by Monte Carlo estimation techniques [Knuth 1975]. Here, we will simply point out one commonly effective way to tinker with a backtracking algorithm.

In our SDR problem, we examined the sets in their given order. Set S_1 has cardinality 4 and so the branching factor at level 1 was 4; S_2 has cardinality 2 and so the branching factor at level 2 was 2; etc. Now backtracking is able to prune one subtree at a time. At level 1 in our problem, this amounts to discarding 1/4 of

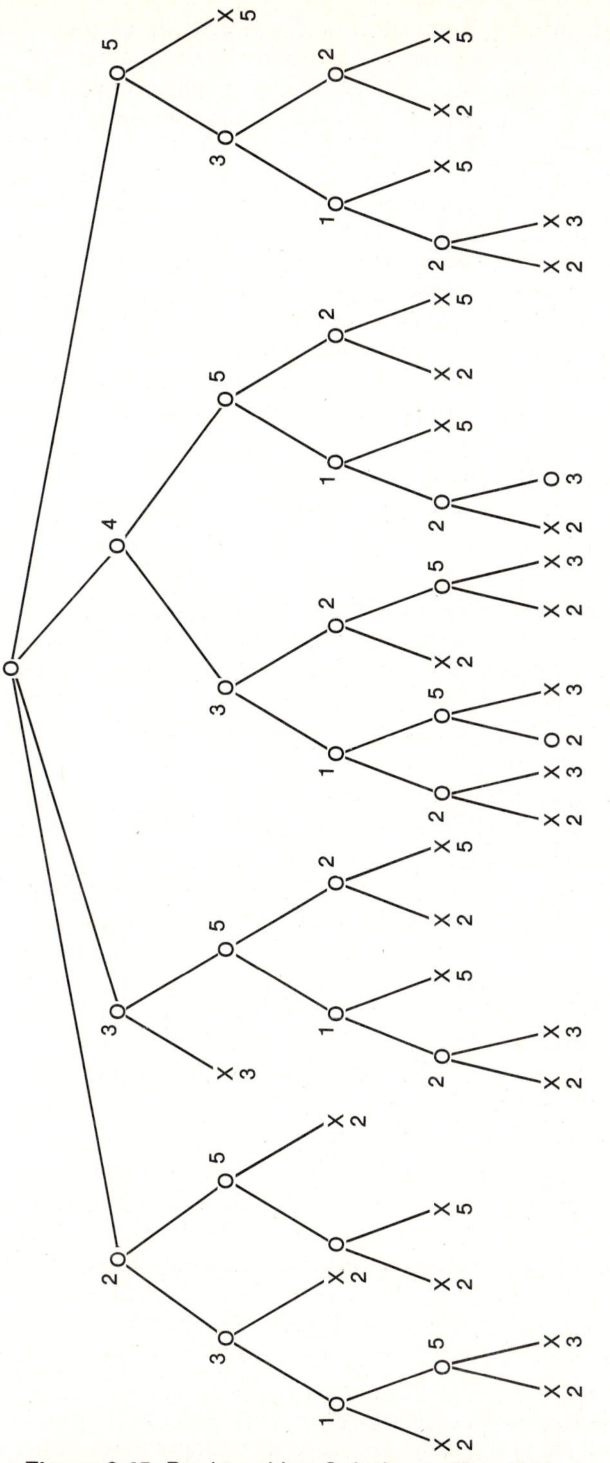

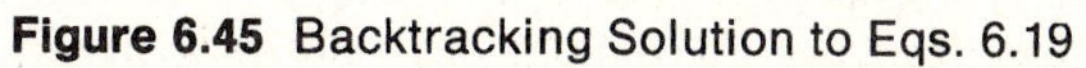

Figure 6.45 Backtracking Solution to Eqs. 6.19

the subtrees; at level 2, it amounts to discarding 1/2 of the subtrees; etc. It is often more effective to rearrange the solution tree so that the nodes of lesser degree are nearer the root. This makes it possible to eliminate larger subtrees with single prunings, rather than smaller subtrees with repeated prunings. In fact, if we do this by relabeling the sets as follows:

$$S'_1 = S_2, \quad S'_2 = S_3, \quad S'_3 = S_4, \quad S'_4 = S_5, \quad S'_5 = S_1$$

then the solution proceeds as in Figure 6.46 rather than as in Figure 6.45. For this trivial example, the reordering reduces the number of nodes that have to be expanded from 30 to 15, and the execution time is reduced in the same ratio. For larger problems the difference can be enormous. The reordering that we illustrated with this example is a static one, wherein the nodes on a given level all correspond to the same set, and so have the same degree. More sophisticated forms of backtracking allow for:

- arranging the levels of search dynamically;
- suspending the search of a subtree S if it appears to be unprofitable, and examining other parts of the solution tree, with the capability of resuming the search of S later.

Although we are happy to have an algorithm to solve the SDR problem, as demonstrated in this section, we note that its complexity is exponential in the number of sets. In Section 7.4.3, however, we will discover more powerful methods for dealing with the problem.

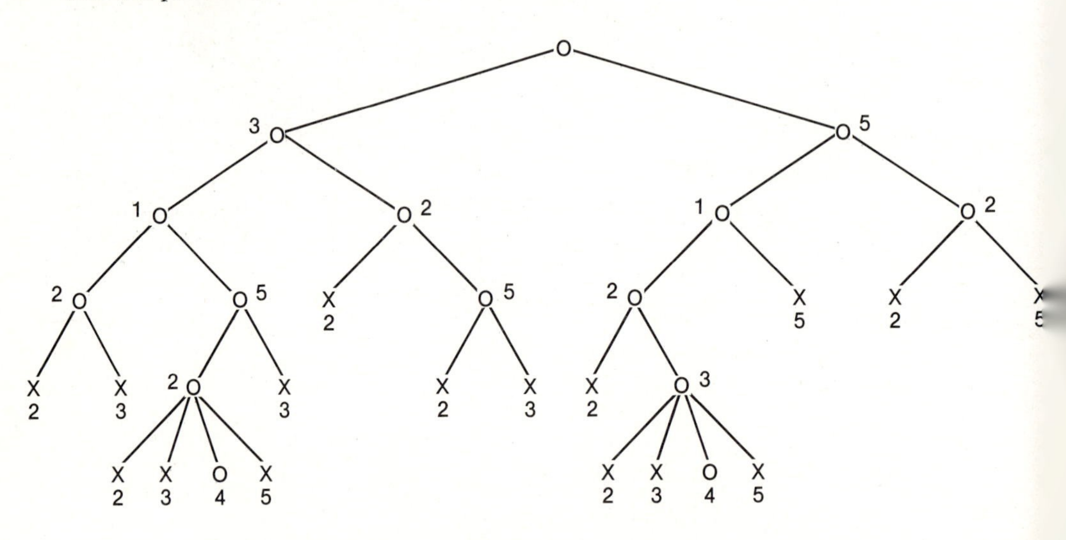

Figure 6.46 A Superior Backtracking Solution to Eqs. 6.19

†6.8.2.2 Nondeterministic Algorithms. One way of viewing our backtracking solution to the SDR problem is that we kept making guesses at the solution until we found it. In order to make such guessing games work properly in a program, under the name of backtracking, we have to be quite careful about various bookkeeping details. A very useful abstraction is obtained by allowing an algorithm to employ the following three idealized functions:

choice(X) – which selects values of a variable X;

failure(*node*) – which causes a path of computation in a solution tree to be abandoned at that node;

success(*leaf*) – which causes the algorithm to terminate, with the solution available via the selected values leading to that leaf.

At a pragmatic level, these functions are implemented in terms of backtracking with a stack, in much the same manner that recursion is implemented with a stack; but it is useful to imagine that they are implemented by either of the following two methods:

A. Whenever there is a choice to be made, the machine clones itself as many times as there are possibilities, and then each of the choices is investigated in parallel by one of these machines.

B. Whenever there is a choice to be made, the machine is able to guess which choice will lead to a solution, and then that course is the one pursued.

An algorithm operating in either of these fashions is called a *nondeterministic algorithm*. The concept of nondeterministic algorithms was pioneered by Floyd [1967], and a review of the subject can be found in Cohen [1979a].

Of course, we don't know how to have a machine duplicate itself indefinitely, nor do we know how to construct a machine that will always make a correct guess. Nonetheless, it seems evident that either capability, A or B, should yield a significant advantage in solving problems. The reason for this is simply that we could then explore a solution tree in time proportional to its depth rather than in time proportional to the exponential number of its nodes. Now, the following type of problem occurs rather frequently: The solution of the problem requires exponential time, but once knowing a soluiion it takes just polynomial time to confirm it. An example of this would be the SDR problem as we have described it. If we are told that a given m-tuple is a solution to this problem, then it requires just polynomial time to verify the assertion. Not knowing the answer though, it requires exponential time to explore all the branches of the solution tree. Nonetheless, since the time to explore any single path is polynomial, a nondeterministic algorithm (or machine), could find the solution in polynomial time. Such a Nondeterministic Polynomial algorithm is said to be an *NP algorithm*.

There are many problems that we know how to solve with *NP* algorithms, but don't know how to solve with *P* algorithms, which compute deterministically in Polynomial time. Such problems are then said to be in the class *NP*. Evidently, the class of *NP* problems properly subsumes the class of *P* problems; that is, the abilities A or B cited above should allow us to solve problems that are in the former class but not in the latter one. This may be so. In fact, although intuition and a variety of circumstantial results indicate that the class *NP* is larger than the class *P*, the best efforts of computer scientists to prove this supposition have come to nil so far. What would such a proof entail? It would require proving that, for even a single problem known to be in *NP*, there is no *P* algorithm for its solution. Even though there are many *NP* problems for which no *P* solutions are known, in none of these cases has the impossibility of a P solution been demonstrated. (Note that the SDR problem is not actually in the class NP. In Chapter 7 we will encounter algorithms of polynomial complexity for its solution; however, these do not constitute such a demonstration.) So we are left with the astonishing conclusion that the seemingly powerful capability to always make a correct guess in the face of uncertainty is of no provable advantage. This leads to the most dramatic question in computer science at this writing: Is $P = NP$?

In discussing NP algorithms and P algorithms, we need to be aware of an important distinction. To frame this matter, we pose our problems in such manner that an algorithm should either find an instance of a solution (Yes), or else inform us that no solution exists (No). A P algorithm will always terminate with one of these responses. However, we cannot expect an NP algorithm to provide a No answer in polynomial time, since the possibility of making the correct guesses does not exist in such a case. In fact an NP problem is, by definition, one for which (i) a Yes answer can be detected by an NP algorithm, and (ii) this answer can be verified by a P algorithm.

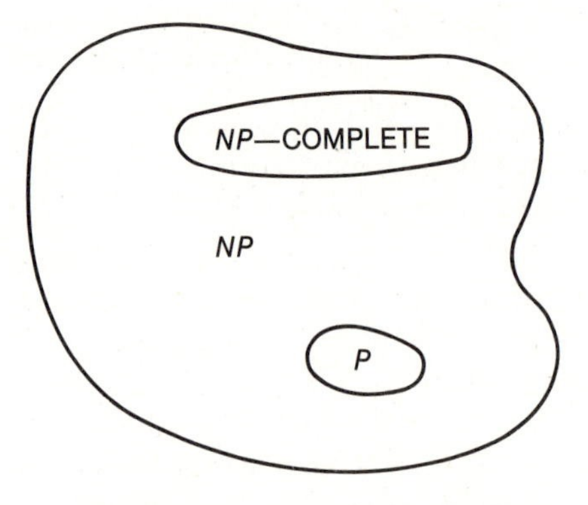

Figure 6.47 The World of *NP*

There is more to the story in the following circumstances, suggesting that indeed $P \neq NP$. It is often possible to transform or reduce one problem X to a different problem Y such that, if we could solve Y in a certain manner, then we could also solve X in this manner. Such techniques have been applied to hundreds of NP problems to show that they are equivalently "hardest" problems in NP. Moreover, these techniques have the character that the reduction can be performed with polynomial complexity in the size of the problem. So if we could solve one of these hardest problems with a polynomial algorithm, then by composing that polynomial algorithm with the polynomial reduction,[4] we could solve any of the other problems in NP with a polynomial algorithm. The class of equivalently hardest problems is known as *NP-complete*. At the present time, it is conjectured that the relation of the sets NP, NP-complete, and P are as shown in Figure 6.47. That no

[4] This illustrates the significance of the observation, made in Section 1.3.2.1, that the class of polynomials is closed under composition.

one has been able to find a P algorithm for even one NP-complete problem strongly suggests that $P \neq NP$. Nonetheless, this is an open question that is the subject of much research; two good references are Garey and Johnson [1979] and Lewis and Papadimitriou [1978].

†6.8.3 Branch-and-Bound

Backtracking is an improvement upon the exhaustive search that underlies DFS; the improvement derives from being able to prune entire subtrees. It is also possible to improve upon exhaustive search with a variation of BFS; this strategy is known as *branch-and-bound*. The same search tree of Figure 6.41 that we used to illustrate BFS and DFS can be used to demonstrate the essential feature of branch-and-bound, which is to *open* nodes for consideration and selectively *close* them as candidates for follow-up. In applying the method to the problem at hand, we will simply use a table of the partial distances to each open node for deciding which is the best candidate. The basic step in branch-and-bound consists of picking the open node with minimum partial distance, closing it, and opening its children. The repetitive application of this process to the tree of Figure 6.41 is illustrated in Figure 6.48.

Close Node	Open Nodes	Distance At
A	*B* – 60 *C* – 20 *D* – 12	12 *D*
D	*K* – 50 *L* – 59	20 C
C	*G* – 52 *H* – 30 *I* – 49 *J* – 36	30 *H*
H	O – 37	36 *J*
J	*P* – 42	37 O
O	*U* – 48 *V* – 50	42 *P*
P	*P* – 42	42 *P*

Figure 6.48 Branch-and-Bound Search

The complexity of branch-and-bound is proportional to the number of nodes that are closed; each such operation requires selecting the open node at minimum partial distance, finding its successors, and computing their partial distances. In our example, note that as soon as the leaf node P is closed on the seventh step, it is sure to be the leaf of minimal distance, and no further confirmatory search is required.

```
procedure BRANCH_BOUND (root: link; var goal: link; var best: integer);

type    prqobj = record
            base: integer;
            ptr: link;
        end;

var     done: boolean;
        next: link;
        datum,defer: prqobj;

begin
   done := false;
   INIT_PRQ_H (pq);
   defer.base := 0;
   defer.ptr := root;
   INSERT_PRQ_H (pq,defer);
   repeat
      REMOVE_PRQ_H (pq,datum);
      if datum.ptr↑.left = nil then         {a leaf}
         done := true
      else begin                           {process children}
         next := datum.ptr↑.left;
         repeat
            defer.base := datum.base + next↑.cost;
            defer.ptr := next;
            INSERT_PRQ_H (pq,defer);
            next := next↑.rite;
         until next = nil;
      end;
   until done;
   goal := datum.ptr;
   best := datum.base;
end;
```

Algorithm 6.12 BRANCH_BOUND

If the implementation of BFS calls for a queue, and the implementation of DFS calls for a stack, what structure is needed for the implementation of branch-and-bound? A little reflection shows that we want to employ a priority queue, in order to efficiently find the open node at minimum distance. For this purpose, we can almost use the algorithms P_QUEUE_H intact, with the definition that the open-node queue objects each consist of a distance and a pointer. Another minor but important point is to reverse the sense of the inequality operator in INSERT_PRQ_H, and to reverse the sense of two inequality operators in REMOVE_PRQ_H, since high priority for this problem means smallest distance. Our corresponding implementation is the procedure BRANCH_BOUND (Algorithm 6.12), with input parameter *root* pointing at the tree to be searched, and with output parameters *goal* and *best* identifying the location and the distance of the winning leaf. It is instructive to compare BRANCH_BOUND with BFS_TREE (Algorithm 6.10). Overall, they are very similar. The principal difference is that in BFS we can never by sure about the relative worth of a node except by extensive comparisons and so must keep searching until the queue is completely empty of prospects, whereas in branch-and-bound we explore the tree with more assurance and are done as soon as we remove a leaf from the priority queue.

Recall from Section 6.8.2 that search can be described in terms of looking for a tuple of values that satisfies some criterion function, subject also to some constraint functions. In branch-and-bound, we try to simplify matters by solving a different problem (X') than that originally given (X). The objective is for X' to have constraints such that its solution encompasses that of X, and for X' to have a criterion function (Φ') that is a good predictor for that of X (Φ). It is important that Φ' be conservative, erring on the side of admitting poor candidates, rather than excluding good candidates. For our sample search problem, Φ' was safe but not very discerning as a predictor; essentially, for any open node, it predicted zero additional distance to reach a leaf. A better example would be that of searching for the shortest highway distance to some location, and using the airline distance from an open node to the destination as a predictor of value. Just as there is a trade-off in backtracking between the effort to refine the constraints that allow pruning and the effort to search subtrees, so in branch-and-bound is there a trade-off between the effort to find a Φ' that shaves the margin of error and the effort to close nodes. Branch-and-bound has been found to be a highly efficient search technique for many problems, and we will examine one such case in Section 7.4.4.3. One of its principal hazards is that the amount of information that must be stored in the priority queue can become rather large. Further discussion of the method can be found in Horowitz and Sahni [1978] and Lawler and Wood [1966].

6.8.4 Games

Games provide particularly appealing instances of search trees. To begin the story, imagine that we are playing the following simple game [Raphael 1976]. There is an initial pile of seven stones, and A and B alternate with each other in removing stones from the pile. The rules are simply that a player must take 1, 2, or 3 stones when it is his turn. The objective is to cause the other player to take the last stone.

The possibilities in this game are diagrammed in Figure 6.49. Here, the information at a non-terminal node is the number of stones still in the pile before a move; the branches have labels corresponding to the number of stones removed on a move; and the leaves are marked A or B, according to whether A or B is the winner in the sequence of moves leading to that leaf. There is something significantly different about this tree. It embodies not just one point of view, as in the case of the trees in the preceding sections, but two opposing points of view. At any given level of the tree, a player is attempting to make a choice that will cause his opponent to lose; but the players alternate with successive levels, so that a see-saw is taking place. In a game-tree such as this, these alternate levels are called *plys*. Since the outcome of a game has always been decided when we reach a leaf, a game tree is best analyzed starting from the leaves and working our way back up to the

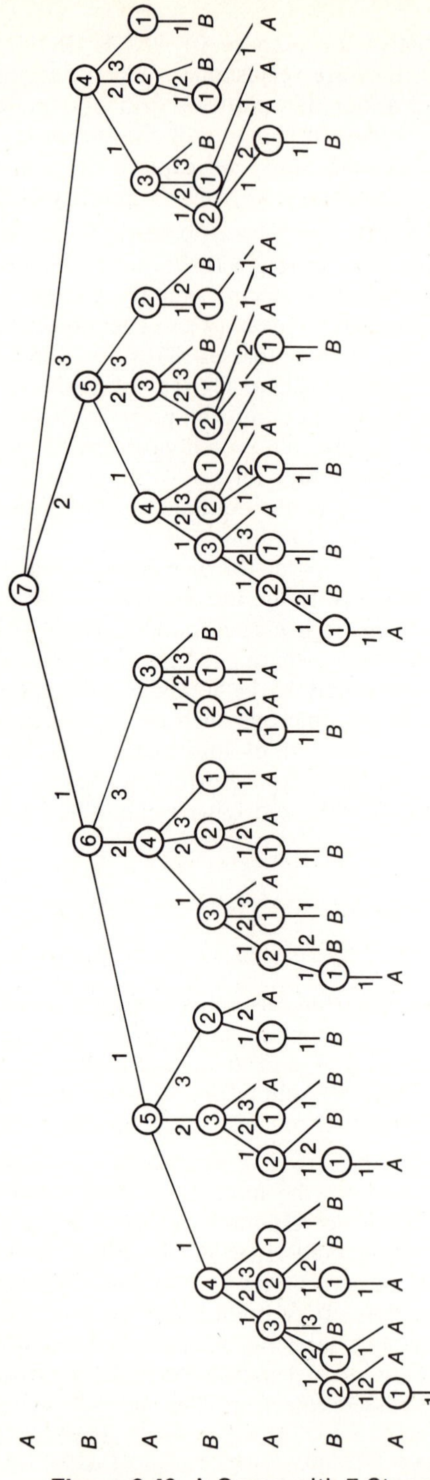

Figure 6.49 A Game with 7 Stones

root, if the size of the tree does not prevent it. To see how this works, consider the subtree from Figure 6.49 that is shown in Figure 6.50:

1. Node *P* is a winning position for *A* and so can be marked with an *A*.
2. At node *Q*, since it is *A*'s turn, he will rationally choose the left branch, forcing *B* to lose; so node *Q* can be marked with an *A*.
3. Node *R* is a winning position for *B* and so can be marked with a *B*.
4. At node *S*, since it is *B*'s turn, he will rationally choose the middle branch, forcing *A* to lose; so node *S* can be marked with a *B*.

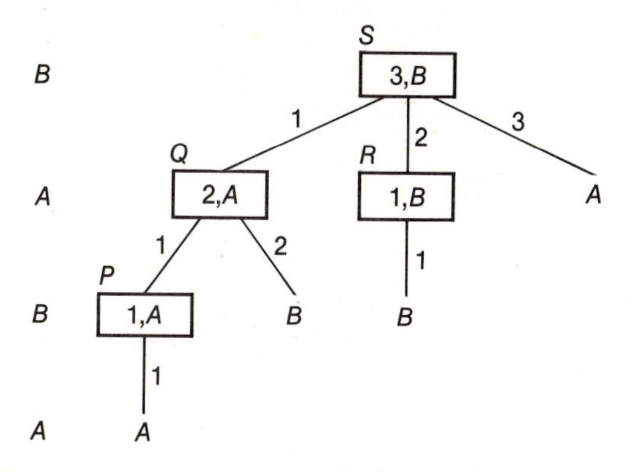

Figure 6.50 Marking Game Tree Nodes from the Leaves Upward

This analysis can be backed up all the way to the root, using the following simple rules:

1. If it is *A*'s (*B*'s) turn at a node and *any* of the children of the node are marked as winning situations for *A* (*B*), then that node is marked as a winning situation for *A* (*B*).
2. If it is *A*'s (*B*'s) turn at a node and *none* of the children of the node are marked as winning situations for *A* (*B*), then that node is marked as a winning situation for *B* (*A*).

The results of applying these marking rules to Figure 6.49 are shown in Figure 6.51, which establishes that whoever moves first can win, provided he removes two stones on the first move and plays rationally thereafter, as indicated by the branches in heavy lines.

At this point, we need to step back from our simple example and make several observations. For one, we can imagine actually generating the entire tree corresponding to a game and then marking the nodes, but this is wasteful on two accounts. The tree may require an enormous amount of storage; furthermore, we probably do not even need it explicitly. It may be possible to generate the nodes sequentially according to some algorithm, in which case the information already obtained from some subtree of a node may make it unnecessary to generate and mark the other subtrees of that node. This may be seen in Figure 6.52, where the left-most subtree (from the root) of Figure 6.51 is reproduced. If the nodes are generated in postorder, then those nodes below the dashed line do not need to be processed at all. For example, from examining the left child, node *P* has been

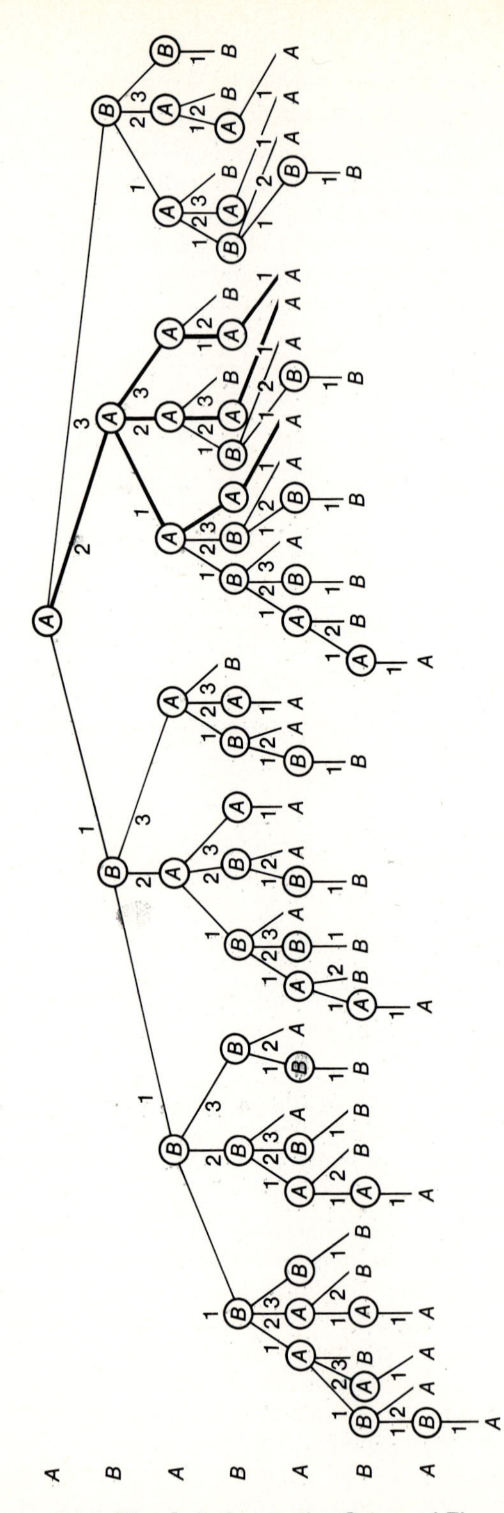

Figure 6.51 The Solution to the Game of Figure 6.49

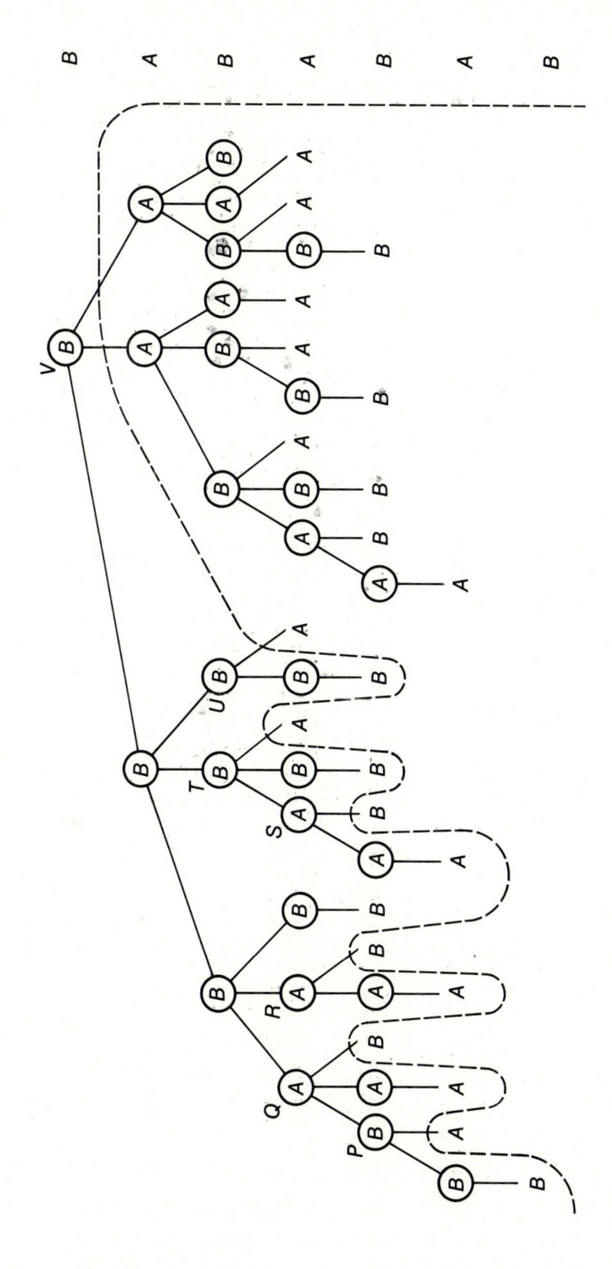

Figure 6.52 Avoidable Subtree Evaluations in Figure 6.51

marked as favoring B, so the right child is irrelevant. Also, once nodes Q, R, and S have been marked as favoring A, their right children can be ignored, and node T and U are similar with respect to B. Finally, at node V, since the left child already favors B, the entire middle and right subtrees can be omitted from consideration.

Our example game is necessarily rather trivial, in order to keep the tree of reasonable size. In fact, it is quite easy to find a strategy that will guarantee a win, without such elaborate analysis. In more complicated games, on the other hand, the application of this principle may be very appropriate. However, such a brute-force approach is completely inadequate for many games – for example, for chess, or even checkers, with the large number of possible moves at each ply and the great number of plys to be followed to reach terminal nodes. In such complicated games, we must start at the root rather than at the leaves and explore a limited number of moves for a limited number of plys. At the frontier of our search in this truncated tree, we need an *evaluation function* to assess how good that potential situation may be. For chess, such a function could measure number and quality of pieces held by each player, quality of board position, special situations such as pins or checks, etc. Since such a function is not a binary one, the marking process then proceeds by *minimaxing*, which is the process of alternately selecting maxima and minima from one level to the next. This will be illustrated in the next section.

Finally, note that there is a lot of wasteful activity in Figures 6.49 and 6.51. The subtree of Figure 6.50 is replicated many times in Figure 6.49, both exactly and with reversed logic. Yet the same analysis is applied in detail each time. Have we encountered any technique that can avoid this? Yes, we have; by using tabulation (see Section 5.4.2.1) to record the values of encoded positions, we can circumvent the exponential behavior exhibited in the figures.

†6.8.4.1 Alpha-Beta Search. In the preceding section, we alluded to the infeasibility of evaluating large game trees from the leaves upward. As a dramatic illustration of this, the complete search tree for chess is estimated to have an average branching factor of 35 and an average height of 100. This corresponds to about $35^{100} \approx 2.5 \times 10^{154}$ leaves to be evaluated. Even if a computer could evaluate each of these possibilities in a nanosecond, it would take 10^{138} years to examine them all. Thus, for efficiently searching large trees, it is important to eliminate the need to search some of the subtrees by using information already obtained – in other words, to "prune" some of the branches. This was illustrated pictorially in Figure 6.52. We now describe this principle more precisely, in the technique known as *alpha-beta search*. It is, in fact, a specialization of branch-and-bound to the case of game trees.

Recall that selection of branches in game trees is based on some evaluation function whose value is maximized/minimized at alternate plys. If we refer to the player at even levels in the tree as the maximizer and the player at odd levels as the minimizer, then the alpha-beta procedure associates extra information with each node, as follows:

1. At maximizer plys, an alpha value is kept with each node as the tentatively highest value attainable at that node.

2. At minimizer plys, a beta value is kept with each node as the tentatively lowest value attainable at that node.

Refer now to Figure 6.53, which shows an excerpt from some larger game tree. The minimizer, at node *P*, will choose the left branch, and so the beta value for node *P* is −2. Backing up to node *Q*, the maximizer can record a tentative alpha value of −2, signifying that he can expect to get at least that much, no matter what else happens. Next, at node *R*, the minimizer will choose the right branch this time for a beta value of 6; and this can be propagated to node *Q* to change its alpha value to 6. Finally, if we examine node *S*, the fact that its value is −1 implies that the beta value of node *T* is less than or equal to −1. From the point of view of node *Q*, there is no need to also examine nodes *U* and *V*, since the right branch from *Q* is already determined to be worse than the middle branch, and it doesn't matter how much worse it is.

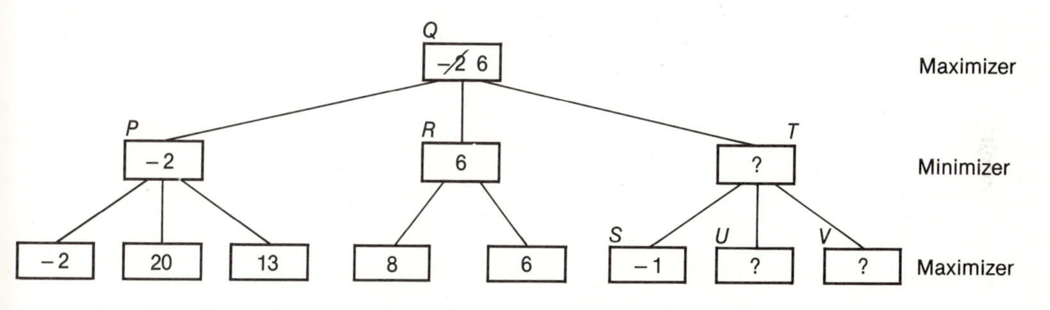

Figure 6.53 Pruning with Alpha-Beta Values

To summarize matters:

1. Alpha values can never decrease, so we discontinue search below any maximizer node if its current alpha value is equal to or greater than the current beta value of *any* of its minimizer node ancestors.
2. Beta values can never increase, so we discontinue search below any minimizer node if its current beta value is equal to or less than the current alpha value of *any* of its maximizer node ancestors.

To illustrate this technique, consider Figure 6.54 as representing some hypothetical game tree in which the leaves, drawn with their values, are generated or scanned from left to right. The tree is then redrawn in Figure 6.55, with the varying alpha-beta values shown in the non-terminal nodes. Branches to those nodes that need to be considered are drawn with heavy lines; branches to those nodes that are pruned are drawn with light lines. Since this searching method can be tricky to understand, and since it is awkward to convey the dynamically varying alpha-beta values in a diagram, you would do well to test your understanding of this method by copying Figure 6.54 and developing on your copy what Figure 6.55 should look like.

In case you are stuck, or in case your tree is beginning to look more butchered than manicured, some remarks about what happens inside the two dotted regions of Figure 6.55 may be helpful. Consider first what happens in the right hand excerpt even though, in time, it occurs after the left hand excerpt. Node *P* has been determined to have a tentative alpha value of 17, but this is greater than the beta value

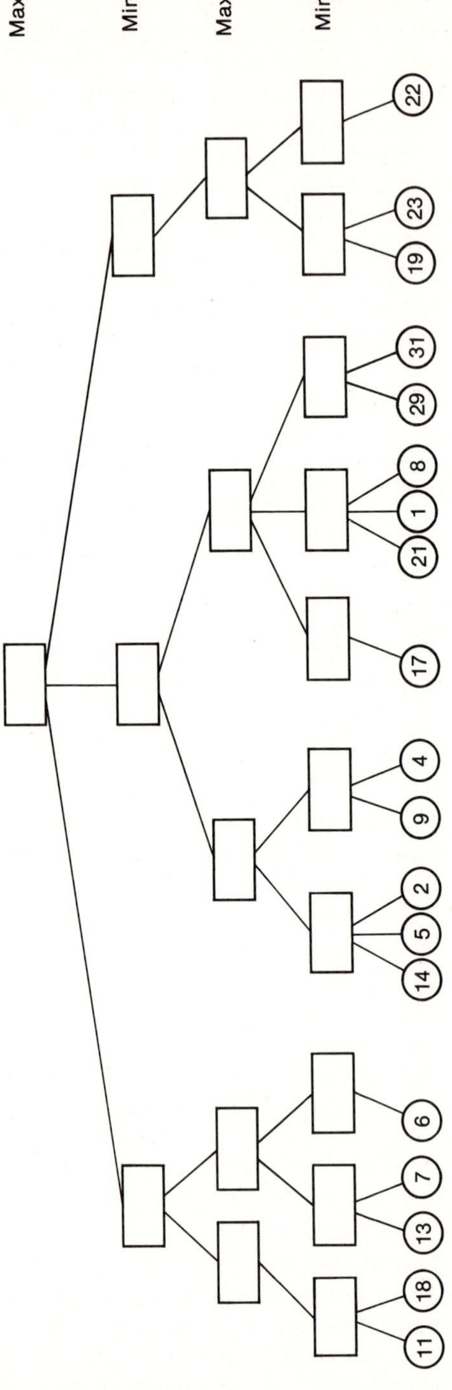

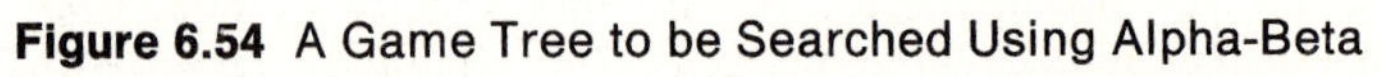
Figure 6.54 A Game Tree to be Searched Using Alpha-Beta

of 5 at node Q. The alpha value can only increase if the middle and right branches of node P are examined. However, they are irrelevant because the minimizer can be certain that the left branch from Q gives a better beta value than the right branch ever will. So prune the two rightmost branches from node P.

Consider next the left hand excerpt at the point in time that it is examined. Node R has been determined to have a tentative beta value of 5. While no tentative values have yet been established for nodes Q or U, node S is already known to have a tentative alpha value of 7. Thus, node T is irrelevant. Even though it may reduce the beta value at node R, when that value is backed up to node S, it will be discriminated against in favor of the better value of 7 that is available from the left branch of S. So prune node T and propagate the beta value of 5 from node R to node U. This alpha value of 5 at node U is only significant as a mark against which to evaluate the contribution from the right branch of U (the alpha value may possibly increase).

How much can be pruned using this technique? It greatly depends upon the actual values in the tree and the order in which the subtrees are examined. In the worst case, there may be no improvement at all. But in the best case, assuming a branching factor b and a depth d, it has been shown [Slagle and Dixon 1969] that the number of leaf evaluations is reduced from b^d to

$$b^{\left\lceil \frac{(d+1)}{2} \right\rceil} + b^{\left\lfloor \frac{(d-1)}{2} \right\rfloor} - 1 \qquad (6.20)$$

In other words, with the optimal sequence of encountering leaf values, alpha-beta search allows the tree to be searched twice as deeply for the same amount of effort expended in ordinary minimaxing without the pruning. What can we expect from alpha-beta if the sequence of leaf values is random? In that case, it has been shown that the depth of search is 4/3 what it would be for ordinary minimaxing [Knuth and Moore 1975].

6.9 OVERVIEW

We began this chapter by citing the pervasiveness of trees, and this should be quite apparent by now. For the most part, we have dealt with explicit tree data structures: how to represent them, how to traverse them, how to associate meaning with them, and how to search them. In the latter topic, moreover, we encountered cases of solution trees where no explicit tree structure even exists.

Trees represent an interesting middle ground between linear data structures (arrays, queues, stacks, strings) and the more general non-linear data structures (Lists and graphs). The unifying principle that every node except the root has in-degree of precisely one has two important consequences. It allows us to find an efficient scheme for representation, via the correspondence between ordered trees and binary trees. It also enables us to develop simple, systematic algorithms for traversing trees, without worrying about cycles. In the extreme case of complete

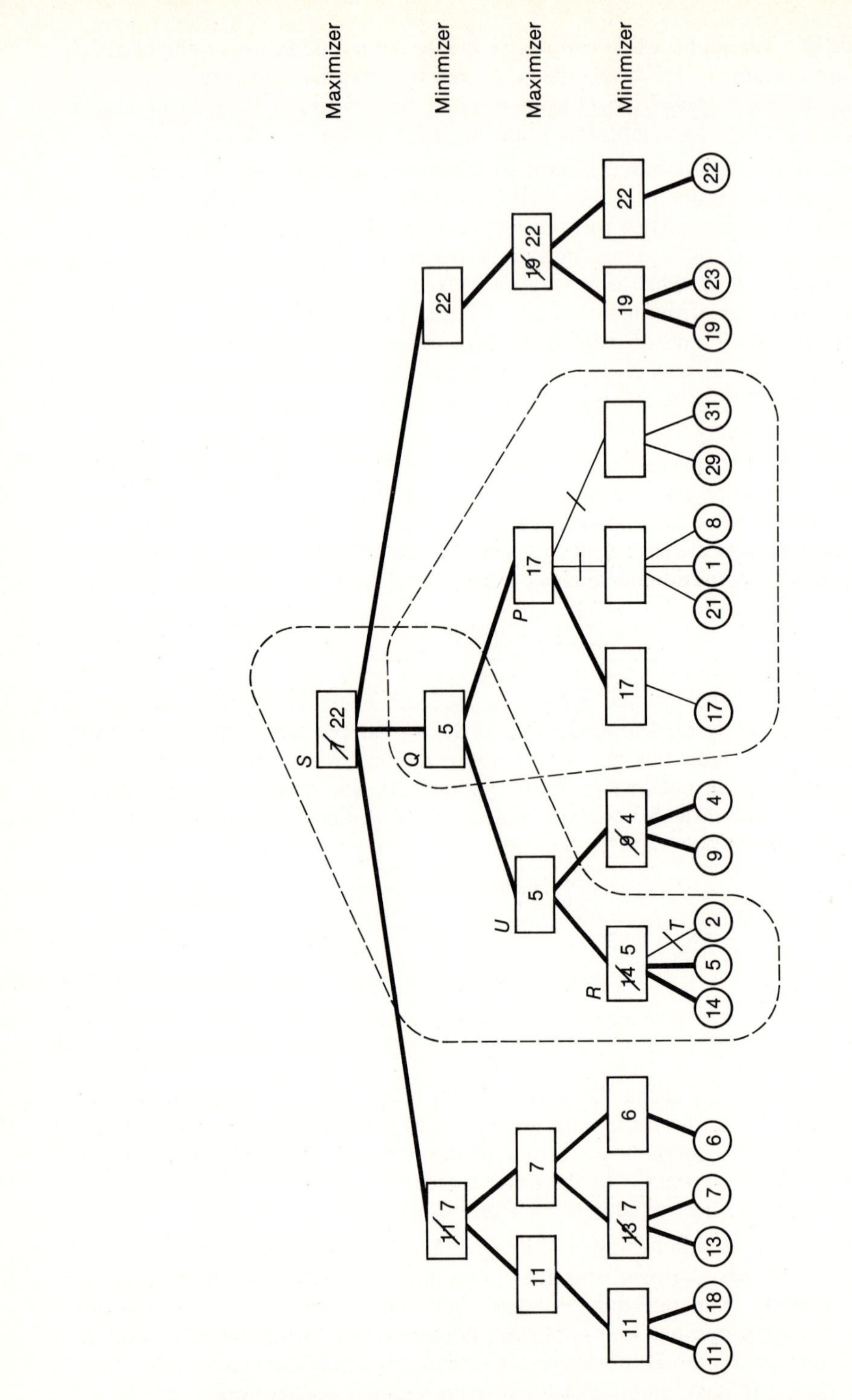

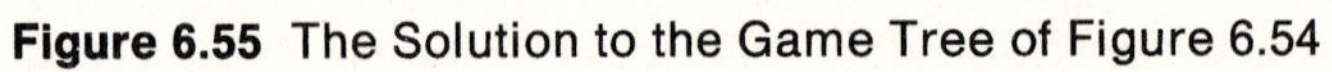
Figure 6.55 The Solution to the Game Tree of Figure 6.54

t-ary trees, the representation collapses to being implicit, without the need of explicit pointers, and this yields important efficiencies in both space and time.

Although this chapter is about trees, it should be reiterated that in some applications, we have actually used trees as powerful means of dealing with sets. One example occurs with priority queues, where we can rephrase the capabilities as:

- add a member to a set, and
- extract the minimum member of the set.

Another occurs with the UNION-FIND algorithm, for which we can rephrase the capabilities as:

- add a member to a set;
- test for membership in a set;
- compute the union of two sets.

Set operations carried out by these mechanisms do not have the limitations that are inherent with built-in set operations in Pascal, where we are restricted to a universal set isomorphic to $0 \,..\, n$, for small n.

In many ways, this chapter has covered only the first half of the subject of trees. When we turn to Searching in Chapter 10, we will find that trees are by far the most important (though not the only) data structure for that purpose. In fact, some authors recognize this de facto situation by including searching as a sub-topic of trees. For us, that approach would have caused this chapter to be intolerably long. More significantly, it is important to look at the subject of searching without being restricted to trees.

In Chapter 5, the last topic that we studied was the intimate relationship between stacks and effective computability. It is intriguing to find another basic issue of computability in our study of trees – that of nondeterministic algorithms and the class NP.

6.10 BIBLIOGRAPHIC NOTES

- Other link inversion traversal schemes, not discussed in Section 6.4.3, can be found in Burkhard [1975], Fenner and Loizou [1984], and Kilgour [1981].

- Permutations have been used as the bases of ranking functions for binary and t-ary trees by a variety of techniques [Knott 1977; Rotem and Varol 1978; Solomon and Finkel 1980; Trojanowski 1978]. Ranking functions based upon feasible sequences can be found in Er [1985], Ruskey [1978], and Ruskey and Hu [1977].

- Branch-and-bound solutions to the computation of time-efficient and space-efficient decision trees are given in Reinwald and Solano [1966, 1967], a dynamic programming solution is that of Schumacher and Sevcik [1976], and an approach combining branch-and-bound with dynamic programming is Martelli and Montanari [1978]. Some heuristics are presented in Ganapathy and Rajaraman [1973], Pollack [1965], Sethi and Chatterjee [1980], Shwayder [1974], and Verhelst [1972]. Yet another approach is to generate decision table code by applying compiler optimization techniques [Myers 1972]. For an excellent review and discussion of methods and results of computing optimal decision trees, consult Moret [1982].

- Good general descriptions of backtracking and suggestions for its efficient implementation can be found in Bitner and Reingold [1975], Fillmore and Williamson [1974], Francez et al. [1977], Golomb and Baumert [1965], Prenner et al. [1972], Purdom et al. [1971], and Wells [1971]. The use of constraints in limiting search is discussed in Freuder [1978, 1982].

6.11 REFERENCE TO TERMINOLOGY

6.12 EXERCISES

Sections 6.1 – 6.2

6.1 Discuss the circumstances under which a genealogical chart is not a tree.

6.2 Convert the trees in Figure 6.56 as indicated:
(a) the ordered tree of (a) to the corresponding binary tree;
(b) the binary tree of (b) to the corresponding ordered tree.

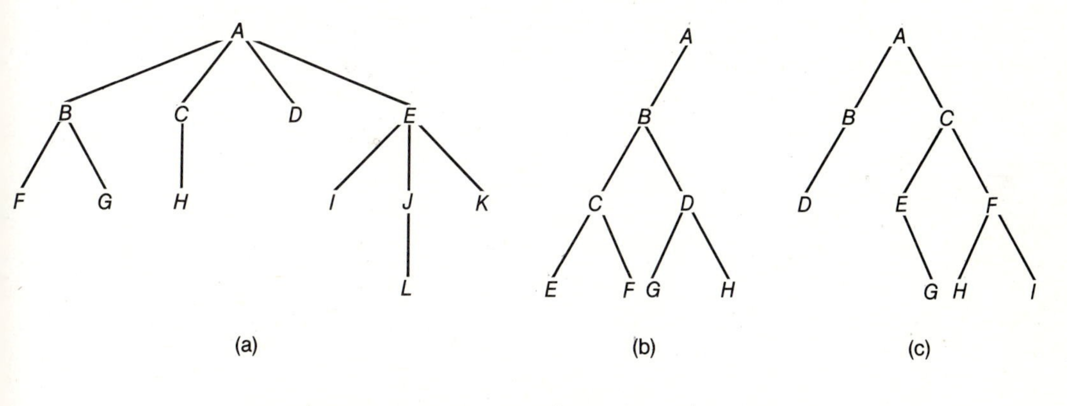

Figure 6.56 Trees for Exercises 6.2, 6.3, and 6.11

Section 6.3

6.3 Traverse the binary tree of Figure 6.56(c) as follows: (a) in preorder, (b) in inorder, and (c) in postorder.

6.4 [Aho et al. 1983] In the following table, the rows correspond to the nature of the extended relationship between two nodes *m* and *n* (see Section 6.1), and the column headings "...order(*m*) < ...order(*n*)" mean that *m* precedes *n* when the binary tree containing *m* and *n* is traversed according to that order. For this table, indicate by T(rue), F(alse), or ? whether the given row and column conditions always, never, or sometimes occur simultaneously.

relationship of *m* to *n*	preorder(*m*) < preorder(*n*)	inorder(*m*) < inorder(*n*)	postorder(*m*) < postorder(*n*)
m left of *n*			
m right of *n*			
m ancestor of *n*			
m descendant of *n*			

††**6.5** [Dasarthy and Yang 1980] In a binary tree B, we can construct the *reflected* binary tree B^R by exchanging the left and right subtrees at each node *except* the root. Further, for an ordered tree T, we can then construct the reflected tree T^R, via the correspondences: $T \rightarrow B \rightarrow B^R \rightarrow T^R$. Thus in Figure 6.57, for the tree $T1$ of (a), such a sequence of transformations yields the tree $T1^R$ of (b).

(a) Construct the sequence of transformations just described, starting with the tree $T2$ of Figure 6.57(c), and arriving at $T2^R$.

(b) An important notion in trees is that of the total path length P in the tree, equal to the sum of the numbers of edges from the root to each node. Thus,

$$P(T) = 3 \times 1 + 4 \times 2 + 2 \times 3 = 17\,, \quad P(T^R) = 2 \times 1 + 3 \times 2 + 3 \times 3 + 4 = 21$$

Prove that for a tree with n nodes, $P(T) + P(T^R) = P(B) + n - 1$. (In our example, we find that $17 + 21 = 29 + 10 - 1$.)

(c) Denoting by $E(T)$ the number of leaf nodes in T, prove that $E(T) + E(T^R) = n$.

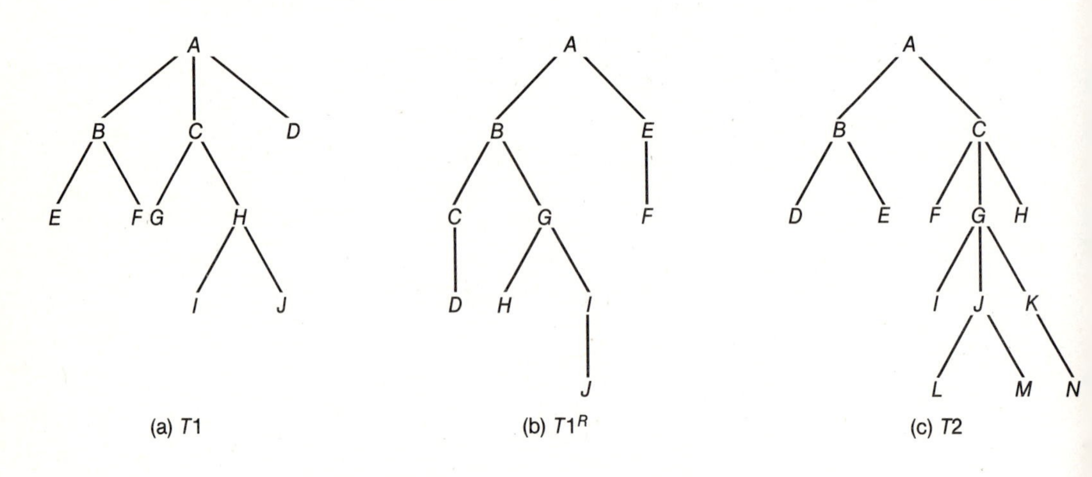

Figure 6.57 Trees for Exercises 6.5 and 6.34

Section 6.4

6.6 Two binary trees are *similar* when they have identical branching structure, which means that either they are both empty, or they are both non-empty and have similar left and right subtrees. Write a function that compares two binary trees for similarity.

6.7 Write a procedure that traverses a binary tree in preorder sequence using a stack. Have your program print out the data contents of the nodes as it visits them.

†**6.8** Write a procedure that traverses a binary tree in postorder sequence using a stack. Have your program print out the data contents of the nodes as it visits them.

6.9 Write a procedure that traverses in preorder sequence a binary tree threaded for inorder traversal.

††6.10 For a binary tree threaded for postorder traversal, write a procedure to perform the postorder traversal.

6.11 [Lindstrom 1973] A generalization of the usual traversal orders for a binary tree that is sometimes useful is *triple-order traversal*: visit node, traverse left subtree, visit node, traverse right subtree, visit node. Suppose that visits to nodes under this scheme are numbered in serial fashion. Use Figure 6.56(c) to demonstrate that we can visit each node just once by retaining only those visits with number equal to 0 (or 1, or 2) mod 3.

†6.12 For the tree of Figure 6.58, add dashed lines showing all of the edges that would be inserted at one time or another if it were traversed by the algorithm MORRIS.

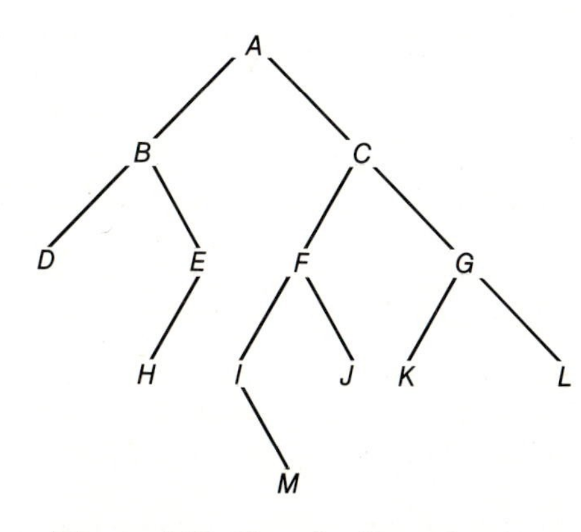

Figure 6.58 Tree for Exercise 6.12

††6.13 Write a version of the algorithm MORRIS that could be used to traverse a binary tree in postorder.

Section 6.5

†6.14 A complete t-ary tree has I internal nodes and X external nodes, with N nodes altogether.

(a) Derive formulas for I and N as functions of X.

(b) Derive formulas for I and X as functions of N.

†6.15 [Tarjan 1983c] By associating non-standard semantics with the links in binary search tree nodes, it is possible to represent a BST in such fashion that any one of the related nodes (parent, left child, or right child) can be accessed in no more than two linking operations.

(a) Illustrate how this can be accomplished.

(b) Sketch the algorithmic statements required for accessing each of the three related nodes.

†**6.16** Write a procedure that reads an ordered tree representation as in Figure 6.17(b) and generates an internal representation in the form of Figure 6.17(d), as preorder sequential with degrees.

††**6.17** Write a procedure that reads an ordered tree representation as in Figure 6.17(b) and generates the corresponding binary tree.

Section 6.6

6.18 The following table shows the Best Actor Awards for 1963 – 1977. Draw the alphabetical BST obtained by inserting them in chronological order, as was done in Figure 6.20.

1963	Poitier	1968	Robertson	1973	Lemmon
1964	Harrison	1969	Wayne	1974	Carney
1965	Marvin	1970	Scott	1975	Nicholson
1966	Scofield	1971	Hackman	1976	Finch
1967	Steiger	1972	Brando	1977	Dreyfus

††**6.19** Write a function analogous to BST_INSERT for inserting a node and updating the threads in a BST threaded for inorder traversal.

††**6.20** [Stephenson 1980] In the usual manner of constructing a BST, new nodes are always inserted at the leaves. It is also possible to grow a BST at the root by using the search key K to split the BST into three components: a left BST containing all nodes with keys less than K, the node K itself, and a right BST containing all nodes with keys greater than K. For the BST of Figure 6.59(a) and the search argument 44, such a splitting operation would produce the three components shown in (b) of the figure.

(a) Write a function analogous to BST_INSERT for constructing a BST in this manner.

(b) Analyze the comparative advantages and disadvantages of the two methods for constructing BST's.

6.21 Draw the expression tree corresponding to

$$(A-(B-C)*(D+E/(F-G)*H)*(I+J)-K)/L$$

†**6.22** Suppose that you have 12 seemingly identical balls and are told that one of them is either heavier or lighter than the others. Draw a decision tree for identifying the odd ball and determining whether it is heavier or lighter, all with just three weighings.

6.23 Given a heap to be used as a priority queue, with contents as shown in Figure 6.60:

(a) What does the restored heap look like after we remove 83 from the root?

(b) What does the restored heap look like after we add 60 to the heap of (a)?

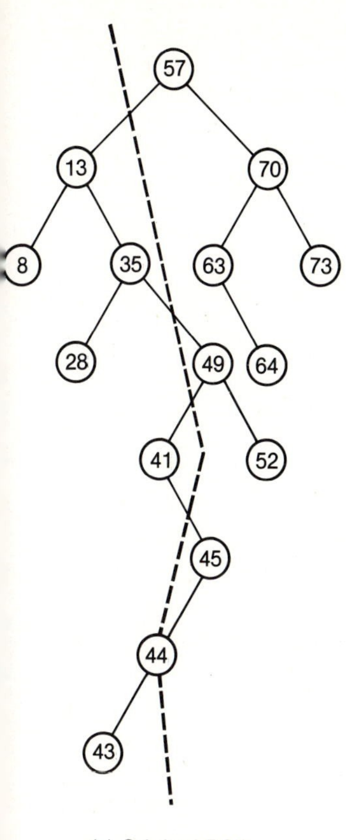

(a) Original BST

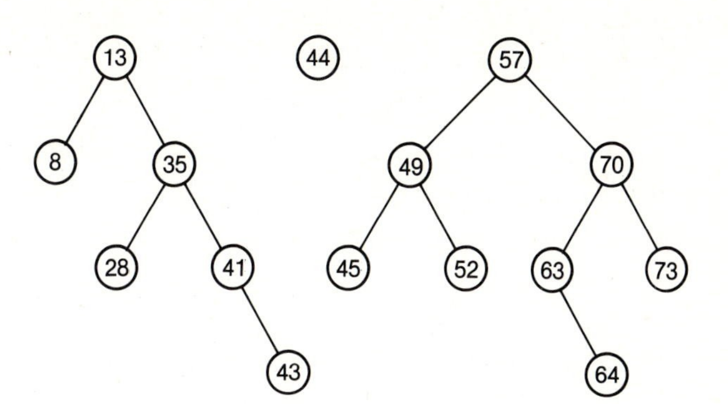

(b) After Splitting BST on 44

Figure 6.59 Trees for Exercise 6.20

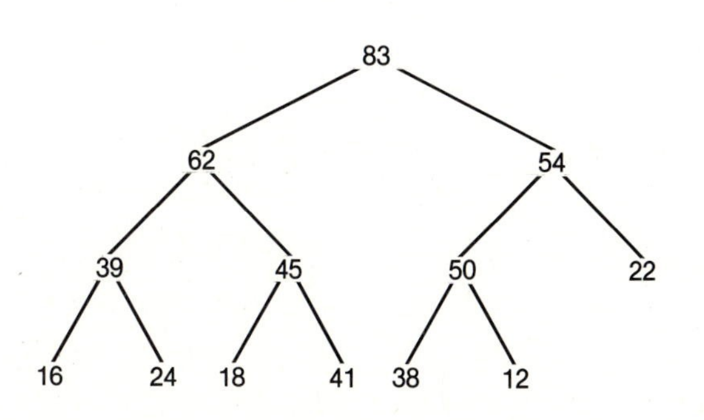

Figure 6.60 Tree for Exercise 6.23

†6.24 [Vuillemin 1980] A *Cartesian tree* is a tree defined on pairs of values (x_i, y_i), with the properties that it is a binary search tree with respect to the x_i, and a priority queue with respect to the y_i. It is simpler, but not essential, to assume that there are no duplicate values in either variable. Then, rephrasing the definition more formally, and using L and R to denote the left and right children of a node N, both of the following are true:

(a) $x_L < x_N$ and $x_N < x_R$

(b) $y_N > y_L$ and $y_N > y_R$

Draw the Cartesian tree built by inserting the following pairs:

(8,35) (21,5) (15,17) (2,22) (12,3) (28,53) (3,48) (6,97) (5,13)

††6.25 [Jonassen and Dahl 1975] One of the shortcomings of implementing a priority queue as a heap (see Section 6.6.4.1) is that when an object is inserted and there are already objects with the same priority, we cannot be certain which of them will be removed first. An alternative scheme using priority trees, or *p-trees*, overcomes this problem, although at a cost $O((\lg n)^2)$. This scheme is based upon binary trees, and is illustrated by Figure 6.61, where the ordering property is such that a right child is always intermediate in value between its parent and its left sibling. If we wish to insert a new object X into this priority queue, we start at T (the root) and apply the following rules:

1. If T is empty or *X.priority* $\geq$ *T.priority*, then insert X with T as its left subtree.
2. Otherwise follow left pointers from T, looking for the first node Y such that *X.priority* $\geq$ *Y.priority*.
3. If there is no such Y, append X as the new left leaf.
4. Otherwise repeat the entire process with the right subtree of Y's parent.

This is almost like ordinary list insertion, except that each item may have an associated sublist. Thus, to add 7 to the tree of (a) in the figure, we would start at 15 and apply rule (2) to get to 4, rule (4) to get to 11, rule (2) to get to 9, rule (2) to get to 5, rule (4) to get to 6, and rule (1) to insert 7 – arriving at the tree shown in (b) of the figure. The highest priority item (lowest value) is in the leftmost leaf. To remove it and regenerate the proper ordering among the nodes in constant time requires that each node contain an additional pointer, to its father. Write procedures for initialization, insertion, and removal in a priority queue implemented via a *p*-tree. Test your program by using it with the following sequence of I(nsert) and R(emove) operations:

I84, I5, I79, I73, I9, I55, R, I31, I22, I53, R, I40, I40, R, I15, I47, R, I47, R

and displaying the *p*-tree structure before and after each removal.

†6.26 Simulate the application of the UNION-FIND algorithm to the following relationships:

1. 1 = 3	5. 14 = 11	9. 12 = 16	13. 19 = 7
2. 2 = 9	6. 4 = 19	10. 14 = 8	14. 8 = 18
3. 18 = 15	7. 17 = 5	11. 17 = 1	15. 10 = 17
4. 6 = 13	8. 6 = 10	12. 2 = 12	16. 18 = 2

Show the resulting trees after each relationship is processed.

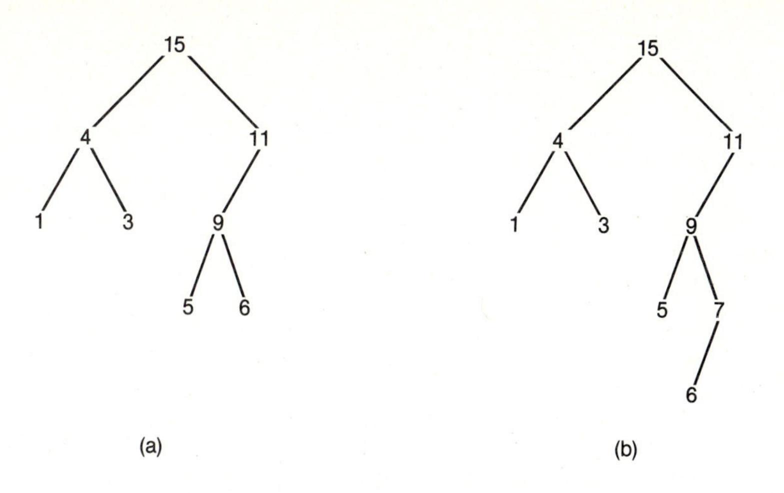

Figure 6.61 Trees for Exercise 6.25

†**6.27** In order to show that UNION without FIND (that is, with FI instead) has complexity $O(n \lg n)$, it is necessary to demonstrate that the height of the tree after a UNION operation is bounded by $\lfloor \lg n$. Prove that this is the case.

Section 6.7

††**6.28** The preorder traversal of a binary tree yields *G E A I B M C L D F K J H*, and the inorder traversal of the same binary tree yields *I A B E G L D C F M K H J*.

(a) Draw the binary tree.

(b) To your tree of part (a), add threads, shown as dotted lines, for postorder traversal.

††**6.29** Draw the labeled free tree that corresponds to the Cayley sequence 6, 8, 1, 2, 12, 1, 12, 1, 5, 8, 12.

††**6.30** Prove that the condition expressed by Eq. 6.18 is both necessary and sufficient for characterizing the leaves of a strictly binary tree.

Section 6.8

†**6.31** Suppose that we wish to search the tree of Figure 6.62 for a leaf at minimum distance from the root.

(a) Trace the order of searching using BFS, as in Figure 6.42.

(b) Trace the order of searching using DFS, as in Figure 6.44.

(c) Trace the order of searching using branch-and-bound, as in Figure 6.48.

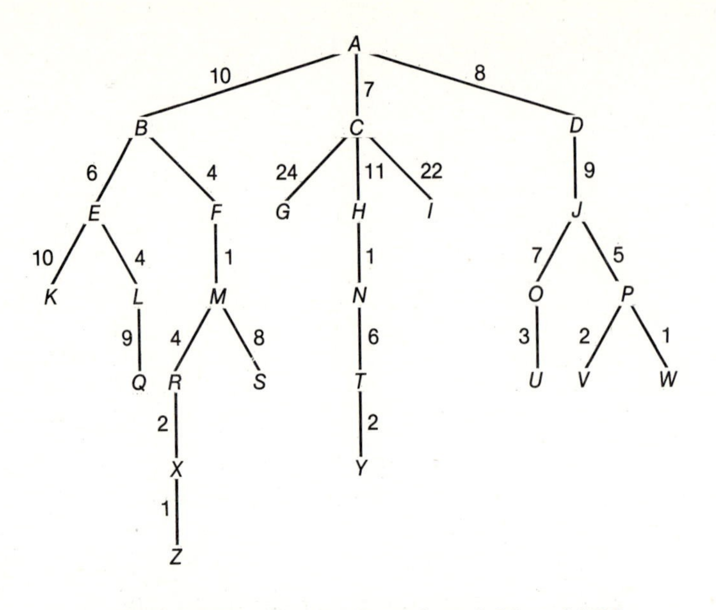

Figure 6.62 Tree for Exercises 6.31 and 6.32

†**6.32** Write a procedure to find the shortest path from the root to a leaf using DFS with recursion instead of a stack. Test your program against the tree of Figure 6.62.

††**6.33** It is very useful to be able to display binary trees on an ordinary line printer in a format that mimics their appearance in drawings. Write a procedure to accomplish this under the following assumptions: the root is to appear at the top of the page, the width of the contents of the nodes is bounded by an input parameter, and trees as large as possible short of overflowing the page width will be printed "prettily." Describe the principles underlying your method, and validate the goodness of your program by applying it to several trees of moderate size and different character (bushy/scrawny, regular/irregular, etc.).

††**6.34** [Kang and Ault 1975] Given a free tree T with n nodes, suppose that we construct an ordered tree by selecting node u as root. Then u will have k subtrees $S_1, S_2, \ldots, S_k$ containing $m_1, m_2, \ldots, m_k$ nodes respectively. Define the "moment" of the oriented tree rooted at u to be max $(m_1, m_2, \ldots, m_k)$. Finally, a *centroid* of a free tree is a node which, when chosen as root, yields an oriented tree of minimum moment. Thus, if the tree $T1$ of Figure 6.57(a) is regarded as a free tree, then the moment of node B is max $(1,1,7) = 7$, that of node C is max $(1,3,5) = 5$, etc.; and both A and C are centroids of $T1$.

(a) Write a function to compute the centroid of a tree, representing the free tree via the standard correspondence between ordered trees and binary trees, where the ordering is irrelevant. Carry out DFS on the tree, starting from the arbitrary choice of root in the representation, and implementing DFS recursively. For each node X in this tree, compute the number of descendants $C(X)$ of that node (counting a node as one of its own descendants). A centroid is the first node encountered in this search for which $C(X) \geq n/2$. Test your program against the tree *T2* of Figure 6.57(c).

(b) Having found one centroid by this algorithm, what can you say about the existence and location of other centroids in the same tree?

††6.35 Write a program to solve the SDR problem by backtracking, where the DFS is conducted via a stack, not via recursion. Apply it to finding all of the SDR's for the following sets:

$$S_1 = \{2,4,5,6\} \qquad S_3 = \{2,6\} \qquad S_5 = \{4,6\}$$
$$S_2 = \{1,4,6\} \qquad S_4 = \{3,6\} \qquad S_6 = \{1,4\}$$

Discuss your choice of data structures, with regard to both the clarity and the efficiency of your program.

††6.36 The *game of 31* is played with a single die according to the following rules. Player *A* begins by orienting the die with one its six faces upward, and the number of pips on the face becomes the initial value. Thereafter, players *B* and *A* alternate in selectively tilting the die so that one of the four side faces (but not the bottom face) becomes the new top face, and the number of pips on the new top face is added to the value. (Remember that the pips on opposite faces sum to seven.) A player who causes the value to reach exactly 31 wins, and a player who causes the value to exceed 31 loses. Write a program to compute the winner of this game, using minimaxing. Have your program count the number of nodes that it expands. Can you think of any ways to improve the efficiency of search?

7

GRAPHS

"The ways ... are dark and intricate,
Puzzled in mazes, and perplex'd with errors;
Our understanding traces them in vain,
Lost and bewilder'd in the fruitless search."

Addison,
Cato, act I, scene 1

A graph is a very general kind of data structure that can be used to represent numerous situations – maps, computer programs, electrical circuits, chemical compounds, sociological relationships, etc. In each of these cases, it is convenient to portray a graph as a set of points with connecting lines. This might suggest that a graph is basically a geometrical object; such an interpretation is misleading, however. A graph is fundamentally a combinatorial object – that is, a set of points and a particular set of connecting lines out of all possible sets of such lines. Because of the generality of graphs and the great diversity of ways that they are used, it is a formidable task to master all of the ideas associated with them. This state of affairs is reflected in the fact that whereas there are hardly any books dedicated to structures such as arrays or stacks or trees, there are numerous books devoted to graphs and their mathematical properties. You may wish to read this chapter in parallel with one of them [§]. This chapter has a more theoretical flavor than the other chapters, reflecting very modestly some of this profusion of concepts from graph theory. It is uncommon to include such material in a book devoted to data structures. We choose to do so because graphs sustain many powerful techniques, yet one can hardly employ them without having some awareness of the basic theoretical ideas that create these possibilities.

The terminology employed for describing graphs and their properties also reflects their generality; this terminology is distressingly non-standard. The most striking evidence of this is that there are two kinds of graph, directed and symmetric. Some authors have the point of view that graphs are basically directed, with the symmetric variety as a special case; others consider graphs to be naturally symmetric, with the directed variety as a special variation. There is some virtue in this dichotomous view, in that many applications are distinctively expressed in terms of just one of these two kinds. But it is also the case that a great number of concepts and applications apply to both kinds. Therefore, our approach is to treat them in parallel as much as possible, indicating to the reader whenever the distinction is important.

The earlier sections of this chapter cover some of the terminology associated with graphs, then the most important means for representing them, and next various ramifications of the most evident feature of graphs – the extent to which they are "connected." This coverage is sufficient to allow us to then discuss in moderate detail, in Section 7.4, a variety of practical applications of graphs. Yet, graphs have such varied and numerous uses that several important topics are not covered in that section. So, in Section 7.5, we endeavor to place these other topics in perspective, if only in summary.

7.1 DEFINITIONS AND TERMINOLOGY

The terminology associated with graphs is extensive and, as mentioned, notoriously non-standardized. This section captures in one place most of the basic terminology; other terms will be introduced as needed. Some readers may prefer to skim it rather quickly, and come back to it as the need arises.

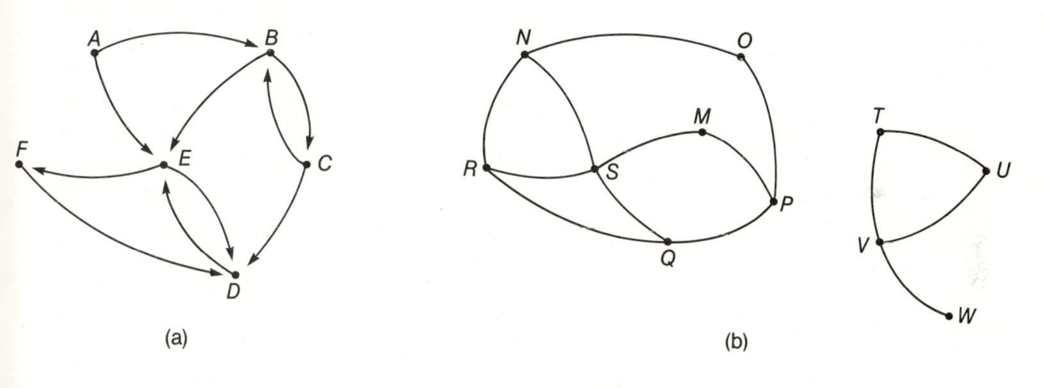

Figure 7.1 Two Graphs

With graphs we are concerned with two sets of entities. The first is the set $V = \{v_1, v_2, \ldots, v_m\}$ of *vertices*, or *nodes*. The second is the set $E = \{e_1, e_2, \ldots, e_n\}$ of *edges*, or *arcs*, which connect pairs of vertices. By an abuse of notation, we will sometimes use V to denote the set of vertices, and other times use V in the sense of $|V|$, the cardinality of V; the same remark applies to E, for the edges. The proper interpretations should always be clear from the context. In Figure 7.1(a), we have the case of a *directed graph*, or *digraph*, as indicated by the arrows; it is common and useful to employ the term arc rather than edge in this case. Vertices connected by an arc are adjacent; more precisely, as an example from (a), B is *adjacent to* E, and E is *adjacent from* B. In Figure 7.1(b), we have the undirected case, which we will simply call graph, and wherein it is useful to employ the term edge. Here, vertices joined by an edge are simply said to be *adjacent* to each other. If we imagine that each edge in (b) really denotes two arcs with opposite orientations, then indeed a graph can be regarded as a special, symmetrical case of a digraph. Conversely, we may regard a digraph as an *orientation* of a graph, wherein a direction has been assigned to each edge; in this case, the graph is then the *underlying graph* of the digraph, wherein the former is obtained by disregarding the directions of the arcs in the latter.

The notion of adjacency is so fundamental that it is often convenient to use the symbol $\Gamma(X)$ to denote all the vertices that are adjacent *from* a given set of vertices X, and likewise the symbol $\Gamma^{-1}(X)$ to denote all the vertices that are adjacent *to* a given set of vertices X. Thus, in (a), $\Gamma\{A\} = \{B,E\}$, and $\Gamma^{-1}\{B, E\} = \{A, B, C, D\}$; in an undirected graph, of course, $\Gamma(X) = \Gamma^{-1}(X)$. The notion of adjacency can be applied to edges as well as vertices. In (a), for instance, the arc BE is adjacent to the arcs ED and EF, at vertex E; in (b), on the other hand, the edges PQ, QR, and QS are all adjacent to one another, at vertex Q. Adjacency is a relation between either pairs of vertices or pairs of edges. There is also a useful relation between the vertices and the edges of a graph, that of incidence; each arc or edge of a graph is *incident* upon precisely two vertices that are its endpoints.

The fact that adjacency (the presence of an arc or an edge between two vertices) is a relation is worth emphasizing. As an example, the graph in Figure 7.2 portrays the "divides" relationship on the set from Section 2.4.1.1. Note that the relation depicted by a digraph is asymmetric. The edges of a graph like that of Figure 7.1(b), on the other hand, always manifest a relation that is symmetric and transitive; that is, the vertices of a graph form disjoint connected *components*. In this case there are two components, and for any pair of vertices in the same component, there exists some *path* of successive edges that connects them. We can specify a path either by listing its sequence of edges or by listing its sequence of vertices. Thus AB, BE, EF, FD and $ABEFD$ describe the same path in (a) of Figure 7.1, but the latter notation is clearly simpler. If the graph in (b) had an appropriate, additional edge, such as OT, then it would be a *connected* graph, with a path between any pair of vertices.

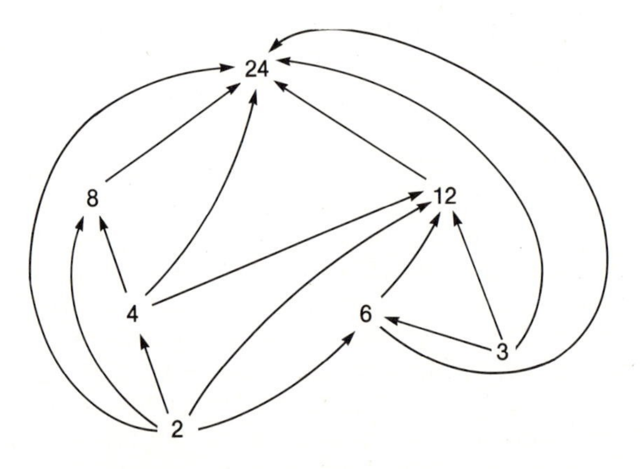

Figure 7.2 A Digraph as a Relation

The concept of connectivity for a digraph is less simple. The example in (a) is said to be *weakly connected* because the underlying graph is connected. However, the more important issue in a digraph is whether it satisfies the condition that from any vertex, we can find paths to every other vertex. In the present case, for example, even though there is a path from A to D ($ABCD$), there is no path from D to A. When a digraph does satisfy this condition, however, it is said to be *strongly connected.* The graph in (a) can be made strongly connected by the addition of an arc from F to A.

In talking about paths in graphs, we may be concerned more with the vertices that we visit, or more with the edges that we traverse, as we will see in Section 7.4.4. In either event though, paths that contain (a) repeated edges or (b) repeated vertices may be disallowed for a given problem. In such cases, where neither (a) nor (b) occurs, the path is said to be *simple*. Implicitly, most of the paths discussed in this chapter are simple ones. Also, if the final vertex of a path is the same as the initial vertex, then the path is a *circuit*, or *cycle*. It is legitimate to have a circuit of length two in a digraph, but in the undirected case we insist that the term is not meaningful unless the length is at least three.

It should be apparent that a tree is really a restricted instance of a graph, satisfying the three conditions:

1. It is connected.
2. It has no circuits.
3. It has a distinguished node, called the root.

As a direct consequence of these conditions, a tree with V vertices must have $V-1$ edges. Because it has a distinguished node, a tree may be thought of as a digraph, with all arcs either pointing away from the root or toward the root. In fact, as we have seen in the preceding chapter, this common polarity allows the arrows to be omitted, unless we wish to emphasize either logical dependency or physical linking.

In the case of a tree, each node except the root has precisely one arc entering it, and the term degree refers to the number of arcs leaving it. In the case of a digraph, we have to distinguish between the *in-degree* ($|\Gamma^{-1}(X)|$) and the *out-degree* ($|\Gamma(X)|$) of a vertex X. For example, in Figure 7.1(a), vertex C has in-degree 1 and out-degree 2, while vertex D has in-degree 3 and out-degree 1. In the undirected case, the *degree* of a vertex is simply the number of edges incident upon the vertex; thus, in (b) of the figure, vertices S and W are, respectively, of degrees 4 and 1. A graph wherein all the vertices have the same degree is said to be *regular*. Note that a 2-regular graph simply consists of one or more cycles.

The graph of Figure 7.3(a) has a new feature, the association of numerical *weights* with its edges. Typically, these weights correspond to distance, time, cost, etc. It is equally feasible to have weights on the arcs of a digraph, perhaps with unequal weights on some opposing arcs. Such might be the case for a map of a city, wherein the nature of one-way streets would cause it to take longer to go from A to B than from B to A. In the graph of Figure 7.3(b), we see symbolic *labels* associated with the arcs rather than weights. Labels are often used to specify which course of action $T(v,i)$ is to be followed, depending upon which vertex v we are at, and what input i we next receive. Whereas there are many examples employing weighted edges in this chapter, it is more convenient to explore the utility of labeled edges in Section 8.5.2, with reference to Finite State Machines.

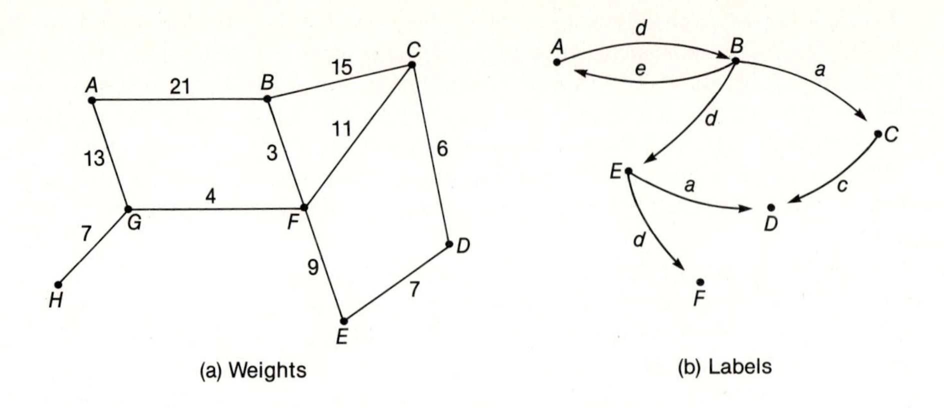

(a) Weights

(b) Labels

Figure 7.3 Edges with Values

Consider next the graphs in Figure 7.4. They illustrate two complications that may arise when dealing with graphs. In the digraph of (a), we have cases of an arc going from a vertex to itself; such an arc is called a *loop*. In the graph of (b), we have multiple edges connecting the same two vertices, yielding a *multigraph*. Note that we may also have loops in graphs and multiple edges in digraphs. Loops pose a minor complication and multiple edges pose a larger one. When a graph has neither of these features, it is said to be a *simple graph*; for most applications, simple graphs are sufficient. Except for some passing references to multigraphs, the graphs in this chapter are always assumed to be simple.

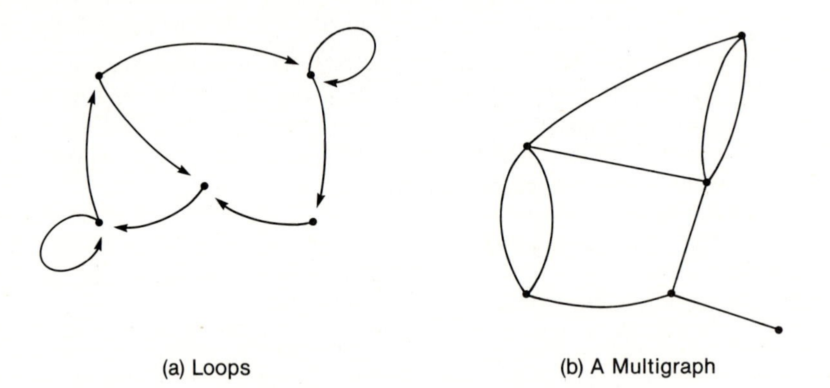

(a) Loops

(b) A Multigraph

Figure 7.4 Non-Simple Graphs

Fortified by these basic definitions, let us conclude this section with some introductory remarks concerning computations with graphs. At the outset, you may ask what makes a graph different in principle from a generalized form of a list, such as a multilist or a List structure. After all, they both seem to consist of nodes and links. There are some important differences, and these distinctions also convey some of the nature of "graph processing." For one, the structure of generalized lists is usually very regular, with each node containing the same number of links to other nodes. The degrees of the vertices in a graph may vary independently, however, from 0 to $V-1$.

More importantly, the edges in graphs are of equal importance with the vertices, whereas in generalized lists they are simply the "glue" that binds the nodes together. Thus, the edges in graphs will often have functions defined upon them, such as weights, labels, etc. Many algorithms on graphs start with a given graph $G=(V,E)$ and derive from it a *subgraph* $H=(V',E')$, wherein $V' \subseteq V$ and $E' \subseteq E$, according to various constraints and conditions. Clearly, the edges in a graph have an importance beyond that of mere glue.

A final remark in this introductory section has to do with the complexity of computations with graphs. With other data structures, we have been able to characterize algorithms operating upon them in terms of one size parameter, as in $O(f(n))$. With graphs, it is necessary to characterize complexity in terms of two size parameters, number of vertices V and number of edges E, or $O(f(E,V))$. Given the value of V, then evidently E can vary from 0 to $C(n,2)$, which is $O(V^2)$. The relative sparsity or density of edges in a graph is significant both for issues of representation and for choice of an algorithm to solve a particular problem. In the maximal case, where there is an edge or arc connecting each of the $C(n,2)$ pairs of vertices (v_i, v_j), then the graph is *complete*. The complete graph on n vertices is commonly denoted by K_n; thus the graph of Figure 7.5 is K_5.

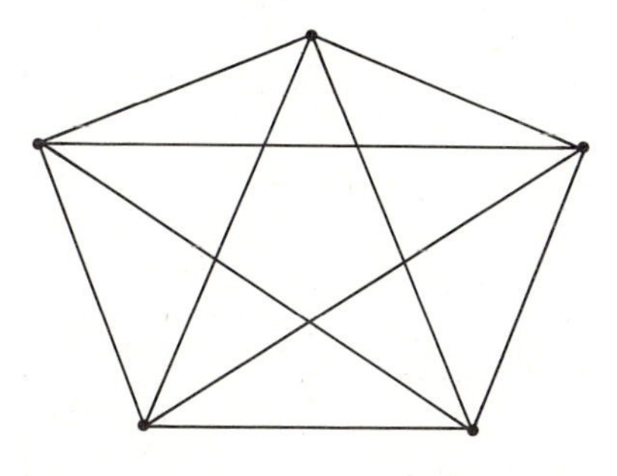

Figure 7.5 The Complete Graph K_5

7.2 OPERATIONS AND REPRESENTATIONS FOR GRAPHS

It is fairly easy to specify the basic operations on graphs by generalizing those that we encountered with trees. To begin with, we need the following operations:

successors(V) – to locate all vertices W_j in $\Gamma(V)$;
predecessors(V) – to locate all vertices U_i in $\Gamma^{-1}(V)$;
vertices(E) – to locate the endpoint vertices V_i and V_j of the edge E.

At a slightly higher level, we need operations for inserting and deleting edges; less commonly, we need operations for inserting and deleting vertices. However, the diversity of uses for graphs is so great that it becomes difficult to generalize to the next higher level of operations. More so than in any other part of this book, each of the major sections of this chapter should be approached as a brand new topic.

With regard to representation, we saw in Section 6.2 that trees could be "regularized" by virtue of a one-to-one correspondence between ordered trees and binary trees. Is such a scheme possible with graphs? The answer is Yes for graphs that are restricted in various ways [Pfaltz 1975; Smyth and Rădăceanu 1974], but such solutions are too limited in application for our purposes. Moreover, in the case of a tree, it was possible to associate directly with each vertex its list of successors. In a graph, however, a given vertex may be a successor (and a predecessor) to several other vertices; so the references between X and $\Gamma(X)$, or between X and $\Gamma^{-1}(X)$, need to be indirect (that is, via links), so that sharing can take place. The usual choices for representing a graph are to use either a set of lists or an array. We will begin by illustrating these two methods and their variations, as applied to the digraph of Figure 7.6. After reflecting upon the issues affecting a choice of representation, we conclude by citing some alternative possibilities.

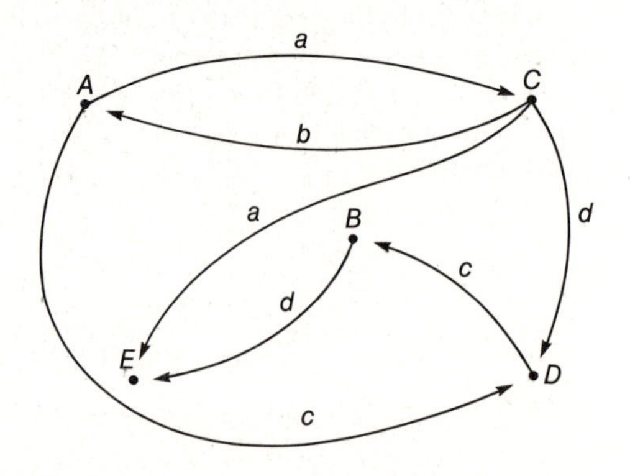

Figure 7.6 An Example for Representation

Figure 7.7 shows an *adjacency structure* for the example digraph. (The term *adjacency list* is often used, but it fails to convey the more specialized nature of the representation.) This structure contains a list of vertex nodes, and each of these vertex nodes serves as a header for a list of edge nodes for that vertex. The amount of information that is stored in each vertex node or edge node would, of course, vary with the given circumstances. In this case, each edge node must specify the identity of the vertex adjacent from the header vertex via that edge, and also the value of the label on that edge. An adjacency structure for an undirected graph would differ from that of Figure 7.7 only in that each edge would have to appear on the edge list for two vertices. It is important to realize that a representation via an adjacency structure is not unique, because of the arbitrary order within each edge list. Therefore, an algorithm applied to two representations of the same graph, different only with respect to their edge list orderings, can yield two dissimilar results. We will see this demonstrated in Section 7.3.1.

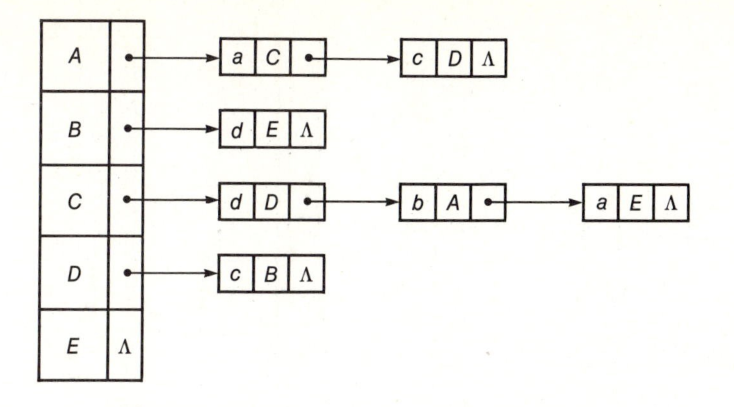

Figure 7.7 Adjacency Structure for Figure 7.6

In Figure 7.7, the vertex list is maintained in an array, and the individual edge lists are maintained as linked lists. Alternatively, the vertex and edge lists might both be in arrays or both be in linked lists. The choice would depend principally upon the relative importance of having random access to the vertex/edge data versus being able to modify the lists of vertices/edges. Figure 7.8 illustrates the use of arrays for both the vertex and edge lists. This structure is sometimes called an *indexed list*.[1] The data values associated with a given entry in the vertex-list array specify (a) how many members belong to that vertex in the edge-list array, and (b) the offset of those members from the beginning of the edge-list array.

The principal alternative to an adjacency structure is the *adjacency matrix*, as illustrated in Figure 7.9 for our example digraph. Such a matrix has one row and one column corresponding to each vertex. Edges correspond to non-null entries; a value in the ith row and jth column indicates relevant information about an edge from vertex i to vertex j – in this case the value of the corresponding label. Thus, in an adjacency matrix, each edge is implicitly determined by a tuple $<v_i, v_j>$. Note that this implied determinacy fails in the case of a multigraph, since there may be several edges with the same tuple values! (This limitation does not apply in the case of an adjacency structure.) For some computational processes, it is useful to store something other than a null where there is no edge; an example of this is storing a very large number instead of a zero, in the case of weights. Of course, in the case of an undirected graph, the adjacency matrix would be symmetric.

How do we choose between an adjacency structure and an adjacency matrix representation? Some of the relevant factors are space, computational efficiency, and flexibility. Let us consider each of these in turn.

Space. The space for an adjacency structure is $O(V + E)$, which is fine when a graph is sparse, but can become very cumbersome (especially with the overhead of

---

[1] We have seen such structures earlier, without making special note of them. Examples include the representation of sparse matrices, in Section 2.8, and the representation of variable length records, in Section 3.3.2 (see Eq. 3.1).

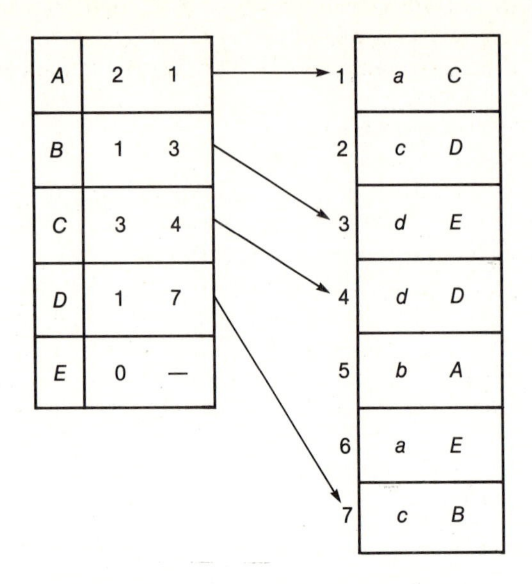

Figure 7.8 Indexed List for Figure 7.6

	A	B	C	D	E
A	0	0	a	c	0
B	0	0	0	0	d
C	b	0	0	d	a
D	0	c	0	0	0
E	0	0	0	0	0

Figure 7.9 Adjacency Matrix for Figure 7.6

the pointers) when the graph is dense with edges. The adjacency matrix always requires $O(V^2)$ space, which is inefficient for a sparse graph and very efficient for a dense one. Particularly if there is extensive auxiliary information associated with each edge in a sparse graph, then it would be inefficient to store that information in the matrix locations, and so an auxiliary edge vector would be required as well. On the other hand, if the edges have no associated weights, labels, etc., then a bit matrix should suffice, and this will almost always be efficient in space.

Computational efficiency. An algorithm that operates on a graph represented as an adjacency structure may have a complexity as low as $O(V + E)$, which may be as low as $O(V)$ for a sparse graph. For the adjacency matrix, however, the corresponding complexity can hardly be less than $O(V^2)$ (see Section 7.5.3). This is counterbalanced by two factors – the capability of accessing information about a random edge in constant time, and the compact manner in which the adjacency matrix can be manipulated.

Flexibility. With an adjacency structure, it is cumbersome to vary the edges incident with a vertex; with an adjacency matrix, it is easy to insert or delete edges. The organization of an adjacency structure makes it straightforward to find $\Gamma(X)$ for a vertex X, but to locate $\Gamma^{-1}(X)$ would require either extensive searching or an auxiliary, inverted list structure. With an adjacency matrix, on the other hand, it is just as easy to find either of the sets Γ and Γ^{-1}.

There are other representations for a graph. The most significant of these alternatives is the *incidence matrix*, containing V rows and E columns. Each column has just two non-zero entries, in the rows corresponding to the two ends of an edge. Incidence matrices do not have the problem of ambiguity for representing multigraphs that adjacency matrices have. In terms of space, an incidence matrix is as good as an adjacency matrix for a sparse graph, $O(V^2)$, but it could require an exorbitant number of entries for a dense graph, $O(V^3)$. An incidence matrix for our example graph is shown in Figure 7.10. Note the use of positive and negative entries to denote the polarity of the arcs; in the case of an undirected graph with no values on its edges, we see that an incidence matrix could be efficiently represented as a bit matrix. For still another representation possibility, see Exercise 7.3.

	1	2	3	4	5	6	7
A	a	c	0	$-b$	0	0	0
B	0	0	d	0	0	0	$-c$
C	$-a$	0	0	b	d	a	0
D	0	$-c$	0	0	$-d$	0	c
E	0	0	$-d$	0	0	$-a$	0

Figure 7.10 Incidence Matrix for Figure 7.6

7.3 CONNECTIVITY

Under the subject of connectivity in graphs, we subsume several related topics related to the notion of *reachability* Γ^*, which means that "we can get to vertex B (for example) from vertex A." The concept is rather straightforward for undirected graphs; we have already seen that the adjacency relation causes the graph to be partitioned into connected components. We have only to start at vertices and search for all their neighbors, a process that can be carried out in several manners. With digraphs, the issue is more complicated because of the distinction between weak and strong connectivity. In the succeeding sections we consider first:

- the implications of various manners of searching a graph, and
- how to find the articulation points of a graph, which are the vertices whose removal would cause a graph to become disconnected.

We then turn to digraphs and investigate:

- how to construct a reachability relation between vertices, and
- how to find the strong components of a digraph.

7.3.1 Search Trees in a Graph

In Section 6.8.1 we examined two different techniques for searching trees, breadth-first (BFS) and depth-first (DFS). These same techniques are used for searching graphs, subject to two complications: We may encounter some vertices more than once in our search, and we may not encounter other vertices at all. In order to solve the first problem, we must mark vertices when they are visited; this is reminiscent of the technique of Algorithms 4.6 (COUNT_LIST) and 4.7 (MARK_LIST). The second problem is solved by looking for unmarked vertices after such a search, and then initiating further searches as needed. Every time that we initiate a new search, we construct a new search tree in the graph. When we are done, the trees of this forest will span every vertex in it, and so they are called *spanning trees*.[2]

In describing the application of BFS and DFS to graphs, we will assume an adjacency structure representation like that of Figure 7.7. The corresponding Pascal syntax is shown in Figure 7.11. Instead of placing a boolean marker in the vertex nodes, we have included the field *data* in which to record the sequence numbers of the visits, and also the field *dad* by which to point to the parent of the vertex in the search tree. Also, we will assume that *vnode* [1].*vid*='A', *vnode* [2].*vid* ='B', etc. Note that the vertices reference the edges via pointers, whereas the edges reference vertices via cursors.

```
type    vndx = 0 .. vmax;
        eptr = ↑enode;
        enode = record
           vno: vndx;
           data: {depending upon the application}
           next: eptr;
        end;
        vnode = record
           vid: char;
           dad: vndx;
           data: {depending upon the application}
           head: eptr;
        end;

var     vlist: array [vndx] of vnode;
```

Figure 7.11 Pascal Syntax for Adjacency Structure

In breadth-first search, we treat vertices X in the order in which they occur in a queue. As we dequeue vertices that are at distance k from the root, we enqueue any vertices in $\Gamma(X)$ that have not yet been visited. Thus, vertices at distance $k+1$

---

[2] In the case of trees, we used the term traversal for a systematic visit to each node, and reserved the term search for a more conditional exploration of the nodes. For graphs, with their much more general structure, we have to use search techniques even for the equivalent of traversal.

```
procedure BFS_GRAPH (vertex: vndx);

var     defer: vndx;
        link: eptr;
        seq: integer;      {a global variable, initially 0}
        vlist: array [vndx] of vnode;
        wait:              {queue type}

begin
   INITQ (wait);
   seq := seq + 1;
   vlist [vertex].data := seq;
   vlist [vertex].dad := 0;
   ENQUEUE (wait,vertex);
   repeat
      DEQUEUE (wait,vertex);
      link := vlist [vertex].head;
      while link <> nil do begin
         defer := link↑.vno;
         if vlist [defer].data = 0 then begin
            seq := seq + 1;
            vlist [defer].data := seq;
            vlist [defer].dad := vertex;
            ENQUEUE (wait,defer);
         end;
         link := link↑.next;
      end;
   until EMPTYQ (wait);
end;
```

Algorithm 7.1 BFS_GRAPH

from the root are not visited until all vertices at distance k have been visited. This search process is expressed in the procedure BFS_GRAPH (Algorithm 7.1), wherein the text of Figure 7.11 is implicitly included, and the implementation of the queue might be via either of the Algorithms 5.1 or 5.2. There are two related issues for our implementation of BFS. One is whether to visit a vertex when it is enqueued or when it is dequeued; the other is how to minimize the enqueuing of vertices that have already been visited. In response to the second issue, and in contrast to the choice employed in BFS_TREE (Algorithm 6.10), it is expedient to visit and mark vertices when they are enqueued, thereby immediately eliminating them from subsequent consideration.

In illustration of the method, suppose that we have the graph of Figure 7.12(a). Then BFS, starting at the first vertex A, will cause one group of vertices to be visited, in the numerical sequence shown in (b) of the figure. A scan of the vertex list will then discover the unmarked vertex I, and initiate a second call to BFS that reaches the remaining vertices. The solid edges in (b) are *tree edges*; they correspond to edges in the graph which were followed to find unmarked vertices. The

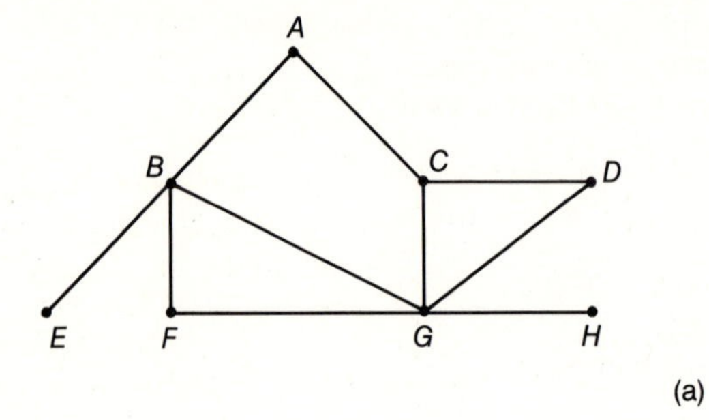

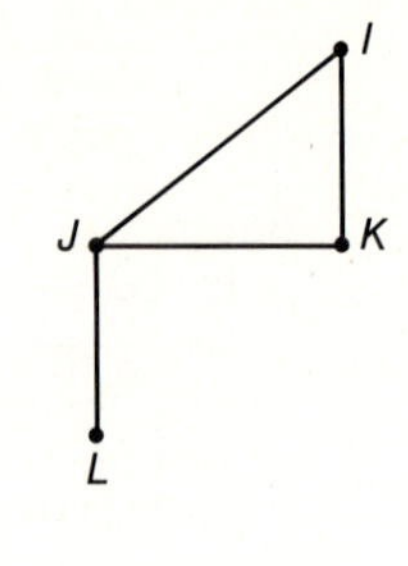

(a)

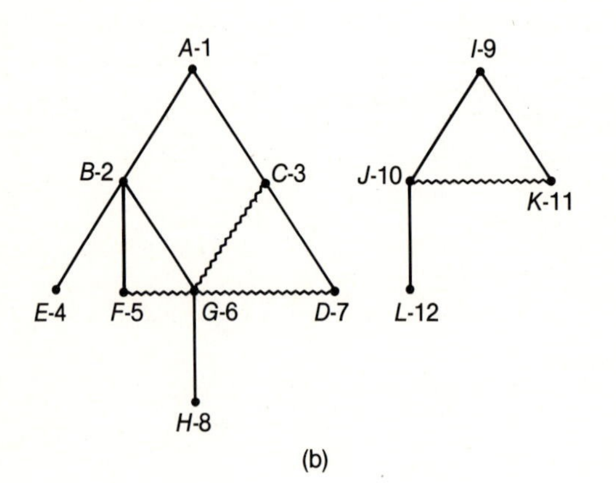

(b)

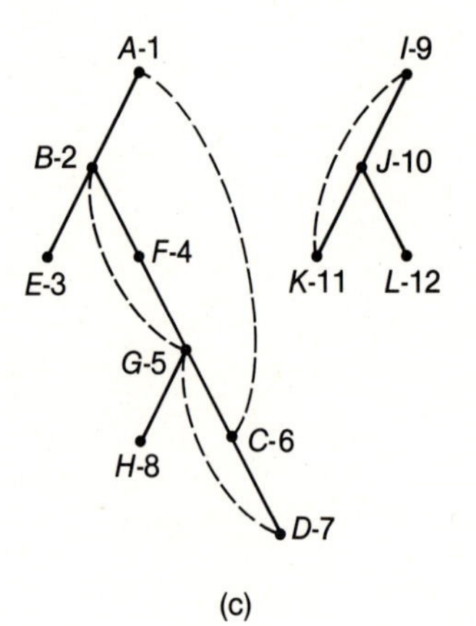

(c)

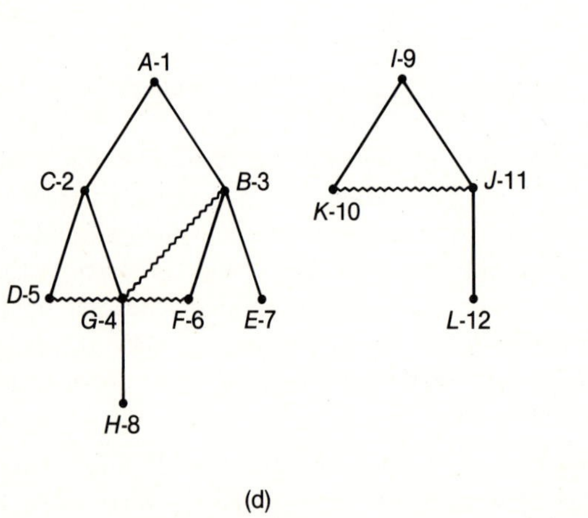

(d)

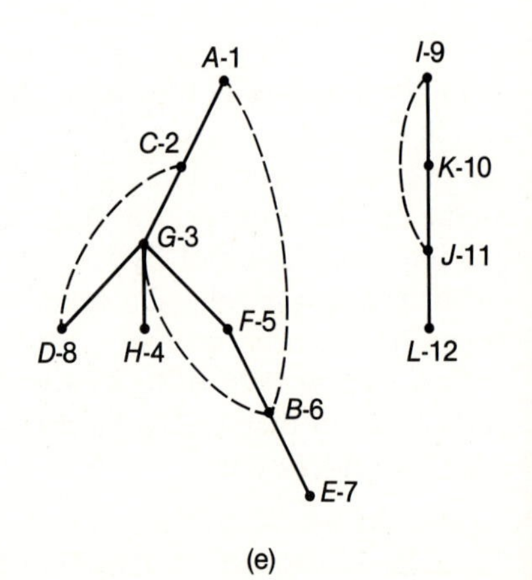

(e)

Figure 7.12 BFS and DFS in a Graph

wiggly lines are *cross edges*; they correspond to the "left-over" edges in the graph. We can observe two facts about cross edges:

- They always occur between vertices that are in a left-right relationship in the spanning tree (see Section 6.1).
- They always link vertices on the same or adjacent levels of the tree.

Depth-first search is best understood as a recursive process. We visit and mark a vertex X, and then we examine the elements of $\Gamma(X)$ one at a time. If a vertex Y in $\Gamma(X)$ is unmarked, we immediately apply DFS to it. This is simply expressed, as in DFS_GRAPH (Algorithm 7.2). As in the case of BFS, the algorithm reflects an adjacency structure representation, per the program text of Figure 7.11, and it records sequence numbers and fathers rather than merely marks. The result of applying DFS(1,0) and then DFS(9,0) to the graph of Figure 7.12(a) is the search forest of (c) in the figure, again displaying the numerical sequence of the visits. DFS search yields tree edges again, but this time the "left-over" edges are *back edges* (dashed lines) rather than cross edges. A back edge of DFS always goes from a vertex to one of its ancestors in the spanning tree; thus, for *any* edge XY in the tree, either X is an ancestor of Y or Y is an ancestor of X. To demonstrate this, assume that there is a cross edge between X and Y. We can arbitrarily assume that X is visited first in the search; but then DFS at X cannot terminate until the edge from X to Y is searched, making Y a child of X, and leading to a contradiction.

```
procedure DFS_GRAPH (vertex,father: vndx);

var     index: vndx;
        link: eptr;
        seq: integer;     {a global variable, initially 0}
        vlist: array [vndx] of vnode;

begin
   seq := seq + 1;
   vlist [vertex].dad := father;
   vlist [vertex].data := seq;
   link := vlist [vertex].head;
   while link <> nil do begin
      index := link↑.vno;
      if vlist [index].data = 0 then
         DFS_GRAPH (index,vertex);
      link := link↑.next;
   end;
end;
```

Algorithm 7.2 DFS_GRAPH

Both BFS and DFS are conceptually simple and can be employed with either an adjacency structure, as we have shown, or with an adjacency matrix. But remember that with the former structure, the order in which vertices are visited will depend upon the order of the edge nodes in their lists. The spanning trees of Figure 7.12(b) and (c) reflect the assumption that the adjacency structures are ordered lexicographically. For comparison, the trees of (d) and (e) in the figure illustrate the results, respectively, of BFS and DFS when the ordering in the edge lists is reversed.

Search techniques such as BFS and DFS are important because they form the basis for many other graph algorithms. In these other processes, we overlay the basic search paradigm with the desired computation, rather than merely marking the vertices as they are visited. In their basic forms, either BFS or DFS is effective for finding the connected components of an undirected graph, in the manner demonstrated. In addition, they can easily detect the presence of circuits in a graph if they reach, via cross edges or back edges, a vertex that has already been marked. When applied to the adjacency structure representation, both BFS and DFS process each vertex just once and examine each edge just twice, so that their complexity is $O(V+E)$. In the case of an adjacency matrix, on the other hand, they both require $O(V^2)$ operations. The algorithms shown here employ queues and stacks implemented in straightforward manners. It is also possible to reduce the storage requirements for these working structures by folding them into the representation of the graph [Tarjan 1983a]. Although we do not pursue that idea here, such a technique is illustrated with relation to topological sorting in Section 7.4.5.1.

What if our only concern is to find the connected components of a graph? We have just seen that we can find them in time $O(V+E)$, using an adjacency structure, and this representation also requires $O(V+E)$ space for storing the graph. However, the edges in a graph express a symmetric and transitive relationship (that is, equivalence classes), and we saw in Section 6.6.4 a way of computing equivalence classes in time almost $O(V+E)$ and in space $O(V)$. That is, we could apply UNION and FIND (Algorithms 6.9) to the edges without even storing them. At the conclusion, we would have one oriented tree for each component of the graph, wherein the edges in these trees would *not* have any certain correspondence to the original edges in the graph. Nonetheless, for a large, dense graph that might have $O(10^3)$ vertices and contain $O(10^6)$ edges, the savings in space would be enormous.

†7.3.1.1 The Number of Trees and Cycles in a Graph. In general, we can construct many different spanning trees for a graph, depending partly upon its representation and, more importantly, upon various criteria that may be applied to the selection of edges. It is sometimes important to be able to determine the total number of distinct spanning trees in a graph, and it might be supposed that a combinatorial search is required to answer the question. In fact, the number can be computed much more directly, via a result known as the *Matrix-Tree Theorem.* To do this, we first construct the *degree matrix* B of the graph, where $b_{i,i} = |\Gamma(i)|$, and $b_{i,j} = -1$ or 0 according as there is or is not an edge (i,j). Then the theorem states that the number of spanning trees is given by the value of the cofactor of any element of B. Thus, for the graph of Figure 7.13(a), the corresponding degree matrix is shown in (b) of the figure. Arbitrarily expanding about $B[2,3]$, we find that the number of spanning trees is three, since the value of the 2,3 cofactor is

$$\begin{aligned}(-1)^{(2+3)} \times \{1 \times [(-1) \times 3 - (-1) \times (-1)] \\ + (-1) \times [0 \times (-1) - (-1) \times (-1)]\} = 3\end{aligned}$$

These three trees are shown in (c) of the figure.

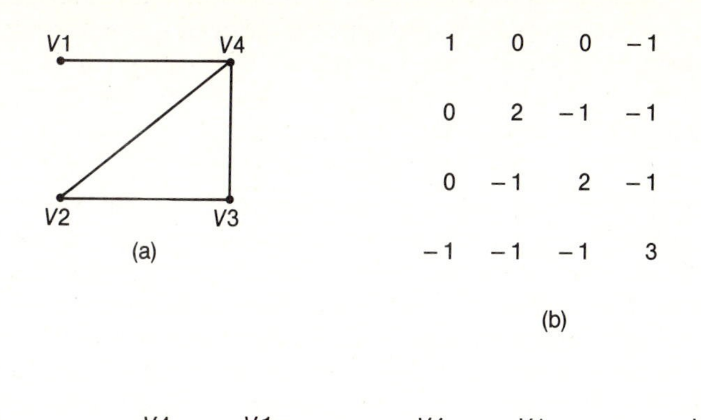

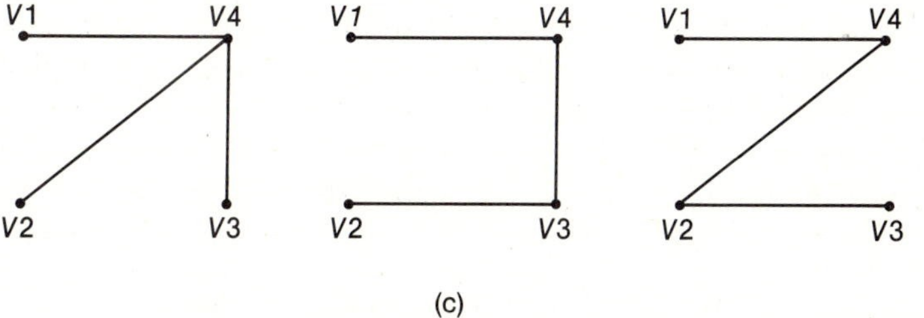

Figure 7.13 Spanning Trees of a Graph

Once we have a spanning tree for a graph, then the addition of *any* other edge must create a cycle. Moreover, each edge induces a cycle that cannot be obtained as a combination of any other cycles. Thus, for a connected graph, there will be $E - V + 1$ *independent cycles.* Any particular cycle in the graph can be expressed as a linear combination of these, where edges are combined using addition modulo 2, although not all linear combinations will yield a cycle. We can generalize this notion to that of a graph G which may not be connected, and which may even be a multigraph. If G has V vertices, E edges, and P components, then the *cyclomatic number* v is defined as $v = E - V + P$. Even for G of the general nature that we have described, v is precisely equal to the maximum number of independent cycles.

†7.3.2 Blocks and Articulation Points of a Graph

By means of spanning trees, we obtain a minimal connectivity among the vertices of the graph. However, there are many instances where such a minimal connectivity is inadequate. In a tree structure, the removal of any interior node would leave the remaining nodes disconnected. In a graph, a vertex whose removal would separate the remainder of the graph is called an *articulation point*, or *cut vertex.* A connected graph that has no articulation points is said to be *bi-connected*, and the maximal bi-connected subgraphs of a graph are called *blocks.* If we imagine that a graph represents a communication network or a railway system, then articulation points represent facilities whose failure or destruction would sever communication. Not only are articulation points strategically "critical"; their presence allows a divide-and-conquer approach to be applied to the analysis of a graph. Many computations involving the use of a graph can be performed more easily by first finding the blocks of the graph, and then applying the computation to the individual blocks.

An equivalent characterization for bi-connectedness is that there are two internally disjoint paths connecting any pair of vertices. The fact that any two vertices in the DFS spanning tree are in an ancestor-descendant relationship allows for an ingenious solution based upon this criterion. More precisely, a node x is an articulation point if it has a subtree wherein none of the nodes have back edges to any ancestors of x. The truth of this condition for x dictates that any path between an ancestor of x and a descendant of x must pass through x. This ingenious use of DFS is due to Tarjan [1972], as illustrated by the program CUT_NODES (Algorithm 7.3); another solution to the problem can be found in Paton [1971]. We begin by finding the DFS spanning tree, recording for each vertex its depth-first sequence DFN(v), as we did in the previous section. This process is equivalent to a preorder processing of the nodes in that tree. We also process the tree nodes in postorder, computing for each a value LOW(v), according to the following rule:

$$\mathrm{LOW}(v) = \min\ \{\mathrm{DFN}(v), \mathrm{DFN}(u), \mathrm{LOW}(w)\} \tag{7.1}$$

where u is any ancestor of v (connected via a back edge), and w is any child of v. In CUT_NODES, the test j < *low* [*vertex*] looks for cases of smaller LOW(w), and the test *vlist* [*index*].*data* < *low* [*vertex*] looks for cases of smaller DFN(u). A complication that comes with either an adjacency structure or an adjacency matrix is that each edge is represented twice, and so the second inspection of an edge must be suppressed if the algorithm is to work properly. This is easily accomplished by the test *vlist* [*vertex*].*dad* < > *index*.

As we work our way in the postorder processing from the leaves of the tree up to the root, the articulation points are precisely those vertices v with a child w such that DFN(v) $\leq$ LOW(w). At the root, this rule will not apply; however, the root is easily seen to be an articulation point in just those cases when it has more than one child. In CUT_NODES, we have simply written out the articulation points. In practice, one might wish to do more; for example, we could record the edges that occur within each block in the following manner. Stack each edge (u,v) the first time that it is encountered; subsequently, when an articulation point is discovered, as above, pop from the stack all edges up to and including (u,v). This group of edges constitutes one block in the graph.

As an illustration of this computation, consider the graph in Figure 7.14(a). In (b) of the figure, the DFS spanning tree is shown starting from vertex A, along with the DFN and the final LOW values. The articulation points are the starred vertices A, F, and I; the resulting blocks are shown in (c) of the figure. Initially, for example, the vertex C is marked (3,3), but the ancestor A with DFN(A) = 1 causes C to be relabeled as (3,1). The vertex B is initially marked (2,2), but the child C with LOW(C) = 1 causes B to be relabeled as (2,1). In similar fashion, the nodes E, G, and H reflect the influence of ancestors, and the nodes D and F reflect the influence of children.

```
program CUT_NODES;
var     flag: boolean;
        i,root,t: vndx;
        low: array [1 .. vmax] of vndx;

function CUT_SCAN (vertex,father: vndx): vndx;
var     index,j: vndx;
        link: eptr;
begin
   seq := seq + 1;
   vlist [vertex].data := seq;
   vlist [vertex].dad := father;
   if father = root then begin
      if not flag then flag := true
      else writeln (root);                {root is a cut-node}
   end;
   low [vertex] := seq;                {initialize LOW(v) to DFN(v)}
   link := vlist [vertex].head;
   while link <> nil do begin
      index := link↑.vno;
      if vlist [index].data = 0 then begin
         j := CUT_SCAN (index,vertex);
         if j < low [vertex] then
            low [vertex] := j;                {LOW(w) < LOW(v)}
         if (j >= vlist [vertex].data) and (vertex <> root) then
            writeln (vertex);                {vertex is a cut-node}
      end else
         if vlist [vertex].dad <> index then     {avoid copy of edge}
            if vlist [index].data < low [vertex] then
               low [vertex] := vlist [index].data;       {DFN(u) < LOW(v)}
      link := link↑.next;
   end;
   CUT_SCAN := low [vertex];
end;

begin
   for i := 1 to vsize do
      vlist [i].data := 0;
   seq := 0;
   for i := 1 to vsize do
      if vlist [i].data = 0 then begin
         flag := false;  root := i;
         t := CUT_SCAN (i,0);
      end;
end.
```

Algorithm 7.3 CUT_NODES

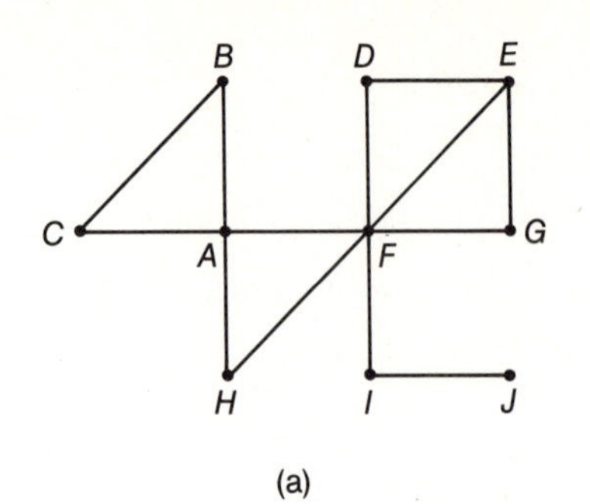

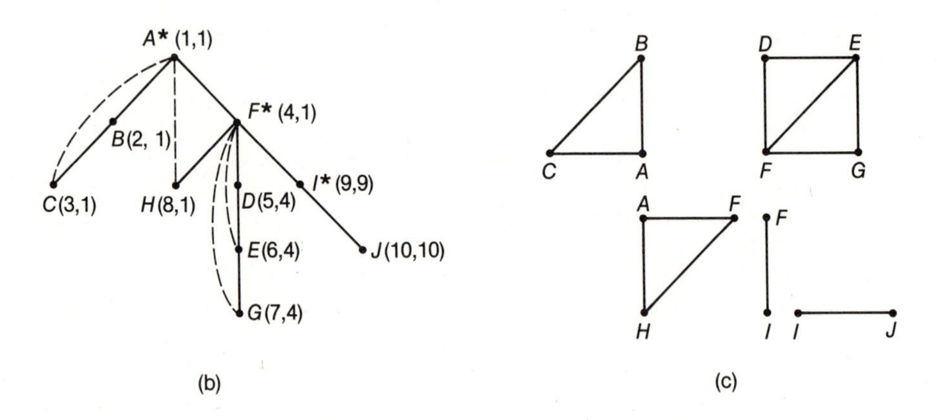

Figure 7.14 Cut Vertices and Blocks

It should be emphasized that CUT_NODES, although it performs a distinctly more sophisticated operation than does plain DFS, is just an elaboration of DFS_GRAPH. In particular, each vertex is still processed just once and each edge is examined just twice, so that the overall complexity for CUT_NODES applied to an adjacency structure representation is $O(V + E)$.

The concept of connectivity can be generalized to the case of a set of cut vertices, the removal of which leaves a graph disconnected. The minimum size of such a set for a graph G is called the *connectivity* $\kappa(G)$; furthermore, for any $k \leq \kappa(G)$, the graph is said to be *k-connected.* Just as bi-connectedness is equivalent to the existence of two internally disjoint paths connecting any pair of vertices, *Menger's Theorem* shows that k-connectedness is equivalent to the existence of k internally disjoint paths connecting any pair of vertices. A complicated but still linear algorithm for finding the tri-connected components of a graph (by DFS again) is given in Hopcroft and Tarjan [1973a]. In a different vein, and analogous to the manner in which a cut vertex separates a graph, we speak of a cut edge, or *bridge*, the removal of which causes a graph to be disconnected; such an edge in Figure 7.14(a) is *FI.* Such edges are easily determined after the articulation points are known (see Exercise 7.11). As with vertices, the notion of edge connectivity can be generalized to the case of a set of edges that disconnects a graph; it is conventional to reserve the term *cut-set* to denote a minimal such set of edges.

7.3.3 Transitive Closure of a Digraph

We turn our attention now to the investigation of search trees in directed graphs. Specifically, suppose that we have the digraph in Figure 7.15(a), and that we apply DFS to it. The result is shown in (b) of the figure. We no longer have just tree edges (solid lines) and back edges (dashed lines). There are cross edges (wiggly lines) and also another category, *forward edges* (dotted lines). The cross edges are between vertices with a left-right relationship, as in BFS, and the forward edges go from a vertex to one of its non-child descendants. An important feature of such a spanning tree is that it does *not* capture all of the reachability relationships among the vertices by partitioning the vertices and edges into equivalence classes, as in the undirected case. For example, since we started from vertex A, the tree conveys that $\Gamma^*(A) = \{A, B, C, F, G\}$. But it fails to convey other reachability relationships, such as F from I. Since the manner in which DFS partitions the vertices of a digraph into spanning trees is dependent upon the starting vertices, then in order to be certain to obtain $\Gamma^*(X)$ for each vertex in a digraph, we must conduct DFS from each vertex. This causes the complexity of computing the reachability relationship in a digraph to be $O(V^2 + EV)$, which in the worst case can be $O(V^3)$.

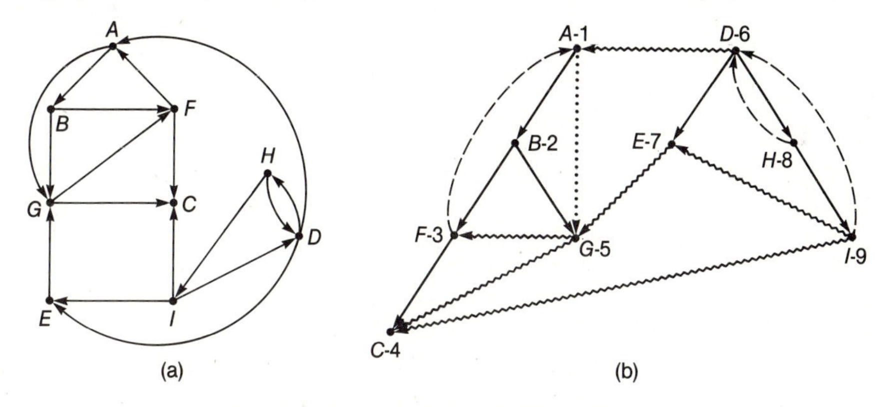

Figure 7.15 DFS in a Digraph

Are there any other solutions? The fact that the reachability relation will typically have a dense set of arcs suggests that an adjacency matrix representation might be efficient. To begin with, suppose that our adjacency matrix A is a boolean matrix, wherein a value of True denotes a directed path of length 1 between the corresponding vertices. Then the matrix A^2 captures information about directed paths of length 2. If we perform boolean multiplication, we simply get a value of True where such a path exists; if we perform integer multiplication, we obtain a count of the number of directed paths of length 2 between the corresponding vertices. In similar fashion, A^i can be used to obtain information about paths of length i. Presume now that we are performing boolean multiplication and addition, and that we compute $A + A^2 + A^3 + \cdots + A^{V-1}$. Since a simple path between any two vertices cannot employ more than $V - 1$ arcs, this boolean sum will evidently represent the union of all paths of all possible lengths, and so we will have computed the reachability relationship, more commonly termed *transitive closure*. The corresponding matrix is called the *path matrix*.

Unfortunately, each of the preceding matrix multiplications is $O(V^3)$, so that the total computation would appear to be $O(V^4)$. But this is not really the case. There are two arguments that demonstrate that it is possible to do better. One of these is a constructive one. If A is *any* boolean matrix and I is the identity matrix, then it is easy to show by induction that

$$I + A + A^2 + \cdots + A^{V-1} = (I + A)^{V-1} \tag{7.2}$$

Since the right hand side can be obtained via lg V repeated squarings (see Exercise 1.16), we can obtain transitive closure in $O(V^3 \lg V)$. However, the other argument yields the astonishing result that the problems of multiplying two boolean matrices and of computing the transitive closure of a boolean matrix are of the same complexity [Aho et al. 1974; Fisher and Meyer 1971]. Thus, we should expect to be able to compute transitive closure in $O(V^3)$.

```
procedure WARSHALL_B (adjacent: adj_mat_b; var path: adj_mat_b);

type    vndx = 0 .. vmax;
        adj_mat_b = array [vndx,vndx] of boolean;

var     i,j,k,vsize: vndx;

begin
   path := adjacent;
   for k := 1 to vsize do
      for i := 1 to vsize do
         if path [i,k] then
            for j := 1 to vsize do
               path [i,j] := path [i,j] or path [k,j];
end;
```

Algorithm 7.4 WARSHALL_B

In fact, a method developed by Warshall [1962], shown as WARSHALL_B (Algorithm 7.4), does just that. It accomplishes this with a series of three nested loops. The rationale for the order of the nesting is rather unobvious. To understand the process, realize that we are finding, for successively larger values of k, paths between the vertices i and j that employ only the first k vertices as intermediate points. Conceptually, we are iterating

$$path_k\,[i,j] = path_{k-1}\,[i,j] \textbf{ or } (path_{k-1}\,[i,k] \textbf{ and } path_{k-1}\,[k,j])$$

to express that there is a path (i,j) employing just the first k vertices as intermediate points if either (a) there is already such a path employing the first $k-1$ vertices, or (b) there are paths (i,k) and (k,j) that employ just the first $k-1$ vertices. This is illustrated in Figure 7.16. Within the actual machine procedure, in order to avoid needless computation of **and**'s and **or**'s, we employ the test **if** $path_k\,[i,k]$. Now the notation $path_k$ and $path_{k-1}$ in the above expression implies that we would need distinct iterated copies of the path array. However, we note that

$$path_k\,[i,k] = path_{k-1}\,[i,k]\,, \quad \text{and} \quad path_k\,[k,j] = path_{k-1}\,[k,j]$$

Thus, during the kth iteration, there is no change in any entry that has either index equal to k, and so the algorithm can operate upon a single copy of the path matrix.

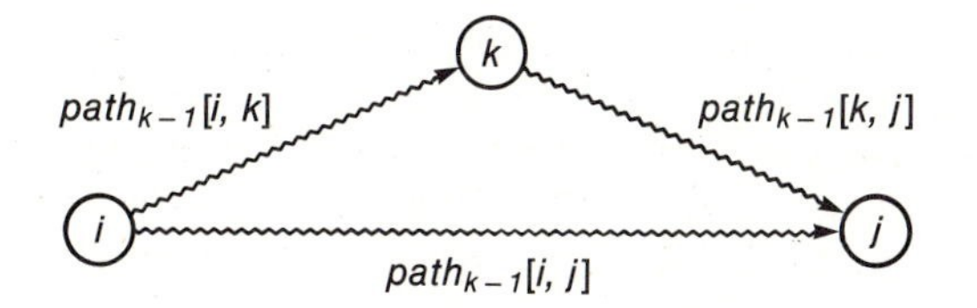

Figure 7.16 Iterated Reachability

Suppose that we have the digraph of Figure 7.17. Then the original value for *path* is shown in Figure 7.18(a), and the results of the five iterations that transform it to the transitive closure are shown in (b)–(f) of the figure. There are many uses for the information in the path matrix. As a simple example, suppose that the original adjacency relationship indicates calling relationships between procedures; for example, from (a) of the figure, *B* calls *C* and *E*. Then $path\,[i,i] = 1$ indicates that the ith procedure is recursive, as in the case of procedures *B*, *C*, *D*, *E* from (f) of the figure.

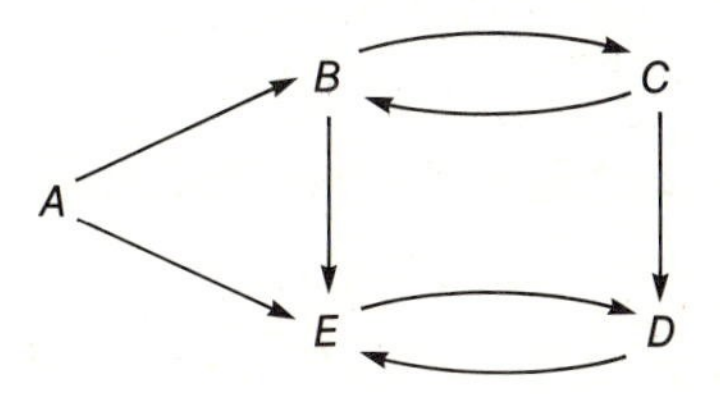

Figure 7.17 An Example for Transitive Closure

Since we have observed that transitive closure is analogous to the multiplication of boolean matrices, we are led back to some of the ideas that we explored in Section 2.5.2. In particular, we saw there that it is often possible to speed up this type of operation by employing sets as variables, thereby gaining access to parallel bit operations at the hardware level. The corresponding embodiment in the present case is WARSHALL_S (Algorithm 7.5), yielding transitive closure in $O(V^2)$. It is

	0 1 0 0 1		0 1 1 0 1		0 1 1 1 1
	0 0 1 0 1		0 0 1 0 1		0 1 1 1 1
(a)	0 1 0 1 0	(c)	0 1 1 1 1	(e)	0 1 1 1 1
	0 0 0 0 1		0 0 0 0 1		0 0 0 0 1
	0 0 0 1 0		0 0 0 1 0		0 0 0 1 1
	0 1 0 0 1		0 1 1 1 1		0 1 1 1 1
	0 0 1 0 1		0 1 1 1 1		0 1 1 1 1
(b)	0 1 0 1 0	(d)	0 1 1 1 1	(f)	0 1 1 1 1
	0 0 0 0 1		0 0 0 0 1		0 0 0 1 1
	0 0 0 1 0		0 0 0 1 0		0 0 0 1 1

Figure 7.18 Trace of Algorithm WARSHALL_B

instructive to compare WARSHALL_S with BOOL_MULT (Algorithm 2.9). They look so similar, and yet they compute such different quantities! As we saw in Chapter 2, there are still other techniques available for reducing the complexity of boolean multiplication, such as RUSSIANS (Algorithm 2.10). This is not quite the final word with respect to efficiency; we will find still another approach to transitive closure in the next section.

```
procedure WARSHALL_S (adjacent: adj_mat_s; var path: adj_mat_s);

type    vndx = 0 .. vmax;
        adj_mat_s = array [vndx] of set of vndx;

var     i,k,vsize: vndx;

begin
  path := adjacent;
  for k := 1 to vsize do
    for i := 1 to vsize do
      if k in path [i] then
        path [i] := path [i] + path [k];
end;
```

Algorithm 7.5 WARSHALL_S

†7.3.4 Strongly Connected Components of a Digraph

As we have seen, DFS does not, by itself, yield equivalence classes of vertices in a digraph. However, there are such equivalence classes, and these are the strongly connected components of the digraph. Many operations upon digraphs can be greatly simplified by finding the strong components as a first step, just as finding the blocks of a graph can simplify matters. There is an important difference, however, between the components of a graph and the strong components of a digraph. The former partition all of the vertices and all of the edges, whereas the latter partition all of the vertices but only some of the arcs.

We saw earlier, with Figure 7.15, that DFS of a digraph yields trees that, in the general case, may contain four types of edges: tree edges, backward edges, cross edges, and forward edges. An important fact about DFS of a digraph is that the cross edges always point from right to left, under the assumption that spanning tree branches are drawn in order of discovery from left to right. The reasoning for this is similar to that in Section 7.3.1, whereby we established that back edges in the undirected case must always go to ancestors. In the present case, cross edges must always go from a vertex with a higher DFS number to one with a lower DFS number.

In a manner remarkably similar to that of CUT_NODES (Algorithm 7.3), DFS can be embellished to perform both preorder and postorder processing of the vertices and yield the strong components in $O(V+E)$. Such an algorithm is due to Tarjan again [1972], and is illustrated by the program STRONG_COMPONENTS (Algorithm 7.6). An alternative approach can be found in Sharir [1981]. Starting at vertex A, we once again compute for each vertex a value LOW(v), as follows:

$$\text{LOW}(v) = \min\{\text{DFN}(v), \text{DFN}(u), \text{LOW}(w)\} \tag{7.3}$$

where u is any ancestor of v (that is, connected via a back edge), *or* where u is any "cousin" of v (connected via a cross edge) leading to such an ancestor, and where w is any child of v. This has the effect that as we process the vertices in postorder, we look for larger and larger subtrees with the property that all nodes of the subtree can reach the root. When we find a vertex x such that LOW(x) is still equal to DFN(x), then we have found the root of a strong component. By stacking vertices when they are first encountered, and then − when this latter condition is met − popping vertices from the stack up to and including x, we capture the components for output. One more thing is needed to make this process work. There may be cross edges from one tree to another tree, as well as cross edges within trees. So that the low DFN values to the left will not cause incorrect values on the right, all the vertices in a strong component are marked as they are removed from the stack.

The action of STRONG_COMPONENTS is illustrated in Figure 7.19 for the digraph of Figure 7.15. The original digraph is reproduced in (a) of Figure 7.19. The spanning trees with the final DFN and LOW values are shown in (b) of the figure, where the starred vertices are the roots of the strong components. The strong components themselves are shown in (c) of the figure. Initially, for example, the vertex F is marked (3,3), but the ancestor A with DFN(A) = 1 causes F to be relabeled as (3,1). The vertex C is initially marked (4,4) and is never changed, so it is a strong component. The vertex B is initially marked (2,2), but the child F with LOW(F) = 1 causes B to be relabeled as (2,1). The vertex G is initially marked (5,5), but the cross edge to F with DFN(F) = 3 causes G to be relabeled as (5,3). In a similar fashion, the vertices H and I reflect their ancestral relation with vertex D; however, the effects of the cross links to the first spanning tree are suppressed.

An important consequence of having found the strong components of a digraph D is that we can then construct its *condensation* D^*. In the condensed graph, each strong component is replaced by a single vertex, and there are no cycles. The condensation of our digraph of Figures 7.15 and 7.19 is shown in Figure 7.20. An

```
program STRONG_COMPONENTS;
var     i,t,top: vndx;
        flag: array [1 .. vmax] of boolean;
        low: array [1 .. vmax] of vndx;
        stack: array [1 .. stkmax] of vndx;

function STRONG_SCAN (vertex,father: vndx): vndx;
var     index,j: vndx;
        link: eptr;
begin
   seq := seq + 1;
   vlist [vertex].data := seq;
   vlist [vertex].dad := father;
   low [vertex] := seq;              {initialize LOW(v) to DFN(v)}
   top := top + 1;
   stack [top] := vertex;
   link := vlist [vertex].head;
   while link <> nil do begin
      index := link↑.vno;
      if vlist [index].data = 0 then begin
         j := STRONG_SCAN (index,vertex);
         if j < low [vertex] then
            low [vertex] := j;                {LOW(w) < LOW(v)}
      end else
         if flag [index] and (vlist [index].data < low [vertex]) then
            low [vertex] := vlist [index].data;     {DFN(u) < LOW(v)}
      link := link↑.next;
   end;
   if low [vertex] = vlist [vertex].data then begin
      repeat
         write (stack [top]);        {stack [top] is part of component}
         flag [stack [top]] := false;
         top := top - 1;
      until stack [top + 1] = vertex;
      writeln;                            {end of strong component}
      vlist [vertex].data := vsize + 1;
   end;
   STRONG_SCAN := low [vertex];
end;

begin
   for i := 1 to vsize do begin
      flag [i] := true;
      vlist [i].data := 0;
   end;
   seq := 0;  top := 0;
   for i := 1 to vsize do
      if vlist [i].data = 0 then
         t := STRONG_SCAN (i,0);
end.
```

Algorithm 7.6 STRONG_COMPONENTS

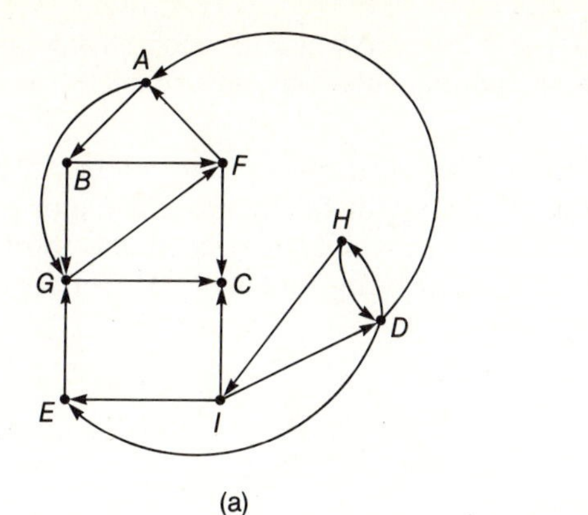

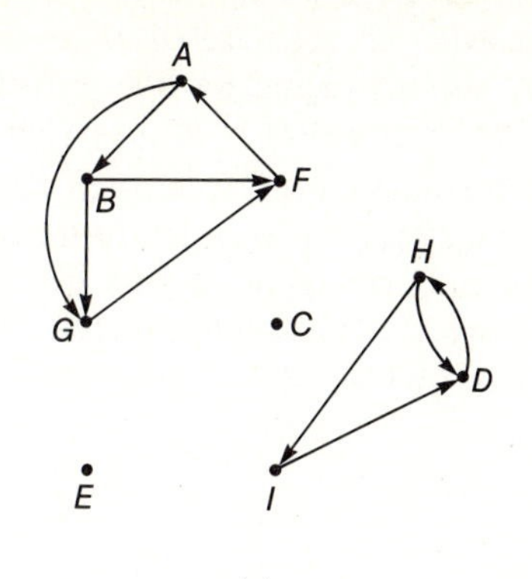

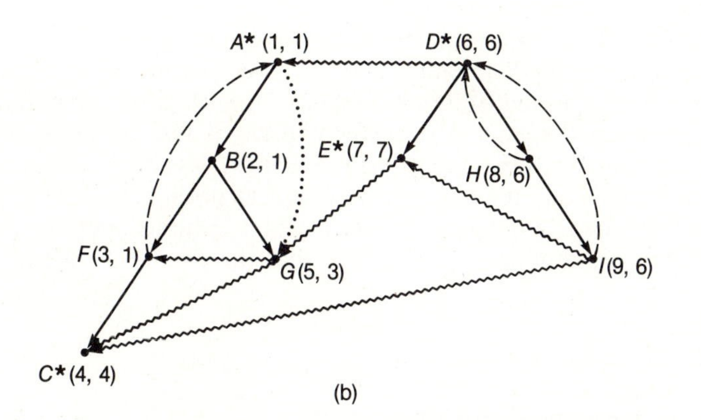

Figure 7.19 Strongly Connected Components

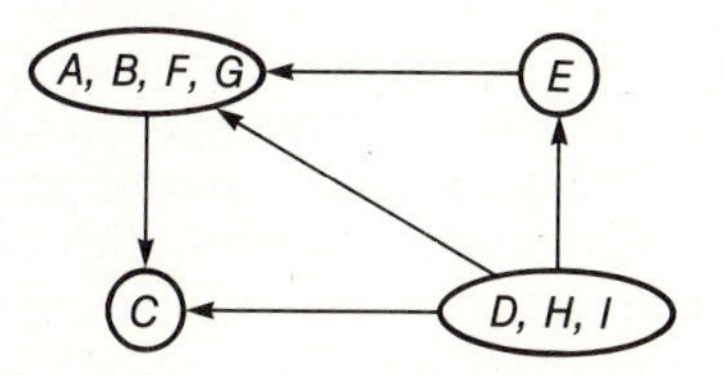

Figure 7.20 Condensation of Figure 7.19

immediate application of this is an alternative method of computing transitive closure [Munro 1971]. We saw that Warshall's algorithm yields the closure in $O(V^3)$ or $O(V^2)$, depending upon the use of parallel bit operations. However, consider the following sequence of operations:

1. Find the strong components, and thus D^*, in $O(V + E)$.

2. Apply Warshall's algorithm to D^*.
3. Construct the closure of D by inserting 1's everywhere in each strong component subarray, and by filling in the remaining subarrays according to the result of the second step – all in $O(V^2)$.

Since the condensation will often have far fewer vertices than the original digraph, the second step may be much faster with D^* than with D. Indeed, the major part of the time may be spent in just filling in the reachability matrix in the third step. While there is a possible reduction in time when using this method, there is also a substantial increase in the programming task.

7.4 APPLICATIONS OF GRAPHS

Graphs can be used for solving so many diverse kinds of problems that it is difficult to do the subject justice at this point. We have tried to choose areas that illustrate a variety of problem types and solution methods for both graphs and digraphs. The first two topics, minimal spanning trees and shortest paths, are fairly conventional. The third section deals with matchings and coverings; less likely to be familiar, this topic is an entree to many interesting and practical problems. The fourth section discusses Eulerian and Hamiltonian traversals of a graph; and the final section concentrates upon the ordering relationships that the arcs of a digraph impose on its vertices.

7.4.1 Minimal Spanning Trees in a Graph

A simple and important use of undirected graphs is the following. G is a connected graph with V vertices, and a set E of weighted edges connecting them. We wish to select a subset of $V-1$ edges that will form a spanning tree connecting the vertices, subject to the criterion that the subset of edges selected will have the lowest possible sum of associated weights. These weights might represent lengths of wire in a circuit or pipe in a house, or they might represent other costs that are not related to distance. In either event, there are commonly real savings associated with finding a set of edges that yield such a *minimal spanning tree* (*MST*) of the network.

There are two principal methods for finding a minimal spanning tree, and they both employ the following principle:

> In the construction of an MST, there will be two sets of vertices, U and its complement $V-U$. If (u,v) is an edge of lowest cost such that $u \in U$ and $v \in (V-U)$, then there must be an MST that contains (u,v).

If we assume the contrary, then let T be some MST for the original graph, and consider the graph H obtained by adding (u,v) to T. H must have a cycle containing the edge (u,v) and another edge $(u',v') \in T$ that connects the same components. Since the edge (u,v) is by definition a lowest cost edge connecting the two components, then we can safely delete edge (u',v') from H to obtain an MST containing the edge (u,v). This confirms the original claim.

One classical use of this principle, by Prim [1957], proceeds along the following lines. We imagine that the vertices are divided among three sets: U containing vertices that are already in the MST, V containing vertices that are not yet in the tree but are in $\Gamma(U)$, and W containing the remaining vertices. We start by placing any single vertex in U. Thereafter, one iteration consists of the following steps:

1. Find the shortest edge that connects a vertex in V with a vertex in U.
2. Add that edge to the tree and update the sets U, V, and W.

We iterate these steps until all the vertices of the graph are included in U. This is conceptually simple, as illustrated by the graph in Figure 7.21(a). Here, if we start with vertex A, the edges are selected in the sequence shown in (b) of the figure.

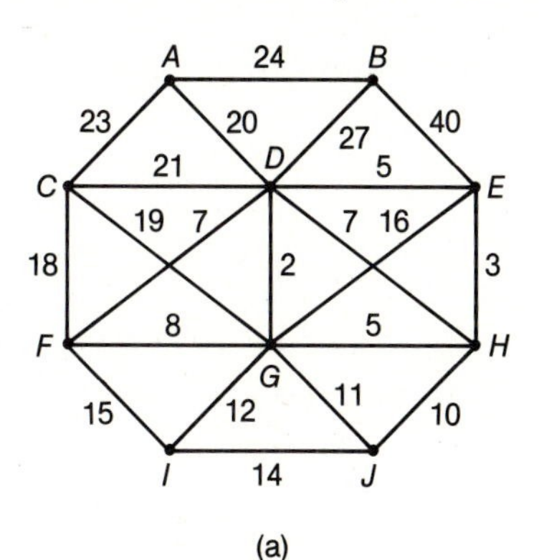

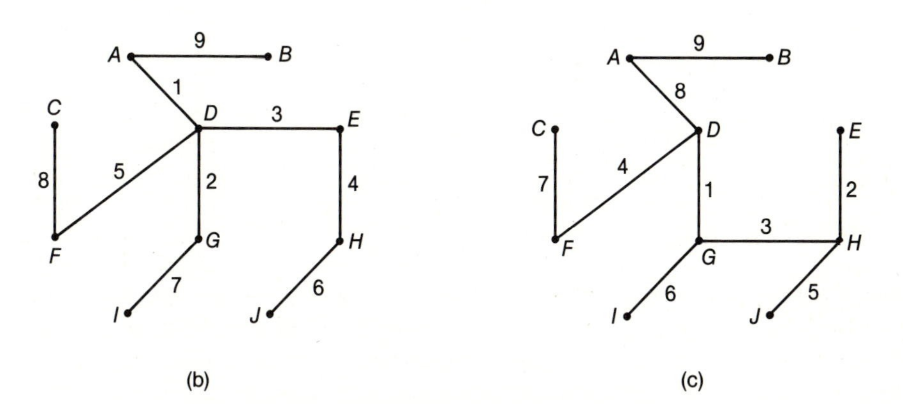

Figure 7.21 Minimal Spanning Trees

The actions "find the shortest edge" and "update the sets U, V, and W" require some attention if we are not to spend an inordinate amount of time examining edges and vertices. The crucial insight for performing these operations efficiently is that, on every iteration, we can associate with each of the vertices v_i in V some

```
procedure PRIM (cost: adj_mat_i; var least: distance;
                        var closest: parent; var sum: integer);

const  inf = {some suitably large number, such as maxint}

type   vndx = 0 .. vmax;
       adj_mat_i = array [vndx,vndx] of integer;
       distance = array [vndx] of integer;
       parent = array [vndx] of vndx;

var    i,j,k,min: integer;
       undone: array [vndx] of boolean;

begin
  least [1] := 0;  closest [1] := 0;  undone [1] := false;
  sum := 0;
  for j := 2 to vsize do begin      {find smallest edge}
    least [j] := cost [1,j];
    closest [j] := 1;
    undone [j] := true;
  end;
  for k := 2 to vsize do begin    {reach other V − 1 nodes}
    min := inf;
    for j := 2 to vsize do          {update tree data}
      if undone [j] and (least [j] < min) then begin
        min := least [j];  i := j;
      end;
    sum := sum + min;
    undone [i] := false;
    for j := 2 to vsize do
      if undone [j] and (cost [i,j] < least [j]) then begin
        least [j] := cost [i,j];  closest [j] := i;
      end;
  end;
end;
```

Algorithm 7.7 PRIM

smallest edge e_i linking it to the set U. Therefore, when we have selected the shortest of these particular edges and thereby moved a vertex X from V to U, we need just examine the effect of this upon the sets $\{e_i\}$, U, V, and W. But this can be simplified even further. We choose to employ an adjacency matrix representation for illustrating Prim's method. As discussed in Section 7.2, this allows us to represent "no edge" by some arbitrarily large number. Then the distinction between the sets V and W vanishes, and we need only update the sets $\{e_i\}$, U, and V. The result is the procedure PRIM (Algorithm 7.7). The progress of the algorithm is illustrated by the partial trace in Figure 7.22, starting from vertex A and thereafter showing successive values of *closest* and *least* – that is, the v_i and their corresponding e_i – and of *sum*.

i	*closest* [*i*]	*least* [*i*]	*sum*	*B*	*C*	*D*	*E*	*F*	*G*	*H*	*I*	*J*
				24	23	20	*	*	*	*	*	*
				A	*A*	*A*	*A*	*A*	*A*	*A*	*A*	*A*
D	*A*	20	20	24	21	20	5	7	2	7	*	*
				A	*D*	*A*	*D*	*D*	*D*	*D*	*A*	*A*
G	*D*	2	22	24	19	20	5	7	2	5	12	11
				A	G	*A*	*D*	*D*	*D*	G	G	G
E	*D*	5	27	24	19	20	5	7	2	3	12	11
				A	G	*A*	*D*	*D*	*D*	*E*	G	G
H	*E*	3	30	24	19	20	5	7	2	3	12	10
				A	G	*A*	*D*	*D*	*D*	*E*	G	*H*
F	*D*	7	37	24	18	20	5	7	2	3	12	10
				A	*F*	*A*	*D*	*D*	*D*	*E*	G	*H*
	...							...				
B	*A*	24	101	24	18	20	5	7	2	3	12	10
				A	*F*	*A*	*D*	*D*	*D*	*E*	G	*H*

Figure 7.22 Partial Trace of Algorithm PRIM

The other classical technique for constructing an MST is by Kruskal [1956]. In this case, we start with all the vertices as separate components, and we examine the edges in increasing order of their cost. For each edge, if it connects two previously distinct components, we include it in the spanning tree; if it connects two vertices already in the same component, so that its inclusion would create a cycle, we discard it. Let us apply this method to the same graph of Figure 7.21(a). The edges are selected in the sequence shown in (c) of the figure. Observe that at the third step, there is a choice between two edges of cost 5. It does not matter which is chosen, and we assume that the edge *GH* is chosen rather than *DE*. As a result, we find in the figure an illustration of the fact that the MST need not be unique with respect to its set of edges. Nonetheless, the value of the MST (101, the sum of the weights) is unique.

Although conceptually simple, the description in the preceding paragraph glosses over two significant sub-problems: how to find the next smallest edge, and how to discover when two vertices are already connected. The first problem can be handled by sorting all the edges before beginning, and this is $O(E \lg E)$, as we will see in Chapter 13. However, we need only $V - 1$ edges, which will in most cases be much less than all E of them. A much better answer to the first sub-problem is to use a priority queue. For the second sub-problem, the resolution is to use UNION-FIND (Algorithms 6.9)!

Having indicated how to solve the associated sub-problems, we leave the detailed algorithm for Kruskal's method as an exercise (see Exercise 7.17).

However, it is valuable to consider here the circumstances under which one would choose between Prim's and Kruskal's methods. It is easy to see that Prim's method as applied to an adjacency matrix is $O(V^2)$; if applied to an adjacency structure in the most obvious fashion, the complexity would still be the same. The use of a priority queue to find the smallest edge connecting U and $V - U$ would reduce this for a sparse graph, but would increase it for a dense graph. Originally, Kruskal's method was not very competitive with Prim's because of the high cost then associated with both of its sub-problems. Since the discovery of efficient means for dealing with these problems, the balance has shifted somewhat. In particular, we will learn in Section 13.2.1.2.1 that a priority queue of the edges can be constructed in $O(E)$ if we process all of them at the beginning. Thereafter, for each iteration of Kruskal's method, finding the next smallest edge is $O(\lg E)$ and testing for "equivalent" vertices is almost $O(1)$. In the extreme case, it might be necessary to examine all the edges, so that the worst-case complexity is $O(E \lg E)$; typically, however, Kruskal's algorithm would perform better than this. A generalization, confirmed by experiment, is that Prim's method is better for a dense graph, while Kruskal's method is better for a sparse graph [§].

Both Prim's and Kruskal's methods illustrate what are known as *greedy algorithms*; this means that they attain globally optimal solutions by means of locally optimal decisions. There are many other problems associated with graphs for whicl this tactic does not work very well, as we will see in Section 7.4.4.3. The methods of Prim and Kruskal represent two extremes: picking the next edge so as to add one vertex to a single tree, and picking the next shortest edge while ignoring the internal nature of the various trees already formed. By taking the latter details into account – for example, via a priority queue for each tree – still more efficient (and more complicated) MST algorithms can be obtained.[3] These methods attain complexity $O(E \lg \lg V)$, and they appear to have average performance $O(V + E)$.

7.4.2 Shortest Paths in Graphs and Digraphs

Another extremely common problem that arises with weighted graphs is that of finding the shortest (minimum time or other cost) path between two vertices. As opposed to our discussion of MST's, the logic of this problem, and therefore the discussion in this section, applies equally well to digraphs. More general than the problem of finding the minimum distance between two particular vertices is a second one of finding the minimum distances between a given *source* vertex and all of the other vertices of the graph. If all the weights have the value 1, then the first problem is trivially solved by BFS (recalling our discussion in Section 7.3.1). In the general case of unequal weights, however, it appears to be no easier to solve the first problem than it is to solve the second. Thus, our interest is in a means for

---

[3] However, an implementation of priority queues in terms of heaps will not serve us in this case, because we need to merge priority queues when we merge the corresponding subtrees, and such an operation is $O(V \lg V)$ with heaps. Some of the other priority queue implementations discussed in Section 6.6.4.1 do not have this drawback.

solving the latter. This can be accomplished by Dijkstra's method [1959]. (His article actually contains an independent exposition of Prim's method as well as the present algorithm.)

The ideas behind Dijkstra's method have a very familiar ring. During the course of the algorithm, we imagine that the vertices are divided among three sets: U containing vertices that are already processed, V containing vertices that are not yet processed but are in $\Gamma(U)$, and W containing the remaining vertices. We start by placing the source vertex v_0 in U; thereafter, one iteration consists of the following steps:

1. Find the shortest edge that connects a vertex in V, via the vertices in U, to v_0.
2. Add that edge to the tree, and update the sets U, V, and W.

We iterate these steps until all the vertices of the graph are included in U. The crucial difference between Prim's method and this process is that the former looked for the next minimum distance vertex from the partial tree, whereas Dijkstra's algorithm looks for the next minimum distance vertex from v_0. Once again, we employ an adjacency matrix representation, and we obtain the procedure DIJKSTRA (Algorithm 7.8), remarkably similar in form to PRIM.

For an example of this method, consider the digraph of Figure 7.23. The corresponding adjacency matrix is shown in Figure 7.24(a), and a trace of DIJKSTRA, with E (the fifth vertex) as the source, is shown in Figure 7.24(b), for successive values of *least* and *father*. By tracing out the final values of *father*, we see that the corresponding spanning tree of shortest paths from E is completely degenerate in this case: $E-B-A-F-C-D$. As in the case of the MST algorithms, the shortest-paths spanning tree need not be unique, but the minimum costs will be unique. In general the spanning tree constructed for this problem will bear no relation to the spanning tree generated for the MST problem. To see this, suppose that we apply DIJKSTRA to the graph of Figure 7.21(a), starting at vertex J. The spanning tree for this case is shown in Figure 7.25; it is indeed very different from those of Figure 7.21(b) and (c).

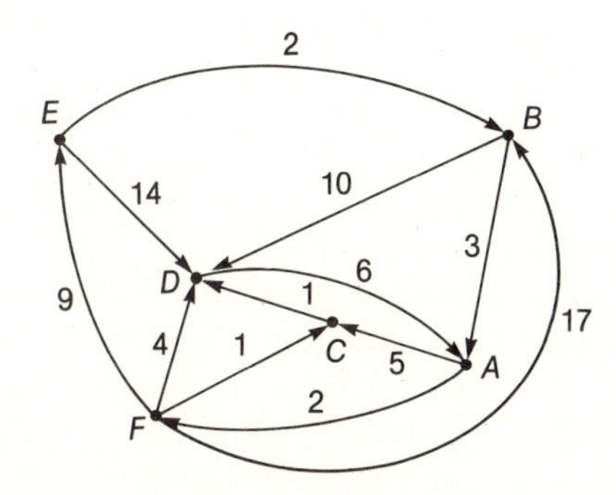

Figure 7.23 An Example for Shortest Paths

Dijkstra's algorithm is remarkably similar in form to Prim's but subtly different, so that it is not as obvious why it works. To understand it, note that we always

```
procedure DIJKSTRA (source: vndx; cost: adj_mat_i;
                    var least: distance;  var father: parent);

const  inf = {some suitably large number, such as maxint}

type   vndx = 0 .. vmax;
       adj_mat_i = array [vndx,vndx] of integer;
       distance = array [vndx] of integer;
       parent = array [vndx] of vndx;

var    i,j,k,vsize: vndx;
       min: integer;
       undone: array [vndx] of boolean;

begin
  for i := 1 to vsize do begin
    least [i] := cost [source,i];
    father [i] := source;
    undone [i] := true;
  end;
  least [source] := 0;  undone [source] := false;
  for k := 2 to vsize do begin       {reach other V - 1 nodes}
    min := inf;
    for j := 1 to vsize do           {find smallest edge}
      if undone [j] and (least [j] < min) then begin
        min := least [j];  i := j;
      end;
    undone [i] := false;
    for j := 1 to vsize do           {update tree data}
      if undone [j] and (min + cost [i,j] < least [j]) then begin
        least [j] := min + cost [i,j];  father [j] := i;
      end;
  end;
end;
```

Algorithm 7.8 DIJKSTRA

select the next closest vertex v to the source such that v can be reached via vertices already in the set U. Then the cost of this path to v via vertices in U must be the minimum cost path to v. Suppose the contrary, that there exists some first vertex w not in U, such that a path from the source to w and then ultimately to v has lower cost, as illustrated in Figure 7.26. But then the distance just to w in such a path must be less than the distance to v, and w would have to have been selected before v, according to the original selection criterion. Since the assumption of such an alternate, lower cost path leads to a contradiction, it cannot exist, and so the process works.

We see that DIJKSTRA, like PRIM, has a complexity of $O(V^2)$ when implemented for an adjacency matrix; once again, for a sparse graph, an implementation based upon an adjacency structure and employing priority queues could yield a lower complexity. If we merely want to find the least distance from the source to a

	A	B	C	D	E	F
A	*	*	5	*	*	2
B	3	*	*	10	*	*
C	*	*	*	1	*	*
D	6	*	*	*	*	*
E	*	2	*	14	*	*
F	*	17	1	4	9	*

(a) Adjacency Matrix

i	*least* [*i*]	*father* [*i*]	A	B	C	D	E	F
			*	2	*	14	0	*
			E	E	E	E	E	E
B	2	E	5	2	*	12	0	*
			B	E	E	B	E	E
A	5	B	5	2	10	12	0	7
			B	E	A	B	E	A
F	7	A	5	2	8	11	0	7
			B	E	F	F	E	A
C	8	F	5	2	8	9	0	7
			B	E	F	C	E	A
D	9	C	5	2	8	9	0	7
			B	E	F	C	E	A

(b) Trace

Figure 7.24 Trace of Algorithm DIJKSTRA

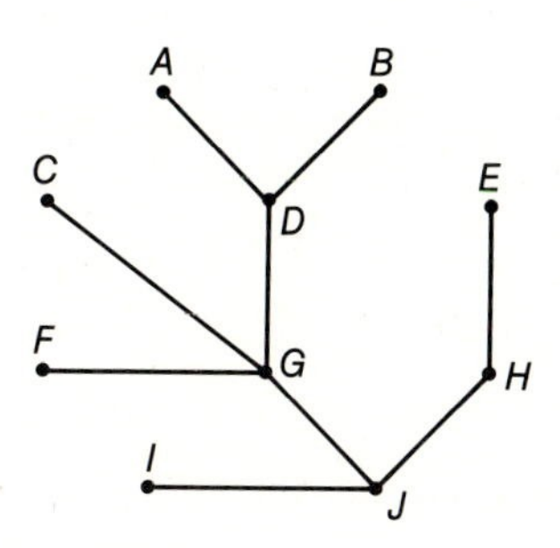

Figure 7.25 Shortest Paths from *J* in Figure 7.21

particular other vertex, then we could revise DIJKSTRA so that it terminated as soon as that vertex had been reached; however, the complexity would still be $O(V^2)$. To go to the other extreme, suppose that we wished to find the matrix of minimum distances between every pair of vertices (v_i, v_j). We could obtain this with DIJKSTRA, starting from each vertex in turn, with a complexity of $O(V^3)$. However, there is an attractive alternative due to Floyd. Although still $O(V^3)$, it is more compact, being entirely analogous to WARSHALL_B (Algorithm 7.4). In Warshall's algorithm, we detect a path from v_i to v_j by iterating (conceptually)

$$path_{k-1}\,[i,j] \textbf{ or } (path_{k-1}\,[i,k] \textbf{ and } path_{k-1}\,[k,j])$$

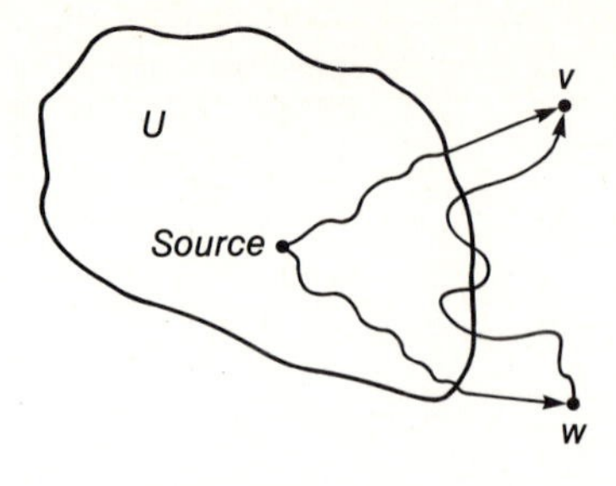

Figure 7.26 Rationale of Dijkstra's Method

In Floyd's algorithm, we obtain the minimum distance from v_i to v_j by iterating (conceptually)

$$\min \{least_{k-1} [i,j], least_{k-1} [i,k] + least_{k-1} [k,j]\}$$

The resulting procedure is FLOYD (Algorithm 7.9). Note that it is conventional to set the diagonal entries in the cost matrix to zero in order to model the underlying reality of the problem. If this were not done, the final diagonal entries would not correspond to shortest paths, but rather to the shortest circuits incident upon these vertices. Analogously to WARSHALL_B, we test for *least* $[i,k] <> \infty$ in order to eliminate unnecessary computations. The result of applying FLOYD to the digraph of Figure 7.23 is illustrated by the trace in Figure 7.27. The initial value of *least* is that of *cost* from Figure 7.24(a), and the final shortest paths are those given by Figure 7.27(f).

```
procedure FLOYD (cost: adj_mat_i; var least: adj_mat_i);

const  inf = {some suitably large number, such as maxint}

type   vndx = 0 .. vmax;
       adj_mat_i = array [vndx,vndx] of integer;

var    i,j,k: vndx;

begin
   least := cost;
   for k := 1 to vsize do
      least [k,k] := 0;
   for k := 1 to vsize do
      for i := 1 to vsize do
         if least [i,k] <> inf then
            for j := 1 to vsize do
               if least [i,k] + least [k,j] < least [i,j] then
                  least [i,j] := least [i,k] + least [k,j];
end;
```

Algorithm 7.9 FLOYD

We stated earlier that using FLOYD is preferable to making V calls on DIJKSTRA. But this once again depends upon the relative density of the graph; for a sparse graph the repeated use of DIJKSTRA could be significantly better. There is another factor that is also important in choosing between these two algorithms. For some applications it makes sense to have edges with negative weights. In these cases, Dijkstra's algorithm does not work properly. Although it can easily be modified to accommodate negative weights (see Exercise 7.20) – as long there are not negative cycles as well – the resulting complexity can then be exponential [Johnson 1973]. Floyd's algorithm handles negative weights with no attendant difficulties, but the case of negative cycles poses an obvious problem.

```
     0  *  5  *  *  2          0  *  5  6  *  2          0  *  5  6  *  2
     3  0  8 10  *  5          3  0  8  9  *  5          3  0  8  9  *  5
(a)  *  *  0  1  *  *     (c)  *  *  0  1  *  *     (e)  7  *  0  1  *  9
     6  * 11  0  *  8          6  * 11  0  *  8          6  * 11  0  *  8
     *  2  * 14  0  *          5  2 10 11  0  7          5  2 10 11  0  7
     * 17  1  4  9  0         20 17  1  2  9  0          8 11  1  2  9  0

     0  *  5  *  *  2          0  *  5  6  *  2          0 13  3  4 11  2
     3  0  8 10  *  5          3  0  8  9  *  5          3  0  6  7 14  5
(b)  *  *  0  1  *  *     (d)  7  *  0  1  *  9     (f)  7 20  0  1 18  9
     6  * 11  0  *  8          6  * 11  0  *  8          6 19  9  0 17  8
     5  2 10 12  0  7          5  2 10 11  0  7          5  2  8  9  0  7
    20 17  1  4  9  0          8 17  1  2  9  0          8 11  1  2  9  0
```

Figure 7.27 Trace of Algorithm FLOYD

†7.4.2.1 Dynamic Programming. In previous sections, we have encountered several algorithmic techniques for contending with the complexity associated with solving problems: divide-and-conquer, backtracking, and branch-and-bound. By reexamining some of the material from the preceding section, we now find another important technique, *dynamic programming*. In the case of divide-and-conquer, we saw how some problems can be broken up into smaller problems that can be solved and composed independently. However, there are instances where we can decompose a problem and solve its parts independently, and yet the resulting sub-solutions cannot be composed independently. In such cases, if two specific conditions apply, then we can use dynamic programming to reduce the exponential costs associated with evaluating a large tree of possibilities. The first necessary condition is that an optimal solution of a sub-problem should always be optimal no matter how that sub-solution is combined in a larger problem. The second necessary condition is that sub-problems should recur in several larger problems; this allows us to compute the solutions for sub-problems just once and then store them in tables, where they can be looked up when needed within larger problems.

Let us reexamine Floyd's algorithm in the light of these remarks. There, for all pairs i,j, we look for

$$\min \{least_{k-1}[i,j],\ least_{k-1}[i,k] + least_{k-1}[k,j]\}$$

over successively larger sets of intermediate vertices $v_1 .. v_{k-1}$. On the kth iteration, the values of $least_{k-1}[i,k]$ and $least_{k-1}[k,j]$ always represent the shortest distances (i,k) and (k,j) over paths wherein the first $k-1$ vertices are intermediate, so that the first of the above conditions applies. Moreover, since

$$least_k [i,k] = least_{k-1} [i,k] \text{ , and } \quad least_k [k,j] = least_{k-1} [k,j]$$

then table entries having k as a subscript will not change on the kth iteration. Thus the intermediate tables, corresponding to the second of the above conditions, can be maintained in the same table where the final answer is developed! The fact that the storage for the solutions for the sub-problems is essentially free is key to the success of dynamic programming in this situation.

The method of tabulation for the transformation of a recursive program to a more efficient one (see Section 5.4.2.1) is related to dynamic programming in a limited sense. In this former technique we also store values in tables so that they can be reused rather than recomputed. Dynamic programming is a more general process in that it involves an optimization using such tabulated values. That Floyd's algorithm is an instance of dynamic programming almost escapes our notice because of the fortuitous manner in which storage is reused. We will encounter other, more distinctive uses of dynamic programming in Sections 7.4.4.3, 8.3.3, 8.6.3, and 10.3.2.1.

7.4.3 Matchings and Coverings in a Graph

Suppose that we have a group of persons and that we must pair them off, perhaps as roommates. We can represent the persons as vertices of a graph in which, for every compatible pair, there is a corresponding edge. Is there an efficient algorithm that will either find a compatible roommate for every person, or else determine that no such pairing exists? We will return to the question after posing it in the terminology of graph theory. A *matching* in a graph is an *independent* subset of its edges (such that no two of the edges are adjacent), and a maximum matching in a graph G is synonymous with the largest possible set of independent edges in G. An important numerical parameter of a graph is the cardinality of a maximum matching, a quantity known as the *edge independence number* I_E of the graph. If a matching is such that it covers, or includes, all of the vertices, then we have a *complete matching*.

We can also inquire as to the minimum number of (not necessarily independent) edges that are required to obtain a *covering* of all the vertices of the graph – that is, a set of edges such that all the vertices are incident to at least one edge in the set. This quantity is known as the *edge covering number* C_E of the graph. By reversing the roles of the vertices and the edges, we obtain two analogous parameters for vertices. One of these is the *vertex independence number* I_V, equal to the cardinality of a maximal independent (non-adjacent) set of vertices in the graph. The other is the *vertex covering number* C_V, equal to the cardinality of a smallest (not necessarily independent) set of vertices that covers all the edges of the graph. It is straightforward to see that, given *any* set S of independent vertices in a graph G, the complementary set of vertices $V - S$ must be a covering of G, and vice-versa. To see this, note that S is an independent set if and only if there exists no edge with both ends in S; however, this is equivalent to the condition that every edge in G has at least one of its ends in the set $V - S$. In particular, this is true for the case of a maximal independent set of vertices and a minimum vertex cover, yielding

$$C_V + I_V = V \tag{7.4}$$

The analysis is slightly more complicated for the edge parameters, but as long as there are no isolated vertices (that is, of degree 0), then also

$$C_E + I_E = V \tag{7.5}$$

These notions are illustrated in Figure 7.28, where the graph in (a) has a maximal matching as shown in (b); thus, we have that $I_E = 3$. In addition, it is easily verified that $C_E = 4$, $I_V = 2$, and $C_V = 5$.

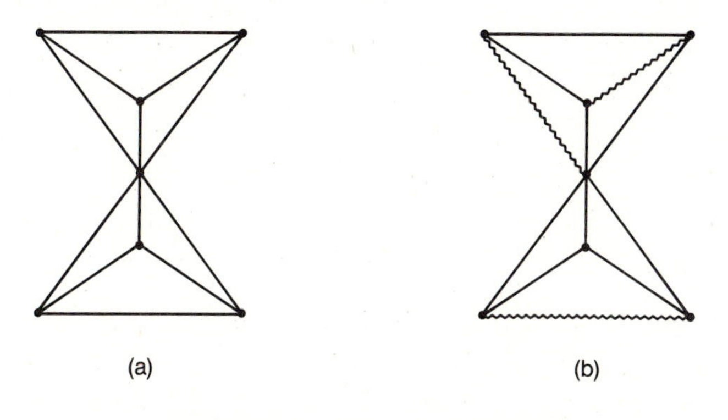

Figure 7.28 Independent Edges

Our original question was how to compute the maximum matching in a graph. There is an efficient algorithm, but it is too complicated for us to consider here. However, there are several variations on the problem of finding a maximum matching. We will begin by introducing one of these simpler variations, and will then illustrate its relevance to the SDR problem first considered in Chapter 6. Section 7.4.3.3 calls attention to an important, alternative point of view for matching problems. Finally, Section 7.4.3.4 briefly deals with matching in the general case.

7.4.3.1 Bipartite Graphs. Suppose that the vertices of our graph comprise two independent sets, U and W; in other words, all edges in the graph are of the form (u,w), with $u \in U$ and $w \in W$, for U and W disjoint sets of vertices, not necessarily of the same cardinality. Graphs of this form are called *bipartite*;[4] a *complete bipartite graph* $K_{m,n}$ is one in which every vertex of U, of cardinality m, is adjacent to

[4] Note that a tree is a bipartite graph.

every vertex of W, of cardinality n. For many applications, a bipartite graph is conveniently represented via an adjacency matrix wherein the rows correspond to elements of U and the columns correspond to elements of W. Thus, for the graph of Figure 7.29(a), such a representation is shown in (b) of the figure.

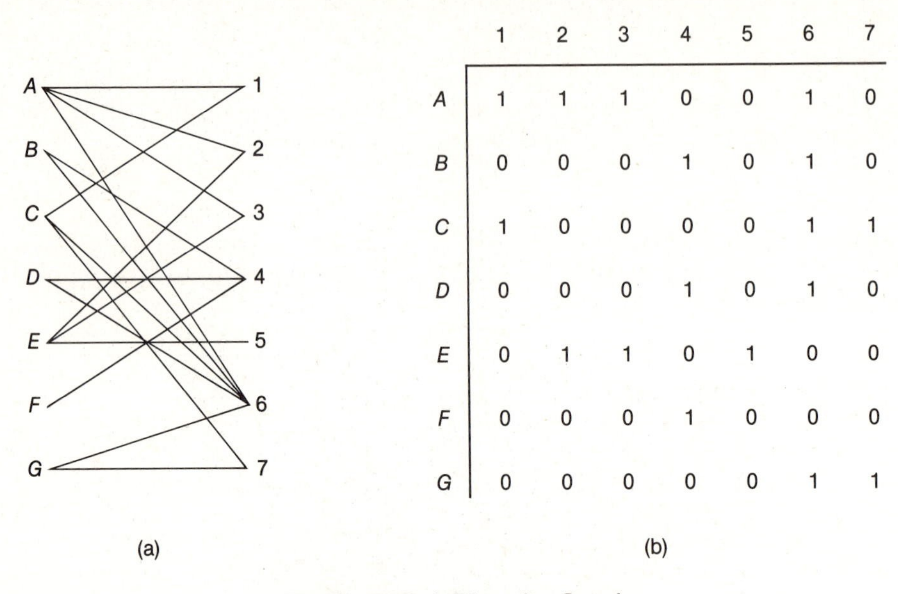

	1	2	3	4	5	6	7
A	1	1	1	0	0	1	0
B	0	0	0	1	0	1	0
C	1	0	0	0	0	1	1
D	0	0	0	1	0	1	0
E	0	1	1	0	1	0	0
F	0	0	0	1	0	0	0
G	0	0	0	0	0	1	1

Figure 7.29 A Bipartite Graph

There are many natural applications of bipartite graphs to matching problems. For example, the two vertex sets in the figure might represent men and women, and the edges might again denote compatibility. Then the issue might be to maximize the number of compatible marriages (with no polygamy). Or perhaps the vertex sets might represent workers and jobs, and the objective could be to try to assign every worker to a job for which he is qualified. Even though our example of Figure 7.29 is small, it can still be tricky to find a maximum matching in it. Before reading the next paragraph, you are encouraged to try to do so.

Happily, the matching problem is fairly simple for bipartite graphs. An underlying reason is that in this case the edge independence number is equal to the vertex covering number; that is,

$$I_E = C_V \tag{7.6}$$

an equality that does not hold in the general case. The method for finding such a maximum matching is to start with a given matching and then repeatedly try to enlarge it by the following strategy. Let the given matching be M, consisting of some subset of the edges; and let O be the remaining edges of the graph. We then construct a path P whose edges are alternately in O and in M. More precisely, we construct such a path starting with a vertex $u_0 \in U$ that is not covered by M. From u_0 we visit and mark unmarked vertices, building a BFS tree. In this tree, in going from an even level of the tree to an odd level, we may have zero, one, or many edges in O to choose from. But in going from an odd level of the tree to an even level, we can have just zero or one edges in M to choose from. If we arrive at a vertex $w_0 \in W$ and there is no edge in M to carry us back to U, then our path consists of j edges from M and $j+1$ edges from O. Such a path P is called an *augmenting path*, and it can be employed to construct a larger matching M'. We do this by deleting from M those edges in $M \cup P$, and then adding to M those edges in $O \cup P$; another way of expressing this is that $M' = M$ XOR P. For the graph of Figure 7.29(a), this process is illustrated in Figure 7.30(a), where the solid lines are in O and the wiggly lines are in the matching M. An augmenting path has been derived by starting from G and building the tree shown in Figure 7.30(b). By reversing the roles of the solid and the wiggly edges in the path $G-7-C-1-A-3$, we obtain the larger matching shown in (c) of the figure. Note that it would have been possible to extend the tree in (b) by adding the edge $2-E$. But that is irrelevant. We are happy to be "stuck" at an unmatched vertex (3), so that we can stop building the tree and construct an augmenting path.

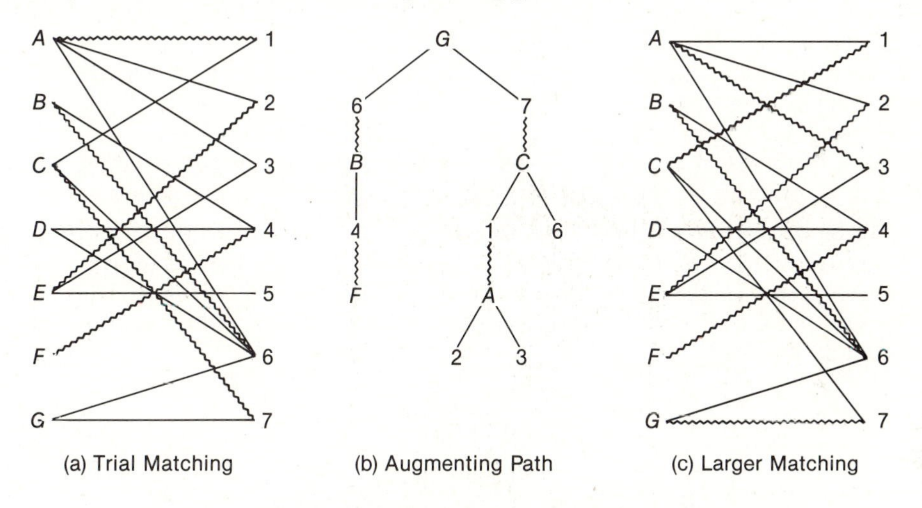

Figure 7.30 Bipartite Matching

If we try to apply this process again, we are unable to find an augmenting path. Such a condition corresponds to the fact that M' is a maximal matching for this graph. What is the complexity of this algorithm? We note first that the number of searches for an augmenting path is $O(V)$, actually $O(\min(U,W))$. For each search, if the graph is represented by an adjacency structure, then the time to build the tree is $O(E)$. Thus, the overall complexity of this method is $O(VE)$. There is a still faster algorithm for this problem, as we will see in Section 7.4.3.3.

†7.4.3.2 Systems of Distinct Representatives Again. The Systems of Distinct Representatives (SDR) problem was introduced in Section 6.8.2.1, where it was solved by means of backtracking. An unfortunate aspect of that approach, of course, it that it has exponential complexity in the number of sets. With graphs, however, we can obtain both theoretical insight about the problem and considerably better methods for solving it. We begin by constructing a bipartite graph that models the statement of the problem. In this graph, the vertex set U corresponds to the sets, the vertex set W corresponds to the members, and an edge (u,w) corresponds to the fact that $w \in U$. With regard to insight, a necessary and sufficient condition for the existence of a solution, in the case of finite sets, is given by *Hall's Theorem*: The union of any k distinct sets from the given collection of sets $\{S_i\}$ should have at least k distinct members [Hall 1935]. In applying this to the graph in Figure 7.29(a), we find that $\bigcup (B,D,F) = \{4,6\}$, so that indeed we cannot expect to find a complete matching. Unfortunately, there are two reasons that cause Hall's Theorem to have more theoretical than practical significance. For one, it is not a constructive criterion for a solution; for another, the application of this condition requires $O(2^n)$ tests for a problem dealing with n sets.

The SDR problem of Eqs. 6.19 is reproduced here as Eqs. 7.7:

$$S_1 = \{2,3,4,5\},\ \ S_2 = \{3,5\},\ \ S_3 = \{1,2\},\ \ S_4 = \{2,5\},\ \ S_5 = \{2,3\} \tag{7.7}$$

The bipartite graph corresponding to these equations is shown in Figure 7.31(a). By repeatedly applying to it the method of the preceding section, we readily obtain a complete matching, such as the one shown in (b) of the figure. For large instances of the SDR problem, the solution based upon the graph structure will be much more efficient than the previous one using an implicit tree structure.

We have used the SDR problem as a vehicle here and in Chapter 6 for illustrating various points about graphs and trees, and we will now take leave of it. However, there is a great deal more to be said on the topic, particularly with regard to generalizations of it. Expositions of these further details can be found in Brualdi [1977] and Korfhage [1974a].

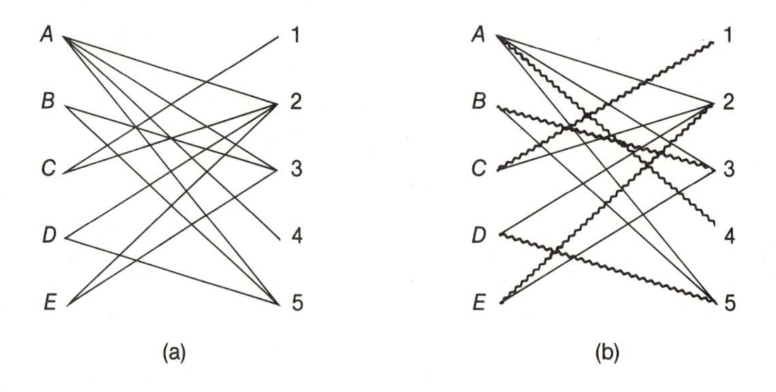

Figure 7.31 SDR Solution by Matching

†7.4.3.3 Networks and Flows. At this point, it is worthwhile to introduce a related, important topic concerning computations on graphs. While we do not have the space to treat it fully, it would be remiss not to at least mention it. The digraph in Figure 7.32(a) is called a *network*. It has a distinguished beginning vertex, the *source* s, and a distinguished ending vertex, the *sink* t. The weights on the edges represent the *capacities* $c(u,w)$ of those edges. We wish to find a function defined on each edge, the *flow* $\phi(u,w)$, such that for all $(u,w) \in E$

$$0 \leq \phi(u,w) \leq c(u,w) \tag{7.8}$$

and such that for all $v \in V$

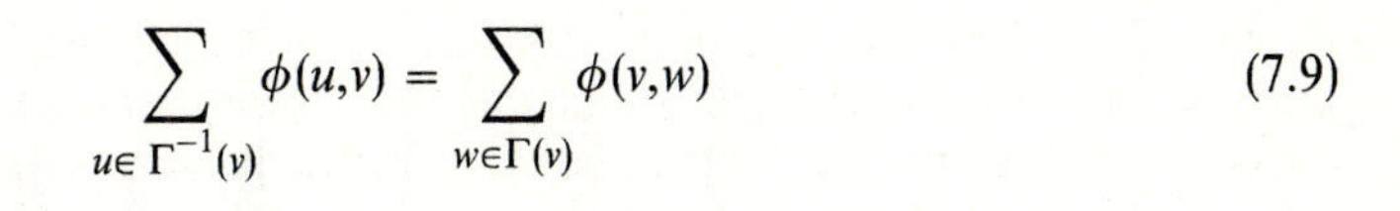

$$\sum_{u \in \Gamma^{-1}(v)} \phi(u,v) = \sum_{w \in \Gamma(v)} \phi(v,w) \tag{7.9}$$

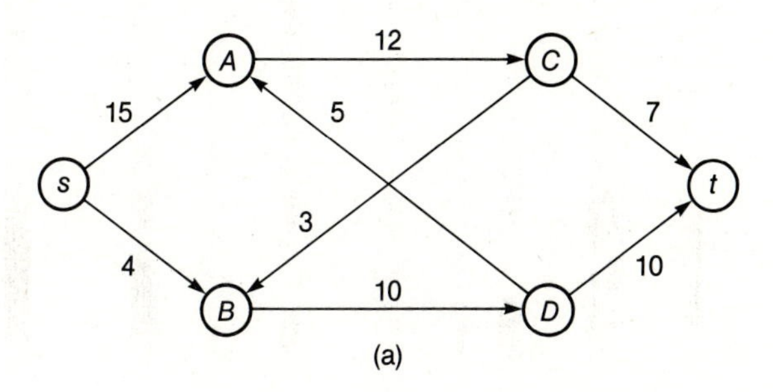

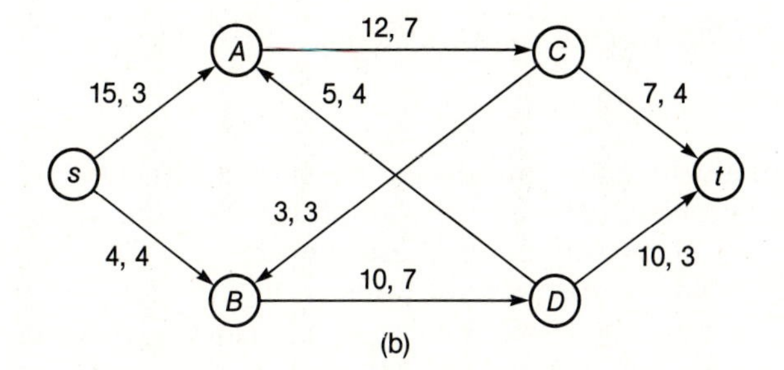

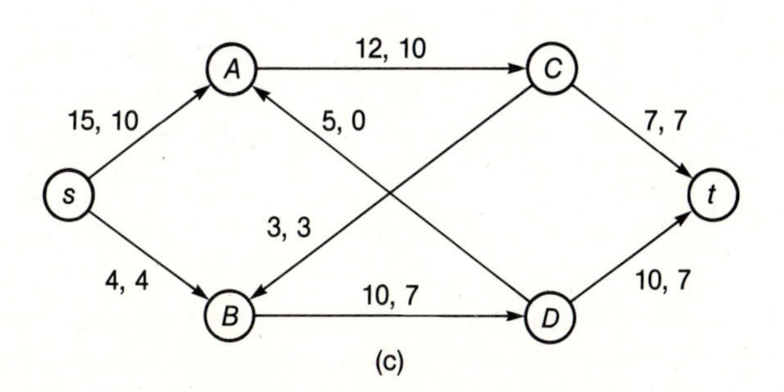

Figure 7.32 Network Flows

Eq. 7.8 expresses that the flow along an edge cannot exceed its capacity. Eq. 7.9 is a conservation condition: The total flow into a vertex must equal the total flow out of it. A problem characterized in this manner can be easily understood in terms of flow of liquid through a pipe. The subject of flows in networks was pioneered by Ford and Fulkerson [1962]. The usual objective is to find values for ϕ that maximize the total flow – that is, the equal amounts of flow leaving the source s and entering the sink t. For instance, a non-maximal flow for the network of Figure 7.32(a) is shown in (b) of the figure. The general method of solution is to iteratively improve such a situation until it is maximal, as illustrated in (c) of the figure. There has been a remarkable history of better and better algorithms for this purpose [§]. We will simply point out that these methods commonly use BFS and cut-sets (see Section 7.3.2) to iteratively find sequences of augmenting flows, analogous to the augmenting paths of the preceding section.

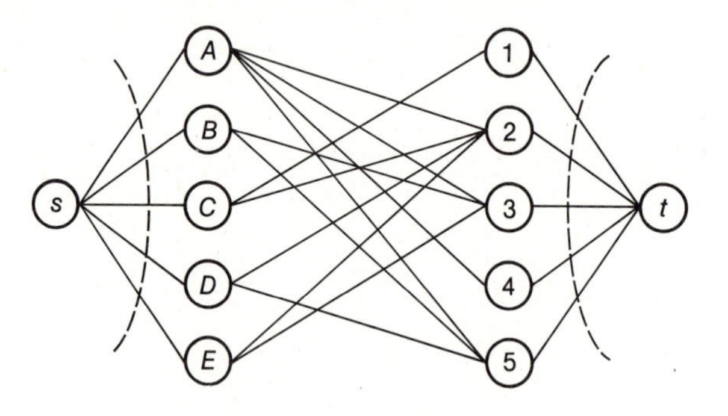

Figure 7.33 Network Model of SDR Problem

One of our motivations for introducing the subject of networks, albeit briefly, is that the matching problem on a bipartite graph can be reduced to a network problem by a very trivial construction. In illustration of this, the matching problem of Figure 7.31 corresponds to the network problem of Figure 7.33. We simply add a source node and a sink node, and we set all the capacities equal to 1; then the value of the maximal flow is equal to the value of the maximal matching. As a result of this correspondence, some of the effective techniques for dealing with network flows can be used to solve the bipartite matching problem. In particular, the algorithm described in Section 7.4.3.1 has complexity $O(VE)$, which can be $O(V^3)$ in the worst case. However, the network of Figure 7.33 is especially simple, leading to a solution for the bipartite matching problem with complexity $O(V^{2.5})$ [Hopcroft and Karp 1973].

†7.4.3.4 Matching in the General Case. There are two principal ways in which to generalize the previous results concerning the matching problem. One is to discard the bipartite restriction. Another is to introduce weights on the edges, and then look for a matching that maximizes the weighted sum of the matching edges. Let us consider both of these in turn.

For the general matching problem, the method of augmenting paths still applies [Berge 1957], except that we may now encounter circuits of odd length. The presence of certain types of odd circuits, known as *blossoms*, makes the analysis much more difficult [Edmonds 1965]. There are several fairly complicated algorithms that master the problem; the best of these has complexity $O(V^{0.5}E)$ [Micali and Vazirani 1980].

Under the heading of weighted matching, there are a variety of distinctive problems. A particularly appealing example, for the bipartite case, is the *Stable Marriage Problem* [Gale and Shapley 1962] (as opposed to the merely compatible marriage situation). Herein, we may suppose that each boy and each girl ranks all the members of the opposite sex in terms of their relative desirability in his or her eyes. There then begins a series of proposals by the boys to the girls on their lists. After every round of proposals, each girl accepts her best suitor, perhaps jilting a previous choice in the process. Boys who are rejected or jilted simply propose to the next choices on their lists in the next round. The final set of matchings, or marriages, is said to be stable if there does not exist any boy-girl pair who mutually prefer each other to their respective spouses. The question arises: Is it even possible for all the eager boys and girls to attain simultaneous, stable connubial bliss? The answer is that a stable situation does always exist. To see this, suppose that Alice and Bob are not married, but that Alice likes Bob better than her husband Arthur, and Bob likes Alice better than his wife Betty. But then, during the courtship sessions, Bob must have proposed to Alice, only to lose out to someone she preferred over him, perhaps Arthur. So instability cannot occur; in fact, there may be several stable solutions [McVitie and Wilson 1971]. The one that we have described is optimal for the men; if the women do the proposing, we may obtain a different solution that is optimal from their point of view; and there may exist still other stable solutions. There are many realistic analogues of the Stable Marriage Problem. One example is the process by which college applicants and colleges become matched every year (in which situation, please note, the colleges do the proposing).

Another example of bipartite weighted matching occurs in matching workers to jobs, with the proviso that the workers have numerically ranked skill levels relative to the different jobs. The objective is to maximize the skills utilized by the workers. This is known as the assignment problem, and the preferred method of solution is the so-called *Hungarian method*, with complexity $O(V^3)$ [Kuhn 1955].

What about weighted matching in the non-bipartite case? To begin with, there may not be an analogue of Stable Marriage. In other words, it may be impossible to obtain a matching among homosexuals that is stable, as in the heterosexual case. For the more general case of finding a maximal weighted matching, the presence of blossoms again makes the solution complicated; nonetheless, it can be attained with complexity $O(V^3)$. Our discussion of matching has necessarily gotten skimpier as we considered more involved variations. Excellent sources for amplifiying these matters are Galil [1986], Lawler [1976], and Papadimitriou and Steiglitz [1982].

7.4.4 Traversals of a Graph or Digraph

Sections 7.4.1 and 7.4.2 discussed finding trees in a graph – in one case to minimize the sum of the weights on the edges of the tree, and in the other case to minimize the distances between pairs of nodes. In this section, we consider two problems relating to paths in a graph:

I. Is it possible to traverse each edge of a connected graph G once and only once?

II. Is it possible to visit each vertex of a connected graph G once and only once?

In both cases, we may insist that our initial and final vertices are the same, so that we have a circuit, or we may be content to have an unclosed path. A cyclic solution to problem I is called an *Eulerian tour*, in which case the graph is said to be *Eulerian*; a non-cyclic solution is called an *Eulerian path*. A cyclic solution to problem II is called a *Hamiltonian cycle*, in which case the graph is said to be *Hamiltonian*; a non-cyclic solution is called a *Hamiltonian path*. The two problems are meaningful for both graphs and digraphs. The nature of these properties, and their independence, may be more easily appreciated by reference to Figure 7.34. There, the graph in (a) is both Eulerian and Hamiltonian, that in (b) is Eulerian but not Hamiltonian, that in (c) is Hamiltonian but not Eulerian, and that in (d) is neither Eulerian nor Hamiltonian.

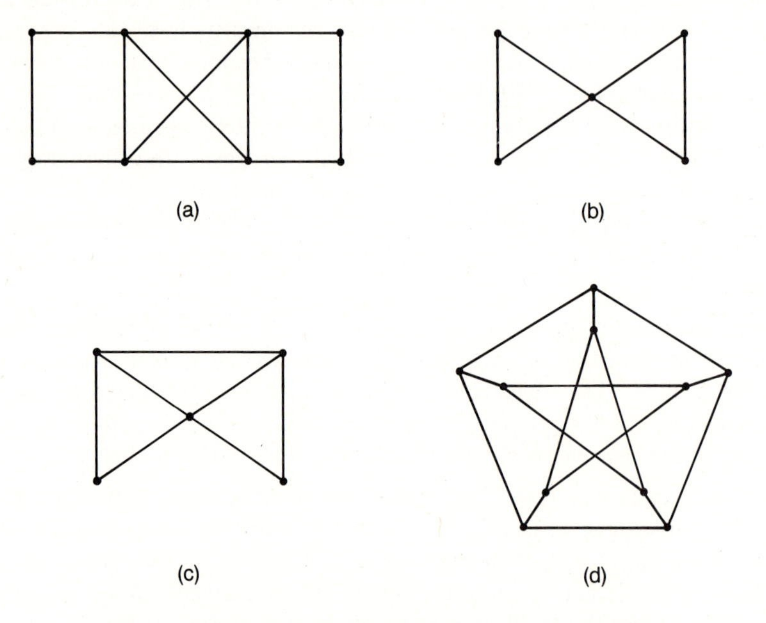

Figure 7.34 Eulerian and Hamiltonian Properties

Although the statements of the two problems have a nice symmetry, their solutions are very different. The first has a very easy solution, and the second is *NP*-complete. Our objectives in this section are rather limited:

- to acquaint the reader with these important aspects of graphs, and
- to relate these problems to some things that we have already learned.

The statements of problems I and II make no mention of weights. If a graph is Eulerian, then the effect of weights is of course irrelevant. For the Hamiltonian problem, however, the influence of weights is very important, giving rise to the Traveling Salesman problem, wherein a Hamiltonian cycle of least cost is sought. That is the third and the most substantial topic of this section.

7.4.4.1 Eulerian Tours. The genesis of graph theory occurred in 1736 when Leonhard Euler solved the following problem: Was there a way in which the townspeople of Königsberg could take a walk that crossed each of the seven bridges over the Pregel River, depicted in Figure 7.35(a), once and just once? Euler showed that such a walk is impossible. It is easy to see why by reference to Figure 7.35(b). This multigraph is derived from (a) by shrinking the land masses to points. If a vertex in a graph is of even degree, then after arriving at it by one edge, we are sure to have another edge by which to leave it; for a vertex of odd degree, however, this is not the case. The net result is that if a graph has no vertices of odd degree, then it is Eulerian, and the tour is easily found. If the graph has two vertices of odd degree, then it admits an Eulerian path with these two vertices as the endpoints.[5] Since Figure 7.35(b) has four vertices of odd degree, the original question about the bridges must be answered in the negative.

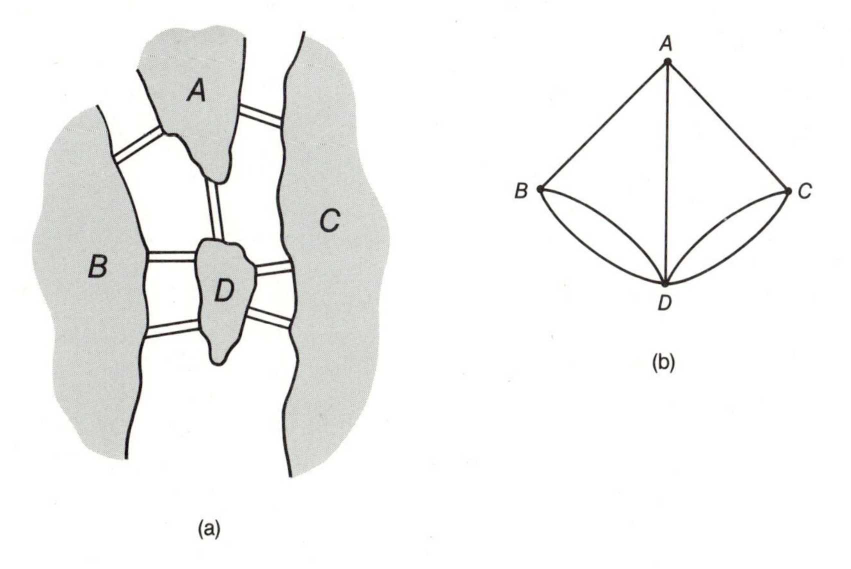

Figure 7.35 The Königsberg Bridges

[5] By counting the number of edges incident to each vertex, we can see that there must be an even number of vertices with odd degree.

We can see from this example that the criterion is equally applicable to graphs and multigraphs (including loops). For digraphs, the requirement is simply that of equality between the in-degrees and out-degrees of each of the vertices. Euler's condition is quite useful in that it is both necessary and sufficient. It is easily evaluated for a given graph G, and if the answer is affirmative then it can also be used to guide the construction of a tour of G: We simply employ the auxiliary condition that whenever there is a choice about which edge to use next, we should not select a bridge – that is, an edge that would disconnect the untraversed portion of the graph (see Section 7.3.2).

Unfortunately, Euler's condition is not likely to be satisfied in many real-life situations. Thus, a postmen must deliver mail along each street even though his route probably contains many intersections (vertices) with odd degree; the same problem is faced in garbage collection and many other services. In these cases, we are forced to traverse some of the edges in the graph more than once. To compound the problem, the graphs for these practical situations are weighted, so that the selection of the repeated edges is non-trivial. This is known as the *Chinese Postman Problem*. The solution is somewhat lengthy, but it involves two concepts that we are already familiar with. We begin by computing the shortest distances between all pairs of vertices. Next, on the subgraph consisting of the nodes of odd degree, we solve a minimum weighted matching problem. The matching identifies which edges should be traversed twice. The details of this approach can be found in Edmonds and Johnson [1973].

7.4.4.2 Hamiltonian Cycles. There is no known succinct property for infallibly characterizing Hamiltonian graphs, as there is for Eulerian graphs. However, there are a variety of sufficient conditions, of which the following is representative: If G is a graph with V vertices such that, for all distinct non-adjacent vertices x and y, the sum of the degrees of x and y is not less than V, then G is Hamiltonian. However, it is easy to find Hamiltonian graphs for which such conditions are not necessary, such as a 2-regular graph, or cycle. When confronted with a graph that does not satisfy any of the various sufficient conditions, we are reduced to combining various heuristics with backtracking in order to resolve the matter [Rubin 1974]. Most heuristics are based upon the following principles:

- Once we have picked the two edges to be used in passing through a vertex, then the remaining edges incident upon that vertex can be eliminated from contention.
- We must never construct a circuit that does not include all the vertices.

Thus, we begin by including any edges incident upon vertices of degree 2; these restrict the inclusion of other edges at other vertices, and either force the inclusion of edges, or at least reduce the number of cases to be examined. We proceed in this manner until either a Hamiltonian cycle has been constructed, or its impossibility has been deduced. In particular, if we start from an independent set of vertices $v_1, v_2, \dots, v_k$, (see Section 7.4.3) then there can be just $2k$ edges through them. This dictates that the number of edges in the graph that cannot occur in a Hamiltonian circuit is given by $t = \sum |\Gamma(v_i)| - 2k$. If $t < V$, we then have obtained a conclusive negative result. For an interesting variation on the problem of Hamiltonian cycles, see Exercise 7.36.

†7.4.4.3 The Traveling Salesman Problem. The *Traveling Salesman Problem* (*TSP*) is the vertex analogue of the Chinese Postman problem, and has many important applications. Besides the obvious cases suggested by the name – that is, minimizing the cost of providing service to V geographically separated facilities – there are others. One common example arises when V different jobs must be scheduled for some production facility, and there is a cost $c_{i,j}$ associated with switching between the ith and jth jobs; the goal here is an optimal cyclical schedule for the jobs that minimizes the aggregate changeover times.

There are some important distinctions between this problem and that of ascertaining if a graph has a Hamiltonian cycle. For one, it is common to assume that there is an edge between every pair of vertices, although it may be infinite in value for some pairs. Thus the issue is not so much to determine if there is a cycle as it is to determine the shortest cycle that visits each vertex once and only once. Another issue is that, for some problems, the weights on the edges will satisfy the triangle inequality of Euclidean plane geometry; that is, the sum of the values of any two edges of a triangle cannot be less than the value of the third edge. For such problems, this property can be used to advantage. Note that there are problems, such as the job scheduling example, for which this need not be the case.

From the preceding discussion, you might easily infer that the Hamiltonian cycle problem (A) and the Traveling Salesman problem (B) are distinct in their complexities. But this would be an erroneous inference. By the process known as *problem reduction*, we can transform (A) to (B), as follows. Wherever there is an edge in (A), let the distance in (B) be 1; wherever there is not an edge in (A), let the distance in (B) be 2. Then look for a solution of (B) such that the total distance is not greater than V, the number of vertices. If there were a polynomial-time algorithm to solve (B), then that coupled with the trivial polynomial-time algorithm for this reduction would yield a polynomial-time algorithm to solve (A). But since (A) is known to be *NP*-complete, this is impossible, and so (B) must be *NP*-complete also. Reductions such as this, though typically more complicated, have been used extensively to establish that hundreds of problems are equivalently "hard" (see Section 6.8.2.2). To illustrate just how hard TSP is, note that a backtracking solution with no pruning would have to examine $(V-1)!$ paths (it doesn't matter where we start). This is worse than the worst complexity illustrated in Table 1.3, and an exact solution for even moderate values of V would require centuries on the fastest known computer.

One of the earlier, serious approaches was to apply dynamic programming. In this formulation, we start at an arbitrary first city, and then successively consider tours on larger and larger sets of cities. Let us denote by $C(S,k)$ the cost of the shortest path that starts at 1, visits (once) each city in the set S, and ends at k. Now, for each such city k, the cost of that shortest path consists of the minimum, over all predecessor cities j, of the quantity $C((S-\{k\}),j)+d_{j,k}$. Starting with the trivial values $C(\{k\},k)=d_{1,k}$, we can then compute the values $C(S,k)$ for all sets of successively larger sizes, and do so for every city in each such set in terms of the $C(S,k)$ on the smaller sets. Finally, we obtain $C((V-\{1\}),1)$, yielding the optimal tour on all the cities. Dynamic programming reduces the time complexity from $O(V!)$ to $O(V^2 2^V)$. Although enormously better than the factorial complexity of ordinary backtracking, it is still exponential; more significantly, the tables of intermediate solutions require $O(V2^V)$ space, a dramatically less auspicious situation than that which prevailed with Floyd's algorithm.

For smaller size instances of TSP, dynamic programming works fairly well, but for larger problems, branch-and-bound has been found to be more successful. As an example of this latter approach, let us suppose that the distances are given by an adjacency matrix A. We begin by subtracting from each entry in every row the value r_i of the smallest entry in that row, to obtain A'. Since one entry from each row of A must occur in the solution, then the solution to TSP on A is the same as $\sum r_i$ plus the solution to TSP on A'. Next, subtract from each entry in every column of A' the value c_j of the smallest entry in that column, to obtain A''. The same reasoning as used before tells us that the solution to TSP on A is the same as $\sum r_i$ plus $\sum c_j$ plus the solution to TSP on A''. In other words, $\sum r_i + \sum c_j$ is a bounding value. Let us denote this transformation process $A \to A' \to A''$ by ϕ. Next, we look for a branching entry $a_{r,s}$ among the zero values in A''. If we do not include $a_{r,s}$ in the tour, then we can effectively replace its value by infinity ∞. If we do include $a_{r,s}$ in the tour, then there are two consequences. One is that we must effectively set $a_{s,r}$ equal to ∞ in order to avoid a cycle of length 2; the other is that we cannot use any further entries in row r or column s. So the choice of whether or not to employ the edge $a_{r,s}$ in the tour corresponds to a branch point. If we do not include it, we can apply ϕ to an altered A''; if we do include it, we can apply ϕ to a submatrix of an altered A''. The branch-and-bound solution to TSP proceeds by alternately closing a branch point and evaluating the bounds associated with the two choices, then picking the open branch with lowest bound for further exploration, etc. Several branching criteria can be applied; a common one is to look for that zero value in A'' whose selection will maximize the increase in the lower bound.

Another successful class of techniques for solving TSP operates by *local search*; with this method, one first obtains an approximate or a partial solution, and then modifies it by local improvements. We shall not pursue local search here. However, the concept of applying approximate solution methods to intractable problems is an important one. With them, it is often possible to come reasonably close to the elusive exact solution, but at far less cost. We will illustrate how some of the concepts arising from more tractable graph problems are very useful for finding approximate solutions to TSP. The simplest method of all is to try a greedy approach, as follows. Start with the shortest edge. Thereafter, consider adjacent edges in order of their length, appending them to the tour if (a) they would not cause any vertex to have degree three or more, and (b) they would not create a cycle (unless that cycle includes all the vertices). Suppose that we had to pack our sample case and visit the following cities: (A)tlanta, (B)ismarck, (D)enver, (H)ouston, (J)acksonville, (L)ouisville, (M)emphis, (O)maha, (P)ortland, (S)an Diego, and (W)ichita. They are depicted in Figure 7.36(a), and the intercity mileages are given in Table 7.1. The greedy method would select the edges in the sequence shown in Figure 7.36(b), for a tour of 8678 miles.

We can generally expect to do better if the triangle inequality is satisfied, as cited at the beginning of this section. In that case, consider the following simple-minded approach. First, find the MST for the graph; then consider the tour obtained by using each edge of the MST twice; and finally introduce "shortcuts" by bypassing the second occurrence of each vertex. Note the relevance of the triangle inequality for guaranteeing that a shortcut will always live up to its name. As

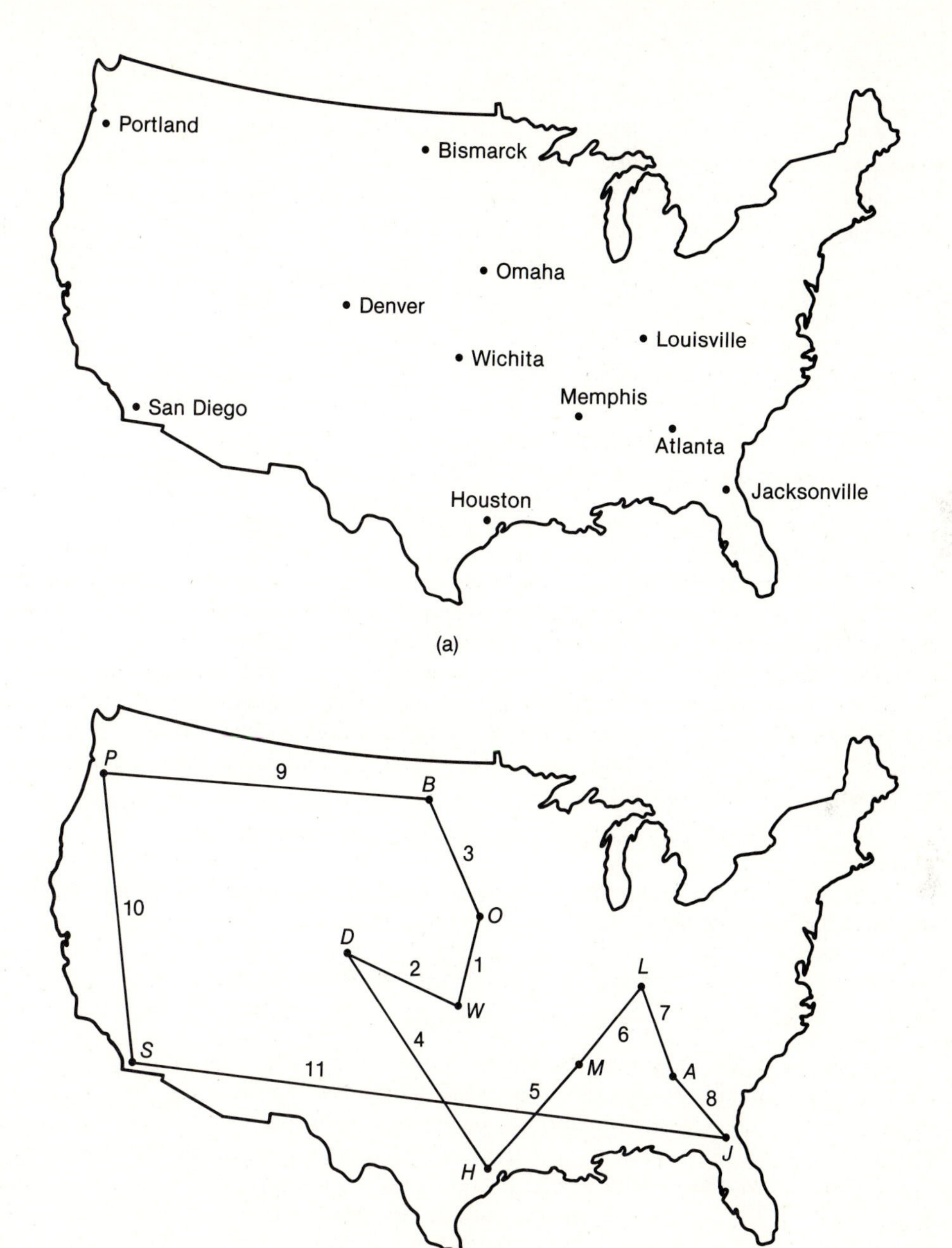

Figure 7.36 The Greedy Heuristic for Solving TSP

	A	B	D	H	J	L	M	O	P	S	W
Atlanta	0	1483	1385	780	307	383	369	962	2569	2106	899
Bismarck	1483	0	668	1383	1790	1106	1209	576	1265	1639	781
Denver	1385	668	0	1014	1692	1118	1038	534	1234	1086	510
Houston	780	1383	1014	0	869	922	557	858	2189	1470	602
Jacksonville	307	1790	1692	869	0	690	672	1269	2876	2319	1202
Louisville	383	1106	1118	922	690	0	367	693	2302	2069	702
Memphis	369	1209	1038	557	672	367	0	633	2240	1778	530
Omaha	962	576	534	858	1269	693	633	0	1648	1619	297
Portland	2569	1265	1234	2189	2876	2302	2240	1648	0	1083	1735
San Diego	2106	1639	1086	1470	2319	2069	1778	1619	1083	0	1373
Wichita	899	781	510	602	1202	702	530	297	1735	1373	0

Table 7.1 Mileage Chart for TSP
(Standard Highway Mileage Guide, Rand McNally & Co, 1982)

applied to the graph of Figure 7.36(a), this method first computes the MST shown by dashed lines in Figure 7.37(a). Now we need to be more specific about various details such as where to start, which edge of the MST to traverse next when there is a choice, which shortcut to take, etc. Let us make the arbitrary assumption that we start with A(tlanta), and the reasonable assumptions that we always choose the shortest adjacent edge in traversing the MST, and that we are likewise greedy in making shortcuts. If we double each edge in the MST and use these assumptions, we obtain the preliminary tour

$$A\ J\ A\ M\ L\ M\ W\ O\ B\ O\ W\ D\ S\ P\ S\ D\ W\ M\ H\ M\ A$$

When we introduce the greedy shortcuts, the repeated values drop out of this sequence, yielding the tour

$$A\ J\ M\ L\ W\ O\ B\ D\ S\ P\ H\ A$$

for a total of 8727 miles, as shown by solid lines in Figure 7.37(a).

In this particular instance, the more sophisticated method failed to outperform the greedy approach! Nonetheless, the MST method is important in that it is relatively simple, and yet guaranteed to produce a tour no worse than twice the optimum. To see this, observe that the optimal tour minus an edge is a spanning tree T, and the weighted value $|\mathrm{MST}|$ cannot exceed the weighted value $|T|$; that is, $|\mathrm{MST}| \le |T|$. But then, twice around the MST cannot exceed $2 \times |T|$, a bound that can only be improved by the shortcuts. If we consider the deviation of our approximate solution from the optimal solution, and take the ratio of the former to the latter, then that ratio is bounded by 1. Thus, the tree method is said to be a *1-approximate* solution.

One of the better heuristics for solving the TSP is a ½-approximate solution, based upon matching. We commence by computing the MST again. Then, on the

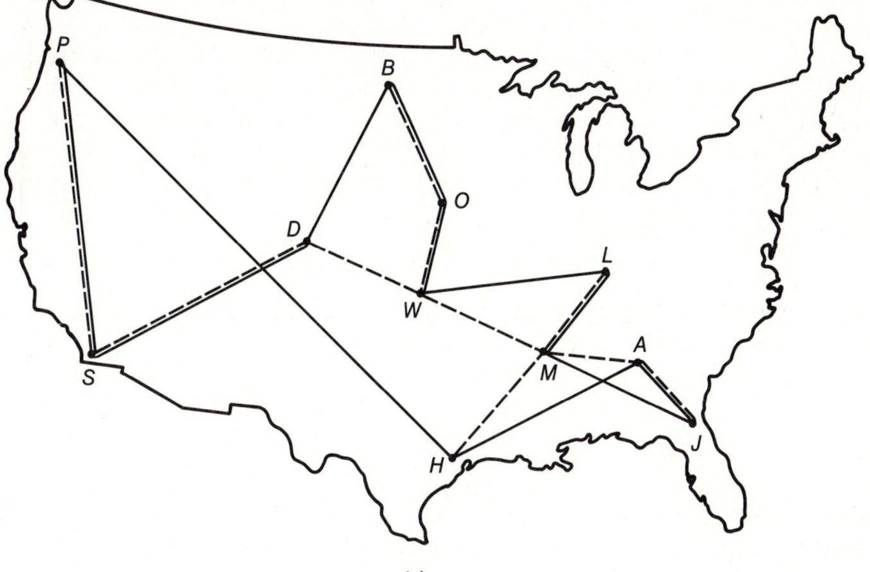

(a)

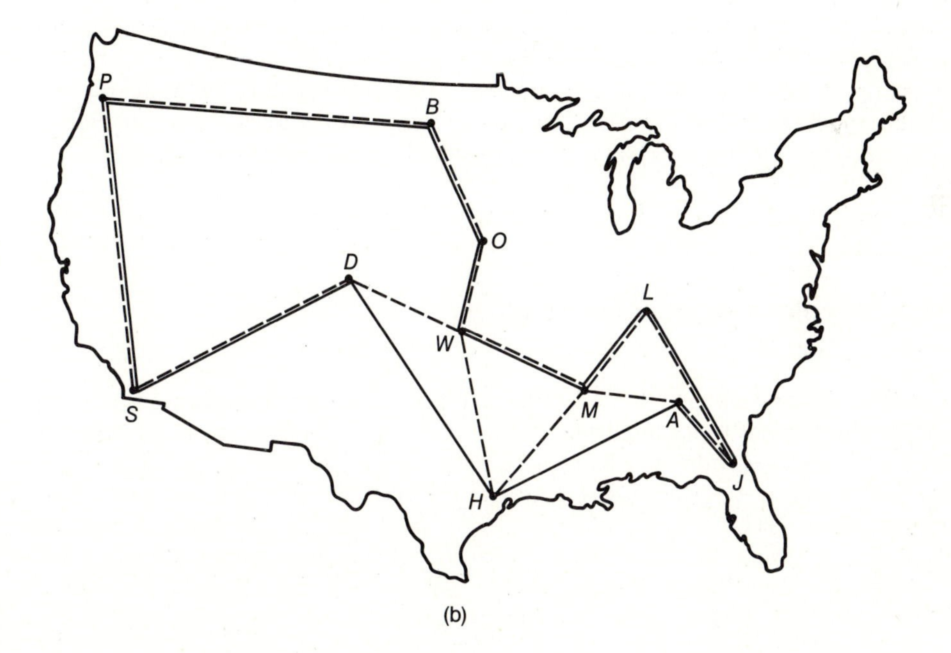

(b)

Figure 7.37 Other Heuristics for Solving TSP

vertices of the MST that are of odd degree, we solve a minimum weighted matching problem. We (i) add these edges M to the MST, (ii) construct an Eulerian tour employing the edges in MST $\cup M$, and (iii) apply shortcuts again. It is fairly easy to show that, just as $|\text{MST}| \le |T|$, so also $|M| \le \frac{1}{2} \times |T|$, which establishes the ½-approximate character of the solution. As applied to our test data, we start with the same MST as before, and note that the vertices of odd degree correspond to Bismarck, Houston, Jacksonville, Louisville, Portland, and Wichita. A minimum weight matching for these is: $B-P$, $H-W$, $J-L$. By adding these matching edges to the MST, we obtain the Eulerian graph shown by dashed lines in Figure 7.37(b). Starting at A again, and with similar assumptions as for Figure 7.37(a), we first construct the preliminary tour

$$A\ J\ L\ M\ W\ O\ B\ P\ S\ D\ W\ H\ M\ A$$

This is already close to a good solution, and we need introduce only one shortcut from D to H and another from H to A, to obtain

$$A\ J\ L\ M\ W\ O\ B\ P\ S\ D\ H\ A$$

for a total of 7995 miles, as shown by solid lines in Figure 7.37(b).

It is possible to construct examples where the 1-approximate and ½-approximate algorithms of the last two paragraphs will actually attain their maximum relative errors. In practice, however, these algorithms tend to yield results much closer to the optimum. We should hasten to add that approximation methods for TSP without the triangle inequality do not have such nice worst-case bounds. In fact, if there were an r-approximate method, for any bounded value of r, then $P = NP$ – a most unlikely result! Our objective in this section has been primarily to introduce TSP and to demonstrate how methods for attacking it are related to other, familiar techniques for dealing with graphs. For the rest, we supply several references [§], and leave the details of algorithms as exercises.

7.4.5 Precedence Relations in a Digraph

We have emphasized that the edges of a graph represent a mathematical relation among the vertices. An important special case of this occurs in a digraph where there are no cycles, otherwise known as a *directed acylic graph* (*DAG*).[6] In a DAG, the arcs represent a *partial ordering* among the vertices. We can represent the presence of an arc from A to B by $A \prec B$. In the case of a *total ordering* (for example, the points on a line) we always have a relation between two distinct objects A and B – either $A < B$ or $B < A$. The nature of a partial ordering relationship is such that there may exist distinct pairs A,B where neither $A \prec B$ nor $B \prec A$, and thus we

---

6 Note that a whereas a tree corresponds to a pure List and a graph to a recursive List, a DAG corresponds to a reentrant List.

cannot construct a unique sequential ordering of our set of objects.[7] As an example, the digraph of Figure 7.2 is a DAG. We may know, for instance, that $4 < 6$; but that doesn't alter the fact that neither integer divides the other, and so there is no partial (divisibility) ordering between them. Given that there are no cycles in a DAG, we can always construct a linear ordering with the property that if $A \prec B$, then A will occur to the left of B in this sequence. In fact, we can in general construct many *topological orderings* that have this property. As an illustration of these notions, consider the digraph of Figure 7.38(a). Two topological orderings of the vertices are $I\,B\,D\,G\,C\,E\,F\,J\,A\,H$ and $C\,E\,G\,A\,I\,B\,F\,J\,D\,H$; there are many others. Note that if we place the vertices in topological order, and then insert the arcs from the original graph, they will all point from left to right. Thus, the effect of a topological ordering is to embed a partial ordering in a total ordering.

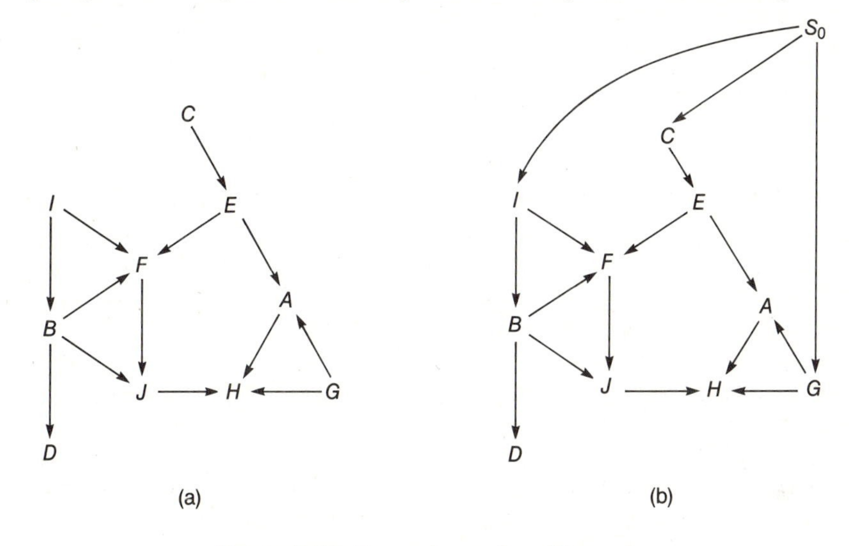

Figure 7.38 Precedence in a Digraph

DAG's are one special case of a digraph. Another important, special case is a *flow graph*, which has a unique entry-point node s_0, from which all other nodes can be reached. The significance of flow graphs is that they can be used to model programs. The more sophisticated methods of detecting errors in programs and of optimizing their compilation all make extensive use of various concepts associated with flow graphs.

In the ensuing three sections, we will first consider how to check for topological orderings in a digraph. This capability is important as an initial step of other, more complicated processes, and our second area of discussion consists of an example in this spirit. Section 7.4.5.3 describes some of the concepts and techniques associated with using flow graphs to analyze programs.

---

[7] Technically, since we do not allow for the reflexive case $A \preccurlyeq A$, what we have described is a *quasi ordering*. But this strict form of partial order is what we want here.

7.4.5.1 Topological Sorting. The process of discovering topological orderings of the vertices of a digraph is known as topological sorting, and the problem presents itself in various guises. For instance, we may be presented with a set of partial orderings, analogous to the equivalence relations of Eqs. 4.6 and 6.5, or we may already have their representation as a graph. Another consideration is that we may already be certain that there are no cycles, or the existence of cycles may be an open and important issue. As one concrete example, suppose that we think of these relationships as signifying "A is defined in terms of B," and that our goal is to write a dictionary. Then it would be desirable to use an algorithm that would either find some topological ordering, or else report that we had circular definitions. For another example, suppose that the relationships expressed facts such as: "Course P of r units is a prerequisite for course Q of s units." Our chief interest then might be to find a sequence of courses that would allow us to graduate in reasonable time. In still another variation, our objective might be to enumerate all possible topological orderings.

The usual approach to the latter type of problem is not to generate permutations, but to use the precedence relations in a clever manner to prune subtrees (in other words, to employ backtracking) [Knuth and Szwarcfiter 1974; Varol and Rotem 1981]. An interesting, alternative technique employs a ternary tree in a manner analogous to the use of a BST for ordinary sorting [Szwarcfiter and Wilson 1978]. In this method, the middle child of a ternary tree node corresponds to the case where neither $A \prec B$ nor $B \prec A$; after all the relationships have been processed, the topological orderings can be obtained by a traversal of the final ternary tree.

Procedures for solving the other types of problems (that is, where enumeration of all possible orderings is *not* the objective) are fairly simple. As a first comment, the technique of DFS is directly applicable to either computing a valid topological ordering, or else reporting that there is a cycle. We simply need modify DFS so that (a) it still marks a node as soon as it reaches it, but (b) it labels the node with its topological value just before exiting. The labels will actually be generated in reverse topological order, but it is trivial to complement them. Note that if this modified form of DFS encounters a node that is marked but not labeled, then a cycle has been detected. A final observation is that we must attend to one other detail in order for DFS to work — we must have a unique node of in-degree zero, from which to start the search. Thus, the method would not work as described for Figure 7.38(a). However, in most cases this can easily be taken care of by inserting a dummy node S_0 that has arcs to the original nodes of in-degree zero, as illustrated in Figure 7.38(b).

In a case where we have a large set of partial ordering relationships with no prior awareness about their nature, a somewhat different approach is called for. We cannot use DFS directly; however, the solution is obtained by a similar process. We need to maintain counts of the in-degrees of the nodes in the digraph, corresponding to the relationships. We then proceed as follows:

(a) Begin by making a list of the nodes with in-degree zero.

(b) Look for any node X on the list, remove it, and decrement the in-degree counts of the nodes in $\Gamma(X)$ by one.

(c) As each of the counts is decremented in step (b), test to see if it is now zero; if it is then add that node to the list.

```
program TOPO_SORT;

label  1;

var    elink: eptr;
       i,k,top,vlink: vndx;

begin
   top := 0;
   for i := 1 to vsize do     {build initial stack}
      if vlist [i].indegree = 0 then begin
         vlist [i].indegree := top;  top := i;
      end;
   for k := 1 to vsize do
      if top = 0 then begin
         write ('  Cycle at remaining nodes');
         goto 1;
      end else begin
         write ('  ',vlist [top].vid);
         elink := vlist [top].head;
         top := vlist [top].indegree;
         while elink <> nil do begin
            vlink := elink↑.vno;
            vlist [vlink].indegree := vlist [vlink].indegree - 1;
            if vlist [vlink].indegree = 0 then begin
               vlist [vlink].indegree := top;  top := vlink;
            end;
            elink := elink↑.next;
         end;
      end;
1: writeln;
end.
```

Algorithm 7.10 TOPO_SORT

(d) If we have processed all n nodes then we are done, else if the list is non-empty then repeat step (b); otherwise, there must remain some node(s) with non-zero counts, indicating that there is a cycle.

Either a queue or a stack can be used for the list; the list order is not important. We can obtain an algorithm that is economical in terms of space by threading a stack where the in-degree values were maintained; that is, once such a field has been determined to contain a zero, it will never be referenced by step (b) again, and so is "free." A program that implements this strategy is TOPO_SORT (Algorithm 7.10). Figure 7.39 illustrates the method as applied to the original digraph of Figure 7.38(a). The structure before the process commences is illustrated in Figure 7.39(a). The program begins by building a stack in the count fields of I,G,C, as shown in (b) of the figure. By the time I and B have been output by the algorithm, the count fields appear as in (c) of the figure, where the link values associated with I

and *B* are no longer meaningful. When the process terminates, it has discovered the topological ordering *I B D G C E F J A H*.

Node	Count	Successors
1—*A*	2	*H*
2—*B*	1	*D F J*
3—*C*	0	E
4—*D*	1	
5—*E*	1	*A F*
6—*F*	3	*J*
7—*G*	0	*A H*
8—*H*	3	
9—*I*	0	*B F*
10—*J*	2	*H*

(a)

top (at 9)

Node	1	2	3	4	5	6	7	8	9	10
	A	*B*	*C*	*D*	*E*	*F*	*G*	*H*	*I*	*J*
Count	2	1	0	1	1	3	3	3	7	2

(b)

top (at 4)

Node	1	2	3	4	5	6	7	8	9	10
	A	*B*	*C*	*D*	*E*	*F*	*G*	*H*	*I*	*J*
Count	2	7	0	7	1	1	3	3	7	1

(c)

Figure 7.39 Progress of Algorithm TOPO_SORT

†7.4.5.2 Critical Path Analysis. Throughout life, we often must complete certain tasks before we can embark upon others. An earlier example of this was the necessity to take certain courses as prerequisites before taking others. A much more complicated example is that of constructing a material object such as a building or an airplane. In such an endeavor, the discrete activities that compose it will have associated time values, and there will often be a strong economic incentive to make the total time from start to finish as short as possible. Moreover, it is often possible to allocate resources so that some number of these activities can be conducted in parallel. Such a situation is readily modelled by a weighted DAG, because the presence of a cycle would correspond to the unreasonable circumstance that an activity would have to be completed before it could be started! Several techniques have been devised for analyzing such projects by the use of graphs. Prominent examples are *PERT* (*Progress Evaluation Review Technique*) and *CPM* (*Critical Path Method*). They typically allow the user to determine the shortest overall time that is possible, given the constituent times and the dependencies; they also identify those activities that are most critical, in the sense that any shortening (lengthening) of their elapsed times may be directly reflected in a shortening (lengthening) of the overall time.

To illustrate these ideas, we will consider the making of an omelette, with several kitchen helpers available as needed. Be forewarned that our motivation is more mathematical than culinary, and we do not guarantee the recipe! As a first step, we need to identify the separate, atomic activities to be performed; for our omelette, these activities and their times are shown in Figure 7.40. Next we need to make a DAG, with activities as vertices, that captures all of the dependencies; in our case, we obtain Figure 7.41(a). It is possible to perform some analysis directly

	Activity	Duration in seconds
A	– Crack eggs	40
B	– Put butter in pan	15
C	– Slice mushrooms	170
D	– Beat eggs	50
E	– Heat butter in pan	90
F	– Add some of melted butter to eggs	10
G	– Add some milk to eggs	15
H	– Saute the mushrooms	40
I	– Reserve mushrooms in side dish	10
J	– Add special seasonings to mushrooms	105
K	– Pour egg mixture into pan	5
L	– Cook one side	90
M	– Add mushrooms to eggs in pan	5
N	– Turn omelette	15
O	– Cook other side	75

Figure 7.40 Omelette Preparation Activities

on this *activity-node* graph. However, it is more common to transform the activity-node graph to an *event-node* graph, wherein the original activities become the edges, and the nodes are events. Each event corresponds to the completion of all activities preceding it, and no successor activity can take place until the event has occurred. Such an event-node graph for our omelette is shown in Figure 7.41(b). In making this transformation, we find that we must often insert *dummy activities*, of zero time duration, in order to prevent false dependencies. For the present case, we need a dummy activity $P1$ between nodes 5 and 6, and another dummy activity $P2$ between nodes 8 and 11. The former is necessary, for instance, because activities G and H both depend upon activity F, and activity H also depends upon activity C; however, G does not depend upon C. Without the dummy activity, events 5 and 6 would collapse into a single event, introducing a false dependency of activity G upon activity C.

Most or all of the work described in the preceding paragraph has to be done by hand; it requires judgement and skill, and it is often accomplished by a series of successive refinements to an initial model of the process. With regard to the transformation from activity-node graph to event-node graph, we would like the latter to have the minimum number of nodes and arcs. There are algorithms to accomplish this transformation, but it turns out that this can be a non-trivial problem in its own right [Corneil et al. 1973].

Now we are ready to start cooking! In essence, we need to compute the longest path through the graph from Start (event 1) to Finish (event 14). In our computation, we begin by having an array of values as in Figure 7.40:

$T_{i,j}$ – the duration of the activity between events i and j.

We then compute, successively, three other arrays of values:

1. ET_j – the *earliest time* at which event j can occur;
2. LT_i – the *latest time* at which event i can occur without causing the final event to be delayed;

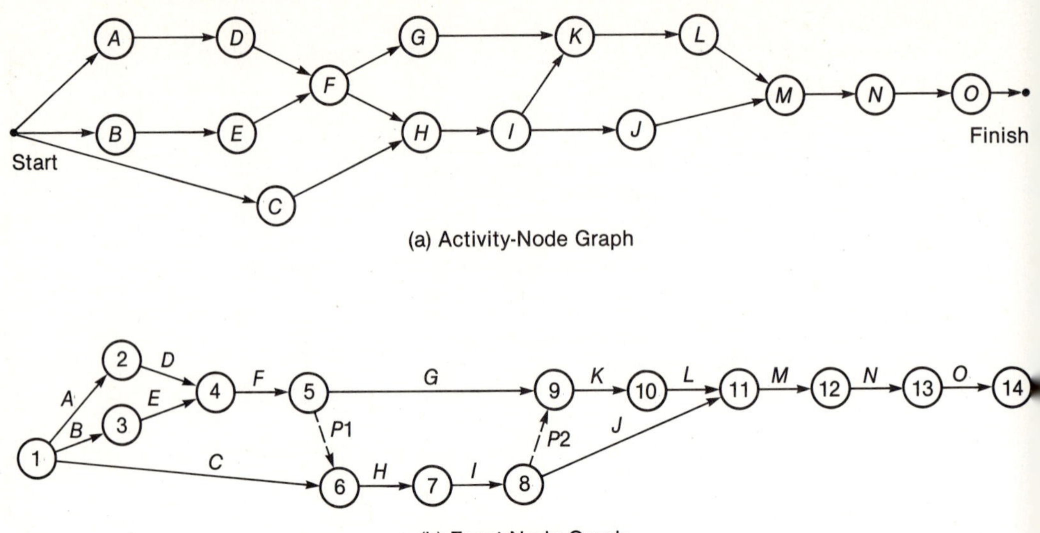

Figure 7.41 Precedence Graphs for Figure 7.40

3. $Float_{i,j}$ – the amount of time to spare in the activity between events i and j.

These calculations require us to process the event-nodes in the proper order. Not surprisingly, this corresponds to their topological ordering, so that a topological sort must be incorporated in the process. Although no cycles should be present, we cannot rule out the possibility that the input data contains errors; therefore, in a large real-life problem, the sort operation should check for this eventuality. For our simple example, we have bypassed this step by assigning event-node numbers that are already in topological order.

The earliest times ET_j are computed in topological sequence by the rule

$$ET_1 = 0 \; ; \quad ET_j = \max_{i \in \Gamma^{-1}(j)} \{ET_i + T_{i,j}\} \tag{7.10}$$

This must be so because the jth event cannot occur until all of the activities originating from predecessor events have been completed. By analogous reasoning, the latest times LT_i are computed in reverse topological sequence using the rule

$$LT_n = ET_n \; ; \quad LT_i = \min_{j \in \Gamma(i)} \{LT_j - T_{i,j}\} \tag{7.11}$$

Having the earliest and latest times for the events, it is finally a simple matter to compute the floats by the rule

$$Float_{i,j} = LT_j - ET_i - T_{i,j} \tag{7.12}$$

The application of Eqs. 7.10 – 7.12 to the data of Figure 7.40 is shown in Figure 7.42. We note that activities A,B,D,E, among others, have non-zero floats, and thus are not so urgent. On the other hand, activities C,H,I,J,M,N,O have zero floats, and thus they are *critical activities*; if any of these are not commenced at their earliest possible times, the Finish time will be delayed. There will always be at least one *critical path* from Start to Finish, consisting entirely of critical edges. One of the principal objectives of this type of analysis is to identify such edges. The corresponding activities can then be closely monitored in an effort to prevent slippage in completing the project. It may even be possible to concentrate more resources on some critical activities in an effort to speed up the project. However, increased attention to a particular critical activity will be beneficial only if that activity lies on all critical paths; in general, there may be more than one critical path, with some critical activities present in only some of the paths.

Event	ET	LT	Activity		Duration	Float
1	0	0	A	(1, 2)	40	110 – 0 – 40 = 70
2	40	110	B	(1, 3)	15	70 – 0 – 15 = 55
3	15	70	C	(1, 6)	170	170 – 0 – 170 = 0
4	105	160	D	(2, 4)	50	160 – 40 – 50 = 70
5	115	170	E	(3, 4)	90	160 – 15 – 90 = 55
6	170	170	F	(4, 5)	10	170 – 105 – 10 = 55
7	210	210	P1	(5, 6)	0	170 – 115 – 0 = 55
8	220	220	G	(5, 9)	15	230 – 115 – 15 = 100
9	220	230	H	(6, 7)	40	210 – 170 – 40 = 0
10	225	235	I	(7, 8)	10	220 – 210 – 10 = 0
11	325	325	P2	(8, 9)	0	230 – 220 – 0 = 10
12	330	330	J	(8,11)	105	325 – 220 – 105 = 0
13	345	345	K	(9,10)	5	235 – 220 – 5 = 10
14	420	420	L	(10,11)	90	325 – 225 – 90 = 10
			M	(11,12)	5	330 – 325 – 5 = 0
			N	(12,13)	15	345 – 330 – 15 = 0
			O	(13,14)	75	420 – 345 – 75 = 0

Figure 7.42 Critical Path Analysis of Omelette

†7.4.5.3 Data Flow Analysis of Programs. Anyone who is familiar with program flowcharts can well appreciate that a program can be modelled by a graph, wherein the nodes represent segments of code, and the edges represent the flow of control between these segments. A segment of code might be as small as a single machine instruction or a single HLL statement. However, it is much more efficient to equate each node with a *basic block* of instructions, with the property that if the first instruction in the block is executed, then so must the remainder of the block be executed. We said earlier that a flow graph of a program has the special property of possessing a unique entry-point node s_0, from which all other nodes can be reached. It is easy to search the graph of a program from its starting location to check for various types of errors, such as the existence of nodes that are not reachable from s_0. However, most of the effort of program analysis is concerned with interactions between the use of variables in the various nodes. Thus, the major topic is global data flow analysis, where the term global refers to the fact that the entire graph (program) is being considered, and the term data refers to that which is under investigation. Because of the multiplicity of possible execution sequences in a program, the aliasing of variables, and the possibility of external procedure calls, such analyses can be non-trivial to perform.

The techniques of global data flow analysis are primarily useful for optimization purposes in compilers, and include:

- *Common expression elimination.* If the same expression is computed in several nodes of a flow graph, and if each of these nodes has a common ancestor, then it may be possible to remove that duplicated code from these nodes to their ancestor.
- *Live variable detection.* Within a block, the values of various variables are computed. If any such value is (is not) used in any successor blocks, then that variable is said to be a *live* (*dead*) *variable* at the conclusion of the block, and its value need (need not) be saved at that point.
- *Available expression detection.* Within a block, the computation of an expression may be redundant if (i) it was previously computed in every predecessor block, and (ii) none of the variables in the expression were subsequently assigned new values.

Typically, a bit vector is associated with each block, with one bit position for each data object. The solution of a data flow problem is related in some fashion to the propagation of these bit values through the nodes of the graph. Historically, there have been two alternative approaches to organizing these calculations. We will illustrate one of these, in the first section, as applied to the computation of dominators. To describe the other technique, we need to introduce the notion of reducibility in the second section.

†7.4.5.3.1 Dominance. A node U in a digraph is a *dominator* of another node W if every path from s_0 to W contains U. Dominance is another type of partial ordering on the nodes of a graph, but it is stronger than the type discussed in Section 7.4.5. In the former case, if $A \prec C$ and $B \prec C$, we could not make any statement about partial ordering between A and B. In the present case, if A dominates C and B dominates C, then either A must dominate B or B must dominate A. To see why this is so, consider any path from s_0 to C that contains A before B. If A did not dominate B, then we could construct another path from s_0 to C, going through A and avoiding B. But that would violate the dominance relation between B and C. Similarly, if B precedes A on any path to C, then B must dominate A. An important consequence of this stronger form of relationship is that, for any node of a graph, its dominators form a linear sequence. Thus, every node has a unique immediate dominator from this sequence, and consequently we can form a dominator tree of the nodes. For the flow graph of Figure 7.43(a), the dominator tree is shown in (b) of the figure. Dominators have several uses in data flow analysis, examples being common expression elimination and the detection of loops. Loops are present, for instance, whenever we have an arc whose head dominates its tail.

Dominators can be computed rather easily by iteratively propagating bit values among the nodes of the flow graph. Intuitively, the computation expresses that if node A is a dominator of node B, then A must be a dominator of all the immediate predecessors of node B. For the present purpose, we find it convenient and sufficient to represent the graph by an array of type *vsets*, containing for each node X

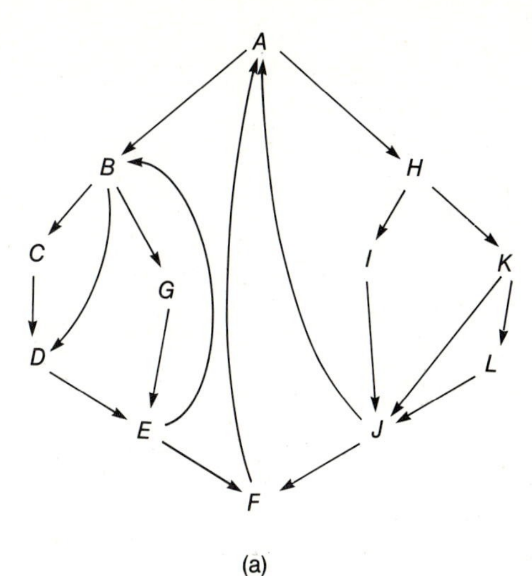

(a)

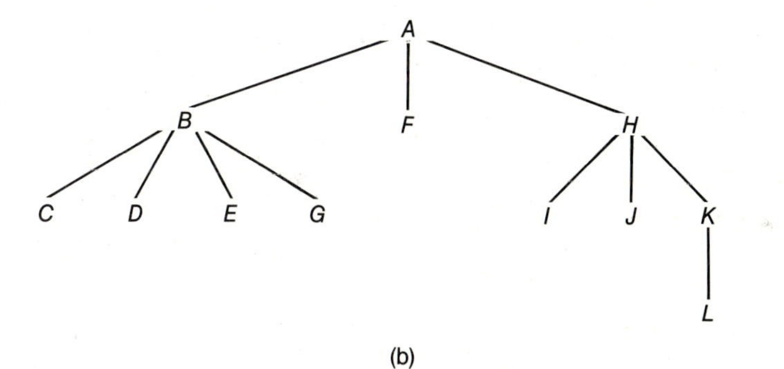

(b)

Figure 7.43 Dominators in a Flow Graph

the information $\Gamma^{-1}(X)$, represented as **set of** 1 .. *vmax*. The dominators of a node form a set of the same type, and the computation is expressed by the procedure DOMINATORS (Algorithm 7.11). It begins by initializing the dominator sets *doms*, and it then processes the nodes in some order, propagating information among these sets. Any processing sequence, as specified by the parameter *domseq*, would eventually produce the same final result. For now, we will simply assume that *domseq* $[i] = i$. When, after an entire iteration, there has been no change in any of the sets in *doms*, then the final values in *doms* contain the sets of dominators for each node. As applied to the flow graph of Figure 7.43(a), it requires two iterations (plus one to determine that there has been no change) in order for DOMINATORS to converge. These two iterates of *doms* are shown in Figure 7.44.

```
procedure DOMINATORS (domseq: vseq; vpred: vsets; var doms: vsets);

type    vndx = 1 .. vmax;
        vseq = array [vndx] of vndx;
        vset = set of vndx;
        vsets = array [vndx] of vset;

var     change: boolean;
        i,j,k: vndx;
        newdom: vset;

begin
  doms [1] := [ ];            {corresponds to the node s0}
  for j := 2 to vsize do
    doms [j] := [1 .. vsize] - [j];
  change := true;
  while change do begin
    change := false;
    for i := 2 to vsize do begin
      j := domseq [i];
      newdom := [1 .. vsize] - [j];
      for k := 1 to vsize do
        if k in vpred [j] then
          newdom := newdom * (doms [k] + [k]);
      if doms [j] <> newdom then
        change := true;
      doms [j] := newdom;
    end;
  end;
end;
```

Algorithm 7.11 DOMINATORS

DOMINATORS is not the fastest algorithm for the purpose; we will discuss its performance in the next section. The best algorithm for computing dominators has complexity $O(E\,\alpha(E))$ [Lengauer and Tarjan 1979], where α is the Ackermann inverse function described in Section 6.6.5.1. DOMINATORS has the two virtues that it is extremely simple, and that it illustrates several important notions in data flow analysis. We will return to this algorithm in the next section, after broaching some other concepts. What is worth noting here is that it is possible to solve the live variable and the available expression problems by processes that are remarkably similar. Such algorithms involve the manipulation of several sets for each node, instead of just one (*doms*); however, the concept in both cases is to scan through all the nodes of the graph, computing new values for these sets until we have an iteration in which none of them has changed.

†7.4.5.3.2 ***Reducibility.*** For a program of any significant size, data flow analysis in terms of basic blocks is too large a computation, and needlessly so. What is

First Iteration	Second Iteration
doms [1] := {}	*doms* [1] := {}
doms [2] := {1}	*doms* [2] := {1}
doms [3] := {1,2}	*doms* [3] := {1,2}
doms [4] := {1,2}	*doms* [4] := {1,2}
doms [5] := {1,2,4}	*doms* [5] := {1,2}
doms [6] := {1,2,4,5}	*doms* [6] := {1}
doms [7] := {1,2}	*doms* [7] := {1,2}
doms [8] := {1}	*doms* [8] := {1}
doms [9] := {1,8}	*doms* [9] := {1,8}
doms [10] := {1,8,9}	*doms* [10] := {1,8}
doms [11] := {1,8}	*doms* [11] := {1,8}
doms [12] := {1,8,11}	*doms* [12] := {1,8,11}

Figure 7.44 Iterations of the Sets *doms*

desired is a technique for partitioning the flow graph into meaningful units that are larger than basic blocks. We encountered one such partitioning of a digraph, the condensed graph, in Section 7.3.4; it is based upon detecting the strong components of the digraph. Some of the earlier data flow analyses were, in fact, based upon nested, strongly connected subgraphs [Lowry and Medlock 1969]. However, in such a partitioning, we have the undesirable feature that a strong component may have multiple entry points.

The concept of an interval, on the other hand, leads to a set of disjoint partitions, each with a single entry point [Allen 1970; Cocke 1970]. An *interval of a node v* is the maximal, single entry subgraph such that v is the only entry node, and all loops contain v. The notion is applied by finding a sequence of *reductions*, or transformations, to the original flow graph, according to various rules.[8] If the reductions can be carried out to the point that the reduced flow graph consists of a single interval, then the original flow graph is said to be *reducible*. Conversely, if the reductions terminate leaving more than one interval, then the original flow graph is said to be *irreducible*.

The definition of what constitutes a reducible flow graph depends upon the allowable transformations, and there is some inconsistency in this regard. The most common definition employs two transformations *T*1 and *T*2, as follows:

- *T*1 – If there is an arc (v,v) in a flow graph, delete it.
- *T*2 – If there is a node v_2 (not s_0) with a single predecessor v_1, then replace v_1 and v_2 and the arc (v_1, v_2) by a single new node node v_0.

---

[8] In addition to condensation and reduction as techniques for simplifying a digraph, there is yet another transformation. It consists of deleting as many arcs as possible without affecting the reachability properties. The result is the *minimum equivalent graph* (*MEG*) of the digraph. Quite aside from its utility for data flow analysis, however, the problem of finding the MEG of a digraph is *NP*-complete.

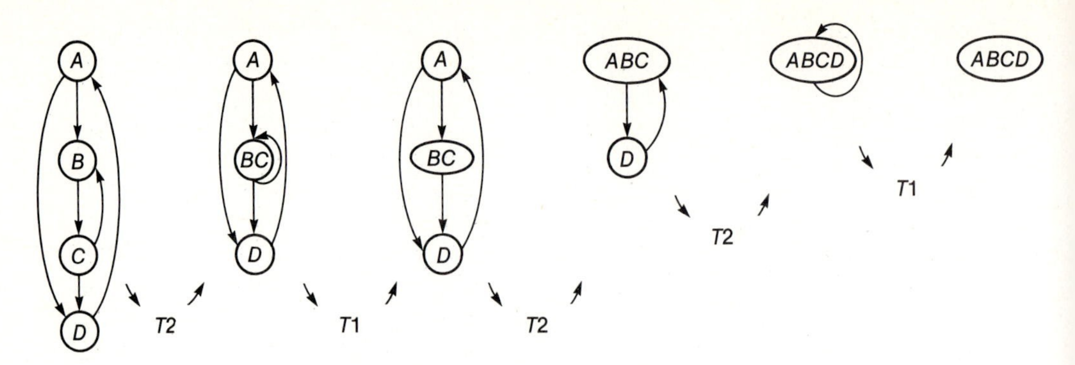

Figure 7.45 Reduction of a Flow Graph

These transformations are illustrated in Figure 7.45, where they are applied in the sequence *T*2, *T*1, *T*2, *T*2, *T*1 to the original flow graph. Note that the first application of *T*1 is essential in order to be able to make the subsequent application of *T*2. Since the final graph consists of a single node, the original graph is a reducible one. An example of a flow graph that is irreducible because neither of these transformations can be applied is shown in Figure 7.46. In fact, this particular example is the paradigm of an irreducible flow graph, in the sense that any irreducible graph contains it as a subgraph.

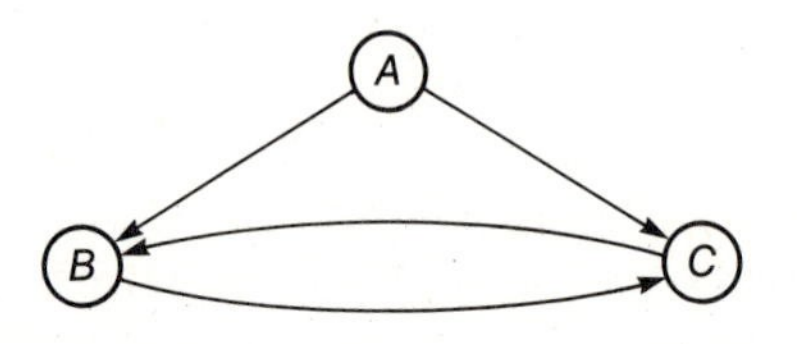

Figure 7.46 Irreducible Flow Graph

In describing the transformations *T*1 and *T*2, we have not made any reference to the intervals cited at the beginning of this section. However, it can be shown that successful reduction to a single node by use of *T*1 and *T*2 is equivalent to reduction in terms of intervals [Hecht and Ullman 1972]. Moreover, reduction in terms of *T*1 and *T*2 is simpler than the direct calculation of intervals. The principal consequences of having a reducible flow graph are:

- Every loop has a unique entry point from the starting block.
- The edges in the flow graph can be partitioned into two sets, *advancing edges* and *retreating edges*; the advancing edges form a DAG in which every node is reachable from s_0, and the retreating edges consist of just those edges whose heads dominate their tails.

These properties are sufficient, as well as necessary. Moreover, the latter can be used as the basis for establishing reducibility. In fact, a flow graph can be tested for reducibility in $O(E)$ time [Gabow and Tarjan 1985]. The cited algorithm employs DFS, and uses a linear variant of UNION-FIND (Algorithms 6.9) to keep track of the necessary information. In contrast to the iterative approach in DOMINATORS, it is essentially based upon interval analysis. An approach combining iterative and interval analysis techniques has also been found to be usually linear [Graham and Wegman 1976].

The concept of reducibility is of practical importance for several reasons. It happens that the iterative procedure DOMINATORS of the previous section works whether a flow graph is reducible or not. Some of the earlier analyses in terms of intervals, on the other hand, either would not work for an irreducible flow graph, or would only work after making complicated adjustments. More recent analyses in terms of intervals do not have this dependency [Allen and Cocke 1976]. Nonetheless, even though reducibility is no longer such a critical factor for performing data flow analysis, it can still make a significant difference in terms of efficiency. To illustrate this, consider again the algorithm DOMINATORS. It iterates until there has been no change in any of the sets of *doms*. If the graph is reducible, however, and if we also process the nodes in a certain order, then we can compute the dominators in one direct pass, without iteration!

The simplification to DOMINATORS just described depends upon a variant of DFS. Given that DFS from s_0 generates a spanning tree of the flow graph, our numbering of the nodes heretofore (see Algorithm 7.2) has corresponded to a preorder traversal of the spanning tree. What we need now is to vary DFS slightly so that it numbers the nodes in reverse postorder sequence; that is, we need to change DFS_GRAPH as follows:

(a) Start with $seq = V$ (the number of nodes) instead of 0, and decrement *seq* rather than increment it.

(b) Label the nodes in postorder – that is, just before exiting DFS_GRAPH, rather than just after entering it. Note that we still need to mark nodes on entry, and so the DFS numbers can no longer serve as marks.

By way of illustration, Figure 7.47 shows both the preorder numbering and the reverse postorder numbering of the nodes in our flow graph of Figure 7.43(a). Now, by inverting the numberings on the nodes, we obtain the desired order of processing the nodes in DOMINATORS. Given that the DFS numbers are stored in the field *data* for each vertex, the inversion can be computed by

```
for i := 1 to vzsize do
   domseq [vlist [i].data] := i;
```

It is not too hard to show that the dominators of a reducible flow graph can always be computed in one direct pass via this sequence, significantly simplifying the algorithm [Hecht and Ullman 1975]. The reason is related to the fact that the retreating edges of a reducible graph will always correspond to back edges in its DFS spanning tree. To recapitulate, by processing the nodes of Figure 7.43(a) in the order *A H K L I J B G C D E F*, just one pass is needed in DOMINATORS to compute the values of *doms*, rather than two plus one as in Figure 7.44.

It is worth reflecting upon the appropriate graph representation to accomplish these operations. When we first discussed DOMINATORS, it might have seemed that an adjacency matrix would be a more serviceable representation in this problem than an adjacency structure. The columns of the matrix would provide Γ^{-1} at no additional storage cost. One factor that would be overlooked by such a choice is the desirability of being able to use set operations rather than the slower boolean operations. We now see that another factor is that of being able to do DFS quickly, via the adjacency structure.

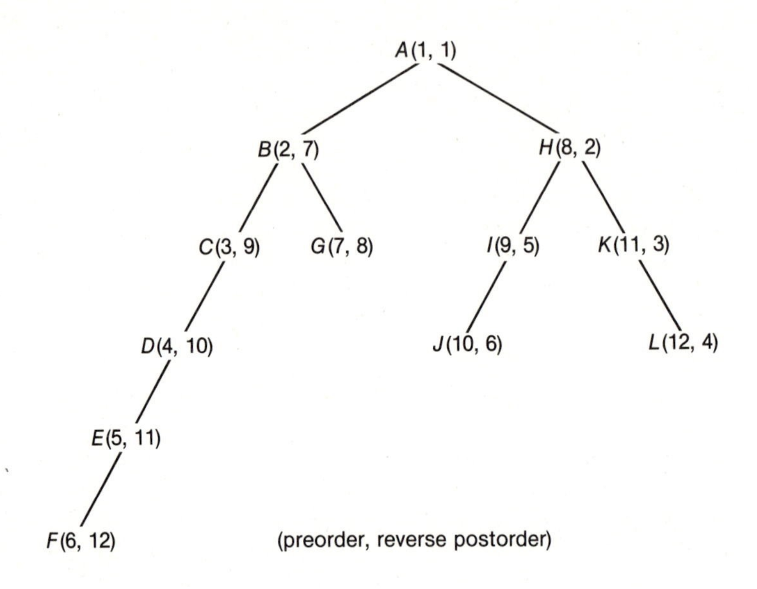

Figure 7.47 Ordering the Nodes in a Flow Graph

DFS also optimizes the performance of other flow analyses, even though it does not always produce a linear algorithm. Its wider significance is related to an additional, important concept – that of *interval depth d*, or *loop-interconnectedness*. This depth is equal to the largest number of retreating edges on any cycle-free path. If DOMINATORS is applied to an irreducible flow graph, then the use of DFS as described in the preceding paragraph will guarantee an upper bound of $d+2$ iterations. In other flow analysis computations (for example, live variables) the use of DFS provides a similar bound.

How do results such as these relate to programs in the real world? Surveys of actual programs are encouraging in two respects. In one examination of a large set of flow graphs, the average value of the depth d was found to be about 2.75 [Knuth 1971a]. A second significant point concerning actual programs is that most of them – 90 percent in one study, and 100 percent in another – do have reducible flow graphs! In fact, it is commonly thought that any program without this property is not well-structured and should be revised.

7.5 OTHER ISSUES RELATING TO GRAPHS

Even with all that has been said, there are many significant matters relating to graphs that we have failed to mention. The purpose of this last section is to briefly acquaint you with these. It may be useful to explain why these items have been relegated to this final section, rather than earlier ones. Sections 7.5.1 and 7.5.2 discuss the two graph issues of coloring and planarity. Although there are many graph theoretical ideas associated with both of these, we find that coloring, on the one hand, is an intractable problem, and planarity, though a linear problem, has very complicated algorithms. Thus, there is less immediate value for us in analyzing the solutions of these problems than there was for those of the preceding section. Sections 7.5.3 and 7.5.4 deal with the complexity of graph algorithms and with graph isomorphism. The former really constitutes a summing-up of many of the ideas in the chapter; the latter is an appropriate finale that hearkens, after all that we have discussed, to the basically combinatorial nature of graphs.

†7.5.1 Graph Colorings

There are a variety of problems that can be formulated in terms of:

- coloring the vertices of a graph in such manner that no adjacent pair of vertices has the same color, or
- coloring the edges of a graph in such manner that no adjacent pair of edges has the same color.

As in the case of traversals of a graph, the vertex-oriented and the edge-oriented problems have very different characteristics.

Historically, vertex coloring has been more significant. An example is the situation wherein final examinations or other sorts of meetings must be scheduled, and where participants have potential conflicts with regard to these schedules. This can be represented by a graph wherein the meetings are vertices, and an edge is drawn between every pair of vertices where there is a conflict (some individual must participate in both meetings). We now look for an assignment of colors to the vertices such that no adjacent pair of vertices has the same color. If distinct colors correspond to unique meeting times, then there will be no meetings that involve conflicts for the participants. An obviously desirable feature is for the number of colors/meeting times to be minimal. The minimum number of colors required for the vertices of a graph is known as the *chromatic number* χ of the graph; if $\chi(G) = k$, then G is said to be *k-chromatic*. Another way of viewing the chromatic number is that it is the minimum number of independent subsets (see Section 7.4.3) into which the vertices of a graph can be partitioned.

For certain types of graphs, the chromatic number is easily determined. For example, K_n is n-chromatic, and any bipartite graph is 2-chromatic. In the general case, let Δ be the largest degree of any of the vertices in a graph. Then it is easy to see that $\chi \leq \Delta + 1$. Thus, begin by coloring an arbitrary vertex, and then repeatedly look for any uncolored vertex and color it; in iterating this latter step until all vertices are colored, we can always be certain of having an unused color, since the number of adjacent vertices is always less than $\Delta + 1$. Graph theorists have obtained tighter bounds on χ. In the general case, however, to determine the precise value of the chromatic number or to compute a minimal assignment of colors to vertices is an *NP*-complete problem. Algorithms employing a variety of heuristics are available [§]. Note, by the way, that the exponential character of these methods can always be mitigated by first finding the blocks of the graph, in effect employing divide-and-conquer. Nonetheless, for any one of these algorithms, it is possible to find input graphs for which they will perform arbitrarily poorly, and this seems to be a fundamental aspect of the problem. For TSP with the triangle inequality, we exhibited both 1-approximate and ½-approximate methods. For vertex coloring, there are no methods known to be r-approximate, for any fixed r. The best known approximation algorithm has $r(V) = V/\lg V$; indeed, it has been shown that if there were an algorithm that was 1-approximate or better, then there would also have to be a 0-approximate algorithm [Garey and Johnson 1976]!

Situations modeled by edge coloring seem to be less common. The minimum number of colors required for the edges of a graph is known as the *chromatic index* χ', or edge chromatic number. It is obvious that $\Delta \leq \chi'$, but a remarkable result known as *Vizing's Theorem* establishes also that $\chi' \leq \Delta + 1$. For a bipartite graph $\chi' = \Delta$ always, but in the general case it can be difficult to ascertain which value applies. Many instances of edge coloring are concerned with bipartite graphs, so that efficient algorithms based upon matching are available. Thus, a coloring of the edges corresponds to a set of disjoint matchings, with a distinct color for each matching. This happy situation is complicated, however, by the fact that many applications involve additional constraints, leading to *NP*-complete problems again.

†7.5.2 Planarity

When confronted with graphs such as those in Figure 7.48(a) and (b), an important issue may be whether they are actually *planar* – meaning that they can be drawn in such manner that the edges do not intersect each other except at the vertices where they are adjacent. The issue is extremely important, for instance, in the fabrication of VLSI components, and it occurs naturally when we are dealing with maps. It also has a fundamental significance for the applicability of divide-and-conquer to a given graph. To be precise, if a graph is planar, then we can be certain of being able to divide it into two components of roughly equal size by removing $O(V^{1/2})$ vertices [Lipton and Tarjan 1979, 1980].

In any discussion of planarity, it is usual to restrict attention to graphs wherein there are no vertices with degree less than 3. A feature of planar graphs of this type is that the edges form a number of closed regions and one infinite region. Now, there are several ways to go about testing a graph for planarity, depending upon our point of view.

A. A relatively simple approach is to try to apply *Euler's formula*

$$V - E + R = 2 \tag{7.13}$$

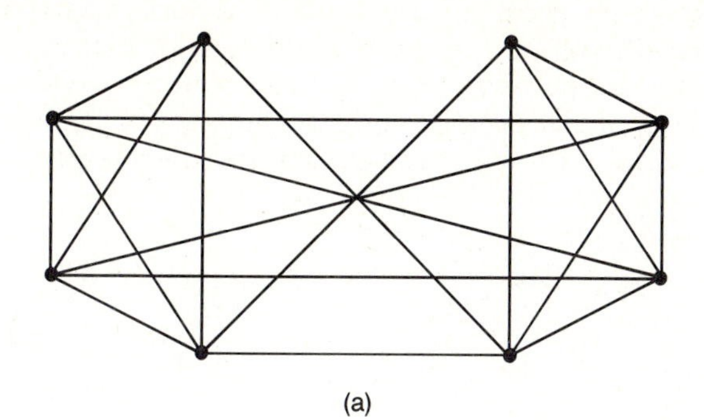

(a)

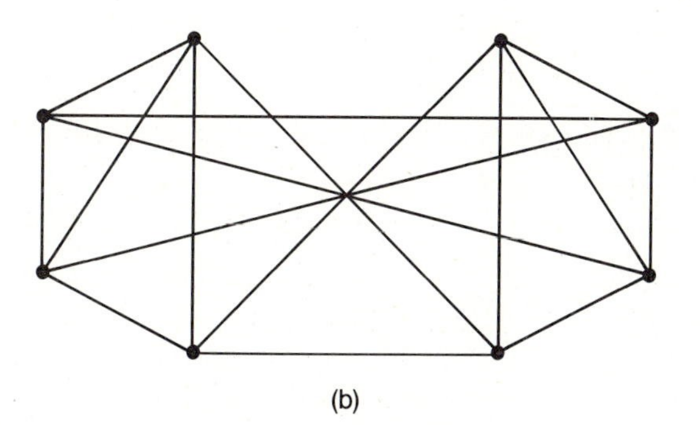

(b)

Figure 7.48 Planarity

which relates the numbers of vertices, edges, and regions in a planar graph.[9] Since we are not considering multigraphs, then each region must be bounded by three or more edges, and so the total number of edges over all the regions cannot be less than $3R$. In this inventory, each edge is counted as belonging to two regions, and so $2E \geq 3R$. Combining this fact with Euler's formula gives us the result that in any planar graph

$$E \leq 3V - 6 \tag{7.14}$$

Thus, when confronted with a particular graph, we can apply the criterion of Eq. 7.14. If it is violated, then the graph cannot be planar. For the graph of Figure 7.48(a), for example, we have 8 vertices and 19 edges, so that it cannot be planar. On the other hand, Eq. 7.14 is satisfied both for Figure 7.48(b), with 8 vertices and 16 edges, and for Figure 7.34(d), with 10 vertices and 15 edges; yet one is planar and the other is not.

---

[9] Note that Euler's formula is actually a special case of the cyclomatic number v (see Section 7.3.1.1), since the value of v equals the number of finite regions; that is, $v = R - 1 = E - V + 1$.

B. Unfortunately, Eq. 7.14 is a necessary condition for planarity, but not a sufficient one. For a graph theorist, therefore, it is very satisfying to learn that *Kuratowski's Theorem* gives an exact characterization of planar graphs. Namely, the non-planar graphs are precisely those that have embedded (as subgraphs) either the complete graph K_5 or the complete bipartite graph $K_{3,3}$, as illustrated in Figure 7.49.[10] (Is Eq. 7.14 relevant for either of these? If not, then is Eq. 7.13?)

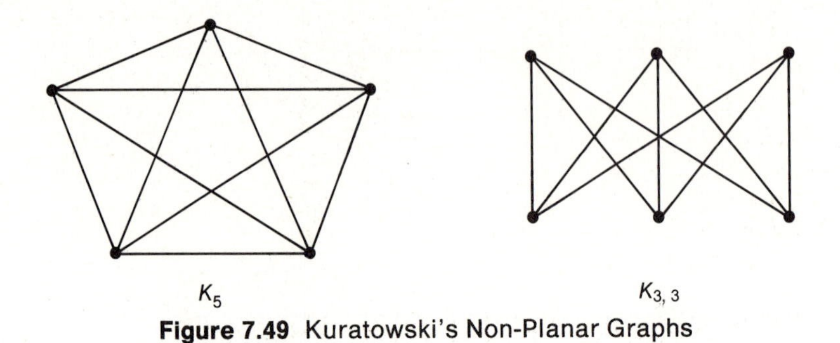

Figure 7.49 Kuratowski's Non-Planar Graphs

C. Although Kuratowski's theorem is conclusive, its computational complexity causes it to have limited value. Happily, there are several (rather complicated) $O(V)$ methods to test for planarity. Once again, an effective first step is to find the blocks of the graph, and then apply one of these algorithms [§].

7.5.3 Complexity of Graph Algorithms

In this section, we will summarize two quite different issues that we have already encountered many times in this chapter. We denote them here as the intrinsic and extrinsic complexity of algorithms for dealing with graphs.

Intrinsic complexity. There are literally hundreds of meaningful problems that can be posed about graphs. Some, such as finding a minimal spanning tree, are very easy; others, such as determining planarity, are quite complicated. Aside from their relative difficulty, they are both tractable problems. In fact, planarity has complexity $O(V)$ and is even more efficient than the minimal spanning tree, with typical complexity $O(E \lg E)$. However, the combinatorial nature of graph problems causes many of them to be *NP*-complete. The two chief instances of this that we have discussed are the traveling salesman problem, and the coloring of the vertices of a graph. The list of problems determined to be *NP*-complete grows every month [§].

---

[10] Actually, in looking for the two forbidden subgraphs of Figure 7.49 in a graph G, we should ignore any vertices of degree 2 in G.

Extrinsic complexity. Anyone who wishes to solve a graph problem on a computer must first decide upon the best choice of representation. Our two most common choices have been the adjacency structure and the adjacency matrix. We have also referred to indexed lists and incidence matrices, as well as sets (Section 7.4.5.3.1) and edge multilists (Exercise 7.3). We have seen several examples wherein the choice of an adjacency structure leads to an $O(V+E)$ algorithm, whereas the choice of an adjacency matrix leads to an $O(V^2)$ algorithm. So the question arises, is this as fundamental a distinction as it appears to be? For any non-trivial problem dealing with a graph, must the use of an adjacency matrix always entail an algorithm of complexity $O(V^2)$? In response, it is possible to find somewhat non-trivial problems for which there are $O(V)$ algorithms, even with an adjacency matrix (see Exercise 7.48). However, the *Aanderaa-Rosenberg conjecture*, which is carefully worded to exclude certain instances, seems to demonstrate that the answer is affirmative [Rivest and Vuillemin 1975; Rosenberg 1973]. Thus, for most problems on sparse graphs, we are well advised to avoid an adjacency matrix in favor of an adjacency structure.

†7.5.4 Graph Isomorphism

Two graphs are *isomorphic* if there is a one-to-one correspondence between their vertex sets such that the adjacency relationships are preserved. In deciding about graph isomorphism, we ignore any values attached to the vertices or edges and consider only the adjacency relationships. Thus, in Figure 7.50, the graphs of (a) and (b) are isomorphic to each other under the mapping: $A \to I$, $B \to K$, $C \to M$, $D \to J$, $E \to L$, $F \to N$; but they are both non-isomorphic to that of (c). (Why?) The issue of graph isomorphism is central to a variety of problems having to do with pattern recognition, such as the following:

- In chemistry, are two molecules, whose structures are modelled by multigraphs, equivalent?
- In information retrieval, what database items match a request?
- In artificial intelligence, to what recognizable objects might parts of a visual scene correspond?

One of the intriguing aspects of this problem is that, in distinction to almost all the other problems relating to graphs, its complexity is uncertain. Technically, it is an *NP* problem, since no polynomial algorithm is known; however, it has not been demonstrated to be *NP*-complete. The reader has the chance to attain fame and glory by resolving the issue! Actually, as with so many graph problems, by either specializing it or generalizing it, we change the complexity picture. Thus, if we restrict ourselves to planar graphs, there is an $O(V)$ algorithm for complexity [Hopcroft and Wong 1974]. On the other hand, if the question is whether a graph $G1$ is isomorphic to a subgraph of another graph $G2$, then the problem is known to be *NP*-complete.

For our stated problem of testing for graph isomorphism, we again need to find good heuristics to employ with a backtracking approach. But first, perhaps we can learn something from our treatment of trees (see Sections 6.7 and 6.7.1). There, we

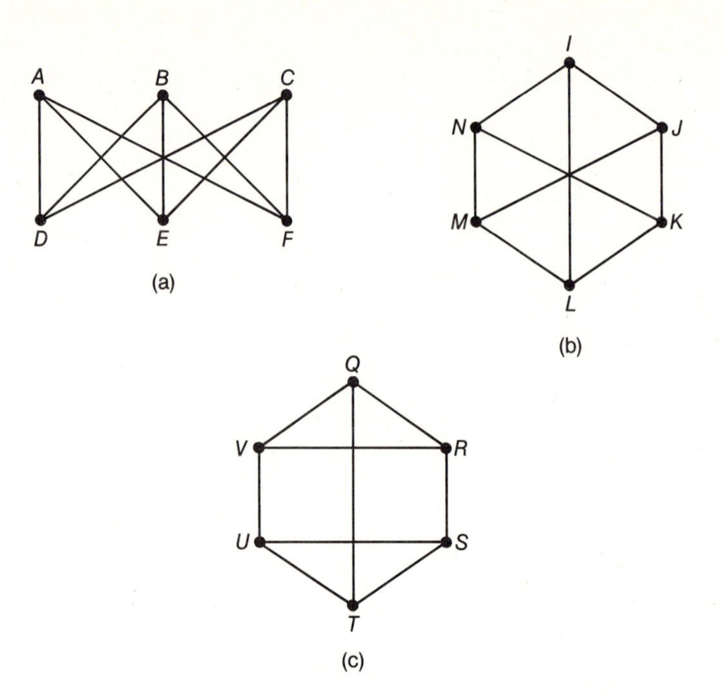

Figure 7.50 Isomorphic and Non-Isomorphic Graphs

were able to completely encode the structure of a tree as either a single number or sequence of numbers, such as a Cayley sequence or a feasible sequence. By now, we have encountered a great number of graph parameters. In addition to the values V and E, we also have the following: the cyclomatic number (Section 7.3.1.1); the vertex connectivity and edge connectivity (Section 7.3.2); the vertex covering number, vertex independence number, edge covering number, and edge independence number (Section 7.4.3); the chromatic number and chromatic index (Section 7.5.1); and the dominance number (Exercise 7.29). Moreover, there are still quite a few others that we have not introduced. Can any two sets of such parameters for two graphs be used to infallibly determine isomorphism? Quite aside from the exponential complexity associated with computing some of these parameters, the answer for the general case is No.

There are several graph isomorphism algorithms, employing a variety of heuristics [§]. We will illustrate the idea with one of these heuristics, which is quite simple and can be very effective. It uses the invariant of a graph known as the *degree spectrum*, which is an ordered list $(d_0, d_1, \ldots, d_{V-1})$ where d_i equals the number of vertices of degree i. For the graph of Figure 7.51, the degree spectrum is (0, 0, 3, 2, 1, 0). Since this graph has six vertices, an unrestricted attempt to find a correspondence between G and any other graph G' with six vertices would have complexity $O(6!) = O(720)$. But by comparing the degree spectrum S of G with the spectrum S' of G', we could immediately discern many non-isomorphic cases. Moreover, for the case $S = S'$, we could accomplish the backtracking analysis with complexity $O(0!\ 0!\ 3!\ 2!\ 1!\ 0!) = O(12)$, since we would only have to look for matches among the three vertices of degree two and the two vertices of degree three. Although the degree spectrum is a highly effective tool in many cases, as with our example, note that that it does not help at all in other cases, such as regular graphs.

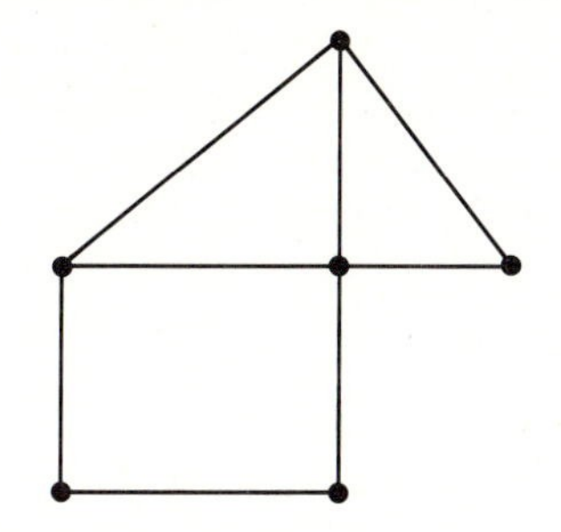

Figure 7.51 Example for the Degree Spectrum

7.6 OVERVIEW

In our catalogue of data structures, graphs unquestionably provide a wider variety of interpretations than any other structure. The notion of a set of objects (vertices) and adjacency relationships among them (edges) is deceptively simple. In fact, as we have seen, the adjacency relationship leads to many others − connectivity, reachability, independence, covering, dominance (in two different interpretations), traversability, reducibility, colorability, planarity, etc. Each of these notions can be used to model problems that are real and significant. This diversity of interpretation and the basically combinatorial nature of graphs have caused this chapter to be more mathematical in content than the others.

Another aspect of this diversity is that we are much more conscious of making choices of data structure representation and of algorithmic method. Thus, for a given problem, are we better off using an adjacency structure, an indexed list, an adjacency matrix, an incidence matrix, sets, or perhaps some other representation? And should we use BFS, DFS, a greedy approach, matching, branch-and-bound, dynamic programming, or some heuristics? (These algorithmic possibilities are not distinct; for example, a given method might simultaneously involve BFS, matching, and heuristics.) For some problems, we are pleased to find that good choices of data structure representation and algorithmic method can have a decided effect upon the efficiency of our solution. Other problems seem to be intrinsically difficult, and the best we can hope for is that a good heuristic will work well for most of the cases.

We have made the point that graphs sustain more variety and complexity than any other data structure that we have studied. It is intriguing to close the circle and point out some strong commonalities between problems couched in terms of graphs and problems couched in terms of the most basic data structure, the array. This duality is visible both in terms of representation (the adjacency matrix) and in terms of theoretical insight (for example, the Matrix-Tree theorem in Section 7.3.1.1). Other examples of co-extensiveness include:

- the relationship between matrix multiplication and transitive closure;
- the related techniques for dealing with sparse matrices and with strong components [Cuthill and McKee 1969; Tarjan 1976];
- the intimate relationship between cut-sets and vector spaces.

This symbiosis works both ways. Arrays yield powerful techniques for dealing with graphs, and graphs yield powerful insights for dealing with arrays.

7.7 BIBLIOGRAPHIC NOTES

- Several good expositions of graph theory are Behzad et al. [1979], Berge [1962], Bondy and Murty [1976], and Harary [1969].

- Discussions of the relative merits of Prim's method and Kruskal's method can be found in Brennan [1982], Jarvis and Whited [1983], and Kershenbaum and Van Slyke [1972]. The method of building MST's with average cost $O(V + E)$ is given in Cheriton and Tarjan [1976].

- An early, significant method for solving network flow with complexity $O(V^3E)$ was Edmonds and Karp [1972]. A steady series of improvements are Dinic [1970] with complexity $O(V^2E)$, Karzanov [1974] and Malhotra et al. [1978] with complexity $O(V^3)$, and Tarjan [1983c] with complexity $O(VE \lg V)$.

- The early, dynamic programming approach to solving TSP was formulated by Bellman [1962] and Held and Karp [1962]. Subsequently, branch-and-bound was employed rather successfully [Held and Karp 1970, 1971]. More recent and highly viable is the technique of local search found in Lin and Kernighan [1973] and Rosencrantz et al. [1977]. The ½-approximate solution that we describe is based upon Christofides [1976]. For a good, up-to-date account of the history and methods of solution for TSP, consult Held et al. [1984].

- Some of the more significant heuristics for the vertex coloring problem are Brélaz [1979], Christofides [1971], Corneil and Graham [1973], Dutton and Brigham [1981], Wang [1974], and Welsh and Powell [1967]. For edge coloring, consult Cole and Hopcroft [1982] and Gabow and Kariv [1982].

- Testing for planarity by application of Kuratowski's Theorem leads to an $O(V^6)$ algorithm [Mei and Gibbs 1970]. Two good methods that are $O(V)$ proceed by successively adding either edges [Hopcroft and Tarjan 1974] or vertices [Even and Tarjan 1976; Lempel et al. 1966] to an internal representation. Both techniques continue until either the entire graph has been represented or non-planarity has been detected. Two other algorithms that have been found good in practice, though not quite linear, are Rubin [1975] and Yeh [1982].

- An assortment of approaches to the graph isomorphism problem are Berztiss [1973], Corneil and Gotlieb [1970], Corneil and Kirkpatrick [1980], Schmidt and Druffel [1976], and Ullman [1976].

- The pioneering account of problems shown to be *NP*-complete is Karp [1972]. A comprehensive catalogue of the situation is Garey and Johnson [1979]; some excellent overviews are Cook [1983], Karp [1986], and Tarjan [1978].

7.8 REFERENCE TO TERMINOLOGY

7.9 EXERCISES

Sections 7.1 – 7.2

7.1 Given the following two adjacency matrices, draw their corresponding graphs.

	A	*B*	*C*	*D*	*E*	*F*
A	0	1	1	0	1	0
B	1	0	0	1	0	1
C	1	0	0	1	1	0
D	0	1	1	0	1	1
E	1	0	0	1	0	0
F	0	1	0	1	0	0

(a)

	G	*H*	*I*	*J*	*K*	*L*
G	0	13	2	0	0	11
H	13	0	8	0	5	0
I	2	8	0	0	7	4
J	0	0	0	0	6	17
K	0	5	7	6	0	0
L	11	0	4	17	0	0

(b)

7.2 For the graph of Figure 7.52, show the representations as:

(a) an adjacency structure,

(b) an indexed list,

(c) an adjacency matrix,

(d) an incidence matrix.

†7.3 The fact that edge nodes are duplicated in the adjacency structure for an undirected graph can be an annoyance. One manner of circumventing this is to maintain the edges in a multilist, with links for the two vertices of each edge. Depict such a representation for the graph of Figure 7.52.

†7.4 The *line graph* of a graph G is the graph $L(G)$ wherein the vertices correspond to edges in G, and wherein two vertices in $L(G)$ are adjacent if and only if those edges in G are incident on a common vertex.

(a) Draw the line graph corresponding to the graph of Figure 7.52.

(b) Derive a formula, based upon properties of G, that counts the number of edges in $L(G)$.

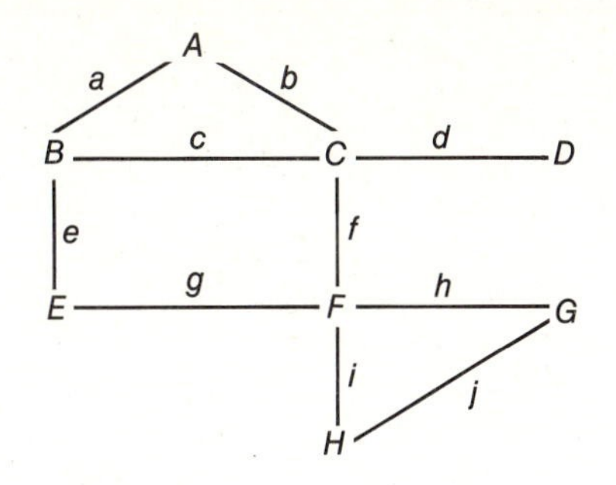

Figure 7.52 Graph for Exercises 7.2, 7.3, 7.4

7.5 Write a procedure that reads a list of records capturing the structure of a graph and generates the corresponding adjacency structure representation. For example, for Figure 7.6 we might have

A: a *C* c *D*
B: d *E*
C: d *D* b *A* a *E*
D: c *B*
E:

Section 7.3

7.6 For the graph of Figure 7.53(a), assuming that the adjacency structure is in lexicographical order, do the following:

(a) Starting from vertex *A*, draw the BFS spanning forest and show the BFS numbers and the cross edges.

(b) Starting from vertex *A*, draw the DFS spanning forest and show the DFS numbers and the back edges.

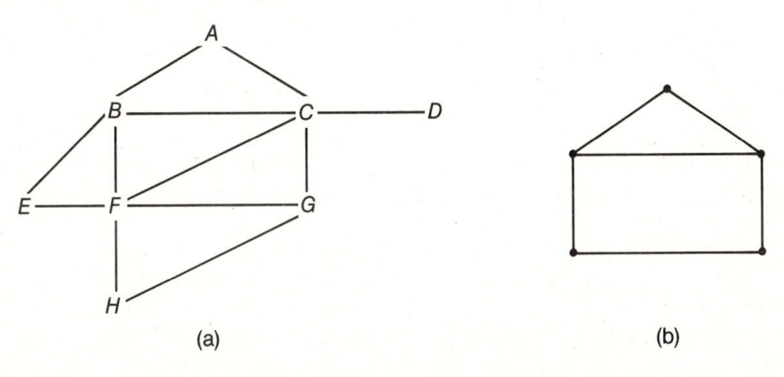

Figure 7.53 Graphs for Exercises 7.6 and 7.8

†7.7 Derive a relationship between the adjacency, incidence, and degree matrices of a graph.

†7.8 Use the Matrix-Tree theorem to compute the number of spanning trees of the graph of Figure 7.53(b). Draw them.

††7.9 Use the Matrix-Tree theorem to derive Cayley's formula (see Section 6.7) for the number of labeled free trees on n nodes.

††7.10 In the graph of Figure 7.54(a), assuming that the adjacency structure is in lexicographical order, do the following:

(a) Starting from vertex A, draw the DFS spanning forest and show the DFS numbers and the back edges.

(b) Add the values of LOW(v) to your figure, indicate the articulation points, and draw the blocks.

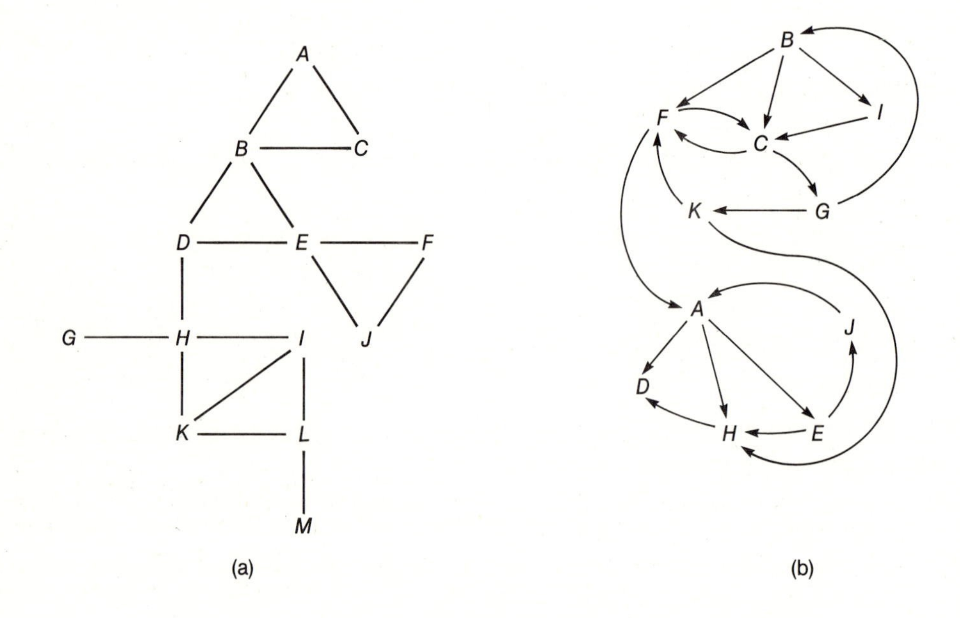

Figure 7.54 Graphs for Exercises 7.10, 7.11, 7.12, 7.13, 7.15

††7.11 In Section 7.3.2 we stated that one can rather easily determine the bridges of a graph after using CUT_NODES; this remark is based on the fact that a bridge will have an articulation point for at least one of its vertices. Describe how the algorithm CUT_NODES can be modified to locate the bridges of a graph explicitly. Demonstrate your technique by applying it to the graph of Figure 7.54(a).

††7.12 Write a procedure to perform DFS on a graph via an explicit stack instead of recursively, assuming that the graph is represented by an adjacency structure again. Test your program against the graph of Figure 7.54(a).

††7.13 In the digraph of Figure 7.54(b), assuming that the adjacency structure is in lexicographical order, do the following:

(a) Starting from vertex A, draw the DFS spanning forest and show the DFS numbers and the other classes of edges.

(b) Add the values of LOW(v) to your figure, and draw the strong components; also, show the condensation graph D^*.

†7.14 Prove the validity of Eq. 7.2.

†7.15 Write a procedure that uses DFS to determine the type of each edge in a digraph – tree, forward, backward, or cross. Test your program against the digraph of Figure 7.54(b).

Sections 7.4.1 – 7.4.2

7.16 For the graph of Figure 7.55(a), do the following:

(a) Starting from node A, find an MST by Prim's algorithm, numbering the edges in the order of their selection;

(b) Find an MST via Kruskal's algorithm, numbering the edges in the order of their selection.

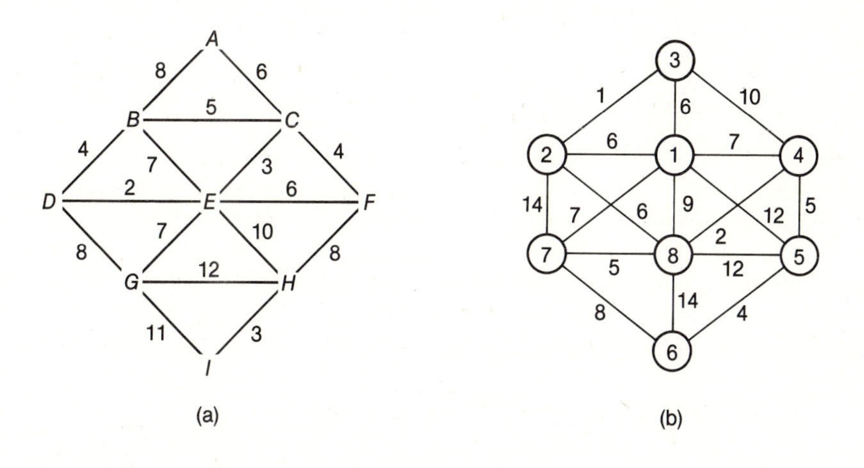

Figure 7.55 Graphs for Exercises 7.16, 7.17, 7.18, 7.19, 7.21, 7.22

†7.17 Write a procedure to find an MST using Kruskal's technique. Test your program against the graph of Figure 7.55(a).

7.18 Compute the shortest distances from node #3 to all the other nodes in the graph of Figure 7.55(b), using Dijkstra's algorithm and tracing the values assumed by the variables *least* and *father*, as in Figure 7.24(b).

†7.19 For the graph of Figure 7.55(b), use branch-and-bound to find the shortest distance from node #3 to node #6. In doing so, you will need to choose between some alternative details of technique. Discuss these alternatives, and compare the use of Dijkstra's algorithm and branch-and-bound for solving this problem.

††7.20 We have cited that Dijkstra's algorithm will fail in the presence of negative edge costs.

(a) Give an example of this phenomenon.

(b) Describe a modification of the algorithm that allows shortest distances to be computed correctly even in this case, as long as there are not also cycles with negative cost.

††7.21 If we want to know the shortest distance between just two specific vertices of a graph, a source and a sink, then we could implement a bi-directional form of Dijkstra's algorithm. With this method, we would alternate between adding an edge from the source end and adding an edge from the sink end. Write a procedure to accomplish this, and test it against the graph of Figure 7.55(b). Can the alternation be terminated when the two search trees meet?

††7.22 The algorithms PRIM and DIJKSTRA, very similar in form, solve two different problems related to finding trees with minimum properties. Consider the same two problems wherein we want the maximal solutions – the spanning tree with maximum weight, and the longest paths between a source vertex and the other vertices. For both PRIM and DIJKSTRA, either show how they can be modified to produce the desired answer, or show why they cannot be so modified. Apply your modifications to the graphs of Figure 7.55(a) (starting at node A) and Figure 7.55(b) (starting at node 3), respectively.

††7.23 Given an $n \times n$ array M of positive integer elements, write a procedure to find a sequence of horizontally or vertically adjacent entries such that (a) it starts at $M[1,1]$ and ends at $M[n,n]$, and (b) the sum of the squares of the differences between adjacent entries is a minimum. As an example, for the matrix $M1$ of Figure 7.56, such a minimum sequence is given by 4, 1, 3, 5, 4, 2, 7, 12, 7 with value 97. Test your program by finding the solution for the matrix $M2$ of the figure.

4	8	10	5	7
1	3	6	9	5
6	5	4	2	7
10	3	8	5	12
4	9	6	13	7

M1

14	6	10	14	20	14	10
19	18	9	1	17	16	12
11	20	17	8	20	9	13
15	9	18	17	2	5	17
18	20	19	3	5	9	10
9	19	6	17	20	15	4
11	15	9	15	17	7	3

M2

Figure 7.56 Two Mazes

Section 7.4.3

7.24 For the graph of Figure 7.28, exhibit a minimum edge cover, a maximal independent vertex set, and a minimum vertex cover.

†7.25 Starting from the unmatched vertex D in Figure 7.30(c), draw the BFS tree to verify that no augmenting path is possible.

†7.26 Use augmenting paths to discover the solution to the SDR problem of Exercise 6.35, reproduced here:

$$S_1 = \{2,4,5,6\} \qquad S_3 = \{2,6\} \qquad S_5 = \{4,6\}$$
$$S_2 = \{1,4,6\} \qquad S_4 = \{3,6\} \qquad S_6 = \{1,4\}$$

Start with the initial matching: $S_1 - 2$, $S_2 - 4$, $S_3 - 6$, $S_4 - 3$, $S_6 - 1$

††7.27 Write a program to solve the maximal bipartite matching problem by constructing BFS trees from unmatched vertices. Test your program against the following bipartite graph:

```
A:  4  8           F:  1  2  3  4  9
B:  5  7           G:  5  6
C:  4  9           H:  9 10
D:  1  3  5        I:  2  8
E:  6  8           J:  7 10
```

††7.28 Write a procedure to find a minimum vertex cover for an arbitrary graph.

††7.29 Whereas a vertex cover of a graph G is a set of vertices S such that all edges of G are incident with at least one vertex in S, a *dominating set* of vertices S is one such that all vertices of G are either in S or adjacent to vertices in S. The cardinality of a minimum (vertex) dominating set for a graph is the (*vertex*) *dominance number* of the graph.

(a) Give an example of a graph such that the minimum dominating set is not an independent set.

(b) Write a procedure to find a minimum dominating set for an arbitrary graph.

††7.30 The famous *8-Queens problem* in chess is that of finding a set of squares where 8 queens can be placed such that none threatens any other. In fact, this problem corresponds to finding a maximal independent vertex set of a graph. Write a program to solve the n-queens problem for an $n \times n$ chessboard.

††7.31 A somewhat different problem than that of Exercise 7.30 is to find a smallest set of squares on a chessboard such that queens placed upon those squares will dominate every square on the board. For example, it is possible to achieve this for an 8×8 chessboard with five queens; that is, the dominance number of the corresponding graph problem is five. Write a program to solve this problem for an $n \times n$ chessboard.

††7.32 Write a program to solve the Stable Marriage Problem. Test it against the data in Figure 7.57, where the men are denoted by upper case letters and the women are denoted by lower case letters. The two matrices represent their orders of preference; for example, man B prefers the women in the order $b\,c\,e\,d\,a\,f$. Use your program to compute both the male-optimal and female-optimal solutions. How might you construct a solution that has neither male nor female bias?

	1	2	3	4	5	6
A	e	a	b	f	d	c
B	b	c	e	d	a	f
C	c	d	e	b	f	a
D	c	b	d	a	f	e
E	b	e	a	c	f	d
F	a	f	e	d	b	c

	1	2	3	4	5	6
a	E	C	F	A	B	D
b	F	C	E	B	A	D
c	A	E	F	B	D	C
d	C	B	D	A	E	F
e	F	D	C	A	B	E
f	B	E	D	F	C	A

Figure 7.57 Marriage Partner Preferences

Section 7.4.4

†7.33 Prove the following facts relating to line graphs (see Exercise 7.4).

(a) If G is Eulerian, then $L(G)$ is both Eulerian and Hamiltonian.

(b) If G is Hamiltonian, then $L(G)$ is Hamiltonian.

(c) Demonstrate that the converses of (a) and (b) are false.

†7.34 An orientation of a complete graph (see Section 7.1) is a *tournament.* In other words, the arc that exists between each pair of vertices can be interpreted as a relative ranking between that pair of "players." Prove that a tournament always has a Hamiltonian path.

†7.35 Write a program to find an Eulerian tour in an Eulerian graph. Test your program against the graph of Figure 7.58. *Hint:* The method described in the text depends upon diagnosing the presence of bridges, an easy capability for the human eye. A more effective algorithm for a machine is one that, for every vertex on an initial tour, endeavors to incorporate (recursively) any detours along unmarked edges from that vertex. Two strategies will help in carrying this out efficiently. One is to allow edges to be deleted from the adjacency structure as they are used. The other is to employ bi-directional linked lists, to facilitate inserting one list within another list.

††7.36 In chess, the knight always moves to the opposite corner of a 2×3 rectangle; as long as it stays on the board, it has eight possible moves, as shown in Figure 7.59(a). A classical problem is to find a *Knight's Tour,* in which it visits every square just once; thus, we have a special case of finding a Hamiltonian path. A solution for the case of a 5×5 chessboard is shown in Figure 7.59(b), where the numbers indicate the sequence of visitation. Write a *non-recursive* program to solve this problem for the $n \times n$ case. Try to find a good heuristic to limit the amount of search. Explain your approach, and try to estimate its effectiveness.

††7.37 Write a program to solve TSP using dynamic programming, and test it against the data of Table 7.1. Your program should display enough information about optimal sub-tours to demonstrate how it works.

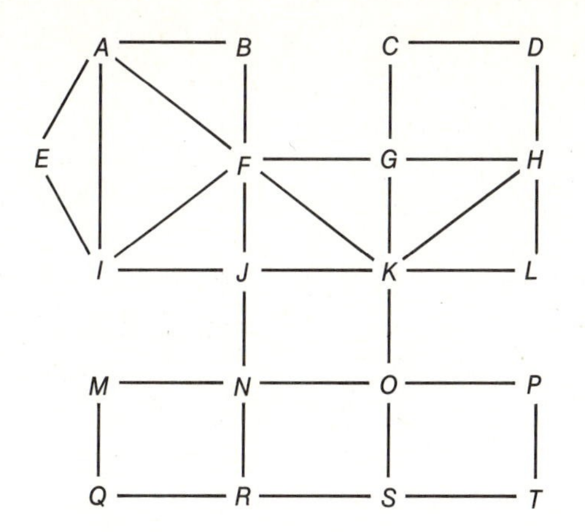

Figure 7.58 Graph for Exercise 7.35

	x		x	
x				x
		Kt		
x				x
	x		x	

(a)

23	10	15	4	25
16	5	24	9	14
11	22	1	18	3
6	17	20	13	8
21	12	7	2	19

(b)

Figure 7.59 Knight's Tour

††7.38 Write a program to solve TSP using branch-and-bound, and test it against the data of Table 7.1. Be sure to describe your criterion for picking branch nodes. Also, your program should display enough intermediate information to demonstrate how it works.

Section 7.4.5

7.39 Find a topological ordering for the digraph of Figure 7.60(a).

††7.40 Write a procedure to discover all the topological orderings of a DAG. Test your program against the digraph of Figure 7.60(a).

†7.41 For the event-node digraph of Figure 7.60(b), compute the early times, late times, and floats. Also, indicate the critical path(s).

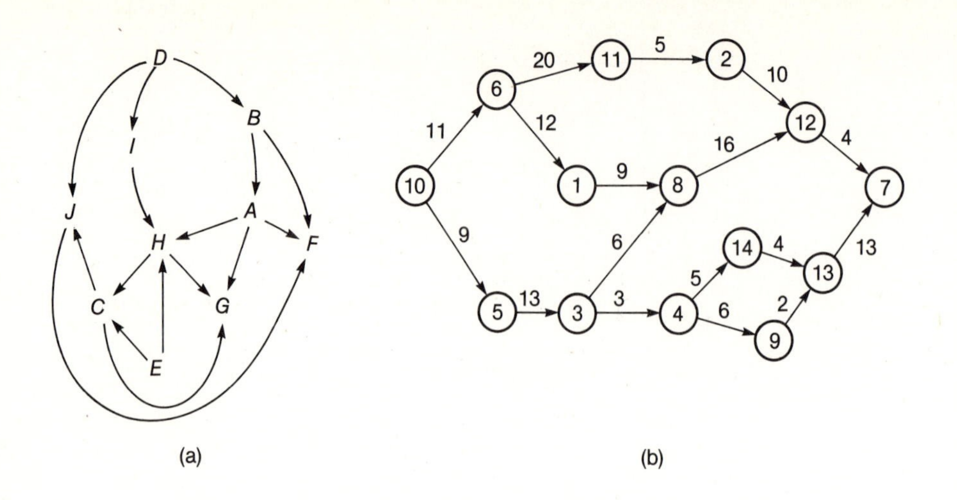

Figure 7.60 Graphs for Exercises 7.39, 7.40, 7.41, 7.42

††**7.42** For the problem of performing critical path analysis on an event-node digraph, first discuss the relative merits of the three graph representations: adjacency structure, adjacency list, and indexed list. Then write a program to perform such an analysis; that is, compute the early times, late times, and floats. Test your program against the digraph of Figure 7.60(b).

†**7.43** For the flow graph of Figure 7.61, do the following:

(a) Draw the dominator tree.

(b) Use variant DFS to label the nodes with the reverse postorder numbering required for efficient use of the algorithm DOMINATORS.

†**7.44** Explain the relationship between the advancing and retreating edges of a reducible flow graph and the four categories of edges discovered by ordinary DFS? How is this relationship different for an irreducible flow graph?

Section 7.5

†**7.45** Write a procedure to find a minimal vertex coloring for an arbitrary graph. Try to find a good heuristic to limit the amount of search. Explain your approach, and try to estimate its effectiveness.

†**7.46** Prove Euler's formula (Eq. 7.13) by induction.

†**7.47** Prove that for every planar graph there must be at least one vertex with degree 5 or less.

†**7.48** For a digraph represented by its adjacency matrix, consider the problem of determining whether it contains a vertex with in-degree $V-1$ and out-degree 0. Write an $O(V)$ procedure to solve the problem.

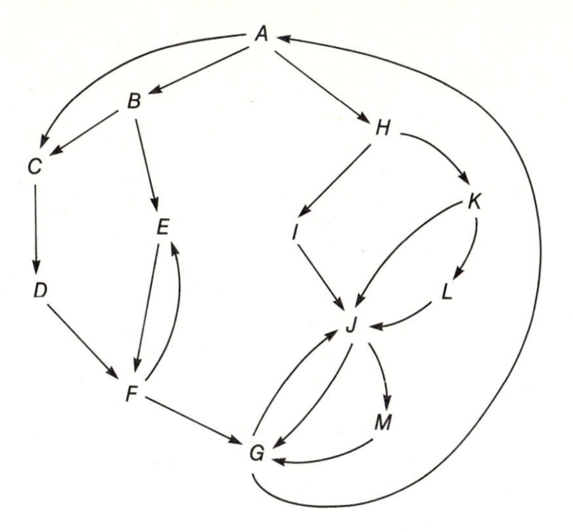

Figure 7.61 Graph for Exercise 7.43

†**7.49** The *complement* of a simple graph U is the graph W with the same vertex set, such that vertices are adjacent in W if and only if they are not adjacent in U.

(a) Show that if a graph G is isomorphic to its complement, then the number of vertices in G is congruent to 0 or 1 (mod 4).

(b) Prove that if a graph is not connected, then its complement must be connected.

(c) Prove that for any graph G with seven or less vertices, either G or its complement must be planar.

(d) Prove that for any graph G with eleven or more vertices, either G or its complement must be non-planar.

8

STRINGS

"... untune that string,
And, Hark! What discord follows."

Shakespeare,
Troilus and Cressida, act I, scene 3

The string is no doubt a familiar data structure to most readers, and familiarity may have bred a measure of indifference. After all, isn't a string simply an array of characters? In terms of implementation, it commonly is. Nonetheless, strings illustrate the adage that "the whole can be greater than the sum of its parts." For instance, when considered solely as a sequence of letters from the alphabet, this paragraph has no meaning; it acquires meaning only via the two-step process: letters aggregated as words, and words aggregated as sentences. Thus, the subject of string processing is not single characters, but rather groups of characters considered as entities. Moreover, note that strings tend to be of widely varying lengths.

This example of composing a paragraph from groups of characters also illustrates another point. Although we may wish to compute with multi-linked structures such as trees and graphs, we are constrained to encode our ideas into a string of symbols for most communication purposes. However, this is not a severe limitation, since it is a trivial matter to encode the description of a graph in a string. More significantly, the common way of expressing an algorithm for *any* possible computation is as a string of symbols in a programming language. Also, as we will see, the performance of that computation can be modelled, in turn, by a sequence of string operations whereby the input (program string) is transformed to the output (result string). Evidently the string, although not as flashy a data structure as the graph, sustains a great deal of power. In fact, the ubiquity of string processing causes our treatment of strings to be far longer than one might naively suppose would be adequate.

We start by looking at strings logically and then physically. Thereafter, we examine first some simpler uses of strings and then some more advanced ones, such as cryptography and pattern matching. This culminates in an expansion of the concept of pattern, via grammars, to encompass a more general type of recognition. We conclude by describing how more general kinds of grammars open the door to still more general types of recognition, and by characterizing the aforementioned model of computation via string transformations.

8.1 STRINGS AND STRING OPERATORS

A string is a sequence (possibly empty) of symbols from some alphabet. From now on, we will speak of characters rather than symbols, since the difference is rather subtle and irrelevant to our purposes. The necessity of distinguishing between a named string and a literal string value gives rise to two common systems of denotation for dealing with strings:[1]

I. Names of strings and values of strings are distinguished by using different alphabets or type fonts (for example, S, bd, s1, 4, etc. as literal values; and α, β, δ, etc. as the names of strings).

II. String values are distinguished by delimiting them within quotation marks (for example, 'S', 'bd', 's1', '4', etc. as literal values; and S, bd, s1, etc. as the names of strings).

One immediate issue is how to specify the length of a string; this is usually indicated as $|\alpha|$ in notation I, and as LENGTH(s1) in notation II. Another immediate issue is how to specify an empty string; this is usually denoted by ε in notation I, and as '' in notation II. Note that an empty string is not the same as a string consisting of a blank character, commonly denoted by 'ƀ'.

Although most programming languages allow for string constants via notation II, it is less common for them to support variables of *type* string. Moreover, in cases where they do, the terminology and notation for expressing operations with string data are woefully non-standardized. The standard definition of Pascal supports string constants in a limited fashion; several implementations of Pascal extend the language to support string variables as well. For the purposes of this book, we make no assumptions, but rather build our string facilities from scratch.

The fundamental operations with strings are concatenation, comparison, insertion, deletion, and substitution. The most basic of these is the *concatenation* of two strings to form a string whose length is the sum of the lengths of the two components. This operation is denoted by various symbols in different programming languages: '||' (PL/1), ',' (APL), '+', or merely juxtaposition (SNOBOL). Using juxtaposition, and for α = is and β = land, we would then have $\alpha\beta$ = island. In Section 8.2.3 we introduce the procedure CONCAT that accomplishes this purpose.

Comparison of strings is performed lexicographically, using the same rules whereby words are ordered in a dictionary. Thus, in comparing two strings

$$\alpha = a_1 a_2 \ldots a_m \quad \text{and} \quad \beta = b_1 b_2 \ldots b_n$$

to determine whether $\alpha < \beta$, $\alpha = \beta$, or $\alpha > \beta$, we examine successive pairs a_i and b_i, starting with $i = 1$, until either:

(a) the first pair is found for which $a_i \neq b_i$, or

(b) no inequalities have been found but one string is longer than the other, or

(c) no inequalities have been found and the strings are of the same length.

---

[1] Note that this necessity does not occur with numerical data. There, for example, '1234' is evidently a numerical constant, and 'R2D2' is implicitly a numerical variable.

In the first case, the ordering between α and β has the sense of the inequality; in the second case, the shorter string precedes the longer one; and in the third case, the strings are equal. Examples are 'plow' < 'pray' and 'pray' < 'prayer'. Comparison of strings is commonly supported directly in HLL's, via the same six relational operators that are used for numerical data.

The (conditional) *substitution* of one string as part of another string involves a subject string κ, a pattern string μ, and a replacement string ν, as follows:

1. κ is searched to determine if it is equivalent to $\alpha\mu\beta$ (where α and β may be null); in case there are multiple instances of μ, the first one is selected.
2. If the search succeeds, then ν is substituted for μ, so that κ is transformed to $\alpha\nu\beta$; otherwise, no action is performed.

We have described substitution in "non-procedural" terms; that is the way it is accomplished in a language specialized for string processing, such as SNOBOL. For our exposition, we will employ the non-standard symbols '¿' to denote testing and '¡' to denote replacement. Then for κ=banana, μ=na, and ν=ndan, we would obtain:

μ ¿ κ ¡ ν = bandanna
ν ¿ κ ¡ μ = banana

In the other notation, let m='an', s='distant', and n='omin'; we would then have:

'ist' ¿ s ¡ 'ec' = 'decant'
m ¿ s ¡ 'inc' = 'distinct'
'ist' ¿ s ¡ n = 'dominant'

The substitution operation is powerful enough that it encompasses two other fundamental operations – inserting one string within another, and deleting a portion of a string. This can be seen from the further examples:

'sta' ¿ s ¡ '' = 'dint'
'nt' ¿ s ¡ 'ntly' = 'distantly'

In general purpose HLL's, substitution is usually broken out into two explicit procedures. Typically, in string processing, a function called INDEX or MATCH is provided to perform the equivalent of '¿', returning an indication of the presence of the pattern string in the subject string. A procedure by the name of SUBSTR is typically provided for performing the actual replacement, at the location determined by INDEX or MATCH. In PL/1 it is actually possible to use SUBSTR on either side of an assignment statement. On the right side, it specifies the selection of a *substring* from a string; on the left side, it specifies the replacement of a substring of a string, as in our previous discussion. Note that the latter usage poses some problems. What if the replacement string does not have the same length delineated by SUBSTR? Ideally, the subject string should be shrunk or expanded to fit the situation; PL/1 instead pads or truncates the replacement string to match the length delineated by SUBSTR. In Section 8.2.3 we introduce the algorithms MATCH_0, SUBSEL, and SUBREP that accomplish these purposes, but without this shortcoming of PL/1.

8.2 REPRESENTATIONS FOR STRINGS

Since strings are sequences of characters from some alphabet, we will first consider how individual characters are commonly represented, and then how sequences can be represented. The choice for the representation of characters in a particular *code set* is not likely to be an accessible parameter for many applications, but it is still an important topic. On the other hand, the choice for the representation of sequences is a significant one, as we will see. Having examined these latter choices, we will subsequently choose one of them, and then map the logical string operations that we discussed in Section 8.1 into Pascal procedures.

Sections 8.2.4 and 8.2.5 are concerned with other aspects of string representation. Since codes are largely arbitrary, it is sometimes possible to construct a code that gains efficiency by squeezing out redundancy in the underlying binary representation. In particular, we will see how to do this with a structure called the Huffman tree. On the other hand, we must frequently be concerned with the likelihood of data being corrupted by errors, usually in communication channels rather than in computers per se. In this case, the resolution is to deliberately introduce redundancy into code sets! As we will see, if this is done in a careful manner, then the correct data values can often be determined despite errors.

8.2.1 Character Code Sets

As we observed in Section 1.1.1, a code set is a mapping from a set of characters to an arbitrary set of bit patterns. All such sets in general use employ a constant number of bits for each character in their set, so that the number of distinct characters for a representation with k bits is evidently 2^k. In the 1950's and 1960's, a prevailing standard code set was the six-bit BCDIC (Binary Coded Decimal Interchange Code). BCDIC was itself derived from the earlier Hollerith code whereby characters are represented by combinations of holes in punched cards. Six-bit codes such as BCDIC are still in use on some computers; they are adequate for representing the 26 upper case letters, 10 digits, a score or more special characters, and a few *control characters* which are used, for example, for directing an output device to perform a carriage return, a line feed, or a horizontal tab. Whereas control characters are not supposed to correspond to a visual symbol, the majority of the bit patterns in a code set are visible for input and output, and they are termed *graphics*.

A six-bit code allows an insufficient number of symbols by present-day standards. In BCDIC, for example, there is no room for the 26 lower case letters. Even with this limitation, however, the demand for a variety of special characters causes the existence of several *duals* in BCDIC – that is, two graphics sharing the same bit pattern, as with '%' and '('. Most computers today utilize either seven-bit *ASCII* (*American Standard Code for Information Interchange*) or eight-bit *EBCDIC* (*Extended Binary Coded Decimal Interchange Code*). With both of these codes, a great deal of deliberation went into assigning characters to bit patterns in an intelligent fashion. Some of the more important considerations were as follows:

- Control characters and graphics should have bit patterns that are easily distinguishable.
- Corresponding letters in upper and lower case should differ in only their high order bits.
- There should be no duals.
- Compatibility with previous codes (such as BCDIC) should be sought-after.
- The consecutive letters of the alphabet should have consecutive bit patterns.

Some of these considerations, particularly the last two, are conflicting. For such reasons, and for a host of personal and national reasons, the designers of EBCDIC and ASCII arrived at the two different code sets displayed in Table 8.1.[2] The most significant difference is that the sequence of the graphics is different in the two codes. These represent distinct *collating sequences* for purposes of arranging character strings in lexicographic order – that is, sorting. Thus, comparisons of strings in the two codes yield different results. In particular, ASCII has the precedence: digits, upper case, lower case; and EBCDIC has the precedence: lower case, upper case, digits. If the choice of collating sequence among lower case, upper case, and digits is a difficult one, the choice of collating sequence among the scores of special characters is much more so. Yet, this sequence has great implications in that it manifests a canonical order for storing and retrieving indexed items within a database. By inspecting Table 8.1, we can observe various other significant features of ASCII and EBCDIC, as follows:

- The first 32 characters in ASCII and the first 64 characters in EBCDIC are control characters.
- The letters of the alphabet are contiguous in ASCII, but broken into three groups in EBCDIC, for compatibility reasons.
- the character for "space" ('ƀ') collates low to all other graphics in both ASCII and EBCDIC;
- EBCDIC still has unassigned code positions.

Many of the control characters are for use in data transmission: ACK (acknowledge), STX (start of text), ETX (end of text), CR (carriage return), LF (line feed), BEL (ring the bell), etc.

The historical development of various character code sets is thoroughly documented in Mackenzie [1980]. We will pursue one final point before moving to the next topic. Consider one of the oldest codes of all, the teletype code (CCITT). This code includes the 26 upper case letters, 10 digits, and various other characters; yet it is a five-bit code! How is this possible? The answer can be seen by looking at any typewriter keyboard. Certain characters are *shift characters* that change the mode of translation of subsequent characters – for example, from lower case to upper case. Thus, teletype code is almost a six-bit code, with one bit stripped off and carried along as context. In point of fact, the five-bit code is used only for data transmission. At the sending location, a shift character is generated whenever the

---

2 One of the major reasons for designing EBCDIC as an eight-bit code was to gain efficiency in representing the decimal data that pervades commercial data processing. The choice of eight bits allows two binary-coded decimal digits (BCD) to be packed into a single byte.

Dec.	Hex.	EBCDIC	ASCII
0	00	NUL	NUL
1	01	SOH	SOH
2	02	STX	STX
3	03	ETX	ETX
4	04	PF	EOT
5	05	HT	ENQ
6	06	LC	ACK
7	07	DEL	BEL
8	08		BS
9	09		HT
10	0A	SMM	LF
11	0B	VT	VT
12	0C	FF	FF
13	0D	CR	CR
14	0E	SO	SO
15	0F	SI	SI
16	10	DLE	DLE
17	11	DC1	DC1
18	12	DC2	DC2
19	13	TM	DC3
20	14	RES	DC4
21	15	NL	NAK
22	16	BS	SYN
23	17	IL	ETB
24	18	CAN	CAN
25	19	EM	EM
26	1A	CC	SUB
27	1B	CU1	ESC
28	1C	IFS	FS
29	1D	IGS	GS
30	1E	IRS	RS
31	1F	IUS	US
32	20	DS	SP
33	21	SOS	!
34	22	FS	"
35	23		#
36	24	BYP	$
37	25	LF	%
38	26	ETB	&
39	27	ESC	'
40	28		(
41	29		)
42	2A	SM	*
43	2B	CU2	+
44	2C		,
45	2D	ENQ	-
46	2E	ACK	.
47	2F	BEL	/
48	30		0
49	31		1
50	32	SYN	2
51	33		3
52	34	PN	4
53	35	RS	5
54	36	UC	6
55	37	EOT	7
56	38		8
57	39		9
58	3A		:
59	3B	CU3	;
60	3C	DC4	<
61	3D	NAK	=
62	3E		>
63	3F	SUB	?

Dec.	Hex.	EBCDIC	ASCII
64	40	Sp	@
65	41		A
66	42		B
67	43		C
68	44		D
69	45		E
70	46		F
71	47		G
72	48		H
73	49		I
74	4A	¢	J
75	4B	.	K
76	4C	<	L
77	4D	(	M
78	4E	+	N
79	4F	|	O
80	50	&	P
81	51		Q
82	52		R
83	53		S
84	54		T
85	55		U
86	56		V
87	57		W
88	58		X
89	59		Y
90	5A	!	Z
91	5B	$	[
92	5C	*	\
93	5D	)	]
94	5E	;	¬
95	5F	¬	_
96	60	-	`
97	61	/	a
98	62		b
99	63		c
100	64		d
101	65		e
102	66		f
103	67		g
104	68		h
105	69		i
106	6A	¦	j
107	6B	,	k
108	6C	%	l
109	6D	_	m
110	6E	>	n
111	6F	?	o
112	70		p
113	71		q
114	72		r
115	73		s
116	74		t
117	75		u
118	76		v
119	77		w
120	78		x
121	79	`	y
122	7A	:	z
123	7B	#	{
124	7C	@	]
125	7D	'	}
126	7E	=	~
127	7F	"	DEL

Dec.	Hex.	EBCDIC
128	80	
129	81	a
130	82	b
131	83	c
132	84	d
133	85	e
134	86	f
135	87	g
136	88	h
137	89	i
138	8A	
139	8B	
140	8C	
141	8D	
142	8E	
143	8F	
144	90	
145	91	j
146	92	k
147	93	l
148	94	m
149	95	n
150	96	o
151	97	p
152	98	q
153	99	r
154	9A	
155	9B	
156	9C	
157	9D	
158	9E	
159	9F	
160	A0	
161	A1	~
162	A2	s
163	A3	t
164	A4	u
165	A5	v
166	A6	w
167	A7	x
168	A8	y
169	A9	z
170	AA	
171	AB	
172	AC	
173	AD	
174	AE	
175	AF	
176	B0	
177	B1	
178	B2	
179	B3	
180	B4	
181	B5	
182	B6	
183	B7	
184	B8	
185	B9	
186	AA	
187	AB	
188	AC	
189	AD	
190	AE	
191	AF	

Dec.	Hex.	EBCDIC
192	C0	{
193	C1	A
194	C2	B
195	C3	C
196	C4	D
197	C5	E
198	C6	F
199	C7	G
200	C8	H
201	C9	I
202	CA	
203	CB	
204	CC	⑀
205	CD	
206	CE	⑂
207	CF	
208	D0	}
209	D1	J
210	D2	K
211	D3	L
212	D4	M
213	D5	N
214	D6	O
215	D7	P
216	D8	Q
217	D9	R
218	DA	
219	DB	
220	DC	
221	DD	
222	DE	
223	DF	
224	E0	\
225	E1	
226	E2	S
227	E3	T
228	E4	U
229	E5	V
230	E6	W
231	E7	X
232	E8	Y
233	E9	Z
234	EA	
235	EB	
236	EC	⑁
237	ED	
238	EE	
239	EF	
240	F0	0
241	F1	1
242	F2	2
243	F3	3
244	F4	4
245	F5	5
246	F6	6
247	F7	7
248	F8	8
249	F9	9
250	FA	|
251	FB	
252	FC	
253	FD	
254	FE	
255	FF	

Table 8.1 EBCDIC and ASCII Character Codes

value of the sixth bit changes from the preceding character; at the receiving location, a sixth bit – the value of which depends upon the most recent shift character – is appended to each incoming character. There may in fact be several shift codes, allowing several modes of operation. Of course, it is important to distribute the characters among the modes so that the expected frequency of shifts between modes is low; for example, all the digits should be in the same mode. In addition, very common characters, such as space, should occur in both modes, again to reduce extra shift characters.

Let's investigate the circumstances under which a shift code (one employing shift characters) is more economical than a non-shift code, for the same alphabet [Karlgren 1963]. To begin with, let's do this for the teletype code. The two shift characters and three other control characters occur in both modes, and the bit pattern '00000' is unused in either mode. The other 26 bit patterns each have two graphics, so that the total alphabet offers $2 \times 26 + 6 = 58$ possibilities. With an unshifted code of six bits, the average character length will be exactly 6; with a shifted code of five bits, the average character length will be $5 \times (1 + P_s)$, where P_s is the probability that a shift between modes will be required. Then the shift code is superior whenever

$$5 \times (1 + P_s) < 6, \quad \text{or} \quad P_s < \frac{1}{5} \tag{8.1}$$

More generally, for an alphabet of N characters, an unshifted code will require $\lceil \lg N$ bits, and a shift code with c characters common to both modes will require $\lceil \lg ((N - c)/2 + c)$ bits. So there will be a net gain in efficiency whenever

$$(\lceil \lg ((N - c)/2 + c)) \times (1 + P_s) < \lceil \lg N \tag{8.2}$$

A variation upon the use of shift characters occurs with the *escape character*. This is analogous to using shift without shift-lock on a typewriter, for the purpose of changing the mode for only the next character. For infrequently used characters, this is superior to the use of a shift code, since it requires two characters instead of three for transmission. The effect is to impart a double length to such characters whenever they occur. Both ASCII and EBCDIC contain an escape character (ESC), although its precise use remains to be specified. In general, ESC followed by any other character, or possibly a sequence of characters, may have a variety of meanings; in particular, ESC followed by another character could signal a shift to an alternate mode.

8.2.2 Data Structure Choices

The choice of a representation for strings requires careful attention to their expected manner of use. We will describe six possibilities and then make some generalizations about their applicability. To illustrate these schemes, let us suppose that we have the sample line

'L1   CMPR   BANANAS,WATERMELONS,12'

This might, for instance, represent one line (or card) containing an instruction in some assembly language. There will be some program that extracts the two fixed-length fields ('L1b̸b̸b̸b̸' and 'CMPRb̸b̸b̸') and the three variable-length fields ('BANANAS', 'WATERMELONS', and '12'), storing each of them in the given string representation.

1	L 1
2	C M P R
3	B A N A N A S
4	W A T E R M E L O N S
5	1 2

Figure 8.1 Fixed-Length String Representation

The simplest method of all is to represent *fixed-length strings* by means of arrays, as shown in Figure 8.1. Here, each string is *padded* with extra blanks on the right (in other words, left justified) to fill its array. A more sophisticated technique is to use *varying-length strings.* A fixed-length array is used as before, but each array also has an associated integer value that specifies the number of meaningful characters in the string; note that there could just as well be meaningful, embedded blanks. This representation is shown in Figure 8.2, and the corresponding Pascal syntax is simply

```
type    string = record
           size: 0 .. maxstring;
           data: array [1 .. maxstring] of char;
        end;
```

1	02	L 1
2	04	C M P R
3	07	B A N A N A S
4	11	W A T E R M E L O N S
5	02	1 2

Figure 8.2 Varying-Length String Representation

The remaining four schemes all address the issue of truly *variable-length strings.* This is important for reasons of storage efficiency, and also because the two simpler representations run the risk (depending upon the application) of being too short for some strings. We have already faced this issue in Section 3.3, in discussing variable-length records. From the techniques presented there, we know that we can delimit variable-length strings using either separators or count fields. The latter are superior for machine processing of data, and so the third representation for our example is as shown in Figure 8.3. The fourth scheme should by now be fairly familiar; it is the indexed list, formally introduced in Section 7.2 for representing the edge list of a graph, and used earlier in Section 2.8 for representing sparse matrices. As applied to our example, it yields Figure 8.4.

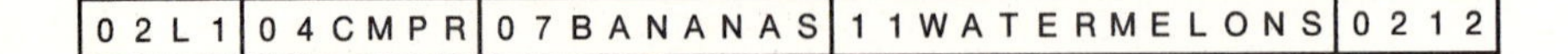

Figure 8.3 Count-Delimited String Representation

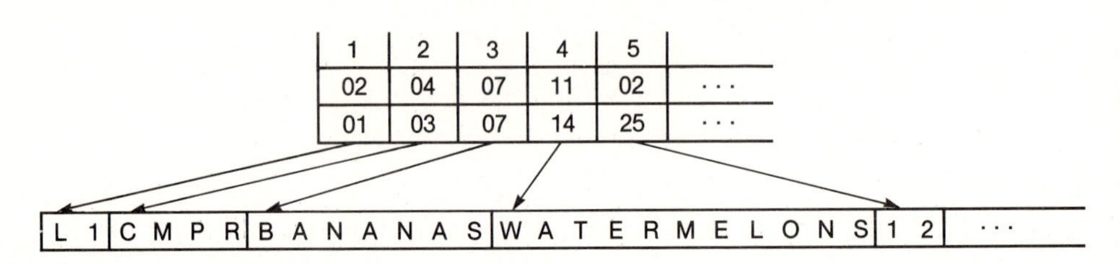

Figure 8.4 Indexed List String Representation

Not surprisingly, the technique that offers the most flexible representation is that of a linked list, and this is shown in Figure 8.5. Here each cell represents a machine word, containing a one byte character and a three byte pointer value. The patent storage inefficiency in such a scheme suggests using a blocked linked list. For the blocking illustrated in Figure 8.6, each cell is a machine double-word containing four one byte characters and a three-byte pointer; the unused byte might contain a fifth character or be used for other purposes.

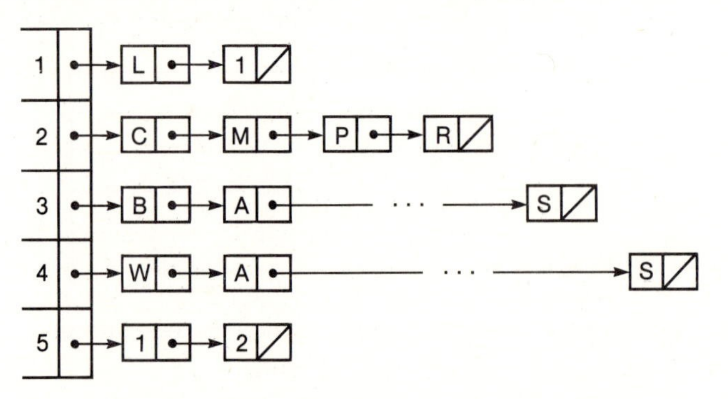

Figure 8.5 Linked List String Representation

Of the various measures that might be applied to these choices for representing strings, three are particularly important: efficiency of storage use, ease of looking-up (matching) an argument string, and ease of modifying (substituting) a given

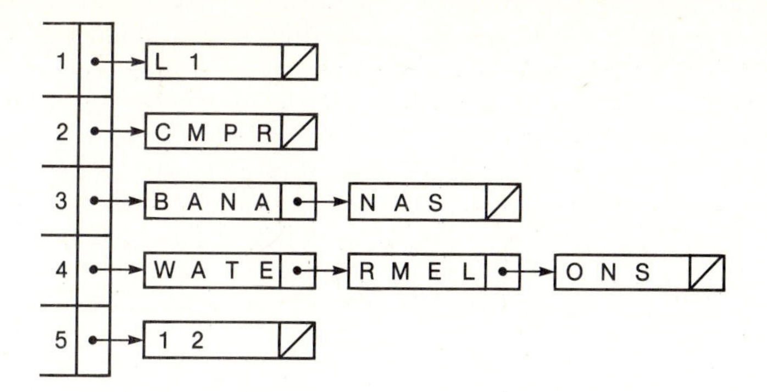

Figure 8.6 Blocked Linked List String Representation

string. When we apply these three criteria to our six representation choices, we obtain Table 8.2. Let's look at the values of some of the entries in the table.

	storage efficiency	ease of look-up	ease of modification
fixed-length	poor	fair	fair
varying-length	poor	good	fair
count delimiters	excellent	fair	poor
indexed list	excellent	good	poor
linked list	fair	poor	excellent
blocked linked list	good	fair	good

Table 8.2 Relative Merits of String Representations

Fixed-length strings evidently do not have much to commend them. Nonetheless, their extreme simplicity causes them to be worthwhile for applications where the intrinsic variability in length is not significant, as with punched cards or line printers. Varying-length strings offer superior performance with only a trivial increment in complexity. They do not save space but they save significantly in time, since processing of irrelevant character positions is avoided. With both of these methods, we find that the presence of unused character positions causes string modification to be reasonably easy in many circumstances.

The count delimiter and indexed list techniques are actually rather similar – the counts being with the data in the former case, and in a separate array in the latter case. However, in processing strings, as opposed to records, it is usually important to have all the descriptive information (counts and pointers) in the latter form; this facilitates dealing with the *i*th string, for example. The indirection also makes it possible to deal with substrings without the necessity of replicating character data, as illustrated in Figure 8.7. The capability can be more useful than is suggested by this humorous example. For instance, systems that interact with people may have hundreds of messages, requiring a large amount of storage, and the words and phrases of these messages typically have a great deal of redundancy. An indexed list can be used to overlap portions of text, with significant savings in storage [Wagner 1973a]. The count delimiter and indexed list techniques are hard to beat in terms of storage efficiency. Their biggest drawback is that string modification becomes extremely expensive unless the replacement string is never longer than the pattern string. However, applications that require insertion and look-up, but not string modification, occur rather frequently. A notable example is in the building and use of symbol tables during assembly or compilation of programs.

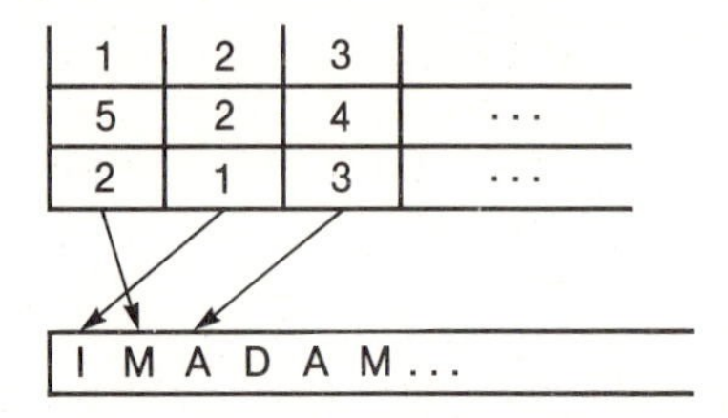

Figure 8.7 Overlapped Messages

The linked list methods trade storage efficiency for ease of string modification. Since a character usually requires one byte and a pointer usually requires three bytes, the efficiency of the simpie linked list representation is only 25 percent. The blocked linked list technique brings the efficiency up to 50 percent or more, depending upon the blocking factor, but causes string modification to become more complicated. It may be necessary to have an "empty" character, such as '#'. Thus, suppose that we wish to change 'DISTANT', in Figure 8.8(a), to 'DOMINANT'. If accomplished as in (b) of the figure, we must shuffle characters around; if accomplished as in (c) of the figure, we must waste block space. Even so, for general string processing the blocked linked list seems to offer a favorable combination of characteristics.

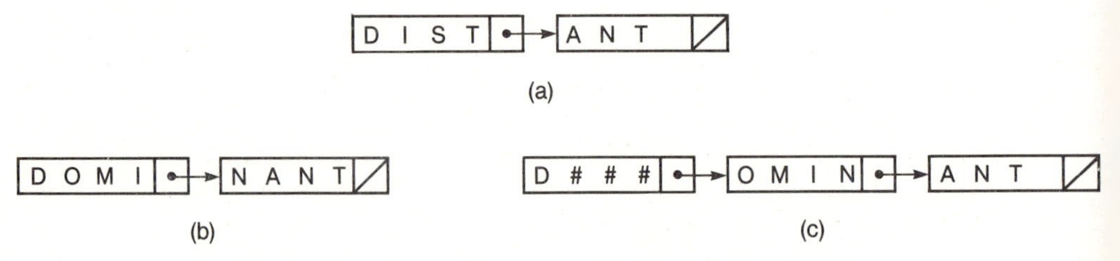

Figure 8.8 Complications with Blocked Linked Lists

As a postscript to the subject of string representations, the addressing capabilities of the underlying machine are a factor that is outside the implementer's control. If the machine is only word-addressable, and if several characters are packed into a word, then the cost of operating upon individual characters can be high. A machine that is addressable by characters (bytes) will perform much better for string processing. Many machines, of course, offer both byte and word addressing.

8.2.3 A Set of String Manipulation Algorithms

For the purpose of illustrating string manipulation algorithms here and in the rest of this chapter, we need to select a representation. The one that we will employ throughout is that of varying-length strings, as was illustrated in Figure 8.2. As mentioned earlier, this choice is inferior for some applications, but in many cases it is a good choice, and it also has the virtue of simplifying the exposition of string algorithms. To begin with, we will employ the definitions:

```
type    extent = 0 .. maxstring;
        string = record
           size: extent;
           data: packed array [1 .. maxstring] of char;
        end;
```

The keyword **packed** is used to specify that characters should be stored densely in words, rather than singly.

```
procedure CONCAT (s1,s2: string; var s3: string);

var     b,i: extent;

begin
   if s1.size + s2.size > maxstring then
      {Overflow}
   else begin
      b := 0;
      for i := 1 to s1.size do
         s3.data [b + i] := s1.data [i];
      b := s1.size;
      for i := 1 to s2.size do
         s3.data [b + i] := s2.data [i];
      s3.size := b + s2.size;
   end;
end;
```

Algorithm 8.1 CONCAT

The procedure CONCAT (Algorithm 8.1) is straightforward, concatenating the contents of strings *s*1 and *s*2 in the string *s*3; note that, with this representation, a test for potential overflow is imperative. The function MATCH_0 (Algorithm 8.2) warrants a modest amount of explanation. It tests for the presence of *pattern* within *text*, returning either a zero if it is not present, or else the index in the text where the first match begins. Within the **repeat** ... **until** loop, a successful comparison of the *j*th text character and the *k*th pattern character causes both indices to be

```
function MATCH_0 (pattern,text: string): extent;

label  1;

var    j,k: extent;

begin
  j := 1;  k := 1;
  repeat
    if text.data [j] = pattern.data [k] then begin
      j := j + 1;
      k := k + 1;
    end else begin
      j := j - k + 2;
      if j + pattern.size <= text.size + 1 then
        k := 1
      else
        goto 1;
    end;
  until (j > text.size) or (k > pattern.size);
1: if k > pattern.size then MATCH_0 := j - pattern.size
                      else MATCH_0 := 0;
end;
```

Algorithm 8.2 MATCH_0

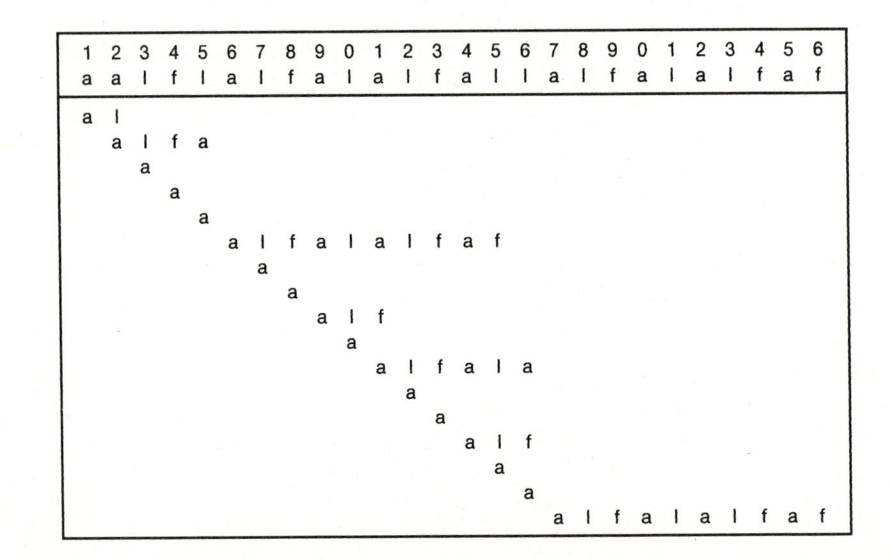

Figure 8.9 Trace of Algorithm MATCH_0

advanced by one; an unsuccessful comparison causes the text cursor to be backed up and the pattern cursor to be reset to one. In looking for the pattern 'alfalalfaf' in the text 'aalflalfalalfallalfalalfaf', MATCH_0 would perform the individual comparisons indicated in Figure 8.9 before returning a value of 17.

```
procedure SUBSEL (s1: string; base,span: extent; var s2: string);

var     i: extent;

begin
   for i := 1 to span do
      s2.data [i] := s1.data [base - 1 + i];
   s2.size := span;
end;
```

Algorithm 8.3 SUBSEL

```
procedure SUBREP (var s1: string; base,span: extent; s2: string);

var     delta,i,p: integer;

begin
   delta := s2.size - span;
   if s1.size + delta > maxstring then
      { Overflow };
   if delta < 0 then
      for p := base + span to s1.size do
         s1.data [delta + p] := s1.data [p];
   if delta > 0 then
      for p := s1.size downto base + span do
         s1.data [delta + p] := s1.data [p];
   for i := 1 to s2.size do
      s1.data [base - 1 + i] := s2.data [i];
   s1.size := s1.size + delta;
end;
```

Algorithm 8.4 SUBREP

The procedure SUBSEL (Algorithm 8.3) selects a substring from the string *s*1, with *base* and *span* specifying the beginning index in *s*1 and the length of the substring; the result is assigned to *s*2. Thus, let *u* be the string 'abcdefghij'; then SUBSEL (*u*,3,4,*z*) would cause *z* to be the string 'cdef'. The procedure SUBREP (Algorithm 8.4) replaces a substring of *s*1 with the string *s*2. There are the same parameters as in SUBSEL, but now *s*1 is the output string and *s*2 is an input string. The first concern is to discover whether the "tail" of the string *s*1 must be moved left/right because the substring to be replaced is longer/shorter in length than *s*2. If so, those characters are relocated appropriately. Finally, the contents of *s*2 are copied into the "hole." Note that replacing a longer substring with a shorter one will leave extra characters at the end of the target *s*1. However this doesn't matter, since $s1.size$ is the determining factor. To illustrate matters, let u be 'abcdefghij' again, and let v be '12345'. Then we would obtain results such as:

for SUBREP (u,3,0,v) , u='ab12345cdefghij'
for SUBREP (u,3,1,v) , u='ab12345defghij'
for SUBREP (u,3,5,v) , u='ab12345hij'
for SUBREP (u,3,7,v) , u='ab12345j'

With regard to complexity, we see that CONCAT, SUBSEL, and SUBREP are linear algorithms; however, the function MATCH_0 is more costly. In fact, for $pattern.size = m$ and $text.size = n$, MATCH_0 is $O(mn)$; for the usual case of $n >> m$, we can see this from the example of $pattern = a^m b$ and $text = a^n$, where a^m represents m concatenations of a. In Section 8.5.1, we will examine ways in which this can be improved.

8.2.4 Minimum Redundancy Codes

The significance of strings is that they carry meanings. In this sense, strings are messages. In a finite collection of strings/messages, some are usually more likely to occur than others. This spread of likelihoods can be viewed at the level of characters, words, or even sentences, as illustrated in Figure 8.10. If we have a set of messages $U = \{m_1, m_2, \ldots, m_N\}$, with respective probabilities $\{p_1, p_2, \ldots, p_N\}$, then the "surprise" associated with receiving any one of the m_i is defined as $-\lg p_i$. These ideas originated with Shannon's Information theory [Shannon 1948], wherein the quantity of information H associated with the entire set of messages U is defined as the average surprise

$$H(U) = -\sum_{i=1}^{N} p_i \lg p_i \tag{8.3}$$

characters	words	sentences
E	the	How are you?
A	bird	Give it to me.
N	futility	It's a double feature.
O	abomination	Grammars describe languages.
Y	oxymoron	The purple door sagged open.

Figure 8.10 Messages in Order of Decreasing Probability

This quantity H, called the *entropy*, is a minimum bound on the number of binary decisions required to discriminate the value of a message. Thus, suppose that we have the candidate messages and probabilities shown in the first two columns of Figure 8.11. A binary decision tree for discriminating which data structure is intended might look like Figure 8.12. An important quantity associated with such a tree is its *weighted path length* (*w.p.l.*). This is obtained by multiplying each frequency by its level in the tree and them summing; it corresponds to the average value for the number of decisions that will be required. For the tree of Figure 8.12, the w.p.l. is

$$3 \times .17 + 2 \times .24 + 4 \times .12 + 3 \times .11 + 4 \times .15 + 3 \times .01 + 2 \times .20 = 2.83$$

Evaluating Eq. 8.3 for the same case, we obtain

$$H = .17 \times 2.56 + .24 \times 2.06 + .12 \times 3.06 + .11 \times 3.18 + .15 \times 2.74 + .01 \times 6.64 + .20 \times 2.32 = 2.59$$

message	probability	code *A*	code *B*
tree	.17	010	010
array	.24	00	001
graph	.12	0110	011
stack	.11	111	100
list	.15	0111	111
queue	.01	110	101
string	.20	10	110

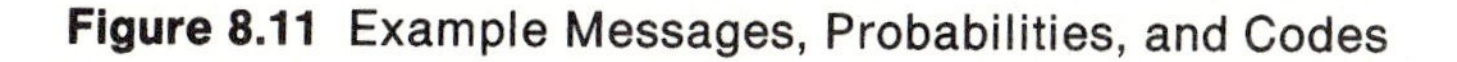

Figure 8.11 Example Messages, Probabilities, and Codes

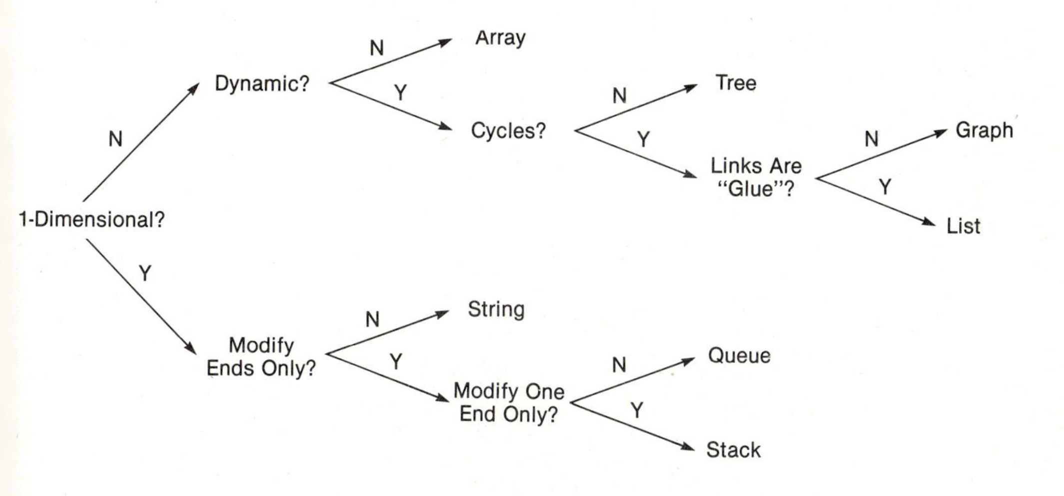

Figure 8.12 A Decision Tree for Data Structures

The definition in Eq. 8.3 has several desirable properties:

- It is always positive.
- It attains its maximum value when all the $p_i = 1/N$. This corresponds to the intuitively reasonable notion that there is the most surprise when all outcomes are equally likely.

- It is additive. If we have two independent sets of messages U and V, with information contents $H(U)$ and $H(V)$, then the information contained in the cross-product of messages from U with messages from V is

$$H(UV) = -\lg pq = -\lg p - \lg q = H(U) + H(V)$$

Since a given set of messages contains a fixed amount of information, we can try to reduce the aggregate storage requirements for their recording or transmission by mapping the messages $\{m_i\}$ into codewords of non-uniform lengths $\{s_i\}$, assigning more likely messages to shorter codes. In general, the codeword symbols can be selected from an alphabet with K symbols. Then the expected character length will be given by $L = \sum p_i s_i$. A fundamental result from information theory states that this average length is bounded from below by $H(U)/\lg K$; that is,

$$L = \sum_{i=1}^{N} p_i s_i \geq \frac{H(U)}{\lg K} \tag{8.4}$$

with the bound being attainable only in those rare cases where the $s_i = -\lg p_i$ are integers. In general, our encoding scheme will have *redundancy*, defined as $1 - H(U)/(L \lg K)$. We are particularly interested in applying this idea to the representation of a set U of characters by binary codewords, for which $K = 2$. An illustration is given by the Code A in Figure 8.11 (representing the decision tree of Figure 8.12) with a redundancy of $1 - 2.59/2.83 = 0.085$. Although this is not the best possible encoding, it is clearly better than any fixed-length code could be. Compare it, for example, with the Code B in Figure 8.11, where we find $L = \sum p_i s_i = s \sum p_i = 3 \times 1 = 3$, and the redundancy is $1 - 2.59/3 = 0.137$.

In the general case of trying to find a set of codes to represent a set of messages, one must be careful to choose a set that can be decoded uniquely, and also instantaneously – that is, without the necessity to look ahead of the current position in the input. Such a code set is said to have the *prefix property*. By way of illustration, the code in Figure 8.13(a) is not uniquely decipherable;[3] the message '010' could be decoded as either 'uw' or 'vu'. The code in (b) of the figure is uniquely decipherable but not instantaneous; the message '0000001' corresponds to 'yyyz', but the 'y' values cannot be determined without scanning ahead each time.

Huffman [1952] found an elegant, yet simple algorithm for constructing a minimum-redundancy code with the prefix property, given a set of messages with associated probabilities. The method proceeds by building a strictly binary tree (see Section 6.2), wherein the message elements are leaves. His construction can be applied either with a set of weights (unnormalized frequencies) or with a set of probabilities (normalized frequencies). We begin by arranging the elements in a list, from bottom to top, in order of increasing frequencies. We then remove the two elements with lowest frequencies f_1 and f_2, and combine them in a new element with frequency $f_1 + f_2$. In the binary tree this new element becomes a parent node to its two summands, and in the list it is inserted so as to maintain the ascending

---

[3] Note that the Morse code, using dots and dashes, does not have the prefix property. How then can a message in Morse code be unambiguously decoded?

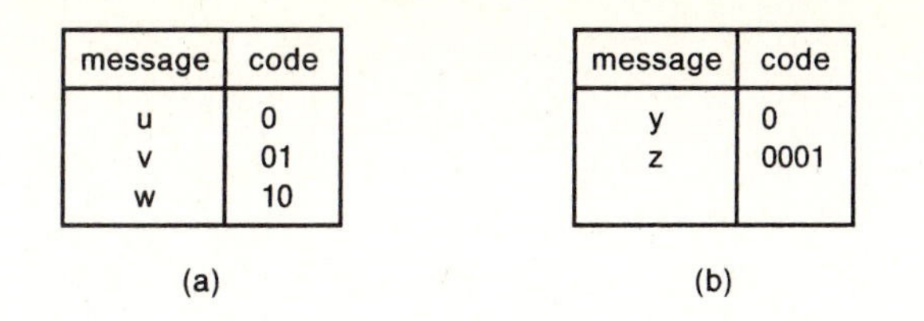

message	code
u	0
v	01
w	10

(a)

message	code
y	0
z	0001

(b)

Figure 8.13 An Ambiguous and a Non-Instantaneous Code

sequence. Then the two elements/nodes with lowest frequencies are selected as before, and the process is repeated. This continues until the list contains just one node, corresponding to the root of the binary tree. Here, we illustrate the algorithm with the data of Figure 8.14 rather than that of Figure 8.11. Figure 8.15 shows successive values for the list and for the tree as the algorithm progresses. When the tree has been completed, a code is immediately forthcoming, by mapping left/right branches in the tree to 0/1 bit values to reach the messages at the leaves. This is shown in Figure 8.15(b), where the (square) terminal nodes are the original data and the (circular) non-terminal nodes are generated by the algorithm. The final code is also summarized in Figure 8.14. Huffman's algorithm yields a tree with the minimum weighted path length (w.p.l.) that can be obtained via an encoding. In our example, it is

$$2 \times 50 + 3 \times (13 + 16 + 26 + 28) + 4 \times (8 + 9 + 11) + 5 \times (6 + 7) = 526$$

message	weight	code	message	weight	code
A	11	0110	N	13	000
C	16	001	O	50	10
D	8	0100	R	9	0101
E	26	110	T	28	111
L	7	01111	Y	6	01110

Figure 8.14 Huffman Encoding for Weighted Messages

Eq. 8.4 stated a lower bound for the average path length, and it can easily be shown that the tree obtained by Huffman's construction has the minimum possible w.p.l. (see Exercise 8.5). In fact, more can be said. A minimum encoding satisfies

$$\frac{H(U)}{\lg K} \leq \sum p_i s_i < \frac{H(U)}{\lg K} + \sum p_i \tag{8.5}$$

[Ash 1965; Gallagher 1968]; thus, for a binary Huffman tree with normalized frequencies, we are assured that

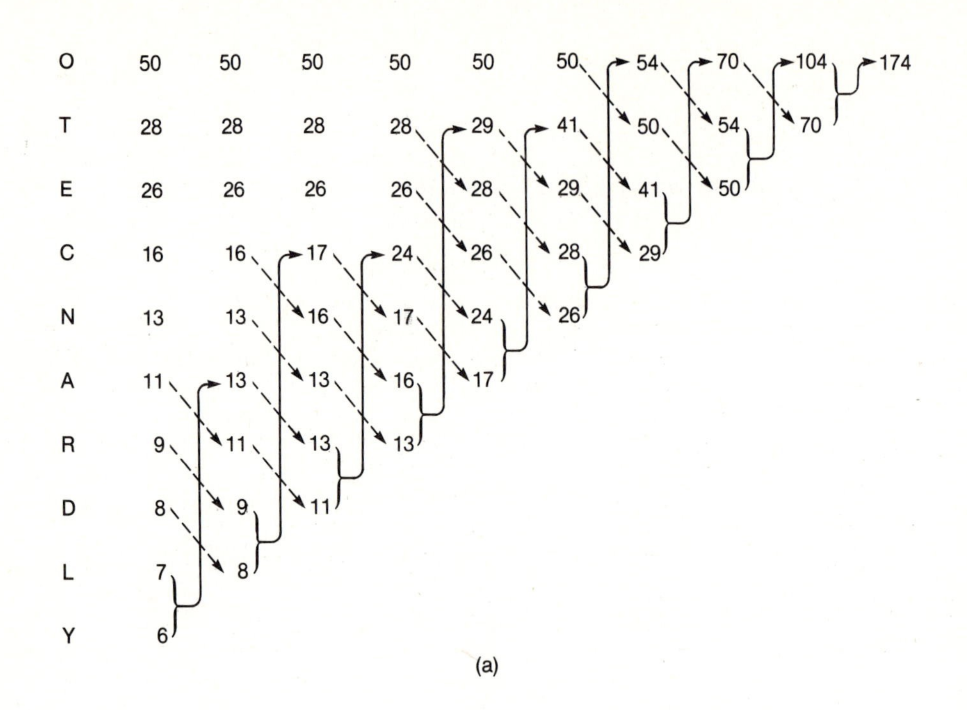

(a)

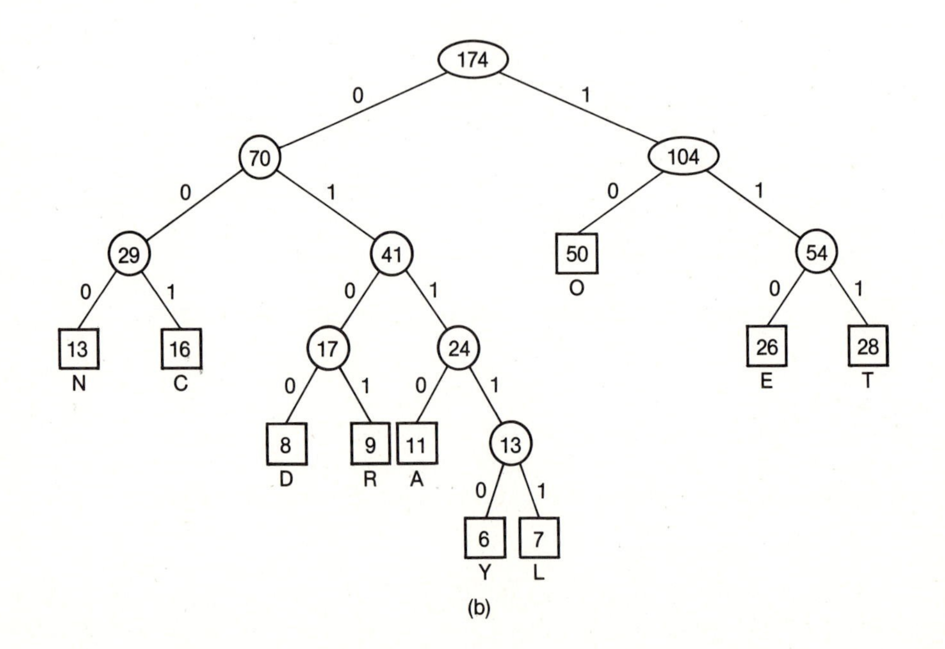

(b)

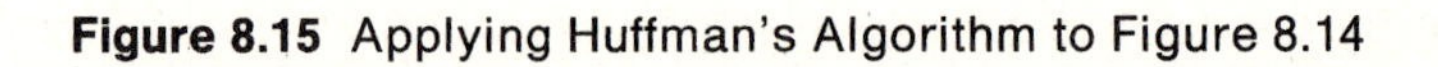

Figure 8.15 Applying Huffman's Algorithm to Figure 8.14

$$H(U) \leq \sum p_i s_i < H(U) + 1 \tag{8.6}$$

In other words, a minimum binary encoding will never cost more than one extra access beyond the limiting entropy value.

Having derived the code of Figure 8.14, how do we decode a message such as '001100100110'? We start at the root of the tree and the beginning of the message, branching according to successive bits until we find the first symbol at a leaf, 'C'. We continually restart at the next bit in the message and at the root of the tree again, finally obtaining the complete message, 'CODE'. Note how the prefix property guarantees a unique decoding.

It should be apparent that the Huffman construction does not yield a unique tree/encoding scheme, although the w.p.l. value is unique. In fact, it may not even yield a unique oriented tree; an alternative tree and code for the data of Figure 8.14 are shown in Figure 8.16. Although the two trees/codes have the same w.p.l., note that the second one is better balanced, with a lesser depth. It is straightforward to modify the Huffman algorithm to guarantee the latter result [Schwartz 1964]. When a non-terminal node has been formed and is to be inserted into the list, there may be other nodes in the list with the same weight. In such a case, the new node should be inserted *after* such nodes. You should verify that such a modification does in fact lead to Figure 8.16. The implementation of Huffman's algorithm is left as a fairly easy programming exercise. Note that, with one complication (see Exercise 8.8), the priority queue is a natural choice of data structure for the necessary operations of inserting a new node and removing a minimum node.

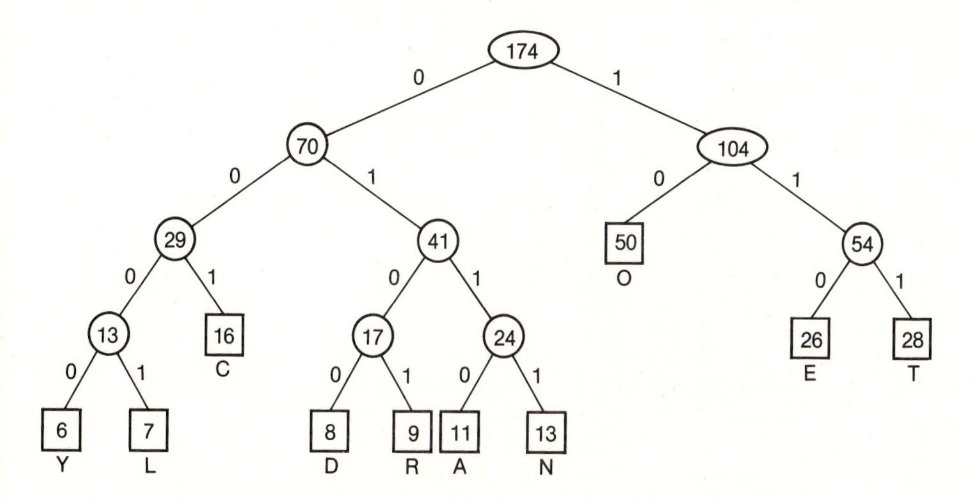

Figure 8.16 Alternative Huffman Tree of Minimum Height

Huffman's algorithm responds to the objective of reducing the storage requirements for data recording and transmission. In fact, the net savings by this method may not be very great unless we are dealing with a rather small collection of messages in which some are much more likely than others. It is often possible to obtain an improved compression of redundancy by considering larger segments of the message string than just individual symbols, as we will see in Section 8.4.1. Another drawback to this method is that the decoding process requires the serial examination of a bit string, which is difficult to implement efficiently on most computers. On the other hand, the logic of Huffman tree construction can be useful in instances unrelated to data compression (see Section 13.4.3).

8.2.5 Error Detecting and Correcting Codes

While the objective in the preceding section was efficiency, in this section it is reliability. We should expect that errors will cause changes in code values and corrupt the associated meanings. This is particularly so when information is transmitted between locations, and noise perturbs the information carrier. A sensible response to this situation is to deliberately provide redundant information with a message. Ordinary discourse contains a great deal of redundancy, thereby enabling humans to detect and correct mistakes in communication in an unsystematic manner.

However, to provide this facility with machines, we need to incorporate redundancy of a more systematic nature, such as a checksum or an odd/even parity check. With such a scheme, the sender computes some redundant information as a function of the data, and attaches it to the message. The receiver recomputes the same redundant information, and compares it to the received redundancy values. At that point, one of three possibilities can be decided upon:

Acceptance – There are, with high probability, no errors.

Correction – Errors are present in locations that can be computed, so that they can be corrected.

Rejection – Errors are present in unknown parts of the message, so that they cannot be corrected.

A central idea for constructing codes that allow *error detection* and *error correction*, as suggested above, is that errors are often independent. In this case, the probability of multiple errors in a given code sequence will be much less than the probability of a single error. Now let B^n be the set of binary n-tuples, and suppose that we have a code C that is a subset of B^n. Two important concepts are the *Hamming weight* of a codeword, defined to be its number of non-zero coordinates, and the *Hamming distance* between any pair of codewords from C, defined to be the number of coordinates in which their values differ. For concreteness, let us consider B^6 and the code C of Figure 8.17. We can regard this code as follows. The data is contained in the leftmost three bits, the fourth bit is an even parity check on the two leftmost data bits, the fifth bit is an even parity check on the first and last data bits, and the sixth bit is an even parity check on the two rightmost data bits. The significant fact is that for any pair of codewords in the set, the minimum Hamming distance is three. This means that three or more independent errors are required in order to change one codeword into another one. In the much more likely event of a single error, we will obtain a faulty codeword Y at Hamming distance one from some word X in C, and at Hamming distance two or more from all the other words in C. It is then reasonable to conclude that the correct value of Y must be X.

message	code C
0	0 0 0 0 0 0
1	0 0 1 0 1 1
2	0 1 0 1 0 1
3	0 1 1 1 1 0
4	1 0 0 1 1 0
5	1 0 1 1 0 1
6	1 1 0 0 1 1
7	1 1 1 0 0 0

Figure 8.17 A Code with 3 Data Bits and 3 Check Bits

What if we have a code such that the minimum Hamming distance between any two codewords is two? In this event, we may receive a faulty codeword Y that is at Hamming distance one from two different codewords. It will not be possible to correct the error, other than with a guess; on the other hand, we can be sure that no single error can get by without our being aware of it. This is the function that use of a single parity bit provides.

In general, as first shown by Hamming [1950], codes with a minimum distance of $d + 1$ enable detection of d errors, and codes with a minimum distance of $2d + 1$ enable correction of d errors. This can be visualized in geometric terms such that each codeword is a point in space. When we speak of detection, we find that d errors are insufficient to reach one codeword from another because they are at Hamming distances $d + 1$. When we speak of correction, we find that each codeword is surrounded by a "sphere" of radius d, and that none of the spheres can intersect because the centers are at Hamming distances $2d + 1$. Thus, as illustrated in Figure 8.18, any codeword with $k \leq d$ errors can safely be corrected to the value of the codeword at the center of one particular sphere. Note that these two distance conditions interact. A code with minimum distance of three can be used either to correct single errors or to detect double errors, but not both. A code with a minimum distance of five can be used either to correct double errors, correct single errors and detect triple errors, or to detect quadruple errors. The choice of whether to opt for more detection or more correction depends upon the application. For example, it is common to have a situation where error detection could be used to signal a request for retransmission. In such cases, we could emphasize rejection (that is, detection without correction) in order to reduce the likelihood of an undetected multiple error. On the other hand, where retransmission is impossible or irrelevant, as in the case of reading corrupted data from a magnetic tape, it would make more sense to opt for as much correction as possible.

One potentially troublesome point is that, by introducing check bits, we have lowered the efficiency, or the *rate*, of the code. In the example of Figure 8.17, we have halved the effective transmission rate by including as many check bits as information bits. What is the trade-off in general terms? If we have codewords with $n = m + r$ bits, where m bits carry the information and r bits provide the checking, how big must r be for a given m, in order to provide single-error correction? It

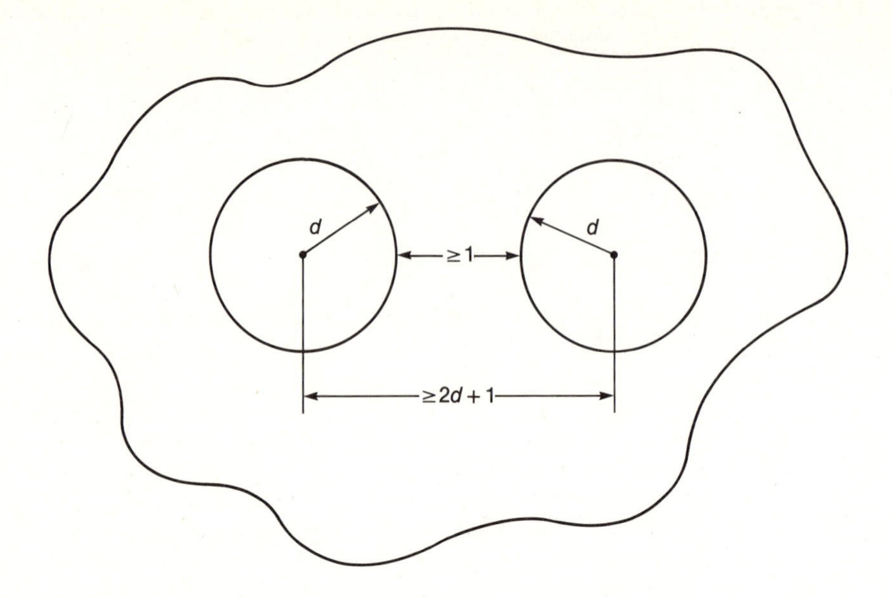

Figure 8.18 Hamming Distances for Correction

must be such that $2^r \geq m + r + 1$; this is so because there must be sufficient information in the r bits to distinguish among the $m + r + 1$ cases:

(a) there is an error in one of the m data bits;

(b) there is an error in one of the r check bits;

(c) there is no error.

This is equivalent to

$$m = n - r \leq 2^r - r - 1 \tag{8.7}$$

When equality holds, we can construct a corresponding *perfect Hamming code*, of length $n = 2^r - 1$ and *size* (that is, number of messages) $2^{2^r - r - 1}$. Some pairs (n,m) for which perfect Hamming codes can be constructed are (3,1), (7,4), (15,11), (31,26), etc. As you can see, efficiency ceases to be an issue as n increases.

One can carry out similar arguments to obtain various upper or lower bounds for multiple-error correcting codes. For example, referring to Figure 8.18 again, suppose that we have codewords of n bits and that we want d-bit error correction. Then the "sphere" about each codeword must contain the codeword itself and all the points reachable in d or fewer errors. The total number of points is $P = 2^n$, and the total number in each sphere is $S = \sum C(n,j)$, for $0 \leq j \leq d$. The ratio P/S is known as the *Hamming bound*, corresponding to the maximum number of distinct messages on n bits with d-bit error correction. For a single-error correcting code, the Hamming bound reduces to $2^n/(1 + n)$; for $n = 2^r - 1$, this tells us that we can have $2^{n-r} = 2^m$ messages, agreeing with the results of the preceding paragraph. One must be careful, however, because the Hamming bound is a necessary but not sufficient condition, and a code satisfying the bound may not exist.

†8.2.5.1 Group Codes. In the preceding section, we showed the existence of single-error correcting codes with good rates. Actually finding such codes and determining how to use them efficiently is another matter. For instance, if we receive a faulty codeword Y that does not match any of the messages of an (n,m) code, we might try comparing Y with each of the 2^m messages to see which it is closest to. For m of even modest size, however, just the storage requirements of this approach render it completely infeasible. Therefore, we want codes for which we can find good encoding and decoding algorithms. Beyond this, if we can solve these problems for single-error correcting codes, can we solve them for multiple-error correcting codes? In this section, we will sketch how *group codes* provide a solution for the single-error case. The demonstration suppresses a great deal of theoretical underpinning which comes from linear algebra and group theory; a fuller treatment can be found in Blahut [1983].

To be specific, what is an example of the Hamming (7,4) code, and how would we use it to correct a faulty codeword? It is effective to represent the coding process as the multiplication of the input vector $I = (i_1, i_2, i_3, i_4)$ by a (4×7) *generator matrix G*, as shown in Figure 8.19(a), yielding a codeword in the desired code C. It is possible for G to have other forms, but the G of the figure makes the encoding particularly simple. The leftmost four columns of G are the identity matrix, and the rightmost three columns of G compute three parity bits to be appended to I, via the multiplication $X = I \times G \pmod 2$. As an example, the input $I = 1011$ would become the codeword $X = 1011010$. An essential feature of this process is that any codeword in C is a linear combination of the four rows of G, causing C to be a subgroup of B^7.

```
1 0 0 0 1 1 0        1 1 0 1 1 0 0
0 1 0 0 1 0 1        1 0 1 1 0 1 0
0 0 1 0 0 1 1        0 1 1 1 0 0 1
0 0 0 1 1 1 1
```

(a) Generator Matrix G (b) Parity-Check Matrix H

Figure 8.19 Coding Matrices for Hamming (7,4) Code

Suppose now that we receive Y instead of X; that is, $Y = X + Z \pmod 2$, for Z an error vector. The value of Z can be determined in an ingenious fashion by using the (3×7) *parity-check matrix H* of Figure 8.19(b). Observe that the rightmost three columns of H are an identity matrix once again, and the leftmost four columns of H are the transpose of the rightmost three columns of G. We begin by computing $S = H \times Y^T \pmod 2$; the quantity S is called the *syndrome*. Now the multiplication of Y^T by H is a mapping from B^7 to B^3. The set C of codewords form a kernel of this mapping, for which $S = 0$. Moreover, the remaining values in B^7 form seven cosets of C, or equivalence classes, each with sixteen members. The significance of the syndrome is that it depends only upon Z and not upon X, since $H \times Y^T = H \times (X + Z)^T = 0 + H \times Z^T$, for X in C. If $S = 0$, then we know that $Z = 0$; if $S \neq 0$, then it specifies a coset of sixteen possible error vectors. As an example, suppose that we receive $Y = 0110101$. Multiplying Y^T by H, we obtain the syndrome $S = 011$. In fact, any of the following Z values

0000011	0100110	1000101	1100000
0001100	0101001	1001010	1101111
<u>0010000</u>	0110101	1010110	1110011
0011111	0111010	1011001	1111100

could have caused this value of S. But since we assume that single errors are much more likely than multiple errors, then the underlined one, known as the *coset leader*, is deemed to be the desired value of Z. So the message is decoded as the first four bits of $X = 0110101 + 0010000 = 0100101$, or as '0100'.

In the process just described, the use of the syndrome to pick a coset leader reduces the number of items to be searched from 2^m to 2^{n-m}. For the case in question – $n = 7$ and $m = 4$ – this is not significant; however, it rapidly does become significant for larger codes, such as (15,11). The solution for the Hamming perfect codes is even more elegant than we have described, in that the syndrome can be used to determine Z without the necessity of storing 2^{n-m} coset leaders. But for an arbitrary (n,m) single-error correcting code, we must find the coset leaders. It can be a sizeable task to determine them (without computing $H \times Z^T$, for every possible Z, and recording the Z of smallest Hamming weight for each value of S). On the other hand, they need be computed only once. The reader encountering these ideas for the first time may find them slightly overwhelming. The significant point to comprehend, however, is that by choosing a code to be a subgroup of B^n, one can fairly directly and elegantly obtain efficient decoding algorithms for singe-error correction.

The construction of codes that can correct multiple errors is an advanced topic, as is the design of algorithms that efficiently decode (that is, accept, correct, or reject) the codewords [§]. Some of the techniques, such as the use of a syndrome as an error-locator function, carry over, but the details become much more complicated. They depend heavily upon arithmetic over finite fields $GF(q)$.

8.3 TEXT PROCESSING

We can look forward to a society that uses less real paper, but it will also be one in which there is assuredly more paperwork. Word-processors and general-purpose computing machines assist us in the preparation and generation of ever more memos, letters, programs, reports, etc. The preparation phase is typically an electronic "cut-and-paste" one, in which we interactively edit the text of a document. We may also invoke programs that detect or even correct misspellings. Finally, in the generation phase, a formatting program processes the text file to yield a document that is aesthetically pleasing. Our discussion of text processing is based upon these three principal themes.

8.3.1 Text Editing

The most common conceptual model of text editing is that the user has a document consisting of lines of characters. A moderate number of contiguous lines (about twenty) are presented to the user on a video screen; at a given instant, a *cursor* indicates a particular character position on a particular line. The user can position the cursor underneath any character position on his screen, and he can also cause the screen contents to *scroll* up or down to reveal lines that are above or below the text on the screen. In addition, since some lines in his document may be too wide for the screen, he can scroll left or right to reveal portions of lines that are off the sides of the screen. The editor program that supports such operations usually has two modes – one in which the user can type in new lines of text, and one in which he can operate upon the existing lines of text. Typical capabilities in the latter mode are:

- to cause the aforementioned scrolling over the two dimensional document – up, down, left, or right;
- to locate occurrences of a given pattern anywhere in the document;
- to insert, change, or delete a specified substring in a line;
- to insert, change, or delete some or all occurrences of a specified substring in the document;
- to insert or delete entire lines;
- to delete a block of lines from the document;
- to move or copy a block of lines from one portion of the document to another.

This model deals in terms of lines that can readily be displayed to the user, and thus we do not expect the lines to be extremely wide. It is common to employ varying-length strings for individual lines, and an array of pointers to keep track of the relative sequence of the lines. Thus, a fragment of a document might look like Figure 8.20, with string data as in (a) and with pointers as in (b). It is easy to see how the editing operations cited above could be supported by the data organization in this figure – using the string manipulation routines of Section 8.2.3, manipulating pointer values, etc.

There are other text editing models. In discussing these models, the issue of lines and lengths is paramount. For instance, suppose that we edit the line with relative number 329 in Figure 8.20, changing 'echo' to 'reverberation'. Suppose also that the resulting line exceeds the limit of the varying-length string implementation. This would cause a failure in a primitive editor. However, other editors would automatically split the line in two, depending perhaps upon the type of the document. Still more sophisticated is to dispense with underlying lines altogether, treating the text file as one long super-string, or stream, of characters. In this model, carriage returns and line feeds can be left in the text, and they can be edited like ordinary characters; however, the editor program does not use them for control when displaying the text to the user, and substring searching can be done in a manner that ignores them. Among other things, this solves the following common problem. If we are looking for a substring with a line-oriented editor, and it happens to span the end of one line and the beginning of the next, then we will not find it. However, this same situation will be treated properly in the case of a stream-oriented editor.

location	string
1300	models. In discussing these models, the issue of
1400	lines and lengths is paramount. For instance, suppose
1500	of the varying-length string implementation. This
1600	in Figure 8.20, changing 'echo' to 'reverberation'.
1700	
1800	that we edit the line with relative number 329
1900	Suppose also that the resulting line exceeds the limit
2000	would cause a failure in a primitive editor. However,

(a) String Storage

line number	326	327	328	329	330	331	332	...
location	1300	1400	1800	1600	1900	1500	2000	...

(b) String Pointers

Figure 8.20 A Text Editing Example

This discussion has been limited to conveying just a few of the more important notions in text editing. Other important topics include:

- the capability of pointing directly at a block of text with a *mouse*;
- the ability to mix text with line-drawings and pictures;
- the editor function of displaying the document so that "What You See Is What You Get" (WYSIWYG).

Readers interested in pursuing these matters can find a comprehensive survey of text editing in Meyrowitz and van Dam [1982].

8.3.2 Spelling Correction

It has long been recognized that there are four typical kinds of spelling mistakes in a document: (a) omission of a letter, (b) insertion of a letter, (c) substitution of one letter for another, and (d) transposition of adjacent letters. These are meaningful categories of errors, in that they correspond to real-world mistakes in the typing of input. But note that their relative importance depends upon the source of the document; for example, we would not expect to find transposition errors when using optical character reading devices.

The four types of errors are important also because they form a basis for a metric of the difference between a pair of strings. More precisely, one can define the *edit-distance* between a pair to be the minimum number of editing changes (insertions, deletions, substitutions, or transpositions) required to transform one string to the other (see Exercise 8.24). This notion is fundamental in attempting to correct spelling errors [Lowrance and Wagner 1975; Wagner and Fischer 1974]. But first, let us deal with the simpler issue of detection.

In any language, we have a higher expectation of encountering some successive pairs of letters – for example, 'TH' or 'ER' – than others – such as 'GY' or 'QZ'. These letter pairs are called *digrams*, and statistics concerning their relative frequency in ordinary English text are readily obtained. A generalization that is also useful is to employ statistics concerning *n-grams*, or successive groupings of n letters. One can detect a great many typical spelling errors simply by scanning the text of a document and flagging words that seem to be exceptional according to these standards [McMahon et al. 1978].

In common practice, it is preferable to use a program that helps in correcting errors by suggesting what was intended. Although the concept of edit-distance is useful in this regard, it is not as powerful as the analogous idea of Hamming distance. With the former, codes are designed so that some minimum distance is maintained between any pair of codewords. In natural language, however, it is trivial to find numerous pairs of words, wherein both words are valid and yet their edit-distance is just one; in such cases, not even detection is possible, much less correction. Fortunately, most random single errors will not produce another valid word, so that one can attempt to find the correct word that is "closest" to an incorrect word, either in terms of edit-distance or some other criteria. It is relatively easy to compensate for errors of insertion and transposition, requiring $O(n)$ trials for a word of length n. To compensate for errors of omission and substitution is more costly, requiring $O(kn)$ trials, where k is the size of the alphabet.

Correction is harder than detection because of the difficulties cited in determining what is the most likely correct word. Correction is also more expensive; a significant part of this cost arises from the need to be able to employ a large dictionary efficiently. Diverse techniques are employed for shoehorning a large dictionary into a computer, and we will not encounter most of these (such as hashing and superimposed coding) until Chapters 10 and 12. But data compression is also important for this purpose (see Section 8.4.1). A discussion of spelling correction in general, with particular emphasis upon the dictionary problem, is Peterson [1980].

8.3.3 Text Formatting

The text that was created via the techniques of the preceding section may have been a program, a letter, a report, a book, etc. In all but the first of these instances, the author would most likely want a printed copy that is formatted in some prescribed and/or pleasing manner. Formatting is a rather broad topic that includes such matters as:

- generating output that is fairly uniform with respect to spacing between words, width of lines, and number of lines per page;
- displaying functionally distinct parts of the document (parts of a letter, section headings, running headers and footers, etc.) in distinctive manners;
- employing special fonts, such as bold or italic, where appropriate;
- capturing information that can be used for automatically generating special document parts, such as a table of contents or an index;

- defining and using *macros* to effect parameterized textual substitution.

Fortunately, there are numerous program tools to assist the author in accomplishing these objectives. In many cases, the author actively directs the process by incorporating verb-like commands (as in the IBM SCRIPT language) or adjective-like descriptors (as in the IBM GML language) with the text. Both of these tools were used, for example, in causing this book to be typeset by computer. Using these tools is really a form of programming in a specialized language, and it is too extensive a topic for us to pursue here. An excellent treatise on text processing functions in general is Kernighan and Plauger [1981].

The first item in the preceding list is somewhat different from the others in that it is accomplished with very little participation by the author, and we will devote our attention to it here. It basically requires three related decision processes that are as old as printing:

1. Between which words of a paragraph should *line-breaking* be performed?
2. When and where should words be hyphenated?
3. If the right margins are to be even and not ragged, where should the extra space be placed within each line?

If these matters are decided poorly, the result is a printed page that is aesthetically displeasing. The three questions are answered in very different fashion by a commercial printer and by a word-processing program. Commercial printing is usually synonymous with typesetting (although movable type has largely disappeared), where the characters are of varying width. Because of this variability, the printer can answer the second and third questions in many different ways, adjusting even the space between letters of a word as well as the space between words of a line. In typical word-processing, on the other hand, character width is a constant, and hyphenation is likely to be impossible. We will discuss both cases in brief, general terms.

The simplest approach used by printers is to keep adding words to a line until no more will fit, using normal spacing, and then to try to expand the spacing to absorb what is left over at the right margin. If this cannot be done without leaving too much space, then the printer can try to shrink the spacing and add one more word to that line. The same approach can be used in typesetting by computer, with the distinction that the spacing resolution may be finer. This simple, "greedy" approach may do well, but it may also lead to poorly set lines later in the paragraph. However, using a computer makes it feasible to look ahead in the text and assess the effects of a more general set of line-breaks − not just those variations attained by moving a word from the beginning of the $(i+1)$st line to the end of the ith line. This is a problem in optimization that is readily amenable to dynamic programming, since the principle of optimality applies with respect to sub-segments of the paragraph. Even so, the time and memory requirements for a straightforward dynamic programming solution make it unacceptable in many applications, and better approaches have been sought. The most conspicuous and thorough solution maintains a list of *feasible breakpoints* as nodes of a digraph [Knuth and Plass 1981]. An arc from node U to node V corresponds to a line of text between these breakpoints, and attached to each such arc is a *penalty* metric. The penalty figure reflects how unsatisfactory that line is; its computation depends in a somewhat subjective fashion upon many factors that we will not describe here. Under this formulation, the solution corresponds to finding the shortest distance from the start node to the end node. There are many less feasible breakpoints than there are words, and breakpoints are even discarded at times. Thus, the complexity of this solution is significantly better than that obtained by dynamic programming over all sub-segments of the paragraph.

Line-breaking and spacing are much simpler problems in the typical word-processing program, but the corresponding solutions are both interesting and of value. Once again, dynamic programming provides a starting point of view from which simpler algorithms are derived. Assume, for instance, that we first apply the simple process described at the beginning of the previous paragraph. If this tentative output has m lines, and if we decide that our solution should have m lines also, then the total amount of spacing in the resultant paragraph, and so also the average interword spacing, are essentially known constants. (This is not quite true when we consider the effects of periods at the ends of lines, and the extra space at the right margin of the last line in the paragraph.) One approach uses properties of the breakpoint indices to limit the range of dynamic search [Achugbue 1981]; another moves words between adjacent lines until the variance of the interword spacing is minimized [Samet 1982].

8.4 STRING TRANSFORMATIONS

In discussing codes in Sections 8.2.4 and 8.2.5, we considered alternate ways to represent a string via recodings of individual characters in the string. Although these recodings might take into account overall statistical properties of the character set, the actual context of a given character occurrence never influenced the recoding process. To illustrate this in plain words, the high conditional probability Pr('h'|'t') that an 'h' might follow a 't' would not be taken into consideration. Our concern in this section is with alternate ways to represent strings, taking into account a larger context, perhaps a few adjacent characters or words or even the entire string. However, these techniques have the property that they are not concerned at all with the meaning of these larger units. String transformations that do operate with "meaningful" substrings are the subject of Section 8.6. The first string transformations that we will consider now are for *compression*, wherein redundancy is squeezed out of data; this is an extension of the ideas in Section 8.2.4. The second class of transformations, although they do not recognize the meaning in a string, have the express purpose of concealing its meaning from unauthorized persons.

8.4.1 Data Compression

To begin with, recall that the objective of a Huffman encoding of a character set is to minimize the redundancy that is usually present. The redundancy arises from the unequal (unconditional) probabilities of characters occurring in an average string. This encoding, by assigning shorter codewords to more probable characters, yields a shorter expected length for messages containing them. One consequence is reduced cost of storage, of course, and another is reduced cost of transmitting such messages over communication lines. The Huffman encoding has a rather simple elegance and is useful in various situations, but it has three practical shortcomings as a compression technique:

1. It cannot detect and eliminate more global forms of redundancy that follow from the conditional probabilities cited in the preceding section.
2. Although the encoding process can be done fairly efficiently, the decoding process requires extensive bit manipulation, which tends to be inefficient on most machines.
3. It requires an a priori knowledge of the probabilities.

In this section, we will survey some techniques that respond to one or more of these difficulties.

There is a type of redundancy that is fairly common and also quite easily compressed. Typically, we see it in text with long sequences of blank characters, or in numbers with long sequences of zeros. It is also very prevalent in pictures, where there are usually large homogeneous areas. An effective scheme in this case is *run-length encoding*. We simply encode a run of K homogeneous values C as a three character sequence: an escape character (see Section 8.2.1), the value of K (as a byte), and the character C itself. Thus, in EBCDIC and postulating '%' as the escape character, if we encountered a sequence of 76 periods, we could replace these 76 periods with '%<.'. Here the '<' corresponds to the fact that '<'=**chr**(76) in EBCDIC (see Table 8.1) and the '.' is the compressed character itself. It is easy to see that run-length encoding has none of the three shortcomings listed above. However, its usefulness is limited to those situations where redundancy occurs in the form of runs; in many applications, such redundancy has already been removed by other means.

Huffman's method uses the unconditional probabilities of single symbols; the simplest extension of this idea is to utilize expectations concerning the occurrence of digrams (see Section 8.3.2). Typically, in this method, the most common digrams would be translated to unused byte values in the character code set. This is particularly easy to do in EBCDIC, since many of the 256 values are commonly unused. Note that with this method we also avoid the problem of having to decode a serial bit string. Of course, it is possible to extend the technique even further to consider groups of n-grams; however, a more effective technique is to look for text fragments of varying size, solely on the basis of their relative frequencies. Note the contrast here:

- Huffman's technique is a fixed-to-variable encoding that minimizes redundancy by converting fixed-length symbols of unequal likelihood to variable-length symbols, composed of equally likely binary values.
- The objective in the present instance is a variable-to-fixed encoding that minimizes redundancy by looking for fragments of variable-length but equal likelihood. These fragments are then translated, via a dictionary, to equiprobable fixed-length encodings [Cooper and Lynch 1982].

In the methods of the preceding paragraph, we saw the need for a dictionary of digrams or other text fragments. The further these methods are carried, the more the size of the resulting dictionary becomes an issue. Thus, although effective for large, relatively static databases [Schuegraf and Heaps 1973], these ideas are not economical for the compression of a transient message. Another issue with the use of such dictionaries is that there will be overlap among the fragments, as illustrated by both 'TH' and 'HE' in 'THE'. It then becomes a significant computation to decide which fragments to employ in order to maximize the compression.

There is in fact no single best compression method; the choice depends upon the nature of the text and the manner in which it is to be used. For the methods described thus far, we have to strike a balance among the four associated costs of (a) preprocessing the text to determine what code to use, (b) generating and carrying along the dictionary, (c) performing the encoding, and (d) performing the decoding. It may be effective to combine two simple methods, perhaps run-length encoding followed by Huffman encoding.

In a different category are dynamic compression schemes that require no preprocessing. Rather, as a message is scanned, statistics about it are used to continually update a data structure according to which the message is compressed. Basically, the same algorithm is used by both sender and receiver, with an identical dynamic dictionary being built for decompression. There are several of these dynamic compression schemes [§]. One principal category is that of dynamic Huffman compression, which is still an encoding of individual characters. The method known as *universal compression* operates on an entirely different principle; it uses the statistics to maintain a dynamic dictionary of *strings*. In its simplest form, this latter scheme corresponds to a variable-to-variable encoding, although it can also be cast into variable-to-fixed form.

8.4.2 Cryptography

By the *encryption* of a message into a *cipher*, we attempt to make it unintelligible to eavesdroppers, wiretappers, spies, etc. At the same time we must have a reverse *decryption* process by which authorized parties can recover the original message from the cipher. The need for such capabilities resided largely with diplomatic and military operations until fairly recently. But we now have phenomena such as electronic mail systems, electronic fund transfers, and databases containing billions of banking and medical records. Moreover, issues of privacy, authenticity, tampering, etc. make cryptographic techniques relevant to a much larger community. Of course, whether it is good to be able to "break" a code depends upon your point of view; so this topic has two perspectives – that of the cryptographer who devises the code, and that of the cryptanalyst, or adversary, who tries to solve it. In discussing these dual perspectives, we will find some insights from both information theory and computational complexity.

Although cryptography has been employed for centuries, its first solid foundation was provided by Shannon [1949]. We begin with his model, shown in Figure 8.21, wherein A sends a message to B over an insecure channel. An adversary may listen to the message traffic on this channel. The sender and the receiver overcome this insecurity by having a *key* The sender applies the key to the *plaintext* message to produce a *ciphertext* message; and the receiver applies the key to the ciphertext

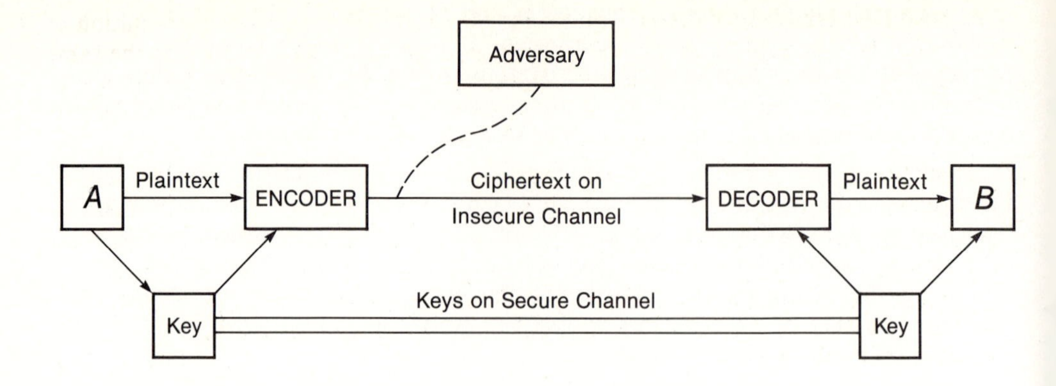

Figure 8.21 A Communication Channel

to recover the plaintext. Even though the adversary may know the general nature of the encryption and decryption processes, he does not know the key and so cannot understand the message. None of this is feasible, of course, unless the key is secret; and so a secure channel is required for the communication of the key(s), as shown in Figure 8.21. It might seem that we have just shifted the problem without solving it; however, we might use a courier as the secure channel and have him transmit a set of keys well in advance. Also, we can try to find clever schemes whereby, although relatively small keys are employed, their effects are magnified by the encryption/decryption processes.

From the preceding paragraph, we infer that there are two issues: to find good encryption/decryption algorithms, and to find good ways to generate and employ keys. Two diverse manners of handling the latter issue – one corresponding to "classical" cryptography, and the other corresponding to recent invention – lead to the treatments in the ensuing two sections. Superimposing cryptographic techniques upon conventional data processing has a substantial cost, and thus the marketplace has adopted them only in certain instances, such as for bank teller machines. However, the cost of not adopting them more generally is potentially much higher, and so they are likely to be very important in years to come. To supplement our coverage of the topic, the encyclopedia of classical cryptography is Kahn [1967], and an excellent extended account of modern developments is Lempel [1979].

8.4.2.1 Private-Key Systems. The most familiar manner of applying a key for encryption purposes is to perform a character-by-character *substitution* of symbols in an output alphabet for symbols in the input alphabet. Commonly, the alphabets are the same, and the key amounts to a permutation of the alphabet symbols, as in:

```
A B C D E F G H I J K L M N O P Q R S T U V W X Y Z
Q W E R T Y U I O P A S D F G H J K L Z X C V B N M
```

Thus, if we apply this substitution to the plaintext 'CRYPTOGRAM', we obtain the ciphertext 'EKNHZGUKQD'. There is another basic encryption method. To apply it, we must first break the message into *blocks* of size n; we then use a permutation of $1 .. n$ as a rule defining a *transposition* of the symbols in each block. For the same plaintext as before, with block-size 5 and with key of (1 5 3 2 4) (see the discussion of cycle notation for permutations in Section 1.2), the corresponding ciphertext would be 'PYTRCARMGO'.

These basic methods are astonishingly poor for concealing ordinary plaintext. In substitution, we see that there are 26! possible transformations for an alphabet of just upper-case letters, and so the complexity of discriminating among them might appear to make for a good code. However, ordinary English text is estimated to have a redundancy of 3.2 bits per character. Although there are $\lg (26!) = 88.4$ bits of *equivocation* introduced by the uncertainty as to which key is in use, this equivocation is reduced by 3.2 bits for each character in the ciphertext. Thus, only 25 to 30 ciphertext symbols (that is, 88.4/3.2) are required, on the average, to dispel ambiguity and allow decryption. This point in analyzing ciphertext where its content becomes unequivocal is called the *unicity point*. The primary clues for solving a substitution cryptogram come from the known, unequal frequencies of single characters, alluded to in our discussions of redundancy and compression. This vulnerability is made worse by the similar phenomena with respect to digrams and n-grams, yielding further clues for the cryptanalyst. Transposition ciphers are perhaps slightly superior to substitution ciphers in that such higher order statistics are obscured; nonetheless, they too readily succumb to a skilled adversary.

Since the inherent redundancy in a message allows simple ciphers to be broken so easily, one possible remedy is to use compression in order to diminish that effect. Indeed, this will push back the unicity point; however, if the adversary has sufficient ciphertext, the eventual outcome will be the same. A more effective solution is to have the key introduce equivocation into the cipher as steadily as the message dissipates it. In fact, this can be done by using a completely random string of symbols as a key. If we map the letters of the alphabet to the integers $0 .. 25$, then encryption is performed character by character, using addition modulo 26. One simply combines successive characters of the message with successive characters of the key. Decryption is accomplished by the inverse process of subtracting (modulo 26) successive characters of the key from successive characters of the ciphertext. This type of code is referred to as a *one-time pad*. It is completely secure against cryptanalysis, since no amount of previous ciphertext provides any clues for interpreting succeeding ciphertext. Unfortunately, it requires large amounts of secure key data at both ends of the communication channel. Thus, it is used only in very special situations, such as the Hot Line between Moscow and Washington.

One technique for bypassing the large key requirements of one-time pads is to have a true key cause the generation of a pseudo-key of much greater length, akin to the manner in which a seed value can be used to control pseudo-random number generation. Although appealing, such generation schemes tend to have dependencies that a skilled cryptanalyst can exploit to find the true key, given sufficient ciphertext. A more effective approach is to combine repeated applications of substitution and transposition in a *product cipher*. As implemented in hardware in the IBM Lucifer system, the substitutions and transpositions are accomplished via *S*(ubstitution)-boxes and *P*(ermutation)-boxes operating upon blocks of symbols [Feistel 1973]. A typical *P*-box with a block of 8 binary inputs and 8 binary outputs is illustrated in Figure 8.22(a); a typical *S*-box with 3 binary inputs and 3 binary outputs is illustrated in (b) of the figure. The effect of an S-box is to convert its n-bit input to a number in the range $0 .. 2^n - 1$, then to permute these possible converted values, and finally to convert the result of the permutation back to binary. Thus, there are $(2^n)!$ possible wirings for an S-box with n inputs. It is not technologically feasible to build S-boxes for large values of n; therefore, neither P-boxes nor S-boxes, used alone, provide cryptographic strength. But their combination does, in the manner illustrated in Figure 8.22(c). The effect of the S-boxes is to *confuse* the single character statistics via complicated, non-linear bit mappings, and the effect of the P-boxes is to *diffuse* these mappings over wide spacings, making their analysis (and also that of n-grams) very difficult. In practice, the P-boxes and the S-boxes have predetermined input-output mappings. Note, however, that the layers of S-boxes really consist of pairs of boxes (S_0, S_1). This is where the keys enter the picture. For every such pair, the selection between S_0 and S_1 is conditioned by a bit in the key. An example of this effect is illustrated by the shading of one member of each pair in Figure 8.22(c).

Figure 8.22 captures the essence of a product cipher, but the actual parameters in Lucifer are quite a bit greater. It calls for P-boxes that permute 128 bits, S-boxes that make substitutions on 4-bit groups, keys that consist of 128 bits, and devices that contain many P and S layers. These same ideas are now embodied in the *Data Encryption Standard* (*DES*) adopted by the National Bureau of Standards [1977] for use by federal and other agencies. The DES is actually a reduced variant of Lucifer, employing a key of 56 bits. This reduction in key size has sparked a great deal of controversy [Diffie and Hellman 1977]. It is argued that even though 56 bits are adequate for a while, advances in technology will make it economically feasible for motivated adversaries to break DES-based ciphers within a decade or so. Only time will settle the question; for now, however, the DES has stood up very well under cryptanalysis.

†8.4.2.2 Public-Key Systems. Cryptography was originally employed by limited numbers of people — diplomats, soldiers, lovers, thieves, etc. — who found it reasonable to exchange secret keys in advance of their communications. As the use of cryptography becomes more widespread via DES or other means, it becomes an overwhelmingly large task to manage the keys and keep them secret (for example, by a master encryption scheme) [Ehrsam et al. 1978; Matyas and Meyer 1978]. Moreover, if there are n parties, then $\frac{1}{2}n \times (n-1)$ keys are required corresponding to the $\frac{1}{2}n \times (n-1)$ possible pairs of communicants, so that the sheer volume of key administration is a nuisance. Finally, there will be numerous situations in which A will wish to send a confidential message to a stranger B, for whom he has no key. An ingenious proposal for solving these problems (and others also, as we will see) is to employ two keys instead of one, in a *public-key cryptosystem* [Diffie and Hellman 1976]. Every user u has his own public encryption key P_u that is maintained in a public directory; he also has his own secret decryption key S_u that is known only to himself. For M a message, C the corresponding cipher, E an encryption algorithm, and D a decryption algorithm, we arrange matters such that

$$C = E(M,P_u) \quad \text{and} \quad M = D(C,S_u) = D(E(M,P_u),S_u) \tag{8.8}$$

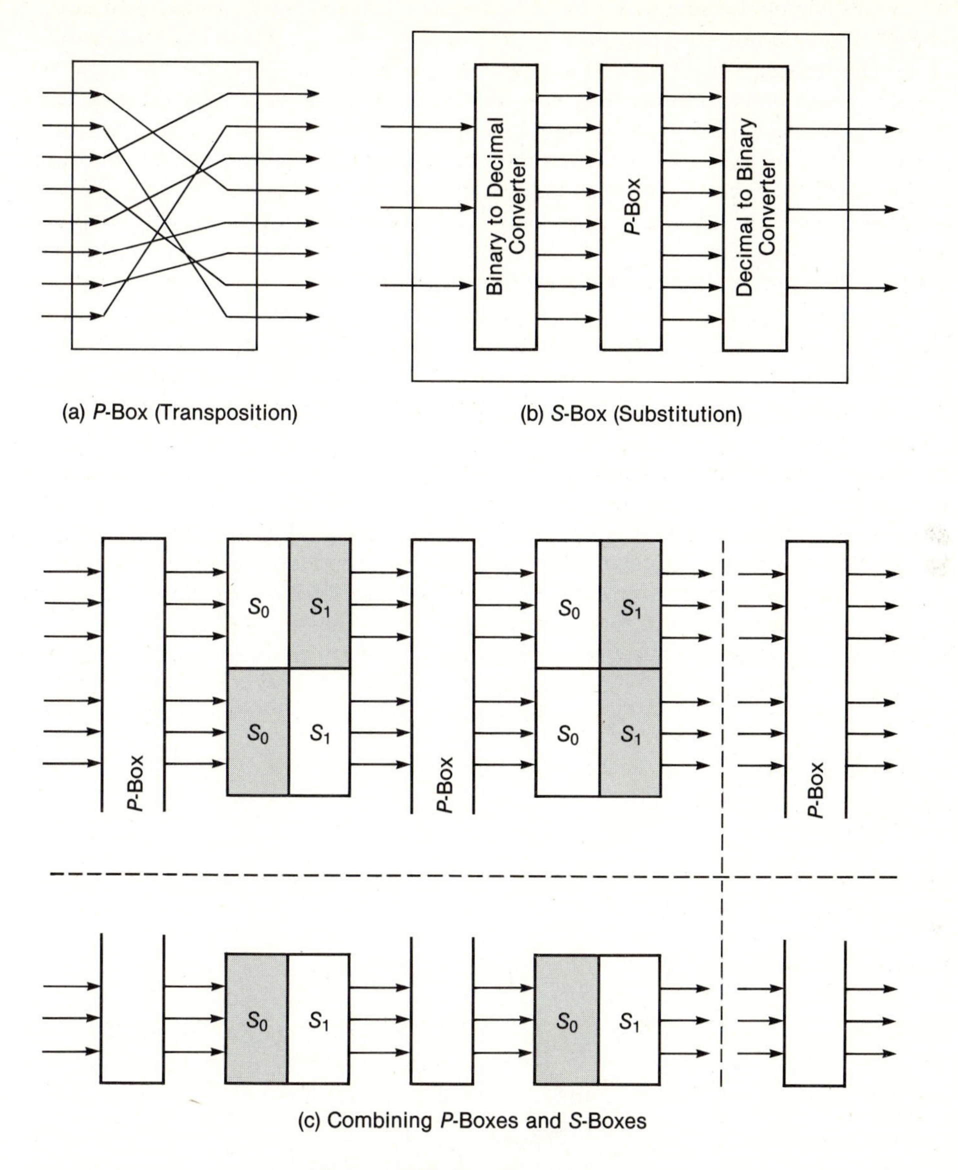

(a) *P*-Box (Transposition)

(b) *S*-Box (Substitution)

(c) Combining *P*-Boxes and *S*-Boxes

Figure 8.22 Product Ciphers

The E and the D algorithms are designed to be easily computable, but to have the property that it is computationally very difficult to invert E and find D. A function f with the property that f^{-1} is much harder to compute than f is called a *one-way function.* A moderate instance of this occurs when dealing with polynomials $y(x)$, where it is easy to compute the value of y corresponding to a value of x, but it is generally much more work to find the value(s) of x corresponding to a value of y. However, for a public-key cryptosystem, we also arrange that E and D

are *trapdoor one-way functions.* This means that with the right sort of knowledge – namely, the value of the secret key – the receiver can "push the hidden button" to spring the one-way function in the opposite direction and perform the decryption. The net result is as follows. If any other user wishes to send a secret message to user u, he simply looks up P_u in the public directory, applies the known algorithm E using the first of Eqs. 8.8, and transmits the message. Even though the algorithms D and E and the key P_u are generally known, no one but u is able to decrypt it using the second of Eqs. 8.8, since only he knows the value of S_u. Finding good trapdoor one-way functions is a challenging quest, and we will get to that issue shortly. But first, we comment about other uses of public-key directories.

A one-way function is useful in cryptography even when it doesn't have the trapdoor feature. With such a function, two users u and v can use their keys P_u and P_v in the public directory to create a private key $S_{u,v}$, and they can then use this key for any subsequent private messages, as in the discussion of the previous section. This technique also makes it possible to use DES without many of the awkward key management problems cited earlier. A candidate function of this sort is exponentiation modulo q, for q a properly chosen prime number and for α a fixed primitive element in the finite field $GF(q)$. Exponentiation has complexity $O(\lg q)$ (see Exercise 1.16), but the best known algorithm for the inverse function of finding the logarithm modulo q has complexity $O(q^{1/2})$. Each user u posts as his public key the value $P_u = \alpha^{S_u} \pmod q$, for some secret value S_u in the set $\{1, 2, \ldots, q-1\}$. Then exponentiation is all that is required for user u to compute

$$S_{u,v} = P_v^{S_u} = \alpha^{S_v S_u} \pmod q$$

and for user v to compute

$$S_{u,v} = P_u^{S_v} = \alpha^{S_u S_v} \pmod q$$

But any other user would have to employ the more costly logarithmic process in order to compute

$$S_{u,v} = P_u^{\log_\alpha P_v} \pmod q$$

As an example, if q is slightly less than 2^{200}, then exponentiation would be $O(200)$, whereas finding the logarithm would be $O(2^{100}) = O(10^{30})$ using the best known method. Further details can be found in Pohlig and Hellman [1978].

There is a more profound benefit to be derived from public-key directories, however. Secrecy is just one of a set of related requirements that occur when computer-based methods replace more conventional ones; it protects against the extraction of information. Every bit as serious is the necessity to protect against tampering with information in a message, or the forging of messages. For example, hard-copy signatures are fundamentally important for bank checks and for legal contracts. If hard-copy documents are to be replaced by electronic messages, there must be corresponding guarantees of *authenticity*, or that:

(a) a message purporting to come from user v really did originate with v, and

(b) nobody else could have performed an electronic cut-and-paste upon it.

Ingeniously, by adding to Eqs. 8.8 the condition

$$M = E(D(M,S_u),P_u) \tag{8.9}$$

for any message M, then D (as well as E) has a unique inverse in the message space. This means that both of the conditions (a) and (b) can then be validated. In order for user v to send a certified message M to user u, he first decrypts M with his S_v and then encrypts the result with u's P_u, obtaining $C = E(D(M,S_v),P_u)$. Upon receipt of C, user u first decrypts C with his S_u and then encrypts the result with v's P_v. He then has the original message; moreover, it could have come only from v, since only v has S_v. There are interesting and subtle ramifications in these matters of authentication; a much fuller discussion can be found in Simmons [1979].

In the quest for trapdoor one-way functions, an obvious place to start is with problems known to be hard to solve, such as the *NP* problems. If the process of trying to invert E to obtain D can be structured in such terms, then intuitively we may have succeeded. Since public-key systems were first described, two well-known trapdoors and a few lesser ones have been discovered. One is based upon an *NP*-complete problem, the *knapsack problem* [Merkle and Hellman 1978]. The other is based upon an *NP* problem, the factorization of large numbers, which will be described in the next section. For both methods, the process of inverting E to obtain D has seemed to be exponentially difficult, as desired. Nonetheless, there are serious pitfalls in proceeding on such bases. It is a fairly common error to infer difficulty of decipherment from the presence of a large number of possibilities. We have already seen one instance where this argument is totally without merit, in our information-theoretic analysis of simple substitution (see Section 8.4.2.1). Analogously, the arguments relating to *NP* problems are worst-case arguments, subject to much simpler exceptions. In fact, a cipher that is *NP*-complete, yet easily broken, has been demonstrated by Lempel [1979]. More recently, the knapsack trapdoor, or at least the basic variation thereof, has been broken [Shamir 1982], reinforcing the observation that it may be inappropriate to utilize arguments based upon computational complexity.

Mathematical arguments are useful in cryptography, but the ultimate demonstration is the pragmatic one that a given cipher be able to resist sustained cryptanalysis. In this regard, we always presume that the method (that is, the E and D algorithms) is completely known, and beyond that we distinguish three levels of threat by an adversary:

- *Unlimited ciphertext* attack is his minimal capability, and a cipher that cannot withstand it is worthless.
- *Known plaintext* attack (where the adversary can obtain corresponding plaintexts and ciphertexts) is harder to defend against. It is also a realistic capability, since encrypted announcements are commonly sent prior to some point in time and then disclosed at a later date. Susceptibility to this form of attack can cause substantial embarrassment or worse inconvenience to the communicants.
- *Chosen plaintext* attack can occur when the adversary is able to plant or stimulate a plaintext and then look for the appearance of the corresponding ciphertext. A cipher must be very strong to withstand this attack.

†8.4.2.2.1 The RSA System. RSA refers to a trapdoor scheme by Rivest, Shamir, and Adleman [1978]. It depends upon the fact that there are good algorithms to determine if a number is prime, but only exponential algorithms to find the actual factors of a number known not to be prime. We begin by finding two large random primes q and r, and then computing their product $n = q \times r$. The next step is to use *Euler's totient function* $\phi(n)$, which is equal to the number of integers less than n and relatively prime to n. For n a prime, $\phi(n) = n - 1$; in the present case with $n = q \times r$, $\phi(n) = (q - 1) \times (r - 1)$. The secret key is then chosen as an integer s that is simultaneously:

(a) larger than either q or r,

(b) less than $\phi(n)$, and

(c) relatively prime to $\phi(n)$.

By a variant of Euclid's algorithm for finding the GCD (greatest common divisor) of two integers, the public key p is computed as the multiplicative inverse of s modulo $\phi(n)$. Finally, both n and p are inserted in the public directory. A message is segmented into blocks M in a manner such that the value of each block can be mapped into the range $0 .. n - 1$. Then each block M is encrypted via $C = M^p \pmod n$; also, each block C is decrypted via $M = C^s \pmod n$. Exponentiations such as this are not as formidable as they might seem, since they can be computed modulo n; as already cited in the preceding section, this can be performed with complexity $O(\lg n)$.

The method is easily illustrated by an example with $q = 47$, $r = 59$, and $s = 157$. From these, we first obtain $n = 47 \times 59 = 2773$, and $\phi(n) = 46 \times 58 = 2668$. The value of p is then computed to be the inverse to s modulo 2668, or $p = 17$. In other words, $p \times s = 2669 \equiv 1$ (modulo 2668).[4] The choice of parameters conveniently allows us to use the correspondence 'ƀ'=0, 'A'=1, ... , 'Z'=26 to map two characters at a time into four digit integers in the range 0 .. 2626. For the message 'PLAY IT AGAIN SAM', the numeric blocks are then

1612 0125 0009 2000 0107 0109 1400 1901 1300

The encryption for each four digit block M is given by

$$C = M^{17} = (((M^2)^2)^2)^2 \times M \pmod{2773}$$

so that the resulting ciphertext is

1908 0164 2072 0317 2287 0170 0982 1281 0446

To decrypt the message, each block C is raised to the 157th power modulo 2773.

The validity of the RSA scheme depends upon the fact that

$$D(E(M,p),s) = M^{ps} \equiv M \text{ (modulo } n) \tag{8.10}$$

It has the nice feature that encryption and decryption really use the same, relatively simple algorithm. Although some misgivings have been expressed about its crypto-

---

4 The notation $a \equiv b$ (modulo n) states that a is *congruent* to b modulo n, meaning that $(a - b)$ is a multiple of n, or $(a - b) \bmod n = 0$.

graphic strength, it is easy to choose the primes q and r in a way that seems to guarantee a strong cipher [Rivest 1978b; Simmons and Norris 1977]. For example, it is recommended that primes q and r of 100 digits each be used; such values can be located in a few seconds on a large computer [Solovay and Strassen 1977]. Moreover, for maximum security, both $(q-1)$ and $(r-1)$ should contain large prime factors, and their GCD should be small. In summary, the cryptosecurity of an RSA cipher is related to the known difficulty of factoring large numbers, in the sense that nobody knows how to attack it except by trying to factor n as a crucial first step in finding s. This is implied security rather than demonstrated security. Recently, however, it has been shown that cryptanalysis of a variant of the RSA method is really equivalent in difficulty to factoring, and this provides increased confidence in its importance.

†8.5 PATTERN MATCHING

In Section 8.2.3 we encountered the problem of looking for a pattern string in a text string, for which we saw a solution with the function MATCH_0 (Algorithm 8.2). MATCH_0 has the disappointing worst-case characteristic of being $O(mn)$, the product of the lengths of the two strings. Indeed, until the mid-1970's, no better algorithm was known. In Section 8.5.1 we will find that several linear algorithms have since been discovered for solving this problem. The remaining sections expound on several manners in which those powerful ideas can be generalized.

†8.5.1 Substring Matching

The results of these sections sustain one of the more dramatic stories in computer science. The account begins in 1970, when Cook proved the theoretical result that if a machine known as a *2DPDA* (*two-way deterministic pushdown automaton*)[5] could recognize a string in *any* amount of time, then a random access machine could recognize the string in linear time. Intrigued by this result and aware of its relevance to the string matching problem, Knuth and Pratt tediously unravelled his proof until they found a way to do substring matching in linear time, via a technique that was independently discovered by Morris. If the Knuth-Morris-Pratt algorithm (KMP) is surprising, a slightly later algorithm by Boyer and Moore (B&M) is even more so. It matches substrings with a performance that is often sub-linear! More recently, still a third linear solution has been discovered. We will

---

[5] A 2DPDA is a machine with two tapes, one of which is read-only for input, and the other of which can be used as a stack. For the substring matching problem, the 2DPDA keeps a record of successfully matched characters using the pushdown tape; when a mismatch occurs, the values of these matched characters can be reconstructed from the pushdown tape, without rescanning that portion of the input tape.

study the KMP algorithm in detail, say something about the other methods, and then step back to evaluate the significance of the various substring matching algorithms from a practical point of view.

†8.5.1.1 The Knuth-Morris-Pratt Algorithm. It is instructive to reexamine MATCH_0 (Algorithm 8.2) and its trace in Figure 8.9. In particular, let us concentrate upon the early part of the trace, as reproduced in Figure 8.23. We are looking for an instance of the substring 'alfalalfaf'. After finding a mismatch between *pattern* [2] and *text* [2], we conceptually move the pattern one position to the right and start again, with *pattern* [1] and *text* [2]. We then find that *pattern* [1 .. 3] matches *text* [2 .. 4], but *pattern* [4] fails to match *text* [5]; so we naively restart with *pattern* [1] and *text* [3]. However, it is really not essential to reexamine *text* [3 .. 4]. We already know what they are; they must, from the previous comparisons, correspond to *pattern* [2 .. 3]. Moreover, in this particular case, *pattern* [4] ('a') matches *pattern* [1], but no other positions *pattern* [2 .. 3], so that *pattern* [1] therefore matches no positions *text* [3 .. 5]. More generally, we can conclude that if:

(i) we have a partial match of $k - 1$ characters ending at *text* [$j - 1$], as in

$$pattern\,[1\,..\,k-1] = text\,[j-k+1\,..\,j-1]$$

(ii) *pattern* [k] fails to match *text* [j], and

(iii) *pattern* [k] matches *pattern* [1] but no intermediate characters in the pattern,

then *pattern* [1] cannot occur anywhere in *text* [$j - k + 1 .. j - 1$]. So we can conceptually slide the pattern all the way past *text* [$j - 1$].

1	2	3	4	5	6	7	8	9	0	1	2	3	4	5	...
a	a	l	f	l	a	l	f	a	l	a	l	f	a	l	...
a	l														
	a	l	f	a											
		a													
			a												
				a											
					a	l	f	a	l	a	l	f	a	f	

Figure 8.23 Partial Trace of Algorithm MATCH_0

This is helpful in some cases, but we need to deal with situations that are more general yet, as when *pattern* [k] occurs in *pattern* [$2 .. k - 1$], which means that it also occurs in *text* [$j - k + 2 .. j - 1$]. We will do this by finding a vector *next* [1 .. m] of displacements such that, upon a mismatch at *pattern* [k], we can use *next* [k] to direct the amount by which we should slide the pattern. Let us defer for a moment the issue of how such a vector can be computed, and follow the consequences of having it available. We are led to the function MATCH_1 (Algorithm 8.5), rather similar in form to MATCH_0, but with an important difference. Now, upon an unsuccessful comparison, we do not backup the index j and reset the index

```
function MATCH_1 (pattern,text: string): extent;

label   1;

type    offset = array [1 .. maxstring] of extent;

var     j,k: extent;
        next: offset;

begin
   SCAN_1 (pattern,next);  {generate next from pattern}
   j := 1;  k := 1;
   repeat
      if text.data [j] = pattern.data [k] then begin
         j := j + 1;
         k := k + 1;
      end else
         if next [k] > 0 then
            k := next [k]
         else if j + pattern.size > text.size then
            goto 1
         else begin
            j := j + 1;
            k := 1;
         end;
   until (j > text.size) or (k > pattern.size);
1: if k > pattern.size then MATCH_1 := j - pattern.size
                        else MATCH_1 := 0;
end;
```

Algorithm 8.5 MATCH_1

k to one; rather we reset k to *next* $[k]$, and j is *never decremented.* This last point is important when dealing with a text file that is too large to fit in main memory, so that it is being accessed via buffers, which could make backup very awkward.

The operation of MATCH_1 is illustrated in Figure 8.24, where (a) displays the value of the vector *next*, and (b) traces the comparisons that are performed. In the vector *next*, a value of zero signifies that comparisons should resume with *text* $[j+1]$ and *pattern* $[1]$. A non-zero value specifies that comparisons should resume with *text* $[j]$ and *pattern* $[next\ [k]]$. The underlined values in (b) of the figure do not correspond to comparisons. They represent places where comparisons have been avoided, by virtue of knowing from previous successful comparisons what the corresponding text values must be. Note that the amount of shift upon a mismatch is given by $k - next\ [k]$; for example, $4 - 0 = 4$ for $j = 5$, $6 - 3 = 3$ for $j = 16$, etc. It is straightforward to demonstrate that MATCH_1 has complexity $O(n)$. We add one to the index variable k a maximum of n times, and we sometimes decrement it, but it always stays positive. Therefore, the maximum number of iterations is bounded by $2n$.

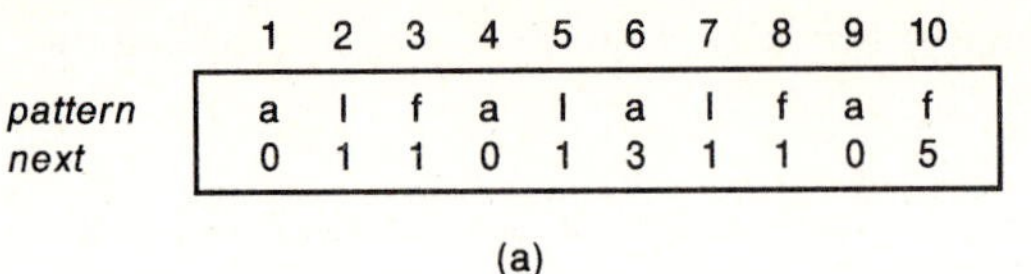

	1	2	3	4	5	6	7	8	9	10
pattern	a	l	f	a	l	a	l	f	a	f
next	0	1	1	0	1	3	1	1	0	5

(a)

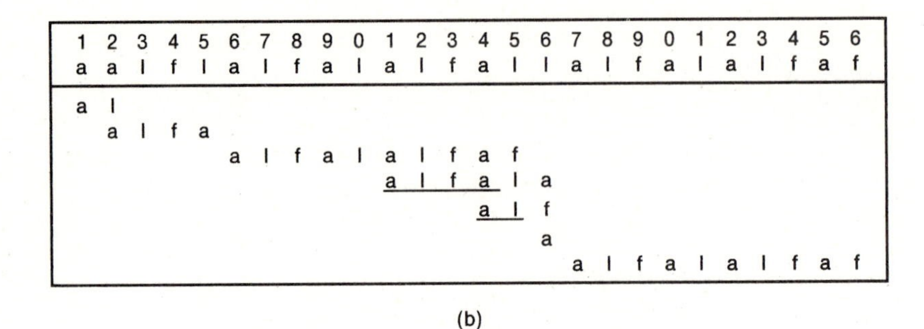

(b)

Figure 8.24 Trace of Algorithm MATCH_1

Examination of Figure 8.24(b) helps us to decide what we need to compute for the vector *next*. When there has been a partial match of $k-1$ characters ending at *text* $[j-1]$, as in

$$pattern\ [1 \mathinner{..} k-1] = text\ [j-k+1 \mathinner{..} j-1]$$

but such that *pattern* $[k] <> text\ [j]$, then we wish to find the largest prefix of *pattern* $[1 \mathinner{..} k-1]$ that matches a suffix of it, and thus also matches some of *text* preceding the cursor j. In other words, we seek the largest $i < k$ such that

$$pattern\ [1 \mathinner{..} i-1] = pattern\ [k-i+1 \mathinner{..} k-1]$$

This means that we need to compare the pattern against itself, in much the same manner as we compared the pattern against the text. It is instructive to retain in another vector *fail* $[1 \mathinner{..} m]$ the values of i just described, with *fail* $[1] = 0$, by definition. For our sample pattern 'alfalalfaf', the values are as shown in Figure 8.25. Thus, *fail* $[9] = 4$ indicates that *pattern* $[1 \mathinner{..} 3] =$ *pattern* $[6 \mathinner{..} 8]$.

	1	2	3	4	5	6	7	8	9	10
pattern	a	l	f	a	l	a	l	f	a	f
fail	0	1	1	1	2	3	2	3	4	5
next	0	1	1	0	1	3	1	1	0	5

Figure 8.25 SCAN Computation for 'alfalalfaf'

Having *fail* $[k]$ and *next* $[k]$, we can compute *fail* $[k+1]$ by the following argument. If *pattern* $[k]$ matches *pattern* $[fail\ [k]]$, then *fail* $[k+1] =$ *fail* $[k] + 1$;

```
procedure SCAN_1 (pattern: string; var next: offset);

var     i,t: extent;
        fail: offset;

begin
  i := 1; t := 0;
  fail [1] := 0;
  next [1] := 0;
  with pattern do
    repeat
      while (t > 0) and (data [i] <> data [t]) do
        t := next [t];
      i := i + 1;
      t := t + 1;
      fail [i] := t;
      if data [i] = data [t] then next [i] := next [t]
                             else next [i] := t;
    until i >= size;
end;
```

Algorithm 8.6 SCAN_1

that is, we have extended the match by one character, as in the case $k = 9$. If *pattern* [k] fails to match *pattern* [*fail* [k]], then we need to try $t = next\,[k]$, or *next* [*next* [k]], or .... In other words, we slide the pattern against itself until we find *pattern* [k] = *pattern* [t]. For example, with $k = 6$ the search within the pattern proceeds to the point that

$$pattern\,[6] = pattern\,[next\,[next\,[6]]] = pattern\,[next\,[3]] = pattern\,[1]$$

The corresponding value of t then determines the next entry in *fail*, by means of $fail\,[k + 1] = t + 1$. Thus, for $k = 6$, we have $fail\,[6 + 1] = 1 + 1$. Moreover, as soon as we find $fail\,[k + 1] = t + 1$, then we also know how to compute $next\,[k + 1]$. Namely, if $pattern\,[t + 1] = pattern\,[k + 1]$, the character in the $(t + 1)$th position must lead to a mismatch, since the character in the $(k + 1)$th position did; in this case, then, we must use a shorter prefix. Otherwise, we can use $next\,[k + 1] = t + 1$.

The logic for computing the vectors *fail* and *scan* is given in the procedure SCAN_1 (Algorithm 8.6).[6] Note that the vector *fail* is never accessed and is not explicitly needed; it is present solely for edification. SCAN_1 can be seen to be

---

[6] Actually, there is a subtle bug in SCAN_1. What happens when $t = 0$, and reference is made to *data* [t] in testing the **while** condition? (Compare the discussion of the algorithm EQUIV in Section 4.2.1.) Happily, a great many Pascal compilers bypass the second test when the first one fails, so that this scenario never occurs. Where this is not the case, a clumsy circumlocution is required.

$O(m)$ by a similar argument to that used with MATCH_1. Specifically, the variable t is incremented by one at most m times, is sometimes decremented, and never goes negative.

MATCH_1 and SCAN_1 constitute the KMP algorithm [Knuth et al. 1977]. The pragmatic value of this method will be addressed in the next section. However, note that the presentation here is designed to stress comprehensibility rather than efficiency. Some refinements that can be added to emphasize efficiency over comprehensibility are:

- inserting special code to speed up the common case of finding a mismatch at the first position of the pattern;
- employing sentinel characters at the ends of the pattern and the text, in order to reduce the overhead in the compound test for termination of the **repeat** loop.

†8.5.1.2 State-of-the-Art of Substring Matching. We usually think of substring matching in terms of aligning the pattern against the left end of the text, comparing characters from left to right, and sliding the pattern to the right on mismatches. Suppose, instead, that we align the pattern against the left end of the text, as before, but then compare characters from right to left. On a mismatch, we still shift the pattern right, but we can now employ other information as well. Specifically, if the character *text* [j] that caused the mismatch does not occur *anywhere* in *pattern*, then we can effectively slide *pattern* all the way past *text* [j], and resume our right-to-left comparison scheme with *pattern* [m] and *text* [$j + m$]. In general, whenever there is a mismatch and the corresponding text character does not occur in the pattern, we can then completely ignore some number of characters in the text. There are several components to the Boyer-Moore (B&M) substring matching algorithm [1977], but what we have just described is the most important one. In the most favorable situation, if we find a mismatch between the last position of the pattern and a position of the text on every comparison, it may take just n/m comparisons to determine that there is no substring match!

Just as with the KMP algorithm, we evidently need a table that tells how much to shift the pattern when a mismatch occurs. In fact, the B&M algorithm employs two tables, *Delta_*1 and *Delta_*2. *Delta_*1 requires one entry for each symbol in the alphabet being employed, with *Delta_*1 [*char*] equal to m if *char* does not occur in *pattern* and otherwise equal to $m - i$, for the largest i such that *char* = *pattern* [i]. *Delta_*2 is very similar to the table *next* in the KMP algorithm, except that it is computed from the right of the pattern instead of the left. It serves the same purpose of precluding $O(mn)$ comparisons should the pattern happen to be highly repetitive (and should *Delta_*1 happen to be ineffectual). With these two tables in hand, the Boyer-Moore algorithm resembles the Knuth-Morris-Pratt algorithm, with the following principal differences:

- On a match, the indices j and k step downward rather than upward.
- On a mismatch, the pattern index k is reset to m, and the text index j is incremented by the greater of *Delta_*1 [*text* [j]] and *Delta_*2 [k].

Thus, suppose that we had *text* = 'pepper nutmeg onion tarragon', and *pattern* = 'tarragon'. Then the *Delta_*1 values for 'a,g,n,o,r,t' would be 3,2,0,1,4,7; and all other *Delta_*1 values would be 8. A trace of the comparisons that would be performed is shown in Figure 8.26, with the periods indicating omitted comparisons. On the first two mismatches, the shift would be determined by *Delta*_1 ['b̸'] = 8, and on the third mismatch by *Delta*_1 ['r'] = 4.

1	2	3	4	5	6	7	8	9	0	1	2	3	4	5	6	7	8	9	0	1	2	3	4	5	6	7	8
p	e	p	p	e	r		n	u	t	m	e	g		o	n	i	o	n		t	a	r	r	a	g	o	n
.	.	.	.	.	.	o	n																				
								.	.	.	.	.	g	o	n												
																.	.	.	.	.	.	.	n				
																				t	a	r	r	a	g	o	n

Figure 8.26 Trace of Boyer-Moore Algorithm

The relative importance of *Delta*_1 and *Delta*_2 depends primarily upon the size of the alphabet in use. With a binary alphabet, it is very unlikely that *Delta*_1 will discriminate very effectively (although this can be overcome by comparing blocks of bits rather than single bits); on the other hand, for a large alphabet such as ASCII or EBCDIC, the work to initialize *Delta*_1 will not be trivial. How good is the B&M algorithm? Although its average behavior is sub-linear, typically requiring just one comparison for every four text characters, its worst case complexity is still $O(n)$. However, we should not be too disappointed, since the worst-case behavior for any string matching algorithm must be $O(n)$ [Rivest 1977].

What can be said about the practical significance of the KMP and B&M algorithms? Drawing upon several different studies [§], we can conclude:

- Most patterns are such that an unsophisticated algorithm like MATCH_0 will detect a mismatch, for a given alignment of the pattern and the text, in just slightly more than one comparison. In the average case, the KMP algorithm may not do much better.
- If the pattern is small, then the overhead of preprocessing it to generate the tables causes these sophisticated techniques to be less efficient than a naive method. This is especially true with the B&M algorithm.
- The previous remark applies also in the case that the penetration (how far into the text the search proceeds) is not large.
- For a small alphabet, KMP may perform significantly better than B&M.
- For B&M the table *Delta*_1 is much easier to compute than *Delta*_2, and it is also far more effective in reducing the number of comparisons with typical text. Thus, it is reasonable to implement B&M using just *Delta*_1, if we are not concerned about worst-case possibilities.
- If the pattern is not too small (that is, $m \geq 5$) and if the alphabet is reasonable in size, then B&M is superior to any other method.

This does not exhaust all the possibilities for substring matching. There are other methods, including another linear one, but they are based upon hashing, and so we must defer their description until Section 10.4.4.

†8.5.2 Finite State Machines

At this juncture, we need to revert to a subject that was postponed when we studied graphs. The labeled digraph of Figure 8.27(a) is called a *transition diagram*; its most common use is to represent a *Finite State Machine* (*FSM*), wherein the nodes represent *states* and the arcs represent *transitions* between states in response to possible values of input. Each arc is labeled with the input value causing that transition, and each node is labeled with the value of the output for that state.[7] Thus, if this FSM is in state 3 and the input 'b' is seen, then it will go to state 1 and output '0'. Formally, an FSM is characterized by a quintuple $(I, S, O, \delta, \lambda)$, where:

I is a set of symbols from an input alphabet;
S is a set of machine states;
O is a set of symbols from an output alphabet;
δ is a mapping from $S \times I$ to S;
λ is a mapping from S to O.

In other words, δ determines the next state as a function of the current state and the input symbol, and λ determines the output symbol (possibly null) as a function of the input symbol. Examples of FSM's from everyday life are elevators and vending machines; each of them reacts in accordance with a set of internal states and a set of external stimuli. Note that the amount of memory that such a device can have of past events is limited by the finiteness of its set of states.

A special variant of an FSM is a *Finite Automaton* (*FA*), which is characterized by a slightly different quintuple $(I, S, S0, \delta, F)$, where:

I is a set of symbols from an input alphabet;
S is a set of machine states;
$S0$ is a distinguished initial state;
δ is a mapping from $S \times I$ to S;
F is a set of final, or *accepting*, states.

The main difference is that whereas an FSM produces various outputs, an FA simply has a set of final states $F \subseteq S$. The principal role of an FA is to decide, via the finite sense of history implied by its state transitions, whether a given input sequence meets certain criteria. Thus, an FA does have a limited form of output, namely "accept" or "reject." An example of an FA is shown in Figure 8.27(b). Starting in state $S0$, and in response to a binary input string, this FA will be in state $S3$ whenever the last three symbols in the input are '101' (that is, if the numeric value is divisible by 5). It is customary, as in the figure, to denote final states by double circles.

In fact, the distinction between FSM and FA is often blurred, depending mostly upon the context of their application. In the present instance, the notion of an FA can appreciably increase our understanding of the KMP substring matching algo-

---

[7] What we are describing is a *Moore machine*, where the output is a function of just the current state. In a *Mealy machine*, the output is a function of the input symbol and the current state. The difference is not significant, since either one can be modelled in terms of the other.

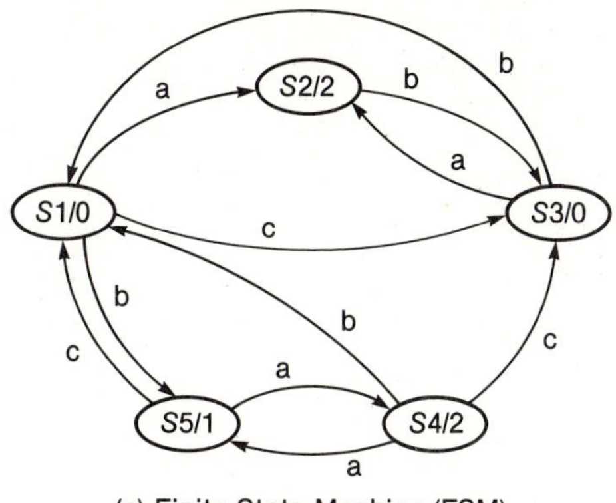

(a) Finite State Machine (FSM)

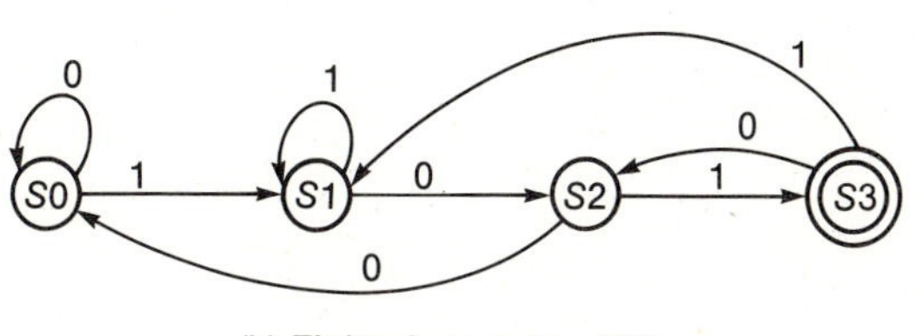

(b) Finite Automaton (FA)

Figure 8.27 FSM and FA

rithm. To see this, consider the machine shown in Figure 8.28. This FA is atypical in that it has precisely two transitions for every input character. If the input corresponds to the desired character, the machine goes to the succeeding state and reads the next input; if the input fails, the machine goes to the designated failure state (dashed lines) with the *same* input. The failure transitions do not have to be labeled, since they correspond to the negations of the successful transitions. State *S*0 is special in that it makes the transition to *S*1 with the next input in all cases. What process does this machine represent? It corresponds to our example of 'alfalalfaf' from Figure 8.25! In other words, the action of SCAN_1 is to construct an FA, as represented by the table *next*, which MATCH_1 then interprets to decide if there is a match. This pictorial representation helps us understand how to construct the ultimate optimization of the KMP algorithm, by having the preprocessing function generate in-line code rather than the vector *next*. In other words, we can just as well "hardwire" the effect of *next* rather than interpret its values. Figure 8.29 shows the code that does this.

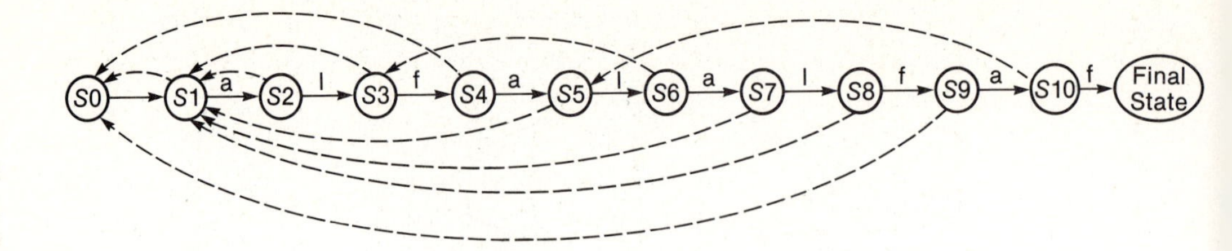

Figure 8.28 FSM for 'alfalalfaf'

```
S0: j := j + 1;
S1: if text [j]  <> 'a' then goto S0;
    j := j + 1;
S2: if text [j]  <> 'l' then goto S1;
    j := j + 1;
S3: if text [j]  <> 'f' then goto S1;
    j := j + 1;
S4: if text [j]  <> 'a' then goto S0;
    j := j + 1;
S5: if text [j]  <> 'l' then goto S1;
    j := j + 1;
S6: if text [j]  <> 'a' then goto S3;
    j := j + 1;
S7: if text [j]  <> 'l' then goto S1;
    j := j + 1;
S8: if text [j]  <> 'f' then goto S1;
    j := j + 1;
S9: if text [j]  <> 'a' then goto S0;
    j := j + 1;
S10: if text [j] <> 'f' then goto S5;
    j := j + 1;
{final state: pattern matched in text}
```

Figure 8.29 In-line Code for 'alfalalfaf'

†8.5.3 Generalizations of Substring Matching

From the discussion of Section 8.5.1.2, it might be concluded that the Knuth-Morris-Pratt algorithm has relatively little practical utility. But such is not the case; it is a paradigm for many generalizations of the matching problem [§] (see also Exercise 8.23). We will now illustrate a particularly useful one, that of finding all occurrences of a fixed set of patterns in a text string. For depicting this process, the notion of an FA is no longer ancillary; it is central.

Suppose that we have a set of words or phrases, and that we wish to find all occurrences of any them in some text. This is a typical requirement in applications involving information retrieval or text editing. We could look for each of these patterns in turn, employing the insights of Section 8.5.1; however, by constructing an appropriate FSM, we can look for them all in parallel, with considerable savings in time. Thus, suppose that our set of words is {'chin', 'ice', 'itch', 'with'}. The essential aspects of such a machine are described by the transition diagram in Figure 8.30. For each state, there are one or more labeled successful transitions, and one unlabeled failure transition (dashed lines). In the figure, we have shown only those failure transitions that do not return to *S*0; the others, returning to *S*0, are implicit. As in the case of Figure 8.28, successful transitions call for the next input character, and failure transitions (except in the case of *S*0) employ the same input character. The provision of failure transitions from the leaves of this tree-like structure reflects the desire to find all occurrences of patterns in the text, even when they overlap.

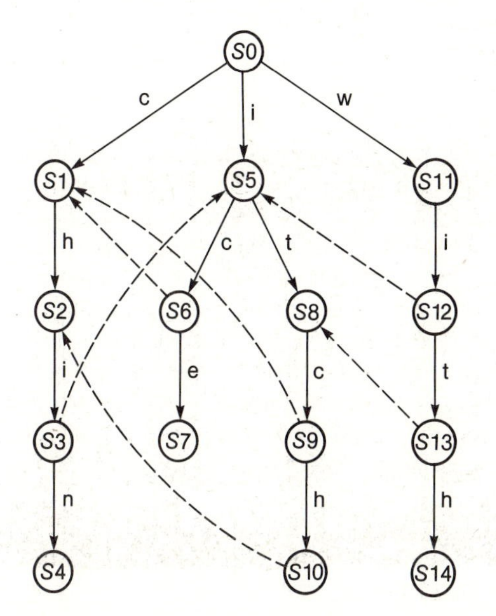

Figure 8.30 FSM for {'chin', 'ice', 'itch', 'with'}

The algorithm to search a text string, using this FSM, is very similar to MATCH_1. A successful comparison of a text position against a state advances the text pointer and the state, as indicated in the transition diagram. In the case of an unsuccessful comparison, a failure state is selected, according to Figure 8.31(a), and the comparison cycle is repeated. Whenever a successful comparison leads to one of the final states {4, 7, 10, 14}, an appropriate output message is generated and the failure transition is made. Thus, in applying this FSM to the input text 'witching', the state transitions would be as shown in Figure 8.31(b), where horizontal progression corresponds to successful transitions and vertical progression to failure transitions, and where underlined transitions would generate output.

state	0	1	2	3	4	5	6	7	8	9	10	11	12	13	14
transition	0	0	0	5	0	0	1	0	0	1	2	0	5	8	0

(a) Failure Transitions

w	i	t	c	h	i	n	g
11	12	13					
		8	9	<u>10</u>			
				2	3	<u>4</u>	
						0	0

(b) Trace of State Transitions

Figure 8.31 Parallel Pattern Search

Of course, there is a glaring omission in the preceding discussion. Given a fixed set of patterns, how do we construct the corresponding FSM? More precisely, it is rather easy to see how to perform the construction by hand, but what is the algorithm for a machine to do it? Not surprisingly, such an algorithm is reminiscent of SCAN_1 in many ways, although the details are different. In SCAN_1, we computed later values of *fail* [*i*] and *next* [*i*] in terms of earlier values of *next* [*i*]. In this case, noting that the successful transitions form a tree, we would compute the failure transitions first for nodes at distance 1 from *S*0 in this tree, then at distance 2, etc. An important question is just how much effort is required for this computation; it can be shown that the complexity is linear in the sum of the lengths of the patterns. In a large application involving bibliographic retrieval, the cost of searching in this manner was found to be approximately independent of the number of keywords specified, and the overall search was speeded up by a factor of 5 to 10 over that of previous methods [Aho and Corasick 1975].

†8.5.4 Suffix Trees

In the preceding sections, we have seen how to improve the efficiency of matching patterns against a text string by preprocessing the patterns. With text editing, for example, this is an appropriate strategy. However, there are other applications in which efficiency is derived by preprocessing the text rather than the patterns. This can be accomplished fairly efficiently with *suffix trees*, which effectively provide indices into a text string *S* [McCreight 1976; Weiner 1973]. In this structure, we must impose the condition that the final character of *S* does not occur anywhere else in *S*. This is easily handled by placing a sentinel value at the end of *S*; thus *S* ='ababc' becomes *S*='ababc$'. In the suffix tree, each edge corresponds to a substring, and each leaf corresponds to the index of the last occurrence of the suffix spelled out by the edges leading to that leaf. The suffix tree for our example *S* is shown in Figure 8.32(a). We see, for instance, that 'ab' occurs twice; one time it is part of 'ababc' starting in the first position, and the other time it is part of 'abc' starting in the third position. As a practical matter, we do not need to store the substrings with the edges; rather we store S once, and then place in each node V a pair of indices. These indices delineate that portion of S corresponding to the in-edge of V (compare Figures 8.4 and 8.7), as shown in Figure 8.32(b) for the suffix tree in (a) of the figure.

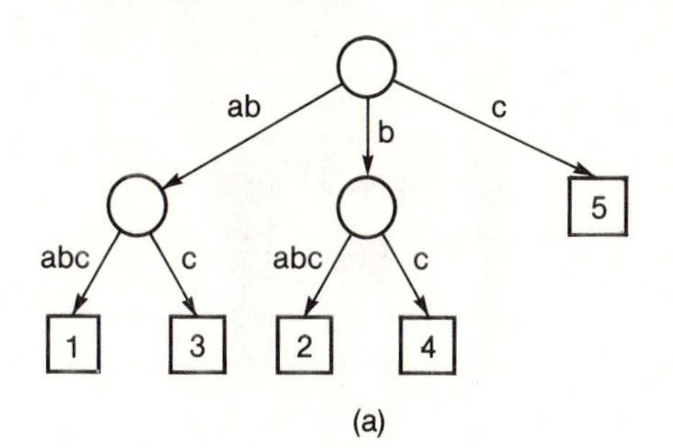

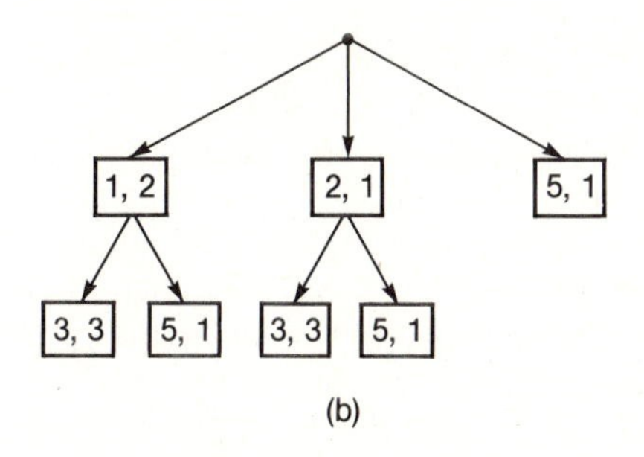

Figure 8.32 Suffix Tree for 'ababc'

With suffix trees, it is possible to efficiently answer questions such as:

- What are all the occurrences of a pattern in a text?
- What is the longest repeated substring in a string?
- What is the longest string that occurs as a substring in two other strings?

Suffix trees can also be used to implement the dynamic dictionary used for universal data compression, as cited in Section 8.4.1 [Rodeh et al. 1981]. Algorithms for the construction of suffix trees are linear in the length of the text string, and substring searches are then linear in the length of the pattern; however, both time and space requirements grow with the size of the alphabet.

8.6 LANGUAGES

The most important purpose of strings, as indicated earlier, is to convey meaning. But meaning depends upon understanding, which brings us to the problem of recognizing a sentence in a language. This recognition really has two parts:

Syntax – Does the given sentence have a valid structure to be meaningful?

Semantics – Can a meaningful interpretation be supplied to the parts of the sentence that have been perceived syntactically?

As an example of this distinction, the sentence "The pencil's purple concepts snored pungently" is impeccable by syntactic standards; but it is nonetheless gibberish when we try to supply semantics. We will not be concerned with semantic issues here; rather, we will demonstrate how the pattern matching ideas of Section 8.5 can be generalized to deal with broader and broader problems of syntactic pattern recognition. Many of these ideas were originally motivated by the study of natural language. Subsequently, it has been found that natural language is only moderately amenable to analysis by these methods. However, the same techniques have been enormously useful for the study of computer languages. Our objective here is merely to show the forest of these activities. It is an extremely dense forest, with perhaps the most extensive theoretical foundation of any in computer science. For extensive details, you may wish to consult Hopcroft and Ullman [1979].

Our first concern is to communicate an appreciation of the mechanisms by which languages can be specified. We will then consider a concrete example of the recognition process for a restricted but important class of languages. After some general discussion about recognition in less restricted classes of languages, we will conclude with some comments concerning the inherent power of expressing computation in terms of string operations.

8.6.1 Grammars

To begin with, a *language* L is simply a set of *sentences*, or strings over some alphabet of symbols. It is perfectly possible for L to be a finite set; however, most languages of interest are infinite sets. A very useful way of specifying a language is by finding a *grammar* G, or set of rules, that characterizes it. We had a glimpse of this previously, when we discussed BNF in Chapter 5. One of the significant features of BNF is that it easily allows the definition of an infinite set of sentences, via recursion.

Given some grammar G, we can use it derive in a systematic fashion all the legal sentences in $L(G)$, the language defined by the grammar. A harder problem is to take a language L and find a grammar G that specifies L and all of L and nothing but L. Although this can often be done, the answer may not be unique; there may be several grammars that generate the same language. Another problem, harder than simply enumerating all the sentences of a grammar, is that of recognizing whether a given string α is in $L(G)$ (without simply searching for α in all of $L(G)$, of course). This latter issue is our principal concern.

At this point, it is useful to compare the discussion of BNF in Section 5.4.1 with the discussion of logical operations on strings in Section 8.1. As you can see, applying a production is simply a matter of performing a string substitution: Given a sentence $\alpha\mu\beta$, we can transform it to $\alpha\nu\beta$ whenever there is a production $\mu \rightarrow \nu$. The BNF grammar for a language must always have a distinguished non-terminal symbol from which any derivation of a sentence starts. We then apply productions, obtaining for a time mixtures of non-terminal and terminal symbols, and eventually winding up exclusively with terminals – that is, a sentence in $L(G)$. Although finite languages may be of limited value, they have some charming uses. The familiar instance shown in Figure 8.33(a) serves as a vehicle for illustrating the substitution process. Starting from <sentence> we can derive a variety of actual sentences. One such is illustrated in Figure 8.33(b), where we apply successively the productions 1, 2, 5, 6, 3, 4, 7, 2, 5, 6.

```
1. <sentence>     ::= <noun phrase> <predicate>
2. <noun phrase>  ::= <noun> | <article> <noun>
3. <predicate>    ::= <verb phrase> | <verb phrase> <noun phrase>
4. <verb phrase>  ::= <verb> | <verb> <adverb>
5. <article>      ::= a | the
6. <noun>         ::= farmer | wife | child | nurse | dog | cat | rat | cheese
7. <verb>         ::= takes | leaves | stands
8. <adverb>       ::= alone
```

(a) BNF for "Farmer in the Dell"

```
<sentence> → <noun phrase> <predicate>
           → <article> <noun> <predicate>
           → the <noun> <predicate>
           → the farmer <predicate>
           → the farmer <verb phrase> <noun phrase>
           → the farmer <verb> <noun phrase>
           → the farmer takes <noun phrase>
           → the farmer takes <article> <noun>
           → the farmer takes a <noun>
           → the farmer takes a wife
```

(b) Derivation Using BNF of (a)

Figure 8.33 A Familiar Finite Language

We are now ready to make some crucial distinctions. What kinds of string substitutions does our grammar specify in its productions; that is, how general in nature are they? A pioneering classification by Chomsky [1959] recognizes four progressively more restricted types of substitution rules, or classes of grammars:

- *Type 0 grammars*, or *phrase-structure grammars*, allow the substitution $\alpha\mu\beta \rightarrow \alpha\nu\beta$ whenever $\mu \rightarrow \nu$ is a production.
- *Type 1 grammars*, or *context-sensitive grammars*, impose the restriction that the length of ν cannot be less than that of μ.
- *Type 2 grammars*, or *context-free grammars*, impose the additional restriction that the left hand side of any production must consist of a single non-terminal symbol. In other words, the applicability of a production does not depend upon particular contexts α and β in which μ occurs.

- *Type 3 grammars*, or *regular grammars*, impose one of the additional restrictions: (a) the right hand side of any production must have the form t or tV, or (b) the right hand side of any production must have the form t or Vt, where t is a terminal symbol and V is a non-terminal symbol.

Corresponding to each class of grammars is a class of languages; thus, we speak of context-sensitive languages (CSL), context-free languages (CFL), and regular languages. Intuitively (and provably) regular languages are properly contained in context-free languages, context-free languages are properly contained in context-sensitive languages, and context-sensitive languages are properly contained in those derived from phrase-structure grammars.

The example in Figure 8.33(a) is a context-free grammar, and we illustrated its use in the derivation of a sentence in Figure 8.33(b). Recall, however, that we are more concerned about recognizing a given sentence as part of $L(G)$ than we are about generating sentences. How is this done? In short, one must be able to deduce from the sentence itself an appropriate sequence of productions that leads from the start symbol to that sentence. This can be tricky, and the difficulty increases enormously as we proceed up the hierarchy from Type 3 to Type 0. In the next section we show how it can be done for regular languages, and in the subsequent section we comment upon the more difficult cases.

†8.6.2 Recognizing Regular Expressions

In Section 8.5 we saw how to recognize fixed patterns or even fixed sets of patterns in a text string. We now wish to recognize variable patterns, as specified by some grammar. For some significant applications, the amount of variability provided by a regular grammar is sufficient. The sentences that can be defined by regular grammars are called *regular expressions* (*R.E.'s*), and they have a comparatively simple structure. For an alphabet I, any symbol $x \in I$ is a regular expression, and further expressions can be composed recursively by the following operations:

Concatenation – If α and β are regular expressions, then so is $\alpha\beta$, or writing α followed by β.

Union – If α and β are regular expressions, then so is $\alpha + \beta$, by which is meant writing either α or writing β.

Closure – If α is a regular expression, then so is α^*, which signifies writing any number of instances (possibly none at all) of α.

It is useful to relate these three operations to familiar ones of ordinary arithmetic, as follows:

regular expressions	arithmetic
union	addition
concatenation	multiplication
closure	exponentiation

This analogy is especially useful because the relative precedence is the same in both columns. Thus, the regular expression '((A+BC)* B+AC)A' denotes (((any number of 'A' or 'BC') followed by 'B') or 'AC') followed by 'A'. Some particular sentences that correspond to this specification are 'BA', 'ABCABA', 'ACA', etc.

We could have defined the same language by means of BNF, as in:

```
<expression> ::= <α> A
<α>          ::= <β> B | A C
<β>          ::= ε | <β> <γ>
<γ>          ::= A | B C
```

where ε denotes the empty string. However, the simpler notation makes it possible to specify a regular expression in one short phrase. Such conciseness is useful, for instance, in specifying a pattern that a text editor should look for. In any event, we now know of two ways to specify a regular language, but how can we recognize one? Finite state machines again provide the answer. In this case, to recognize an expression of the form '((A+BC)* B+AC)A', we need the machine shown in Figure 8.34. It is different from those we have seen before, in that it has no failure transitions; however, it does have ε-transitions, which are transitions that can occur without any input! The reason for this is that we have to deal with a nondeterministic situation. Both the union and the closure operators allow for alternate paths to the final state; the ε-transitions provide the mechanism whereby we can pursue these alternate paths in parallel in order not to miss a valid expression.

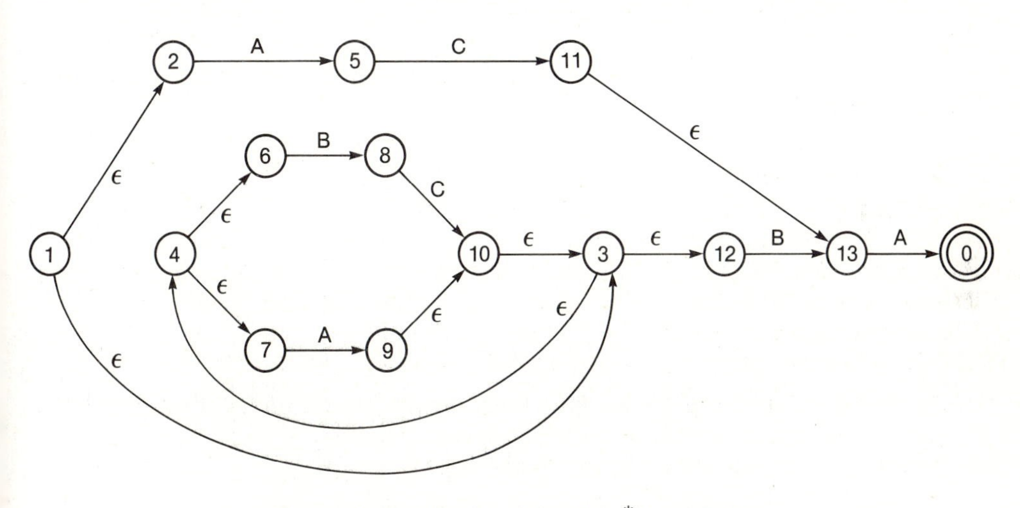

Figure 8.34 NFA for '((A+BC)*B+AC)A'

In fact, the machine in Figure 8.34 is an example of a *Nondeterministic Finite Automaton* (*NFA*). Such machines have one or both of the characteristics:

- There are ε-transitions.
- The transition labels for some nodes are not distinct, so that the same input symbol may evoke transitions to any of several other states.

Remarkably, although an NFA seems to be "more" than an FA, it really is not; there is a straightforward procedure, given an NFA, to construct an equivalent FA. This procedure entails two steps:

1. The ε-transitions are eliminated by constructing the ε-closure – that is, by taking the transitive closure of the transition diagram under the ε's.
2. An FA is generated whose states are the powerset of the states of the NFA. If the NFA has n states, then the equivalent FA could have 2^n states, of course, but the actual number is very often much less.

The construction just described is significant because it shows that there are two distinct strategies that we could employ to build a regular expression recognizer:

- We already know how to build an interpreter for an FA; so we could (i) do the construction, and then (ii) build such an interpreter.
- We could build an interpreter for the NFA.

Now constructing the FA from the NFA is straightforward, but it can be costly, so that the first route makes sense only when the resulting FA will be used many times. When the FA will be used only a few times the second route is better, and that is the method that we will use here. Also, this will allow us to demonstrate some techniques that are much more instructive than the details of building the FA from the NFA.

We begin by considering Figure 8.34 again. It appears that there is some arbitrariness about the use of ε-transitions, and that some of them might have been omitted. Toward the end of this section, we will comment on how we obtained this diagram from the regular expression '((A+BC)* B+AC)A', and why it has the form that it does. Our interpreter will examine the text string without ever backing up; for each input character X, we will build a set S_i of states, where each S_i is obtained from S_{i-1} in two stages:

1. The initial value of S_i is computed as those states of the NFA that we can transit to from states in S_{i-1}, according to the value of X.
2. The final value of S_i is computed as the ε-closure of the initial value of S_i.

This sounds rather complicated, but a clever choice of data structure leads to a fairly simple algorithm, as you will soon see. We will use a deque, more precisely an output-restricted deque. Relative to a given input character X, we will remove and examine each of the states $u \in S_i$ in the left end of the deque:

(a) if u is a final state, we have found a regular expression;

(b) if X causes a non-ε-transition from u to another state v, we insert v in the right end of the deque, as part of the initial value of S_{i+1};

(c) if u is a state with one ε-transition v (or two ε-transitions v and w), we insert it (them) in the left end of the deque, as part of the ε-closure of S_i.

By this process, we are both adding to and subtracting from the final value of S_i on the left, until ultimately it has disappeared, leaving just the initial value of S_{i+1} on the right. One other thing is necessary – that we keep the growing and shrinking value of S_i separate from the growing value of S_{i+1}. This can be accomplished by putting a special marker value between them in the deque. When we remove a value from the left end of the deque and find that it is the marker, then we know that S_i is exhausted; so we are ready to work with the next text character and the initial value of S_{i+1}; but first we reinsert the marker at the right end to keep S_{i+1} separate from S_{i+2}.

Having fixed the nature of the interpreter, we also need to fix the nature of the representation for the NFA. For this purpose, and with the transition diagram as we have constructed it, each state can be represented by a record with one label field and two transition fields; the entire NFA can be represented by an array of these states. The values of such an array for the NFA of Figure 8.34 are shown in Figure 8.35(a). We adopt the following conventions for programming convenience:

- *state* = 1 is the initial state and *state* = 0 is the final state;
- the marker corresponds to *state* = −1;
- for states with just one ε-transition, we duplicate the value of that transition.

Regarding the manner of implementation of the deque, it could of course be a linked list (see Exercise 5.3) or a circular array (see Exercise 5.4). The operations for our output-restricted deque are then available as:

INITDQ − to initialize a deque;
ENQ_L − to insert a value at the left end of the deque;
ENQ_R − to insert a value at the right end of the deque;
DEQ_L − to remove a value from the left end of the deque.

	1	2	3	4	5	6	7	8	9	10	11	12	13
label		A			C	B	A	C				B	A
*next*1	2	5	4	6	11	8	9	10	10	3	13	13	0
*next*2	3	0	12	7	0	0	0	0	10	3	13	0	0

(a) Encoded Form of NFA of Figure 8.34

Examine States from Deque							Accept
$\underline{1}$	$\underline{3}$	12	$\underline{4}$	7	$\underline{6}$	2	B
13	$\underline{8}$						C
10	$\underline{3}$	12	$\underline{4}$	$\underline{7}$	6		A
$\underline{9}$	$\underline{10}$	$\underline{3}$	$\underline{12}$	4	7	6	B
$\underline{13}$	8						A
$\underline{0}$							

(b) Trace of Transitions for 'BCABA'

Figure 8.35 Interpretation of an NFA

Putting the pieces all together, the function RE_COGNIZER (Algorithm 8.7) searches for an occurrence of *pattern* in *text*, beginning at *start*. If there is no match beginning at *start*, the function returns a zero; if there is a match, the function returns the index in *text* of the end of the pattern. For example, with the pattern encoded as in Figure 8.35(a), and with *text* ='CABBCABAABCBAC', RE_COGNIZER would fail to find a match for *start* = 1,2,3; but for *start* = 4, it would find a match. In doing so, it would make the transitions and accept the input characters as shown in Figure 8.35(b), where the underlined transitions correspond to the correct sequence of "guesses." As a result, RE_COGNIZER would return a value of 8, signifying that 'BCABA' in *text* [4 .. 8] is an instance of '((A+BC)* B+AC)A'.

```
function RE_COGNIZER (pattern: fsm; text: string; start: extent): extent;

type    state = record
           ch: char;
           next1,next2: 0 .. maxstate;
        end;
        fsm = array [1 .. maxstate] of state;

var     dq: deque;
        found: boolean;
        i,j: integer;
        pattern: fsm;
        stat: state;

begin
   RE_COGNIZER := 0;
   found := false;  j := start;
   INITDQ (dq);
   ENQ_L (dq,1);  ENQ_R (dq,-1);        {start and marker symbols}
   repeat
      DEQ_L (dq,i);
      if i < 0 then begin               {marker}
         j := j + 1;
         ENQ_R (dq,-1);                 {recycle marker}
      end else if i = 0 then begin      {final state}
         found := true;
         RE_COGNIZER := j - 1;
      end else begin
         stat := pattern [i];
         if stat.ch = text.data [j] then
            ENQ_R (dq,stat.next1)
         else if stat.ch = ' ' then begin
            ENQ_L (dq,stat.next1);
            if stat.next1 <> stat.next2 then
               ENQ_L (dq,stat.next2);
         end;
      end;
   until found or (j > text.size) or (dq.count = 1);
end;
```

Algorithm 8.7 RE_COGNIZER

What is the complexity of recognizing a regular expression of length m in a string of length n? As a first step, we draw upon the fact that for a regular expression of length m, the number of states in an NFA for recognizing it can be bounded by $2m$. Moreover, (a) no input character is matched against any state more than once, and (b) no state has more than two transitions. Thus, the complexity of this matching problem is $O(mn)$. Crucial to this bound is the nature of the transition diagram as we have drawn it. In essence, we are computing the ε-closure every time we need it, but the cost of each such computation is strictly bounded. By contrast, if ε-transitions are contracted – that is, if an NFA with partial or complete ε-closure is used – then the complexity may actually increase because conditions (a) and (b) may no longer be true.

We promised to describe how the transition diagram of Figure 8.34 was obtained from the regular expression '((A+BC)* B+AC)A'. In brief, this is done by building bigger machines from smaller ones, where there is a rule for each of the operations – concatenation, union, and closure. The most elementary machine is one that recognizes a character, as in Figure 8.36(a). For concatenation, we merge a final state with a succeeding initial state to obtain the machine in (b) of the figure. For union, we need an initial state with two ε-transitions, and we also introduce an ε-transition from the final state of one alternative to the final state of the other alternative, as in (c) of the figure. Lastly, for closure, we make the construction shown in (d) of the figure, where we make an initial state out of what was the final state, and then introduce a new final state.

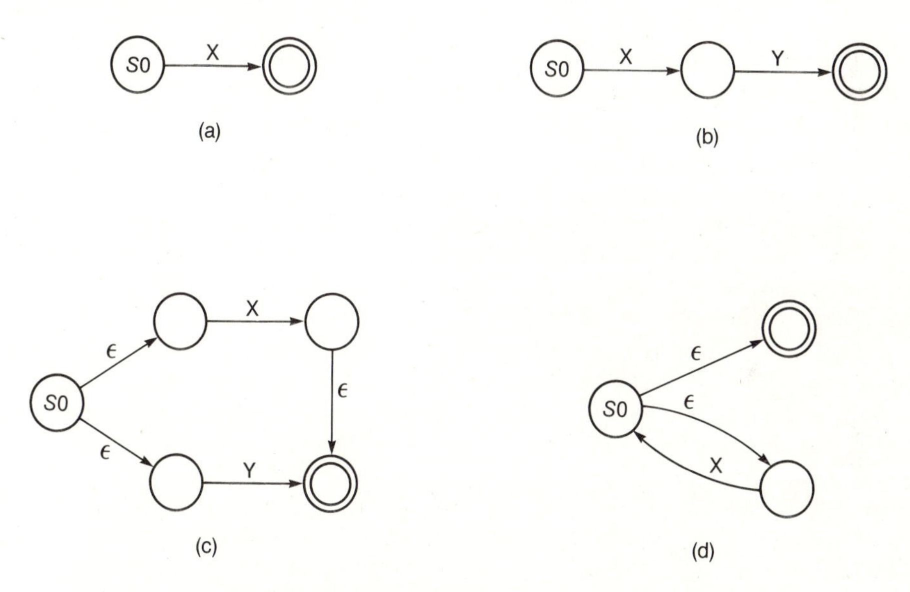

Figure 8.36 Composition Rules for NFA's

The pattern matching method that we have just described is used in text editors, where the cost of constructing the equivalent FA would far outweigh the benefit of having it [Thompson 1968]. There are other applications where the reverse is true. This is well exemplified in the process of scanning the text of a program to find the tokens (see Section 5.2.3.3). Tokens are easily described using regular expressions. Identifiers are usually a letter followed by some optional number of letters, digits, and special characters. Numbers are composed from digits and also {+ - . , etc.}. Just as there is a straightforward procedure to construct an FA equivalent to an NFA, so is it possible to construct an NFA that will recognize a given regular expression, by following the technique of our construction for '((A+BC)* B+AC)A'.

These two steps are usually combined with a third one for minimizing the number of states in the FA, since it could have 2^n of them if the NFA has n states. An optimized FA for finding program tokens is one of the easier and major components of any compiler.

Our final remark serves as a climax to our discussion, and also as prelude to the next section. We employed FSM's in an ad hoc manner for the purpose of recognizing regular expressions. In fact, not only can FSM's recognize all regular expressions; the cognitive power of FSM's extends precisely to sentences generated by a Type 3 grammar, and no further! In the next section, we will encounter analogous characterizations of the other classes of grammars in terms of what is required in order to recognize their languages.

†8.6.3 Parsing in General

Pattern recognition by now has become a familiar two-step:

1. We translate the pattern to some representation.
2. We interpret that representation against some input string.

For simple substring matching, the first step is fairly simple; for regular expression recognition, it is straightforward but no longer simple; and for recognizing sentences higher up in the Chomsky hierarchy, the first step can be a large task with many subtleties. We will content ourselves in this section with describing how the distinctions among the four types of grammars are significant, and what sorts of recognition mechanisms are required.

Context-free grammars (CFG's) are the next most difficult after regular grammars. Happily, they suffice (almost) for HLL's as we know them. Two instances where they are inadequate for the purpose are that of enforcing that variables must be declared before they are used, and that of monitoring that the actual parameters in a procedure call match the formal parameters of the procedure. However, such issues can be dealt with by other parts of a compiler. The fact that most of a programming language can be characterized by a CFG expressed in BNF has a very important consequence. Specifically, there are algorithms to perform the first step above in a clean fashion, culminating in tables that can then be interpreted to guide the parsing (that is, recognition of the syntactic components) of a program. The output of a parser usually takes the form of a parse tree, such as those we described in Section 6.6.2.2. As it turns out, even unrestricted CFG's are troublesome for programming languages for reasons having to do with efficiency and ambiguity. Both of these items merit a descriptive paragraph.

The first parsers for CFL's employed backtracking and were rather inefficient. A major improvement came with the realization that they can be parsed using dynamic programming to find longer and longer valid substrings. This leads to algorithms of complexity $O(n^3)$, for an input string of length n. More astoundingly, it can be shown that this problem is equivalently hard to the familiar ones of matrix multiplication and transitive closure [Valiant 1975a]. The latter parallel should not be too surprising in the light of the ε-closure discussion in the preceding section. Since parsing is such an important issue for programming, it is common to describe

HLL's by CFG's that are restricted in various fashions in order to simplify and speed up the parsing process. (Recall that a given language may be specifiable by many different grammars.) As a consequence of these restrictions, it is common to find parsers for HLL's that operate linearly for almost all programs.

Another reason for having restricted context-free grammars is to avoid *ambiguity* in the derivation of the parse tree. Sometimes, the ambiguity is not serious, as when the BNF production

<expression> ::= <expression> + <expression>

would allow the derivation of either $(x+y)+z$ or $x+(y+z)$ for the expression $x+y+z$. In any event, this is easily made unambiguous by including extra productions, along the lines of Figure 5.16. The infamous dangling **else**, in the case of the BNF production

```
<if_stmt> ::= if <condition> then <stmt>
            | if <condition> then <stmt> else <stmt>
```

is more of a problem, since the statement

if A **then** **if** B **then** C **else** D

can be parsed as either

if A **then** (**if** B **then** C **else** D), or **if** A **then** (**if** B **then** C) **else** D

with quite different meanings. It is possible to augment the productions so that this is unambiguous also, but the resulting grammar in this case is distinctly harder to understand. Moreover, whenever we augment the grammar with extra productions to remove ambiguity, the parsing process takes significantly longer. It is often simpler and more convenient to allow the grammar to be ambiguous, but to *disambiguate* it by applying various rules in other parts of the compiler [Aho et al. 1975]. As a capstone to this discussion, some CFL's are inherently ambiguous, making it impossible to find an unambiguous CFG for them.

We promised to characterize languages of Types 0, 1, and 2 in terms of their recognition mechanisms. Briefly put, the story is as follows:

- Context-free languages can be recognized by a *pushdown automaton* (*PDA*); this is essentially an FSM enhanced with an infinite stack.
- Context-sensitive languages can be recognized by a *linear bounded automaton* (*LBA*); this is essentially an FSM enhanced with a finite rewritable tape that originally contains the input.
- Phrase-structure languages can be recognized by a *Turing machine*; this is essentially an FSM enhanced with an infinite, rewritable tape that originally contains the input.

To sum it up, the notion of pattern recognition embraces matters from the most prosaic, as exemplified by the algorithm MATCH_0, to the most fundamental in computer science.

†8.6.4 String Processing as a Model of Computation

We have seen ample evidence that the simple notion of string substitution is powerful enough to support very complex processes, such as the compilation of programs. It is useful at this point to recall the programming language LISP (see Section 4.4.4). LISP was, in fact, modelled very deliberately upon the *lambda calculus* [Landin 1964] as a means of expressing recursive computations. As we saw in Section 5.4.3, this notation is powerful enough to represent any function that is computable. Another formalism that has been demonstrated to have the same power as that of lambda calculus is that of *Markov algorithms* [Tremblay and Sorenson 1984]. We will not try to describe them here, partly for reasons of space, but also because we have already illustrated the essence of this algorithmic notation in our discussion of string substitution at the very beginning, in Section 8.1. The analogy with Lists is completed when we realize that the language SNOBOL [Griswold et al. 1971] is a string-processing language closely modeled upon the Markov formalism. It includes all of the string substitution capabilities that we have described in this chapter, and many more. In particular, it is easy in SNOBOL to specify patterns that are as general as any that can be defined via BNF [Gimpel 1973]. SNOBOL is very useful for certain types of calculations, and it possesses the same theoretical power as List-processing languages. Nonetheless, HLL's based upon strings seem not to be as generally useful as those based upon Lists. In part, this is due to the lack of standardization with respect to string notation and string operations. More compellingly, whereas it is often natural to think of computations in List-processing terms, it is less natural to think of them in string-processing terms.

8.7 OVERVIEW

Wherever we turn in dealing with strings, we are reminded that they sustain meaning that is expressed via patterns. Most of the ways of dealing with strings that we have discussed reflect this fact:

- transforming strings to more efficient representations that still retain all the information;
- transforming strings to representations that can retain the meaning even in the face of errors;
- transforming strings to disguise the meaning;
- recognizing meaningful phrases within strings.

The operations just described are all based upon string transformations. This is true even for the recognition problem, which is usually couched in terms of recognizing which transformations will have a desired effect. It is remarkable that the concept of string transformation is so effective over such a wide range of applications, even though the notation for expressing it is so poorly standardized.

In earlier chapters, we encountered two types of searching – one in which we looked for a specific value of a key in a data structure, and one in which we looked for the optimization of some criterion function. By the time we finished the last of the topics on the preceding list, we had discovered a third, more general type of search. This hidden power in string processing accounts for the election of strings as our ultimate data structure.

8.8 BIBLIOGRAPHIC NOTES

- Much material on single-error correcting codes, such as the construction of a generator matrix G and parity-check matrix H for a given (n,m) pair, can be found in Berlekamp [1968], Blahut [1983], and Peterson and Weldon [1972]. These also contain a wealth of information about more general kinds of codes.

- For discussions of dynamic Huffman coding, consult Gallagher [1978], Knuth [1985], and Vitter [1985]. Universal compression is described in Ziv and Lempel [1977, 1978], and an efficient variable-to-fixed implementation is given in Welch [1984]. Yet another dynamic compression scheme is that of Bentley et al. [1986].

- Two broader applications of the KMP matching technique are comparing polygons for similarity [Manacher 1976], and matching arbitrary patterns in two dimensions [Baker 1978b; Bird 1977c]. The summary conclusions about string matching are drawn from Davies and Bowsher [1986], Horspool [1980], and Smit [1982].

8.9 REFERENCE TO TERMINOLOGY

8.10 EXERCISES

Sections 8.1 – 8.2

8.1 What are the results of the following string operations, given that I='SISS', P='ISSI', and S='MISSISSIPPI'?

(a) 'SPIS' || I

(b) 'MIS' ¿ S ¡ I

(c) I ¿ S ¡ P

(d) P ¿ S ¡ 'UDDY'

8.2 Indicate by T(rue) or F(alse) the results of the following string comparisons, both in EBCDIC and in ASCII.

(a) 'Aa1' < = 'aA1'

(b) 'Aa10' < 'Aa2'

(c) 'blah' = 'blah '

(d) 'X(1)' > = 'X(l)'

8.3 Let u='abce' and v='aababcabcdabcde'. Trace the operation of MATCH_0 (u,v), as in Figure 8.9. How many character comparisons are made?

8.4 We have the following frequencies for symbols in a set of strings:

A – .18	D – .16	G – .06
B – .07	E – .23	H – .03
C – .11	F – .04	I – .12

Compose a Huffman tree of minimum height, and also the corresponding binary codes for the symbols. What is the weighted path length of the coding tree?

†**8.5** Prove that the tree obtained by Huffman's algorithm must have a minimum weighted path length.

†**8.6** [Schwartz and Kallick 1964] Show how the ideas of Exercise 6.30 can be used to obtain a *canonical* Huffman tree in which the weights appear at the leaves in ascending order from left to right. For the data of Exercise 8.4, what is the canonical tree, what is the corresponding code, and what is the w.p.l.?

†**8.7** Huffman t-ary trees can be constructed similar to Huffman binary trees, with the t smallest weights being combined each time. We have a set of messages with frequencies as follows:

A – 15	D – 13	G – 70	J – 25	M – 9
B – 7	E – 51	H – 6	K – 80	N – 11
C – 64	F – 4	I – 75	L – 5	

Construct a Huffman ternary tree of minimum height over the alphabet (0,1,2) for these messages, show the codes for the messages, and compute the w.p.l.

†**8.8** Write a program to compute a Huffman tree for a given set of symbols and frequencies. In doing so, you will have to decide whether it is important to construct the tree of minimum height; the heap implementation of a priority queue does not handle this requirement very well. There are other possibilities, as exemplified by the p-tree of Exercise 6.25. After writing your program, test it against the data of Exercise 8.4.

8.9 Prove that the minimum Hamming distance for a group code is equal to the minimum weight of its non-zero codewords.

†**8.10** Applying the Hamming bound,

(a) What is the maximum number of possible messages, if we wish to have a code of sixteen bits with double-error correction?

(b) What is the minimum number of bits required to send five messages and have single-error correction? Find a code that satisfies this objective.

††**8.11** For the (7,4) code of Figure 8.19,

(a) What are the codeword values?

(b) What are the coset leaders for each of the non-zero syndromes?

††**8.12** Describe how the syndromes for the (7,4) code of Figure 8.19 can be used to effect error correction without using coset leaders.

Sections 8.3 – 8.4

††**8.13** Write a set of procedures to extract statistics from a file of English text; these might include, for example, counts of individual characters, word counts, sentence counts, etc. State your assumptions about recognizing word breaks (blanks, hyphen, end-of-line, etc.) and sentence breaks (period, semi-colon, etc.), and demonstrate that your procedures handle them properly. Describe how such statistics can be used, separately and in combination, to make judgements about issues such as compression and readability. Apply your procedures to three differ-

ent types of input text – adult, juvenile, and technical prose – and summarize your conclusions.

††8.14 Write an algorithm to do line-breaking of paragraphs by dynamic programming, and apply it to various test paragraphs. As part of doing this, you will have to choose a cost function that your solution minimizes; explain the rationale for your choice.

†8.15 We discussed fixed-to-variable, variable-to-fixed, and variable-to-variable encodings. When might a fixed-to-fixed encoding be applicable, and how might it be accomplished?

†8.16 Write functions to implement the RSA encryption/decryption scheme, presuming that the parameters n,p,q,r,s are integers that fit in the word of your underlying machine. Test these by decoding the following message, where the parameter values are the same as those employed in Section 8.4.2.2.1.

1510 0731 2049 1904 0741 1964 0962 2624 2417 1908 2326 0363
2624 0542 1655 1717 1567 0219 0521 1684 1007 1787 2342

††8.17 Write functions to implement RSA encryption/decryption under the more realistic assumption that multi-precision arithmetic is required.

††8.18 Prove the validity of Eq. 8.10.

Sections 8.5 – 8.6

††8.19 Use the Knuth-Morris-Pratt algorithm to do the following:

(a) Compute the failure transitions *fail* and *next* for the pattern 'pollopolop', as in Figure 8.25.

(b) For *text*='pollopollopolloppollolop', trace the values of the indices over *pattern* and *text*, as in Figure 8.24.

(c) Draw the equivalent FSM, as in Figure 8.28.

†8.20 Construct the FSM (by hand) for searching in parallel for the words {AAB, ABAB, ABC, BAA, BBC, CAB, CBC, CCAA}. Show the FSM as in Figure 8.30, and also the failure transitions as in Figure 8.31(a).

†8.21 Write a procedure analogous to MATCH_1 to do parallel searching for several patterns, using the FSM approach. Apply your program to the data of Figures 8.30 and 8.31.

††8.22 Write a program analogous to SCAN_1 that generates the FSM (that is, the nodes and their success and failure transitions) for a given set of patterns. (*Hint*: Write one procedure that generates the success transitions, and then a second one that scans the success transitions to generate the failure transitions.) Give some thought to your choice of data structure. It should be possible to take the structure encoding any given set of patterns and add other patterns to it, without having to reorganize everything. Test your program by applying it to the data of Exercise 8.20.

††8.23 Write a function that searches an input string and finds the first palindrome therein. Your algorithm should scan the string and stop as soon as it finds such a palindrome.

††8.24 [Hirschberg 1975] Given a string $A = a_1a_2 \ldots a_n$, then $S = a_{i1}a_{i2} \ldots a_{ip}$ is a subsequence of A when $1 \leq i1 < i2 < \cdots < ip \leq n$; thus S ='bcfk' is one of many possible subsequences of A ='abcdefghijk'. An important issue in comparing two strings for their "closeness" is to determine the *longest common subsequence* (*LCS*) between them. For example, with A='xyzwtwxzx' and B='ywxzxyxw', the LCS is 'ywxzx'. This problem has many important applications. One is that of computing the edit-distance between two text strings. Another is that of comparing strands of genetic material to determine their evolutionary distance, regarded as the number of mutations required to produce one strand from another strand. Although it is not the fastest method, a fairly simple algorithm for the problem can be developed via the following recursive function definition:

```
if (A [j] = B [k]) then f(j,k) := 1 + f(j-1,k-1)
                   else f(j,k) := Max (f(j,k-1),f(j-1,k))
```

with $f(j,k) = 0$ at the low boundaries. This definition expresses the length of the LCS on prefixes of the two strings in terms of the lengths on shorter prefixes, with the final LCS length determined by $f(m,n)$. It is straightforward to express the above formulation iteratively rather than recursively, using the technique of dynamic programming (see Section 7.4.2.1).

(a) Apply this process, by hand, to find the LCS of the strings 'abbcabacb' and 'cacbcbbac'.

(b) Write a procedure to compute and display the LCS of two strings, and test your program against the data of part (a).

(c) What are the time and space requirements of your program? Can you find a way to reduce the space requirement?

††8.25 Suppose that we call RE_COGNIZER with the same pattern and the same text as in Section 8.6.2, but with *start* = 8. Trace the corresponding state transitions and other data as in Figure 8.35(b).

††8.26 Construct an NFA that can be used for recognizing regular expressions of the form '(0+1)((01)* +1)* 1', as in Figure 8.34. Also construct the corresponding array of state information, as in Figure 8.35(a).

††8.27 In order to search *text* to find the leftmost occurrence of a regular expression, no matter where it occurs, we need (a) to enhance the algorithm RE_COGNIZER, and (b) to construct a somewhat different NFA. Describe what is required for (a) and (b), then implement these requirements, and finally apply your results to the data of Exercise 8.26.

9

STRUCTURE and COMPLEXITY

"Structure without life is dead.
But Life without structure is un-seen."

John Cage,
Silence, Lecture on Nothing

We have studied in considerable detail the data structures: array, set, record, list, queue, stack, tree, graph, and string. In this brief chapter, we present a more general essay on their nature. To begin with, consider the following questions:

- Are any of these structures more fundamental than the others? Is there any way to relate them to one another?
- More generally, what theoretical bases can we find for the use of data structures? What are the advantages and shortcomings of these bases?
- From a practical point of view, how do we choose a good implementation for a data structure?

Of course, this list of questions is by no means comprehensive. Over the past years, there have been numerous attempts to deal with questions such as these, leading to elegant formal methods in some cases. Unfortunately, because of their formality and because of lack of consistency among the approaches, few programmers have deemed it worth the effort to master such concepts. Our objective is to present the essential characteristics of a few of the more promising ideas. Some other useful points of view include d'Imperio [1969], Fleck [1978], Korfhage [1974b], and Mealy [1967].

9.1 BUILDING DATA STRUCTURES

We begin by referring to the summary of the advantages and limitations of arrays (see Section 2.6). After all, in those cases where none of the shortcomings apply, there is little reason to look beyond the array data structure. But many problems, of course, are not so tractable. Thus we find the need to use, alone or in combination, the several other structures discussed in this book. Is the diversity that we have seen really necessary? Is any one of these structures powerful enough to subsume all the others? In terms of computability, we have previously alluded to four structures that have been employed as universal data types:

1. Arrays have been used in APL, and their theoretical adequacy and power have been developed in Array Theory. (See Section 2.9 and Gull and Jenkins [1979] for a discussion of this).
2. Sets have been used in SETL (see Section 2.4.3).
3. Lists have been used in LISP. (For a discussion of this, see Section 4.4.4 and McCarthy [1963]).
4. Strings have been used in SNOBOL (see Section 8.6.4).

However, the issue here is the narrower and more difficult one of representational power. This is analogous to the issue of comparing the power of various programming control structures (**goto**, **repeat** ... **until**, etc.), in that the choices of data structure and its representation can affect the complexity of a computation; but it is complicated in a way that comparison of control structures is not. The difficulty arises in trying to separate two aspects of a data structure:

(a) the specification of its semantic intent – the "what," and

(b) the details of its realization – the "how."

This latter point is less of an issue with control structures, since it is their nature to express "how"; so the issue there is simply concern for the power and convenience of alternative constructs for "how," rather than confusion of "what" and "how."

In the ensuing three sections, we begin by reexamining the role of pointers in data structuring. Then we examine some results concerning the explicit representation of one data structure by another. Lastly, we consider the interesting case of implicit data structures.

9.1.1 Pointers Reconsidered

We have stressed that programming with pointer variables is hazardous (see Section 4.5.1). Their improper use is a frequent source of errors; moreover, the errors thus created are typically much harder to diagnose than are other sorts of errors. The pointer issue is worth reexamining since it relates directly to the difficulty cited in the preceding section – that of trying to distinguish between the semantic specification of a data structure and the details of its implementation.

If we think about it, we realize that pointers are used for three principal purposes:

1. They express as *connectors* that we want to tie together other structures.
2. They express as *relators* that two nodes bear some semantic relationship to one another.
3. They bind a variable to a particular value.

The latter usage may arise implicitly, in the disciplined context of passing a parameter to a procedure by reference (as opposed to value); it may also arise explicitly, as when referring to the head of a list or to the root of a tree. But the use of a pointer (that is, a location) to effect such a binding is a consequence of the way in which the structure has been declared. We could alternatively have a manner of declaration in which the binding was accomplished using a name rather than a location [Kieburtz 1976].[1]

The major difficulty in using pointer variables stems from the confusion between using them as connectors and as relators. Indeed, there is ample reason for such confusion, since a pointer may be serving both purposes at once; an example of this is the use of pointers to connect and relate the nodes of a BST. On the other hand, the fact that one node follows another on a sequential linked list may convey no essential relationship. (The only thing that I have in common with the person next to me in the grocery line is that we both wish to purchase food.) At the other extreme, we could have an r-regular graph, with the vertices represented by an array of nodes, and with each of these vertices adjacent to $r - 1$ other vertices. In such a case, it would be natural and efficient to express these fundamental relationships via links to the adjacent vertices.

The one pointer mechanism can serve the two purposes, connector and/or relator. But which of these is meant to apply in a given instance often cannot be discerned by looking at code employing pointers, any more than one can easily tell by looking at some assembly code what is intended. In both of these cases, the problem is that the level of expression is too low to sustain the true meaning. An apt example of this in the case of pointer-based data structures is the following. Consider two record structures – one for bi-directional linked lists, and one for binary trees. Either structure will have, in addition to its ordinary data fields, two pointer fields to other records of its type. However, there is nothing to distinguish which of the two very different logical structures this one physical structure embodies, other than by the haphazard manner in which the programmer supplies names to the structure.

Unfortunately, there are no magic answers to these difficulties. What is needed is a method of abstracting above the level of operations with pointer variables. In Section 9.2 we will confront the important topic of data abstraction in general. When pointers must be used there are only a few remedies, each with its shortcomings. One is to provide an environment where explicit pointer freeing is not allowed. This is done at the cost of significant run-time overhead, as we will see in Chapter 11. Another proposal allows for explicit pointer freeing, but again with compensating overhead, this time via a "bump" imposed upon dynamic structures, and called a *tombstone* [Lomet 1985]. The tombstone remains even when the dynamic structure is discarded, and thus is able to catch and invalidate subsequent references to the structure. Many users work in environments where these methods are not available. Their only recourse is to adopt their own disciplined programming mechanisms, of which pointer rotations are a good example.

---

1 A similar remark applies to a fourth use of pointer variables, not listed above. In our discussion of inverted lists (see Section 4.3.1), we found that there were two possibilities – to use locations (either pointers or cursors), or to use keys (names).

†9.1.2 Data Encodings

The concept of a *data encoding*, wherein one data structure is represented in another one, is not completely novel to us. We have already seen several instances of it. The most pervasive one is that of encoding a multi-dimensional array in a line (a one-dimensional array), reflected in our discussion of storage allocation functions in Section 2.2.1. Another rather elegant one is that of encoding any ordered tree as a corresponding binary tree (see Section 6.2); still others include the encoding of any ordered tree in a line (see Sections 6.5.2 and 6.5.3). In general terms, we speak of a *guest structure* G, which is to be encoded in a *host structure* H. To accommodate the most general case, it is conventional to regard both G and H as graphs, with G being *embedded* in H. A primary issue with any data structure is the set of usage patterns characterizing access from one atomic item to another. In the embedding, vertices in G become vertices in H, but edges in G become paths in H, with the costs of traversing paths representing a dilation of the access costs in H over those in G [Rosenberg 1978]. This dilation can occur with respect to both space and time, where the former may partly be due to the overhead of pointers. Restricting our attention to the time dilation, the concepts that we have been describing can be expressed as $G \leq_T H$ whenever G can be encoded in H such that no adjacent nodes in G have path length greater than T in H. More generally, T may be some function $T(n)$, where n characterizes the size of G in the usual way.

One of the issues to which these ideas have been successfully applied is that of loss of proximity between array elements under various encodings (see Section 2.7 for a related discussion). In the preceding paragraph, we alluded to the usage patterns of access within a data structure. In a d-dimensional array, an element in general has $2d$ immediate neighbors. For $d > 1$, when the array is represented in the conventional manner by a linearizing storage allocation function, it has been rigorously shown that there is an unbounded loss of proximity in at least some of the dimensions [Rosenberg 1975]. This is easy to visualize intuitively when we consider that an element in a 2-dimensional array cannot "squeeze" n^2 neighbors (from the array) into $2n$ neighbors (on the line). In many cases, this loss of proximity may not be serious. For example, patterns of array usage are often confined to traversals in a single dimension, as in ordinary matrix multiplication, so that dilation in the other dimensions is irrelevant. Also, the effects of the dilation will only become significant when the array is so large that it must be decomposed, explicitly or implicitly, into sub-arrays for processing.[2] However, it is easy to find examples where both of these issues do matter. One instance is that of multiplying large matrices by Strassen's method (see Section 2.5.1.1), which proceeds by recursively decomposing matrices into sub-matrices.

We might ask what would be the effect of having a host H of more general character than a line – perhaps a binary tree. (In such an encoding, the vertices of G are understood to be embedded at the leaves of H). Even in this case, for G an

---

[2] By implicit decomposition, we refer to the effects of virtual memory. In such an environment, there is always the hazard of degradation in performance when data accesses must cross page or cache boundaries (see Section 12.2.2).

$n \times n$ matrix, it has been shown that loss of proximity is still unbounded; more precisely, in this case $T(n) \geq (\lg n - 2) / 3$ [Lipton et al. 1976]. So far, we have been speaking of the worst-case loss of proximity. When we consider the average loss of proximity, however, the situation is different. Arrays encoded as lines must still have unbounded loss of average proximity, but arrays can be encoded as binary trees in such a manner that the average loss in proximity is bounded [DeMillo et al. 1978]. In fact, there is a result of immediate practical use. Consider two possible ways of encoding a two-dimensional array, as illustrated in Figure 9.1. The encoding in (a) is via a 2-tree (a binary tree), and the encoding in (b) is via a 2^2-tree (a *quaternary tree*).[3] The encoding in (b) has been shown to be superior to that in (a) in the following respects [Wood 1978]:

- Under reasonable assumptions about relative costs of primitive machine operations, access time will be 30 percent higher with (a) than with (b).
- The binary encoding of (a) requires 50 percent more pointer locations than the quaternary encoding of (b).
- Average loss in proximity will be 75 percent worse with (a) than with (b).

Evidently, 2^2-trees are considerably superior to 2-trees for the encoding of two-dimensional arrays. Even more generally, it has been shown that for encoding a d-dimensional array in a tree, the choice of a 2^d-tree as a host is always nearly optimal [Rosenberg 1979].

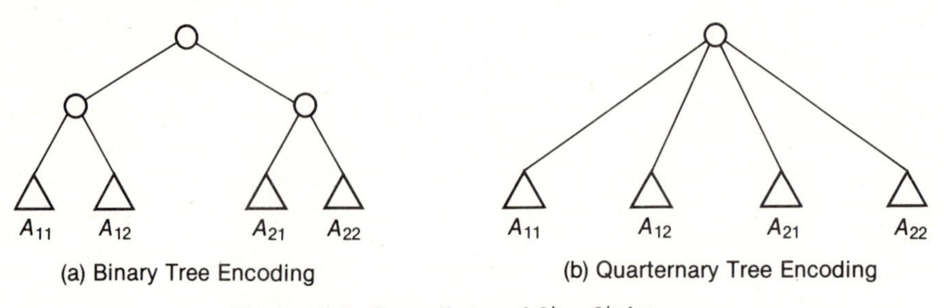

Figure 9.1 Encodings of $2^k \times 2^k$ Arrays

†9.1.3 Implicit Data Structures

The notion of order among data values is often a crucial issue in a data structure. One example of this is a BST, wherein recursively all the values in the left/right subtrees of a node are smaller/greater than the value at the node itself; here the ordering is explicitly maintained via the use of pointers. An even more basic example is that of an array whose elements are in sequence; in this case the ordering is maintained among the array locations, and no pointers are required. A third example is the heap. The ordering in this elegant structure is partial, not total, but again

---

[3] Quaternary trees are conventionally termed *quad trees*. We will say a little bit about them in Section 12.4.3.1.

the ordering is maintained among the data locations rather than via pointers. Data structures such as the ordered array and the heap are called *implicit data structures*. Since they don't use pointers, they are efficient in terms of space; they also avoid the problems cited in Section 9.1.1. In this section we will meet some more exotic examples in this useful category. In order to appreciate the discussion, you may wish to skim Sections 10.2.2 and 10.3.1, if you are not already familiar with the material therein.

To begin with, we note some performance characteristics of the ordered array and the heap. Three measures are significant for our purpose:

- the complexity of searching for an arbitrary item;
- the complexity of inserting or deleting an item;
- the complexity of finding a distinguished (minimum or maximum) item.

Drawing upon what we know already and/or anticipating some of the subject matter of Chapter 10, the complexities are as follows:

structure	search	insert/delete	distinguished
ordered array	$O(\lg n)$	$O(n)$	$O(1)$
heap	$O(n)$	$O(\lg n)$	$O(1)$

In particular, we see that the product of the search and the insert/delete complexities is $O(n \lg n)$ for both structures, and that both are imbalanced with respect to these two capabilities. For a BST, the search time is $O(\lg n)$ and so is the insert/delete time (inclusive of the associated search time), yielding a product of $O(\lg n)^2$. However, this increased efficiency is purchased at the expense of additional storage for the pointers. This suggests the question: Are there any implicit data structures such that (1) the product of the complexities of search and insert/delete is better than $O(n \lg n)$, and/or (2) there is better balance between the complexities?

One such structure is the *bi-parental heap*, or *beap*. It is like a heap except that each child must satisfy the partial ordering relationship with respect to two parents. An example of a beap with example data obeying such an ordering is shown in Figure 9.2(a). In terms of implementation, however, we perceive a triangular matrix, more particularly a diagonal shell matrix as discussed in Section 2.7.1. This is apparent from Figure 9.2(b), shown with array locations. The storage allocation formula for such a representation is reproduced here from Eq. 2.23:

$$\text{loc}\,(A\,[i,j]) = b + \binom{i+j}{2} - i = b + \frac{(i^2 + 2ij + j^2 - 3i - j)}{2} \qquad (9.1)$$

However, the manner of using a beap is to travel (up,down,left,right) between adjacent nodes, and the formulas for such transitions are fairly simple. The beap is treated as though each diagonal were a separate block, with the ith diagonal containing i elements. The bi-parental ordering is such that the kth element of the jth block is less than both the kth and $(k + 1)$th elements of the $(j + 1)$th block. These ordering constraints in a beap are stronger than in a heap, and they make it possible to search for an arbitrary item X with time complexity $O(n^{1/2})$. Any such search is initiated at the top right node in Figure 9.2(b), and always proceeds either leftward or downward, as follows:

(a) if $X < a_{i,j}$ then move left;

(b) if $X > a_{i,j}$ then move downward, and also move left if $a_{i,j}$ is beyond the fringe diagonal.

Since the longest path that can be traversed in this manner is $O(n^{1/2})$, we have the cited result. The technique for insertions and deletions is analogous to that for a heap, except that the longest path is once again $O(n^{1/2})$. In other words, the beap is an implicit data structure for which the complexities of search and insert/delete are balanced, and such that their product is $O(n)$.

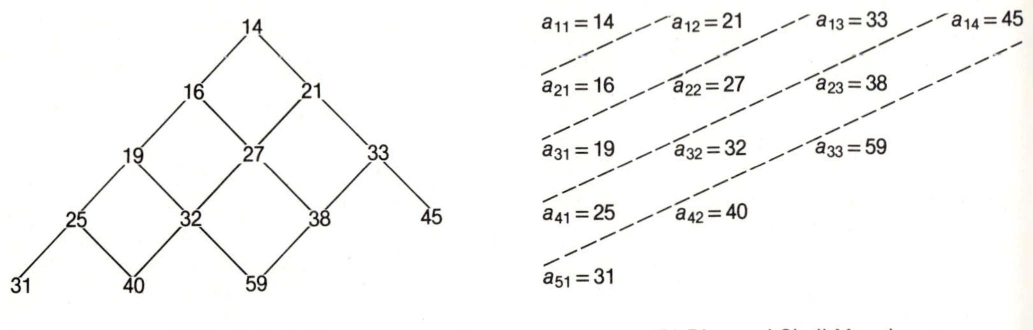

(a) Beap Ordering

(b) Diagonal Shell Mapping

Figure 9.2 Bi-Parental Heaps (Beaps)

But this is just the beginning of the story! Consider next the data structure illustrated in Figure 9.3. It is a sequence of blocks such that (1) the ith block has i elements, and (2) each element in the ith block is less than every element in the $(i + 1)$th block. But also, the ith block is a *rotated list* – that is, a cyclic shift of a sorted list. A crucial feature of our intended use of such a structure is that the elements in a block must all be distinct. Assuming that this is so, note that we can then always find the minimum element in a block $B[s .. t]$ in $O(\lg i)$ comparisons. We simply need apply a variant of binary search (see Section 10.2.2). With this variant we first compute $m = (s + t)$ **div** 2; we then look for the minimum in $B[s .. m]$ if $B[m] < B[t]$, or in $B[m + 1 .. t]$ if $B[m] > B[t]$.

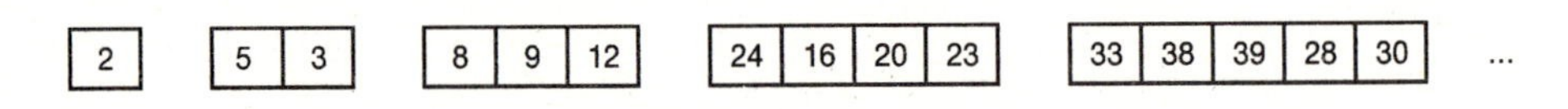

Figure 9.3 Rotated Lists

Because we can find the minimum element in a block in $O(\lg i)$ time, we can also find any arbitrary element X in the data structure of Figure 9.3 in $O(\lg n)$ time, by the following process:

(a) First apply ordinary binary search, discovering that X must be in either one of two consecutive blocks.

(b) Next apply the variant method of binary search on the larger rotated list to find its minimum element Min_i.

Depending upon the comparison of X and Min_i, then proceed as follows:

(c) If $X \geq Min_i$, re-apply the variant method to find X in the larger block.

(d) If $X < Min_i$, apply the variant method twice to the smaller block, finding first its minimum Min_{i-1} and then X.

Finally, we can insert or delete an element X in $O(n^{1/2} \lg n)$ time. The technique to perform insertion is as follows. We begin by finding the block i to which X belongs. This can be found in $O(\lg n)$ time by searching in the manner described in the preceding paragraph. We then perform a "hard exchange," in which X is inserted in its proper place. This requires $O(n^{1/2})$ data shifts in the worst case, since that is the magnitude of the largest block. As a result of the insertion of X, we can expect that the former maximum element Max_i in that block may now have to be relocated to the $(i + 1)$th block, in turn bumping Max_{i+1} to the next block, etc. However, each of these bumping operations is an "easy exchange": The minimum and maximum in the new block are found in $O(\lg i)$ time once again, and then the old maximum is displaced by a new minimum – without any data shifts! The process for deletion in a rotated list is completely analogous. The summary accounting for insertion/deletion is $O(n^{1/2} \lg n)$ comparisons and $O(n^{1/2})$ moves. In other words, for the rotated lists structure of Figure 9.3, the product of the complexities for searching and insertion/deletion is $O(n^{1/2} (\lg n)^2)$.

The beap and the rotated lists structure and others as well, including a beap *of* rotated lists, are described in Munro and Suwanda [1980]. Table 9.1 summarizes the complexities for the implicit data structures that have been cited in this section. There are still other possibilities; as an example, we can have rotated lists of elements that are (recursively) rotated lists [Frederickson 1983].

structure	search	insert/delete
ordered array	$O(\lg n)$	$O(n)$
heap	$O(n)$	$O(\lg n)$
beap	$O(n^{1/2})$	$O(n^{1/2})$
rotated lists	$O(\lg n)$	$O(n^{1/2} \lg n)$
beap of rotated lists	$O(n^{1/3} \lg n)$	$O(n^{1/3} \lg n)$

Table 9.1 Complexities of Implicit Data Structures

9.2 MASTERING COMPLEXITY

As our starting point, let us consider the following parable by Simon [1962]. There once were two watchmakers, Hora and Tempus, who both made highly regarded timepieces. However, their methods of operation differed. Tempus constructed his watches by carefully assembling 1,000 components. Hora, on the other hand, first constructed 100 sub-assemblies of 10 components each, then assembled these into 10 larger units of 10 sub-assemblies each, and finally obtained a finished watch by putting these 10 units together. Since their watches were so highly regarded, they received frequent phone calls from eager customers. Unfortunately, whenever they answered their phones, the assembly that was being worked upon would fly apart, making it necessary to restart after the phone call. As the demand for their products increased and their phones began to ring more often, a strange thing happened. Hora prospered, but Tempus was driven out of business.

We can see why this happened when we compute their respective probabilities of finishing a watch between phone calls. Let $p = .01$ be the probability that a call occurs while adding a part to an assembly. In Hora's case, he has to make 111 assemblies altogether. The probability of his finishing any of his 10-part assemblies without interruption is $(1 - .01)^{10} = 0.9$, and he will have lost the effort of assembling 5 components, on average, whenever it is necessary to restart. Now Tempus has to perform just one assembly of 1,000 components, but his probability of accomplishing this without interruption is $(1 - .01)^{1000} = 44 \times 10^{-6}$. Moreover, he will have assembled $1/p = 100$ components, on average, before an interruption. Summarizing these figures,

- Tempus makes just 1/111 as many assemblies as Hora.
- Tempus loses 100/5 = 20 times as much work as Hora per interruption.
- Tempus has to restart $0.99^{10} / .99^{1000} = 20{,}000$ times more frequently than Hora.

By multiplying these three ratios, we find that it takes Tempus about 4,000 times longer than Hora to obtain one finished watch. No wonder his business failed!

Simon presents several other conclusions from his parable, two of which are particularly noteworthy. First, in order to master complexity it is crucial to superimpose structure upon it. Second, an eminently useful structure for this purpose is a hierarchy, or tree. One of the most obvious features in biology is the hierarchical organization of living creatures into stable "building blocks" – first by cells, then by tissues, then by organs, etc. If we relate biological assemblages to those of the watchmakers, it is strikingly clear that evolution works as well as it does because it models Hora rather than Tempus.

In programming also, we are incapable of mastering complexity except by decomposing it via structure. With respect to data structures, one can cite several objectives of such an approach:

- We hope first of all to obtain a higher-level point of view that will help us better understand and solve certain problems. Thus, to the undiscerning eye, a heap might be just an array used in some strange fashion. But viewed in terms of the notion of a priority queue, it is much more.

- By structuring data in coherent and meaningful fashion, we also hope to gain some leverage for achieving reliability in our programming. In particular, a formal treatment of data structures provides the opportunity of conjoining them with other formal constructs that can facilitate proof of correctness.

- If we are successful in separating the issue of semantic specification from that of implementation, then we have the opportunity to select at a later time whichever representation is best for a given set of operating circumstances.

Mechanisms for attaining these objectives are the abstract data types (ADT's) discussed in Section 1.1.2. At the very least, an ADT specifies both the set of permissible values that a variable of this type may assume and also the permissible operations on instances of ADT's. It may or may not include mechanisms for facilitating proofs of correctness, or for automatically choosing an optimal representation. A variety of methods have been employed for specifying ADT's. In the next section we characterize these methods, and then illustrate one of them in brief detail.

†9.2.1 The Specification of Abstract Data Types

The earliest formal techniques for the specification of data types had some of the flavor of the data encodings described in Section 9.1.2. In particular, data structures were commonly modelled by graphs because of their generality [Earley 1971]. However, such schemes were primitive in the sense that they did not bundle a data structure and its operations into a package. The language Simula was the first to provide facilities for constructing such packages of data types and associated operations, calling them *classes* [Dahl and Nygaard 1966]. As with Pascal, however, the representation details are completely visible in Simula, so that there is no protection against misuse of a data structure. Some examples of languages that do provide facilities for defining and using protected ADT's are Alphard via *forms* [Shaw et al. 1977], CLU via *clusters* [Liskov et al. 1977], and Mesa and Modula via *modules* [Geschke et al. 1977; Wirth 1985]. The provision for ADT's as *packages* in Ada is destined to have even more impact [U.S. Dept. of Defense 1983]. The methods of specifying data abstraction in these languages are explicit; that is, the semantics of the new data type are modelled constructively, in terms of operations upon more basic data types. With this technique, it is also straightforward to incorporate axiomatic assertions for establishing proof of correctness. In cases such as these, the method is termed *axiomatic specification*; the classic description of such a process is Hoare [1972b].

From a purist viewpoint, the preceding constructive approach toward ADT's is just a modelling of desired behavior, not a theoretical specification of the desired abstract properties. The explicit approach has some practical drawbacks as well, related to the fact that the model is essentially a program. The intent of abstraction is to reduce matters to easily comprehended units. But a program is likely to become too long and to contain details that are irrelevant to the intended abstraction. These facts, in conjunction with the combinatorial buildup of interaction among the program parts, can soon thwart easy comprehension. Finally, such a program model of an ADT is likely to bias one's perspective about how that ADT should ultimately be implemented.

By appealing to some notions of abstract algebra, however, it is possible to remove the "how" from specifications. By way of introduction, an *algebra* is characterized in terms of four entities:

1. A set, called the *carrier* of the algebra; typical carriers are the boolean values True and False, the set of integers, the set of character strings, etc.
2. Various operations upon the carrier; typical operations for these carriers include, respectively: AND, OR, NOT; addition and multiplication; concatenation and comparison.
3. The presence of some distinguished constant elements from the carrier.
4. Some number of axioms relating the first three items.

Depending upon the richness of the carrier and operations and axioms, one can obtain many different kinds of algebraic systems [Stanat and McAllister 1977]. Some examples are semigroups, monoids, groups, rings, lattices, fields, etc.

The axioms of an algebra for ADT's usually have to express relations simultaneously involving several carriers, as we will see momentarily.[4] The corresponding terminology is to refer to these different carriers as *sorts*; and so the *algebraic specification* technique is in terms of a *many-sorted algebra*. There have been two major expositions of algebraic specification. One is known as *ADJ* [Goguen et al. 1978], and the other is known as *ADT* [Guttag 1977]. We employ the notation of the latter to illustrate in Figure 9.4 the algebraic specification of a stack. It is a very time-honored example for readers unfamiliar with these techniques (and a very time-worn example for some other readers).

Let us examine Figure 9.4. You may wish to compare it with the informal specification of a stack that was presented in Section 5.2.1. After the introduction of the ADT that is being defined (via the label **type**), it has a declarative section (via the label **syntax**) that specifies the domains and ranges of the five stack operations. For example, PUSH takes as arguments a *Stack* and an *element*, and then returns a *Stack*. The final section (via the label **semantics**) defines the "what" of *Stack* in terms of relations, or axioms, that must hold between the various operations. In both form and intent, the organization in Figure 9.4 can be likened to that of a program with its heading, declarative part, and procedural part. An important distinction, however, is that in this case the procedural part contains just functions, and these functions have no side effects. The fact that the heading of the ADT *Stack* is parameterized by *element* causes *Stack* to be a *generic data type*. As a consequence, there is no necessity to have separate *Stack* ADT's for each distinct type of stackable item.

The crucial feature of the specification in Figure 9.4 is that it in fact defines an algebra, of the many sorts: *Stack*, *element*, and *Boolean*. As such, it can be manipulated algebraically to derive proofs of theorems from the axiom-relations. Moreover, the specification is concise, and any properties algebraically proved

---

4 There is an important distinction here. While both axiomatic specification and algebraic specification incorporate axioms, the former yields a constructive definition, and the latter yields a non-constructive one.

```
type Stack [element]

syntax
   NEWSTK → Stack
   PUSH (Stack,element) → Stack
   POP (Stack) → Stack
   TOP (Stack) → element ∪ {UNDEFINED}
   ISNEW (Stack) → Boolean

semantics
   declare stk: Stack; item: element;
      POP (NEWSTK) = NEWSTK
      POP (PUSH (stk,item)) = stk
      TOP (NEWSTK) = UNDEFINED
      TOP (PUSH (stk,item)) = item
      ISNEW (NEWSTK) = TRUE
      ISNEW (PUSH (stk,item)) = FALSE
```

Figure 9.4 Algebraic Specification of a Stack

about it do not depend in any way upon extraneous details of representation. The idea here is first to prove the correctness of the simple, abstract specification. Then, when the abstract description is mapped to a concrete one, all that is required for establishing the correctness of the resulting implementation is to demonstrate that this mapping is a homomorphism that preserves the necessary algebraic properties. The details of the agenda described in the two preceding sentences can become fairly complex, but they can also be partially automated [Guttag et al. 1978a]. The essential point is that such an agenda factors the proof-of-correctness problem into two stages, and this constitutes a significant advantage.

This algebraic specification gives us a set of axioms rather than a model. In all fairness, however, it would be hard to imagine how these axioms were originally conceived, other than through the imagery of a model. Although there is no bias of representation, there is one in the choice of identifiers; for example, the terms POP, PUSH, etc. strongly suggest the intent. Moreover, the stack is just about the simplest data structure that we can define in this manner. If we were to illustrate the technique with a more complicated structure, such as a BST, and if the identifiers were to be nonsensical, then it would be a much harder task to understand the "what" of the structure. In short, systems of axioms have been termed "systems designed to reason about not to reason in"; finding the right set of axioms for specifying an ADT can require a great deal trial and error. Note that on the one hand, the absence of a model is one of the important features of this technique; on the other hand, the implementor of such an ADT then has no guidelines as to how to proceed, which may be a source of difficulty in some cases.

In addition to the practical considerations just discussed, there are some theoretical issues relating to the use of algebraic specifications. In any axiom system we must be concerned with completeness, consistency, and power. A set of axioms about an ADT is *complete* if any true statement characterizing the ADT can be derived from the axioms; the set is *consistent* if it is impossible to derive contradictory statements from the axioms. In practice, the issue of completeness is the more pressing one. As an example, does the given set of axioms completely specify the behavior of the ADT under various boundary conditions? For example, what is the proper interpretation of applying a POP to an empty stack? Also, our specification in Figure 9.4 really needs to be expanded to deal with Stacks of bounded size, imposing another boundary condition. Lastly, with regard to power, we find that some ADT's can be completely specified only via the introduction of axioms employing *hidden operators*, or even *hidden sorts*. These hidden entities are not visible or accessible to the user of the ADT, but the specification axioms are necessarily incomplete without them.

In this section, we have been concerned simply with introducing some of the increasingly important concepts about data structure specification. For a more general survey of specification techniques consult Liskov and Zilles [1975]. For illustrations of the algebraic specification of a wide variety of ADT's – including stacks, queues, binary trees, BST's, sets, and strings – consult Guttag et al. [1978b]. Finally, for a good survey of all aspects of the issue of data abstraction, see Ford [1979].

9.3 CHOICE OF DATA STRUCTURE IMPLEMENTATION

We learned in the preceding section of the many advantages gained by describing the solution of a problem at a very high level, incorporating abstract data structures. Work in this direction will very likely cause a substantial transformation in what it means to program in years to come. However, two developments must take place before such techniques come into widespread use. We have alluded to one of them, the automation of some of the logical processes involved in deriving a specification. It is also important that computers assist in automatically choosing representations that will yield efficient overall programs. The automation is desirable both to relieve the burden on the programmer, and to bypass the potential for human clerical error. Before describing the relatively few results in automated selection, let us consider how people deal with the matter.

To begin with, this concern does not arise for the majority of FORTRAN users. They operate with only the most basic data structure, the array, and usually have no reason to employ anything other than the standard representation via sequential storage. As the logical data structures become more complicated, however, possibilities for representation become more numerous. And when a problem requires several logical data structures, each with its choices for representation, we have the familiar phenomenon of combinatorial explosion in ensuring that they interface properly. At present it falls upon the user to sort out these possibilities. This is very much an art, and explains why it may be profitable to write a book about Data Structures. One important point relates to a generalization about programming. It is often possible to trade space for time. As the following examples illustrate, one must be very careful in applying that generalization to a choice of data structure representation:

- In deciding to use a linked list rather than an array to represent a dynamic ordered sequence, it is true.
- In deciding to use a bi-directional list rather than a simple linked list, it is false at the level of list operations – that is, both space and time increase with the former – but very likely to be true at the higher level of the problem that is to be solved.
- In using one of the representations of Section 2.8 for a very sparse matrix, it is absolutely false; the sequential allocation representation method can take orders of magnitude more space *and* time.
- There are so many ways to represent trees that we simply leave it to the reader to sort out the possibilities and their consequences.
- The two principal representations for a graph are the adjacency structure and the adjacency matrix. Applied to the extremes of graph density, the generalization is false; but there are very likely some intermediate situations where it is true. By the way, you should feel pleased if you recognize that this is basically the same statement as the earlier one about sparse matrices.

One of the very first efforts in automated choice of representation took the approach of incorporating just one standard possibility for each structure, and then applying some of the techniques of data flow analysis (see Section 7.4.5.3) to optimize the resulting program [Schwartz 1975]. A later, more ambitious effort employed a library of alternative possibilities for each logical data structure, and then attempted to analyze the user's high-level program to ascertain which combinations of representations would most likely yield the best performance. The selection program depended upon a variety of heuristics that in many cases achieved reasonably good results. In many cases, however, the heuristic would guess incorrectly about the intent of the user program, and then the quality of the final program could be extremely bad [Low 1978]. By using a more formal approach, in which the selection program is allowed to better "understand" the user program, there is hope of avoiding such bad outcomes [Rowe and Tonge 1978].

The success of automated efforts at selection ultimately depends upon being able to use one of three means for extracting the intentions of a user program. The most desirable possibility is for the selection program to be able to make a correct analysis on its own, but this appears to be extremely difficult. In lieu of or in conjunction with analysis, there is the option that the user interactively assist in the process. Unfortunately, the user often has either no ideas or incorrect ideas about what is really likely to happen. The last option is to rely upon test runs employing alternative representations. This is likely to be unsatisfactory because the test data may predict poorly the results with typical data, and also because of the combinatorial growth in cost of cases to be tried. In fact, it may be unwise to beat one's head against the issue of having one best representation, and then having to compute numerous conversions to interface properly. Rather, it may be much more efficient at times to have redundant representations that incorporate more than one view of a structure, and do not require any conversions.

9.4 REFERENCE TO TERMINOLOGY

10

SEARCHING

"Seek not the things that are too hard for thee,
Neither search the things that are above thy strength."

Ecclesiasticus 3: 21

The notion of searching is familiar to us both in everyday life and from earlier topics in this book. In fact, we have encountered in previous chapters three very different paradigms of searching:

1. The most common use of the term is that we have a set of records, and that one field of each record has a value (the key) that uniquely identifies it. We are then presented with an input key value, for which we are to find the corresponding record. We have seen such a set of values maintained as an array in Section 2.1.2 and also as a linked list in Section 4.2.1.

2. A different interpretation is that we wish to search for a value that optimizes some criterion function, possibly also subject to some constraint function(s). In particular, we saw in Section 6.8 the use of breadth-first search, depth-first search, and other techniques for exploring solution trees.

3. We encountered still another interpretation when we discussed pattern matching in strings in Section 8.5. In its simplest form, that of looking for the occurrence of *pattern* as a substring of *text*, this does not appear to be significantly different from the first paradigm. However, as the specification of the pattern becomes more and more general in nature, as in the case of a regular expression or a sentence in a context-free language, we find that the relatively simple idea expressed by the first paradigm has grown to become a very powerful concept.

Search can also be understood in a very narrow sense, as exemplified by using an index value to retrieve a desired value from an array. Indeed, as we will see when we study hashing, this is not a completely ridiculous interpretation. In addition to encountering imprecision relative to the paradigm of searching, we also encounter it with respect to the domain of searching. We speak at various times of searching a table or a file or a database. What distinctions are intended in these cases? The conventional sense of these three search domains is as follows:

- A table of data is an ephemeral set of values held in main memory during the course of a calculation, with just one key field per item.
- A file of data is a permanent set of values that resides in secondary memory, so that it must be retrieved in order to be used. There is usually just one key field per item.
- A database is a set of related files in secondary memory. The records typically have many key fields per item and many items for each key value; so retrieval is no longer a matter of finding the single record whose single key matches the given key.

Most of this chapter will be concerned with the first search paradigm, of looking for the occurrence of a key in a table of data (but not necessarily an array!) in main memory. Implicitly, every item is a record with the key as just one field, but we will almost always deal with just keys, for the sake of simplicity. We will develop this paradigm of searching under four different categories: linear data structures, tree structures, hash tables, and digital structures. At the end of this chapter, we will allude briefly to still other searching paradigms; however, we will not really be finished with the topic of Searching until we study Secondary Memory in Chapter 12.

10.1 THE ISSUES INVOLVED

As we confront the task of searching, we find that there are a substantial variety of choices among interrelated data structures and algorithms. Depending upon the circumstances, almost every one of the methods that we will discuss can be the best one for a given situation. We will make some comparative comments as we proceed through the various methods, and then present an overall comparison in the Overview. The factors to which we have just alluded are principally:

- How large is the table?
- What action is required if the search succeeds? if it fails?
- Which actions are required against the table − look-up? insertion? deletion?
- Is there any a priori knowledge of the relative likelihoods p_i for searches on the various keys K_i?
- Is there a possibility of equal keys?
- For a given method, what is its efficiency?
- For a given method, what other criteria are important for deciding when it is appropriate to use?

Situations in which it it necessary to allow for equal keys tend to be less common. They are also contrary in spirit to the first paradigm, with which we are mostly concerned. So we will ignore that possibility, obtaining the welcome bonus that our algorithms are thereby relieved of the clutter that equal keys sometimes introduce. A comparatively trivial issue is whether the keys are alphabetic or numeric in character; we will see examples of both types. The bottom line in most of our discussions will be the efficiency of a given method, as measured by the average number of comparisons required between key values. We will refer repeatedly to the two quantities:

CS_n – the average number of comparisons in searching a table of size n when the search *succeeds*;

CF_n – the average number of comparisons in searching a table of size n when the search *fails*.

In order to obtain rigorous answers to questions concerning efficiency, we will need the material in the next two sections, dealing with harmonic numbers and with path length properties of trees.

10.1.1 Harmonic Numbers

The *harmonic series* defined by

$$H = 1 + \frac{1}{2} + \frac{1}{3} + \cdots + \frac{1}{n} + \cdots \tag{10.1}$$

is a divergent one that is frequently encountered in mathematics. The partial sums given by the first n terms of Eq. 10.1 are known as *harmonic numbers* H_n. They occur in diverse applications. As an example, suppose that we are recording a sequence of random independent values about some phenomena, such as the heights of adult persons passing by. How many times should we expect to see someone taller than anyone seen previously? The first person is automatically taller than any predecessors, the second person is the taller of the first two with probability 1/2, the third person is the tallest of the first three with probability 1/3, ... , and the nth person is the tallest of the first n with probability $1/n$. So the total number of cases of "tallest so far" when observing n random independent values is given by $H(n)$. In more mathematical terms, the average number of left-to-right maxima in a sequence of n elements is given by H_n; and the same argument can be applied for observing minima rather than maxima. Now recall that the canonical representation of a permutation P in cycle notation (see Section 1.2) is itself a unique parenthesis-free permutation Q, with one cycle in P for every left-to-right minimum in Q. So as one surprising and rewarding consequence of our knowledge of harmonic numbers, we learn that the average number of cycles in a random permutation on n elements is given by H_n.

Although the harmonic series diverges, it does so very slowly. (Yet remarkably, if each term i^{-1} in Eq. 10.1 is replaced with i^{-s} for any $s > 1$, then the corresponding series converges!) Just how slowly the values of H_n diverge is conveyed by the following data [Boas and Wrench 1971]:

$H_n > 5$ only for $n \geq 83$
$H_n > 10$ only for $n \geq 12367$
$H_n > 15$ only for $n \geq 1835421$
$H_n > 20$ only for $n \geq 272400600$
...

Fortunately, if we need the value of H_n for some large n, we can approximate it quite well by

$$H_n = \ln n + \gamma + \frac{1}{2n} - \frac{1}{12n^2} + \frac{1}{120n^4} + \cdots \quad (10.2)$$

[Knuth 1973a], where $\gamma = 0.57721 \ldots$ is *Euler's constant*. Thus, $H_n = O(\ln n)$.

10.1.2 Path Length Properties of Trees

We will commonly represent the search process by a binary tree (even in some cases where there is no explicit tree structure) such that each node denotes a distinct search outcome. An important notion is that of an *extended binary tree*, wherein leaves are appended wherever possible to the nodes of the original tree. The original nodes are then called *internal nodes* (denoted by circles), and the appended nodes are called *external nodes* (denoted by squares). The resulting tree is a strictly binary one, with each of the original nodes having degree two. This process is illustrated in Figure 10.1, with a binary tree in (a) and the corresponding extended tree in (b). The original nodes now constitute n internal nodes, each with two non-nil pointers, and there are x external nodes. Since the $2n$ pointers point to $n + x - 1$ of the nodes in the extended tree, we must then have $x = n + 1$. Extended trees have many uses (see Sections 6.7.1 and 8.2.4); their significance in this chapter is that the external nodes will be used to denote distinct unsuccessful outcomes of searches.

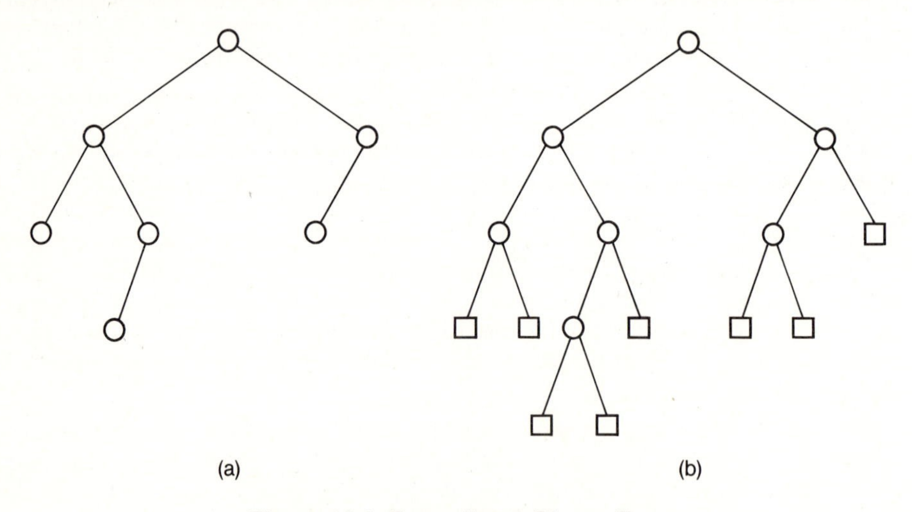

Figure 10.1 Extending a Binary Tree

An important notion in any tree is that of path length, which is the sum of the lengths of the paths from the root to each node. More particularly, we will be speaking of *internal path length I* and *external path length E* in binary trees, where the sums are restricted to internal and external nodes, respectively. Thus, in Figure 10.1(b), we find

$$I = 2 \times 1 + 3 \times 2 + 1 \times 3 = 11, \quad \text{and} \quad E = 1 \times 2 + 5 \times 3 + 2 \times 4 = 25$$

An important relation between these two quantities for binary trees is

$$E = I + 2n \tag{10.3}$$

To see this, suppose that we convert an external node at level k to an internal node at level k and two external nodes at level $k + 1$, as shown in Figure 10.2. The net change in E is $-k + 2 \times (k + 1)$, and the net change in I is $+k$; thus the net change in $(E - I)$ is $+2$, and Eq. 10.3 is easily established by induction.

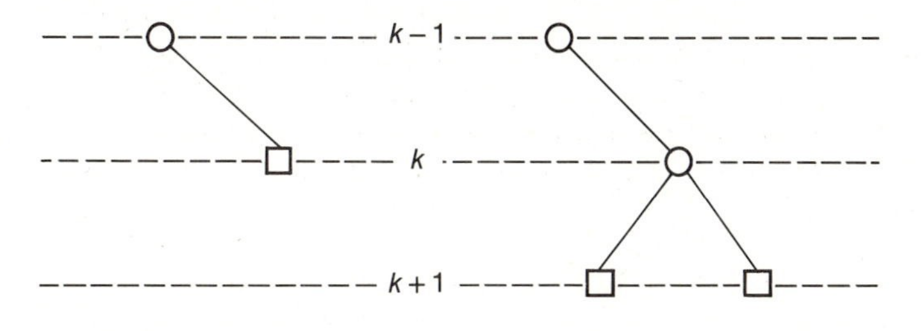

Figure 10.2 Change in Path Lengths, I and E

For our purposes, we will be concerned with the minimum, average, and maximum values of the path lengths for various binary trees having n internal nodes. The maxima, over all binary trees, are readily seen to occur when the tree is completely degenerate – that is, when each internal node has at least one external node as a child. The precise average values depend upon the set of binary trees under consideration. But assuming that all successful outcomes are equally likely and likewise that all unsuccessful outcomes are equally likely, then these averages correspond, in fact, to our parameters CS_n and CF_n. In order to compute the former value, we need to include the cost of the comparison at the root for each internal node and divide by n; in the case of failure, we have simply the average over the $n + 1$ external nodes. That is, for equally probable situations,

$$CS_n = \frac{I + n}{n}, \quad \text{and} \quad CF_n = \frac{E}{n + 1} \tag{10.4}$$

Moreover, combining Eqs. 10.3 and 10.4, we find that

$$CS_n = \left(1 + \frac{1}{n}\right) CF_n - 1 \tag{10.5}$$

When do the minimum values occur? A very convenient characterization is that the minimum path lengths will occur for just those trees where the external nodes all lie on either one level or two adjacent levels (see Exercise 10.4), resulting in a *completely balanced binary tree* (but not necessarily a complete binary tree). In such a case, with j of the x external nodes on level $k - 1$ and $x - j$ of them on level k, we must have $j \times 2^{-k+1} + (x - j) \times 2^{-k} = 1$ (see Eq. 6.18), whence $x + j = 2^k$. Since also $x < 2^k \leq 2x$, we have shown that $k = \lfloor \lg x = \lfloor \lg (n+1)$; thus, a binary tree on n internal nodes and with minimum path length must have height $\lfloor \lg (n+1)$.

10.2 SEARCHING LINEAR DATA STRUCTURES

The two types of (unrestricted) linear data structures that we have studied are one-dimensional arrays and linked lists, and searching was illustrated with both of them. In the array case we dealt with an unordered sequence of keys, and in the linked list case we dealt with an ordered sequence of keys. In the three sections that follow, we will reexamine these two basically different situations in some detail. We consider first the case of unordered keys, then a workhorse method for ordered keys, and finally some other techniques that can be used with ordered keys.

10.2.1 Sequential Search

We saw two versions of sequential search in Section 2.1.2, SEARCH_A and SEARCH_B (Algorithms 2.1 and 2.2). Although a pragmatic modification causes the latter to have a significantly better constant factor than the former, the two algorithms have the same computational complexity. What is that complexity? Let us assume for now that the probabilities p_i of searching for the keys K_i are all equal to $1/n$, for a table of size n. Then the quantity CS_n for successful search will be $n/2$, on the average; however, the quantity CF_n for unsuccessful search must always be n. There are several avenues for improving upon this. Presuming still that the p_i are all equal, and in the expectation that unsuccessful searches are common, then we are somewhat better off if the keys are ordered, as in SEARCH_LIST (Algorithm 4.1) in Section 4.2.1. This allows us to always terminate the search for K as soon as we reach a key K_i such that $K_i \geq K$. In other words, CF_n will now have an average value of $n/2$ also. However, note that the worst case still requires n comparisons, for both success and failure, so that sequential search is $O(n)$. We will presently see a variety of better methods for taking advantage of ordered keys.

On a different tack, if the probabilities p_i are not equal, we can find other avenues for improvement. Suppose that the values of the p_i are known, and that they do not vary with time. Then we can optimize matters by arranging our sequence of keys from most probable to least probable (see Exercise 10.7). In other words we have, after relabeling them, $K_1, K_2, \ldots, K_n$ such that $p_1 \geq p_2 \geq \cdots \geq p_n$, and this minimizes the expected value

$$CS_n = 1 \times p_1 + 2 \times p_2 + \cdots + n \times p_n \tag{10.6}$$

The relevance of this approach is apparent from *Zipf's Law*, which demonstrates repeatedly the validity of the following observation with respect to natural phenomena: The nth most likely value seems to occur with probability proportional to $1/n$ [Zipf 1949].[1] For such data, we would have

$$p_1 = \frac{c}{1},\ p_2 = \frac{c}{2},\ \ldots,\ p_n = \frac{c}{n} \tag{10.7}$$

where $c = 1/H_n$ (the reciprocal of the nth harmonic number). This combined with Eq. 10.6 leads immediately to $CS_n = n/H_n$. Since $H_n = O(\ln n)$, we see that pre-ordering of data that satisfies Zipf's law speeds up search by a factor of $(\ln n)/2$. Similar improvements can be noted for other probability distributions. In particular, there is another empirical observation known as the 80-20 rule: 80 percent of the activity deals with 20 percent of the data, with the same rule applying recursively to the data in that 20 percent, etc. [Heising 1963]. For a set of keys conforming to this statistic and pre-ordered accordingly, it can be shown that $CS_n = 0.122n$ [Knuth 1973b].

Although the approach just described can work very well for applications with known and static probabilities, it does not help for those cases where the p_i are unknown in advance or where they vary in time. For these dynamic probabilities, we can employ a *self-organizing list*, wherein the chronological sequence of requests causes the keys to be continually reordered in the list:

- For example, when the key K_i is retrieved, we can employ the *move-to-front* heuristic, moving K_i to be K_1 and shifting $K_1 .. K_{i-1}$ to the rear, in anticipation that K_i is likely to be a target again fairly soon.
- A less drastic strategy is the *transposition* heuristic, whereby K_i is swapped with its predecessor K_{i-1} in the list.

The transposition strategy has been shown to have some theoretical advantage. If there is no correlation among the requests, it yields asymptotically fewer comparisons than *any* other reorganizing heuristic [Rivest 1976a]. However, it is fairly common for there to be such correlation, leading to situations where move-to-front yields better performance. A good example of this is seen with the pattern of references to variables in a local section of a program. An extreme example where transposition performs poorly is the case of several items being permuted repeatedly near the end of the list, with none of them making any progress toward the front of the list. Another problem with the transposition heuristic is that its superiority is asymptotic. Convergence to asymptotic behavior may be slow, and a more meaningful measure may be *amortized performance*, wherein the cost is averaged over the actual sequence of requests. From this perspective, the move-to-front heuristic will often be more effective, since it may converge more quickly toward a low-cost ordering of the list. Thus, we see that there are several reasons for the move-to-front heuristic to be preferred in practice [§]. In comparing these two heuristics, however, we cannot overlook the issue of whether the sequential search is being conducted in an array or in a linked list. With a linked list, either strategy is cheap

---

[1] Zipf found this to be true of words in natural language, population figures of cities, etc. Also, the most common words tend to be the shortest ones, yielding some minimization of effort – that is, built-in minimal-redundancy.

and easy; with an array, transposition is still cheap, but move-to-front has $O(n)$ complexity.

Although the search methods in the remainder of this chapter will have lower complexities, they will usually have higher constant factors. Therefore, for small tables, and particularly where the search probabilities are unequal, one of the techniques described in this section may often be the method of choice.

10.2.2 Binary Search

We consider now the case in which there is an ordered set of keys in an array. In applying sequential search, by key comparisons, to such an array, every comparison divides the table into one element that may or may not be the desired value, and the remainder of the table that may contain the desired value. A much more effective technique is to use divide-and-conquer, such that each comparison either locates the desired value or else splits the remainder of the table into two halves, only one of which need be searched. This approach, known as *binary search*, is comparatively simple and is one of the truly venerable computing techniques. Yet, remarkably, even experienced programmers seem to have trouble in getting it right the first time. You are encouraged to try to do so before proceeding.

In this algorithm for searching, we once again use a function that returns either the location of the sought-after key value, or else a zero to signify that it is absent. Our function in this case is SEARCH_BINARY (Algorithm 10.1), employing three local variables: *lo* and *hi* delimit the subrange of the array where the input key must occur if present, and *i* is computed (using integer division, **div**) as the midpoint of that range. The algorithm actually makes two comparisons for every iteration, which affects the constant factor but not the complexity class; in some circumstances, this can be finessed by using a 3-way compare instruction. Suppose now that we invoke SEARCH_BINARY to search for 93 in the table of Figure 10.3; the corresponding trace of the variables *lo, hi, i, tbl* [*i*] is shown in Figure 10.4(a). Similar trace sequences for input arguments of 58 and 20 are shown in (b) and (c) of the figure. Note the importance of the **while** condition in the case of $key = 20$; because this value is not in the table, the condition $lo > hi$ ultimately causes the search to terminate.

i	*tbl* [*i*]	*i*	*tbl* [*i*]	*i*	*tbl* [*i*]	*i*	*tbl* [*i*]
1	3	8	33	15	61	22	87
2	8	9	34	16	62	23	89
3	11	10	39	17	69	24	93
4	15	11	47	18	74	25	96
5	17	12	50	19	78	26	97
6	24	13	52	20	81		
7	28	14	58	21	83		

Figure 10.3 Binary Search Data

```
function SEARCH_BINARY (key: integer; tbl: table): integer;

{given the key, the function returns the value 0 if it is not in
 the table, and returns the index of the key in the table if it is}

label   1;

const   n = {size of the table}

type    table = array [1 .. n] of integer;

var     i,hi,lo: 0 .. n;

begin
   SEARCH_BINARY := 0;
   lo := 1;  hi := n;
   while hi >= lo do begin
      i := (lo + hi) div 2;
      if key > tbl [i] then
         lo := i + 1
      else if key < tbl [i] then
         hi := i - 1
      else begin
         SEARCH_BINARY := i;
         goto 1;
      end;
   end;
1:
end;
```

Algorithm 10.1 SEARCH_BINARY

lo	*hi*	*i*	*tbl* [*i*]
1	26	13	52
14	26	20	81
21	26	23	89
24	26	25	96
24	24	24	93

(a) *key* = 93

lo	*hi*	*i*	*tbl* [*i*]
1	26	13	52
14	26	20	81
14	19	16	62
14	15	14	58

(b) *key* = 58

lo	*hi*	*i*	*tbl* [*i*]
1	26	13	52
1	12	6	24
1	5	3	11
4	5	4	15
5	5	5	17
6	5	–	–

(c) *key* = 20

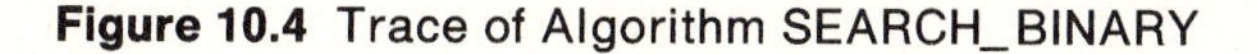

Figure 10.4 Trace of Algorithm SEARCH_BINARY

Binary search is sometimes called logarithmic search because it has complexity $O(\lg n)$. We can see this easily by drawing the binary tree traced by the search process for various arguments, as in Figure 10.5. The logarithmic height can be established by an inductive argument on the subrange size, $hi - lo + 1$. The external nodes are not drawn, but adding them shows that the tree is completely balanced, and thus has the minimum possible path lengths. By evaluating I and E

for this tree and applying Eqs. 10.4, we find that $CS_n = 4.00$ and $CF_n = 4.81$. In the general case and with the assumption that all keys are equally likely to be accessed, it can be shown that the average numbers of comparisons for binary search are approximated by

$$CS_n = \left(1 + \frac{1}{n}\right) \lg (n + 1) - 1 \,, \quad \text{and} \qquad CF_n = \lg (n + 1) \tag{10.8}$$

The imprecision in these formulas is slight (≈ 0.086); a more precise treatment can be found in Reingold and Hansen [1983]. Eqs. 10.8 do more than confirm that binary search on an ordered table has average performance of lg n. With sequential search, the worst case is n, twice its average cost of $n/2$. The worst case with binary search corresponds to failure, for which the cost is only slightly worse than the average performance!

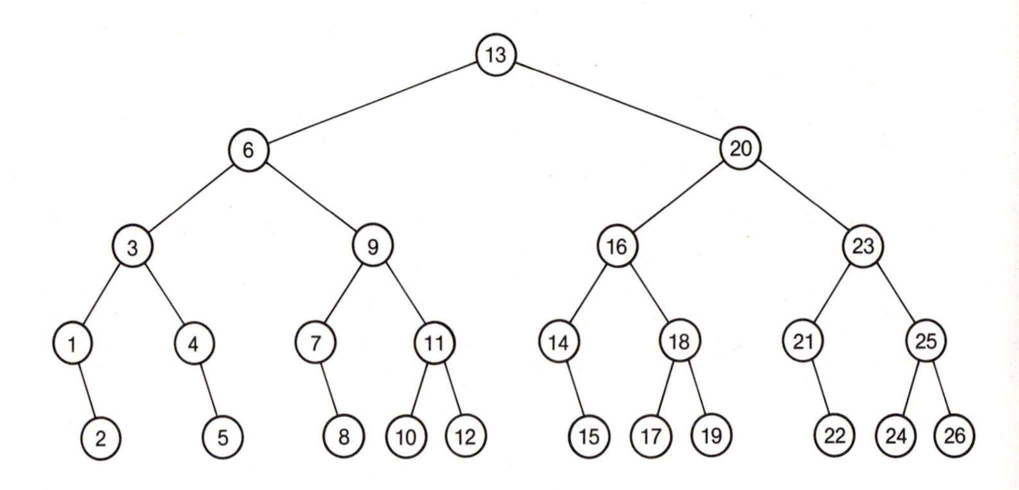

Figure 10.5 Tree Followed by SEARCH_BINARY

The principal disadvantage of binary search is that it is ill-suited to a table where the contents must be modified by insertions or deletions. This is because the method depends upon the table being in an array, so that index arithmetic can be performed; and both insertion and deletion may require that half the table (on the average) be shifted in order to open or close a hole in the array. Thus, this method would work very well for a telephone directory that is issued once a year, but would be quite unsuitable for the guest listing in a large hotel. In most other respects, if insertions and deletions are not an issue, binary search is a very good method.

†10.2.3 Other Methods for Ordered Tables

For some computing machines, the division step in each iteration of binary search may be a source of significant inefficiency. With *Fibonacci search*, it is possible to avoid this and derive successive sub-intervals entirely by subtraction. Just as binary search is most easily understood in terms of completely balanced trees, Fibonacci search is most easily understood in terms of Fibonacci trees. Each such tree contains F_{n-1} nodes, and has as left child a Fibonacci tree with $F_{n-1} - 1$ nodes and as right child a Fibonacci tree with $F_{n-2} - 1$ nodes. As an example, the Fibonacci tree with 20 nodes is shown in Figure 10.6. Each new subrange can be computed from that of its parent by using the two properties:

1. The difference between a node and its two children is the same (and is a Fibonacci number), both to the left and to the right.
2. If the difference between a node and its parent is F_n, then the next difference on the left is F_{n-1}, and the next difference on the right is F_{n-2}.

Analysis of Fibonacci search shows it to require only about 4 percent more comparisons than binary search on the average (see Exercise 10.11). Because the subranges are of unequal sizes, however, Fibonacci trees are less well balanced, and the worst-case performance is severely degraded. In fact, although the average cost of Fibonacci search is only 4 percent greater than that of binary search, the worst case can have a cost of 44 percent more comparisons, as we will see in Section 10.3.3.1. Stated in other terms, we have already seen that the worst case of binary search is not significantly worse than the average case; in Fibonacci search, however, the worst case is 40 percent worse than the average case [Overholt 1973].

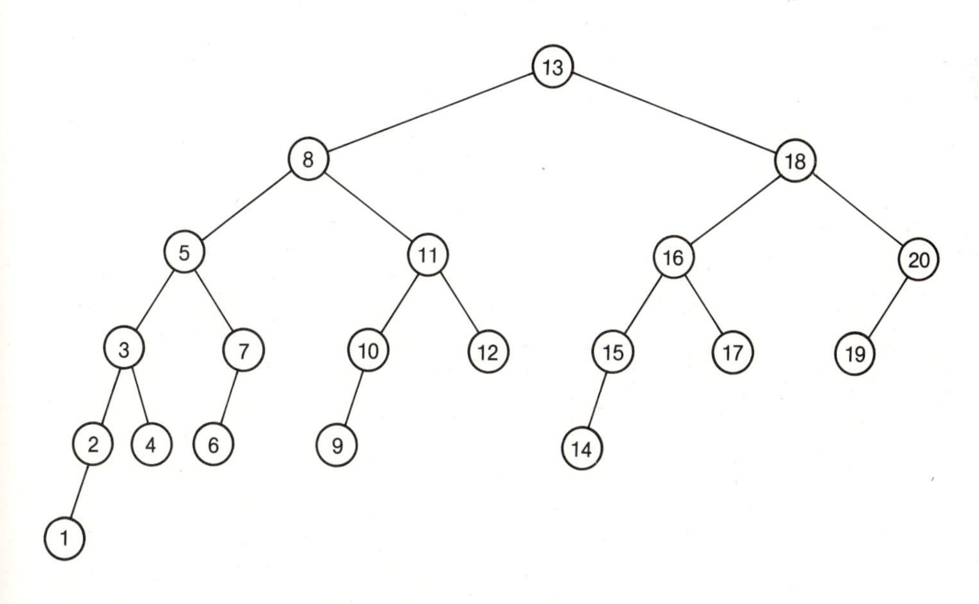

Figure 10.6 A Fibonacci Tree

Human beings learn to be quite efficient in searching, as when looking for a word in a dictionary, or for a name in a telephone book. Clearly, we use a method more sophisticated than binary search. In fact, we employ a predictive element, basing our next search location upon how nearly correct the previous search location was. We can attempt the same thing with an algorithm, leading to the method of *interpolation search*. If the current search interval in an ordered table is *lo* .. *hi*, then a good guess as to the location of an input key K is given by

$$lo + \left\lceil \left(\frac{K - K_{lo}}{K_{hi} - K_{lo}} \times (hi - lo - 1) \right) \qquad (10.9)$$

(The use of $(hi - lo - 1)$ rather than $(hi - lo)$ causes the search to converge better near the boundaries.) Thus, for an input value of $K = 93$, interpolation search would first examine location

$$1 + \left\lceil \left(\frac{93 - 3}{97 - 3} \times (26 - 1 - 1) \right) = 24$$

in Table 10.3, as compared to location 13 on the first trial with binary search.

Interpolation search has been demonstrated to have average complexity $O(\lg \lg n)$ [Perl et al. 1978]; this demonstration is fairly complex and not readily apparent. However, imagine that we are performing ordinary binary search, wherein the path length is $O(\lg n)$, and that we then discover a way to perform binary search on the correct path for finding the input key – for an overall complexity of $O(\lg \lg n)$! It's not that simple, since we don't know the correct path until after we have found the key. Nonetheless, this "quadratic" view of binary search provides a useful insight about interpolation search [Perl and Reingold 1977]. As a standard against which to measure all other methods for searching an ordered table, interpolation search is optimal if the distribution of key values is fairly uniform [Yao and Yao 1976]. This latter result is reasonable because, if the distribution were absolutely uniform, then interpolation would always compute the exact location on the first try.

Unfortunately, the distribution of key values is usually far from being uniform, with the unpleasant result that the worst-case behavior of interpolation search is $O(n)$. (This can be overcome by employing alternate cycles of binary and interpolation search.) Another consideration about this method is that its complexity has a large constant factor because of the overhead of the interpolation computations. Consequently, the table has to be very large before this technique is significantly better than binary search. Despite these rather discouraging remarks, interpolation search is sometimes worth the trouble. This is particularly so when it can save even one access to secondary memory, or when the keys are such that the basic cost of a comparison is high.

10.3 SEARCHING TREE STRUCTURES

In the preceding section, we found that thinking of binary search and Fibonacci search in terms of trees greatly enhanced our understanding and analysis of them. The principal drawback with these methods was their inflexibility with respect to insertions and deletions. Thus, it is very plausible to think of employing explicit tree structures in order to obtain flexibility. There is another trade-off as well. In binary search and Fibonacci search, consider how often we recompute the next left child or right child, even though they are always the same for a given table. Although the explicit tree structure costs more in terms of space for pointers, it saves the time spent in blindly repetitive address calculations.

Felicitously, we are already familiar with many of the basic ideas about BST's from our study of them in Section 6.6.1. Our first task at this point is to extend those ideas by considering the problem of deletion from BST's, and then to analyze the efficiency of random BST's. After that we will look for improvements upon the basic scheme. Analogous to sequential search, there are methods appropriate to static trees wherein the keys have unequal probabilities, and where insertion and deletion are not an issue. In a different cateory, there are a variety of methods for dealing with the potential imbalance in trees that vary dynamically.

10.3.1 Random BST's

In Section 6.6.1 we saw how to "grow" BST's, adding new nodes as leaves in such a manner that we could at any time retrieve all the nodes in the tree in proper sequence by performing an inorder traversal. The function for doing this, BST_INSERT (Algorithm 6.6), has a great deal of symmetry and is fairly simple.[2] When we consider how to delete a node from a BST, we find that it is a bit more complicated. We are constrained to adjust the pointers in the tree in such fashion that an inorder traversal of the reduced BST will encounter the remaining nodes in proper sequence. In fact, there are two ways to do this – by "promoting" either the predecessor or the successor of the node to be deleted; what we mean by promoting will become clear shortly. Note that as human agents we can easily use an overview to select whichever is easier in the particular circumstances. However, it would be uneconomical to embody this approach in a machine algorithm. We will elect to present a deletion algorithm that proceeds by first finding the inorder successor of the node X to be deleted. Where is the successor of X? A little thought shows that we must go right from X and then proceed as far left as we can until we find a **nil** left pointer. After we start to travel leftward, any node Y that we encounter with a non-**nil** left pointer cannot be the successor of X, since there then exists some other node Z that follows X but precedes Y.

---

[2] Recall that it is more than just an insertion algorithm; it is really a search algorithm that automatically performs an insertion if the input key is not already in the tree.

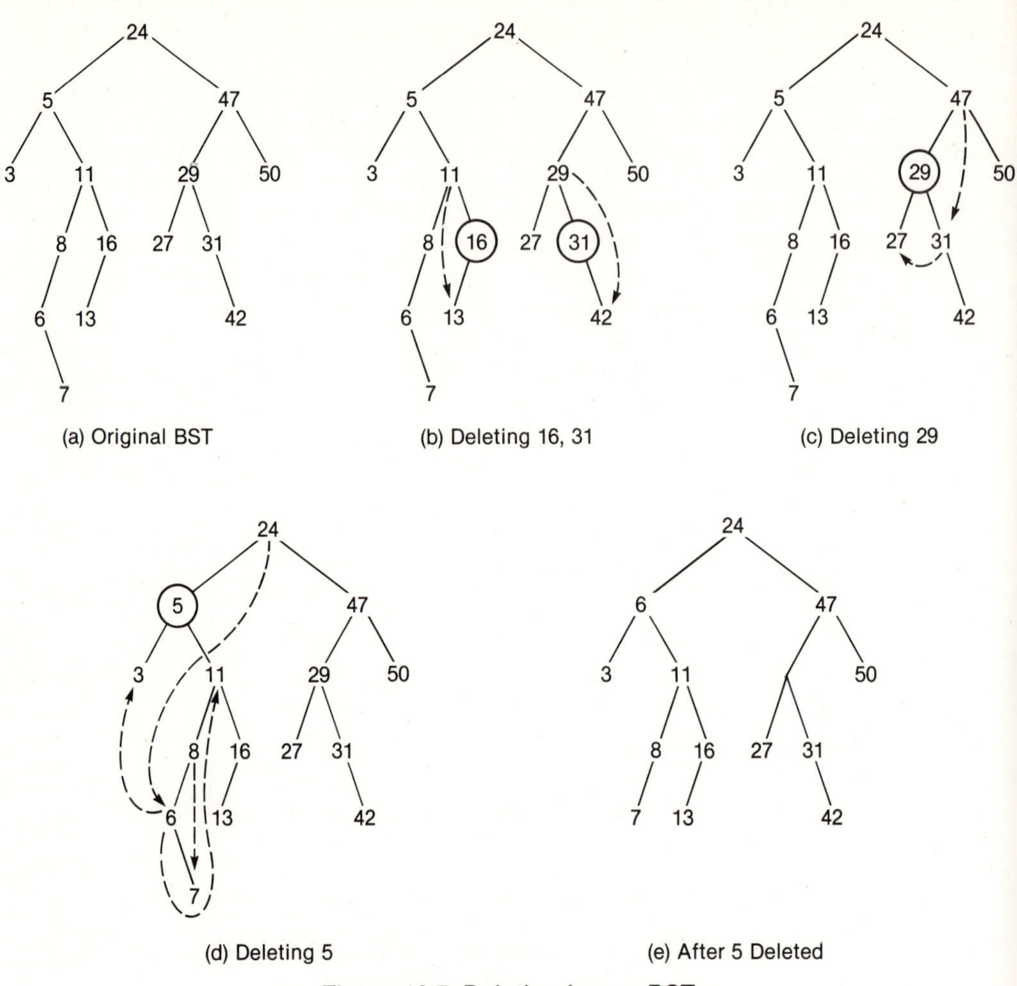

Figure 10.7 Deletion from a BST

In order to illustrate the deletion process, let us imagine that we have built the BST shown in Figure 10.7(a) as a result of the following sequence of insertions:

24 47 29 5 11 16 31 13 27 3 8 50 6 42 7

Now there are actually two very simple cases, corresponding to when one (or both) of the pointer values in a node X is **nil**; in those cases, we simply cause the father of X to point to the only child of X. Thus, suppose that we wish to delete either 16 or 31; the changed pointer values for these two deletions are shown by the dashed lines in Figure 10.7(b). If we look now at the procedure BST_DELETE (Algorithm 10.2), we find those cases represented and dealt with by the first four lines in the body of the code. When the node to be deleted has two non-**nil** pointer values, however, we must find its successor, as described previously. For the case of deleting 29 from (a), we make the adjustments illustrated in Figure 10.7(c); here, *tptr↑.left* = **nil** in BST_DELETE, and so the corresponding **if** statement is not executed. The most complicated possibility is illustrated by the deletion of 5 from (a), for which the necessary adjustments are illustrated in Figure 10.7(d), and the resulting BST is completely redrawn in (e). In this case, the variable *tptr* successively takes the values 11,8,6 until a **nil** left pointer is encountered, with the variable *sptr* then having the value 8. Note that the input argument *nptr* is called by reference, since it is one of the pointer variables that must be reassigned.

```
procedure BST_DELETE (var nptr: link);

{nptr points to the node to be deleted from the tree}

type    link = ↑node;
        node = record
           key: {the value to be used for ordering}
           left: link;
           rite: link;
        end;

var     sptr,tptr: link;

begin
   if nptr↑.left = nil then
      nptr := nptr↑.rite
   else if nptr↑.rite = nil then
      nptr := nptr↑.left
   else begin
      tptr := nptr↑.rite;
      if tptr↑.left <> nil then begin
         repeat
            sptr := tptr;
            tptr := tptr↑.left;
         until tptr↑.left = nil;
         sptr↑.left := tptr↑.rite;
         tptr↑.rite := nptr↑.rite;
      end;
      tptr↑.left := nptr↑.left;
      nptr := tptr;
   end;
end;
```

Algorithm 10.2 BST_DELETE

BST's and their associated algorithms are very convenient for searching, insertion, and deletion. How efficient are they? In the case of binary search, the completely balanced character of the implicit search tree guarantees logarithmic behavior. For dynamically varying BST's, there is the hazard that they may become very imbalanced. Fortunately, the imbalance is not likely to be bad, in a probabilistic sense. We will show that BST's grown with random insertions behave only 39 percent worse than completely balanced trees. For the case of deletions, only partial analyses exist, but we will see that these are reassuring, nonetheless.

We assume that CS_n and CF_n are average values over all possible random BST's with n nodes – that is, over all $n!$ orderings of the input keys. The simplest way to establish the result for the case of random insertions is to note that the number of comparisons when finding a key must be one more than the number of comparisons when it was first inserted. Averaging these over CF_0 (for the first node inserted), CF_1 (for the second node inserted), ... , CF_{n-1} (for the last node inserted), we have

$$CS_n = 1 + \frac{CF_0 + CF_1 + \cdots + CF_{n-1}}{n} \tag{10.10}$$

Combining this with Eq. 10.5 we get

$$(n+1)\ CF_n = 2n + CF_0 + CF_1 + \cdots + CF_{n-1} \tag{10.11}$$

The next step is to subtract from this equation the corresponding equation with $(n-1)$ in place of n, yielding the recurrence equation

$$(n+1)\ CF_n - nCF_{n-1} = 2 + CF_{n-1} \tag{10.12}$$

which is readily solved as

$$CF_n = CF_{n-1} + \frac{2}{n+1} = 2H_{n+1} - 2 \tag{10.13}$$

Finally, combining this with Eq. 10.5 again, we have

$$CS_n = 2\left(1 + \frac{1}{n}\right)H_n - 3 \tag{10.14}$$

Since H_n is approximated by $\ln n$ (see Eq. 10.2), then CS_n is approximated by $2 \ln n$, or about $1.386 \lg n$. In other words, search in a BST grown by random insertions will, on the average, cost just 39 percent more comparisons than for one that is completely balanced. This is all the more remarkable when we learn that if the average is taken over all binary trees, rather than over all BST's, the average path length does not grow as $\ln n$, but rather as $n^{1/2}$ [Knuth 1973a]!

One of the earliest derivations of these results about BST's and about the path length properties in Section 10.1.2 is by Hibbard [1962]. Hibbard also established the result that a random deletion from a random BST leaves a random BST. In order to clarify the meaning of this last statement, we need to define what is meant here by random. Although we speak of a set of distinct keys $\{K_1, K_2, \ldots, K_n\}$ we can just as well, for the present purpose, speak of the integers $S_n = \{1, 2, \ldots, n\}$. The trees formed by insertion and deletion operations on the $\{K_i\}$ will be isomorphic to the trees formed by insertion and deletion operations on permutations of S_n. In this manner, the problem of dealing with random trees is converted to the problem of dealing with random permutations (see Section 6.7.1). As an example, if we compute the 24 BST's generated by S_4, we find the 14 distinct trees of Figure 10.8, with frequency of shapes: 1, 1, 2, 1, 1, 3, 3, 3, 3, 1, 1, 2, 1, 1. We can reverse the point of view and decide about the randomness of any set of BST's on n nodes by comparing their shape distribution with that obtained by growing all $n!$ BST's on S_n.

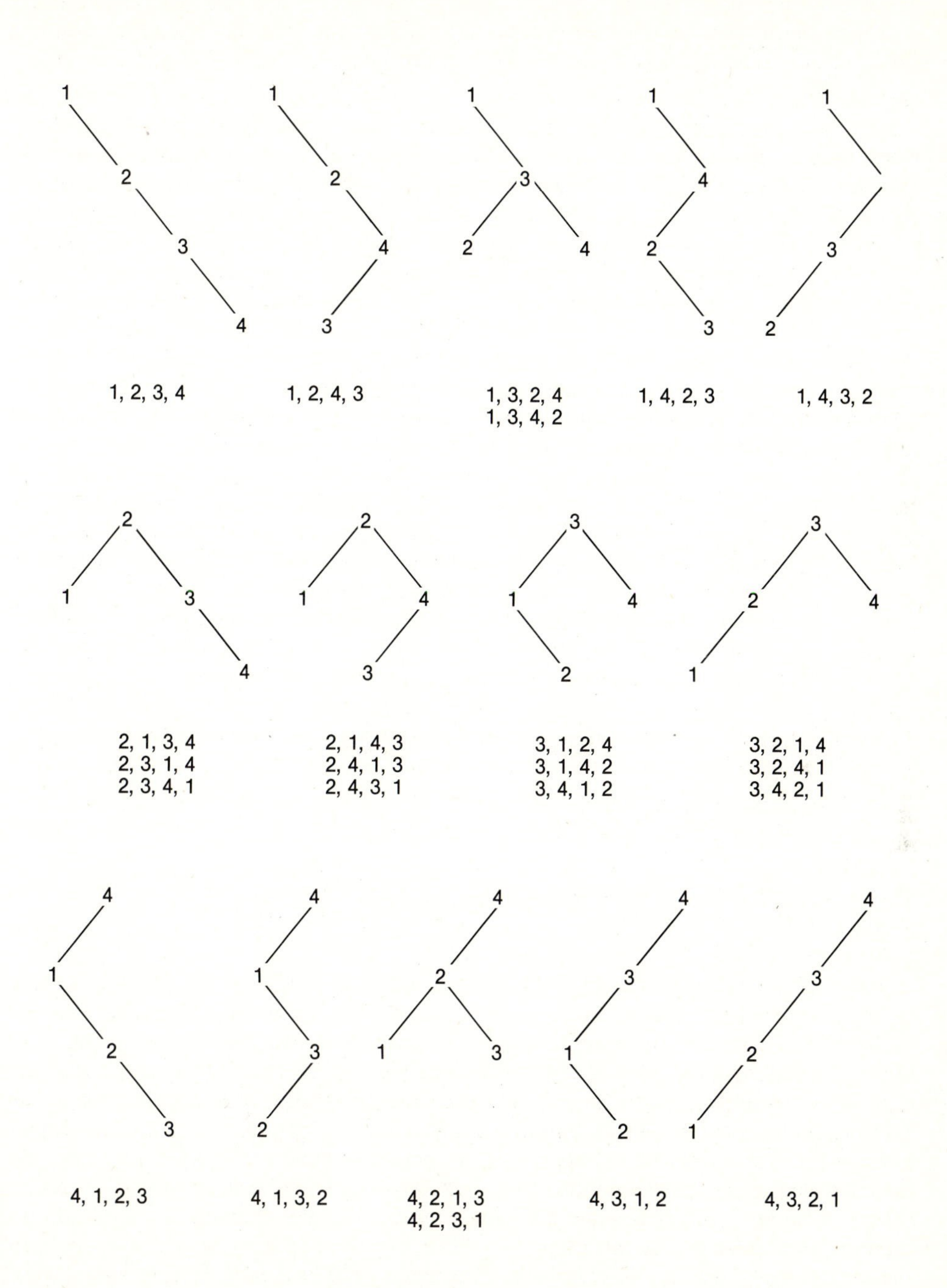

Figure 10.8 Shape Distribution of BST's on 4 Nodes

This is the manner of proving the assertion at the beginning of the paragraph. More precisely, if we tabulate the composition of each of the $n!$ random insertion sequences with each of the n possible random deletions, we find that the resulting BST's on $n - 1$ nodes have the same shape distribution as the $(n - 1)!$ BST's on S_{n-1} (see Exercise 10.14).

Does this mean that a sequence of random, interspersed insertions and deletions is guaranteed to be random? No; in fact, after a sequence of random insertions and one deletion, the BST obtained by just one more random insertion is no longer random! Succinctly, the problem is that after the deletion, one of the gaps into which the next insertion might be made has relative width $2/(n + 1)$, and all the other gaps have relative width $1/(n + 1)$. Also, recall that our deletion algorithm is asymmetrical, always promoting the successor and never the predecessor. We should anticipate that this bias will cause the root of the BST to move inexorably to the right, and thus lead to increased average search length after many insertion/deletion pairs. Early analyses of the exact behavior of random BST's were complex and not definitive [Knuth 1977]. It was subsequently shown by simulation [Eppinger 1983] that, paradoxically, the average path length improves (for a while, anyway)! These experiments also showed that after a very large number of insertion/deletion pairs, the average path length steadily worsens, particularly for larger BST's. Finally and very significantly, this same study demonstrated that the use of a *symmetrical deletion* algorithm always causes the average path length to become *better* than random. The symmetrical effect can be obtained either by strictly alternating between predecessor and successor, or by using a random number generator to "flip a coin." More recent analytical results confirm the observed phenomena by proving that, after a great many insertions and asymmetrical deletions, the average search length approaches $O(n^{1/2})$ [Culberson 1985]. There is as yet no corresponding theoretical basis for the observed phenomena that symmetrical deletion improves matters.

10.3.2 Static BST's with Unequal Frequencies

In the case of sequential search for keys with unequal frequencies of access, we saw in Section 10.2.1 several methods for using these frequencies to reduce the average search time. Similar opportunities present themselves with BST's. It is useful in this case to associate p_i's $(i = 1 .. n)$ with successful search terminating at an internal node, and to associate q_i's $(i = 0 .. n)$ with unsuccessful search terminating at an external node. Search terminating at a node labeled q_i corresponds to an argument key that falls between the keys K_{i-1} and K_i located at nodes labeled p_{i-1} and p_i; the node labeled q_0 (q_n) corresponds to an argument key that is less than K_1 (greater than K_n). Now consider the two BST's in Figure 10.9, where the first row of adjoining numbers tabulates the path lengths. Then, for the hypothetical values of p_i, q_i in the second row, we see that the overall average *weighted path length* (see Section 8.2.4) is 1.8 in (a) of the figure and 2.2 in (b) of the figure; thus, the better balanced tree of (a) is superior. However, this comparative advantage is easily reversed if we use the hypothetical values of p_i, q_i in the third row, leading to average weighted path lengths of 1.9 for (a) and 1.8 for (b). Note that these path length values are a combination of both CS_n and CF_n.

We see from Figure 10.9 that the optimal shape for a BST varies with the values of the p_i and q_i. The determination of the optimal shape, given a set of frequencies, affords a pretty illustration of dynamic programming, as we will see in the next section. Following that, we will discuss several methods for computing quasi-optimal solutions. Then, in the last two sections, we will reconsider the problem of optimality from entirely different viewpoints.

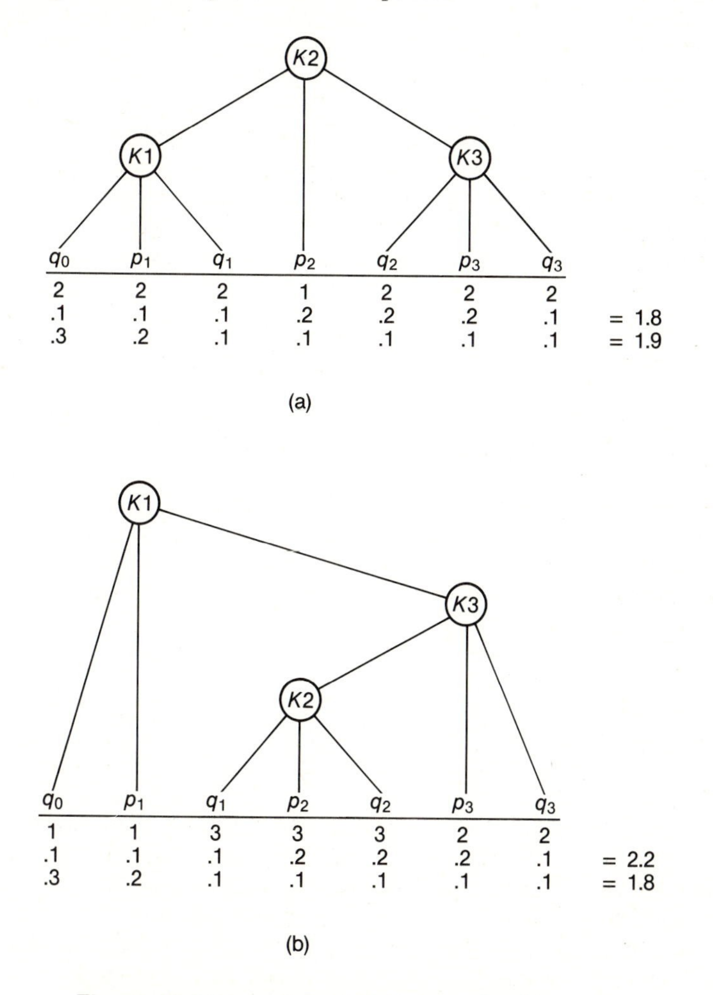

Figure 10.9 Variation of Path Length with p_i, q_i

10.3.2.1 Optimal BST's. It would be very natural at this point to wonder why the computation of optimal BST's presents an issue. In Section 8.2.4 we saw Huffman's simple but elegant construction for finding a code tree with minimal weighted path length. How is this different? In fact, there are two significant differences:

- In Chapter 8, the input data was associated with just the external nodes, but now we have input data (frequencies) at both internal and external nodes.
- Our binary tree is now a BST, with the requirement that the keys must be maintained in inorder sequence.

We might simply generate all the possible BST's for the given set of data, compute their weighted path lengths, and retain the best one. But recall that there are $C(2n,n)/(n+1)$ such BST's (see Eq. 6.14), and so this approach is completely impractical. We are saved, however, by the principle of optimality (see Section 7.4.2.1). For any optimal tree T, its descendants TL and TR must also be optimal BST's. If not and (for example) TL is not optimal, then by finding the optimal version TL' and constructing T' from TL' and TR, we have T' superior to T, which is a contradiction. So we can start with single internal nodes and then proceed by successively constructing larger BST's from smaller ones. Since we can tabulate and reuse the values for the smaller trees over and over again, this computation is not exponential after all. As with the Huffman construction, we can work with either (normalized) probabilities or (unnormalized) frequencies. We will illustrate matters with the latter. In doing this computation, we will be concerned with subtrees $T_{i,j}$ spanning the leaves from q_i to q_j, and for which we have the following three quantities:

$w_{i,j}$ – the sum of the weights in $T_{i,j}$; note that $w_{i,i} = q_i$, and that for $j - i = 1$, then $w_{i,j} = q_i + p_j + q_j$.

$c_{i,j}$ - the cost (that is, weighted path length) of $T_{i,j}$; note that $c_{i,i} = 0$, and that for $j - i = 1$, then $c_{i,j} = w_{i,j}$.

$r_{i,j}$ – the root of the optimal $T_{i,j}$ spanning q_i to q_j; note that for $j - i = 1$, then $r_{i,j} = j$.

In the general case, since the depth of the vertices in the subtrees TL and TR is increased by one when they are combined in T, we have the formula

$$c_{i,j} = w_{i,k-1} + p_k + w_{k,j} + c_{i,k-1} + c_{k,j} \tag{10.15}$$

relating the cost of $T_{i,j}$ with root at k to the values on the corresponding subtrees. The sum of the first three terms is simply $w_{i,j}$, and the essential calculation is to find the value of k that minimizes $c_{i,j}$, as follows:

$$c_{i,j} = w_{i,j} + \min_{i<k\leq j} (c_{i,k-1} + c_{k,j}) \tag{10.16}$$

To illustrate matters, suppose that we have the following set of frequencies:

$$\begin{array}{c} p_1 = 2,\ p_2 = 4,\ p_3 = 1,\ p_4 = 3,\ p_5 = 1 \\ q_0 = 2,\ q_1 = 3,\ q_2 = 1,\ q_3 = 3,\ q_4 = 2,\ q_5 = 7 \end{array} \tag{10.17}$$

The computation can be laid out as in the tableaux of Figure 10.10, where each box contains the values of $w_{i,j}$, $c_{i,j}$, and $r_{i,j}$ for the indicated pair i,j. As an example of the optimization, consider the calculation of $c_{1,5}$. It is the minimum of the cases:

$$\begin{aligned} w_{1,5} + c_{1,1} + c_{2,5} &= 25 + 0 + 33 = 58 \\ w_{1,5} + c_{1,2} + c_{3,5} &= 25 + 8 + 24 = 57 \\ w_{1,5} + c_{1,3} + c_{4,5} &= 25 + 17 + 10 = 52 \\ w_{1,5} + c_{1,4} + c_{5,5} &= 25 + 32 + 0 = 57 \end{aligned}$$

00	11	22	33	44	55
w = 2	w = 3	w = 1	w = 3	w = 2	w = 7
c = 0	c = 0	c = 0	c = 0	c = 0	c = 0
r =	r =	r =	r =	r =	r =

01	12	23	34	45
w = 7	w = 8	w = 5	w = 8	w = 10
c = 7	c = 8	c = 5	c = 8	c = 10
r = 1	r = 2	r = 3	r = 4	r = 5

02	13	24	35
w = 12	w = 12	w = 10	w = 16
c = 19	c = 17	c = 15	c = 24
r = 2	r = 2	r = 4	r = 5

03	14	25
w = 16	w = 17	w = 18
c = 28	c = 32	c = 33
r = 2	r = 2	r = 4

04	15
w = 21	w = 25
c = 43	c = 52
r = 2	r = 4

05
w = 29
c = 67
r = 4

Figure 10.10 Computation of an Optimal BST

from which we conclude that $c_{1,5} = 52$. Moreover, since this minimum occurs for $k = 4$, then $r_{1,5} = 4$ is the root of the optimal subtree $T_{1,5}$ spanning q_1 to q_5. The final optimal BST is shown in Figure 10.11(a), in the same style as Figure 10.9, thereby confirming the final value of $c_{0,5}$. In this final tree, it is straightforward to see from the tableaux that $r_{0,5} = 4$. Moreover, this has the further consequence that the left subtree of K_4 is $T_{0,3}$ spanning the leaves q_0 to q_3; so we look for the value $r_{0,3} = 2$ and find that the root of $T_{0,3}$ is K_2.

This calculation can be expressed rather concisely, as shown in the program OPT_BST (Algorithm 10.3). The algorithm has three nested loops, one for computing the subtrees of successively greater widths, one for computing all the subtrees of a given width, and one for minimizing a given subtree. Thus, the complexity is apparently $O(n^3)$ for both time and storage. However, it can be shown that the roots of the subtrees satisfy the property

$$r_{i,j-1} \leq r_{i,j} \leq r_{i+1,j} \tag{10.18}$$

and this allows a reduction of the search interval in the inner loop. To see this informally, note that the tree $T_{i,j}$ can be obtained from $T_{i,j-1}$ by adding p_j and q_j and

```
program OPT_BST;

const  size = {number of internal nodes}

type   ndx = 0 .. size;

var    h,i,j,k,m,min: integer;
       p,q = array [ndx] of integer;
       cost,weight: array [ndx,ndx] of integer;
       root: array [ndx,ndx] of ndx;

begin
   for i := 0 to size - 1 do begin
      j := i + 1;
      weight [i,j] := q [i] + p [j] + q [j];
      cost [i,j] := q [i] + p [j] + q [j];
      root [i,j] := j;
   end;
   for h := 2 to size do begin
      for i := 0 to size - h do begin
         j := i + h;
         weight [i,j] := weight [i,j - 1] + p [j] + q [j];
         k := root [i,j - 1];
         min := cost [i,k - 1] + cost [k,j];
         for m := k + 1 to root [i + 1,j] do
            if (cost [i,m - 1] + cost [m,j]) < min then begin
               k := m;
               min := cost [i,m - 1] + cost [m,j];
            end;
         cost [i,j] := weight [i,j] + min;
         root [i,j] := k;
      end;
   end;
end.
```

Algorithm 10.3 OPT_BST

re-optimizing. Intuition suggests that the root could move right in this process, but should never move left. A similar remark applies to $T_{i+1,j}$. By proving Eq. 10.18 rigorously, it can be shown that both the time and space requirements for this calculation are reduced to $O(n^2)$ [Knuth 1971b]. This shortcut is reflected in the algorithm OPT_BST. With regard to our example of Figure 10.10, since $r_{0,3} = 2 = r_{1,4}$, then we need consider only the case $k = 2$ in computing $c_{0,4}$.

We can observe the separate impact of the p_i and the q_i by recomputing the optimal BST for the data of Eqs. 10.17, but in one case treating the p_i as identically zero, and in another case treating the q_i as identically zero. The resulting "leaf" form of the BST (for $p_i = 0$) is shown in Figure 10.11(b), and the resulting "node" form of the BST (for $q_i = 0$) is shown in Figure 10.11(c). We see that the three trees in the figure are all quite different.

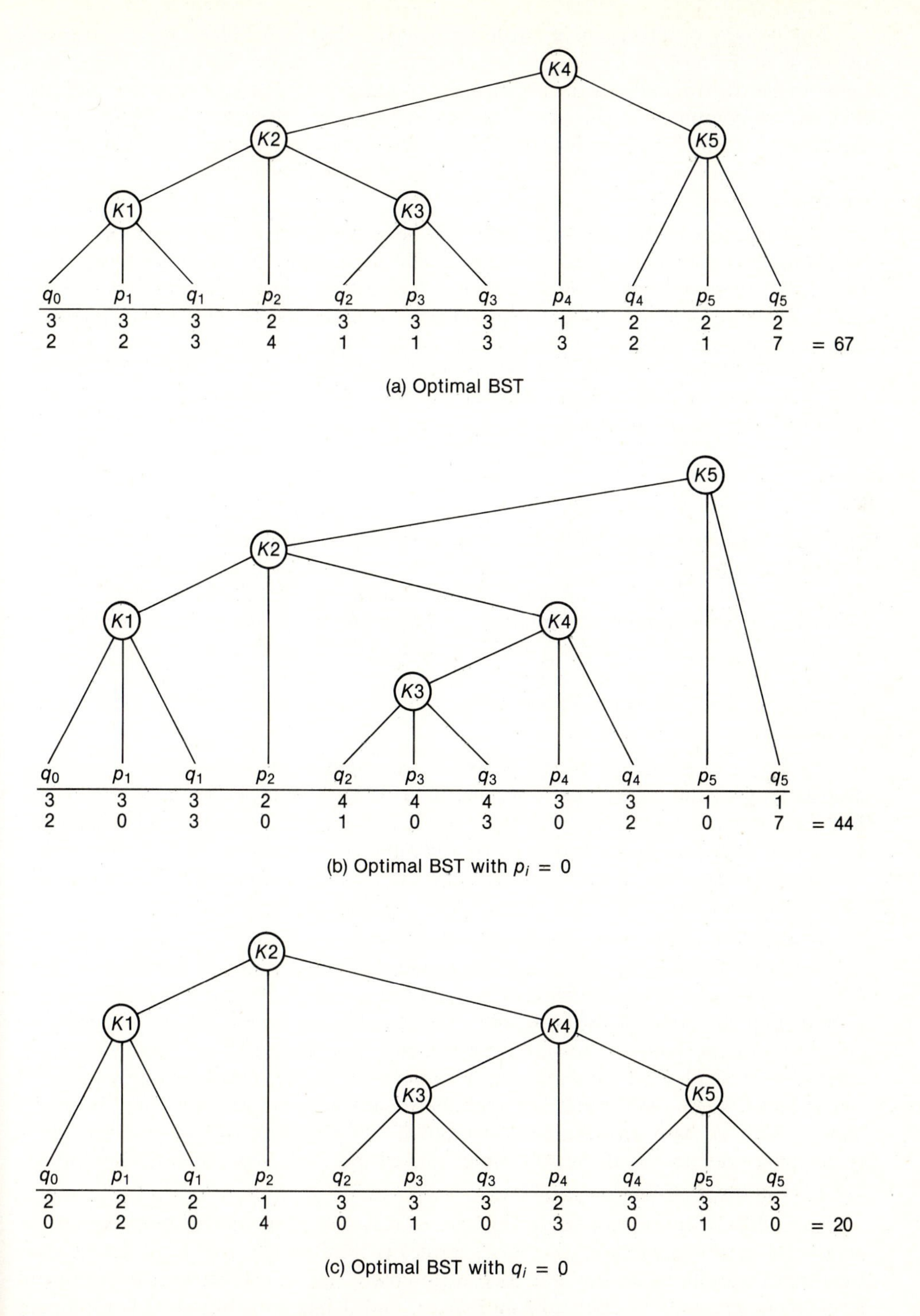

(a) Optimal BST

(b) Optimal BST with $p_i = 0$

(c) Optimal BST with $q_i = 0$

Figure 10.11 Optimal BST's

For certain problems, it is natural to regard the probabilities p_i of successful search as all being identically zero, as when the values K_i are boundaries separating items to be distributed into an ordered set of categories. In this case, the optimal BST can be computed in $O(n \lg n)$ time and $O(n)$ space. However, both the original algorithm for this [Hu and Tucker 1971] and a subsequent refinement [Garsia and Wachs 1977] are fairly complicated, in terms of both implementation and proof of correctness.

The problem of the optimal BST can be generalized by assigning other cost functions, by constraining the maximum height of the tree, by using multiway trees, etc. In all these various possibilities, how does the problem of computing an optimal alphabetic tree (that is, with traversal constraints on the node ordering) compare with the problem of computing an optimal non-alphabetic tree? Do the constraints always make the problem harder, as in this case, or do they sometimes make it easier, by reducing the number of cases to be investigated? In fact, both situations can occur; an example of the latter is given in Itai [1976].

†10.3.2.2 Quasi-Optimal Methods. For large sets of keys, not even the quadratic method of Algorithm 10.3 is very satisfactory, particularly with regard to space. Also, the p_i are not usually all zero, and so the $O(n \lg n)$ method cited near the end of the last section is often not applicable. Therefore, a number of heuristic methods have been proposed for finding BST's that may be slightly less than optimal, by means of algorithms that are $O(n \lg n)$ or even $O(n)$ [§]. When we consider that the probabilities p_i, q_i are often known only approximately, this becomes a very good trade-off.

As an initial approach to the problem, we might try inserting keys in order of decreasing probabilities p_i; for the same data of Eqs. 10.17, this method yields the BST of Figure 10.12(a), with a cost of 69. It is not hard to see that this *monotonic heuristic* is a poor one that can lead to a completely degenerate BST, having correspondingly large cost. Even in the average case, this heuristic yields BST's that are no better than random BST's − that is, with an average cost of $1.4 \lg n$.

It would be nice if we could employ divide-and-conquer, first finding the root of the final BST by some criterion, and then recursively applying that same criterion to the two subtrees. Several such criteria have been tried. For one, we can pick the root so that the sums of the weights in the two subtrees are balanced as closely as possible; for the same data again, this heuristic yields the BST of Figure 10.12(b), with a cost of 72. This *balanced heuristic* can be implemented in $O(n)$ time and space, and it yields BST's that are probabilistically as good as completely balanced ones − that is, with an average cost of $\lg n$. Nonetheless, this method can yield moderately poor results if the root thus selected has itself a particularly low probability, as in our example.

In another variation of balancing, the root is picked in such a manner that the maximum of the weights of the two subtrees is minimized; for our example, this happens to produces the optimal BST, with cost of 67. This *min-max heuristic* can also be implemented in $O(n)$ time and space, and it has been found to be generally superior to the balanced heuristic.

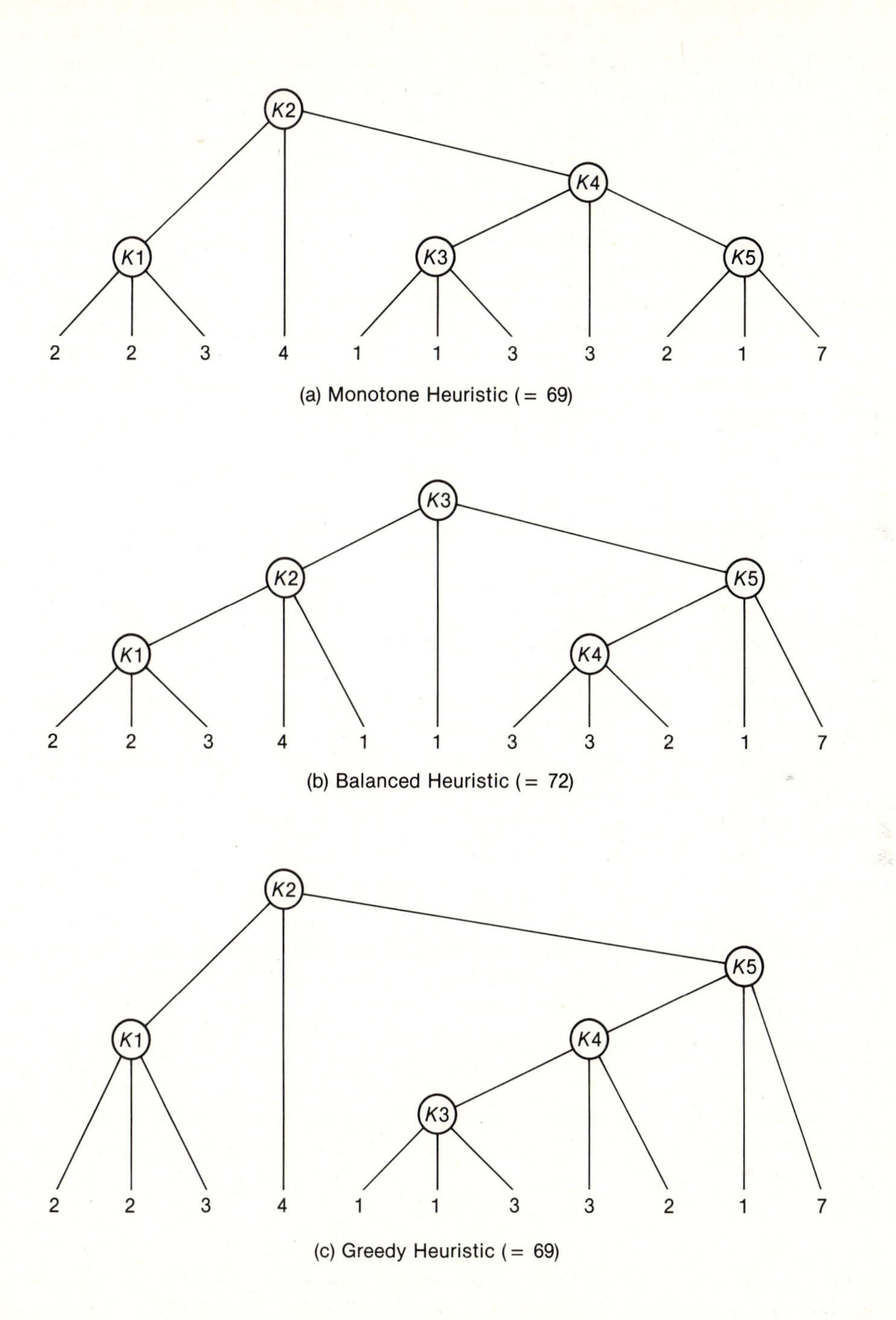

Figure 10.12 Quasi-Optimal BST's

A completely different approach is to employ a *greedy heuristic*. In this method, the tree is built from the bottom rather than the top by repeatedly (a) looking for a triple q_{i-1}, p_i, q_i with the property that its sum is a local minimum, scanning left to right, and then (b) replacing the triple with one external node (as in Huffman's method). The result of the greedy heuristic applied to the same example data is again the BST of Figure 10.12(c), with a cost of 69. This technique can also be implemented in $O(n)$ time and space, and experiments suggest that it yields even better results than the balanced or min-max heuristics.

To put things in perspective, the quasi-optimal BST's obtained by methods such as these are typically only a few percent inferior to the optimal BST's, indicating that they are pragmatically quite acceptable. Even so, if we have a static set of items from which an optimal or quasi-optimal BST might be constructed, we should consider the possibility that the same set of items might better be handled in an array, using ordinary binary search. Whether or not an optimal or quasi-optimal BST will buy as much as it costs depends upon how heavily the BST will be used and how widely the p_i, q_i values are skewed. (We will illustrate the comparative performance of binary search and an optimal BST for a realistic set of data in Section 10.3.2.4.) This is not the last word about optimal BST's. In the succeeding two sections, we will examine the issue from other points of view.

†10.3.2.3 Information-Theoretic Considerations. It is interesting to examine the issue of optimal BST's from a theoretical point of view. In Section 8.2.4 we introduced the notion of the entropy $H(U)$ associated with a set of messages $U = \{m_i\}$ of varying probabilities p_i. One of the principal results described there is that, for K the number of code symbols, the average codeword length is bounded from below by $H(U)/ \lg K$, or (Eq. 8.4)

$$L = \sum_{i=1}^{N} p_i s_i \geq \frac{H(U)}{\lg K}$$

Moreover, for a minimum binary encoding with normalized frequencies, we also had (Eq. 8.6)

$$H(U) \leq \sum p_i s_i < H(U) + 1$$

Consider next the case of an optimal BST with the p_i identically zero, with normalized q_i and with $H = -\sum q_i \lg q_i$. In that case, it has been shown that

$$H(U) \leq \sum q_i s_i < H(U) + 2 \qquad (10.19)$$

[Gilbert and Moore 1959]. In other words, the imposition of the alphabetic constraint in going from a minimum binary encoding to a leaf form of an optimal BST causes the upper bound to increase by just one more comparison, on the average. Other authors have since discovered even better bounds for optimal BST's, and also for various types of quasi-optimal BST's. For example, with C_{opt} denoting the cost of optimal BST's, it has been shown that

$$\begin{aligned} H/\lg 3 \le H - \lg H - (\lg e - 1) \le C_{\text{opt}} \le C_{\text{wb}} \le H + 2 \\ H/\lg 3 \le H - \lg H - (\lg e - 1) \le C_{\text{opt}} \le C_{\text{mm}} \le H + 2 \end{aligned} \tag{10.20}$$

where C_{wb} and C_{mm} denote the cost of the balanced and min-max quasi-optimal BST's of the preceding section [Bayer 1975]. The bound $H/\lg 3$ is not as tight as the other lower bound, but it has an easy intuitive interpretation. Namely, a BST corresponds to a ternary search tree with the information removed to a leaf node; then the term $H/\lg 3$ follows from Eq. 8.4.

†10.3.2.4 An Alternative – Median Split Trees. If we step back from the problem of finding the optimal shape for a BST to support efficient searching, we could say that there is a conflict between two objectives:

- balancing the tree, and
- placing frequently accessed items near the root.

A thoughtful way to overcome this is to allocate *two* key values at each node of the tree, with one reflecting the first objective, and the other reflecting the second objective. Such search trees are called *split trees*, with one key serving as the target of a successful match, and the other key serving to split unsuccessful matches to the left and to the right. We might ask what would be the optimal form of a split tree, given a set of p_i, q_i. The computation to determine an optimal split tree is evidently of complexity $O(n^5)$ [Huang and Wong 1984]. However, the original proposal for this type of tree uses the lexical median of the set of keys as a splitting value [Sheil 1978]. The resulting structure is called a *median split tree*, and it can be constructed in $O(n \lg n)$ time. A median split tree is either empty or else consists of:

(a) a root containing Kp_i (the key with highest frequency of access in the tree) and Ks_i (the median value of the keys $K \neq Kp_i$);

(b) a left subtree that is a median split tree containing the remaining keys K such that $K \neq Kp_i$ and $K < Ks_i$;

(c) a right subtree that is a median split tree containing the remaining keys K such that $K \neq Kp_i$ and $K \geq Ks_i$;

It might be objected that both the space for an extra key and the time for an extra comparison would make such a method less efficient than one based upon pure BST's, or would at least cause attempts to compare this method with other methods to be suspect. As far as time is concerned, the extra comparison will in many cases be insignificant within the overall computation associated with a node.[3] It is the number of distinct node accesses (the path length) that is usually most important. The extra space is also likely to be insignificant for a real application. Moreover, using the median as the split value allows us to obtain a net space saving in all cases! This is because the resulting tree can then be compactly represented as

---

[3] Recall that binary search, as commonly implemented (Algorithm 10.1), also involves two comparisons at each node of the search tree.

a complete binary tree stored in an array. There is one complication. In a complete binary tree, as opposed to a completely balanced binary tree, all the leaves at level k should be to the left of leaves at level $k-1$. In order to force this condition, we do not choose the median as split value; rather, for a set of n ordered keys, we use a *pseudo-median* according to the following pattern:

n	1	2	3	4	5	6	7	8	9	10	11	12	13	14	15	16	17	...
$f(n)$	1	2	2	3	4	4	4	5	6	7	8	8	8	8	8	9	10	...

Note that this also takes care of the fact that the median is not well-defined for an even number of items.

i	word	p_i	F_i	i	word	p_i	F_i	i	word	p_i	F_i
1	a	.068	5	10	from	.013	26	19	of	.106	2
2	and	.084	3	11	had	.015	22	20	on	.020	16
3	are	.013	24	12	he	.028	10	21	that	.031	7
4	as	.021	14	13	his	.020	15	22	the	.204	1
5	at	.016	18	14	I	.015	20	23	this	.015	21
6	be	.019	17	15	in	.062	6	24	to	.076	4
7	but	.013	25	16	is	.029	8	25	was	.029	9
8	by	.015	19	17	it	.026	12	26	with	.021	13
9	for	.028	11	18	not	.013	23				

Table 10.1 26 Most Common Words in English Text

By way of illustration, consider Table 10.1, wherein the 26 most common words in typical English text have been taken from Kučera and Francis [1967] and listed in lexical order, along with their normalized relative frequencies p_i, and also their frequency rank order F_i. If ordinary binary search is performed, then the structure of the search tree is that of Figure 10.5, and we readily find that $CS_n = 4.43$. (This is markedly inferior to the value $CS_n = 4.00$ in Section 10.2.2, where the 26 keys were assumed to have equal likelihood of access.) If the optimal BST is constructed, as shown in Figure 10.13(a), then $CS_n = 3.24$. Finally, if the pseudo-median split tree is constructed, as shown in Figure 10.13(b) with nodes written as Kp_i/Ks_i, then $CS_n = 2.95$. Thus, there can be substantial advantage in separating the issues of lexical ordering and frequency ordering. Note that the median split tree is simultaneously a heap with respect to the frequencies and a complete BST with respect to the key splitting! This is similar to the Cartesian tree of Exercise 6.24, in that one structure embodies both a BST and a priority queue, but it is different in that here we are dealing with only one variable, and also in that this priority queue is a heap. We have seen that the interaction of lexical and frequency orderings can lead to serious degradation for optimal BST's. However, it has been shown that this is much less likely to occur with split trees; they are relatively stable about their optimal conjunctions of lexical/frequency orderings.

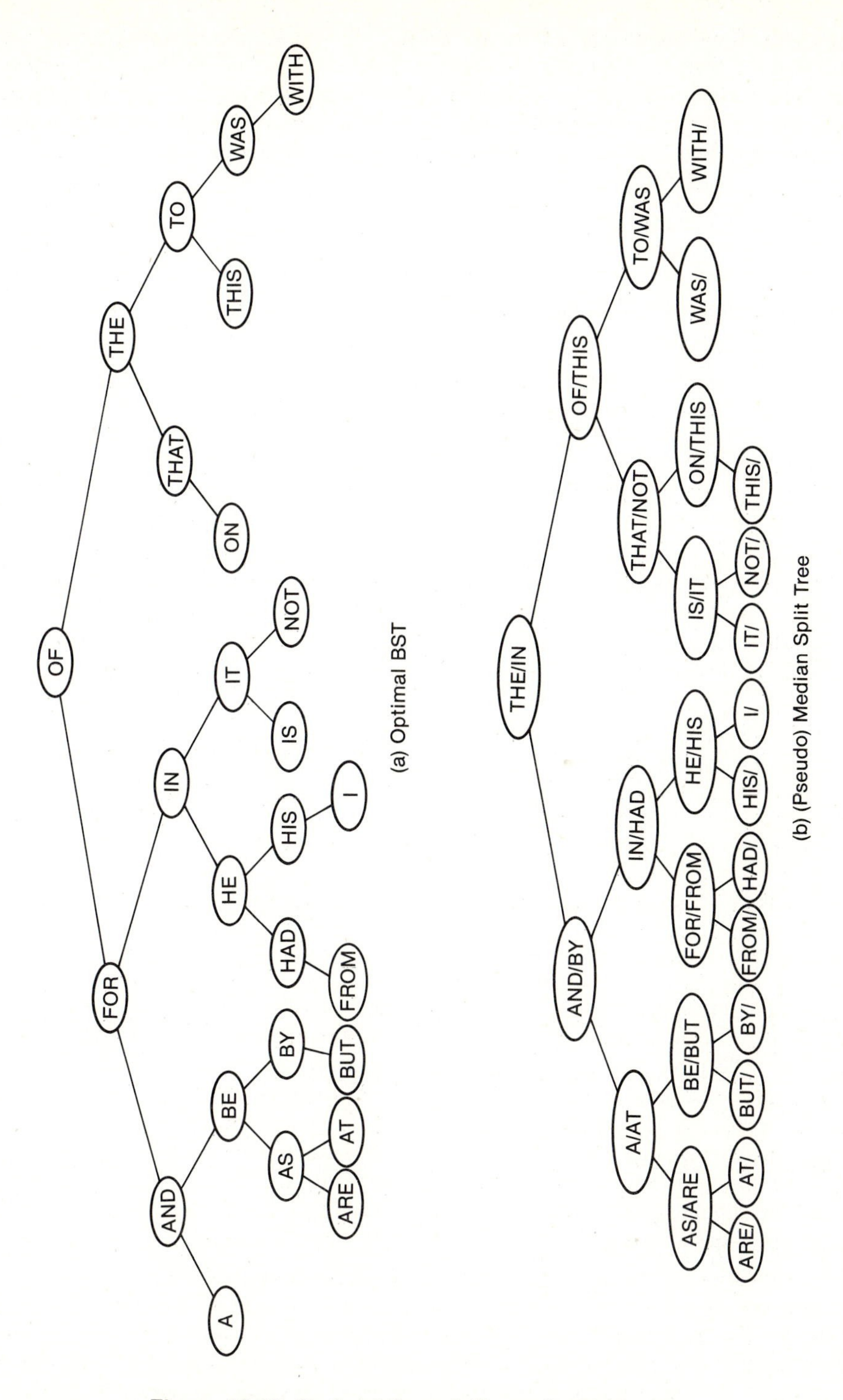

Figure 10.13 Optimal Search Trees for Table 10.1

As a final comment about the construction of split trees, we have not taken into account the effects of unsuccessful searches. However, it is important to consider the q_i only when their values are known to be highly skewed. In many cases their values will be very uncertain compared to those for the p_i, and in other cases it will be reasonable to assume that they are not highly skewed. Thus, omitting their influence from the computation is unlikely to be a serious matter.

10.3.3 Dynamically Balanced BST's

For the Best Actresses data of Figure 6.19, we obtained the BST of Figure 6.20 when we used BST_INSERT (Algorithm 6.6) repeatedly. What if we now try this with another list of Best Actresses, as given in Figure 10.14? The resulting BST in this case is shown in Figure 10.15; it illustrates how easily a random input sequence can lead to an unbalanced tree with very poor search characteristics. In fact, this eventuality is a realistic one, since many BST's are not grown randomly. There is no possibility of pre-constructing an optimal BST in these cases. Instead, the tree is reorganized dynamically whenever insertions or deletions cause it to become imbalanced. As we will see, depending upon the criteria that are used to characterize the balance of the tree, there are several methods for deciding when and how to do this restructuring.

1944	Bergman	1949	de Havilland	1954	Kelly
1945	Crawford	1950	Holliday	1955	Magnani
1946	de Havilland	1951	Leigh	1956	Bergman
1947	Young	1952	Booth	1957	Woodward
1948	Wyman	1953	Hepburn	1958	Hayward

Figure 10.14 Academy Awards for Best Actress

As an extreme measure, we might insist that the BST be completely balanced at every step. Unfortunately, the original algorithm for enforcing this condition has complexity $O(n)$ for each rebalancing, and requires two stacks [Martin and Ness 1972]. Although it is possible to reduce the workspace required, it is still the case that the tree needs to be rebalanced for a high proportion of insertions, and the rebalancing can have global consequences. This latter point is illustrated in Figure 10.16, where (a) depicts a complete binary tree before insertion of node A, and (b) depicts the rebalanced tree after insertion. Note that it was necessary to alter the position of every single node in the tree in order to rebalance it.

Felicitously, we can obtain a great deal by settling for less than perfection. The first and still most common technique is that of balancing (recursively) the heights of the two subtrees of every node; we will discuss this method in the first section. Following that, we will examine a technique that balances the weights of the two subtrees; and then we will consider several other alternatives, some of which just respond to local imbalance without guaranteeing any global criteria.

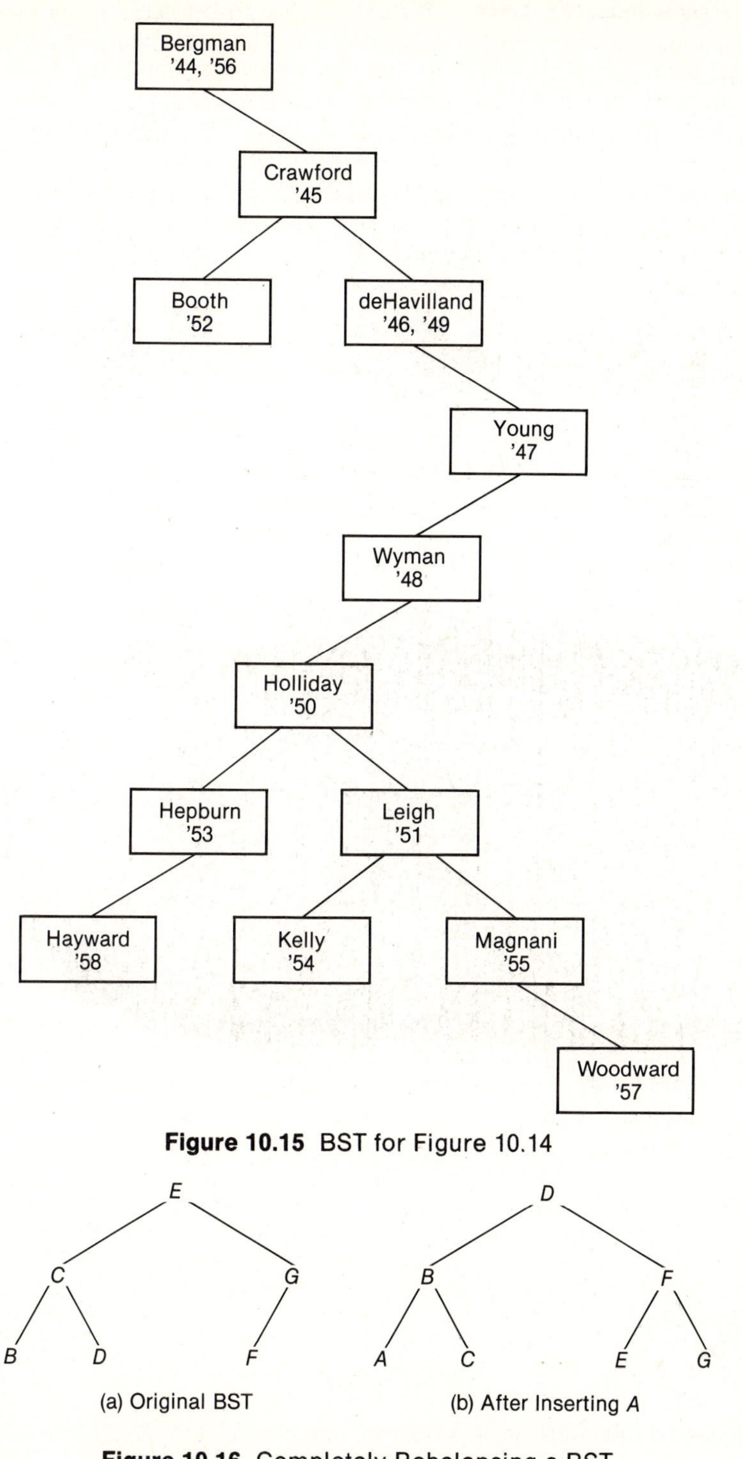

Figure 10.15 BST for Figure 10.14

(a) Original BST

(b) After Inserting *A*

Figure 10.16 Completely Rebalancing a BST

10.3.3.1 Height-Balanced Trees. Height-balanced trees were discovered by two Russian mathematicians, Adel'son-Vel'skii and Landis, from whom their more common name of *AVL trees* derives [Adel'son-Vel'skii and Landis 1962]. They have the property that for every node the *balance factor*, or height of left subtree minus height of right subtree, is −1, 0, or +1. Thus, in Figure 10.17, (a) is an AVL tree, but (b) is not because the AVL property is violated at node *K*. In order to manipulate AVL trees, it is necessary to retain the value of the balance factor with each node, which requires a minimum of two bits of extra storage. It is common to speak of a node with a balance factor of +1, 0, or −1 as being left heavy, balanced, or right heavy.

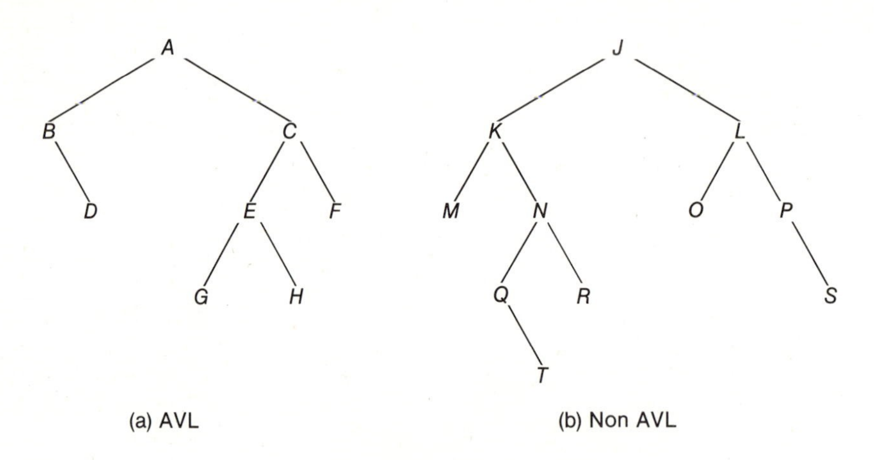

Figure 10.17 Example Binary Trees

Just how unbalanced can a binary tree be and yet retain the AVL property? This question is readily answered by turning it around and constructing *mintrees* of successively greater heights; that is, for a given value of height *h*, we want the AVL tree T_h with the minimum number of nodes. Each such mintree must consist of a root, one subtree that is the AVL mintree of height $h-1$, and another subtree that is the AVL mintree of height $h-2$. The mintrees $T_1 - T_4$ are, for example, as shown in Figure 10.18. We see that the number of nodes $n(T_h)$ is given by the recurrence relation

$$n(T_h) = 1 + n(T_{h-1}) + n(T_{h-2}) \tag{10.21}$$

This is remarkably similar to the recurrence relation for Fibonacci numbers, $F_n = F_{n-1} + F_{n-2}$; and we find that the successive values of $n(T_h)$ – 1, 2, 4, 7, 12, ... – are each just one less than a value in the Fibonacci sequence 1, 1, 2, 3, 5, 8, 13, ...; thus, we have that

$$n(T_h) = F_{h+2} - 1 \tag{10.22}$$

Not surprisingly, the mintrees of AVL type are also called *Fibonacci trees*. We have already encountered them in Section 10.2.3, with T_5 illustrated in Figure 10.6.

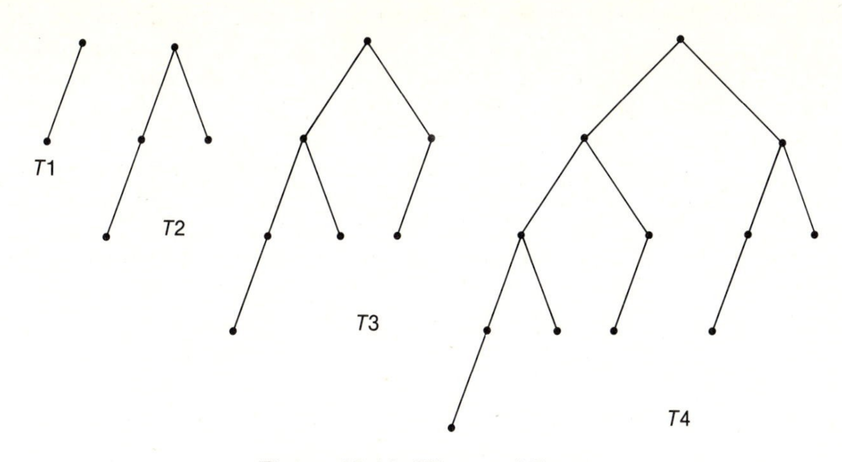

Figure 10.18 Fibonacci Trees

AVL trees are quite good as BST's. One important reason is that the path length for an AVL tree containing n items can never exceed by more than 44 percent the path length of a completely balanced tree containing those n items [Adel'son-Vel'skii and Landis 1962; Foster 1965]. To show this, we note that a closed form solution of Eq. 10.21 can be obtained on the basis of our earlier closed form Fibonacci solution in Eq. 1.29. Since we have just shown that the number of nodes n in an AVL tree of height h cannot be less than $F_{h+2} - 1$, then

$$n + 1 \geq \frac{r_1^{h+2} - r_2^{h+2}}{\sqrt{5}} > \frac{r_1^{h+2}}{\sqrt{5}} - 1 \qquad (10.23)$$

where r_1, r_2 are given in Eqs. 1.26, and where the second inequality follows from the fact that $r_2 < 1$. Substituting the value of r_1, taking logarithms to the base 2, and simplifying yields

$$h < 1.44 \lg (n + 2) - 0.33 \qquad (10.24)$$

for the promised result. This is the worst-case figure; in fact, we will see that the average path length is lg n plus a small constant.

All of the preceding might be somewhat academic were it not for another important feature of AVL trees – that it is relatively simple to perform rebalancing, when it becomes necessary to do so. If an insertion causes a tree to lose its AVL property, then a few local readjustments are sufficient to restore the AVL property. This is in contrast to the global readjustments that were required in Figure 10.16. In Figure 10.19, nodes are drawn as circles and show their balance factors, and subtrees are drawn as triangles and show their height. Looking in the figure, we see:

(a) an AVL tree;

(b) the tree after adding a new node and causing imbalance;

(c) the tree after rebalancing.

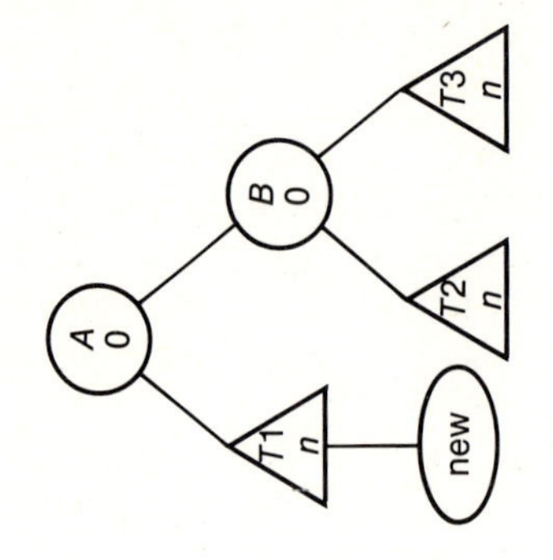

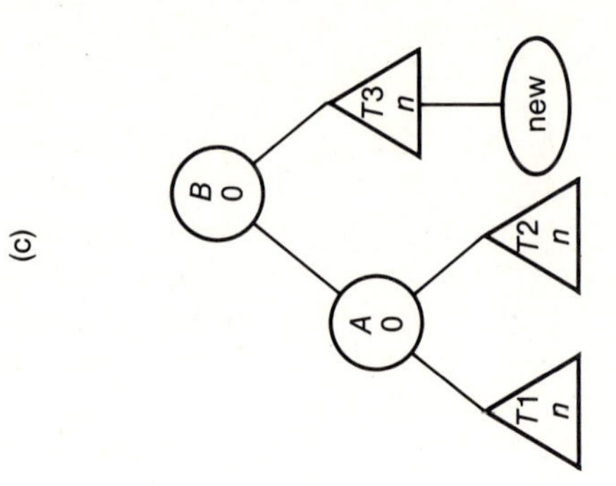

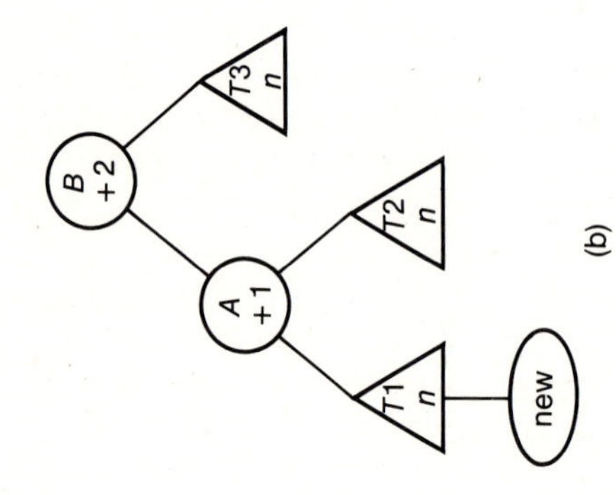

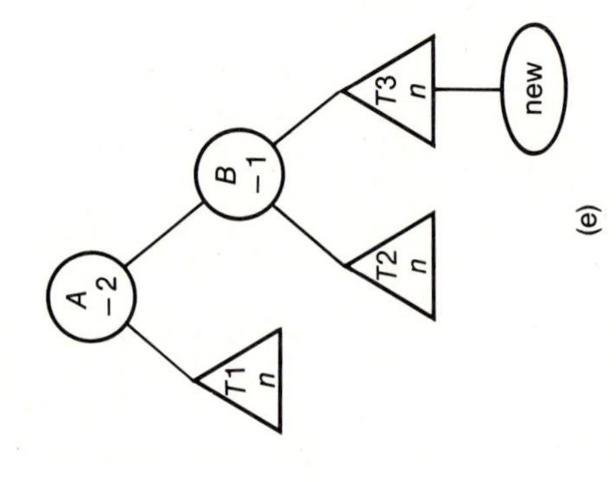

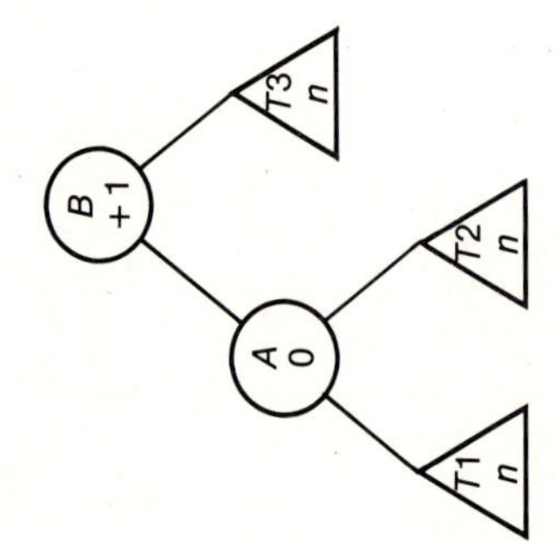

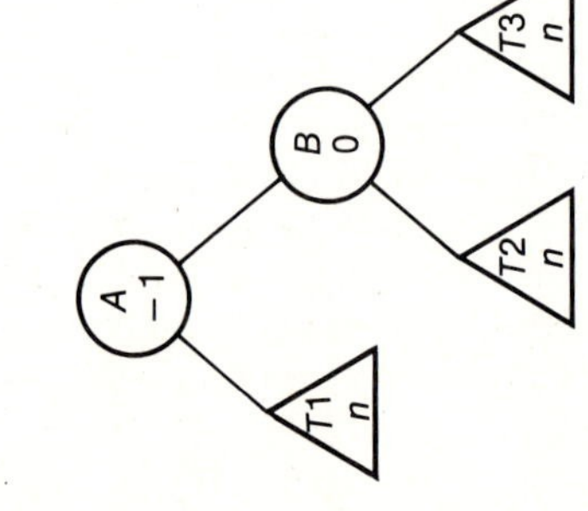

Figure 10.19 Single Rotations

The type of rebalancing illustrated in this sequence is called a *single right rotation*. It has two important features:

1. It preserves the in-order traversal of the tree: *T*1, *A*, *T*2, *B*, *T*3.
2. The height of the tree at the root is the same after rebalancing as it was before the new node was added.

The last point is at the heart of the matter. If the tree shown in Figure 10.19 is really a subtree in a larger tree that has the AVL property, then the fact that the height of the subtree is invariant under rebalancing means that the balance factors of the ancestor nodes cannot be affected. Only the balance factors between the root of the subtree and the point of insertion are subject to change. Moreover, a little reflection shows that the root of the affected subtree, known as the *critical node*, is that closest ancestor to the new node that has a non-zero balance factor. There is a mirror-image case of a *single left rotation*, illustrated in Figure 10.19(d) – (f). Note that single rotations rebalance trees in which the balance factor has the same sense for a critical node and its child, either left-left for a single right rotation, or else right-right for a single left rotation. Single rotations require changes in just two pointer values.

In order to implement AVL trees, we define nodes as

```
type   link = ↑node;
       node = record
          key: { the value to be used for ordering }
          tilt: -1 .. +1;
          left,right: link;
       end;
```

The actions of single right and single left rotation are then reproduced by the procedures ROTATE_LL and ROTATE_RR (Algorithms 10.4). Be careful to observe that the suffixes '_LL' and '_RR' refer to the sense of imbalance, which is opposite to the sense of the corrective rotation.

```
procedure ROTATE_LL (dad,son: link);
begin
   dad↑.tilt := 0;
   son↑.tilt := 0;
   dad↑.left := son↑.rite;
   son↑.rite := dad;
end;

procedure ROTATE_RR (dad,son: link);
begin
   dad↑.tilt := 0;
   son↑.tilt := 0;
   dad↑.rite := son↑.left;
   son↑.left := dad;
end;
```

Algorithms 10.4 ROTATE_LL and ROTATE_RR

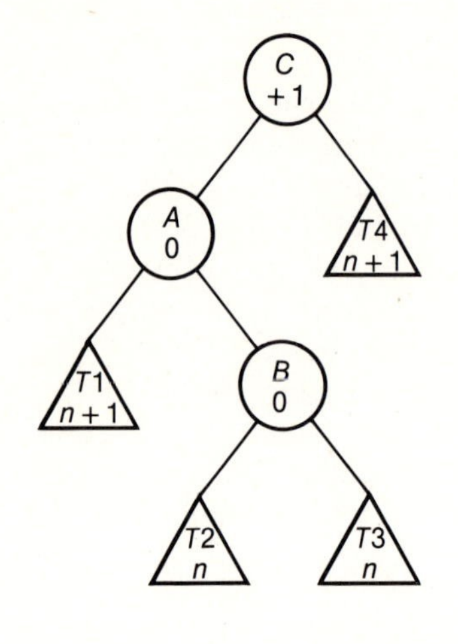

(a)

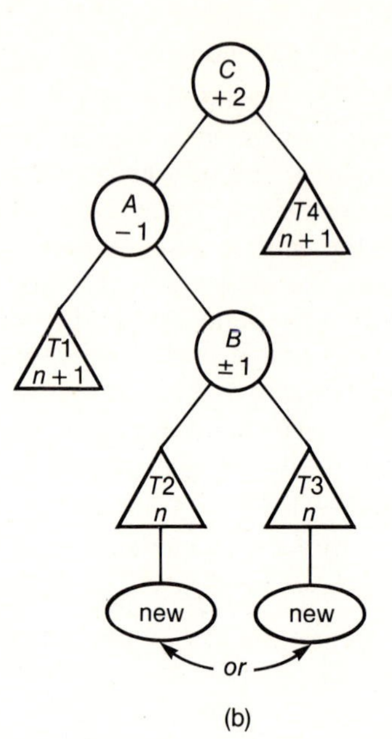

(b)

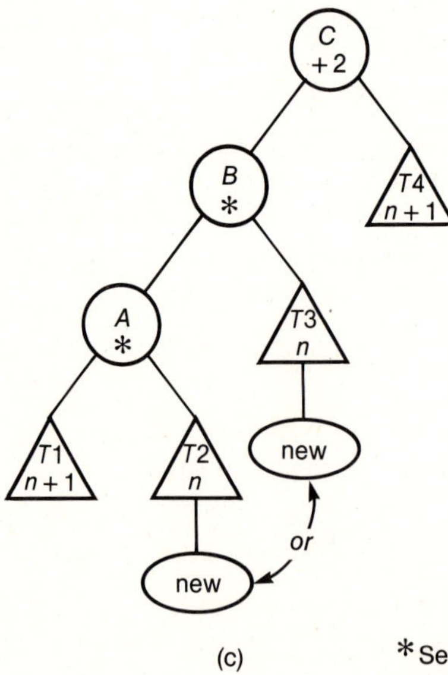

(c)

*See text for explanation.

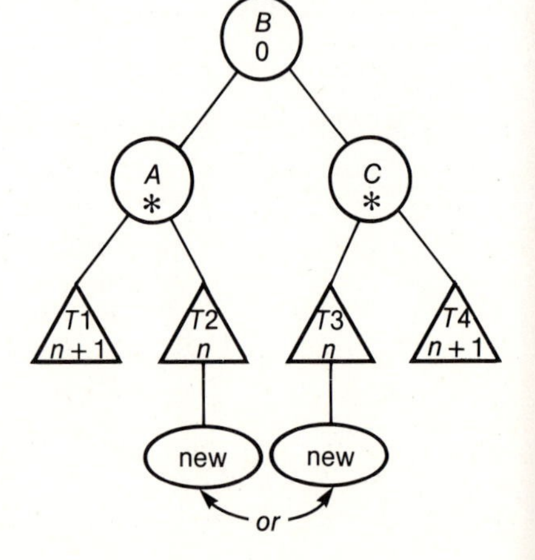

(d)

Figure 10.20 Double Right Rotation

```
procedure ROTATE_LR (dad: link; var son: link);

var     gson: link;

begin
   gson := son↑.rite;
   son↑.rite := gson↑.left;
   dad↑.left := gson↑.rite;
   gson↑.left := son;
   gson↑.rite := dad;
   case gson↑.tilt of
         -1: begin
                  son↑.tilt := +1;
                  dad↑.tilt := 0;
              end;
         0: begin
                  son↑.tilt := 0;
                  dad↑.tilt := 0;
              end;
         +1: begin
                  son↑.tilt := 0;
                  dad↑.tilt := -1;
              end;
   end;
   gson↑.tilt := 0;
   son := gson;
end;
```

Algorithm 10.5 ROTATE_LR

When the sense of the balances of the critical node and its child are opposite, then we have a more complicated situation that requires a double rotation. This is illustrated in Figure 10.20, wherein we see:

(a) an AVL tree;

(b) the tree after adding a new node as a child of either $T2$ *or* $T3$, causing the balance at node B to be +1 (for $T2$) or −1 (for $T3$), and causing imbalance at node C;

(c) the tree after performing a left rotation at node A, causing the balance at nodes A and B to be either 0 and +2 (for $T2$) or +1 and +1 (for $T3$);

(d) the rebalanced tree, after performing a right rotation at node B, causing the balance at nodes A and C to be either 0 and −1 (for $T2$) or +1 and 0 (for $T3$).

Here, the critical node is heavy to the left and its child is heavy to the right; this left-right combination is rebalanced by performing a single left rotation at the child and then a single right rotation at the critical node. The composite effect is called a *double right rotation*, as illustrated in procedure ROTATE_LR (Algorithm 10.5). There is, of course, the mirror image case of right-left imbalance; the composite rebalancing for it is termed a *double left rotation*. Note that, as with the single

```
procedure AVL_INSERT (var nptr,rptr: link);

label  1;

var    kkey: {same type as link↑.key}
       del: -1 .. +1;
       dad,gdad,ptr,qtr,son: link;

begin
{Phase I - locate insertion point for new node}
  if rptr = nil then begin
    rptr := nptr;
    goto 1;
  end;
  gdad := nil;
  dad := rptr;
  qtr := nil;
  ptr := rptr;
  kkey := nptr↑.key;
  while ptr <> nil do begin
    if ptr↑.tilt <> 0 then begin
      gdad := qtr;
      dad := ptr;
    end;
    if kkey = ptr↑.key then begin
      nptr := ptr;
      goto 1;
    end else begin
      qtr := ptr;
      if kkey < ptr↑.key then ptr := ptr↑.left
                         else ptr := ptr↑.rite;
    end;
  end;
```

Algorithm 10.6 AVL_INSERT (1 of 2)

rotations, tree height is preserved; so also is the inorder traversal: *T*1, *A*, *T*2, *B*, *T*3, *C*, *T*4.

The complete algorithm for inserting a new node in an AVL tree is given in the procedure AVL_INSERT (Algorithm 10.6), which uses the rotation procedures of Algorithms 10.4 and 10.5 and also an analogous procedure ROTATE_RL. In order to identify those nodes for which the balance factors may need to be changed after the insertion, we could use a stack. Much more efficient is the use of the variables *dad* and *gdad* to simply record the identity of the critical node. Though slightly long, AVL_INSERT is straightforward, with logic that parallels what is depicted in Figures 10.19 and 10.20. If we now build a BST for the data of Figure 10.14, using AVL_INSERT rather than BST_INSERT, the tree will grow as in Figure 10.21. In the top part of the figure, the tree is shown as it appears just prior to each rotation, and the names on the nodes have been abbreviated to the first two letters. Also, critical nodes are circled and wiggly arrows pointing to transformed

```
{Phase II - insert as child of qtr, and rebalance}
   if kkey < qtr↑.key then qtr↑.left := nptr
                     else qtr↑.rite := nptr;
   if kkey < dad↑.key then begin
      son := dad↑.left;  del := +1;
   end else begin
      son := dad↑.rite;  del := -1;
   end;
   ptr := son;
   while ptr <> nptr do
      if kkey < ptr↑.key then begin
         ptr↑.tilt := +1;  ptr := ptr↑.left;
      end else begin
         ptr↑.tilt := -1;  ptr := ptr↑.rite;
      end;
{If tree is balanced then adjust and return, else rotate}
   if dad↑.tilt = 0 then
      dad↑.tilt := del
   else if dad↑.tilt + del = 0 then
      dad↑.tilt := 0
   else begin
      if del = +1 then begin
         if son↑.tilt = +1 then ROTATE_LL (dad,son)
                          else ROTATE_LR (dad,son);
      end else begin
         if son↑.tilt = -1 then ROTATE_RR (dad,son)
                          else ROTATE_RL (dad,son);
      end;
      if gdad = nil then rptr := son
      else if dad = gdad↑.left then gdad↑.left := son
      else if dad = gdad↑.rite then gdad↑.rite := son;
   end;
1:
end;
```

Algorithm 10.6 AVL_INSERT (2 of 2)

trees are labeled with the type of imbalance. The final tree at the bottom is comparable to Figure 10.15.

The story of deletions in AVL trees is somewhat analogous to that of insertions, but a little more complicated. If the AVL property is destroyed by a deletion, then the property can be restored by applying the same LL, RR, LR, or RL rotations as for insertion. However, it may be necessary to apply not just one such rotation, but $O(\lg n)$ of them. In order to see this possibility, imagine that the rightmost node is deleted from a Fibonacci tree (see Figures 10.6 or 10.18). We leave the details of the complete algorithm for AVL deletion as an exercise (see Exercise 10.22).

Our final concern has to do with the efficiency of the algorithms for search, insertion, and deletion in AVL trees. This depends significantly upon the average

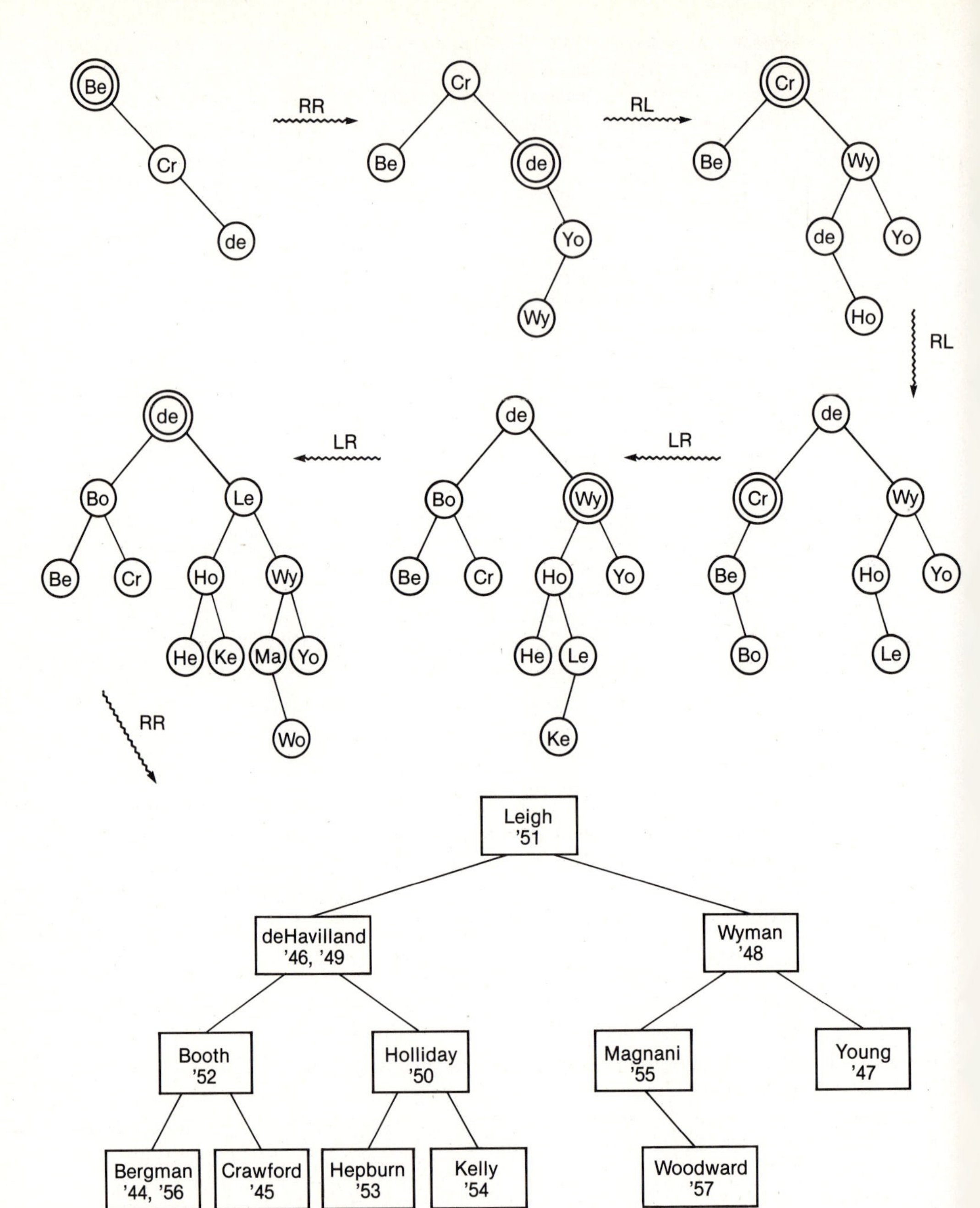

Figure 10.21 Growth of AVL Tree for Figure 10.14

frequency of single and double rotations under random sequences of insertions and deletions, and also upon the average length of the path that is retraced when adjusting balance factors. Extensive simulations indicate the average values shown in Table 10.2 [Karlton et al. 1976]. We see that deletions, although somewhat more complicated to implement, are less likely to incur rebalancing. But most importantly, the average value for the path length in an AVL tree is empirically found to be approximated by $\lg n + c$, where $c \approx 0.25$.

	Insertions	Deletions
no rebalancing	.535	.785
single rotations	.233	.132
double rotations	.232	.083
traceback length	2.78	1.91

Table 10.2 AVL Rebalancing Statistics

If there are advantages to using trees with the AVL property (height of left subtree minus height of right subtree equal to $-1 \,..\, 1$), then what might be the case for trees where the balance factor is allowed to be $-2 \,..\, 2$, $-3 \,..\, 3$, or $-k \,..\, k$? These generalizations of AVL trees are called *height-balanced HB* [*k*]*trees* [Foster 1973]. On the one hand, the worst-case height increases as k increases [Karlton et al. 1976]; thus,

$$\text{for } k = 2,\ h = 1.81 \lg n - 0.71:$$
$$\text{for } k = 3,\ h = 2.15 \lg n - 1.13:$$
$$\text{etc.}$$

as compared to Eq. 10.24 for $k = 1$. On the other hand, the frequency of rebalancing is less, declining from .465 for $k = 1$ (see Table 10.2) to about 0.2 for $k = 2$. The optimal value of k depends upon the relative importance of searches, insertions, and deletions in a given application – being a trade-off between increased average search length and decreased cost of restructuring. However, one comparison via simulation strongly suggests that HB [1] trees (pure AVL trees) are often better than their generalizations [Baer and Schwab 1977].

Just as HB [*k*] trees are a generalization of AVL trees, *one-sided height-balanced* (*OSHB*) *trees*, are a specialization of AVL trees. For these, the condition is imposed that the balance factor is never positive (or negative). Their motivation is that the balance factor can then be stored in just one bit. Whether or not this is significant depends very much upon the details of the implementation. Although there are algorithms for performing insertion and deletion in OSHB trees with the same $O(\lg n)$ complexity as for HB trees, they are considerably more complicated [Räihä and Zweben 1979; Zweben and McDonald 1978]. If it is really important to find a balancing scheme that requires just one bit per node, then we will find better ways to accomplish this in Section 10.3.5.

†10.3.3.2 Weight-Balanced Trees. In the preceding section, we saw how to obtain BST's with good performance by imposing the criterion of height-balance. Similar success has been obtained by imposing the criterion of *weight-balance*, in two different manners. In the original method, for a tree T with left and right subtrees T_L and T_R, the node balance of a node T is defined as 1/2 if T is an external node, and as $\beta(T) = |T_L| / |T|$ otherwise, where $|T|$ denotes the number of external nodes in T [Nievergelt and Reingold 1973]. Obviously, we must have $0 < \beta(T) \leq 1$. Then T is said to be of *bounded balance* α, or in BB [α], if

(i) $\alpha \leq \beta(T) \leq 1 - \alpha$;

(ii) both T_L and T_R are also in BB [α].

Although originally characterized as "bounded balance," this criterion is now commonly described as "weight-balance." But the reader should beware on this point. The term "weight-balance" was in fact originally applied to a different method that is now less widely in vogue. In this other method, the weight is stored at each node X, and rotations are applied in a fashion to reduce the value of the internal path length at X whenever possible [Baer 1975]. Trees constructed by this method have the same worst-case search length of 1.44 lg n as AVL trees, and a worst-case value of internal path length that is better than for either AVL trees or BB [α] trees [Gonnet 1983]. Unfortunately, a rotation at one node according to this criterion can cause imbalance at other nodes, and lead to a "chain-reaction" of rotations both upward and downward. Thus, we turn our attention to BB [α] trees.

A tree in BB [1/2] is a complete binary tree with a full complement of 2^h leaves. Some other examples of weight balanced trees are shown (without external nodes) in Figure 10.22, with each node displaying its value of β. Note that the BB [α] category of a tree is *not* the same as the value of β at the root of the tree. Curiously, there can be no trees with $1/3 < \alpha < 1/2$. If there were such a tree, it would have to have subtree(s) not in BB [1/2]. Let T be a smallest such subtree. Then the subtrees of T are both in BB [1/2], and have $2^L - 1$ and $2^R - 1$ internal nodes, respectively. However, $L \neq R$ since T is not in BB [1/2]. In that case, the balance of T is $\beta(T) = 2^L / (2^L + 2^R) = 1 / (1 + 2^{R-L})$. If $L < R$ then $\beta(T) \leq 1/3$, and if $L > R$ then $\beta(T) \geq 2/3$. Thus there cannot be a tree T in BB [α] with $1/3 < \alpha < 1/2$.

How are weight-balanced trees related to height-balanced trees? In answer, there is no relationship; neither class is properly contained in the other. For example, the tree of Figure 10.22(c) is BB [1/3], and we learned in the preceding paragraph that this is the best that can be obtained, short of completely balanced trees. But it is obvious that this tree is not height-balanced (and neither is the BB [1/4] tree of (b) in the figure). In the other direction, let T be a tree such that T_L is a Fibonacci tree of height h and T_R is a complete binary tree with 2^h leaves. Then the ratio $|T_L| / |T|$ can be made smaller than any α, for h sufficiently large. So T is then height-balanced but not weight-balanced.

The crucial property of height-balanced trees is that balance can be maintained globally, in the face of insertions and deletions, via simple rotations. A similar property exists for weight-balanced trees, but it is not so elementary. In the case of insertions, a BB [α] tree can be maintained as such via the same single or double rotations as for height-balanced trees, whenever $0 < \alpha < 1 - 2^{-1/2}$. The case of deletions is more complicated, leading to the bounds $2/11 < \alpha < 1 - 2^{-1/2}$ (approximately, $0.182 < \alpha < 0.293$) [Blum and Mehlhorn 1980]. Moreover, the height of weight-balanced trees is logarithmic in the number of nodes, and also the rotations can be applied in logarithmic time. The effects of rotations upon the node balances

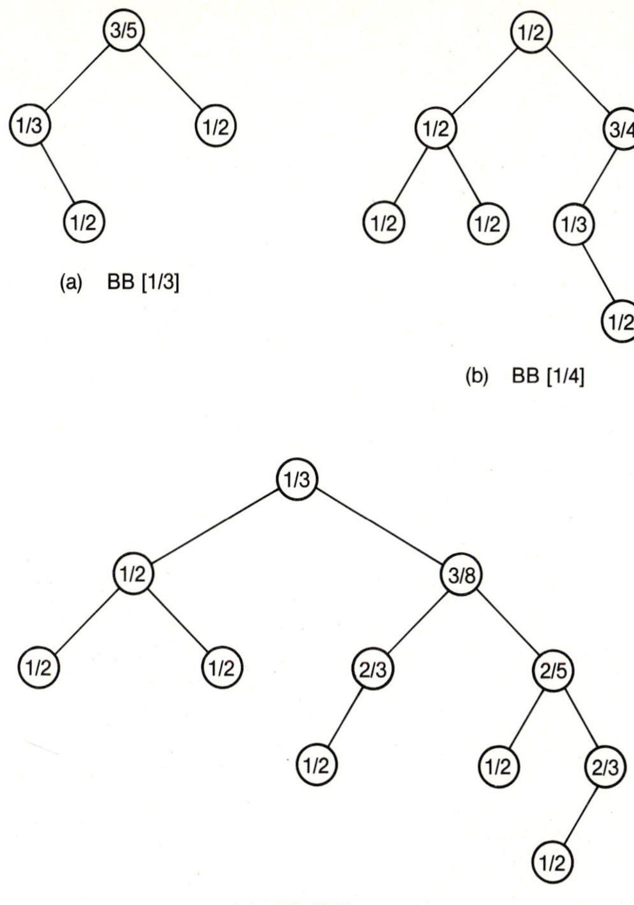

Figure 10.22 BB [α] Trees

is illustrated in Figure 10.23; the derivation of the formulas therein are left as an exercise (see Exercise 10.24).

How do weight-balanced trees compare with height-balanced trees in terms of performance? This question has several answers:

- Even for the (best possible) case of BB [1/3] trees, the average search length is 1.09 lg n and the worst search length is 1.70 lg n, as compared with lg n and 1.44 lg n for HB [1] trees.

- Weight-balance is certainly a more expensive criterion, both in terms of the time required to perform divisions and in terms of the space required to store the balance information. But note that it is much more useful to store the weight $|T|$ and to compute the β values as needed, rather than to store $\beta(T)$.

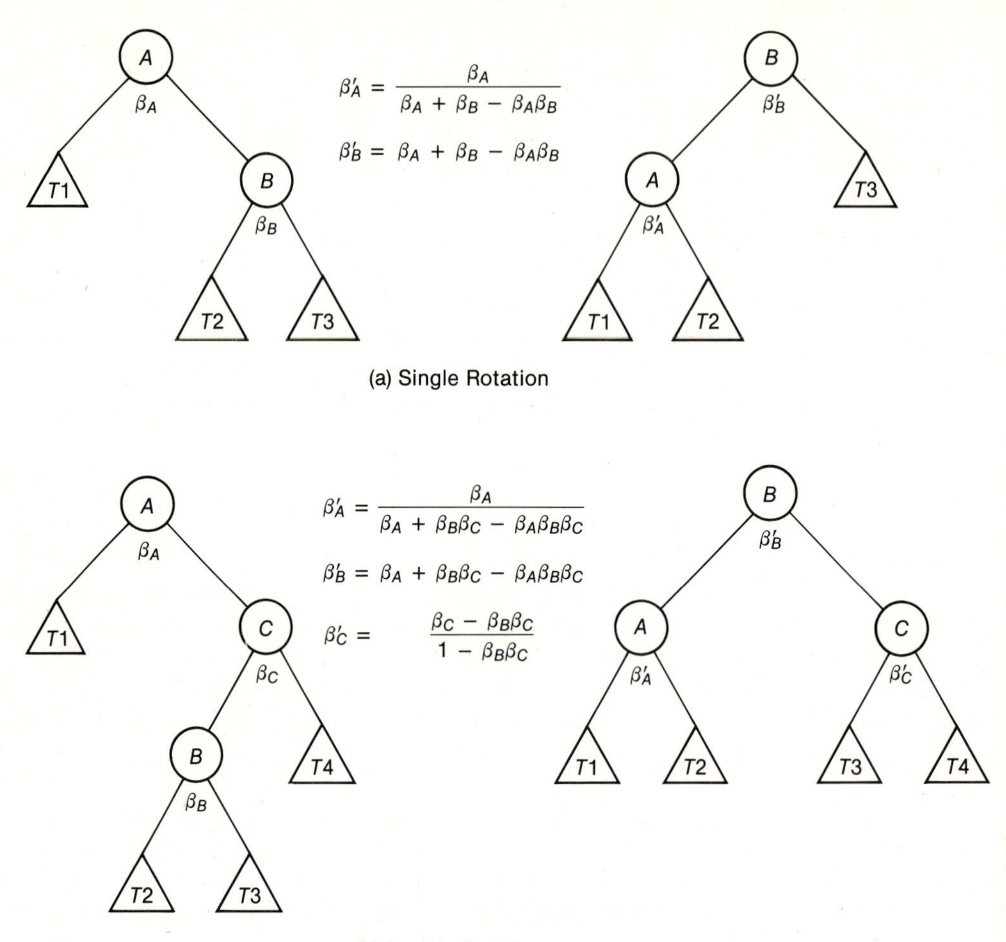

Figure 10.23 Weight Balance Transformations

- Although it costs more space to store weights than to store height differentials, the weight information has the additional advantage that it can be quite useful for finding an item in a BST according to its rank. Thus, suppose that we wish to retrieve the jth item out of the n items stored in a BST. An algorithm for this need simply compare the argument j against the weight w of the left subtree of a node X; as a result,

  (a) if $j < w$ then proceed to the left subtree;
  (b) if $j = w$ then X is the jth node;
  (c) if $j > w$ then proceed to the right subtree with $j := j - w$.

- Height-balancing requires a retracing of part of the insertion path to restore balance, after the point of insertion is determined. Weight-balancing, on the other hand, can be performed as the search proceeds top-down from the root.

- One of the principal motivations for the weight-balancing method was to be able to "fine-tune" the performance by using a stringent (relaxed) value of α, according as searches (insertions) are more important. Although it is also possible to relax HB [1] to HB [k], the consequences in that case are abrupt rather than gradual.

- Overall, the additional complications of weight-balancing do not seem to be as cost-effective as the simpler techniques of height-balancing. They require a bit more time and produce slightly inferior results [Baer and Schwab 1977; Walker and Wood 1976]. The differences are slight, however, and the choice between them might reasonably depend upon the importance of satisfying rank queries, as described above.

†10.3.3.3 Restructuring Without Balance Criteria. The methods of the two preceding sections have relied upon the retention of balance criteria at each node. The essential point of those methods is that whenever an insertion or a deletion causes the criterion to be violated at any node(s), then it can always be efficiently restored by means of rotations. It is possible to use the same rotations without reference to explicit balance criteria. The two obvious ways to do this are analogous to the move-to-front rule and transposition rule for linear search (see Section 10.2.1). A transposition can be accomplished by one rotation, and a move-to-root can be accomplished by a series of rotations. One advantage of this approach is the savings in space and time for storing and manipulating the balance data. Another is that the rotations can be applied even in the case of search, and not just with insertions and deletions; thus the resulting BST might be able to converge steadily toward its optimal form. In fact, the transposition rule "flirts with disaster" when applied to BST's [Allen and Munro 1978]. The performance of the move-to-root rule is distinctly better, but it can very easily lead to monotonic trees with $O(n)$ worst-case search times (see Section 10.3.2.2). Whether or not this is a serious possibility depends upon the entropy of the keys in the BST (see Section 10.3.2.3) [Bitner 1979]. If the entropy is high (the access probabilities are fairly uniform), then the shape of the tree becomes important and the move-to-root rule does not perform too well. But if the entropy is low, as it is for example with Zipf's law, then the keys with high access probabilities will all tend to be near the root, so that this approach is reasonable. Even so, there is another problem with the practical implementation of such self-organizing BST's. They tend to cause many more rotations than do the methods of the two previous sections. One technique for bounding the cost of restructuring to an amortized value of $O(\lg n)$ is to split the original BST into two BST's that are then concatenated [Sleator and Tarjan 1983] (see also Exercise 6.20).

†10.3.4 **Multiway Trees.** Although several criteria were employed for balancing search trees in the preceding section, one property was kept inviolate, that the search trees should always be binary. The effects of the different balancing criteria were reflected in the varying heights of the subtrees, although height was not always the criterion per se. A different strategy is to insist that subtrees should always be equal in height, but allow the width or *arity* (that is, branching factor) of the nodes to vary. Such trees are called *multiway trees.* As in the case of the trees of the preceding section, by imposing conditions upon the manner in which the arity is allowed to vary, it is possible to define closed classes of trees, such that a specified property is maintained under insertions and deletions. Consequently, one can analyze such a class of trees and obtain various properties about it. The original notion of multiway trees balanced in this fashion corresponds to that of B-trees having large arity, for use with secondary memory. We will study them in Section 12.3.4. Here we will consider the viability of trees of low arity, for dynamic searching in main memory.

The simplest case that we encounter is that of *2-3 trees*,[4] in which each node is either a 2-node containing one key and two children, or a 3-node containing two keys and three children. Search and insertion for a key K both begin at the root. In the case of insertion, this process carries us to an external node X, and the insertion proper proceeds bottom-up from that point. If the parent of X is a 2-node, then K is placed therein and the 2-node becomes a 3-node. But if the parent of X is a 3-node, then the insertion of K causes *node-splitting*; in this process, the 3-node is replaced by two 2-nodes, and a key K' is promoted upward in the 2-3 tree into its parent node. The promotion may cause a similar split and promotion in the parent node, and this process can continue all the way to the root. Balancing by splitting is conceptually easy to follow, as we can see by applying the method to our Best Actress data of Figure 10.14. The corresponding growth to the final 2-3 tree is shown in Figure 10.24. Splittings occur with the insertions of de Havilland, Wyman, and Leigh. The last of these also splits its parent, causing the entire tree to grow in height and to acquire a new root node. Subsequent splittings occur for Magnani and Hayward.

If we consider how to implement 2-3 trees, we are led to adopt a node structure in the nature of

```
type  link23 = ↑node23;
      node23 = record
         full: boolean;
         k1,k2: integer;
         p0,p1,p2: link23;
      end;
```

In order to insert a new value, we need to use a stack to retain pointers along the path from the root to the point of insertion. Subsequently, in the procedure for inserting a key into a node X, if the insertion causes X to split, then the pointer to the parent of X can be retrieved from the stack, and the procedure can recursively call itself to insert a promoted key into the parent. (Note that pointers as well as

---

[4] 2-3 trees are B-trees of order 3, as we will see in Chapter 12.

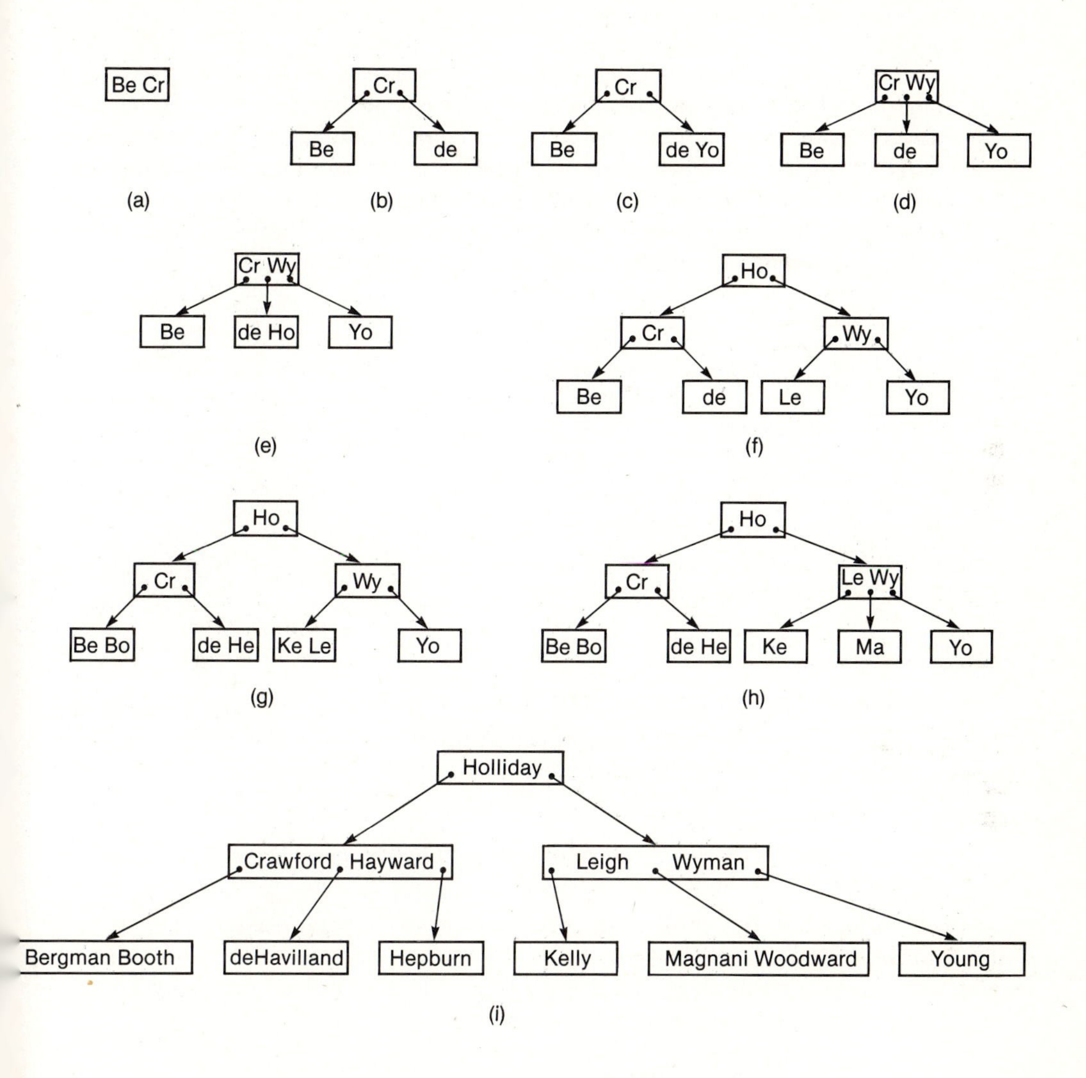

Figure 10.24 Growth of 2-3 Tree for Figure 10.14

keys are promoted upward during splits.) The details of an algorithm to do this are left as an exercise (see Exercise 10.26).

It was fairly straightforward to compare various balancing criteria for binary search trees. In order to compare these previous techniques with 2-3 trees, however, we need to ask more general questions:

I. In terms of space, for a binary tree with n keys, there are n nodes, but in a 2-3 tree with n keys, there can be anywhere from $n/2$ to n nodes. Is it possible to obtain bounds better than (0.5, 1.0) for the average storage efficiency of random 2-3 trees?

II. The normal expectation is that one key comparison is required to search a 2-node and two key comparisons are required to search a 3-node. In terms of time, are we more concerned about the average number of key comparisons required, or are we more concerned about the average number of nodes that will be accessed? Either of these measures might be the more significant one, depending upon underlying details of implementation. What shapes of 2-3 trees are optimal with respect to the two measures?

The answer to the first question – the average number of nodes N_n in a random 2-3 tree with n keys – can be obtained by a very pretty combinatorial technique by Yao [1978], known as *fringe analysis.* Since most of the keys must occur at the lower levels of the tree, it is effective to concentrate our attention upon the subtrees at those levels. Thus, the only two possibilities for subtrees at the very lowest level are 2-nodes and 3-nodes. An arbitrary 2-3 tree T is said to be of *class* $(1; a,b)$ if its subtrees of height one consist of a 2-nodes and b 3-nodes. As an example, the 2-3 tree of Figure 10.24 is of class (1; 4,2). In a tree with n keys, and therefore $n + 1$ external nodes, we must have

$$2a + 3b = n + 1 \tag{10.25}$$

Denoting by $N(T)$ the number of nodes in a particular 2-3 tree T, there are $a + b - 1$ keys in the internal nodes above the lowest level, so that the number of nodes, $N(T) - a - b$, above the lowest level must satisfy

$$\frac{(a + b - 1)}{2} \leq N(T) - (a + b) \leq (a + b - 1) \tag{10.26}$$

Let $\Pr_n(a,b)$ be the probability of obtaining a tree of class $(1; a,b)$ after n random insertions. Also define A_n to be the average value of a for a random 2-3 tree with n keys, and similarly for B_n with respect to b. Then averaging over all 2-3 trees with n keys, and using Eq. 10.26, we obtain

$$\frac{3(A_n + B_n)}{2} - \frac{1}{2} \leq N_n \leq 2(A_n + B_n) - 1 \tag{10.27}$$

Now if T is a 2-3 tree with $n - 1$ keys, of class $(1; a,b)$, then a random insertion into T will yield a tree either of class $(1; a - 1,b + 1)$ or of class $(1; a + 2,b - 1)$. The former case will happen with probability $2a/n$, and the latter with probability $1 - 2a/n$. Accordingly,

$$A_n = \sum \Pr_{n-1}(a,b)\left(\frac{2a}{n}(a-1) + \left(1 - \frac{2a}{n}\right)(a+2)\right)$$
$$= \sum \Pr_{n-1}(a,b)\left(a - \frac{6a}{n} + 2\right) \qquad (10.28)$$
$$= \left(1 - \frac{6}{n}\right)A_{n-1} + 2$$

We find that the first few values for this recurrence are $A_1 = 1$, $A_2 = 0$, $A_3 = 2$, etc.; and the general solution for $n \geq 6$ is given by $A_n = 2(n+1)/7$. With this result and Eq. 10.25, we also find that $B_n = (n+1)/7$, for $n \geq 6$. Combining these latter two formulas with Eq. 10.27 leads to the improved bounds on N_n

$$0.64n < \frac{9}{14}n + \frac{1}{7} \leq N_n \leq \frac{6}{7}n - \frac{1}{7} < 0.86n \qquad (10.29)$$

for all $n \geq 6$.

This calculation of the bounds (0.64, 0.86) can be regarded as a first-order analysis, with the bounds (0.5, 1.0) being a zero-order analysis. By considering all classes of subtrees of height two on the bottom fringe, it is possible to conduct a second-order analysis, leading to improved bounds (0.70, 0.79). However, this analysis and others of still higher order become exponentially more difficult to conduct [Eisenbarth et al. 1982].

With regard to the second question raised above, concerning the optimal shape of 2-3 trees, elegant answers have been obtained for both measures – number of key comparisons [Rosenberg and Snyder 1978] and number of node accesses [Miller et al. 1979]. As it turns out, the best 2-3 for our data of Figure 10.14 is the same under either measure (see Exercise 10.27), and has the form shown in Figure 10.25. However, such a coincidence occurs only for some 16 values of n within the range 2 .. 31. In general, striving for the objective of minimum number of node accesses leads to "bushy" trees containing a large number of 3-nodes. On the other hand, striving for the objective of minimum number of comparisons leads to "scrawny" trees, with 3-nodes permitted only on the leftmost path from the root to the leaves. Unfortunately, these answers to the second question raised above are somewhat academic for dynamic tree search; they refer to the best possible 2-3 trees, not to 2-3 trees as they occur randomly in practice.

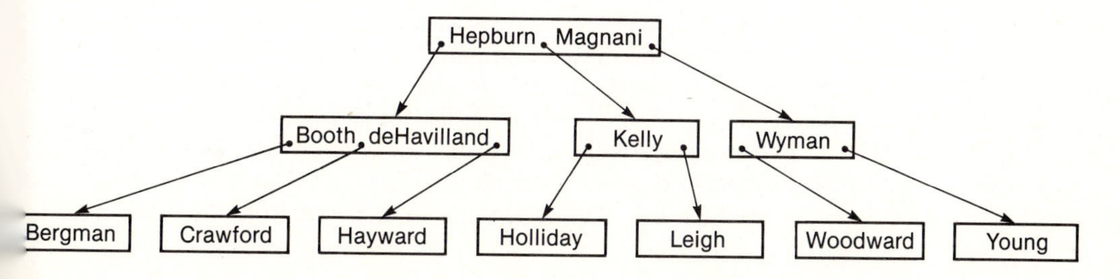

Figure 10.25 Optimal 2-3 Tree for Figure 10.14

†10.3.5 A Unifying Perspective

We have now discussed several tree structures suitable for dynamic searching. There are still several others. In this last section on the subject we will introduce one more tree structure, by means of which we are able to illustrate some surprising commonality among many of the methods. To begin with, let us reconsider the 2-3 trees of the last section. Although that section expressed the attitude that we would be willing to spend (and possibly waste) extra space in tree nodes, it is still true that programs are commonly constrained to be economical in their use of main memory. It is easy to do this for a 2-3 tree by *binarizing* it, and converting every 3-node to two 2-nodes. For example, the binarized version of Figure 10.24 is shown in Figure 10.26. This latter figure is drawn in a manner emphasizing that the original solid links have not changed, but now some dashed links have been inserted between keys in the same 3-node. Frequently the solid links are described as "vertical" links, and the dashed links are drawn and described as "horizontal" links. Note that a data structure for this representation still needs just one boolean value in each node. In this case, the boolean value for a node indicates whether the right link from that node is horizontal or vertical.

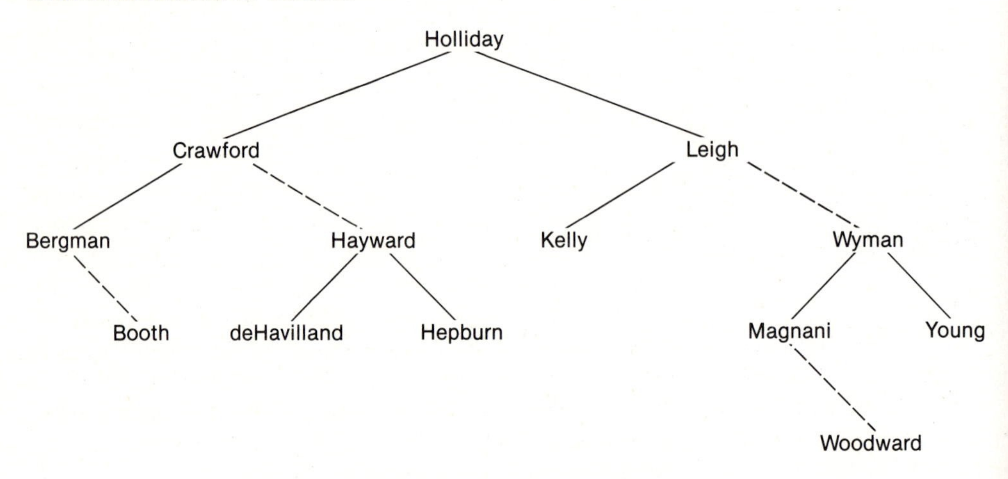

Figure 10.26 Binarized Form of Figure 10.24

The fact that the left links in binarized 2-3 trees do not likewise have a dual interpretation suggests the tree structure known as a *symmetric binary B-tree* (*SBB tree*), in which either link may be either horizontal or vertical [Bayer 1972]. In non-binarized form, this corresponds to a *2-3-4 tree*,[5] with rules for insertion and rebalancing by splitting that are analogous to those for a 2-3 tree. A very important property of the splitting rules is that there can never be two horizontal links in succession on any path from the root. Evidently, we now need two boolean values in each node, one for each link. This is similar to the situation for AVL trees,

---

[5] 2-3-4 trees are B-trees of order 4, as we will see in Chapter 12.

where we needed two bits to represent the three possible values of balance factor at a node. This suggests the question, "How well do SBB trees, using the same 2-bit quantity of balance information, perform compared to AVL trees?"

First, note that there are SBB trees that are not AVL trees. It is easiest to illustrate this with reference to Figure 10.26, the binarized form of a 2-3 tree, where we see that the AVL property does not hold at the node for Leigh. SBB trees are still logarithmic, but in the longest comparison path we can find alternating horizontal and vertical links. As a result, the worst case is given by $2 \lg n$, as compared to $1.44 \lg n$ for AVL trees (see Eq. 10.24). On the other hand, there seems to be less of splitting reorganization in SBB trees than there is of rotational reorganization in AVL trees.

Now let us make the following alteration in our conception of SBB trees. Think of the horizontal links as being red and the vertical links as being black, and then use *one* bit in each node to indicate the color of its link to its parent. This formulation is that of *red-black trees*. By this invention, many of the methods for constructing balanced trees can be shown to share certain themes. Among these are that (i) every path from the root to a leaf must contain the same number of black links, and (ii) no path from the root can ever encounter two red links in succession. Depending upon the rules used to redress exceptions to (ii), when they arise, we can obtain a variety of methods. One particularly simple rule is to rebalance from the top-down on insertions, always splitting a 4-node (that is, one with two red links) into two 2-nodes. But such a splitting involves nothing more than *color flips* of three links and possibly a single or double rotation! These matters are illustrated in Figure 10.27, where the solid links denote black and the dashed links denote red. In each of the cases (a) and (b) and (c), we see a 2-3-4 tree on the left, then the binarized form of the tree, then the effects of a split, and finally the corresponding 2-3-4 tree after the split. When the 3-node containing D and E is oriented as in (a) of the figure, only the color flips are required. But if the 3-node is oriented the other way, as in (b) of the figure, we see that a single rotation is required as well as the flips. Finally, in (c) of the figure, we see a case requiring flips and a double rotation. The beautifully simple reason that this is guaranteed to work is that since 4-nodes are split on the way down, then it will always be possible to insert a value with its parent if necessary (that is, change the color of that link to red), because its parent must be a 2-node or a 3-node.

This colorful approach has many more nuances and possibilities than we have space to describe in detail, and the original paper is well worth reading [Guibas and Sedgewick 1978]. We simply make these final observations:

- There are other possibilities besides the top-down balancing method just described. A very efficient bottom-up alternative, never requiring more than $O(1)$ rotations for either insertion or deletion, is that of Tarjan [1983b].

- Search (without insertion) in a red-black tree is "color-blind" ordinary BST search, in which the colors of the links can simply be ignored.

- Although 2-3-4 trees are not AVL trees, they properly include AVL trees. A nice way to demonstrate this is with a construction that transforms an AVL tree to a 2-3-4 tree by coloring its links. As an example, consider the AVL tree of

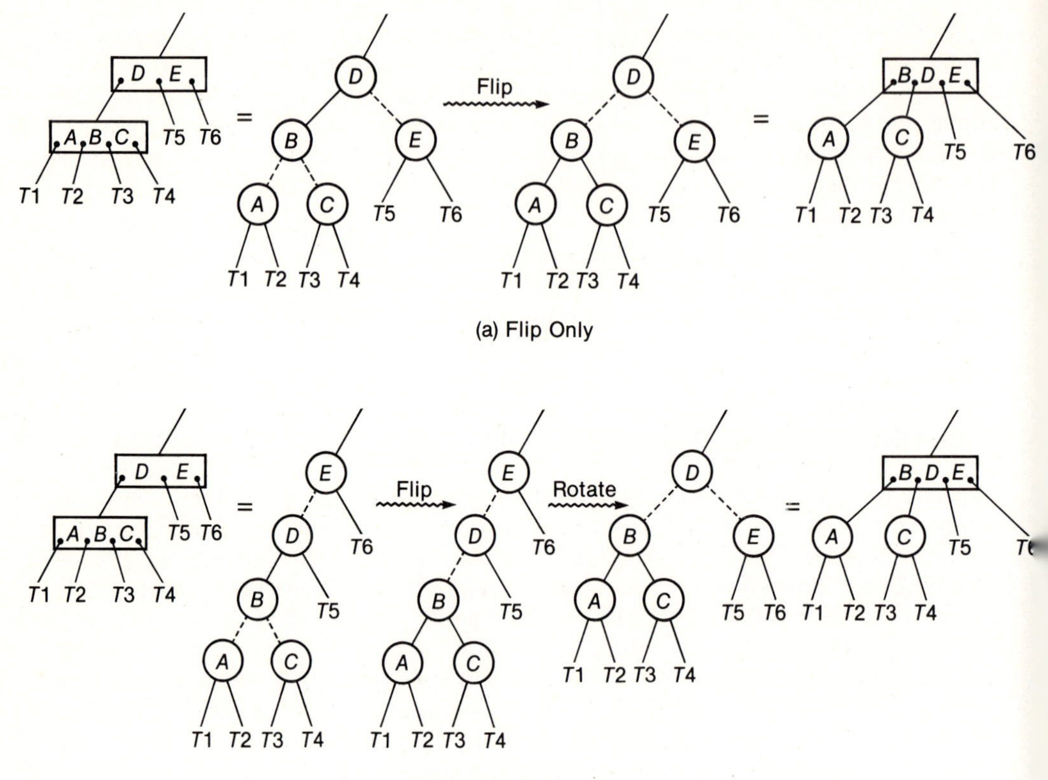

(a) Flip Only

(b) Flip and Single Rotation

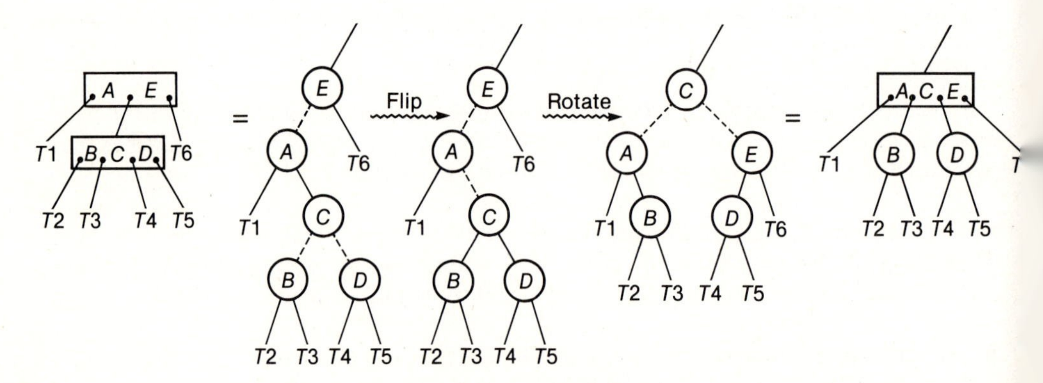

(c) Flip and Double Rotation

Figure 10.27 Top-Down Splitting in Red-Black Trees

Figure 10.21, and define the height of a node as the length of the longest path to an external node. Then apply the color red to any link connecting a parent of even height and a child of odd height. In Figure 10.28(a), the original AVL tree is redrawn showing the height values and the colors; the corresponding 2-3-4 tree is shown in (b) of the figure.

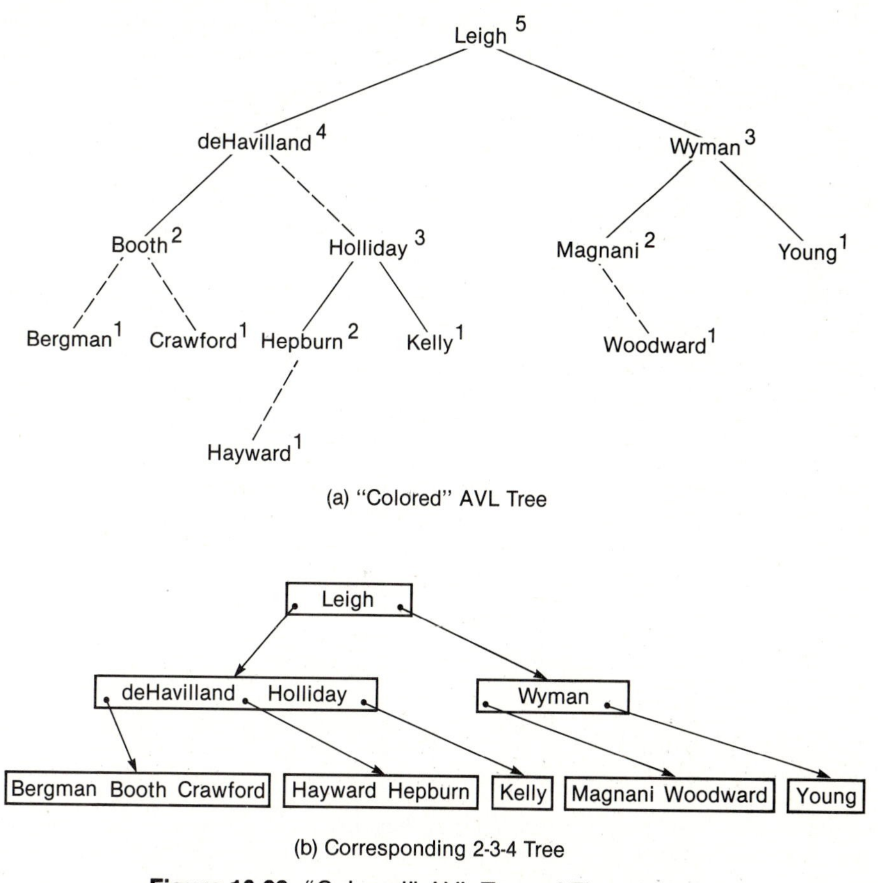

(a) "Colored" AVL Tree

(b) Corresponding 2-3-4 Tree

Figure 10.28 "Colored" AVL Tree of Figure 10.21

10.4 HASHING

Binary search and the explicit tree search methods that we have studied are all of complexity $O(\lg n)$. Thus their performance is fairly good for tables of moderate size, but the inexorable growth causes these methods to be less satisfactory for very large tables. A radically different approach is to proceed not by comparisons between key values, but by finding some function $h(K)$ that can directly yield the location of K in the table. In fact, the storage allocation formulas that map array elements to memory locations as functions of their indices provide examples of this facility (see Sections 2.2.1 and 2.7). An important aspect of such storage allocation functions is that they are one-to-one from a limited domain of index values to a corresponding range of memory locations. But in the present case we are usually dealing with a very large potential *name space* of keys and a much smaller actual *address space* of table locations.

These ideas are readily illustrated in terms of the mapping from the set of all possible identifiers in a programming language to a compiler symbol table. For example, there are over 10^9 legal six-character identifiers in FORTRAN, and many more in Pascal. Of course, only a minuscule proportion of these will actually occur in any given program; thus, a symbol table of about 10^3 locations is typically adequate. Mappings $h(K)$ for such situations are called *hash functions*, with the property that we can expect $h(K_i) = h(K_j)$ for many different pairs i,j. With the numbers from our FORTRAN example, we see that any hash function must inevitably map a minimum of at least 10^6 *synonym* keys, out of all possible ones, to some table locations. The objective, then, is to find a hash function that, when applied to any typical set of keys, will produce relatively few *collisions*, – that is, occurrences of synonyms. Note that it is crucial to store the key K itself at a hash table location, since there is no unique reverse mapping $h(K) \rightarrow K$ to determine which synonym is present. (See Exercise 10.35 for a method of partially subverting this requirement.)

Finding hash functions that minimize collisions is just one aspect of the problem, and we will consider this matter in Section 10.4.1. But we must still deal with those synonyms that do occur, in the process known as collision resolution, in Section 10.4.2. After these two principal concerns, we devote the remaining sections to some other issues relating to hashing.

10.4.1 Hash Functions

Over the years, about half a dozen distinct hashing techniques have been employed. In practice, the method of division has been found to be distinctly superior to all the rest. Therefore, except for some preliminary mention of the other techniques, we will concentrate our attention upon hash functions using division. As we said in the preceding paragraph, an important criterion for a hash function is that it should minimize collisions. A second important factor is that it be relatively fast and simple to compute if it is not to lose its advantage over comparison-based methods. Thirdly, $h(K)$ should usually be a function of all the bits in the machine representation of K. A technique that violates this latter principle is to extract some subset of the bits in K in order to compose $h(K)$. Extraction is acceptable when it is known in advance that the discarded bits convey very little distinguishing information; the hazard in the general case is that the discarded bits may be just the ones needed to thwart the generation of synonyms.

In addition to extraction and division, there are techniques that employ folding, radix transformation, algebraic coding, and multiplication. Folding is the combining of multi-word keys into single-word quantities, typically by exclusive-OR'ing; it is used singly and also as a prelude to the other techniques. The radix transformation and algebraic coding techniques are of theoretical interest but computationally expensive and less effective than division, so they are seldom employed. Nonetheless, it is instructive to consider the rationale for algebraic coding. In Section 8.2.5 we saw that by constructing codes with redundancy in an appropriate manner, it is possible to create codeword clusters. This clustering property can then be used to facilitate error detection and correction in codewords. In hashing, we find that actual sets S_i of keys usually do *not* have the character of being randomly drawn from the universe U of possible keys. Rather, they tend to exhibit natural clustering. It is often possible to obtain many other words from a given word by changing just one letter; a good example of this is provided by the word "band." Given that clusters tend to occur, we find a fourth important criteria for a hash function – that it should separate clusters. In fact, there is a great deal of similarity between the methods that algebraic coding employs for separating clusters and the methods cited in Section 8.2.5.1 for generating clusters via group codes. More precisely, both employ arithmetic over finite fields $GF(q)$.

The next hashing technique to consider is multiplication. Although less popular than division, it is still a very viable method. It entails multiplying the key K either by itself or by some constant, and then using some portion of the bits from the product as the hash table location. When the choice is to multiply K by itself, we have the *mid-square method.* If K is 20 bits then the product is 40 bits, wherein the middle 10 bits satisfy the criterion that they are a function of all the original bits of K. The method also satisfies the criteria of simplicity, but it does have two drawbacks. One is that degenerate keys, with many leading or trailing zeros, will be reflected in hash values containing many zeros; the other is that the size of the hash table is constrained to be a power of two.

A much safer multiplicative method, avoiding both the degeneracy and the constraint on table size, is to compute $h(K) = \lfloor(M \times ((C \times K) \bmod 1))$. In this expression, M is the size of the table and $0 < C < 1$. It is important to choose C with some circumspection in order to avoid various ill effects, such as causing an alphabetic key K to be synonymous with other keys obtained by permuting the characters of K. An example of a value which has been found to be theoretically sound is $C = .6180339887\ldots$[6] [Knuth 1973b].

We come now to the method of hashing by division. The hash function is computed simply as $h(K) = K \bmod M$, using 0-origin indexing and for a table of size M. Although the formula is applicable for tables of any desired size, it is nonetheless important to choose the value of the divisor M with care, as with the choice of C for multiplicative hashing. For instance, if M were even, then all even (odd) keys would be mapped to even (odd) table locations – a severe bias. More generally, a good rule is to choose M to be a prime number, but to avoid primes that divide $r^k \pm 1$, for the case that a and k are small and r is the radix of the character set (presuming alphabetic keys). To illustrate the simplest case of the reason for this restriction, suppose that characters are treated as integers to the radix r, and that M

---

[6] This value of C is called the *golden ratio*. It is the reciprocal of $r_1 = \frac{1}{2}(1 + \sqrt{5})$, obtained in Section 1.3.2.3 (Eqs. 1.26) as one of the roots of the Fibonacci recurrence equation.

is a prime that divides $r - 1$. Another way of expressing the latter fact is as a statement of *congruence*; r is said to be congruent to 1 modulo M, or $r \equiv 1 \pmod{M}$ (see also Section 8.4.2.2.1). Note that if $r \equiv 1$ (modulo M), then also $r^k \equiv 1$. Now consider the case of $h(K)$ applied to the alphabetic key $K = a_n a_{n-1} \ldots a_0$. We find that

$$
\begin{aligned}
h(K) = h\left(\sum_{i=0}^{n} a_i r^i\right) &= \left(\sum a_i r^i\right) \bmod M \\
&= \sum\left((a_i \bmod M)\,(r^i \bmod M)\right) \\
&\equiv \sum (a_i \bmod M) \text{ (modulo } M) \\
&= \left(\sum a_i\right) \bmod M
\end{aligned}
\tag{10.30}
$$

In other words, this $h(K)$ will compute the same hash value for any permutation of the characters of K. Similar clustering effects occur for other small values of a and k.[7] In practical terms, for a byte oriented character set, one should avoid choosing M to be a prime close to 256^k, as in the example $65537 = 256^2 + 1$. There is one final comment concerning the choice of divisor M. The foregoing has stressed the choice of M as a suitable prime. In fact, a value of M that is non-prime, but that has no small primes $p < 20$ as factors is often just as satisfactory [Lum et al. 1971].

We have described several hash function methods. By what standard(s) can they be evaluated for their efficacy? A very common one is to compare their performance against that of *random hashing*. This corresponds to the assumption that every input key is equally likely to be hashed to any one of the hash table locations, disregarding collisions. For a table of size M and a set of keys of cardinality n, the probability that a single key will hash to any particular location is $1/M$, and the probability $p(i)$ that a given table location will correspond to i synonyms can be expressed in terms of the binomial distribution as

$$p(i) = \binom{n}{i}\left(\frac{n}{M}\right)^i\left(1 - \frac{n}{M}\right)^{n-i}$$

In most cases of interest, we will have that $n >> 1$ and $M >> 1$, with the average density of hashing being given by n/M. In such cases, where the likelihood of "hitting" a given location with any one key is rare and the overall probability n/M of a hit is not large, it is convenient to approximate $p(i)$ by the *Poisson distribution*

$$P\left(\frac{n}{M}, i\right) = \frac{e^{-n/M}}{i!}\left(\frac{n}{M}\right)^i \tag{10.31}$$

The Poisson probability distribution has the appearance of a skewed normal distribution, with the amount of skew dependent upon the first parameter. A few values of $P(i)$ are shown in Table 10.3, for $n/M = 0.5$ and for $n/M = 1.0$. Examin-

---

[7] This is essentially the same reasoning by which one can show that a poor choice of C, in multiplicative hashing, can lead to clusters among permutations of an alphabetic key K.

ing this table and disregarding the effects of collision resolution, we see that the overall likelihood of finding synonyms (that is, $i > 1$) at any one location is 0.09 for a hash table that is half-full ($n/M = 0.5$), and 0.26 for one that is full ($n/M = 1.0$). It is reasonable to evaluate any given hashing method by comparing its performance to that of this random hashing criterion. By this standard, the division method has been found to be quite good, subject to the restriction from the preceding paragraph concerning choice of divisor; surprisingly, it often performs even better than random hashing! The reason for this lies with our earlier remark that typical sets of input keys do not conform to the assumptions for random hashing. Rather, they commonly contain clusters such as {SUM1, SUM2, SUM3, ...}; and the division method tends to exploit such non-randomness to separate the clusters.

i	0.5	1.0	i	0.5	1.0
0	.60653	.36788	4	.00158	.01533
1	.30327	.36788	5	.00016	.00307
2	.07582	.18394	6	.00001	.00051
3	.01264	.06131	7		.00007

Table 10.3 Sample Poisson Values $P\left(\frac{n}{M}, i\right)$

There is much more to be said about hash functions and how to choose among them [§]. We have cited the division method as being generally superior. But for a large application that relies extensively upon hashing, one dare not ignore the statistical nature of the sets of input keys; the performance of any of the methods can be greatly influenced by it.

10.4.2 Collision Resolution

The second major issue in hashing is that of resolving collisions among synonyms. Indeed, as long as the hash function is not a poor one, the choice of collision resolution technique tends to be distinctly more important for success of hashing performance. In the previous section we referred to the Poisson model to predict the likelihood that there would be collisions at any one location. Suppose that we ask, instead, about the likelihood of collisions anywhere in the table. The probability of this is high, even in the event that the table is relatively empty. An appealing illustration of this is the famous *birthday paradox*: In an assembly of 23 persons, there is a better than even chance that some two of them will have exactly the same birthday of the year! In more prosaic terms, hashing just 23 keys into a hash table of size 365 will, with probability 0.5072, produce at least one collision.

There are four basic methods of collision resolution, two of which depend upon the idea of maintaining linked lists of synonyms, and two of which depend upon the idea of computing a sequence of hash table locations until an empty slot is found. In all of these, the comparative measure is the number of *probes* – that is, the number of memory locations that must be examined in order to determine the location of a key in the table. We will examine these basic methods in Sections 10.4.2.1 and 10.4.2.2, and then evaluate their performance in Section 10.4.2.3. However, there is more to the story. Specifically, in the last two sections we will examine first the issues of deletion and overflow in hash tables, and then ways of rearranging hash tables to enhance performance.

In order to illustrate matters, we need to introduce some sample keys and to choose a hash function. For all of our illustrations, the table size will be $M = 13$, and the prevailing definitions will be those of Figure 10.29. Into this table, we will successively insert the keys from Figure 10.30. The hash function $h_1(K)$ will be implemented as HASH := *key* **mod** *hsiz*, for which the values are also shown in the figure. By assuming that $K = 0$ does not occur naturally, we can mark all hash table locations as initially empty by initializing them to zero. Since the operations of search and insertion are so closely related, we will present algorithms that (a) search for an item and insert it if necessary (unless this would cause table overflow), and (b) return either the location of the item in the table, or a -1 in the case of overflow. They are easily modified if one wishes to have algorithms that perform just one of the two operations

```
const  hsiz = 13;

type   hash_ndx = 0 .. 12;
       hash_link = -1 .. 12;
       hash_item = record
          key: integer;
          data: {depending upon the application}
          link: hash_link; {necessary for some methods}
       end;
       hash_table = array [hash_ndx] of hash_item;
```

Figure 10.29 Type Definitions for Hashing

j	K_j	$h_1(K_j)$	j	K_j	$h_1(K_j)$
1	119	2	7	109	5
2	85	7	8	147	4
3	43	4	9	38	12
4	141	11	10	137	7
5	72	7	11	148	5
6	91	0	12	101	10

Figure 10.30 Sample Keys with Initial Hash Values

10.4.2.1 Chaining. There are two variants of chaining. In the simpler of these, the locations in the hash table serve as list heads, and all the keys that hash to a given location are maintained dynamically in a linked list. This method is commonly called *separate chaining*. Of course, there is further variability if we allow for different methods of maintaining the linked synonym lists, such as FIFO, LIFO, or by key value. But in most implementations of separate chaining, the individual lists will tend to be so short that there is little reason not to make the simplest choice, which is LIFO. For the example keys of Figure 10.29, the resulting hash table will be as shown in Figure 10.31.

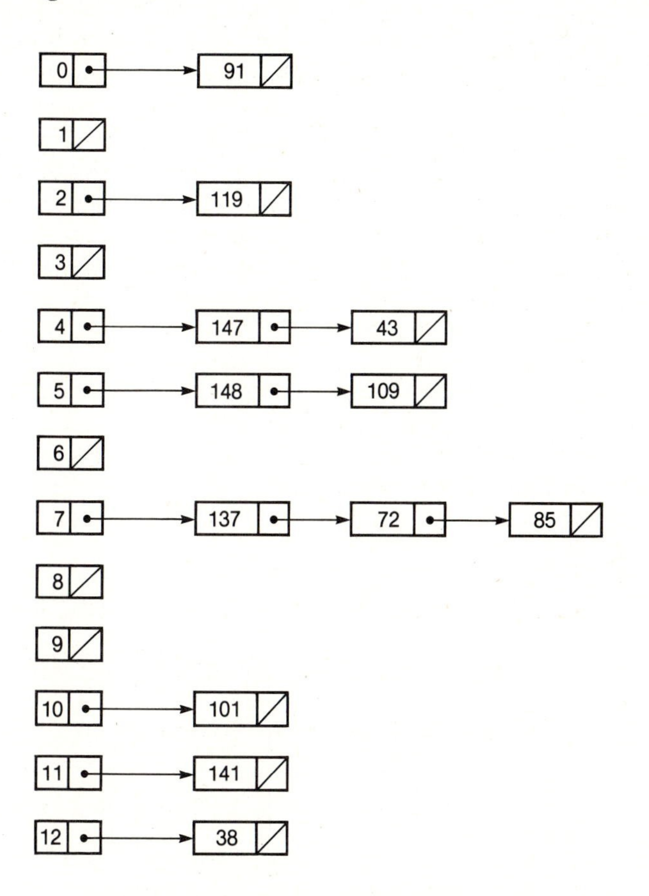

Figure 10.31 Separate Chaining

As we will see in Section 10.4.2.3, the method of separate chaining has the best performance of any of the collision resolution methods. However, it is frequently inconvenient to dedicate the hash table entries to the role of list heads, especially if the number of entries in the hash table is relatively moderate. This leads to the other chaining method, known as *internal chaining*. In this case, the linking among synonyms is within the hash table itself, via cursor fields that are all initialized to

−1 (for **nil**).[8] The method requires one global cursor value *finger*, initialized to the value *hsiz* − 1 and used in resolving collisions. Search commences at the location $h(K)$. If the location is empty then K is inserted there; otherwise that location and others linked to it are probed in search of K. If K has not been found before a **nil** cursor value is encountered, then the value of the global cursor *finger* is used to initiate a search for an empty table location. When (and if) such a location i is found, then K is inserted there and the last cursor value in the linked list is updated to the value i.

For example, after the insertion of the first eight keys from Figure 10.29, the resulting hash table will appear as in Figure 10.32(a), with linked lists for $h(K) = 4$ and $h(K) = 7$. For the next key (38) the location $h(38) = 12$ is already occupied and the link field for location 12 is **nil**, so the variable *finger* is employed to find the empty location 9. Note that this has caused the linked lists for 7 and 12 to *coalesce*, as shown in (b) of the figure. Indeed, because of this characteristic phenomenon, the method of internal chaining is more commonly known as *coalesced chaining*. Figure 10.32(c) displays the final appearance of the hash table after all the keys have been inserted. It also shows the number of probes required to insert each key and, in parentheses, the lesser number of probes required to subsequently find some keys. The detailed algorithm to accomplish coalesced chaining as we have just described it is the function HASH_COALESCE (Algorithm 10.7). In this algorithm note that the effect of repeatedly using *finger* to find the next empty table location is bounded in its potential cost. Its value starts at *hsiz* − 1 and always decreases toward zero; thus the average cost per entry, in a table that is reasonably full, cannot be more than one extra probe per access.

i	*Key*	*Link*
0	91	−1
1		−1
2	119	−1
3		−1
4	43	10
5	109	−1
6		−1
7	85	12
8		−1
9		−1
10	147	−1
11	141	−1
12	72	−1

(a)

i	*Key*	*Link*
0	91	−1
1		−1
2	119	−1
3		−1
4	43	10
5	109	−1
6		−1
7	85	12
8		−1
9	38	−1
10	147	−1
11	141	−1
12	72	9

(b)

i	*Key*	*Link*	*Probes*
0	91	−1	1
1	0	−1	
2	119	−1	1
3	101	−1	4(2)
4	43	10	1
5	109	6	1
6	148	−1	3(2)
7	85	12	1
8	137	−1	4(4)
9	38	8	2(2)
10	147	3	3(2)
11	141	−1	1
12	72	9	2(2)

(c)

Figure 10.32 Illustration of Coalesced Chaining

[8] Note that in assembly language, it may be possible to conserve additional space by using short cursors rather than full-length pointers.

```
function HASH_COALESCE (arg: integer; var htbl: hash_table): hash_link;

var     finger: hash_ndx;  {a global variable, initially hsiz − 1}
        i: hash_ndx;

begin
  i := HASH (arg);
  if htbl [i].key = 0 then begin
    htbl [i].key := arg;
    htbl [i].link := -1;
    HASH_COALESCE := i;
  end else begin
    while (htbl [i].key <> arg) and (htbl [i].link <> -1) do
      i := htbl [i].link;
    if htbl [i].key = arg then
      HASH_COALESCE := i
    else begin
      while (htbl [finger].key <> 0) and (finger > 0) do
        finger := finger - 1;
      if htbl [finger].key <> 0 then   {table is full}
        HASH_COALESCE := -1
      else begin                       {insert arg in table}
        htbl [finger].key := arg;
        htbl [finger].link := -1;
        htbl [i].link := finger;
        HASH_COALESCE := finger;
      end;
    end;
  end;
end;
```

Algorithm 10.7 HASH_COALESCE

We defer discussion about the expected complexities of the chaining methods until Section 10.4.2.3. However, it is appropriate to point out now some avenues for improving upon these two basic methods of resolution. With separate chaining, we may be able to eliminate the necessity of storing the entire key in each node. This becomes possible when we find a quantity $g(K)$ such that K is uniquely determined as a function of $g(K)$ and $h(K)$. For this, the quantities $g(K) = K \text{ div } M$ and $h(K) = K \bmod M$ are likely candidates. Moreover, it is possible to modify internal chaining so that the chains do not coalesce (see Exercise 10.35), thereby gaining the same advantage for this method also. A different tactic for improving upon coalesced chaining is to reserve a part of the table area outside of the range of the hash function; such a region is called a *cellar*. All collisions are chained to the cellar until it is full, and only after that to the main hash area. If the proportion of the table memory reserved for the cellar is small (as in ordinary coalesced chaining, where there is no cellar), then coalescing will begin to happen early, with an increase in the average number of probes. On the other hand, too large a cellar will, by diminishing the range of the hash function, also increase the average number of probes. The optimum occurs when the hash and cellar areas are apportioned approximately in the ratio 0.86 : 0.14; however, this varies somewhat with the influence of other factors [Vitter 1982].

10.4.2.2 Open Addressing. In many applications, any pointer overhead at all is unacceptable. This leads to the technique as known as *open addressing*, in which a sequence of table locations is inspected until either the desired key or an empty slot is found. The original technique for doing this simply calls for starting at the location $h_1(K)$ and examining locations sequentially (mod M). This is called *linear probing*. After the first seven keys from Figure 10.29 have been inserted, the hash table will appear as in Figure 10.33(a). When the key 147 is presented, it will be inserted in location 6, after failing to find an empty slot in locations 4,5. Before 147 was inserted, there were clusters of keys in locations 4,5 and 7,8. After the insertion of 147, these two clusters have been combined into one large *primary cluster*. Any keys that subsequently hash to locations near the beginning of the cluster unavoidably require a relatively large number of probes, and the clustering phenomenon gets worse with increasing cluster size! In order for hashing to work well, we need to have the "holes" distributed randomly; however, linear probing propagates primary clusters that thwart this property. Ultimately, when all the keys have been inserted, the hash table will appear as in Figure 10.33(c). Once again, appended to each entry in (c) is the number of probes required for its insertion.

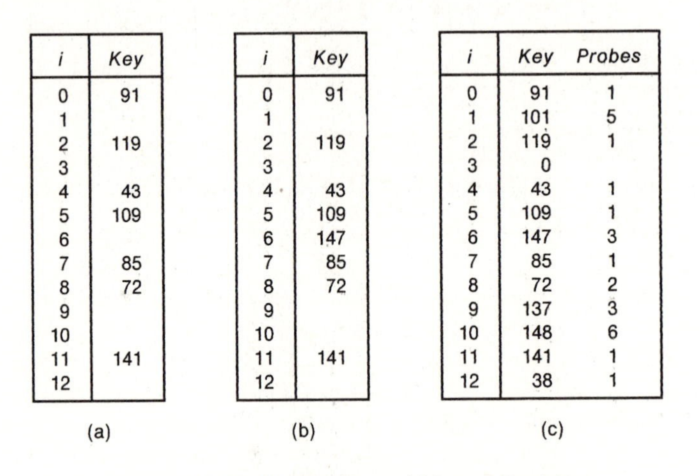

i	*Key*
0	91
1	
2	119
3	
4	43
5	109
6	
7	85
8	72
9	
10	
11	141
12	

(a)

i	*Key*
0	91
1	
2	119
3	
4	43
5	109
6	147
7	85
8	72
9	
10	
11	141
12	

(b)

i	*Key*	*Probes*
0	91	1
1	101	5
2	119	1
3	0	
4	43	1
5	109	1
6	147	3
7	85	1
8	72	2
9	137	3
10	148	6
11	141	1
12	38	1

(c)

Figure 10.33 Illustration of Linear Probing

At first glance, we might try to redress the primary clustering problem by computing successive probe locations as $h_i(K) = h_1(K) + (i - 1) \times c$ rather than $h_i(K) = h_1(K) + (i - 1)$. Although this does eliminate primary clustering, it does not prevent the formation of *secondary clusters*. The basic problem with this attempt is that any two keys that probe a given location will then probe the identical sequence of successor locations (as when we walk in another person's footsteps on the beach).

What is needed is for the values in the *probe sequence* for a key to be random in character; in fact, the term random probing is sometimes employed. But what we look for, practically speaking, is a probe sequence that is simple to compute, yet sufficiently scrambled that it thwarts clustering. The sequence should also access every location in the table, since that may be necessary as the table becomes full.

A method that is good in all of these respects is that known as *double hashing*. In this case the value of the increment to $h_1(K)$ is determined from an auxiliary hash function $h_0(K)$, and the probe sequence is computed as

$$h_i(K) = (h_{i-1}(K) + h_0(K)) \mod hsiz \quad (\text{for } i = 2, 3, \ldots) \qquad (10.32)$$

The value of h_0 should not be zero, of course, and should be relatively prime to the table size, thereby guaranteeing access to each location. In practice, it works well to use a function such as $h_0(K) = 1 + K \mod (hsiz - 2)$. This form of double hashing is particularly good when *hsiz* and *hsiz* − 2 are twin primes.

K_j	$h_1(K_j)$	$h_0(K_j)$
119	2	10
85	7	9
43	4	11
141	11	10
72	7	7
91	0	4
109	5	11
147	4	5
38	12	6
137	7	6
148	5	6
101	10	3

(a)

i	*key*	*Probes*
0	91	1
1	72	2
2	119	1
3	101	3
4	43	1
5	109	1
6	137	3
7	85	1
8		
9	147	2
10	148	4
11	141	1
12	38	1

(b)

Figure 10.34 Illustration of Double Hashing

The application of this method is illustrated in Figure 10.34, for *hsiz* = 13 and *hsiz* − 2 = 11. In (a) of this figure, the values K and $h_1(K)$ are reproduced from Figure 10.30, and the values of $h_0(K)$ are appended. We can see, for example, that the probe sequence for the key 38 is

12 5 11 4 10 3 9 2 8 1 7 0 6

Figure 10.34(b) displays the final locations of the keys in the hash table, along with the corresponding number of probes required for their insertions. The algorithm to

```
function HASH_DOUBLE (arg: integer; var htbl: hash_table): hash_link;

var     found: boolean;
        hcnt: hash_ndx;    {a global count of table entries}
        i,j: hash_ndx;

begin
  found := false;
  i := HASH (arg);  j := INCR (arg);
  while (htbl [i].key <> 0) and (not found) do
    if htbl [i].key <> arg then
      i := (i + j) mod hsiz
    else
      found := true;
  HASH_DOUBLE := i;
  if not found then begin
    if hcnt = hsiz - 1 then        {table is full}
      HASH_DOUBLE := -1
    else begin                     {insert arg in table}
      hcnt := hcnt + 1;
      htbl [i].key := arg;
    end;
  end;
end;
```

Algorithm 10.8 HASH_DOUBLE

accomplish this is the function[9] HASH_DOUBLE (Algorithm 10.8), wherein $h_0(K)$ is implemented as INCR := $1 + key$ **mod** $(hsiz - 2)$. A critical detail in this implementation is the use of *hcnt* to keep track of the number of entries. In particular, by never allowing *hcnt* to exceed $hsiz - 1$, we guarantee that there will always be at least one empty location for forcing termination of the **while** loop in the event that a key is not in the table.

10.4.2.3 Evaluation of Resolution Methods. The significant aspect of searching by hashing is that its average performance depends upon the ratio n/M, for n the number of items and M the table size, rather than upon just n. This ratio is denoted α, the *load factor*. We have already seen it, in effect, in the discussion of the Poisson distribution in Section 10.4.1. In the present section our principal concern is the average number of probes for each of the four collision resolution methods, in terms of *PS* (successful searches) and *PF* (unsuccessful searches). Approximate formulas for each of the eight cases are derived in Knuth [1973b]. For the most part, we are content to quote the formulas and comment upon them.

---

[9] An algorithm for linear probing is not shown; with the proviso that $h_0(K) = 1$ for all K, it would be identical to HASH_DOUBLE.

α	PS	PF	PS	PF	PS	PF	PS	PF
.25	1.12	1.03	1.14	1.04	1.17	1.39	1.15	1.33
.50	1.25	1.11	1.30	1.18	1.50	2.50	1.39	2.00
.75	1.38	1.22	1.52	1.49	2.50	8.50	1.85	4.00
.90	1.45	1.31	1.68	1.81	5.50	50.50	2.56	10.00
	(a) Separate Chaining		(b) Coalesced Chaining		(c) Linear Probing		(d) Random Probing	

Table 10.4 Values of $PS(\alpha)$ and $PF(\alpha)$

To assist in their comprehension, all eight of them are evaluated for several values of α, in Table 10.4.

The first method that we discussed was that of separate chaining. It can be somewhat misleading to compare this method with the other three, since in fact one can have $\alpha > 1$ in this case. Nonetheless, for separate chaining, the approximate formulas are

$$PS = 1 + \frac{\alpha}{2}, \quad \text{and} \quad PF = e^{-\alpha} + \alpha \tag{10.33}$$

These expressions apply even when $\alpha >> 1$. Thus, for $n >> M$, the average length of each list will be α, and we should expect to search half of a list, on average, before finding an item. For coalesced chaining, the approximate formulas are

$$PS = 1 + \frac{\alpha}{4} + \frac{e^{2\alpha} - 1 - 2\alpha}{8\alpha}, \quad \text{and} \quad PF = 1 + \frac{e^{2\alpha} - 1 - 2\alpha}{4} \tag{10.34}$$

We can see from Table 10.4 that both chaining methods are superior to either open addressing method. In particular, even as α approaches one, the expected number of probes with coalesced chaining is still close to just two! Next, the approximate formulas for linear probing are

$$PS = \frac{1 + (1 - \alpha)^{-1}}{2}, \quad \text{and} \quad PF = \frac{1 + (1 - \alpha)^{-2}}{2} \tag{10.35}$$

Inspection of Table 10.4 confirms that linear probing, while satisfactory for small α, is extremely poor as α approaches one. In fact, the average values of PS and PF at this limit are, respectively, $\pi M/\sqrt{8}$ and $M/2$.

For the case of double hashing, recall that the intent is to generate a probe sequence that is random in character. This is commonly described by employing the concept of *uniform hashing*, wherein the probe sequence is equally likely to be any of the $M!$ permutations $(0 \mathinner{\ldotp\ldotp} M - 1)$. This has the consequence that the $C(M,n)$ possible empty/full configurations are all equally likely to occur. It is instructive to compute the expected values of PS and PF under such idealized circumstances. Suppose that a hash table of M locations has a loading factor α, and that we conduct an unsuccessful search for an entry. Then the probability of an initial collision (and at least a second probe) is α, and the probability p_i of i successive collisions and at least an $(i+1)$th probe is α^i. We can compute PF as the sum of the probe lengths k weighted by the probabilities q_k that exactly k probes are required – that is, $\sum k \times q_k$. Thus,

$$\begin{aligned} PF &= q_1 + 2q_2 + 3q_3 + \cdots \\ &= q_1 + q_2 + q_3 + \cdots \\ &\quad\;\; + q_2 + q_3 + \cdots \\ &\quad\;\;\quad\;\; + q_3 + \cdots \\ &\quad \cdots \\ &= p_1 + p_2 + p_3 + \cdots = \sum \alpha^i = \frac{1}{1-\alpha} \end{aligned} \tag{10.36}$$

Now, for each key that is in the table, the number of probes required to find it is the same as the number of probes required in the unsuccessful search preceding its insertion.[10] Averaging this quantity over all values of PF as the table grows from 0 entries to $n-1$ entries, we find

$$PS = \frac{1}{n}\sum_{i=0}^{n-1} PF_i \approx \frac{M}{n}\int_0^{\alpha} \frac{dx}{1-x} \approx -\frac{1}{\alpha}\ln(1-\alpha) \tag{10.37}$$

If we examine double hashing closely, we find that the probe sequences are far from being random. In fact, they are always arithmetic progressions determined by $h_1(K)$ and $h_0(K)$. Thus the likelihood of having the same probe sequences for two keys under double hashing is $O(1/M^2)$; yet the likelihood of having the same probe sequences under uniform hashing is $O(1/M!)$. So it is somewhat surprising to find that both in theory and in practice, the performance of double hashing closely approximates that of random probing, as expressed in Eqs. 10.36 and 10.37 [Guibas and Szemerédi 1978]. The average values of PS and PF as α approaches one are, respectively, $\ln M$ and $M/2$.

In comparing coalesced chaining, linear probing, and double hashing, we find that the probe sequences of double hashing approximate those of random probing, the probe sequences of linear probing are significantly inferior, and the probe sequences of coalesced chaining are significantly superior. The improvement of coalesced chaining over that of random probing comes, of course, at the expense of carrying along additional information in the form of the links. In general, we might be tempted to conclude that either chaining method requires more space than either open addressing technique. However, this is not always true. Observe that separate chaining requires space for M pointers of size P and n records of size $R+P$, whereas open addressing requires space for M table slots of size R. When $R >> P$ then separate chaining may be more efficient in space. For example, suppose that $M = 200$, $n = 150$, $P = 1$, and $R = 24$. Then separate chaining would require

---

[10] The validity of this remark depends upon the details of the hashing scheme (compare this with Section 10.3.1). It is true for linear probing and double hashing, but not true for coalesced hashing.

$200 \times 1 + 150 \times 25 = 3950$ units of storage, and open addressing would require $200 \times 24 = 4800$ units of storage.

Overall, hashing has some distinct advantages and some distinct disadvantages relative to comparison-based searching methods. When we can afford to trust in the laws of probability, then for large values of n (and reasonable values of α), a good hashing scheme usually requires less probes (on the order of $1.5-2.0$) than does any other method that we have examined thus far, including search in a binary tree. On the other hand, we should realize that hashing may perform abominably, requiring $O(n)$ probes in the worst case. Thus, we would not care to use it where timely responsiveness is critical, as in an air-traffic control system. Two other problems with hashing are (i) the need to have some a priori estimate of the maximum number of items to be accommodated in the hash table, and (ii) ways to handle deletions. These problems are somewhat related, and we will discuss responses to both of them in the next section. For now, we note that where there is not an advance estimate of the number of items, separate chaining would be recommended, since overflow is then not a problem. Finally, none of the advantages of ordered relationships are available in a hash table. For example, we cannot process the items in the table sequentially. Neither can we conclude, after an unsuccessful search, anything about items that are "close" to the one that we sought.

10.4.2.4 Deletions and Rehashing. When we first have the need to delete a value K_i from a hash table that has been generated by coalesced hashing or open addressing, we encounter a surprising fact. If K_i precedes any other value K_j in a probe sequence, then we cannot simply discard K_i. If we did, then subsequent probes for K_j, on encountering the "hole" left by K_i, would conclude that K_j was not present. We can see the truth of this in any of the Figures 10.32, 10.33, or 10.34. The solution is that we need to regard each hash table location as being in one of three states: empty, occupied, or deleted. Then as far as searches are concerned, a deleted cell is treated just like an occupied one. In the case of insertions, we can arrange to use the first empty or deleted location that is encountered in the probe sequence. Observe that this problem does not arise with deletions from the lists of separate chaining. Also, with linear probing it is fairly simple to relocate values backward in their probe sequence when a deletion occurs, so that no "deleted" values are introduced (see Exercise 10.37).

For coalesced hashing and double hashing, however, the problem of deletions is more serious. Although the introduction of a tag value for marking deletions will make it possible for the algorithms HASH_COALESCE and HASH_DOUBLE to work properly, that is only a partial solution. There is still the problem that if deletions are common, then unsuccessful searches will begin to require $O(M)$ probes in order to detect that a value is not present. (Exercise 10.38 presents a more subtle problem.) When a hash table overflows absolutely, or when its performance becomes too degraded because of deletions, the only recourse is to rehash it into another table of a more appropriate size. The value of α at which this becomes worthwhile can be characterized in terms of the expected savings in subsequent accesses [Hopgood 1968]. Note that since deleted entries will not be rehashed, then the new table might be either larger or smaller, or even the same size. Rehashing is a simple matter if the new table area is distinct from the old table area; however, one may wish to rehash into a new table area that is not distinct. An algorithm to accomplish this, using a boolean array to distinguish relocated/unrelocated values, is the subject of Exercise 10.39.

†10.4.2.5 Hash Table Rearrangement. If we peruse Table 10.4, we observe that when the load factor is high then open addressing, by either linear or random probing, is distinctly worse for unsuccessful searches than it is for successful ones. The reason is not hard to see. It is the familiar issue that we cannot detect an unsuccessful search in an unordered list until we reach the end of the list. For the moment, let us suppose that the keys had been arranged in sequence by decreasing value, and that they had then been hashed into the table from this sequence. As a result, the probe sequence of any key K must consist of keys that are already present and larger than it. So we could detect an unsuccessful search for a key K_j whenever, in the probe sequence for key K_j, we encountered another key K_i such that $K_j > K_i$. (By assumption, if K_j were present, it would have been inserted before K_i). Moreover, such a situation would relieve the necessity of the compound termination condition that we see in the **while** loop of HASH_DOUBLE.

In fact, it is not necessary that the keys have been inserted in decreasing order of their values. The technique known as *ordered hashing* compensates for this via the following search/insertion algorithm [Amble and Knuth 1974]. When a new key K_j is to be inserted, we can follow its probe sequence until either an empty slot is found or else a smaller key K_i is found. In the latter event, K_j "bumps" K_i from its location, and K_i is directed to proceed further along *its* probe sequence. The entire affair has been likened to a game of musical chairs, wherein many keys may be bumped before matters settle down. This logic is captured in the function HASH_ORDERED (Algorithm 10.9), which you should compare carefully with HASH_DOUBLE. The application of this method to the keys of Figure 10.29 is shown in Figure 10.35. Things proceed uneventfully for the first few keys. When the key 72 is presented, it collides with 85; but it is smaller and so we proceed to location 1. However, when the key 147 is presented, it bumps the key 43 from location 4. The subsequent probe sequence for 43 is 2, 0, 11, 9 (since $h_0(43) = 11$); but because locations 2, 0, 11 are already occupied by keys larger than 43, we do not stop looking until location 9. Later, the key 137 bumps 85 along to location 3. The real chase comes when the key 148 is presented; it bumps 109 from location 5 to location 3, in turn bumping 85 to location 12, in turn bumping 38 to location 10. On the final insertion, the key 101 bumps 38 from location 10 to location 8.

0	1	2	3	4	5	6	7	8	9	10	11	12
91	72	119	85 109	43 147	109 148		85 137	38	43	38 101	141	38 85

Figure 10.35 Illustration of Ordered Hashing

It is easy to see that this scheme must work when insertions are performed by decreasing order of the key values. Therefore, we know how to generate at least

```
function HASH_ORDERED (arg: integer; var htbl: hash_table): hash_link;

var     hcnt: hash_ndx;     {a global count of table entries}
        i,j: hash_ndx;
        k: integer;

begin
  i := HASH (arg); j := INCR (arg);
  while arg < htbl [i].key do
    i := (i + j) mod hsiz;
  if arg = htbl [i].key then
    HASH_ORDERED := i
  else begin
    if hcnt = hsiz - 1 then                    {table is full}
      HASH_ORDERED := -1
    else begin                                  {insert arg in table}
      while htbl [i].key <> 0 do begin
        if arg > htbl [i].key then begin       {bump the key}
          k := htbl [i].key;
          htbl [i].key := arg;
          arg := k;
        end;
        i := (i + INCR (arg)) mod hsiz;
      end;
      hcnt := hcnt + 1;
      htbl [i].key := arg;
      HASH_ORDERED := i;
    end;
  end;
end;
```

Algorithm 10.9 HASH_ORDERED

one arrangement of the table for which ordered hashing is viable. Remarkably, no matter what input permutation of the keys is employed, the algorithm HASH_ORDERED will always generate the same final hash table! To see this, suppose that there are in fact two or more table arrangements. Then let K_j be the largest key with a different location in two distinct arrangements. Necessarily, all the keys $K_i > K_j$ have identical locations in all possible arrangements, by the manner in which K_j was chosen. But then, in the probe sequence for K_j – in any arrangement – all the keys greater than K_j reside in fixed locations, and any keys less than K_j must occur later in the probe sequence. Accordingly, K_j must reside in the first probe location not occupied by larger keys, and must do so for all arrangements. This contradicts the existence of K_j and thus the possibility of more than one hash table arrangement.

Ordered hashing was introduced with the motive of improving the performance of unsuccessful searches. It is fairly easy to see that it does so. To begin with, since we have seen that the final hash table arrangement is independent of the insertion sequence, let us presume that the keys have been inserted in sequence by decreasing value, as suggested at the beginning of this section. This amounts to ordinary double hashing, and we have already seen (Eq. 10.37) that in this case $PS = (-1/\alpha) \times \ln(1 - \alpha)$. But since this corresponds to the unique sequence in the ordered hash table, then PS for ordered hashing must have the same value. In the case of an unsuccessful search for a key K, the significant observation is that the number of probes PF is the same as it would have been if K *did* occur in the table in its proper place, after any keys $K_i > K$ in its probe sequence. In other words, for ordered hashing, $PF = PS$. What about the cost, during randomly ordered insertions, of relocating items? Although the average cost of insertions is the same as in the case of double hashing, the probability distribution is not the same. In particular, some insertion sequences can require $O(n^2)$ "demotion" iterations in the algorithm HASH_ORDERED. Our final observation is that if an unsuccessful search is always followed by an insertion, as in typical compiler and assembler applications, then there is not much reason to employ the method. But when there are relatively many unsuccessful searches compared to the number of successful searches, then ordered hashing is strongly recommended. Note the implication of these last two statements – the advantage of the method will be gained via a variant of HASH_ORDERED that searches but does not insert.

We have seen that ordered hashing does not improve matters for successful searches. Is there any technique that does? In fact, there have been several approaches to this problem. One of these is illustrated in Figure 10.36(a). A new key K_0 has the probe sequence indicated in the first row of the diagram, where circles denote occupied locations and squares denote empty locations. We see that five probes would be required to find an empty location for K_0. Shown vertically are the probe sequences for the keys K_a, K_b, ... that occupy the locations along K_0's sequence. Although the locations are shown as being distinct, they need not be, of course. What really counts is whether, by bumping one of the keys out of K_0's sequence, we can reduce the aggregate probe lengths of all the keys. The first choice would be to bump K_a by one if the next location in its probe sequence were empty, but that is not the case here. The second choice would be either to bump K_a by two or K_b by one, but this does not help either. However, on the next diagonal, by bumping K_c by one to an empty location, there is a change of $+1$ for accessing K_c and -2 for accessing K_0. All in all, this method has been shown to lead to an average $PS = 2.49$ as α approaches one, and to an expected worst case cost of $O(n^{1/2})$ [Brent 1973].

A more general approach is illustrated in (b) of Figure 10.36. In this diagram, search is not limited just to the probe sequences of those keys on K_0's sequence. Rather, a binary tree of choices is explored. Whenever the probe sequence of a key K_i finds that location occupied by another key K_j, then the next locations in the sequences for both keys are examined. (Once again, note that the locations corresponding to these nodes need not be distinct.) The sense of the figure is that the probe sequence for the bumping key K_i continues to the left, and that the probe sequence for the bumped key K_j extends to the right. For the case illustrated in the figure, the optimum strategy would be to bump the key X from node A to node B and the key Y from node B to node C, thus allowing the insertion of K_0 at node A. This method has been shown to lead to an average $PS = 2.13$ as α approaches one, and to an expected worst case cost of $O(\lg n)$ [Gonnet and Munro 1979].

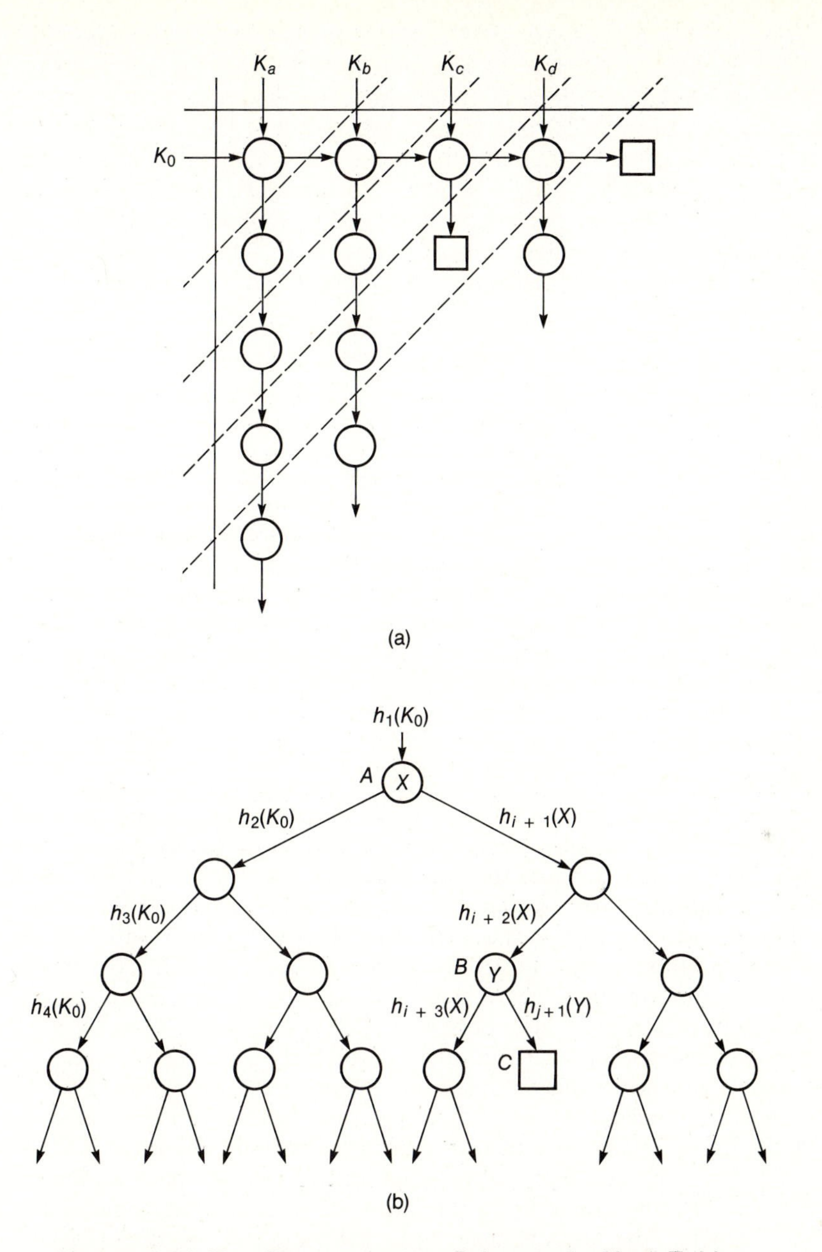

Figure 10.36 Two Rearrangement Schemes for Hash Tables

There is a limitation with either of the two methods illustrated in Figure 10.36, in that probe sequences are explored only in a forward direction. This causes some of the arrangements that they compute to be sub-optimal. The computation of an optimal arrangement (apparently yielding 1.83 for the average value of PS as α approaches one) would also, in effect, have to allow for exploring probe sequences in a backward direction [Lyon 1978; Rivest 1978a]. Such a computation would correspond, in fact, to solving the assignment problem; this was cited in Section 7.4.3.4 as one of the variations of computing a minimum weighted matching for a bipartite graph. In practice, one would seek to adapt the amount of rearranging activity to the expected savings in subsequent accesses, along the lines depicted in Figure 10.36. Is it likely to be worthwhile to rearrange hash tables to reduce the average value of *PS*? For the symbol table for a compiler, it might well be, since there the ratio of subsequent (successful) searches to initial (unsuccessful) searches can be high; and for a fixed dictionary, it almost certainly would be.

†10.4.3 Hashing Optimality

In our evaluation of open hashing performance in Section 10.4.2.3, we found that the average value of *PS* is $O(\log n)$, and that the worst-case value of *PS* is $O(n)$. Subsequently, in Section 10.4.2.5, we saw how to improve these values by means of collision resolution methods that rearrange the hash table. By these rearrangements, the average value can be reduced to $O(1)$ (a constant), and the worst-case value can be reduced to $O(\log n)$. In this section we consider the question of the absolutely best hashing performance that can be obtained. These improvements are obtained both via the choice of hashing function and via the choice of collision resolution method. There are several variations on this theme, all of them sustaining the central idea that it is possible to use a hash table with $O(1)$ worst-case performance.

In order to discuss these matters, we will speak of a universe U of possible key values and a subset S of keys, chosen from U and to be hashed into a table of size M. Also, the size $|U|$ is N and the size $|S|$ is n. Now the most desirable situation would be to find a *perfect hashing function* that would engender no collisions, and so would map each key in S into a distinct location in the table with a single probe. It is extremely unlikely that an arbitrary hashing function will have this property. As an illustration, suppose that $n = 30$ and $M = 40$. Then there are $40^{30} \approx 10^{48}$ mappings from S into the table; only $40 \times 39 \times \cdots \times 11 = 40!/10! \approx 2 \times 10^{41}$ of these do not have collisions, however. In other words, only about two in every 10 million will be perfect for these values of n and M. Nonetheless, Sprugnoli [1977] discusses two heuristics for finding for such a function, once having been presented with some fixed, unchanging set S. We can impose the additional condition that $M = n$ — that is, that there be no empty table slots; in this case we have a *minimal perfect hash function*. In one attack upon this problem, a hash value is constructed using the first character, the last character, and the length of the key [Cichelli 1980]. Various heuristics are then employed to guide a backtracking search for an assignment of values to the characters that will produce a minimal perfect hash function. In one example of this method, a minimal perfect hash function is obtained that maps the reserved words of Pascal into the range 2 .. 37; for example, with 15 for 'B' and 13 for 'N', this function hashes 'BEGIN' to 33.

For small, static sets of keys, as with the reserved words in an HLL, the idea of a perfect or minimal perfect hash function can be extremely worthwhile. As a general approach to hashing, however, the idea has some practical shortcomings. It is totally unsuited for a varying set of keys, where a single insertion makes it necessary to compute an entirely new hash function. Moreover, even for static sets of keys, the methods just described have limited applicability except for small n. One reason is because of the use of heuristics with exponential complexity; thus, we may not be able to ascertain in any reasonable amount of time whether a solution exists for a given set S, much less the value of a solution. Another reason is that the methods can generate hash constants so large with respect to the fixed word size of the underlying machine that they cannot reasonably be employed. Nonetheless, the search for perfect and minimal perfect hash functions has attracted a large amount of effort [§].

In addition to the pragmatic results outlined in the preceding paragraphs, some remarkable theoretical results have been obtained concerning the possibility of hashing a sparse table; by this, we mean hashing an arbitrary subset S from a universe U of size N to a table of size M, where M is suitably less than N. For $M > 2$ and $N \leq 2M - 2$, as an example, it is always possible to determine (with a single probe!) whether or not any given member of U is present in the table. This is possible by means of an ingenious assignment of keys to table locations, such that examination of the location specified by $h(K)$ has one of three results:

(a) K is there and so is present in the table;

(b) some different key from U is there, such that we can infer that K is somewhere else in the table;

(c) some different key from U is there, such that we can infer that K is absent from the table.

On the one hand, this result is true for *any* subset of elements of U (as long as $N \leq 2M - 2$). On the other hand, it may not actually retrieve K if it is present; rather, the result has the effect of determining set membership. This unusual demonstration is coupled with further conclusions concerning the sufficiency of $O(1)$ probes (but not single probes), subject to restrictions on the relative values of M and N [Yao 1981]. These restrictions are removed in Fredman et al. [1984], where it is shown how hashing can be used to store and retrieve a sparse subset of items from a universe U in a table M with $O(1)$ worst-case performance – regardless of the relative values of M and N!

Thus far, we have viewed the question of hashing optimality as one of trying to find a hash function h for which the worst-case performance will not be too bad, no matter what subset S of U is presented to it. More precisely, we look for an h such that, averaged over all sets of input keys, the number of collisions produced by h is bounded relative to the size of the set. The approach known as *universal hashing* uses separate chaining and deals not with a single hash function, but with a set H of hash functions [Carter and Wegman 1979]. One chooses an h at random from H and then averages the expected number of collisions over all the members of H, rather than over all the possible input sets S. The effect of this is to provide relief, in a technical sense, for the possible worst-case behavior that any single hash function can have for certain inputs. In other words, universal hashing guarantees that the expected time to process *any* input sequence is linear in the length of the sequence. For a suitable prime p, one example of a class H of universal hash functions is given by H: $h_{s,t}(K) = (s \times K + t) \bmod p$. The idea is that one chooses a function from H at random and then monitors its operation on the input set S at hand. In the event of unsatisfactory performance, one just randomly chooses another function from H.

Alas, we must note that the results described in the two preceding paragraphs do not come without cost. In both cases, although the expected time complexities of the methods are guaranteed to be $O(1)$, the cost in the size of the information (that is, program and/or data) required to specify them is unbounded. (We are reminded of the unlimited growth of hash constants in some of the perfect hashing methods.) Quantitative discussions of these compensating costs can be found in Mairson [1983] and Mehlhorn [1982a].

†10.4.4 Predictive Hashing

The conventional use of hashing is for determining the location of an item in a table or file. Sometimes we encounter situations wherein an item is very unlikely to be present and where it is not disastrous to mistakenly decide that it is, as long as we don't decide that it is not present when it really is. This leads to a different and powerful use of hashing for predicting whether an item is *likely* to be present in a table or file. Actually, the idea is to be able to compute rather quickly, and with no error, whenever a value is *not* present. We accept, however, that the computation may erroneously predict that an item is present when it is not. In other words, this method will filter out all the values that are really present, but will also filter out some number of *false drops* – that is, values that seem to match the criteria but really do not. Thus, suppose that we are checking a credit card number to see if the card is suspect. In the vast majority of cases no action is required. However, the cost of looking for the card number in a large reference file is likely to be high; the complete file may not even fit in main memory. So it is better to be able to determine quickly when a complete search is not required, even at the expense of occasionally being misled that a number is in the file and looking for it without finding it.

For the situation just described, we employ a large bit table $b_0 b_1 \dots b_{M-1}$ and a set of hash functions $h_1, h_2, \dots, h_s$. These functions are chosen to be completely independent of each other, but each of them hashes input keys into the range $0 \,..\, M-1$. The hash table (the bit values) is generated by applying each hash function to each key in the file. For a given key K_i, the effect will be to set to one those bits addressed by the union of $h_1(K_i), h_2(K_i), \dots, h_s(K_i)$. When the entire set of keys has been hashed to this bit array, then b_k will have the value one only if some hash function applied to some key returned the value k. Now when an input key K is presented, we simply test whether $b_{h_j}(K) = 1$ for all $1 \le j \le s$. If the test fails for any j, then K cannot be in the file and we can proceed with other matters. Otherwise, we should assume that K is present and search for it in the file. For maximum effectiveness, the parameters s and M for this *Bloom filter* [Bloom 1970] should be chosen such that approximately half of the M hash bits get set to one. We will analyze a closely related situation very shortly, from which it can be seen that for a file of N records, the probability of getting a false drop is approximated by $(1 - e^{-\frac{sN}{M}})^s$. Moreover, even if there are a moderate number of false drops in the "hits" to the file, that is much less significant than the time that is saved by not doing a full search for the majority of items that are not in the file. In situations for which this approach is appropriate, the hash table is typically large, but not too large to fit in main memory, whereas a conventional hash table for the file would not fit in main memory.

In the method just described, we constructed a large hash table that could be used as a predictor for all the items in a table or file. A closely related approach can be used for speeding up the search for a string pattern in a text file. In this scenario, we have a large, fairly static text file that is to be searched many times, perhaps a file used for information retrieval. Such a file is typically organized in terms of text lines (see Figure 8.20). Rather than laboriously searching for an input pattern in each line of such a file, we can construct a small hash table for each line, as a predictor for substrings that occur in that line [Harrison 1971]. In particular, we construct a *hashed k-signature* by applying a hash function h to each of the substrings $a_i a_{i+1} \dots a_{i+k-1}$ of length k in that line. The range of h is $0 \mathinner{..} m-1$, and the hash table is a bit table $b_0 b_1 \dots b_{m-1}$. After the signature is constructed for a line, then b_j in that signature will have the value one only if h applied to some substring in that line returned the value j. Now when an input pattern is presented, we first compute the hashed k-signature of all its substrings of length k. Then the pattern cannot be in a text line if, for any $0 \le j \le m-1$, the jth bit of the pattern signature is one and the jth bit of the line signature is zero, whereupon we can skip with certainty to the next text line. If the signature of the text line does "cover" that of the pattern, however, we must employ conventional pattern matching on that line.

Of course, there may be false drops. Let us estimate the probability of this, using 2-signatures and assuming that there is no correlation among substrings of length two – that is, digrams. (From our mention of digrams in relation to spelling correction in Section 8.3.2, we know that this assumption is not really justified.) The probability that any single digram in a line of text will not hash to a particular location in the bit table is $(1 - 1/m)$. For an average number t of digrams in a text line, the probability that none of them will hash to that particular location is therefore $(1 - 1/m)^t$; and the probability that at least one of them *will* hash to that location and set it to one is $(1 - (1 - 1/m)^t)$. Therefore, if the pattern has s digrams, the probability that each of them will hash onto one of these locations in the line signature having value one is $\Pr = (1 - (1 - 1/m)^t)^s$. Finally, since $(1 - 1/m)^m \approx e^{-1}$, we can substitute $e^{-t/m}$ for $(1 - 1/m)^t$ and rewrite this as

$$\Pr = \left(1 - e^{-t/m}\right)^s \tag{10.38}$$

(The analysis of false drops for a Bloom filter is almost identical.) As an example, suppose that we have a 12-character pattern (with 11 adjacent pairs) and an 80-character text line (with 79 adjacent pairs). Then for a hash table of 64 bits, $\Pr = (1 - e^{-79/64})^{11} = .02275$. In other words, for these parameters, the signature test allows almost 98 percent of the non-matching substrings to be discarded without further testing.

The signature method is certainly useful for a large static text file that will be searched often, but it is not practical for spontaneous searching of text files. Moreover, it requires that extra space be allocated with each text line for its signature. Our last example of predictive hashing responds to both of these objections. It is in fact a third $O(n)$ method for general substring matching (see Section 8.5.1), by Karp and Rabin [1981]. In this algorithm (K&R), hashing is used to construct a *fingerprint* of a pattern. In order to be useful, the fingerprint function must be so concise and easily computable that there is a savings in comparing fingerprint values rather than directly comparing substrings. It should also, of course, yield a small percentage of false drops. With this scheme, we need to construct the fingerprint of the pattern just once. But since we have to construct the fingerprints of many successive substrings of the text, we need some method that allows for very efficient "updating" of the fingerprint from one substring to the next.

In the K&R substring matching method, the characters a_i of a substring are treated as digits d_i relative to the radix r of the character set. Then the fingerprint of a substring $D = d_i d_{i+1} \ldots d_{i+m-1}$, of length m, is defined by

$$\phi(D) \equiv d_i r^{m-1} + d_{i+1} r^{m-2} + \cdots + d_{i+m-1} \text{ (modulo } p) \qquad (10.39)$$

where p is a large prime. For $p < 2^{32}$, we see that comparing fingerprints reduces to comparing full-word integers in common machine architectures. What is ϕ for D', the successor to D, when we shift right one place? The crux of this method is that we can compute $\phi(D')$ fairly simply by

$$\phi(D') \equiv (\phi(D) - d_i r^{m-1}) \times r + d_{i+m} \text{ (modulo } p) \qquad (10.40)$$

An important reason that Eq. 10.40 is easy to evaluate is that, for prime p, the modulus operation can be applied after each operation rather than at the end of the evaluation. Now observe that ϕ is a hash function, but we do not need a hash table like that required in the signature method. Rather, the fast update of Eq. 10.40 takes its place!

One more thing is required in order for the K&R method to be useful. The probability of a false drop has to be suitably small. In Karp and Rabin [1981] it is shown that for a text string of length n and a suitable choice of prime p, this probability is $2.511/n$ and the expected complexity of looking for a match is $O(n)$. Since we know that any hashing function can yield very bad performance for certain inputs, their method also incorporates a notion akin to that of uniform hashing (see Section 10.4.3). In particular, if the number of false matches with a given pattern/text combination is excessive, then one can interrupt the process, randomly choose a different suitable prime, and then continue the process with the new definition of ϕ. In conclusion, note that good performance for the K&R algorithm depends upon two capabilities that are not required with the earlier KMP and B&M algorithms; we must be able to do multiplication and modulus operations quickly, and we must be able to obtain random prime numbers easily.

10.5 DIGITAL SEARCHING

Most of our searching methods have been based upon binary comparisons of keys. Hashing was a notable exception, substituting properties of key transformations for the natural ordering among the keys. Now let's suppose that instead of organizing the data, we organize the search space. We can do this by regarding a key in terms of its representation as a sequence of "digits" – characters or actual digits or bits – and then using the values in this sequence to guide our search. Indeed, we do this very naturally when we use the thumb-indices of a large dictionary to find the first entries for each letter of the alphabet. We will examine two rather different ways of operating with the digits of the key. The first conforms to the thumb-index analogy; the second combines elements of digital searching with those of BST's.

10.5.1 Tries

The word *trie* comes from the word re*trie*val and is pronounced like "try" so that it will not be confused with tree. It is particularly appropriate for alphabetic keys, where the radix is 27, allowing for a space character. For illustrative purposes, however, that is too "branchy," and so we will use just the eight most common letters {e, t, a, o, i, n, s, t}. In particular, we will compose examples from the 26 most common words that employ only these (non-blank) letters, as shown in Table 10.5 (and as opposed to Table 10.1 in Section 10.3.2.4). Ordinary words do not have the prefix property (see Section 8.2.4), and we can see several instances of this in the table; for example, 'the' is a prefix of 'then' and 'these'. When using tries, therefore, it becomes necessary to employ some distinct terminator character to discriminate such cases. We will employ '≠' for that purpose. At each node of a trie for our example words, we will make a nine-way branch, corresponding to the nine possible values '≠, a, e, h, i, n, o, s, t' of the examined character. This process is illustrated in Figure 10.37, where the value used for branching at the jth level is the jth character of the argument key. Since the initial portions of the keys are determined by the search path, there is a choice between storing an entire key at a leaf (as in the figure), or just the suffix portion of a key. One or the other is required, however, in order to prevent a partial match from being falsely interpreted as a complete match.

i	*word*	*i*	*word*	*i*	*word*	*i*	*word*
1	the	8	it	15	not	22	its
2	to	9	as	16	an	23	into
3	a	10	his	17	one	24	than
4	in	11	on	18	she	25	these
5	that	12	at	19	has	26	then
6	is	13	I	20	no		
7	he	14	this	21	so		

Table 10.5 26 Most Common Words Using {e, t, a, o, i, n, s, h}

Two things are apparent from Figure 10.37. First, this structure allows us to make more elaborate discriminations and so find keys faster, on average, than is possible with a BST. In particular, if there are n keys and we are performing m-way branching on their digits, then with the best of circumstances we should be able to

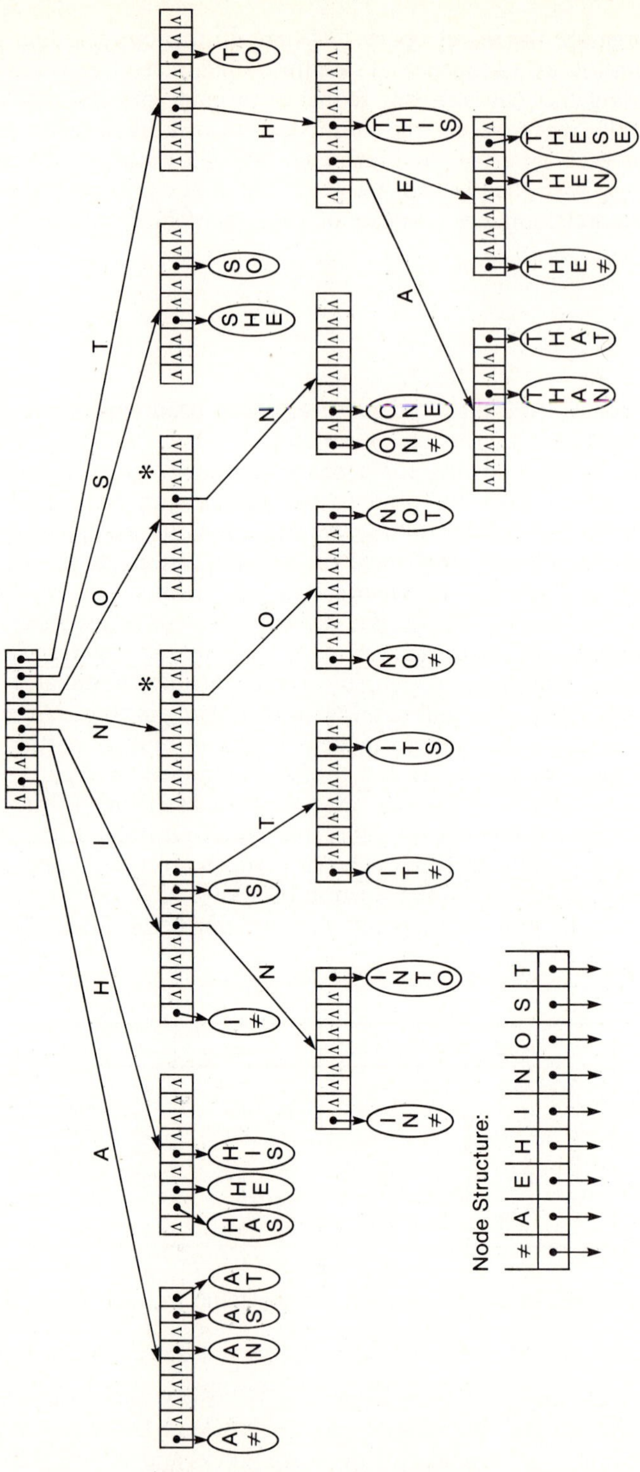

Figure 10.37 An Example Trie

discriminate among them with $\log_m n = \lg n / \lg m$ tests. In the case of a full alphabet of 27 characters, this would suggest that only $1/\lg 27 \approx 0.21$ as many tests would be needed as with ordinary binary comparisons. Even in the worst case, moreover, the number of tests is bounded by the number of characters in the longest key, and this is far less than the $O(n)$ worst-case for unbalanced BST's. Another feature of Figure 10.37 is that, in fact, many of the branch possibilities are empty. This increases the actual number of discriminations required, and also leads to extravagant use of space in tries. A realistic expected value for the number of nodes, under the assumption that the keys are random, can be shown to be $n/\ln m$ [Knuth 1973b]; accordingly, the average amount of space is $mn/\ln m$. There are several avenues to explore for reducing the wasted space that we see in Figure 10.37.[11] But first, let us take up the matter of implementing tries.

Dealing with tries in an HLL like Pascal reveals some interesting problems. A fundamental one is that the pointers in Figure 10.37 may refer either to other nodes containing vectors of pointers or to nodes containing keys. Since the keys are likely to be of widely varying length, they might preferably be placed in a string table rather than in the trie nodes. But that doesn't alter the fact that the pointers must be able to reference two very different sorts of structures, for which the remedy is to use variant records. In our case, we will have one variant that contains a vector of pointers, and another variant that contains an alphabetic key. The reason for using a vector of pointers is that the multiway branch can thereby be accomplished in one machine operation, by indexing the vector with the character at hand. We will use '≠' .. 'Z' as the index type for the vector of pointers. The value '≠' is arbitrarily chosen as the terminator character because it closely precedes the range 'A' .. 'Z' in the EBCDIC character set; a different choice would doubtless be made for ASCII (see Table 8.1).

Incorporating these observations, we arrive at the function TRIE_INSERT (Algorithm 10.10) for searching a trie, inserting *arg* if it is not already there, and (in any case) returning a pointer to the node containing *arg*. Note that there are two circumstances under which an argument key will be inserted. The simpler case occurs when one of the appropriate pointers is **nil** and so a new *word* node must be created and attached to the trie. A trickier situation occurs when a pointer chain terminates with an unequal match between *arg* and the key K at a leaf. In this case, it is first necessary to insert intervening *vect* node(s) up to the point of the earliest level j at which *arg* and K differ in the jth position; and then the trie pointers must be updated to reflect this.[12]

In selecting the representation in Figure 10.37 and in developing the algorithm TRIE_INSERT, we were guided by the desire to be able to build a trie dynamically. We may have a simpler situation where just searches need be performed, and not insertions, as in the case of the reserved words of an HLL. In that case, we

---

[11] The non-contiguity of the alphabetic characters in EBCDIC is particularly distressing at this point. It exacerbates the phenomenon of wasted space in tries by interspersing extra unused pointer positions in the nodes.

[12] In TRIE_INSERT, we could have written **new**(*r*,*vect*) and **new**(*s*,*word*) in order to preclude wasted space (see Figure 4.10). For the sake of simplicity, this was not done.

```
function TRIE_INSERT (arg: key_id; var tbl: trie_ptr): trie_ptr;

const  first = '≠'; last = 'Z';

type   alf = first .. last;
       key_range = 1 .. key_max;
       key_id = packed array [key_range] of char;
       nodetype = (vect,word);
       trie_ptr = ↑trie_node;
       trie_node = record
          case tag: nodetype of
             vect: (ptrs: array [alf] of trie_ptr);
             word: (key: key_id);
       end;

var    ch: alf;
       done: boolean;
       i,j: key_range;
       p,q,r,s: trie_ptr;

begin
   done := false; i := 1; q := tbl;
   while done = false do begin
      done := true;
      case q↑.tag of
         vect: if q↑.ptrs [arg [i]] <> nil then begin
            p := q; q := q↑.ptrs [arg [i]];
            done := false; i := i + 1;
         end else begin        {hang a new word node from vect node}
            new (s); s↑.tag := word;
            q↑.ptrs [arg [i]] := s;
            s↑.key := arg;
            TRIE_INSERT := r;
         end;
         word: if arg = q↑.key then   {found it}
            TRIE_INSERT := q
         else begin            {need new vect node(s) and a new word node}
            i := i - 1; j := i;
            repeat
               new (r); r↑.tag := vect;
               for ch := first to last do
                  r↑.ptrs [ch] := nil;
               p↑.ptrs [arg [j]] := r;
               j := j + 1; p := r;
            until arg [j] <> q↑.key [j];
            r↑.ptrs [q↑.key [j]] := q;
            new (s); s↑.tag := word;
            r↑.ptrs [arg [j]] := s;
            s↑.key := arg;
            TRIE_INSERT := r;
         end;
      end;
   end;
end;
```

Algorithm 10.10 TRIE_INSERT

might represent the trie as a two-dimensional array, where each member of the array is either a keyword or else an index of another column in the array, according to the following definitions:

```
type   col_ndx = 1 .. col_max;
       member = (link,word);
       trie_member = record
          case tag: member of
             link: (cursor: 0 .. col_max);
             word: (key: key_id);
       end;
       trie_a = array [alf,col_ndx] of trie_member;
```

An algorithm to perform searching in such a structure is likewise much simpler than Algorithm 10.10. Figure 10.38(a) exhibits an array representation corresponding to the original trie of Figure 10.37.

It is certain that we can expect to have a shorter search path with a trie than with a BST. How this will affect search times is less clear. It depends largely upon the relative speeds of doing character extraction and word comparison on the underlying machine, and so is mostly outside of our control. However, a major concern with using tries has always been how to implement them efficiently in terms of space. Some of these efforts are summarized in the following paragraphs.

A. Tries were first proposed by Fredkin [1960] and also by de la Briandais [1959]. These two proposals have a significant difference. The former presents tries as we have described them. The latter characterization retains just the non-void siblings within a node, and then transforms this ordered tree with nodes of variable degree to the corresponding binary tree. When this transformation is applied to Figure 10.37, we obtain the binary tree in Figure 10.39. Now there is less wasted space, but it is no longer possible to accomplish fast branching by indexing on an array of pointers. Exactly how much space is saved depends upon several factors. The savings will be greater as the sparsity of the vector increases. Don't forget, though, that each non-void entry now requires space for a digit label and two pointers, as opposed to just one pointer in Figure 10.37. Because the fast multi-branching is lost, the representation in Figure 10.39 is generally less popular. However, it is possible to recoup some of the loss by familiar techniques. One is to link sibling nodes in decreasing order of their expected usage. Another might be to replace linked lists of siblings by BST's of siblings.

B. Trie nodes are usually space efficient near the root and less so further away from the root, as in Figure 10.37. A sensible response to this is to employ a hybrid data structure that is like a trie near the root, but reverts to linked lists or BST's near the leaves, when the number of children becomes less than some value b. As cited at the beginning of this section, the average number of nodes for a random trie is $n/\ln m$. Employing a hybrid random trie in this manner, the node requirement is approximately $n/(b \ln m)$, for b and m small and n large [Knuth 1973b]. The optimal overall strategy is to switch at about $b = 6$, thereby reducing the number of nodes by a factor of six [Sussenguth 1963].

C. In realistic sets of alphabetic keys for information retrieval, we often encounter words that have identical prefix portions – for example, physical, physician, physi-

	1	2	3	4	5	6	7	8	9	10	11	12	13	14	15
≠	—	A	—	I	—	—	—	—	IN	IT	NO	ON	—	—	THE
A	2	—	HAS	—	—	—	—	—	—	—	—	—	14	—	—
E	—	—	HE	—	—	—	—	—	—	—	—	ONE	15	—	—
H	3	—	—	—	—	—	SHE	13	—	—	—	—	—	—	—
I	4	—	HIS	—	—	—	—	—	—	—	—	—	THIS	—	—
N	5	AN	—	9	—	12	—	—	—	—	—	—	—	THAN	THEN
O	6	—	—	—	11	—	SO	TO	—	—	—	—	—	—	—
S	7	AS	—	IS	—	—	—	—	—	ITS	—	—	—	—	THESE
T	8	AT	—	10	—	—	—	—	INTO	—	NOT	—	—	THAT	—

(a) Normal

	1	2	3	4	5	6	7	8	9	10	11	12	13
≠	—	—	—	—	—	—	HE	AN	TO	AS	IS	AT	HIS
A	A	—	8	—	10	12	—	—	—	—	—	—	—
E	2	—	THEN	—	—	—	—	—	—	—	—	—	—
H	—	7	—	—	—	—	—	THAN	—	HAS	13	THAT	—
I	I	—	IN	—	11	IT	—	—	—	—	—	—	—
N	3	ONE	—	NO	—	—	—	—	INTO	—	—	—	—
O	4	—	ON	—	—	NOT	—	—	—	—	—	—	—
S	5	THESE	—	SO	—	—	SHE	—	—	—	—	—	—
T	6	—	—	9	ITS	—	THE	—	—	—	—	—	THIS

(b) Reversed

Figure 10.38 Array Forms of Trie of Figure 10.37

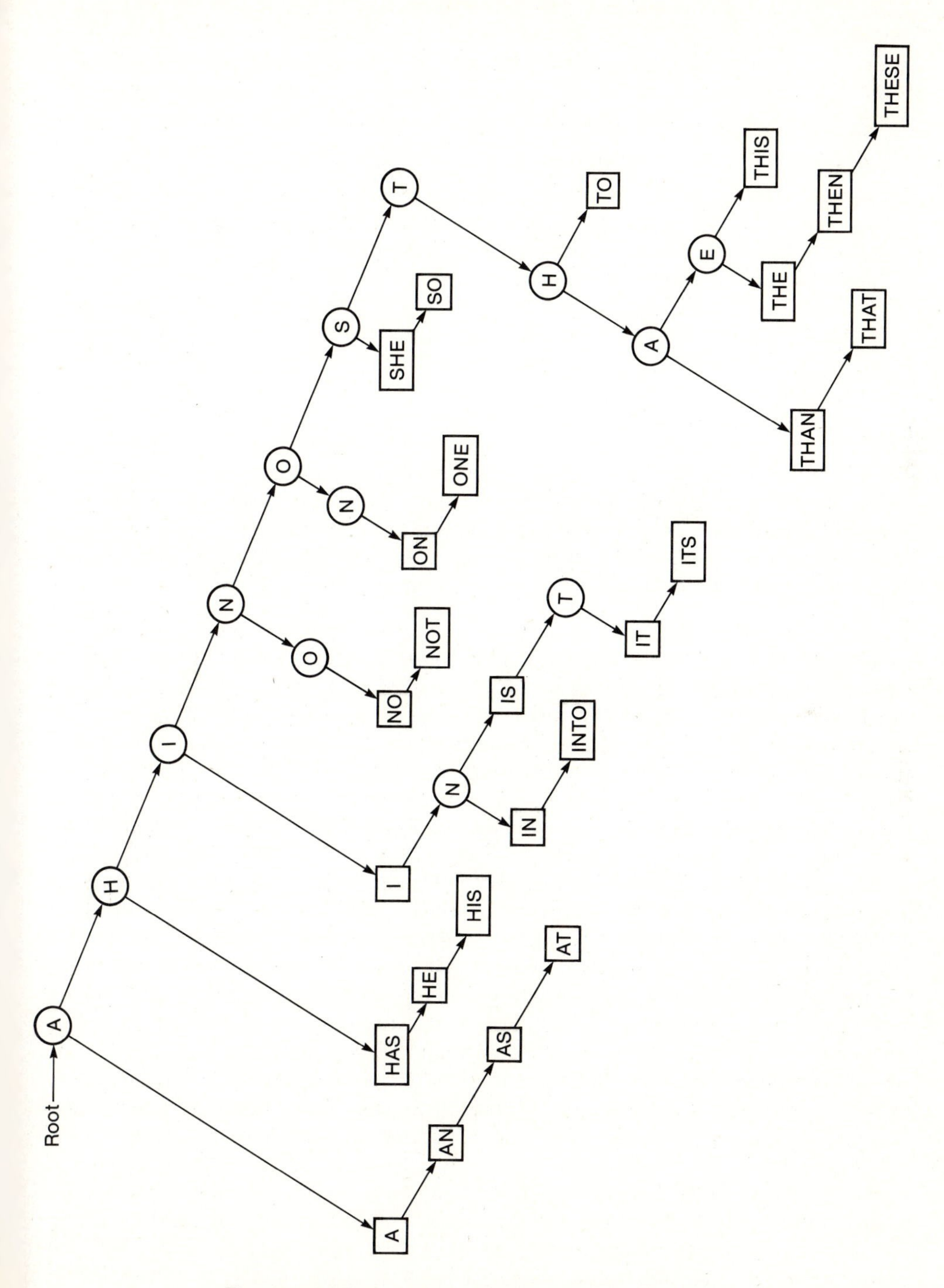

Figure 10.39 Tree Form of Trie of Figure 10.37

cist, physics. Because of this non-random property, many more trie nodes are required to discriminate such words than we would otherwise expect. In particular, it causes "one-way" branching; we see two such nodes (marked with *'s) in Figure 10.37. It is not hard to "collapse" tries so that one-way nodes are deleted. We simply incorporate in each node an additional field that specifies how many digits should be skipped over until finding one that is significant for discrimination.

D. It was natural to build the trie in Figure 10.38(a) by examining the characters from left to right. But there are other possibilities. For example, by examining the characters from right to left, we can construct the trie in Figure 10.38(b), which requires only thirteen nodes of pointers rather than fifteen. Can we discover an optimal sequence of character positions to test and thus construct the optimal trie, as we did the optimal BST in Section 10.3.2.1? Unfortunately, this problem and several alternate phrasings of it have all been shown to be *NP*-complete [Comer and Sethi 1977]. Therefore, in lieu of exact answers, we look for heuristics. The problem of finding an optimal sequence of character positions for discriminating between words has been investigated in the context of finding optimal rules for abbreviation of words. In an excellent study of this matter, many rules were tried, and one of the simplest was found to be generally superior [Bourne and Ford 1961]. Specifically, a good rule is simply to skip over all the characters in the even-numbered positions. In particular, this discards the second characters of words. Second characters are very commonly vowels, and accordingly provide less discriminatory power than do characters in other positions.

E. Lastly, there are techniques for retaining the branching structure of a trie, but "squeezing" out the excess space. Examine Figure 10.38 again, and imagine that we slice such an array into its columns. Then suppose that we slide these columns up and down beside a large empty vector of slots in such manner that there are no multiple entries in any row, and as few empty rows as possible. We can then superimpose the vertically shifted columns upon the vector of slots, and this elongated vector can be used in lieu of the two-dimensional array, with subsequent savings in space. The result is known as a *compacted trie*. It is illustrated in Figure 10.40, where (a) is the original trie for the words {APE, ATE, PAT, PEA, PET, TAP, TEA}, and where (b) shows a compacted trie for the same words; the values above the compacted trie mark the beginnings in (b) of the corresponding columns from (a). Exact and approximate algorithms for finding compacted tries in this manner are given in Al-Suwaiyel and Horowitz [1984], and they tend to reduce the space requirement by 70 percent. The exact algorithm is exponential in the number of trie nodes examined. However, the simplest of the approximate algorithms compacts almost as well in practice and yet has complexity $O(mn)$, for m the branching factor and n the number of nodes. The goodness of the compacted result depends much more heavily upon m than upon n. Interestingly, repeated use of the KMP string matching technique (see Section 8.5.1.1) is central to all of these algorithms. Of course, the technique of compaction is useful only for static tries. Another way of squeezing space out of tries is to construct *compressed tries*, in which the essential point is to replace vectors of pointers by vectors of boolean indicators [Maly 1976]. This typically reduces storage requirements by an order of magnitude, with no diminishment of accessing speed. The resulting structure is very cumbersome to update; so it too is suitable only for static tries.

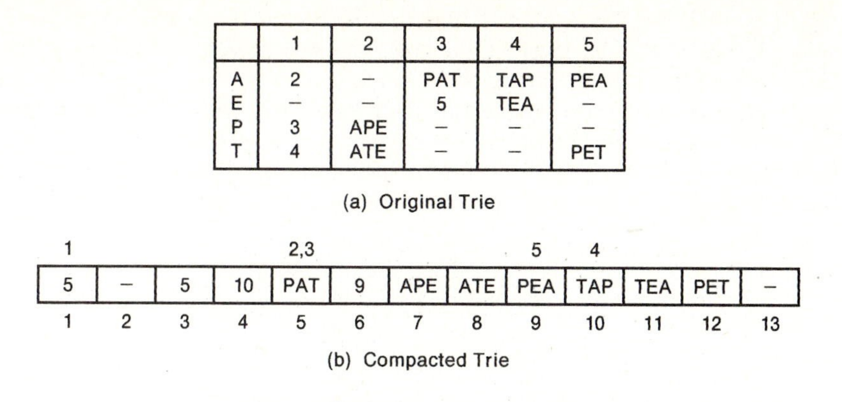

	1	2	3	4	5
A	2	–	PAT	TAP	PEA
E	–	–	5	TEA	–
P	3	APE	–	–	–
T	4	ATE	–	–	PET

(a) Original Trie

1				2,3				5	4			
5	–	5	10	PAT	9	APE	ATE	PEA	TAP	TEA	PET	–
1	2	3	4	5	6	7	8	9	10	11	12	13

(b) Compacted Trie

Figure 10.40 Compacting a Trie

Now that we have dealt at length with the issue of space in tries, what can be said about their usefulness as compared with other structures for searching? First, they are particularly useful for dealing with long, variable-length keys. Most trie searches on such keys need examine only the first few characters. Moreover, in the event of an unsuccessful search, we will know the longest partial match. By contrast, methods based upon key comparisons or hashing may cost more because of the need to deal with the entire key; also, hashing is useless for indicating partial matches. A significant hazard with unbalanced BST's and with hashing is their $O(n)$ worst-case behavior. This is far less of a problem with tries. We have already mentioned that the longest path can be no longer than the longest key. The possibility of this happening depends upon non-randomness in the distribution of digits in the keys. Unlike the BST case, however, it is completely independent of the sequence in which the keys are inserted. For a given set of keys, the same trie will be obtained for any sequence of insertions!

†10.5.2 Binary Digital Searching

In contrasting tries with BST's, we might conclude that comparison searching is intrinsically binary and that digital searching is intrinsically multiway. This is not true, however. Multiway comparison trees were introduced in Section 10.3.4; we will now encounter a binary form of digital searching. In this method, the bit representation of a key is used rather than its character representation. That makes it more appropriate for implementation in assembly language than in an HLL, where bit extraction is awkward. We can illustrate the concept nonetheless, using the hypothetical mapping from characters to bits illustrated in Figure 10.41(a). Under this mapping, the keys of Table 10.5 would appear as in (b) of Figure 10.41. An algorithm for inspecting the binary digits from left to right and searching/inserting in a binary tree would be very similar to BST_INSERT (Algorithm 6.6). When the search has reached a node X, the first step is to compare the argument key with the key at X. If they are equal, the argument has been found. Otherwise, for X at the ith level of the tree, the search goes left or right from X, according to whether the ith bit of the argument has the value 0 or 1. When the words of Figure 10.41(b) are inserted in their listed sequence, from more probable to less probable, we obtain the *binary digital search tree* of Figure 10.42. It is somewhat disconcerting at first glance; it resembles an ordinary BST with some keys out of place, as though it might have been constructed by a novice.

	binary	octal		binary	octal
a	000	0	n	100	4
e	001	1	o	101	5
h	010	2	s	110	6
i	011	3	t	111	7

(a) Binary/Octal Encoding of {e, t, a, o, i, n, s, h}

	word	octal		word	octal		word	octal		word	octal
1	the	721	8	it	37	15	not	457	22	its	376
2	to	75	9	as	06	16	an	04	23	into	3475
3	a	0	10	his	236	17	one	541	24	than	7204
4	in	34	11	on	54	18	she	621	25	these	72161
5	that	7207	12	at	07	19	has	206	26	then	7214
6	is	36	13	I	3	20	no	45			
7	he	21	14	this	7236	21	so	65			

(b) Words and Octal Equivalents

Figure 10.41 Binary Representation of the Words of Table 10.5

We learned in the preceding section that the shape of a trie is dependent upon the distribution of the digits in the keys, but is independent of the order of insertion. This is in contrast to BST's, in which the shape is independent of the key values, but very dependent upon the order of insertion. Since binary digital search trees are intermediate in character to tries and BST's, it is not completely surprising to learn that their shapes depend upon both of these factors. The good news is that their dependence upon order of insertion is much less than with BST's. Therefore, as with tries, the worst-case performance of binary digital search trees is much better than that of BST's. We can observe that this is so by taking the keys from Figure 10.41(b) and building an ordinary BST with them, as in Figure 10.43. This latter tree is badly unbalanced, with an average path length of $152/26 = 5.846$. By contrast, the tree of Figure 10.42 has an average path length of $111/26 = 4.269$. What if the keys are distinctly non-random, such that there are many instances of equality among the prefix portions of their binary representations? In this case we could first hash the keys to scramble their bit values, and then proceed as before. In fact, the original description of binary digital searching is couched in these terms [Coffman and Eve 1970].

Whereas in trie searching the keys are at the leaves, in binary digital searching they are at the nodes; thus, this latter method requires many more key comparisons

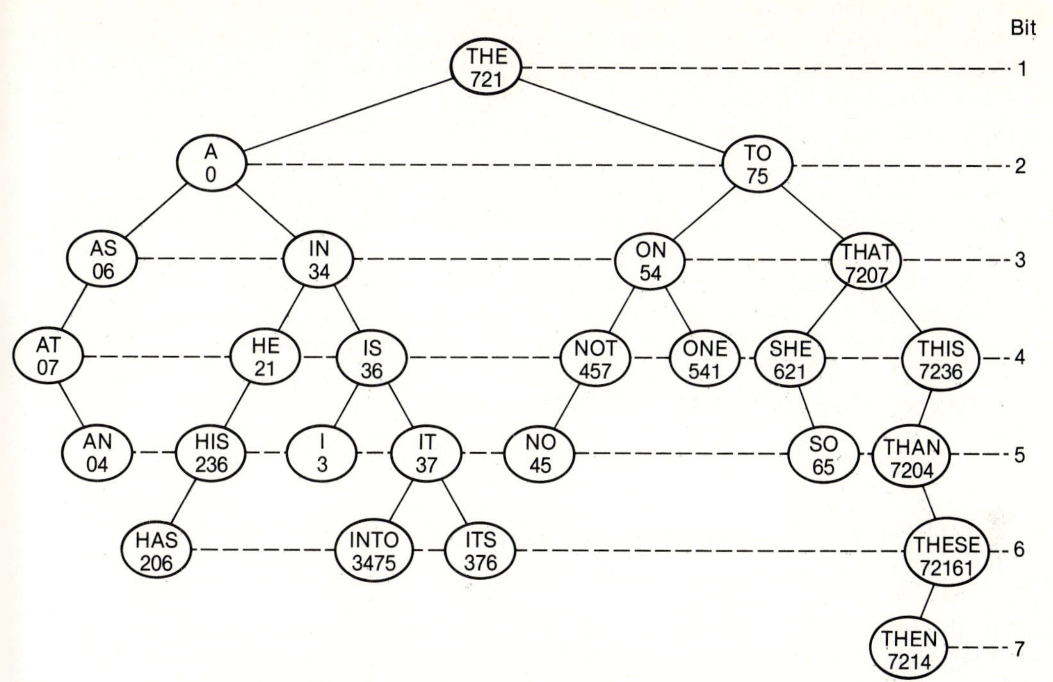

Figure 10.42 Digital Binary Search Tree for Figure 10.41

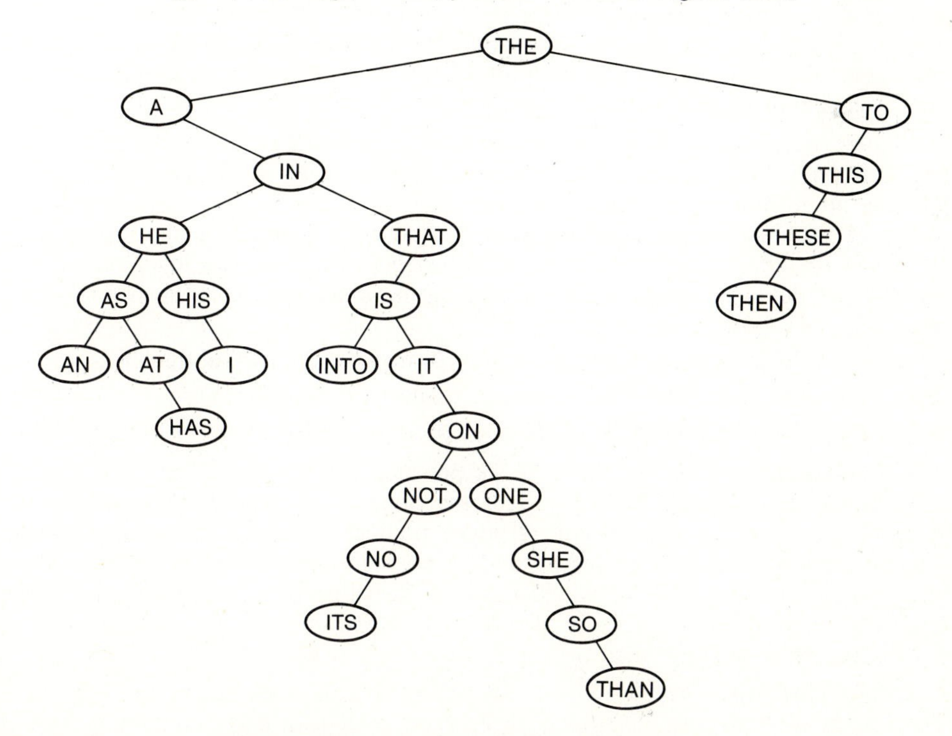

Figure 10.43 Ordinary BST for Figure 10.41

than trie searching does. An example of a digital search method that does not have this drawback is the elegant technique known as *Patricia* (Practical Algorithm to Retrieve Information Coded in Alphanumeric) [Morrison 1968]. On the way down in the search path from the root, the keys are examined from left to right, and one-way branching is eliminated because each node has a field specifying the index of the next bit that is significant for discrimination. The sequence of examined bit values on the way down then corresponds to just one legitimate entry. The last node along any valid, unique sequence does not have a downward link to an external node containg the key, as in a trie, but rather an upward link to one of the nodes on the search path – with the unique key matching the search stored therein. This means that comparisons do not have to be made against keys on the way down, but only after following a back pointer; and this is easily recognized because it leads to a node with a smaller bit index. So Patricia requires just one type of node and just one full key comparison per search!

†10.6 OTHER PARADIGMS OF SEARCH

In the beginning of this chapter, we cited three paradigms of searching that had been encountered throughout the book. We called attention to them at that point expressly for the purpose of distinguishing the paradigm of this chapter from other, familiar possibilities. We now return to the subject. There are, in fact, yet other types of search that one may want to perform; corresponding to all these possible paradigms, there is a substantial body of study. Our intent here is simply to give a brief overview of them.

Range search. The objective in this case is to find *all* the values that lie between two limiting values, L(ower) and U(pper). This is fairly easily accomplished by building upon familiar methods. One approach would be to first sort all the input values. It would then be straightforward to find both L and U in the sorted array via binary search, and then return all the values between those two locations. Alternatively, we could construct a BST of the input values and then traverse the BST selectively, as follows:

(a) if the value at a node X is greater than L, traverse the left subtree of X;

(b) if the value at a node X falls between L and U, output X;

(c) if the value at a node X is less than U, traverse the right subtree of X.

Closest-match search. In this case we presume that the search will not succeed in finding an exact match, and so we seek the value in the table that is closest to the search argument. An appropriate response to this situation is to preprocess the original input values x_i to ranges by finding the midpoints y_i between them. Then binary search on the table of y_i will indicate the value of x_i that is closest to the input argument. We have already seen this paradigm, in more complicated form, in our discussion of spelling correction in Section 8.3.2.

Multi-dimensional search. This is the issue that can cause search to "blow-up." There is the obvious case of looking for an exact match for a key containing several attributes or dimensions. But also, all the other paradigms, such as range searching and closest-match searching, generalize to it as well. Multi-dimensional search could be explored at this juncture, with some profit. In many cases of practical interest, however, the quantity of multi-dimensional data is so large that the issues of secondary memory are very significant. Accordingly, we defer discussion of this topic to Section 12.4.

10.7 OVERVIEW

When viewed in all its paradigms, the notion of search, in the sense of looking for the correct or the best answer to a problem, is broad enough to encompass much of computing. What is the best way to search greatly depends upon the relative costs of those two basic resources, time and space. Consider the case of finding the value of $\sin(x)$. If memory is relatively more precious, then it is better to rely solely upon an approximation formula to evaluate $\sin(x)$. But if computing cycles are relatively more precious, then it is better to store tabular values that can be used to expedite the numeric calculation of $\sin(x)$. Trade-offs like this assumed great importance in the infancy of computing, when cycles and memory were both comparatively dear. The issue is still important in many instances, as witness the immense potential benefit of trading space for time with the techniques of tabulation (see Section 5.4.2.1) and dynamic programming (see Section 7.4.2.1). Stated simply, we should always remember that it is sometimes better to recompute, and sometimes better to search for a precomputed value in a table.

Recomputing is one way of recasting the problem of search. The use of *associative memory* is yet another way. With machines having this form of memory, one can specify a desired value of an attribute and then access all records possessing this property, via one operation of parallel search over all the records in the memory [Gotlieb and Gotlieb 1978; Pfaltz 1977]. Indeed, hashing provides a mapping from a key value to a location value and so has much of the flavor of *associative search*, except that it is complicated by the occurrence of synonyms. One can also look at inverted lists as providing associative retrieval.

Returning to the narrower view of search that we have explored in this chapter, let us reflect in broad terms upon four typical techniques for this purpose: binary search, search trees, hashing, and digital search. Most of our discussion has been directed at the time complexities for conducting searches and insertions/deletions in the associated structures. However, just as we found a time-space trade-off in the preceding paragraphs, we find another trade-off at this lower level of problem solving. Not including insertions and deletions, there are three costs to consider:

$P(n)$ – the preprocessing time to build the search structure
$S(n)$ – the space required for the search structure
$Q(n)$ – the time required for querying the search structure

Table 10.6 shows these three costs for each of the four searching techniques. We can see that binary search is superior in terms of space and competitive in terms of query time; it is nonetheless inappropriate, even for a static set of data, when only a few queries will be conducted, because of the relatively high preprocessing cost.

Of course, the table tells only part of the story. Besides the neglected issues of insertion/deletion, there are others: the relative significance of average as opposed to worst-case performance, the importance that the structure manifest the order relationship between keys, etc. There is clearly no one best search method. The choice depends both upon the requirements of the application and upon the characteristics of the data (see Exercise 10.46). Moreover, as we particularly saw in the discussion of digital search, it is quite possible that the best solution is a combination of methods.

Method	P(reprocess)	S(pace)	Q(uery)
Binary Search	$O(n \lg n)$	$O(n)$	$O(\lg n)$
Search Trees	$O(1)$	$O(3n)$	$O(\lg n)$
Hashing	$O(n)$	$O(n/\alpha)$	$O(1)$
Digital Search	$O(1)$	$O((nm)/(b \ln m))$	$O(\log_m n)$

Table 10.6 Costs of Search Techniques

10.8 BIBLIOGRAPHIC NOTES

- For analyses and comparisons of the move-to-front and transposition heuristics for self-organizing lists, consult Bentley and McGeoch [1985], Bitner [1979], and Sleator and Tarjan [1985]. For a general discussion of self-organizing linear search, see Hester and Hirschberg [1985].

- Exposition and comparison of various heuristics for constructing quasi-optimal binary search trees can be found in Fredman [1975], Korsh [1981, 1982], Mehlhorn [1975, 1977], and Walker and Gotlieb [1972].

- A good theoretical discussion of hashing functions can be found in Knott [1975], and a comprehensive evaluation of their performance against a variety of representative inputs can be found in Lum et al. [1971]. For a more detailed discussion of the paradoxically good behavior of the division method consult Ghosh and Lum [1975].

- Examples of different approaches to the construction of perfect and minimal perfect hash functions can be found in Cormack et al. [1985], Jaeschke [1981], Sager [1985], and Yang and Du [1985].

10.9 REFERENCE TO TERMINOLOGY

address space, 516
† amortized cost, 469
arity, 508
AVL tree, 494
balance factor, 494
† balanced heuristic, 486
† binarizing, 512
† binary digital search tree, 548
binary search, 470
† Bloom filter, 536
† bounded balance BB [α], 504
† cellar, 523
closest-match search, 550
coalesced chaining, 522
collision, 516
† color flip, 513
† compacted trie, 546
completely balanced tree, 467
† compressed trie, 546
critical node, 497
double hashing, 525
double rotation, 499
extended binary tree, 466
external node, 466
external path length, 467
† false drop, 536
Fibonacci search, 473
Fibonacci tree, 494
† fingerprint, 538
† fringe analysis, 510
† greedy heuristic, 488
harmonic number, 465
harmonic series, 465
hash function, 516
† hashed k-signature, 537
height-balanced tree, 503
internal chaining, 521
internal node, 466
internal path length, 466
interpolation search, 474
linear probing, 524
load factor, 526
† median split tree, 489
† min-max heuristic, 486
† mintree, 494
† monotonic heuristic, 486
move-to-front heuristic, 469
multi-dimensional search, 550
multi-way tree, 508
name space, 516
node-splitting, 508
open addressing, 524
† ordered hashing, 530
† perfect hashing function, 534
† Poisson distribution, 518
primary clustering, 524
probe, 519
probe sequence, 525
random hashing, 518
range search, 550
† red-black tree, 513
secondary clustering, 524
self-organizing list, 469
separate chaining, 521
single rotation, 497
† split tree, 489
† symmetric binary B-tree, 512
† symmetrical deletion, 480
synonym, 516
2-3 tree, 508
† 2-3-4 tree, 512
transposition heuristic, 469
trie, 539
† uniform hashing, 527
† universal hashing, 535
† weight-balanced tree, 504
weighted path length, 480
Zipf's Law, 468

10.10 EXERCISES

Section 10.1

†10.1 Prove the following facts about harmonic numbers:

(a) $1 + \frac{m}{2} \le H_{2m} \le 1 + m$

(b) $\sum_{i=1}^{n} H_i = (n+1)H_n - n$

10.2 Compute the values of the internal and external path lengths for the BST in Figure 10.15 and for the BST at the bottom of Figure 10.21.

10.3 Derive expressions for the internal and external path lengths of an extended binary tree that has n nodes and is degenerate – that is, each internal node has at least one external node as a child.

†10.4 Prove that an extended binary tree with all of its leaves on at most two adjacent levels has the minimal value of path length for any such tree with the same number of nodes.

†10.5 Derive (a) a relationship between the number of external nodes and the number of internal nodes in an extended t-ary tree, and (b) a relationship between the external path length and the internal path length in an extended t-ary tree.

Section 10.2

10.6 Name four things that one might do (not all at the same time) to improve the performance of sequential search.

†10.7 In sequential search with known and unequal probabilities,

(a) Prove that the sequence $p_1 \ge p_2 \ge \cdots \ge p_n$ yields the minimum average time for searching.

(b) What sequence yields the maximum average search time? Derive a relationship between the minimum and maximum average search times.

††10.8 In sequential search with known and unequal probabilities, one can optimally arrange the keys in decreasing order of these probabilities. When the probabilities are not known in advance, one remedy is the move-to-front self-organizing heuristic. Prove that the asymptotic cost (number of comparisons) for the latter can never be worse than that for the optimal static ordering by more than a factor of two.

10.9 Using the data of Figure 10.3, show the execution of SEARCH_BINARY for (a) *key* = 33 and (b) *key* = 75, tracing the values of *lo*, *hi*, *i*, and *tbl* [*i*] as in Figure 10.4.

†**10.10** How would you generalize Fibonacci search so that it works for any size table? Write an algorithm for this general case of Fibonacci search, and test your program by applying it to the same input data and input arguments used in the text for binary search (see Figures 10.3 and 10.4).

††**10.11** Derive expressions for the internal and external path lengths of Fibonacci trees, and calculate the asymptotic values of these expressions.

Sections 10.3.1 – 10.3.2

10.12 Presume the following sequence of I(nsert) and D(elete) operations for a binary search tree:

I 32 I 17 I 14 I 47 I 35 I 20 I 4 I 51 I 38 I 40 I 16 D35 I 28
I 57 I 62 I 39 I 45 I 25 I 22 I 23 I 24 D51 I 18 D20 I 35 D22

Draw the tree as it appears immediately before and immediately after each of the four deletions (that is, eight sketches of the tree), with deletions performed according to BST_DELETE.

†**10.13** How many permutation sequences on 1 .. 10 will yield the following cases of BST's:

(a) for Figure 10.44(a)?

(b) for Figure 10.44(b)?

(c) for completely degenerate trees (each internal node has at least one external node as a child)?

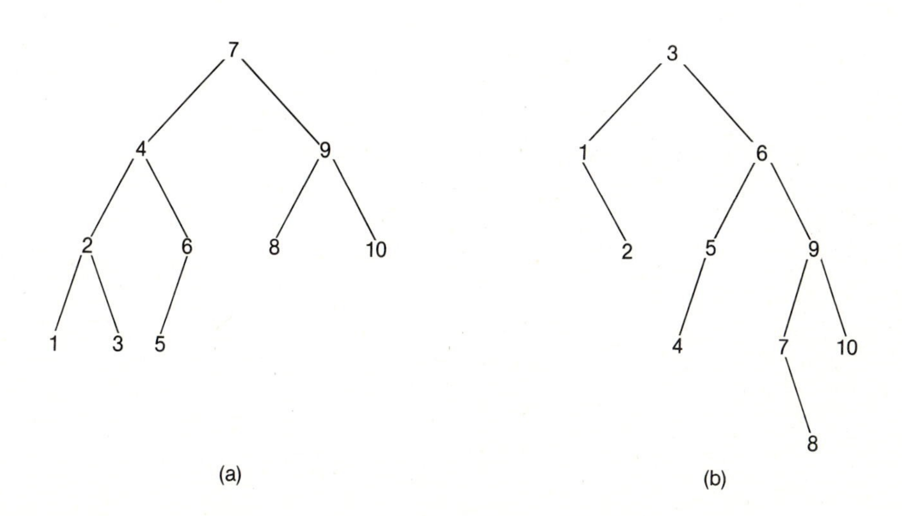

Figure 10.44 Trees for Exercise 10.13

††10.14 Suppose that we have a random permutation of {1,2,3,4} and that we perform the following sequence of operations:

(a) insert the first three elements into a BST;

(b) randomly delete one of these three elements from the BST per BST_DELETE;

(c) insert the left-over element into the BST.

Do this for all possible permutations and deletions, and compare the shape distribution of the final BST's with that of random BST's on three elements.

†10.15 Compute (by hand) the optimal BST for the following frequencies:

$$p_1 = 1,\ p_2 = 3,\ p_3 = 2,\ p_4 = 4,\ p_5 = 5$$
$$q_0 = 4,\ q_1 = 5,\ q_2 = 1,\ q_3 = 2,\ q_4 = 4,\ q_5 = 3$$

†10.16 For the frequencies in Exercise 10.15, compute the quasi-optimal BST's (and their costs) according to the four heuristics – monotonic, balanced, min-max, and greedy – of Section 10.3.2.2.

††10.17 The balanced and min-max heuristics for quasi-optimal BST's are very similar. Write a better-than-$O(n^2)$ algorithm that can be used to compute either tree, along with its associated cost. First, test your program against the data of Exercise 10.15 Next, use your program to compute the balanced tree and the min-max tree for the data of Table 10.1 in Section 10.3.2.4 (where all the $q_i = 0$).

††10.18 Assume that the words in Table 10.5 of Section 10.5.1 obey Zipf's Law (see Section 10.2.1), and then construct the median split tree for them. Compute the resulting value of CS_n. What is the value of CS_n for binary search on these words, under the same assumption of Zipf's Law?

Sections 10.3.3 – 10.3.5

†10.19 By definition, the AVL mintree T_h contains the minimum number of nodes $n(T_h)$ for any AVL tree of that height. Does it also have the maximum (internal) path length for any AVL tree that contains $n(T_h)$ nodes? (*Hint*: Consider the case of $n = 20$.)

†10.20 The Best Actor Awards for 1944 – 1958 have the sequence shown in the following figure.

(a) Generate the BST for the sequence.

(b) Generate the AVL tree for the sequence, showing the tree just prior to each rotation, according to AVL_INSERT.

1944	Crosby	1949	Crawford	1954	Brando
1945	Milland	1950	Ferrer	1955	Borgnine
1946	March	1951	Bogart	1956	Brynner
1947	Colman	1952	Cooper	1957	Guinness
1948	Olivier	1953	Holden	1958	Niven

†10.21 Derive an expression for the minimum proportion of nodes in an AVL tree that must have zero balance factors.

††10.22 Analyze the problem of deletion from AVL trees, and construct figures showing how the various cases should be handled. (*Hint*: You can first reduce the problem of deleting a node X at an arbitrary position to that of deleting a leaf, by finding the successor Y to X and then exchanging them.) Use your analysis to write an algorithm that does AVL deletions, and test your program by deleting Leigh from the tree of Figure 10.21.

†10.23 Prove that Fibonacci trees are BB [1/3].

††10.24 In Figure 10.23, derive the formulas shown for the new balance factors in terms of the original balance factors, after the rotations.

††10.25 For the data of Figure 10.14, construct the corresponding BB [1/4] tree, showing the tree before and after each rotation, and displaying the balance factors at each node.

††10.26 Analyze and diagram the various cases for splitting a node in a 2-3 tree. Then write an algorithm to accomplish search and insertion in a 2-3 tree. Test your program by inserting the values 1 .. 20 into an originally empty tree, displaying the tree immediately after each insertion that has affected more than a single node.

10.27 What is the comparison cost (sum over all keys of the number of comparisons required) for the 2-3 tree of Figure 10.24? for that of Figure 10.25? What are these costs directly related to?

†10.28 The first step in performing a second-order fringe analysis of 2-3 trees is to classify the subtrees of height two that can occur. Show the subtrees that result from such a classification.

††10.29 [Aho et al. 1974] From time to time, we have alluded to the need for a representation of priority queues such that not only the operations of insertion and removal can be performed in $O(\lg n)$ time, but also that of merging queues. Describe in detail how 2-3 trees can be used to provide such an implementation.

†10.30 Construct the 2-3-4 tree obtained by applying the top-down method of splitting and rotations to the data of Figure 10.14. Show the tree before and after each split and/or rotation.

†10.31 Name the motion pictures for which the actresses of Figure 10.14 won their Academy Awards.

Section 10.4

†10.32 Prove that the step from the first to the second line in Eq. 10.30 is valid when M is a prime; also, show by a counterexample that it is not valid when M is not a prime.

†10.33 Obtain characterizations of poor multipliers for multiplicative hashing.

†10.34 Presume that we have the following sequence of input keys

185 99 145 71 197 129 72 172 48 108 142 122

for a table of size 13, and that we use double hashing with $h_1(K) = K \pmod{13}$ and $h_0(K) = 1 + K \pmod{11}$. Then display the following data:

(a) the contents of each hash table location, and the number of probes required for the corresponding insertion, using the above algorithm;

(b) the same quantities as in (a), but with linear probing − that is, with $h_0(K) = 1$;

(c) the same quantities as in (a), but with coalesced chaining;

(d) the final insertion location of each key when ordered hashing is used.

†10.35 Describe how to implement internal chaining so that lists do *not* coalesce. One motive for doing this is to be able to save space by storing abbreviated keys (for example, K div M) at table locations. Another is to facilitate the process of deletion. Modify HASH_COALESCE to incorporate the ideas of no coalescing and abbreviated keys, and then test your program against the example data of Figure 10.29.

†10.36 [Maurer 1968] The earliest collision resolution method for overcoming primary clustering was that known as *quadratic residue search*, according to the probe sequence

$$h_{i+1}(K) = (h_1(K) + a \times i + b \times i^2) \bmod (hsiz) \quad (\text{for } i = 1, 2, \ldots)$$

Aside from the question of how well it approximates random probing, there is also an issue as to whether this will probe every table location. Derive relations among a, b, and *hsiz* that affect how much of the table is probed.

10.37 Write an algorithm that performs deletions from a hash table constructed by linear probing, and that rearranges the table in the process so that valid probe sequences are maintained. Test your program by deleting the entries from the table of Figure 10.33, in the sequence in which they were originally inserted.

†10.38 Consider the case where double hashing is employed and deletions are performed. What should be done about the value of the global variable *hcnt* that is used in HASH_DOUBLE? Explain the reasoning behind your answer.

†10.39 [Bays 1973] Write an algorithm to rehash a hash table in situ, as mentioned in Section 10.4.2.4. First, test your program by applying it to the data of Figure 10.34, rehashing the table contents to **array** [0 .. 18] in place of **array** [0 .. 12]. For the new hash functions, use $h_1(K) = K \pmod{19}$ and $h_0(K) = 1 + K \pmod{17}$. Second, test your program again by rehashing the table contents back to **array** [0 .. 12].

†10.40 For very large hash tables, a serious drawback can be the time required to initialize them. Describe a method whereby initialization can be avoided (at the expense of using extra space).

††10.41 Write a function that implements the Karp and Rabin substring matching algorithm. Employ an auxiliary function to convert characters to integers in a suitable range, try using $p = 33554393$, and test your program against the data of Section 8.5.1.1.

Sections 10.5 – 10.7

10.42 We wish to keep track of all twelve 4-character substrings that occur in 'POPOLLOPPOLOOPO', using a trie. First show the trie that we would have if we branched on the substring characters from left to right, and then show the trie that we would have if we branched on the substring characters from right to left. Presuming that trie nodes are not overlapped, how many nodes are required in the two cases?

††10.43 Find the most compacted form that you can for the trie of Figure 10.38(a). How does this compaction affect the cost of searching the trie with an input key?

††10.44 Write an algorithm to do trie deletion, and test your program by deleting 'TO' from the trie of Figure 10.37.

††10.45 If we enlarge the alphabet used in Figure 10.41(a) to that of Figure 10.45, we can then encode the words in Table 10.1 of Section 10.3.2.4. Use this encoding to construct the binary digital search tree for those words, assuming that they are inserted in order of decreasing probability.

	binary		binary		binary		binary
a	0000	f	0100	n	1000	t	1100
b	0001	h	0101	o	1001	u	1101
d	0010	i	0110	r	1010	w	1110
e	0011	m	0111	s	1011	y	1111

Figure 10.45 Alphabet for Exercise 10.45

†10.46 For the paradigm of search studied in this chapter, give a general analysis of how to choose a particular method. Your presentation should be fairly complete, comprising a few pages. You might choose to employ a decision table as part of your analysis.

11

MANAGING PRIMARY MEMORY

"Memory [is] like a purse – if it be overfull
that it cannot shut, all will drop out of it.
Take heed of a gluttonous curiosity to feed
on many things, lest the greediness of the appetite
of thy memory spoil the digestion thereof."

Thomas Fuller,
Holy and Profane States: of Memory

Our discussions of computational efficiency have focused mostly on execution time, with an occasional nod to memory requirements, even though the limits imposed by a finite memory size are certainly more rigid than the usual constraints of time. The earlier chapters in this book might lead one to believe that he can always get as much space as he needs, either by explicitly asking for it, as with **new** in Pascal, or simply because the program needs it, as in LISP or APL. Fortunately, memory is a *reusable* resource. So this attitude will work – but only if there is some means to effectively recycle the chunks of memory that programs discard during execution. In discussing this problem, we find that the dynamic data structures that can cause us to run out of memory space can also be important tools for managing it.

The problem is a complex one, with many contributing factors. We will begin by painting, in the next section, a broad picture of what the issues are. As we will see, perhaps the most significant of these issues is whether the pieces of memory are all of one size or of various sizes. The two major sections of this chapter correspond to this dichotomy.

An additional point is that we will be describing memory management algorithms in Pascal, even though in practice they would largely be implemented in assembly language. But Pascal imposes some restrictions upon pointer operations; for example, only the two most basic relational operators $\{=, <>\}$ are allowed, and not $\{<, <=, >=, >\}$. Thus, although we will sometimes model situations in terms of pointer variables, at other times we will employ cursors (see Section 4.1.1) in order to sidestep these restrictions.

11.1 MEMORY MANAGEMENT ISSUES

The issues that concern us in this chapter recur at several different levels when we use a computer. At most or all of these levels, the matter is out of our hands, with "the system" providing the services that we need. For instance, most of our work may be done under one operating system. If this system provides multiprogramming services on one underlying machine to a set of users, then it must apportion the available memory space among these users, with the active requirements for each member of this set tending to fluctuate dynamically. At a lower level, one such user may be using some HLL, or editor, or other system program. The execution environment for each of these programs must, in turn, divide the piece of memory pie given to it by the system among the procedures and data that constitute that total program. As we go to deeper levels, with our own program executing, we may have to solve a memory resource problem that mimics, with smaller pieces, what transpired at a higher level. We will explore these matters further under the heading of "The Environment."

At each level, the system and/or the user must make various choices that direct how this dividing-up process is to be regulated. We will investigate these choices under the heading of "Memory Management Policies." For now, the relevant points are two: Depending upon the user's relationship to the environment, he may be responsible for some or all of these choices; and a poor set of policies can have dire consequences, making computation very inefficient or even impossible.

11.1.1 The Environment

The most conspicuous part of our programming environment is usually determined by the HLL's in which we do the bulk of our work. It is the built-in characteristics of these languages that shape the memory management problem in our eyes. For instance, various languages allow the requisition of space in any of three distinct fashions, as follows:

1. *Static Allocation.* When a program is to be executed, the fixed, total memory requirement for that program has already been calculated by the compiler, and so memory in this amount is obtained from the system before the program is loaded and given control. This is the only possible manner of using memory in FORTRAN, for instance. As long as the operating system can supply the necessary total requirement, there is no memory management problem at the user program level.

2. *Automatic Allocation.* Languages such as ALGOL, Pascal, and PL/1 are *block-structured.* This means that they can (recursively) have nested sub-procedures, each with their own set of local variables. To reduce the memory demand on the system, space for the local variables of any such procedure is automatically obtained on procedure entry and automatically released on procedure exit. In this manner, sibling procedures can share from a common

pool of working memory. The pool is administered via a run-time stack (see Section 5.2.3.1), and there is relatively little problem.

3. *Dynamic Allocation.* Many languages – ALGOL, APL, LISP, Pascal, PL/1, and SNOBOL, for example – support the ability to requisition space dynamically; it is this facility that raises the memory management problem. The request for space may be explicit (as with **new** in Pascal), or it may be implicit (as in APL or LISP). Similarly, the release of space may be explicit or implicit. Also, the size of the request may be a constant (as with LISP), or it may be a variable amount (as with APL or Pascal). Fixed-size units of memory are commonly termed *cells*, and variable-sized units are usually called *blocks*. In order to keep track of which memory locations are in use and which are not, the user program and the run-time environment divide the responsibility in manners that vary with the language. APL and LISP, for instance, do it all for the user; in Pascal, the responsibility is shared; and in PL/1, the burden is even more upon the user program. Unfortunately, as more responsibility is shifted away from the system to the user, this added burden is not only complex, but also highly error-prone!

Note that all three allocation policies may be in use at one time. For instance, a Pascal program has a static requirement equal to the total size of all its code segments plus the amount needed for global variables. As the program executes, sub-procedures will automatically acquire and release space for parameters and local variables on the the run-time stack. Finally, any user calls to **new** or **dispose** will dynamically use space from the Pascal heap.

The issue of whether we are dealing in fixed-size cells or variable-size blocks makes a great deal of difference for memory management. We will look at the former case in Section 11.2, and then deal with the latter case in Section 11.3. It would be misleading, however, to suggest that the items we have cited so far are the only environmental factors. An extremely important issue is how the areas of dynamic memory may reference one another with pointer variables, as illustrated by the following examples:

- Memory mamagement in a multiprogramming operating system is not trivial. The jobs that the system must schedule tend to have widely varying requirements for both amount and duration of memory occupancy. Nonetheless, the different jobs do not reference one another, and this greatly simplifies matters.

- In the programming environment of APL or SNOBOL, the pointer links to areas of dynamic memory form a bipartite graph; pointers are from system "names" in a symbol table to dynamic objects, or vice versa. Thus, although dynamic objects can reference one another, these references are disciplined by the symbol table.

- In the most complicated cases, a dynamic object may contain pointers directly to other dynamic objects. This may be slightly less complex when, as in LISP, the number of such references is limited to two. In ALGOL or Pascal, however, the possibilities for multi-linking can vary widely from one dynamic block to the next.

To recapitulate, the chief environmental issues are:

- modes of memory usage – static, automatic, and dynamic;
- responsibility – user, system, or shared;
- fixed-size cells versus variable-size blocks;
- pointer "connectivity."

To restate the problem in its worst form, there may be dynamic memory objects of variable sizes, containing variable numbers of pointer links to each other. The moment of truth in memory management comes when we must shift all of these objects in memory and correctly reestablish all the pointer references to reflect these shifts. Fortunately, some of the programming environments that we have been describing yield situations that are much simpler to manage than this.

11.1.1.1 Virtual Memory. There is another environmental factor whose presence causes the memory management problem to be completely recharacterized, and that is whether we are operating with virtual memory. At this point we will be brief and consider only the logical nature of this facility; the physical realization of virtual memory depends upon secondary memory, which is the subject of Chapter 12.

The entire rationale for memory management is that the machine has a fixed, inflexible amount of main memory. Since even one memory location in excess of this limit spells disaster, we must be niggardly and strive to contain our total memory appetite to what is available. Now virtual memory gives a computer the *functional appearance* of having much more main memory available than is really present in the hardware. This fiction is maintained at some cost (paid to the operating system), as we will see in Chapter 12; however, this cost is amply compensated by the fact that user programs can now become much simpler. What, then, of the battle to hold the breach against a mythical limit?

There are two answers to this question. The first is that many user programs do not operate in virtual memory environments, and so these concerns are still vital. The second is that even with virtual memory, some management policy is required for dynamic allocation. In fact, the policies will be not be very different in either case. The result of poor policies in one case is catastrophic degradation of performance (that is, program failure); in the virtual memory case it is progressive degradation of performance.

11.1.2 Memory Management Policies

Whatever the environment in which memory must be managed, and no matter how responsibility is shared among the system and the user, policies must be chosen and implemented to cover three major issues: memory organization, memory allocation, and memory reclamation. At this point we will just introduce each of these problems; the details of specific solutions will be developed in Sections 11.2 and 11.3.

At any instant in time, some cells and/or blocks of dynamic memory will be in use and others will be free. How should these two sets of memory areas be organized? Should they all be linked together in one list? or should there be a linked list of just the free areas? or should there be several lists, corresponding to various sizes of blocks? If there is a single list, should it be maintained as a stack? or a queue? or by order of the block addresses? or by order of block sizes?

Given a definite memory organization policy, the next question is how a request for a block of a specific size should be serviced. Should we simply allocate the first block of adequate size from the free storage list? Or should we try to respond in some more sophisticated fashion, for possibly better overall performance? If we do not find a block of exactly the desired size, what do we do with the excess memory in the block that is chosen for allocation?

The number of meaningful combinations of an organization policy with an allocation policy is great enough that it requires care to discriminate among the combinations. Nonetheless, the implementation details tend to be relatively straightforward. On the other hand, storage reclamation can be fairly tricky. In part, this stems from the asymmetrical attitude we express toward memory blocks (or anything that we "need"). When we need something, we are impatient to have it immediately; when we no longer need it, we are more likely to forget about it than to make an explicit effort to return it. Thus, in writing a program with pointer variables, we cannot forget **new** where it is required, but we may remember **dispose** only as an afterthought, if at all. So the first problem in storage reclamation is that it may be non-trivial to answer the question: Which memory blocks are still in use and which no longer are (and therefore should really be considered free)? In answering this question, the environment is very important. Storage reclamation also has another component. Once it has been determined which blocks are no longer in use, it is necessary to make them explicitly available as part of the free pool. In fact, the variety of methods that are employed for solving this problem, including special techniques of organization, account for much of this chapter.

11.2 FIXED-SIZE CELLS

In this section we restrict our attention to the case when all memory requests are of one fixed size. What happens when, in addition, these cells never reference one another? The memory management for such a situation is very simple. We can organize our Free pool as a stack. Requests can always be satisfied by the top cell on the stack; cells that are released can be pushed back on the stack. Indeed, we described just such a simplified mechanism in Section 4.1.3. Note the assumption, in this scheme, that cells are explicitly pushed on the stack, and not abandoned when no longer needed.

In practice, there are two issues that complicate memory management for cells. One is that it is common to abandon cells that are no longer needed, and the other is that each cell may contain pointers to other cells. Cells are *the* data structure in languages that operate on Lists, such as LISP; and the majority of the literature on the topics of this section is best understood in the context of memory management for LISP-like systems. The logical structure and various physical representations of cells for these List processing environments were explored in Section 4.4.1; recall that such a cell never contains more than two pointers to other cells, so that pure Lists are binary trees.

List-processing languages in general, and LISP in particular, assume all of the responsibility for reclaiming memory, with no cooperation required of the user program. They must therefore have a mechanism for discovering which cells are no longer in active use. If a pointer variable P is pointing at cell X, and if the value of P is changed so that it no longer points at X, then cell X cannot automatically be returned to the Free pool, for X may still be pointed at by some other List cell. Two distinct approaches are used to solve this problem.

In one of these, called *garbage collection*, no effort is expended until the time arrives when a request for a cell cannot be satisfied because the Free pool is exhausted, or almost so. At that juncture, the normal course of user computation is suspended, and the system performs a phase of following all the pointers that lead to active memory cells, *marking* those cells as being in use. After the active cells have been marked, the system performs a second phase of incorporating the unmarked (and therefore unused) cells into the Free pool, thereby allowing them to be reused. Except in the case when no garbage cells have been found, the system then honors the memory request that precipitated this activity and returns control to the user program. We will look at these matters in detail in Section 11.2.1.

An alternative approach is for the system to try to keep track of which cells are in active use by maintaining, for each cell or each sub-List, a *reference count* of the number of pointers to that cell or sub-List. Then, whenever one of these counts is decremented to zero, that cell or sub-List can be reclaimed by the Free pool. We will look at this approach in Section 11.2.2.

11.2.1 Garbage Collection

As stated above, garbage collection basically consists of a marking phase followed by a collection phase. We will begin by exploring these two phases. Later on, we'll step back to consider first some of the difficulties associated with garbage collection, and then some sophisticated variations that have been developed in response to these difficulties. These variations deal with such matters as compaction, hybrid methods, and parallel garbage collection.

11.2.1.1 Marking. You might well be having a sensation of deja vu at this point. After all, we discussed basically the same problem in Section 4.4.3.1; we also encountered a generalization of it in Section 7.3.1, in connection with depth-first search of a graph. In the context of garbage collection, however, there are some important distinctions. One difference is the importance of efficiency, since garbage collection can constitute as much as $10-30$ percent of program execution. Other issues are related to the environment in which garbage collection is conducted.

For one, in our earlier, brief characterization of marking, we ignored a simple but important detail. The marking phase must initialize the marks of *all* the cells of memory to "unused" before it begins to mark active cells as "used." Fortunately, because the cells are all of the same size, it is easy to sweep through memory to perform this initialization. Another issue is that although pure Lists are binary trees, reentrant and recursive Lists are graphs. In order to find all the active cells, or nodes of this graph structure, we must do a search from each "base" pointer into the structure. Where these base pointers are to be found depends upon the environment, but the same algorithm for searching is applied to each of them. Taking these comments into account, we will proceed to discuss marking under the assumptions that:

1. The initialization has already been performed.
2. Any algorithm that we discuss is applied to each base pointer.

In Section 4.4.3.1 we first examined the recursive algorithm COUNT_LIST (Algorithm 4.6) for examining all the cells of a List, and then raised the issue of efficiency. We saw in Sections 5.4.2 and 6.4.1 that a very common manner of eliminating recursion in the interest of efficiency is to introduce an explicit stack. However, this technique presents us with a dilemma in the case of garbage collection. The marking that precedes collection is invoked when the Free pool is almost exhausted. If the marking algorithm then uses a stack, that stack may require $O(n)$ entries, for a memory with $O(n)$ cells. There may not be that much available space for the garbage collector to do its thing!

An ingenious resolution to this dilemma is to use link inversions, as we saw in MARK_LIST (Algorithm 4.7). The information that would otherwise be retained in a stack is therewith retained in the link fields of the List itself. Although MARK_LIST has complexity $O(n)$, it visits each cell three times. Because of this and the inherent overhead in the rotations, it is slower than an algorithm that simply uses a stack. A compromise solution is to combine stack traversal with link inversions, employing the first technique until the stack becomes full, at which point we fall back upon the second technique for a while.

There are other ways too. In Section 4.4.3.1 we pointed out that the Schorr-Waite algorithm could require space for an explicit tag bit in each node, depending upon the representation for cells. Lindstrom [1973] has shown how to mark a List without employing any tag information at all, but this technique has an average complexity of $O(n \lg n)$ and a worst-case complexity of $O(n^2)$. An algorithm by Wegbreit [1972] is $O(n)$ and does not require any tag bits in the cells. This method employs link inversion again, but it records tag information in a bit stack only as needed; in practice, the size of this bit stack can be fixed, and yet still be adequate for all but extreme cases. Moreover, stack entries (and revisits) are required for just those cells in which both CAR and CDR reference sub-Lists. Even so, careful analysis of the operations required to implement a variety of marking algorithms shows that the Schorr-Waite algorithm is commonly faster – unless, of course, there is space for a pointer stack, thereby eliminating link inversions [Baer and Fries 1977].

Still other possibilities are obtained if we consider why certain List structures cause various marking algorithms to perform poorly. As an example, Wegbreits's algorithm will stack each cell of the List in Figure 11.1, but no stacking is really required if we look ahead in the List. Rather than presume, for a List cell with two successor links, that we must stack one and follow the other, we can first check to see that both of the cells pointed to are unmarked (and not an atom). Since stacking is faster than link inversion and since this technique reduces the stack depth in some cases, it is worthwhile [Kurokawa 1981]. Nonetheless, even this method will fail to secure any advantage if, for instance, the List is a balanced binary tree.

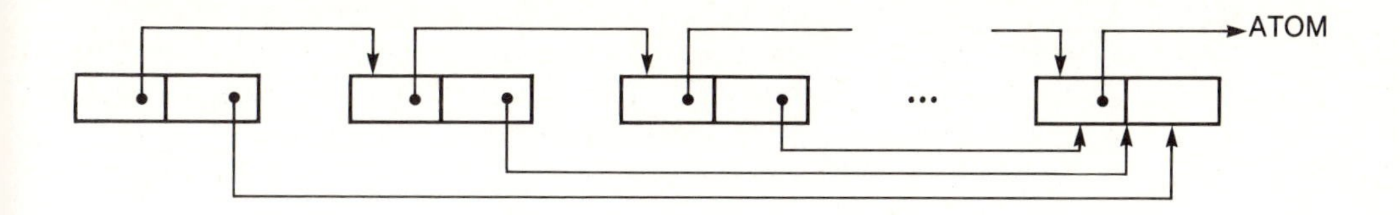

Figure 11.1 Wasted Marking Effort

In summarizing this discussion of marking, we find that a simple stack algorithm provides the best performance, but that there is the hazard of running out of space. Although this may be less significant with virtual memory, it is frequently important to use methods that do not have this drawback, even at the cost of decreased performance. Of these methods, MARK_LIST is particularly noteworthy because it serves as a model for other algorithms with Lists. Also, note that MARK_LIST operating upon List cells with two link fields requires one bit of tag information to discriminate between the links. For marking fixed-size List cells with m link fields, the algorithm can be generalized to use lg m bits of tag information. MARK_LIST and the alternative techniques cited in this section all have the feature that for unrestricted Lists, they require either more than linear time or more than bounded workspace. If we disregard tricks of implementation (as in MARK_LIST), we are left with the interesting theoretical question: Is it possible to mark unrestricted Lists in linear time and with bounded workspace?

11.2.1.2 Collection. The second phase of garbage collection may be quite simple; it might consist of just scanning all of memory and linking together the unmarked cells. Such a method is given by COLLECT_0 (Algorithm 11.1). The area of memory to be collected is represented as a global array of cells, and cursors are employed rather than pointer variables, in anticipation of studying more complicated reclamation schemes later on. The collection is conducted downward from *hi* to *lo* so that the resulting Free-list will be ordered by ascending addresses. This allows subsequent allocations of cells from Free to come from the lower end of memory. Note that collection also turns off mark bits, in anticipation of the marking phase of the next garbage collection cycle. In COLLECT_0 we have ignored some considerations that might prompt more complicated reclamation policies; these will be explored in Section 11.2.3.

```
procedure COLLECT_0;

type    cursor = lo .. hi;
        cell = record
           mark: boolean;
           case isatom: boolean of
              true: (data: char);
              false: (head,tail: cursor);
        end;

var     free,p: cursor;
        store: array [cursor] of cell;

begin
   free := 0;
   for p := hi downto lo do
      with store [p] do
         if mark then
            mark := false
         else begin
            isatom := false;
            tail := free;
            free := p;
         end;
end;
```

Algorithm 11.1 COLLECT_0

11.2.2 Reference Counters

With reference counters, either every cell or every List (and sub-List) has a field in which the number of references to that cell or List is dynamically maintained. It is considerably more economical to maintain these counts at the sub-List level, in the header nodes. Such a List structure, with its counts, is illustrated in Figure 11.2(a). Here we see Lists *U*, *V*, *W*, *X* with reference counts of 1, 2, 1, 4 in their header cells. Suppose that, in this figure, the reference to the List *U* is released. The reference count for *U* then goes from 1 to 0. However, before deallocating the cells on List *U*, it is necessary to trace out the "closure" of *U*, to decrement the reference counts of Lists referred to from cells of *U*. Note that this process is very similar to the marking process in garbage collection; it can be carried out recursively, or by using a stack, or by a more sophisticated method. The decrementing ultimately reduces the Lists of (a) in Figure 11.2 to those of (b), leaving Lists *U* and *W* freed, while Lists *V* and *X* still have non-zero counts. There is no periodic collection process, as with garbage collection. Rather, as soon as a reference counter goes to zero, all of the corresponding cells are added to the Free-list immediately after their references are checked.

Imagine that we are using reference counters, and that we deallocate a tree by setting its root pointer to NIL. For a tree of appreciable depth, the scheme just

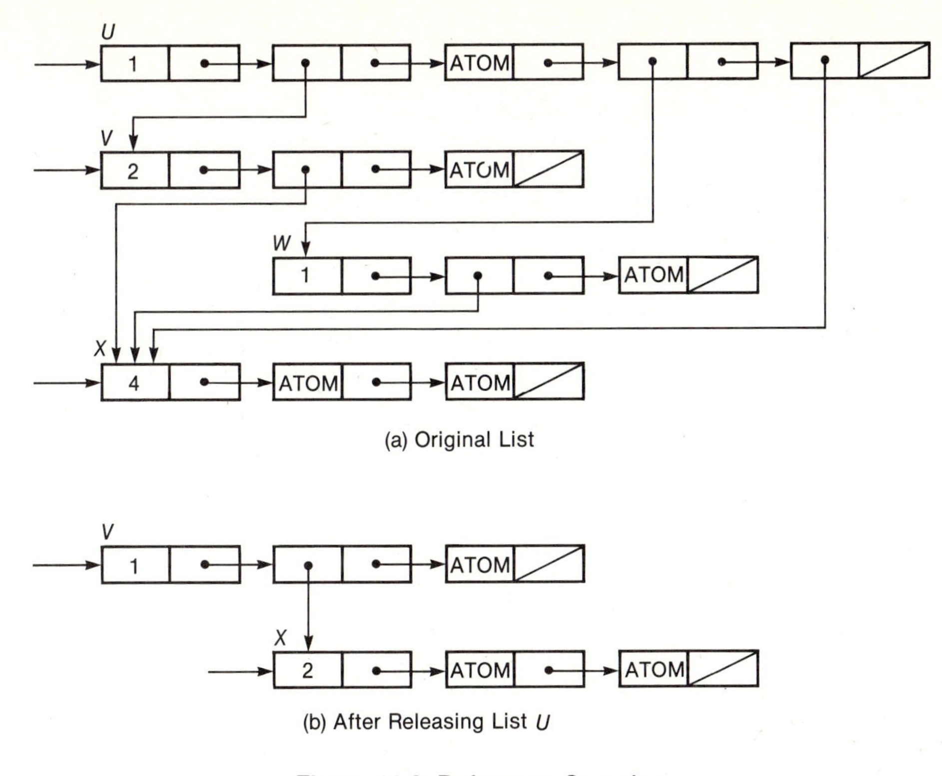

Figure 11.2 Reference Counting

described can cause a significant cascade of dereferencing activity. The List processing language SLIP introduced an ingenious variation of reference counting that simultaneously eliminates both this burst of activity and also any need for a stack for finding the closure [Weizenbaum 1963, 1969]. When a List *U* is deallocated, its successor Lists are not traced immediately. Rather, the cells of *U* are added to the end of the Free-list – that is, Free is maintained as a queue – and references from cells of *U* are not checked until those cells reach the front of Free.

11.2.3 Compaction

Either with garbage collecting or with reference counting, the cells in active use will eventually become interspersed with the Free-list cells throughout the memory available to the List processing environment. In some cases this dispersion needs to be counteracted by *compacting* the active cells into a contiguous storage area. As one example, available memory for a process may consist of two dynamic areas that grow from the opposite ends of a region (see Figure 5.13). Indeed, dynamic memory for Pascal is often administered in this fashion, with the run-time stack and the heap being the two areas. If such a heap area is used for List cells, then it may be important to restrain the sprawl of the heap so that the stack may have sufficient space for expansion.

Another instance arises when the system is operating with virtual memory. As the active cells become interspersed with the Free cells throughout a large address space, program execution will generate more and more page faults (see Section 12.2) in order to retrieve cells. The only manner in which to hold down the large inefficiency of execution caused by these faults is, once again, to compress the active cells into contiguous pages.

We will discuss one particular method for compacting fixed-size cells and then a class of different methods. The first and simpler technique, exchanging cells, relies upon a conventional, initial marking phase, and it especially reflects the stack/heap situation. The second class of methods involves relocation of entire Lists. These latter methods have wider applicability; also, they can be used to compact memory *without* an initial marking phase.

11.2.3.1 Exchanging Cells. With this method we employ two cursors, p and q, that start at opposite ends of memory and move toward each other until they meet. First the cursor p is incremented until it references an unmarked cell, and then the cursor q is decremented until it references a marked cell. This pair of cells is exchanged and the cycle is repeated, until eventually p and q meet. Such a process physically relocates the free and active cells into two disjoint areas; however, some additional logic is needed to adjust the inter-cell links so that they retain the proper connectivity. The technique for accomplishing this is to place in each old active cell location a link, known as a *forwarding address*, to the new active cell location. Then, when the swapping phase is concluded, a second pass through just the active cells can retrieve updated link values via these forwarding addresses.

A procedure for accomplishing what has been described is COLLECT_1 (Algorithm 11.2); it requires several comments:

- *Store* [*lo*] and *store* [*hi*] are reserved as marker locations, so that the algorithm can be guaranteed to work properly in degenerate cases.
- The Free-list is regenerated, in order of ascending addresses as in COLLECT_0, during the swapping phase rather than in a separate phase.
- Mark bits are turned off (as in COLLECT_0), in anticipation of the next garbage collection cycle.
- In the old active locations, the head cursor is used as the forwarding address, and the tail cursor is used to link the Free-list.
- The algorithm requires one-and-a-half passes through memory.

Its operation can be seen with the List shown in Figure 11.3(a). The same List is shown in (b) of the figure, scattered in hypothetical memory locations between $lo = 0$ and $hi = 21$. After the swapping phase is concluded, the relevant List cells appear as in (c) of the figure; for example, the active cell originally in location 13 is now relocated to location 5. Finally, Figure 11.3(d) shows the contents of the old and new List cells after the pointers have been updated in the second phase of COLLECT_1.

```
procedure COLLECT_1;

type    cursor = lo .. hi;
        cell = record
           mark: boolean;
           case isatom: boolean of
              true: (data: char);
              false: (head,tail: cursor);
        end;

var     free,p,q: cursor;
        store: array [cursor] of cell;

begin
   free := 0;
   p := lo;  store [p].mark := true;
   q := hi;  store [q].mark := false;
   repeat
{match active cell from one end with free cell from other end}
      repeat
         p := p + 1;
      until not store [p].mark;
      repeat
   { build new Free-list as we go }
         store [q].tail := free;
         free := q;
         q := q - 1;
      until store [q].mark;
      if p < q then begin
   {swap active cell with free cell, leave forwarding address}
         store [p] := store [q];
         store [q].mark := false;
         store [q].isatom := false;
         store [q].head := p;
      end;
   until p >= q;
{use forwarding addresses to update links, as required}
   for p := lo + 1 to q do begin
      store [p].mark := false;
      if not store [p].isatom then begin
         if store [p].head > q then
            store [p].head := store [store [p].head].head;
         if store [p].tail > q then
            store [p].tail := store [store [p].tail].head;
      end;
   end;
end;
```

Algorithm 11.2 COLLECT_1

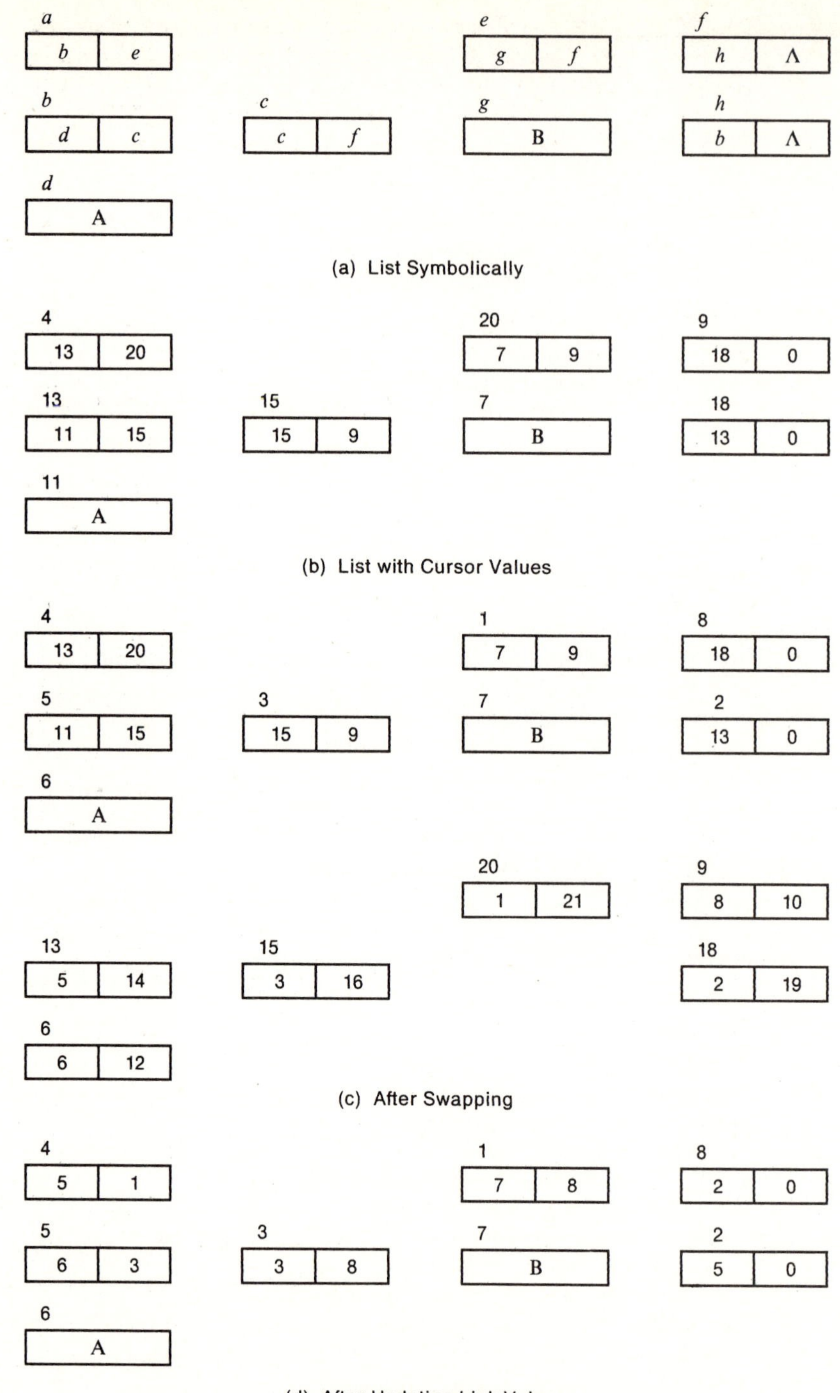

Figure 11.3 Progress of Algorithm COLLECT_1

11.2.3.2 Relocating Lists. There are two unsatisfactory features about COLLECT_1. First, it scans all of the addressable List space (which can be quite large under virtual memory). Second, the physical sequence of the cells of a List after collection will most likely bear no relation either to (a) the logical sequence of the cells, or (b) the physical sequence of those cells before collection. By relocating entire Lists, rather than operating upon cells, it is possible:

- to limit the work to the size of the Lists rather than the memory size;
- to obtain desirable properties in the address sequence of cells in the new List;
- to dispense with a separate marking phase.

Studies of the empirical properties of Lists in LISP show that most such Lists contain long linear segments [Clark 1979; Clark and Green 1977]. Therefore, it may be desirable, when compacting a List, to "linearize" it by causing cells to become physically adjacent to predecessors as much as possible.

The most widely used technique for compaction under these considerations is to move a List that is dispersed in one area of memory to a fresh area. A variation is to copy the List, rather than move it. The distinction is that the moving process may destroy the old List, whereas the copying process will leave the old List intact. Note that the utility of both of these techniques is certainly not restricted to the cause of memory management. But for memory management, an important issue once again is the potential shortage of working storage at the instant when moving or copying needs to be performed. Some of the techniques for overcoming this hazard are the familiar ones of forwarding addresses and link inversions. In our discussion of marking algorithms for Lists (see Section 11.2.1.1), we encountered an apparent requirement for either more than linear time or more than bounded workspace. Yet for the more complicated operations of moving or copying a List, we will find that linear time and bounded workspace are simultaneously achievable. This is so because, in both cases, we are able to employ the doubled space (for the original and for the copy) to record temporary values during the construction of the new List. Of course, relocation cannot be guaranteed to yield compaction unless the new area is contiguous. One method for insuring this is to divide the List memory into two *semi-spaces* and to alternate their usage, relocating active Lists from one semi-space to the other when performance monitoring dictates it [Fenichel and Yokelson 1969].

†11.2.3.2.1 Moving Lists. The problem is to move an arbitrary List from one memory area to another. As with marking, we wish to avoid recursion in the interest of efficiency, and we are precluded from using an explicit stack since that might consume more space than is available at this juncture. The challenge is to find an algorithm that is $O(n)$ in time (for a List with n cells) and that requires just a constant amount of workspace. Two earlier algorithms attain this goal [Cheney 1970; Reingold 1973], but with the requirement that each cell of the List be visited twice. A study of List-processing programs found that only about 1/3 of CAR's and 3/4 of CDR's typically have sub-Lists [Clark and Green 1977]. This led to an algorithm by Clark [1976] that we will present here. It achieves better performance by following tail pointers before following head pointers. Assuming that these proportions are independent, then this algorithm will only revisit about 1/4 of the

List cells in typical cases. Moreover, the relocated Lists become *CDR-linearized*, which is important with virtual memory.

As a cell is visited,

(a) its contents are moved to a new location;

(b) a forwarding address is placed in the head link at the old location;

(c) when the head link points to a non-atomic sub-List, then the tail link at the old location is used as part of an implicit stack for recording cells that must be revisited.

The algorithm for this is the function MOVE_LIST. It uses the procedure NEWCELL to obtain and initialize new cells, as follows:

```
procedure NEWCELL (var ptr: link);
begin
   new (ptr);
   ptr↑.mark := true;
   ptr↑.isatom := false;
end;
```

In the **repeat** ... **until** loop, the algorithm chains through an "outer" List, setting the forwarding addresses and developing the implicit stack, all within the pointer fields at the old locations. In the **while** loop, cells in the stack are picked off for processing, unless the associated sub-Lists have already been moved. In many applications of this algorithm, it is even possible to dispense with the mark field, using machine address values to distinguish original cells from new cells.

The operation of MOVE_LIST is illustrated in terms of the List of Figure 11.3(a) again, with the actual trace displayed in Figure 11.4. The original List is shown in (a). At the conclusion of the first pass over the outer List, the situation is as shown in (b), wherein cells n,o,p,q have been allocated for the new List. Note the forwarding addresses in the old List, and also the stack of deferred sub-Lists associated with cells f and a. The pass over the sub-List from cell f yields the situation shown in (c), with deferred sub-Lists associated with cells h and a. At the conclusion of the pass over the sub-List from cell h, the situation is as shown in (d), wherein all of the cells in the new List have by now been allocated; however, there are still deferred sub-Lists associated with cells c and a. The final pass finds no new cells, but adjusts pointer values in cells n and u to yield the situation shown in (e). Upon termination, we find that:

- The original List has been destroyed.
- Both List cells and atomic cells have been relocated.
- The new List is CDR-linearized.
- MOVE_LIST returns with a pointer to the new List.

†11.2.3.2.2 ***Copying Lists.*** Since algorithms for copying a List must not destroy the original List, they are somewhat more complicated. An important requirement, again, is that these schemes have a bounded requirement for working storage. There has been a succession of algorithms with complexities diminishing from $O(n^2)$ to $O(n \lg n)$ to $O(n)$ [§]. One of the latter, by Robson [1977a], requires no mark bits and has no dependency (as have some) upon either the address ordering or the

```
function MOVE_LIST (list: link): link;

label   1;

type    link = ↑cell;
        cell = record
           mark: boolean;
           case isatom: boolean of
              true: (data: char);
              false: (head,tail: link);
        end;

var     endlist: boolean;
        atom,copy,left,rite,next,temp,top: link;

begin
   next := list;
   NEWCELL (copy);
   list := copy;
   MOVE_LIST := copy;
   top := nil;
1: repeat
      endlist := true;
      left := next↑.head;  rite := next↑.tail;
      next↑.head := copy;  copy↑.head := left;
      if left↑.isatom then begin
         NEWCELL (atom);
         atom↑.isatom := true;  atom↑.data := left↑.data;
         copy↑.head := atom;  left↑.isatom := false;
         left↑.head := atom;  left↑.tail := nil;
      end else if not left↑.mark then begin
         next↑.tail := top;  top := next;
      end;
      if rite = nil then
         copy↑.tail := rite
      else if rite↑.head↑.mark then
         copy↑.tail := rite↑.head
      else begin
         endlist := false;
         NEWCELL (copy↑.tail);
         copy := copy↑.tail;  next := rite;
      end;
   until endlist;
   NEWCELL (copy);
   while top <> nil do begin
      next := top↑.head↑.head;
      temp := top;  top := top↑.tail;
      if next↑.head↑.mark then
         temp↑.head↑.head := next↑.head
      else begin
         temp↑.head↑.head := copy;
         goto 1;
      end;
   end;
end;
```

Algorithm 11.3 MOVE_LIST

a: b e		e: g f	f: h #				
b: d c	c: c f	g: B	h: b #				
d: A							

(a) *top* = #

a: n #		e: o f	f: q a	n: b o		o: p q	q: h #
b: d c	c: c f	g: p #	h: b #			p: B	
d: A							

(b) *top* = *f*

a: n #		e: o f	f: q a	n: b o		o: p q	q: r #
b: d c	c: c f	g: p #	h: r a			p: B	r: b #
d: A							

(c) *top* = *h*

a: n #		e: o f	f: q a	n: b o		o: p q	q: r #
b: s c	c: u a	g: p #	h: r a	s: t u	u: c q	p: B	r: s #
d: t #				t: A			

(d) *top* = *c*

a: n #		e: o f	f: q a	n: s o		o: p q	q: r #
b: s c	c: u a	g: p #	h: r a	s: t u	u: u q	p: B	r: s #
d: t #				t: A			

(e) *top* = #

Figure 11.4 Trace of Algorithm MOVE_LIST

contiguity of List cells. Although it is somewhat slower than the other algorithms, the lack of restrictions makes it more useful for the general case of copying a List. The ideas behind Robson's technique are interesting, and we will sketch these ideas without presenting the algorithm explicitly.

The method proceeds in two phases. In the first phase, the cells of the old List are scanned and cells of the new List are generated. At the conclusion of this phase, the head fields of the old List cells have forwarding addresses, as in MOVE_LIST, but the tail fields of the old List cells contain special marks. The original contents of cells from the old List have been copied into their counterpart cells in the new List. Atomic cells are *not* copied; to do so would likely cause unnecessary duplication, since their values can be shared.

As cells of the old List are scanned, one of four constant mark values − denoted by *marks* [i] ($i = 0,1,2,3$) − is stored in each tail field. These mark values symbolically encode information about forward and backward pointers in the original List cell contents. In scanning a List and following either head or tail pointers, a pointer is a *forward pointer* if it points to an unexamined sub-List, and a *backward pointer* if it points either to an atom or to a sub-List that has been examined. Obviously, this depends upon the order in which pointers are followed −

head and then tail, or tail and then head. The choice employed, systematically and recursively, in the first phase is head and then tail.

The meaning attached to the four constant, symbolic values in the *marks* array is as follows:

marks [0] – The original head and tail pointers of a cell having this value are both backward pointers.

marks [1] – The original head pointer of a cell having this value is a backward pointer, and the original tail pointer is a forward pointer.

marks [2] – The original head pointer of a cell having this value is a forward pointer, and the original tail pointer is a backward pointer.

marks [3] – The original head and tail pointers of a cell having this value are both forward pointers.

Note that the forward pointers discovered in the first phase define a spanning tree for the structure, with the cells on this tree being visited in preorder. In the second phase the List is scanned again; but this time the pointers are followed, systematically and recursively, in the order tail and then head. As cells are scanned in this phase, two things are done simultaneously:

1. The original contents of the old List cells are restored from their counterparts in the new List.
2. The correct pointer values for the new List cells are inserted, using the forwarding addresses from the old List cells.

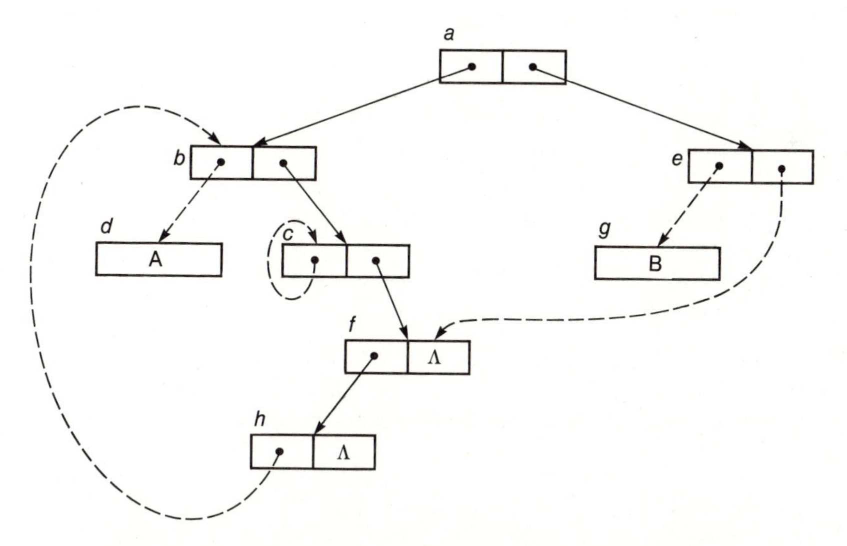

Figure 11.5 Forward and Backward Pointers (Robson)

We can illustrate these ideas by describing the operation of the algorithm upon the sample List of Figure 11.3(a) again, redrawn as Figure 11.5. By applying the definition (following head pointers before tail pointers), we find that the solid lines in the figure are forward pointers and that the dashed lines in the figure are backward pointers. At the conclusion of the first phase, the situation is as shown in Figure 11.6(a), where the marks $\{m0, m1, m2, m3\}$ in the tails of the original List cells indeed correspond to the four cases for the pointers in those cells, according to Figure 11.5. At the conclusion of the second phase, the situation is as shown in Figure 11.6(b).

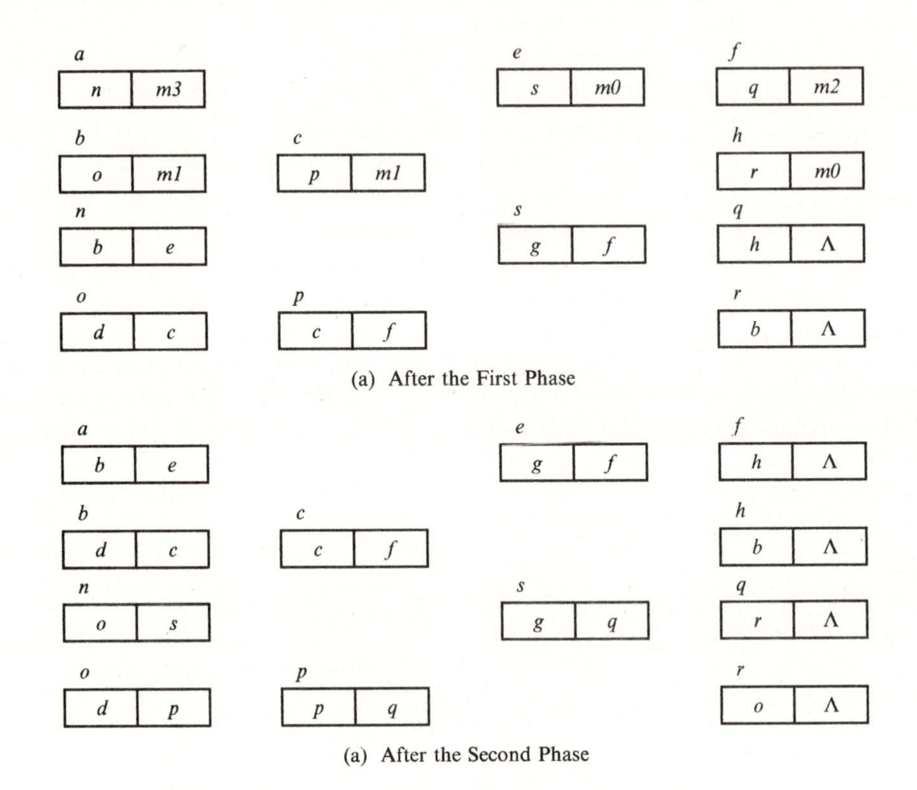

Figure 11.6 Progress of Robson's Copy Algorithm

11.2.4 Garbage Collection versus Reference Counters

There are some important caveats attached to both garbage collecting and reference counting, particularly in the straightforward versions that we have described so far. For instance, it is imperative with either scheme that the implementation leave no loopholes such that a List is deallocated while a pointer variable still references it; this creates a dangling reference which, if then used, can create havoc (see Section 4.5.1). This problem can arise in garbage collection if base pointers, that may for an instant reside in temporary registers, are missed in the marking phase. It can also arise with reference counters if the bookkeeping is done improperly. It is usually very difficult to ferret out program errors of this sort, for two reasons. First, the system will usually not manifest a malfunction until much later in time, when the evidence is diluted or lost. Second, the state of the system that invoked the error may not be reproducible. Many of the other difficulties associated with garbage collection and reference counting are more complementary in nature, so let's consider these in turn.

With garbage collection, the danger of developing a dangling reference is compounded because the state of the system upon initiation of marking is unpredictable. At that instant, some List structures may be ill-formed, perhaps because the user program is in the middle of constructing the Lists, or because the user program is doing its own link inversions upon a List, etc. A different and significant problem with the use of garbage collection is that when it is invoked, the user task stops until the marking and collection cycle is completed. In the A.I. environment, where List processing is the general method of choice, this can have severe consequences. It is not feasible to control a robot in real-time, for example, with the expectation that it may have to "freeze" for substantial intervals (perhaps $10-20$ seconds) while garbage collection takes place.

Still another problem arises with garbage collection when the Free-list becomes nearly exhausted. At this point, the collection process will be invoked more and more often, and reclaim less and less space. Therefore, it is a good idea to have the garbage collector count the number of cells reclaimed, and – if that number is less than some limit – abort the job immediately rather than thrash itself to an ungraceful termination. Alternatively, it is often possible to vary the amount of space allocated by the system, either initially or dynamically. Under the assumption that computing cost is proportional to the product of storage size and execution time, we can then ask what is the optimal amount of storage, such that we are neither paying for too much unused memory, nor wasting too much time in garbage collection instead of in useful computation. If M is the available memory size, and n is the average number of cells still in use after each collection, then let $\rho = n/M$. Also, let c_1 be the cost of marking and unmarking a cell in use, and let c_2 be the cost of collecting a cell not in use, where we expect to find $c_1 >> c_2$. Then the average cost per cell returned to Free is given by

$$C = \frac{c_1 n + c_2(M-n)}{M-n} = \frac{c_1 \rho}{1-\rho} + c_2 \tag{11.1}$$

For $\rho = 1/4$, this yields $C = c_1/3 + c_2$; but for $\rho = 3/4$, we find that $C = 3c_1 + c_2$. In other words, the cost per liberated cell rises sharply as ρ increases. A more detailed analysis shows curves that have shallow cost minimums in the range $0.6 \le \rho \le 0.8$, but that escalate steeply as ρ approaches 1.0 [Hoare 1974]. A subsequent analysis with somewhat different assumptions suggests that it is better to operate with ρ closer to 0.5 [Campbell 1974].

The reference counter method avoids the abrupt pause associated with garbage collection, because the reclamation is incremental. However, there is a high cost involved in performing the bookkeeping. There is the obvious cost of finding space for counts rather than just mark bits. At the List-header level there is ample room, but at the level of individual cells this may be a severe problem. The cost in terms of execution overhead is even worse. Thus, consider the work associated with the statement $p :=$ {pointer expression}:

(a) decrement the count of the List $p\uparrow$;

(b) if this count is zero, free the List $p\uparrow$;

(c) evaluate the expression and then increment the count for that List;

(d) finally, assign the pointer value to p.

Moreover, if the above statement is $p := p$, then even this simple-minded sequence is insufficient to prevent the reference by p on the left-hand side from being lost before it is needed by the right-hand side.

Another major difficulty associated with reference counters is that they are unable to cope with circular, or recursive, Lists since the counts therein can never go to zero. This is illustrated by Figure 11.7, wherein the two Lists U and V mutually prevent their reclamation. Thus, even ordinary sequential lists of the circular and bi-directional type cannot be managed by reference counts, which is a serious handicap. One rather unsatisfactory remedy is to have the user explicitly free such recursive Lists. A second solution is to isolate circular structures via header nodes, and then count just the external references to such a structure [Bobrow 1980; Friedman and Wise 1979]. The next section provides still another remedy.

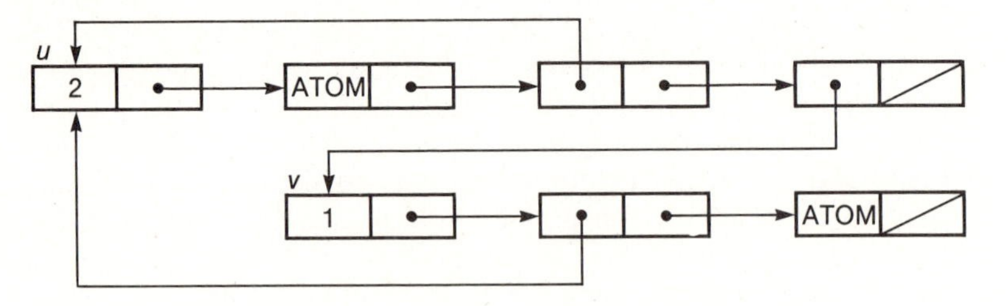

Figure 11.7 Reference Counting Circularity

A different perspective on the relative merits of garbage collection and reference counting can be obtained by examining how their costs are assessed. In a multiprogramming environment, the time penalty for the former can fall upon everyone, regardless of the nature of the particular programs. The situation is somewhat fairer with reference counting, where the overhead for maintaining proper counts is always charged directly to the program that is using them.

Clearly, neither of the straightforward methods that we have examined for reclaiming unused memory is entirely satisfactory. In the next two sections, we will investigate some fancier techniques that offer ways to overcome the principal difficulties associated with garbage collection and reference counting.

†11.2.5 Hybrid Reclamation

As we have seen, one problem associated with garbage collection is the large amount of time required to mark and reclaim all of memory. A related problem is the impact that such a computation can have upon the feasibility of real-time applications. Since reference counting has neither of these drawbacks, a useful idea is to employ a hybrid scheme wherein counting is the primary method, but garbage collection is used occasionally. Collection is essential in this hybrid scheme both for reclaiming the circular structures that reference counting cannot detect, and for providing compaction of the active cells. Although this hybrid of garbage collection and reference counting is feasible, it fails to take into account some of the other shortcomings of counting. In particular, we have seen that this method is costly in terms of space for the counts, and also with respect to the time spent in continually updating them.

The scheme just described can be substantially improved by making use of the observation [Clark and Green 1977] that, in typical LISP programs, about 90–98 percent of the reference counts are one! Therefore, it is much more economical to keep track of just those items with counts of zero and counts of greater than one. In order to do so, the counts are placed in hash tables, using a technique known as *hash linking* [Bobrow 1975], which we will explain briefly. Suppose that we have a set of keys and a table T, and that for most keys the table locations are adequate to store the associated information. However, we find that some small proportion of the keys require additional information to be associated with them. In such a case, we can either use a bit flag at the corresponding table address A, or store some exceptional value at A, signifying that special treatment is required. Then a hash function h is applied to A, and $h(A)$ serves as an implicit link to an entry in an auxiliary table T', without requiring space to store an explicit link at A to the entry in T'. As an illustration of the utility of this technique, suppose that we wish to maintain counts in a table T of 16-bit words (allowing a range of 0 .. 65535), and that some small percentage of the counts will reach or exceed the upper limit. This is easily handled with hash linking by storing counts *less than* 65535 just as they are, but storing 65535 in any location A_j where the inequality fails. For the latter cases, we compute $h(A_j)$ to direct us to an entry in a snall hash table T', where that entry in T' contains space for a key A_j and its count value.

We will now consider a hybrid reclamation scheme [Deutsch and Bobrow 1976] that uses hash linking to maintain three tables, as follows:

1. *Multiple Reference Table* (*MRT*) – Each entry corresponds to an address and a corresponding count of two or more.
2. *Zero Count Table* (*ZCT*) – Each entry corresponds to an address for which the corresponding count is zero. An address can be in this table either because the corresponding datum is truly unreferenced, or because the datum is referenced only externally – that is, from a program variable or from the run-time stack.
3. *Variable Reference Table* (*VRT*) – Each entry corresponds to an address referenced externally, as described for the ZCT.

Note that the large majority of data, with reference counts of one, will not appear in either the MRT or the ZCT. Conversely, we can determine that the count is one whenever the corresponding address does not appear in either table.

The use of the hash tables solves the problem of excessive space for reference counts, but it does not respond to the problem of time spent in updating them. The answer here is to generate a sequential file (see Section 12.3.1) of reference count transactions, rather than applying them as they occur. This file can then be read at suitable intervals, and the transactions can be applied to the hash tables in batches. A transaction of type *allocation* of a new datum causes an address to be placed in the ZCT. For a transaction of type *pointer creation*:

(a) if the datum is in the ZCT, then delete it (the count is now one);

(b) else if the datum is in the MRT, then increment it unless the count is at its maximum;

(c) else enter it in the MRT with default count of two.

Finally, for a transaction of type *pointer destruction*:

(d) if the datum is not in the MRT, then enter it in the ZCT (the count was one);

(e) else (the datum is in the MRT), then delete it if the count is two;

(f) else do nothing if the count is at its maximum, else decrement it.

As a result of processing a sequence of transactions against the hash tables, if any datum D has an entry in the ZCT but not in the VRT, then after decrementing the counts of data to which it refers, D can safely be recycled back to Free.

The foregoing hybrid scheme was designed specifically for use with a second level of memory (see Section 12.1). A large measure of the efficacy of this approach comes as a result of the transactions being accumulated in primary memory before being written out, so that many of them can be cancelled against one another without ever being written to the file. This can be seen from observation again [Clark and Green 1977]. For example, it is very common to have an allocation transaction for an address followed by a pointer creation transaction for it, whereby the datum is "nailed down"; the net result is no change in the hash tables. Another example is that of a datum created and rapidly abandoned, again resulting in no change. Where the List-processing program is compiled, then the methods of global data flow analysis (see Section 7.4.5.3) can be used to further advantage; they can detect a variety of situations that lead to cancellation, and so require no transaction posting at all [Barth 1977].

It is also possible to implement a form of hybrid reclamation without recourse to secondary memory. With this scheme, a one-bit reference count is kept with each datum, such that a value of one denotes multiple references [Wise and Friedman 1977]. Once this condition applies to a datum, it can be reclaimed only by marking and garbage collection. But as discussed above, multiple references are relatively infrequent. Moreover, by maintaining and consulting a table of the most recent activity, it is possible to reduce the number of instances where a multiple reference is recorded and a datum is "lost." Another useful benefit of this technique is that the bit used for the reference count can also be employed as a tag during the marking phase of garbage collection.

†11.2.6 Parallel Garbage Collection

By providing a measure of incremental reclamation, the hybrid scheme of the previous section can significantly reduce the total amount of time spent in garbage collection. However, another problem still remains – collection engenders a pause that can completely disrupt a real-time application. In response to this, there have been several proposals to interleave the activity of the user process with that of the collection process. Some of these are of the mark-and-collect variety, as in Section

11.2.1, and others are of the relocation variety, as in Section 11.2.3.2. We will look at both of these in turn.

In the paradigm for parallel garbage collection, there are two distinct processors, with the *mutator* doing the useful work of the user, and the *collector* reclaiming cells soon after they are abandoned. Since the mutator may cause the pointers from a cell to change after the cell has been marked but before marking has terminated and collection has begun, some new ideas are required. A very elegant solution to this problem employs three colors – white, gray, and black – with which to mark cells [Dijkstra et al. 1978]. Marking begins by graying the roots of the mutator graph and the Free-list. Thereafter, the basic marking operation is to find a gray cell X and then to gray any of its white descendants, at the same time blackening X. In essence, a white cell is unmarked, a gray cell is marked but its descendants are not, and a cell that is black has both itself and its descendants marked. Also, the mutator must cooperate by graying any white cell that it acquires. The marking phase eventually alternates with a collection phase, during which white cells are recognized as "quick garbage" and returned to the Free-list, and black cells are whitened. Black cells that have in fact been abandoned are "slow garbage"; they will fail to be marked in the next cycle, and so be reclaimed at that time.

A mutator-collector parallel garbage collector is *not* a simple algorithm, because of the delicate possibilities for interaction between the two processes. For instance, marking must be prohibited from altering the pointer topology of Lists, as happens in MARK_LIST (Algorithm 4.7). In one detailed description of this method, marking is performed via repeated linear scans of memory in search of gray cells, which is clearly inefficient. However, the issue there was not efficiency in the first place [§]; rather, it was to obtain an algorithm for which correctness could be demonstrated [Gries 1977]. An example of a more efficient mutator-collector is provided by Kung and Song [1977]. By employing four colors, it avoids the necessity of having to mark the Free-list as well as the mutator graph. It presumes the availability of space for a deque, thereby attaining respectable marking efficiency.

For the relocating variant of reclamation, recall from Section 11.2.3.2 that two semi-spaces E and F are employed. The user process runs in E until it becomes full, then active data is moved from E to F, then operation resumes in F until it becomes full, then active data is moved from F to E, etc. By itself, this does not eliminate the pause, but the following scheme does [Baker 1978a]. In equilibrium, as the user program is running, some number of cells have been copied from *fromspace* to the bottom end of *tospace* via a pointer B. If the user program requires a new cell, it is allocated from the top end of *tospace* via a pointer T. Interleaved with user program operations are collection operations that scan the cells in *tospace* from the bottom end via another pointer S. When the pointer S reaches a cell in *tospace* with a link X to a cell in *fromspace*, the collector moves that cell to the bottom end of *tospace* (via pointer B), updates the link X, and leaves a forwarding address in the old cell location. After a while, the pointer S will have caught up with the pointer B, and the moving activity will have incrementally cleaned out *fromspace*, at which point the two spaces can "flip." A further embellishment comes from the observation that young objects have a high mortality rate, but old objects die hard, and so it is a waste of time to keep moving the latter. Therefore, it is worthwhile to operate with several smaller segments of memory rather than two large semi-spaces, separating objects into different segments according to their age, and eventually not examining segments filled with old objects [Lieberman and Hewitt 1983].

The mutator-collector approach described at the beginning of this section would appear to be quite different from the relocation method just described. But think of the cells still in *fromspace* as being white, of those copied to *tospace* but with descendants that have not yet been examined as being gray, and of those copied and examined as being black. We see that the two approaches do in fact share some very basic concepts of graph marking. One of the significant distinctions in the relocation approach is that the graph is scanned in breadth-first order; the cells in *tospace* serve as a queue for this purpose, and no explicit stack is required.

11.3 VARIABLE-SIZE BLOCKS

In order to convey the nature of the problem with variable-size blocks, let us investigate the consequences of some particular, arbitrary assumptions concerning storage organization, allocation policy, and deallocation policy. Suppose that we have a memory of twelve units (initially empty) and that we are presented with a series of requests involving allocation and deallocation, yielding the states shown in Figure 11.8(a). In order to portray what is happening, we label empty blocks with the number of units they contain, and active blocks with the name of the item they contain. In general, when a request for R units is matched against a block containing S units, we will allocate the rightmost R units to the request, and the leftmost $(S - R)$ units as a smaller empty block. The Free space of empty blocks is maintained as a linked list, with returned blocks being inserted at the front. The reason for allocating from the right will be described in Section 11.3.1.1; the reason for maintaining Free-space as a stack is that it is the simplest way to manage a linked list. One final point is that we will encounter situations where there are two or more contiguous empty blocks; for now, we will presume that they are left in that state. Figure 11.8(a) speaks for itself. When we try to obtain space for E, we fail because memory has become checkerboarded with active blocks and small empty blocks. There are actually five unused units of memory, but they are unavailable to us because unused memory has become *fragmented* into useless blocks. Coping with fragmentation causes memory allocation to be a problem for blocks, whereas allocation was trivial for cells.

The example in Figure 11.8(a) is based upon some definite but simplistic policies of organization (a stack), allocation (first-fit), and deallocation (do nothing). Now let us consider another example, using some different policies. In particular, suppose that requests for variable-size allocations are always honored by rounding them up to the nearest multiple of some standard size *Bstd*, say 1000 units. This example typifies the way in which an operating system would respond to requests for storage for program tasks. It is illustrated in Figure 11.9 for a hypothetical series of requests, and with a total available memory of 10,000 units. Here, we are unable to satisfy the request for 900 units for E even though there are 2100 unused units of memory. In this case, the unused but unavailable memory locations occur

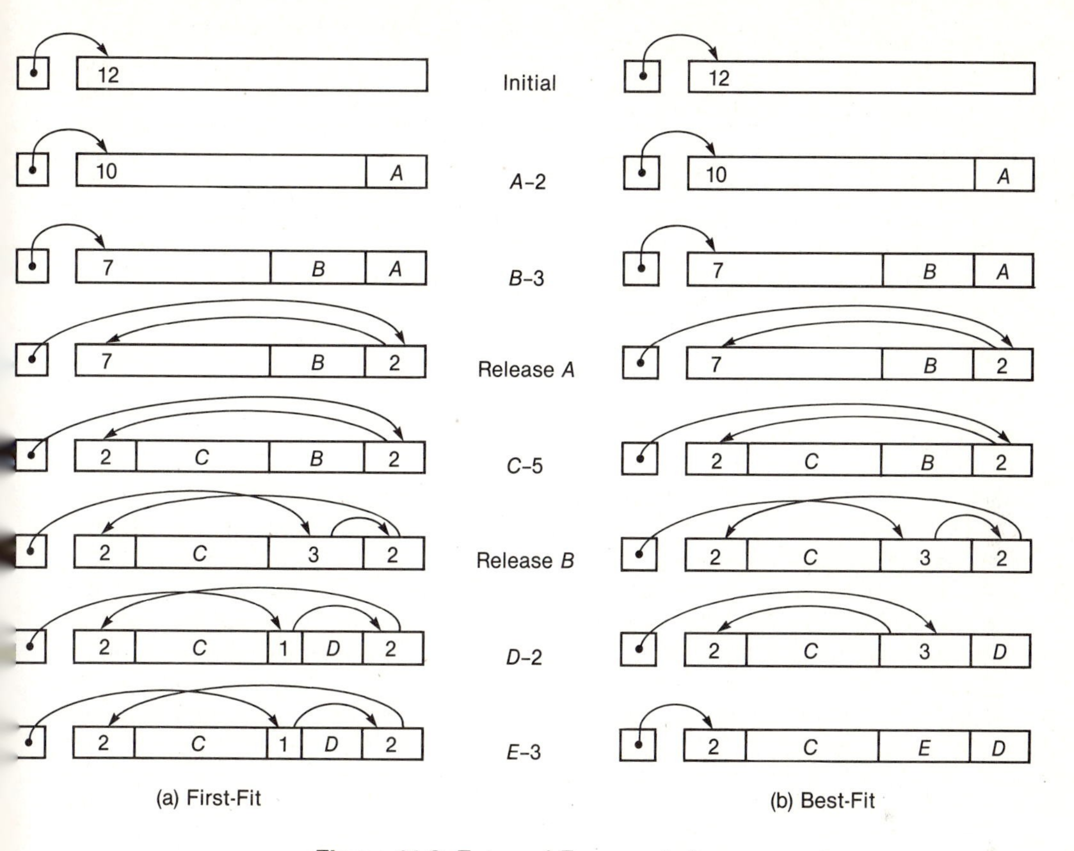

Figure 11.8 External Fragmentation

within allocated blocks, and so the phenomenon is termed *internal fragmentation*. The phenomenon portrayed in Figure 11.8 is termed *external fragmentation*.

We can regard the examples of Figure 11.8 as having a basic block size *Bstd* = 1. Then it is easy to see that as we vary *Bstd* from small values to large values, the external fragmentation will decrease but the internal fragmentation will increase. Moreover, it has been observed that the increase in internal fragmentation sharply exceeds the decrease in external fragmentation [Randell 1969].

In this section, we will examine several variations in each of the three policies – organization, allocation, and reclamation. Initially, we will restrict our attention to various manners of dealing with memory as one storage pool. Subsequently, we will look first at a class of methods known as buddy systems, and then at the use of multiple storage pools.

The number of combinations of policies soon becomes cumbersome to grasp even conceptually, much less in terms of performance characteristics. Memory management strategies are generally measured with respect to two performance parameters – the degree to which they are able to satisfy various sequences of stor-

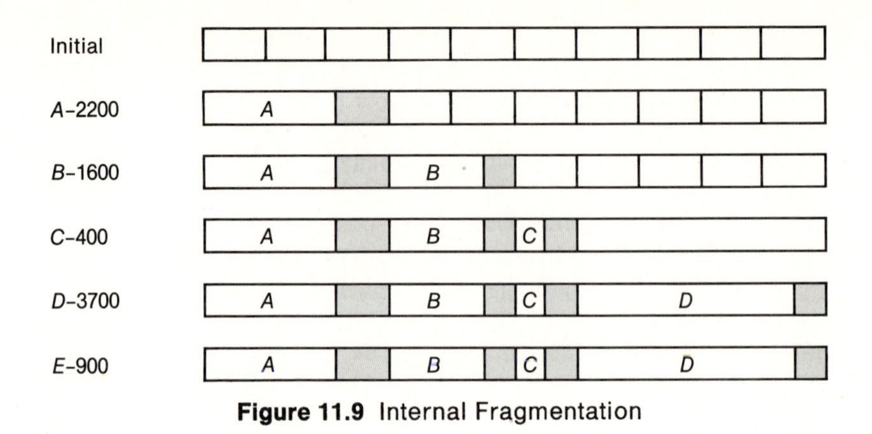

Figure 11.9 Internal Fragmentation

age requests from a finite available memory, and their execution overhead. In order to fully characterize such sequences of requests, we must consider:

- the distribution of request sizes;
- the distribution of arrival times of these requests;
- the distribution of occupancy times of these requests.

Clearly, to measure each of the sizable number of combinations of policies against a representative set of request sequences is a large task. So we conclude with a section that will hopefully bring some order out of chaos for the reader, drawing upon several excellent published analyses and simulation studies.

11.3.1 Single Storage Pool

The idea here is that blocks of memory are strung together as one sequential linked list, with various possibilities for organizing that list. When a request is received for a block of a given size, the allocation policy must actually perform two tasks:

1. select a free block from which to satisfy the request;
2. decide what to do about the difference between the request size and the selected block size.

The policy of reclamation includes actions that can happen either at storage release time, or when an allocation request cannot be satisfied. The former type of action is suggestive of the incremental reclamation of storage with reference counts; the latter type is analogous to a compaction phase of garbage collection.

11.3.1.1 Organization. Our meaningful unit of storage is now a block rather than a cell; therefore, we need to examine what must be included in the structure of a block. As a minimum, an unused block would need the format shown in Figure 11.10(a), and an active block might have either the format shown in (b) or (c) of the

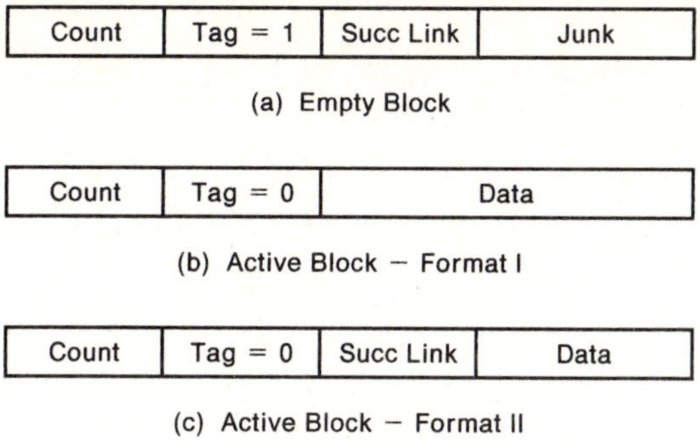

Count	Tag = 1	Succ Link	Junk

(a) Empty Block

Count	Tag = 0	Data

(b) Active Block – Format I

Count	Tag = 0	Succ Link	Data

(c) Active Block – Format II

Figure 11.10 Memory Block Formats

```
type   cursor = lo .. hi;
       block1 = record
          count: cursor;
          case tag: boolean of
             false: (data: {string of data bytes});
             true:  (succ: cursor;
                        junk: {string of empty bytes});
       end;
       block2 = record
          count: cursor;
          case tag: boolean of
             false: (succ: cursor;
                        data: {string of data bytes});
             true:  (succ: cursor;
                        junk: {string of empty bytes});
       end;
```

Figure 11.11 Pascal Syntax for Memory Blocks

figure. In Pascal terms we would have either *block*1 or *block*2, as illustrated in Figure 11.11.

One of the first consequences that follows from these formats is that an unused block must have a minimum size *bmin* that is large enough to contain the *count*, *tag*, and *succ* fields; an allocation policy must never split off an empty block smaller than this limit. It is also easy to see from these formats why – in splitting an empty block into a reduced empty part and an active part, as in Figure 11.8 – we make the active part on the right. By so doing, we have only to reduce the count to reestablish the empty block; if we made the active part on the left, we would also have to reestablish the tag and link fields. The choice between the *block*1 and the *block*2 alternatives depends upon whether or not our linked list of blocks is to be just a Free-list, or should include all the blocks in memory. The *block*1 format will speed up searching for an empty block because the list is shorter. The *block*2 format, with all the blocks in order of address, can facilitate the process of reclamation, but it requires both more space and more time. In the *block*1 case, it is possible to maintain the Free-list in several ways. In Figure 11.8, we employed a stack; you may recall that in SLIP a queue is used (see Section 11.2.2). A common choice is to maintain the Free-list by address, although the block size is sometimes used as the criterion.

11.3.1.2 Allocation. As we have said, an allocation policy includes both selecting an empty block and possibly having to dispose of an excess in that block. Let's consider the problem of excess capacity first. One possibility is to simply include the excess in the allocated block. Indeed, that is what happens when memory is allocated in multiples of a fixed block size *Bstd*, as in Figure 11.9, and it leads to internal fragmentation. This is also what must happen if the excess is too small, as we discussed in the previous section. Note that this manner of handling the excess may necessitate extra information in an active block, to distinguish *data* from *junk*. The other way of handling excess capacity is the one illustrated originally in Figure 11.8; namely, we split the excess off into a new and smaller unused block, leading to external fragmentation.

Allocation is essentially the process of searching a list to find a block that is large enough. We see that external fragmentation complicates allocation in two ways. It simultaneously causes this list to be longer and the entries in the list to be smaller, both of which increase the search overhead. In our example of Figure 11.8(a), the allocation selection policy specified the first unused block that was large enough, no matter how much larger; this is known as *first-fit*. It would appear that such a policy is imprudent, causing us to be unable to allocate 3 units to *E* because we had previously split a 3-unit block to satisfy *D*, when a 2-unit block would have worked just as well. This suggests that a better policy might be *best-fit*, whereby we would look for the smallest unused block that is just large enough to satisfy the request. Indeed, if we apply such a policy to that same series of requests, as shown in (b) of Figure 11.8, we are rewarded with greater success. However, it is easy to construct a counter-example where best-fit fails and first-fit succeeds, as illustrated in Figure 11.12. More generally, a problem with best-fit is that it may rarely find a block of exactly the desired size, and so will split an empty block into an active part and a *splinter*, an empty block so small that it is of little practical value. Over a period of time, if Free-list accumulates many such splinters, it may both worsen execution overhead and reduce memory availability.

Note that if the linked list is maintained by address, then the process of searching for a best-fit means searching the entire list (unless we find an exact-fit), and so will be more expensive than searching for a first-fit. For this reason, the Free-list might be maintained by block size to shorten the searching process of best-fit. What happens if we use the first-fit method with a Free-list ordered by block size? It depends upon whether the blocks are in increasing or decreasing order of size. If they are in increasing order, first-fit becomes best-fit; if they are in decreasing order, first-fit will succeed (or fail) on the very first try, yielding a policy known as *worst-fit*. This policy, which always splits up the largest unused block, is not necessarily a bad one; it definitely tends to oppose the formation of small fragments.

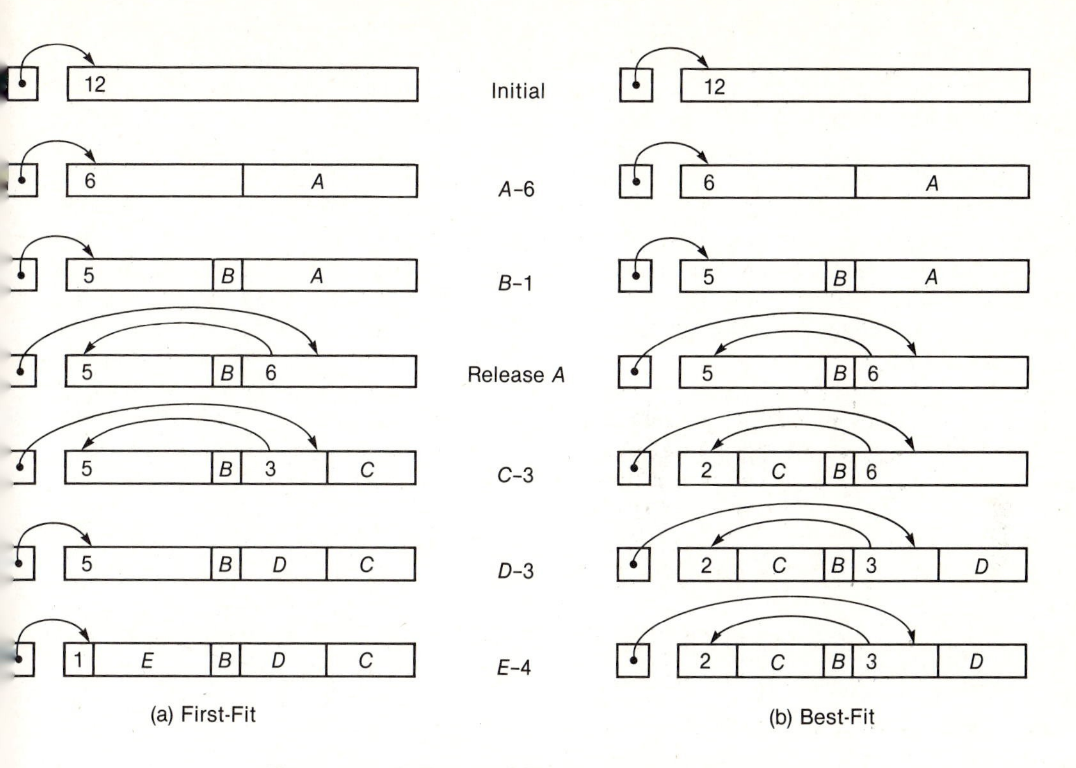

Figure 11.12 External Fragmentation, Again

Let's attempt to apply intuition again, as when we decided to try best-fit rather than first-fit. If first-fit is applied to a lengthy series of allocation and deallocation requests, then the continual activity at the front end of the Free-list can be expected to bias Free toward having more small blocks at the front and more large blocks at the rear. This in turn will cause any requests for large blocks to have long searches. It would seem that an improvement upon this situation would be to have each search cycle begin at that point in the list where the previous search cycle ended. In such a *next-fit* policy, the distribution of block sizes in the list should be more random, and the average search length should be shorter. In fact, as we will see in Section 11.3.4.2, the observed results with next-fit need careful interpretation.

Our final allocation policy derives from the optimal stopping policy for Markov chains, and is dramatically illustrated by the following hypothetical situation. You are presented with a sequence of choices, one after the other. If you could "spread them out" and go back and forth, it would be easy to pick the best. However, you are required to examine them in sequence, with no knowledge about the values of the still unseen choices. As each choice is paraded before you, you can pass on it, which eliminates it from further consideration, or you can select it, which concludes the game. An example of this might be a motorist trying to pick a motel without going back over his tracks.

To illustrate the principle in a different manner, suppose that you are playing the following card game. The value of the cards in the deck is considered to run, from lowest to highest: 2,3, ... , ace of clubs; 2,3, ... , ace of diamonds; and so on, for hearts and then spades. The dealer shuffles the cards, takes the first one, and then begins to look at the other cards one at a time. As he looks at each card in turn, the dealer compares it with the one in his hand, retaining the higher one and discarding the lower one. Obviously, by the time he reaches the end of the deck, he will be holding the ace of spades. What is your role in this game? You are watching him as he does this, but you cannot see the faces of the cards, only his actions in exchanging one card for another. Nonetheless, you are asked to identify the ace of spades when it comes by, not after the fact. If you were challenged to play this game with odds of 3 to 1 in your favor, would it be a favorable bet? Surprisingly, it would be!

The unaided probability of identifying the ace of spades as the cards go by you, face unseen, is certainly just 1/52. So how is this a favorable bet? A key observation is that a candidate for best must be better than any that has been seen so far. Your strategy is:

1. to allow S out of the total of N to go by, simply noting the best candidate in this initial segment from 1 to S; and then
2. to pick the first candidate after that point.

What is the probability that this strategy will find the best candidate X in the jth position, if you allow S of them to go by? It is the joint probability $\Pr(S,j)$ of the two events that:

(a) X occurs in the jth location, and

(b) there will be no candidates in the interval S to $j-1$.

The probability of event (a) is given by $1/N$. Also, if Y is the best candidate in the first $j-1$ positions, then the probability of event (b) that Y will occur within the first S positions, so that no candidates occur between S and $j-1$, is given by $S/(j-1)$. In other words, $\Pr(S,j) = (1/N) \times (S/(j-1))$. Summing this over the likelihoods of finding the best candidate in positions $S+1$ through N, we obtain

$$\sum_{j=S+1}^{N} \frac{1}{N}\frac{S}{j-1} = \frac{S}{N}\left(\frac{1}{S} + \frac{1}{S+1} + \cdots + \frac{1}{N-1}\right) = \frac{S}{N}(H_{N-1} - H_{S-1}) \qquad (11.2)$$

For large values of N, the value of S that maximizes this summation is closely approximated by $N/e \approx 0.368N$, and this strategy will succeed in correctly identifying the best candidate with probability $1/e \approx 0.368$. In other words, for the card game, if you picked the first candidate, as indicated by an exchange of cards on the dealer's part, after the nineteenth card, you would have a better than even chance of winning with the 3 to 1 odds. If the game is instead to try to identify one or both of the two of clubs and the ace of spades, at even money, the prospects are even more favorable.

As applied to the storage allocation problem, this is called the *optimal-fit* policy. It suggests (1) examining 0.368 of the blocks on the Free-list and recording the block Y in this sample that is closest in size to the request, and (2) picking the first block X thereafter that gives a closer fit than Y. Compared to first-fit, we would expect it to require more searching but to give a better fit; compared to best-fit, we would expect it to require less searching but to yield, on the average, a poorer fit. This is a very pretty method, but its validity rests upon certain assumptions that do not always apply with the storage allocation problem:

- that the blocks in the Free-list are statistically independent in terms of size;
- that the number of blocks is both large and known;
- that it is impossible to return to a block once it is passed over [Leung 1982b].

When the latter assumption is false there is some benefit, because it may happen that no candidate block is found after the sample, and yet a candidate existed in the sample. In the original description of optimal-fit, reversion to a candidate from the sample was employed about 25 percent of the time, and the method was found to be generally superior to first-fit [Campbell 1971]. However, as we will see in Section 11.3.4.2, the first assumption above is usually not true with first-fit − that is, the block sizes are not independent. Therefore, the observed results with optimal-fit also need careful interpretation.

Except for some very different storage organizations that we will examine in Sections 11.3.2 and 11.3.3, the methods that we have described here encompass most of the techniques used in organizing memory for dynamic allocation of variable-size blocks. Still, there are other possibilities. For example, Free-list might be organized as a binary search tree (see Exercises 11.10 and 11.11). However, this introduces overhead that may not be worthwhile unless Free-list is fairly long. Extra space is required for the tree pointers, thereby increasing *bmin*. Also, time must be spent maintaining the pointers and (possibly) keeping the tree in balance. Still another idea is to have the allocation policy take into account the anticipated release times of already allocated blocks [Beck 1982].

11.3.1.3 Reclamation. With fixed-size cells, we found that it is sometimes necessary to compact them in order to reduce their dispersion in memory. In the case of variable-size blocks, a more pressing need is to counteract the trend toward fragmentation of memory. This was evident in the examples of Figures 11.8 and 11.12, where the reclamation policy was the trivially simple one of pushing deactivated blocks onto a stack. There are two approaches that can be used for the purpose. One idea is to determine, upon the return of a block, if either adjacent block in memory is also an empty block. If so, they can be *coalesced* into one larger block. (The terms "collapsed" and "consolidated" are also used.) Although effective, coalescing has its limitations. Therefore, the more drastic step of compaction may be required; however, compaction is considerably more complicated with blocks than it is with cells. We will now look at coalescing and compaction in turn.

11.3.1.3.1 Coalescing. The goal in coalescing is to merge adjacent empty blocks. The basic problem in implementing it is to find the two blocks that are adjacent to a given block and, if necessary, adjust the chain of Free-list pointers. When a block at location Q of size C is returned, it is simple to investigate the block that follows it in memory, by looking in or around location $R = Q + C$ (taking into account prefix space). If the block at R is empty, it is also simple to combine it with the block at Q. However, it is not so simple to adjust the relevant Free-list pointer to point to Q instead of R:

- If the Free-list is in arbitrary sequence, then we must search the entire list to find the predecessor to R, which will typically require $O(n)$ probes.
- If the Free-list is maintained by address, then the block at location Q *is* the predecessor of the block at location R. However, the operation of inserting the block Q (or any block) into such an ordered Free-list will have required $O(n)$ comparisons, so that we are no better off.

One apparent solution is to organize the empty blocks as a bi-directional list, in arbitrary sequence. Then, when a block Q is returned, and if the succeeding block R in memory is also empty, we can combine Q and R and adjust the pointers, all in constant time. However, what we have described still only accounts for coalescing with an empty neighbor block on the right. The problem of finding and coalescing with an empty neighbor block on the left is a bit more complicated. We first have to find the beginning of the left neighbor block, in order to test if it is empty; and the bi-directional list does not help with this, unless the Free-list is maintained by location. (If it is, we can link to the predecessor of Q, and then test to see whether it extends as far as Q, or if there is an intervening active block.) Unfortunately, we saw with the second case above that it costs $O(n)$ operations to maintain the Free-list by location.

Is there any solution that can deactivate a block and coalesce on both sides, and do so in constant time? There is, but at the expense of requiring additional information in active blocks as well as empty blocks. Note that we should not mind having extra information in empty blocks, since most of their space is unused anyway. With regard to active blocks, on the other hand, the additional overhead may be a substantial proportion of the allocation or it may be insignificant. A very effective manner of including additional information in active and empty blocks to facilitate coalescing is to use *boundary tags*. Such a scheme is illustrated in Figure 11.13, wherein each block has a suffix containing *count* and the boolean value *empty*; this suffix can easily be interrogated by any procedure working in another block to its immediate right. Note that an empty block requires several items of information, while the only essential extra information for an active block is a duplicate of its tag. With boundary tags, when a block Q is deactivated, we can find the adjacent block R on the right by using Q's count, as before. We can also test the suffix of the block P to the left of Q; if P is active, there is nothing further to do; but if P is empty, we can use the duplicate count value in P's suffix to reach the beginning of P. Since the Free-list is bi-directional, we can combine Q with P and/or R and restructure the list, as appropriate, all in constant time.

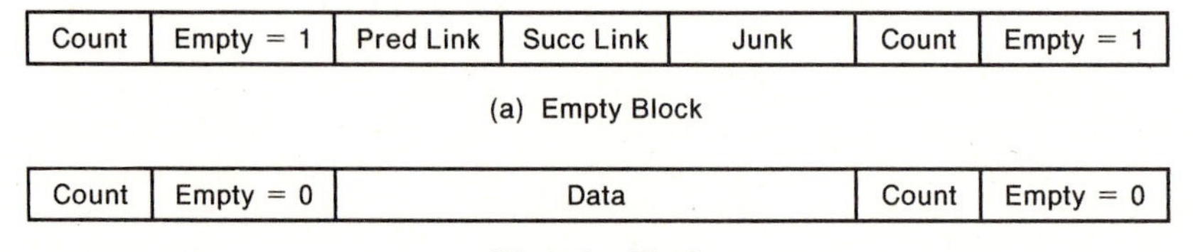

Figure 11.13 Boundary Tag Formats

```
const  bdry_size = 1;
       bmin = 3;

type   cursor = lo .. hi;
       itemicity = (boundary,fill,links);
       item = record
          case itemicity of
             boundary: (count: integer;
                             empty: boolean);
             fill: (byte: char);
             links: (pred,succ: integer);
       end;

var    free: integer;
       store: array [cursor] of item;
```

Figure 11.14 Boundary Tag Item Formats

Of course, it is unlikely that we can allocate a one-bit suffix in an active block without sacrificing an entire word, or at least an entire byte. Thus, it is common to show the same suffix form, containing duplicate values of *count* and *empty*, for both active and empty blocks. It is awkward to illustrate the boundary tag method in Pascal if we try to represent entire blocks via variant records. However, we can do almost as well if we use variant records to represent *items* within blocks. In particular, we will use the global information shown in Figure 11.14, such that an item is one of the three types: *boundary*, *fill*, or *links*. For the sake of simplicity, a *boundary* item has the same format for prefix and suffix and for both empty and active blocks; however, our algorithms will not use the *count* information in the suffix item of an active block.

Cursor	Itemicity	Contents
lo	*boundary*	*count* = 1 , *empty* = 1
lo + 1	*links*	*pred* = 0 , *succ* = *lo* + 4
lo + 2	*boundary*	*count* = 1 , *empty* = 1
lo + 3	*boundary*	*count* = −1 , *empty* = 0
lo + 4	*boundary*	*count* = *hi* − *lo* − 6 × *bdry_size* , *empty* = 1
lo + 5	*links*	*pred* = *lo* , *succ* = 0
hi − 1	*boundary*	*count* = *hi* − *lo* + 6 × *bdry_size* , *empty* = 1
hi	*boundary*	*count* = −1 , *empty* = 0

Figure 11.15 Initialization for FIRST-FIT and COALESCE

We now present algorithms to do first-fit allocation and also deallocation with coalescing, using these formats. *Store* is considered to be an array of items, and *free* identifies the head of our bi-directional, non-circular Free-list. We assume that the items in the first six and the final two locations of *store* are initialized as shown in Figure 11.15. The contents of $lo + 3$ and *hi* are dummy active blocks needed for the coalescing process; note that with a block size of -1, the same *boundary* item serves as both prefix and suffix. The small empty block from *lo* to $lo + 2$ serves as the head of the Free-list. Its size and position guarantee its permanence – that is, it will never be either allocated or coalesced. By using *bdry_size* to parameterize the size of a *boundary* item, we facilitate transcribing these algorithms to assembly language, should that be desired. We are not so concerned about introducing a similar parameter for the size of a *links* item, since that can easily be provided for by the choice of *bmin*.

```
function FIRST_FIT (n: integer): integer;

var     done: boolean;
        p,q,size: integer;
        u: item;

begin
   p := free;  done := false;
   FIRST_FIT := 0;                   {in case no space is available}
   repeat
      size := store [p].count;
      if size < n then begin
         p := store [p + 1].succ;
         done := (p = 0);
      end else begin
         if (size = n) or (size - n < bmin) then begin
            store [p].empty := false;
            store [store [p + 1].pred + 1].succ := store [p + 1].succ;
            store [store [p + 1].succ + 1].pred := store [p + 1].pred;
            store [p + size + bdry_size].empty := false;
            FIRST_FIT := p;
         end else begin
            q := size - n - 2 * bdry_size;
            store [p].count := q;  store [p + q + bdry_size].count := q;
            q := p + size - n;
            u.count := n;  u.empty := false;
            store [q] := u;  store [q + n + bdry_size] := u;
            FIRST_FIT := q;
         end;
         done := true;
      end;
   until done;
end;
```

Algorithm 11.4 FIRST_FIT

The function FIRST_FIT (Algorithm 11.4) searches the Free-list for the first block that is not less than the desired size *n*, returning either the address of that block, or a zero if there is none. If a block is found such that it has size *n* or such

```
procedure COALESCE (q: cursor);

var     glued: boolean;
        p,r,size: integer;

begin
   glued := false;
   store [q].empty := true;
   size := store [q].count;
   if store [q - 1].empty then begin
      p := q - store [q - 1].count - 2 * bdry_size;
      size := size + store [p].count + 2 * bdry_size;
      glued := true;
      q := p;
   end;
   r := q + size + 2 * bdry_size;
   if store [r].empty then begin
      size := size + store [r].count + 2 * bdry_size;
      if glued then begin
         store [store [r + 1].pred + 1].succ := store [r + 1].succ;
         store [store [r + 1].succ + 1].pred := store [r + 1].pred;
      end else begin
         store [store [r + 1].pred + 1].succ := q;
         store [store [r + 1].succ + 1].pred := q;
         store [q + 1].pred := store [r + 1].pred;
         store [q + 1].succ := store [r + 1].succ;
         glued := true;
      end;
   end;
   if not glued then begin
      r := store [free + 1].succ;
      if r <> 0 then
         store [r + 1].pred := q;
      store [q + 1].succ := r;
      store [q + 1].pred := free;
      store [free + 1].succ := q;
   end;
   store [q].count := size;
   store [q + size + bdry_size] := store [q];
end;
```

Algorithm 11.5 COALESCE

that its size is in excess of n by less than *bmin*, then the entire block is removed from the the Free-list and allocated. If the excess size of this block equals or exceeds the minimum, then it is split. The procedure COALESCE (Algorithm 11.5) is called with the address q of the block Q. It first checks the block P on the left, coalescing if appropriate. It next checks the block R on the right. If R is to be coalesced and P already was, then R is de-linked as a distinct block on the Free-list;

if R is to be coalesced and P was not, then the appropriate link adjustments are made. Finally, if Q was not coalesced with either P or R, then it is inserted at the front of the Free-list.

The process of coalescing has several virtues. It reclaims memory incrementally rather than in the spasmodic style of garbage collection. It can also be accomplished quickly in time and with little space overhead. In particular, since blocks are not relocated, we do not have to worry about updating pointer values. Note that there are alternative ways to coalesce, if we separate the issues of what to do (that is, coalesce) and when to do it. The usual policy with regard to "when" is at deallocation time. One alternative policy is to coalesce at allocation time; if an allocation request causes an empty block to be split, then the resulting smaller empty block can be tested for coalescing with an adjacent empty block at that time. Still another alternative policy is not to coalesce at either allocation or deallocation, but to wait until an allocation request fails. At that time, all the blocks in memory can be scanned in address sequence, to simultaneously coalesce adjacent empty blocks and also regenerate the Free-list.

†11.3.1.3.2 Compaction. Unfortunately, coalescing cannot by itself prevent situations where memory may be only 50 percent utilized, and yet unable to satisfy a reasonable request. For example, memory could consist of alternating active and empty blocks all of size X, and the request could be for a block of size $X + 1$. In such situations, we need to compact the active blocks toward one end of the dynamic memory area, leaving the remainder as one large free block. In the discussion of compaction in Section 11.2.3.1, we were able to employ the regular structure of cells to advantage in two ways. First, COLLECT_1 (Algorithm 11.2) was able to swap active and empty cells between locations at opposite ends of memory, since all cells are of the same size. Second, it was straightforward to update pointers by means of forwarding addresses left in the old locations, since the detection of pointer values within cells obeyed easily computable rules.

The irregular structure of blocks makes swapping impossible; also, the detection of pointers within blocks can be difficult. Since the latter issue depends heavily upon details of implementation, we will not pursue it here. We simply note, in passing, two different approaches to the problem. One is to program for each block type (that is, record) a corresponding routine that knows how to find the pointers in such a block. Another is to make each block self-describing (see Section 3.3), and then use an interpreter to extract pointers. An interesting discussion of this problem can be found in Wodon [1969].

We turn from the issue of detecting pointers within blocks to that of computing the compaction. Since swapping is impossible, the general technique is that of *sliding compaction*, wherein all of the active blocks slide to one end, squeezing out the empty blocks in the process. The earliest algorithms for doing this were rather expensive in either time or space; so compaction of blocks, with associated pointer adjustment, was often regarded as a means of last resort. Several methods traded space for time by specifying that each block should contain extra space that would always be available to the compactor. We will refer to such an area within each block as the *utility field.* Compaction can then be conducted with three left-to-right, or *lo* to *hi*, passes over the blocks, as follows:

(a) As each active block Q is reached in the first scan, its forwarding address is stored in its utility field. The value of the forwarding address is easily computed as the value of the present address of Q minus the sum of the space in all the *holes* (empty blocks) to the left of Q.

(b) As each active block is reached in the second scan, the pointers are extracted and updated, using the forwarding addresses in the blocks to which they refer. Any pointers to the blocks from outside the dynamic memory area are also updated at this point.

(c) Now that all pointers are updated, the third scan can safely relocate each block, using its forwarding address again.

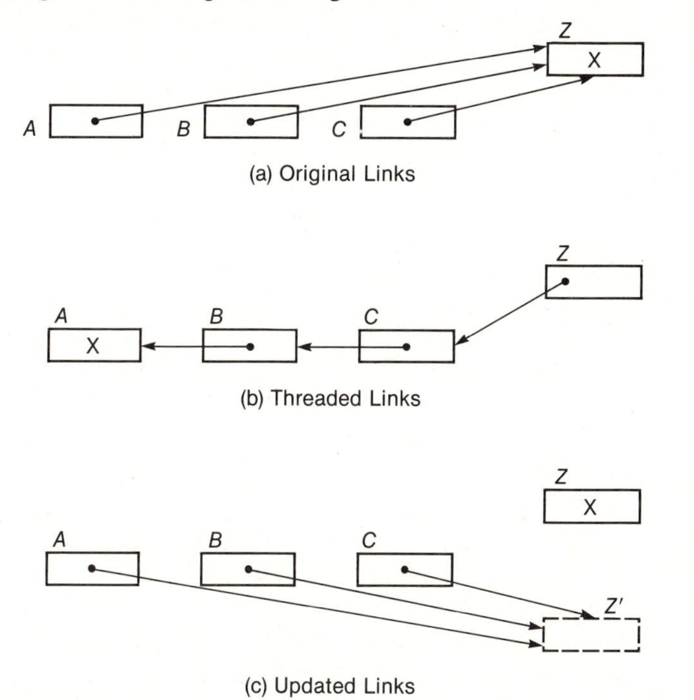

Figure 11.16 Pointer Transformations for Compaction

A significant improvement over earlier methods is a linear algorithm by Morris [1978] that requires just two passes, and also one extra bit for each pointer field. The essence of the method is the reversible transformation illustrated in Figure 11.16. We see in (a) of the figure a block at location Z that is referenced by several pointers. In (b) the tree pointers of (a) are *threaded* to form a sequential list, with the initial location Z now acting as list head, and with the non-pointer item X that originally resided at Z now serving to terminate the list. Subsequently, the forwarded location of the block is computed to be Z', after which the list in (b) is converted back to a tree in (c), with the pointer values being updated to the value Z'. Since all the pointers have now been updated, there is no further need to access them in their original locations; thus, it is safe to conclude the process by sliding the block to Z'.

There is one complication in performing the sequence of transformations shown in Figure 11.16 without an extra scan. It depends upon the links all being *up-pointers* – that is, pointing in the direction from *lo* to *hi.* This allows the updating to be applied as soon as the block at *Z* is reached, thereby restoring the information X that may be required in order to interpret the contents of the block. However, this complication can be remedied by treating the up-pointers in one scan, and then treating the *down-pointers* in a second scan from *hi* to *lo*. Morris's algorithm actually compacts memory by sliding active blocks from *lo* toward *hi* at the same time that it processes the down-pointers, and it presupposes a previous marking phase, as in garbage collection. We will illustrate the sequence of events during compaction using, instead, a variation by Jonkers [1979].[1] It does not depend upon prior marking, it does not require an extra bit per pointer, it uses two *lo* to *hi* scans, and it compacts memory from *hi* toward *lo*. Figure 11.17(a) depicts memory checkerboarded with active and empty blocks, and containing both up-pointers and down-pointers to block *Q*. There are pointers to the other blocks as well, but they are omitted in the interest of clarity. By the time that the first scan reaches *Q*, the up-pointers to *Q* have been threaded, as in (b). But now the sum of the holes to the left of *Q* is known, and the up-pointers can be updated, as in (c). Note that this also restores the contents of the header for block *Q*, thereby facilitating the interpretation of its contents. The first scan then continues to the end of the memory region and threads the down-pointers to *Q* as it does so, as in (d). Now when *Q* is reached in the second scan, it is safe to update all the down-pointers originating from blocks to the right, as in (e). Moreover, all blocks to the left of *Q* will have been relocated, and so *Q* can also be moved to its new location, as in (f).

The discussion of compaction in this section would appear to be very different from that of Section 11.2.3. They actually have much in common. In particular, one view of compaction in the earlier section was as a means of reclaiming garbage, following one of a variety of marking algorithms. The compaction techniques of this section are also relevant for garbage collection. We do not explicitly discuss the marking of multi-linked blocks, since it is the familiar business of searching a graph. But note that if blocks contain utility fields, these fields also provide an easy solution to the problem of finding space for a stack. Marking techniques based upon the utility field approach are described in Thorelli [1972]. But there is an even stronger common ground between compaction as discussed earlier and as treated here. Even for compacting fixed-size cells, the techniques of this section are sometimes preferred to that of COLLECT_1. This is so because of the sliding nature of the compaction. The original physical memory sequence of the cells of a List can be important in some applications, and COLLECT_1 jumbles this sequence.[2] Sliding compaction, on the other hand, preserves the so-called *genetic ordering* of the original physical sequence [Terashima and Goto 1978].

---

[1] For still another variation see Martin [1982].

[2] Recall that the list-moving method of Section 11.2.3.2.1 has a different type of virtue; it provides a linearizing compaction.

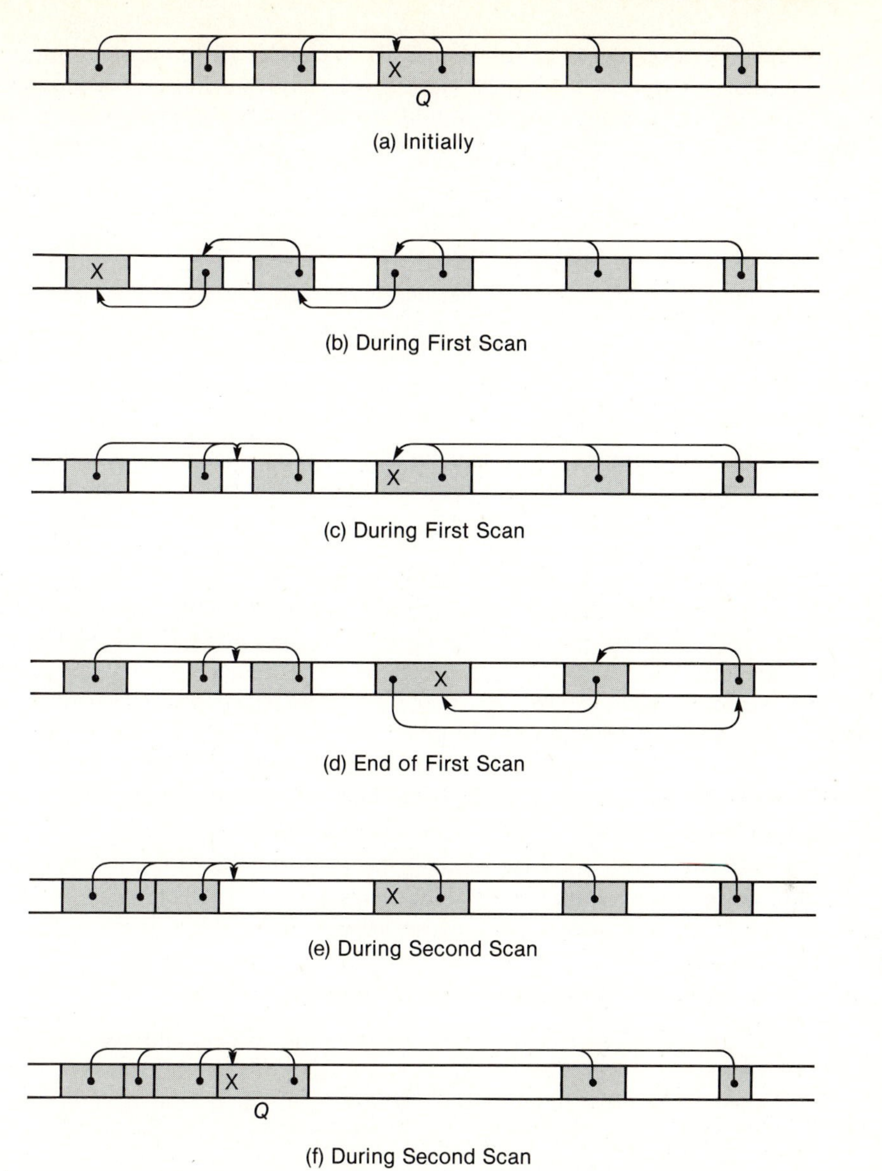

Figure 11.17 Progress of Jonkers' Compaction Algorithm

11.3.2 Buddy Systems

If we reflect upon what we have encountered so far in managing storage for variable-size blocks, it appears that allocation is moderately expensive, because it involves searching the Free-list, and reclamation is very expensive whenever compaction is required. Both of these problems can be side-stepped by choosing a different form of storage organization that leads to simpler algorithms for allocation and reclamation. The idea is that blocks should only exist in a fixed number of sizes $s_1 < s_2 < \cdots < s_m$, and that a split should always break a block B of size s_i into two *buddies* B_L and B_R of sizes s_{i-1} and s_{i-K}. Thus,

$$s_i = s_{i-1} + s_{i-K} \tag{11.3}$$

Subsequently, whenever B_L and B_R are both free, they can be recombined to reconstitute the original block. Moreover, neither B_L nor B_R can recombine *except* with its buddy. Reclamation is thus efficient because buddies always have a fixed address relationship, making it easy for a block to determine if its buddy is available for recombination. Allocation is made efficient by maintaining separate bi-directional lists for each block size s_i. (Why bi-directional?)

The original and simplest buddy system is the *binary buddy system*, corresponding to $K = 1$ in Eq. 11.3 [Knowlton 1965]. In this case, it is easy to see that blocks always split by dividing in half. With any of the buddy systems, it is important to be able to locate the buddy of a block quickly. For binary buddies, we can see that this is simply a matter of regarding the addresses of the blocks as binary numbers. The addresses of two buddies – for example, 'abc00000' and 'abc10000' – will always agree in their prefix portions, be opposite in one bit position, and have all zeros in their suffix portions. Thus, we can find the buddy of a block by simply inverting a particular bit position. Another way of regarding this is that the split of a block of size $s_i = 2^i$ at location L will give rise to two blocks of size $s_{i-1} = 2^{i-1}$, at locations L and $L + 2^{i-1}$. These matters are illustrated in Figure 11.18, which exhibits a hypothetical snapshot of a dynamic memory area organized as binary buddies. In this figure we can observe the following details:

- Blocks that have been split are denoted by empty circles, allocated blocks are denoted by solid circles, and empty blocks are denoted by rectangles.
- With each block is shown its address, in binary on the upper levels and in decimal on the lower levels.
- All empty blocks of a given size are linked together.

Details about the effectiveness of this organization will be addressed in Section 11.3.4. In general terms, however, we can see that this method engenders both internal fragmentation (any request must be rounded up to the next largest size $s_i = 2^i$) and external fragmentation (it may be impossible to satisfy a request, even though there are unallocated buddies with aggregate space in excess of the request). If the request sizes all happen to be slightly in excess of a power of two (such as 9, 17, 33, etc.) then the internal fragmentation for a binary buddy system can approach 50 percent. The problem is that the set of allowable sizes $\{s_i\}$ is too coarse. A resolution for this is to vary K in Eq. 11.3.[3] In particular, for $K = 2$, we have as $\{s_i\}$ the familiar Fibonacci numbers, yielding the *Fibonacci buddy system* [Hirschberg 1973]. When $K > 2$, we encounter *generalized Fibonacci buddy systems* [Hinds 1975]; for example, $K = 3$ leads to block sizes $\{1, 2, 3, 4, 6, 9, 13, 19, \ldots\}$.

---

[3] More accurately, specification of a solution for Eq. 11.3 depends not only upon a value for K, but also upon values for the K initial sizes $s_1, s_2, \ldots$.

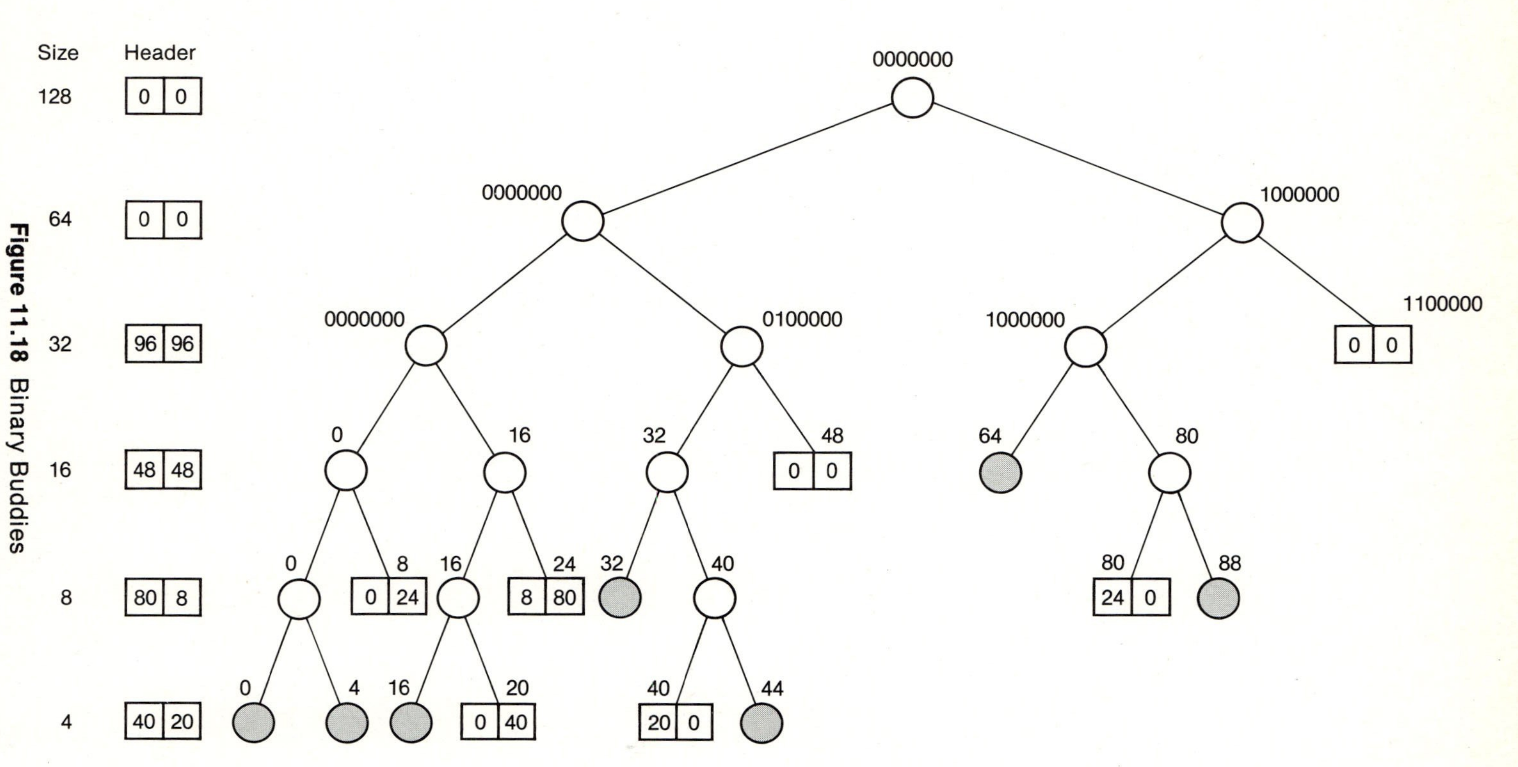

Figure 11.18 Binary Buddies

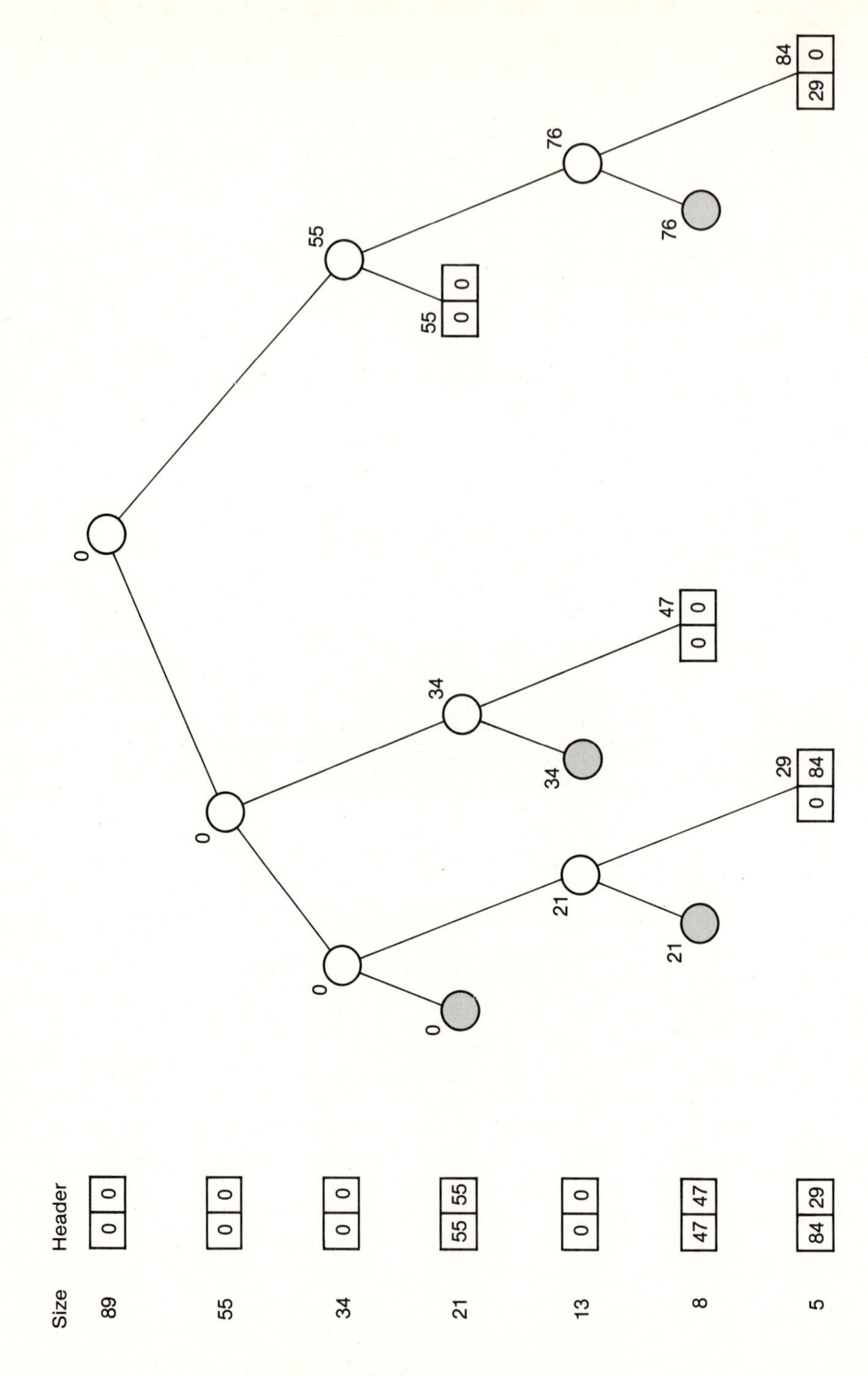

Figure 11.19 Fibonacci Buddies

Let us consider how a generalized Fibonacci buddy system might be implemented. As a starting point, Figure 11.19 is a hypothetical snapshot of an ordinary Fibonacci buddy organization analogous to Figure 11.18. It is easy to locate the binary buddy of a block, but the logic for computing a buddy block in the generalized case is apparently not so simple:

- If a block B is a left buddy of size s_i at location L, then its right buddy is of size s_{i-K+1} at location $L + s_i$, and they combine to form a block of size s_{i+1} at location L.
- If a block B is a right buddy of size s_i at location L, then its left buddy is of size s_{i+K-1} at location $L - s_{i+K-1}$, and they combine to form a block of size s_{i+K} at location $L - s_{i+K-1}$.

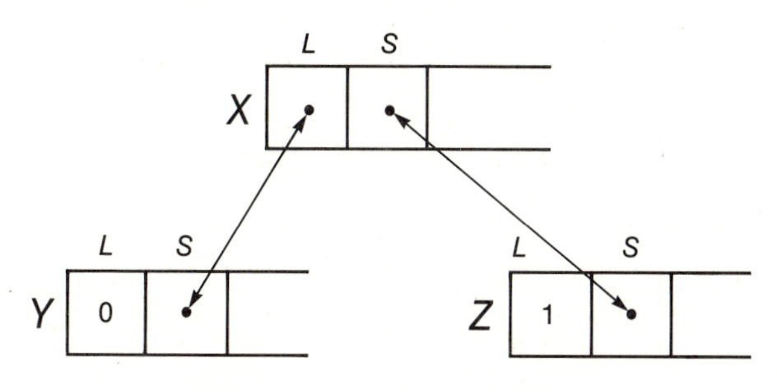

Figure 11.20 Tagging Buddies

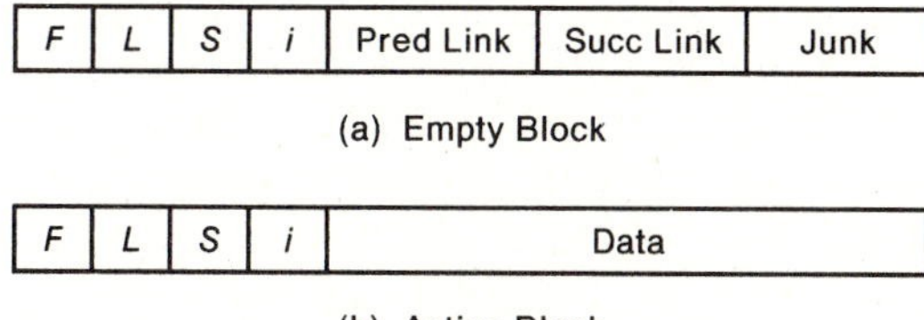

Figure 11.21 Buddy Block Formats

In fact, it is possible to keep track of the buddies elegantly and simply, as illustrated in Figure 11.20, by means of two boolean values L(eft) and S(ave) in each block [Cranston and Thomas 1975]. When a block X splits into a left buddy block Y and a right buddy block Z, where Y is by convention the larger of the two, then we assign $L_Y := 0$ and $S_Y := L_X$ on the left, and $L_Z := 1$ and $S_Z := S_X$ on the right. Recombination is accomplished by discarding the L bits of the offspring and assigning $L_X := S_Y$ and $S_X := S_Z$. In addition to the L and S bits, we need other information in the blocks. Each block requires, of course, a boolean value F(ree). It also needs the value of i, as an encoding of the size, for indexing into a vector of sizes s_i. Note that it is quite easy to pack F, L, S, i together on most machines. Finally, each empty block must have space for its two bi-directional pointers. Combining these items, we obtain the pictorial formats shown in Figure 11.21 and

```
const  K = {1 for binary, 2 for Fibonacci, etc.}

type   cursor = lo .. hi;
       sizcod = 1 .. sizmax;
       itemicity = (fill,links,tags);
       item = record
          case itemicity of
             fill:  (byte: char);
             links: (pred,succ: integer);
             tags:  (free,left,save: boolean;
                          code: sizcod);
       end;
       list = record {header for a list of size s_i}
          size: integer;
          pred,succ: integer;
       end;

var    lists: array [sizcod] of list;
       store: array [cursor] of item;
```

Figure 11.22 Pascal Syntax for Buddy System Data

the Pascal formats shown in Figure 11.22. In the latter figure, the values of *lists* [*i*].*size* must be initialized to the values corresponding to the choice of K − for example, the ordinary Fibonacci numbers for $K = 2$.

The logic of requesting a block under the buddy system is spelled out in the function RQST_BUDDY (Algorithm 11.6). It first looks for the smallest adequate size with a non-empty list.[4] If that size is too large then a block from that list is split, and this process is iterated with the buddy closer in size (with the unused buddy being inserted in the proper list). Three auxiliary routines of a straightforward nature are not shown but are required, as follows:

1. DETACH (*p*: *cursor*) − which deletes the block located at *p* from its doubly linked list. If either the predecessor or the successor link is zero (indicating the list head), then the size code in *store* [*p*] can be used to index the proper list.
2. ATTACH (*i*: *sizcod*; *p*: *cursor*) − which inserts the block located at *p* in the *i*th doubly linked list.
3. SET_TAGS (*p*: *cursor*; *a,b,c*: boolean; *s*: *sizcod*) − which assigns the parameters *a,b,c,s* to the tags in the block located at *p*.

The reverse process is illustrated by the procedure RTN_BUDDY (Algorithm 11.7). The returned block is iteratively combined with any buddy blocks that are completely empty, and finally the largest possible combined block is inserted in its proper list. Note that the algorithms RQST_BUDDY and RTN_BUDDY will

[4] In practice, one would have to decide whether to adjust the parameter *n* in either RQST_BUDDY or in the caller in order to account for the space required by the header tags.

```
function RQST_BUDDY (n: integer): integer;

var     i,j: integer;
        p,q: cursor;

begin
   RQST_BUDDY := 0;              {in case no space is available}
   if n <= lists [sizmax].size then begin
      i := 1;
      while n > lists [i].size do
         i := i + 1;              {find smallest adequate size}
      j := i;
      while lists [j].succ = 0 do
         j := j + 1;           {find non-empty list}
      if j <= sizmax then begin
         p := lists [j].succ;
         DETACH (p);
         while (j > i) and (j - K >= 1) do begin        {split}
            q := p + lists [j - 1].size;
            SET_TAGS (q,true,false,store [p].save,j - K);
            SET_TAGS (p,true,true,store [p].left,j - 1);
            if i > j - K then begin           {use larger buddy}
               ATTACH (j - K,q);
               j := j - 1;
            end else begin                    {use smaller buddy}
               ATTACH (j - 1,p);
               j := j - K;  p := q;
            end;
         end;
         store [p].free := false;
         RQST_BUDDY := p;
      end;
   end;
end;
```

Algorithm 11.6 RQST_BUDDY

work for any value of K, with proper initialization of *lists* [i].*size*. However, for the case of $K = 1$ (that is, binary buddies), one might choose to simplify them slightly. In accordance with the objective stated at the beginning of this section, buddy system organizations are generally able to allocate and deallocate blocks of storage faster than any of the methods of Section 11.3.1. (However, what would happen if the activity consisted alternately of requests and returns of a block of smallest size?) We will say more about this, and about the relative merits of the method for various values of K, in Section 11.3.4.

```
procedure RTN_BUDDY (p: cursor);

var     buddy: item;
        done: boolean;
        j,j0: sizcod;
        p0,q: cursor;

begin
   done := false;  store [p].free := true;
   p0 := p;  j0 := store [p0].code;
   while (store [p].code < sizmax) and (not done) do begin
      j := store [p].code;
      if store [p].left then begin
         q := p + lists [j].size;  buddy := store [q];
         if not ((buddy.free) and (buddy.code = j - K + 1)) then
            done := true
         else begin
            DETACH (q);
            SET_TAGS (p,true,store [p].save,buddy.save,j + 1);
         end;
      end else begin
         q := p - lists [j + K - 1].size;  buddy := store [q];
         if not ((buddy.free) and (buddy.code = j + K - 1)) then
            done := true
         else begin
            DETACH (q);
            SET_TAGS (q,true,buddy.save,store [p].save,buddy.code + 1);
            p := q;
         end;
      end;
   end;
   if done then ATTACH (j,p)
            else ATTACH (sizmax,p);
end;
```

Algorithm 11.7 RTN_BUDDY

11.3.3 Multiple Storage Pools

One of the oldest ideas for organizing storage to satisfy requests of different sizes is still one of the best, albeit somewhat more complicated [Ross 1967]. It is to maintain separate lists of blocks of various sizes, as in the buddy system. As with buddies, if the list with the optimum size for a request is empty, then a block from a larger size list may be split. One difference between this method and the buddy system is that now recombination does not follow such simple rules; in practice, boundary tags might be used for the purpose. Another difference is that the set of sizes can be chosen arbitrarily, to try to match the actual pattern of request sizes. If the number of distinct sizes is moderately large, then it would be sensible to organize the list heads as a binary search tree, thereby guaranteeing logarithmic rather than linear search times. The issue of overhead is not important in this case because the tree structure is superimposed upon the list heads rather than upon the individual blocks (compare the remark in the last paragraph of Section 11.3.1.2). Note that with multiple storage pools, as with buddy systems, allocation policy is a matter of finding the right list as opposed to selecting an item from a list.

If the pattern of request sizes is accurately known, as is often the case – for example, the sizes requested by an operating system for its various standard data structures – then the multiple storage pool idea can work very well. In cases where these sizes are not known, however, the sizes "in stock" may correspond very poorly, and thus lead to fragmentation that is actually much worse than with a single storage pool. An effective way to deal with this is to have the storage allocation system vary its inventory of block sizes dynamically, as a function of the recent history of requests [Leverett and Hibbard 1982; Oldehoeft and Allan 1985].

11.3.4 Analyses and Comparisons

At the very beginning of our discussion of variable-size blocks, we stressed the extreme difficulty of obtaining precise measures of the goodness of various policies of organization, allocation, and reclamation. For one, there are a very large number of possible combinations of these policies. For another, orthogonal to this combinatorial complexity are the issues of:

- the distribution of request sizes;
- the distribution of arrival times of these requests;
- the distribution of occupancy times of these requests.

Although theoretical results are meager in comparison to what is known for other areas, such as searching and sorting, they are nonetheless interesting and helpful. However, most of the available wisdom about choosing an optimal combination of policies derives from a variety of simulation experiments. In the next two sections, we will discuss these two approaches in turn.

†11.3.4.1 Theoretical Results. Suppose that we have a storage policy that is in equilibrium, such that there are M empty blocks and N active blocks; then let p be the probability that a request for a block of a given size cannot be matched exactly, so that an empty block must be split. In such an equilibrium situation, it can be shown that $M = pN/2$ (see Exercise 11.14). For the not uncommon situation where $p \approx 1$, this yields $M = N/2$, otherwise known as the *fifty-percent rule.* With these circumstances, in other words, there will tend to be half as many empty blocks as active blocks.

Now let M,N,p retain their meaning, and denote by f the average size of an empty block and by r the average size of an active block. The effective storage utilization can then be expressed as $\rho = rN/(fM + rN)$. It can be shown that in equilibrium $f = r$, and so $\rho = 1/(1 + \frac{1}{2}p)$. For $p \approx 1$ again, this yields $\rho = 2/3$, otherwise known as the *two-thirds rule* [Gelenbe 1971]. In such an equilibrium situation, in other words, storage utilization will be about two-thirds.

Although the two preceding results are generalizations that do not take into account much of the dynamic variability in storage policies, they are nonetheless helpful in interpreting the behavior of such policies. Of a different nature, a number of more precise results have been obtained by Robson. They characterize the worst-case amount of memory required to satisfy a sequence of storage allocations and deallocations, under the assumption that coalescing is performed but not compaction. More formally, let $N(M,n)$ be the smallest amount of memory N such that:

(i) the size of an individual block never exceeds n, and

(ii) the total amount of allocated space never exceeds M.

Robson [1971] has shown that $N(M,2) = \lfloor(3M - 1)/2$. In other words, even when blocks are requested only in sizes one and two, then no matter what allocation policy is used, it is possible to have memory just two-thirds full and yet not be able to satisfy a request. Note that this result, although consonant with the two-thirds rule of the preceding paragraph, is very specific and much stronger. Exact values for other values of n are not so easily obtained; however, Robson has shown that with $N(n) = \lim_{M\to\infty} N(M,n)/M$, then

$$0.5 \lg n \leq N(n) \leq .84 \lg n + O(1) \tag{11.4}$$

The preceding results indicate the limits that can be obtained with *any* storage allocation policy. What can be said about specific policies? Robson [1977b] has also shown that first-fit is not far from optimal, with lower and upper bounds (analogous to Eq. 11.4) of $0.5 \lg n$ and $\lg n$. For best-fit, on the other hand, Robson demonstrates a sequence of requests such that Mn words are needed – that is, $N(n) \geq n$.

Turning to the buddy systems, there is the following analogous result [Knuth 1973a] for binary buddies:

$$r \leq N(2^r) \leq 2(r + 1) \tag{11.5}$$

A more practical question concerns the relative usefulness of buddy systems for various values of K in Eq. 11.3. Recall that the rationale for Fibonacci buddies was that providing more block sizes would serve to reduce the internal fragmentation. It has been shown analytically that this does occur over a broad range of request size distributions, with typical internal fragmentation (expressed in terms of overallocation) of 1.24 for $K = 2$, as opposed to 1.33 for $K = 1$ [Peterson and Norman 1977; Russell 1977].

Although it was not stated and may not have been apparent, all but the last of the results cited in this section are derived solely through combinatorial reasoning. None of the probabilistic concerns cited at the outset play any part in this section, although they do so in the next. There are many other pretty combinatorial results pertaining to storage allocation, often in terms of the well-known *bin-packing* problem. A good introduction to these more general results is Coffman [1983].

†11.3.4.2 Experimental Results. Since the analysis of storage allocation is intractable in its full generality, we must fall back upon well-conceived and carefully executed simulations for guidance in choosing among dynamic storage policies. There are really two types of simulations. Some are primarily directed at tuning a particular system [§], and others are concerned to obtain more general conclusions. We will not say much about the former here but just abstract from some of them, for the benefit of the interested reader. Two features are of particular interest:

1. In actual practice, the distribution of block sizes is usually very irregular, characterized by several sharp peaks.
2. The most effective way to deal with this irregularity seems to be to use multiple storage pools.

The input parameters to a simulation have already been cited: policies for storage organization, allocation, and reclamation; and distributions characterizing request sizes, arrival times, and occupancy times. With regard to output, there are two principal figures of merit. One is a measure of the efficiency of memory utilization, and the other is a measure of the speed of the algorithms that implement the different policies. There is no difficulty in measuring time, but the measurement of storage efficiency must be somewhat indirect. We know that the two ways in which memory becomes unavailable are through internal fragmentation and external fragmentation. The first of these is easily computed as the excess of what is allocated over what was requested; but the second is a relative matter. Empty blocks that are too small for one series of requests may be just fine for a different series. Therefore, external fragmentation is usually computed by running until a request cannot be satisfied, and then computing the total percentage of unallocated memory at that point.

The fifty-percent rule tells something about the degree of external fragmentation. In practice, however, the ratio M/N is often closer to 40 percent than to 50 percent. This is partly due to the systematic splitting of active blocks from the right end of empty blocks (see Section 11.3.1.2). It is also a consequence of the fact that the release sequence of active blocks is not random, but rather is correlated with their age. These observations, found in Shore [1977], follow from an earlier experiment measuring the relative amounts of external fragmentation under first-fit and best-fit [Shore 1975]. In this earlier study, the difference in storage efficiency for the two allocation policies was not great (only about 3 percent), and it varied with the nature of the request size distributions.[5] Storage efficiency also varied with the frequency of requests that were large compared to the average request. A useful conclusion is that when this frequency is large, then first-fit is to be preferred over best-fit, and vice-versa. The reason is that first-fit, by preferentially allocating from one end of memory, tends to encourage the formation of large available blocks at the other end. There are also two slightly subtle corollaries to this conclusion. The next-fit allocation policy systematically eliminates the bias toward one end of memory in first-fit, and the optimal-fit policy assumes that no such bias exists. In fact, the elimination of bias can cause next-fit to have storage utilization inferior to

---

[5] These included uniform, normal, exponential, and hyperexponential distributions.

that of either first-fit or best-fit [Bayes 1977]. Also, the effects of this bias can cause first-fit to typically outperform optimal-fit after all [Page 1982].

There are also interesting experimental results concerning external fragmentation in buddy systems. We saw in the preceding section that Fibonacci buddies definitely have less internal fragmentation than binary buddies, typically 24 percent overallocation as compared with 33 percent. Unfortunately, they accomplish this by introducing split-off blocks that are smaller and less useful. Simulations show that, in fact, the *sum* of the internal and external fragmentations is relatively constant [Peterson and Norman 1977]. This total fragmentation seems to be in the range $35-45$ percent, no matter what buddy system is employed!

Remember, though, that storage utilization is only half of the story. Let us turn now to the issue of how quickly dynamic storage can be managed with various combinations of policies. One early simulation compared three very different policies[6] – first-fit, binary buddy, and multiple storage pools [Purdom et al. 1971]. In terms of storage utilization, multiple storage pools were slightly better than first-fit, and both were much better than binary buddy. With regard to speed, however, binary buddy was always much faster than first-fit and often faster than multiple storage pools.

Nielsen [1977] conducted an extremely ambitious and thorough series of simulation experiments. First, he constructed a base test load of storage requests founded upon a mixture of distributions, and then he developed 17 other test loads as variations of the base load. He also combined organization, allocation, and reclamation policies in various manners to obtain 35 distinct dynamic storage policies. Rather than conduct $18 \times 35 = 1890$ experiments, he began by applying all 35 policies to the base test load. After analyzing those results, he selected 7 of the best storage policies and then applied them to the other 17 test loads in a second phase. The 35 policies fell into 6 categories according to the method of storage organization, as follows:

- I all blocks in one list ordered by address
- II a Free-list ordered by address
- III a Free-list organized as a stack or a queue
- IV multiple storage pools
- V binary buddies
- VI a Free-list ordered by size

The individual policies within these categories tested allocation strategies of first-fit, best-fit, and next-fit. The reclamation strategies included garbage collection, coalescing, and compaction.

The first phase yielded the following general conclusions:

- Reclamation is slower with just the Free-list organized by address than it is with all the blocks ordered by address, but allocation is faster.
- Next-fit is slightly inferior with respect to storage utilization, but it is dramatically faster.

---

[6] The probability distributions employed here were Poisson for arrival, geometric for size, and exponential for life.

- Organizing the Free-list as a stack or a queue is a poor idea in terms of both storage utilization and speed.
- Multiple storage pools are decidedly effective in terms of both storage utilization and speed.
- Buddy systems are very fast but are the worst in terms of storage utilization.
- A Free-list ordered by size provides acceptable storage utilization, but it is non-competitive in speed with the other organizations.
- A good dynamic storage policy can typically provide better than 80 percent storage utilization (except for buddy systems).

The detailed results from the first phase led Nielsen to choose the following 7 particular policies for more extensive testing in the second phase:

A	organization I	next-fit	coalesce upon allocation
B	organization I	next-fit	coalesce upon deallocation
C	organization II	next-fit	coalesce upon deallocation
D	organization II	next-fit	garbage collect and compact
E	organization IV		garbage collect
F	organization V		combine upon deallocation
G	organization V		combine only when out of space

Policy *E* performed the best both in terms of storage utilization and speed. Policy *B* performed surprisingly well except when storage was heavily used, leading to somewhat longer allocation searches. In the two buddy system strategies, policy *G* was distinctly superior to policy *F*, which frequently would combine buddies and then immediately have to split them again. The wisdom of deferring recombination was also reflected in the superiority of policy *B* to policy *A*. Finally, neither policy *C* nor *D* was as good as either policy *A* or *B*. In other words, these experiments indicate that linking all blocks into one address-ordered list is better than just linking empty blocks into a Free-list. Nielsen's overall ranking of the policies was as follows: *E*, *G*, *B*, *F*, *A*, *D*, *C*.

As ambitious and comprehensive as Nielsen's results are, it is wise to exercise some caution in selecting a policy for dynamic storage management. Just as in the case of choosing a hashing function, the selection depends a great deal upon the particular application. The degree of ambiguity in these matters is well illustrated by the question, "Which is relatively better, first-fit or best-fit?" We saw with the theoretical treatment of the previous section that best-fit has a disastrous worst case compared to that of first-fit. However, such worst-case behaviors are not encountered in practice. With regard to the experimental side, there is poor agreement. Some find best-fit to be better, and others find that first-fit is superior. The latter conclusion is related to the earlier cited tendency to generate large blocks at one end; this tendency has the paradoxical effect that it also causes first fit to yield a psuedo-best fit!

11.4 OVERVIEW

The objective in this chapter is simple to state. It is the dynamic management of pieces of memory so that a user program will always be able to obtain a piece when it needs it, and be able to do so economically. However, the problem is not a trivial one to solve, as evidenced by the great number of approaches that have been tried. This diversity reflects the fact that the successful use of modern programming environments, with ever larger address spaces and with increasing use of dynamic structures, is critically dependent upon efficient solutions to the problem. Although this chapter is organized principally along the dichotomy between fixed and variable size pieces of memory, many of the same concerns – marking, pointer updating, etc. – can be found in both contexts. An excellent alternative survey of many of these pervasive issues is provided by Cohen [1981]. Hopefully, it is clear by now why we have chosen to treat this subject after that of searching. An efficient implementation of memory management depends, after all, upon skillful use of the techniques of Chapter 10.

Sections 11.2.4 and 11.3.4 already distill many of the significant conclusions about alternative ways to solve the memory management problem, so we will simply conclude with a few remarks of a more general nature. First, we cannot obtain a solution "for free." We must plan, except in rare circumstances, to spend extra memory resource if we do not want to see the storage manager usurp most of the cycles of the computer. In the case of garbage collection, we saw in Section 11.2.4 that an efficient equilibrium point occurs when the actual requirements are only about two-thirds of the total available space. Remarkably, we saw the same operating ratio of two-thirds in our discussion of management of blocks in Section 11.3.4.1. The two-thirds ratio is of course only a generalization, but we can expect to run into severe degradation when we operate much beyond it. Much of the ability to crowd this ratio successfully, to better than 80 percent, depends upon tailoring the memory management strategy to the environment in which it will be used. This is reminiscent of the importance of analyzing an application before adopting a hash function. Our final advice concerns the benefits of being "lazy." One extreme opinion on the topic of memory management is that it is profitable to trivialize the allocation problem by combining or compacting blocks of memory as frequently as possible. (The analogous point of view for cells is to use reference counts.) In quite a few cases, as evidenced in the investigations of Section 11.3.4.2, it is really more economical to defer such activity until it cannot be avoided.

11.5 BIBLIOGRAPHIC NOTES

- One early algorithm for copying a List is $O(n^2)$ in time without mark bits, and still another is $O(n \lg n)$ in time by using mark bits [Lindstrom 1974]. The earliest $O(n)$ algorithm requires that the new List be allocated in a contiguous block of storage; moreover, it also requires arithmetic upon the pointer values

[Fisher 1975]. There is a later $O(n)$ algorithm with better performance that again requires contiguity [Clark 1978].

- There are several measures by which to assess the relative advantage of parallel garbage collection over serial garbage collection. These matters are discussed in Hickey and Cohen [1984] and Wadler [1976].

- Experiments conducted with memory management for the purpose of tuning particular systems are Bozman et al. [1984] directed at the IBM VM/SP operating system, Hanson [1977] directed at a SNOBOL4 system, Margolin et al. [1971] directed at the IBM CP/CMS operating system, and Marlin [1979] directed at a Pascal system.

11.6 REFERENCE TO TERMINOLOGY

automatic allocation, 561
† backward pointer, 576
best-fit, 588
binary buddies, 600
blocks, 562
† boundary tags, 592
buddy system, 600
† CDR-linearization, 574
cells, 562
† coalescing, 591
† collector, 583
† compacting, 569
† down-pointer, 598
dynamic allocation, 562
external fragmentation, 585
Fibonacci buddies, 600
† fifty-percent rule, 607
first-fit, 588
† forward pointer, 576
† forwarding address, 570
garbage collection, 565
† genetic ordering, 598
† hash linking, 581
holes, 597
internal fragmentation, 585
marking, 565
† mutator, 583
next-fit, 589
† optimal-fit, 590
† priority search tree, 615
reference counting, 565
† semi-space, 573
† sliding compaction, 596
splinter, 588
static allocation, 561
† two-thirds rule, 608
† up-pointer, 598
worst-fit, 588

11.7 EXERCISES

Section 11.2

11.1 If the algorithm COLLECT_1 is used to compact the following scattered List, then what will be the contents of the old and the new List locations after the compaction? Show your results in the style of Figure 11.3.

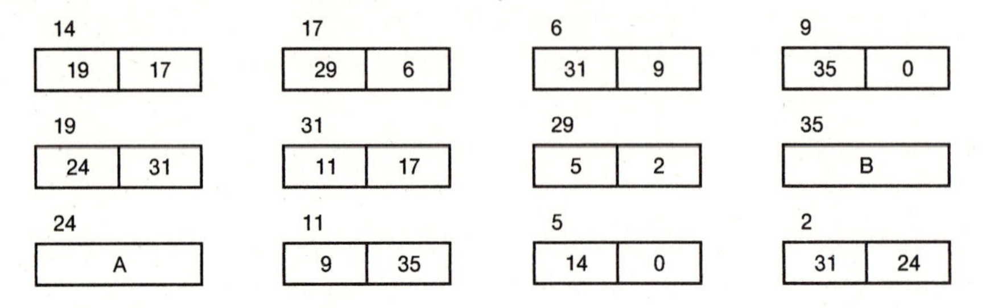

††11.2 [Dijkstra 1976] A generalization of COLLECT_1 is the problem of the *Dutch National Flag*. Imagine that we have a row of cans, each of which contains a single red or white or blue pebble. The object is to exchange pebbles between cans until their contents are: all those with red pebbles, then all those with white pebbles, then all those with blue pebbles. The two permissible operations are (i) to inspect the contents of a can, and (ii) to exchange the contents of two cans. Write a procedure that mimics this situation by operating upon a one-dimensional array. Your algorithm should use only a few working registers, should never inspect a given pebble more than once, and should strive for the minimum number of exchanges. Demonstrate the correctness of your program by applying it to a few sets of cans with random contents, and also to some degenerate cases – for example, all red or white or blue pebbles, pebbles already sorted, etc. What can you say about the average number of exchanges performed by your algorithm?

†11.3 Trace the operation of the algorithm MOVE_LIST on the following List, showing the symbolic values of the pointers in the old List and in the new List at each iteration, as in Figure 11.4.

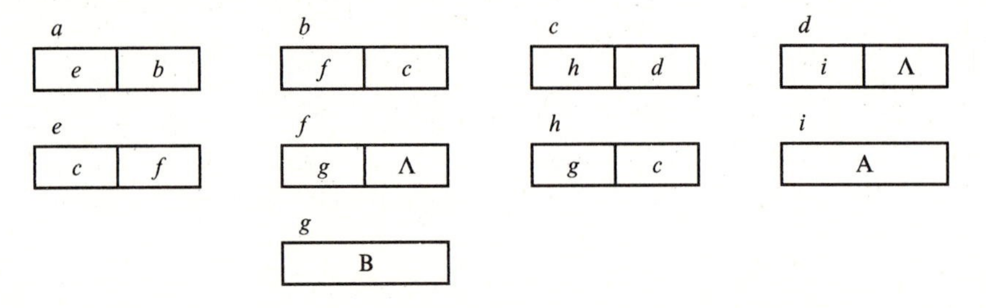

†11.4 Assume that Robson's List-copying technique is applied to the accompanying List.

(a) Redraw the List to show the forward and backward pointers, in the style of Figure 11.5.

(b) Show the contents of the old List after the first phase, as in Figure 11.6(a), and the contents of the new List after the second phase, as in Figure 11.6(b).

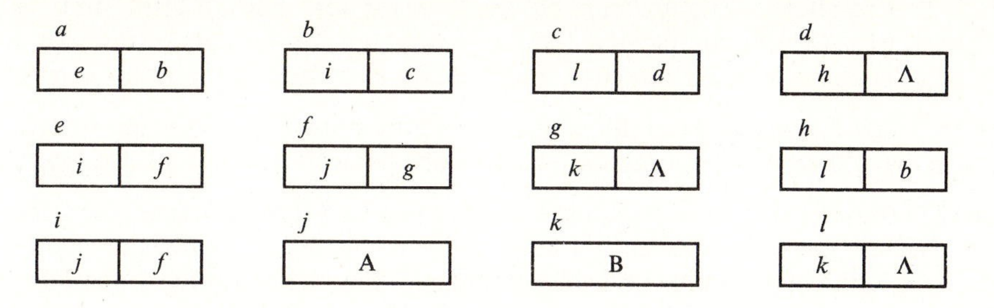

†11.5 Derive the expected number of exchanges performed by the algorithm COLLECT_1, assuming that the expectation of a cell being free is given by the probability f.

††11.6 Write a procedure that implements Robson's List copying algorithm. Test your program by using it to copy the List of Figure 11.3(a).

Section 11.3

11.7 Explain as concisely as possible the terms external and internal fragmentation, and the distinction between them.

11.8 Explain as concisely as possible the terms coalescing and compaction, and the distinction between them.

11.9 Suppose that we have a memory of the indicated number of units, and the following sequence of allocations and deallocations:

A − 4 units	E − 1 unit	H − 3 units
B − 7 units	F − 3 units	release F
release B	release A	I − 2 units
C − 1 unit	G − 1 unit	release D
D − 1 unit	release E	release G

Draw pictures of memory, showing the locations of A, B, etc., and the disposition of free storage at the conclusion of this sequence. (*Note*: Give some thought to displaying this data in a clear fashion.)

(a) Do so for a first-fit strategy with 15 units, LIFO return, no coalescing.

(b) Do so for a best-fit strategy with 15 units, LIFO return, no coalescing.

(c) Do so for a binary buddy strategy with 16 units.

(d) Do so for a Fibonacci buddy strategy with 13 units, splitting the larger buddy to the left.

†11.10 [McCreight 1985] Organizing memory blocks in a binary tree presents two problems. The first is that we need to be able to retrieve blocks along two different dimensions − location and size. The Cartesian tree of Exercise 6.24 might be used for this. However, it does not solve the second problem, that the resulting binary tree can become very imbalanced. The *priority search tree*, using rebalancing techniques from Section 10.3.3, solves both problems. In a priority search tree used for memory management, location is a primary dimension of organization, and the size of the largest node (block) in the left subtree is a secondary dimension of organization. The resulting structure can be used to support both first-fit and best-fit allocation with $O(\lg n)$ complexity. Describe in detail the formats of the tree nodes and the rules to be used for insertion and deletion in order to obtain this capability.

††11.11 Write procedures to allocate and reclaim storage blocks using first-fit, for the case that the blocks are organized as a priority search tree, as in Exercise 11.10.

††11.12 Assume that memory blocks contain just two types of items, the first type being a header that contains both a label and a count of the number of pointers in that block, and the second type being pointers to the beginning locations of blocks in the memory region. Write a program to implement Jonkers' compaction algorithm for such blocks. Test your program against the memory blocks shown scattered in locations 1 through 50 in the following table. Display the memory contents after both passes of the algorithm.

location	items
3	*A* – 3, 15, 3, 40
9	*B* – 2, 40, 3
15	*C* – 1, 15
21	*D* – 4, 27, 9, 3, 27
27	*E* – 0
34	*F* – 2, 9, 40
40	*G* – 5, 9, 15, 9, 40, 34

11.13 Prove that splitting and recombination of Fibonacci buddies cannot be accomplished with less than two bits per block.

†11.14 [Knuth 1973a] Suppose that memory is checkerboarded with M empty blocks and N active blocks, of the four types:

H – a hole (that is, an empty block)
A – an active block between two holes
B – an active block between a hole and an active block
C – an active block between two active blocks

Also, let p be the probability that a request for a block of a given size cannot be matched exactly, so that an empty block must be split. Assuming that blocks are released at random, show that if the storage policy is in equilibrium, such that the value of M tends to remain constant under insertions and deletions, then $M = pN/2$.

††11.15 Write a set of programs with which to conduct your own simulation experiments with dynamic memory algorithms. In addition to particular allocation and reclamation algorithms, such as Algorithms 11.4–11.7, you will need to develop (a) procedures to generate requests of various sizes and lifetimes, (b) a driver program to control the simulation, and (c) auxiliary procedures to gather and display pertinent data.

12

ISSUES WITH SECONDARY MEMORY

"Teach me not the art of remembering, but the art of forgetting, for I remember things I do not wish to remember, but I cannot forget things I wish to forget."

Cicero,
Themistocles in *De Finibus*,
Bk ii, Ch 32, Sec 104

It is a familiar observation that when the dimensions of a phenomenon change by orders of magnitude, then we have not just a qualitatively different phenomenon, but a completely different one. This is clearly so when we compare travelling between two locations by foot, and by car, and by airplane. It is also a conspicuous feature in the transition from primary memory to secondary memory for a computer. In all the preceding chapters, the fact that primary memory is directly addressable, fast, volatile, and relatively expensive was responsible for numerous choices about data structures and algorithms in the interests of efficiency.

Secondary memory is not directly addressable from within a program; data must be explicitly transmitted from secondary memory to primary memory before it can be used. Secondary memory may be very fast by human standards, but it is several orders of magnitude slower than primary memory. For any computation that depends heavily upon the use of secondary memory, this difference will be directly reflected in an execution time that is very much greater. On other side of the coin, the data in secondary storage can persist for long periods; so the greatly reduced cost over that of primary memory makes it the only viable medium when we must retain large volumes of data.

With secondary memory, sizes as well as speeds typically vary by several orders of magnitude from those of primary memory. We will see that this causes the quest for optimum performance to lead to representation choices that are very different from some choices made in earlier chapters. This will be notably true, for example, in the way we use trees, and in the way we deal with overflow when hashing. Also, pointers are powerful agents for constructing data structures in primary memory, but "bare" pointers are generally unacceptable in secondary memory.

Secondary memory actually serves another purpose as well, that of providing a reservoir of working memory during large calculations. Thus, during operations upon large arrays that cannot all fit in main memory at the same time, we might partition the arrays and then explicitly transfer sub-arrays back and forth between primary and secondary memory during the calculation. Or if a program is so large that it will not all fit in main memory at the same time, then we might repeatedly *overlay* one piece of program (that is no longer needed) with another piece of program. If an excess of needed working memory over available primary memory were the only problem, then by using virtual memory (to be described in Section 12.2) we could practically make that reason disappear. However, the second need still remains – to be able to save or archive data over a period of time. For this, there is no substitute for having non-volatile secondary storage.

Our first concern will be to describe the principal types of secondary storage, for the benefit of readers not already acquainted with them. Section 12.2 is then devoted to an account of virtual memory. The major part of this chapter is Section 12.3, wherein we explore several alternative schemes for allocating files of data to secondary memory. Finally, in Section 12.4, we consider the important topic of multi-attribute files, which are the basis for various database organizations.

12.1 STORAGE DEVICES

The general character of all storage devices is that performing input from a device to main memory or output from main memory to a device involves two time intervals, as follows:

1. There is a delay time while finding the location of the information on the storage medium; the length of this delay depends upon the device (and the location), but not upon the quantity of information to be transferred.
2. There is a transfer time for actually sending the information; this transfer time depends both upon the device and upon the quantity of information that is to be transmitted.

In almost all cases, the rate of data transfer, expressed in bytes per second, is at least an order of magnitude slower than the corresponding rate for accessing data from main memory, and the delay time is usually several orders of magnitude worse than the transfer time. With these factors, it is important to minimize having the computer wait for the completion of input/output, or I/O. There are two means for accomplishing this.

One is to transmit a large block of information on each I/O operation, thus amortizing the delay time per byte of data transferred. Another means, available in all except the simplest of current machines, is to attach the storage devices to *channels*, which are in reality computers dedicated to performing the I/O. A channel can run independently of the CPU, after the CPU has presented it with a special program that specifies what is required of it. Thus, the CPU and the channels on a computer can be running simultaneously, and the CPU is not required to sit and wait until I/O is completed. There is one situation where the CPU may have to wait for the channel to finish an operation – when they both try to access main memory at the same time. Whenever the channel needs to do I/O of an item of data in the main memory, it usurps control from the CPU for just long enough to accomplish it. This is called *cycle stealing*, and is transparent to the user. Although there are a variety of storage devices, we will concentrate our attention upon tapes, disks, and drums since they are by far the most important devices.

12.1.1 Tapes

The most common size of magnetic tape for computers is 1/2 inch in width and 2400 feet long. Data is recorded as bits along a number of parallel tracks, usually eight for data and one for parity (see Section 8.2.5). With this arrangement one byte, or character, can be recorded at a time across the width, and so the important parameter is density of recording along the length. This is designated in terms of *bpi*, or bits per inch (although it would perhaps be more meaningful to speak of bytes per inch). Recording densities have steadily increased over the years, with 800, 1600, and 6250 bpi now being common. A fundamental fact about tapes is that they do not move except when performing I/O. Therefore, any operation using a tape must first accelerate it from rest to its operating speed (typically, 125 inches per second), then do the data transfer, and finally decelerate it to rest again. This means that for typical figures of 1600 bpi and 125 inches per second, we have a data transfer rate of 200,000 bytes/second. The starting and stopping have several consequences. One is a delay time on the order of 20 milliseconds before the next record can be read or written, and another is a necessarily unused area on the tape, or *inter-record gap* (IRG), between successive blocks of data. There is also a more subtle consequence. It is not possible to change a block of data on the tape unless it is the last block, because there is no guarantee of controlling the tape motion with sufficient precision to over-write a block and yet accurately maintain the IRG for reading the next block. In other words, we can read a tape or write it, but not perform some interspersed sequence of these operations; thus, a process involving change to data on tape necessitates rewriting an entirely new tape.

The IRG typically varies in size from 3/10 to 3/4 inch, depending upon the characteristics of the tape drive. If we are not careful about the size of the blocks, or *physical records*, we may wind up with a tape that consists of mostly blank IRG's and relatively little data. One extreme (and unrealistic) alternative would be to write one physical record as long as the tape. With a length of 2400 feet and a recording density of 1600 bpi, we could store more than 46 million bytes on one tape. This would be enough for about 23 copies of the entire text of this book. For a more realistic objective, suppose that we wanted to store the data of punched cards as discrete physical records. Each card has 80 columns and can be recorded as 80 bytes. With the same density of 1600 bpi, this amounts to 0.05 inch for each card image. For the typical case of 0.6 inch IRG's, we are left with the situation illustrated in Figure 12.1, and with a tape holding only 44,300 card images, or 3.5 million bytes, for less than 8 percent of its maximum storage capacity.

The resolution for this situation is to group some number of *logical records* (cards in this case) into one physical record. This number of logical records per physical record is called the *blocking factor*. Suppose that we employed a blocking factor of 20. In that case the physical record length would be 1.0 inches, and the tape could hold 18,000 physical records (but 360,000 logical card records) for 63

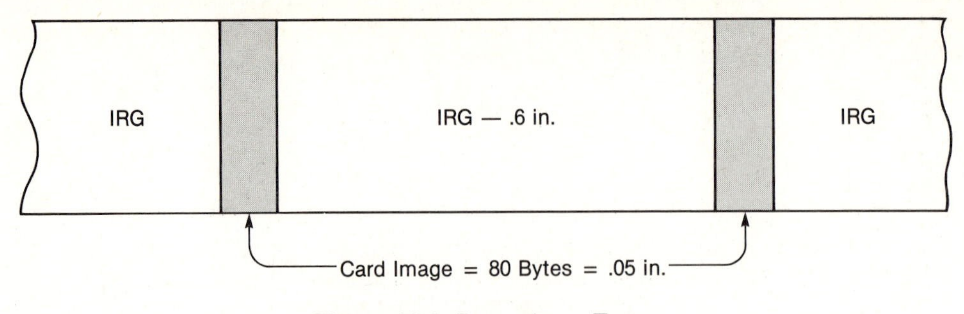

Figure 12.1 Records on Tape

percent of its maximum storage capacity. A large blocking factor helps us in terms of tape capacity, and it also helps to amortize the delay time per byte of data, as mentioned in Section 12.1. However, there is another side to the coin. We must have a correspondingly large block of main memory, called a *buffer*, for completing the data transfer. In practice, the choice of size for I/O buffers reflects a compromise between attaining reasonable I/O performance and not consuming too much primary memory.

12.1.2 Disks and Drums

Tapes are very useful for storage if we use them in the mode of reading or writing records in successive positions. But since it typically takes about two minutes to scan a tape from beginning to end, it is hopelessly ineffective to try to retrieve random records from a tape – the average delay is an intolerable one minute for each record. By contrast, disks and drums are *direct-access devices*, with the property that it is feasible to access any of their storage locations at random. Disks are much more common and also more generally useful than drums, so we will mostly talk about them. We will be describing typical large-capacity disks that are employed with a medium-sized or large computer, not the small floppy disks that are now so common with personal computers. These large disks can typically hold 100 million bytes of data.

A disk consists of a number of platters, typically between six and thirty, stacked one above another on a spindle. Data is recorded on both the top and bottom surfaces of each platter except for the two outermost surfaces, and there is usually one read/write head for each surface. All the heads are physically ganged together in a comb-like arrangement, which causes them to move in lock-step between the outer periphery of the platters and the center. The data on each surface is recorded in concentric *tracks* (not in a spiral, as with a phonograph record). There are typically 200 to 800 tracks, plus a few spare ones in case a track becomes unusable, and each of these is composed of several *sectors*. Finally, the collection of tracks at the same radial distance on all the surfaces is termed a *cylinder*. Figure 12.2 illustrates the features just described.

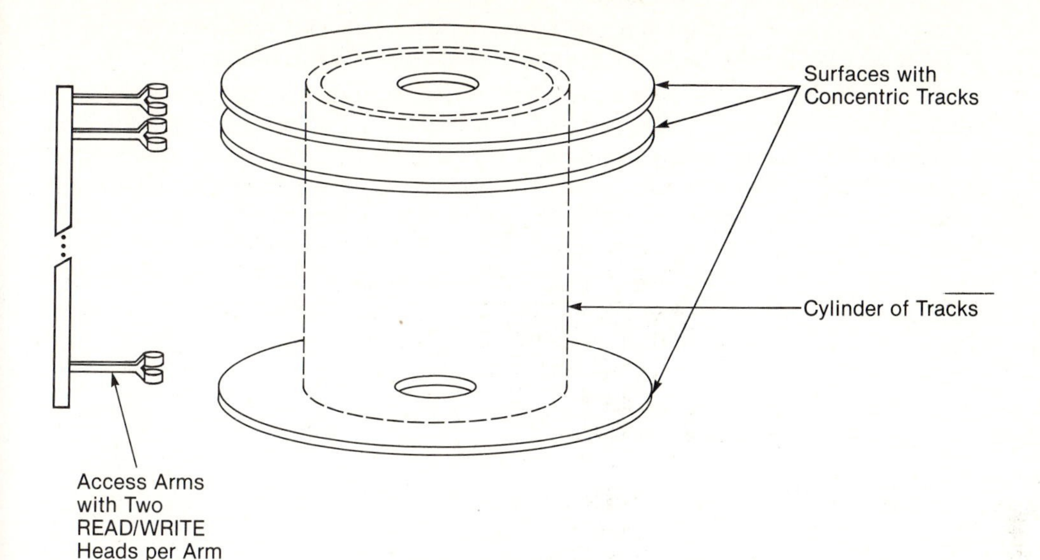

Figure 12.2 Disk Storage

We can see that it is natural to regard the location of an item of data on a disk as being determined by a three-level address: cylinder number, track (that is, surface) number, and angular position. In fact, access to a disk location is specified by: (a) using the cylinder number to control the radial positioning of the read/write heads, (b) using the track number to select the proper head, and then (c) using a coordinate related to angular position. The delay time for accessing a disk location thus has two components:

- a *seek time* to accomplish the radial positioning, if the read/write heads are not already at the proper cylinder;
- a rotational *latency* while waiting for the correct angular position to occur under the heads.

The seek time is significantly larger, because it involves mechanical motion of the heads over some number of cylinders; representative minimum/average/maximum values are 10/30/55 milliseconds. At typical rotational speeds of 3600 rpm, the average latency, on the other hand, is 8.3 milliseconds. Finally, for a typical recording density of about 13,000 bytes/track and with the same 3600 rpm, the data transfer rate would be 800,000 bytes/second.

Just as with tapes, we look for ways to use disks efficiently. Blocking can again be used for improving both storage utilization and average access rate, by the same reasoning used with tapes. There is one difference, however, in that the blocking is pre-defined by the sector sizes. For some disks, there is just one immutable sector size, and the user simply packs as many logical records in a sector as possible. With the larger and more expensive disks, it is common to be able to pre-format tracks to have sectors of customized sizes. This pre-formatting may not be under the control of the end-user; on the other hand, there is another factor that he more likely can control. By allocating his data on a single cylinder, or at least on consecutive cylinders, the user can make the seek time non-existent, or at least minimal.

Drums typically have several hundred tracks around the circumference of a rotating drum, with one read/write head permanently positioned over each track, as in Figure 12.3. Thus, drum locations are determined by two-level addresses, as opposed to the three levels for disks. The total capacity of a drum is significantly smaller than that of a disk, being on the order of 5 million bytes. Drums tend to have smaller latencies than disks, due to higher rotational speeds; even more significantly, they have no seek delays. As we will see in Section 12.2, this combination of characteristics makes them well-suited for supporting virtual memory.

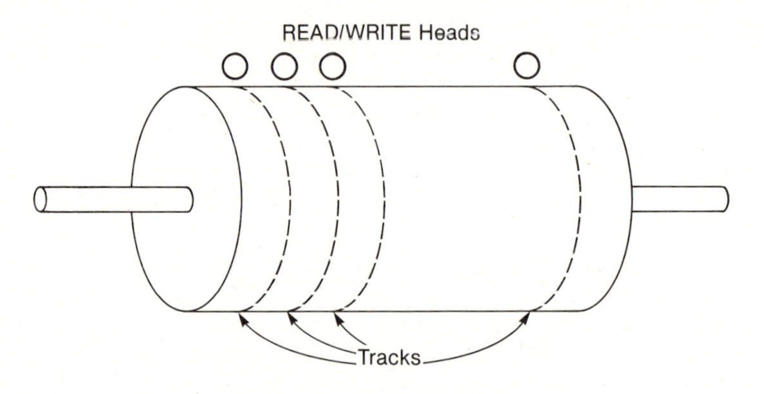

Figure 12.3 Drum Storage

†12.1.2.1 Disk Fragmentation. A single disk for the IBM 3350 contains over 16,000 tracks of about 19,000 bytes each. Allocation of data will typically be in terms of entire tracks, for very large blocks of data that may require from one to a dozen tracks. Over a period of time, as tracks are allocated and deallocated, the storage on the disk will become fragmented into varying-size *extents* – that is, sets of logically contiguous tracks on the same cylinder. Some of these extents will be occupied and some will be empty, in a manner analogous to the fragmentation of main memory, but now on a much larger scale. A severe consequence of external fragmentation in main memory is that we may be unable to find a large enough contiguous extent. With disk space this is not a problem, however, because we can spread a large data block over several extents that are chained together. Instead, we encounter a different problem – the extended time required to access the separate extents. This is especially severe when the tracks must be spread over two or more cylinders, thus requiring additional seek delays. Theoretical models of disk fragmentation in terms of the geometric distribution and of Markov chains can be found in Leung [1982a, 1983].

In order to limit the cumulative degradation in performance, it is expedient to reorganize the entire contents of a disk periodically. A common technique for doing this is just to copy all the data, in logical sequence, from the fragmented disk onto a new disk; this is such a lengthy operation that it must be done at off-hours. In an alternative, pragmatic approach, only about 10 percent of the extents are selectively relocated, so this can be interwoven with normal processing. Yet the reduction in fragmentation is substantially equivalent to that obtained with the slower, naive process [Franaszek and Considine 1979].

12.1.3 Storage Devices – A Reprise

The nature of tapes is such that they usually retain data for just one user or process over long periods of time, and they are retrieved from a tape library when required by that user or process. It is not uncommon for a computing center to have just a few tape drives, but a library containing thousands of tape reels. At the other extreme, drums cannot be removed, and they are used to retain data for many processes for relatively short periods of time. The average computing center has either no drums or just one, which is then used for special purposes. Disks are a good compromise. It is often possible to exchange disk packs in a disk drive. Also, while some disks are used to retain data for many users or processes, others are used to retain data that is private to a single user or process. Because of these features and because they are intermediate in performance to tapes and drums, disks are the most versatile and useful of the storage devices. Typically, a computing center may have a dozen disk drives and a library of several score disk packs, some public and some private. A representative comparison of the values for average delay and access speed is shown in Table 12.1 for typical main memory, drum, disk, and tape. The two delay figures represent the average values for (a) locating an arbitrary block of data, and (b) beginning to access the next block of data in physical sequence. Note that all of these values are an order of magnitude better than those for a typical personal computer, and at least an order of magnitude inferior to those of state-of-the-art devices with large computers. The principal intent of the table, however, is to illustrate relative speeds rather than absolute speeds.

	Average Delay (milliseconds)		Access Speed (microseconds/byte)
	(a)	(b)	
main memory	0	0	0.050
drums	5	5	0.300
disks	30	8	1.250
tapes	10^5	20	5.000

Table 12.1 Representative Timing Figures

There are many variations upon the ideas presented here, as illustrated by disks with several sets of read/write heads, "electronic" disks that have no mechanical arms at all, drums that do have movable read/write heads, etc. More significant than these, however, is the point that since tapes and disks can be removed from the machine and stored in libraries, we can effectively have a tertiary level of storage. This third level is of indefinitely large capacity, but with correspondingly larger delays to allow for human intervention. Some applications need to have a third level of storage that is more automatic and has shorter delays. One such storage device is the IBM 3850 Mass Storage System. It can backup a disk storage unit with as much as 472 billion bytes of data, stored in 4,000 tape cartridges, and it has the capability of streaming data between the disk and a selected tape cartridge at high speed.

12.2 VIRTUAL MEMORY

If the memory requirements for a problem exceed the main memory that is available to us, then we can explicitly shuffle portions of our data or program between main memory and secondary memory, as we described at the beginning of this chapter. But this is a very unpleasant route to have to take. It is cumbersome to program, resulting in a solution that has no flexibility with regard to alternative memory configurations, and it is simply a distraction so far as our principal endeavor is concerned [Sayre 1969]. Virtual memory, if available, relieves us of these difficulties. With it, we are able to use a program-address space that can be much larger than the memory-address space available to us.[1] The hardware and the system software then contrive to swap blocks of data between main and secondary memory as needed, pushing out a block that hopefully won't be needed again soon, in order to make room for the block that is now required.

If the parameters of the computing system are chosen with care, virtual memory can work very well. But if they are not chosen with care, and the amount of swapping becomes excessive, then the several orders of magnitude difference in access speeds illustrated in Table 12.1 spell disaster. In the next section we will describe how virtual memory is accomplished, and call attention to the most important factors determining its effectiveness. Following that, we will illustrate how the presence of virtual memory does not completely relieve the user of care; rather, it presents strong implications about how he should organize a large problem for efficient machine solution.

---

[1] A less common situation that is sometimes confused with this one is that of a program-address space that is smaller than the memory-address space, because the machine architecture develops an address of restricted size (perhaps 16 bits) when decoding instructions. In such cases the issue is not to map a large logical address space to a small physical address space, but rather to map many small logical address spaces to one large physical address space.

†12.2.1 Implementation Issues

We have said that the system can, by a combination of hardware and software, bring absent blocks into main memory *on demand.* A basic issue is whether the blocks should be of fixed or variable size. Blocks of variable size, or *segments,* correspond to logical units of programming, such as structured data items, compiled procedures, etc. On the other hand, blocks of fixed size, or *pages,* correspond to convenient physical units of data transfer. With the former we encounter the familiar phenomenon of external fragmentation, and with the latter that of internal fragmentation (see Section 11.3). We saw in Chapter 11 that the problem of managing primary memory in order to accommodate variable-size blocks is much more difficult than that of managing fixed-size blocks. So when there are no other issues, we find that virtual memory is almost always implemented with pages, in the interest of simplicity.

However, it is also very common for a computer with virtual memory to be operating in a multiprogramming mode, in which it is servicing several users simultaneously; additionally, it is common for these users to wish to share programs and data. The conduct of this multi-user activity (and the related issue of protecting the shared objects from misuse) depends upon the concept of logical segments. Therefore, in order to satisfy both logical and physical considerations, virtual memory is commonly implemented in terms of segments that are then partitioned into pages. In this case there is a need for a segment table and also a number of page tables, one for each segment.

The details of the organization just described are conveyed by Figure 12.4, where a program address is shown as consisting logically of a segment identifier 3, a page identifier 14, and a displacement 159 within the page. The translation of the program address is carried out in two phases. First, the value 3 is found in the segment table. In our case, it is present, and the corresponding table entry points to a page table; if the reference had been to segment 6, then the setting of the *presence bit* would have signalled its absence. In the latter case, (i) the data in the pointer field would indicate the location of the segment in secondary memory, (ii) a page table for that segment would be allocated, (iii) the entry in the table for segment 6 would be updated to reflect this change, and (iv) the translation would then proceed in normal fashion.

The second translation step is similar to the first. The page identifier 14 becomes an offset in the page table for segment 3, and the corresponding entry points to the location of that page in main memory at location 18000. If the reference had been to the second page of that segment, then the setting of the presence bit would have signalled its absence. In this latter case, (i) the data in the pointer field would indicate the location of the page in secondary memory, (ii) the page would be swapped into a *page frame* in main memory, (iii) the entry in the table for page 2 would be updated to reflect this change, and (iv) the translation would then proceed in normal fashion. At the conclusion of the translation steps described in these two paragraphs, the data is finally accessed at location 18000 + 159 = 18159.

The translation process just described requires several comments. Even when there is no *segment fault* or *page fault*, corresponding to the circumstance that data is not already in main memory, it would seem that the amount of work required for

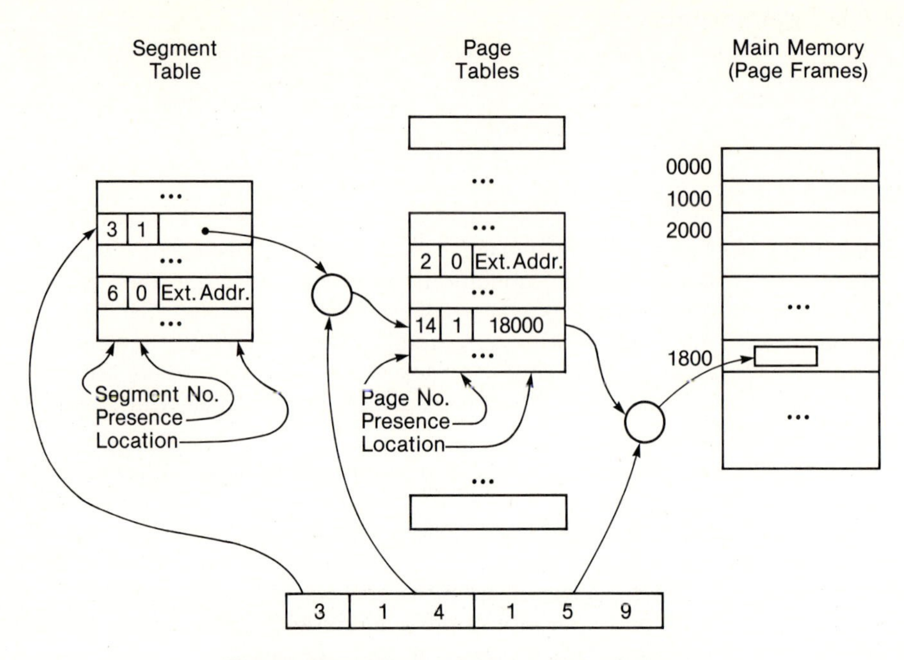

Figure 12.4 Virtual Address Translation

decoding addresses is three times that required in the absence of virtual memory, making this feature uneconomical in practice. In fact, although the segment and page tables are usually just arrays in main memory, special hardware is provided to accomplish the translation, and the net overhead is commonly just a few percent. Also, for a single user system, there is no need for segments, which simplifies the translation. Unavoidably, however, there is the potential that the computer will spend almost all of its time waiting for a needed page to be swapped in. There are three steps involved in thwarting this:

1. Make the access ratio between secondary and main memory as low as possible.
2. Adopt a policy for replacing pages that will tend to minimize the likelihood of subsequent page faults.
3. Multiprogram, so that while waiting upon a page for one user, the machine can be executing the program of another user.

With regard to the first point, a common tactic has been to use a drum as the paging device, although of late this role is sometimes taken over by disks with very high performance. The second and third points are more complicated and very interrelated. Consider, for example, the paging behavior of a single user's program with relation to the fraction f of its total pages that are in main memory. If f is close to 1, then page faults will be relatively infrequent; if f is small, then a fault will occur very quickly. Overall, the incidence of faulting as a function of f is shown in Figure 12.5, where the shaded area represents the variation induced by various choices for page replacement strategies. It is clear that although the choice of such a strategy is important, it is much less significant than having a substantial proportion of a program's pages already in main memory. Even though the precise value of this proportion varies from one program to the next, the general phenomenon indicated by the figure always exists; and the minimum number of pages that should be present before it is sensible for a program to start executing is called its *working set*[2] [Denning 1968]. In a multiprogramming environment, each of the programs manifests this same need to have its working set resident in main memory. Thus, as an initial fact of life, the very act of multiprogramming drastically expands the minimum amount of main memory required.

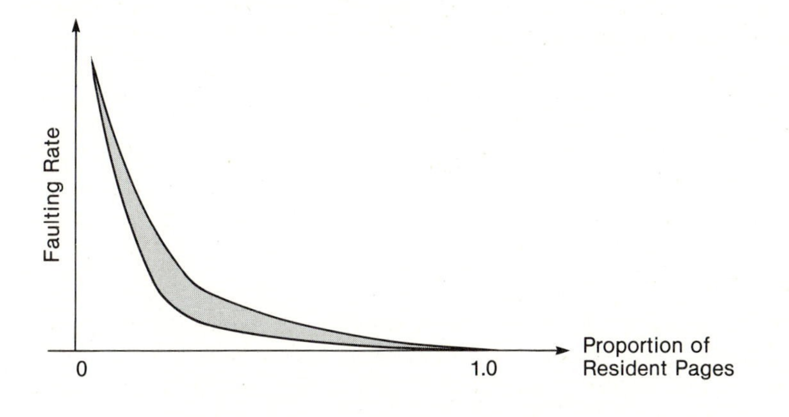

Figure 12.5 Page Faulting Behaviour

Assuming that we do have an adequate amount of main memory, then two policies interact very strongly:

- selecting the page to be replaced;
- choosing which program to schedule for execution next, when the one that was executing cannot proceed. (This may be because of a page fault, an incomplete I/O operation, the expiration of a time quantum, or some other reason.)

When these policies are poorly coordinated, the executing program will engender a page fault rather quickly, leading to another pair of decisions with similar bad consequences, and degenerating into what is termed *thrashing*. At that point the system spends almost all of its time juggling pages and never doing any useful work. We will not discuss scheduling policies further, but it should be clear that they are very much related to the page replacement policies.

Several replacement policies have been studied, including random selection, organizing pages as a circular queue and replacing their contents in cyclical fashion (see Exercise 12.2), and various other strategies. One that works well and is commonly used is to replace the page that was *least recently used* (*LRU*). The LRU

---

2 What constitutes the working set for a program depends upon the time interval over which its behavior is observed. It is obviously a monotonic function of the length of the interval; moreover, it is fairly easy to conclude that a plot of the function is concave downward.

algorithm requires the effect of a list wherein the identifier of a page is moved to the front of the list whenever the page is referenced (analogously to the move-to-front heuristic of Section 10.2.1). In practice, special hardware in the machine provides the LRU function at high speed, without the necessity to explicitly manipulate such a list. Another effective strategy is to try to capture sufficient data to be able to identify the working set, and then to release pages that have dropped out of the working set.

In order to assess the effectiveness of these various policies, we can ignore the multiprogramming issue and ask the following question: If we had perfect hindsight, what replacement policy applied to the stream of addresses generated by a program would result in the minimum number of page faults? This question can be answered by the artifice of first generating the stream of addresses and then computing from that stream the optimal policy. Such an experiment was performed. It yields, not an implementable policy (since we cannot expect to have the necessary vision in practice), but one against which other policies can be measured [Belady 1966]. Briefly stated, a good policy such as LRU is found to lead to a faulting rate that differs from the optimum by only about 30 percent.

At this point, let us recapitulate some of the various factors that affect how well virtual memory will work. A system designer must balance the effects of total main memory, access ratio between main and secondary memory, the multiprogramming load (that is, maximum number of active users), working set sizes, scheduling policy, and replacement policy. Some comments are in order about the relative significance of some of these. In particular, it is much less effective to have a good replacement policy than it is to have a page allocation of adequate size for the working set. And even if both of these factors are satisfactory, a high access ratio will still vitiate the entire scheme. A clever way of capitalizing upon the importance of the access ratio is to introduce a high-speed *cache memory* between the CPU and the main memory, giving two levels of virtual access. A cache memory will typically be about 1/10 the size but about 10 times as fast as the main memory. Yet it can enable a computer to operate within 80−90 percent of the performance that it would have if the entire main memory were of the higher speed [Liptay 1968; Smith 1982]!

The low access ratio of a cache memory serves another useful purpose. Page sizes for virtual memory are typically 1K or 4K bytes. This has two harmful effects. One is substantial internal fragmentation. Another is that much of that large block of data may not be referenced and so is superfluous; yet we paid the cost of fetching it, and it takes up valuable space in main memory.[3] Although the large page size would appear to be inefficient, it is only relatively so; because of the high access ratio, a smaller choice for the page size would yield worse overall performance. The numbers change in the case of a cache, however. Typical cache sectors are 64 or 128 bytes in size, and the efficiency of their use tends to be high.

An extensive discussion of virtual memory can be found in Denning [1970]. We turn our attention, in the next section, to the user side of the matter.

---

[3] Note that this is an additional argument against a virtual memory scheme based solely upon segments.

†12.2.2 Efficient Use of Virtual Memory

Ideally, the presence of virtual memory would be transparent to our programs in their use of an artificially large address space. In fact, it is important for working sets not to become too large, but rather to migrate through the address space in nice clusters. This translates into having programs that manifest a high degree of *locality* – that is, the addresses generated over a period of time should not cross too many page boundaries. It is for this reason that the CDR-linearization discussed in Section 11.2.3.2.1 is significant. Still another consequence of operating with virtual memory is illustrated by the semi-spaces described in Section 11.2.3.2. Further analysis of the related roles of garbage collection and virtual memory can be found in Baecker [1972].

Although the design techniques just cited are important, they are not under control of the average user. So we will focus, instead, upon the remarkable consequences that simple variations in ordinary programming can have upon performance. These effects have been commonly appreciated for many years; we will confine our discussion to one example from a more recent treatment. Specifically, let us consider the program MAT_MAT (Algorithm 2.4) for multiplying two matrices, with $m = n = p$ for the sake of simplicity. The executable code is then

```
for i := 1 to n do
   for j := 1 to n do begin
     sum := 0;
     for k := 1 to n do
        sum := sum + A [i,k] * B [k,j];
     C [i,j] := sum;
  end;
```

In the ordinary case, with all data in main memory, the multiplications are the dominant steps and the complexity is $O(n^3)$.

But now let the sizes be such that each matrix A,B,C resides on several pages of k elements each, so that each requires n^2/k pages. Furthermore, let us assume that

$$n < k << n^2 \qquad (12.1)$$

Since the time to service a page fault is several orders of magnitude greater than the time for performing a multiplication, the page faults now become the dominating steps (see Section 1.3.2.2) that we should count in analyzing this version of matrix multiplication. Finally, recall that the conventional method of storing matrices is in row-major order (see Section 2.2.1). In that case the nested loops of the algorithm are such that the elements $A\,[i,k]$ and also the elements $C\,[i,j]$ will be accessed in the order in which they occur in storage. Thus, there will be n^2/k faults associated with accessing each of them. However, the references to the elements $B\,[k,j]$ will cause n^2/k faults for every complete cycle through the inner loop, or n^4/k faults for the entire program. The total number of faults is is therefore $(n^4 + 2n^2)/k$ – which is less than n^3, by Eq. 12.1.

These circumstances can be dramatically improved by first computing the transpose T of B, as follows:

```
for i := 1 to n do
   for j := 1 to n do
      T [j,i] := B [i,j];
```

The revised multiplication step for MAT_MAT is then

```
sum := sum + A [i,k] * T [j,k]
```

During the transposition, the matrix B will generate n^2/k page faults, and the matrix T will generate a like number for each value of i, or n^3/k faults in all. In the matrix multiplication per se, A and C will still cause $2n^2/k$ faults between them, and the matrix T will generate n^2/k faults for each value of i – or n^3/k faults in all. Adding these up, the final fault count is $(2n^3 + 3n^2)/k$, and this is less than $2n^2$, by Eq. 12.1. In other words, simply by first transposing B, we have reduced the complexity by an order of magnitude. This can be more fully appreciated by making a plausible assumption – for example, $k = 512$ and $n = 256$, which yields 8,400,000 faults without transposition and 66,000 faults with transposition. A fuller treatment of this example, and other examples as well, can be found in Moffatt [1983].

12.3 FILE ORGANIZATIONS

If the operating economics of virtual memory were favorable enough, we would never have to be concerned about the issues we address in this section. We would not need to maintain files as distinct entities in secondary memory. Instead, we could regard them as always being directly addressable in our large virtual memory when we needed them, and the same kinds of data structuring that we have used heretofore could in principal be applied without any change. However, the operating economics of virtual memory do not yet sustain such a casual attitude. For the time being, for a file in secondary storage, we must first identify the records from the file that we wish to access, and then explicitly copy them back and forth.

Since it is common to be dealing with many thousands or even millions of records, and since each individual access to secondary memory is orders of magnitude slower than ordinary computational steps, it is imperative to organize the data so that just a few accesses are required. In almost all cases, this organization is based upon the primary key associated with each record. This necessitates searching, and so it might be tempting to try to use storage addresses directly, in order to avoid the searching problem. But these addresses have an an artificial device-dependency, and are generally awkward to employ for most practical situations. Even worse, the data on secondary storage devices will almost inevitably be subject to reorganization, causing physical addresses to lose their validity.

Accepting that records are identified by their keys, one of the major issues is whether we should:

1. simply deal with the keys in their records;
2. employ a subset of the key values in a *sparse index*;
3. employ all of the key values in a *dense index*.

Assuming that the keys constitute just a small fraction of the total storage requirement, we can expect that the use of an index will reduce the overall number of storage accesses, since most of the search can then be conducted within the index in main memory. The use of a dense index has two additional advantages. One is that there is more freedom about where the records are actually placed, since every record is pointed to from the dense index by its key. Another is that variable-length records are thereby easily accommodated. In the common case that an index is employed, it will often be inefficient to fetch or retain in main memory the entire set of indices for a large file; rather, the search will proceed by accessing a block of typically hundreds of index entries, searching it, and then making subsequent access(es) as a result.[4]

Quite apart from the relationship between the index entries and the final record(s) that are sought, there are some choices concerning the index entries themselves. For one, since these entries are understood to be keys in sequence, the redundancy between successive key values is usually high. Thus, it is possible to employ *key compression* techniques that are considerably more efficient than the compression techniques discussed in Section 8.4.1. Typically, this involves suppressing leading characters that can be derived from the preceding keys in the sequence. The advantage of compression, of course, is that it accommodates having many more key values in a block. It has several disadvantages, however, one being the additional computation required for decompression, and another that we will mention very shortly. Still another choice is whether a block of indices should have the structure of a simple list, or perhaps that of a tree. In the former case, one could then employ either sequential or binary search of the block. Other techniques from Chapter 10 apply in the latter case, of course. The choices as to compression and structure are not independent. Thus, binary search of a sequential list structure is more effective than ordinary sequential search, and so is tree search, given the usual size of the index blocks. When the keys are compressed, however, sequential search is the only possibility. The interplay of factors in designing indices for files draws upon our previous studies in several ways, and it is one of the principal themes of this chapter. A further treatment of some of the particular points addressed in this paragraph can be found in Maruyama and Smith [1977].

In the following two sections, we will examine file organizations, or access methods, that correspond in natural fashion to the basic types of storage devices, tape and direct-access. Sections 12.3.3 and 12.3.4 then discuss the two principal ways in which tree structures are built in secondary memory. Lastly, we examine some more recent techniques that guarantee a small, fixed number of accesses.

---

[4] With or without an index, there is another possibility. Some disk storage devices are able to scan a track and search for a record with a specified key, thus obviating the need for search of a block in main memory. However, the circumstances in which this capability exists and can be put to use are relatively less common.

12.3.1 Sequential Files

This is the simplest organization, and the only one that can be used with data stored on tape. It depends upon the records being in key sequence within the file, so that they can be processed one after the other in their physical sequence. In reality, there is a distinction to be made, depending upon whether or not keys are present and relevant for the operation being performed. The use of keys implies that the presence or absence of a record with a given key can be significant, and we are then truly performing *sequential access*. It is also possible to perform the same operation upon each record in the physical sequence, regardless of its key value. In this case, we are performing *serial access*. This distinction becomes inescapable when we reach the last record in our file. With sequential access, it is common to rely upon a signal from the data, in the form of a sentinel record with an artificial key. With serial access, we must rely upon an indication from the device that no more records exist; in the case of tape, this signal from the device is called an *end-of-file* (*EOF*).

In the earliest days of computing, sequential and serial access were the only file organizations, reflecting the fact that tape and punched cards were then the only physical file media. Even though other possibilities now exist, sequential access is still very useful for applications where data is accumulated, sorted, and then *batch processed* at the convenience of the system, as opposed to responding in a timely manner to requests from users. Batch processing is appropriate in the preparation of account statements and bills every month, in doing payroll calculations, etc. Note, by the way, that even though we can have much fancier file organizations with a disk than with a tape, what we sometimes want on a disk is nothing more than sequential access. However, the definition of sequential access files retains a feature deriving from their origin with tapes and cards: They cannot be modified, only read or written. In terms of computation, there is not a great deal to be said with regard to sequential files, because their organization is so simple. (But see Exercise 12.4, which demonstrates that this is not entirely true.)

For searching ordered files in main memory, we saw that binary search was much more effective than sequential search. Binary search applied to blocks of data on tape, however, would involve costly backward and forward motion and would perform worse than sequential search. There is a different, fairly obvious technique for reducing the amount of search in that sort of situation. If we are looking for a particular key K somewhere in a set of sequential blocks, we can access blocks and just examine the last key K_j in each block until $K \leq K_j$; when that happens, K must be in that block, and we can look for it by either sequential or binary search. This method is called either *jump search* or, for obvious reasons, *block search* [Shneiderman 1978]. The performance of jump search depends upon the relative costs c_j of jumping and c_s of searching a block, and also upon the number of records N and the size of the blocks B. We should expect to jump over half of the blocks, for a cost of $N/2B$, and we can assume sequential search within the final block, for a cost of $B/2$. Then the total cost is

$$C = c_j \frac{N}{2B} + c_s \frac{B}{2} \qquad (12.2)$$

We can look for the minimum value of C by differentiating this equation with respect to B and setting the result equal to zero. From this process, we find the optimum value of B and the corresponding minimum value of C as

$$B = \left(\frac{c_j N}{c_s}\right)^{1/2}, \quad \text{and} \quad C = \left(c_j c_s N\right)^{1/2} \tag{12.3}$$

In the case of tape, c_j is so much higher than c_s that the advantage of jump search over sequential search is scarcely noticeable. But there are other cases of sequential files where binary search is either inefficient (as with sequential files on disk) or impossible (as with compressed indices). For these, the square root complexity of jump search is quite respectable – not as good as the logarithmic complexity of binary search, but much better than the linear complexity of sequential search.

12.3.2 Random Access Files

Random access files depend upon direct-access devices for implementation, and the term *random access* can easily be misinterpreted. It should not be thought of in terms of independence of access time as a function of the key, since in fact the seek and rotational delays cause the access behavior not to be random with respect to where the key is located. Rather, the term signifies a method for dealing with keys that appear in random sequence from the key space. Thus, whereas sequential access is appropriate for applications such as account billing or payroll, random access would be the method of choice for an application such as inventory control, where it is important to maintain up-to-date status of stock on hand. In some rare cases where the key space is not too large and the user can control the assignment of keys, it may be possible to use disk addresses directly as keys, as mentioned in Section 12.3. For example, a manufacturer might assign disk addresses as part numbers (and might regret it when the need arose to obtain a disk with a different address structure). Such situations are very uncommon, however, and the standard way of implementing random access is via hashing.

There are some important differences between our use of hashing in Chapter 10 and its application to secondary memory. For one, it is no longer relevant that the hash function be simple to compute. For another, the optimal manner of handling collisions is different. Principally, however, it is expedient to partition storage into blocks called *buckets*, with each bucket containing some fixed number of *slots* for synonymous keys. Thus, the hash function is used to compute a bucket number, and then that entire bucket is read into main memory and searched for the desired key. Depending upon the nature of the search outcome, retrieval and search of additional bucket(s) may be required. The principal objective is no longer to limit the number of key probes, but rather to limit the number of bucket accesses. It is usually advantageous to have a moderately large bucket size, and this will in fact tend to *increase* the average number of key probes (equal to the product of the number of slots and the average number of accesses). However, the larger buckets will tend to absorb the fluctuations from the average, leading to less accesses and thus reduced overall cost.

It is implicit in the above discussion that sequential search is employed when looking for a key in a bucket. In reality, the keys might be maintained in order within a bucket, thus allowing binary search. Since bucket sizes tend to be moderate, however, and since it is usually too costly to maintain such ordering within buckets, the choice of sequential search is a reasonable one. On the other hand, it is sometimes plausible to load the keys into the buckets in decreasing order of probability of reference. As in previous discussions (see Section 10.2.1), this can be very effective in reducing the average number of accesses during sequential search.

In our study of collision resolution in Chapter 10, we encountered two chaining techniques – separate and coalesced – and two open addressing techniques – linear probing and random probing. Of these four methods, linear probing definitely yielded the worst performance; the choice among the other three methods depended upon various factors. When we reconsider these techniques in the context of secondary memory, we find that random probing is distinctly the worst method, since it implies disk accesses with significant delay times. Linear probing, on the other hand, implies accesses to buckets in successive logical tracks in the same cylinder. So linear probing, conventionally referred to simply as open addressing in this context, is one of the two acceptable and commonly used techniques for dealing with bucket overflow.

The other method of choice is a variation of separate chaining. In Chapter 10 each home address contained just a pointer and no keys. In this case, the home buckets are called the *prime area*, and each such bucket can contain several keys, as well as a pointer. In the event of bucket overflow, synonyms are stored in buckets in an *overflow area*, and these buckets are chained to buckets in the prime area. The chaining in the overflow area is between records rather than between buckets, but this should not create excessive overhead in a well-designed system having a low percentage of overflow entries. In the typical situation of a disk having 20 surfaces, $16-19$ of the tracks in each cylinder might be treated as distinct prime buckets, and the remaining $1-4$ tracks in a cylinder might be treated as an overflow area for retaining the overflow chains from the prime buckets.

In this section, we have lightly sketched some of the issues having to do with random access; in the ensuing section, we will look more closely at some of the details. One curious aspect of all this is that we are encountering hashing in secondary storage as an addendum to hashing in main memory. In fact, the history of hashing is just the reverse! It was devised originally as a means of providing random access to secondary storage, and subsequently adopted for searching main storage [Morris 1968]. Two excellent, pioneering references that demonstrate the original emphasis are Buckholz [1963] and Peterson [1957].

†12.3.2.1 Random Access Parameters. In our closer look at random access, we will find that the determination of an optimal set of design parameters is a fairly complicated business, for which both simulation and analysis techniques have been employed. Two of the most critical parameters are B, the number of buckets, and S, the number of slots in each bucket. In terms of these and the loading factor α, the principal figures of merit in evaluating a particular design are:

OP – the percentage of records that overflow from their home bucket, and

AA – the average number of bucket accesses that are required.

In Section 10.4.1 the Poisson distribution was used to predict the number of synonyms that will hash to a given location, as a function of the loading factor $\alpha = n/M$ (see Eq. 10.31). In this case, we wish to know the likelihood that a bucket will overflow. The total available memory is $M = BS$, and the average loading per bucket is $\mu = n/B = \alpha S$. Then the distribution of bucket occupancies can be approximated by the Poisson distribution as

$$P(\mu,i) = \frac{e^{-\mu}\mu^{i}}{i!} \tag{12.4}$$

where M is presumed to be fixed, with S varying. As an example, Table 12.2 displays $P(\mu,i)$ for a range of i, for the values $\mu = 5$ and $\mu = 8$. The overflow can be found by summing terms of Eq. 12.4 for which $i > S$.

i	5	8	i	5	8	i	5	8
0	.007		6	.146	.122	12	.003	.048
1	.034	.003	7	.104	.139	13	.001	.030
2	.084	.011	8	.065	.139	14		.017
3	.140	.029	9	.036	.124	15		.009
4	.176	.057	10	.018	.099	16		.005
5	.176	.092	11	.008	.072	17		.002

Table 12.2 Sample Poisson Values $P(\mu,i)$

Recall that the Poisson model reflects the assumption that the hash function completely randomizes the assignment from key space to address space, and that the use of division for a hash function will often yield results that are better than predicted by this random model. On the other hand, as we also discussed in Chapter 10, the divisor should be chosen with some circumspection. For that matter, the effectiveness of any particular hash function depends upon the nature of the set of given keys, considered as a subset from the entire key space. Suppose that hashing by division is employed and yields relatively poor performance for a particular set of keys. Then there will be an increase in the collision rate. This is of far more consequence with secondary storage than with main memory, since it can lead to an increase in the average number of costly bucket accesses; therefore, it can be worthwhile to expend effort to compute a better hash function.

As an example of a situation where extra care may be warranted, consider the case where the keys consist of digits expressed as EBCDIC characters; thus, we would have '0' = 11110000, '1' = 11110001, ... , '9' = 11111001 (see Table 8.1). When four-character groups are treated as 32 bit integers, then for some choices of divisors, congruential relationships will cause distinctly worse than random clustering of synonyms (compare Section 10.4.1). This effect is aggravated when the keys are non-random (such as sequential numbers) and for small bucket sizes S. An effective manner to cope with this phenomenon in such cases is to use two division steps [Clapson 1977]. The first one employs a "good" divisor for the purpose of smoothing the keys; the second one is a conventional division by B for the purpose of mapping into the address space.

Turning from the issue of choosing a hashing function to that of handling collisions, we can single out two factors that are particularly important:

- the choice of number of bucket slots S, and
- the choice between chaining and open addressing.

In fact, the values for both the overflow percentage OP and the average number of accesses AA are decreasing functions of S (and of B as well). As a primitive means of visualizing the effects of these choices, Figure 12.6 displays two collision patterns, one for a bucket size of one, and another where the bucket size has been doubled and the hash function has been adjusted correspondingly. For $S = 1$ in (a) of the figure, we can see that the average value of OP is $4/11 = 0.36$; if chaining is employed the value of AA is $16/11 = 1.45$, and if open addressing is employed the value of AA is $24/11 = 2.18$. For $S = 2$ in (b) of the figure, we can see that the average value of OP is $2/11 = 0.18$; if chaining is employed the value of AA is $13/11 = 1.18$, and if open addressing is employed the value of AA is $14/11 = 1.27$. These reductions in OP and AA correspond to what we would expect, since statistical variations should tend to cancel out with larger values of S. The extent to which this is true is illustrated by Figure 12.7, where the value of AA with open addressing is plotted as a function of α for several values of S. We see that AA decreases dramatically as S increases from 1 to 20. But of course we can only increase S within the constraint that the available memory $M = BS$. Eventually, the space and data transmission costs associated with a large buffer impose limits upon the effective size for S.

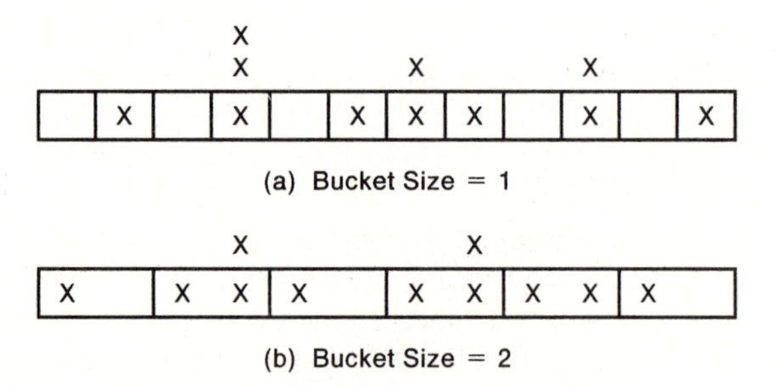

Figure 12.6 Two Collision Patterns

Both simulation and analysis have been applied to such questions as finding optimum bucket sizes, deciding between open addressing and chaining, and dealing with other random access issues [§]. The principal conclusions are as follows:

- At the outset, we cannot attach the same significance to α in chaining that we do in open addressing, since the former case does not take into account the space allocated for the overflow area.
- In fact, whereas α can never be greater than 1.0 in open addressing, it is possible and even reasonable to have $\alpha > 1.0$ with chaining, since the overflow area can be arbitrarily large.

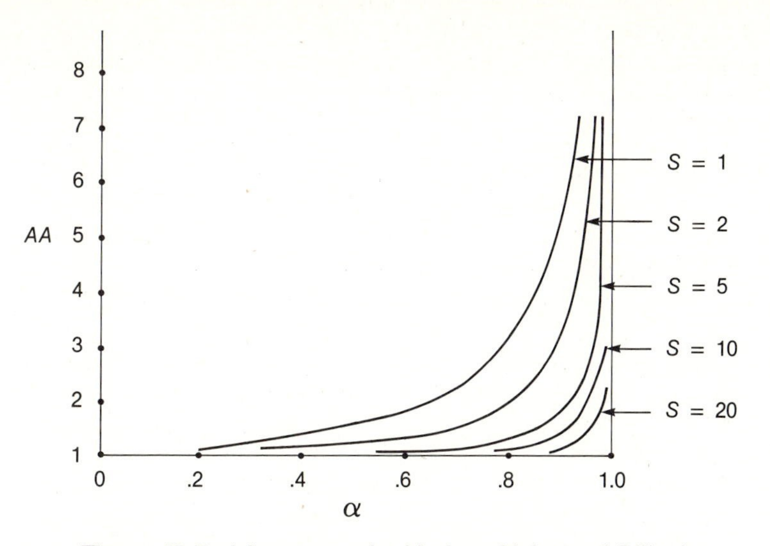

Figure 12.7 *AA* versus α for Various Values of S(lots)

- A common rule of thumb is to make a bucket the size of a track. Although this is a good first approximation, it can be better for some combinations of device and application parameters to have a bucket be either more or less than a single track.
- For small S, or as α approaches 1.0, open addressing is inferior to chaining.
- For $S \geq 10$, the value of AA is good with both overflow methods. Open addressing has the virtue of being simpler, and tends to be slightly faster. Chaining is less susceptible to statistical variations; it also can be pushed to yield very good space utilization, for $\alpha \approx 1.5$ and $S \geq 10$.

As a final point, if we are contemplating the use of overflow chaining, there is an additional issue that must be taken into consideration — the effects of insertions and deletions. For example, suppose that we wish to design a random access file that will hold 64,000 records distributed among 8,000 buckets, with $S = 10$ and $\alpha = 0.8$. Then, from Table 12.2, we can expect to encounter as overflow:

corresponding to $i = 11$, $1 \times 0.072 \times 8000 = 576$ records
corresponding to $i = 12$, $2 \times 0.048 \times 8000 = 768$ records
corresponding to $i = 13$, $3 \times 0.030 \times 8000 = 720$ records
etc.

for a total of 3,384 overflow records. Since these amount to only about 5 percent of the 64,000 original records, we might be tempted to allocate 95 percent of the tracks on a cylinder as a prime area and 5 percent of the tracks as an overflow area. But we must realize that whereas a deletion has only a 5 percent chance of removing a record from the overflow area, an insertion has more than a 28 percent chance of encountering a full track (from summing terms in Table 12.2 for $i \geq 10$) — thereby adding a record to the overflow area! Thus, the overflow area will exhibit substantial net growth until equilibrium is reached, and so the initial file design must anticipate this situation. In the example just cited, this would correspond to allocating 15 – 20 percent of the tracks in a cylinder for overflow. A detailed treatment of this issue, along with graphs and tables to assist in planning a file layout, can be found in Olson [1969]; an even more complete analysis can be found in van der Pool [1973a].

12.3.3 Indexed Sequential Files

For many applications with files, it is satisfactory to "give up" sequential access in order to obtain random access.[5] But it is worth reflecting upon what has been lost. Keys that are missing or duplicated in an input file may be significant. They are trivially recognizable in sequential processing, but not in random processing. A similar remark applies to near misses between keys. For many applications, therefore, it is important to be able to obtain both sequential *and* random access. As an example, credit card issuers must be able to access their files sequentially in order to prepare monthly account statements; they also must be able to access their files randomly in order to check for cardholders exceeding their credit limits, for lost or stolen cards, etc. A file organization with this capability is the *indexed sequential access method* (*ISAM*). The idea is conveyed by Figure 12.8, wherein we have a sparse index, each of whose entries corresponds to the last key in a block of data.

The file might be small enough that the entire index could reside in main memory and thus could be binary searched, or the file might be so large that the index would also be partitioned into blocks. In the latter case, we might use jump search on the index. More likely, however, we would prefer to introduce a second level of indexing, as in Figure 12.9, that could reside in main memory. The total cost of finding a record is then the sum of: (i) an access to a lower-level index block, (ii) an access to a data block, and (iii) the costs of searching within the two index blocks and the data block. With respect to (iii), note that the comments in Section 12.3 apply; that is, within each block we can choose among sequential search, binary search, tree search, jump search, etc.

When we look at the issue of using a disk to implement ISAM with two levels of indexing, we find a very natural match: The first-level index should direct the search to the proper cylinder, and the first track in each cylinder should contain a second-level index directing the search to the proper track in that cylinder. Alternatively, one might consider using a single level of indices along with interpolation search, rather than two levels of indices. Although this can reduce the number of index accesses from 2.0 to an average between 1.1 and 1.7, for typical sets of keys, there is no guarantee against a particular set of keys having an average that is greater than 2.0 [Ghosh and Senko 1969]. In particular, such a set of keys could then cause an extra disk seek.

---

[5] Note that although we cannot obtain sequential access on a random access file, we can obtain serial access.

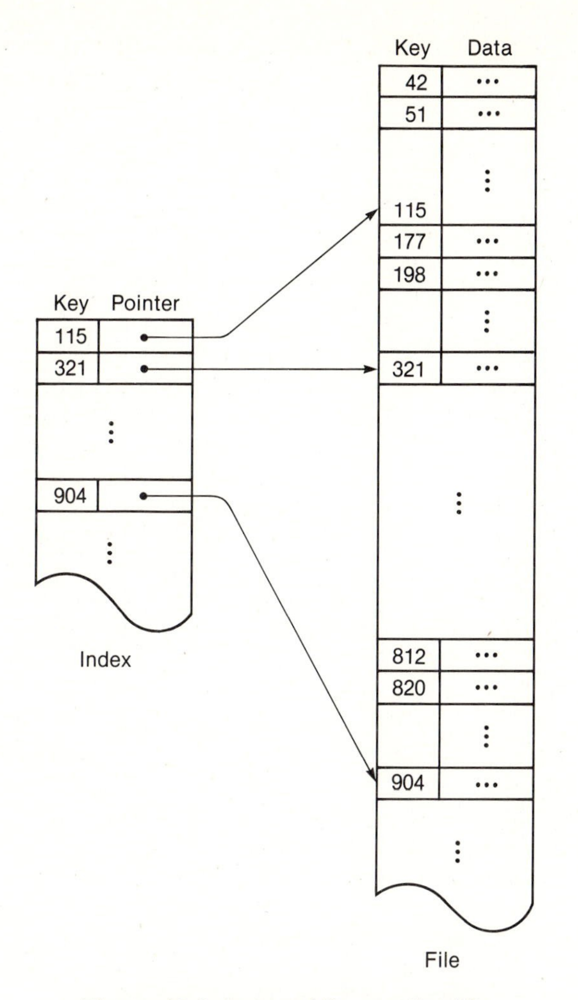

Figure 12.8 Indexed Sequential File

The structures in Figures 12.8 and 12.9 serve very well for a file that is static, or comparatively so. In reality, it is also necessary to allow for the possibility of insertions, and also deletions. In part, insertions can be handled by allowing extra initial space in the ISAM blocks, but eventually this must lead to overflow. The method of handling overflow in ISAM is similar to the technique of separate chaining into overflow areas in the case of random access. To be precise, each track index entry would contain the following data:

(a) the *highest* key for the associated track T (in either prime or overflow area);

(b) the prime track number T;

(c) the *highest* key for T in the overflow area (same as (a) if there are no overflow keys for T);

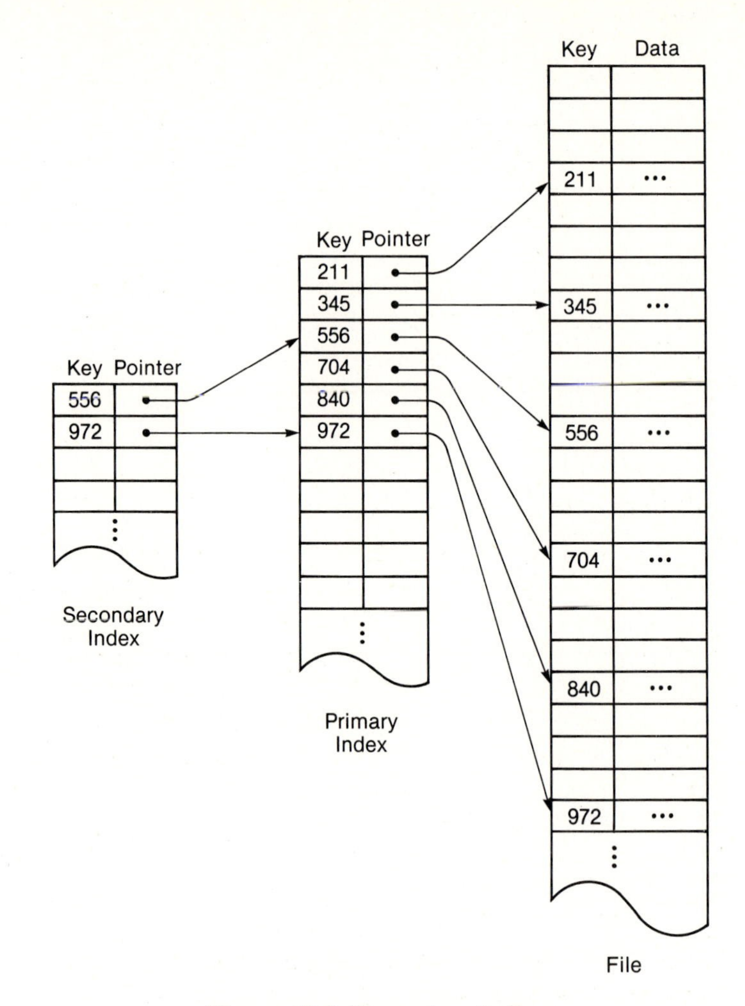

Figure 12.9 Secondary Indices

(d) the overflow track and record numbers for the *lowest* key for T in the overflow area (same as (b) if there are no overflow keys for T).

This is illustrated in Figure 12.10(a). For example, the highest key for track 1 is 285, and it has not overflowed, so the prime and the overflow entries for track 1 have the same key and pointer values. On the other hand, track 2 has overflow entries; this is conveyed by the dissimilar entries for prime and overflow for track 2, where track r is understood to be an overflow track. Note that the overflow record in track r with key 549 carries a pointer linking it back to its home track.

With the situation shown in (a) of the figure, if the key 427 were to be presented, the prime track 2 would be searched; but if the key 533 were presented, then the overflow chain beginning at track r and record 1 would be searched. On the other hand, if the key 168 were presented and not found in track 1, then the

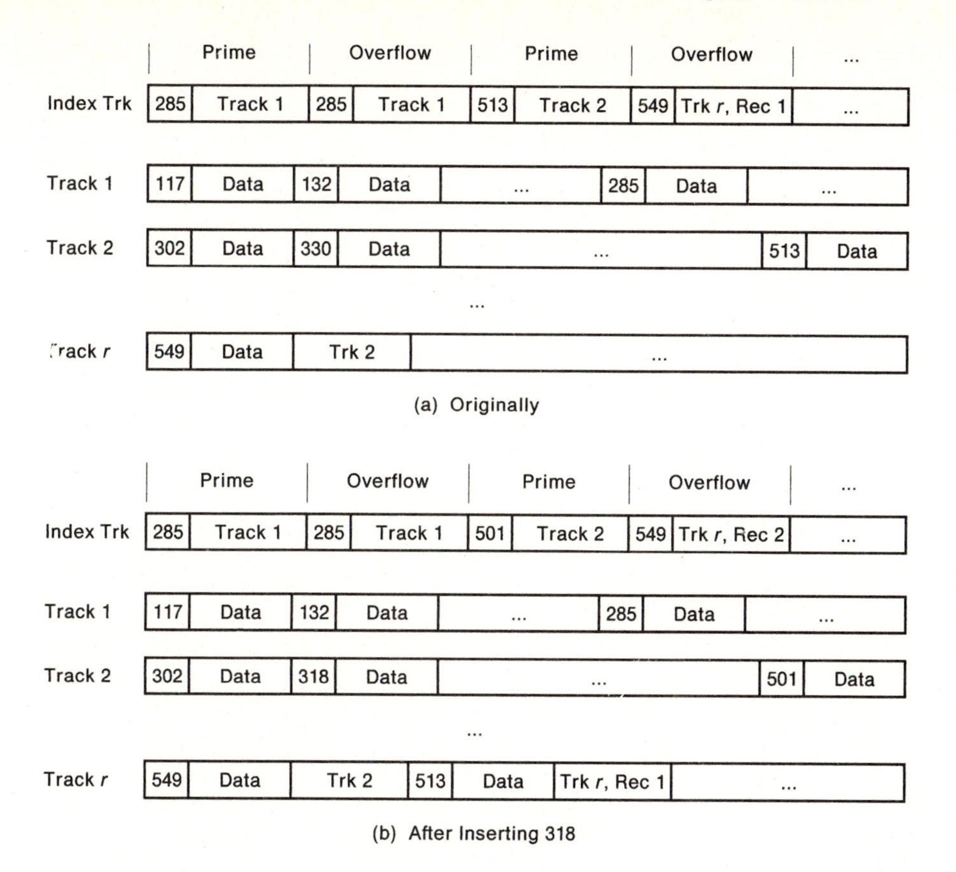

Figure 12.10 ISAM Details

replicated value of 285 in that track index would signify that the overflow area need not be searched. In other words, a search in ISAM examines either the prime area or the overflow area, but never both. This is different from random access, where the prime area is always searched first and then, if that fails, the overflow area is examined second. Figure 12.10(b) illustrates the effect of inserting 318. Since the prime tracks are maintained in key sequence, this insertion causes the record with key 513 to be moved from prime to overflow. The primary index value for track 2 is then adjusted to be 501 to reflect this change. Meanwhile, 549 remains as the highest overflow key for track 2, but now 513 becomes the lowest overflow key for track 2. Note that the data in the overflow tracks is maintained in linked list form, with the end of a list denoted by the appropriate prime track number.

As long as overflow can be contained within the same cylinder, ISAM performance is quite acceptable. When the overflow area on a particular cylinder is full, however, and further insertions must be chained to a separate overflow cylinder, performance can rapidly degrade. The resolution is to reorganize the contents of the disk. One must then decide how to balance the cost of reorganization against the cumulative degradation of performance caused by the extra accesses; several analytical models have been described for estimating this trade-off [Shneiderman 1973; Tuel 1978].

12.3.4 Tree-Structured Files

Searching an ISAM file corresponds, in large part, to searching a multiway tree, wherein each node can have many children (see Section 10.3.4). Moreover, in the absence of insertions, it has the pleasing property of requiring just two accesses to retrieve any item. Unfortunately, these characteristics are soon lost when insertions are common, and the search path to an item involves overflow chaining. Let us then ask the general question: How feasible is it to use tree searching techniques when the data occupies secondary storage? At the outset, we have two choices about the nature of our links between nodes:

- If we are relying upon virtual memory to implement a large, transitory tree, then ordinary pointer variables will work.
- In the absence of virtual memory, or if the large tree is to endure after the computation, then we must use explicit secondary storage addresses rather than pointer variables.

In primary memory, a principal concern in dealing with binary trees was to minimize wasted storage for empty pointer values; the resulting BST's can be characterized as skinny and deep. Suppose that we apply the same reasoning in the case of secondary memory. Then for a BST with a million nodes, even if it is completely balanced, the path length to the leaves is twenty since $10^6 \approx 2^{20}$. If each inter-node reference were to cause a disk access, the cost would be insupportable. But with balanced and comparatively bushy and shallow multiway tree of order 32, for example, the number of references would be reduced to five, since $10^6 \approx 32^5$. Sections 12.3.4.1 and 12.3.4.2 explore efficient ways in which to implement multiway trees. Before that, however, we consider more carefully the viability of binary trees in secondary memory.

The high number of accesses cited in the preceding paragraph is misleading; it does not take into account that closely related nodes will tend to cluster on a page. Suppose, in fact, that we are growing a BST, and that its nodes spread over more and more pages (or blocks). The simplest strategy is to assign successive nodes to successive locations within a page, allocating a new page whenever the current one becomes full. We can illustrate the results of this approach by the following example. If we have 2048 keys, then the argument of the preceding paragraph suggests a total of 11 accesses, for a completely balanced BST; by comparison, the use of Eq. 10.14 suggests a total of 14 accesses for a random BST. In fact, for a page size of 32 keys and for a random BST, it has been shown that this sequential allocation strategy would entail an average of just 7 accesses [Muntz and Uzgalis 1970]. Even better than this naive strategy, however, is the following grouped allocation strategy. Whenever a new node is to be assigned a location, it is placed in the same page as its father if there is room; otherwise, it is placed in a brand-new page. With this strategy, for n the number of keys and b the number of keys per page, the average number of page accesses is approximated by $H_n/(H_b - 1)$ [Knuth 1973b].

For our same example (that is, 2048 keys, page size of 32 nodes, and random BST), this strategy entails just three accesses, on the average. Now the average number of accesses in a complete t-ary tree is optimal, of $O(\log_t n) = O(\ln n/\ln t)$; so we see that the grouped allocation strategy is actually close to this in performance.

A little reflection suggests a drawback. The method tends to cause the allocation of a large number of pages that remain partially empty. A resolution for this is to allow just k unfilled pages at any one time. Then when a node cannot fit in its father's page, it is assigned to one of these k pages. (Note that $k = 1$ corresponds to sequential allocation, and $k = \infty$ corresponds to grouped allocation.) Simulations suggest that a value of $k = 8$ is almost as good as $k = \infty$, but without the correspondingly poor storage utilization [Sprugnoli 1981].

These results are certainly encouraging. Nonetheless, they are inadequate to recommend the use of BST's in secondary storage, in most instances. One reservation is that these results are averages, and the number of accesses in the worst case can be horrendously higher. Also, any insertions or deletions or rebalancings in BST's seriously compound the number of additional accesses. So we turn instead to a method that is stable with respect to the cost of search, and also with respect to the costs of insertion, deletion, and rebalancing.

12.3.4.1 B-Trees and B$^+$-Trees. We will use the definition that a *B-tree of order m* is a tree with the following properties:

1. The root is a leaf, or else has j sons and contains $j-1$ keys, where $m \geq j \geq 2$.
2. The internal nodes have j sons and contain $j-1$ keys, where $m \geq j \geq m/2$.
3. The leaves have no sons and contain $j-1$ keys, where $m \geq j \geq m/2$.
4. The leaves are all on the same level.

The original definition of B-trees of order m is in terms of $2m \geq j \geq m$ [Bayer and McCreight 1972]; that definition and the one employed here are both in current vogue. Our choice is motivated by the fact that the balanced trees that we discussed in Section 10.3.4 are, in fact, B-trees of low order. The definition $m \geq j \geq m/2$ encompasses both 2-3 trees as B-trees of order 3 and 2-4 trees as B-trees of order 4. The definition $2m \geq j \geq m$ encompasses 2-4 trees as B-trees of order 2, but it fails to encompass 2-3 trees.

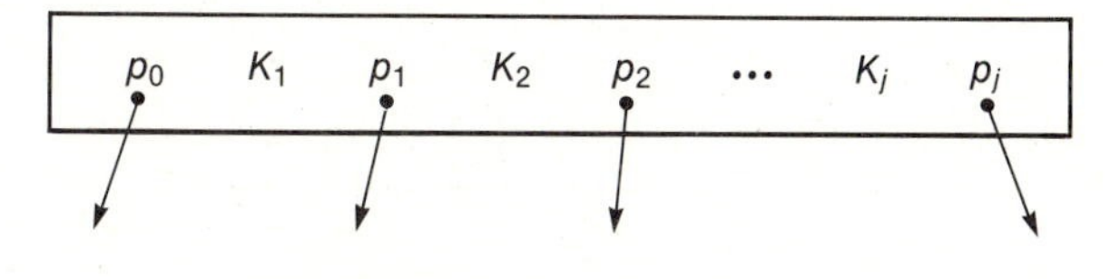

Figure 12.11 A B-Tree Node

The logical structure of a B-tree internal node is shown in Figure 12.11. If an argument key K is not found (by sequential or binary search) in this node, and if K falls between K_i and K_{i+1}, then search continues in the son pointed to by p_i. A concrete example of a B-tree of order 5 is shown in Figure 12.12. If search in a B-tree terminates unsuccessfully at a leaf and if K is then to be inserted in the tree,

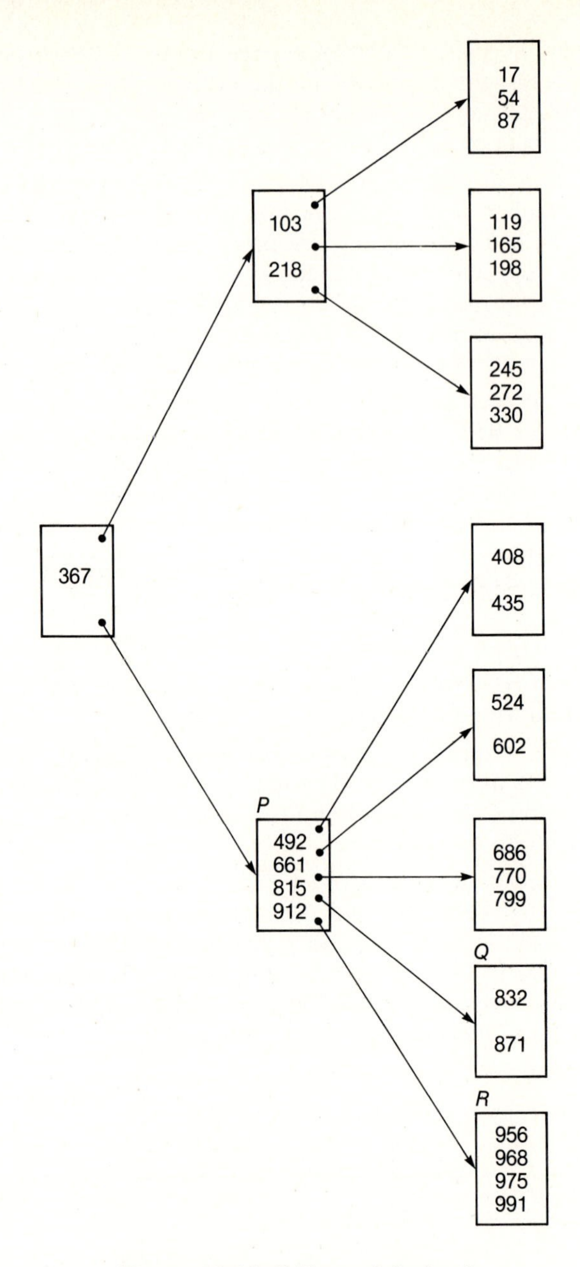

Figure 12.12 B-Tree of Order 5

there may well be space for it in the leaf. But if there is no room because the leaf node is full, then

(a) *K* is logically inserted in the proper order;

(b) the full node is split and half of its contents are relocated into a newly allocated node;

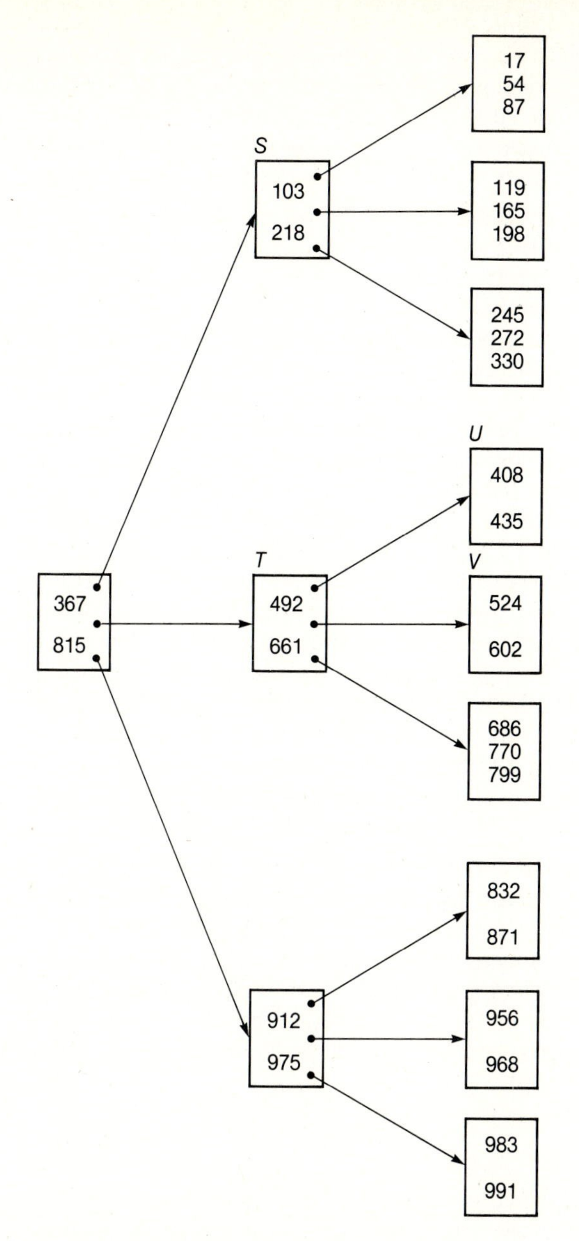

Figure 12.13 Insertion of 983 in Figure 12.12

(c) the median key value is removed and migrated up to the parent node.

As a result of the last step, the parent node will need to find room for the migrated key, and also a new pointer. If the parent is already full, then it will itself undergo a split according to the same rules (a) – (c). Finally, if a split occurs at the root, the B-tree grows *upward* one level, with *two* new nodes being allocated. In illustration,

Figure 12.13 depicts the result of adding 983 to the B-tree of Figure 12.12. Node R is forced to split, causing a key to migrate up to node P and an additional pointer to be inserted in P. But P has no room for another key/pointer pair; so it also splits, in turn affecting the root. It is easy to see that since splits migrate median key values upward, they serve to balance the B-tree with respect to width.

When a value is deleted from a B-tree, the process that takes place is the reverse of what happens during insertion, with one additional twist. A key may be deleted from a leaf Q as long as it remains half-full. When that condition is violated, then the first recourse is to pick either of the closest siblings of the affected node, and to rebalance the contents between the two nodes. However, if the sibling Q' is just half-full also, then the two half-full nodes are joined as one almost full node Q''. Because of this joining, the parent node must shed a pointer and migrate a key downward into Q''; in fact, the deletion from Q guarantees that there will be space in Q'' for the extra key. As with splitting, joining can be repeated upward to the root. The twist in this operation occurs when the key K_i to be deleted is in an internal node P rather than a leaf. In this case, we look for the successor K_j to K_i in some descendant of P, swap K_i into the descendant node and K_j into P, and then delete K_i from the descendant. In fact, we see from the nature of the B-tree structure that the successor must be located in the first position of a leaf. (Whether this is the leftmost or the uppermost position in a picture depends upon the orientation of the picture.) These interactions are illustrated by the deletion of 367 from the B-tree of Figure 12.13. The deletion initially causes the successor to 367 (that is, 408) to be swapped into the root. Since the node U is then too sparse, it is joined with node V, pulling 492 from node T into the combined node. This in turn leaves node T too sparse; so it must be joined with node S, pulling 408 from the root into that combined node. The final B-tree is then as shown in Figure 12.14.

It is important to determine the maximum number of accesses required to find a key in a B-tree. We can see that a B-tree of order m must have at least two nodes at level one, and at least $2(\lceil(m/2))^{j-1}$ nodes at each level $j > 0$. Now think of the leaves as internal nodes, and imagine that there are external nodes at one level below the leaves. Then a B-tree of n total internal nodes, with its leaves at level h, must have a minimum of $n+1$ external nodes at level $h+1$. But these $n+1$ external nodes correspond to the n keys in the B-tree of height h. Thus, we find that $n+1 \geq 2(\lceil(m/2))^{h-1}$, or

$$h \leq 1 + \log_{\lceil(m/2)}\left(\frac{n+1}{2}\right) \qquad (12.5)$$

In practice, m is usually chosen to be in the range $50-300$. The exact choice depends both upon the record size for the given application and, not surprisingly, upon the characteristics of the underlying secondary storage medium. If the record sizes are either large or variable, it is common to employ indirection – that is, place pointers to data records in the nodes, rather than the actual records. This has the effect of causing an extra access. But without this step, extra accesses would doubtless be required anyway, since the large records would effectively reduce the attainable branching factor m. A final point about the choice of node size is that it is common to design B-trees so that the size of a node corresponds to the size of a page in virtual memory. This allows the fast paging hardware to assume responsibility for fetching and retaining the required pages/nodes in main memory.

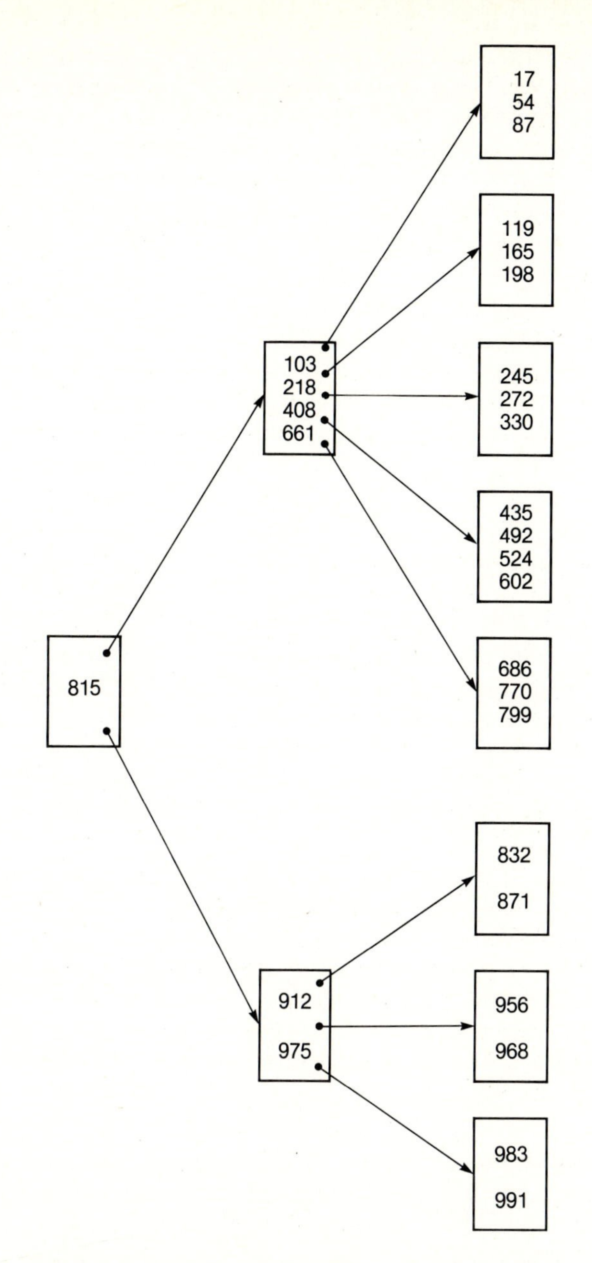

Figure 12.14 Deletion of 367 from Figure 12.13

Disregarding the possibility of indirection, let us employ Eq. 12.5 to evaluate $h(n,m)$ over the indicated range of $50-300$ for m, and for various values of n. What we find are relatively flat curves; for example,

$$h(10^4, 100) \leq 3 \qquad h(10^4, 200) \leq 2$$
$$h(10^6, 100) \leq 4 \qquad h(10^6, 200) \leq 3$$

Thus a cost of just three accesses is representative for searching a B-tree with a million keys; moreover, if the root node is kept in main memory at all times, just two accesses are required. What about the number of accesses required for insertion and deletion? When conducting the top-down search, the h nodes on the search path would be retained in memory; then the bottom-up insertion or deletion processes would require no more than $O(h)$ additional accesses. In fact, the average number of additional accesses is much less. To illustrate this for the case of insertions, we note two facts:

- The minimum number of keys in a B-tree of order m with p nodes is $1 + (\lceil(m/2) - 1)(p - 1)$.
- For a tree with p nodes, the number of splits is given by $p - h$ (allowing for the creation of two new nodes each time that the root splits).

Dividing the latter by the former, we find that the average number of splits is less than $1/(\lceil(m/2) - 1)$.

We might be able to obtain even fewer splits by the following strategy. In the example of adding 983 to the B-tree of Figure 12.12, it would have been possible to "overflow" 956 to node Q; this would have perturbed nodes P, Q, R somewhat, but not as much as with the splitting operation. In similar fashion, when keys are deleted in a B-tree, it is possible to "underflow" with a neighbor rather than perform joining operations. Still more generally, rather than rotate just one p,K pair from (to) a node on overflow (underflow), we could attempt to balance the number of p,K pairs in two adjacent sibling nodes. Even without this overflow technique, however, we see from the preceding paragraphs that the algorithms for search, insertion, and deletion in B-trees of reasonable order are all of low complexity. They are also straightforward as to logic, but fairly tedious in their details [Wirth 1976].

A closer scrutiny of B-trees suggests several ways in which their performance might be improved. We will defer most of these ideas until Section 12.3.4.2, but one variation is so important that we will describe it now. Our discussion of the B-tree of Figure 12.12 was entirely in terms of random access. Suppose that we also wished to perform sequential access upon the same set of keys. It is relatively easy to do so with a preorder traversal of the B-tree; however, the resulting performance compares unfavorably with that of sequential access in an ISAM file. The *B^+-tree* offers a resolution for this unsatisfactory state of affairs. It is based upon two simple ideas:

- The internal nodes should be used only for indexing, with all real data stored at the leaves (thus, some keys will occur both in internal nodes and in leaves).
- Each leaf should contain a pointer whereby the leaves can be chained together in logical sequence.

With the provision of a header node, it is then trivial to access the keys of a B^+-tree sequentially. It is also cheaper in terms of space, requiring just one node in main memory at any instant, rather than all the nodes on the path from the root to the current node. This new structure is illustrated in Figure 12.15, for the same data of Figure 12.12. You should compare the two figures to note the differences. B^+-trees have another significant advantage beyond their principal one of expediting sequential access; namely, deletion is simplified. If the key to be deleted occurs in both an internal node and a leaf, we need simply remove it from the leaf, and the value in

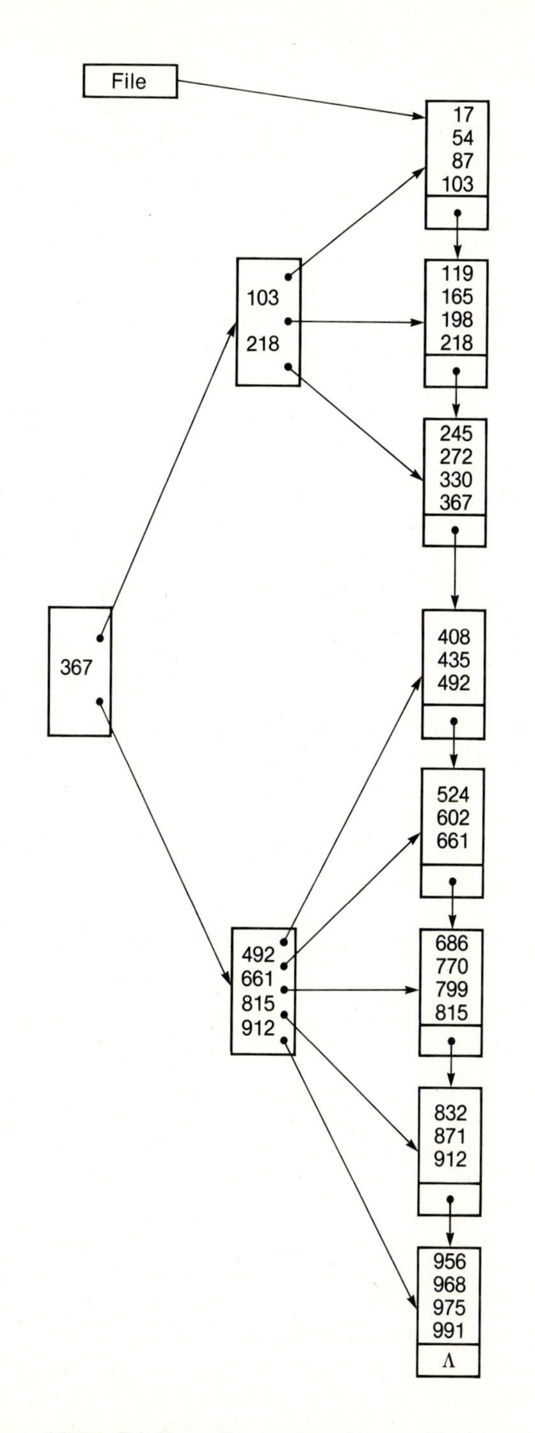

Figure 12.15 B^{+}-Tree Corresponding to Figure 12.12

the internal node can be left intact – it still serves to direct the search path to the proper son! In other words, any key value that serves to separate two leaves is permissible, whether it exists in a leaf or not.

The characteristics of B^+-trees are so good that they have become somewhat of a standard for file organization. This is exemplified by IBM's *Virtual Storage Access Method* (*VSAM*). The implementation details and the terminology of VSAM are different, but the organization is nonetheless that of a B^+-tree. We sketch the major differences, as follows:

- The basic node of data storage is the *control interval*, located at the bottom level of the tree, and with the format shown in Figure 12.16. Control intervals usually have the size of a disk track. Since all data records are retrieved via the control information, it is easy to handle variable-size records. Also, in the processes of insertion and deletion, the free area is maintained as one contiguous block. A group of control intervals in one disk cylinder is a *control area*.
- The level just above the control intervals is that of the *sequence set*. Typically, each node in the sequence set corresponds to one control area and is stored in the same cylinder as its control area, thereby reducing seek activity. Links between the nodes in the sequence set are used to facilitate sequential processing. The levels above the sequence set constitute the *index set*.
- Compression is applied to both the keys and the pointers, allowing more of them to be stored in a node and thereby gaining a higher branching factor.

We will say a bit more about B-trees in the next section; a good general survey of the topic is Comer [1979]. Further details about VSAM, in particular, can be found in Keehn and Lacey [1974] and Wagner [1973b].

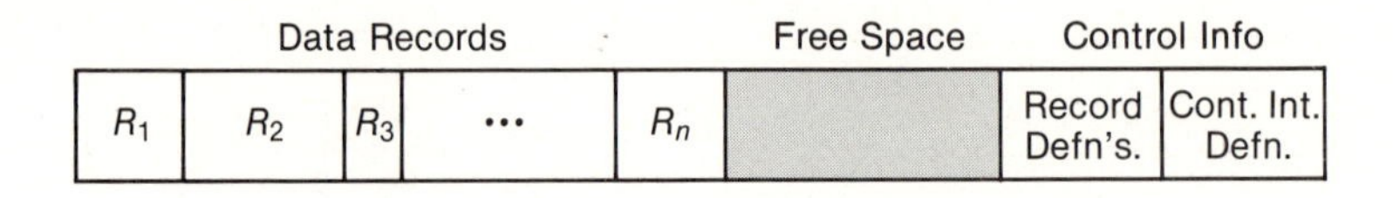

Figure 12.16 Format of the VSAM Control Interval

†12.3.4.2 Additional B-Tree Considerations. With B-trees, reorganization is done dynamically, as contrasted with the off-line reorganization that is required with ISAM, and this causes them to have superior performance in most cases. But a B-tree does have an Achilles' heel, having to do primarily with inefficient use of storage. This is partly because of the use of pointers, but also because of unused space within the nodes. To appreciate the first of these reasons, suppose that we are able to treat the tree of Figure 12.15 as a static structure, in which nodes will seldom be reorganized. Then we can economize on pointers as in Figure 12.17, allocating sibling nodes in sequential locations. As a result, we can increase the branching factor. Then, for some combinations of the parameters (number of keys, node size, pointer size, etc.), a static structure like that of Figure 12.17 may have a shorter height than that of the corresponding B-tree. By including one overflow pointer (not shown) in each leaf node, the possibility of handling insertions exists.

For a file with only moderate numbers of insertions and deletions, the reduced number of accesses with this structure might more than compensate for the overhead of occasional reorganizations [Held and Stonebraker 1978].

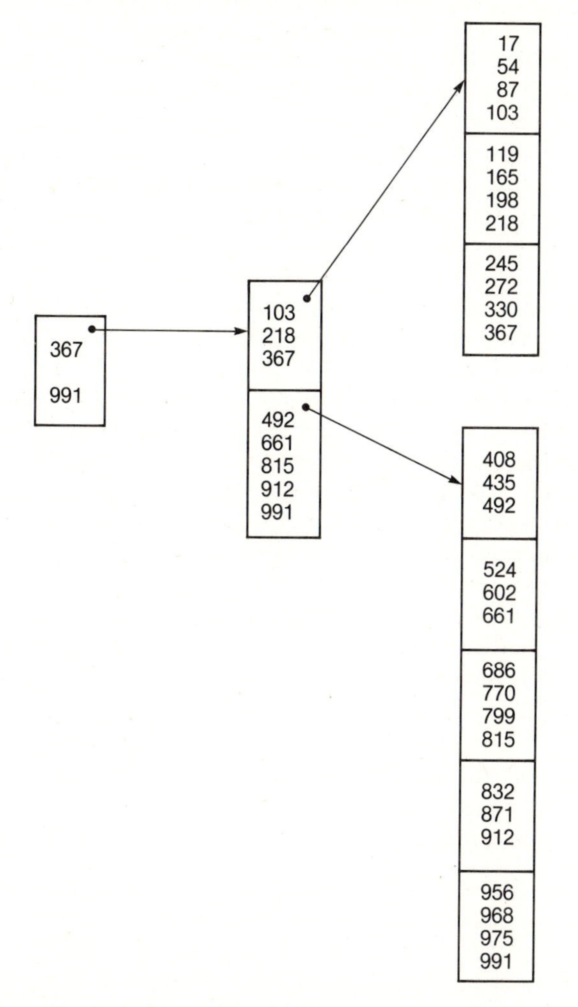

Figure 12.17 A Static File Corresponding to Figure 12.12

With respect to the issue of unused space in B-trees, an immediate observation is that since the leaves have no children, then we may as well employ an alternate format for them, one without space for pointers. A more fundamental issue is that of discovering where in the $50-100$ percent range their average storage efficiency actually lies. The fringe analysis technique provides an elegant solution to this problem (see Section 10.3.4). As a matter of fact, such an analysis for B-trees of typical order m is simpler than it is for 2-3 trees. This is so because a much higher proportion of the keys reside in the bottom layer of the fringe, and therefore it suffices to analyze just that layer and ignore the others. By this means, for a B-tree obtained by random insertions, it has been shown that the average storage efficiency is $\ln 2 = 69$ percent [Yao 1978].

If we are concerned with worst-case storage efficiency or if we wish to improve the average efficiency, then we can think of increasing the minimum proportion of fullness above 1/2, thereby obtaining a *dense multiway tree* [Culik et al. 1981]. The case of B*-trees, with a minimum proportion of 2/3, is particularly common, and is implemented as follows. Overflow in a node Q (unless Q is the root) is handled by attempting first to redistribute keys and pointers between Q and a non-full left or right sibling Q', in order to balance their contents (compare this with the discussion of "overflow" and "underflow" on page 648). Only if both sibling nodes are full is splitting performed. In this case, a new node Q'' is allocated, and the contents of the full node Q and a full sibling Q' are redistributed so that Q, Q', and Q'' each have at least $(2m - 1)/3$ children apiece. Note that this not only increases storage efficiency, but also improves the average search length, since the resulting tree may have a shorter height.

Still another means of increasing storage efficiency is suggested by the fact that in B^+-trees, we can employ any "key" values at the upper levels of the tree, as long as they properly separate the keys at the lower levels. For the common case of alphabetic keys, this leads to the concept of *prefix B-trees* [Bayer and Unterauer 1977]. The idea is to compress separator keys into minimal prefix strings of characters. Since the number of prefix characters required in order to distinguish between a consecutive pair of keys will vary for different pairs, this suggests the possibility of adjusting the breakpoints between nodes in a fashion that minimizes the aggregate prefix lengths. The rationale for this is that shorter prefixes can enable a higher branching factor, and thus once again a tree with possibly shorter height.

†12.3.5 Extendible Hashing

One way of viewing B-trees is that they are "elastic," being able to grow and shrink to conform to the storage requirement, without imposing a costly worst-case penalty. The hashing schemes that we examined in Section 12.3.2 have an excellent $O(1)$ average performance under reasonable operating conditions, but they are unacceptable in some applications because of their very poor worst-case cost. Elasticity is not present in hash tables except by costly rehashing (see Section 10.4.2.4), and even then the worst-case feature does not go away. Of rather recent invention are several hashing schemes, designed specifically for secondary memory, where these failings are removed. We will describe one of these methods in modest detail, and then comment about another.

The concepts in *extendible hashing* [Fagin et al. 1979] are reminiscent of those employed in constructing binary digital search trees in Section 10.5.2. In order to describe the method, we will initially use the keys in their natural form, ignoring the hashing aspect until later. The technique employs a directory filled with pointers to leaf pages that hold the actual data. Associated with the directory is a parameter d, the *depth*, that indicates how many leading bits of a key are to be used. When a

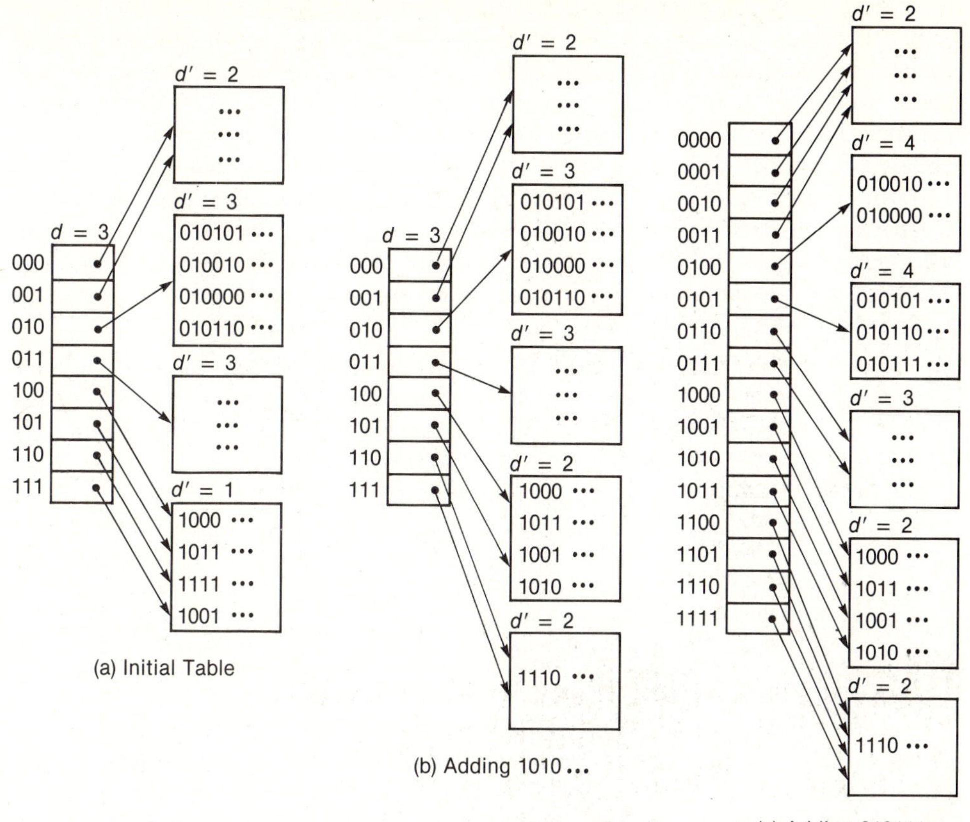

(a) Initial Table

Figure 12.18 Illustration of Extendible Hashing

key is presented, its first d bits are used to index an entry in the directory that contains the pointer to the leaf page for that key, as shown in Figure 12.18(a). In the figure, we see that $d = 3$ and so the directory has eight slots. In general, there may be more than one pointer from the directory to a given leaf page, as with the pointers for '000' and '001' in the figure. The central idea in extendible hashing is that it can never take more than two secondary memory references to find an item of data. The first of these accesses the correct directory page P (presuming that the directory is typically far too large to fit in main memory), and the second uses the appropriate pointer in P to fetch the desired leaf page.

How is this two-access figure maintained when pages overflow, without the usual overhead of chaining or open addressing? When an insertion exceeds the capacity of a page, which we assume here to be four for illustrative purposes, then d', the *local depth*, of that page becomes important. Suppose that we add the key '1010...' to the structure of Figure 12.18(a). The directory uses the initial bits '101' to point to the appropriate page. The fact that $d' = 1 < d$ for this page indicates that keys beginning with '100', '110', and '111' also reside there, and that there are other pointers to this page corresponding to such key values. So the response is to split the page on the value of the second bit of its keys, just as a B-tree page is split when it becomes full. There is a difference, of course, in that the new pages in a B-tree will both be half-full, whereas here the contents may split unevenly. After the page has split, the table appears as in (b) of Figure 12.18, with the directory updated. Consider next the consequence of adding '010111...' to the table of Figure 12.18(b). Now the directory uses '010' to point to the appropriate page, and it must be split again. This time, however, the fact that $d' = 3 = d$ serves as a signal that the value of d must be incremented, and the size of the directory must be doubled. The final effect is shown in (c) of Figure 12.18. We see that the number of accesses to find a key is still just two.

One of the nice features of this scheme is that the structure can also contract, when warranted by a deletion, thus creating a hash table that is as elastic as a B-tree. The scheme is also reminiscent of the binary buddy system that we studied in Section 11.3.2, since splitting and recombination are based upon leading bits. Still another advantage of extendible hashing is that, if the directory entries are based upon the leading bits of the keys (and not hashed keys, which we will come to momentarily), then it is possible to process the hash file (in a weak sense) sequentially! More precisely, the leaf pages are in the correct natural order. So sequential processing can be obtained by fetching each one in turn and sorting its relatively small number of items.

How well does extendible hashing work in a real application? There are two principal issues to consider. One is that it could perform very poorly with a bad set of keys, such that their prefixes are all very similar. This is where hashing comes into the picture. By using hashed keys instead of the keys themselves, the prefix bits become randomly distributed, particularly so if a technique like universal hashing is used (see Section 10.4.3), and the splittings subsume the role of collision resolution. One slight drawback, of course, is that this curtails the possibility of weak sequential processing. A second area of concern with extendible hashing is the size of the directory. It can theoretically become extremely large in the worst case; however, analysis indicates that this "never" happens in a probabilistic sense. Both simulations and usage suggest that extendible hashing is very competitive with B-trees. In terms of storage utilization, the average value is the same, being $\ln 2 = 69$ percent. With regard to secondary accesses, the number is always just two, as opposed to three or four for large B-trees.

There are other hashing schemes that attain performance comparable to that of extendible hashing by different techniques. To give just one example, in the method known as *dynamic hashing* [Larson 1978], the directory is maintained as a binary tree rather than as the "squashed trie" of extendible hashing. This causes the directory to grow and shrink less abruptly, and it also means that the total space for the directory is probably less, even allowing for the pointer overhead. Nonetheless, there is no longer any guarantee that one access will be sufficient to find the correct portion of the directory.

12.4 MULTI-DIMENSIONAL SEARCH

In Chapter 10 and in the earlier parts of this chapter, we have encountered a remarkable variety of techniques for searching for a record that matches a given key value. Unfortunately, these many methods are, in themselves, inadequate for a variety of other important paradigms of search. Some of these other paradigms were cited at the beginning and at the end of Chapter 10, particularly in Section 10.6. It happens that a number of data structures and algorithmic techniques suited to these other purposes are available. Some of them are of comparatively recent invention, and it would not be surprising to see further, substantial growth of capability in these areas. In this section, we will try to convey a modest appreciation of the issues and of the possibilities. The most pressing issue is where the underlying data records have *secondary keys* in addition to the *primary keys* by which they are uniquely identified. Effective means for dealing with this issue are important because they underpin the vast enterprise known as database, which we will not address [§]. Search in terms of just one key reflects underlying many-to-one relationships that can be described in terms of trees, and for which a single index structure is sufficient. Search in terms of several keys reflects the more complicated case of underlying many-to-many relationships. Here the natural description is in terms of graphs, and one solution is to provide a separate index structure for each secondary key.

There are several progressively more complicated ways in which one can *query* a set of records having multiple keys. Some of these other ways are as follows:

- *simple queries* – for example, to find all students who are majoring in Computer Science;
- *boolean queries* – for example, to find all male students who are married and without children;
- *range queries* – for example, to find all students between the ages of 20 and 25;
- *closest-match queries* – for example, to find the student with hometown closest to Wichita, Kansas.

In the most general case, a boolean query can contain *conjunction* (AND), *disjunction* (OR), and *negation* (NOT). Very commonly, of course, there are queries in which *no* operators are applied to one or more keys; that is, any values of those keys are acceptable. This corresponds to a *partial-match query*; it is conventional to denote unspecified attributes in such a query by '*'. Thus, for a crossword-puzzler, 'H * S *' might be any member of the set of words {HASP, HISS, HOSE, HOST, HUSH, HUSK}. As we will see, the various methods for multi-dimensional searching are not all equally adept at handling these four possibilities – conjunction, disjunction, negation, and partial-match.

Although it is possible to conduct any of the queries just cited by performing a search of the entire data file and applying the appropriate tests to each record, that is precisely what we would rather not do, except in the case when the data file is very small. And we particularly wish to avoid this when the data file is so large that it resides in secondary memory. In our survey of multiple-dimensional search, Section 12.4.1 treats search that is conducted via multiple sets of indices, and

Section 12.4.2 explores some sophisticated variants of hashing. The last section describes two data structures that are useful for multi-dimensional binary search.

12.4.1 Multiple Sets of Indices

Two structures that have long been used for searching on multiple keys are the *inverted files* and *multilists* encountered in Chapter 4. There we introduced and illustrated them. Here we will examine them more critically for their relative performance with respect to space, query time, and update time.

The relative suitability of inverted files depends very much upon the number of attributes (that is, keys), the nature of the values assumed by these attributes, and the type of query to be conducted. Recall from Section 4.3.1 that with this structure, index information about the data is maintained in a separate file of inverted lists. This is a great advantage when the inverted file is smaller than the data file itself and can be retained in primary memory. In that case, simple queries and boolean queries can be performed efficiently by first operating upon the inverted file, and then retrieving just the pertinent records from the data file in secondary memory. In order for this to pay off, it is important that there be neither too few nor too many values for an attribute. For example, consider the attribute sex, with values male and female. The lists for male and for female would be very large, so searching on this attribute would not significantly reduce the proportion of the data file that must be retrieved. At the other extreme, consider the attribute salary, with discrete values from $300.00 to $1000.00. Unless these values are grouped into ranges, we are faced with the unsatisfactory situation that there are likely to be as many distinct lists for salary value as there are records in the data file. Inverted files are very commonly used, because of the convenience that they provide for many and varied types of boolean queries. However, this convenience is purchased at the price of having inverted lists for each attribute, and the aggregate size of the inverted file may come to exceed the size of the data file. The inverted file will often no longer even fit in primary memory, thereby vitiating one of its main advantages. In this case, it can become a major issue to organize the inverted file in a manner that minimizes the number of secondary accesses to it! We will refer to this problem in the next section, but first let us consider the use of multilists.

First of all, recall that there is much less of a problem with space when using multilists (see Section 4.3.2). On the other hand, queries against multilists will be somewhat slower because of the necessity to thread through the data file. For simple queries, this can be acceptable. Also, a conjunctive query can be performed rather efficiently by following the links for the list with the smallest number of records and discarding those records for which the conjunction fails. However, searching a multilist with a disjunctive query is very inefficient, requiring the search of a list for each term in the disjunction.

The issue of update efficiency for inverted files and multilists cannot be resolved quite as summarily as the issues of space and query efficiency. Suppose that we wish to change the value of an attribute. Recall that it is common to link records in a multilist with forward pointers to physical locations. This is all the more important if we wish to minimize accesses to secondary storage. So changing the value of an attribute requires searching two link lists and changing the appropriate pointer values. With bi-directional lists, this can be done fairly readily. In the case of inverted files, it is more common to employ logical pointers (in terms of primary key values). Although this causes data retrieval to be somewhat slower, it allows the contents of the inverted file to be unaffected by any relocation of records in the data file. Changing the value of an attribute, however, requires that the list for the old value be searched, followed by a deletion, and then an insertion in the new list. Depending upon the details of implementation, these update operations might require more or less work than those required for the multilist.

12.4.1.1 Bitmaps. We have seen that an inverted file provides more flexible query capability than a multilist, but that a serious problem is the large amount of space that may be required for the inverted lists. One remedy is to just partially invert the data file (that is, invert on only certain attributes), but this may not be satisfactory in many applications. For attributes that have only a small number of values, an effective alternative is to employ a *bitmap* [§]. This is a matrix B with one row for each record and one column for each value of each attribute, so that $B[i,j] = 1$ if the ith record has the jth attribute value. Whereas a small number of values for an attribute is inefficient for an inverted file, it works very well with bitmaps. Consider a file of n records that have the attribute *class*, with values {freshman, sophomore, junior, senior}. Inverted lists on this attribute would require a minimum of $n \lg n$ bits to store either n pointers or n keys, whereas a bitmap for this attribute would require just $4n$ bits. (The four values could be encoded in two bits, of course, but it is better to retain them unencoded to facilitate query processing.) In other words, a bitmap B is likely to be preferable whenever there are less than $\lg n$ values for an attribute. In addition to conserving space, bitmaps greatly facilitate boolean queries. A fairly obvious reason for this is that conjunctions and disjunctions can be performed directly on the columns of B, without the necessity of scanning inverted lists and comparing their entries. A more subtle reason is that now negated queries are easily obtained by complementing the appropriate bit, whereas negated queries against an inverted file require the merging of all the complementary inverted lists.

†12.4.2 Multiple-Key Hashing

Just as hashing eliminates the need for an index when searching on a single key, so all the more does it eliminate the need for the multiple sets of indices employed in inverted files. Hashing also helps solve another problem. If a partial-match query is fairly general, many records may satisfy the request. Suppose for example that 10 percent of the records in a large data file satisfy a query, and that a file "page" contains 20 records. If the records $\{R_i\}$ satisfying the query are distributed randomly throughout the file, then the probability that none of the 20 records in a page will be accessed is $(1 - (0.9)^{20}) = 0.12$. So 88 percent of the pages will have to be accessed in order to retrieve the 10 percent of the $\{R_i\}$ that satisfy the query.

The performance will be little better than that of searching the entire data file! As we will see, hashing can be used to mitigate this effect.

To begin with, suppose that a string of bits $b_1 b_2 \dots b_w$ of width w is used to address a bucket of records. Then a straightforward technique is that of *partitioned hashing*, in which a hash function h_i is applied to each key K_i, such that the range of h_i is v_i bits, and $\sum v_i = w$. These hash values can then be concatenated to provide one composite hash value for the entire set of keys. In general the v_i may vary, and it is appropriate to assign longer bit fields to keys that are more commonly used in queries, and also to keys with greater numbers of values. Both of these allocations have the effect of reducing the number of accesses to secondary memory against those keys. Moreover, by choosing the hash functions properly, we can try to form *clusters*, consisting of groups of records having similar attribute values. In one investigation, a mixed approach using inversion and hashing was found to reduce the number of secondary accesses by a factor of two or three [Rothnie and Lozano 1974]. A word of caution is that the success of this approach is relative to the intrinsic clustering of the data values and to the nature of the queries conducted against them.

Hashing provides still another advantage. What happens with an inverted file as a partial-match request becomes more specific? The number of records that are retrieved will almost certainly decrease, but the amount of work will increase with each attribute that must be examined! Considering that rather precise queries are common, it would be nice to have a method such that fewer retrievals coincided with less work. Let us assume that we use partitioned hashing with k attributes, and with the same number of bits v for each attribute − that is, $w = kv$. Then the search space is reduced by a factor of 2^v for each attribute that is specified. Conversely, if t is the number of unspecified attributes, then the number of hash buckets to be searched is proportional to $n^{t/k}$.

Rivest has shown how to extend this to handle negation as well as conjunction, in a method called *associative block design* (*ABD*). To set the background, we will restrict the discussion to binary attributes. (It is straightforward to encode non-binary attributes as binary ones.) Then an ABD (k,w) is characterized by a table with $b = 2^w$ rows and k columns, where the values '0, 1, *' signify, respectively, that an attribute is absent, present, or arbitrary. In such a table,

(a) Each row has w bit values and $k - w$ asterisks.

(b) For any two rows, there is at least one column that is different with respect to the bit values (0,1).

(c) Every column contains $b\,(k - w)/k$ asterisks.

These properties are illustrated in the ABD(4,3) of Figure 12.19. The significance of such a design is that each row corresponds to a list of records answering that description and maintained in a corresponding hash bucket. With hash functions properly chosen to yield this partitioning, the number of buckets that must be searched is a decreasing function of the number of unspecified attributes. The intent of condition (a) is to restrict the maximum size of each bucket, the intent of condition (b) is to guarantee that lists are disjoint, and that of condition (c) is to restrict the worst-case behavior. For the 81 possible queries on $\{0, 1, *\}^4$, Figure 12.20 tabulates the number of buckets (lists) that must be searched as a function of t, the number of unspecified attributes. For example, the query '* * 1 *' would require searching of the five buckets 2, 4, 5, 6, 7, and so would any other query with three unspecified attributes. However, the query '1 * * 0' would require searching of just the three buckets 1, 4, 8, and so would any other query with two unspecified attributes. In the case of just one unspecified attribute, 8 of the possible 32 such queries would need to search only one bucket (for example, '0 1 * 0' with bucket 5), and the other 24 would require searching of two buckets (for example, '0 1 * 1' with buckets 2 and 3).

Bucket	Bit Position 1	2	3	4	Bucket	Bit Position 1	2	3	4
1	*	0	0	0	5	0	1	*	0
2	*	1	1	1	6	1	0	*	1
3	0	*	0	1	7	0	0	1	*
4	1	*	1	0	8	1	1	0	*

Figure 12.19 Associative Block Design (4,3)

The significant fact in Figure 12.20 is the close correspondence between the computed averages in the third column and the theoretical values in the fourth column. That is, the number of lists to be searched decreases as t decreases, again in proportion to $n^{t/k}$. Now the construction of associative block designs is a non-trivial combinatorial problem [Rivest 1976b]. For many parameter pairs (k,w), no corresponding ABD (k,w) exists; an instance of this is the pair (5,4). Our example ABD(4,3) is too small to be practical per se. However, given an ABD (k,w), it is possible to use it as a basis for larger ABD's, of type (rk,rw) and also of type (k^r, w^r). Aside from the difficulty in finding ABD's, one of their principal drawbacks is the complexity of the hash function computation. However, this cost is very worthwhile for data files stored in secondary memory because of the large reductions in the number of accesses. Related combinatorial designs for partial-match retrieval are given in Burkhardt [1976a, 1976b].

t	No. Queries	Avg. No. Buckets	$8^{t/4}$
4	1 × 1 = 1	8	8.000
3	4 × 2 = 8	5	4.757
2	6 × 4 = 24	3	2.828
1	4 × 8 = 32	56/32 = 1.75	1.682
0	1 × 16 = 16	1	1.000

Figure 12.20 Retrieval Costs for ABD(4,3)

†12.4.2.1 Superimposed Codes. In Section 10.4.4 we saw several variations on the theme of predictive hashing. The essence of those methods was the multiple use of hash function(s). Each hash computation would turn on a small number of bits in a large boolean vector, and the multiple hash values were superimposed by OR'ing them together in this vector. This is the basis for a method of information retrieval that antedates all the others in this chapter. In the context of partial-match retrieval (rather than text searching, as in Chapter 10) it is known as *superimposed coding* [Mooers 1951]. The analogy between the text searching point of view and the partial-match point of view can best be understood by referring to the Bloom filters discussed earlier. In that technique any key present in a file is hashed onto a large bit vector T with each of several independent hash functions, and this operation is done for each key in the file. Subsequently, in order to predict if a specific key K is in the file, the same hash functions are applied to K. If *any* of the bit locations that must be turned on for K to be present are not found turned on, then K assuredly cannot be in the file. On the other hand, the outcome that they are all turned on does not guarantee that K is in the file; the key K might be a false match, or *false drop*.

In the case of a Bloom filter, one bit vector T serves as a predictor for the occurrence of keys in the entire file. In the present context, we are hashing the presence of binary attributes in a record R_i, and so we associate with each record a bit vector P_i that is the superimposed encoding of the attributes of that record. When presented with a conjunctive query, we hash the attributes that are specified and then compare this vector Q of superimposed codes with the vectors $\{P_i\}$. Any record R_i potentially satisfies the query if the ones in its P_i include all of those in Q. Of course, since an R_i may be a false drop, it is always necessary to verify that it does indeed match the query specifications. However, the possibility for error exists only in one direction; that is, no valid record will be missed. The trick in using superimposed coding is to properly adjust two principal parameters − the width w of the vector Q, and the number of bits k that are turned on in Q for each attribute. When these are well chosen, there are just a few false drops, and the fact that the bulk of the non-matching records never need to be accessed amply compensates for the cost of the false drops.

In many ways, the vectors $\{P_i\}$ are like the bitmaps that we encountered in Section 12.4.1.1, and some of those same bit processing techniques are applicable here. There are also important differences. Superimposed codes do not support disjunction and negation, as do bitmaps; on the other hand, they can efficiently encode thousands of binary attributes in less than a hundred bits. A comprehensive, up-to-date account of superimposed coding and a realistic application of it are given in Roberts [1979]. In a typical large information retrieval system, even the compression provided by superimposed codes may not relieve the necessity of having the $\{P_i\}$ in secondary memory. An effective solution in this case is to structure the codes in two levels, analogous to the use of a secondary index in ISAM, thereby sharply reducing the number of secondary accesses [Sacks-Davis and Ramamohanarao 1983].

†12.4.3 Structures for Generalized Binary Search

In dealing with attributes of data, we find that there are various modalities. The most important of these are:

- *qualitative data* – the possible values are descriptive only, such as male for sex, Protestant for religion, etc.;
- *ordinal data* – a discrete number of possible values can be ranked, but not measured against one another, such as sophomore for class, blue for color, etc.;
- *quantitative data* – some metric such as time or length exists for comparing any two values, such as years for age, miles for distance, etc.

Most of our treatment of multi-dimensional search has until now been concerned with data that has many dimensions, or attributes, each of which is qualitative, or perhaps ordinal. The structures that we examine now are particularly well suited for dealing with data that has few dimensions, each of which is quantitative. The simplest case, of course, is the familiar one of geometrical space of two or three dimensions. For this reason, search employing these structures is commonly characterized as *geometric search*. In the same vein, typical search paradigms for these structures are range-search and closest-match search, as described in Section 10.6. Several data structures have been devised for these purposes; we will describe just two of the most common ones. They represent two different manners in which to generalize the technique of binary search. A broader treatment of structures for these purposes is found in Bentley and Friedman [1979].

†12.4.3.1 Quad Trees. The term *quad tree* actually describes several structures that recursively decompose a region of two-dimensional space into four sub-regions, or quadrants. As originally proposed and still commonly used, the recursion proceeds on the locations of points in this space [Finkel and Bentley 1974]. For a large class of applications, it is more useful to decompose space into successively smaller squares, as illustrated in Figure 12.21. The shaded regions and the clear regions in (a) of this figure represent two classes of data in those areas, such as binary pixel values. The quad tree representation of the entire region is shown in (b) of the figure. It is conventional to attach the four child quadrants of a node in the order N(orth)W(est), N(orth)E(ast), S(outh)W(est), S(outh)E(ast). Recursive decomposition proceeds until each square is homogeneous. The leaves are tagged as being black or white, according to the value of the data in that area, and internal nodes are tagged as being gray. More efficient in many cases, however, is to terminate the recursion at some threshold, and then apply a gray-scale value to the leaves. The regularity of decomposition that we see in Figure 12.21 is beneficial in that it might be used to good purpose via a parallel processing mechanism. It can also be a source of complication when, for example, the natural form of input consists of rectangles that overlap the quadrant regions. One of the principal reasons for using quad trees to represent regions is that they can significantly reduce the space required to store data. The space for a two-dimensional array of values is $O(n^2)$. For many types of two-dimensional images, however, the space requirement for the corresponding quad tree is $O(n)$.

(a) Region Image

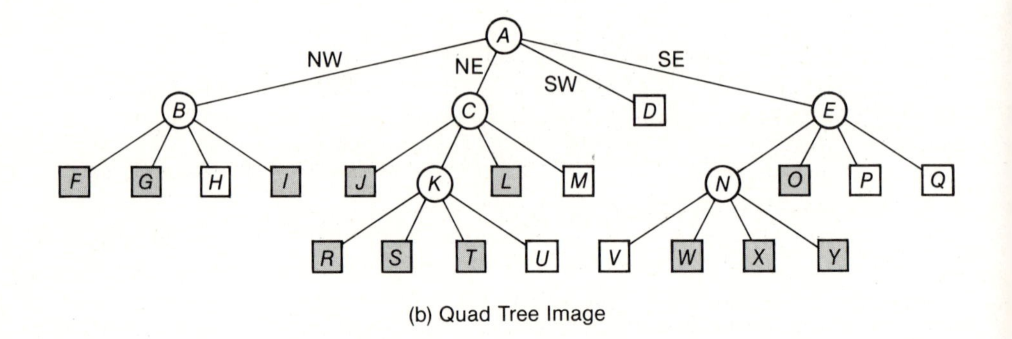

(b) Quad Tree Image

Figure 12.21 The Quad Tree Structure

The use of quad trees for storing point data is different in character and easily described. In this case each node might represent a city, with its latitude and longitude as the two keys. Then, when presented with the latitude and longitude of a search location, each iteration of an algorithm analogous to binary search would discard three quadrants and look in the remaining quadrant. We will not pursue their use in this regard, since the structure of the next section has been found to be much better for many purposes. An extensive survey of quad trees and their representations is Samet [1984].

†12.4.3.2 *k*-d Trees. The *k-d tree* (*k*-dimensional tree) is a binary tree such that the left (right) subtree of a node contains items with keys having values less than (equal to or greater than) the value of a key stored at the node. (It is important to accommodate the case of equality, since there may be many non-unique secondary key values.) The decisive feature with *k*-d trees is that the comparison relation is computed with different attributes, or keys, at successive levels of the tree. If the keys were geographic coordinates, for instance, then latitude might be employed at odd levels and longitude at even levels. Felicitously, *k*-d trees are useful for database types of search as well as for geometric search paradigms [Bentley 1979a]. We will employ the data of Figure 12.22 to try to illustrate the flexibility they bring to the former type of search. The data in the figure might pertain to a history of accomplishments by some precocious undergraduates. Each record contains values for the attributes of name, age, and class. The simplest way to implement *k*-d trees is according to the original proposal, whereby the attributes are used cyclically [Bentley 1975]. An instance of a *k*-d tree built by cycling on them in the order of class, age, name, and then class again is shown in Figure 12.23(a).

Record	Name	Age	Class
1	Hoare	21	junior
2	Ullman	20	freshman
3	Knuth	21	senior
4	Tarjan	18	freshman
5	Codd	20	freshman
6	Graham	20	junior
7	Hoare	24	junior
8	Graham	19	sophomore
9	Tarjan	19	sophomore
10	Knuth	20	freshman
11	Bentley	24	senior
12	Tarjan	17	freshman
13	Yao	18	sophomore

Figure 12.22 Multi-dimensional Data

In practice, there are several ways to improve upon the *k*-d tree construction of Figure 12.23(a). One is to employ a threshold, as with quad trees, to terminate branching when there are only a few items left in a subtree. Another is to look for a way to obtain more balanced trees. Clearly, whichever attribute is used at a given level, the optimal choice of an attribute value is the median of those in that tree. Even so, the cyclic choice of attributes can easily lead to comparatively unbalanced subtrees. A way to avoid this is to employ *adaptive partitioning*, which means to employ at each root of a subtree that attribute having the maximum dispersion of values in that subtree [Friedman et al. 1977]. For this, each node must carry along an explicit *discriminator*, or index, of the attribute to be used for the next level in the tree. Applying this idea to the data of Figure 12.22 leads to the better *k*-d tree of Figure 12.23(b), with the discriminator values (1) *name*, (2) *age*, and (3) *class* shown with each node. Note that an attribute may be employed two times in a row; an instance of this is *age* in the case of records #4 and #9. Also, we can

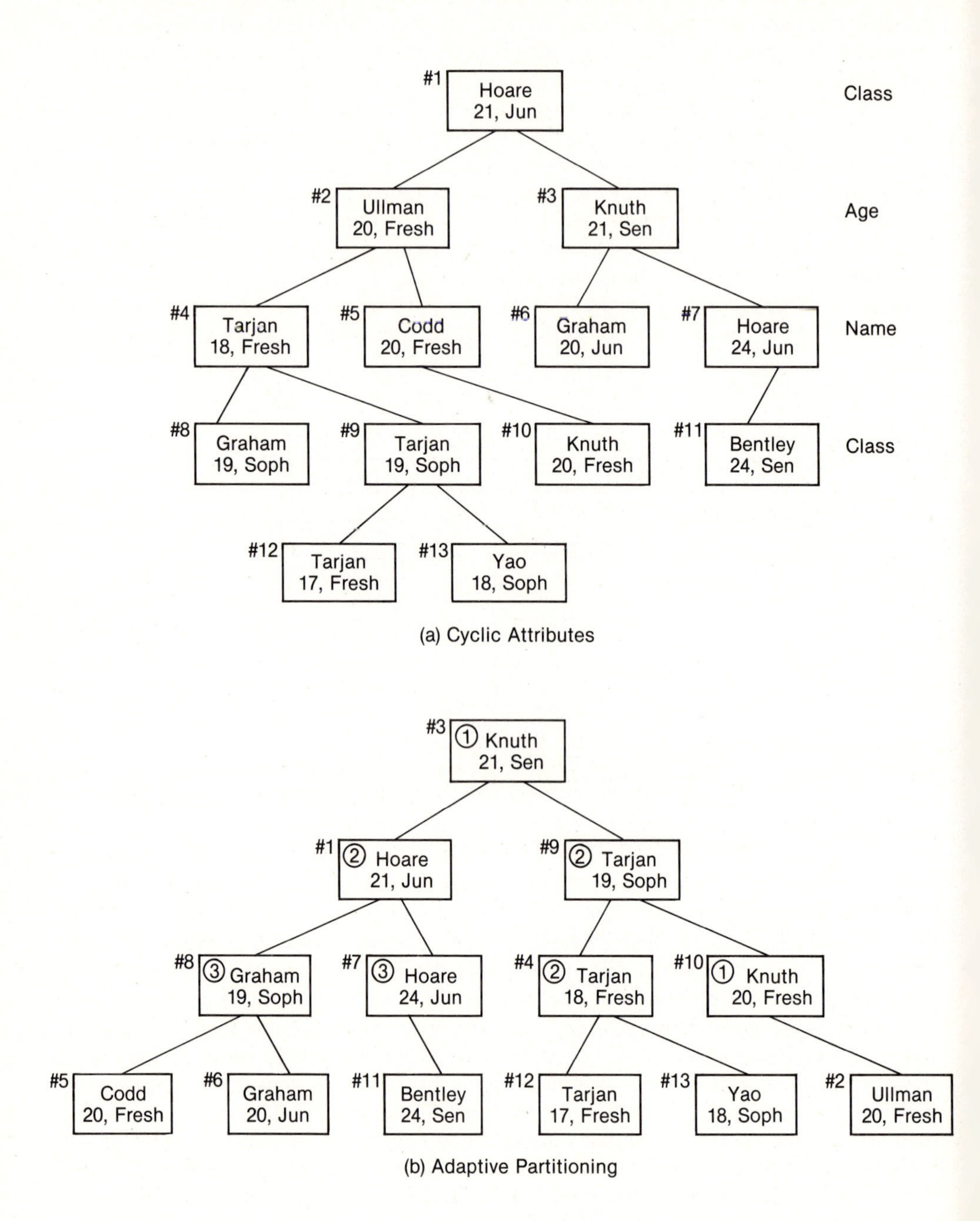

Figure 12.23 Examples of a *k*-d Tree

expect to see records on a given level of the tree employing different attributes for discrimination at the next level; an example of this is records #7 and #8 using *class*, #4 using *age*, and #10 using *name*.

The adaptive partitioning approach causes a k-d tree to be sensitive to the data from which it is built, and this is one of its particular advantages. Even so, a k-d tree can be somewhat inefficient for queries with respect to just one dimension. The problem is that there may be many dimensions, and branching might occur on the desired dimension at just every kth level of the tree. Thus, the work to compute a partial-match with just one key specified may be 2^k times what it would be in a BST on that key. The good news, on the other hand, is that k-d trees share an important characteristic with the hashing techniques of Section 12.4.2. Specifically, the work associated with a partial-match query goes down exponentially with the number of attributes that are specified. With respect to range queries and closest-match queries, k-d trees evidently have an average cost of $O(\lg n)$.

There are some limitations to k-d trees, a principal one being a paucity of good methods for using them dynamically. It is fairly easy to insert new nodes, and a random k-d tree has the same expected value for maximum path length of $1.386 \lg n$ as does a random BST (see Eq. 10.14). However, deletions present more of a problem. Moreover, there are not as yet any good methods for rebalancing k-d trees, and this is certainly an important issue for dynamic situations.

12.5 OVERVIEW

In Chapter 1 we stated that data structures are often fundamentally more significant than algorithms for determining how efficiently or conveniently a task can be performed. The consequences of choosing between algorithms are typically expressed in varying complexity classes, and ultimately these differences prevail. But the constant factors are also important. This is particularly true with secondary memory, where the constants may vary by many orders of magnitude. The influence of these constant factors upon the choice of data structure is substantial, and it accounts for the variety of structures in this chapter. One can avoid deciding between all of these structures by relying upon virtual memory, but this only hides the issue and does not solve it, as we illustrated in Section 12.2.

In the progression of the file organizations in Section 12.3, we find parallels to much of the previous course of this entire book. The earliest file organization (and the only one for many years) was the sequential file; its analogues in primary memory are the array and queue and stack. The first way of responding to the need for dynamic structures in secondary memory was via hashing, which typically relies upon linked lists (explicitly or implicitly) of synonyms. Another response was via indexed sequential files, which are trees. And just as structures for maintaining tree balance are important in primary memory, they are also vital in secondary memory with B-trees. Lastly, although the issue was beyond the scope of this book and thus barely exposed, the requirement to deal with multi-dimensional data has analogues with graphs. In particular, some database models make use of the structure known as a *hypergraph*. Succinctly, whereas a graph conveys relationships between pairs of vertices via edges, a hypergraph is a generalization that conveys relationships among sets of vertices.

12.6 BIBLIOGRAPHIC NOTES

- Simulation is employed in Lum et al. [1971] as the basis for answering questions about optimum bucket sizes, for deciding between open addressing and chaining, and for responding to other random access issues. Analytical answers to some of these questions can be found in Severance and Duhne [1976] and van der Pool [1972, 1973b].
- The problem of designing files with multiple attributes so that they provide good performance for many kinds of queries is a very difficult one, and it has inspired a variety of ideas far beyond what we have room to describe. Among the more interesting approaches are those of Abraham et al. [1968], Bolour [1979], Bose and Koch [1969], Chow [1969], Ghosh [1972], Hsiao and Harary [1970], Lum [1970], Schkolnick [1975], Shneiderman [1977], and Wong and Chiang [1971].
- Data structures texts that treat the subject of database are Gotlieb and Gotlieb [1978] and Tremblay and Sorenson [1984]. Texts devoted entirely to the topic are Date [1981, 1983] and Ullman [1982].
- For alternative methods of employing bitmaps, particularly with regard to minimizing the number of accesses to secondary memory, and for analyses of their performance, consult Burke and Rickman [1973], Pfaltz et al. [1980], and Vallarino [1976].

12.7 REFERENCE TO TERMINOLOGY

12.8 EXERCISES

Sections 12.1 – 12.4

12.1 How many logical records of 100 bytes each can be stored on a tape that is 2000 feet long with a recording density of 1600 BPI (a) if the blocking factor is 5? (b) if the blocking factor is 40?

12.2 [Belady et al. 1969] We can model the behavior of a paging algorithm against the execution of a given program as follows. Let the pages that are successively referenced by the program be given by a string of page numbers, as for example: 1 2 3 4 1 2 5 1 2 3 4 5. Suppose now that a FIFO replacement algorithm is used, and that we have slots A,B,C for three pages in main memory. Then the history of the page slots in time will be as follows, where a period indicates an empty slot and an underscore indicates the most recent reference.

A :	$\underline{1}$	1	1	$\underline{4}$	4	4	$\underline{5}$	5	5	5	5	$\underline{5}$
B :	.	$\underline{2}$	2	2	$\underline{1}$	1	1	$\underline{1}$	1	$\underline{3}$	3	3
C :	.	.	$\underline{3}$	3	3	$\underline{2}$	2	2	$\underline{2}$	2	$\underline{4}$	4

We can see that this set of circumstances incurs nine page faults: 1, 4, 5 in A and 2, 1, 3 in B and 3, 2, 4 in C. Suppose that we now try to improve matters by allocating four page slots instead of three. Trace the paging activity for this case, as above, and describe what happens.

12.3 Describe briefly the essential differences between serial and sequential access.

†12.4 [Dijkstra 1976] Even though batch processing is a venerable style of computation, it engenders the *File Update Problem.* Even after many years of existence, it is frequently solved in a clumsy fashion. This is a pity, because it has clean and elegant solutions. In this problem, there are two sequential files as input:

1. An Old Master File, consisting of one record per key, and (for our purposes) containing an account key and an account balance in each record.
2. A Transaction File, consisting of possibly many records per key. Each record is one of three types: (I)nsertion, specifying that a new account with the given key and a zero balance is to become part of the Master File; (U)pdate, applying a positive or negative increment to the balance; or (D)eletion, specifying that the given record for that key is to be removed from the Master File.

It is neither possible nor efficient to update the Old Master File directly, and so we construct as output a New Master File, consisting of one record per key, with balances reflecting the contributions from the two inputs. Artificially high keys are used as sentinels to mark the ends of all three files.

The reason that solutions to this problem are often clumsy has to do with their manner of dealing properly with exceptional conditions. In particular, various combinations of missing and repeated keys in the two input files make it tricky to synchronize matters. Thus, an attempt to insert a key already present in the Master file, or to delete a key not already present, signals an error, as does an attempt to update a key that is not currently valid. However, the transaction file may contain a succession of records such that a key is deleted, then reinserted, then updated several times, then deleted again, etc. Write a program to perform Sequential File Update, and test it against the following input:

Old Masters: 5, 21 / 8, 9 / 10, 7 / 18, 31 / 999, 0
Transactions: U, 8, 3 / D, 8 / U, 8, 2 / I, 8 / U, 8, 40 / I, 10 / D, 15 / U, 18, −1 / U, 18, 11 / U, 18, −4 / I, 24 / U, 24, 5 / I, 999

12.5 Describe briefly the essential differences between indexed-sequential and direct access.

12.6 What are the significant differences between using hashing for main memory and using it for secondary memory?

12.7 For the following two patterns of collisions, compute the corresponding values of overflow percentage *OP*, and also the average number of accesses *AA*, both with chaining and with open addressing.

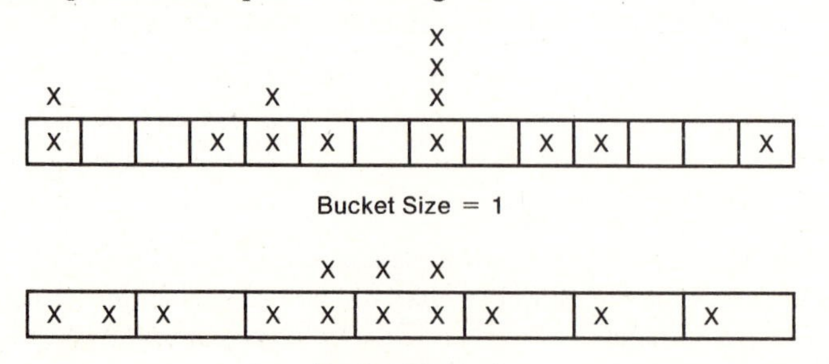

†**12.8** Assume that the keys 1 .. 29 are inserted, in that sequence, into initially empty B-trees, for the cases (a) and (b) below. Draw the trees as they appear immediately after each insertion that has affected more than a single node. For this exercise, when equality of balance is not possible, always split off nodes with greater numbers of entries to the left. Take care to be exact in applying the various rules.

(a) Do this for a B-tree of order 6.

(b) Do this for a B*-tree of order 6.

††**12.9** The "other half" of Exercise 10.26 is deletion from a 2-3 tree. Analyze and diagram the various cases for this, making note of any arbitrary algorithmic choices. Then write the program and test it in the following manner. Start with the 2-3 tree obtained by inserting 1 .. 20 as in Exercise 10.26, and then try four patterns of deletions. For each pattern, start counting with the first item and then delete exactly 13 items, each time selecting the next item to be deleted as the mth of the remaining items, in the style of the Josephus problem (see Exercise 4.7). Do this for $m = 2, 3, 5$, and 8. What are the final 2-3 trees for the four cases?

††**12.10** Write an algorithm to perform search and insertion for extendible hashing, such that if search fails then the item is inserted. Presume that initially the depth of the directory is $d = 2$, and do not consider the possibility that the directory may require more than one "page." Also assume that leaf pages hold just four items and that they are initially empty. Test your program against a random sequence of 40 insertions, and display the contents of the directory and the hash table just before and just after each split.

††**12.11** Prove the following about an ABD (k,w) design:

(a) Each column contains a total of $\frac{bw}{2k}$ bit values.

(b) For any $0 \leq u \leq w$, there are $\binom{w}{u}$ rows which agree in exactly u positions with any given record in $\{0,1\}^k$.

(c) $\frac{k}{w} \leq \frac{wb}{2(b-1)}$

†**12.12** Draw the k-d tree that is obtained for the data of Figure 12.22 when the attributes are employed in the cycle: name, age, class, etc.

††**12.13** Write an algorithm to do insertion into a k-d tree. Test your program by applying it to the data of Figure 12.22, using the cycle: name, age, class, etc.

13

SORTING

"Light shone, and order from disorder sprung."

Milton,
Paradise Lost, Bk III

"Better late than never, as Noah remarked
to the Zebra, which had understood
that passengers arrived in alphabetical order."

Bert Leston Taylor,
The So-Called Human Race

The advantages of having items ordered according to the values of their keys are very compelling. We find data arranged this way in dictionaries, in libraries, in timetables, and in countless other places. Much of the motivation for having this orderliness stems from the needs of humans. For example, although hashing can be very efficient as a means of searching for an item with a computer, it is decidedly inconvenient for use by people. Sorting is also commonly used as a preprocessing step for expediting subsequent searches with computing machines. Thus, whether for the sake of people or machines or both, this need for order is reflected in the commonly accepted statistic that computers spend more than one-quarter of their time performing the sorting function.

Sorting is a fundamental process, and it also illustrates very nicely the practical benefits of many of our previous studies. Thus, even though much of the story of sorting relates to discoveries now one or two decades old, and which are treated definitively in Knuth [1973b], it behooves us to give it the special attention of this chapter. Our objective is to be thorough, though not nearly so complete as Knuth, and to bring the subject up to date in the areas where there is recent invention.

Just as in the case of searching, we need to begin with a few mathematical concepts, dealing in the present case with some properties of permutations. After that, most of Section 13.2 is drawn from the "classical" material on sorting described in the preceding paragraph. More precisely, it discusses *internal sorting* methods that can be used when main memory is large enough to hold all the data to be sorted. A problem that is related to sorting, yet simpler, is that of selection, as in the example of finding the third largest item from a set; this is the topic of

Section 13.3. When main memory is not large enough to hold all the data to be sorted, some very different methods in Section 13.4 for *external sorting* are appropriate. The final topic is an active area of current research, that of methods for parallel sorting.

13.1 THE ISSUES INVOLVED

Given a sequence of items that have keys, we say that they are sorted if $K_i \leq K_j$ whenever $i < j$. When we are dealing with numeric keys, the proper ordering between pairs of keys is clear. The situation for alphabetic keys is less obvious, being crucially dependent upon the collating sequence of the character set (see Section 8.2.1). But there are few differences in principle between alphabetic keys and numeric ones, and for the most part we we will employ numeric keys in the interests of simplified exposition. We can regard a sequence that is in order as the identity permutation, and a sequence S that is not in order as some permutation P applied to the identity. Then sorting amounts to finding the inverse permutation P^{-1} that should be applied to the sequence S so that it will be in order. A very useful concept in this regard is that of the number of inversions in a permutation, to be discussed in Section 13.1.1.

It is possible, of course, that values of keys may be repeated within a sequence; such a case would occur, for example, when sorting a group of transactions based upon account numbers. However, this is somewhat of a distraction from our principal objective of elucidating the various methods; so we will not treat the case of repeated key values in any systematic fashion. In fact, we will commonly use the following sequence in the course of illustrating a variety of methods:

$$33\ \ 41\ \ 7\ \ 15\ \ 55\ \ 87\ \ 28\ \ 22\ \ 9\ \ 46\ \ 32 \tag{13.1}$$

There is one aspect of the repeated-key case that cannot be ignored, however. Suppose that we have the data items

$$3\ \ 1_1\ \ 5\ \ 1_2\ \ 4_1\ \ 2_1\ \ 4_2\ \ 2_2\ \ 1_3$$

where equal keys are distinguished by subscripts corresponding to their relative positions originally. Then it may be important that the sorted sequence should retain this secondary ordering, as in

$$1_1\ \ 1_2\ \ 1_3\ \ 2_1\ \ 2_2\ \ 3\ \ 4_1\ \ 4_2\ \ 5$$

If a sorting technique is guaranteed to preserve this secondary ordering, it is said to be a *stable sort*. Although stability is important in some applications, it is irrelevant in others. The latter fact is a fortunate one, since several of the sorting methods that are fastest are also unstable.

The principal criteria for comparing sorting methods are, as heretofore, time complexity foremost, and space complexity secondarily. For searching, most of our discussions centered on the number of comparisons required in order to locate a record with a given key. An important difference now is that the output of a sort is a permutation of the input, and so we need to measure work in terms of moving data as well as comparing keys. Moreover, some sorting algorithms perform the same amount of work regardless of the actual input; that is, they are oblivious (see Section 1.3.2.2). On the other hand, many methods are not oblivious, so that their minimum and maximum complexities are very different from their average complexities. This sometimes gives rise to what could be termed "pathologies," or perverse behaviors, associated with certain combinations of sorting method and input permutation. We will find that the time complexities of the sorting methods do not vary greatly, with $O(n^2)$ and $O(n \lg n)$ being most typical. In practice, the size n is often very large, so that even this modest difference becomes extremely significant.

```
type   index = 0 .. size;  {size = n}
       item = record
          key: integer;
            ...
       end;
       items = array [index] of item;
```

Figure 13.1 Type Definitions for Sorting

Sorting is conveniently characterized in terms of permuting the elements of an array from an input sequence to an output sequence. With this in mind, we will presume throughout this chapter that the type definitions of Figure 13.1 apply. Given that n may be very large and that arrays are highly efficient in use of storage, this is also by far the most natural characterization. When we account for the movement of records, however, and particularly if the records are large, then two other possibilities might be considered – the use of linked lists, and the use of a table for indirection. By way of illustration, suppose that we have the array elements shown in Figure 13.2(a). Then the sorted array would be, of course, as shown in (b). The effect of sorting the same data using cursors as links is shown in (c) of the figure. Finally, we see in (d) of the figure the use of a table for indirection; sorting via this latter technique is called an *address table sort*. In employing this last method, it may happen that the records are long but the keys are short. It would probably be better in that case to operate upon direct copies of the keys rather than indirectly upon the keys in the original records; this variation is known as *key sorting*. For many (but not all) of the sorting methods, we can always incorporate one of these structures if it is warranted, so we lose little and gain simplicity in exposition by sticking with the array representation.

As a concluding note, output in the form of a linked list or an address table may be adequate, or we may still need to physically permute the records. The problem of generating the rearrangement corresponding to an address table is closely related to the generation of the inverse of a permutation, using its cycle structure (see Exercise 2.9). The problem of generating the rearrangement corresponding to a linked list is the subject of Exercise 13.5.

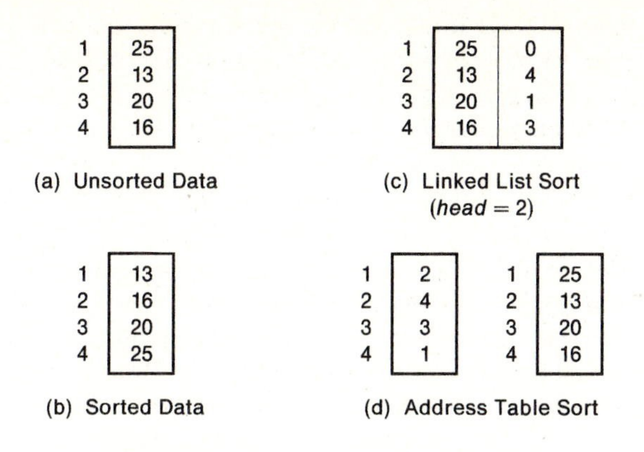

Figure 13.2 Structures for Sorting

13.1.1 Inversions

If a sequence is not in order, it is useful to quantify its relative unsortedness. A convenient measure for this is the number of inversions by which the corresponding permutation differs from the identity. There is an *inversion* for every pair (j,i) such that $j > i$ and j is to the left of i. Moreover, for a given permutation, let b_k represent the number of inversions in which k is the second member of a pair. The sequence $b_1, b_2, \dots, b_n$ is called the *inversion table* of the permutation. Thus the permutation 2 7 9 4 8 5 3 6 1 would have the inversion table 8 0 5 2 3 3 0 1 0 where, for example, $b_5 = 3$ because of the three inversions (7,5), (9,5), and (8,5). The inversion table entries must clearly have the property that $0 \le b_k \le n - k$. The greatest number of inversions in a permutation will occur for $n, n-1, \dots, 1$; it will have the corresponding inversion table $n-1, n-2, \dots, 0$. Summing these entries, we find that the maximum is $O(n^2/2)$; the average number of inversions in a permutation is easily found to be $O(n^2/4)$. Inversions have the remarkable property that it is easy to go in the opposite direction, constructing the permutation corresponding to a given inversion table. We simply start with b_n and work our way to the left, dropping each value k into the permutation sequence in the manner dictated by b_k. To illustrate using our original example,

for $b_8 = 1$, place 8 with 9 yielding 9 8
for $b_7 = 0$, place 7 with 9 8 yielding 7 9 8
for $b_6 = 3$, place 6 with 7 9 8 yielding 7 9 8 6
for $b_5 = 3$, place 5 with 7 9 8 6 yielding 7 9 8 5 6
etc.

In constructing a random permutation of 1 .. n, we have to be careful that the generated elements are distinct. If we define a random permutation in terms of its inversion table, however, we can take advantage of the fact that the b_k are independent of one another. For example, what is the average number of maxima seen in scanning a permutation from right to left? (In our example there are four such maxima, at 1, 6, 8, 9.) Now for any such maximum k, all the values $j > k$ must occur to the left of it; in other words, for that value of k, b_k has its maximum value of $n - k$. The average number of right-to-left maxima is then equal to the sum of the independent probabilities that $b_k = n - k$, which is

$$1 + \frac{1}{2} + \frac{1}{3} + \cdots + \frac{1}{n}$$

This sum is instantly recognizable as the nth harmonic number H_n. In fact, from our discussion of harmonic numbers in Section 10.1.1, we see that this is really a familiar problem. In that section we recounted that permutations can be expressed in cycle notation in a canonical manner (see Section 1.2) by arranging for each cycle to begin with its smallest element, and then writing the cycles in decreasing order of these first elements. In this fashion, our sample permutation 2 7 9 4 8 5 3 6 1 becomes (5 8 6) (4) (1 2 7 3 9). Recall that we can omit the parentheses and write this as 5 8 6 4 1 2 7 3 9, because the parentheses (and thus the cycles) can be reconstructed by looking for left-to-right minima. But looking for minima is isomorphic to looking for maxima, and looking from left to right is isomorphic to looking from right to left. In other words, in analyzing permutations in terms of inversions, we once again discover that the average number of cycles in a random permutation on n elements has the value H_n.

13.2 INTERNAL SORTING

We have spoken of the variety of sorting methods. How many are there, really? From one point of view, there are just five generic methods. Four of them operate via comparisons between pairs of keys in one manner or another, and we will describe them first. The fifth generic method can be lumped under the category of distribution sorting, and we treat it distinctly from the other methods, in Section 13.2.2. These generic methods are "no-frills" offerings that have the virtues of simplicity and low programming effort. However, most of them have complexity $O(n^2)$; and so for large n, it is worthwhile to consider "brand-name" offerings that are not as simple but have lower complexity. There are scores of such sorting methods. Generally, though, we will examine just one efficient counterpart for each of the generic methods.

13.2.1 Comparison-Based Methods

The comparison-based methods are: insertion sorting, selection sorting, exchange sorting, and merge sorting. At first acquaintance, the distinctions among the first three of these will seem to be rather illusory, in that the operations of insertion, selection, and exchanging can be found to occur in all three of them. Indeed, some of the earlier surveys of sorting methods (such as Martin [1971]) employ classifications different than those employed here. However, the distinctions that we will be making are useful ones that are by now well accepted. Before proceeding, we should ask whether these methods (and distribution sorting) are really the only generic methods. The answer is, not quite.

We are already familiar with the possibility of using BST's for the purpose of sorting (see Section 6.6.1); this method even has good complexity (see Section 10.3.1). Nonetheless, because of the space requirement for two link variables with each key, it is unlikely to be used for large values of n. Another method is *enumeration sorting*. Imagine that a list of unique values of numerical grades has been posted, and that we wish to determine our relative rank in the class. We can ascertain the rank by using that list to count j, the number of grades that are greater than ours. Our rank is then given by $j + 1$. Indeed, every student in the class can determine his rank in the class in the same fashion. Note that we have not actually permuted the data items by this process. Rather, the array of rank values that we obtain is related to the auxiliary array of values in an address table sort. To be precise, the permutation specified in the counting case is the inverse of the permutation specified in the address table case. It is easy to see that enumeration sorting is $O(n^2)$, so that it is neither better nor worse than the generic methods that we have cited. Since there does not seem to be any way to improve enumeration sorting so that it is better than $O(n^2)$, as with the other methods, it is rarely accorded equal status with them. (However, we will see an exception to this in Section 13.5.)

13.2.1.1 Insertion Sorting. Insertion sorting is easily understood in the familiar terms of repeatedly picking up playing cards and inserting them into the proper position in a partial hand of cards, thereby maintaining the cards in order. Let us apply this process to our sample input of Eq. 13.1. Matters progress as illustrated in Figure 13.3, with the numbers below (above) the diagonal constituting the sorted (unprocessed) portions of the input. The work for each new number K_j (just above the diagonal) consists of comparing it with numbers K_i to its left until we find $K_i < K_j$, or until we reach the left end of the list. Rather than test for both eventualities each time, it is better to put a sentinel at the left end. Corresponding to this, we have the procedure INSERT_SORT (Algorithm 13.1), wherein the text of Figure 13.1 is implicitly included. The method would also sort properly if the comparison were $K_i \leq K_j$, rather than $K_i < K_j$. But then, for equal keys, the execution time would increase; more significantly, the method would change from being stable to being unstable.

For random data, each of the n keys must be compared against a sequence to its left of average length $n/2$, and each of those searches will be of average length $n/4$. Moreover, compares and moves are interspersed in this algorithm. Thus, insertion sort entails $O(n^2/4)$ comparisons and $O(n^2/4)$ moves. We can obtain a more meaningful picture, however, by reflecting upon the work performed by the inner loop. Each comparison that results in a move is the result of an inversion in the input permutation, and each such move reduces the number of inversions by one. Since the average number of inversions is $O(n^2/4)$, we thus have direct confirmation of the expected complexity of insertion sort. Of greater significance, we see that since the work is proportional to the number of inversions, then insertion sort will perform much better than average with input data for which the degree of

33	41	7	15	55	87	28	22	9	46	32
33	41	7	15	55	87	28	22	9	46	32
7	33	41	15	55	87	28	22	9	46	32
7	15	33	41	55	87	28	22	9	46	32
7	15	33	41	55	87	28	22	9	46	32
7	15	33	41	55	87	28	22	9	46	32
7	15	28	33	41	55	87	22	9	46	32
7	15	22	28	33	41	55	87	9	46	32
7	9	15	22	28	33	41	55	87	46	32
7	9	15	22	28	33	41	46	55	87	32
7	9	15	22	28	32	33	41	46	55	87

Figure 13.3 Trace of Insertion Sort

```
procedure INSERT_SORT (var data: items);
const  ninf = {a large negative value as sentinel}
var    i,j: index;
         rcrd: item;
begin
   data [0].key := ninf;
   for i := 2 to size do begin
      j := i - 1;  rcrd := data [i];
      while rcrd.key < data [j].key do begin
         data [j + 1] := data [j];
         j := j - 1;
      end;
      data [j + 1] := rcrd;
   end;
end;
```

Algorithm 13.1 INSERT_SORT

unsortedness (the number of inversions) is low.[1] In fact, because of its extreme simplicity and because it performs so well in this case, insertion sort as in Algorithm 13.1 is the recommended method for data that is nearly sorted.

In analyzing the performance of any algorithm, we must be very careful to understand the assumptions underlying the analysis. The importance of this is illustrated when we examine insertion sort more closely, seeking ways in which to improve it. Since the search is conducted on an ordered array, we might try replac-

---

[1] The number of inversions is not the only possible measure of unsortedness. Other measures of disorder are discussed in Section 13.2.4.

ing the sequential search with binary search, leading to the method known as *binary insertion*. This would reduce the overall complexity of the search from $O(n^2)$ to $O(n \lg n)$. Unfortunately, there is no corresponding reduction in the complexity of the moves, so this approach has limited practical utility. In fact, for the occasions when insertion sort is most appropriate – that is, with data that is nearly in order – binary search might even be less efficient than sequential search. There is a significant way to improve the performance, however. We should recognize that the process of inserting an element into an array by shifting some of the array contents is much less efficient than inserting an element into a linked list, which requires changing two link values. By the latter approach, although we still have $O(n^2/4)$ comparisons, we have only $O(n)$ moves! Although this modification is very worthwhile (see Exercise 13.4), it still does not overcome the $O(n^2)$ barrier. That is the subject of the next section.

13.2.1.1.1 Shellsort. In order to break the $O(n^2)$ barrier with insertion sorting (and for that matter with any of the generic methods), we need to reduce the number of inversions by more than one on each iteration. A method that accomplishes this in the present case is *Shellsort*, named after its discoverer [Shell 1959]. It is also called *diminishing increment sort*, which captures the essence of the method – to perform insertion sorts with a series of increments h_s that diminish to one on the last pass. In the earlier stages, each move of an element from the ith to the $(i + h_s)$th position can have the effect of eliminating several inversions. Since the last pass employs an increment of one, it is equivalent to ordinary insertion sorting, and so the output of the pass must necessarily be sorted. Because of the previous stages, however, this last pass will encounter relatively few inversions.

We illustrate the technique for our example data, employing increments of 5, 3, 1. Each pass with a particular h_s consists logically of h_s distinct insertion sorts, conducted upon values that are h_s apart in the data. This is not as complicated as it may sound, as can be seen by reference to Figure 13.4. In (b) of the figure, we have offset the five chains corresponding to $h_3 = 5$ on five lines, and in (c) and (d) of the figure we see the final values of this pass. The sequence is now said to be 5-sorted. The next pass uses $h_2 = 3$, and parts (e) and (f) of the figure show the corresponding chains before and after sorting. The sequence at this point is said to be 3-sorted. In fact, the transition from (e) to (f) has required just four upward moves, but it has reduced the number of inversions from 18 to 8. The chains for $h_1 = 1$ are shown before sorting in (g) and after sorting in (h). The detailed procedure to perform all of this is SHELLSORT (Algorithm 13.2). In reducing the above description to code, it is expedient to have each pass scan the array just once from left to right, rather than trying to isolate h_s chains each time. Thus, the algorithm rotates among the distinct chains as it proceeds, rather than following the sequence just described. The logical effect is identical though.

Two related and unresolved issues about Shellsort are the optimum choice of a sequence of increments, and its complexity. These matters are explored masterfully in Knuth [1973b], and the remainder of this section draws heavily upon it. Suppose, to begin with, that we have just two increments, the last being $h_1 = 1$. Then it can be shown that the optimum choice for h_2 is approximately $1.72n^{1/3}$, yielding an average performance of $O(n^{5/3})$. However, it is more effective to employ

(a)	33	41	7	15	55	87	28	22	9	46	32
	33					87					32
		41					28				
(b)			7					22			
				15					9		
					55					46	
	32					33					87
		28					41				
(c)			7					22			
				9					15		
					46					55	
(d)	32	28	7	9	46	33	41	22	15	55	87
	32			9			41			55	
(e)		28			46			22			87
			7			33			15		
	9			32			41			55	
(f)		22			28			46			87
			7			15			33		
(g)	9	22	7	32	28	15	41	46	33	55	87
(h)	7	9	15	22	28	32	33	41	46	55	87

Figure 13.4 Trace of Shellsort

```
procedure SHELLSORT (var data: items);

const  t = 3;    {for this example}

var    done: boolean;
       h,j,s: index;
       i: integer;
       incr: array [1 .. t] of index;
       rcrd: item;

begin
   incr [1] := 1;  incr [2] := 3;  incr [3] := 5;
   for s := t downto 1 do begin
      h := incr [s];
      for j := h + 1 to size do begin
         done := false;  i := j - h;  rcrd := data [j];
         while (i > 0) and (not done) do
            if rcrd.key >= data [i].key then
               done := true
            else begin
               data [i + h] := data [i];
               i := i - h;
            end;
         data [i + h] := rcrd;
      end;
   end;
end;
```

Algorithm 13.2 SHELLSORT

a greater number of increments. The original description of Shellsort suggested the sequence $\lfloor(n/2)$, $\lfloor(n/4)$, $\lfloor(n/8)$, ... However, it has been shown that if a sequence of h_s satisfies such a divisibility property with respect to any set of divisors, then it cannot yield an average performance better than $O(n^{3/2})$. Moreover, the worst-case performance with such a sequence is $O(n^2)$. For maximum effectiveness, the h_s should be relatively prime to one another; in this case, there is more mixing among the data items, which leads to a faster reduction in the number of inversions. In this mixing, a remarkable property becomes significant. If we have a sequence that has already been j-sorted and we then k-sort it, the output of this latter pass is still j-sorted! We leave the proof of this fact as an exercise (see Exercise 13.7), but its truth can be seen in Figure 13.4.

Despite considerable research, no one knows even the optimal number of increments to employ for a sequence of size n, much less the optimal set of values. Knuth suggests using $h_1 = 1$ and $h_{s+1} = 3h_s + 1$, stopping with h_t when $h_{t+2} \geq n$; the sequence in this case is 1, 4, 13, 40, ... This suggestion and several others seem to yield a performance that can be approximated either as $O(n \lg^2 n)$ or as $O(n^{5/4})$, with some evidence that the exponential form is closer to reality. There is still the tantalizing possibility, however, that some sequence may be found which will yield an $O(n \lg n)$ average performance.

13.2.1.2 Selection Sorting. With this method we repeatedly look for the smallest remaining key and then move it to its final position. It is instructive to compare the effect of insertion sort with that of selection sort. With the former we examined one new key each cycle and maintained the growing output in correct relative order, but could not be sure that any item was in its final location until the last cycle. With selection sort we examine the entire (remaining) input each cycle, and we always know that the initial portion of the output contains its final values. This is illustrated with our example data in Figure 13.5, wherein the numbers below (above) the diagonal constitute the sorted (remaining) portions of the input. The corresponding procedure is SELECT_SORT (Algorithm 13.3), with the text of Figure 13.1 implicitly included once again.

Selection sorting requires about twice as many comparisons as insertion sorting, on the average, since each outer loop examines the entire remaining sequence, yielding $O(n^2/2)$ comparisons. However, it requires just $O(n)$ moves. This latter fact suggests that selection sort might be appropriate when the underlying records are large. Nonetheless, the method is still $O(n^2)$ overall. This shortcoming is more significant here than it was with insertion sorting, because selection sorting is an oblivious method. That is to say, selection sorting will execute its $O(n^2/2)$ comparisons and $O(n)$ moves even if the input is already sorted! Thus, it is not a good method to apply to input data that is nearly in order.

13.2.1.2.1 Heapsort. With ordinary insertion sorting, we saw a fundamental limitation due to the necessity to make as many data moves as there are inversions. The fundamental shortcoming with ordinary selection sorting, on the other hand, is that we are obtaining a great deal of information in each outer loop, but then ignoring it and reconstructing the same information again in the next cycle. One way to

33	41	7	15	55	87	28	22	9	46	32
7	41	33	15	55	87	28	22	9	46	32
7	9	33	15	55	87	28	22	41	46	32
7	9	15	33	55	87	28	22	41	46	32
7	9	15	22	55	87	28	33	41	46	32
7	9	15	22	28	87	55	33	41	46	32
7	9	15	22	28	32	55	33	41	46	87
7	9	15	22	28	32	33	55	41	46	87
7	9	15	22	28	32	33	41	55	46	87
7	9	15	22	28	32	33	41	46	55	87
7	9	15	22	28	32	33	41	46	55	87
7	9	15	22	28	32	33	41	46	55	87

Figure 13.5 Trace of Selection Sort

```
procedure SELECT_SORT (var data: items);

var     i,j,k: index;
        lo: integer;
        rcrd: item;

begin
   for i := 1 to size - 1 do begin
      k := i;  rcrd := data [i];  lo := rcrd.key;
      for j := i + 1 to size do
         if data [j].key < lo then begin
            k := j;  lo := data [j].key;
         end;
      data [i] := data [k];  data [k] := rcrd;
   end;
end;
```

Algorithm 13.3 SELECT_SORT

redress this situation would be to employ divide-and-conquer, splitting our original data into $n^{1/2}$ groups of $n^{1/2}$ items each, and using a work area of size $n^{1/2}$. We begin by placing the smallest item from each group in a corresponding work location. Then we repeatedly (a) select the smallest item from the work area, and (b) replace it with the next largest item out of the group from which it originated. Such a method is called *quadratic selection sort*, and has complexity $O(n^{3/2})$. Better still, however, is to organize our comparisons as a tournament, in the manner shown in Figure 13.6 for our example data. In other words, we could place our data at the leaves of a complete binary tree and make a series of pairwise comparisons, always promoting the smallest value to be the parent. By this process, the smallest key will be promoted to the root. Then, when we remove the lowest key from the root, we can determine the next "winner" with just $\lceil \lg n$ further comparisons. Indeed, such a method is feasible, and is termed a *tournament sort*. However, it requires space for $O(n)$ internal nodes in addition to the $O(n)$ leaves, and we must be careful to mark the empty nodes as promotions drain the tree. The latter effect is illustrated in Figure 13.7.

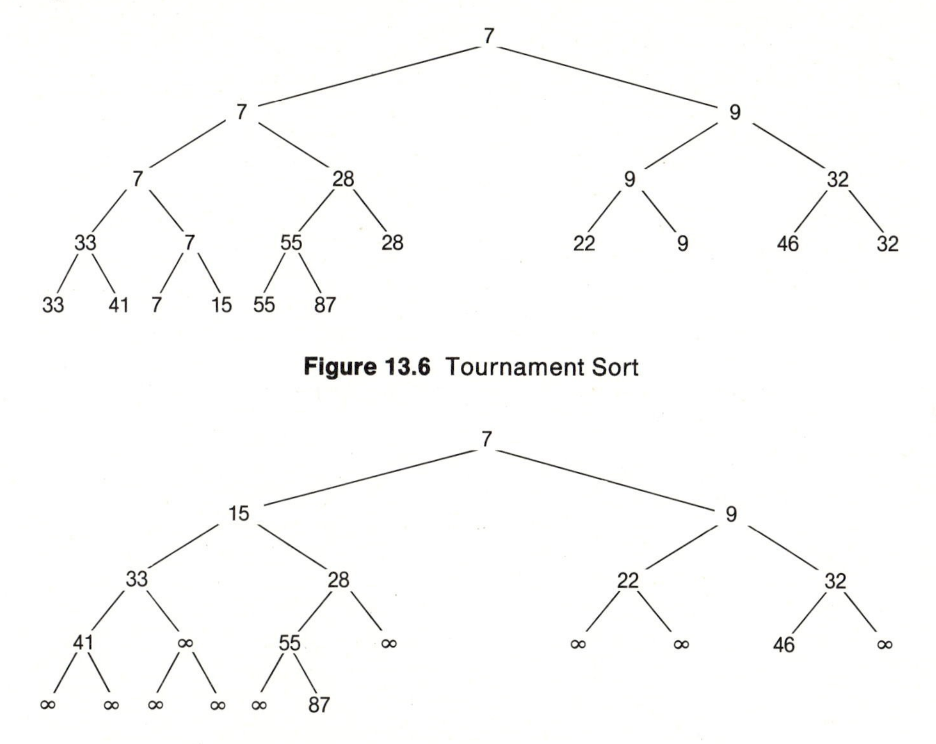

Figure 13.6 Tournament Sort

Figure 13.7 A Tournament with Promotions

An ingenious method that attains the effect of a tournament sort without the shortcomings just described is *Heapsort*. It operates, as the name suggests, by employing the heap data structure of Section 6.6.4. To be precise, we regard our array of data as a complete binary tree, with the data at all of the nodes, and not just the leaves. The method has two phases. In the first we convert the tree to a heap by iteratively applying the heap condition to each internal node, starting at the last and working our way up to the root. Thus, our example data as a complete binary tree is shown in Figure 13.8(a). In (b) of the figure we begin applying the heap condition at location 5 (value 55), and repeatedly apply it until we get to location 1. The following exchanges take place:

15 and 22, 7 and 87, 41 and 55, 41 and 46, 33 and 87

Note how the exchange of 41 and 55 forces a subsequent exchange of 41 and 46. At the conclusion of the first phase, we then have the heap as in (c) of Figure 13.8.

It may seem strange that we have applied the heap condition in the sense of promoting the largest value each time, rather than the smallest. Even stranger

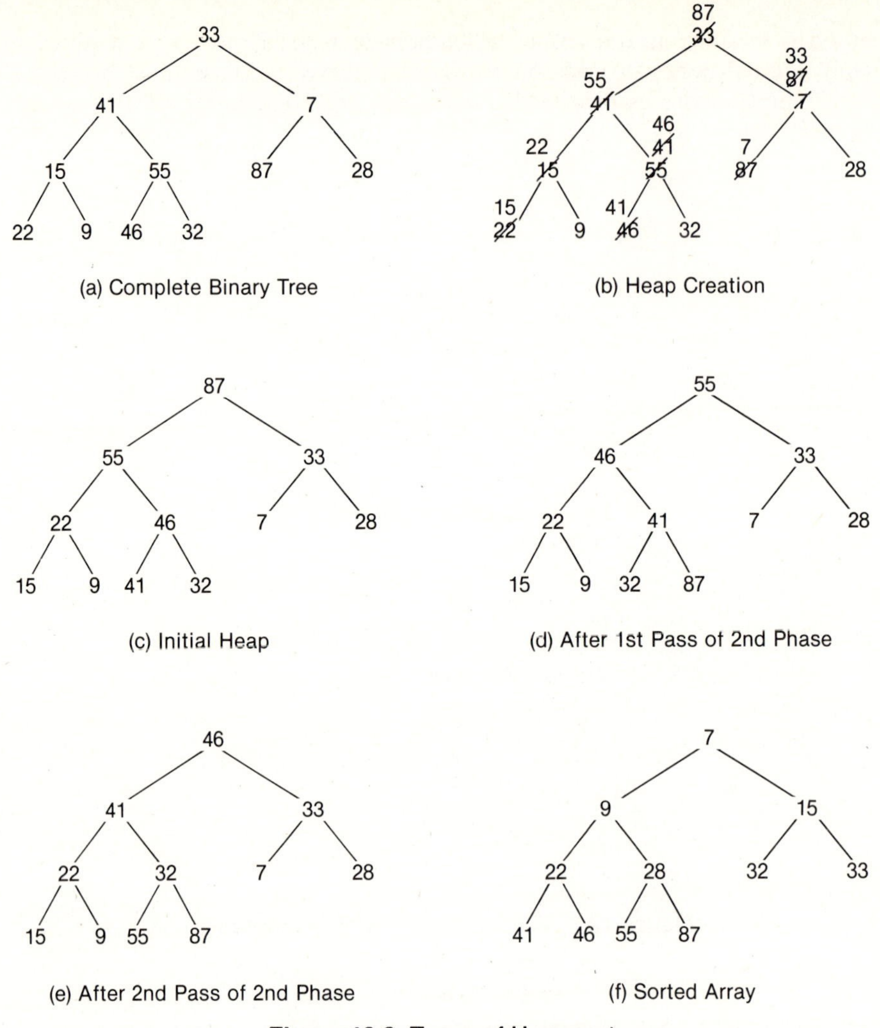

Figure 13.8 Trace of Heapsort

perhaps, the second phase of Heapsort proceeds by repeatedly truncating the heap, exchanging the value at the root with the value at the truncated position, and then restoring the heap property. Thus, the first pass in the second phase exchanges 87 and 32, and then restores the heap property by the further exchanges:

32 and 55, 32 and 46, 32 and 41

leading to the situation in Figure 13.8(d). The second pass of the second phase exchanges 55 and 32, and then restores the heap property by the further exchanges

32 and 46, 32 and 41

All of this leads to the situation shown in (e) of the figure, and eventually we obtain the sorted arrangement shown in (f) of the figure. In fact, this mechanism is exactly

```
procedure HEAPSORT (var data: items);
var     i: index;
        rcrd: item;

procedure SIFT (left,rite: index);
label  1;
var     j: integer;
begin
   j := 2 * left;  rcrd := data [left];
   while j <= rite do begin
      if j < rite then
         if data [j].key < data [j + 1].key then
            j := j + 1;
      if rcrd.key >= data [j].key then
         goto 1;
      data [left] := data [j];
      left := j;  j := 2 * j;
   end;
1: data [left] := rcrd;
end;

begin
   for i := size div 2 downto 1 do
   {transform original tree into heap}
      SIFT (i,size);
   for i := size - 1 downto 1 do begin
   {swap root (largest) with last and restore heap}
      rcrd := data [i + 1];
      data [i + 1] := data [1];
      data [1] := rcrd;
      SIFT (1,i);
   end;
end;
```

Algorithm 13.4 HEAPSORT

the same that we used for removing an item from a priority queue implemented as a heap. It is also the basis for accomplishing the first phase of Heapsort; we just vary the subrange of the array upon which we operate!

Putting all of this together leads to the procedure HEAPSORT (Algorithm 13.4), where the sub-procedure SIFT is almost identical to REMOVE_PRQ_H (Algorithm 6.7). One might easily suppose, because of all the data motion, that Heapsort is not very efficient. Not only that, in converting our original array of values to a heap, we have actually increased the number of inversions, from 27 to 38. Nonetheless, for large n, Heapsort is the most efficient method that we have encountered so far. Both the heap creation phase and the selection phase consist of $O(n)$ calls upon the procedure SIFT, and each such call can involve no more than $O(\lg n)$ exchanges along a path from an internal node to a leaf. (Note that, for a series of n related exchanges, we do not actually perform $3n$ moves, but rather $n + 2$

moves.) Thus Heapsort is $O(n \lg n)$, even in the worst case; that is, it is a $\Theta(n \lg n)$ sorting method. In fact, the first phase can be shown to be $O(n)$ (see Exercise 13.11). This is not very relevant for sorting with a heap, since the second phase is still $O(n \lg n)$, but it is significant for other applications of heaps.

There is a distinction between tournament sort and Heapsort that is a bit subtle and sometimes significant. With the former, we know exactly the number of comparisons and promotions that are required. Namely, there are $n - 1$ for setting up the tournament and $\lceil \lg (n - 1)$ for promoting a winner out of the tournament. With the latter, we know that the number of comparisons (and exchanges) is $O(n)$ for setting up the heap and $O(\lg n)$ for promoting a winner out of the heap; however, we do not know the *exact* values. Consequently, if our focus is on developing a good algorithm, we would probably prefer to use a heap; on the other hand, if our focus is on getting accurate counts in developing complexity bounds, we should employ a tournament. Instances where this distinction matters can be found in Sections 13.3 and 13.4.2.

Although analysis of the average complexity of Heapsort is incomplete, the average amount of computation is found to be fairly stably approximated by $n \lg n$. Thus, the best case of Heapsort for 8 items is exemplified by 8 7 6 3 2 4 5 1, with 21 comparisons and 13 exchanges. Yet the corresponding worst case, as exemplified by 1 5 2 6 4 3 7 8, is not that much worse; it requires 29 comparisons and 24 exchanges. These results also illustrate a general feature of the method, that performance is better for input data that tends toward descending order than it is for data that tends toward ascending order.

13.2.1.3 Exchange Sorting. In the generic form of exchange sorting, we repeatedly compare pairs of elements, exchanging them if they are out of order, until no out-of-sequence pairs remain. The most common method for doing this is to start at the beginning of the sequence and compare K_i and $K_i + 1$ for successive values of i from 1 to $n - 1$. This will sweep the largest value to the last position. The entire process is then repeated for values of i from 1 to $n - 2$, then from 1 to $n - 3$, etc. The observed behavior has been likened to that of bubbles rising in a liquid, with the result that this method is called *bubble sort*. We observe that successive cycles can terminate with successively smaller values: $n - 1$, $n - 2$, etc. In fact, we can do even better by keeping track of the last location *bound* where an exchange occurred during a cycle of the outer loop. Because no exchanges occurred thereafter, the remainder of the sequence must be order; so *bound* $- 1$ is an appropriate right-hand limit for comparisons on the next cycle of the outer loop. With this refinement, a trace of bubble sort upon our example data is shown in Figure 13.9; included in the trace is the value of *bound* after each cycle of the outer loop. The corresponding procedure is BUBBLE_SORT (Algorithm 13.5).

For estimating the efficiency of bubble sort, we find that inversions are useful in two ways. Since each basic exchange operation reduces the number of inversions by just one (as in insertion sorting), and since the average number of inversions is $O(n^2/4)$, we can see that bubble sort is basically an $O(n^2)$ method. However, each exchange involves *three* moves, so that the average number of moves is actually $O(3n^2/4)$ – far inferior to either insertion or selection sorting. The estimation of the average number of comparisons is more complicated, since it depends upon the

bound	1	2	3	4	5	6	7	8	9	10	11
	33	41	7	15	55	87	28	22	9	46	32
10	33	7	15	41	55	28	22	9	46	32	87
9	7	15	33	41	28	22	9	46	32	55	87
8	7	15	33	28	22	9	41	32	46	55	87
7	7	15	28	22	9	33	32	41	46	55	87
6	7	15	22	9	28	32	33	41	46	55	87
3	7	15	9	22	28	32	33	41	46	55	87
2	7	9	15	22	28	32	33	41	46	55	87
0	7	9	15	22	28	32	33	41	46	55	87

Figure 13.9 Trace of Bubble Sort

```
procedure BUBBLE_SORT (var data: items);

var     bound,i,j: index;
        rcrd: item;

begin
   bound := size;
   repeat
      j := 0;
      for i := 1 to bound - 1 do
         if data [i].key >= data [i + 1].key then begin
            rcrd := data [i];
            data [i] := data [i + 1];
            data [i + 1] := rcrd;
            j := i;
         end;
      bound := j;
   until bound = 0;
end;
```

Algorithm 13.5 BUBBLE_SORT

average number of iterations of the **repeat** ... **until** loop. In this regard, it is useful to look at the complete inversion table. We find that each outer iteration of bubble sort reduces each non-zero value of b_i by one. For example, with reference to Figure 13.9, the initial value of the inversion table is 2 7 2 5 4 5 0 0 2 0 0, after the first pass it is 1 6 1 4 3 4 0 0 1 0 0, etc. Thus, the number of outer cycles is determined by the largest expected value among the b_i. This can be shown to lead to the result that the average number of comparisons is given by $n \times (n - \ln n)/2$. So in number of comparisons, bubble sort is inferior to insertion sorting and of no significant advantage over selection sorting. All in all, considering both comparisons and moves, we see that bubble sort is inferior to either insertion sort or selection sort, despite its catchier name.

Once again, we can look for ways to improve upon the basic method. In examining Figure 13.9, we notice an asymmetry: large values propagate to the right quickly, but small values (for example, 9) propagate to the left slowly. This observation has inspired the *cocktail shaker sort*, which is basically bubble sort with alternation of direction on successive passes. Although this method seems to perform marginally better than bubble sort, it does not overcome the basic $O(n^2)$ character of the method [Wirth 1976]. A better idea is to incorporate diminishing increments into bubble sort, yielding complexity analogous to that of Shellsort [Dobosiewicz 1980]. But the best way to use exchanges is that of the next section.

13.2.1.3.1 Quicksort. The method we now describe was dubbed *Quicksort* by its inventor Hoare [1962]. This title is well-deserved, since it was then and still is the fastest known method for internal sorting based upon comparisons of keys. It is also known as *partition-exchange sort*, since that term captures the basic idea of the method, as follows. One of the items is selected as a *partitioning element*; the remaining items are compared with it, and a series of exchanges is performed. At the conclusion of this series of exchanges, the original sequence has been partitioned into three subsequences:

(a) all the items less than the partitioning element;

(b) the partitioning element in its *final* place;

(c) all the items greater than the partitioning element.

At this stage, we have finished with (b) and can recursively apply Quicksort to the items in (a), and also to the items in (c); when the recursion terminates, the entire sequence will be sorted.

If we pay close attention to the description in the preceding paragraph, we note that there are two distinct processes that have to be spelled out: how to select the partitioning element at each stage, and how to perform the exchanges. For now, we will simply choose the first element in a sequence as its partitioning element, and concentrate our attention upon the exchanges. This latter process is conducted with the aid of two cursors, i starting from the left of the sequence and j starting from the right. First i is incremented until it references an item greater than the partitioning element, and then j is decremented until it references an item less than the partitioning element. This pair of items is exchanged and the cycle is repeated, until i and j cross. When they do, the point at which they cross identifies the proper place to insert the partitioning element in order to obtain the three subsequences described in the previous paragraph. More precisely, the cycle terminates with $i = j + 1$. At this point, we have *data* [*left* + 1 .. *j*] less than the partitioning element and *data* [*j* + 1 .. *rite*] greater than the partitioning element; thus, an exchange of the items referenced by *left* and *j* achieves the desired partitioning. This mechanism is spelled out in the procedure QUICKSORT (Algorithm 13.6); you would do well, before continuing, to compare it with the procedure COLLECT_1 (Algorithm 11.2) of Section 11.2.3.1.

Once again, we illustrate matters with our example data. Note that QUICKSORT has as input parameters a pair of indices delimiting the subrange of *data* to

```
procedure QUICKSORT (var data: items; left,rite: index);

var     i,j: integer;
        part,rcrd: item;

begin
  i := left; j := rite + 1; part := data [left];
  repeat
    repeat
      i := i + 1;
    until data [i].key >= part.key;
    repeat
      j := j - 1;
    until part.key >= data [j].key;
    if i < j then begin
      rcrd := data [i];
      data [i] := data [j];
      data [j] := rcrd;
    end;
  until i >= j;
  data [left] := data [j]; data [j] := part;
  if left < j -1 then
    QUICKSORT (data,left,j - 1);
  if i < rite then
    QUICKSORT (data,i,rite);
end;
```

Algorithm 13.6 QUICKSORT

which the current procedure invocation applies. Accordingly, the trace in Figure 13.10 is segmented vertically according to recursive calls, with the first line of each segment showing the corresponding values of the parameters *left* and *rite*. The underlined items in each line are those referenced by *i* and *j* (or by *left* and *j*), and the circled items are those that are in their final place, either because of an exchange, or because they are sequences consisting of a single item. The efficiency of Quicksort is illustrated by the fact that only four exchanges are performed in the first procedure invocation, and yet the number of inversions has been reduced from 27 to 15. On occasion, we see that *left* and *j* reference the same item, as indicated by the double underline for 41 in the sixth invocation in Figure 13.10. The resulting exchange is indeed wasteful, but less so than it would be to insert a test for equality.

All that we have said about Quicksort so far is by way of introduction, to convey the basic principles of the method. To use it practically, one needs to introduce several refinements. In fact, since it seems to be the best method, it has been the target of numerous suggested refinements. Since some of these suggestions are of dubious benefit, some discretion is required in choosing among them. In the remainder of this section we will first describe the more important refinements, and then discuss the efficiency of Quicksort.

left	*rite*	1	2	3	4	5	6	7	8	9	10	11
1	11	33	41	7	15	55	87	28	22	9	46	32
		33	32	7	15	55	87	28	22	9	46	41
		33	32	7	15	9	87	28	22	55	46	41
		33	32	7	15	9	22	28	87	55	46	41
		28	32	7	15	9	22	33	87	55	46	41
1	6	28	32	7	15	9	22	33	87	55	46	41
		28	22	7	15	9	32	33	87	55	46	41
		9	22	7	15	28	32	33	87	55	46	41
1	4	9	22	7	15	28	32	33	87	55	46	41
		9	7	22	15	28	32	33	87	55	46	41
		7	9	22	15	28	32	33	87	55	46	41
3	4	7	9	22	15	28	32	33	87	55	46	41
		7	9	15	22	28	32	33	87	55	46	41
8	11	7	9	15	22	28	32	33	87	55	46	41
		7	9	15	22	28	32	33	41	55	46	87
8	10	7	9	15	22	28	32	33	41	55	46	87
		7	9	15	22	28	32	33	41	55	46	87
9	10	7	9	15	22	28	32	33	41	55	46	87
		7	9	15	22	28	32	33	41	46	55	87

Figure 13.10 Trace of Algorithm QUICKSORT

To begin with, the procedure as shown masks a bug. We see from Figure 13.10 that the sort is accomplished via an initial call specifying the bounds of the input array as parameters. Depending upon the actual data values, however, either i or j could run off the ends of the array in the initial pass. Thus, sentinel values are needed at both ends in order to guarantee the termination of the inner **repeat** ... **until** loops.

A more profound point is that we have shown Quicksort as a recursive procedure. This has the usual benefits of perspicuity and brevity, at the expense of efficiency. Since efficiency is much more important in a procedure that may be heavily used, we should convert it to an iterative procedure, using a stack to record pairs of indices that correspond to sub-arrays yet to be sorted. Moreover, the procedure QUICKSORT exhibits tail recursion (see Section 5.4.2). Therefore, the corresponding iterative procedure need push just one pair of indices onto the stack, and then loop to sort the sub-array corresponding to the other pair of indices. In our simplified version, we have always sorted the leftmost sub-array before the rightmost sub-array. It is not hard to find an input sequence such that this rigid policy would require a working stack of size $O(n)$. This is easily remedied, however, if we compare the relative sizes of the two subsequences, and then always save the larger subsequence and sort the smaller subsequence first. By this device, we can be sure that the size of the stack is $O(\lg n)$.

As the subsequences become smaller and smaller, the comparatively elaborate machinery of Quicksort becomes counter productive, so it is better to switch to a simpler method for small sequences. Since by then we are dealing with items that are almost sorted, it is an ideal situation for applying insertion sort to finish the task. The best cutover value at which to make this switch depends, in practice, upon details of implementation and the underlying machine; typically, it has been observed to be in the range $6-15$. Even better than invoking insertion sort separately for each small subsequence is to simply ignore such sequences during Quicksort, and then make one call on insertion sort after Quicksort terminates! The number of residual inversions is the same in either case, and the overhead of numerous distinct procedure calls is thereby avoided.

The nature of our last basic refinement to Quicksort is best motivated by the following question. What will happen if we apply Algorithm 13.6 to a sequence that is already completely sorted? The first and smallest item will become the partitioning element, and j will subsequently be decremented n times in search of a smaller value, with the result that the first item will be exchanged with itself. This will be followed by the call QUICKSORT(*data*,2,*n*), with $n-1$ comparisons, etc $-$ for a total complexity of $O(n^2)$. Data that is already sorted, or nearly so, is a very significant possibility; yet this highly touted method is totally inefficient for such a case. What went wrong? The answer has to do with the issue that we bypassed when beginning to discuss Quicksort; it lies with the choice of the partitioning element. For this method to work well, the partitioning element should on the average divide its sequence into two subsequences of comparable size. By definition, the median of a sequence would accomplish exactly this. A pragmatic technique that works well is to choose the partitioning element as the median of a small sample $-$ commonly as the median of the three elements at the first, middle, and last locations in the sequence. Although this will not eliminate the worst-case complexity of $O(n^2)$, it will make it much less likely to occur.

The refinements discussed in the preceding paragraphs are summarized in the following considerations:

- Sentinels need to be placed at either end of the input array.
- Iteration should be substituted for recursion.
- The subsequence to be stacked should always be the longer one.
- Small subsequences should be deferred for one final invocation of insertion sort.
- The partitioning element should be chosen with discretion, perhaps with the median-of-three technique.

A more detailed discussion of these and other issues relating to practical implementation of Quicksort can be found in Sedgewick [1978].

We turn now to the issue of the efficiency of Quicksort. We stated at the beginning of this section that it is the fastest known method based upon comparisons of keys. It is not hard to see why this might be so, since the two main inner loops are simply $i := i + 1$ and $j := j - 1$. Detailed proofs of its $O(n \lg n)$ average complexity are rather elaborate [Sedgewick 1977]. An easier, informal approach comes from noting the close correspondence of Quicksorting a random permutation to that of constructing a BST from the same random permutation. The root of the BST corresponds to the partitioning element, with each other item in the tree being compared with the root during its insertion. The same remarks apply with respect to the left (right) child of the root and all the other nodes in the left (right) subtree of the root; likewise, they apply at successively lower levels in the BST. This is illustrated, for our example data, by the BST of Figure 13.11. This argument can be made more precise, along the lines of the derivation of Eqs. 10.10 – 10.14 in Section 10.3.1. The result is completely analogous; the expected number of comparisons for Quicksort applied to a random input sequence is given by $1.386n \lg n$. Be aware that a rigorous proof of this result depends upon the input subsequence for each pass being a random permutation. It is not uncommon to tinker with Quicksort in an attempt to improve it, and inadvertently destroy the property of randomness in the subsequences.[2] For several such cases, it has been shown that the "improvement" in fact degrades performance.

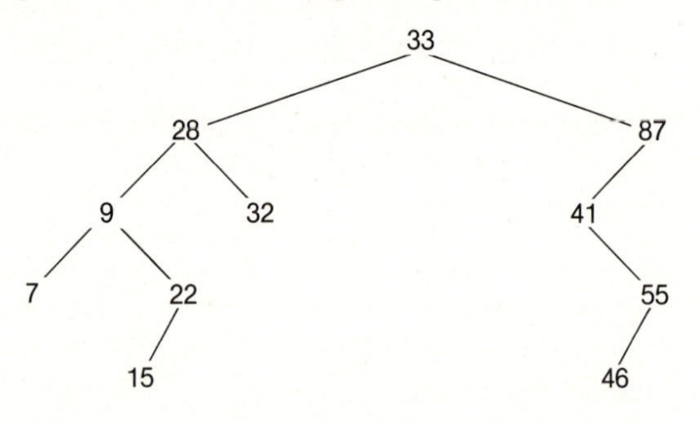

Figure 13.11 BST Analogous to Quicksort

How does Quicksort compare with Heapsort, the other $O(n \lg n)$ algorithm? Quicksort has commonly been found to be about twice as fast as Heapsort, owing largely to its fast inner loops. Another important advantage is that it easily allows the incorporation of a simpler sorting method to handle small subsequences. There are two words of caution though. For one, Heapsort is $O(n \lg n)$ in the worst case. With Quicksort, although the median-of-three approach can reduce the likelihood of quadratic worst-case complexity, the possibility still exists, just as it does with random BST's. Finally, Heapsort operates in situ, requiring a small, bounded amount of working storage, whereas Quicksort requires an $O(\lg n)$ stack.

13.2.1.4 Merge Sorting. Another way of thinking about Quicksort is that it is an application of divide-and-conquer. It has good average performance because the

---

[2] This matter is particularly sticky when equal keys are present. It then matters greatly whether the inner loops terminate on equality or continue until inequality.

partitioning element on the average divides input sequences into two subsequences of approximately equal size. Merge sorting is a method in which divide-and-conquer is applied without leaving anything to chance, by recursively dividing input sequences into two subsequences that are invariably of the same size. Thus, the complexity of merge sort is $O(n \lg n)$ even in the worst-case. Unfortunately, this method also tends to require a fair amount of working storage, thereby reducing its appeal as an internal sorting method. Nonetheless, it has two features that cause it to be highly important. For one, it is a stable $O(n \lg n)$ method, and the other two $O(n \lg n)$ methods, Heapsort and Quicksort, are not. Even more significantly, it is *the* method that we must employ, eventually at least, when the volume of the data forces us to use external sorting methods.

Output *W*	Input *U*	Input *V*
	17 23 38 ...	14 24 32 ...
14	17 23 38 ...	24 32 41 ...
14 17	23 38 39 ...	24 32 41 ...
14 17 23	38 39 55 ...	24 32 41 ...
14 17 23 24	38 39 55 ...	32 41 44 ...

Figure 13.12 The Merging Process

Before discussing merge sorting, we need to focus upon the process of merging two ordered input sequences to form one ordered output sequence. In fact, this is a familiar concept, although previous examples were encumbered with various, particular details. An example was the addition of polynomials represented as linked lists, using POLYADD (Algorithm 4.2) in Section 4.2.2. The essentials of merging are illustrated in Figure 13.12, where the basic step is to compare the first items of two input sequences U and V, and to promote the smaller one to the output sequence W. This is mirrored in the procedure MERGE (Algorithm 13.7), where input arrays U of size p and V of size q are combined to yield an output array W of size r. A significant aspect of merging is that it is linear in the combined sizes of the two inputs, since each comparison results in the production of one of the $r = p + q$ outputs. Implemented in the obvious manner with arrays, however, it requires $O(n)$ space both for the input sequences and for the output sequence. Although there are methods for merging arrays with a bounded amount of workspace, they tend to be impractical. A better resolution is to employ linked list techniques. The inclusion of cursors with each record

```
type  item = record
          key: integer;
          link: index;
            ...
      end;
```

will usually be less costly than doubling the entire data space. And there is the additional, significant advantage that cursor assignments can then be employed, rather than costly record moves. If it is necessary to conclude with the records physically in sequence, we can resort to the technique of Exercise 13.5.

```
procedure MERGE (U: items; p: index; V: items; q: index;
                        var W: items; var r: index);

const  inf = {a large positive value as sentinel}

var    i,j,k: index;

begin
   i := 1;  U [p + 1].key := inf;
   j := 1;  V [q + 1].key := inf;
   r := p + q;
   for k := 1 to r do
      if U [i].key <= V [j].key then begin
         W [k] := U [i];  i := i + 1;
      end else begin
         W [k] := V [j];  j := j + 1;
      end;
end;
```

Algorithm 13.7 MERGE

Assuming that all the cursor fields have been initialized to zero, our sorting technique will be to divide the input array of records into two sub-arrays (larger on the left, if there are an odd number of items), recursively sort both sub-arrays, and then merge them. This process is spelled out in the procedure MERGE_SORT and the sub-procedure MERGE_LIST (Algorithm 13.8). Although the details are dissimilar, you should be able to recognize that MERGE_LIST is indeed the linked list analogue of the procedure MERGE. Two of its input parameters are cursors p and q, pointing to the beginnings of two linked lists of records in *data*; and it returns output parameter r, the initial cursor for the merged combination. For MERGE_SORT, the input parameters *left* and *rite* specify the subrange of the array *data* to be sorted; and the output parameter *head* is the initial cursor for the sorted array. A trace of the action of Algorithm 13.8 upon our sample data is given in Figure 13.13. The figure shows the contents of the link fields for the records *data* [*left* .. *rite*], and also the corresponding value of *head*. The initial index parameters supplied to MERGE_SORT are of course 1, 11; however, the trace output in the figure reflects the order in which the recursion "unwinds" with its results.

The form of MERGE_SORT suggests the following recurrence equation

$$T(n) = 2T(n/2) + cn \tag{13.2}$$

where the first term reflects the costs of the two recursive calls to sequences of size $n/2$, and the second term reflects the fact that merging is linear in the combined sizes of its two inputs. It is fairly easy to establish from this that

$$T(n) = an \lg n + b \tag{13.3}$$

from which we can infer that merging is indeed $O(n \lg n)$. We could not apply this argument to Quicksort, since there the partitioning does not always yield

```
procedure MERGE_SORT (var data: items; left,rite: index;
                      var head: index);

var     headl,headr,midl,midr: index;

procedure MERGE_LIST (var data: items; p,q: index; var r: index);
var     s: index;
begin
   if data [p].key <= data [q].key then begin
      r := p;  p := data [p].link;
   end else begin
      r := q;  q := data [q].link;
   end;
   s := r;
   while ((p > 0) and (q > 0)) do
      if data [p].key <= data [q].key then begin
         data [s].link := p;  s := p;  p := data [p].link;
      end else begin
         data [s].link := q;  s := q;  q := data [q].link;
      end;
   if p > 0 then data [s].link := p;
   if q > 0 then data [s].link := q;
end;

begin
   midl := (left + rite) div 2;  midr := midl + 1;
   if (rite - left < 2) then headl := left
                    else MERGE_SORT (data,left,midl,headl);
   if (rite - left < 3) then headr := midr
                    else MERGE_SORT (data,midr,rite,headr);
   if (rite - left < 1) then head := headl
                    else MERGE_LIST (data,headl,headr,head);
end;
```

Algorithm 13.8 MERGE_SORT

left	*rite*	*head*	1	2	3	4	5	6	7	8	9	10	11
			33	41	7	15	55	87	28	22	9	46	32
1	2	1	2	0									
1	3	3	2	0	1								
4	5	4				5	0						
4	6	4				5	6	0					
1	6	3	2	5	4	1	6	0					
7	8	8							0	7			
7	9	9							0	7	8		
10	11	11										0	10
7	11	9							11	7	8	0	10
1	11	3	2	10	9	8	6	0	11	7	4	5	1

Figure 13.13 Trace of Algorithm MERGE_SORT

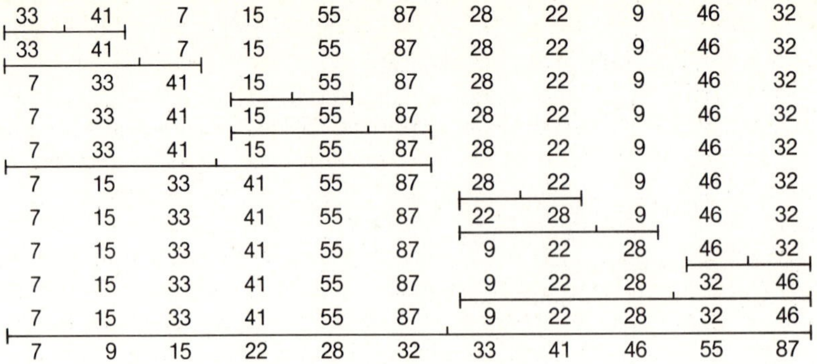

33 41 7 15 55 87 28 22 9 46 32
33 41 7 15 55 87 28 22 9 46 32
7 33 41 15 55 87 28 22 9 46 32
7 33 41 15 55 87 28 22 9 46 32
7 33 41 15 55 87 28 22 9 46 32
7 15 33 41 55 87 28 22 9 46 32
7 15 33 41 55 87 22 28 9 46 32
7 15 33 41 55 87 9 22 28 46 32
7 15 33 41 55 87 9 22 28 32 46
7 15 33 41 55 87 9 22 28 32 46
7 9 15 22 28 32 33 41 46 55 87

(a) Top-Down Recursive Merging

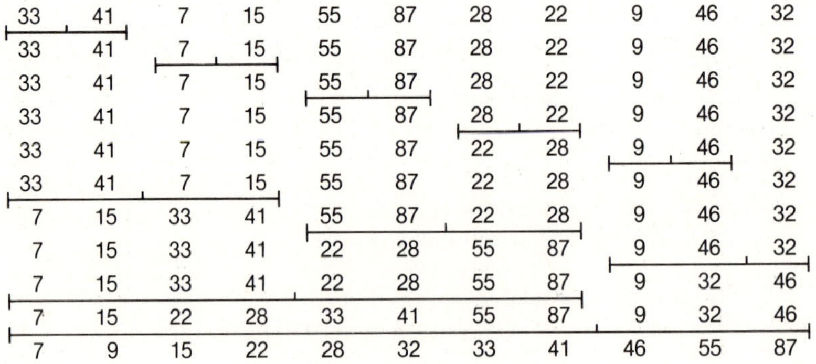

33 41 7 15 55 87 28 22 9 46 32
33 41 7 15 55 87 28 22 9 46 32
33 41 7 15 55 87 28 22 9 46 32
33 41 7 15 55 87 28 22 9 46 32
33 41 7 15 55 87 22 28 9 46 32
33 41 7 15 55 87 22 28 9 46 32
7 15 33 41 55 87 22 28 9 46 32
7 15 33 41 22 28 55 87 9 46 32
7 15 33 41 22 28 55 87 9 32 46
7 15 22 28 33 41 55 87 9 32 46
7 9 15 22 28 32 33 41 46 55 87

(b) Bottom-Up Straight Merging

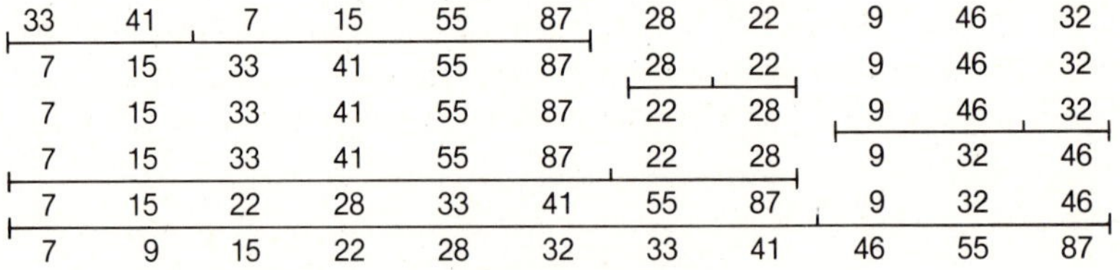

33 41 7 15 55 87 28 22 9 46 32
7 15 33 41 55 87 28 22 9 46 32
7 15 33 41 55 87 22 28 9 46 32
7 15 33 41 55 87 22 28 9 32 46
7 15 22 28 33 41 55 87 9 32 46
7 9 15 22 28 32 33 41 46 55 87

(c) Natural Merging

Figure 13.14 Alternative Merge Patterns

subsequences of equal length. Nonetheless, it is instructive to compare the recursive formulations of Quicksort and merge sort. They both represent divide-and-conquer solutions. In Quicksort, all of the work goes into splitting the original sequence into subsequences that are then joined trivially by juxtaposition. In merge sort, on the other hand, the splitting is performed very simply, and all of the work goes into joining the resulting parts. In the terms in which we usually think of divide-and-conquer, merge sort is much more typical; yet they are both instances of the paradigm, coming at the problem from opposite directions.

As with Quicksort, if we intend to implement merge sorting for extended use, we should introduce refinements for the sake of efficiency. Some examples of these might be exchanging recursion for iteration, applying insertion sort to small initial subsequences, etc. In the course of making these changes, we might also choose to merge bottom-up rather than in the top-down manner of Algorithm 13.8. In this case, unless n is a power of two, we will merge different sequences than previously. Even if n is a power of two, it is simpler to merge all pairs of one-item sequences first, then all pairs of two-item sequences, etc. The difference is illustrated in Figure 13.14, where (a) shows the logical effect of the top-down merge from Figure 13.13, and (b) shows the logical effect of a bottom-up merge on the same data.

There is yet another important variation of merge sorting. The methods discussed so far are oblivious to any pre-existing order in the input, and are called *straight merging*. The "order" with which we are concerned here is that expressed by the runs in the input sequence. A *run* is a maximal subsequence $K_r \ldots K_t$ such that $K_r \leq K_s \leq K_t$ for all $r < s < t$. Although a random permutation will have runs with an average length of about 2, we may be dealing with non-random input, with runs of substantial length. We can take advantage of this order by looking for and merging naturally occurring runs, with the expectation that fewer merge passes will be required overall. This technique is called *natural merging*, and it constitutes an alternative bottom-up approach to the problem. The logical effect of applying natural merge to the same data as before is illustrated in (c) of Figure 13.14.

The traces in Figure 13.14 illustrate some shortcomings associated with these techniques. In both (b) and (c), we see that the later passes may not have a partner with which to merge. If we are merging by copying back and forth between two areas, this will lead to unproductive copying of "bachelors"; in any event, it will lead to sequences of varying length. This latter phenomenon is even worse in (c), since we can expect that the initial runs will vary considerably in length. All in all, merge sorting is slightly inferior as an internal sorting method. It has been found to be about as fast as Heapsort (that is, half as fast as Quicksort), but it cannot be reasonably performed except with $O(n)$ working storage. The real utility of merge sorting will become apparent when we discuss external sorting in Section 13.4.

13.2.2 Distribution Methods

The preceding methods are all based upon comparisons between pairs of keys. We will see in Section 13.2.3 that this leads to the fundamental lower bound $\Omega(n \lg n)$. The methods of the present section are able to break this bound by means of performing other kinds of operations upon the keys. In all cases, some arithmetic function of the key value is used to map the key to one of a number of *buckets*. The effect is to allow multi-way decisions instead of just two-way decisions based upon comparisons. This is the sorting analogue to the use of tries in searching, wherein we find a method of very different character from the usual methods based upon binary comparison trees. After one or more functional applications of a distribution method, the last distribution of the keys among the buckets yields all of the keys in sorted sequence. This general principle gives rise to several different methods: radix sorting, radix exchange sorting, and value distribution sorting.

13.2.2.1 Radix Sorting. *Radix sorting* corresponds to the method of sorting used with electro-mechanical card sorting machines before computers became so powerful and ubiquitous. In more familiar terms, it is analogous to the use of tries as data structures for searching. Using our familiar example data of Eq. 13.1, each key K_i can be expressed in radix ten as $K_i = T_i \times 10 + U_i$, with $0 \leq T_i, U_i \leq 9$. The basic operation of radix sorting is to distribute each key into one of ten buckets, corresponding to the ten possible values for a digit in a particular position of each key. In our case, we have only tens and units digits. Although it may not be obvious at first, we need to begin with the least significant digit (LSD), and end with the most significant digit (MSD). The distribution of our eleven keys on the value of their units digits is shown in Figure 13.15(a). In terms of a card sorter, we see ten card pockets; in terms of data structures, we see ten queues. In either interpretation, we next collect and concatenate the contents of the ten sequences into one sequence

$$41 \quad 22 \quad 32 \quad 33 \quad 15 \quad 55 \quad 46 \quad 7 \quad 87 \quad 28 \quad 9 \tag{13.4}$$

We then apply the distribution operation to the tens digits, being careful to treat leading blanks as zeros, with the result shown in Figure 13.15(b). Since the keys have only two digits, we have only to collect the contents of the ten queues/pockets once again, and we have a sorted output. Radix sorting is stable. Indeed, the stability between successive passes is an essential reason that the method works.

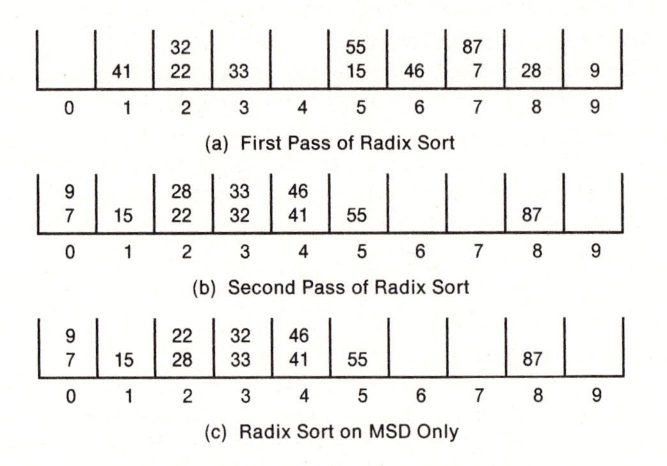

(a) First Pass of Radix Sort

(b) Second Pass of Radix Sort

(c) Radix Sort on MSD Only

Figure 13.15 Illustration of Radix Sort

We have alluded to the implementation of radix sort in terms of queues. In the present case the radix value was $r = 10$, but other values are possible. We must be careful about the possibility of data such that all of the records are distributed to the same queue on a given pass; this would lead to an $O(nr)$ space requirement for the queues. A better strategy is to allocate a link field in each record, and to use $2r$ locations to identify the head and the tail for each queue. This yields an improved space $O(n + r)$ requirement. An algorithm to perform radix sorting would then consist of alternate phases: distribution, wherein the items are distributed among the r queues; and collection, wherein the contents of these queues are concatenated into one list again. The work associated with each distribution is $O(n)$, and that associated with each collection is $O(r)$. If the keys consist of p "digits," then the total complexity is evidently $O(p(n + r))$. For cases where both p and r are fixed and not too large, we have found an $O(n)$ sorting method.

The method just described for decimal keys can be generalized to other kinds of data. If the keys are binary, then it would be inefficient to employ $r = 2$, since the resulting value of p would cause too many passes to be required; clearly, radix sort is not an improvement over comparison-based sorts unless $p < \lg n$. For binary keys, it is better to extract b bits at a time, and to distribute the data among $r = 2^b$ buckets. However, if the range of the key values is much greater than n, then even this approach may not be feasible, in terms of either space or time. Note that we can also apply this approach to alphabetic strings, or even to enumerated types such as *date* in Section 3.1.2; in this latter case, the value of r will be different for each pass, but that is a fairly simple matter to take care of. We leave the detailed implementation of a radix sorting algorithm as an exercise; the operations of distribution and collection of linked-records in the queues do not, after all, involve anything very new to us. However, one comment about such an endeavor is worthwhile. Although it is possible to extract bits or digits from keys in HLL's such as Pascal, the costs of doing so will almost certainly vitiate any advantage that radix sorting might have – at this level of programming. The one circumstance that might counteract this would be if we were to extract bytes ($r = 256$), since some compilers are clever enough to find simple translations for such extractions.

Radix sorting, as described thus far, requires that we process the keys from LSD to MSD. If the range of the keys is large, however, we should note two undesirable consequences. One is that so many passes are then required that the method becomes non-competitive. The other is that the activity of the earlier passes will tend to be irrelevant, being of consequence only in the unlikely event that we have keys that are equal with respect to all of their higher-order "digits." A very worthwhile approach for such cases is to first perform a radix sort on k of the MSD's, thereby partitioning the data into r^k buckets, and then apply insertion sort to each bucket [MacLaren 1966]. Be careful here, for the radix sort of the k MSD's must still proceed from the least to the most significant of the MSD's! As a concrete example, in sorting n four-byte integers, we might do a radix sort on the two high-order bytes, and then apply a comparison-based sort to each resulting bucket.[3] We can expect to accomplish this latter phase efficiently since each bucket

---

[3] This "sophisticated" approach comes more naturally than you might suppose. It is the technique that you might use for sorting playing cards into order by rank within suit. It is also the technique that the Postal Service uses for classifying mail by Zip Code, with the additional advantage that the second phases can be off-loaded to the corresponding Post Offices.

is small, and since not many inversions can occur in any of the buckets. By way of illustration, Figure 13.15(c) shows the effect of doing a radix sort on just the MSD of the example data. If we now collect the contents of these queues as

$$7 \quad 9 \quad 15 \quad 28 \quad 22 \quad 33 \quad 32 \quad 41 \quad 46 \quad 55 \quad 87 \tag{13.5}$$

we find that the number of inversions has been reduced from 27 to 2. To put matters more precisely, if radix sort is applied to the first k of the "digits," then the expected number of inversions remaining is $n(n-1)/(4r^k)$ — if the values of the keys have a uniform distribution. If the latter condition is not fulfilled, then this technique is subject to the degenerate possibility that most of the n keys may wind up in just one of the final buckets, so that the second phase is no longer efficient. A good rule of thumb for coping with deviations from uniformity is to choose r and k such that $n/r^k \leq 0.1$.

13.2.2.2 Radix Exchange Sorting. *Radix exchange sorting* is unlike the other distribution methods in two ways: It specifically operates upon the binary *representations* of the keys, and it operates in situ [Hildebrandt and Isbitz 1959]. We begin by examining the leftmost bit of each key, and rearranging the data so that all keys with a zero in this position are placed to the left, and all keys with a one in this position are placed to the right. We then apply the method recursively to the two subsequences, using the next bit to the right. The method of rearranging each time is a familiar one. It is the exchange method that we have seen both in COLLECT_1 (Algorithm 11.2) in Section 11.2.3.1, and also in QUICKSORT (Algorithm 13.6) in Section 13.2.1.3.1. A principal difference in this case is that the partitioning value of 2^b may not actually occur in the data. For keys that are uniformly distributed, radix exchange is another $O(n \lg n)$ method, with performance comparable to that of Quicksort (which it actually predates). However, it rapidly degenerates whenever the assumption of uniformity fails to hold. In particular, it performs very poorly when there are many equal keys, or even when most of the keys have the same value in some bit positions. Note that this can easily occur with numeric data having leading zeros, or with alphabetic character codes.

13.2.2.3 Value Distribution Sorting. If the analogue of radix sorting is trie searching, then the analogue of *value distribution sorting* is hash searching. We seek to map keys directly to their final locations via an order-preserving function F — that is, one such that $F(K_i) \leq F(K_j)$ whenever $K_i < K_j$. Such a method has long been known, under the name of *address calculation sorting* [Isaac and Singleton 1956]. If the keys are uniformly distributed over the range $K_{lo} .. K_{hi}$, then we can allocate B buckets, with the range of the jth bucket defined as

$$K_{lo} + \frac{(j-1) \times (K_{hi} - K_{lo})}{B} \quad \text{to} \quad K_{lo} + \frac{j \times (K_{hi} - K_{lo})}{B} \tag{13.6}$$

As with hashing, we can anticipate collisions. The best way to handle them is to maintain each bucket as a linked list. We can either maintain each list in order as keys are distributed to individual buckets, or we can perform a comparison-based sort upon each bucket at the conclusion of the distributions. There is an obvious resemblance to radix sorting coupled with insertion sorting, except that the distribution is determined by one arithmetic function applied to the entire key rather than by multiple radix distributions. There is the impediment, once again, that $O(n)$ space is required. There is also the practical hazard that non-uniformly distributed keys may occur frequently. In such cases, the method can easily degenerate, with most of the keys falling into one bucket, so that we wind up with a quadratic method rather than a linear one. A technique for combatting this degeneration is to use a cumulative distribution function of the key values, thereby allowing the construction of a more accurate address function F. This is fine if such a function can be determined in advance, but not very cost effective if it must be constructed for every set of data to be sorted. One proposal for confronting this issue employs a double level of distribution, where one of the levels is determined by sampling the input [Noga and Allison 1985].

More recently, this approach has attracted attention in the form of *distributive partitioning* [Dobosiewicz 1978]. The crucial difference with this method is that for predictive purposes, only the *minimum*, *median*, and *maximum* key values in the input need be determined. With these data at hand, the method proceeds by dividing both of the intervals *minimum .. median* and *median .. maximum* into $n/2$ sub-intervals of equal length. The keys are then distributed into these sub-intervals. After that, if any sub-interval has received more than one key, the same process is applied recursively to it. For a variety of distributions of the input keys (for example, uniform or normal), this method has been shown to have $O(n)$ average complexity. Moreover, for *any* input distribution, it has a worst-case complexity of $O(n \lg n)$, by an argument similar to that for Eqs. 13.2 and 13.3 with merge sorting, in Section 13.2.1.4. An essential part of this argument depends upon the fact that the median can be determined in linear time, as we will see in Section 13.3. Even though linear, that process is somewhat complicated; nonetheless, several experiments indicate that distributive partitioning is commonly faster than Quicksort.

The conclusions of the preceding paragraph are so provocative that it is helpful to step back and try to place them in perspective. Since we have an $O(n)$ expected sorting method, why might it not be the method of choice? Three factors contribute to the answer:

- As with merge sorting, the method requires $O(n)$ space.
- The details of its implementation are fairly complicated, owing largely to the nature of the median-finding process.
- The method is still somewhat controversial.

As noted in previous discussions, the complexity of an algorithm depends upon the model of computation that is employed. Thus, we will see in the next section that comparison-based sorting is necessarily $\Omega(n \lg n)$. An essential aspect of distributive partitioning is that of being able to include a floor operator in the computational model; this enables one to compute n-way branches efficiently [Schmitt 1983]. Implicit here is the assumption (usually justified) that the key can be treated as a single-precision real number. (This has the unexpected result that the floating-point performance of the underlying machine then becomes an issue!) Just as the success of Quicksort has inspired many variations, so has the success of distributive partitioning engendered variations, usually in combination with one or more comparison-based techniques (see Section 13.2.4).

13.2.3 Theoretical Considerations

We have now encountered several sorting methods that are $O(n^2)$, and several others that are $O(n \lg n)$. Implicit throughout has been the contention that sorting is $\Omega(n \lg n)$. In this section, our first order of business is to demonstrate the true sense of this implied statement. The result will be a lower bound on the number of comparisons needed to sort n items. The existence of such a lower bound confers no guarantee that a sorting method conforming to it exists, or that we can find it if it does. So we will follow the presentation of the lower bound with two sections wherein we look at methods and results that approach the lower bound in practice.

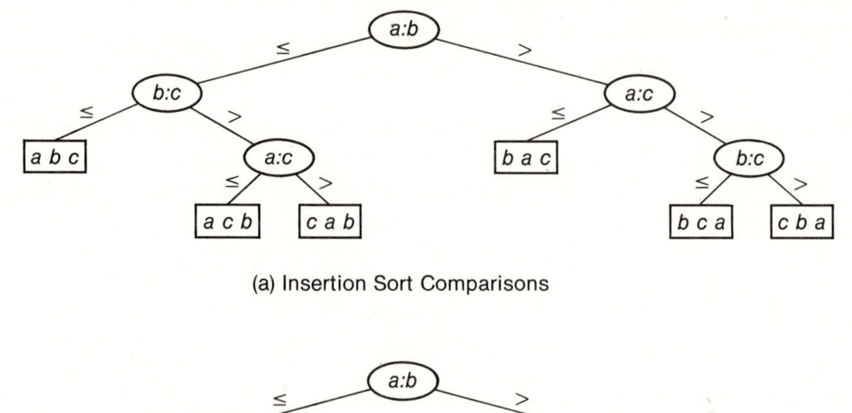

(a) Insertion Sort Comparisons

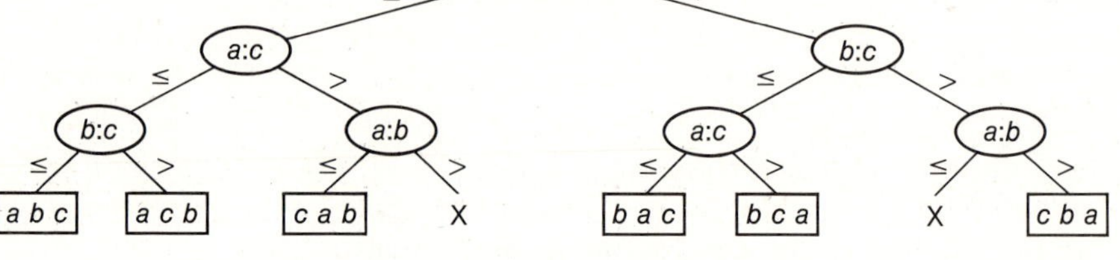

(b) Selection Sort Comparisons

Figure 13.16 Sort Comparison Trees

A useful manner of depicting sorting by comparisons is via a decision tree. In this tree, a node with a label *a:b* represents the comparison of two items, with the left branch corresponding to the outcome $a \leq b$, and the right branch corresponding to the outcome $a > b$. We have seen decision trees before, in Figure 6.24 of Section 6.6.3, and in Figure 8.12 of Section 8.2.4. Nodes in the present decision trees have just two outcomes rather than three. However, we can increase our understanding by allowing for the realistic case $a \leq b$ rather than just $a < b$. The tree of Figure 13.16(a) depicts the comparisons made by insertion sort in ranking three elements *a,b,c*. The effect of the tree is to "unwind" the loops of the algorithm and show each comparison explicitly. In interpreting a comparison tree such as this, it is important to realize that the labels are associated with the items and not the locations, although the sorting method may cause items to be moved as a result of a comparison. For example, if $a > b$, then the insertion sort algorithm will cause the sequence at the node on the right branch from the root to become $b\ a\ c$.

Figure 13.16(b) depicts the tree of comparisons made by selection sort for the same input. Note that this tree contains two extra comparisons and two leaves marked as X, to denote impossible outcomes; their occurrence reflects that selection sort is an oblivious technique. For either tree in Figure 13.16, there are 6 possible leaves, or outcomes, corresponding to the 3! input permutations. In general, for any such decision tree on n inputs, there must be $n!$ leaves. We also know from Section 10.1.2 that the minimum height for a binary tree with x leaves is $\lfloor \lg x$. Accordingly, our decision tree with $n!$ leaves has a minimum height of $\lfloor \lg (n!)$. By observing that

$$n! > n\,(n-1)\,(n-2) \ldots \frac{n}{2} > \left(\frac{n}{2}\right)^{n/2} \tag{13.7}$$

we then obtain $\lg (n!) > (n/2) \lg (n/2)$, or $\lg (n!) = \Omega(n \lg n)$. In other words, no method of sorting n items can discriminate among the $n!$ possible orderings in less than $\Omega(n \lg n)$ comparisons. By using Stirling's formula for $n!$, we obtain a more precise value for the *Information Theoretic Bound*

$$\begin{aligned} L(n) &= \lceil \lg (n!) = n \lg n - \frac{n}{\ln 2} + 0.5 \lg n + O(1) \\ &= n \lg n - 1.443n + O(\lg n) \end{aligned} \tag{13.8}$$

on the minimum number of comparisons $L(n)$ to sort n items.

†13.2.3.1 Sort Optimality. The Information Theoretic Bound $L(n)$ yields a minimum value for the maximum number of comparisons required to sort n items in the worst case. That still leaves us with the task of finding a sequence of comparisons that has this *minimax* property; the redundant comparisons in Figure 13.16(b) readily suggest how an injudicious sorting method could far exceed the bound. We have already alluded to a technique that focuses upon comparisons, downplaying other considerations, and that is the binary insertion method (see Section 13.2.1.1). Let us see how well this method performs for $n = 6$. It is fairly easy to see that the maximum number of comparisons in building an ordered sequence with successive lengths 2, 3, 4, 5, 6 is 1, 2, 2, 3, 3 – for a worst case total of 11 compares. But $L(6) = 10$. In general, the maximum value for binary insertion is given by

$$B(n) = \sum_{k=1}^{n} \lceil \lg k = n \lceil \lg n - 2^{\lceil \lg n} + 1 \tag{13.9}$$

Except for $n < 5$, $B(n)$ is always in excess of $L(n)$, and the excess grows steadily.

However, it is possible to sort 6 elements with a maximum of 10 comparisons. To do so, we first make three pairwise comparisons, leading to the digraph depicted in Figure 13.17(a). In this and subsequent digraphs the relation $x < y$ is denoted by placing x to the left of y, and so the arrows can be omitted. The second step is to

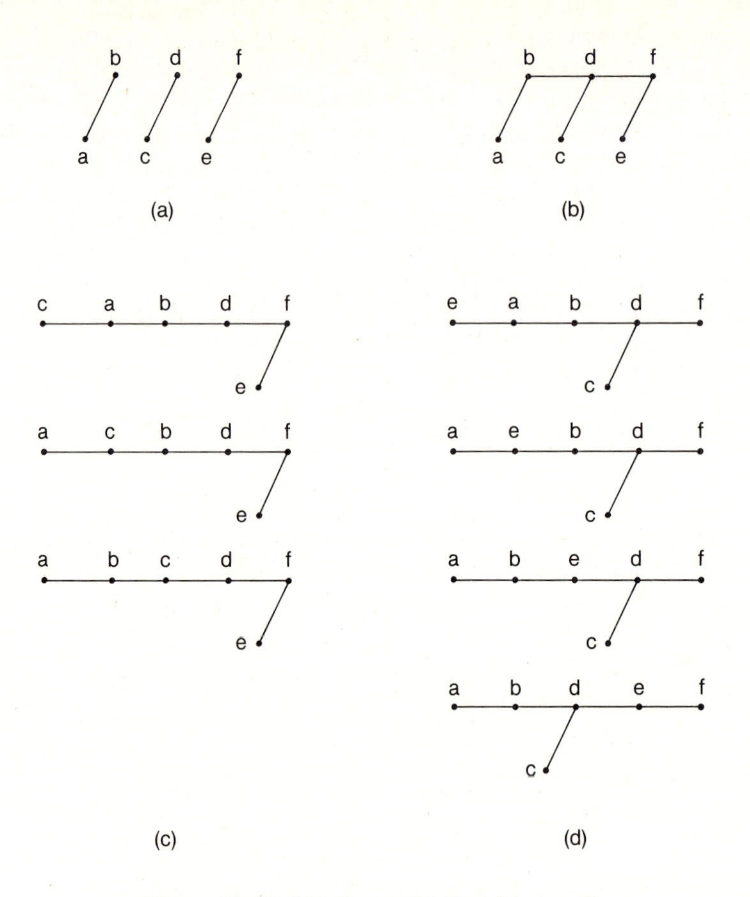

Figure 13.17 Minimum Sorting for $n = 6$

sort the top three elements with a maximum of three comparisons, leading to the (possibly relabeled) configuration shown in (b) of the figure. The final step of merging c and e into the sequence a, b, d, f is the crucial one. If we first insert c, then we will require a maximum of two comparisons and obtain one of the three configurations shown in (c) of the figure, leaving e to be inserted with a maximum of three comparisons. The three steps then total $3 + 3 + 5 = 11$. It is better to first insert e. This requires exactly two comparisons and leads to one of the four configurations depicted in (d) of the figure; in either event, the element c can then be inserted with two more comparisons. Altogether, the three steps establish that $L(6) = 3 + 3 + 4 = 10$.

The method just described can be extended recursively to handle any number of elements; it is known as the *Ford-Johnson algorithm* [Ford and Johnson 1959], and also as *merge insertion*. As an example, suppose that we wish to sort 17 elements by this method. We first make 8 pairwise comparisons to obtain eight pairs $b_i < a_i$, leaving the odd element as b_9; next we apply the method recursively to the a_i, arriving at the situation represented by the graph of Figure 13.18(a). As in the case of

Figure 13.17, we now merge the remaining b_i into the sorted chain $b_1 a_1 .. a_8$ in such a manner as to maximize the efficiency of the binary search at each stage – by causing the number of relevant items in the chain to be $2^k - 1$, or somewhat less. Figure 13.18(b) shows the appropriate order of insertion, and also the number of comparisons, in parentheses, for each b_i. The total number of comparisons is 8 for the first step, 16 for the second (recursive) step, and evidently 26 for the third step, for 50 altogether. By contrast, $B(17) = 54$, and $L(17) = 49$.

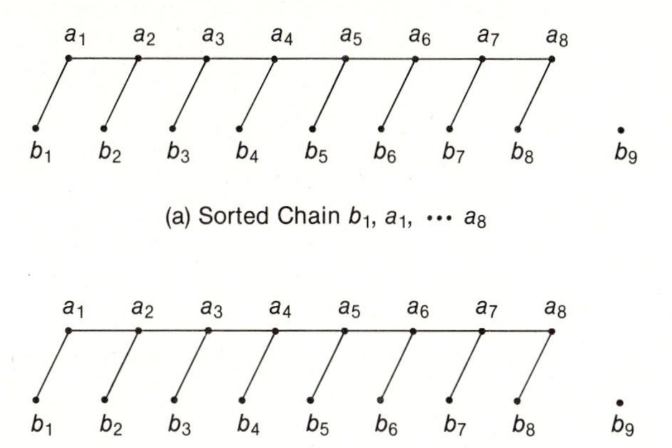

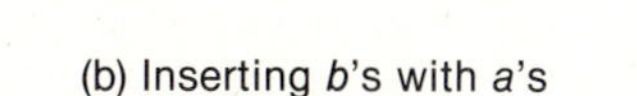

(b) Inserting b's with a's

Figure 13.18 Merge Insertion

The insertion order sequence follows the pattern $b_3, b_2; b_5, b_4; b_{11}, b_{10}, \ldots, b_6; \ldots$. By characterizing it more precisely (see Exercise 13.19), it is possible to show that the number of comparisons in merge insertion is given by

$$
\begin{aligned}
F(n) &= \sum_{k=1}^{n} \left\lceil \lg \left(\frac{3k}{4} \right) \right\rceil \qquad (13.10) \\
&= n \lg n - c(n)\, n + O(\lg n)
\end{aligned}
$$

where $1.329 \le c(n) \le 1.415$. It is interesting to study the values of $L(n)$, $F(n)$, and $B(n)$ for n from 2 to 22, as recorded in Table 13.1. It has been shown that $F(n) > L(n)$ for all $n \ge 22$ [Hwang and Lin 1969]. Nonetheless, Eq. 13.10 is so close to the Information Theoretic Bound of Eq. 13.8 that we have to wonder whether merge insertion is the best attainable method, or if there exists a better minimax method for some values of n. In fact, the Ford-Johnson algorithm misses being optimal for infinitely many $n \ge 189$ [Manacher 1979].

The minimax behavior that we have just studied is often of less concern than an examination of *minimean* behavior – that is, measuring the average number of comparisons of various algorithms over all inputs, and trying to find a particular algorithm that minimizes this average. This is a potentially harder problem in that it may require a knowledge of the probability distribution for various inputs. Assuming that all permutations of an input sequence are equally likely, however, we find that the problem is actually a familiar one. We wish to find a sorting method that guarantees that all leaves of the comparison tree lie on two adjacent levels, thereby minimizing the external path length (see Section 10.1.2). For $n < 6$, merge insertion is minimean optimal, as well as minimax optimal; for $n = 6$, although the process of Figure 13.17 is minimax optimal, it is not minimean optimal. The discovery of a method that is minimean optimal for $n = 6$, and no worse than minimax optimal, is left as an exercise (see Exercise 13.17). For large n, it has been speculated that a minimean solution may fail to be a minimax solution.

n	2	3	4	5	6	7	8	9	10	11	12	13	14	15	16	17	18	19	20	21	22
$L(n)$	1	3	5	7	10	13	16	19	22	26	29	33	37	41	45	49	53	57	62	66	70
$F(n)$	1	3	5	7	10	13	16	19	22	26	30	34	38	42	46	50	54	58	62	66	71
$B(n)$	1	3	5	8	11	14	17	21	25	29	33	37	41	45	49	54	59	64	69	74	79

Table 13.1 Values of $L(n)$, $F(n)$, $B(n)$

†13.2.3.2 Merge Optimality. The circumstances of merging – that it operates upon two files already in sequence, and that it is so fundamental to sorting when n is large – single it out for special analysis. To dispel possible confusion, recall the distinction between *linear merging* (Algorithm 13.7) and merge-sorting (Algorithm 13.8), where the former is implicitly a basic step in the latter process. We have seen that the maximum number of comparisons in merging two ordered files U: $u_1, u_2, \ldots, u_n$ and V: $v_1, v_2, \ldots, v_m$ is given by $n + m - 1$. Denoting by $M(n,m)$ the number of comparisons for any optimal, alternative merging method, then evidently $M(n,m) \leq n + m - 1$. But suppose that $m = 1$. Then it requires just $\lceil \lg (n+1)$ comparisons to merge the solitary item with the other file, and so $M(n,1)$ is much less than what can be obtained via linear merging. Perhaps information theory can guide us here, as it did in the discussion of sort optimality. In merging U with n elements and V with m elements, there are $C(n+m,m)$ possible outcomes, corresponding to the m ways in which the v_i can be placed in the output file of size $n + m$. For $m = n$, we find that $M(n,m) \geq \lg C(n+m,m) = 2n - 0.5 \lg n + O(1)$, from application of Eq. 13.8. Which is more accurate – the upper bound of $2n - 1$ from linear merging, or the lower bound of $2n - 0.5 \lg n$ from information theory?

The answer to this question is that $M(n,n) = 2n - 1$. For $m = n$, the Information Theoretic Bound is weak, and linear merging is actually optimal. To see why no fewer comparisons will suffice in the worst case, let the two sequences U and V be chosen such that $u_i < v_j$ whenever $i \leq j$ and $u_i > v_j$ whenever $i > j$. Then the output sequence must be $u_1 < v_1 < u_2 < v_2 < \cdots < u_n < v_n$. Moreover, each of the $2n - 1$ comparisons $u_1{:}v_1$, $v_1{:}u_2$, $u_2{:}v_2$, ... , $u_n{:}v_n$ must have been made. Without comparing $v_1{:}u_2$, for example, the above sequence would be indistinguishable from $u_1 < u_2 < v_1 < v_2 < \cdots < u_n < v_n$. And without comparing $u_2{:}v_2$, it would be indistinguishable from $u_1 < v_1 < v_2 < u_2 < \cdots < u_n < v_n$.

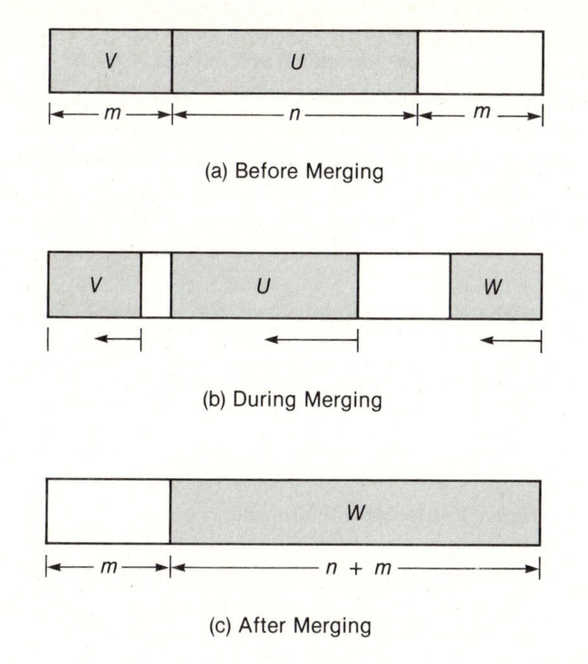

Figure 13.19 Merging $(n + m)$ Items in $(n + 2m)$ Space, $n \geq m$

From the optimality of binary insertion when $m = 1$ and the optimality of linear merging when $m = n$, we are led to the *Hwang-Lin algorithm* [Hwang and Lin 1972], also known as *binary merging*, which combines the best features of these two approaches. Suppose that we wish to merge file U with n elements and file V with m elements, where $n \geq m$. Binary merge is usually programmed to examine the two input files from right to left and write the output file in the same direction. With this technique, we are able to use the diminishing values of n and m to keep track of the unprocessed portions of U and V. Moreover, if m is much less than n, we can obtain significant efficiency of space by using the technique illustrated in Figure 13.19, thereby performing the merge in a total of $n + 2m$ space. The rationale of binary merge is to partition U into $m + 1$ segments of about $\lfloor(n/m)$ elements each, and to compare v_m with u_p, which is chosen to be the last element of the *next-to-last* segment of U. As a result of the comparison,

- If $u_p > v_m$, then the elements $u_p \mathinner{..} u_n$ are written out, and the method resumes with $v_1 \mathinner{..} v_m$ and $u_1 \mathinner{..} u_{p-1}$.
- If $u_p \leq v_m$, then binary search (requiring an additional t comparisons) is used to find the largest index q such that $u_q < v_m$; the values v_m, $u_{q+1} \mathinner{..} u_n$ are written out; and the method resumes with $v_1 \mathinner{..} v_{m-1}$ and $u_1 \mathinner{..} u_q$.

To optimize the efficiency of binary search in the second of these two cases, we choose $t = \lfloor\lg (n/m)$, and then $p = n + 1 - 2^t$, causing the size of the last segment of U to be $2^t - 1$.

We will illustrate these matters for the case $n = 35$ and $m = 5$. Rather than portray actual input values, we will simply make arbitrary decisions as to the outcome of each comparison step, and thus the consequent action. Figure 13.20 describes the sequence of events, showing for each step the values of m, n, t, p, and the output values, and also the value of q if it is relevant. It is easy to see that for this example there are 8 comparisons made by the main loop and a total of 11 comparisons made in the binary search, for a total of 19 comparisons altogether. Linear merge, on the other hand, would require about twice as many comparisons.

n	m	t	p	Compare	q	Output
35	5	2	32	$u_{32} > v_5$		$u_{32} .. u_{35}$
31	5	2	28	$u_{28} < v_5$	30	$v_5\ u_{31}$
30	4	2	27	$u_{27} < v_4$	27	$v_4\ u_{28} .. u_{30}$
27	3	3	20	$u_{20} < v_3$	23	$v_3\ u_{24} .. u_{27}$
23	2	3	16	$u_{16} > v_2$		$u_{16} .. u_{23}$
15	2	2	12	$u_{12} < v_2$	15	v_2
15	1	3	8	$u_8 > v_1$		$u_8 .. u_{15}$
7	1	2	4	$u_4 < v_1$	5	$v_1\ u_6\ u_7$
5	0					$u_1 .. u_5$

Figure 13.20 Binary Merging Example

Let us denote the complexity of binary merge as $H(n,m)$. Then we can see that it satisfies the recurrence equation

$$H(n,m) = \max\big(H(n - 2^t,m) + 1,\ H(n,m - 1) + t + 1\big) \qquad (13.11)$$

reflecting the two possible outcomes of each comparison, and assuming the worst-case eventuality that binary search will alway terminate with $q = n$. The solution of Eq. 13.11 is

$$H(n,m) = m + \lfloor\left(\frac{n}{2^t}\right) - 1 + mt \qquad (13.12)$$

where $t = \lfloor \lg (n/m)$. It is straightforward to see that for $m = 1$, Eq. 13.12 yields $H(n,1) = \lceil \lg (n + 1)$, which is the same as the best performance via ordinary binary insertion. Likewise, it is straightforward to see that for $m = n$, Eq. 13.12 yields $H(n,n) = 2n - 1$, which is the same as the best performance via linear merging. The Hwang-Lin algorithm does indeed capture the best aspects of the two more basic methods. It also works well for intermediate values of m, although it is not always optimal. We should note that when m and n are close in value, then the roles of "smaller" and "larger" may oscillate between the two files U and V. So each step of binary merging should begin by comparing m and n to determine the sense of the merging logic.

As we have said, binary merging is not always optimal. The determination of the optimal values $M(n,m)$ is a difficult problem in the general case. It is fairly easy to extend the result that $M(m,m) = 2m - 1$ to show that $M(m+1,m) = 2m$. This can also be generalized to show that $M(m+d,m) = 2m + d - 1$ whenever $m \leq n \leq \lfloor(3m/2) + 1$, so that linear merge is optimal over a large range of d [Stockmeyer and Yao 1980]. At the other extreme – that is, the determination of $M(n,d)$ for small values of d – only isolated results are known.

13.2.4 Translating Theory into Practice

The difficulty of finding the best sorting algorithm for all situations can be better appreciated when we step back to list some of the qualities that it ought have:

- It should have good average performance and good worst-case performance.
- It should be stable.
- It should use minimum storage.

There is also another less obvious quality:

- It should respond with better performance to inputs that have a measure of pre-sortedness, with the complexity improving from $O(n \lg n)$ to $O(n)$ as we go from random input to input that has a high degree of pre-sortedness.

This last issue can be very influential in evaluating different methods.

Since the answers that we obtain about these concerns will vary considerably with the yardstick used for measuring order, we need to say a little about various measures. The one that we have used most frequently is the number of inversions. If we consider an input such as

$$n+1, n+2, \dots, 2n, 1, 2, \dots, n$$

its measure is $O(n^2)$. Yet this sequence is intuitively nearly sorted, and in fact can easily be put in order via merging. So inversions have shortcomings as a measure. Since runs provide a good measure for natural merging, are they appropriate in general? Once again we find a counter-example, as demonstrated by

$$2, 1, 4, 3, \dots, n, n-1$$

which has $O(n)$ runs. Yet this sequence is easily placed in order via insertion sort in just $O(n)$ time.

Still another possible measure is the minimum number of compound delete-insert operations required to sort a sequence. This number, in turn, is equal to n minus the length of the *longest ascending subsequence* (*LAS*) in the sequence. For our example data

33 41 7 15 55 87 28 22 9 46 32

the longest ascending subsequences are all of length 4 (for example, 7 15 28 32); in other words, $11 - 4 = 7$ such compound operations would be required. Unfortunately, the realization of an efficient sorting method based upon this measure is another matter. There are also some other less common measures [Manilla 1985], but let us instead return to the central issue of choosing among sorting methods.

If we look at comparison-based methods pragmatically, some of the highlights are as follows:

- Insertion sort is one of the simplest (thereby having an excellent constant factor), and it is particularly appropriate whenever the input has relatively few inversions. It is also stable.

- Heapsort has $O(n \lg n)$ complexity in both the average and the worst case; however, it is not stable and it tends to be only half as fast as Quicksort.

- Quicksort is one of the two methods more commonly preferred, primarily because of its speed. This is counterbalanced by its $O(n^2)$ worst-case complexity and its lack of stability. Since it is the winner in terms of raw, average speed, it has been the target of numerous attempts (not always successful) at improvement. These attempts have focused on making it even faster, making it stable, overcoming its worst-case complexity, etc. [§].

- Merging is the other of the two methods more commonly preferred. Although not quite as fast as Quicksort, it has the advantages of stability and of $O(n \lg n)$ complexity in both the average and worst case. Straight merging is usually not as good as natural merging because it does not capitalize on pre-sortedness. A recommended technique, in fact, is to convert Algorithm 13.8 so that it does natural merge. The inferior features of merging are the amount of space required and the amount of data movement. One proposal for merging with reduced data movement suggests using balanced trees, of either the AVL or 2-3 variety [Brown and Tarjan 1979].

On the theoretical side, some of the more important insights are those concerning pre-sortedness, cited earlier. From Section 13.2.3, the Ford-Johnson and Hwang-Lin algorithms are concerned with minimizing comparisons, which they do admirably. They are not equally good with respect to data movement, however, and we know that this is a significant part of the cost of sorting. Historically, the Hwang-Lin algorithm was designed for external sorting with tapes. For this, it does have practical significance, since the issues of space and data movement are then absorbed within the larger paradigm.

The distributive methods are in a special category, of course, since they are not restricted by the Information Theoretic Bound. The simplest distributive method is radix sort, which clearly merits consideration when the keys are short. The more general question is, "With arbitrary keys, should one aim for an $O(n)$ sort via distributive partitioning?" As we have seen, this approach requires more space, and there is also the hazard of getting an $O(n^2)$ result if the chosen algorithm fails to cope with a particular input distribution.

In the final analysis, if the sorting requirement is large, it may be worthwhile to go to the trouble of implementing a *hybrid sorting* method that couples two or more methods. We have seen this idea before – for example, in coupling Quicksort with a final insertion sort, and in one of the variants of radix sorting. A particularly common idea is to combine distributive partitioning with a comparison-based method. The goal is to dispense with the median-finding process, and yet to attain $O(n)$ expected complexity and $O(n \lg n)$ worst-case complexity [§].

†13.3 SELECTION

We all know, in computing or in real life, how to effectively identify the item or person that wins a contest. Techniques for properly identifying runners-up are much less well known. For instance, in the typical situation that the winner has been determined by a randomly composed tournament of comparisons, the second best is very likely *not* the one who lost to the winner on the final round. Half of the time, the second best will have been eliminated by the winner in an earlier round of the tournament. This is the reason for seeding top-rated players in sports contests, thereby making it highly likely that the best players will reach the finals.

The problem of finding the second best was discussed earlier, and it can be done in $O(n + \lg n)$ time (see Exercise 4.19). What about the more general problem of finding the kth best? One possibility is to sort all the items and then simply extract the kth best, but this approach requires $O(n \lg n)$ work, most of which is wasted in the general case. For small, constant values of k, either of the selection sorts, SELECT_SORT or HEAPSORT, will do the job simply and efficiently. We can simply insert a test to terminate after the kth iteration. With HEAPSORT, we do not even require that k be a constant. As long as $k \leq (n / \lg n)$, then we can build the heap in $O(n)$ time and select the k smallest elements in $O(n + k \lg n) = O(n)$ time. It should be apparent that, by symmetry, all of the remarks in this paragraph apply equally well to finding the $(n - k + 1)$th element. The most difficult case occurs for $k = \lceil (n/2)$, which corresponds to the median.

The major result that we will develop in this section is that, in fact, there are $O(n)$ algorithms for all of these selection problems. But either they are somewhat complicated and/or they have large constant factors. So first let us look at a very pretty technique discovered by Hadian and Sobel [1969]. We begin by making a tournament of $n - k + 2$ items, using $n - k + 1$ comparisons. Since the largest item is greater than $n - k + 1$ others, it cannot be the kth largest. So for each of the remaining $k - 2$ items, we replace the largest item in the tournament and recompute the tournament, using $\lceil \lg (n - k + 2)$ comparisons. We then finish off by finding the desired item as the second largest item in the final tournament. Adding up all of these leads to

$$V_k(n) \leq n - k + (k - 1) \lceil \lg (n - k + 2) \tag{13.13}$$

as a minimax bound $V_k(n)$ on the cost for finding the kth largest of n items. Note that we were careful to employ a tournament rather than a heap, since we were anxious to get precise upper bounds on the number of comparisons. The values predicted by this construction are optimal for small values of k and n; a few such values are shown in Table 13.2.

In the two preceding paragraphs, we have described first some practical approaches to solving the selection problem and then a more theoretical approach.

n	$V_1(n)$	$V_2(n)$	$V_3(n)$	$V_4(n)$	$V_5(n)$	$V_6(n)$
2	1	1				
3	2	3	2			
4	3	4	4	3		
5	4	6	6	6	4	
6	5	7	8	8	7	5

Table 13.2 Values of $V_k(n)$

Is there anything to add to the story? There is, and it begins with Quicksort. Suppose that we are looking for the kth smallest element. Then let us apply Quicksort, with the result that the partitioning value winds up in the jth location. If $k = j$, we are done; if $k < j$, we should look in the left partition; and if $k > j$, we should look in the right partition [Hoare 1971]. It is that simple! Moreover, since we use just one of the two partitions each time, there is no longer any need to employ either recursion or a stack. It can be shown that this method has average complexity $O(n)$ (see Exercise 13.26). Unfortunately, the example of trying to find the smallest item from input such as $n, 1, 2, \ldots, n-1$ shows that it has $O(n^2)$ worst-case complexity, just as with ordinary Quicksort.

Let us now concentrate upon the case of finding the median. The Quicksort variation is linear on the average, but quadratic in the worst case. The Hadian-Sobel method is close to optimal for small values of k, but we can see that it requires $O(\frac{1}{2}n \lg n)$ comparisons for finding the median. Thus, we can appreciate the significance of more recent methods that compute the median (or any other kth best value) with worst-case linear complexity. The idea is to choose a partitioning element for the Quicksort variation in such a manner that the two partitions cannot be degenerate, thus guaranteeing linear performance. To do this, we first pick some small, odd number r and then divide the original sequence of items into $2q + 1$ groups, each containing r items apiece (inserting dummy items if required). The second step is to sort each of the $2q + 1$ small groups to find their medians. Thirdly, we make a recursive application of this entire method to the set of medians, thereby discovering the *median of medians, mm.* At this point we have the situation depicted in Figure 13.21 for the case $r = 7$. In this figure the open circles denote the medians, and the open square denotes the median of medians. The points other than *mm* fall into four regions A,B,C,D with:

$4q + 3$ items that must be greater than *mm* in region B
$4q + 3$ items that must be less than *mm* in region C
$6q$ items with unknown relationship to *mm* in regions A and D

In our Quicksort variation we now choose *mm* as the partitioning element, and then recursively continue the search in regions A,B,D or in regions A,C,D. In either event, we are left with no more than $(10q + 4)/(14q + 7) < 5/7$ of the original items that need to be searched.

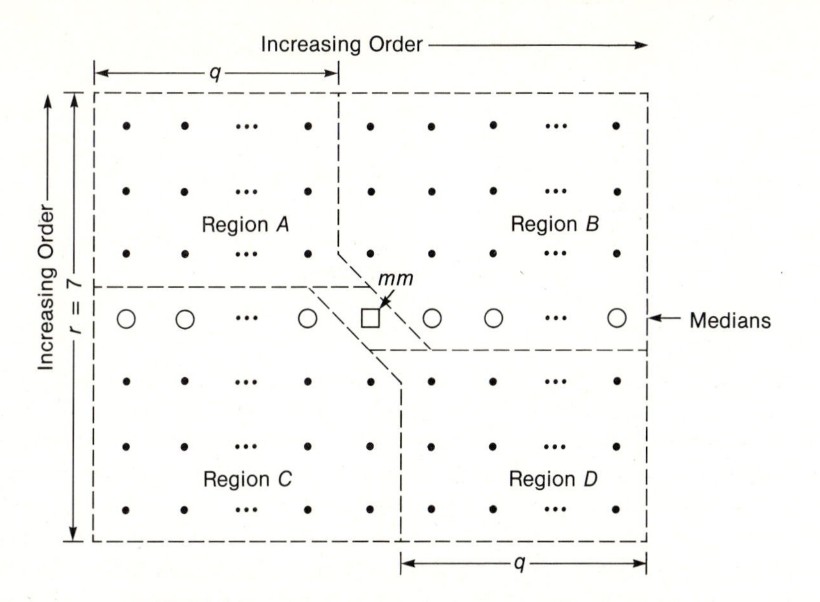

Figure 13.21 The Median of Medians Construction

We will now show that this process never requires more than $20n$ comparisons, so that we indeed have a linear algorithm for selection. The bookkeeping to establish this must include the comparisons for:

(a) the sorting of the $2q + 1$ small groups;

(b) the recursive sorting of the $n/7$ medians to find the median of medians;

(c) the partitioning of the original data about *mm*;

(d) the recursive sorting of the $5n/7$ (maximum) items in the relevent partition.

For (a) we know from Table 13.1 that $r = 7$ items can be sorted with 13 comparisons; thus, all the groups can be sorted in $13n/7$ comparisons.. For (b) we can find the median of medians in $20n/7$ comparisons, by our inductive hypothesis. The partitioning (c) can trivially be performed in n comparisons. And finally, applying our hypothesis again, the sort of the smaller set of items can be accomplished in $100n/7$ comparisons. Adding these gives us a total of $(13 + 20 + 7 + 100)n/7 = 20n$ comparisons, as promised!

The accounting in our demonstration was very loose in order to make the exposition easier. We also neglected the possibility that there may be repeated data items. Improvements for the purposes of handling duplicate values and of attaining better bounds are left as exercises (see Exercises 13.27 and 13.28). The best bound in the original version of this technique was $5.43n$ comparisons [Blum et al. 1973]; this was subsequently improved to about $3n$ comparisons [Schönhage et al. 1976]. Both of the cited constructions have high constant factors. More useful is a method based upon sampling; although not guaranteed to be linear in all cases, it works very well in practice [Floyd and Rivest 1975].

13.4 EXTERNAL SORTING

In many real-life applications that require sorting, the number of items far exceeds the capacity of primary memory, and so it becomes imperative to employ sorting methods that make efficient use of secondary memory – that is, tapes or disks – to accomplish the process. We have seen, in Chapter 12, that a dominating concern in using these devices efficiently is to minimize the number of separate accesses that are required. Also, both of these storage mediums have a physical structure that causes certain accessing behaviors to be strongly preferred – sequential access in the case of tapes, and minimal number of seek operations with disks. The weight of all of these considerations will now cause us to completely revise some opinions derived in the case of internal sorting.

The usual paradigm of external sorting is first to construct sorted *initial runs* by employing familiar sorting techniques in internal memory, and then to complete the sort by successively merging these into larger and larger runs. At the outset, one might question the necessity of these basic assumptions. With virtual memory, we might simply apply one of the techniques already studied, and hope for the best. This is not a completely ridiculous idea if the number of items is only moderately large, and it is worth considering briefly. The most important issue is that the pattern of references to the data should have a high degree of locality. Thus, Shellsort or a distributive sort would be very poor in this regard. However, one of the best methods for internal sorting, Quicksort, is also very good with respect to locality. Quicksort with virtual memory (or Quicksort applied directly to data in secondary memory) is just barely feasible for moderately large values of n [Brawn et al. 1970]; however, it does not compare favorably with the better variations of the sort-merge paradigm, particularly as n increases. Moreover, its worst-case $O(n^2)$ behavior is intolerable in this context.

It is very typical in large sorting applications for the records to be big. It might seem particularly appropriate, therefore, to use a key sort (see Section 13.1). Appearances can be deceiving though. The use of an address table with a large amount of data can usurp a significant amount of primary memory better used for the original data. And paradoxically, even though it may be possible to sort the keys very fast, the final pattern of secondary accesses to rearrange the records in order may lead to a total performance far worse than would occur without key sort [Hubbard 1963]!

Our first concern in the succeeding sections is to explain multiway merging, the basic version of the sort-merge paradigm. Subsequent sections explore various avenues for improving this basic approach – first by obtaining better initial runs, then by employing more sophisticated merge patterns that take into account the idiosyncrasies of secondary memory devices.

13.4.1 Multiway Merging

Most of the early invention with regard to external sorting was directed toward efficient uses of tapes, since they were by far the more prevalent medium when these problems were first confronted. The subsequent prevalence of disks does not render these ideas irrelevant, since we know that it is often useful to employ a disk as a sequential access device. Thus, although our discussion in this and the next two sections is in terms of the number t of tapes employed as input – or the *order of merge*, t – much of it is relevant for disks also, and we will tidy up matters in Section 13.4.3.2. Suppose that we have four tapes $T1$, $T2$, $T3$, $T4$, and that $T4$ contains r runs, where $r = 57$. We will also assume for now that all the runs have the same length m; that is, the total number of items to be merged is $n = m \times r$. One possibility is to first distribute the runs as evenly as possible from $T4$ to $T1$, $T2$, $T3$; then merge the runs from $T1$, $T2$, $T3$ back to $T4$; then distribute the new runs of length $3m$ back to $T1$, $T2$, $T3$; etc. Four distributions and four merges are plainly sufficient to complete the process, since the number of distinct runs is reduced by a factor of three each time, and $\lceil \log_3 57 = 4$. Altogether, we have made 8 *passes* (read/write operations) over each item, although the distributions seem to contribute less to the solution than the merges. It is convenient to depict this pattern of activity as in Figure 13.22, where successive lines show the contents of $T1$, $T2$, $T3$, $T4$ at successive stages of the merging operation. The meaning of an entry such as $9^6 3^1$ for $T4$ is that $T4$ currently contains 6 runs of length $9m$ and 1 run of length $3m$.

$T1$	$T2$	$T3$	$T4$
–	–	–	1^{57}
1^{19}	1^{19}	1^{19}	–
–	–	–	3^{19}
3^7	3^6	3^6	–
–	–	–	$9^6\ 3^1$
$9^2\ 3^1$	9^2	9^2	–
–	–	–	$27^2\ 3^1$
27^1	27^1	3^1	–
–	–	–	57^1

Figure 13.22 Merging with 3 Input and 1 Output Tapes

We can employ the same four tapes more usefully in a *balanced merge*, wherein there are always the same number of tapes for input and for output, with their roles being alternated. Suppose that we have the same initial runs on $T4$, and that we begin by distributing them to $T1$, $T2$. Then the first runs from $T1$, $T2$ are merged and written on $T3$; the second runs from $T1$, $T2$ are merged and written on $T4$; and this alternation to $T3$, $T4$ continues. When the input on $T1$, $T2$ is exhausted, then $T3$, $T4$ become the input tapes and $T1$, $T2$ become the output tapes; when the input on $T3$, $T4$ is exhausted, the roles are switched again; etc. After the initial

$T1$	$T2$	$T3$	$T4$
–	–	–	1^{57}
1^{29}	1^{28}	–	–
–	–	$2^{14}\ 1^{1}$	2^{14}
$4^{7}\ 1^{1}$	4^{7}	–	–
–	–	8^{4}	$8^{3}\ 1^{1}$
16^{2}	$16^{1}\ 9^{1}$	–	–
–	–	32^{1}	25^{1}
57^{1}	–	–	–

Figure 13.23 Balanced 2-way Merging

distribution, six merging phases are plainly sufficient to complete the process, since the number of distinct runs is reduced by a factor two each time, and $\lceil \log_2 57 = 6$. Figure 13.23 depicts the pattern of merging activity in this case. Although there are more merges than before, we have eliminated the useless copying, and the total of 7 passes is a distinct improvement over the previous 8. Actually, by rotating which tape receives the output and by copying just 2/3 of the items from the output tape each time, we could have improved the 3-way merging scheme to the point that it outperformed this balanced 2-way merging scheme. But for $2t$ tapes, where $t \geq 3$, balanced merging will always be the better alternative.

Although simple, these two examples convey several important points. First, we are led to compare the efficiency of various merging schemes in terms of the total number of passes over the data. Secondly, if there are n items and they are in initial runs of size m, then balanced multiway merging with $2t$ tapes requires $\lceil \log_t (n/m)$ passes. In looking for better ways to accomplish merging, one obvious approach is to use larger values of t, and another is to start with larger values of m – in other words, larger initial runs. In fact, we will find that sophisticated merging patterns overcome the apparent dilemma encountered in this section – that we must settle for either wasteful copying (Figure 13.22) or reducing the order of merge (Figure 13.23).

†13.4.1.1 Buffer Management. The multiway merging scheme that we have just examined is a combination of input, trivial computation, and output. We have stressed that for efficiency, it is important to minimize the number of distinct accesses. There is more to it than that. While an input buffer is being filled, no computation can safely be performed with its contents. Therefore, it is conventional to use *double buffering*, wherein the contents of buffer A are available for use while buffer B is being filled with the next block of data from the input. As long as buffer B is filled and ready when the computation finishes with buffer A, then their roles can be switched with no loss in time. Similar remarks apply to the use of output buffers and to the use of pairs of buffers for multiple input streams. Thus,

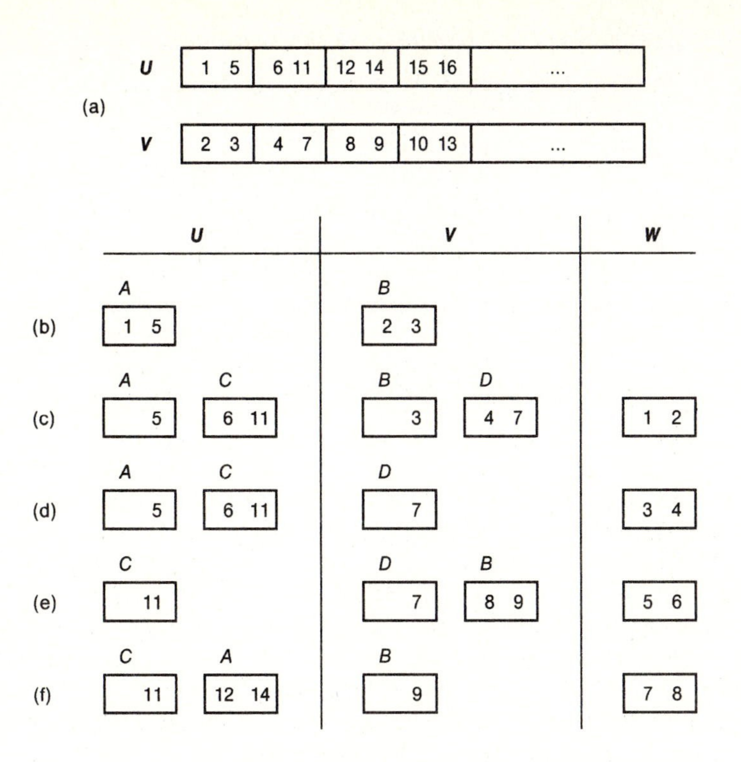

Figure 13.24 The Insufficiency of Paired Buffers

for multiway merging of order t, one would want 2 buffers for each input and 2 buffers for output, for a total of $2t + 2$.

However, simply having $2t + 2$ buffers allocated in pairs is not a good enough strategy. The merging process should, at any time, be able to find m items to fill the next output buffer, and should not have to wait for an input buffer to be filled in order to do so. The example in Figure 13.24 demonstrates that, in fact, this may not be possible if the $2t$ input buffers are simply assigned in pairs to the t inputs. In (a) of the figure we see the contents of input tapes U and V, in blocks of size two. The remainder of the figure traces the double buffering activity, with buffers A and C dedicated to tape U and buffers B and D dedicated to tape V. Of course, double buffering would also be used for the output buffers for tape W, but we disregard this and simply show the output blocks. As we follow the progress of the merging activity, we observe

(b) initial loading of buffers A and B from U and V;

(c) loading of buffers C and D from U and V;

(d) emptying of buffer B;

(e) emptying of buffer A and reloading of buffer B from V;

(f) emptying of buffer D and reloading of buffer A from U.

Now the merging process is delayed because the next block is needed from tape V; however, this must be loaded into buffer D, which was just depleted on this step and will not be reloaded until the next step.

There is a resolution for this type of situation, and that is to anticipate which of the active input buffers will be the first to be depleted. In the technique of *forecasting*, one simply looks at the last items in these buffers, and deduces from the smallest of those values which input will first need replenishing. With this method the pool of $2t$ buffers becomes a set of *floating buffers*, with many of them possibly being assigned to a single input for some interval. Suppose that this policy were in effect upon reaching the state toward the bottom of Figure 13.24. Then, upon comparing the 9 in buffer B with the 11 in buffer C, the next input would have been directed from tape V to the available buffer A, thereby avoiding the delay.

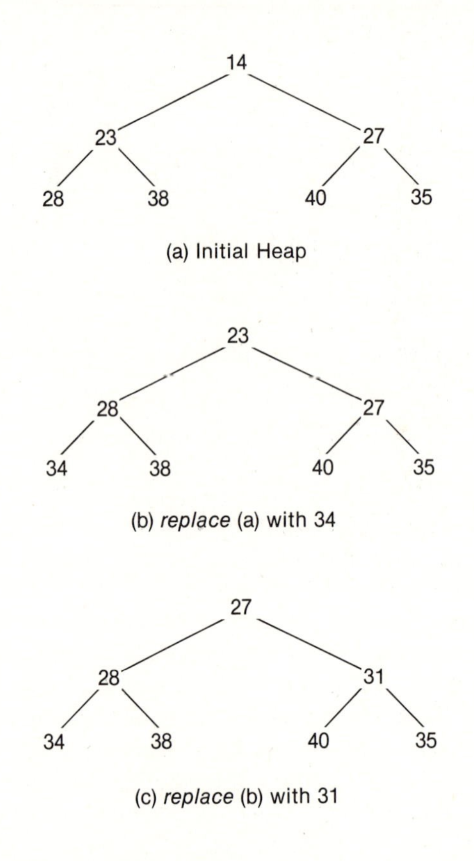

Figure 13.25 The Heap *replace* Operation

13.4.2 Replacement Selection

Suppose that we have space in primary memory for a buffer of size *m*, to be used for producing initial runs. The obvious approach is to repeatedly (a) fill the buffer with the next *m* items, (b) sort them with some efficient method from Section 13.2, and (c) write out the run of length *m*. A much better scheme is to use the buffer as a heap, along with a new priority queue operation:

replace(pq,min,next) – to remove the smallest item from *pq*, assigning it to *min*, and to insert *next* in *pq*, restoring the heap property as required.

In illustration of the *replace* operation, suppose that we have the heap shown in Figure 13.25(a), with $m = 7$. Output of 14 and input of 34 leads to the situation shown in (b) of the figure; output of 23 and input of 31 leads to the situation shown in (c); etc.

Let us now assume that $m = 4$, and use this operation with the input sequence shown in Figure 13.26(a), in the technique known as *replacement selection.* In generating runs, as shown in (b) of the figure, we repeatedly select the smallest of the current items in the buffer. The underlying mechanism for this is, of course, the heap strategy of Figure 13.25;[4] however, for long records it would probably be preferable to use a level of indirection, storing pointers in the heap rather than the actual records. Also, we must not select any item from the buffer if it is smaller than the last value that has been output in the current run. Items in this category (marked with *'s in the figure) are ineligible for the current run, and must wait for the next run. This requirement is easily implemented by keeping track of the current run number; keys of eligible items are then prefixed with the current run number, and keys of ineligible items are prefixed with the next run number.

We observe from Figure 13.26 that although the buffer size is four, the lengths of the first two initial runs are six and nine. There is nothing particularly contrived about this example. It is in the nature of replacement selection that, for random input, it generates initial runs with an average length of twice the buffer size. The practical results are even better than this theoretical value,. because it is fairly common for the input to be already partially sorted (see Section 13.2.4). In this event, the method will perform even better than predicted by theory, generating initial runs that may be much longer than $2m$ (see Exercise 13.31). All of this is important because, as we have seen in the preceding section, longer runs mean fewer runs, and this can shorten the merging phase. Another advantage of replacement selection is that it lends itself very well to overlapping of input, computation, and output. On the other hand, we should note two slight disadvantages. The runs produced are not of fixed length; neither can we divide the number of items *n* by a chosen buffer size *m* to obtain some known number of final runs *r*. Both of these matters may cause some inconvenience in the ensuing merge phase.

---

[4] Note that since our interest is in a good, convenient algorithm and not in precise counts of comparisons, we choose to use a heap rather than a tournament (see Section 13.3).

37 63 21 89 14 40 66 18 03 43 69 10 22 72 24 76 98 01 84 27 59 ...

(a) Input Sequence

Buffer (m = 4)	***Output***
37 63 21 89	
37 63 14* 89	21
40 63 14* 89	21 37
66 63 14* 89	21 37 40
66 18* 14* 89	21 37 40 63
03* 18* 14* 89	21 37 40 63 66
03* 18* 14* 43*	21 37 40 63 66 89
	(First run completed)
03 18 14 43	
69 18 14 43	03
69 18 10* 43	03 14
69 22 10* 43	03 14 18
69 72 10* 43	03 14 18 22
69 72 10* 24*	03 14 18 22 43
76 72 10* 24*	03 14 18 22 43 69
76 98 10* 24*	03 14 18 22 43 69 72
01* 98 10* 24*	03 14 18 22 43 69 72 76
01* 84* 10* 24*	03 14 18 22 43 69 72 76 98
	(Second run completed)
01 84 10 24	
27 84 10 24	01
27 84 59 24	01 10

...

(b) Generating Initial Runs

Figure 13.26 Replacement Selection

13.4.3 Merge Patterns

We will be examining patterns of merging in which intermediate runs of varying lengths are created. If at some point in this process we think of the existing sets of runs as leaves in a t-ary tree, then Huffman's algorithm (see Section 8.2.4) suggests a simple and elegant solution to the problem of minimizing the amount of work required to merge them. That is, one would always combine at the deepest level of the tree the contents of those tapes containing the least amount of data. Unfortunately, this simple perspective ignores the idiosyncrasies of the two chief external mediums, tape and disk. These generate other concerns, as we will see in the following two sections.

†13.4.3.1 Tape Sorting. To begin with, we cannot do t-way merging with tapes unless we have at least $t + 1$ of them − t for input and 1 for output. Thus, there is a pragmatic upper limit for any user who must depend upon the computing facilities available to him. A more fundamental fact about tapes is that they are efficient only when used as sequential access devices. In fact, the methods that we are describing use them as queues, but with a strong additional restriction − that the queue be completely filled before it is emptied.[5] Moreover, after a tape is written, it must be rewound before it can be read, and this can take a significant portion of a minute. Therefore, it is important that successive merge passes leave their output on tape in such fashion that there be no waste tape motion, and that they deliver the most work per pass. Although balanced multiway merging is quite respectable, it is not optimal in this respect, as we will now see.

Let us reconsider the same set of four tapes *T*1, *T*2, *T*3, *T*4 and the same set of 57 runs that we discussed in Section 13.4.1. We found there that 3-way merging was inferior to balanced multiway merging because of the unproductive nature of the distributive, or copying, passes. Is there a more efficient way to employ 3-way merging, using those same four tapes? There is, and since we are by now familiar with the format established in Figures 13.22 and 13.23, the easiest recourse is to demonstrate the technique by a similar figure. In the method of *polyphase merging* depicted in Figure 13.27, we begin by distributing unequal numbers of runs from *T*4 to *T*1, *T*2, *T*3. We then merge from *T*1, *T*2, *T*3 to *T*4 until *T*3 becomes empty, producing 13 runs of length $3m$ on *T*4; then *T*3 and *T*4 are rewound, and the next merge step produces 7 runs of length $5m$ on *T*3; etc. Note that we now have a fifth column in the figure, showing the amount of data that is processed at each step, as a fraction of the number of initial runs. There are altogether 7 merge steps in this example, the same as for multiway merging. In that case, however, each of the 57 initial runs was processed 7 times; now those 57 runs have been processed an average number of times equal to

$$\frac{57 + 39 + 35 + 36 + 34 + 31 + 57}{57} = 5.07$$

The trick here is to wind up at the last step with exactly one run on each of input tapes, and then conclude with a t-way merge of these t runs for the final output. It was not just luck that we succeeded in this case. Rather, the value 57 is one of a series of numbers that are perfect for the purpose of doing polyphase merging with four tapes. We can rather easily discover what those numbers are by building a table backwards, as shown in Figure 13.28. In this scheme, we let $a > b > c$ represent the numbers of runs on the non-empty tapes at successively higher levels. This condition implies that the largest number in a row must be the same as the smallest number in the next row, since a step must end when the tape with the smallest number of runs is depleted. In fact, we have this relation and two others, as follows:

[5] There are also tape merging schemes that use tapes as stacks, by reading tape backward as well as forward. Although these have a slight advantage in some cases, we will not pursue them here.

*T*1	*T*2	*T*3	*T*4	File Fraction
—	—	—	1^{57}	(Initial)
1^{24}	1^{20}	1^{13}	—	57/57
1^{11}	1^{7}	—	3^{13}	39/57
1^{4}	—	5^{7}	3^{6}	35/57
—	9^{4}	5^{3}	3^{2}	36/57
17^{2}	9^{2}	5^{1}	—	34/37
17^{1}	9^{1}	—	31^{1}	31/57
—	—	57^{1}	—	57/57

Figure 13.27 Polyphase Merging for $t = 4$

$$a_n = c_{n+1}\,, \quad b_n = a_{n+1} - a_n\,, \quad c_n = b_{n+1} - a_n \tag{13.14}$$

from which we find that

$$a_n = a_{n-1} + a_{n-2} + a_{n-3} \tag{13.15}$$

with initial conditions $a_1 = 1$, $a_2 = 2$, $a_3 = 4$. In other words, this method will work with $r = 9, 17, 31, 57, 105, \ldots$. The scheme can also be generalized for any number of tapes $p + 1$, yielding a p-way polyphase merge, for which the perfect initial values are the *pth order Fibonacci numbers*

$$f_n^{(p)} = f_{n-1}^{(p)} + f_{n-2}^{(p)} + f_{n-3}^{(p)} + \cdots + f_{n-p}^{(p)} \tag{13.16}$$

Some examples of these values for different values of p are shown in Table 13.3.

Level	*a*	*b*	*c*	Total
0	1	0	0	1
1	1	1	1	3
2	2	2	1	5
3	4	3	2	9
4	7	6	4	17
5	13	11	7	31
6	24	20	13	57
7	44	37	24	105
		...		

Figure 13.28 Perfect Polyphase Distributions for $t = 4$

An obvious question at this point is what to do if the number of initial runs does not match one of the values in the desired column of Table 13.3. The easy answer is that we should insert a number of *dummy runs* equal to the difference. However, the issue of where they should be inserted is a more subtle one. To begin

Level	$p=2$	$p=3$	$p=4$	$p=5$	$p=6$
1	2	3	4	5	6
2	3	5	7	9	11
3	5	9	13	17	21
4	8	17	25	33	41
5	13	31	49	65	81
6	21	57	94	129	161
7	34	105	181	253	321
8	55	193	349	497	636

Table 13.3 *p*th Order Fibonacci Numbers

with, we do not really need to insert the dummies; rather, we can just use counters to keep track of the numbers of these fictitious runs on each tape. Then we note that merging a dummy run with a real run amounts to copying, and that merging two dummy runs amounts to simply decrementing two counters. So there is much advantage in dividing the total number of required dummy runs equally (in some sense) among the tapes in the initial distribution. The details are more intricate than this simple observation suggests, with the surprising result that it is sometimes better to operate with more than the minimum number of dummy runs and passes [Shell 1971]!

$T1$	$T2$	$T3$	$T4$	$T5$
—	—	—	—	1^{85}
1^{30}	1^{26}	1^{19}	1^{10}	—
1^{20}	1^{16}	1^{9}	—	4^{10}
1^{11}	1^{7}	—	3^{9}	4^{10}
1^{4}	—	2^{7}	3^{9}	4^{10}
—	$1^{4}*$	2^{7}	3^{9}	4^{10}
10^{4}	—	2^{3}	3^{5}	4^{6}
10^{4}	9^{3}	—	3^{2}	4^{3}
10^{4}	9^{3}	7^{2}	—	4^{1}
10^{4}	9^{3}	7^{2}	$4^{1}*$	—
10^{3}	9^{2}	7^{1}	—	30^{1}
10^{2}	9^{1}	—	26^{1}	30^{1}
10^{1}	—	19^{1}	26^{1}	30^{1}
—	$10^{1}*$	19^{1}	26^{1}	30^{1}
85^{1}	—	—	—	—

Figure 13.29 Cascade Merging for $t=5$

We have alluded previously to two sources of wasted tape motion, copying and rewinding. Rewinding is actually much more of a culprit than is copying (see Exercise 13.29), and polyphase merging as we have described it still has this problem. In each merge step, in fact, the tape last depleted and the tape just filled both have to be rewound by sizeable amounts. There are variations of polyphase sorting that directly confront this issue. However, it is more instructive to examine briefly the pattern known as *cascade merging*. As with polyphase merging, we start with a perfect distribution of initial runs on the tapes. To illustrate this method, we will use five tapes rather than four; a viable distribution of initial runs in this case is 30, 26, 19, 10. We see in the ensuing pattern, as shown in Figure 13.29, that a given merge step has sub-steps. In this case, for example,

a first sub-step does 4-way merging from *T*1, *T*2, *T*3, *T*4 to *T*5
a second sub-step does 3-way merging from *T*1, *T*2, *T*3 to *T*4
a third sub-step does 2-way merging from *T*1, *T*2 to *T*3
a final sub-step copies from *T*1 to *T*2

The number of runs that are copied (marked with *'s) is so small as to be of little consequence.

We see that this method employs merges of orders $t, t-1, \dots, 2$ and that it always processes all of the runs on each step. This might seem to place it at a disadvantage compared to polyphase, which always does merges of order t and processes just a fraction of the runs at each step. Nonetheless, for $t > 6$, cascade merge is asymptotically superior to polyphase merge. The reason is that the tapes containing the most initial runs are written earlier in each step, and can then be rewound while the tapes with lesser numbers of runs are being written; thus, much of the rewind activity is overlapped with useful computation.

	$t = 4$	$t = 6$	$t = 8$	$t = 10$
Balanced Merge, $t/2$	1.000 lg r	0.631 lg r	0.500 lg r	0.431 lg r
Ordinary Merge, $t-1$	1.262 lg r	0.861 lg r	0.712 lg r	0.631 lg r
Polyphase Merge, $t-1$	1.042 lg r	0.598 lg r	0.528 lg r	0.509 lg r
Cascade Merge, $t-1$	1.042 lg r	0.622 lg r	0.479 lg r	0.407 lg r

Table 13.4 Asymptotic Numbers of Tape Passes

Let us summarize this matter of merge patterns by tabulating their asymptotic behavior, in terms of fractional number of runs processed, for various values of t. We do this in Table 13.4 for balanced multiway merging, for multiway merging with copying, for polyphase merging, and for cascade merging. It is important to realize that these are asymptotic, theoretical numbers. In many computing environments, for example, balanced multiway merge and polyphase merge may differ only slightly in their efficiency. Moreover, a fortuitous number of initial runs, or perhaps the characteristics of a particular device, can easily tip the balance. Nonetheless, when external sorting is a major activity, it is sensible to investigate alternatives such as these, with the possibility of saving substantial amounts of time.

†13.4.3.2 Disk Sorting. Many of the limitations with tape do not apply with disks. One need not have $t + 1$ disks to do t-way merging; in fact, just two will suffice, one for the inputs and one for the output. Neither do we have to contend with rewinding. So there is much more flexibility in composing merge patterns, and one might be encouraged to employ large merge orders, thereby decreasing the number of passes. But now we discover a different kind of limitation. If the order of merge is high, then space must be allocated for buffers for each of the inputs. Since the buffers are obtained by dividing up some fixed amount of space t ways, this leads to smaller buffers as t gets larger. Now transmission time is a decreasing function of the merge order, as we wished, but seek time is an increasing function of the merge order, since smaller buffers require more seeks to fill them. In other words, to do a t-way merge of n items will require time proportional to $(St + T)n$, where S and T are constants related to the seek and transmission costs, and where normally $S < T$. These dependencies usually yield an operating curve with a moderately shallow minimum. For a given computing environment, it is fairly easy to obtain usable estimates for the relative importance of seek and transmission times, and to thereby locate a good operating point.

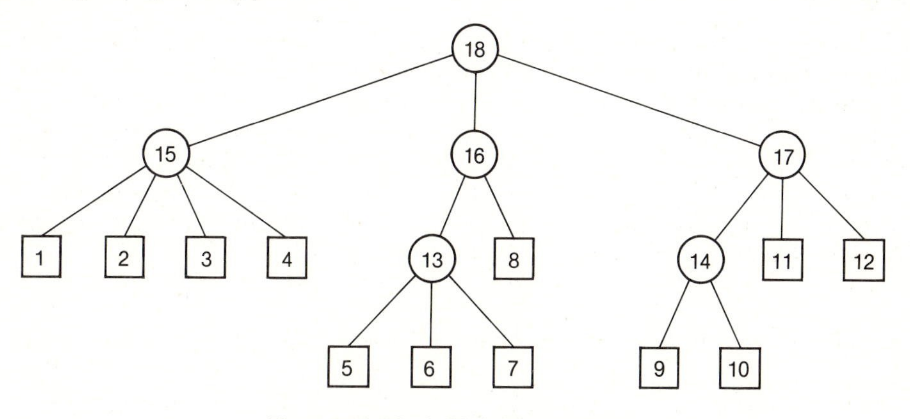

Figure 13.30 A Disk Merge Tree

An idealized model of the situation just described is given by the cost function

$$C = S \times D + T \times E \qquad (13.17)$$

To see the significance of the variables D and E, let us draw a tree representing a hypothetical merge sequence, as in Figure 13.30, where the leaves all contains initial runs of length m. If we compute the costs as tabulated in Figure 13.31, then the value of E for this merge tree is 29, which we recognize as external path length. But what is D? It is the *degree path length*, which can alternatively be expressed as the sum, over all leaf nodes, of the degrees of the internal nodes on the path from the leaf to the root. Thus, D for the tree of Figure 13.30 can be obtained as:

$$4 \times (4 + 3) + 3 \times (3 + 2 + 3) + 1 \times (2 + 3) + 2 \times (2 + 3 + 3) + 2 \times (3 + 3) = 85$$

If we have values for S and T, then we can construct an optimal merge tree by using the principle of optimality in a fashion reminiscent of, but different from, the principle that we used for building optimal binary search trees in Section 10.3.2.1 (see Exercise 13.38).

Node	Cost
13	$(3S + T) \times 3m$
14	$(2S + T) \times 2m$
15	$(4S + T) \times 4m$
16	$(2S + T) \times 4m$
17	$(3S + T) \times 4m$
18	$(3S + T) \times 12m$
Total	$(85S + 29T) \times m$

Figure 13.31 Cost Computation for the Tree of Figure 13.30

†13.5 PARALLEL SORTING SCHEMES

For the preceding sections of this chapter, most of the results were discovered well before the 1970's. Although the concerns of this section likewise date from that time, they also reflect more recent invention. Our starting point is the Information Theoretic Bound of $O(n \lg n)$ from Section 13.2.3. If sorting is so important, then perhaps we can circumvent this bound by having many processors operating in parallel. In particular, we inquire whether n processors can be employed in such a fashion that the time is reduced to $O(\lg n)$? The first order of business in looking for answers to such questions is to define the model of computation, and we will speak to that very shortly. From first principles, however, we are able to see that no comparison-based method can hope to do better than $O(\lg n)$ time. This is so because there are that many levels in the comparison tree, and the tests on each level depend upon the test results from preceding levels, but no assemblage of processors can produce results any faster than dictated by this number of levels.

Before describing models of parallel computation, it might be well to explain why we tolerate the notion of having n processors, where n could be very large. One reason is the historical one that these issues were first raised in the context of building fast switching, or permutation, networks. This is a somewhat simpler problem than sorting, and an important one, for which n is commonly of reasonable size. So it has practical appeal. Another, obvious reason is that the enormous advances in VLSI fabrication techniques now make such devices plausible. Finally, even if some of the ideas are not yet feasible, the unrestricted models of parallel computation have theoretical importance in their own right.

There are two broad models for parallel computation. In the *network model*, the processors are autonomous, having their own memories, and communicating via a network of connections. In the *shared memory model*, all the processors can communicate freely via their shared memory. In almost all of the former models, the links tend to be few in number and very regular in their topology. These features are conventionally imposed because of their practical significance; the end result is that these models are less powerful than the shared memory models, due to the constricted communication among the processors. There are many variations upon both of these models, reflecting very significant concerns. Examples of these are the quantity of information that must be exchanged among processors (the network model), the handling of memory contention (the shared memory model), and the cost of setting up a computation (both models). It is curious that, in either model, attempts to parallelize the more efficient $O(n \lg n)$ serial sorting methods have not succeeded. It seems as though they are inherently serial to some degree. Thus, it is easy to apply multiple processors to the early steps of merging or later steps of Quicksort, but seemingly not possible to do so with the final steps of merging or initial steps of Quicksort. The methods that have responded well to parallelization are some of the more lowly $O(n^2)$ methods!

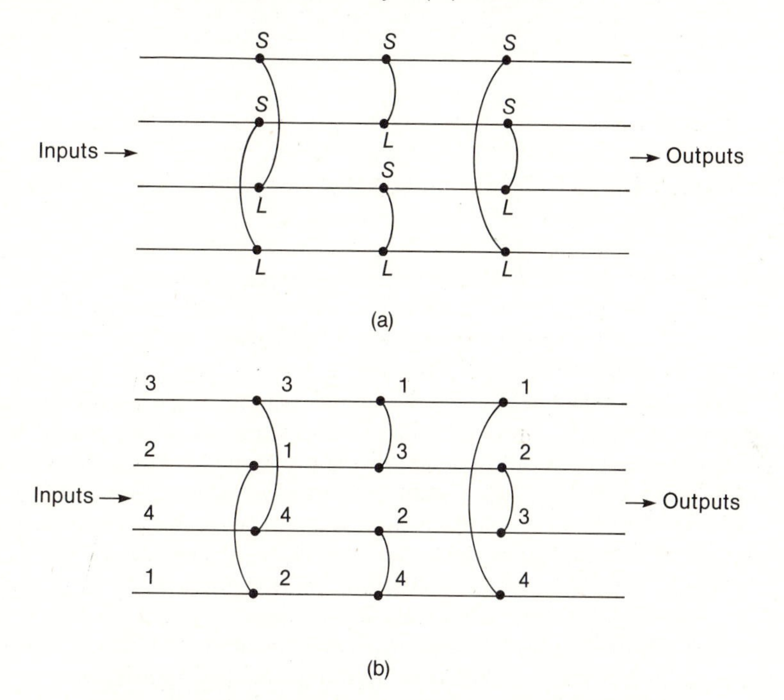

Figure 13.32 Sorting with a Network of Comparators

In speaking of network models, we need to distinguish between those that are intended to serve a wide variety of computational purposes and those that are designed strictly for sorting. The logic required for sorting is extremely simple, and so it is comparatively easy to design a network when that is the only operation required of it. The basic logical unit required is a *comparator* with two inputs A and B, and two outputs S and L, such that the output S receives the smaller of the two inputs, and the output L receives the larger of the two. A useful convention for representing a network of such comparators is depicted in Figure 13.32(a), with the inputs on the left and the outputs on the right. A comparator is a vertical bridge between a pair of inputs; it will cause that pair to be exchanged, if necessary, so that the S output is above the L output. Thus, Figure 13.32(b) illustrates the action of this network in sorting the input sequence 3, 2, 4, 1. Note that two comparisons are performed in parallel each time, and that three time steps are required.

Using comparators in sorting networks is like doing bubble sort comparison-exchanges in parallel. With $O(n)$ comparators, we could hope to translate the $O(n^2)$ character of that method into an $O(n)$ parallel sorting method. How much better can we do in reality? In this regard, Batcher [1968] demonstrated two different schemes that sort n items in $O(\lg^2 n)$ time by using networks of $O(n \lg^2 n)$ comparators. A more recent result uses a graph-theoretic construction to demonstrate that a network of $O(n \lg n)$ comparators can sort n numbers in $O(\lg n)$ time [Ajtai et al. 1983]. Unfortunately, whereas Batcher's schemes admit of practical implementation, this more recent method does not at present.

If the paradigm of most network models is the comparison-exchange of bubble sort, the paradigm of most shared memory models is enumeration sorting! Since the processors can freely compare any pair of values, then counting can be used to determine the ranks of the items. To cite the power of this technique, we know that serial computation requires $n - 1$ comparisons to find the maximum of n items. Yet in the shared memory model of computation, it has been shown, by another graph-theoretic construction, that n processors can find the maximum in time $\lg \lg n + c$, for c a constant [Valiant 1975b]! Related arguments there and elsewhere show how to apply enumeration to the problems of sorting and merging. These methods do attain our goal of having n processors sort n items in $O(\lg n)$ time. However, the final remark at the end of the previous paragraph applies here also – it is not presently feasible to implement these methods.

The preceding remarks appear to leave the issue of fast parallel sorting unresolved. Although the theoretical outlook is good, those methods with best asymptotic performance seem to have unreasonably high costs, in either the network or the shared memory model. Moreover, the economics of building special purpose devices has never generated more than limited enthusiasm. It is only a matter of time until parallel computing architectures begin to proliferate though. At that point, it is likely that economics will dictate the adoption of general purpose network architectures, perhaps *shuffle-exchange networks* [Stone 1971] or *cube-connected-cycles* [Preparata and Vuillemin 1979], to name just two. The issue will then become that of discovering what parallel sorting algorithms can best be adapted to these general purpose schemes for parallelism.

13.6 OVERVIEW

In several ways, this final chapter is broader in scope than any of the others. Computer science is now several decades old, and the topic of sorting has played a central role from the very earliest years until the present. The number of published sorting algorithms, with all their variations, is very large. And although the problem statement of sorting is relatively simple, compared to that of searching, the choice of which method to use is not so simple. The numerous alternatives have been classically used to illustrate the benefits of various computing trade-offs at all levels of pedagogy. Thus, sorting teaches us about the "engineering" side of computer science. At the same time, as the discussion of Section 13.5 reveals, sorting is a very active area of research in contemporary computer science.

The broad scope is also apparent when we contrast some of the real-world concerns (buffer management, and merge patterns that cater to tape and disk behaviors) with some of the theoretical results. In the latter regard, there is pleasing symmetry in the following observation. For each of the issues – sorting optimality, merging optimality, and selection optimality – a pair of investigators have made major contributions by using very pretty combinatorial analysis and sophisticated data structures. We refer, of course, to the algorithms by Ford and Johnson, Hwang and Lin, and Hadian and Sobel. The virtue of breadth in this final sense – of having one's feet planted both in the real world and in theory – is a fitting note on which to close.

13.7 BIBLIOGRAPHIC NOTES

- Some Quicksort variations include sampling to determine the partitioning element [Frazer and McKellar 1970], computing the mean rather than the median to determine the partitioning element [Motzkin 1983], and exploiting pre-sortedness [Dromey 1984].

- One proposal for hybrid sorting is essentially address calculation sorting followed by Heapsort, thus bounding the worst-case complexity [Meijer and Akl 1980]. Another is a combination of distribution and merging [van der Nat 1980]. And still another employs three phases: distribution, then Quicksort on each bucket, and finally insertion sorting to clean up remaining inversions [Allison and Noga 1982].

13.8 REFERENCE TO TERMINOLOGY

13.9 EXERCISES

Sections 13.1 – 13.2.2

13.1 What is the inversion table for the permutation 5 3 7 2 1 9 8 6 4?

†13.2 Write an algorithm to compute a permutation, given its inversion table. Test your program against the inversion table 7 6 6 4 0 2 2 1 0. What is the complexity of your program?

†13.3 In enumeration sorting, how are the final counts related to the permutation P^{-1} that is needed to rearrange the input values in order? Write an algorithm that accomplishes this rearrangement.

13.4 Write a version of insertion sort that uses a linked list, using cursors rather than pointer variables. Test your program against the data of Eq. 13.1, displaying the cursor values after each major iteration.

†13.5 Assume that cursors have been employed in performing a linked list insertion sort, as in Exercise 13.4. Write an algorithm that will permute the resulting records (in the final array, after that sort) to their proper sequence, using as little working storage as possible. What is its complexity? Test your program under the assumption that the input data to the linked list insertion sort was that of Eq. 13.1, displaying the cursor values after each major iteration.

13.6 Sort the following input via a Shellsort, using increments of 5,3,1 and showing the sequence of the keys after each pass.

74 95 26 66 36 24 1 60 70 2 25 22 31

††**13.7** [Gale and Karp 1972] Prove that a sequence that is first j-sorted and then k-sorted still remains j-sorted.

13.8 Demonstrate either that selection sort is stable or that it is not stable.

13.9 Show the effect of transforming the sequence of keys from Exercise 13.6 into a heap. Then perform a Heapsort, displaying the heap after each sift-up operation.

†**13.10** Write an algorithm to perform tournament sorting. Test your program against the input from Exercise 13.6.

†**13.11** Prove that the complexity of initially creating the heap in Heapsort is $O(n)$.

13.12 Sort the sequence of keys from Exercise 13.6 via Quicksort. Show the values of the parameters *left* and *rite* for each invocation, and show the sequence of the keys after each exchange.

†**13.13** Write a version of Quicksort incorporating all of the basic refinements discussed in Section 13.2.1.3.1, and implementing the median-of-three function as a sub-procedure. Test your program against three sample sets of data, each of size about one hundred; try it with data in order, data in reverse order, and data in random order. Compare its execution times against these test inputs with those of Algorithm 13.6 for the same inputs.

13.14 Use merging to sort the sequence of keys from Exercise 13.6, doing so for:

(a) a two-way top-down recursive merge,

(b) a two-way bottom-up straight merge,

(c) a natural merge.

Show the sequence of the keys after each pass, as in Figure 13.14.

13.15 Sort the sequence of keys from Exercise 13.6 via a radix sort, showing the sequence of the keys after each pass.

Sections 13.2.3 – 13.3

††**13.16** Draw the comparison trees that correspond to applying Heapsort and Quicksort to a sequence of three elements a,b,c. Your trees should be done in the style of Figure 13.16.

††**13.17** What is the external path length for the comparison tree corresponding to the method of Figure 13.17? Demonstrate a minimean sorting method for six elements that has a smaller external path length.

††**13.18** [Knuth 1973b] Given a digraph G as in Figure 13.17, one can define the efficiency of G as $E(G) = n! \,/\, (2^k T(G))$, where k is the number of comparisons made in obtaining the configuration G, and $T(G)$ is the number of ways in which G can be topologically sorted (see Exercise 7.40). Initially $k = 0$ and $T(G) = n!$, so that $E(G) = 1$. In the final graph (a line) $T(G) = 1$, so that the efficiency depends upon the number of comparisons made to complete the sort. Since $F(6) = 10$, from Table 13.1, the final graph for this merge insertion has an efficiency of $6!/2^{10} = 45/64$. With reference to Figure 13.17(b), calculate the efficiency of the graph obtained by inserting c before e, and the efficiencies of the graphs obtained by inserting e before

c (the values of $T(G)$ can easily be computed by hand). The significance of this process is that a comparison always leads to a graph of lower efficiency; therefore, it can be determined a priori that inserting c before e could never lead to a graph with final efficiency of 45/64, as above, whereas inserting e before c could do so.

††13.19 Obtain a formula that describes the insertion order sequence for merge insertion. Starting from this formula, derive the summation form of Eq. 13.10.

†13.20 For the following input files, trace the action of binary merge as in Figure 13.20; however, show the actual comparisons and actual outputs that result from merging these inputs.

U: 15 19 20 25 28 31 37 42 44 48 51 52 54 55
56 61 63 67 69 72 73 76 78 83 85 89 90 96
V: 23 57 79 88

††13.21 Write a program to perform binary merging. Test it by applying it to the data of Exercise 13.20, and printing out the same values asked for in that exercise.

†13.22 Write an algorithm to find the length L of the longest ascending subsequence of a sequence. Test your program against the sequence

23 11 24 25 14 15 17 22 12 26 13 21 16

What is the complexity of your program? Finally, revise your algorithm so that it actually finds an instance of such a longest subsequence of length L.

†13.23 [Pohl 1972] The problem of finding the maximum (or the minimum) in an array of n elements by a sequence of comparisons can be characterized as follows. To simplify matters, assume that the elements all have distinct values. Then the elements of the array are in one of two disjoint sets: A containing elements that could be the maximum, and B containing elements that cannot be the maximum. Any comparison must be of one of three forms:

$a\,?\,a$ between elements from set A
$a\,?\,b$ between elements from sets A and B
$b\,?\,b$ between elements from set B

Initially, set A has cardinality $N_A = n$ and set B has cardinality $N_B = 0$. The three types of comparisons alter the cardinalities as follows:

	a ? a	a ? b		b ? b
		a < b	a > b	
ΔN_A	-1	-1	0	0
ΔN_B	$+1$	$+1$	0	0

Since the goal is to have $N_A = 1$ and $N_B = n - 1$, then the best we can do is always make comparisons of the form $a\,?\,a$, and a minimum of $n - 1$ of these will be required to reach the desired final state.

In Section 2.5.1 we saw how to find both the minimum and maximum values in an array of n elements at a cost of $3/2n - 2$ comparisons, using the recursive procedure MIN_MAX (Algorithm 2.8). Analyze this problem afresh in terms of four disjoint sets:

A – containging elements that could be either the minimum or the maximum
B – containing elements that could be the minimum but not the maximum
C – containing elements that could be the maximum but not the minimum
D – containing elements that can be neither the minimum nor the maximum

with initial cardinalities $N_A = n$, $N_B = 0$, $N_C = 0$, $N_D = 0$. Construct a table containing an analysis of all possible comparisons (like that above), and then demonstrate that a minimum of $3/2n - 2$ comparisons are required.

†13.24 According to Table 13.2, the value of $V_2(5)$ is 6. Even so, show how to find the two largest of five items, without necessarily knowing which is greater, in just five comparisons.

††13.25 [Hyafil 1976] An upper bound on the complexity of selection is given by Eq. 13.13. Prove that a lower bound is given by

$$V_k(n) \geq n - k + (k-1)\left\lceil\left(\frac{\lg n}{k-1}\right)\right.$$

(*Hint*: Use a technique like that of Exercise 13.23.)

††13.26 Prove that in using the ordinary variation of Quicksort to perform selection (that is, without linear median-finding), the average complexity is $O(n)$.

††13.27 Demonstrate whether or not the linear median-finding construction will work for $r = 5$. What about $r = 3$? Finally, show the effect of repeated data values upon the choice of r.

††13.28 Demonstrate an improved bound for linear median-finding, either by using a larger value of r and/or by using more careful techniques than those employed in the text.

Sections 13.4 – 13.5

13.29 Suppose that we are merging n runs with three tapes, and that the initial distribution is 1 run on $T1$ and $n - 1$ runs on $T2$. Is any copying required? How many passes will be required?

13.30 What would be the initial runs obtained via replacement selection, assuming a buffer size of 5, for the following input sequence?

56 12 68 22 76 29 80 31 81 30 77 24 70 15 59
02 44 86 26 65 04 41 78 13 48 82 14 46 77 07

†13.31 Under what circumstances will replacement selection transform the input sequence to a single initial run, thereby accomplishing the sort without any need of subsequent merging operations?

†13.32 If we define a random input sequence of elements $x_1, x_2, \ldots, x_n$ in terms of a random permutation of $1 \,..\, n$, then what is the expected length of the first run encountered in the input to replacement selection?

††13.33 Write an algorithm to perform replacement selection. Test your program against the data of Exercise 13.30.

†13.34 Generate a table, like that of Figure 13.28, showing perfect polyphase distributions for $t = 6$. Then generate the analogue of Figure 13.27, showing how 65 initial runs would actually be merged.

††13.35 Investigate the action of polyphase merge on 17 initial runs with four tapes. Label the runs in their initial locations on $T1$, $T2$, $T3$; then use a merge tree to keep track of their activity throughout the merging process. Use this to draw conclusions about the disposition of dummy runs.

††13.36 Write an algorithm to perform polyphase merging, assuming that tapes are modelled by arrays. You may ignore the issue of dummy runs by assuming a perfect initial distribution, but your algorithm should be general enough to handle any reasonable number of tapes. Test your program against three initial distributions ($n > 100$ in each case) for each of the cases $t = 3$, $t = 5$, $t = 8$.

†13.37 Describe in moderate detail how one might best do sorting if just *two* tapes were available.

††13.38 Suppose that we have 24 initial runs of equal sizes. Using Eq. 13.17, compute and draw the optimal merge patterns corresponding to three different sets of assumptions: $S = 1$ and $T = 1$, $S = 1$ and $T = 0$, $S = 0$ and $T = 1$.

†13.39 The sorting network of Figure 13.32 uses six comparisons to sort four numbers. Try to find a network that sorts four numbers in fewer comparisons.

LIST of ALGORITHMS

BIBLIOGRAPHY and REFERENCES

There are three types of references, as follows:

1. General references of a significant nature for the study of data structures; they may have been cited numerous times or not at all. These are listed with [•].
2. Specific references that are cited in the text just a few times. These are listed with the section numbers in which they appear.
3. Incidental references that are not cited in the text, but that provide noteworthy background material. These are listed without any special marking.

Abraham, C.T., Ghosh, S.P., and Ray-Chaudhuri, D.K. (1968) File Organization Based on Finite Geometries, *Information and Control 12*, 143-163. [12.6]

Achugbue, J.O. (1981) On the Line Breaking Problem in Text Formatting, Proceedings of ACM SIGPLAN-SIGOA Symposium on Text Manipulation, *ACM SIGPLAN Notices 16: 6*, 117-122. [8.3.2]

ACM (1976) Proceedings of Conference on Data: Abstraction, Definition, and Structure, *ACM SIGPLAN Notices 11* (Special Issue).

ACM (1979) Curriculum '78: Recommendations for the Undergraduate Program in Computer Science, *ACM Communications 22*, 147-166. [Preface]

Adel'son-Vel'skii, G.M. and Landis, E.M. (1962) An Algorithm for the Organization of Information, *Soviet Math. Doklady 3*, 1259-1263. [10.3.3.1]

Aho, A.V. and Corasick, M.J. (1975) Efficient String Matching: An Aid to Bibliographic Search, *ACM Communications 18*, 333-340. [8.5.3]

Aho, A.V., Hopcroft, J.E., and Ullman, J.D. (1974) *The Design and Analysis of Computer Algorithms*, Addison-Wesley. [•]

Aho, A.V., Hopcroft, J.E., and Ullman, J.D. (1983) *Data Structures and Algorithms*, Addison-Wesley. [•]

Aho, A.V., Johnson, S.C., and Ullman, J.D. (1975) Deterministic Parsing of Ambiguous Grammars, *ACM Communications 18*, 441-452. [8.6.3]

Aho, A.V. and Ullman, J.D. (1977) *Principles of Compiler Design*, Addison-Wesley. [6.6.2]

Ajtai, M., Komlós, J., and Szemerédi, E. (1983) An $O(n \log n)$ Sorting Network, *Proceedings 15th ACM Symposium on Theory of Computing*, 1-9. [13.5]

Allen, A.O. (1975) Elements of Queueing Theory for System Design, *IBM Systems Journal 14*, 161-187. [5.1.3.1]

Allen, B. and Munro, J.I. (1978) Self-Organizing Binary Search Trees, *ACM Journal 25*, 526-535. [10.3.3.3]

Allen, F.E. (1970) Control Flow Analysis, *ACM SIGPLAN Notices 5: 7*, 1-19. [7.4.5.3.2]

Allen, F.E. and Cocke, J. (1976) A Program Data Flow Analysis Procedure, *ACM Communications 19*, 137-147. [7.4.5.3.2]

Allison, D.C.S. and Noga, M.T. (1982) Usort: An Efficient Hybrid of Distributive Partitioning Sorting, *BIT 22*, 135-139. [13.7]

Al-Suwaiyel, M. and Horowitz, E. (1984) Algorithms for Trie Compaction, *ACM Transactions on Database Systems 9*, 243-263. [10.5.1]

Amble, O. and Knuth, D.E. (1974) Ordered Hash Tables, *Computer Journal 17*, 135-142. [10.4.2.5]

Angluin, D. (1976) The Four Russians' Algorithm for Boolean Matrix Multiplication is Optimal in Its Class, *ACM SIGACT News 8: 1*, 29-33. [2.5.3]

Arden, B.W., Galler, B.A., and Graham, R.M. (1961) An Algorithm for Equivalence Declarations, *ACM Communications 4*, 310-314. [4.2.3]

Arlazarov, V.L., Dinic, E.A., Kronrod, M.A., and Faradžev, I.A. (1970) On Economical Construction of the Transitive Closure of an Oriented Graph, *Soviet Math. Doklady 11*, 1209-1210. [2.5.3]

Ash, R. (1965) *Information Theory*, Wiley-Interscience. [8.2.4]

Atkinson, L.V. (1979) Pascal Scalars as State Indicators, *Software Practice and Experience 9*, 427-431. [4.2.1]

Atkinson, L.V. (1984) Jumping About and Getting into a State, *Computer Journal 27*, 42-46. [4.2.1]

Auslander, M.A. and Strong, H.R. (1978) Systematic Recursion Removal, *ACM Communications 21*, 127-134. [5.6]

Baase, S. (1978) *Computer Algorithms: Introduction to Design and Analysis*, Addison-Wesley. [2.5.3]

Backus, J. (1960) The Syntax and Semantics of the Proposed International Algebraic Language of the Zurich ACM-GAMM Conference, *Proceedings International UNESCO Conference on Information Processing*, Paris, 125-132. [5.4.1]

Baecker, H.D. (1972) Garbage Collection for Virtual Memory Systems, *ACM Communications 15*, 981-986. [12.2.2]

Baer, J.L. (1975) Weight-Balanced Trees, *Proceedings National Computer Conference*, 467-472. [10.3.3.2]

Baer, J.L. and Fries, M. (1977) On the Efficiency of Some List Marking Algorithms, *Proceedings IFIP Congress*, 751-766. [11.2.1.1]

Baer, J.L. and Schwab, B. (1977) A Comparison of Tree-Balancing Algorithms, *ACM Communications 20*, 322-330. [10.3.3.1, 10.3.3.2]

Baker, H.G. (1978a) List Processing in Real Time on a Serial Computer, *ACM Communications 21*, 280-294. [11.2.6]

Baker, T.P. (1978b) A Technique for Extending Rapid Exact-Match String Matching to Arrays of More Than One Dimension, *SIAM Journal of Computing 7*, 533-541. [8.8]

Barnard, T.J. (1969) A New Rule Mask Technique for Interpreting Decision Tables, *Computer Bulletin 13*, 153-154. [2.11]

Barth, J.M. (1977) Shifting Garbage Collection Overhead to Compile Time, *ACM Communications 20*, 513-518. [11.2.5]

Batcher, K.E. (1968) Sorting Networks and Their Application, *Proceedings Spring Joint Computer Conference*, 307-314. [13.5]

Bayer, P.J. (1975) Improved Bounds on the Costs of Optimal and Balanced Binary Search Trees, *M.I.T. Project MAC Tech. Memo. 69.* [10.3.2.3]

Bayer, R. (1972) Symmetric Binary B-Trees: Data Structure and Maintenance Algorithms, *Acta Informatica 1*, 290-306. [10.3.5]

Bayer, R. and McCreight, E. (1972) Organization and Maintenance of Large Ordered Indexes, *Acta Informatica 1*, 173-189. [12.3.4.1]

Bayer, R. and Unterauer K. (1977) Prefix B-Trees, *ACM Transactions on Database Systems 2*, 11-26. [12.3.4.1]

Bays, C. (1973) The Reallocation of Hash-Coded Tables, *ACM Communications 16*, 11-14. [10.10]

Bays, C. (1977) A Comparison of Next-fit, First-fit, and Best-fit, *ACM Communications 20*, 191-192. [11.3.4.2]

Beck, L.L. (1982) A Dynamic Storage Allocation Technique Based on Memory Residence Time, *ACM Communications 25*, 714-724. [11.3.1.2]

Beckman, F.S. (1980) *Mathematical Foundations of Programming*, Addison-Wesley. [5.4.3, 6.6.5.1]

Behzad, M., Chartrand, G., and Lesniak-Foster, L. (1979) *Graphs and Digraphs*, Wadsworth Publishers. [7.7]

Belady, L.A. (1966) A Study of Replacement Algorithms for a Virtual Storage Computer, *IBM Systems Journal 5*, 78-101. [12.2.1]

Belady, L.A., Nelson, R.A., and Shedler, G.S. (1969) An Anomaly in Space-Time Characteristics of Certain Programs Running in a Paging Machine, *ACM Communications 12*, 349-353. [12.8]

Bellman, R. (1962) Dynamic Programming Treatment of the Travelling Salesman Problem, *ACM Journal 9*, 61-63. [7.7]

Bellmore, M. and Nemhauser, G.L. (1968) The Traveling Salesman Problem: A Survey, *Operations Research 16*, 538-558.

Bentley, J.L. (1975) Multidimensional Binary Search Trees Used for Associative Searching, *ACM Communications 18*, 509-517. [12.4.3.2]

Bentley, J.L. (1979a) Multidimensional Binary Search Trees in Database Design, *IEEE Transactions on Software Engineering SE-5*, 333-340. [12.4.3.2]

Bentley, J.L. (1979b) Decomposable Searching Problems, *Information Processing Letters 8*, 244-251.

Bentley, J.L. (1980) Multidimensional Divide-and-Conquer, *ACM Communications 23*, 214-229.

Bentley, J.L. and Friedman, J.H. (1979) Data Structures for Range Searching, *ACM Computer Surveys 11*, 397-409. [12.4.3]

Bentley, J.L., Haken, D., and Saxe, J.B. (1980) A General Method for Solving Divide-and-Conquer Recurrences, *ACM SIGACT News 12: 3*, 36-44.

Bentley, J.L. and McGeoch, C.C. (1985) Amortized Analyses of Self-Organizing Sequential Search Heuristics, *ACM Communications 28*, 404-411. [10.8]

Bentley, J.L., Sleator, D.D., Tarjan, R.E., and Wei, V.K. (1986) A Locally Adaptive Data Compression Scheme, *ACM Communications 29*, 320-330. [8.8]

Berge, C. (1957) Two Theorems in Graph Theory, *Proceedings National Academy of Science 43*, 842-844. [7.4.3.4]

Berge, C. (1962) *Theory of Graphs and its Applications*, Methuen-Wiley. [7.7]

Berlekamp, E.R. (1968) *Algebraic Coding Theory*, McGraw-Hill. [8.8]

Berry, D.M., Erlich, Z., and Lucena, C.J. (1976) Correctness of Data Representations: Pointers in High Level Languages, Proceedings of Conference on Data: Abstraction, Definition, and Structure, *ACM SIGPLAN Notices 11* (Special Issue), 115-119. [4.5.1]

Berry, D.M. and Schwartz, R.L. (1979) United and Discriminated Record Types in Strongly Typed Languages, *Information Processing Letters 9*, 13-18.

Berztiss, A.T. (1973) A Backtrack Procedure for Isomorphism of Directed Graphs, *ACM Journal 20*, 365-377. [7.7]

Berztiss, A.T. (1975) *Data Structures – Theory and Practice* (2nd ed.), Academic Press.

Betteridge, T. (1974) An Analytical Storage Allocation Model, *Acta Informatica 3*, 101-122.

Bird, R.S. (1977a) Notes on Recursion Elimination, *ACM Communications 20*, 434-439. [5.6]

Bird, R.S. (1977b) Improving Programs by the Introduction of Recursion, *ACM Communications 20*, 856-863. [5.6]

Bird, R.S. (1977c) Two Dimensional Pattern Matching, *Information Processing Letters 6*, 168-170. [8.8]

Bird, R.S. (1980) Tabulation Techniques for Recursive Programs, *ACM Computer Surveys 12*, 403-417. [5.6]

Birkhoff, G. and MacLane, S. (1977) *A Survey of Modern Algebra* (4th ed.), Macmillan. [2.3.2]

Bitner, J.R. (1979) Heuristics That Dynamically Organize Data Structures, *SIAM Journal of Computing 8*, 82-110. [10.3.3.3, 10.8]

Bitner, J.R. and Reingold, E.M. (1975) Backtrack Programming Techniques, *ACM Communications 18*, 651-656. [6.10]

Blahut, R.E. (1983) *Theory and Practice of Error Control Codes*, Addison-Wesley. [8.2.5.1, 8.8]

Bloom, B.H. (1970) Space/Time Trade-offs in Hash Coding with Allowable Errors, *ACM Communications 13*, 422-426. [10.4.4]

Blum, M., Floyd, R.W., Pratt, V., Rivest, R.L., and Tarjan, R.E. (1973) Time Bounds for Selection, *Journal Computer and System Sciences 7*, 448-461. [13.3]

Blum, N. and Mehlhorn, K. (1980) On the Average Number of Rebalancing Operations in Weight-Balanced Trees, *Theoretical Computer Science 11*, 303-320. [10.3.3.2]

Boas, R.P. and Wrench, J.W. (1971) Partial Sums of the Harmonic Series, *American Mathematical Monthly 78*, 864-870. [10.1.1]

Bobrow, D.G. (1975) A Note on Hash Linking, *ACM Communications 18*, 413-415. [11.2.5]

Bobrow, D.G. (1980) Managing Reentrant Structures Using Reference Counts, *ACM Transactions on Programming Languages and Systems 2*, 269-273. [11.2.4]

Bobrow, D.G. and Raphael, B. (1964) A Comparison of List-Processing Computer Languages, *ACM Communications 7*, 231-240. [4.4.4]

Bolour, A. (1979) Optimality Properties of Multiple-Key Hashing Functions, *ACM Journal 26*, 196-210. [12.6]

Bondy, J.A. and Murty, U.S.R. (1976) *Graph Theory with Applications*, Elsevier North-Holland. [7.7]

Bookstein, A. and Fouty, G. (1976) A Mathematical Model for Estimating the Effectiveness of Bigram Coding, *Information Processing and Management 12*, 111-116.

Bose, R.C. and Koch, G.G. (1969) The Design of Combinatorial Information Retrieval Systems for Files with Multiple-Valued Attributes, *SIAM Journal of Applied Mathematics 17*, 1203-1214. [12.6]

Bourne, C.P. and Ford, D.F. (1961) A Study of Methods for Systematically Abbreviating English Words and Names, *ACM Journal 8*, 538-552. [10.5.1]

Boyer, R.S. and Moore, J.S. (1977) A Fast String Searching Algorithm, *ACM Communications 20*, 762-772. [8.5.1.2]

Bozman, G., Buco, W., Daly, T.P., and Tetzlaff, W.H. (1984) Analysis of Free-Storage Algorithms – Revisited, *IBM Systems Journal 23*, 44-64. [11.5]

Brawn, B.S., Gustavson, F.G., and Mankin, E.S. (1970) Sorting in a Paging Environment, *ACM Communications 13*, 483-494. [13.4]

Brélaz, D. (1979) New Methods to Color the Vertices of a Graph, *ACM Communications 22*, 251-256. [7.7]

Brennan, J.J. (1982) Minimal Spanning Trees and Partial Sorting, *Operations Research Letters 1*, 113-116. [7.7]

Brent, R.P. (1973) Reducing the Retrieval Time of Scatter Storage Techniques, *ACM Communications 16*, 105-109. [10.4.2.5]

Brinck, K. and Foo, N.Y. (1981) Analysis of Algorithms on Threaded Trees, *Computer Journal 24*, 148-155. [6.4.2]

Brown, M.R. (1978) Implementation and Analysis of Binomial Queue Algorithms, *SIAM Journal of Computing 7*, 298-319. [6.6.4.1]

Brown, M.R. (1979) A Partial Analysis of Random Height-Balanced Trees, *SIAM Journal of Computing 8*, 33-41.

Brown, M.R. and Tarjan, R.E. (1979) A Fast Merging Algorithm, *ACM Journal 26*, 211-226. [13.2.4]

Brualdi, R.A. (1977) *Introductory Combinatorics*, Elsevier North-Holland. [7.4.3.2]

Brzozwski, J.A. (1964) Derivatives of Regular Expressions, *ACM Journal 11*, 481-494.

Buchholz, W. (1963) File Organization and Addressing, *IBM Systems Journal 2*, 86-111. [12.3.2]

Bunch, J.R. and Rose, D.J. (eds.) (1976) *Sparse Matrix Computations*, Academic Press. [4.3.3.1]

Burke, J.M. and Rickman, J.T. (1973) Bitmaps and Filters for Attribute-Oriented Searches, *International Journal Computing and Information Sciences 2*, 187-200. [12.6]

Burkhard, W.A. (1975) Nonrecursive Traversals of Trees, *Computer Journal 18*, 227-230. [6.10]

Burkhard, W.A. (1976a) Hashing and Trie Algorithms for Partial Match Retrieval, *ACM Transactions on Database Systems 1*, 175-187. [12.4.2]

Burkhard, W.A. (1976b) Partial Match Retrieval, *BIT 16*, 13-31. [12.4.2]

Burstall, R.M. and Darlington, J. (1977) A Transformation System for Developing Recursive Programs, *ACM Journal 24*, 44-67. [5.4.2]

Burstall, R.M. and Feather, M. (1978) Program Development by Transformation: An Overview, *Proceedings of "Les Fondements de la Programmation,"* IRIA-SEFI, France, 45-55.

Campbell, J.A. (1971) A Note on an Optimal-Fit Method for Dynamic Allocation of Storage, *Computer Journal 14*, 7-9. [11.3.1.2]

Campbell, J.A. (1974) Optimal Use of Storage in a Simple Model of Garbage Collection, *Information Processing Letters 3*, 37-38. [11.2.4]

Carter, J.L. and Wegman, M.N. (1979) Universal Classes of Hash Functions, *Journal of Computer and System Sciences 18*, 143-154. [10.4.3]

Cheney, C.J. (1970) A Nonrecursive List Compacting Algorithm, *ACM Communications 13*, 677-678. [11.2.3.2.1]

Cheriton, D. and Tarjan, R. E. (1976) Finding Minimum Spanning Trees, *SIAM Journal of Computing 5*, 724-742. [7.7]

Chomsky, N. (1959) On Certain Formal Properties of Grammars, *Information and Control 2*, 137-167. [8.6.1]

Chow, D.K. (1969) New Balanced-File Organization Schemes, *Information and Control 15*, 377-396. [12.6]

Christofides, N. (1971) An Algorithm for the Chromatic Number of a Graph, *Computer Journal 14*, 38-39. [7.7]

Christofides, N. (1976) Worst Case Analysis of a New Heuristic for the Traveling Salesman Problem, *Algorithms and Complexity: New Directions and Recent Results* (ed. Traub, J.F.), Academic Press, 441. [7.7]

Cichelli, R.J. (1980) Minimal Perfect Hash Functions Made Simple, *ACM Communications 23*, 17-19. [10.4.3]

Clapson, P. (1977) Improving the Access Time for Random Access Files, *ACM Communications 20*, 127-135. [12.3.2.1]

Clark, D.W. (1976) An Efficient List-Moving Algorithm Using Constant Workspace, *ACM Communications 19*, 352-354. [11.2.3.2.1]

Clark, D.W. (1978) A Fast Algorithm for Copying List Structures, *ACM Communications 21*, 351-357. [11.5]

Clark, D.W. (1979) Measurements of Dynamic List Structure Use in LISP, *IEEE Transactions on Software Engineering SE-5*, 51-59. [11.2.3.2]

Clark, D.W. and Green, C.C. (1977) An Empirical Study of List Structure in LISP, *ACM Communications 20*, 78-87. [11.2.3.2, 11.2.3.2.1, 11.2.5]

Cocke, J. (1970) Global Common Subexpression Elimination, *ACM SIGPLAN Notices 5: 7*, 20-24. [7.4.5.3.2]

Coffman, E.G. (1983) An Introduction to Combinatorial Models of Dynamic Storage Allocation, *SIAM Review 25*, 311-325. [11.3.4.1]

Coffman, E.G. and Eve, J. (1970) File Structures Using Hashing Functions, *ACM Communications 13*, 427-432,436. [10.5.2]

Cohen, D.I.A. (1978) *Basic Techniques of Combinatorial Theory*, John Wiley & Sons. [6.7]

Cohen, J. (1979a) Non-Deterministic Algorithms, *ACM Computer Surveys 11*, 79-94. [6.8.2.2]

Cohen, J. (1981) Garbage Collection of Linked Data Structures, *ACM Computer Surveys 13*, 341-367. [11.3.4.1]

Cohen, N.H. (1979b) Characterization and Elimination of Redundancy in Recursive Programs, *Proceedings 6th ACM Symposium on Principles of Programming Languages*, 143-157. [5.6]

Cole, R. and Hopcroft, J. (1982) On Edge Coloring Bipartite Graphs, *SIAM Journal of Computing 11*, 540-546. [7.7]

Comer, D. (1978) The Difficulty of Optimum Index Selection, *ACM Transactions on Database Systems 3*, 440-445.

Comer, D. (1979) The Ubiquitous B-Tree, *ACM Computer Surveys 11*, 121-137. [12.3.4.1]

Comer, D. and Sethi, R. (1977) The Complexity of Trie Index Construction, *ACM Journal 24*, 428-440. [10.5.1]

Cook, S.A. (1983) An Overview of Computational Complexity, *ACM Communications 26*, 401-408. [7.7]

Cooper, D. and Lynch, M.F. (1982) Text Compression Using Variable-to-Fixed-Length Encodings, *Journal of American Society for Information Scence 33*, 18-31. [8.4.1]

Coppersmith, D. and Winograd, S. (1982) On the Asymptotic Complexity of Matrix Multiplication, *SIAM Journal of Computing 11*, 472-492. [2.5.1.1]

Cormack, G.V., Horspool, R.N.S., and Kaiserworth, M. (1985) Practical Perfect Hashing, *Computer Journal 28*, 54-58. [10.8]

Corneil, D.G. and Gotlieb, C.C. (1970) An Efficient Algorithm for Graph Isomorphism, *ACM Journal 17*, 51-64. [7.7]

Corneil, D.G., Gotlieb, C.C., and Lee, Y.M. (1973) Minimal Event-Node Network of Project Precedence Relations, *ACM Communications 17*, 296-298. [7.4.5.2]

Corneil, D.G. and Graham, B. (1973) An Algorithm for Determining the Chromatic Number of a Graph, *SIAM Journal of Computing 2*, 311-318. [7.7]

Corneil, D.G. and Kirkpatrick, D.G. (1980) A Theoretical Analysis of Various Heuristics for the Graph Isomorphism Problem, *SIAM Journal of Computing 9*, 281-297. [7.7]

Cranston, B. and Thomas, R. (1975) A Simplified Recombination Scheme for the Fibonacci Buddy System, *ACM Communications 18*, 331-332. [11.3.2]

Culberson, J. (1985) The Effects of Updates in Binary Search Trees, *Proceedings 17th ACM Symposium on Theory of Computing*, 205-212. [10.3.1]

Culik, K., Ottmann, T., and Wood, D. (1981) Dense Multiway Trees, *ACM Transactions on Database Systems 6*, 486-512. [12.3.4.2]

Cuthill, E. and McKee, J. (1969) Reducing the Bandwidth of Sparse Symmetric Matrices, *Proceedings ACM National Conference*, 157-172. [7.6]

Dahl, O.J. and Nygaard, K. (1966) SIMULA – an ALGOL-Based Simulation Language, *ACM Communications 9*, 671-678. [9.2.1]

Dahlquist, G. and Björck, A. (1974) *Numerical Methods*, Prentice-Hall. [1.6]

Dasarthy, B. and Yang, C. (1980) A Transformation on Ordered Trees, *Computer Journal 23*, 161-164. [6.12]

Date, C.J. (1981) *An Introduction to Database Systems* (3rd ed.), Addison-Wesley. [12.6]

Date, C.J. (1983) *An Introduction to Database Systems: Volume II*, Addison-Wesley. [12.6]

Davies, G. and Bowsher, S. (1986) Algorithms for Pattern Matching, *Software Practice and Experience 16*, 575-601. [8.8]

de la Briandais, R. (1959) File Searching Using Variable Length Keys, *Proceedings Western Joint Computer Conference*, 295-298. [10.5.1]

DeMillo, R.A., Eisenstat, S.C., and Lipton, R.J. (1978) Preserving Average Proximity in Arrays, *ACM Communications 21*, 228-231. [2.11, 9.1.2]

Denning, D.E. (1984) Digital Signatures with RSA and Other Public-Key Cryptosystems, *ACM Communications 27*, 388-392.

Denning, P.J. (1968) The Working Set Model for Program Behavior, *ACM Communications 11*, 323-333. [12.2.2.1]

Denning, P.J. (1970) Virtual Memory, *ACM Computer Surveys 2*, 153-189. [12.2.2.1]

Deutsch, L.P. and Bobrow, D.G. (1976) An Efficient, Incremental, Automatic Garbage Collector, *ACM Communications 19*, 522-526. [11.2.5]

Diffie, W. and Hellman, M. (1976) New Directions in Cryptography, *IEEE Transactions on Information Theory IT-22*, 644-654. [8.4.2.2]

Diffie, W. and Hellman, M. (1977) Exhaustive Cryptanalysis of the NBS Data Encryption Standard, *Computer 10: 6*, 74-84. [8.4.2.1]

Dijkstra, E.W. (1959) A Note on Two Problems in Connexion with Graphs, *Numerische Mathematik 1*, 269-271. [7.4.2]

Dijkstra, E.W. (1976) *A Discipline of Programming*, Prentice-Hall. [1.8, 11.7, 12.8]

Dijkstra, E.W., Lamport, L, Martin, A.J., Scholten, C.S., and Steffens, E.F.M. (1978) On-the-Fly Garbage Collection: An Exercise in Cooperation, *ACM Communications 21*, 966-975. [11.2.6]

d'Imperio, M.E. (1969) Data Structures and their Representation in Storage, *Annual Review of Automatic Programming 5*, Pergamon Press, 1-75. [9.]

Dinic, E.A. (1970) Algorithm for the Solution of a Problem of Maximal Flow in a Network with Power Estimation, *Soviet Math. Doklady 11*, 1277-1280. [7.7]

Dobkin, D. and Lipton, R.J. (1976) Multidimensional Searching Problems, *SIAM Journal of Computing 5*, 181-186.

Dobosiewicz, W. (1978) Sorting by Distributive Partitioning, *Information Processing Letters 7*, 1-6. [13.2.2.3]

Dobosiewicz, W. (1980) An Efficient Variation of Bubble Sort, *Information Processing Letters 11*, 5-6. [13.2.1.3]

Dreyfus, S.E. (1969) An Appraisal of Some Shortest Path-Algorithms, *Operations Research 17*, 395-412.

Dromey, R.G. (1984) Exploiting Partial Order with Quicksort, *Software Practice and Experience 14*, 509-518. [13.7]

Dutton, R.D. and Brigham, R.C. (1981) A New Graph Coloring Algorithm, *Computer Journal 24*, 85-86. [7.7]

Dwyer, B. (1981) One More Time – How to Update a Master File, *ACM Communications 24*, 3-8.

Earley, J. (1970) An Efficient Context-Free Parsing Algorithm, *ACM Communications 13*, 94-102.

Earley, J. (1971) Toward an Understanding of Data Structures, *ACM Communications 14*, 617-627. [9.2.1]

Edmonds, J. (1965) Paths, Trees, and Flowers, *Canadian Journal of Mathematics 17*, 449-467. [7.4.3.4]

Edmonds, J. and Johnson, E.L. (1973) Matching, Euler Tours, and the Chinese Postman, *Mathematical Programming 5*, 88-124. [7.4.4.1]

Edmonds, J. and Karp, R.M. (1972) Theoretical Improvements in Algorithmic Efficiency for Network Flow Problems, *ACM Journal 19*, 248-264. [7.7]

Ehrsam, W.F., Matyas, S.M., Meyer, C.H., and Tuchman, W.L. (1978) A Cryptographic Key Management Scheme for Implementing the Data Encryption Standard, *IBM Systems Journal 17*, 106-125. [8.4.2.2]

Eisenbarth, B., Ziviani, N., Gonnet, G.H., Mehlhorn, K., and Wood, D. (1982) The Theory of Fringe Analysis and Its Application to 2-3 Trees and B-Trees, *Information and Control 55*, 125-174. [10.3.4]

Elgot, C.C. and Snyder, L. (1977) On the Many Facets of Lists, *Theoretical Computer Science 5*, 275-305.

Elson, M. (1975) *Data Structures*, Science Research Associates.

Eppinger, J.L. (1983) An Empirical Study of Insertion and Deletion in Binary Search Trees, *ACM Communications 26*, 663-669. [10.3.1]

Er, M.C. (1985) Enumerating Ordered Trees Lexicographically, *Computer Journal 28*, 538-542. [6.10]

Even, S. (1979) *Graph Algorithms*, Computer Science Press.

Even, S. and Tarjan, R.E. (1975) Network Flow and Testing Graph Connectivity, *SIAM Journal of Computing 4*, 507-518.

Even, S. and Tarjan, R.E. (1976) Computing an *st*-Numbering, *Theoretical Computer Science 2*, 339-344. [7.7]

Fagin, R., Nievergelt, J., Pippenger, N., and Strong, H.R. (1979) Extendible Hashing – A Fast Access Method for Dynamic Files, *ACM Transactions on Database Systems 4*, 315-344. [12.3.5]

Falkoff, A.D. and Iverson, K.E. (1973) The Design of APL, *IBM Journal of Research and Development 17*, 324-334. [2.9]

Faloutsos, C. (1985) Access Methods for Text, *ACM Computer Surveys 17*, 49-74.

Feistel, H. (1973) Cryptography and Computer Privacy, *Scientific American 228: 5*, 15-23. [8.4.2.1]

Feldman, J.A. and Rovner, P.D. (1969) An ALGOL-Based Associative Language, *ACM Communications 12*, 439-449. [2.11]

Fenichel, R.R. and Yochelson, J.C. (1969) A LISP Garbage-Collector for Virtual-Memory Computer Systems, *ACM Communications 12*, 611-612. [11.2.3.2]

Fenner, T.I. and Loizou, G. (1981) A Note on Traversal Algorithms for Triply Linked Binary Trees, *BIT 21*, 153-156. [6.5.1]

Fenner, T.I. and Loizou, G. (1984) Loop-Free Algorithms for Traversing Binary Trees, *BIT 24*, 33-44. [6.10]

Fillmore, J.P. and Williamson, S.G. (1974) On Backtracking: A Combinatorial Description of the Algorithm, *SIAM Journal of Computing 3*, 41-55. [6.10]

Finkel, R.A. and Bentley, J.L. (1974) Quad Trees – A Data Structure for Retrieval on Composite Keys, *Acta Informatica 4*, 1-9. [12.4.3.1]

Fischer, M.J. (1972) Efficiency of Equivalence Algorithms, *Complexity of Computer Computations*, (eds. Miller, R.E. and Thatcher, J.W.), Plenum Press, 153-167.

Fischer, M.J. and Meyer, A.R. (1971) Boolean Matrix Multiplication and Transitive Closure, *Proceedings 12th IEEE Symposium on Switching and Automata Theory*, 129-131. [7.3.3]

Fischer, M.J. and Paterson, M.S. (1974) String Matching and Other Products, *M.I.T. Project MAC Tech. Memo. 41.*

Fisher, D.A. (1975) Copying Cyclic List Structures in Linear Time Using Bounded Workspace, *ACM Communications 18*, 251-252. [11.5]

Fleck, A.C. (1971) Towards a Theory of Data Structures, *Journal of Computer and System Sciences 5*, 475-488.

Fleck, A.C. (1978) Recent Developments in the Theory of Data Structures, *Computer Languages 3*, 37-52. [9.]

Floyd, R.W. (1967) Nondeterministic Algorithms, *ACM Journal 14*, 636-644. [6.8.2.2]

Floyd, R.W. and Rivest, R.L. (1975) Expected Time Bounds for Selection, *ACM Communications 18*, 165-173. [13.3]

Ford, L.A. and Johnson, S.M. (1959) A Tournament Problem, *American Mathematical Monthly 66*, 387-389. [13.2.3.1]

Ford, L.R. and Fulkerson, D.R. (1958) Network Flow and Systems of Distinct Representatives, *Canadian Journal of Mathematics 10*, 78-85.

Ford, L.R. and Fulkerson, D.R. (1962) *Flows in Networks*, Princeton University Press. [7.4.3.3]

Ford, R. (1979) A Survey of the Development and Implementation of Data Abstractions, *University of Pittsburgh Computer Science Dept. Report 79-3*. [9.2.1]

Forsythe, G.E., Malcolm, M.A., and Moler, C.B. (1977) *Computer Methods for Mathematical Computations*, Prentice-Hall. [1.6]

Foster, C.C. (1965) Information and Storage Using AVL Trees, *Proceedings ACM National Conference*, 192-205. [10.3.3.1]

Foster, C.C. (1973) A Generalization of AVL Trees, *ACM Communications 16*, 513-517. [10.3.3.1]

Fraenkel, A. (1979) Paired Sequential Lists in a Memory Interval, *Information Processing Letters 8*, 9-10. [5.3]

Franaszek, P.A. and Considine, J.P. (1979) Reduction of Storage Fragmentation on Direct Access Devices, *IBM Journal of Research and Development 23*, 140-148. [12.1.2.1]

Francez, N., Klebansky, B., and Pnueli, A. (1977) Backtracking in Recursive Computation, *Acta Informatica 8*, 125-144. [6.10]

Franta, W.R. and Maly, K. (1977) An Efficient Data Structure for the Simulation Event Set, *ACM Communications 20*, 596-602. [5.6]

Franta, W.R. and Maly, K. (1978) A Comparison of Heaps and the TL Structure for the Simulation Event Set, *ACM Communications 21*, 873-875.

Frazer, W.D. and McKellar, A.C. (1970) Samplesort: A Sampling Approach to Minimal Storage Tree Sorting, *ACM Journal 17*, 496-507. [13.7]

Frederickson, G.N. (1983) Implicit Data Structures for the Dictionary Problem, *ACM Journal 30*, 80-94. [9.1.3]

Fredkin, E. (1960) Trie Memory, *ACM Communications 3*, 490-499. [10.5.1]

Fredman, M.L. (1975) Two Applications of a Probabilistic Search Technique: Sorting $X+Y$ and Building Balanced Search Trees, *Proceedings 7th ACM Symposium on Theory of Computing*, 240-244. [10.8]

Fredman, M.L., Komlós, J., and Szemerédi, E. (1984) Storing a Sparse Table with $O(1)$ Worst Access Time, *ACM Journal 31*, 538-544. [10.4.3]

Freuder, E.C. (1978) Synthesizing Constraint Expressions, *ACM Communications 21*, 958-966. [6.10]

Freuder, E.C. (1982) A Sufficient Condition for Backtrack-Free Search, *ACM Journal 29*, 24-32. [6.10]

Friedman, D.P. and Wise, D.S. (1979) Reference Counting Can Manage the Circular Environments of Mutual Recursion, *Information Processing Letters 8*, 41-45. [11.2.4]

Friedman, J.H., Bentley, J.L., and Finkel, R.A. (1977) An Algorithm for Finding Best Matches in Logarithmic Expected Time, *ACM Transactions on Mathematical Software 3*, 209-226. [12.4.3.2]

Gabow, H.N. (1976) An Efficient Implementation of Edmonds' Algorithm for Maximum Matching on Graphs, *ACM Journal 23*, 221-234.

Gabow, H.N. and Kariv, O. (1982) Algorithms for Edge Coloring Bipartite Graphs and Multigraphs, *SIAM Journal of Computing 11*, 117-129. [7.7]

Gabow, H.N. and Tarjan, R.E. (1985) A Linear-Time Algorithm for a Special Case of Disjoint Set Union, *Journal of Computer and System Sciences 30*, 209-221. [7.4.5.3.2]

Gale, D. and Karp, R.M. (1972) A Phenomenon in the Theory of Sorting, *Journal of Computer and System Sciences 6*, 103-115. [13.9]

Gale, D. and Shapley, L.S. (1962) College Admissions and the Stability of Marriage, *American Mathematical Monthly 69*, 9-15. [7.4.3.4]

Galil, Z. (1979) On Improving the Worst Case Running Time of the Boyer-Moore String Matching Algorithm, *ACM Communications 22*, 505-508.

Galil, Z. (1980) Finding the Vertex Connectivity of Graphs, *SIAM Journal of Computing 9*, 197-199.

Galil, Z. (1986) Efficient Algorithms for Finding Maximum Matchings in Graphs, *ACM Computer Surveys 18*, 23-38. [7.4.3.4]

Galil, Z., Micali, S., and Gabow, H. (1982) Priority Queues with Variable Priority and an $O(EV \log V)$ Algorithm for Finding a Maximal Weighted Matching in General Graphs, *Proceedings 23rd IEEE Symposium on Foundations of Computer Science*, 255-261.

Gallager, R.G. (1968) *Information Theory and Reliable Communication*, John Wiley & Sons. [8.2.4]

Gallager, R.G. (1978) Variations on a Theme of Huffman, *IEEE Transactions on Information Theory IT-24*, 668-674. [8.8]

Galler, B.A. and Fischer, M.J. (1964) An Improved Equivalence Algorithm, *ACM Communications 7*, 301-303. [4.2.3]

Ganapathy, S. and Rajaraman, V. (1973) Information Theory Applied to the Conversion of Decision Tables to Computer Programs, *ACM Communications 16*, 532-539. [6.10]

Garey, M.R. and Johnson, D.S. (1976) The Complexity of Near-Optimal Graph Coloring, *ACM Journal 23*, 43-49. [7.5.1]

Garey, M.R. and Johnson, D.S. (1979) *Computers and Intractability – A Guide to the Theory of NP-Completeness*, W.H. Freeman & Co. [6.8.2.2, 7.5.3]

Garey, M.R., Johnson, D.S., and Tarjan, R.E. (1976) The Planar Hamiltonian Circuit Problem is *NP*-Complete, *SIAM Journal of Computing 5*, 704-714.

Garsia, A.M. and Wachs, M.L. (1977) A New Algorithm for Minimum Cost Binary Trees, *SIAM Journal of Computing 6*, 622-642. [10.3.2.1]

Garwick, J.V. (1964) Data Storage in Compilers, *BIT 4*, 137-140. [5.3]

Gelenbe, E. (1971) The Two-Thirds Rule for Dynamic Storage Allocation Under Equilibrium, *Information Processing Letters 1*, 59-60. [11.3.4.1]

Gersting, J.L. (1982) *Mathematical Structures for Computer Science*, W.H. Freeman & Co.

Geschke, C.M., Morris, J.H., and Satterwaite, E.H. (1977) Early Experience with Mesa, *ACM Communications 20*, 540-553. [9.2.1]

Ghandour, Z. and Mezei, J. (1973) General Arrays, Operators, and Functions, *IBM Journal of Research and Development 17*, 335-352.

Ghosh, S.P. (1972) File Organization: The Consecutive Retrieval Property, *ACM Communications 15*, 802-808. [12.6]

Ghosh, S.P. and Lum, V.Y. (1975) Analysis of Collisions when Hashing by Division, *Information Systems 1*, 15-22. [10.8]

Ghosh, S.P. and Senko, M.E. (1969) File Organization: On the Selection of Random Access Index Points for Sequential Files, *ACM Journal 16*, 569-579. [12.3.3]

Gilbert, E.N. and Moore, E.F. (1959) Variable-Length Binary Encodings, *Bell System Technical Journal 38*, 933-967. [10.3.2.3]

Gimpel, J.F. (1973) A Theory of Discrete Patterns and Their Implementation in SNOBOL, *ACM Communications 16*, 91-100. [8.6.4]

Goguen, J.A., Thatcher, J.W., and Wagner, E.G. (1978) An Inital Algebra Approach to the Specification, Correctness, and Implementation of Abstract Data Types, *Current Trends in Programming Methodology, Vol. IV* (ed. Yeh, R.T.), Addison-Wesley, 80-149. [9.2.1]

Goldberg, I.B. (1967) 27 Bits are Not Enough for 8-Digit Accuracy, *ACM Communications 10*, 105-106.

Golomb, S.W. and Baumert, L.D. (1965) Backtrack Programming, *ACM Journal 12*, 516-524. [6.10]

Gonnet, G.H. (1983) Balancing Binary Trees by Internal Path Reduction, *ACM Communications 26*, 1074-1081. [10.3.2.2]

Gonnet, G.H. and Munro, J.I. (1979) Efficient Ordering of Hash Tables, *SIAM Journal of Computing 8*, 463-478. [10.4.2.5]

Goodman, S. and Hedetniemi, S. (1973) Eulerian Walks in Graphs, *SIAM Journal of Computing 2*, 16-27.

Goodman, S.E. and Hedetniemi, S.T. (1974) On Hamiltonian Walks in Graphs, *SIAM Journal of Computing 3*, 214-221.

Gotlieb, C.C. and Gotlieb, L.R. (1978) *Data Types and Structures*, Prentice-Hall. [10.7, 12.6]

Gotlieb, L. (1981) Optimal Multi-way Search Trees, *SIAM Journal of Computing 10*, 422-433.

Graham, S.L. and Wegman, M. (1976) A Fast and Usually Linear Algorithm for Global Flow Analysis, *ACM Journal 23*, 172-202. [7.4.5.3.2]

Gries, D. (1971) *Compiler Construction for Digital Computers*, John Wiley & Sons. [6.6.2]

Gries, D. (1977) An Exercise in Proving Parallel Programs Correct, *ACM Communications 20*, 921-930. [11.2.6]

Gries, D. (1979) The Schorr-Waite Graph Marking Algorithm, *Acta Informatica 11*, 223-232.

Griswold, R.E., Poage, J.F., and Polonsky, I.P. (1971) *The SNOBOL4 Programming Language* (2nd ed.), Prentice-Hall. [8.6.4]

Guibas, L.J. and Sedgewick, R. (1978) A Dichromatic Framework for Balanced Trees, *Proceedings 19th IEEE Symposium on Foundations of Computer Science*, 8-21. [10.3.5]

Guibas, L.J. and Szemerédi, E. (1978) The Analysis of Double Hashing, *Journal of Computer and System Sciences 16*, 226-274. [10.4.2.3]

Gull, W.E. and Jenkins, M.A. (1979) Recursive Data Stuctures in APL, *ACM Communications 22*, 79-96. [9.1]

Guttag, J.V. (1977) Abstract Data Types and the Development of Data Structures, *ACM Communications 20*, 396-404. [9.2.1]

Guttag, J.V., Horowitz, E., and Musser, D.R. (1978a) Abstract Data Types and Software Validation, *ACM Communications 21*, 1048-1064. [9.2.1]

Guttag, J.V., Horowitz, E., and Musser, D.R. (1978b) The Design of Data Type Specifications, *Current Trends in Programming Methodology, Vol. IV* (ed. Yeh, R.T.), Addison-Wesley, 60-79. [9.2.1]

Haberman, A.N. (1973) Critical Comments on the Programming Language Pascal, *Acta Informatica 3*, 47-57. [1.6]

Hadian, A. and Sobel, M. (1969) Selecting the *i*th Largest Using Binary Errorless Comparisons, *Colloquia Mathematica Societatis Janos Bolyai 4*, 585-599. [13.3]

Hall, M. (1948) Distinct Representatives of Subsets, *AMS Bulletin 54*, 922-926.

Hall, M. and Knuth, D.E. (1965) Combinatorial Analysis and Computers, *American Mathematical Monthly 72* (part 2), 21-28.

Hall, P. (1935) On Representatives of Subsets, *London Mathematics Society Journal 10*, 26-30. [7.4.3.2]

Hall, P.A.V. and Dowling, G.R. (1980) Approximate String Matching, *ACM Computer Surveys 12*, 381-402.

Hamming, R.W. (1950) Error Detecting and Error Correcting Codes, *Bell System Technical Journal 29*, 147-160. [8.2.5]

Hamming, R.W. (1971) *Introduction to Numerical Analysis*, McGraw-Hill. [1.6]

Hanson, D.R. (1977) Storage Management for an Implementation of SNOBOL4, *Software Practice and Experience 7*, 934-941. [11.5]

Harary, F. (1969) *Graph Theory*, Addison-Wesley. [7.7]

Harrison, M.C. (1971) Implementation of the Substring Test by Hashing, *ACM Communications 14*, 777-779. [10.4.4]

Hecht, M.S. and Ullman, J.D. (1972) Flow Graph Reducibility, *SIAM Journal of Computing 1*, 188-202. [7.5.5.3.2]

Hecht, M.S. and Ullman, J.D. (1974) Characterizations of Reducible Flow Graphs, *ACM Journal 21*, 367-375.

Hecht, M.S. and Ullman, J.D. (1975) A Simple Algorithm for Global Data Flow Analysis Problems, *SIAM Journal of Computing 4*, 519-532. [7.4.5.3.2]

Heising, W.P. (1963) Note on Random Addressing Techniques, *IBM Systems Journal 2*, 112-116. [10.2.1]

Held, G. and Stonebraker, M. (1978) B-Trees Re-examined, *ACM Communications 21*, 139-143. [12.3.4.2]

Held, M., Hoffman, A.J., Johnson, E.L., and Wolfe, P. (1984) Aspects of the Traveling Salesman Problem, *IBM Journal of Research and Development 28*, 476-486. [7.7]

Held, M. and Karp, R.M. (1962) A Dynamic Programming Approach to Sequencing Problems, *SIAM Journal 10*, 196-210. [7.7]

Held, M. and Karp, R.M. (1965) The Construction of Discrete Dynamic Programming Algorithms, *IBM Systems Journal 4*, 136-147.

Held, M. and Karp, R.M. (1970) The Traveling Salesman Problem and Minimum Spanning Trees, *Operations Research 18*, 1138-1162. [7.7]

Held, M. and Karp, R.M. (1971) The Traveling Salesman Problem and Minimum Spanning Trees: Part II, *Mathematical Programming 1*, 6-25. [7.7]

Hellman, M.E. (1979) The Mathematics of Public-Key Cryptography, *Scientific American 241: 2*, 146-157.

Herlestam, T. (1978) Critical Remarks on Some Public-Key Cryptosystems, *BIT 18*, 493-496.

Hester, J.H. and Hirschberg, D.S. (1985) Self-Organizing Linear Search, *ACM Computer Surveys 17*, 295-311. [10.8]

Hibbard, T.H. (1962) Some Combinatorial Properties of Certain Trees with Applications to Searching and Sorting, *ACM Journal 9*, 13-28. [10.3.1]

Hickey, T. and Cohen, J. (1984) Performance Analysis of On-the-Fly Garbage Collection, *ACM Communications 27*, 1143-1154. [11.5]

Hildebrandt, P. and Isbitz, H. (1959) Radix Exchange – An Internal Sorting Method for Digital Computers, *ACM Journal 6*, 156-163. [13.2.2.2]

Hinds, J.A. (1975) An Algorithm for Locating Adjacent Storage Blocks in the Buddy System, *ACM Communications 18*, 221-222. [11.3.2]

Hirschberg, D.S. (1973) A Class of Dynamic Memory Allocation Algorithms, *ACM Communications 16*, 615-618. [11.3.2]

Hirschberg, D.S. (1975) A Linear Space Algorithm for Computing Maximal Common Subsequences, *ACM Communications 18*, 341-343. [8.10]

Hoare, C.A.R. (1962) Quicksort, *Computer Journal 5*, 10-15. [13.2.1.3.1]

Hoare, C.A.R. (1971) Proof of a Program: FIND, *ACM Communications 14*, 39-45. [13.3]

Hoare, C.A.R. (1972a) Notes on Data Structuring, *Structured Programming* (Dahl, O.J., Dijkstra, E.W., and Hoare, C.A.R.), Academic Press, 83-174.

Hoare, C.A.R. (1972b) Proof of Correctness of Data Representations, *Acta Informatica 1*, 271-281. [9.2.1]

Hoare, C.A.R. (1974) Optimization of Store Size for Garbage Collection, *Information Processing Letters 2*, 165-166. [11.2.4]

Hoare, C.A.R. and Wirth, N. (1973) An Axiomatic Definition of the Programming Language Pascal, *Acta Informatica 2*, 335-355.

Hopcroft, J.E. and Karp, R.M. (1973) An $n^{5/2}$ Algorithm for Maximum Matchings in Bipartite Graphs, *SIAM Journal of Computing 2*, 225-231. [7.4.3.3]

Hopcroft, J. and Tarjan, R.E. (1973a) Dividing a Graph into Triconnected Components, *SIAM Journal of Computing 2*, 135-158. [7.3.2]

Hopcroft, J. and Tarjan, R.E. (1973b) Algorithm 447: Efficient Algorithms for Graph Manipulation [H], *ACM Communications 16*, 372-378.

Hopcroft, J. and Tarjan, R.E. (1974) Efficient Planarity Testing, *ACM Journal 21*, 549-568. [7.7]

Hopcroft, J.E. and Ullman, J.D. (1973) Set Merging Algorithms, *SIAM Journal of Computing 2*, 294-303. [6.6.5.1]

Hopcroft, J.E. and Ullman, J.D. (1979) *Introduction to Automata Theory, Languages, and Computation*, Addison-Wesley. [8.6]

Hopcroft, J.E. and Wong, J.K. (1974) Linear Time Algorithm for Isomorphism of Planar Graphs, *Proceedings 6th ACM Symposium on Theory of Computing*, 172-184. [7.5.4]

Hopgood, F.R.A. (1968) A Solution to the Table Overflow Problem for Hash Tables, *Computer Bulletin 11*, 297-300. [10.4.2.4]

Horowitz, E. and Sahni, S. (1976) *Fundamentals of Data Structures*, Computer Science Press. [•]

Horowitz, E. and Sahni, S. (1978) *Fundamentals of Computer Algorithms*, Computer Science Press. [6.8.3]

Horspool, R.N. (1980) Practical Fast Searching in Strings, *Software Practice and Experience 10*, 501-506. [8.8]

Housden, R.J.W. (1975) On String Concepts and Their Implementation, *Computer Journal 18*, 150-156.

Hsiao, D. and Harary, F. (1970) A Formal System for Information Retrieval from Files, *ACM Communications 13*, 67-73. [12.6]

Hu, T.C. and Tucker, A.C. (1971) Optimal Computer Search Trees and Variable-Length Alphabetical Codes, *SIAM Journal of Applied Mathematics 21*, 514-532. [10.3.2.1]

Huang, S.H.S. and Wong, C.K. (1984) Generalized Binary Split Trees, *Acta Informatica 21*, 113-123. [10.3.2.4]

Hubbard, G.U. (1963) Some Characteristics of Sorting in Computing Systems Using Random Access Storage Devices, *ACM Communications 6*, 248-255. [13.4]

Huffman, D.A. (1952) A Method for the Construction of Minimum-Redundancy Codes, *IRE Proceedings 40*, 1098-1101. [8.2.4]

Hwang, F.K. and Lin, S. (1969) An Analysis of Ford and Johnson's Sorting Algorithm, *Proceedings 3rd Princeton Conference on Information Sciences and Systems*, 292-296. [13.2.3.1]

Hwang, F.K. and Lin, S. (1972) A Simple Algorithm for Merging Two Disjoint Linearly Ordered Sets, *SIAM Journal of Computing 1*, 31-39. [13.2.3.2]

Hyafil, L. (1976) Bounds for Selection, *SIAM Journal of Computing 5*, 109-114. [13.9]

Hyafil, L. and Rivest, R.L. (1976) Constructing Optimal Binary Decision Trees is *NP*-Complete, *Information Processing Letters 5*, 15-17. [6.6.3]

Imbrasha, M. and Rajaraman, V. (1978) Detection of Logical Errors in Decision Table Programs, *ACM Communications 21*, 1016-1025. [2.11]

Inglis, J. (1974) Inverted Indexes and Multi-list Structures, *Computer Journal 17*, 59-63.

Isaac, E.J. and Singleton, R.C. (1956) Sorting by Address Calculation, *ACM Journal 3*, 169-174. [13.2.2.3]

Itai, A. (1976) Optimal Alphabetic Trees, *SIAM Journal of Computing 5*, 9-18. [10.3.2.1]

Iverson, K.E. (1964) Formalism in Programming Languages, *ACM Communications 7*, 80-88. [2.9]

Iverson, K.E. (1980) Notation as a Tool of Thought, *ACM Communications 23*, 444-465. [2.9]

Jaeschke, G. (1981) Reciprocal Hashing: A Method for Generating Minimal Perfect Hashing Functions, *ACM Communications 24*, 829-833. [10.8]

Jarvis, J.P. and Whited, D.E. (1983) Computational Experience Using Minimum Spanning Tree Algorithms, *Operations Research Letters 2*, 36-41. [7.7]

Jensen, K. and Wirth, N. (1984) *Pascal User Manual and Report* (3rd ed.), Springer-Verlag. [1.4.1]

Johnson, D.B. (1973) A Note on Dijkstra's Shortest Path Algorithm, *ACM Journal 20*, 385-388. [7.4.2]

Johnson, D.B. (1975) Priority Queues with Update and Finding Minimum Spanning Trees, *Information Processing Letters 4*, 53-57.

Johnson, D.B. (1977) Efficient Algorithms for Shortest Paths in Sparse Networks, *ACM Journal 24*, 1-13.

Johnson, D.B. (1982) A Priority Queue in Which Initialization and Queue Operations Take $O(\log\log D)$ Time, *Mathematical Systems Theory 15*, 103-106. [6.6.4.1]

Johnson, W.L., Porter, J.H., Ackley, S.I., and Ross, D.T. (1968) Automatic Generation of Efficient Lexical Processors Using Finite State Techniques, *ACM Communications 11*, 805-813.

Jonassen, A. and Dahl, O.J. (1975) Analysis of an Algorithm for Priority Queue Administration, *BIT 15*, 409-422. [6.12]

Jones, D.W. (1986) An Empirical Comparison of Priority-Queue and Event-Set Implementations, *ACM Communications 29*, 300-311. [5.6]

Jones, J.P. (1974) Recursive Undecidability – An Exposition, *American Mathematical Monthly 81*, 724-738.

Jonkers, H.B.M. (1979) A Fast Garbage Collection Algorithm, *Information Processing Letters 9*, 26-30. [11.3.1.3.2]

Kahn, A.B. (1962) Topological Sorting of Large Networks, *ACM Communications 5*, 558-562.

Kahn, D. (1967) *The Code-Breakers*, Macmillan. [8.4.2]

Kam, J.B. and Ullman, J.D. (1976) Global Data Flow Analysis and Iterative Algorithms, *ACM Journal 23*, 158-171.

Kambayashi, Y., Yajima, S. and Nakatsu, N. (1982) Data Compression Procedures Based on the Similarity of Strings, *Systems – Computers – Controls 13*, 29-37.

Kang, A.N.C. and Ault, D.A. (1975) Some Properties of a Centroid of a Free Tree, *Information Processing Letters 4*, 18-20. [6.12]

Kang, A.N.C., Lee, R.C.T., Chang, C.L., and Chang, S.K. (1977) Storage Reduction Through Minimal Spanning Trees and Spanning Forests, *IEEE Transactions on Computers C-26*, 425-434.

Karlgren, H. (1963) Representation of Text Strings in Binary Computers, *BIT 3*, 52-59. [8.2.1]

Karlton, P.L., Fuller, S.H., Scroggs, R.E., and Kaehler, E.B. (1976) Performance of Height-Balanced Trees, *ACM Communications 19*, 23-28. [10.3.3.1]

Karp, R.M. (1972) Reducibility Among Combinatorial Problems, *Complexity of Computer Computations*, (eds. Miller, R.E. and Thatcher, J.W.), Plenum Press, 85-103. [7.7]

Karp, R.M. (1975) On the Computational Complexity of Combinatorial Problems, *Networks 5*, 45-68.

Karp, R.M. (1986) Combinatorics, Complexity, and Randomness, *ACM Communications 29*, 98-111. [7.7]

Karp, R.M., Miller, R.E., and Rosenberg, A.L. (1972) Rapid Identification of Repeated Patterns in Strings, Trees, and Arrays, *Proceedings 4th ACM Symposium on Theory of Computing*, 125-136.

Karp, R.M. and Rabin, M.O. (1981) Efficient Randomized Pattern-Matching Algorithms, *Aiken Computer Laboratory Report TR-31-81*, Harvard University. [10.4.4]

Karzanov, A.V. (1974) Determining the Maximal Flow in a Network by the Method of Preflows, *Soviet Math. Doklady 15*, 434-437. [7.7]

Keehn, D.G. and Lacey, J.O. (1974) VSAM Data Set Design Parameters, *IBM Systems Journal 13*, 186-212. [12.3.4.1]

Kendall, D.G. (1953) Stochastic Processes Occurring in the Theory of Queues and Their Analysis by the Method of the Imbedded Markov Chain, *Annals of Mathematical Statistics 24*, 338-354. [5.1.3.1]

Kennedy, K. and Schwartz, J.T. (1975) Introduction to the Set-Theoretic Language SETL, *Computers and Mathematics with Applications 1*, 97-119. [2.11]

Kernighan, B.W. and Plauger, P.J. (1981) *Software Tools in Pascal*, Addison-Wesley. [8.3.2]

Kershenbaum, A. and Van Slyke, R. (1972) Computing Minimal Spanning Trees Efficiently, *Proceedings ACM National Conference*, 518-527. [7.7]

Kieburtz, R.B. (1976) Programming Without Pointer Variables, Proceedings of Conference on Data: Abstraction, Definition, and Structure, *ACM SIGPLAN Notices 11* (Special Issue), 95-107. [4.5.1, 9.1.1]

Kilgour, A.C. (1981) Generalized non-Recursive Traversal of Binary Trees, *Software Practice and Experience 11*, 1299-1306. [6.10]

King, P.J.H. (1966) Conversion of Decision Tables to Computer Programs by Rule Mask Techniques, *ACM Communications 9*, 796-801. [2.3.3.1]

Kirk, H.W. (1965) Use of Decision Tables in Computer Programming, *ACM Communications 8*, 41-43. [2.11]

Kirkpatrick, D. (1974) Determining Graph Properties from Matrix Representations, *Proceedings 6th ACM Symposium on Theory of Computing*, 84-90.

Kleinrock, L. (1975) *Queueing Systems Volume I: Theory*, John Wiley & Sons. [5.1.3.1]

Knott, G.D. (1975) Hashing Functions, *Computer Journal 18*, 265-278. [10.8]

Knott, G.D. (1977) A Numbering System for Binary Trees, *ACM Communications 20*, 113-115. [6.10]

Knowlton, K.C. (1965) A Fast Storage Allocator, *ACM Communications 8*, 623-625. [11.3.2]

Knuth, D.E. (1971a) An Empirical Study of FORTRAN Programs, *Software Practice and Experience 1*, 105-133. [7.4.5.3.2]

Knuth, D.E. (1971b) Optimum Binary Search Trees, *Acta Informatica 1*, 14-25. [10.3.2.1]

Knuth, D.E. (1973a) *The Art of Computer Programming, Vol. 1: Fundamental Algorithms* (2nd ed.), Addison-Wesley. [•]

Knuth, D.E. (1973b) *The Art of Computer Programming, Vol. 3: Searching and Sorting*, Addison-Wesley. [•]

Knuth, D.E. (1974) Structured Programming with **go to** Statements, *ACM Computer Surveys 6*, 261-301. [1.4.1, 6.4.1]

Knuth, D.E. (1975) Estimating the Efficiency of Backtrack Programs, *Mathematics of Computation 29*, 121-136. [6.8.2.1]

Knuth, D.E. (1976a) Big Omicron and Big Omega and Big Theta, *ACM SIGACT News 8: 2*, 18-24. [1.3.2.2]

Knuth, D.E. (1976b) Mathematics and Computer Science: Coping with Finiteness, *Science 194*, 1235-1242.

Knuth, D.E. (1977) Deletions that Preserve Randomness, *IEEE Transactions on Software Engineering SE-3*, 351-359. [10.3.1]

Knuth, D.E. (1981) *The Art of Computer Programming, Vol. 2: Semi-Numerical Algorithms* (2nd ed.), Addison-Wesley.

Knuth, D.E. (1985) Dynamic Huffman Coding, *Journal of Algorithms 6*, 163-180. [8.8]

Knuth, D.E. and Moore, R.W. (1975) An Analysis of Alpha-Beta Pruning, *Artificial Intelligence 6*, 293-326. [6.8.4.1]

Knuth, D.E., Morris, J.H., and Pratt, V.R. (1977) Fast Pattern Matching in Strings, *SIAM Journal of Computing 6*, 323-350. [8.5.1.1]

Knuth, D.E. and Plass, M.F. (1981) Breaking Paragraphs into Lines, *Software Practice and Experience 11*, 1119-1184. [8.3.2]

Knuth, D.E. and Szwarcfiter, J.L. (1974) A Structured Program to Generate All Topological Sorting Arrangements, *Information Processing Letters 2*, 153-157. [7.4.5.1]

Korfhage, R.R. (1974a) *Discrete Computational Structures*, Academic Press. [7.4.3.2]

Korfhage, R.R. (1974b) On the Development of Data Structures, *ACM SIGPLAN Notices 9: 12*, 14-22. [9.]

Korsh, J.F. (1981) Greedy Binary Trees are Nearly Optimal, *Information Processing Letters 13*, 16-19. [10.8]

Korsh, J.F. (1982) Growing Nearly Optimal Binary Search Trees, *Information Processing Letters 14*, 139-143. [10.8]

Korsh, J.F. and Laison, G. (1983) A Multiple-Stack Manipulation Procedure, *ACM Communications 26*, 921-923. [5.3]

Krarup, J. and de Werra, D. (1982) Chromatic Optimisation: Limitations, Objectives, Uses, References, *European Journal Operations Research 11*, 1-19.

Kruse, R.L. (1984) *Data Structures and Program Design*, Prentice-Hall.

Kruskal, J.B. (1956) On the Shortest Spanning Subtree of a Graph and the Traveling Salesman Problem, *AMS Proceedings 7: 1*, 48-50. [7.4.1]

Kučera, H. and Francis, W. (1967) *Computational Analysis of Present-Day American English*, Brown University Press. [10.3.2.4]

Kuhn, H.W. (1955) The Hungarian Method for the Assignment Problem, *Naval Research Logistics Quarterly 2*, 83-97. [7.4.3.4]

Kung, H.T. and Song, S.W. (1977) An Efficient Parallel Garbage Collection System and Its Correctness Proof, *Carnegie-Mellon University Computer Science Dept. Report.* [11.2.6]

Kurokawa, T. (1981) A New Fast and Safe Marking Algorithm, *Software Practice and Experience 11*, 671-682. [11.2.1.1]

Landin, P.J. (1964) The Mechanical Evaluation of Expressions, *Computer Journal 6*, 308-320. [8.6.4]

Langdon, G.G. (1984) An Introduction to Arithmetic Coding, *IBM Journal of Research and Development 28*, 135-149.

Larson, P.A. (1978) Dynamic Hashing, *BIT 18*, 184-201. [12.3.5]

Lawler, E.L. (1976) *Combinatorial Optimization: Networks and Matroids*, Holt, Rinehart, and Winston. [7.4.3.4]

Lawler, E.L. and Wood, D.W. (1966) Branch-and-Bound Methods: A Survey, *Operations Research 14*, 699-719. [6.8.3]

Lecarme, O. and Desjardins, P. (1974) Reply to a Paper by A.N. Haberman on the Programming Language Pascal, *ACM SIGPLAN Notices 9: 10*, 21-27. [1.6]

Lecarme, O. and Desjardins, P. (1975) More Comments on the Programming Language Pascal, *Acta Informatica 4*, 231-243.

Lehman, D.J. (1977) Algebraic Structures for Transitive Closure, *Theoretical Computer Science 4*, 59-76.

Lempel, A. (1979) Cryptology in Transition, *ACM Computer Surveys 11*, 285-303. [8.4.2, 8.4.2.2]

Lempel, A., Even, S., and Cederbaum, I. (1966) An Algorithm for Planarity Testing of Graphs, *Proceedings International Symposium on Theory of Graphs*, Rome, 215-232. [7.7]

Lengauer, T. and Tarjan, R.E. (1979) A Fast Algorithm for Finding Dominators in a Flowgraph, *ACM Transactions on Programming Languages and Systems 1*, 121-141. [7.4.5.3.1]

Leung, C.H.C. (1982a) A Simple Model for the Performance Analysis of Disc Storage Fragmentation, *Computer Journal 25*, 193-198. [12.1.2.1]

Leung, C.H.C. (1982b) An Improved Optimal-Fit Procedure for Dynamic Storage Allocation, *Computer Journal 25*, 199-206. [11.3.1.2]

Leung, C.H.C. (1983) Analysis of Disc Fragmentation Using Markov Chains, *Computer Journal 26*, 113-116. [12.1.2.1]

Leverett, B.W. and Hibbard, P.G. (1982) An Adaptive System for Dynamic Storage Allocation, *Software Practice and Experience 12*, 543-555. [11.3.3]

Lew, A. (1982) On the Emulation of Flowcharts by Decision Tables, *ACM Communications 25*, 895-904. [2.11]

Lewis, H.R. and Papadimitriou, C.H. (1978) The Efficiency of Algorithms, *Scientific American 238: 1*, 96-109. [6.8.2.2]

Lewis, T.G. and Smith, M.Z. (1982) *Applying Data Structures* (2nd ed.), Houghton Mifflin.

Lieberman, H. and Hewitt, C. (1983) A Real-Time Garbage Collector Based on the Lifetimes of Objects, *ACM Communications 26*, 419-429. [11.2.6]

Lin, S. and Kernighan, B.W. (1973) An Effective Heuristic Algorithm for the Traveling Salesman Problem, *Operations Research 21*, 498-516. [7.7]

Lindstrom, G. (1973) Scanning List Structures without Stacks or Tag Bits, *Information Processing Letters 2*, 47-51. [6.4.3, 6.12, 11.2.1.1]

Lindstrom, G. (1974) Copying List Structures Using Bounded Workspace, *ACM Communications 17*, 198-202. [11.5]

Liptay, J.S. (1968) Structural Aspects of the System/360 Model 85: The Cache, *IBM Systems Journal 7*, 15-21. [12.2.1]

Lipton, R.J., Eisenstat, S.C., and DeMillo, R.A. (1976) Space and Time Hierarchies for Classes of Control Structures and Data Structures, *ACM Journal 23*, 720-732. [9.1.2]

Lipton, R.J. and Tarjan, R.E. (1979) A Separator Theorem for Planar Graphs, *SIAM Journal of Applied Mathematics 36*, 177-189. [7.5.2]

Lipton, R.J. and Tarjan, R.E. (1980) Applications of a Planar Separator Theorem, *SIAM Journal of Computing 9*, 615-627. [7.5.2]

Liskov, B.H., Snyder, A., Atkinson, R., and Schaffert, C. (1977) Abstraction Mechanisms in CLU, *ACM Communications 20*, 564-576. [9.2.1]

Liskov, B.H. and Zilles, S.N. (1975) Specification Techniques for Data Abstractions, *IEEE Transactions on Software Engineering SE-1*, 7-19. [9.2.1]

Liu, C.L. (1968) *Introduction to Combinatorial Mathematics*, McGraw-Hill. [1.6, 6.7]

Lomet, D.B. (1985) Making Pointers Safe in System Programming Languages, *IEEE Transactions on Software Engineering SE-11*, 87-96. [9.1.1]

Low, J.R. (1978) Automatic Data Structure Selection: An Example and an Overview, *ACM Communications 21*, 376-385. [9.3]

Lowrance, R. and Wagner, R.A. (1975) An Extension of the String-to-String Correction Problem, *ACM Journal 22*, 177-183. [8.3.2]

Lowry, E.S. and Medlock, C.W. (1969) Object Code Optimization, *ACM Communications 12*, 13-22. [7.4.5.3.2]

Lueker, G.S. (1980) Some Techniques for Solving Recurrences, *ACM Computer Surveys 12*, 419-436. [1.3.2.3]

Lum, V.Y. (1970) Multi-attribute Retrieval with Combined Indices, *ACM Communications 13*, 660-665. [12.6]

Lum, V.Y., Yuen, P.S.T., and Dodd, M. (1971) Key-to-Address Transform Techniques: A Fundamental Performance Study on Large Existing Formatted Files, *ACM Communications 14*, 228-239. [10.8, 12.6]

Lynch, M.F. (1973) Compression of Bibliographic Files Using an Adaptation of Run-Length Coding, *Information Storage and Retrieval 9*, 207-214.

Lynch, M.F. (1977) Variety Generation – A Reinterpretation of Shannon's Mathematical Theory of Communication, and Its Implications for Information Science, *Journal Amererican Society for Information Science 28*, 19-25.

Lyon, G. (1978) Packed Scatter Tables, *ACM Communications 21*, 857-865. [10.4.2.5]

Mackenzie, C.E. (1980) *Coded Character Sets, History and Development*, Addison-Wesley. [8.2.1]

MacLaren, M.D. (1966) Internal Sorting by Radix Plus Sifting, *ACM Journal 13*, 404-411. [13.2.2.1]

MacVeigh, D.T. (1977) Effect of Data Representation on Cost of Sparse Matrix Operations, *Acta Informatica 7*, 361-394. [2.11]

Madnick, S.E. (1967) String Processing Techniques, *ACM Communications 10*, 420-424.

Mairson, H.G. (1983) The Program Complexity of Searching a Table, *Proceedings 24th IEEE Symposium on Foundations of Computer Science*, 40-47. [10.4.3]

Malhotra, V.M., Kumar, M.P., and Maheshwari, S.N. (1978) An $O(V^3)$ Algorithm for Finding Maximum Flows in Networks, *Information Processing Letters 7*, 277-278. [7.7]

Maly, K. (1976) Compressed Tries, *ACM Communications 19*, 409-415. [10.5.1]

Manacher, G. (1976) An Application of Pattern Matching to a Problem in Geometrical Complexity, *Information Processing Letters 5*, 6-7. [8.8]

Manacher, G. (1979) The Ford-Johnson Sorting Algorithm is Not Optimal, *ACM Journal 26*, 441-456. [13.2.3.1]

Mannila, H. (1985) Measures of Presortedness and Optimal Sorting Algorithms, *IEEE Transactions on Computers C-34*, 318-325. [13.2.4]

Margolin, B.H., Parmelee, R.P., and Schatzoff, M. (1971) Analysis of Free-Storage Algorithms, *IBM Systems Journal 10*, 283-304. [11.5]

Marlin, C.D. (1979) A Heap-Based Implementation of the Programming Language Pascal, *Software Practice and Experience 9*, 101-119. [11.5]

Martelli, A. and Montanari, U. (1978) Optimizing Decision Trees Through Heuristically Guided Search, *ACM Communications 21*, 1025-1039. [6.10]

Martin, J.J. (1982) An Efficient Garbage Compaction Algorithm, *ACM Communications 25*, 571-581. [11.3.1.3.2]

Martin, W.A. (1971) Sorting, *ACM Computer Surveys 3*, 147-174. [13.2.1]

Martin, W.A. and Ness, D.N. (1972) Optimizing Binary Trees Grown with a Sorting Algorithm, *ACM Communications 15*, 88-93. [10.3.3]

Maruyama, K. and Smith, S.E. (1977) Analysis of Design Alternatives for Virtual Memory Indexes, *ACM Communications 20*, 245-254. [12.3]

Matyas, S.M. and Meyer, C.H. (1978) Generation, Distribution, and Installation of Cryptographic Keys, *IBM Systems Journal 17*, 126-137. [8.4.2.2]

Maurer, W.D. (1968) An Improved Hash Code for Scatter Storage, *ACM Communications 11*, 35-38. [10.10]

Mayne, A. and James, E.B. (1975) Information Compression by Factorising Common Strings, *Computer Journal 18*, 157-160.

McCarthy, J. (1960) Recursive Functions of Symbolic Expressions and Their Computation by Machine, Part I, *ACM Communications 3*, 184-195. [4.4.4]

McCarthy, J. (1963) A Basis for a Mathematical Theory of Computation, *Computer Programming and Formal Systems* (eds. Braffort, P. and Hirshberg, D.), North-Holland, 33-70. [9.1]

McCormack, W.M. and Sargent, R.G. (1981) Analysis of Future Event Set Algorithms for Discrete Event Simulation, *ACM Communications 24*, 801-812. [5.6]

McCreight, E.M. (1976) A Space-Economical Suffix Tree Construction Algorithm, *ACM Journal 23* (1976), 262-272. [8.5.4]

McCreight, E.M. (1985) Priority Search Trees, *SIAM Journal of Computing 14*, 257-276. [11.7]

McMahon, L.E., Cherry, L.L., and Morris, R. (1978) Statistical Text Processing, *Bell System Technical Journal 57*, 2137-2154. [8.3.2]

McVitie, D.G. and Wilson, L.B. (1971) The Stable Marriage Problem, *ACM Communications 14*, 486-492. [7.4.3.4]

Mealy, G.H. (1974) Data Structures: Theory and Representation, *Proceedings IFIP Congress*, 322-325. [9.]

Mehlhorn, K. (1975) Nearly Optimal Binary Search Trees, *Acta Informatica 5*, 287-295. [10.8]

Mehlhorn, K. (1977) A Best Possible Bound for the Weighted Path Length of Binary Search Trees, *SIAM Journal of Computing 6*, 235-239. [10.8]

Mehlhorn, K. (1982a) On the Program Size of Perfect and Universal Hash Functions, *Proceedings 23rd IEEE Symposium on Foundations of Computer Science*, 170-175. [10.4.3]

Mehlhorn, K. (1982b) A Partial Analysis of Height-Balanced Trees Under Random Insertions and Deletions, *SIAM Journal of Computing 11*, 748-760.

Mei, P.S. and Gibbs, N.E. (1970) A Planarity Algorithm Based Upon the Kuratowski Theorem, *Proceedings Spring Joint Computer Conference* 91-93. [7.7]

Meijer, H. and Akl, S.G. (1980) The Design and Analysis of a New Hybrid Sorting Algorithm, *Information Processing Letters 10*, 213-218. [13.7]

Merkle, R.C. and Hellman, M.E. (1978) Hiding Information and Signatures in Trapdoor Knapsacks, *IEEE Transactions on Information Theory IT-24*, 525-530. [8.4.2.2]

Meyrowitz, N. and van Dam, A. (1982) Interactive Editing Systems: Part I, *ACM Computer Surveys 14*, 321-352. [8.3.1]

Micali, S. and Vazirani, V.V. (1980) An $O(|v|^{0.5}|E|)$ Algorithm for Finding Maximum Matching in General Graphs, *Proceedings 21st IEEE Symposium on Foundations of Computer Science*, 17-27. [7.4.3.4]

Miller, J.C.P. and Brown, D.J.S. (1966) An Algorithm for the Evaluation of Remote Terms in a Linear Recurrence Sequence, *Computer Journal 9*, 188-190. [5.6]

Miller, R.E., Pippenger, N., Rosenberg, A.L., and Snyder, L. (1979) Optimal 2,3-Trees, *SIAM Journal of Computing 8*, 42-59. [10.3.4]

Minsky, M.L. (1967) *Computation: Finite and Infinite Machines*, Prentice-Hall. [5.4.3]

Moffat, A. (1983) The Effect of Paged Memory upon Algorithm Performance, *ACM SIGACT News 15: 2*, 45-52. [12.2.2]

Montalbano, M. (1962) Tables, Flow Charts, and Program Logic, *IBM Systems Journal 1*, 51-63. [6.6.3]

Montalbano, M. (1974) *Decision Tables*, Science Research Associates. [2.11]

Montangero, C., Pacini, G., and Turini, F. (1977) Two-Level Control Structure for Nondeterministic Programming, *ACM Communications 20*, 725-730.

Mooers, C.N. (1951) Zatacoding Applied to Mechanical Organization of Knowledge, *American Documentation 2*, 20-32. [12.4.2.1]

More, T. (1973) Axioms and Theorems for a Theory of Arrays, *IBM Journal of Research and Development 17*, 135-175. [2.9]

Moret, B.M.E. (1982) Decision Trees and Diagrams, *ACM Computer Surveys 14*, 593-623. [6.6.3, 6.10]

Morin, T.L. and Marsten, R.E. (1976) Branch-and-Bound Strategies for Dynamic Programming, *Operations Research 24*, 611-627.

Morris, F.L. (1978) A Time- and Space-Efficient Garbage Compaction Algorithm, *ACM Communications 21*, 662-665. [11.3.1.3.2]

Morris, J.M. (1979) Traversing Binary Trees Simply and Cheaply, *Information Processing Letters 9*, 197-200. [6.4.3]

Morris, R. (1968) Scatter Storage Techniques, *ACM Communications 11*, 38-44. [12.3.2]

Morrison, D.R. (1968) PATRICIA – Practical Algorithm to Retrieve Information Coded in Alphanumeric, *ACM Journal 15*, 514-534. [10.5.2]

Motzkin, D. (1983) Meansort, *ACM Communications 26*, 250-251. [13.7]

Munro, J.I. (1971) Efficient Determination of the Transitive Closure of a Directed Graph, *Information Processing Letters 1*, 56-58. [7.3.4]

Munro, J.I. and Suwanda, H. (1980) Implicit Data Structures for Fast Search and Update, *Journal of Computer and System Sciences 21*, 236-250. [9.1.3]

Muntz, R. and Uzgalis, R. (1970) Dynamic Storage Allocation for Binary Search Trees in a Two-Level Memory, *Proceedings 4th Princeton Conference on Information Sciences and Systems*, 345-349. [12.3.4]

Muthukrishnam, C.R. and Rajaraman, V. (1970) On the Conversion of Decision Tables to Computer Programs, *ACM Communications 13*, 347-351. [2.11]

Myers, H.J. (1972) Compiling Optimized Code from Decision Tables, *IBM Journal of Research and Development 16*, 489-503. [6.10]

National Bureau of Standards (1977) *Data Encryption Standard*, Publication 46. [8.4.2.1]

Naur, P. (1975) Programming Languages, Natural Languages, and Mathematics, *ACM Communications 18*, 676-683.

Naur, P. et al. (1960) Report on the Algorithmic Language ALGOL 60, *ACM Communications 3*, 299-314. [5.4.1]

Nielsen, N.R. (1977) Dynamic Memory Allocation in Computer Simulation, *ACM Communications 20*, 864-873. [11.3.4.2]

Nievergelt, J. and Reingold, E.M. (1973) Binary Search Trees of Bounded Balance, *SIAM Journal of Computing 2*, 33-43. [10.3.3.2]

Nilsson, N.J. (1980) *Principles of Artificial Intelligence*, Tioga Publishing, Palo Alto. [6.8]

Noga, M.T. and Allison, D.C.S. (1985) Sorting in Linear Expected Time, *BIT 25* 451-465. [13.2.2.3]

Oldehoeft, R.R. and Allan, S.J. (1985) Adaptive Exact-Fit Storage Management, *ACM Communications 28*, 506-511. [11.3.3]

Olson, C.A. (1969) Random Access File Organization for Indirectly Addressed Records, *Proceedings ACM National Conference*, 539-549. [12.3.2.1]

O'Neil, P.E. and O'Neil, E.J. (1973) A Fast Expected Time Algorithm for Boolean Matrix Multiplication and Transitive Closure, *Information and Control 22*, 132-138.

Overholt, K.J. (1973) Efficiency of the Fibonacci Search Method, *BIT 13*, 92-96. [10.2.3]

Page, I.P. (1982) Optimal Fit of Arbitrary Sized Segments, *Computer Journal 25*, 32-33. [11.3.4.2]

Papadimitriou, C.H. (1976) On the Complexity of Edge Traversing, *ACM Journal 23*, 544-554.

Papadimitriou, C.H. and Steiglitz, K. (1982) *Combinatorial Optimization – Algorithms and Complexity*, Prentice-Hall. [7.4.3.4]

Parnas, D.L. (1972a) A Technique for Software Module Specification with Examples, *ACM Communications 15*, 330-336.

Parnas, D.L. (1972b) On the Criteria To Be Used in Decomposing Systems into Modules, *ACM Communications 15*, 1053-1058.

Parnas, D.L. and Clements, P.C. (1986) A Rational Design Process: How and Why to Fake It, *IEEE Transactions on Software Engineering SE-12*, 251-257.

Paterson, M.S. and Hewitt, C.E. (1970) Comparative Schematology, *M.I.T. Project MAC Conference on Concurrent Systems and Parallel Computations*, 119-127. [5.4.3]

Paton, K. (1971) An Algorithm for the Blocks and Cutnodes of a Graph, *ACM Communications 14*, 468-475. [7.3.2]

Perl, Y., Itai, A., and Avni, H. (1978) Interpolation Search – A Log Log *N* Search, *ACM Communications 21*, 550-553. [10.2.3]

Perl, Y. and Reingold, E.M. (1977) Understanding the Complexity of Interpolation Search, *Information Processing Letters 6*, 219-222. [10.2.3]

Perlis, A.J. and Thornton, C. (1960) Symbol Manipulation in Threaded Lists, *ACM Communications 3*, 195-204. [6.4.2]

Peterson, J.L. (1980) Computer Programs for Detecting and Correcting Spelling Errors, *ACM Communications 23*, 676-687. [8.3.2]

Peterson, J.L. and Norman, T.A. (1977) Buddy Systems, *ACM Communications 20*, 421-431. [11.3.4.1, 11.3.4.2]

Peterson, W.W. (1957) Addressing for Random-Access Storage, *IBM Journal of Research and Development 1*, 130-146. [12.3.2]

Peterson, W.W. and Weldon, E.J. (1972) *Error-Correcting Codes* (2nd ed.), M.I.T. Press. [8.8]

Pfaltz, J.L. (1972) Graph Structures, *ACM Journal 19*, 411-422.

Pfaltz, J.L. (1975) Representing Graphs by Knuth Trees, *ACM Journal 22*, 361-366. [7.2]

Pfaltz, J.L. (1977) *Computer Data Structures*, McGraw-Hill. [2.13, 10.7]

Pfaltz, J.L., Berman, W.J., and Cagley, E.M. (1980) Partial-Match Retrieval Using Indexed Descriptor Files, *ACM Communications 23*, 522-528. [12.6]

Pippenger, N. (1978) Complexity Theory, *Scientific American 238: 6*, 114-124.

Pohl, I. (1967) A Method for Finding Hamilton Paths and Knight's Tours, *ACM Communications 10*, 446-449.

Pohl, I. (1972) A Sorting Problem and Its Complexity, *ACM Communications 15*, 462-464. [13.9]

Pohlig, S.C. and Hellman, M.E. (1978) An Improved Algorithm for Computing Logarithms over *GF(p)* and Its Cryptographic Significance, *IEEE Transactions on Information Theory IT-24*, 106-110. [8.4.2.2]

Pollack, S.L. (1965) Conversion of Limited-Entry Decision Tables to Computer Programs, *ACM Communications 8*, 677-682. [6.10]

Pollack, S.L., Hicks, H.T., and Harrison, W.J. (1971) *Decision Tables: Theory and Practice*, John Wiley & Sons. [2.11]

Pooch, U.W. (1974) Translation of Decision Tables, *ACM Computer Surveys 6*, 125-151. [2.11]

Pooch, U.W. and Nieder, A. (1973) A Survey of Indexing Techniques for Sparse Matrices, *ACM Computer Surveys 5*, 109-133. [2.11]

Prenner, C.J., Spitzen, J.M, and Wegbreit, B. (1972) An Implementation of Backtracking for Programming Languages, *Proceedings ACM National Conference*, 763-771. [6.10]

Preparata, F.P. and Vuillemin, J. (1981) The Cube-Connected Cycles: A Versatile Network for Parallel Computation, *ACM Communications 24*, 300-309. [13.5]

Prim, R.C. (1957) Shortest Connection Networks and Some Generalizations, *Bell System Technical Journal 36*, 1389-1401. [7.4.1]

Purdom, P.W., Brown, C.A., and Robertson, E.L. (1981) Backtracking with Multi-Level Dynamic Search Rearrangement, *Acta Informatica 15*, 99-113. [6.10]

Purdom, P.W., Stigler, S.M., and Cheam, T.O. (1971) Statistical Investigation of Three Storage Allocation Algorithms, *BIT 11*, 187-195. [11.3.4.2]

Quine, W.V., Paradox (1962) *Scientific American 206: 4*, 84-96. [2.4.1]

Rabin, M.O. (1976) Probablistic Algorithms, *Algorithms and Complexity: New Directions and Recent Results* (ed. Traub, J.F.), Academic Press, 21-39.

Rabin, M.O. (1977) Complexity of Computations, *ACM Communications 20*, 625-633.

Räihä, K.J. and Zweben, S.H. (1979) An Optimal Insertion Algorithm for One-Sided Height-Balanced Binary Search Trees, *ACM Communications 22*, 508-512. [10.3.3.1]

Randell, B. (1969) A Note on Storage Fragmentation and Program Segmentation, *ACM Communications 12*, 365-369,372. [11.3]

Raphael, B. (1976) *The Thinking Computer — Mind Inside Matter*, W.H. Freeman & Co. [6.8, 6.8.4]

Read, R.C. and Corneil, D.G. (1977) The Graph Isomorphism Disease, *Journal of Graph Theory 1*, 339-363.

Reingold, E.M. (1972) On the Optimality of Some Set Algorithms, *ACM Journal 19*, 649-659.

Reingold, E.M. (1973) A Nonrecursive List Moving Algorithm, *ACM Communications 16*, 305-307. [11.2.3.2.1]

Reingold, E.M. and Hansen, W.J. (1983) *Data Structures*, Little, Brown, & Co. [•]

Reinwald, L.T. and Solano, R.M. (1966) Conversion of Limited-Entry Decision Tables to Optimal Computer Programs I: Minimum Average Processing Time, *ACM Journal 13*, 339-358. [6.10]

Reinwald, L.T. and Solano, R.M. (1967) Conversion of Limited-Entry Decision Tables to Optimal Computer Programs II: Minimum Storage Requirement, *ACM Journal 14*, 742-755. [6.10]

Rivest, R.L. (1976a) On Self-Organizing Sequential Search Heuristics, *ACM Communications 19*, 63-67. [10.2.1]

Rivest, R.L. (1976b) Partial-Match Retrieval Algorithms, *SIAM Journal of Computing 5*, 19-50. [12.4.2]

Rivest, R.L. (1977) On the Worst-Case Behavior of String-Searching Algorithms, *SIAM Journal of Computing 6*, 669-674. [8.5.1.2]

Rivest, R.L. (1978a) Optimal Arrangement of Keys in a Hash Table, *ACM Journal 25*, 200-209. [10.4.2.5]

Rivest, R.L. (1978b) Remarks on a Proposed Cryptanalytic Attack on the M.I.T. Public-Key Cryptosystem, *Cryptologia 2*, 62-65. [8.2.2.1]

Rivest, R.L., Shamir, A., and Adleman, L. (1978) A Method for Obtaining Digital Signatures and Public-Key Cryptosystems, *ACM Communications 21*, 120-126. [8.4.2.2.1]

Rivest, R.L. and Vuillemin, J. (1975) A Generalization and Proof of the Aanderaa-Rosenberg Conjecture, *Proceedings 7th ACM Symposium on Theory of Computing*, 6-11. [7.5.3]

Roberts, C.S. (1979) Partial-Match Retrieval via the Method of Superimposed Codes, *IEEE Proceedings 67*, 1624-1642. [12.4.2.1]

Roberts, F.S. (1984) *Applied Combinatorics*, Prentice-Hall. [1.6]

Robson, J.M. (1971) An Estimate of the Store Size Necessary for Dynamic Storage Allocation, *ACM Journal 18*, 416-423. [11.3.4.1]

Robson, J.M. (1973) An Improved Algorithm for Traversing Binary Trees Without Auxiliary Stack, *Information Processing Letters 2*, 12-14. [6.4.3]

Robson, J.M. (1974) Bounds for Some Functions Concerning Dynamic Storage Allocation, *ACM Journal 21*, 491-499.

Robson, J.M. (1977a) A Bounded Storage Algorithm for Copying Cyclic Structures, *ACM Communications 20*, 431-433. [11.2.3.2.2]

Robson, J.M. (1977b) Worst Case Fragmentation of First Fit and Best Fit Storage Allocation Strategies, *Computer Journal 20*, 242-244. [11.3.4.1]

Rodeh, M. (1982) A Fast Test for Unique Decipherability Based on Suffix Trees, *IEEE Transactions on Information Theory IT-28*, 648-651.

Rodeh, M., Pratt, V.R., and Even, S. (1981) Linear Algorithm for Data Compression via String Matching, *ACM Journal 28*, 16-24. [8.5.4]

Rosenberg, A.L. (1973) On the Time Required to Recognize Properties of Graphs: A Problem, *ACM SIGACT News 5: 4*, 15-16. [7.5.3]

Rosenberg, A.L. (1974) Allocating Storage for Extendible Arrays, *ACM Journal 21*, 652-670. [2.11]

Rosenberg, A.L. (1975) Preserving Proximity in Arrays, *SIAM Journal of Computing 4*, 443-460. [2.11, 9.1.2]

Rosenberg, A.L. (1978) Data Encodings and Their Costs, *Acta Informatica 9*, 273-292. [9.1.2]

Rosenberg, A.L. (1979) Encoding Data Structures in Trees, *ACM Journal 26*, 668-689. [9.1.2]

Rosenberg, A.L. and Snyder, L. (1978) Minimal-Comparison 2,3-Trees, *SIAM Journal of Computing 7*, 465-480. [10.3.4]

Rosenberg, A.L. and Stockmeyer, L.J. (1977) Hashing Schemes for Extendible Arrays, *ACM Journal 24*, 199-221.

Rosenkrantz, D.J., Stearns, R.E., and Lewis, P.M. (1977) An Analysis of Several Heuristics for the Traveling Salesman Problem, *SIAM Journal of Computing 6*, 563-581. [7.7]

Ross, D.T. (1967) The AED Free Storage Package, *ACM Communications 10*, 481-492. [11.3.3]

Rotem, D. (1975) On a Correspondence Between Binary Trees and a Certain Type of Permutation, *Information Processing Letters 4*, 58-61.

Rotem, D. (1981) Stack Sortable Permutations, *Discrete Mathematics 33*, 185-196.

Rotem, D. and Varol, Y.L. (1978) Generation of Binary Trees from Ballot Sequences, *ACM Journal 25*, 396-404. [6.10]

Rothnie, J.B. and Lozano, T. (1974) Attribute Based File Organization in a Paged Memory Environment, *ACM Communications 17*, 63-69. [12.4.1.1]

Rowe, L.A. and Tonge, F.M. (1978) Automating the Selection of Implementation Structures, *IEEE Transactions on Software Engineering SE-4*, 494-506. [9.3]

Rubin, F. (1974) A Search Procedure for Hamilton Paths and Circuits, *ACM Journal 21*, 576-580. [7.4.4.2]

Rubin, F. (1975) An Improved Algorithm for Testing the Planarity of a Graph, *IEEE Transactions on Computers C-24*, 113-121. [7.7]

Rubin, F. (1976) Experiments in Text File Compression, *ACM Communications 19*, 617-623.

Rubin, F. (1979) Cryptographic Aspects of Data Compression Codes, *Cryptologia 3*, 202-205.

Ruskey, F. (1978) Generating *t*-ary Trees Lexicographically, *SIAM Journal of Computing 7*, 424-439. [6.10]

Ruskey, F. and Hu, T.C. (1977) Generating Binary Trees Lexicographically, *SIAM Journal of Computing 6*, 745-758. [6.10]

Russell, D.L. (1977) Internal Fragmentation in a Class of Buddy Systems, *SIAM Journal of Computing 6*, 607-621. [11.3.4.1]

Sacks-Davis, R. and Ramamohanarao, K. (1983) A Two Level Superimposed Coding Scheme for Partial Match Retrieval, *Information Systems 8*, 273-280. [12.4.2.1]

Sager, T.J. (1985) A Polynomial Time Generator for Minimal Perfect Hash Functions, *ACM Communications 28*, 523-532. [10.8]

Samet, H. (1982) Heuristics for the Line Division Problem in Computer Justified Text, *ACM Communications 25*, 564-571. [8.3.2]

Samet, H. (1984) The Quadtree and Related Hierarchical Data Structures, *Computer Surveys 16*, 187-260. [12.4.3.1]

Sayre, D. (1969) Is Automatic "Folding" of Programs Efficient Enough to Displace Manual?, *ACM Communications 12*, 656-660. [12.2]

Schkolnick, M. (1975) The Optimal Selection of Secondary Indices for Files, *Information Systems 1*, 141-146. [12.6]

Schmidt, D.C. and Druffel, L.E. (1976) A Fast Backtracking Algorithm to Test Directed Graphs for Isomorphism Using Distance Matrices, *ACM Journal 23*, 433-445. [7.7]

Schmitt, A. (1983) On the Number of Relational Operators Necessary to Compute Certain Functions of Real Variables, *Acta Informatica 19*, 297-304. [13.2.2.3]

Schönhage, A., Paterson, M.S., and Pippenger, N. (1976) Finding the Median, *Journal of Computer and System Sciences 13*, 184-199. [13.3]

Schoor, A. (1982) Fast Algorithm for Sparse Matrix Multiplication, *Information Processing Letters 15*, 87-89. [4.3.3.1]

Schorr, H. and Waite, W.M. (1967) An Efficient Machine-Independent Procedure for Garbage Collection in Various List Structures, *ACM Communications 10*, 501-506. [4.4.3.1]

Schuegraf, E.J. and Heaps, H.S. (1973) Selection of Equifrequent Word Fragments for Information Retrieval, *Information Storage and Retrieval 9*, 697-711. [8.4.1]

Schuegraf, E.J. and Heaps, H.S. (1974) A Comparison of Algorithms for Data Base Compression by Use of Fragments as Language Elements, *Information Storage and Retrieval 10*, 309-319.

Schumacher, H. and Sevcik, K.C. (1976) The Synthetic Approach to Decision Table Conversion, *ACM Communications 19*, 343-351. [6.10]

Schwartz, E.S. (1964) An Optimum Encoding with Minimum Longest Code and Total Number of Digits, *Information and Control 7*, 37-44. [8.2.4]

Schwartz, E.S. and Kallick, B. (1964) Generating a Canonical Prefix Encoding, *ACM Communications 7*, 166-169. [8.10]

Schwartz, J.T. (1975) Automatic Data Structure Choice in a Language of Very High Level, *ACM Communications 18*, 722-728. [2.11, 9.3]

Sedgewick, R. (1977) The Analysis of Quicksort Programs, *Acta Informatica 7*, 327-355. [13.2.1.3.1]

Sedgewick, R. (1978) Implementing Quicksort Programs, *ACM Communications 21* 847-857. [13.2.1.3.1]

Sedgewick, R. (1983) *Algorithms*, Addison-Wesley. [•]

Sethi, I.K. and Chatterjee, B. (1980) Conversion of Decision Tables to Efficient Sequential Testing Procedures, *ACM Communications 23*, 279-285. [6.10]

Severance, D.G. (1974) Identifier Search Mechanisms: A Survey and Generalized Model, *ACM Computer Surveys 6*, 175-194.

Severance, D. and Duhne, R. (1976) A Practitioner's Guide to Addressing Algorithms, *ACM Communications 19*, 314-326. [12.6]

Shamir, A. (1982) A Polynomial Time Algorithm for Breaking the Basic Merkle-Hellman Cryptosystem, *Proceedings 23rd IEEE Symposium on Foundations of Computer Science*, 145-152. [8.4.2.2]

Shannon, C.E. (1948) A Mathematical Theory of Communication, *Bell System Technical Journal 27*, 379-423 and 623-656. [8.2.4]

Shannon, C.E. (1949) Communication Theory of Secrecy Systems, *Bell System Technical Journal 28*, 656-715. [8.4.2]

Sharir, M. (1981) A Strong-Connectivity Algorithm and Its Applications in Data Flow Analysis, *Computers and Mathematics with Applications 7*, 67-72. [7.3.4]

Shaw, M. (1980) The Impact of Abstraction Concerns on Modern Programming Languages, *IEEE Proceedings 68*, 1119-1130.

Shaw, M., Wulf, W.A., and London, R.L. (1977) Abstraction and Verification in Alphard: Defining and Specifying Iteration and Generators, *ACM Communications 20*, 553-564. [9.2.1]

Sheil, B.A. (1978) Median Split Trees: A Fast Lookup Technique for Frequently Occurring Keys, *ACM Communications 21*, 947-958. [10.3.2.4]

Shell, D.L. (1959) A High-Speed Sorting Procedure, *ACM Communications 2: 7*, 30-32. [13.2.1.1.1]

Shell, D.L. (1971) Optimizing the Polyphase Sort, *ACM Communications 14*, 713-719. [13.4.3.1]

Shneiderman, B. (1973) Optimum Data Base Reorganization Points, *ACM Communications 16*, 362-365. [12.3.3]

Shneiderman, B. (1977) Reduced Combined Indices for Efficient Multiple Attribute Retrieval, *Information Systems 2*, 149-154. [12.6]

Shneiderman, B. (1978) Jump Searching: A Fast Sequential Search Technique, *ACM Communications 21*, 831-834. [12.3.1]

Shneiderman, B. and Scheuermann, P. (1974) Structured Data Structures, *ACM Communications 17*, 566-574.

Shore, J.E. (1975) On the External Storage Fragmentation Produced by First-Fit and Best-Fit Allocation Strategies, *ACM Communications 18*, 433-440. [11.3.4.2]

Shore, J.E. (1977) Anomalous Behavior of the Fifty-Percent Rule in Dynamic Memory Allocation, *ACM Communications 20*, 812-820. [11.3.4.2]

Shortt, J. (1978) An Iterative Program to Calculate Fibonacci Numbers in $O(\log n)$ Arithmetic Operations, *Information Processing Letters 7*, 299-303. [5.6]

Shwayder, K. (1974) Extending the Information Theory Approach to Converting Limited-Entry Decision Tables to Computer Programs, *ACM Communications 17*, 532-537. [6.10]

Shwayder, K. (1975) Combining Decision Rules in a Decision Table, *ACM Communications 18*, 476-480. [2.3.3]

Siklóssy, L. (1972) Fast and Read-Only Algorithms for Traversing Trees Without an Auxiliary Stack, *Information Processing Letters 1*, 149-152. [6.4.3]

Simmons, G.J. (1979) Symmetric and Asymmetric Encryption, *ACM Computer Surveys 11*, 305-330. [8.4.2.2]

Simmons, G.J. and Norris, M.J. (1977) Preliminary Comments on the M.I.T. Public-Key Cryptosystem, *Cryptologia 1*, 406-414. [8.2.2.1]

Simon, H.A. (1962) The Architecture of Complexity, *Proceedings of the American Philosophical Society 106*, 467-482. [9.2]

Slagle, J.R. and Dixon, J.K. (1969) Experiments with Some Programs that Search Game Trees, *ACM Journal 16*, 189-207. [6.8.4.1]

Sleator, D.D. and Tarjan, R.E. (1983) Self-Adjusting Binary Trees, *Proceedings 15th ACM Symposium on Theory of Computing*, 235-245. [10.3.3.3]

Sleator, D.D. and Tarjan, R.E. (1985) Amortized Efficiency of List Update and Paging Rules, *ACM Communications 28*, 202-208. [10.8]

Smit, G. de V. (1982) A Comparison of Three String Matching Algorithms, *Software Practice and Experience 12*, 57-66. [8.8]

Smith, A.J. (1982) Cache Memories, *ACM Computer Surveys 14*, 473-530. [12.2.1]

Smith, H.F. (1965) *Numerical Development of Harmonic Series for the Coordinates of the Moon*, Ph.D. Thesis, Columbia University. [2.11]

Smyth, W.F. and Rădăceanu, E. (1974) A Storage Scheme for Heirarchic Structures, *Computer Journal 17*, 152-156. [7.2]

Snyder, L. (1977) On Uniquely Represented Data Structures, *Proceedings 18th IEEE Symposium on Foundations of Computer Science*, 142-146.

Solntseff, N. and Wood, D. (1977) Pyramids: A Data Type for Matrix Representations in Pascal, *BIT 17*, 344-350. [2.11]

Solomon, M. and Finkel, R.A. (1980) A Note on Enumerating Binary Trees, *ACM Journal 27*, 3-5. [6.10]

Solovay, R. and Strassen, V. (1977) A Fast Monte-Carlo Test for Primality, *SIAM Journal of Computing 6*, 84-85. [8.4.2.2.1]

Soule, S. (1977) A Note on the Nonrecursive Traversal of Binary Trees, *Computer Journal 20*, 350-352.

Spira, P.M. and Pan, A. (1975) On Finding and Updating Spanning Trees and Shortest Paths, *SIAM Journal 4*, 375-380.

Sprugnoli, R. (1977) Perfect Hashing Functions: A Single Probe Retrieving Method for Static Sets, *ACM Communications 20*, 841-850. [10.4.3]

Sprugnoli, R. (1981) On the Allocation of Binary Trees to Secondary Storage, *BIT 21*, 305-316. [12.3.4]

Stanat, D.F. and McAllister, D.F. (1977) *Discrete Mathematics in Computer Science*, Prentice-Hall. [9.2.1]

Standish, T.A. (1980) *Data Structure Techniques*, Addison-Wesley. [•]

Stephenson, C.J. (1980) A Method for Constructing Binary Search Trees by Making Insertions at the Root, *International Journal Computer and Information Sciences 9*, 15-29. [6.12]

Stockmeyer, L.J. and Chandra, A.K. (1979) Intrinsically Difficult Problems, *Scientific American 240: 5*, 140-159.

Stockmeyer, P.K. and Yao, F.F. (1980) On the Optimality of Linear Merge, *SIAM Journal of Computing 9*, 85-90. [13.2.3.2]

Stone, H.S. (1971) Parallel Processing with the Perfect Shuffle, *IEEE Transactions on Computers C-20*, 153-161. [13.5]

Stone, H.S. (1973) *Discrete Mathematical Structures and Their Applications*, Science Research Associates.

Stonebraker, M. (1974) The Choice of Partial Inversions and Combined Indices, *International Journal Computer and Information Sciences 3*, 167-188.

Strassen, V. (1969) Gaussian Elimination is not Optimal, *Numerische Mathematik 13*, 354-356. [2.5.1.1]

Strong, H.R. (1971) Translating Recursion Equations into Flowcharts, *Journal of Computer and System Science 5*, 254-285. [5.4.3]

Stubbs, D.F. and Webre, N.W. (1985) *Data Structures with Abstract Data Types and Pascal*, Brooks/Cole Publishing. [•]

Sussenguth, E.H. (1963) Use of Tree Structures for Processing Files, *ACM Communications 6*, 272-279. [10.5.1]

Sussenguth, E.H. (1965) A Graph-Theoretic Algorithm for Matching Chemical Structures, *Journal of Chemical Documentation 5*, 36-43.

Suzuki, N. (1982) Analysis of Pointer "Rotation," *ACM Communications 25*, 330-335. [4.4.3.1]

Szwarcfiter, J.L. and Wilson, L.B. (1978) Some Properties of Ternary Trees, *Computer Journal 21*, 66-72. [7.4.5.1]

Tarjan, R.E. (1972) Depth-First Search and Linear Graph Algorithms, *SIAM Journal of Computing 1*, 146-160. [7.3.2, 7.3.4]

Tarjan, R.E. (1974a) Testing Flow Graph Reducibility, *Journal of Computer and System Sci. 9*, 355-365.

Tarjan, R.E. (1974b) Finding Dominators in Directed Graphs, *SIAM Journal of Computing 3*, 62-89.

Tarjan, R.E. (1975) Efficiency of a Good But Not Linear Set Union Algorithm, *ACM Journal 22*, 215-225. [6.6.5.1]

Tarjan, R.E. (1976) Graph Theory and Gaussian Elimination, *Sparse Matrix Computations* (eds. Bunch, J.R. and Rose, D.J.), Academic Press, 3-22. [7.6]

Tarjan, R.E. (1978) Complexity of Combinatorial Algorithms, *SIAM Review 20*, 457-491. [7.7]

Tarjan, R.E. (1979) Applications of Path Compression on Balanced Trees, *ACM Journal 26*, 690-715.

Tarjan, R.E. (1983a) Space-Efficient Implementations of Graph Search Methods, *ACM Transactions on Mathematical Software 9*, 326-339. [7.3.1]

Tarjan, R.E. (1983b) Updating a Balanced Search Tree in $O(1)$ Rotations, *Information Processing Letters 16*, 253-257. [10.3.5]

Tarjan, R.E. (1983c) *Data Structures and Network Algorithms*, SIAM, Philadelphia. [•]

Tarjan, R.E. and Yao, A.C.C. (1979) Storing a Sparse Table, *ACM Communications 22*, 606-611.

Tenenbaum, A.M. and Augenstein, M.J. (1981) *Data Structures Using Pascal*, Prentice-Hall. [•]

Terashima, M. and Goto, E. (1978) Genetic Order and Compactifying Garbage Collectors, *Information Processing Letters 7*, 27-32. [11.3.1.3.2]

Thompson, K. (1968) Regular Expression Search Algorithm, *ACM Communications 11*, 419-422. [8.6.2]

Thorelli, L.E. (1972) Marking Algorithms, *BIT 12*, 555-568. [10.3.1.3.2]

Tremblay, J.P. and Manohar, R. (1975) *Discrete Mathematical Structures with Applications to Computer Science*, McGraw-Hill.

Tremblay, J.P. and Sorenson, P.G. (1984) *An Introduction to Data Structures with Applications* (2nd ed.), McGraw-Hill. [•]

Trojanowski, A.E. (1978) Ranking and Listing Algorithms for *k*-ary Trees, *SIAM Journal of Computing 7*, 492-508. [6.10]

Tucker, A. (1984) *Applied Combinatorics* (2nd ed.), John Wiley & Sons. [1.6, 2.5.1]

Tuel, W.G. (1978) Optimum Reorganization Points for Linearly Growing Files, *ACM Transactions on Database Systems 3*, 32-40. [12.3.3]

Ullman, J.D. (1972) A Note on the Efficiency of Hashing Functions, *ACM Journal 19*, 569-575.

Ullman, J.D. (1982) *Principles of Database Systems* (2nd ed.), Computer Science Press. [12.6]

Ullman, J.R. (1976) An Algorithm for Subgraph Isomorphism, *ACM Journal 23*, 31-42. [7.7]

U.S. Dept. of Defense (1983) *Reference Manual for the Ada Programming Language*, ANSI/MIL-STD-1815A. [1.1.2, 9.2.1]

Valiant, L.G. (1975a) General Context-Free Recognition in Less Than Cubic Time, *Journal of Computer and System Science 10*, 308-315. [8.6.3]

Valiant, L.G. (1975b) Parallelism in Comparison Problems, *SIAM Journal of Computing 4*, 348-355. [13.5]

Vallarino, O. (1976) On the Use of Bit Maps for Multiple Key Retrieval, Proceedings of Conference on Data: Abstraction, Definition, and Structure, *ACM SIGPLAN Notices 11* (Special Issue), 108-114. [12.6]

van der Nat, M. (1980) A Fast Sorting Algorithm, a Hybrid of Distributive and Merge Sorting, *Information Processing Letters 10*, 163-167. [13.7]

van der Pool, J.A. (1972) Optimum Storage Allocation for Initial Loading of a File, *IBM Journal of Research and Development 16*, 579-586. [12.6]

van der Pool, J.A. (1973a) Optimum Storage Allocation for a File in a Steady State, *IBM Journal of Research and Development 17*, 27-38. [12.6]

van der Pool, J.A. (1973b) Optimum Storage Allocation for a File with Open Addressing, *IBM Journal of Research and Development 17*, 106-114 [12.3.2.1]

van Emde Boas, P., Kaas, R., and Zijlstra, E. (1977) Design and Implementation of an Efficient Priority Queue, *Mathematical Systems Theory 10*, 99-127. [6.6.4.1]

Varol, Y.L. and Rotem, D. (1981) An Algorithm to Generate all Topological Sorting Arrangements, *Computer Journal 24*, 83-84. [7.4.5.1]

Vaucher, J.G. and Duval, P. (1975) A Comparison of Simulation Event List Algorithms, *ACM Communications 18*, 223-230. [5.6]

Verhelst, M. (1972) The Conversion of Limited-Entry Decision Tables to Optimal and Near-Optimal Flowcharts: Two New Algorithms, *ACM Communications 15*, 974-980. [6.10]

Vitter, J.S. (1982) Implementations for Coalesced Hashing, *ACM Communications 25*, 911-926. [10.4.2.1]

Vitter, J.S. (1985) Design and Analysis of a Dynamic Huffman Coding, *Proceedings 26th IEEE Symposium on Foundations of Computer Science*, 293-302. [8.8]

Vose, M.R. and Richardson, J.S. (1972) An Approach to Inverted Index Maintenance, *Computer Bulletin 16*, 256-262.

Vuillemin, J. (1978) A Data Structure for Manipulating Priority Queues, *ACM Communications 21*, 309-315. [6.6.4.1]

Vuillemin, J. (1980) A Unifying Look at Data Structures, *ACM Communications 23*, 229-239. [6.12]

Wadler, P.L. (1976) Analysis of an Algorithm for Real Time Garbage Collection, *ACM Communications 19*, 491-500. [11.5]

Wagner, R.A. (1973a) Common Phrases and Minimum-Space Storage, *ACM Communications 16*, 148-152. [8.2.2]

Wagner, R.A. and Fischer, M.J. (1974) The String-to-String Correction Problem, *ACM Journal 21*, 168-173. [8.3.2]

Wagner, R.E. (1973b) Indexing Design Considerations, *IBM Systems Journal 4*, 351-367. [12.3.4.1]

Walker, A. and Wood, D. (1976) Locally Balanced Binary Trees, *Computer Journal 19*, 322-225. [10.3.3.2]

Walker, W.A. and Gotlieb, C.C. (1972) A Top-Down Algorithm for Constructing Nearly Optimal Lexicographic Trees, *Graph Theory and Computing* (ed. Read, R.C.), Academic Press, 303-323. [10.8]

Wang, C.C. (1974) An Algorithm for the Chromatic Number of a Graph, *ACM Journal 21*, 385-391. [7.7]

Warshall, S. (1962) A Theorem on Boolean Matrices, *ACM Journal 9*, 11-12. [7.3.3]

Wegbreit, B. (1972) A Space-Efficient List Structure Tracing Algorithm, *IEEE Transactions on Computers C-21*, 1009-1010. [11.2.1.1]

Weide, B. (1977) A Survey of Analysis Techniques for Discrete Algorithms, *ACM Computer Surveys 9*, 291-313. [1.3.2.2]

Weiner, P. (1973) Linear Pattern Matching Algorithms, *Proceedings 14th IEEE Symposium on Switching and Automata Theory*, 1-11. [8.5.4]

Weizenbaum, J. (1963) Symmetric List Processor, *ACM Communications 6*, 524-536. [11.2.2]

Weizenbaum, J. (1969) Recovery of Reentrant List Structures in SLIP, *ACM Communications 12*, 370-372. [11.2.2]

Welch, T.A. (1984) A Technique for High-Performance Data Compression, *Computer 17: 6*, 8-19. [8.8]

Wells, M.B. (1971) *Elements of Combinatorial Computing*, Pergamon Press. [6.10]

Welsh, D.J.A. and Powell, M.B. (1967) An Upper Bound for the Chromatic Number of a Graph and its Application to Timetabling Problems, *Computer Journal 10*, 85-86. [7.7]

Welsh, J., Sneeringer, W.J., and Hoare, C.A.R. (1977) Ambiguities and Insecurities in Pascal, *Software Practice and Experience 7*, 685-696. [1.6]

Winograd, S. (1970) On the Number of Multiplications Necessary to Compute Certain Functions, *Communications in Pure and Applied Mathematics 23*, 165-179. [2.13]

Winston, P.H. (1977) *Artificial Intelligence*, Addison-Wesley. [6.8]

Wirth, N. (1973) *Systematic Programming: An Introduction*, Prentice-Hall. [2.13]

Wirth, N. (1975) An Assessment of the Programming Language Pascal, *IEEE Transactions on Software Engineering SE-1*, 192-198. [1.6]

Wirth, N. (1976) *Algorithms + Data Structures = Programs*, Prentice-Hall. [•]

Wirth, N. (1985) *Programming in Modula-2* (3rd ed.), Springer-Verlag. [1.1.2, 9.2.1]

Wirth, N. (1986) *Algorithms and Data Structures*, Prentice-Hall.

Wise, D.S. (1976) Referencing Lists by an Edge, *ACM Communications 19*, 338-342. [4.1.4]

Wise, D.S. (1979) Morris's Garbage Compaction Algorithm Restores Reference Counts, *ACM Transactions on Programming Languages and Systems 1*, 115-120.

Wise, D.S. and Friedman, D.P. (1977) The One-Bit Reference Count, *BIT 17*, 351-359. [11.2.5]

Wise, D.S. and Watson, D.C. (1976) Tuning Garwick's Algorithm for Repacking Sequential Storage, *BIT 16*, 442-450. [5.3]

Wodon, P.L. (1969) Data Structure and Storage Allocation, *BIT 9*, 270-282. [11.3.1.3.2]

Wong, E. and Chiang, T.C. (1971) Canonical Structure in Attribute Based File Organization, *ACM Communications 14*, 593-597. [12.6]

Wood, D. (1978) A Comparison of Two Methods of Encoding Arrays, *BIT 18*, 219-229. [9.1.2]

Wright, W.E. (1981) Binary Search Trees in Secondary Memory, *Acta Informatica 15*, 3-17.

Wulf, W.A., Shaw, M., Hilfinger, P.N., and Flon, L. (1981) *Fundamental Structures of Computer Science*, Addison-Wesley.

Wyman, F.P. (1975) Improved Event-Scanning Mechanisms for Discrete Event Simulation, *ACM Communications 18*, 350-353. [5.6]

Yang, W.P. and Du, M.W. (1985) A Backtracking Method for Constructing Perfect Hashing Functions from a Set of Mapping Functions, *BIT 25*, 148-164. [10.8]

Yao, A.C.C. (1978) On Random 2-3 Trees, *Acta Informatica 9*, 159-170. [10.3.4, 12.3.4.2]

Yao, A.C.C. (1981) Should Tables be Sorted?, *ACM Journal 28*, 615-628. [10.4.3]

Yao, A.C.C. and Yao, F.F. (1976) The Complexity of Searching an Ordered Random Table, *Proceedings 17th IEEE Symposium on Foundations of Computer Science*, 173-177. [10.2.3]

Yeh, D. (1982) Improved Planarity Algorithms, *BIT 22*, 2-16. [7.7]

Zipf, G.K. (1949) *Human Behavior and the Principle of Least Effort*, Addison-Wesley. [10.2.1]

Ziv, J. and Lempel, A. (1977) A Universal Algorithm for Sequential Data Compression, *IEEE Transactions on Information Theory IT-23*, 337-343. [8.8]

Ziv, J. and Lempel, A. (1978) Compression of Individual Sequences via Variable-Rate Encoding, *IEEE Transactions on Information Theory IT-24*, 530-536. [8.8]

Zweben, S.H. and McDonald, M.A. (1978) An Optimal Method for Deletion in One-Sided Height-Balanced Trees, *ACM Communications 21*, 441-445. [10.3.3.1]

INDEX

A 6
B 7
C 8
D 9
E 0
F 1
G 2
H 3
I 4
J 5